A Guide to the Phonics Units of Study, Grades K–1

Lucy Calkins and Natalie Louis

Photography by Peter Cunningham

Illustrations by Marjorie Martinelli

HEINEMANN ◆ PORTSMOUTH, NH

MW00637493

To the colleagues who emerged from all corners to lend their artistic talents to this series: Lisa Hernandez Corcoran, Kimberly Fox, Tim Steffen, Suzanne Korn, Hilary Andaya, Barry Rothman, Graham Holley, Valerie Geschwind, and Elizabeth Valway. And especially to Marjorie Martinelli, who pulled it all together.

Heinemann
361 Hanover Street
Portsmouth, NH 03801–3912
www.heinemann.com

Offices and agents throughout the world

Cataloging-in-Publication data is on file with the Library of Congress.

ISBN-13: 978-0-325-10535-2

Editors: Karen Kawaguchi and Anna Gratz Cockerille
Production: Elizabeth Valway
Cover and interior designs: Jenny Jensen Greenleaf
Photography: Peter Cunningham
Illustrations: Marjorie Martinelli and Kimberly Fox
Composition: Publishers' Design and Production Services, Inc.
Manufacturing: Steve Bernier

Printed in the United States of America on acid-free paper
22 21 20 19 18   VP   1 2 3 4 5

Contents

A Note to Our Readers

WELCOME, COME IN. How I wish that I could be alongside you as you open the books and the boxes of this phonics curriculum. How I'd love it if Natalie and I or one of the coauthors could be your personal tour guide, showing you all its special features. I'd take you to the online resources (denoted by 🖱) right away, so you could see the loving care we've invested in ensuring that everything you'll need is here for you, in both black-and-white and color versions. I'd help you understand the rhyme and reason behind the Resource Pack (denoted by 📦), pointing out that we color-coded materials to make it easier for you to see which resource matches which unit and grade. I'd take you to favorite sessions and extensions, too, pausing to delight in the photos along the way. What beautiful kids, and what engagement, what joy we have in store for you!

Most of all, though, I'd love to be with you as you teach this curriculum. I want to learn from the way in which your teaching brings these pages to life. A few months ago, several hundred teachers and literacy coaches came to the Teachers College Reading and Writing Project for our very first conference on Units of Study in Phonics. We loved hearing their recommendations and felt so lucky when we could incorporate their suggestions right into our drafts. How we wish that as you also become part of our circle of thought, we could incorporate your suggestions into the written units. Alas, as I write this, Heinemann is at the door, waiting to pull the manuscript from my hands. The day has come when my colleagues and I need to pass this curriculum from our hands to yours. Know from the start that we fully expect you to add your own spin. The Units of Study in Phonics are intentionally sparse so that you can easily incorporate favorite games, songs, and activities into each unit. We recognize this is still a community effort, and a work in progress. Please, make videos of your teaching and share them with your colleagues, your kids' parents, and with the community that gathers on the Units of Study Facebook pages!

You should know that all of us at the Teachers College Reading and Writing Project have fallen head-over-heels in love with this curriculum. Three decades ago, I was the junior partner in Don Graves's break-the-mold research on children's writing. That research helped a generation of researchers to reimagine educational research. Grave's work was a game-changer, showing the world that educational research need not be dry and voiceless. Since that groundbreaking research, many other researchers have written articles and books that are also filled with the voices of young people and that are written to be read by teachers, following in the tradition that Graves's work began.

The coauthors, Natalie, and I hope that the Units of Study in Phonics break the mold of phonics curriculum in a similar way. We have our fingers crossed that these units will set a new standard for readability, teachability, and effectiveness. We hope that you'll regard this curriculum as a gift, because that is what we have intended.

As you look over the books in an effort to orient yourself to the curriculum, let me give you a bird's-eye view of what you'll see.

- **There are five units for each grade, K–2.** Each unit is designed to be taught roughly at the same time as the corresponding reading and/or writing unit of study and to last five to six weeks, keeping pace with those units. It's likely that you'll have some time left in your school year after you finish the fifth unit. To respond to the gap between the end of this unit and the end of your year, you'll find teaching suggestions in the Unit 5 online resources so that unit works like an accordion, stretching or contracting to accommodate your students' needs and the time you have left in the school year. These resources provide a menu of If. . .Then. . . options for your instruction. It's likely there are additional phonics concepts you'll want to teach, either because your students are ready for new work or because there is work they need to revisit.

These final weeks or months in your school year can also give you time to teach any topics in your school's curriculum you have yet to cover. ✴

- **Each unit contains distinct bends, or parts.** Any one of these bends can be detached and taught at a slightly different time. For example, after one bend in a unit, you might decide to add some repeated practice of the content you've just taught. Each bend ends with a celebration, and there is a larger, end-of-unit celebration.

- **Each bend contains approximately six sessions.** A session is a day of phonics instruction, although there will be a few times when you decide to extend a session so that it lasts across two days. A bend in the unit, then, supports approximately a week and a half of teaching.

- **Each session contains a micro-lesson (an abbreviated minilesson) that channels kids to do some work.** That work is generally done right there on the carpet, with children working with partners or with a cluster of several others—this is known as a **rug club**. After this semi-independent work time, the phonics session ends with a brief **share**. A day's phonics session lasts twenty minutes.

- **For each session, we include two or three extensions, most of which are optional, that you can do to build on each day's phonics instruction.** These extensions are usually designed to be done while children line up to go home or when there is an extra five minutes before a special starts. They tend to involve kids in singing a song, chiming in to a shared reading, playing a round of a game— all activities that tend to not require you to organize materials. Some extensions, such as those on star names in kindergarten Unit 1, *Making Friends with Letters*, and those that introduce high-frequency words are particularly important.

- **We offer support in coaching into the work that students do during each session and in leading small groups.** In addition, you'll be given help leading more than sixty assessment-based small groups. You'll lead these groups outside of phonics time, most often during reading and writing workshop. Intervention teachers might draw on these small groups as well, during intervention time. As Patricia Cunningham writes in *Month-by-Month Phonics for First Grade* (2008) of word study, "Students don't know something until they use it in their reading and writing" (108). These small groups aim to support students

in transferring what they are learning in phonics time to their ongoing reading and writing work.

- **There is a fun storyline to each unit.** In one unit, kids are detectives, researching the mystery of the silent *E*. In another, kids are word scientists, studying and using the alphabet chart. In yet another, kids are given a super power—word-part power. They learn phonograms— onsets and rimes—while becoming Super Readers. The stories in these units align with the stories that engine the reading and writing units themselves.

- **The curriculum includes assessments that allow you to track your students' growth.** These are designed to be lean so that you have time to study the findings. The assessments will help you detect any hint of a problem and quickly attend to it. The goal is for you to be able to respond with agility to indications that extra teaching or further assessments are needed.

In Chapter 1, this *Guide* overviews the principles that undergird this phonics curriculum. Chapter 2 is probably the most important chapter of the *Guide*. This chapter overviews phonics development and helps you understand the developmental progression that the series supports. This chapter includes a section on effective ways to support English language learners in phonics. Chapter 3 orients you to the methods and materials used in this curriculum. This chapter overviews the parts of a workshop and will be most important for those of you who do not already know the structure of a workshop, although this chapter will also help you know ways in which parts such as minilessons and shares during phonics workshop differ from those in reading and writing units of study. It will also introduce you to new parts, such as rug time and extensions. This chapter overviews the standby methods that are used again and again in this phonics curriculum, such as sorting and "Making Words." Chapter 3 also suggests a schedule to fit your phonics instruction into the day. Chapter 4 overviews the ideas that we hope will inform your small-group phonics instruction. Chapter 5, "Assessing Your Students' Phonics Development," builds on Chapter 2 and overviews the assessments that will help you to watch over your students' growth.

A word about the evolution of this curriculum: My colleagues and I have always known that it is important for a school to adopt a planned, sequenced curriculum in phonics. Over the years, the schools we know best have adopted phonics programs such as *Phonics They Use* (Cunningham 2016), *Words Their Way* (Bear et al. 2016), Fountas & Pinnell *Phonics* (2017), and *Fundations*® (Wilson Language Training 2012). We've become expert in those approaches and we value them. We have not written this because we found fault with those approaches. But over the past few years, we came to believe that the lack of transference between phonics, reading, and writing could no longer be ignored. We believe that transference will be more omnipresent, and your teaching will be easier and more coherent, if you follow the same paradigm for your reading and writing *and* phonics instruction.

Although each book in this series has a set of official coauthors, the truth is that the entire organization has worked on all of the books. You'll see the collaboration that informs each book detailed in the Acknowledgments pages, but you should know from the start that Natalie Louis has joined me as a senior author of the series. She and I have supported all the coauthors and made sure we have a coherent curriculum and voice across all the units. Then, too, any one book may have poems by Mike Ochs and Georgia Heard, art by a whole team of TCRWP artists including our brilliant Marjorie Martinelli and also Elizabeth Franco, Lisa Corcoran, Kim Fox, Tim Steffen, Valerie Geschwind, and many others. Each book will also have spunky, fun curricular ideas from a collection of colleagues, state-of-the-art phonics research from others, book recommendations from yet others, photographs from our world-famous photographer, videos from a score of colleagues, insights gleaned from pilot teaching by a dozen staff developers, and writing help from the team of writers.

We hope that you join the Units of Study Facebook groups, bringing your stories and insights and questions so that we can continue the conversation as you proceed through this curriculum, bringing it to life with your talent and love and above all, with your children.

All our love,
Lucy, Natalie, and the TCRWP Phonics Team

CHAPTER 1

Principles Undergirding This Phonics Curriculum

Y OU ARE A CRUCIAL FACTOR in determining a child's eventual success in learning to read and write. The extraordinary and beautiful thing is that when a child is given the gift of a wonderful teacher during the first few years of school, there is an enormous likelihood that the youngster will grow into an avid reader and writer.

However, if you are the best reading and writing workshop teacher in the world, and yet do not teach your children phonics, that is not enough. If your children cannot get words onto and off the page, they will not write letters advocating for a class turtle, nor will they stay up late reading by flashlight. Many of your children need you to teach phonics directly, according to a research-based sequence of instruction, using methods that have emerged from decades of practice and study. And for some aspects of phonics, just six to ten hours of instruction across *the entire year* can make the difference. So phonics is an area where more is not better, but *wiser* is better. This guide and this series aim to help you teach wiser phonics, not more phonics, and to teach phonics in such a way that your energy for teaching and your children's energy for literacy grows.

Always, it is important to remember that decisions about teaching and curriculum are decisions about values. In choosing a way to teach phonics, you are choosing the messages you want to send to children—and because phonics is a vital part of a child's earliest schooling experience, those messages will shape your children's understanding of school, of reading and writing, of themselves as learners, and of learning itself.

PHONICS INSTRUCTION SUPPORTS CHILDREN'S READING AND WRITING; TO BE USEFUL, PHONICS MUST BE TRANSFERRED.

To start, it is important to remember that the goal of phonics instruction is to support kids' progress as readers and writers. Every message you send during phonics instruction needs to be angled to support transfer to reading and writing. Your goal is not for your kids to become linguistic scholars, able to pontificate about the six syllable types or the eight sounds that an *O* can make. Instead, phonics instruction only matters because it enables reading and writing.

This commitment to teaching phonics in ways that give your kids wings as readers and writers has important implications for the nature of your phonics instruction. It means that the pace and content of your instruction needs to align to the work your children do as readers and writers. Instead of starting kindergarten by teaching one letter a week, for example, you'll want to quicken the pace of that instruction, knowing that your children can cement their knowledge of letter-sound correspondences as they use that knowledge to label their drawings during writing time. The demands that books pose will also influence the pace of your phonics instruction. If you keep in mind that level C books contain contractions and that children reading level E books will need to draw on a knowledge of long vowels, then it is clear that your phonics curriculum cannot proceed slowly enough that children master one bit of content before proceeding to another. And if your phonics instruction aims to keep pace with your children's reading and writing development, you won't be able to give equal time to all twenty-six letters, the thirty-seven most common phonograms, and to each and every blend!

Even something as simple as the sequence in which you teach high-frequency words will be affected by your commitment to teach in ways that align with your reading and writing instruction. You'll presumably still draw on Fry's list of 250 high-frequency words, but you'll tweak the sequence in which you teach those words so that when children are writing Small Moment stories, they learn to spell *said* and *went*, and when they are writing How-To books, they learn to spell *how* and *put*.

It is not just the content of your phonics curriculum that will shift when your teaching is designed to support transfer to reading and writing—the kind of work you ask of children will shift as well. During a phonics unit on short vowels, your children will still spend time doing the sorting work that can help them distinguish one short vowel from another, but to help transfer, you'll also ask children to look over the writing they've done recently, making sure that every syllable of every word contains a vowel. Have they chosen the correct short vowel? You'll tell them that checking for this requires careful listening for the small nuanced differences between the short *I* and the short *E*, for example. When teaching with the transfer of phonics skills to reading and writing in mind, the work the children do during and especially near the end of phonics time is more apt to look like, feel like, and even *be* reading and writing.

PHONICS INSTRUCTION BENEFITS CHILDREN WHEN IT FOLLOWS A RESEARCH-BASED SEQUENCE.

This curriculum relies on proven, research-based practices, drawing on the work of Adams, Bear, Beck, Blevins, Cunningham, Ehri, Fountas, Fry, Helman, Hiebert, Ganske, O'Connor, Pinnell, Rasinski, Scanlon, Snowball, Yopp and Yopp, and others. We also bring to this curriculum a deep respect for the important work of Reading Recovery™ and of the late Marie Clay. How fortunate we are that these meticulous researchers have collected data on things such as the varying degrees of challenges children encounter when learning the twenty-six letters and the six syllable types. We make no claim to having done this original research, but it is with enormous gratitude that we stand on the shoulders of these researchers.

The sequence of these Units of Study in Phonics follows a pathway that is widely supported in this research. We detail that pathway later in this *Guide*, but for now, suffice it to say that whether children are studying the Units of Study in Phonics or Bear's *Words Their Way* (2016) or Cunningham's *Phonics They Use* (2016) or *Fundations* (2012), or Fountas and Pinnell's *Phonics* (2017), or any one of many other programs, the sequence of topics they study will not be widely different. Always, children first develop phonemic awareness: learning to segment words into phonemes, to blend phonemes into word parts and words, and to rhyme and play with language. Simultaneously, children learn the alphabetic principle—learning letter names and sounds and formation. They also become immersed in concepts of print. By late fall, kindergartners progress to learning rimes (word families such as *-at: rat, cat*) and digraphs (*SH, TH, CH*); in the late winter, they study short vowels and begin to learn vowel flexibility. Blends will be important, too. Many of those topics will need to be revisited before kindergarten is over, and again in first grade. Throughout all of this, kids learn high-frequency words—about fifty of them during kindergarten. The progression unfolds further in first grade.

Researchers have some differences of opinion—should students develop phonemic awareness prior to any involvement with phonics (with visible letters) or can phonemic awareness develop in synchrony with phonics knowledge? How much emphasis should be given to word families (rimes) as opposed to letter-by-letter cumulative word solving? These differences of opinion are relatively small, however, compared to the consensus that emerges among people who know and study about phonics instruction. We are grateful for this research base.

Of course, any curriculum developed by the team at the Teachers College Reading and Writing Project will also draw on decades of research and practice in the teaching of reading and writing more broadly. Given that phonics is important only insofar as it transfers to and informs literacy writ large, we think it is essential that a phonics curriculum draw on this broad, deep, applied knowledge of how students develop as writers and readers, speakers and listeners.

This phonics curriculum is also informed by a dedication to a growth mind-set, and it is steeped in knowledge of child development. This means the curriculum is infused with a commitment to giving young children opportunities to take risks, try again, talk, explore, pretend, move, play, question, invent, sing, and laugh. It also is shaped by our knowledge of you, our readers. My colleagues and I have gone to great lengths to develop a curriculum that reflects our firsthand knowledge of the many competing demands on you as you work with your quirky, boisterous crew of students in our increasingly complex profession.

PHONICS INSTRUCTION BENEFITS CHILDREN WHEN IT SUPPLEMENTS AND DOES NOT REPLACE READING AND WRITING INSTRUCTION.

In a recent article titled "What Really Matters in Teaching Phonics Today: Laying a Foundation for Reading," James Cunningham (2017) overviews the history of phonics within the U.S. over the past two decades. He points out that in 1997, an initiative of Congress created Reading First (and the larger policies imbued in Leave No Child Behind), which brought systematic phonics front and center in schools across the country. As Cunningham reports, the official federal evaluation of this well-funded and large-scale initiative to teach reading through systematic phonics programs found "no consistent pattern of effects over time in the impact estimates for reading instruction in grade one or in reading comprehension in any grade" (Cunningham 2017; Gamse et al. 2008). Sixty-seven percent of the children who grew up entirely under the regime of systematic phonics scored below proficient levels of reading (Cunningham 2017, 7), leading Tucker to conclude that the adoption of a systematic phonics curriculum led to "almost no improvement in student performance" (Tucker 2014).

In his article summarizing this history, Jim Cunningham questions what went wrong and what one can conclude. He writes, "Is phonics/decoding truly foundational?" (2017, 7). He answers:

Yes, but it is not the building. That is the right lesson to learn from the disappointing results of Reading First (7) . . . The lack of success for Reading First was not because it taught phonemic awareness and phonics/decoding, but because it neglected to teach reading and writing at the same time. This error has been corrected in the college and career readiness standards where reading foundations, reading, writing, and meaning vocabulary are all to be taught in parallel starting in kindergarten. However, the dual challenges this change presents to school and district leadership today are 1. that teachers have less time to teach phonics than during Reading First and 2. that the phonics taught must transfer to reading and writing. (9)

Specifically, Jim Cunningham suggests that phonics needs to be contained within twenty minutes a day—a recommendation that one also finds in New York State's newest iteration of the Common Core State Standards (15).

Even if you quibble with that recommendation, increasing the time allotment by as much as 25%, it still remains true that phonics instruction needs to be lean and efficient. Every minute you spend teaching phonics (or preparing phonics materials to use in your lessons) is less time spent teaching other things.

You will see that Units of Study in Phonics recommends twenty minutes for explicit phonics instruction, with time outside of phonics for small-group instruction in phonics. We also recommend that during transitional moments during your day, you revisit phonics and high-frequency words through a song, a chant, a game. In the Units of Study in Phonics books, each session (or day) contains some optional extensions, most of which can be taught as your class lines up for lunch or packs up to go home. Those are good times to play "I Spy" with high-frequency words or to sing the alphabet to the tune of "Row, Row, Row Your Boat."

CHILDREN BENEFIT FROM BEING TAUGHT NOT ONLY ITEM KNOWLEDGE (SUCH AS BLENDS AND DIGRAPHS), BUT ALSO THE STRATEGIES AND PURPOSES THAT ALLOW THEM TO DRAW ON THAT ITEM KNOWLEDGE AS THEY READ AND WRITE.

Readers, will you pause for a moment to list every blend, digraph, and trigraph that exists in the English language? Then, will you make a list of the *R*-controlled vowel sounds? While you are at it, will you take a moment to record all the six different syllable types?

How'd you do? Chances are that this exercise wasn't easy for you. The significant thing, however, is that you probably had no trouble reading the previous paragraph, even though the words in it contained blends and digraphs (*TR*, *BL*, *PH*, *TH*, and *WH* to name a few) and several *R*-controlled vowels (in *record* and *different*, for starters). The paragraph also contains examples of both open and closed syllables (*mo-ment*, for example), as well as consonant *-le* syllables (*syllable* has one!). My point is that although item knowledge of phonics can be helpful, people rely on a variety of strategies as well as item knowledge to read and write.

In Units of Study in Phonics, children are taught the most high-utility phonics, and they are taught to use what they know to be problem solvers, word scientists, super-power readers, and writers. The content that is taught in phonics is a mix of item knowledge and skills and strategies.

Marie Clay has pointed out that, "Almost nobody considering the young child learning beginning mathematics is going to think in terms of how many arithmetical items he knows. Almost everybody will be thinking, 'What mathematical operations can he carry out?'" She suggests a similar shift in thinking needs to occur in literacy (1979, 13).

When teaching blends, for example, the important thing is for youngsters to understand that two letters combine to make one sound. Sometimes one of those letters is hard to hear, so careful listening helps. There are some letters that are often the second letter in a blend—*L*, *R*, for example. Teachers will want to teach children blends that come at the start of words, and blends that come at the ends of words. But it is not necessary for a teacher to teach every possible blend, nor to assess whether a child masters every possible blend. As Pat Cunningham writes in *Phonics They Use*, "There are systems and patterns to the way letters in English represent sounds. Our instruction should point out these patterns. Children who see a new word and ask themselves how that new word is like the other words they know can discover many patterns on their own" (2016, 41).

Imagine that you pull alongside a child and note that he has spelled *blue* like this: *bue*. You can think, "Oh my goodness, this child needs me to reteach the blend unit" and you can proceed to review all of the blends. Alternatively, you can think, "This child needs to learn to reread honestly, accurately, actually seeing what he has written. If he rereads *bue*, he'll see that he left out one of the letters in the initial blend, and he will especially see this if you have taught children that often when blending, there is a letter (usually the second letter) that gets lost, and therefore it is important to listen for the hard to hear sounds.

The point, of course, isn't about blends—it is about the content of your phonics curriculum. Item knowledge is important, but it is equally important for youngsters to know how, when, and why they can use that knowledge. It helps to let kids in on the rationale that informs your teaching. That is, instead of drawing children into a sorting activity by simply saying, "I have a really fun sort for you to do," it helps to explain that just as grown-ups sometimes do push-ups to get stronger muscles, readers also need stronger muscles—and the muscles that especially matter to readers are *ear muscles*. One way to develop stronger ear muscles is for readers to sort picture cards based on small differences between, for example, a word that begins with a single consonant and a similarly spelled word that begins with a blend.

CHILDREN BENEFIT MOST FROM PHONICS WORK THAT IS ENGAGING; PHONICS NEED NOT BE TAUGHT THROUGH WORKSHEETS BUT CAN INSTEAD INVOLVE SINGING, PRETENDING, INVENTING, TALKING, WRITING, AND SPELLING.

In his article "What Really Matters in Teaching Phonics Today," Jim Cunningham (2017) points out that there is not necessarily a connection between what we teach and what our students learn. When teaching is dull, rote, repetitive—and he points out that phonics instruction is often all of the above—then students will be disengaged and all the teaching in the world won't add up to a great deal of learning.

There are many ways in which these units support high levels of student engagement. First, as I'll discuss in detail later, each unit sweeps children up into the power of a good story. Mabel, the elephant who is the class mascot in kindergarten, is found lying on the cold floor. The custodian must not have realized where her bed is! Will children help to label her bed so that after this, she never sleeps on the cold floor? Mabel likes to sleep with other *M* objects—can the children help to tuck her in with lots of things that start with *M*? Mabel loves learning her alphabet—but do the children have other stuffed animals who may want to come to ABC School? Mabel provides the first storyline for kindergarten, and her friend the lion, Rasheed, is equally important to first-graders.

In another unit, you gather the children on the rug, and remark that somehow, they all look a little different—taller, stronger, more *super*—inviting the kids to remind you that they are now Super Readers. You'll go on to reveal an important message, "You know that the job of a Super *Reader*, like the job of any superhero, never ends, right? Your power sticks with you all day long," and suggest that students use their pointer power to help them write during phonics workshop. Children then acquire word-part power and use lassos, like those Wonder Woman uses, to scoop up the rimes in words. Later they are given vowel shields and work to activate their short-vowel power. Soon after the start of first grade, children are engaged in

solving the mystery of the silent *E*, and before long, Rasheed is given a hard hat and he and the children learn about constructing buildings—and long words—out of smaller chunks (including vowel teams).

The storyline of this curriculum will draw students into a study of phonics, but it is equally important that during phonics time, children are learning phonics in ways that are developmentally appropriate. They disperse to do a "beats walk" throughout the classroom, touching things in the room and clapping or stomping the beats in that item's name. They use magnetic letters on top of pictures to label the objects in their picture books. They assemble high-frequency word cards and small animals to construct sentences such as, "I see the lion." They invent better icons for their alphabet charts, replacing the keyword for *B*, *ball*, with *Batman* or *butterfly* and replacing the keyword *egg* with an elephant or whatever other picture they invent. When a great wind blows all the pictures from the alphabet chart, they reconstruct it, drawing on all they know about letters and sounds. They walk through the halls of their school, checking whether every syllable of every bit of environmental print contains a vowel. They help Rasheed, the first-grade mascot, edit his writing (poor Rasheed needs a lot of help with vowel teams!) and then they do similar work on their own writing. They chant and sing and pretend-write in the air and on their legs to develop automaticity with high-frequency words, and later they invent their own ways to learn those words (perhaps inventing little songs to help them remember the spelling of some words or making the words out of pipe cleaners).

Units of Study in Phonics contain the usual collections of picture cards, word cards, nursery rhymes, and decodable texts, but our pledge to you is that if you are expected to print or scissor a teaching tool, we've made every effort to be sure that you reuse that tool repeatedly.

Part of this revolves around a commitment to keep children's work as engaging as possible. Instead of channeling them to circle the number of syllables in pictures on ditto sheets, we're more apt to suggest that they plop their backpacks in front of them, and work with a partner to touch each part of each child's backpack, clapping the syllables to *zipper*, *pocket*, *strap*, and *applesauce*. Instead of asking them to fill in blanks on a ditto, we give them a story that a fictional child has written and ask kids to work with partners to help that child fix up her draft. The good news is that these activities require you to do less duplicating, scissoring, sorting, orchestrating. Our hope is that when teaching phonics this way, your energy goes up, and your children's energy does likewise.

ALL OUR TEACHING, AND ESPECIALLY OUR TEACHING OF SOMETHING AS FOUNDATIONAL AS PHONICS, MUST BE FLEXIBLE ENOUGH AND HAVE SCOPE ENOUGH TO SUPPORT ALL THE MEMBERS OF A LEARNING COMMUNITY.

There was a time in education when "differentiation" was the end goal, in and of itself. We were asked to show how every day's lesson included a high, middle, and low track. The more skilled students wrote sentences, the less skilled circled the right answer. The 2017 U.S. Supreme Court decision, *Endrew F. v. Douglas County School District*, has been a game changer, pointing out that differentiation is not a goal, but one possible means to the goal. Among other things, this unanimous decision signaled that IEPs need to be crafted to enable each child to make significant progress, appropriate to his or her circumstances. The court decision reminds us that it is not lawful to "be satisfied with *de minimis* progress" for some children. The goal needs to be to offer opportunities for all children to engage in successful and ambitious learning.

The principles of Universal Design for Learning make it clear that providing access for all kids is what matters most. The goal of "supporting all learners" cannot mean shuttling kids into opposite corners of the room, providing one group with invitations to engage in work that calls for thinking and imagination while simultaneously channeling another group to work on repetitive, low-level, test-like drills, or to work with a teacher providing such intense "scaffolding" that the child rarely has an opportunity to work with independence. Slotting learners into ability tracks is not apt to give all learners access to the best possible education, if for no other reason than that all of us benefit when we are part of a supportive, rich learning community.

The goal is to give each child an education that is aligned to that child's particular, individual ways of representing knowledge and of engaging with texts, and that takes each child the distance. The workshop environment itself is designed to provide learners with the mix of choice and high expectation that provides the flexibility, responsive teaching, inclusivity, and rigor that each learner needs. At its best, the simple, consistent structure of a reading, writing, or phonics workshop allows you to be alert to the variations in your students' needs. Because there is time every day for students to work with each other, you can observe as children work in partnerships and "rug clubs" and make the adaptations that can allow each learner to be successful.

Your bottom-line assumption needs to be that it is important to provide students with a variety of ways to express what they know. For example, although most of your students will be able to make good use of whiteboards to explore ways in which letter combinations work, some students will benefit more from doing the same work with tiles or magnetic letters fastened to magnetic boards. And, in order to sustain effort, many students will benefit from the invitation to work collaboratively. You can provide options for physical action by allowing kids to work on the meeting area rug or a low-to-the-floor table. Although all your students will be encouraged to apply what they learn during phonics to their work with paper and markers during writing time, some will benefit from working on an iPad or with voice-activated technology.

The most important way in which the Units of Study in Phonics support all learners is by building in flexibility and choice. Because children are often applying what they learn in phonics to their reading and their writing, and because that reading and writing work will by definition be at the learner's just-right level, much of the work that students do during phonics time will already be adjusted so that each child can work within his or her zone of proximal development. That is, if students are asked to take a book from their book baggie and to look through that book for examples of something you just taught, one child will be looking through a level D book, another, a level H book. And if you ask children to reread their writing, checking over their use of blends and digraphs, some children will be rereading writing booklets in which they've written only labels onto drawings, while others will be rereading paragraphs in six-page booklets.

Other invitations issued during phonics work time also invite learners to work at the level that is right for that child. "Take one of these words that you know well and try adding endings to it—see what new words you can create. Here is a list of possible endings, although you can also think of your own." One child turns *play* into *playing*, while another turns *play* into a whole collection of words including *playground* and *playmate*. Another day, you'll ask students to sort word cards into jars. Some students will have words and pictures on those cards, while others will rely on pictures only. For children who do this work easily, you'll say, "You'll see we have included some blank cards. If you have time, make up your own words to add to your collection." Children can also receive support from each other because you will have strategically assigned them to partnerships and "rug clubs" that can provide that support.

On the other hand, it remains true that these Units of Study in Phonics are designed to sweep your whole class up into super-engaging and deeply collaborative studies of letters and sounds. There is a way in which this work is whole-class. We understand this represents a trade-off. It means you will not maintain parallel ability-based tracks. There are some advantages to that sort of old-fashioned differentiation. In the end, however, we decided our priority is to help you lead a super-engaging study of phonics, one that will gather all learners together and help them join in a shared study. For those of you who know our writing curriculum, think about the power and beauty that comes from children engaging in a shared unit on Small Moment stories. For those who know our reading curriculum, think of the high energy in your classroom created by their shared work in the *Word Detectives* or *Super Powers* units. Our goal has been to tap into that sort of energy when teaching phonics, while creating a phonics program that provides the same scope and same levels of engagement as our best K–2 writing and reading units.

Meanwhile, we know that responsive small-group instruction will be utterly crucial, allowing you to provide precursor instruction to the kids who need that, and allowing you to also make sure that your whole-class teaching has traction with all children. A separate book, *Small Groups to Support Phonics*, will help you lead those groups. You will do that during the writing workshop, the reading workshop, choice time, and other stolen moments throughout your day.

CHAPTER 2

Anticipate, Observe, and Support Phonics Development (including English Learners)

T O SUPPORT YOUR STUDENTS' early phonics development, you need to understand how children tend to develop. The challenge is that their development will occur along many interconnected strands. For example, you'll benefit from understanding that starting very early on, children are developing concepts of print. They learn to read books from front to back, top to bottom, left to right, and they learn to read those little blobs of print. You'll benefit, too, from knowing a bit about how children's phonological and phonemic awareness develops, and from understanding that alongside that evolution, kids also progress in their knowledge of letters and of letter-sound connections. Meanwhile, children will need to learn more high-frequency words. That learning includes beginning to do more with their growing repertoire of familiar words. Kids will also need to learn more about words themselves. You and I may forget how much there is to learn—but young kids do not know about digraphs, phonograms, contractions, and diphthongs. Of course, all of this learning comes together to help students be more resourceful word solvers on-the-run as they read and write. In this chapter, each strand of phonics development is addressed separately, even though that is not how development occurs.

Strands of Early Phonics Development

- Phonological awareness, phonemic awareness
  - Rhyming
  - Segmenting, syllabication of two-syllable words, and blending
- Concepts about print
- Letter-sound correspondence
  - Sequence of letter study
  - Letter formation pathways
  - Learning letters and how to use an alphabet chart

- Hearing and recording all sounds in words, starting with initial sounds

- Digraphs and blends

- Phonograms, blending, and word building

- Short vowels

- Long vowels

- Inflectional endings

- Contractions

- Vowel teams, including diphthongs

- Multisyllabic words

- *R*-controlled vowels

- High-frequency words

Note that at the end of this chapter, we provide a section on supporting English learners with the teaching of phonics.

PHONOLOGICAL AWARENESS/PHONEMIC AWARENESS

For those of us who teach children, it seems rather obvious to say that spoken words are composed of sounds. This concept, however, is surprisingly obscure to children who take in spoken words as wholes. Once the child is aware that a spoken word is made up of sounds, she has what is referred to as "phonological awareness." It is phonological awareness that allows a child to hear the difference between *bat* and *brat*. There are subtopics to phonological awareness, and they include rhyming, blending and segmenting, and manipulating and deleting sounds.

Phonemic awareness is a subset of phonological awareness. Phonemic awareness is a term that refers to the child's ability to segment words into the building block of sounds. That is, a word such as *make* is composed of three phonemes: /m/-/ā/-/k/. Phoneme awareness skills include the ability to isolate the first, middle, or last phoneme in a word; the ability to segment a word into its individual phonemes; and the ability to take a word (*rat*) and to remove and add a phoneme (take the R from *rat*, add an S, and what do you have?). That is, children who have phonemic awareness understand the building blocks of a word and can rearrange phonemes to make new words. Phonemic awareness is an essential part of invented spelling.

Both phonemic awareness and phonological awareness are often incorrectly confused with phonics; phonics is actually an instructional approach that teaches the relationship between letters and sounds. It is possible for a child to have strong phonological and/or phonemic awareness without having letter-sound knowledge. On the other hand, it is possible for a child to know the letter names and sounds without having strong phonological and/or phonemic awareness skills. Such a child might know that the letter S makes the /s/ sound but may not know that the words *sit* and *kiss* contain the /s/ sound within them.

Phonological awareness—the broader term that encompasses phonemic awareness—plays a big part in providing children with the foundation they need to make progress in learning phonics and in learning to read and write. Most children begin developing phonological awareness well before the start of kindergarten. This strand of development actually starts when the infant hears her caregiver's voice and, hearing the voice, turns expectantly to see that beloved person arrive at the cribside. The sound of "Good morning, sweetie" becomes associated with Grandma, Mom, or Dad arriving at the bedside, with all the blessings that ensue. A child's engagement with sounds continues to develop. The toddler learns to associate the *whoo-wee, whoo-wee* sound of a fire truck with the streak of red as the truck passes by, and to link the sound of *woof-woof* with the companionable presence of a furry friend. Sounds conjure up meanings—and vice versa. A page of Richard Scarry's truck book leads two youngsters to enjoy making all the wonderful noises of bulldozers and fire trucks, and the book of farm animals leads them to make a cacophony of *moos* and *baas*. All of this is part of phonological awareness, as the youngster learns that sounds can be represented on the page, and the page can conjure up sounds.

A child's phonological awareness is also evident in any approximated writing that the child does. Pre-schoolers, even, will sometimes role-play writing. A child may make a pretend menu for her make-believe restaurant, or she may make a story or a letter to a friend even before she knows a single alphabet letter. Her words might look like squiggles, but a well-informed adult can see lots of evidence of phonological awareness in the way that the child does this work. For example, when the child reads his attempt at writing, it is telling if there is even a rough correspondence between the stream of oral language and the presence of print on the page. It is a big deal if the child "reads" her approximation of writing by looking at marks on the page and saying words to accompany those marks. It is a big deal if the stream of print is broken into words. When the child reads this writing, an informed adult takes note whether the oral version seems attached to the written version, with one spoken word roughly matching each patch of print. And it is a sign of strong phonological awareness if you ask a youngster, "What do you want to write?" and he tells you the message in a word-by-word fashion.

"Please-can-I-have-a-bike? I-*really*-need-one." If you press on, asking, "What do I write first?" and the child tells you to start with "Please," that doesn't just show good manners—that shows phonological awareness.

Before a child can learn much as a reader and a writer, the child needs to grasp that words are sequential collections of speech sounds, and that written language involves taking what someone has said and putting that on the page. Many—even most—kindergartners will come to school with enough of a foundation in phonological awareness that everything you teach will enhance and add onto that foundation. You'll know that the child has this foundation because as you begin to teach letters and sounds, the child will accumulate that knowledge. The child will learn letters as you teach them, grasping something about how to make those letters and about the sounds those letters represent. You may, however, have some students who seem to be like Teflon™. Your letter-sound instruction doesn't stick. A knowledge of letters doesn't seem to cumulate. Chances are, those children need more rudimentary grounding in phonological awareness. That is, although some children will come to school with a foundation of phonological awareness, others will need direct explicit instruction to develop that foundation. They will need this intervention very early in their school careers.

Phonological development is so essential that it is very important for you to be vigilant in watching for signs that children will need you to back up and provide them with early support. One way to be vigilant about this is to know that you needn't worry too much about phonological development for a child who is showing lots of signs of having this well under control. The child who can complete rhymes that you begin, join you in making new verses to rhyming songs, who can stretch out a word to record the initial sounds and who learns letters and sounds quickly doesn't need you to obsess over her phonological development.

But the child who seems like a Teflon learner during phonics instruction needs for you to not postpone assessing and supporting this aspect of her development. These children need to spend time hearing sounds, noting whether the sounds they hear come at the start or the middle or the end of a word, blending sounds to make words, clapping syllables, exploring rhyme. The good news is that even for children who do need explicit help developing their phonological development, a good portion of this can be done without devoting large blocks of time to this goal. Research by O'Connor (2014) and Ryder, Tunmer, and Greaney (2008) has shown that students learn both blending and segmenting in six to ten hours of instruction. We provide more detailed help on this topic in the assessment chapter of this *Guide*, in the first kindergarten units, and in *Small Groups to Support Phonics*.

There will inevitably be those children for whom additional, explicit instruction is needed. If you find that a student, even with much small-group support, is not developing a strong foundation of phonological awareness, you might decide to collaborate with an Orton-Gillingham or similarly trained specialist in your district, to provide that student with additional support using specialized techniques such as multisensory instruction. Instructors who use a multisensory approach engage students in using hearing, sight, touch, and movement to help them recognize, remember, and connect letters and words in a variety of contexts. For example, students are encouraged to looking in the mirror as they say sounds to notice the movement of their mouth. They also learn to listen for and link speech sounds to the letters that they see, or write letters for the sounds that they hear; to use sight to look at words dictated by the teacher to notice where a speech sound occurs in a word; and to use touch and movement to trace, copy, and write the letter or letters that match a corresponding sound. All of these activities build brain pathways that connect speech with print in children who do not naturally develop phonological awareness during regular classroom activities.

But know from the start that the question is not whether support for phonological awareness matters: it absolutely does. The question is only how to assess which children need a lot of this support and then, how much of this is best taught as the focus for whole-group instruction and how much is best taught within small-group instruction. There is also a question as to whether phonological and phonemic awareness need to be taught prior to any instruction in letter names and sounds, or whether those can coexist. Although some kindergarten teachers devote the first month of kindergarten to just the job of helping all kids hear sounds in words with no emphasis yet on recording any of those sounds, we agree with authorities who argue that there is a two-way reciprocal relationship between phonemic awareness and decoding, with decoding instruction supporting phonemic awareness as well as the reverse. Beck and Beck (2013) write, "Decoding instruction does not need to wait for a requisite level of phonemic awareness; they can both be taught and can support and reinforce each other" (31). In Units of Study in Phonics, we embrace the notion of supporting phonemic awareness alongside letter-sound work for a variety of reasons, including the fact that we regard alignment between phonological development and reading and writing curriculum as a priority. We recognize that if students devote the first month of school exclusively to oral work—orally rhyming, blending, and segmenting without yet working with letter-sound correspondence—by extension, this suggests their phonics instruction will not keep pace with kids' work within the reading and writing workshop.

Most importantly, when students participate in a daily writing workshop, they are given many opportunities to develop their phonological awareness skills, as they stretch out words, saying the word really slowly and pausing on each sound, then working to isolate that sound, then rereading to blend the sounds they've recorded thus far and to isolate the next sound. They are getting phonological and phonemic awareness practice.

Rhyming

Most phonics programs place a great premium on rhyme. We encourage you to find lots of ways across your day to immerse your students in poems, nursery rhymes, riddles, and songs. After all, there could be no down side to "Eeny meeny miny moe, catch a tiger by the toe. If he hollers let him go!" If you ask a child to say another word that sounds like *go* and he replies, "Toe! Catch his toe!" then this child is beginning to get the idea that words have common sounds. This is a precursor to the work we do in the units of this program to develop phonemic awareness and phonological awareness in words. For that reason, we include work with rhyme in these units, although it is a relatively small part of the total phonics curriculum.

There are some researchers who worry that when children learn to read by leaning *too much* on rhyme, they are lured away from relying on phonics. These researchers would prefer if students learned to read without too much support from predictable texts, picture support, or rhyme, because that way they'd learn to rely on phonics. This is a debatable question—others disagree with their attempts to teach reading in ways that strip away the support of meaning and syntax. Units of Study in Phonics attempts to strike a balance, for while we believe that to teach for transfer, it is important for kids to learn to read within authentic language, we agree that some texts that are written for novice readers have so much rhyme, repetition, and picture support that children have few opportunities to draw on the phonics concepts they are learning. We value early reading books such as the Ready Readers series, developed by Elfrieda Hiebert, that aim to channel kids to use phonics knowledge while also reading meaningful texts. And we note with interest the research produced by Wiley Blevins (2017), which suggests that perhaps the emphasis on rhyme has been overstated. Although research has found that strong readers are kids with finesse in rhyming, Blevins suggests that research may overstate the causal power of work with rhyme, when in fact those children's strength may come from their immersion in nursery rhymes, stories, and their comfort with language play as much as their specific skill with rhyme.

While the jury is still out on whether work with rhyme is as crucial to kids' phonological development as many have believed, we feel confident that inviting kids into playful, meaningful exploration of sounds in context is helpful. Engaging kids in repetitive work with familiar poems and nursery rhymes is an easy, accessible, child-friendly way to help them become at home with language, while also learning to hear similarities and small differences in the way words sound. That is important because to read and write, children need to grasp that two words that may sound almost the same are, in fact, entirely different words, with different meanings, and different spellings. The difference between *sat* and *sad* might seem inconsequential to someone who is new to the English language, but the different final sounds in those two words matter. Work with rhyme helps children become attuned to small differences in words that are otherwise very similar.

Segmenting and Blending

Meanwhile, it is also important that your children are progressing in their abilities to segment and to blend. These are important and related skills in phonological development. Kids learn about segmenting first at the more global level as they begin to recognize that within a stream of talk, there are a number of individual words. It is not critical that the child can count the exact number of words in a sentence—for example, if the child hears *all of a sudden* as only two words, *allova* and *sudden*, that isn't cause for concern. But it is important that children develop the ability to break a stream of language into meaningful chunks, or words. That is, at first the child will say a speech stream, "I love my rabbit." Then, as the child develops more phonological awareness, she can hear that speech stream as being made of a few words. If you ask, "What do I write first?" she can isolate the first word: *I.*

Soon the child will also hear if some of those words are composed of syllables. She'll recognize that *rabbit* has two syllables, two beats. She can focus in on just the first of those two syllables, saying to herself, "First I should write *rab.*"

Then the next step, one that O'Connor estimates should begin to happen in November of kindergarten, involves the child learning to segment, which means slowing pronunciation of two- or three-phoneme words. Of course, for children to listen for sounds in words to write with invented spelling, they must learn to segment so they can isolate particular sounds in a word. Therefore, if you lead a writing workshop, many of your children will begin doing this long before November. Isolation, hearing an individual phoneme in a word, is an initial stage of developing full phonemic segmentation and blending. It is segmenting, then, that allows children to hear the first sound in a word to draw on letter-sound knowledge to record that sound. It is segmenting and isolation, again, that allows the child to hear the final sound in a word as well as the first sound. Full segmentation and blending means a child can say each sound in a single-syllable word and put sounds together to pronounce words.

All of this may sound easier than it actually is for the young child. For example, when you ask a child to isolate the first sound in a word, you are asking the child to take something he says and to figure out what was the first thing he said in that word. One way to get children to do this is to have them listen to several words that all start with the same first sound and then to listen also to a word that starts differently. So we might say *jacket, jelly, jump, ham*—and then we ask, "Which one is different?" If children have trouble with that, you'll want to do that work repeatedly. You could also show those words, and point out, "This first letter is different. It makes a different sound." This reinforces the idea of where that sound comes from. You can also get kids to do the talking—*jacket, jelly, jump*. Then say, "How does that feel? Now say *ham*. How does that feel? It makes a bunch of air come out of your mouth. *Ham* starts in a different way than the other words you just said."

This work happens throughout Unit 1, *Making Friends with Letters*, in the kindergarten Units of Study in Phonics when Mabel, the mascot elephant, has lots of *M* stuff in her bed, or when kids look at pictures and decide which of those pictures belong in the *M* book.

It's a more complicated step to divide the pictures into piles based on whether they make the sound of one of two letters. The main work is still the same—isolating the initial sound. Lots of kids will do this very easily. You'll say *monkey, moon* and they'll chime in with *man, money, marshmallow*, and recognize that *donuts* and *dragons* start differently. That shows you they're having no trouble with this skill.

The work of isolating sounds does not require that kids attach that sound to a letter and record that letter—that work is the work of letter-sound correspondence. That work, of course, is required when we ask kids to label. They first need to say the word, to isolate the sound, and then they need to attach a letter to it and even more, to make that letter.

In writing workshop, teachers are encouraged to be sure that it is the child who says *bike* slowly and then isolates the initial /b/ sound. One often sees well-intentioned teachers doing that work for kids, saying, "b/ /b/, what letter says /b/?" as if the teacher is setting kids up to do the work. In fact, that teacher has just done the most important work and she'd be far better off to say to a child, "Say the word *bike*. Say it again. What sound do you hear and feel in the beginning?" What sound do you hear at the start of the word *bike*?"

It is not necessary for kids to master the challenge of isolating and hearing initial sounds before they begin to learn letter names and sounds, nor before they embark on the effort to also hear final sounds. One thing you will notice is that sometimes kids actually confuse beginning and ending sounds—when trying to hear the first sound in *bike* they may say /k/ and even write a *K*. That is happening because the ending sound is, in a way, the most recent sound the child hears as he goes from saying to writing. Point out to this child that he has missed the beginning of the word, and help this child know that yes indeed, he has heard a sound—it's just the final sound.

More often, however, kids will latch onto isolating and hearing initial sounds. If they are writing a story, they will record one sound for each word. "I went to the store" becomes *I W T S* or the label for the sun in his picture is just the letter *S*. At this point, it is time (or past time) to teach the youngster to hear more sounds. Final sounds are especially important because once kids hear first and final sounds, they are shifting from writing letters to writing words, and are working with word boundaries. As soon as kids write with initial and ending sounds, it is time to teach them to leave spaces between their words.

It is important to know that doing this work correctly is almost irrelevant. The child will hear a final /k/ sound and spell it as a *C*. No problem. Now is not the time to aim toward mastery, nor is this really work on letter-sound correspondence. The major learning that is happening as kids begin to isolate, hear, and even to record final sounds is the work of phonemic awareness.

In teaching kids to hear final sounds, you'll find that some kids blur right through the endings of words. They don't find it easy to isolate the sounds because they aren't articulating them. You can ask this child to say *fit* and the child says the sound of /f/. That's a youngster who could benefit from some emphasis on articulating ending sounds. Say, "That word is *fiT*. Can you say the word *fiT*? Say the ending."

Some children have a hard time hearing final sounds. It is common for a phonics curriculum to produce words for children and to ask them to determine whether a particular sound within those words—say the /p/ sound—comes at the beginning of the word, in the middle or at the end. The *P* is early in *pole*, late in *hop*, and some kids need practice figuring that out. In the units we attempt to make listening for ending sounds more concrete and easier to understand. A series of three empty boxes are shown for the word *make*. Children are asked to point to each box saying the sounds in *make*. This activity allows children to realize that the letter *K* is the last sound in the word. It also is a means of teaching how phonemes in a word are blended together to read a word. Remember, at this time we are not asking children to name the letter that represents the sound of the letter *K*. Naming the letter that represents the sound in the box will come later. Now, they are merely locating where they hear the sound.

After establishing an understanding of how to listen for ending sounds using the boxes, directions are given that provide less support. "You are to listen to these words and determine where, in the word, you hear the /p/ sound, for example, *pole and hop*, as mentioned above." Then kids are sent off to touch items in the classroom, saying the name of each item in a way that highlights the final sound: *tabLe*, *ruG*, and so forth.

Two things happen when kids begin to hear medial sounds. Typically, they will hear medial consonants first—and those tend to occur in multisyllable words: *little* (/l/-/d/-/l/). Vowels make up a huge part of the middle of words, and if you teach vowels early, you'll find that kids hear them, especially in single-syllable words. You can teach kids that every syllable has at least one vowel, and certainly every word has a vowel. Encourage kids to add vowels, knowing that it will take them a long time to get those vowels right. There is no reason to postpone instruction on vowels until the day when kids can begin to master them—but do expect to see approximations. By spring of kindergarten, most students are able to isolate beginning, medial, and final sounds in sequence which is full segmentation and means the child is ready to write a letter for each of these sounds.

Most of your children will probably respond to engaging, developmentally appropriate instruction in this. Even children who seem to have entered the kindergarten year with what at first may appear to be zero understanding of phonics will begin to accumulate knowledge and skills. Watch for children who do not seem to learn their *ABCs* and remember that chances are good those children need more preliminary help with phonological awareness.

CONCEPTS ABOUT PRINT

It is not unusual for a parent or a teacher to say, "All of a sudden, he just took off as a reader! One day he wasn't reading and then poof! Like magic, he *was* reading." The truth is that this statement says more about the adult than the child because no, reading development does not occur overnight. When an adult thinks it does, that suggests that the adult may not be aware of the preliminary steps that the child has been taking over time. A good many of those preliminary steps involve the child developing concepts of print that allow her to eventually take flight as a reader.

Think about it. A child is handed a book that is written in English. To be able to read that book, the child needs to turn the book right side up, to notice the cover, then the title page, then page one, and so on. She needs to start on the left and read down the page, reading left to right across the page and making a return sweep to the next line. She needs to know that blobs of print represent words, and that one blob of print is one word. She needs to develop a concept of word (what Donald Bear refers to as *COW*). This concept is demonstrated when the beginning reader can point accurately to a few lines of familiar text, showing that the child has one-to-one correspondence (Clay 1979; Uhry 1999; Bear et al. 2016).

Children will develop concepts of print across all the work you do with reading and writing, as well as phonics. As children come to know familiar books through frequent repeated readings of them in read-aloud and shared reading, they will soon be able to read those books on their own, approximating reading in such a way that watching, you might think they were actually decoding the text. Rereading books, poems, and songs that the child has read before and mastered helps the child coordinate spoken language with print, demonstrating and consolidating her knowledge of how print works. She'll acquire directionality, reading from top to bottom and left to right. She'll become proficient with the return sweep. For a time, words may all run together, boundaries between them blurring, but as the child learns a few high-frequency words, those help to anchor her pointing, as does her emergent knowledge of a few letters and their corresponding sounds.

In writing as in reading, it is easy to watch children's progress as they develop a concept of print. They'll progress from random marks on a page to representational drawings with written labels that are distinct from the drawing. You'll notice that even before children represent any actual letters, their pretend writing will look distinctly different from their drawings. As children learn letters, you'll channel them to label their drawings using initial sounds, and soon, recording as many sounds as they hear. Once a child is able to record more than one sound for a word, you'll channel that child to write sentences in addition to labels. Watch for directionality, encouraging children to write from top to bottom, and from left to right. You should see some letter-to-sound matching, and some evidence of a concept of word as children add spaces between some of their words.

At some point, a child's developing concept of print can get in the way of their writing development because they may begin to recognize that their approximations aren't right, and to yearn to write correctly. Although you'll encourage them to be brave spellers, to write words as best they can, to work with independence, you can also celebrate that their concern for conventions reflects a step ahead in their emerging concept of print.

LETTER-SOUND CORRESPONDENCE

Not every language has an alphabet composed of letters as in English. In the Mandarin writing system, each symbol represents a whole meaning. In some Japanese writing systems, each symbol represents a syllable. In most Western languages, symbols represent *phonemes*, or sounds. The term *the alphabetic principle* refers to the fact that to learn to read and write in a language that relies on symbols to represent phonemes, people need to learn to match a symbol to a phoneme. Understanding the alphabetic principle is critical in learning to read and write English. To assess the child's knowledge of this principle, you can ask a child to read or write a nonsense word. The important thing to note is whether the child reads or writes one symbol for each phoneme. To demonstrate a grasp of the alphabetic principle, the important thing is not that the child matches the *correct* letter to a sound—in fact, the symbol the child records can simply be a squiggle. That squiggle still shows the child grasps that each phoneme is recorded in a mark on the page.

In addition to grasping the alphabetic principle, children need letter-sound knowledge. Phonics programs differ in how they introduce letters and sounds, the pacing of this introduction, the sequence of letters, the emphasis on letter-groups or word parts, the emphasis placed on spelling. But there is consensus around many things.

There is agreement that children need to be able to identify the names of letters and to identify letters in different fonts and cases—and they should be able to identify a letter whether it occurs in isolation or within a string of letters. They need to be able to make letters efficiently and they need to know the sound(s) associated with each letter. How do children learn all this? Again, there is a great deal of consensus within the field that these things are important, while there are still some differences of opinion on how they should be taught.

When teaching a letter's sound, people generally agree that it is important for the child to say a word that starts with that letter, saying that word slowly, listening for the first sound. Children can then be shown the letter that makes that sound. They can say the letter, make the letter in the air or on the page, name the letter, and say the sound associated with the letter. They can talk about what they notice when looking at the letter. Is it tall? Does it contain sticks? Curves? Holes? They can decide which of several items do or do not begin with that letter, and which items do or do not end with that letter. The teacher will, of course, return to this work later, reviewing it many times.

Our first instruction in letter-sound correspondence is embedded within a name study. Children learn specific letters: their names, features, and associated sounds. From the start of kindergarten, children learn that letters have names, are associated with sounds, and are formed a certain way. This instruction implicitly supports phonological awareness and phonemic awareness because it conveys the message that letters and letter patterns represent the sounds of spoken language. Children also listen for first sounds, sorting items that do and do not have this first sound.

Researchers generally agree that it is helpful to teach letters in first-sound activities, such as learning the letter while hearing it as the first sound in a word. Consider, for example, alphabet cards that pair a letter with the first sound of an object. When students learn the alphabet by studying their own and each other's names, they are learning letters by working with the words that are the most meaningful of all to them. Engagement is high, and learning is personal and interpersonal.

There are trade-offs, however. Names are irregularly spelled; they are almost opposite to controlled texts. Then, too, learning letters by associating them with first sounds in names doesn't help children recognize that the /b/ sound, for example, is not just heard at the start of *Bob* or of *ball*, but also at the end of *tub*. Therefore, work with letters-as-first-phonemes needs to be balanced with other work.

As mentioned earlier, learning a letter involves learning the letter's name, its form, and the sound it makes. In kindergarten Unit 1, *Making Friends with Letters*, of the phonics series, the study of names supports not only letter knowledge but also kids' abilities to segment words into syllables and further, to isolate the initial sound. This unit, then, doubles as support for developing phonological awareness and support for learning the alphabetic principle.

Sequence of Letter Study

As O'Connor emphasizes, research is clear that teaching letters in alphabetical order is not the best way to proceed. The two letters that students are most apt to confuse—*B* and *D*—are close to each other in the alphabet and yet should be taught at very different times to make confusion less likely. Then, too, *E* and *I* are the two vowels that are most easily confused—they also need to be separated from each other.

Although there is a lot of consensus on the best sequence for studying letters, there are also some debates. Speech pathologists often emphasize the letters that are easiest to make in your mouth. Occupational therapists argue for students to first learn the letters that are easiest to make on the page. For example, straight-line letters are easier to make than curved letters.

Because we highlight that phonics is for writing, we prioritize letters that are used frequently when writing. We also value whether the name of the letter helps kids to learn that letter's sound. We agree with those who argue that it is wise to begin with high-utility letters—*M, S, T, R*.

We teach vowels on the early side because we want to equip kids with what they need to make words, and every word requires a vowel. Vowels will also require more time to learn, so starting on that work early makes sense to us. We're okay with kids messing about with vowels long before they grasp the full complexity of them. For all those reasons, we tend to agree with researchers who argue that it makes sense to teach a vowel every four or five letters. Beck and Beck (2013), for example, advise that the easiest way to avoid confusion between short-vowel sounds is to provide some distance between the introductions of each vowel. It is easier for children to distinguish *A* and *I* than other vowels, so those are good ones to teach early in the sequence. Beck and Beck, in fact, point out that when looking across three program sequences, two of the three support introducing the vowel *A* within the first four days of letter-sound instruction (47).

The temptation when teaching letters is to teach every single letter, giving equal time to each of those letters. Somewhere in our childhood, many of us came to believe that "a letter a day—or a week—keeps the doctor away." The problem is that the knowledge base upon which phonics instruction is based has developed since then, and expectations for children's reading and writing have escalated too. Although a teacher can feel like it is the ultimate in responsibility for her instruction to plod through the entire alphabet, with children doing similar activities for each and every letter, it is not in fact clear that that is the conscientious, dutiful, responsible thing to do. Remember, most kindergartens expect children to be reading level C/D books by the end of the year. You probably can't still be teaching the alphabet five months into kindergarten if you hope to see that sort of progress during the first year of school.

You'll see that we depart from teaching a letter a week, or even teaching a letter a day, and we encourage you to do so as well. First, you'll see that we devote several days of instruction to the first letter that kids study and similar lengths of time to the next letter. That's because at that point, kids are not simply learning particular letters, they are also learning *how* to learn letters, and grasping concepts such as the fact that there are right ways to make a letter, and that one can study a letter. (What letters are tall? Short? Have tails?) This instruction can also highlight the important pronunciation lessons that kids need to learn so that they don't grow up thinking that a *d* makes the sound "duh" rather than the shorter, more abbreviated /d/.

Meanwhile, once kids have learned a dozen or so letters, we know that things can proceed more quickly. They will have grasped many of the concepts that you embed in your letter instruction. That is, they'll be more comfortable listening to words that begin (or end) with the focused sound. They'll have grasped the

major ideas behind handwriting: top to bottom, left to right, continual strokes most of the time. They'll have learned that most but not all letter names can be linked to the sound associated with that letter.

A second reason that we suggest you deviate from the letter-a-week instruction is so that you can teach your students some other things, returning later to address any letters that still cause confusion. Once youngsters have learned a handful of letters, they need time for consolidated review. They need to *own* what they have been taught, because there can be a big difference between you teaching something and your kids actually feeling like they control that information. The good news is that assessing students' knowledge about letters of the alphabet is easily done, and if more direct instruction and more review is needed, that teaching is not particularly difficult to provide. The best way for youngsters to consolidate and review what they know about letters and sounds is for them to put their knowledge to use as they engage in reading and, especially, in writing. Doing so enhances the transfer of learning to real literacy tasks.

M. J. Adams states, "There is however, no sense in which phonemic awareness training should increase classroom 'drill and skill.' On the contrary, explicit phonemic awareness training is about developing in children the attentional and metacognitive control that renders unnecessary the drill and skill of traditional phonics" (76). You'll see that we begin the year teaching letters in a systematic letter-by-letter way and then shift toward teaching kids to use what they know about letters to begin writing as best they can while using the alphabet chart as a resource as they write.

Letter Formation Pathways

You will need to decide how much time you want to devote to helping kids study the features of letters. That instruction can consume days and weeks. You'll want to think about how much you care whether kids can sort letters into piles—those with holes, those without holes, those with straight lines, those with curvy lines—and about how much time you want to devote to helping kids study the various fonts that can be used to make a particular letter. You will see that we teach kids to study letters in these ways to learn them. Part of the study of a name or a letter in Units of Study in Phonics involves channeling children to notice things such as whether a letter is tall or small, has a tail or does not have a tail. Later when kids observe and notice things about the alphabet, they'll return to descriptions of particular letters, this time noticing the differences and similarities between upper- and lowercase letters.

Still, all in all, we do not prolong this focus as much as some do. We tend to focus on the end product of all this discussion—that is, on helping children write letters efficiently. If a child can look at a letter— say, a *K*—and take a mental picture of that letter in such a way that she can proceed to make that letter without needing to look back and forth between your model and her emerging replica, we think that child won't need to devote a lot of time to sorting and discussing the features of letters. If you help the child follow a letter formation pathway to make a letter, that work (for many, but not all children) will encompass a certain amount of study of the letter.

Although it is important for kids to learn to use efficient and consistent motions to form letters, and we support the use of a formation pathway to help children learn to make letters the "right" way, we also believe that in the end, it is not necessary to drill every child on the correct formation of every letter. After children learn recommended pathways for an armload of letters, they begin to grasp the important principles: writing from left to right, top to bottom, more pull and less push, and when possible, keeping the pen on the page rather than lifting it constantly.

Learning Letters and How to Use an Alphabet Chart

It's important not only that kids learn a repertoire of letters but also that they learn how to learn more letters and to learn more about letters. It's important that this learning can continue outside the phonics classroom and outside the teacher's control. For this reason, it is important to explicitly teach kids how to read and rely on an alphabet chart. In many classrooms, kids know how to chant the parts of the alphabet chart: *A*-apple-/ă/, but they don't necessarily know how to use alphabet charts, nor do they feel inclined to do so. That's a missed opportunity since there is a wealth of important knowledge embedded in an alphabet chart: upper- and lowercase letters, letter-sound correspondence, the features of a letter, whether a letter is a vowel or consonant, and so forth. Children who are taught to care about and use an alphabet chart have their own private tutor close at hand as they read and, especially, as they write.

Of course, as kids learn letters of the alphabet, they are also learning concepts about how letter-sound relationships work. Long before kids are explicitly taught the several sounds a particular vowel makes, for example, kids will begin to grasp that some letters say their own names and others do not, that some make more than one sound (and that reading letters involves trying one way that the letter sounds and then another way), and that letters come in upper- and lowercase and sometimes the upper- and lowercase look the same and sometimes they don't.

HEARING AND RECORDING ALL SOUNDS IN WORDS, STARTING WITH INITIAL SOUNDS

As mentioned earlier, it is important first for kids to learn to isolate and hear initial sounds, then final sounds, and lastly, medial sounds. It is also easier for children to use letters to write than to use them to read. When writing, the child always knows the meaning, so the work with letters and sounds is always contextualized. That is not the case for reading. A child who has spotty knowledge of letters and sounds can feel very much at sea when attempting to decode an unknown word. That is especially difficult if there isn't a picture or sentence context that supplies meaning. The implication of this is that when kids first learn a letter, they're apt to apply that letter to their writing long before they use that letter to support their reading.

Early in kindergarten, many kids can, with help, say a word such as *bed* slowly, listening for the first sound, and then record that sound—a *B* for *bed*. Of course, children will not always use the correct letter for a sound, although their miscues are often logical, if incorrect, as when the child uses a *Y* for the /w/ sound (relying on the name of the letter *Y*) or, applying similar logic, an *H* for the /ch/ digraph sound.

As mentioned earlier, when kids are first listening to words, it is typical for them to begin by hearing one phoneme only and usually it will be the one at the start of the word. As kids are taught more, as they read and write more and as they learn more about letters and sounds, their approximations will begin to more closely match the actual spelling of a word.

But our point for now is that it is far easier to hear and record and work with sounds at the *start* of a word than at the end of the word. After explicitly teaching kids to hear sounds at the start of a word, children will be able to label objects in their writing by using a single letter to represent that initial sound. So at first *bed* is written with just a *B* and then with a *BD*. Following is a chart that explains how sounds are produced for individual consonants and vowels.

M	/m/ is a continuous sound and can be voiced for several seconds without distortion.
T	/t/ makes a stop sound and should only be voiced momentarily.
G	The /g/ sound associated with the word *goat* makes a stop sound and should only be voiced momentarily. You will want to teach that the letter *G* makes more than one sound.
R	/r/ is a continuous sound and can be voiced for several seconds without distortion.
L	/l/ is a continuous sound and can be voiced for several seconds without distortion.
N	/n/ is a continuous sound and can be voiced for several seconds without distortion.
I	All vowels have a continuous sound. You will especially want students to listen for the short vowel in the middle of words.
W	Keep in mind that the sound associated with /w/ is not in its name.
S	/s/ is a continuous sound and can be voiced for several seconds without distortion.
D	/d/ makes a stop sound and should only be voiced momentarily. Two of the most challenging letters are *D* and *B*. One way to teach *D* is to ask what comes after *B*, which is a *C*. You can make a *D* out of a *C*. Or draw a *bed*, with the *B* as the front headboard and the *D* as the backboard. Researchers say that if kids are confusing *D* and *B*, not to worry, it is normal. You will want to teach these at least a week apart.
F	/f/ is a continuous sound and can be voiced for several seconds without distortion.
A	All vowels have a continuous sound. You will especially want students to listen for the short vowel in the middle of words.
V	/v/ is a continuous sound and can be voiced for several seconds without distortion.
P	/p/ makes a stop sound and should only be voiced momentarily.

K	/k/ makes a stop sound and should only be voiced momentarily.
X	/x/ makes a stop sound and should only be voiced momentarily.
E	All vowels have a continuous sound. You will especially want students to listen for the short vowel in the middle of words.
B	/b/ makes a stop sound and should only be voiced momentarily.
Z	/z/ is a continuous sound and can be voiced for several seconds without distortion.
J	/j/ makes a stop sound and should only be voiced momentarily.
O	All vowels have a continuous sound. You will especially want students to listen for the short vowel in the middle of words.
C	The /c/ associated with the word *cat* makes a stop sound and should only be voiced momentarily. You will want to teach that the letter *C* makes more than one sound.
H	Keep in mind that the sound associated with /h/ is not in its name.
U	All vowels have a continuous sound. You will especially want students to listen for the short vowel in the middle of words.
Q	Keep in mind that the sound associated with /q/ is not in its name.
Y	Keep in mind that the sound associated with /y/ is not in its name.

DIGRAPHS AND BLENDS

Once children have learned the sounds that many individual letters make, they can begin to work with two of those letters together. This understanding amounts to more than just learning more sounds. There is conceptual work to be done because now the child, as a reader, needs to learn that he sees *two* letters and doesn't tackle each in isolation but instead, puts the two together so as to do something with them.

Many agree that it is best to teach this concept by teaching digraphs first, as the message is clear to children that when reading or spelling a digraph, it is not one letter but *two* letters in combination that make a single sound. You essentially teach digraphs by asking kids to memorize them. There is no way for a child to make the digraph sounds by combining the letter sounds. Usually people start with the three or four most common digraphs: *SH*, *TH*, *CH*, and sometimes *WH*. It's common to teach these as a batch, all at once, because you are really teaching the concept and they all work the same way. Others suggest teaching one every other day. Occasionally a child will confuse *sh* and *ch* since they sound a bit the same, but if you do some mouth work

with that child, that will help him to grasp the difference. There are other common confusions. Children will substitute the letter *H* for *CH*, relying on the name rather than the associated sound of an *H*. Some substitute a *J* for a *CH*, spelling *chin* like this: *jin*. You'll teach the *WH* blend last, because it is difficult to discern the difference between words that begin with a *WH* and those that start with a *W*.

Generally, people teach these digraphs with an emphasis first on their role at the start of a word. It is helpful to teach words in which the rime is a word. Students can learn that when *CH* is added to the word *at*, a new word is made (Ganske 2014, 168). If children have been learning to add consonant letters to the rime *op* to make words such as *hop* and *pop*, they now learn they can also add digraphs to *op* and make *chop* or *shop*.

Of course, digraphs are also found in the middles and at the ends of words, but sometimes that instruction is postponed until later. There are less frequent digraphs such as *CK* (which only comes at the middle or end of a word). You might wonder if *CK* is a blend rather than a digraph—know that it is *not* a blend because the two letters make one sound. It is unusual because it makes one sound and that one sound is the sound of both letters. Some other unusual and less common digraphs include *PH* and *GH*.

A question comes up when teaching digraphs—and this is actually a larger question when teaching the English spelling system. What about the exceptions? The child who studies that the ch digraph can be associated with the /ch/ sound as in *cheese* will come back with questions: "What about *Charlotte* or *machine* or *school*?" The answer is that you will teach kids the most common sounds that a letter or letter cluster makes, and then you'll invite kids to read and write, and in so doing, to explore the whole wide world of possibilities. Children need to grow up knowing that there are outliers to every pattern. In the end, the child will develop an ear and an eye for which exceptions are permissible, and which ones are not.

Because the conceptual work of combining two letters to make one sound is so important, it's helpful when instruction in digraphs paves the way for instruction in blends. Beginning consonant blends can be grouped into four major categories: both letters represent continuous sounds (*SL, SN, SM, FL*); one continuous sound and one stop sound (*SC, SK, SP, ST, SW, BL, CL, GL, PL, BR, OR, FR, GR, PR*); tricky blends (*DR* and *TR*), and three-letter blends (*STR, SCR, SPL, SPR*). The continuous sound blends are easiest to hear because you can stretch each sound without disturbing either one. Most blends are a combination of one stop and one continuous sound. The continuous sound is often easier to hear from the stop sound.

Some letters in a blend are harder to hear than others. This is especially true of some of the *R* blends such as *tr* and *dr*. The hard part about these is that *D+R* would normally sound like /der/ but instead we say /dr/, which feels more like /jr/. Then, too, there are small differences when saying *tree* versus when saying /chrē/ and for that reason, some children confuse these. This confusion tends to manifest especially in kids' writing, when they spell *truck* as *chruck*, or *drive* as *jrive*. You'll see small-group instruction in *Small Groups to Support Phonics* that addresses these particular mix-ups.

As mentioned earlier, your instruction in blends and digraphs will focus first on initial blends and digraphs, then move to final blends and digraphs, and only after that, to medial blends and digraphs. This might sound confusing—you might wonder if initial blends are different than final blends and the answer is *yes*. Many of the blends that one tends to find at the start or middle of a word do not work at the ends of words. For example, you wouldn't end a word with *BL* (we do have a way to handle that, which is to add a final *E*, as in *bubble*, but that essentially loses the blend of the *BL*). Similarly, you would never see an English word that ends with *PR*. The flip side is also true. There are ending blends that don't appear at the start of words, such as *FT* (*left*), *LT* (*felt*), *LF* (*shelf*), *LP* (*help*), *XT* (*next*), *NT* (*went*), and *PT* (*wept*).

Most children can learn blends and digraphs easily and will quickly see these everywhere. *Brown Bear, Brown Bear* becomes a book of blends and *Sheep in a Jeep* becomes a digraph book with blends. If a child does have trouble, it can help to describe these almost as a math problem: $b + l = $ /bl/.

You'll need to encourage kids to listen for and include blends in their own writing. They will write *bu* for *blue* and you'll want to say to them, "There is more to hear in *blue*. Say *blue* and really listen. There are two sounds in the beginning of *blue*." Become accustomed to saying, "Listen harder. This is a two-letter, two-sound beginning. You heard one of them, but you missed the other. It can be tricky to hear both, but you can do it." Help children know that when a word begins with a blend, they needn't read the word by making each sound in isolation, for example, reading *black* by saying /b/ /l/ /ă/. Instead, the child needs to put the first two sounds together: /bl/.

It is especially problematic if the child tries to read *black* by saying to himself /buh/-/luh/. That is, blending becomes especially tricky if you haven't guarded with care against children adding a *schwa* sound to their understanding of the sound the consonant makes. It is true that some consonants have sounds that are difficult to say without adding the *schwa* (*B* and *T* are examples). But if blending seems more difficult than you think it should be, listen closely to see if it's that misplaced *schwa* that is causing the learner trouble.

PHONOGRAMS, BLENDING, AND WORD BUILDING

Some clarification of terms can help before a discussion of these topics. A *phonogram* is a sequence of letters that includes the vowel and the letters that follow it. It's a sequence that's common to many words. Phonograms may occur in single-syllable words (*at, in, eat, or, ug, ump*), as well as in multisyllable words (*chopsticks*). Cunningham's research has identified the forty-four most common phonograms. People use the term *word family* in at least two distinct ways. Words with the same root word (*play, playmate, playground*) are considered one word family, as are words that share a common phonogram (*boat, coat, throat, float*). Finally, a *rime* consists of a vowel and any consonants that follow it. In the word *rime*, the rime is *ime*. That is, you can use *rime* and *phonogram* interchangeably.

Different phonics researchers give varying amount of priority to students learning phonograms. Pat Cunningham and Tim Rasinski regard this work as absolutely essential to the kindergarten child's development. Marilyn Adams, along with researchers Richard Wylie and Donald Durrell, emphasizes that teaching children just the thirty-seven rimes (*ack, at, it, ell, ing,* and so forth) can allow them to produce 500 words. Wylie and Durrell (1970) also point out that the 1,437 words in the spoken vocabulary of primary-aged children are built out of only 272 rimes.

Instruction in phonograms is usually combined with instruction in "making words," because children learn that they can take *at* and add a whole host of consonants, blends, or digraphs to make all sorts of other words. Think for a moment of the power of this. A study of phonograms exponentially increases kids' word power.

There are a few big things to know about teaching phonograms. First, for schools that are channeling children to begin reading level C books in late winter of kindergarten, instruction in phonograms needs to begin in late fall/early winter of kindergarten, although this remains an instructional focus across a good deal of kindergarten and first grade. Work with phonograms builds on and supports the work that you do with initial consonants and with initial blends and digraphs because you work with onsets and rimes. The initial consonant or blend digraph is the onset. Students are learning then that words can be spelled and read in parts. Youngsters can become more efficient readers and writers when they do not need to read or write in a letter-by-letter way.

That is, when teaching phonograms, you teach children that they can read and write by thinking about word parts or spelling patterns. To read *cat*, the child reads the C, and then the *-at*. That becomes especially important when the word is not *cat* but *cat-erpillar*. When reading multisyllabic words, being able to chunk—*cat-er-pil-lar*—makes progress much faster. The advantage is that, when hoping to write "My dog ate my dad's underpants," the child will not need to tone the message down and write simply, "My dog was bad."

As children explore phonograms, they must learn to hear that small differences in sounds make gigantic differences in meaning. It is at this point that kids' work with *rhyme* (spelled *rhyme*, not *rime*) takes on a written dimension. Written rhyme becomes more important. That is, at first, when kids learn to generate rhyme, this was oral work only and this phonological awareness skill prepares kids for work that will be done with spelling patterns. As they learn phonograms, they begin to write in rhyme. We say to them, "When you hear that two words sound the same, it is a good guess that they are apt to be spelled the same." That, of course, is not always true but with CVC words, it tends to be so. It is meanwhile important to know that whereas blends are taught and learned by phonics, by decoding, phonograms are taught and learned by analogy. That is, now you teach, "What you know about words can help you figure out new words. For example, if you know how to spell *back*, you can figure out how to spell *sack* or *tack* or *track*." Cunningham (1975–76) refers to this as mediated word recognition. She writes that "readers mediate the identification of unfamiliar words by comparing the unknown word to known words and word parts" (127–43).

There is a progression to this work. Generally, it is easiest for kids to start by taking a few high-frequency VC words that they know well—*it*, *at*, *an*, *in*—and realize those words give them power to make many more words. That process involves adding consonants to the start of those words. This is work that Pat Cunningham refers to as "making words" and Tim Rasinski (2008) incorporates into his word ladders, which tend to be a slightly more advanced version of this. Teachers teach making words by giving kids whiteboards or magnetic letters and saying something to them such as, "Start by writing the word *at*. Put a *B* in front. What do you have? Yes, *bat*. Now take away the *B* and add a *C*, what do you have? Yes, *cat*."

After doing this with VC word parts that double as high-frequency words, you'll move on to teach other VC rimes (or word parts). For example, you'll do similar work with *-op*, *-ag*, *-et*, *-ut*, and so forth. Note that these all contain short vowels. You might ask why this work is done first with word parts that revolve around short vowels. Whereas the long vowel sounds have many different ways that their sounds are made, the short-vowel sound tends to be made similarly each time. More specifically, usually the short vowel comes in a closed syllable, which means that the vowel is closed by two consonants, one on either side of it.

Once kids have tapped into the power of making words from VC word parts, the next big step forward in their work with phonograms will occur when they begin to explore VCe word parts. That work is considerably more advanced because it requires a base knowledge of long as well as short vowels. We'll discuss this later, then, after an initial discussion of short and long vowels.

This discussion of phonograms has not included any mention of why some phonics experts give less homage to the importance of phonograms than do others. It is worth noting that in her book *Teaching Word Recognition: Effective Strategies for Students with Learning Difficulties*, O'Connor (2014) includes a section titled "The Problem with Word Families." In this section, she suggests that often good readers enjoy working with word families, but poor readers who practice word families "as the dominant approach to reading" may fail to notice the sequence of letters because what they notice is that the words in a collection of related word all end the same. She argues that the predictable patterns in words can signal to these readers that they do not need to pay attention to letters after the initial consonant, so although the instruction may appear to a teacher to be working because children produce the correct word, they are actually rhyming and not, in her eyes, reading. She argues that when children see those same words away from the context of the word family, they don't always have the word-solving skills they need.

O'Connor and others who argue similarly (this would include Beck) tend to emphasize letter-by-letter blending, referring to this as "cumulative blending." The child reads *cat* by saying the sound associated with the first consonant, then the child says the sound associated with the vowel and blends that sound with the earlier one to create /că/. Then the child reads on. This sort of cumulative blending relies more on work with short vowels out of the context of a rime.

Our position is that yes, readers do need to work with short vowels in isolation, as well as when they are embedded in a word part. It is easier for them to learn *AT* or *IN* or *OP* than for the child to learn the short /ă/, /ĭ/, /ŏ/, but there will be times when a reader encounters a word and needs to decode it in a left-to-right, letter-by-letter way. A knowledge of short vowels in isolation is important to that work, and it is for this reason that we include a kindergarten Unit of Study in Phonics called *Vowel Power*.

On the other hand, in this debate, we tend to lean more toward the emphasis that Cunningham, Rasinski, Fountas and Pinnell, and others place on the value of phonograms than on the worry that kids will give individual letters short shrift by relying on word families. After all, to write as well as to read long words, the ability to break those words into chunks and to spell chunk by chunk will give kids enormous power when they want to record words such as *sandwich*, *fireplace*, and *macaroni*.

SHORT VOWELS

There are various opinions about the best time to begin instruction that high-lights short vowels. Phonics programs that aim to teach one topic at a time and to teach to mastery tend to postpone instruction in short vowels because young children are not apt to master the topic early on. It's complex. We made a different decision. As mentioned earlier, because every single word contains a vowel, we recommend you teach a vowel as the fourth or fifth letter that you teach. The reason to do this is also, for us, that yes, vowels *are* complex, and therefore we want children to have extra time to use and confuse them before they are expected to master them. Also, because vowels are complex, we prefer to distribute that instruction over a longer period of time so that we don't teach one vowel in close proximity to another.

We find it helpful for kids to know from very early on that the alphabet can be divided into vowels and consonants. Similarly, we recommend telling children early on that vowels are a bit tricky because they make more than one sound. They make what is called the *short* sound (like the /ă/ in *at*) and they also say their own letter names. Those are lessons that we teach in the first month of kindergarten while children are involved in a name study. The children's names will inevitably contain vowels, so we teach them in an exposure sort of way, not expecting mastery.

Short vowels will be easier for kids to learn than long vowels because there are so many ways to repre-sent any given long-vowel sound. As mentioned earlier, short *A* and short *I* are good vowels to teach first because they are easy to discriminate, one from the other. It is easiest to teach these first within a study of phonograms. As kids take a high-frequency word such as *it* and add consonants to the start of that word, they are implicitly learning about the short *I* and as they do similar work with *at* and *up*, education in short vowels continues. The vowel is almost always short in any CVC word.

We recommend that you give children a good solid grounding in CVC word families before launch-ing into a study of short vowels outside of word families. This work asks students to look at words not as comprised of two units (the onset *B* and the rime *AG*) but instead, as three units or phonemes (*B-A-G*). Students can come to recognize not only the CVC pattern, but also the CCVC pattern (when the word starts with a blend or digraph) and to anticipate that the vowel within such a pattern will be short.

You'll see that it is in the second half of kindergarten that we suggest you highlight short vowels. It is important to teach kids that word parts such as *-at, -an, -ap*, contain an *A* that sounds like /ă/. In that way, you'll help kids isolate the short vowel phoneme. You'll teach one or two short vowels at a time, making sure to contrast vowels that are distinct from one another. That is, you'll channel students to compare the short *A* to a short *I* first, and you'll steer clear of asking students to contrast the short *E* and the short *I*.

After introducing students to two contrasting short-vowels sounds, it is important to give them oppor-tunities to practice distinguishing, sorting, and using those two sounds. You can channel students to sort using printed words or using pictures, perhaps putting the picture of a cat at the head of one column, of a hill at the top of a second column, and a picture of a nut at the head of a third column (Bear, 169).

You'll start with simple three-letter words that students know from their work with word families, and then move to more complex words involving blends, digraphs, and several syllables.

In a leveled library, very early levels of text, such as levels A, B, C, and D, are full of CVC words, so your introduction of CVC words should roughly coincide with your children's work with those books. Children's work with level A and B texts relies less on decoding and more on picture and pattern support, so it will be their work with level C and D books (more than level A and B books) that requires some knowledge of short vowels.

Then, too, kids need to use short vowels to write in such a way that people can read their writing. As they say words slowly, stretching them out, aiming to record each sound they hear with a letter, they'll need to draw on a knowledge of vowels. That is, if the child writes only *SN* for *sun*, that will be hard for a reader to decipher. The interesting thing is that kids tend not to write with CVC words all that much—but that doesn't mean they won't need short vowels to write. In a healthy writing workshop, kids will write with lots of words such as *dinosaur*, *breakfast*, *away*, and *soccer*. All of those words—and work with any word—require work with vowels.

Short-vowel work receives a spotlight also when your instructional focus shifts to long vowels. This will probably occur fairly early in first grade. Your focus on long vowels will include a revisiting of short vowels as youngsters learn to shift between CVC words and CVCE words.

LONG VOWELS

At first glance, it might seem that long vowels are simpler than short vowels. You say the name of the vowel. There is an *A* in *ate*, an *O* in *hope*, an *I* in *nice*. After all, what could be simpler than using a vowel when the sound with which it's associated is the same as its name? For short vowels, there isn't the same easy match between the letter's name and the associated sound. However, as it turns out, the fact that short vowels don't say their own name is a small challenge compared to the many challenges children encounter when working with long vowels. For once a child learns to associate *A*, *E*, *I*, *O*, and *U* with their associated short-vowel sounds, the relationship between a letter and a short-vowel sound tends to be a consistent one, with one letter making one sound except for the instances such as *R*-controlled vowels.

Meanwhile, although it is true that the sound made by a long vowel is straightforward, figuring out which letters to put on the page to make that sound is far from simple! First, letters do not just make a short and a long sound. Listen, for example, to the sounds of the *A* in these words: *cat, star, came, war, saw, father, stay*. Then, too, take even the instances when a word contains the long *A* sound, for example, as in *date, acorn, weight, steak, play, bait, they*. Each of those words is spelled very differently, and yet each makes the long *A* sound. So, while hearing long vowels is easy, there is more work to be done than simply finding the vowel and saying its name.

It is a big deal for beginning readers to learn first, that vowels have more than one sound, including the most common short-vowel sound and the long, "say their own name" sound. Children will need to learn that the silent *E* at the ends of words acts as a signal, cueing them into the presence of a long vowel earlier in the word. O'Connor points out that about 5% of the most common words could be sounded out if students knew the silent-*E* marker.

Children can be introduced to the long-vowel sound by learning that vowels make several sounds and one of them is the sound of the vowel's own name. In kindergarten, children will typically spell *ape* as *ap*, and then early in first grade, they are taught about the silent *E* that turns a vowel from short to long. (This doesn't work all of the time, but it is a helpful pattern for kids to learn, as long as they know from the start that there are many exceptions.) That is, whereas in kindergarten, the important thing to learn is just that vowels have two sounds, and readers benefit from trying a vowel one way, then another, in first grade, children learn about the CVCe spelling pattern. Learning about the silent *E* provides children with continued work in phonograms and in short vowels, because children will tend to learn long vowels as they appear in phonograms, and as alternatives to short vowels. That is, this teaching will remind kids of CVC as well as CVCe work. Children will write the word *hop*, then add a letter to turn *hop* into *hope*. When teaching children about the silent *E*, it is helpful to mix words with and without silent *E*, as well as words with silent *E* that do and do not have a long-vowel sound, so that students get practice approaching these words with flexibility, learning to think about whether this is an instance when the pattern works in a predictable way.

The good thing is that this learning will pay off in the texts that kids are reading. The books that are written for early readers contain lots of CVC words, and lots of CVCe words. There are also a lot of CVVC words, and that vowel pattern is one that children need to learn in first grade as well. The payoff is big when you teach those patterns.

INFLECTIONAL ENDINGS

The term *inflectional endings* refers to the modifications that are made in a word by adding an ending or altering the base to indicate a grammatical change such as a change in number (*one child, many children*) or in tense (*I am going. I went.*). To make a word into a comparative or superlative word, inflectional endings are added to the word (*fast, faster, fastest*). To show past tense, the inflectional ending *-ed* is often added to a verb. Plurals and possessives, too, result in the addition of an inflectional ending (*one dog, two dogs, the one dog's leash, the two dogs' leashes*).

Obviously, children will continue learning about inflectional endings for most of their elementary school careers. They will not master this topic in first grade! Still, it is important early on for children to understand that *run, runs,* and *running* are versions of the same word. It is helpful for children to begin to learn that sometimes when an ending is added to a word, this involves dropping the final *E* in the word or doubling the last letter. There are few exceptions to the principle that when adding an ending onto a CVC word, the last consonant is doubled. Through word sorts, children can discover some of the guiding principles that inform inflectional endings. They can divide words into those in which there is no change when adding an ending, those in which the *E* is dropped, and those in which the consonant is doubled. Once the sort is complete, children can subdivide the categories into short, long, and other vowels. When that task is complete, ask them to think about the guiding principles that might inform what one does before adding an inflectional ending. You can draw their attention to a set of words such as *hope, hoping,* contrasting those with *rub, rubbing.*

CONTRACTIONS

Level D books contain contractions, so you cannot wait too long before acquainting your children with this form of an abbreviation. You'll want to explain that contractions are made up of two or more words that are combined, with two or more letters being removed in the process. The removed letters are replaced by an apostrophe which acts as a placeholder, marking the spot where the letters were removed. You'll probably want children to study families of contractions, such as those that involve the word *not* (*hasn't, couldn't, isn't,* and so forth) and those that involve the word *will* (*I'll, he'll, we'll*).

VOWEL TEAMS, INCLUDING DIPHTHONGS

Many suggest that vowels are challenging for children because they are commonly found in the middle of words (Beck and Beck 2013). Research tells us that struggling readers pay the most attention to the beginning of words, a little less attention to the ends of words, and the least attention to the middle, where vowel teams usually reside (McCandliss, Cohen, and Dehaene 2003). Early in first grade, children need to be taught that middles matter. Once children turn their attention to the middles of words, they'll find themselves working with vowel teams. This is an important development for first-graders because the words children will encounter in their books will require them to be flexible with vowels, and especially with vowel teams.

Early in first grade, readers discover that a long *E* sound isn't often represented with a CVCe pattern (which is the case for other long vowels). Instead, the long *E* is apt to be represented with either the vowel team *EE* or with the vowel team *EA*. Once children are a bit more experienced as readers, you'll teach them *AI, AY,* and *OA,* a collection of vowel digraphs that usually produce a long-vowel sound. A popular way to teach the sound of vowel digraphs is "When two vowels go walking, the first one does the talking. It says its name. The second vowel keeps its big mouth shut." (Or, "The second vowel keeps quiet.")

The term *diphthong* refers to another sound made by a vowel team. A diphthong starts as one vowel sound and moves to another, causing a subtle change within the sound. Try vocalizing the sound represented by the letters *OI* in words like *coin* or *boil*. You can feel your jaw moving. In contrast, your mouth stays still when you make the sound represented by the letters *ee* in *see* or *keep*. While this is an interesting little fact for teachers, we don't feel that it's necessary for children to use the term *diphthong*. We aim to keep our language simple and clear when teaching children, and the term *vowel team* suffices when describing any group of letters that together represent a vowel sound.

Earlier, I mentioned the phrase, "When two vowels go walking, the first one does the talking." In reality this rule doesn't actually work consistently, and your readers will notice this in many of the high-frequency words they see in their books, such as *friend* and *great*, or the past tense of *read*. Donna Scanlon, Kimberly Anderson, and Joan Sweeney (2017) suggest that a more accurate version of this rule would be, "When two vowels go walking, somebody says something." Regardless, it's more effective to encourage children to be flexible, than to teach any set of rules.

Donna Scanlon and her colleagues have taught us that it helps to teach children to see the vowels in words as decision points and to try one vowel sound, and then another, thinking about which option would make sense. Scanlon refers to this strategy as *vowel flexing*. To teach children to vowel flex, it can be helpful to give them a little order of operations. Teach them to first try the long sound of the first vowel, and then the short sound of the first vowel before doing the same with the second vowel. This is a surprisingly effective strategy and means that children don't necessarily need to remember all the possible sounds a vowel team can make. You'll find that we don't cover every possible combination of letters that produce a vowel sound, for instance, *ie* and *ui* are not explicitly taught, but with this vowel-flexing strategy, readers will usually be able to figure out the sounds those vowel teams make inside words.

There are some vowel teams that kids will not be able to solve using vowel flexing. In those instances, children simply need to know the sounds these vowel teams make. This is true for diphthongs like *OU*, *OW*, *OI*, and *OY*. First-graders learn that these vowel teams make a whole new sound that they'll need to remember. You'll teach children that the vowel teams *OU*, *OW*, and *OO* each represent at least two different sounds, such as /o͝o/ in *book* and /o͞o/ in *school*. You may question teaching vowel teams in this order, particularly diphthongs like *ou* and *ow* that are considered more complex. You'll find that diphthongs such as these are very common in the books first-graders are reading, and teaching these sounds early on will allow children more time to consolidate their learning. Children will later go on to study less common vowel teams *OI/OY*, *EW/UE*, and *AU/AW* taught in pairs that represent the same sound.

MULTISYLLABIC WORDS

As early as kindergarten, children are holding books that contain two- and sometimes, three-syllable words, although in early kindergarten there will be a lot of picture support for those words. The number of multisyllabic words increases dramatically as children move through levels F and on, and the picture support decreases. This challenges readers to work more efficiently to problem solve these longer, tougher words. At earlier stages of reading,

students are taught to be flexible with individual letters and sounds; now, these same readers must learn to be flexible with word parts, especially when solving longer words.

Strong readers are remarkably efficient and flexible in their ability to decode words. In Elizabeth L. Kaye's study of proficient readers (2006), students demonstrated more than sixty different ways of solving words and almost all of these involved using word parts. This, of course, is the fastest way to use visual information when problem solving a multisyllabic word, especially when children are working to read longer stretches of text in more complex books.

But to work with such efficiency, readers have to know a lot about the way words work and must be able to apply this knowledge within texts. Specifically, readers must have a firm understanding of all three parts of the alphabetic principle if they are going to be able to do the word work necessary with longer words. This includes the central understanding that letters have sounds associated with them, and that these letters and letter clusters can change sounds, as in vowel teams like *OW* in words like *now* and *know*. Children also need to realize that there is not always a one-to-one correspondence between the letters that they see and the sounds they hear, as in words like *high*.

Across the phonics units, you'll encourage students to experiment with ways to break multisyllabic words they read (and write). You'll also demonstrate to young readers in ways that teach them to identify parts they know as they move left to right across a word. For example, you'll show students that compound words are comprised of two simpler words and that contractions contain snap words they know well. It's important that you demonstrate how to break words into parts in a variety of ways: looking across longer words from start to end, breaking off a word's inflectional ending, breaking a word between its onset and rime, and breaking a word apart by syllables, perhaps drawing on a knowledge that one breaks double consonants apart in the middle in words like *kitten*. You will notice a deliberate attempt across the phonics lessons to teach children to study a particular feature in a fairly familiar word before working with that feature in an unknown word.

During rug time, across phonics sessions in first grade, you'll invite children to break words by literally cutting them apart and taping those parts back together, or by doing a little demolition, breaking letter cubes apart before building those words back up. As readers, children are learning print strategies that ask them to do just that—break words into parts and blend those parts back together as they try to solve words in their books. By giving kids word cards and scissors, or snap cubes labeled with letters, we hope to make the concepts of segmenting and blending more concrete.

Because reading and writing are reciprocal processes, children will also have opportunities to apply this phonics knowledge to both read and spell longer words. You'll teach writers to clap the syllables to spell words part by part, as well as to stretch longer words aloud, listening for parts and using analogy to draw on words they know to spell unknown words. For example, a child might hear *and* in *standing* or recognize the sound /sh/ or phonogram *AKE* in *milkshake*. In this way, you'll help children move away from sounding out and recording words letter by letter, to be equally efficient when spelling longer words.

R-CONTROLLED VOWELS

Some may question why teaching *R*-controlled vowels occurs so early in our curriculum. Hayes and Flanigan (2014) examined the research of Edward Fry and found that many words in the text read by beginners have *R*-controlled vowel patterns. Fry analyzed a corpus of 17,000 high-frequency words in an effort to determine the frequency of spelling patterns. He found that for vowels, the *R*-controlled vowel was one of the spelling patterns that was most frequent. He recommended teaching the *R*-controlled vowel feature early (120).

Words that contain *R*-controlled vowels are difficult for beginning readers because some of these words tend to look like CVC words (e.g., *car, for*), but the short vowels in these words don't work like the novice reader expects. The *R* changes the sound of the vowel so that whereas *cat* has three sounds or phonemes, *car* has only two. The vowel combines with the *R*—hence the term "*R*-controlled vowel." The good news is that once readers master a word such as *car*, the phonogram from *car* can be used much like the rime in other known words to unlock new words: *star, far*. In the same way, the *or* from *for* can be used to read words such as *horn* and *torn*.

When it comes to writing words, many children will ignore the *R*-controlled vowel in a word, writing *brd* for *bird*. As you read through this *Guide* and examine the sessions in each unit of the TCRWP Units of Study in Phonics, you will notice that one of the key principles we teach is that *every word or every syllable in a word contains at least one vowel*. When writers internalize this principle, they begin to put vowels in words they write.

The *R* after a vowel alters the vowel sound. Take the word *cat*. Insert an *R* before the *T*, and the sound of the *A* changes. In the new word that is made, the original /că/ sound is altered. The new word is not /că/-/r//t/ but cart /c/ /är/ /t/. Some call the *R* a bossy letter, some call it a robber (because the *R* following a vowel robs the sound from the vowel before it).

You'll want to teach students to listen for the sound of *OR* as in *for* and *AR* as in *farm*. But listening and attempting to differentiate sounds won't always work with *R*-controlled vowels. The presence of an *R* in *IR*, *ER*, and *UR* often makes sounds that are indistinguishable, one from the next. Beck and Beck (2013) caution, "The graphemes *ER*, *IR*, and *UR*, as in *her, sir*, and *fur*, all represent the same /er/ phoneme" (43). Therefore, a writer might write *hur* or *hir* when trying to write the word *her*. Who can hear a difference in *bird* and in *herd*? It can be impossible to spell those words by listening for differences in the sounds alone. For students to decide whether *bird* is spelled with an *ir* or an *er*, they need to rely on which looks right to them. The more children read, the better they will become at deciding which version of a word looks correct. For any phoneme with one sound, but many ways to spell it, learning to try different possibilities for representing that phoneme is a crucial reading and writing strategy.

You might be thinking, "How in the world do I teach words with *R*-controlled vowels to beginning readers? They would never understand the technical language in the previous paragraphs." As you examine and teach the Units of Study in Phonics, you will notice that words with *R*-controlled CVC patterns (*her*, *for*) are taught as *snap words* in the same way high-frequency words with spelling patterns that do not conform to phonics rules (*was*, *the*) are taught. Children are exposed to several teaching procedures that enable them to memorize the words. They write the words and check a model to see if they are correct. And, they are given many opportunities to encounter the words in meaningful text. Once students learn the sounds and/or the spelling pattern associated with the *AR*, *ER*, *IR*, *OR*, and *UR* in some high-frequency words that they know well, they can use the sounds of these phonemes to solve words when these same phonemes appear in other one-syllable words or syllables of longer words.

HIGH-FREQUENCY WORDS

Meanwhile, it is never too early for children to begin to "own" a few high-frequency words. Estimates suggest that twenty-five of the most common words make up nearly one-third of the text that beginning readers see and that the hundred most common words make up nearly half of the words in print (Fry, Kress, and Fountoukidis 2000, 2015). The value of students learning to recognize these words in a snap cannot be overstated.

Some people refer to these as *sight words* and some as *high-frequency words*. The children who work with TCRWP's Units of Study in Reading and Writing grow up learning to call these *snap words*, in reference to the fact that they are words they can use "in a snap." There is widespread agreement that kindergartners benefit from learning about fifty high-frequency words that year, and first-graders accelerate and learn one hundred more high-frequency words—for a total of 150 of these words by the end of first grade.

We have drawn on a few word lists to derive the list of fifty—or 150—words to teach. *The Reading Teacher's Book of Lists* is one important source (Kress and Fry 2015), as are the research reports by Hanna and colleagues (1966) and the research conducted by Hillerich (1978), which focuses on the most commonly used words in children's writing. Pat Cunningham's research is a favorite resource for teachers and for us. Cunningham has small, grade-specific books that suggest the high-frequency words that are best taught at each grade level. She includes also high-utility words—words such as *phone* that may not be high in frequency, but that are useful for teaching a particular phoneme (in that case, the initial digraph *PH*).

You'll find only very small differences between the lists of high-frequency words that one source or another recommends, and the truth is that you can make your own decisions over whether you teach *look* in September or in November. Stay within the guidelines forwarded by Fry, Dolch, and Cunningham, and make sure that you teach the words early on that will be foundational to later instruction—whether that instruction is in reading, writing, or phonics. Make sure also that your instruction in high-frequency words aligns to your assessment of them.

The particular sequence that we set forward in Units of Study in Phonics is informed by all of those concerns. For starters, we know that tens of thousands of teachers rely on the high-frequency word assessment that is available at no cost on the TCRWP website. In these phonics units, the sequence of words on that list has been tweaked a bit to be sure that young writers are given the high-frequency words they are apt to need for their writing. The first fifty words that we forward in *Units of Study in Phonics* are also words that are assessed in the assessment lists, A and B, on that high-frequency word assessment. The next hundred words are assessed on lists C–F.

Again, we especially highlighted words that we knew would pay off in children's writing and in their reading. For example, we know that kindergartners will write books that contain lots of labels—whether those are part of a unit that highlights a collection of nature objects or that highlights show-and-tell objects that kids bring from home, we know that youngsters will make good use of high-frequency words such as *look, at,* and *see.* We also know that when kindergartners write personal narratives, they'll make good use of past tense verbs such as *was, had,* and *went,* and of pronouns. When kids are doing procedural writing during the third kindergarten writing unit, *How-To Books: Writing to Teach Others,* the phonics unit highlights high-frequency words students are apt to use then such as *can, do,* and *got.*

Then, too, we highlight the words that Marie Clay has suggested are useful for children reading books at levels A–D. Her list includes *I, a, is, in, am, to, come, like, see, the, my, we, at, here, on, up, look, go, this, it,* and *me.*

We also recommend that you include some concrete words in your high-frequency word instruction— words such as *Mom* and perhaps *soccer* or the *Mets.* It should be obvious why this is important. When teaching children high-frequency words, you want to be sure they understand what it means to learn a word, and if all the words you are highlighting come from the Dolch or Fry list, most of those words are elusive, slippery concepts such as *the, was, at, on.* How helpful it will be to children if you intersperse words that have concrete, tangible meanings, and that are dear to children's hearts: hence the inclusion of words like *Mom, soccer,* the *Mets,* or other words that are locally important.

We sequence instruction in high-frequency words so that students have the words they need for later phonics instruction. All their instruction in phonograms will rely on analogy as the primary method of instruction. You'll want to say to your children, "The words you know have power. You can make so many more words from those words." To do that instruction in the late fall of kindergarten, you'll want your children to "own" VC words such as *an, at, it,* and *in.* You'll soon progress to teaching kids that many CVC words are power words—readers and writers can remove the first consonant and add another to make a new word. Again, you will want your kids to have a bank of words in which that work will pay off: *will* and *all* become very useful indeed once your instruction takes that turn. We also try to teach words together that have a similar pattern.

The important thing to know, in any case, is that there are many reasons why this or that high-frequency word might be taught at a particular time, and those reasons do not revolve solely around the logic of the words' spelling because in some instances, you'll teach these words by memory and by logic. Many of these words *are* easily decoded—words such as *at, but*—and others, while in theory, decodable, actually rely on phonics patterns that are not usually taught early on, making the words less decodable for the early readers who will encounter them frequently. Think, for example, of *look* and *like.* Eventually, children will learn the phonics that informs the spelling of those words, but there are important reasons for them to become acquainted with those words long before they can understand the rationale for their spelling. Other words on the high-frequency word lists contain parts that are easily decoded—and parts that are best learned by memory. The word *from* is an example—children will find the spelling of that word to be logical save for the presence of the O, and you may as well teach that letter to children.

It works best to teach kids just a few snap words each week so that each new word can be practiced both in isolation and also in the context of lists, books, and stories. Many people agree on an approximate number of three to five words a week, with fewer at first. We recommend you teach only half a dozen high-frequency words during your first phonics unit because children need to know a bit about phonemic awareness, concept of word, and letter/sound relationship before they can really begin learning high-frequency words. Later, children can learn closer to three or four words a week. You will see that sometimes we spotlight high-frequency words within a session, but other times we don't detail how this instruction will go, leaving it to you to follow templates for high-frequency word instruction. You'll quickly develop a pattern for teaching high-frequency words and you'll want to rely on that pattern of instruction repeatedly.

The rule of thumb is that to teach kids these words, it helps to give them different ways to interact with the word. Kids see the word, spell the word, study the features of the word, clap the word's syllables, imprint the word on their brains, write the word without looking, check the word, and so forth. Diane Snowball (1999) has detailed these steps: *look, say, spell, cover, write, check.*

Research has shown the importance of children saying the word aloud as they study the word, then say the letters aloud in sequence (Carnine et al. 1997, 2004). In *A Fresh Look at Phonics* (2017), Wiley Blevins argues that when teaching high-frequency words, it's helpful to incorporate as much meaning as possible, using sight, sound, and meaning to learn these words. It is important, then, that students *read* the high-frequency word in context (which usually means a sentence) and that they not only *study, spell* the word, *cover, write,* and *check* the word, but they also *use* the word. That is, they first read the word in a sentence, and they end their initial study of the word by generating the word within a sentence. Most of all, they then use that word as much as possible in meaningful ways, noticing the word's meaning and/or function (e.g., the word *to* cues the reader that a group of words will be added that tells about direction).

It is helpful for students to revisit high-frequency words every day until they have really learned those words. The good thing about these words is they actually *are* high in frequency, so you needn't go to terribly great lengths to give kids lots of opportunities to experience the payoff that comes from knowing even just a handful of words with automaticity. While we have listed fifty high-frequency words in kindergarten and a hundred more in first grade, it is important to remember that especially during reading instruction, both shared and independent, kids are getting exposure to a collection of high-frequency words that far surpasses those that you will teach explicitly. You can increase the chances that implicit learning will happen by prompting and coaching students to notice and name words they see over and over. Even just tiny bits of increased awareness will help your students collect high-frequency words with increasing independence.

Most of all, during both your reading and writing workshop, you will want to encourage your children to think and use words they know in a snap, working with those words with automaticity. Coach them to not sound out those words, to not stretch them out to hear the sounds. Instead, say, "Wait a minute, you know that word! You can write it in a snap. Try it, you'll see." The child will then write the word, and you can coach her to check it. If it isn't yet right—no problem. The child studies the word again, imprints it in her mind by taking a mental picture, and then writes the whole word, start to finish, once again, again checking her efforts afterward. You can also teach and prompt the children to use snap words. This is much easier for children if they have used phonics analysis as part of how they learned a snap word in the first place.

SUPPORTING ENGLISH LANGUAGE LEARNERS IN PHONICS

You may find yourself rejoicing as you note that your English language learners respond beautifully to phonics instruction. Typically, these students will have some success learning to identify letters and to match them to sounds, and often they can develop quick word recognition. They might even show remarkable progress in fluency and accuracy. The problem—and this is alarmingly common—is that too often, they are learning to do this in the absence of comprehension. What is even more alarming is that this absence of comprehension can often go undetected and manifest itself in different, deeper ways as the child progresses into more complicated texts, especially in the content areas.

Luckily, there are quick and easy steps you can take to make sure that phonics instruction is not an isolated or abstract activity for English language learners. In fact, researchers have a consensus around this: to promote language acquisition in general, you'll want to involve children in a rich classroom culture of talk and play, of interactive read-alouds and interactive writing, of structured and unstructured conversations with peers and with you. Be wary, therefore, when pull-out instruction which is meant to give extra support gets in the way of English language learners receiving this critical social support. And be absolutely sure that your English language learners are integrated into the social fabric of your classroom, and especially, are working in strong partner-relationships during reading, writing, and phonics time. You may find instances when triads are especially helpful, perhaps grouping one child who is in the silent stage of language learning with a pair of English-proficient partners.

We suggest that you focus very deliberately on embedding phonics instruction into your writing workshop, and on bringing writing into phonics time. The good thing about this reciprocity is that when a child is using letters and sounds to represent words that capture that child's life story, his or her interests and language and thoughts, then the child will be working with phonics within a context that is saturated in meaning.

You'll want to build English vocabulary around the writing that your children are doing and embed phonics instruction into that work. For example, if a child has drawn a bit of his life, you will want to study those pictures and encourage the child to talk more about what he has put onto the page. For example, if you see some stick figures on the paper, you'll ask, "Who is in your story?" and then help this child label "Mom" or "Abuela." Then you can work on the phonics within the name. While this sort of within-writing support is critical for all your learners, it is even more so for English learners since it allows meaning to drive the phonics. When *they* decide what should go on *their* page, English learners control their meaning and can work with sound-symbol connections within that context.

Interactive writing, similarly, is a time to extend phonics instruction for *all* young learners. To make it truly powerful for English learners, you'll want to tuck in some quick and easy vocabulary instruction. That is, you will want to make sure that you provide phonics support for words that are meaningful to your children. A simple and quick way to do this is to do an internet search for images of words you'll be using and have these ready to display. For example, if you're writing interactively about animals, you'll want pictures of an elephant, a panda, a fish, and a crocodile ready to show your English learners for when you practice those words. Vocabulary instruction during phonics work, in addition to providing context, actually deepens retention of the phonics you're trying to teach. In other words, as you're making the continuous /f/ sound for *fish* and inviting English learners to join you, it is critical to be holding the picture of the fish up for all to see.

Pictures alone won't be as effective as when you also have gestures to go with new words. As you invite kids in joining you to make the continuous /f/ sound for *fish*, for example, bring your palms together and make the gesture for swimming and invite them to do the same. The word *crocodile* means so much more if instead of merely showing the picture you also use your hands and face to mimic the menace of this predator, pointing to teeth and snapping your jaws. In *Visible Learning and the Science of How We Learn*, Hattie and Yates (2014) provide compelling research that shows that using gestures, rather than adding an extra task to what you're doing (or asking kids to do), "actually *reduce[s]* the cognitive load on verbal and memory systems" (142).

While phonological awareness is critical for all children, it will be much more so for English learners. To someone who is new to a language, it is often challenging to isolate where one word ends and another begins in oral language—what new speakers often hear is a steady hum and those syllables, words, and sentences sound mushed together. All the syllable segmenting and onset-rime work that you would do to teach phonological awareness through song and play is especially critical for ELLs who are in the silent phase of language acquisition.

So too, is learning to manipulate the sound system of English crucial. There are many phonemes that exist in English but not in other languages and vice versa. While it is unrealistic and impossible for you to know beforehand the exact sounds that each English learner will need extra support with, there are indeed critical ways to help your English learners with recognizing the sounds that exist in English but may not exist in this child's native language. The most important thing you can do is to *listen* when your ELL speaks to assess the sounds that he or she is confusing and coach immediately. Ask the child to study your mouth and even the placement of your tongue as you make a sound—invite him or her to copy you and practice isolating the tricky sound. Even a small bout of deliberate, multisensory oral practice, either tucked into a one-on-one conference or as part of small-group work, will reap tremendous benefits in helping with pronunciation. And while it may appear to be just that: teaching pronunciation—this oral coaching is actually doing much more. When a child says "Seet down" instead of "Sit down," this can have an impact on writing and spelling because that child may be unable to isolate how the long *E* is different from the short *I*. The ability to hear a sound is critical to encoding (writing) it.

In most cases, knowing how to read and write in a primary language allows for quicker transfer of these skills to a second language. But it is also true that the stages of English spelling development and error patterns may look different when children have learned to read and write in a different language. Children who are used to reading a pictorial script such as Chinese, for example, may remember the letters making up a word, but confuse their order because reading Chinese characters does not require identifying sounds in sequence. Therefore, early learners may write the word *table* as *t-b-a-l-e* until phonological segmenting is firmly in place. Similarly, readers of Arabic, Hebrew, and Urdu are accustomed to reading and writing text from right to left, so what may look like mirror writing or reverse spelling might actually indicate a child's confusion with text directionality in English. Again, it is unrealistic (and often unnecessary) to know all the rules of all other languages to anticipate the exact root of the errors you see. The important thing is to recognize that these errors reveal complex processes of acquisition and transition and *not*—as too many unfortunate classroom anecdotes of ELL experiences reveal—a sign of deficiency.

As with all learning, don't demand mastery—search for and celebrate approximation. Research on second language acquisition talks about the "affective filter" or the self-consciousness that gets in the way of ELLs trying out new words and sounds. But classroom teachers recognize when that filter comes down: during play with friends, during songs and whole-class call-outs, during the privacy of a turn-and-talk when we, the teachers, are not breathing down their necks. For ELLs to truly embrace this new language and its culture, our classrooms need to protect the spaces for play. And song. And talk. This phonics curriculum provides many examples of all of these, and you and your students will surely integrate your own favorites into the culture of your classroom as well.

CHAPTER 3

Nuts and Bolts

Structure, Methods, Schedule, Materials, and
Social Systems for Your Phonics Instruction

ALTHOUGH THESE UNITS OF STUDY in Phonics have been designed to be taught alongside the Teachers College Reading and Writing Project's Units of Study in either reading or writing (or both), they'll work well as long as you are teaching your youngsters to write and inviting them to spell as best they can. If you are working with either a reading or a writing workshop, this curriculum will build on the methods and structures you already use.

STRUCTURE

The phonics workshop, like the reading and writing workshop, has a predictable and simple structure. Every day, you'll teach, assess, and coach students in phonics, doing all this in about twenty minutes. When teaching phonics, there are a handful of specific teaching methods that will weave through much of your instruction, including sorting, dictation, interactive editing, and a version of shared reading that many teachers refer to as "Guess the Covered Word." Although those activities will differ from day to day, there will still be a lot of predictability and consistency across the broad structure of your phonics workshop as a whole.

The structure of workshop teaching has been around for decades and remains the same whether the workshop is in science, writing, or phonics. Either way, the decision to teach through a workshop approach is a decision to provide small bits of intense and direct explicit instruction (a minilesson), followed by much more time for guided practice, and then for students to work with some independence on work they care about while you coach through one-to-one and small-group interactions. That is, each day contains the combination of whole-class, small-group, and one-to-one instruction and also provides opportunities for independent practice.

Although the content changes from day to day and the specific methods that you use to teach and to engage kids change, the predictable structure remains. This predictability is by design, because the fact that one day is similar to another frees you from constant choreography and allows you to teach more responsively. You can understand the environment of a workshop if you think about a pottery workshop, a painter's studio, a researcher's laboratory, a scholar's library. Each of those environments is deliberately kept simple and predictable because it is the work at hand that is changing and complex.

During each day's phonics instruction time, your students will follow a similar schedule and that schedule will resemble the schedule for a reading and a writing workshop, only every portion of the workshop lasts about half as long as it does in a full reading or writing workshop.

Each day's phonics instruction time will include:

- Minilesson (including connection, teaching, active engagement/link)
- Rug time (children work in partners or clubs while you coach)
- Share
- Extensions (optional, quick activities to be tucked into transition moments across the day)

Whether you are teaching a reading workshop, a writing workshop, or a phonics workshop, there are only a handful of methods that you will use repeatedly. The good news is that this means that as you teach and receive coaching in workshop methods within any discipline, that coaching will make you a more skilled teacher across subjects. This means that your immersion in the phonics units will help you develop expertise on methods of teaching that you can draw upon across every part of your day.

A Minilesson

The workshop begins with a brief minilesson—in the phonics units of study, we sometimes call these micro-lessons to highlight the fact that they are markedly briefer than the minilessons that occur within a fifty-minute-long reading or writing workshop. Minilessons are generally given in the classroom meeting space, with kids sitting in assigned rug spots, each beside a long-term partner. This is a time for teacher-led, explicit instruction, so instead of seating students in a circle, you will probably pull them as close as possible. We recommend a few long rows—perhaps four—rather than more shorter rows, because this arrangement allows you to reach your kids more easily. You'll want to sit in a low chair, front and center. If you use technology, don't allow it to displace you by getting you to stand instead of sitting close, or to teach from the periphery, with the screen replacing you.

The goal of a minilesson is to equip students with a strategy that they can use anytime they encounter not only a particular letter or pattern, but other similar words (and sounds). For example, in one lesson you'll teach kids that sometimes letters stick together and their sounds blend together like S and T, making /st/, as in *star*. You won't list every possible combination of consonant clusters, but instead you'll teach children how to notice these parts in words, using blends to read and write new words. In the minilesson, you'll demonstrate how you do this and invite kids to work alongside you.

While the content of minilessons changes from day to day, the architecture remains largely the same. Most reading and writing minilessons contain four component parts (connection, teaching, active engagement, link), but within the abbreviated phonics workshop, we typically combine the active engagement with the link. (We also sometimes add some of the link into the share at the end of the session.)

Connection (approximately 1 minute)

Minilessons begin with a two-part connection. The first part connects the day's teaching to the ongoing work that children have been doing in writing, reading, or phonics time. The main job of this part is to recruit kids' interest.

In the second part of the connection, you name the teaching point of the day. An effective teaching point is crystal clear and usually conveys how that day's session will help children learn something that will take them far. For example, your teaching point might be, "Today I want to remind you that letters can work together to make new sounds, like when an *S* and an *H* come together in *shop*. You can look out for these letters and sounds to help you read and spell tough words." Teaching points generally include a goal and a step-by-step strategy for achieving the goal.

The best way to get a quick sense for the teaching point for any one day's minilesson is to skim the section at the start of every session titled "In This Session." That section always begins with the phrase, "Today you'll . . ." and that first blurb crystallizes the focus for that day's minilesson, capturing that day's teaching point.

Teaching (2–3 minutes)

In the teaching portion of the minilesson, you recruit the kids to join you as you demonstrate the step-by-step way you go about doing something, usually the strategy you shared in the teaching point. For example, you may start a sort or a hunt for words. Although you are usually demonstrating how to do something during this interval, kids learn the most if they are almost doing that work alongside you, so you often launch this by saying, "Will you help me as I . . ." or "Let's work together to . . ." Although you invite kids' participation, once you have kids seeing themselves as participants in the work, you often pull ahead of them and demonstrate the strategy you are teaching, before passing the baton to them in the active engagement portion of your brief minilesson.

Active Engagement/Link (2–3 minutes)

In the active engagement, students try to do what you just demonstrated, or they continue the work you and they began together. Everyone participates—sometimes working with a partner, sometimes working on his or her own. Before signaling to the kids to get started, you might help them think about what they are about to do, saying, "Give me a thumbs up when you have thought of some other words you could add to this list." Once many children have signaled that they have an idea, you will then say, with great urgency, "Turn and talk!" or "Add to your list!"

Youngsters quickly become accustomed to these brief invitations for them to try whatever you've just demonstrated, and it takes just seconds for them to shift from listening or watching to actually doing something or saying something to a partner. Sometimes, then, you may call for several turn-and-talks within a single minilesson. The key is to keep these brief, and to refrain from following them with whole-class conversations. If you do want a student to report back after the partnership conversations, we have found it is often most expeditious for you to do the recap, saying something like, "I heard some of you saying . . ." There may be times when you didn't actually hear what you wish you'd heard, in which case you might say, "I bet many of you were saying . . ."

Sometimes during the active engagement section of a minilesson, children will do a bit of writing. This will usually involve dry erase boards, and often, the writing is done collaboratively by members of a partnership or a rug club. For example, early in the year, first-graders study the names of members of their rug club. To do that, the name is written on a whiteboard and then, the four members of the club share the pen, circling and underlining parts of the name as they point out phonics principles they note in the name under review. In that instance, a group of four children share the job of writing and marking up a single name. Sometimes children do a bit more writing than that, but the writing that children do inside of phonics time will never amount to more than a sentence or, at the most, two.

To abbreviate the writing that kids need to do and channel them to think specifically about phonics, you'll often tell them, "My neighbor, Gerty, who sometimes comes by in the evenings for help with her writing, brought me this piece last night. Will you help me think about how to help her?" If the class helps as a whole, or if partners work together and then you collect ideas from them, all of that can pave the way for the next portion of the minilesson, which is a work time.

The best way to get a quick glimpse into the work that students will be doing during any one day's session is to read the second portion of the "In This Session" blurb at the start of each session's overview. This blurb summarizes, first your teaching point, and then, the work that kids will be doing once the minilesson is over. Usually kids will do some work that continues or extends whatever you taught them during that day's minilesson. They may, for example, begin a sort while they are with you in the minilesson and then continue that sort more independently while in their "rug clubs."

Rug Time

After the minilesson, instead of sending kids off to work independently in spots around the room, you'll keep them close by in your meeting area, often clustering them in partnerships or small groups, which we refer to as *rug clubs*. Time is precious, especially during phonics, so it works well to have fewer transitions. Keeping kids huddled together can save you some valuable minutes.

You'll decide how to pair your children into lasting partnerships. There are advantages to making these ability-based, as when reading partners also become phonics partners. There are also advantages to making these heterogeneous, which may mean that your writing partners become phonics partners. Either way, know that although it might serve students well to pair them with a familiar reading partner and with someone who is working at similar levels of ability, there are also advantages to pairing children who have varied strengths. You'll want to establish partnerships based on your knowledge of the readers and writers in your own class and the dynamic that best suits them.

Expect that the groups you establish will be long-lasting, perhaps even stretching across multiple units, and changing to respond to your collected data and observations. It serves kids well to develop a familiarity when working alongside an established group of peers. With time, rug club members will build a strong rapport with one another, encouraging teamwork, questioning, and risk taking.

You'll find that across any given unit of study in phonics, students will work in either partnerships or in rug clubs, working to apply a growing repertoire of strategies for studying letters, sounds, and word parts. This allows you an opportunity to study what kids know and need and to offer feedback that nudges them to do a bit more. One day, you might prompt rug clubs to listen for the blends at the start of a word, adding them to familiar phonograms to generate and write words on whiteboards. Another day, you'll ask clubs to read from their just-right book baggies to search and use blends to solve and check words, jotting them on Post-its® to study and sort with their clubmates. On another day, they'll listen for these sounds in their own writing, checking each other's words and fixing them up to include the right letters. Expect students to plan, talk, and help each other to learn more about the ways words work.

Share

The share is an abbreviated version of the close of reading and writing workshops. Sometimes the share is an invitation for partnerships to share their work with their larger rug club, and sometimes you draw on the work of a few individual students to make a point to the whole class. Sometimes the whole class participates in a shared song, chant, game, or call-and-response activity based on the work of the day.

Other times, you'll use the share to offer students some additional practice with a particular phonics feature. You might close the workshop with a shared reading of a short text or a quick interactive writing to transfer the phonics work into reading and writing.

You might also extend the focus of the lesson by exploring an exception. For example, after studying words with the long-vowel CVCe pattern, you may offer students a chance to examine words with a silent

E that do not make a long-vowel sound, such as *have*. You'll use these opportunities to remind children to be flexible as readers, using their knowledge of words and patterns to problem solve unknown words.

Extensions

You'll see at the end of nearly all sessions that we suggest a few extensions you could do to give students further opportunities to solidify their understanding of that day's instruction. These are meant to be done at other times of day, often during times of transition. For example, an extension might channel kids to chant a rhyme in which they manipulate initial phonemes or sing a song in which they practice rhyming patterns—while they line up for lunch. Other extensions suggest ways to bring that day's phonics work into reading or writing workshop.

Keep in mind that the extensions we suggest do not necessarily need to be done on the same day as the session with which they are associated. Also, they are not necessarily meant to be taught only once. For example, the chant "Willoughby Wallaby Woo" that students learn in an early extension in the first kindergarten phonics unit is meant to be revisited over and over across the unit and perhaps the whole year. Think of the extensions as ways to keep the phonics work you do during phonics time alive for your students so that they are more likely to transfer their phonics learning to their reading and writing.

Some extensions are more important to the unit's ongoing work than others, and you'll need to plan ahead so you make sure to incorporate these. For example, the Star Name extensions in kindergarten Unit 1, *Making Friends with Letters*, are crucial, because these become the place you teach new letters and sounds rather than in the sessions themselves. Extensions also often introduce new high-frequency words, making them particularly important. Such extensions will display a special "snap word" icon so you can spot them easily.

SPECIAL METHODS IN A PHONICS CURRICULUM

Whether you are teaching in configurations that are whole class, small groups, or one-to-one, there are a handful of methods that you will return to again and again in your phonics curriculum. Just as it is helpful in the reading and writing workshop to hone your skills at teaching or leading groups, at guided reading using learning progressions to help kids self-assess and set goals, at engaging in shared reading—so, too, it is helpful to hone your skills in the activities that will be cornerstones of your phonics curriculum.

In this section, we especially address the use of these activities and accompanying materials:

- "Guess the Covered Word/Word Part"
- Word sorts
- Making words
- Interactive writing and dictations

"Guess the Covered Word"

"Guess the Covered Word" is a method of teaching that gets students to practice word-solving work while engaging in the reading process. When you use this method to teach phonics, you strategically cover up words or parts of words in a text that you and your students read together. To solve a covered word (or word part), students will need to draw on information from a number of sources, using all that information to help them figure out what has been covered. That is, the readers weigh syntax and meaning as they come up with a conjecture about what the word might be, and then as you unveil some of the letters in the word, they draw on visual information as well. The fact that you have covered words or parts of words means you create words that will be hard for the whole class to solve, and that allows you to demonstrate and coach kids on the process of solving those tricky words.

In *Month by Month Phonics for First Grade*, Cunningham (2008) suggests that it can help to use two sticky notes to cover the word, one sticky note covering the first letters of the word up to the first vowel, and the other sticky note covering the rest of the word. She suggests cutting the sticky notes so that the paper is exactly as long as the word, allowing the students to use word length as a source of information.

Whether you do as Cunningham suggests or just use a single Post-it to cover the word and tear or fold bits of it as you reveal parts of the word, you will want to encourage your children to guess the word while it is covered, and you'll want to record the students' guesses. Then you'll gradually reveal the covered part of the word, and give students the opportunity to guess again, using all of the available sources of information to guess: the context of the sentence, the visual features of the word, and the word's length.

When you go to cover some words, make sure that you are covering important words. Covering words that are small details and not as critical to the text will not help students draw on the big gist of the text as they word solve. Cover words that hold a lot of meaning. For example, if a sentence said, "She wore a rose sweater," you'd probably want to cover the word *sweater* rather than the word *rose*. The word *sweater* holds a lot of meaning and is probably reflected in the illustration, thus offering students a chance to use different sources of information. Of course, if you decide that *rose* is very important to the story and allows students to word solve in ways that use a phonics concept you are highlighting, then by all means, cover it.

Covering the entire word can be effective for students who are apt to look at the starts of words when they read, drawing on just that part of the word to guess the entire word without checking to make sure the ending letters match their guess. You'll want these readers to generate more than one possibility for what the covered word might say and then to look at the letters as you reveal them to see which of those possibilities is supported by the letters. Coach students to use all of these sources while helping them make informed guesses. For example, say, "Would that make sense and does that sound right?" as you plug one of their guesses into the sentence. Then say, "Does that look right?" as you guide them to be sure they are checking their conjecture against the revealed letters.

You will not only cover words (or parts of words) that are important to the text, but also ones that channel students to work with the phonics features you want them to practice. The point of this work is to give students repeated practice in work they need to do. This means that you are not just trying to cover up "hard" words. Covering a wide variety of word types will not offer your children focused practice. If you want students to work on blends, be sure all the words you cover have blends, for example.

If you are working on blends, leaving the starting blend uncovered and covering the rest of the word will force students to read the blend and guess what might be next, making sure their guess makes sense and sounds right. In this way, students will use meaning and the starting part of the word—the blend— to guess the ending. Once you uncover the word, they will check their guess.

If you are doing this teaching with a small group of students, you'll want to gather students who have similar needs. Scan your running records or review your notes on your kids, looking for students with similar needs. Perhaps a few of them need to be reminded that their word solving should be informed by a focus on meaning. Does it make sense to plug that word into the text? That is, perhaps these students seem to rely especially on the actual letters—on the visual information—and they continue reading even if the word they generate fits with some of the letters but doesn't make sense with the content of the text.

If those are the needs that you are addressing, you'll want to plan your "Guess the Covered Word" activity in such a way that it channels students to generate possibilities for the covered word based on meaning. On the other hand, if students present themselves differently, your priorities could be just the opposite.

Your knowledge of the levels of books they are reading (and approaching) will tell you about phonics work that they need to do. If readers are moving from level C to D, for example, they will need to practice reading CVC words, and they will need to rely on snap words. Your knowledge of your kids and of the challenges posed by different levels of text complexity will help you decide which words pose particularly important challenges for these readers. If they are reading books that are a bit harder, you may want to help them work with prepositional phrases (without, of course, labeling them as such!).

You can also cover words or parts of words in students' own independent books, getting them to work with partners and essentially go through the same process you did with the group. Or you might have students cover up words for each other and play teacher as they read together. The ultimate goal is to support more active engagement in the reading process and to get students to use and orchestrate all three sources of information—syntax, meaning, visual information—to make an attempt and then check it.

Word Sorts

Sorting is an efficient and engaging way to channel kids to see patterns in the way that letters and sounds work and to make generalizations about those patterns. The potent thing about a sort is that children are engaged in hands-on, manipulative activity. They are given an opportunity to learn by doing. Then, too, instead of you doling out rules to your students, students examine words, listening for sounds and isolating parts. Out of this work, they generate their own knowledge of patterns. That is, their work is analytical instead of synthetic. It will usually be more interesting for children when they have opportunities to come to their own generalizations and conclusions about how words tend to go.

To understand sorting, it is helpful to realize many people use the same routine whether students are sorting based on very simple or more complex principles. Although the content of the work will differ for more emergent or more proficient readers, the process of sorting is the same whether students are emergent readers working with initial sounds in words or transitional readers who are wrestling with different vowel patterns.

Whatever the content of a sort, there are things one does early on to support children in sorting, then things one does later on, followed by things one does toward the end of sorting. For starts, well before the sort begins, teachers "stack the deck," to borrow a phrase from Donald Bear, whose work with sorting sets the standard for us all. The phrase "stack the deck" refers to the fact that after you decide on the purpose of the sort, you control the letters, sounds, or words children will study so that they will be channeled to do the work you determine they should be doing.

Before discussing the step-by-step process of sorting, let's consider, for a moment, the different kinds of sorts. When setting up the sort, you need to decide whether this is an open or a closed sort, and whether you are sorting sounds, patterns, or concepts.

The Nature of the Sort: Open vs. Closed Sorts

Open sorts are open ended, which means that the children aren't told preset categories into which they divide their cards. They simply have a set of picture or word cards, and they work to categorize them into different groups based on what they notice. In an open sort, children read through the word or picture cards (or the letter cards) and develop their own categories. These letters have circles, these don't. These letters are tall, these are not tall. These are consonants, these are vowels.

In a *closed sort*, you will provide headers and the children sort into these categories. Usually in that instance, all of the items in the sort will go under one of the provided headings, although there could be a category for "neither" or "outliers."

It is easier to begin with closed sorts. For example, if you are using sorts to help students think about vowel patterns, a closed sort can allow children to analyze a set of words, contrasting first the long and short sounds, and then contrasting different long-vowel patterns. This will be especially helpful when they get to diphthongs. A closed sort provides the memorable headers that will help children remember these various vowel combinations as they attempt new and challenging words in their own writing. When a child wants to write the word *joyful*, she can write it two ways, *joiful* and *joyful*. Then she will recall the headers and word cards from the /oi/ or /oy/ sort and choose the one that looks right.

Kinds of Things Being Sorted: Sound Sorts, Pattern Sorts, Concept Sorts

Sorts can also be categorized by the thing that is being sorted. In *sound sorts*, students are usually given picture cards without the words written out. Learners pay attention to the sounds (the phonemes) in the word. For example, the picture of a boy goes in the pile for "begins with a B" and the picture of a cat goes in the pile for "begins with a C." Students say the name of the picture (referred to as the keyword) and then place the picture under the appropriate letter heading. More advanced students might do a sound sort with the long- and short-vowel sounds, putting the photo of a lion in one column, the photo of a pin in another. Or they might sort words containing two short-vowel sounds, as when they put the picture cards showing a pin in one pile, and a can in another pile.

Pattern sorts revolve around different kinds of patterns. In these sorts, too, the words are often written out. For example, kids who are in the alphabetic stages benefit from taking a collection of words such as these: *fan, fat, pan, rat*, and sorting them by word family. Yes, they can just look at the spellings to put *rat* and *fat* into the same pile, and that may seem obvious, but for these kids, that can be fruitful work. It is especially fruitful for them if the children abide by Donald Bear's saying, "Say it as you lay it." Bear points out that it is important to train kids into saying every word as they sort that word.

Sometimes the work that students do in a pattern sort doesn't revolve so much around the actual act of sorting words, so much as the act of figuring out the logic behind why the words in each category are spelled as they are. For example, imagine a sort of verbs with *-ing* endings that reveals that sometimes the final consonant is doubled and sometimes it isn't. The challenge in that sort is not so much putting the words in which the final consonant is doubled into one column and those where it is not doubled into the other column. Instead, the challenge is to try to figure out what other patterns in those two columns might allow kids to produce the guiding generalization.

Because the goal of a sort is often for children to analyze the words and come to a realization about the underlying patterns or ways that the letters, sounds, or words work, it is especially important for children to have conversations as they engage in these sorts. Adults will want to ask kids questions such as, "What are you making of this?" and "What ideas are you growing about this" and "How can what you are learning from this sort help you when you are reading and writing?" The talk that accompanies the sort is crucial.

Concept sorts are designed to support concept development and vocabulary. For example, a classic one of these is that students put all the words that are synonyms of *angry* in a pile. The children then organize these words so they rise in intensity from *peeved* to *furious*. In the K–1 Units of Study in Phonics, we haven't channeled children into concept sorts—that will be a part of the second-grade curriculum.

The Step-by-Step Process of Sorting

Often the sort begins with a teacher setting some word cards or picture cards out on the table, saying, "Let's go over these cards to be sure all of you can read them and you know what they mean." Then the children read the words or the picture cards, and there is a discussion about the word. For example, in one example in *Words Their Way*, when Bear and his colleagues (2016) are previewing word cards, they come to the word *bare* and a child describes the word as related to a person who has no hair and is bald. The teacher in that instance extends the conversation to include the concept of *bare feet*. The goal is to make sure that before children sort words, the words become familiar to them.

Often the next thing that happens in a sort is that the teacher might ask students to study the words and to discuss what they notice about them. Teachers might nudge students to study the words with their eyes and with their ears. "What do your ears tell you?" some teachers ask.

Then the teacher gets students started in the sort. Depending on the amount of support the teacher wants to give students in the sorting, the teacher might start and show students how to sort the first item. If this is a picture of a word and the children are asked to decide if the picture represents a word with a short or a long *I*, the teacher might pick up the picture of a spider and say "*Spi-der, spiiiii-der.*" Then, referring to the keyword at the top of that column, the teacher might say, "I hear a long *I*, like in *rice*. Should we put this picture under the picture of rice? *Rice, spider*. They both have a long *I*, don't they?" The teacher might move on to support a second word before leaving the kids to continue this work.

Alternatively, once children have learned to sort, you could simply launch the kids in doing this work with a partner and then you could watch what they do. If the children start shuffling cards into piles silently, not saying the words aloud, you could coach them to remember the advice, "Say it as you lay it."

Either way, once words have been sorted, you will definitely want to nudge kids to look back on the results of their sorts and to think about what they notice. You will probably ask them to check what they have done. Do all the words go in the piles they've put them into? Be sure kids know that the process of checking involves rereading each column.

As kids do this work, be sure that you don't hide the fact that there will be some words that don't go in either category. There are long *I* words, short *I* words, and "other." The English language is full of exceptions, so from the start, welcome conversation about oddball words.

Remember that the most important thing about these sorts is that they generate conversations. Ask children to talk with their partner about what they notice about the words in a column. Channel them to ask each other, "How are these words alike? How are the words over here different? What patterns do we notice?" Ask, also, about the ideas kids now have about whatever the principle is that they've been working with. If the sort was about vowel teams, ask, "What conclusions about the vowel teams do you come to?" "What do you notice about the way these words all sound?" "What do you notice about the way they look?"

When sorting, it is helpful to avoid telling the students the rules. The sort allows students to come to their own conclusions if you lead them through careful questioning.

Making Words

In *Phonics They Use*, Cunningham (2016) provides a sample making-words lesson in which the children have the vowels *A* and *I* and the consonants *C, H, N, P,* and *S*. The teacher has large cards with these letters that match the smaller cards held by the children. These have the uppercase letter on one side and the lowercase letter on the other, with consonants in black and vowels in red. The children use these cards to create three-letter words and learn that by changing the vowel they can create new words (e.g., from *nap* to *nip*). The teacher might say, at one point, "You have the word *nap*. You take a short nap. Change the vowel to make a word for a small bite." Then, after a minute, "You have *nip*. Change the first letter to . . ." By continuing to add and remove letters, you lead children to create a series of three- and four-letter words from these few letters. After making words, children sort their words into patterns including beginning letters, endings, and rhymes.

This activity invites kids to manipulate letters in ways that allow them to make discoveries about how words go. Some refer to this kind of teaching as guided discovery. This activity is informed by the belief that to understand phonics principles, it helps if learners discover those principles on their own, with some guidance, of course.

A making-words lesson is angled to teach a phonics principle. That is, the sequence of words that the teacher asks the children to make helps guide them to learn about a particular phonics principle. For example, Cunningham suggests that a making-words activity designed to support vowels might lead children to make this progression of words: *an, and, Dan, has, had, sad, sand, hand, hands*. These words can be sorted by beginning letter (such as *S or H*), or ending sound, such as *-ad, -an,* or *-and*.

Meanwhile, all making-words lessons teach children that small changes can make big differences in words. As learners move from word to word, they are learning to see words as being made up of parts, and that the order of letters really matters.

Also, because you move students from one word to the next by giving directions that tell children which part of the word to pay attention to and what kind of change to make, the learner begins to learn how to pay attention to words. In other words, when the teacher says, "Use three letters to spell the word *cat*," and then says, "Change the vowel to make *cut*," followed by, "Add one letter to the end of the word to make *cute*," the children who follow those directions learn how to think about words. They are discovering that changing just the vowel in the word can make a completely different word. And, then while changing *cut* to *cute* by adding one letter to the end, kids are learning that the addition of the letter *E*, which they cannot hear, can change the sound of a vowel. These kinds of connections help children gain a more flexible understanding of words and can help make them braver as writers and readers.

Most making-words lessons have three distinct parts. In the first part, children are led to make a series of about ten words. While Pat Cunningham often has children make the words using a set of selected magnetic letters, we often accomplish this same work using a whiteboard. While magnetic letters are extra supportive because one can physically manipulate the letters, distributing little piles of magnetic letters to each of your thirty children can mean a lot of preparation time. That said, you'll probably decide to give a few of your children the added support of working with magnetic letters.

After children have a chance to make a word on their own, you'll post the correct word as a way to give every child feedback. This also gives children practice in checking their work. It is important to make sure that one word is correct before building upon it.

The second part of a making-words lesson invites children to sort words by the phonics principles they have in common. For example, they could sort words by vowel teams, such as *eat*, *beat*, *seat* or *oat*, *boat*, *coat*, or they might sort words that have a common digraph, such as *shot*, *shine*, *shut*.

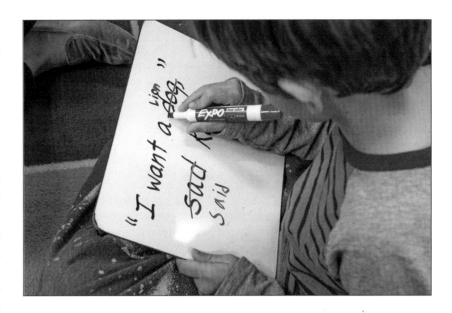

This step is done to help synthesize and make more explicit the learning that the teacher hopes children will carry away with them from any given making-words session. Cunningham also ends her making-words lessons with a secret word, in which kids think of one that can be made from all the letters they've been given. The secret word is challenging and adds scope to the lesson as a whole

The final part of the making-words lesson invites children to imagine using their new phonics discoveries as readers and writers. This is the transfer part of the lesson. This can be done by saying something like, "Imagine it is reading or writing workshop and you needed to read/write this word . . . which word that we made today could help you read or write this word?" When children are asked to transfer their learning to reading, they need to see the target word in a sentence. When they are trying to transfer their learning to writing, they need to hear the target word in a spoken sentence.

Interactive Editing and Dictations

You will notice that interactive editing is one of the mainstay activities that thread through the sessions and the small groups in this phonics series. Whereas we would love to ask kids to edit their own writing for instances when they neglected to write with a blend, a short vowel, or with any one of a number of other things, the problem with that being a mainstay of your phonics classroom is that if you channel kids to pull their most recent story or report from their folders, chances are good that if the child rereads his or her writing, looking for instances when he or she neglected to use a particular phonics principle, that principle won't be evident in the first few lines of the child's writing. The youngster may not have used blends or short vowels or those snap words in the particular passages that she turns to at that moment.

To engineer things so that kids are given practice with the particular phonics concept you have just taught, we pretend that "someone" has written a piece of writing in which that phonics principle needs help. The short vowels are all wrong, or they are missing altogether. Can the youngster help? This activity works especially well because, of course, it makes it more likely that a child will also reread his or her own writing, looking for what works and what doesn't work.

A variation of this is the dictation. Especially as children get older and their writing becomes more fluent, you can also give your kids phonics practice by asking them to take a second and to record something that you dictate to the child. The text can be something you strategically compose to give the youngster the practice he or she needs.

PHONICS ACROSS THE WHOLE DAY

Although phonics time itself will be brief, the good news is that because kids transfer their phonics to their ongoing reading and writing, your students will have no lack of opportunity to practice the phonics they are learning. For example, you'll teach kids that the alphabet contains upper- and lowercase letters, and channel them to notice the use of upper- and lowercase letters on a page from a beloved book. That instruction will then support each child's work during the writing workshop, when the alphabet will be kept close at hand. "Whoopsie," you'll say to one writer. "You've got some uppercase letters thrown into your story in some weird places. See if you can reread and fix that."

Later that day, perhaps your kids will help compose a letter of thanks to the custodian for fixing a crack in the window. As the class works together to decide which words they can write "in a snap" and which require them to say the word slowly, listening for first and later sounds, they're again applying their phonics instruction. All of that work is phonics practice.

The time children spend working on their own important reading and writing projects will be critical to their overall literacy development and specifically to their emerging phonics skills. The truth is that although you may feel daunted by the gigantic list of early literacy concepts that your children need to learn during kindergarten and first grade, it is important to keep in mind that just because kids need to *learn* each of those skills, that doesn't necessarily mean you need to *teach* each of those skills.

Think of a newcomer to this country and of the way he or she picks up customs, language, and ways of being. That newcomer will learn through every pore, at every moment. In the same way, your youngsters will learn from being immersed in the culture of literacy and from being wrapped in the sounds, drama, purposes, and identities that are part of living a literate life. Your teaching will guide, accelerate, and extend that learning, but your kids will learn from each other as well as from you, and they'll learn from all their work and play with written and spoken texts.

How to Fit Phonics into Your Daily Schedule

Teachers sometimes ask us how to fit phonics into their daily schedule, which is already jam-packed with reading, writing, math, read-aloud, and other subjects and activities. Remember that the phonics lesson should only take about twenty minutes a day, along with quick extension activities that you can shoehorn into transitional moments.

Here is one possible schedule that has worked for some teachers. There are many other options that work equally well.

8:30	Morning meeting with interactive writing
8:45	Reading workshop
9:30	Phonics
9:50	Shared reading
10:05	Special
10:45	Math
11:30	Lunch
12:15	Read-aloud
12:30	Writing workshop
1:15	Science or social studies
2:00	Choice
2:45	Phonics extension

The chart below summarizes the approximate amount of time allotted to each subject or activity. This will vary, of course, based on the requirements of your school and district and your students' needs.

Subject/activity	Minutes
Reading	45–60
Writing	45–60
Phonics	20
Read-aloud	15
Shared reading	15
Interactive/shared writing (often merges with morning meeting and/or science/social studies)	10–15
Math	45
Choice/science	45
Phonics extensions/transitions	5–10
Specials/other	40–45

MATERIALS

When teaching phonics, it is easy to feel like your time outside of class is consumed with printing, cutting, filing, and sorting, and inside class, with distributing and collecting little cards and objects and bingo boards and sheets. You'll do yourself a big favor if you develop systems that streamline your work and your students' work with materials. Of course, any system will require more work up front, but these systems will also save you time in the long run.

Getting Your Materials Ready Prior to a Unit

Before starting a unit, you will want to locate, print, prepare, and organize all the materials for the upcoming unit. To do that, look at the Getting Ready sections in each session for detailed information on materials. We suggest you read through these before you teach the unit to see what materials will be required. Also, you will see a complete list of all that you'll need to teach in each unit in the online resources. Note that in these Getting Ready sections in the sessions and in the online resources, we've clarified whether you'll need a class set of a particular material, a set for partners (which means half a class set), a set for clubs (which means a quarter of a class set), or a single teacher copy. For a list of materials for small-group instruction, check the list that accompanies *Small Groups to Support Phonics.*

If you have the Resource Pack that accompanies your grade-level units, many of the cards and other materials you'll need will already be printed. Whether you have the Resource Pack or are printing out everything from the online resources, you will want to think about how you'll store all the sheets and cards. We imagine that you may want to develop an accordion file and/or a notebook for each unit, or for each phonics principle/bend of a unit. Many teachers and staff developers slide most printouts inside plastic covers. They allow kids to write on them with erasable pens, so these handouts can be recycled. Others prefer to leave pages with kids. In this case, use the plastic sleeves to store half a dozen copies of each handout.

You will also want to equip your classroom with the materials that span every unit. For this phonics curriculum, magnetic letters would be useful for some small groups, but there's no need to provision your whole class. Most of the time, partners can work together on a shared whiteboard, but sometimes, each student will need his or her own whiteboard. Students also need whiteboard markers and erasers. We like the markers with erasers attached, but socks work well as erasers, with the added advantage of being good storage spots for markers. We also find that having a few pocket charts—at least one smaller and one larger—can help make quick visual displays to enhance learning.

Plan Systems of Distribution and Collection

It will help you to think carefully about the distribution and collection of materials. We have found that for young kids, you don't really want them holding a set of word cards (or anything else) if you hope their eyes are watching what you are doing. If students need to bring materials to the meeting area, as they will need to do whenever their writing folders or their reading baggies are important for a particular phonics workshop, then you'll want to ask them to sit on those materials until they are needed. Otherwise, you'll tend to distribute materials during the session when the moment comes that students need those materials. You'll want a streamlined system for distributing materials right within a session, while all your children are sitting closely together on the rug. We find that most of the time, the best system is to have preassigned row leaders who know exactly where the materials are always kept for their row of kids, and they can reach those materials right from their spot on the carpet. For example, when you need every partnership to have a whiteboard, you simply say, "Row leaders, will you distribute whiteboards?" and the row leaders reach to a nearby bin for the material they need for their row, and send these materials along the row of kids. Later you say, "Row leaders, will you collect whiteboards?" and the reverse happens. You'll want to avoid dispersing the whiteboards, then the markers, then the erasers as separate actions. Instead, find a way to combine all the related equipment, perhaps by keeping each whiteboard in a baggie with a marker and an eraser, or perhaps by clipping the sock and marker to each board. It will also be easiest if the whiteboards (and other materials) do not have numbers or names.

Those tips go beyond the use of whiteboards. If you need to get a baggie of picture cards to each child or each partnership, we suggest you disperse them systematically as you do with whiteboards. Row leaders can know that the materials are always in the bin near where each row leader sits, and that bin always contains sets of objects. If each child needs picture cards, a paper clip, and a rubber band, then the items that each child needs are all in a baggie and each child takes one baggie. When you need to disperse materials to clubs, you may find it helps to have a club bin, with each bin numbered and clubs knowing which is theirs.

MANAGING THE SOCIAL SYSTEM THAT UNDERGIRDS YOUR PHONICS INSTRUCTION

It will be crucial for children to work most of the time in partnerships or in foursomes, which we refer to as *rug clubs* because these generally work on the rug. You'll decide on the best way to group children—we tend to support pairings in which students' abilities are mixed, but not so mixed that one child functions as the teacher to the other(s). That is, it is helpful if students whose phonics skills are more developed are able to buttress the learning of those whose phonics skills are less strong, but it is not helpful for one student to

dominate so that less proficient students get few opportunities to do the work that they need to do. In Unit 1, *Talking and Thinking about Letters*, of grade 1 phonics, there are special considerations to take into account and it will be important to read the instructions prior to establishing those partnerships.

Your partnerships and rug clubs will presumably last for at least the length of a unit, and then you'll adjust them based on your observations. To streamline the conversations that children have in their partnerships, it will help for you to number each partner. That way, you can say, "Will Partner 1 start and . . ." You'll also probably want to label the members of each club—1, 2, 3, or 4. That way you can help groups get started faster by saying, "Start with Club Member 3 and . . ."

You may want to quietly arrange the numbers so that Partner 1 or Rug Club Member 1 has the strongest phonics skills, so that in times when you want that person to go first, you can make that happen by suggesting Partner/Rug Club Member 1 start. In times when you would prefer that person *not* go first, you can channel Partner 2 to go first.

Of course, children have spots on the rug where they sit, with partners sitting hip to hip and clubs usually comprised of partners in front of (or behind) you. We recommend fewer and longer rows, so you can reach more students. You may also want to teach the middle row of kids to get out of their rug spots and work at a nearby table to give yourself a central aisle from which you can easily reach kids at work.

CHAPTER 4

Small-Group Work in Phonics

E ARLIER IN THIS *GUIDE*, I argued for the importance of keeping your explicit instruction in phonics brief, and then returning to that instruction during transition moments of your day to sing a song, play a game, review high-frequency words, or to otherwise revisit the content of your phonics instruction. You will also teach phonics within your shared reading and interactive writing and during your reading and writing workshop.

This chapter will teach you our most current thinking about small groups in phonics. This thinking is embodied in the sixty-two small groups that fill the pages of *Small Groups to Support Phonics*. Know from the start that some of your small groups will be prompted by assessments that alert you to a child who needs additional help with particular phonics content. For example, if some of your children lag in their letter-sound knowledge, you'll want to provide them with additional opportunities to learn this, and therefore you'll provide small-group instruction for these children. Small groups will also be a way to provide your more proficient students with next-step instruction, and to be sure your whole-class instruction has traction.

THE NUTS AND BOLTS OF PHONICS SMALL GROUPS

We suggest that you think about your small groups in support of phonics as similar to all the other small-group instruction that you teach. We know that you already take every opportunity to provide your students with one-to-one and small-group instruction in reading and writing that both supports the goals of your units and provides particular students with the specific, focused instruction they need. Your phonics small groups will be similar.

When to Teach Small Groups in Phonics

The good news is that workshops are deliberately designed so that they provide you with a context in which you can observe and teach responsively. The predictable, consistent structures of workshop instruction and your emphasis on your kids being able to "carry on" without always needing you to provide minute-to-minute, next-step instructions enable responsive teaching.

However, if you think about the phonics workshop itself, as we have described it, you will probably feel uneasy about the idea of fitting small groups into those workshops, and rightly so. My colleagues and I took years to write just Unit 1 in Units of Study in Phonics—and the reason it was so belabored was that we were torn between competing priorities. It took us years of trial and error to make peace with the fact that important trade-offs would need to be made. Specifically, the only way for a phonics workshop to allow you to provide small-group instruction during that workshop would be for the phonics workshop to be longer than we (and research) believe is necessary, and furthermore for the phonics workshop to channel kids to work on phonics in the same self-sustained way in which they work on their reading and writing.

You'll see that we finally settled on the plan that your small groups in phonics will occur during your reading and writing time. That is, we suggest that your small-group work in phonics take its place alongside small-group work in everything else—in elaboration and structure and voice and clarity and writing process and reading-writing connections and summary, inference, questioning, monitoring for sense, growing theories about characters, and all the rest.

Whew! That's a lot of competition for your limited time to lead small groups! We fervently advise you to *not* let phonics instruction overwhelm all the other important instruction that also needs to be given during those workshops.

This doesn't mean that you won't have some opportunities to pull off more limited, on-the-run responsive teaching during phonics time itself. In a sense, half of every phonics time provides you with opportunities to observe, coach, and teach responsively. That is why we've embedded coaching tips into almost every session.

But the teaching you can do while the whole class engages with any one day's phonics instruction is by design, curtailed. We all know that if your charge is to keep your entire class of twenty-five six-year-olds working for ten minutes on some phonics principle—say, generating a list of words that end with *at*—that is not a context in which you can help a few youngsters who need help with a phonics principle you taught a month earlier.

Just be sure that when you include phonics small groups in your reading and writing workshops, you take care to balance your attention, so your children receive whatever support you think they most need. For example, probably a good proportion of your English language learners will benefit more from small-group work supporting comprehension or vocabulary than from additional work in phonics. Then, too, chances are good that some of your children above all need opportunities to orally rehearse the writing they're about to do. One of our great fears is that by discussing phonics small-group work in some detail, without also developing comprehension in small groups or writing-with-detail small groups, we will inadvertently create an imbalance in your classroom that makes your instruction less, not more, responsive to kids.

Of course, the special power of teaching phonics right smack in the midst of your reading and writing workshop is that this teaching will support students transferring their phonics knowledge into these contexts. That is, if you've taught several lessons during phonics about different short-vowel sounds, and then you notice students who are still omitting vowels from their writing entirely, it will be powerful to gather those students into a small group during writing time and coach them to bring their phonics knowledge into their writing.

The Timing of Small Groups in Phonics

Think of these small groups as lasting five to seven minutes on average, occasionally extending to ten minutes if students are given extensive opportunities to try the work with coaching and feedback. Sometimes when the groups last as long as ten minutes, you'll step away from them midway, after engaging the students in the new work. You can check in with a second group before returning to the first. When small groups are kept brief, it means that you can perhaps follow up one day's small group with another one, a few days later. This also means that kids are not pulled away too much from their ongoing reading and writing to pursue an agenda that you set, rather than their own intentions.

Keeping your small groups brief will require you to take a hard look at your teaching practice and consider places where you might make adjustments. You might film yourself teaching a small group and then play that film, noting places where your teaching runs long. Or you might invite a colleague in to watch you and time what you do, and then share her honest feedback. Perhaps you're accustomed to beginning your small groups by spending a few minutes quizzing students to see if they recall your earlier teaching and you decide to bypass that step. Maybe you regularly ask kids to share their ideas with you one by one, and you instead channel them to share their ideas in partnerships. Whatever your close study turns up, keep in mind that every minute of time you shave off your phonics small groups is an additional minute of time that children get to spend reading, writing, and making meaning off of texts.

Management and Materials for Small Groups

If your small group in phonics requires you to spend more time printing and scissoring and filling little baggies with stuff than you spend teaching the group, something is the matter! The small groups that we suggest are designed so that often they reuse the same materials that you are using with the whole class and in any case, they involve the least amount of materials possible. We have created most of the materials you'll need, and you'll find them in the online resources, and also available in printed form in the grade-level Resource Pack.

During the reading and writing workshop, you'll find it awkward to carry along phonics materials so that you are ready to lead quick small groups. You'll probably want your small-group materials to be stored in a place where you can also imagine leading small groups. Most TCRWP staff developers prefer to lead small groups in the meeting area, often with kids facing the wall, so we can face both the kids and the class beyond them. That way the kids see nothing but us, and we can meanwhile keep an eye on the class. We generally tell kids to sit close enough that we can touch their knees. It's easy for us to scoot back to create a bit more rug space when the moment comes in which kids need to lay their materials out in front of them. Some teachers prefer kidney tables and don't mind the distance these tables create between teacher and students.

When leading small groups, we find it is best to only distribute materials when it is time for kids to use those materials. So if the small group starts with us channeling kids to review something in partners, with each partner holding a chart, we distribute those charts. Then if we want the kids to attend to us for two minutes, we collect the papers that partners are holding, and perhaps write on a whiteboard to give the kids a visual focus. Midway through the small group, if we want kids to focus on their work and not be all-eyes-on-us, we know that distributing materials to them can help kids shift their focus.

Generally, you will want enough materials so that kids can work with partners on whatever work you're asking them to tackle. If they are editing a hypothetical child's writing or sorting some words, if there is only one set of materials for every partnership, you guide kids to work together in a way that channels them to articulate their thinking. The fact that they are talking with a partner allows you to listen in to their thinking without having to interview a child, which can lead you to be roped into a long back-and-forth with that one child. When partners help each other and talk about how to accomplish a task, you are able to tune in to their conversation when you want, and move on easily to listen in on a different partner conversation.

The Composition of Groups—and Their Relation to Assessments

As mentioned earlier, just as a medical doctor tracks key indicators to make sure a child is growing well, you'll track a few key indicators that will let you know when some of your children need an extra leg-up in phonics. We discuss those assessments in Chapter 5, but for now, suffice it to say there will be times when you lead small-group work in phonics to address youngsters who have specific needs that aren't being met by the curriculum alone.

But it is not the case that all your phonics small groups will be designed for kids who need to catch up. Instead, phonics small groups can be like any other small groups—they can ensure that your whole-class instruction transfers to students' independent work, and they can help students go from one level of work to the next. So if you are teaching a phonics unit on the silent E in which you teach children that words are spelled in ways that signal when a vowel is long, then during the writing workshop you may decide to convene a brief small group to ask, "What's up? Why am I not seeing you signaling when your words contain long vowels?" That is, some of your small groups will represent your effort to make sure that your whole-class phonics instruction is sticking, influencing what your students do during other parts of the day as readers and writers.

All your students deserve some small-group instruction. For some, help with comprehension will be especially important, or with using writerly techniques that a mentor author uses, or with using academic language to talk about a character's personality. For others, small-group work in contractions or digraphs or short vowels or high-frequency words will matter more. But either way, small groups are meant as assessment-based instruction designed to take kids farther, and all children will receive some of this instruction.

It is important that your small groups are flexible. Rather than grouping students together into small groups by color or by bird name (despite the creative labels, we all knew that the *Bald Eagles* were reading at a higher level than the *Seagulls*), you'll want the membership of your small groups to respond to your students' needs. Kids develop in idiosyncratic ways. You will not want to create a long-lasting ability-based small group composed of all your youngsters who are reading and writing below grade level. As we wrote earlier, the end goal is not differentiation for the sake of it. Instead the goal is to accelerate each child's learning, to give each child an education that is aligned to that child's particular, individual ways of representing knowledge and of engaging with texts, in a way that is rigorous and compelling and subject to revision, as children change and grow.

IT IS HELPFUL FOR CHILDREN TO BE AS ACTIVE AND INTERACTIVE AS POSSIBLE DURING SMALL GROUPS.

Small groups fulfill a different but complementary function to minilessons. During your minilessons, a fair proportion of instruction involves your children listening to you. In small groups, the priority needs to be for children to be active and interactive and for you to listen to them. Your direct talking to kids might occupy 10% of the total time in a small group, but no more. Mostly, you take a back seat. You get learners doing something they wouldn't have done without you, and you shift between observing, coaching, and scaffolding. The goal is to get them working independently, so they do one thing, then the next, without waiting for your support and feedback at every step.

Because you can only coach if you can set children up with a lot of semi-self–directed work to do, instead of asking them to work with one word and then wait for you to give them the next word, you're more apt to distribute a set of six picture cards and invite students to work through the entire set. If a child works with just one of those cards and then looks to you for support with the next card, be ready to signal, "Keep going." You may want to have a clipboard on hand just so you can say, "Keep going while I watch you work." Be ready to embrace approximation. To keep your children working with support of a partner, not needing you to confirm each action, you will need to allow kids to work as best they can, imperfectly, before you coach into their work. That is, if the activity you imagine involves a child picking up one magnetic letter after another, saying its name and sound, then placing the letter on an alphabet chart, you may need to allow children to simply match magnetic letters with the letters on the chart for a bit, skipping the step of naming the letter or producing its sound. That way you encourage children to not expect your assistance with each letter. Once the child is carrying on with independence, you can coach that youngster to add another step to the activity. "Say the letter's name." you can coach.

Then, too, if a child finishes that work early, you'll want to have ongoing work on hand for the child to turn to. We generally suggest you ask students to bring their book baggie or writing folder with them to the small group, because when they finish early, they can always try to bring the phonics principle they just practiced to bear on their ongoing work.

The important thing to remember is that you will want to do everything possible to decentralize small groups so that as many children as possible are working alongside each other. Although it may be tempting to keep kids on a tighter leash so you can be sure their work doesn't contain errors, you need to accept that approximation is how people learn. Think of how children learn to play a sport or to play a musical instrument: there will inevitably be a lot of imperfect work along those learning pathways, and learning anything in literacy will be no different. In small groups, you'll launch kids to work as best they can, knowing their work will be approximations, and you will coach into their work in ways that lead not to correctness, necessarily, but to continual improvement. We'll explore this concept in more depth later, but for now, know that small groups provide an opportunity for your students to learn through singing, talking, acting out, reading and writing books, jotting on a whiteboard, and manipulating magnetic letters, words, pictures, objects, and the like. They need to be active and interactive, so you can observe and coach.

YOU'LL BENEFIT FROM HAVING A PREDICTABLE PLAN FOR HOW SMALL GROUPS TEND TO PROCEED.

I recommend that your small groups follow a predictable structure, or architecture. Let me explain. As you know, for almost two decades now, every minilesson that my colleagues and I have ever written has followed a consistent architecture. That architecture is based on important principles such as the value of gradually releasing scaffolds as kids become more independent, and teaching through demonstration, followed by guided practice, and then independent practice. The architecture of minilessons has hard-wired the pattern of "I do, we do, you do" into every day's instruction.

I believe it has been helpful to rely on this architecture. Youngsters know what to expect when they participate in a minilesson. You can invent new minilessons or discuss ways to adapt an existing minilesson with your colleagues, using the consistent architecture and the shared vocabulary to support your analytic thinking about the minilesson.

As you will see, we have designed a similar but different architecture for small-group work, and we hope this architecture will be equally helpful.

In doing this, we have again tried to be sure the teaching is founded on solid principles about how kids learn. First and foremost, we've tried to be sure that the small groups are *not* similar to minilessons. This is a different, separate form of teaching, and for us, it is especially crucial that you get learners doing something they wouldn't have done without you and your coaching.

We recommend that within a five- to seven-minute small group, you include some, but not all, of the following component parts. You'll see in our small-group write-ups that we often combine parts or skip them altogether, depending on what kind of instruction the group calls for.

- **Rally Them.** You convey the reason for the teaching that you are about to do, building students' commitment to the work and their sense of how it will fit with their ongoing work. This usually involves saying a few sentences.

- **Activate Phonics.** You involve students in a quick warm-up that gets them doing some work that reminds them of prior phonics learning. For example, students may work in pairs to reread a vowel chart.

- **Launch Them.** You detail the work students will do to engage with the phonics principle. Then the kids get started.

- **Work Side by Side.** You may play an active role in the work, supporting students' work.

- **Challenge Them.** You may intercede to either lift the level of the work all students do, or to channel them to continue the work, only now with less support.

- **Teach toward Tomorrow.** You convey ways in which the content of the small group can affect students' ongoing work as readers or writers. You may channel them to apply the phonics principle to their ongoing reading and writing.

Rally Them

Think about how you start your small-group work. Might your pattern be to start with, "I've called you over to do some sorting," or "You need to practice your vowels," or "Let's play a word game"? We've come to believe that those aren't the ideal ways to start a small group. We suggest that when possible, you try to rally your kids around the importance of the group.

Think of this as your opportunity to give the tiniest keynote address imaginable. For instance, if you gathered a group of students who needed to remember to use the correct vowel when writing, you might start the group by saying, "Writers, I know you've been studying vowel power during phonics time. But here's the thing. Vowel power is also super-important when you write because *every* word needs at least one vowel. To make your writing easy for people to read, you need to use the correct vowel. When you want to say, 'I'll give you a *hat*,' you wouldn't want to mix up the vowels and accidentally say, 'I'll give you a *hit*.'"

Another time, you might want kids to think about medial vowels, saying, "If you think about a sandwich, there are usually two pieces of bread—and the good part is what's in the middle: cheese, tuna, chicken, PB and J. Imagine if your sandwich had nothing in the middle, if it was only bread. That wouldn't even be a sandwich! What's in the middle matters, right? That's true for sandwiches, and it is also true for words."

If the work you'll ask children to do seems like a game, we don't recommend you say, "Let's play a game." Instead, we suggest you talk about the value of the work you are asking students to do. You might say, "The books you are reading lately have a LOT of big words, don't they? To help make your word-solving muscles even stronger, I have a game I want to suggest."

Regardless of what technique you try, you'll want to keep the rally brief, so it takes up less than thirty seconds of your small group.

Activate Phonics

A phonics small group often includes a time early on when you want to remind the students of some phonics content you have already taught them. That way, when you ask kids to apply or practice that content, it is fresh in their minds. We think that it is best if you don't spend time reiterating that phonics content or going over it with them. Small groups are more potent if instead, you set kids up to activate that knowledge themselves, perhaps by reviewing it with each other, by reading over a chart, and so forth.

You will see that we have developed a handful of methods to help students activate their phonics knowledge. Perhaps the simplest way is to distribute copies of a familiar chart, perhaps the "Blends and Digraphs" chart, and invite students to reread it together, doing so in a way that reminds them of the salient features of that concept. You could opt to lead them in that reread, but we think that when possible, it is best to decentralize that work. If you give a copy of the chart to each partnership and ask the kids to work together to reread and review the sheet, you are then free to listen in and coach.

Of course, there are many phonics principles your class could be reviewing. The small group may be designed to channel students to use high-frequency words in sentences, in which case you might suggest they simply read over a list of those words, sorting them into two piles: "Words I Can Read in a Snap" and "Words I'm Still Learning." Another time, you might pass out scraps of paper numbered 1 through 5, and then show students a set of picture cards that illustrate a particular phonics concept (e.g., picture cards of words with different short-vowel sounds), and ask them to jot down the word for each picture. After they do that, you might point out the correct spelling of each word and ask students to check which of the vowels they'd had a harder time with.

This portion of your small-group work has an additional benefit. While students are activating their phonics knowledge, you get an opportunity for formative assessment. Imagine if you asked students to write a series of words containing *R*-controlled vowels: *star*, *dirt*, *butter*. You could take note of which students wrote the *R*-controlled vowels correctly, which chose the wrong vowel sounds, and which omitted the vowel entirely. That on-the-run assessment could give you insight into how you'd coach kids as they work in the small group. Perhaps one child will need reminders to check the vowel sound to make sure it's correct, while another will need reminders to include a vowel. This quick assessment can also let you know if the work is a bit too easy for a child in the group, in which case you might send that child back to his reading/writing spot. Conversely, it can let you know if the work is perhaps too challenging and if a student would benefit from a more foundational small group.

One way to make it more likely that kids are engaged and active in this portion of your small group is to be sure that each child or partnership has hold of the resources. That is, if a vowel chart is reviewed during the "Activate Phonics" part of the small group, it is best if each partnership has a copy and partners are encouraged to read through it in pairs. If the teacher instead leads and all children chime in, often some kids just float along on the group's conversation.

Launch Them

Think of this as your chance to get kids going on the work at hand. The launch is generally brief, though it occasionally includes a bit of new teaching that you'll ask students to draw on as they read or write.

You might share with students some writing done by another child (we often use our imaginary neighbor, Gerty, whose writing tends to be riddled with the kinds of predictable errors we're seeing in kids' writing). You then invite them to reread the writing on the lookout for Gerty's errors, correcting them. Another day, you will involve the group in doing a sort, or in labeling copies of a familiar picture book.

Try hard to make the launch more about getting started and doing than it is about giving long-winded directions.

Work Side by Side

Sometimes, you'll find that when you launch kids into their work, you help them get started by doing a bit of demonstration or some heavier coaching. We call this portion of the lesson working side by side, because it will feel more like you're doing the work alongside the kids.

We recommend you keep this chunk of the lesson brief, just a minute or so. That way, kids will still have a good deal of time to try the work on their own, with your support. For instance, if your small group is about noticing that even though past-tense words may have endings that sound different, but the endings of the words can still be spelled the same, you might show students how you began the job of correcting a text that contains misspelled endings, and then have them correct *playd*, *wantid*, and *lookt* on their own.

When you're planning out the small groups you'll teach, think carefully about the level of scaffolding your students will need. If a group calls for you to work side by side with students at first, and you feel your students are ready to give it a go on their own or in partnerships, you might bypass this stage and instead launch students directly into the work.

Challenge Them

At this part of the lesson, you decrease the level of scaffolding and/or rally kids to tackle another step in their work. If up to this point, you've been doing a bit of demonstration, showing students how you edit Gerty's writing for predictable errors, this is the moment where you'll hand additional pages of Gerty's writing over to students, inviting them to continue the work of reading her writing, noticing errors, and correcting them.

It should feel as if all kids are active during this part of a small group. Previously, group members may have sorted picture cards according to their short vowel, and now you ask students to record words on a whiteboard. You might send children off in partnerships to do a beats walk, touching objects around the classroom and then clapping or snapping the beats. "Carpet: two claps. Dinosaur: three claps." Then again, you might channel kids to pull out their own writing, turn to a page where they need to add words, say the words slowly and catch the first sound, and then write the letter that makes that sound. Regardless of how you ask kids to participate, it should feel like kids are the ones doing the heavy lifting.

We recommend that usually children work in pairs, since this allows you access to check in with one child after another without necessarily engaging each child in a more belabored Q & A. This will allow you to shift your attention from one child to another more quickly, and to coach based on what you see. This coaching will tend to involve lean prompts (e.g., "Do that again!" "Check this one. Reread it."), as well as next-step direction, and will not tend to involve back-and-forth discussions.

Along with other prompts, you might include some that channel kids to self-assess their work. "Is that a real word or a pretend word?" "Does that make sense and look right?" It is helpful to nudge your students to self-assess when you notice an error, as well as at times when the work is well done. This keeps children self-monitoring, and makes it less likely that kids will rely on your questions as a way to know that there is something they need to monitor.

You can be certain that the time will come when you coach a child to try something, and it falls flat. Most likely, that time will come in your first few days of teaching phonics small groups. In this case, it's great to try a different sort of coaching, or to try coaching similarly with a different word/sentence. There will be times when your repeated attempts at coaching don't yield anything from a child. In this situation, it is often wise to say, "Do you want to see me do it? Watch me," and to then offer a brief demonstration, showing the child how you do what it is you had been hoping the child would do. Afterward, you might debrief and name for the student what you did.

Teach toward Tomorrow

If you are familiar with the Units of Study in writing and reading, the "Teach toward Tomorrow" section of the phonics small groups will feel especially similar to the link in your minilessons. This is your opportunity to remind students of what they've learned and to set them up to continue applying the focus principle to their ongoing reading and writing work. If students just edited Gerty's writing for short vowels, you might say, "Writers, this work with Gerty's writing should help you with *your* writing—today and every day. You'll see I've marked a page of your writing with a pink Post-it. Before you continue with today's writing, will you reread that page, checking that you've included short vowels when needed? You'll need to do a bit of fixing up. Then, continue your writing, but keep these tricky short vowels in mind as you work."

If students were reading a shared text, paying attention to the middles of their words, you might say, "You look ready to get going on some reading! Be sure to check the *whole* word from start to end, and remember, the middles matter! Right now, take out one of the books from your baggie and start reading on your own. When you read words in a sentence, and something doesn't make sense, you can tell yourself to try again. Get started!"

You might also ask the members in the group to teach others what they learned. Partnerships that just studied tricky pairs of high-frequency words could teach one another how they'll remember their tricky sets of words.

One way to increase the likelihood that the work kids do in a small group makes a lasting impact is if there's an artifact that remains long after the group is over. A reminder Post-it or a minichart can help. After a small group on double-checking yourself using another strategy, you might leave behind a Post-it that says, "Does it look right? *Sl-eep. Sleep!*"

Other Supports

At the end of many phonics small-group lessons, you'll see a box that overviews additional supports. These boxes contain several categories of supports: replications, prerequisites, extensions, and related lessons from elsewhere in the curriculum that could provide additional support to the members of your small group.

Replicate: Here you'll find suggestions for ways you can teach a similar small group, with new phonics content. For instance, if you've just taught a small group on writing with digraphs, you'll find a suggestion for how you could reteach that lesson using a new text to support writing with blends. The texts and materials you need to do that replication are often included in the online resources.

Preteach ▼: You may find yourself in the midst of teaching a group and realize that one or more students don't yet have the prerequisite skills to participate successfully in the group. If you've just begun the group, you might want to send the child back to his independent work, and if you are well into the group, you might just let him continue to participate. Either way, plan to meet with the child again to provide more foundational support. In the Preteach section, we list resources you can draw upon, including sessions and extensions from units, to help you plan this kind of instruction.

Note that we code these resources like this: "Gr 1, Unit 2, Sess. 3, Ext. 1: Watching Out for Words with a Long *A* Sound and Silent *E*" indicates Grade 1, Book 2, Session 3, Extension 1.

Extend ▲: The *Extend* suggestions provide additional supports or added challenge for teaching the same phonics concept. For instance, you might follow up a small group in which students sort words with different long-vowel patterns with a lesson that asks students to draw on that knowledge to engage in some shared editing. These are coded in the same way as the preteach resources.

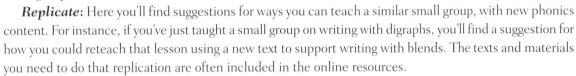

OTHER SUPPORTS

Replicate: You can replicate this group as you teach new high-frequency words. Add new words to children's word pouches and invite them to try this exercise so that they get practice reading and using the new words in the context of a sentence.

▼ **Small Group 46:** "Learning Words in a Snap"

▼ **Gr K, Unit 1, Sess. 16, Ext. 1:** Building Sentences

▼ **Gr K, Unit 1, Sess. 16, Ext. 2:** Making a New Book for the Classroom Library

▲ **Gr K, Unit 2, Sess. 6, Ext. 2:** Making a Class *R* Book

Keep in mind that everyone need not stay with a small group for the entire time. Sometimes, you'll begin a group by checking in on what students already know, as when you ask children to read over a list of words containing digraphs. If you note early in the group that one of the children you've gathered seems to have aced these, you might send that child off to read or write while you teach the remaining children.

BALANCING PHONICS SMALL GROUPS WITHIN YOUR READING AND WRITING WORKSHOPS

During a reading or writing workshop, the teacher's role resembles that of the circus performer who rushes about, giving a few more turns to spinning plates. The performer gets one plate spinning, then another, then another. Soon there are several plates spinning all at once. David Spathaky had a particular knack for this. He holds the Guinness World Record for spinning 108 plates simultaneously in Bangkok, Thailand, in 1996.

It's easy for a teacher to feel as if you've got 108 plates spinning during your reading and writing workshops. You've got twenty-eight students in front of you, each with individual needs. In one short time period, you need to help some students cultivate strong reading and writing habits—reading multiple books, writing across pages, rereading and revising when finished. You meanwhile need to support other students coming up with something to say or read. You're helping still more students to write with clear structures, or with elaboration, or with voice. And, you're helping all students strengthen their grasp of conventions, so their writing becomes increasingly easy to read. It will be challenging to attend to all these important goals, while you also help students become more proficient in phonics.

In one day's writing workshop with your kindergartners, for instance, you could teach a small group on generating ideas for information books, another on elaborating on facts, and yet another small group on hearing and writing more sounds in words. Similarly, within any one day's reading workshop, you might lead a guided reading group designed to help a small group of students move up a reading level, and then help another group of readers to grow ideas about characters or to monitor for meaning or to determine what lesson the characters are learning. Then you might help yet another group become more flexible with *R*-controlled vowels.

The good news is that even if the phonics small groups that you lead during the reading and writing workshop are not perfect, the fact that this instruction occurs during reading and writing time sends a huge message to your students.

THE SPECIAL ROLE—AND CHALLENGE—OF COACHING WITHIN SMALL GROUPS

In his book *Visible Learning*, researcher John Hattie (2009) reports on a mega-study in which he reviewed findings on how we can help learners escalate their achievement in any field—golf, music, writing, teaching, or vowel flexibility. Hattie found that a lot of things that we expected would pay off actually have a negligible effect on student learning, and that there are just a handful of methods that actually make an absolutely gigantic, head-spinning difference. Learners progress when they believe that their teacher has absolute confidence in their abilities to do so. When teachers see more in a learner than that learner sees in himself or herself, that accelerates achievement.

Then, too, learners progress when they receive feedback. And it is not just any feedback that matters, it is the feedback that is given by a teacher who watches learners in the act of attempting to do something that is ambitious and yet within their grasp. The teacher watches, thinks about next steps, and then gives feedback to help the learner progress toward those next steps.

Best of all, the teacher continues to watch, and if the learner does not progress, the teacher regards that as feedback on her teaching, and thinks, "How could I do a better job of helping this learner move forward?"

So feedback is a very big deal. And it is especially helpful if it is delivered close to the activity itself, and if the learner has time to correct his or her practice right away based on the feedback.

This means that it is really helpful for teachers to be prepared to coach as students work with partners, and that is equally true whether this occurs during the active engagement section of a minilesson, during rug time, or during students' ongoing engagement as readers and writers. It is especially helpful if teachers think of lean prompts they can say frequently enough that kids internalize those prompts and begin to say them to themselves. "Look all the way across the word." "Double-check the ending." "Check to see if that makes sense."

In all the small groups we have detailed, you get students engaged in doing some work and in talking with a partner or a rug club about what they are doing, and that visible learning allows you to listen in on a child's thinking, and to be in a position to coach.

Assessing Your Students' Phonics Development

WHEN TEACHING, it helps to have crystal clear goals for your students and a way to track your students' progress toward achieving those goals so that you can teach responsively. John Hattie's research provides mountains of data to support this (2009). He collected data from studies involving twenty million students to understand the ways that instruction most effectively accelerates students' progress. His results show that one of the most important things teachers can do is to work toward crystal clear goals for students and to track and be informed by students' progress toward those goals.

THE NATURE AND NORMS OF ASSESSMENT

To think about an assessment system that could best undergird Units of Study in Phonics, my colleagues and I reviewed assessments used by many existing phonics programs. Time and again, we found ourselves thinking, "Is this realistic to expect teachers to do?" We wondered how possible it is to conduct, say, eight separate assessments on each of your twenty-five (or more) children just to learn each child's level of phonemic awareness—and to then do the same for half a dozen other phonics skills. And then there is the rest of reading and writing to assess, as well! Our concern was that if the system for collecting data was overwhelming, you might spend all your time and energy simply giving assessments. In that case, you wouldn't have time or the energy to mine those assessments for insights that could guide your teaching, let alone to do the responsive teaching that your children need! We worried, too, that if you have more assessments to complete than you could possibly pull off, you might do some and not others. The result might be that you'd end up with an overall assessment package that's unbalanced and therefore unhelpful. We concluded that a more streamlined phonics assessment option is essential.

We found ourselves asking a second question also: "Do phonics assessments have to be so test-like? Can they be more engaging and more similar to the phonics work children do as they read and write?" We concluded that we would try to make the assessments close to the phonics work that children do in reading, writing, and phonics time.

A Guide to the Phonics Units of Study, Grades K–1

Finally, to develop assessments, we needed to figure out the norms against which these assessments gauge progress. To say a five- or six-year-old is "on track" in phonics, whose standards would we rely on? Kindergarten is optional in many parts of this country, and when it does exist, it is sometimes half day and sometimes full day. Perhaps for that reason, most phonics assessments are relatively unspecific until late first grade and sometimes until second grade. The diffuse standards are complicated by the fact that the Common Core State Standards are no longer widely accepted across the United States. States that do embrace those standards have for the most part revised them. This makes it challenging to find a single iteration of the standards that can become a basis for assessment.

Still, there are some grounds for saying a child is or is not "on track." For starts, one can look at the revisions to the Common Core. New York State's latest iteration of them, which is similar to the revisions we are seeing in many states, expects kindergarten students to develop a foundation in phonological awareness, a knowledge of the alphabetic code, and strong concepts of print. Kindergartners are expected to write in such a way that they produce the primary sound for most consonants and short-vowel sounds, and to spell simple words phonetically, drawing on a knowledge of letter-sound relationships. The newest revision of New York State's version of the Common Core also suggests that kindergartners should be able to decode short-vowel words with common spellings. This version doesn't ask kindergartners to show control of blends or digraphs.

By first grade, New York's newest revision of the CCSS expects kids to know letter-sound correspondence for common blends and digraphs, to decode long-vowel sounds using both the silent *E* and vowel teams, and to be able to decode regularly spelled one- and two-syllable words. First-graders are expected to use conventional spelling for words with common spelling patterns and for some frequently occurring irregular words, and to spell untaught words phonetically. They are expected to recognize simple suffixes (*-s, -ed*), and to become familiar with the basics of end punctuation. That adds up to a tall order!

Another way to think about expectations is to think about the levels of text complexity that students are expected to handle at certain grade levels, and the implications those levels have on what students need to know and be able to do in phonics. Of course, different school districts will align themselves with different progressions of levels of text complexity. Many of the districts with which we work especially closely expect children who are on benchmark to leave kindergarten reading level D books and to leave first grade reading level I books. Your school district may have different expectations for reading levels, in which case your expectations for phonics can be altered in corresponding ways. Usually, however, differences of opinion revolve around the question of what should be asked of kindergartners. There is more of a consensus that children are on track if they leave second grade able to read level M books, making it more important that first-graders reach benchmark levels close to level I. The larger point is that it is possible to use text levels, the characteristics of those texts, and the work readers need to be able to do to read those texts as a standard for phonics development.

The following chart provides a snapshot of the big work readers need to do at corresponding phases of development and reading levels. It can help you set expectations for phonics based on what you expect children to be able to do in reading. The first column lists the phases of reading development described by researchers such as Frith (1985) and Ehri (1994). Phases I and II are mostly the work of kindergarten, and Phase III, the work of first grade. We've included the reading levels that coincide with each phase. The column on the right is our effort to specify the work readers need to do completely at those particular levels of text and those phases of development.

The Big Work for Readers at Various Phases of Development

Phase of Reading Development	Approximate Grade Level(s)	Corresponding Reading Levels	Major Reading Behaviors and Skills
Phase I (Logographic Stage)	Kindergarten	A–B	• The child does not necessarily recall letters/words from one day to the next, but she knows a small collection of about 7 high-frequency words. She can find these words in a text. • The child does not yet attend to salient features when learning new words and needs many exposures to a word in order to learn it. • The child matches spoken words to printed words.
Phase II (Rudimentary Alphabetic) Transitional	Kindergarten	C–D	• The child knows more high-frequency words, around 20, and doesn't need to see words as many times to learn them. • The child knows most letters and sounds. • The child attends to beginnings and endings in words. • When reading, the child begins to integrate sources of information, making sure words look right, sound right, and make sense.
Phase III (Alphabetic)	First Grade	E–H	• The child is able to learn words after a few exposures. • The child knows all letters/sounds and is becoming aware of irregularities of some letters and their sounds in words. The child understands some letters combine to make sounds in words (blends, digraphs, vowel teams). • The child attends to internal parts of words, as well as beginnings and endings. • The child checks through words, syllable by syllable, rather than letter by letter.

Of course, the other question one needs to ask is what the purpose is for assessing kindergarten and first-graders in their phonics development. We argue that the purpose of these assessments is to check whether a child is developing phonics skills, and whether the skills are developing progressively so that you can shift your vigilance to other aspects of her development. It is also helpful for you to be able to see when phonics instruction isn't sticking so that you can give that youngster an extra hand now, rather than waiting. This heads-up, then, should not lead to poor grades on a report card or to a child being labeled, but instead, it can lead to a child receiving extra, targeted help.

For students for whom reading, writing, speaking, and listening appear to be progressing at pace, a detailed analysis of each minute portion of that child's knowledge of phonics is not usually necessary, as long as the child's knowledge base is growing every day. On the other hand, if a student's progress is worrying or puzzling you, you may want to conduct more detailed assessments to better understand what may be going on. But chances are good that if you notice early on that a child needs some shoring up in a particular area, a rapid response from you can make a world of difference. These efficient assessments will give you the information you need, in most cases, while still being realistic in their demands on your and your students' time.

A SUMMARY OF THE RECOMMENDED ASSESSMENTS

After studying and trying out lots of possible phonics assessments and variations of them, we've compiled efficient, engaging assessments to accompany this series—five that you will use with every kindergarten child and, assuming those children "test out" of those five assessments, two that you'll use for children once they are in first grade. Of course, some first-graders will need to be tested on the initial five assessments. Each assessment focuses on a different aspect of phonics development, and each will help you ascertain whether the child is making progress in that area and whether she is roughly on par for the grade and for the time of year. You will see that we recommend giving these assessments toward the end of particular phonics units, roughly speaking.

What follows are the nuts and bolts of using the phonics assessment tools. As you study these, keep in mind the goal is for these assessments to provide signals that indicate when a child's progress in phonics is not what you'd hope for so that you can remedy matters straight away. Note that if you follow the Units of Study for Teaching Reading, some of the tools will be familiar, because they are suggested reading assessments as well. You'll be able to mine the results from these to support both your phonics and your reading instruction, further streamlining the assessment process.

Following is a list of assessment tools for kindergarten and first grade, followed by a more detailed explanation of each assessment. An asterisk indicates an assessment that is also recommended in the Units of Study for Teaching Reading. Of course, we also hope you are conducting other reading and writing assessments, including especially running records of your children's reading.

Kindergarten Assessment Tools

Assessing Letter-Sound Correspondence: "Do You Know Your *ABCs*?"*

- Identifying letter names of upper and lowercase letters

- Identifying sound(s) associated with each letter

Assessing Concepts About Print: "Help Your Teacher Read a Book"*

- Demonstrating knowledge of the "rules of the road" of print: text orientation, directionality, spacing, letter versus word, and the stop-and-go marks of punctuation

Assessing Phonological Awareness, Blending, and Segmenting: "Robot Talk"

- Combining parts of compound words, syllables in words, and individual phonemes into a whole word
- Segmenting compound words, syllables in words, and individual phonemes in words

Assessing Developmental Spelling: "Help Mabel Label a Picture Book: *A Birthday Party*"

- Recording initial consonants, final consonants, medial short vowels, and blends and digraphs when writing labels for items in pictures of a wordless book

Assessing Snap Words: "Emptying Your Snap Word Pouch"*

- Reading high-frequency and other important words with automaticity
- Writing high-frequency and other important words with automaticity

First-Grade Assessment Tools

Assessing Developmental Spelling: "Help Rasheed Label a Picture Book: *My Dog Max*"

- Recording features in a format that matches expectations for end of kindergarten/start of first grade: initial consonants, final consonants, medial short vowels, and blends and digraphs when writing labels for items in pictures of a wordless book

Assessing Developmental Spelling: "Help Rasheed Write a Picture Book: *My Stick Ball Game*"

- Recording CVCe words, endings, advanced blends and digraphs, CVVC words, diphthongs, and *R*-controlled vowels to fill in the blanks in sentences for a picture book.

Assessing Snap Words: "Blacking Out Your Word Wall"*

- Reading high-frequency and other important words with automaticity
- Writing high-frequency and other important words with automaticity

Assess letter-sound correspondence, concepts about print, or phonological awareness only if a child demonstrates weakness in one of these areas, or if he or she did not pass the assessment in kindergarten.

Explaining the Assessment Tools

Assessing Letter-Sound Correspondence: "Do You Know Your *ABC*s?"

This assessment tool is used to determine whether children know the names of the letters, the sounds of the letters, and how each letter looks in both upper- and lowercase form. As indicated previously, this assessment may be familiar to some of you since it is also recommended as part of Units of Study for Teaching Reading.

It used to be that kindergarten teachers assumed that kindergarten was the place where children learned their *ABCs*. These days, a fair percentage of you will find that half of your incoming kindergartners already control a hefty collection of letters. Some researchers have shown that when children enter kindergarten knowing ten or more letters, chances are very good that they'll quickly learn the rest of their letters and sounds.

You will want to collect letter-identification information on all your students at the start of the year. You might use the system we recommend in the Units of Study for Teaching Reading; you'll find those materials included in the assessment tools. In this assessment, you show each child uppercase and lowercase letters, out of order, and with no picture support, and you ask them to name each letter and say its sound. Also included in the tools are scoring recommendations and implications.

We recommend devising a system so that you keep information on each student's letter knowledge readily available as you confer. For example, you could decide to keep a record sheet that is shared with (and discussed with) the child. This could take the form of an alphabet chart for each student, with that chart being kept in each child's folder. On each student's alphabet chart, you could highlight the letters that child has *named* correctly and highlight the keyword picture for each letter that the child has *sounded* correctly. Because this will be kept close at hand, you can regularly record instances when you notice the child has learned another letter. This chart will help to guide your conferences, nudging you to engage the child in working with letters he or she does not yet know.

When you identify children who have very little knowledge of the alphabet, it's crucial that you don't wait before giving those children extra opportunities to work with the alphabet. In our book *Small Groups to Support Phonics*, you'll find practical suggestions for small-group work to support letter knowledge and letter-sound correspondence. In addition, tap the power of environmental print, shared texts, and especially children's writing to help them learn more about the alphabet as soon as possible. You might also assess that child's phonological awareness, blending, and segmenting, because chances are good that this child will also need some shoring up in this area.

You will also want to use the data from your group as a whole to identify patterns to inform your instruction in the first phonics unit. If you notice, for example, that most children in your class know most of their letters and sounds, you'll progress through the first unit at a faster clip than if many students know very few letters.

Children who know all the representative letter sounds no longer need this assessment. They are on track, or ahead, and you have learned already what you need to know from this test. For those who are not yet demonstrating this, continue to pull out this assessment at frequent intervals, marking off more representative letters as you see the child use them. A knowledge of sound-letter correspondence will be critical for all your children, but don't be alarmed over a little confusion (such as letter *b–d* mixups that linger a bit).

Assessing Concepts About Print: "Help Your Teacher Read a Book"

We sometimes see kindergarten teachers who spend the first month of the school year meeting with individual children to figure out what each knows before they launch their planned curriculum. We caution against this! Don't postpone beginning your phonics instruction until you've given each and every assessment. With concepts about print in particular, we recommend assessing for this after you've taught Unit 1, *Making Friends with Letters*, likely about six weeks into the school year. Even if your students come to school unsure how to handle books, chances are they'll pick up this concept and so much more, simply through immersion in their daily work. The concepts about print information that you would gather at the very start of the year won't really have a bearing on how you'll proceed through Unit 1, anyhow, so just start.

If you teach the Units of Study for Teaching Reading, you may be familiar with the full, thirteen-point assessment recommended in those materials. That assessment uses a series of questions, based on the work of Marie Clay. One option is to follow that full assessment. You can find this at the Teachers College Reading and Writing Project Website, in the assessments section, or in the online resources of this book.

However, it is probably not necessary to give the full assessment to each child. You can instead ask children a few questions that reveal their levels of text awareness. As you circulate from child to child during reading time, you might ask:

- "Can you help me read this book? Where should I start?" (left-to-right directionality)

- Read a page, point to the last line, and say, "Now where should I go?" (turn the page, top to bottom)

- Find a page with multiple lines of print. Read the first line, then point to the last word. Ask, "Now where should I go?" (return sweep)

- Show a page and ask, "Can you show me a word?" Then ask, "Can you show me a letter?" (concept of word, concept of letter)

If the child answers these questions correctly, you might stop there, because the child's concepts about print are on track. If you still have concerns, give the full assessment to pinpoint specific areas of trouble. You'll find more specific considerations about scoring and analyzing your children's scores at various points in the year with the assessment tools. In *Small Groups to Support Phonics*, you'll find suggestions for targeted concepts about print instruction to help children who need it.

Assessing Phonological Awareness, Blending, and Segmenting: "Robot Talk"

As discussed in Chapter 2, "Anticipate, Observe, and Support Phonics Development," children need to be able to orally blend parts of compound words, syllables, and individual phonemes into words and to segment words into those same word parts. These phonological skills provide a necessary foundation for readers and writers. Only when children are able to hear parts of words and blend them together to say a word can they solve words as readers (blending). Only when they can hear a word and segment it into parts orally can they record the spellings of a word as they write (segmenting).

We recommend giving this assessment to children individually, perhaps first to children you think might struggle with phonemic awareness. You will probably start giving this assessment in the fall of kindergarten. In the first part of the assessment, you say a series of action words, broken apart into phonemes, so that you sound like a robot. The child's job is to blend those phonemes back together, say the word, and do the action. You'll start with a blending task of medium difficulty, and, based on whether the child can do this correctly, you'll give him a harder or an easier challenge. We recommend starting with the mid-level difficulty as this can abbreviate the assessment for children who have no problem with their phonological skills and given that this assessment is done one to one with each child, it's helpful to save moments when you can.

Segmenting is part two of the assessment. Its procedure is nearly identical to the blending portion of the assessment, only in reverse. This time, you show a child a picture card featuring an activity. The child's job will be to segment the word, saying it in robot talk. You will assess the child's ability to do this, and then, for fun, you'll put the word together, and do the action.

If a child's skill in blending is weak, we recommend not assessing segmenting for now. We have found that most children who struggle with blending are not ready for segmenting. Support the child in blending and give the segmenting assessment once her blending skills are stronger. You'll find small groups to support blending, segmenting, and phoneme manipulation in Chapter 1 of *Small Groups to Support Phonics*. You'll also see extensions that support these skills in the early units. Have the child repeat these extensions as often as possible, perhaps with a partner during times of transition. You might also recruit the child's parents to engage in robot talk or other blending games at home. Be sure you reassess within another few weeks. If a teacher in your school has had training with Orton-Gillingham, ask that teacher for extra support or coaching.

Assessing Developmental Spelling: "Help Mabel/Rasheed Make a Picture Book"

As you teach children about the ways letters work together, you will need to check to see if they can write certain key features of words correctly. This assessment will show the extent to which children have mastered the phonics features, rules, and elements. It will show you whether children are transferring their phonics instruction to their writing (of course, you will also want to look at their everyday writing, too!).

In the kindergarten version of this assessment, Mabel's book, *My Birthday Party*, you ask children to label drawings, which is something they presumably do every day in the writing workshop. The labels you will ask for have been carefully selected to reveal the child's facility with particular phonics concepts. We expect you will use this assessment several times over the course of the year, comparing a child's results each time to check for growth. You may use the same assessment each time, because young children often thrive on repetition, and familiarity with the story won't affect the results of the assessment. However, you are welcome to use the same words we chose, and place them in a story of your own. If you write a true story from your class, that will surely engage your youngsters!

For first grade, we have developed two assessments, both featuring Rasheed. The first, *My Dog Max*, assesses end-of-kindergarten (start of first grade) phonics features, the same features as those that are assessed in Mabel's story. Children will be labeling drawings, as in the kindergarten assessment. Whether and how you use this version is up to you. If you know most of your students are comfortable with these phonics concepts, and if they are already writing sentences rather than labeling, you might skip this version

FIG. 5–1 Tommy's assessment

altogether. Or, you might only give it to a small group of children who haven't mastered the kindergarten phonics knowledge.

For the second first-grade assessment, *My Stick Ball Game,* we have chosen a different set of words, selected to assess children's understanding of the phonics concepts you hope they will master by the end of the school year. For this assessment, children will fill in the blanks in sentences (rather than writing labels), so this first-grade assessment, like kindergarten, is aligned to what they'll be doing in the writing workshop. As with the kindergarten assessment, if you give this assessment more than once, it's fine to use the same story. Or, if you wish, you can place the words we chose into a story of your own, or you can choose new words that test the same features. Either way, you'll be able to use our scoring system so that the results of each assessment are comparable.

Included with the assessment tools are the particulars of when we suggest giving these assessments, how to score them, and how to analyze the scores so you understand if children are on track at various points in the school year. We invite you to use these assessments in ways that will give you the most valuable information, depending on the needs of your students. If you'd like to give them more or less frequently, that's perfectly fine. We intend this set of assessment tools not to be a rigid system or something that will take up inordinate amounts of precious instructional time, but to be an engaging, helpful way for you to

FIG. 5–2 Julian's assessment

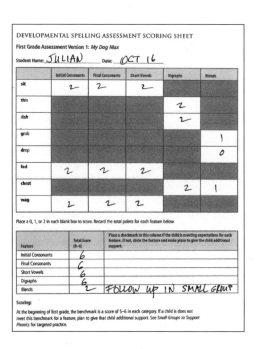

DEVELOPMENTAL SPELLING ASSESSMENT SCORING SHEET

Kindergarten Assessment: *A Birthday Party*

Student Name: Tommy   Date: May 1

	Initial Consonants	Final Consonants	Short Vowels	Digraphs	Blends
dress					1
pet	2	2	2		
chips				2	
wish				2	
frog					2
box	2	2	2		
clap					1
thanks				2	
hug	2	2	1		

Place a 0, 1, or 2 in each blank box to score. Record the total points for each feature below.

Feature	Total Score (0–6)	Place a checkmark in this column if the child is meeting expectations for this time of year, based on the benchmarks chart. If not, circle the feature and make plans to give the child additional support.
Initial Consonants	6	✓
Final Consonants	6	✓
Short Vowels	5	✓ (review short a, short u)
Digraphs		✓
Blends		✓ (review -dr, -cl)

DEVELOPMENTAL SPELLING ASSESSMENT SCORING SHEET

First Grade Assessment Version 1: *My Dog Max*

Student Name: JULIAN   Date: OCT 16

	Initial Consonants	Final Consonants	Short Vowels	Digraphs	Blends
sit	2	2	2		
thin				2	
dish				2	
grab					1
drop					0
fed	2	2	2		
chest				2	1
wag	2	2	2		

Place a 0, 1, or 2 in each blank box to score. Record the total points for each feature below.

Feature	Total Score (0–6)	Place a checkmark in this column if the child is meeting expectations for each feature. If not, circle the feature and make plans to give the child additional support.
Initial Consonants	6	
Final Consonants	6	
Short Vowels	6	
Digraphs	6	
Blends	2	FOLLOW UP IN SMALL GROUP

Scoring:

At the beginning of first grade, the benchmark is a score of 5–6 in each category. If a child does not meet this benchmark for a feature, plan to give that child additional support. See *Small Groups to Support Phonics* for targeted practice.

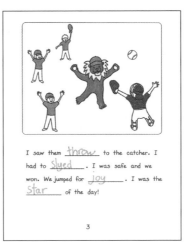

Panel 1: I played stic ball. The ball flow to me. I Swog but I missed. Our teem was losing the game . Their players were too good.

Panel 2: Then it was my turn to hit again. I wated for the ball. I hit the ball and it went flying . I got to therd base. My coch yelled, "Go homr (home)!"

Panel 3: I saw them throw to the catcher. I had to slyed . I was safe and we won. We jumped for joy . I was the star of the day!

FIG. 5–3   Grace's assessment

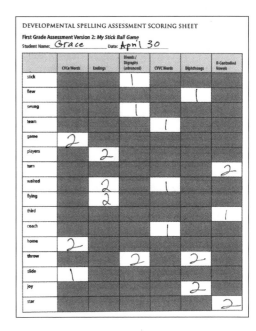

DEVELOPMENTAL SPELLING ASSESSMENT SCORING SHEET

First Grade Assessment Version 2: *My Stick Ball Game*
Student Name: Grace   Date: April 30

	CVCe Words	Endings	Blends/Digraphs (advanced)	CVVC Words	Diphthongs	R-Controlled Vowels
stick			1			
flew						
swung			1			
team				1		
game	2					
players		2				
turn						2
walked		2				
flying		2				
third						1
coach				1		
home	2					
throw				2	2	
slide	1					
joy					2	
star						2

Place a 0, 1, or 2 in each blank box to score. Record the total points for each feature below.

Feature	Total Score (0–6)	Place a checkmark in this column if the child is meeting expectations for each feature. If not, circle the feature and make plans to give the child additional support.
CVCe Words	5	✓
Endings	6	✓
Blends / Digraphs (advanced)	4	
CVVC Words	3	
Diphthongs	5	✓
R-Controlled Vowels	5	✓

Benchmarks Chart

Time of Year Assessment is Given	Benchmarks
After Unit 2	• CVCe Words: 5–6 • Endings: 0–2 • Blends /Digraphs: 0–2 • CVVC Words: 0–2 • Diphthongs: 0–2 • R-Controlled Vowels: 0–2
After Unit 3	• CVCe Words: 5–6 • Endings: 5–6 • Blends /Digraphs: 5–6 • CVVC Words : 0–2 • Diphthongs: 0–2 • R-Controlled Vowels: 0–2
After Unit 5, Bend 1	• CVCe Words: 5–6 • Endings: 5–6 • Blends /Digraphs: 5–6 • CVVC Words: 5–6 • Diphthongs: 5–6 • R-Controlled Vowels: 5–6

check on your students' phonics progress and plan next steps. You'll be able to use the results of the developmental spelling assessments to plan a wealth of customized instruction. You'll be able to see at a glance which phonics features your students struggle with, using this information to understand which concepts to reinforce for your whole class, for small groups, and for individual students.

Assessing Snap Words: "Emptying Your Snap Word Pouch/Blacking Out Your Word Wall"

Occasionally throughout the year, you will need to be sure each student is learning to read and write high-frequency words with automaticity. By the end of kindergarten, you will have taught your children about fifty high-frequency words. For you to feel assured that they are "on course," your hope should be that they can read nearly all of these words easily and correctly, and that they can spell approximately 75% of them correctly and easily, so around thirty-seven words. Ideally, of course, children will master all fifty of these words, but mastery takes time, so the important thing is that you see progress over time.

We recommend beginning to assess students' snap word knowledge after Unit 3, *Word-Part Power*, of kindergarten and continuing to assess for this throughout kindergarten and first grade. Conduct this assessment periodically and informally, as you pull alongside children during reading and writing independent work times every two or three months. In kindergarten, you'll use children's snap word baggies or pouches, the same ones they regularly use to store the snap words they are learning. Each child will have in his or her pouch the class word wall words that he or she doesn't yet know in a snap. When a child shows he can read a word in a snap, place a blue dot in the corner (for blue sky!). This signifies that the child is well on the way to mastering this word. Then, ask the child to write the word. If he can write it in a snap, he no longer needs to store the word in his pouch; he has learned the word with automaticity. Record this word on his snap word assessment sheet. You might do this in front of the student, in a celebratory way, congratulating him on how many words he now knows. You might also decide to remove the snap word card from his pouch (because he now holds it in his head). If he cannot yet write it, leave it (with the blue dot) in his pouch.

For first-grade students, you'll assess using their individual word walls, using the same process as described above. Only, rather than removing words from children's pouches, you'll cross them off of their individual word walls. Hence the name, "Blacking Out Your Word Wall." The first time you give this assessment, we recommend using a word wall filled with the kindergarten snap words. The results will help inform your decision on whether or not to skip assessing kids during Unit 1 and instead begin after Unit 2. By the end of first grade, the aim is for students to be able to read about 150 words easily and correctly, and to be able to write about 110 of these (75%) easily and correctly. Again, what is most important is that children show growth over the school year.

If students are not keeping pace with learning snap words, we suggest turning to the snap word lessons in *Small Groups to Support Phonics*. Also, be sure these students have plenty of time to play the snap word games suggested in unit extensions. Make sure they take their snap word pouches home for additional practice.

Using Reading Assessments, Including Running Records, to Gain Insights on Children's Phonics Development

We won't include a full write-up of all possible reading assessments here, but certainly it is worth mentioning that your reading assessments, such as running records, are another valuable source of information you can mine to understand your students' phonics development. If you have access to *A Guide to the Reading Workshop: Primary Grades*, you'll see a full write-up on how to administer and evaluate running records there.

As we recommend in *A Guide to the Reading Workshop: Primary Grades*, you'll need to study what students do when they are faced with a challenge, so make sure you continue to assess until you reach a child's instructional level. When a child makes errors, you'll be able to see what sources of information she is and is not relying upon, and you'll be able to teach into areas of weakness. While children definitely struggle with using meaning and language structure as sources of information to help them read tricky words, sometimes they struggle with using information. For example, the child may not be decoding all the way to the end of the word and may need help attending to endings. Or, he may be decoding letter by letter, and may need help using word parts or spelling patterns to decode. Also, you'll be able to glean insights into any phonics features that are tripping a child up and may be preventing him from moving up levels. For example, if a child struggles with digraphs or blends, he may get stalled when attempting to move to level E books. When reading assessments reveal these kinds of patterns, you'll have plenty of resources to draw upon in this phonics series.

RECOMMENDED SCHEDULE FOR ASSESSMENT

Kindergarten

Use This Tool . . .	Assessment Tool
During Unit 1	• **Assessing Letter-Sound Correspondence:** "Do You Know Your ABCs?"
After Unit 1	• **Assessing Phonological Awareness, Blending, and Segmenting:** "Robot Talk" • **Assessing Concepts About Print:** "Help Your Teacher Read a Book"
After Unit 2	• **Assessing Developmental Spelling:** "Help Mabel Label a Picture Book" (1st time) • Use previous assessment tools as needed. Use the Letter-Sound Identification assessment to check on children's growing letter-sound knowledge, and phonological assessments as needed.
After Unit 3	• **Assessing Developmental Spelling:** "Help Mabel Label a Picture Book" (2nd time) • **Assessing Snap Words:** "Emptying Your Snap Word Pouch"
After Unit 4	• Use all previous assessment tools, as needed.
After Unit 5 (before If . . . Then . . . phonics projects)	• **Assessing Developmental Spelling:** "Help Mabel Label a Picture Book" (3rd time) • **Assessing Snap Words:** "Emptying Your Snap Word Pouch" • For children who have yet to reach proficiency levels, return to relevant assessment tools.

First Grade

Use This Tool . . .	Assessment Tool
During Unit 1	• **Assessing Snap Words:** "Blacking Out Your Word Wall" • **Assessing Developmental Spelling:** "Help Rasheed Label a Picture Book: Version 1: *My Dog Max*" OR • **Assessing Developmental Spelling:** "Help Rasheed Write a Picture Book: Version 2: *My Stick Ball Game*" • For children who have yet to reach proficiency levels on other kindergarten assessments, return to relevant assessment tools.
After Unit 2	• Assess snap words for children who are not keeping pace with learning snap words.
After Unit 3	• **Assessing Developmental Spelling:** "Help Rasheed Write a Picture Book: Version 2: *My Stick Ball Game*" • **Assessing Snap Words:** "Blacking Out Your Word Wall"
After Unit 4	• Assess snap words for children who are not keeping pace with learning snap words.
After Unit 5, Bend I	• **Assessing Developmental Spelling:** "Help Rasheed Write a Picture Book: Version 2: *My Stick Ball Game*" • **Assessing Snap Words:** "Blacking Out Your Word Wall"

ASSESSING LETTER-SOUND CORRESPONDENCE

"Do You Know Your ABCs?"

Materials

- Print or copy the Letter Identification scoring form, one per student.
- Print or copy the Letter Identification student forms, one copy of the uppercase letters and one copy of the lowercase letters.
- You will need one blank piece of paper or an index card to cover parts of the letter identification pages.

Procedure

1. Place the uppercase letters student copy in front of the child. Show only one row of letters at a time.
2. Ask, "Can you name these letters? Can you say the sounds of each letter?"
3. If the child needs help getting started, or knowing how to proceed, you may point to each letter.
4. If the child does not automatically say the letter name and sound at the same time, let the child name the letters then ask him or her to return to the beginning of the sheet, and say the sound for each letter.
5. Repeat this process for the lowercase letters.

Scoring

Place a check mark in the column if the child identifies the letter or sound correctly. If a child names a letter or sound incorrectly (for example, says B instead of D), record the letter sound the child says (record B in the "No reply or not correct" column for letter D). Count the check marks (correct letters or sounds) and total them onto the score sheet. When assessing vowel sounds, students may say the long vowel sound of the vowel because those are taught first (the long sound is the same as the letter name), but if the child produces either the long or the short sound, judge that as acceptable.

Interpreting the Scores

Following are benchmarks to help you interpret your students' scores on this assessment. You'll see two separate categories, one for letter identification, and one for letter sound. In the chart below, level 3 indicates the child is meeting grade-level expectations for that time of year. Level 4 indicates the child is exceeding grade-level expectations, and levels 1 and 2 indicate the child needs further support in this area. As explained above, you'll no longer give this assessment to children who know all of their letters and sounds, so you won't give this assessment to each child during each month listed below. Use the table to give you a general sense of how your students are progressing at a particular time of year, and not as an indicator of how often you need to assess.

Letter-Sound Identification Benchmarks

	SEPTEMBER	NOVEMBER	JANUARY	MARCH	JUNE
Letter ID	1 = 6 or below 2 = 7–11 3 = 12 4 = 13+	1 = 11 or below 2 = 12–17 3 = 18–29 4 = 30+	1 = 17 or below 2 = 18–29 3 = 30–41 4 = 42+	1 = 29 or below 2 = 30–41 3 = 42–54 4 = N/A	1 = 39 or below 2 = 40–53 3 = 54 4 = N/A
Letter Sound	1 = 1 2 = 2 3 = 3 4 = 4	1 = 4 or below 2 = 5–8 3 = 9–13 4 = 14+	1 = 8 or below 2 = 9–14 3 = 15–19 4 = 20+	1 = 12 or below 2 = 13–19 3 = 20–26 4 = N/A	1 = 14 or below 2 = 15–25 3 = 26 4 = N/A

Letter Identification Assessment

Name: _____   **Date:** _____

Name of Letter	Sound of Letter	No Reply or not correct	Name of Letter	Sound of Letter	No reply or not correct
A			a		
W			w		
P			p		
K			k		
F			f		
Z			z		
U			u		
J			j		
O			o		
H			h		
B			b		
			a		
M			m		
Q			q		
L			l		
Y			y		
C			c		
I			i		
X			x		
S			s		
N			n		
D			d		
T			t		
V			v		
R			r		
G			g		
E			e		
			g		

Known letters: Uppercase _____   Lowercase _____   Known Letter Sounds: _____

List unknown letters:

What do you notice: (Does not know names, but recognizes in words; knows names, but no letter-sound match; reversed letters; stright line known, curved unknown, etc.)

Note: The lowercase letters *a* and *g* appear twice to see if children recognize them in different fonts. A child only needs to correctly identify the letter name/sound for one version of these letters to score a point. Make a note if a child does not correctly identify the letter name/sound for one version and make plans to support the child with that version of the letter.

Letter Identification (page 1)

A	W	P	K	F	Z
U	J	O	H	B	
M	Q	L	Y	C	
I	X	S	N	D	
T	V	R	G	E	

May be photocopied for classroom use. © 2018 by Lucy Calkins and Colleagues from the Teachers College Reading and Writing Project from Units of Study in Phonics (Heinemann: Portsmouth, NH).

Letter Identification (page 2)

a	w	p	k	z
u	j	o	h	b
m	q	l	y	c
i	x	s	n	d
t	v	r	g	e
				g

ASSESSING CONCEPTS ABOUT PRINT

"Help Your Teacher Read a Book"

Earlier, in our summaries of the recommended assessments, we suggested that you needn't give all children a full concepts about print assessment, such as the thirteen-point version that can be found on the TCRWP website and in the online resources for Units of Study in Phonics. Rather, we recommend informally asking the following four questions to individual students at some point after you teach the first unit:

- **"Can you help me read this book? Where should I start?"** (*left-to right directionality*)
- Read a page, point to the last line, and say, **"Now where should I go?"** (*turn the page*)
- Find a page with multiple lines of print. Read the first line then point to the last word. Ask, **"Now where should I go?"** (*return sweep*)
- Show a page and ask, **"Can you show me a word?"** Then ask, **"Can you show me a letter?** (*concept of word, concept of letter*)

If children can answer these four questions soon after you teach the first unit, don't worry, their concepts about print understanding is on track. If a child is able to answer three out of the four, you might wait a month then assess again, using a different book and these same four questions.

For children who only answer one or two of the questions correctly the first time you give the assessment, or who are not able to answer all four questions by early December, you might consider giving the full thirteen-point assessment to pinpoint specific areas of confusion, such as left to right directionality, or concept of word. With these results, you can plan small group intervention to support these children.

If you do give the thirteen-point version, you'll find a scoring guide along with those materials in the online resources, and a set of benchmarks to help you interpret those scores at different times of the year.

ASSESSING PHONOLOGICAL AWARENESS, BLENDING, AND SEGMENTING

"Robot Talk"

Materials

- Print the "Phonological Awareness Assessment Guide," and copy one per student. ✳
- Print the segmentation picture cards. ▱

Procedure for Blending:

1. Sit one-on-one with a child. Say, "I am going to talk like a robot and say a word, sound by sound. You put the sounds together and say the word. And then, you'll act out that word—sing, if the word is *sing*, or hum if the word is *hum*."

2. Begin with row 5 in the "Phonological Awareness Assessment Guide." Say the example word in a sound-by-sound, robot-like way to the child, leaving a pause between each of the two phonemes: /g/—/o/. Then say, "That word was go" and pretend to go.

3. Choose one of the test words and say it in a sound-by-sound, robot-like way. Then ask, "What word was I saying? Can you figure that word out and act it out?" If the child gets this right, you can move on to row 6. You do not have to give the child another word from row 5. If not, try another word from row 5, to see if the child can blend the word on a second (or even third) try.

4. If the child correctly blends a row 5 word, repeat the process with a word from the row 6 list (*run, rub,* or *shake*). As before, ask the child to figure out the word, and then do the action. If a child is able to blend a word from this row with three phonemes, she has passed the blending test. You may stop here, and you do not have to give this assessment again.

5. If the child cannot do the work of row 5, go to row 1 (*skateboard, daydream,* or *tiptoe*). Compound words are often the simplest words to blend because each word part carries meaning. Talk like a robot, and ask the child to blend two words into one compound word. If the child can't blend the word from row one, stop assessing and start supporting!

6. If a child can blend a word from row 1, assess whether she can blend syllables into words, a skill that is harder than blending parts of a compound word, but easier than blending individual phonemes. Give the child a word from row 2 (*relax, open,* or *dancing*). If she can do this, give her a word from row 3 (*exercise, protecting,* or *carrying*). These rows test whether a child can blend syllables into words. The words in row 2 are slightly easier, because they have two syllables, while the row 3 words have three syllables.

7. If a child can blend a word from row 3, try a word from row 4. Onset/rime blending is more difficult than syllable blending but easier than phoneme blending.

To score this assessment, place a check mark in the right hand column if the student can correctly blend a word from that row, along with the date, if you wish. When the student receives a check mark in row 6, the assessment is complete.

Procedure for Segmenting:

As we noted previously, if a child's skill in blending is weak, we recommend not assessing segmenting for now. We have found that many children who struggle with blending are not ready for segmenting. Support the child in blending, and give the segmenting assessment once her blending skills are stronger.

We recommend giving the segmenting portion of this assessment a week or so after you give the blending portion. For each row, you'll give the child an example, segmenting a word and showing how you do the activity the word represents. Then, you'll ask the child to choose a word to segment from a set of two cards. Then you'll do the activity. Note that some of the activities in the pictures might be difficult for children to determine from the picture alone. In this case, you might name the two activities before the child chooses. But be sure not to say them in robot talk, of course.

1. Sit one-on-one with a child. Say, "I want *you* to talk like a robot this time. I am going to show you some pictures of kids doing things. I'll give you an example, and then it will be your turn. You'll choose one of two pictures, and you'll say what the kid in the picture is doing like a robot, sound by sound. Once you say it like a robot, I will do what the word says. You can boss me around!"

2. Ask the child to choose a word from the row 5 list. Ask them to say their chosen word in a sound-by-sound, robot-like way. Once they say their word, you act it out. Assess whether the child has segmented the word accurately. The words are correctly segmented for you on the blending sheet, if you would like to use this as a check.

3. If the child gets the row 5 word right, repeat the process with a word from the row 6 list. Ask the child to give you robot directions and then you do the action. If a child is able to segment a word from this row (a three-phoneme word), she has passed the segmenting test.

4. If the child cannot do the work of row 5, go to row 1. Again, ask the child to choose a picture and talk like a robot. This time the child will be segmenting a compound word into its two component words. If a child can segment a word from row 1, after you act out the word, check row 2 and row 3. These rows test whether a child can segment words into syllables.

5. Then, check row 4. This row tests whether the child can segment words into onset/rime. Ask the child to segment a word from this row. The child who can do this is on his or her way, and just needs some support to learn to segment words into phonemes.

6. If the child can't do row 1, stop assessing and start supporting! Be sure you reassess within another few weeks.

When we field-tested this assessment, we noticed that some children were not able to blend or segment a word from row 5 at first try, but when we started with row 1 and progressed through the rows in numerical order, they were able to blend or segment words all the way through row 6. With the extra examples and scaffolding provided by the earlier rows, they were able to show their good phonological awareness. If a child struggles to blend from row 5 at first, you might give this row another try if the child is successful at rows 1–4.

Scoring:

For children whose phonological awareness is progressing normally, you can expect phases of growth through exposure to language and through your reading, writing, and phonics instruction. Below is a chart that indicates when you can expect children to demonstrate proficiency in the different levels of phonological awareness indicated by this assessment. Note that this assessment is not meant as a formal diagnostic tool, but rather as a way to identify children who would benefit from extra support with blending or segmenting at a particular time of year.

Once a child is able to blend or segment a word from row 6, you do not have to give that portion (blending or segmenting) of the assessment again, even if the child does this early in the school year. The child has met expectations for blending or segmenting.

Row	Expectations for Proficiency
1	By the end of Unit 2
2	By the end of Unit 2
3	By the end of Unit 2
4	By the end of Unit 3
5	By the end of Unit 4
6	This row indicates that the child has met expectations. If a child can blend and segment a word from this row, you do not need to give this assessment again.

PHONOLOGICAL AWARENESS ASSESSMENT GUIDE

Student Name: _____

PART I: BLENDING

Row	Choose one word from the following rows. Say the word segmented into parts, in robot talk. Ask the child to say the word and do the action.	Check if Correct/Date
1	[skateboard, daydream, or tiptoe] Say: "skate . . . . .board" Say: "day . . . . .dream" Say: "tip . . . . .toe"	
2	[relax, open, or dancing] Say: "re . . . . .lax" Say: "o . . . . .pen" Say: "danc . . . . .ing"	
3	[exercise, protecting, or carrying] Say: "ex . . . . .er . . . . .cise " Say: "pro . . . . .tect . . . . .ing " Say: "car . . . . .ry . . . . .ing"	
4	[sing, skip, wave] Say: "s . . . . .ing" Say: "sk . . . . .ip" Say: "w . . . . .ave"	
5	[eat, see, or say] Say: "ea . . . . .t" Say: "s . . . . .ee " Say: "s . . . . .ay"	
6	[run, rub, or shake] Say: "r . . . . .u . . . . .n" Say: "r . . . . .u . . . . .b" Say: "sh . . . . .a . . . . .ke"	

PART II: SEGMENTING

Use the example card to give the child an example from each row. Then, ask the child to choose one of the remaining two cards for the row, and then say the action word segmented into parts, in robot talk.

Row		Check if Correct/ Date
1	[daydream, skateboard, or tiptoe] 1-a 1-b 1-c	
2	[dancing, relax, or open] 2-a 2-b 2-c	
3	[carrying, exercise, or protecting] 3-a 3-b 3-c	
4	[wave, sing, or skip] 4-a 4-b 4-c	
5	[eat, see, or say] 5-a 5-b 5-c	
6	[run, rub, or shake] 6-a 6-b 6-c	

KINDERGARTEN ASSESSING DEVELOPMENTAL SPELLING

"Help Mabel Label a Picture Book"

Materials

- Copy and assemble the assessment booklet *A Birthday Party* for each student. ✻
- Print the Story Guidesheet. ✻
- Print the Developmental Spelling Scoring Assessment Sheet, and make one copy for each child. ✻

Procedure

1. Give each child a copy of *A Birthday Party*. Ask them to write their names on the back of the booklet.
2. Refer to the Story Guidesheet. Read the transcript of the story, repeating the noted words and asking the children to write those words where indicated on the booklet. Encourage children to say the words slowly to listen for the sounds (like they do in writing workshop). Do not stretch the words for children.
3. Collect the booklets, score them using the Developmental Spelling Scoring Assessment Sheet, and make plans to follow up with students who need additional support.

Teacher Version

Student Version

STORY GUIDESHEET

Developmental Spelling Assessment: "Help Mabel Label a Picture Book"

A Birthday Party

Hand out a copy of A Birthday Party, *one per student. Ask students to write their names on the back. Then, read the following introduction:*

"Mabel drew the pictures for her story about a birthday party, but she hasn't written any of the words yet. Will you help her write words to go with her pictures and her story? As I read it, I'll ask you to write some labels to help Mabel. You can write them right on your copy of Mabel's story. The title of her story is *A Birthday Party*."

As you read the script for each page, emphasize the words children will write, bolded below. Pause after you read each bolded word to give children time to write. If needed, you may read the script for each page more than once, or you may repeat bolded words.

"Let's start on page 1. It was Mabel's birthday. She put on her best **dress**. She put a hat on her **pet**. Then she put out the **chips**."

Once children have finished writing the words for page 1, ask them to turn to page 2.

"Turn to page 2. She closed her eyes. Her friends said, 'Make a **wish**.' She wished for a new pet. She really wanted a **frog**. She opened the **box**."

Once children have finished writing the words for page 2, ask them to turn to page 3.

"Turn to page 3. Mabel's wish came true. One friend said, 'Let's all **clap** for Mabel.' Mabel said, '**Thanks**.' Then she gave her new pet frog a **hug**. The End."

KINDERGARTEN

Scoring

Once you have collected the filled-in booklets from each child, score each as follows:

- Mark 2 points if the feature being tested is correct, even if every part of the word is not correct. For example, if the word is *pet*, and the child writes *pit*, the child would get two points for the initial consonant, and two points for the final consonant.

- Mark 1 point if the feature of the word is incorrect, but still, the guess makes sense according to phonics principles. (In the example above, the child would get one point for the short vowel *i*, because she made a guess that shows she has some understanding that a vowel goes here, even though she wrote the wrong vowel.)

- Mark 0 if the child did not write the feature at all, or if what is written is not yet following any discernible logic. (For example, if the child wrote *ptt* or *pt* for the word *pet*, she would score a 0 for the short vowels category.)

DEVELOPMENTAL SPELLING ASSESSMENT SCORING SHEET

Kindergarten Assessment: *A Birthday Party*

Student Name: _____ **Date:** _____

	Initial Consonants	Final Consonants	Short Vowels	Digraphs	Blends
dress					
pet					
chips					
wish					
frog					
box					
clap					
thanks					
hug					

Place a 0, 1, or 2 in each blank box to score. Record the total points for each feature below.

Feature	Total Score (0–6)	Place a check mark in this column if the child is meeting expectations for this time of year, based on the benchmarks chart. If not, circle the feature and make plans to give the child additional support.
Initial Consonants		
Final Consonants		
Short Vowels		
Digraphs		
Blends		

May be photocopied for classroom use. © 2018 by Lucy Calkins and Colleagues from the Teachers College Reading and Writing Project from Units of Study in Phonics (Heinemann: Portsmouth, NH).

Interpreting the Scores

The benchmarks for proficiency with each feature vary, depending on the time of year you give this assessment. The chart below will help you set expectations and know when to plan additional support for students, depending on when you give this assessment.

Benchmarks Chart

Time of Year Assessment Is Given	Benchmarks
After Unit 2	• Initial Consonants: 5–6 • Final Consonants: 5–6 • Short Vowels: 0–2 • Digraphs: 0–2 • Blends: 0–2
After Unit 3	• Initial Consonants: 5–6 • Final Consonants: 5–6 • Short Vowels: 5–6 • Digraphs: 3–4 • Blends: 0–2
After Unit 5 (before If . . . Then . . . phonics projects)	• Initial Consonants: 5–6 • Final Consonants: 5–6 • Short Vowels: 5–6 • Digraphs: 5–6 • Blends: 3–4

FIRST GRADE ASSESSING DEVELOPMENTAL SPELLING

"Help Rasheed Label/Write a Picture Book"

Materials

- Copy and assemble the assessment booklet, either *My Dog Max* or *My Stick Ball Game*, for each student.
- Print the Story Guidesheet.
- Print the Developmental Spelling Assessment Scoring Sheet and make a copy for each child.

Procedure

1. Choose the version of the assessment you will give, depending on the time of year and your students' level of proficiency. Version 1, *My Dog Max*, assesses end-of-kindergarten phonics features, with kindergarten style writing (labels), but with a first-grade storyline. You might use this at the start of the year to see what your students remember from kindergarten. The version 2 assessment, *My Stick Ball Game*, tests phonics features students will learn across the first-grade year. You might give it several times during the school year to assess students' understanding of these first-grade skills.

2. Give each child a copy of the three-page story booklet. Ask them to write their names on the back of the booklet.

3. Refer to the Story Guidesheet. Read the introduction on the set up the activity. Read the transcript of the story, repeating the noted words and asking the children to write those words where indicated on the booklet. Encourage students to say the words slowly to hear the sounds (like they do in writing workshop). Do not stretch the words for students.

4. Collect the booklets, score them using the Developmental Spelling Assessment Scoring Sheet, and make plans to follow up with students who need additional support.

FIRST GRADE ASSESSMENT VERSION 1: *MY DOG MAX*

Teacher Version

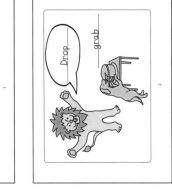

Student Version

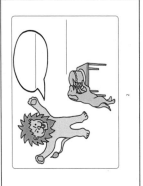

STORY GUIDESHEET

Developmental Spelling Assessment: "Help Rasheed Label a Picture Book"

My Dog Max

Hand out a copy of My Dog Max, *one per student. Ask students to write their names on the back. Then, read the following introduction:*

"Rasheed drew the pictures for his story about teaching his dog, Max, some tricks, but he hasn't written any of the words yet. Will you help him write words to go with his pictures and his story? As I read it, I'll ask you to write some labels to help Rasheed. You can write them right on your copy of Rasheed's story. The title of his story is *My Dog Max.*"

As you read the script for each page, emphasize the words children will write, bolded below. Pause after you read each bolded word to give children time to write. If necessary, you may read the script for each page more than once.

"Let's start on page 1. Rasheed was teaching his dog, Max, some tricks. **'Sit,'** Rasheed said. Max did it. Rasheed put a **thin** piece of cake in his dog **dish.**"

Once children have finished writing the words for page 1, ask them to turn to page 2.

"Turn to page 2. Max tried to **grab** the whole cake. **'Drop** it,' Rasheed said. Max did."

Once children have finished writing the words for page 2, ask them to turn to page 3.

"Turn to page 3. Rasheed **fed** Max a treat. He rubbed his **chest.** 'Good dog,' Rasheed said. Max began to **wag** his tail."

FIRST-GRADE SPELLING ASSESSMENT ONE: LABELS

May be photocopied for classroom use. © 2018 by Lucy Calkins and Colleagues from the Teachers College Reading and Writing Project from Units of Study in Phonics (Heinemann: Portsmouth, NH).

DEVELOPMENTAL SPELLING ASSESSMENT SCORING SHEET

First Grade Assessment Version 1: *My Dog Max*

Student Name: _____ Date: _____

	Initial Consonants	Final Consonants	Short Vowels	Digraphs	Blends
sit					
thin					
dish					
grab					
drop					
fed					
chest					
wag					

Place a 0, 1, or 2 in each blank box to score. Record the total points for each feature below.

Feature	Total Score (0–6)	Place a check mark in this column if the child is meeting expectations for each feature. If not, circle the feature and make plans to give the child additional support.
Initial Consonants		
Final Consonants		
Short Vowels		
Digraphs		
Blends		

Scoring:

At the beginning of first grade, the benchmark is a score of 5–6 in each category. If a child is does not meet this benchmark for a feature, plan to give that child additional support. See *Small Groups to Support Phonics* for targeted practice.

FIRST GRADE ASSESSMENT VERSION 2: MY STICK BALL GAME

Teacher Version

I played *stick* ball. The ball *flew* to me. I *swung* but I missed. Our *team* was losing the *game*. Their *players* were too good.

1

Then it was my *turn* to hit again. I *waited* for the ball. I hit the ball and it went *flying*. I got to *third* base. My *coach* yelled, "*Go home!*"

2

I saw them throw to the catcher. I had to slide. I was safe and we won. We jumped for joy. I was the star of the day!

3

Student Version

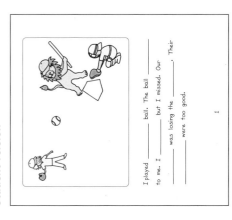

I played _____ ball. The ball _____ to me. I _____ but I missed. Our _____ was losing the _____. Their _____ were too good.

1

Then it was my _____ to hit again. I _____ for the ball. I hit the ball and it went _____. I got to _____ base. My _____ yelled, "Go _____!"

2

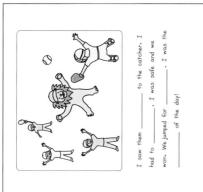

I saw them _____ to the catcher. I had to _____. I was safe and we won. We jumped for _____. I was the _____ of the day!

3

STORY GUIDESHEET

Developmental Spelling Assessment: "Help Rasheed Write a Picture Book"

My Stick Ball Game

Hand out a copy of My Stick Ball Game, one per student. Ask students to write their names on the back. Then, read the following introduction:

"Rasheed drew the pictures for his story about playing stick ball, but he hasn't finished writing some of the words. Will you help him fill in some words to complete his sentences? As I read it, I'll ask you to fill in the words to finish the sentences and help Rasheed. You can write them right on your copy of Rasheed's story. The title of his story is *My Stick Ball Game*."

As you read the script for each page, emphasize the words children will write, bolded below. Pause after you read each bolded word to give children time to write. If necessary, you may read the script for each page more than once.

"Let's start on page 1. I played **stick** ball. The ball **flew** to me. I **swung** but I missed. Our **team** was losing the **game**. Their **players** were too good."

Once children have finished writing the words for page 1, ask them to turn to page 2.

"Turn to page 2. Then it was my **turn** to hit again. I **waited** for the ball. I hit the ball and it went **flying**. I got to **third** base. My **coach** yelled, 'Go **home**!'"

Once children have finished writing the words for page 2, ask them to turn to page 3.

"Turn to page 3. I saw them **throw** to the catcher. I had to **slide**. I was safe and we won. We jumped for **joy**. I was the **star** of the day!"

FIRST-GRADE SPELLING ASSESSMENT TWO: FILL IN WORDS IN SENTENCES

DEVELOPMENTAL SPELLING ASSESSMENT SCORING SHEET

First Grade Assessment Version 2: *My Stick Ball Game*

Student Name: _____ Date: _____

	CVCe Words	Endings	Blends / Digraphs (advanced)	CVVC Words	Diphthongs	R-Controlled Vowels
stick						
flew						
swung						
team						
game						
players						
turn						
waited						
flying						
third						
coach						
home						
throw						
slide						
joy						
star						

Place a 0, 1, or 2 in each blank box to score. Record the total points for each feature below.

Feature	Total Score (0–6)	Place a check mark in this column if the child is meeting expectations for each feature. If not, circle the feature and make plans to give the child additional support.
CVCe Words		
Endings		
Blends / Digraphs (advanced)		
CVVC Words		
Diphthongs		
R-Controlled Vowels		

Benchmarks Chart

Time of Year Assessment is Given	Benchmarks
After Unit 2	• CVCe Words: 5–6 • Endings: 0–2 • Blends /Digraphs: 3–4 • CVVC Words : 0–2 • Diphthongs: 0–2 • R-Controlled Vowels: 0–2
After Unit 3	• CVCe Words: 5–6 • Endings: 5–6 • Blends /Digraphs: 5–6 • CVVC Words : 0–2 • Diphthongs: 0–2 • R-Controlled Vowels: 0–2
After Unit 5, Bend I	• CVCe Words: 5–6 • Endings: 5–6 • Blends /Digraphs: 5–6 • CVVC Words: 5–6 • Diphthongs: 5–6 • R-Controlled Vowels: 5–6

APPENDIX: ASSESSMENT TOOLS

ASSESSING SNAP WORDS

"Emptying Your Snap Word Pouch/Blacking Out Your Word Wall"

Materials

- Use each student's set of word wall words, on small cards. These are usually the whole-class words, but individualized sets of words are possible too, as needed by each student. These are the same word cards students use in the units.
- For kindergarten, a baggie or pouch for the word cards (this is the same baggie or pouch students regularly use to store their snap words, as suggested in the units).
- For first grade, students' individual word walls, as suggested in the units.

Procedure

1. For kindergarten, take a word out of the child's snap word baggie. For first grade, point to a word on the child's individual word wall. Check to see if the card has a dot in the corner. A dot signifies that the child can read the word in a snap. Because the word is still in the child's pouch or on the child's wall, this indicates she cannot yet write it in a snap.

2. If the word card has no dot in the corner, ask the child to read it in a snap. If the child reads it correctly, add a dot to the corner of the card.

3. If the word card already has a dot in the corner, ask the child to write the word. If the child writes the word correctly, remove the card from the baggie or the word wall permanently—no more work on that word is needed.

4. For kindergarten, record that word on the child's snap word assessment sheet. You might review these words from time to time.

5. For both grades, once a word is removed from your collection because you now have it in your brain, you might say something like, "I took this word from your word wall or a card to help you. Forever now, make sure that you are getting these words correct in your reading and writing."

KINDERGARTEN SNAP WORD ASSESSMENT SHEET

Student Name: _____

When you remove a snap word from a child's pouch or wall and declare it mastered—that is, the child can read and write it with automaticity—record that word below.

1.	2.	3.	4.	5.
6.	7.	8.	9.	10.
11.	12.	13.	14.	15.
16.	17.	18.	19.	20.
21.	22.	23.	24.	25.
26.	27.	28.	29.	30.
31.	32.	33.	34.	35.
36.	37.	38.	39.	40.
41.	42.	43.	44.	45.
46.	47.	48.	49.	50.

Attach additional sheets as needed, as the child's bank of snap words grows.

Scoring:

The goal for the end of kindergarten is for children to be able to read about 50 words with automaticity, and to write about 35 words with automaticity.

The goal for the end of first grade is for children to be able to read about 150 words with automaticity, and to write about 110 words with automaticity.

What is most important is that children are growing their banks of snap words over time. Make plans to support children who do not add new words to this list each time you assess.

May be photocopied for classroom use. © 2018 by Lucy Calkins and Colleagues from the Teachers College Reading and Writing Project from Units of Study in Phonics (Heinemann: Portsmouth, NH).

References

Adams, M. J. 1990. *Beginning to Read: Thinking and Learning about Print.* Cambridge, MA: MIT Press.

———. 2003. "Alphabetic Anxiety and Explicit, Systematic Phonics Instruction: A Cognitive Science Perspective." In S. Neuman and D. Dickinson, *Handbook of Early Literacy Research*. New York: Guilford Press.

Bear, D. R., M. Invernizzi, S. Templeton, and F. R. Johnston. 2016. *Words Their Way: Word Study for Phonics, Vocabulary, and Spelling Instruction.* New York: Pearson.

Beck, I. L., and M. E. Beck. 2013. *Making Sense of Phonics.* New York: Guilford Press.

Blevins, W. 2017. *A Fresh Look at Phonics.* Thousand Oaks, CA: Corwin.

Calkins, Lucy. 1994. *The Art of Teaching Writing.* Portsmouth, NH: Heinemann.

———. 2001. *The Art of Teaching Reading.* New York: Pearson.

———, et al. 2016. Units of Study in Opinion/Argument, Information, and Narrative Writing, K–8. Portsmouth, NH: Heinemann.

———, et al. 2017. Units of Study for Teaching Reading, K–8. Portsmouth, NH: Heinemann.

Carnine, D. W., J. Silbert, E. J. Kame'enui, and S. G. Tarver. 1997, 2004. *Direct Instruction Reading.* New York: Pearson.

Clay, Marie. 1979. *Reading: The Patterning of Complex Behavior.* Portsmouth, NH: Heinemann.

———. 2017. *Concepts About Print.* Portsmouth, NH: Heinemann.

Cunningham, J. W. 2017. "What Really Matters in Teaching Phonics Today: Laying a Foundation for Reading." North Billerica, MA: Curriculum Associates, LLC.

Cunningham, P. M. 1975–1976. "Investigating a Synthesized Theory of Mediated Word Identification." *Reading Research Quarterly* 11 (2): 127–43. Hoboken, NJ: Wiley-Blackwell/International Literacy Association.

———. 2008. *Month-by-Month Phonics for First Grade.* Greensboro, NC: Carson-Dellarosa.

———. 2016. *Phonics They Use: Words for Reading and Writing.* New York: Pearson.

Cunningham, P. M., and J. W. Cunningham. 1992. "Making Words: Enhancing the Invented Spelling-Decoding Connection." *The Reading Teacher* 46 (2): 106–15.

Dolch, E. W. 1948. *Problems in Reading.* Champaign, IL: Garrard Press.

Ehri, L. C. 1994. "Development of the Ability to Read Words: Update." In *Theoretical Models and Processes of Reading*, edited by R. Ruddell, M. and H. Singer. Newark, DE: International Reading Association.

Fountas, I. C., and G. S. Pinnell. 2003. *Phonics Lessons.* Portsmouth, NH: Heinemann.

Frith, U. 1985. "Beneath the Surface of Developmental Dyslexia." In *Surface Dyslexia: Neuropsychological and Cognitive Studies of Phonological Reading*, edited by K. Patterson, J. Marshall, and M. Coltheart, 301–30. London: Erlbaum.

Fry, E. B., J. E. Kress, and D. L. Fountoukidis. 2000 and Fry, E. B., and J. E. Kress. 2015. *The Reading Teacher's Book of Lists.* San Francisco: Wiley.

Fundations. 2012. Oxford, MA: Wilson Language Training.

Ganske, Kathy. 2014. *Word Journeys.* New York: Guilford Press.

Gamse, B. C., R. T. Jacob, M. Horst, B. Boulay, and F. Unlu. 2008. *Reading First Impact Study: Final Report* (NCEE 2009-4038). Washington, DC: National Center for Education Evaluation and Regional Assistance, Institute of Education Sciences, U.S. Department of Education.

Hanna, P. R., J. S. Hanna, R. E. Hodges, and E. H. Rudorf. 1966. "Phoneme-Grapheme Correspondences as Cues to Spelling Improvement." Washington, DC: U.S. Department of Health, Education, and Welfare.

Hattie, J. 2009. *Visible Learning*. New York: Routledge/Taylor & Francis Group.

Hattie, J., and G. Yates. 2014. *Visible Learning and the Science of How We Learn*. New York: Routledge/Taylor & Francis Group.

Hayes, L., and K. Flanigan. 2014. *Developing Word Recognition*. New York: Guilford Press.

Helman, L., D. R. Bear, S. Templeton, M. Invernizzi, and F. Johnston. 2011. *Words Their Way with English Learners: Word Study for Phonics, Vocabulary, and Spelling*. New York: Pearson.

Hiebert, E. Ready Readers series. New York: Pearson.

Hillerich, R. 1978. *A Writing Vocabulary of Elementary Children*. Springfield, IL: Charles C. Thomas.

Kaye, E. L. 2006. "Second Graders' Reading Behaviors: A Study of Variety, Complexity, and Change." *Literacy Teaching and Learning: An International Journal of Early Reading and Writing* 10 (2): 51–75.

McCandliss, B. D., L. Cohen, and S. Dehaene. 2003. "The Visual Word Form Area: Expertise for Reading in the Fusiform Gyrus." *Trends in Cognitive Sciences* 7, (July).

New York State P-12 Common Core Standards for English Language Arts & Literacy. 2010, 2011.

O'Connor, Rollanda E. 2014. *Teaching Word Recognition: Effective Strategies for Students with Learning Difficulties*. New York: Guilford Press.

Ryder, J. F., W. E. Tunmer, and K. T. Greaney. 2008. "Explicit Instruction in Phonemic Awareness and Phonemically-Based Decoding Skills as an Intervention Strategy for Struggling Readers in Whole Language Classrooms." *Reading and Writing* 21: 349–69.

Rasinski, T. V. 2008. *Word Ladders*. New York: Scholastic.

Scanlon, D., K. Anderson, and J. Sweeney. 2017. *Early Intervention for Reading Difficulties*. New York: Guilford Press.

Snowball, D., and F. Bolton. 1999. *Spelling K–8 Planning and Teaching*. Portland, ME: Stenhouse.

Tucker, M. S. 2014. *Fixing Our National Accountability System*. Washington, DC: The National Center on Education and the Economy.

Uhry, J. 1999. "Invented Spelling in Kindergarten: The Relationship with Fingerpoint Reading." *Reading and Writing: An Interdisciplinary Journal*, 11: 441–64.

U.S. Supreme Court. 2017. *Endrew F. et al. v. Douglas County School District*.

Wylie, R. E., and D. D. Durrell. 1970. "Teaching Vowels through Phonograms." *Elementary English* 47 (6): 787–91.

Yopp, H. K., and R. H. Yopp. 2000. "Supporting Phonemic Awareness in the Classroom." *The Reading Teacher* 54 (2): 130–43. Newark, DE: International Reading Association.

Index

Playing with Phonics

Lucy Calkins, Amanda Hartman, and Valerie Geschwind

Photography by Peter Cunningham

Illustrations by Valerie Geschwind and Marjorie Martinelli

HEINEMANN ◆ PORTSMOUTH, NH

To Georgia Heard, for inspiring us to hear the poetry in everyday sounds.

Heinemann
361 Hanover Street
Portsmouth, NH 03801–3912
www.heinemann.com

Offices and agents throughout the world

The authors and publisher wish to thank those who have generously given permission to reprint borrowed material:

"Forest Orchestra" copyright 2018 by Georgia Heard. Forthcoming in *BOOM, BELLOW, BLEET* to be published by Boyds Mills Press in 2019. Reprinted by permission of Curtis Brown, Ltd.

"Apple" by Nan Fry. Used by courtesy of David Fry.

Cataloging-in-Publication data is on file with the Library of Congress.

ISBN-13: 978-0-325-10521-5

Editors: Tracy Wells and Anna Gratz Cockerille
Production: Elizabeth Valway
Cover and interior designs: Jenny Jensen Greenleaf
Photography: Peter Cunningham
Illustrations: Valerie Geschwind, Marjorie Martinelli, and Kimberly Fox
Composition: Publishers' Design and Production Services, Inc.
Manufacturing: Steve Bernier

Printed in the United States of America on acid-free paper
22 21 20 19 18 VP 1 2 3 4 5

Acknowledgments

THE STORYLINE FOR THIS BOOK emerged during a think tank with Natalie Louis, where she offered her inventive, creative support. We leaned on Natalie's guidance for help with the intricacies of the phonics content in this book, and also on our colleague, Joe Yukish. We thank them both.

Others helped in dramatic ways as well. Kelly Boland Hohne wrote key sessions in our final bend, helping us to fashion that last portion of this unit in such a way that the methods could be tweaked and used again to teach beyond the confines of this unit. Kelly, thank you for your brilliant clarity, and for writing sessions that took the book from good to great.

We are also grateful to Georgia Heard, poet extraordinaire. Mid-way through this book, we consulted with Georgia, our former colleague and our friend, and her ideas, energy, and delight spurred us on. We are especially grateful to her for sharing her poetry with us.

Amanda and Lucy are grateful to Valerie who did the lion's share of the art for this book. That effort required endless time, and detailed, careful, attentive work. Valerie also brought her miraculous artistic touch to this effort, and the beauty of these pages are a testimony to her talent and care. Marjorie Martinelli worked with Valerie to help provide the tools you'll need to bring this book to life, and we thank her as well.

This unit, like all the units in the Units of Study in Phonics series, stands on the shoulders of the entire community at the Teachers College Reading and Writing Project. We are especially grateful to Natalie Louis, who joined Lucy at the helm of this project and worked endlessly to imbue the series with her prodigious knowledge. We are grateful to all the primary staff developers who helped us ground this effort in research and best classroom practices: Rebecca Cronin, Rachel Rothman-Perkins, Christine Holley, Allyse Bader, Shanna Schwartz, Celena Larkey, Elizabeth Franco, Jennifer DeSutter, Angela Báez, Samantha Barrett, Emma Bemowski, Nancy Brennan, Arlene Casimir-Siar, Lisa Hernandez Corcoran, Marjorie Martinelli, Kimberly Fox, Jessica Greiss, Lizzie Hetzer, Beth Hickey, Lisa Hourigan, Ann Keyser, Katherine Lindner, Sarah Mann, Casey Maxwell, Marie Mounteer, Sarah Picard Taylor, Nicole Santariga, Jessica Someck, Dani Sturtz, Cheryl Tyler, Elise Whitehouse, and Cynthia Williams.

We would like to thank the schools and teachers at PS 212 in Manhattan; Coleytown Elementary School in Westport, CT; Ridgebury Elementary School in Ridgebury, CT; and McCarthy-Towne school in Acton, MA for inviting us into their rooms to try out numerous lessons and small groups to help us think and grow our best ideas for how to help kindergarteners grow stronger as readers and writers. Bryan Andes, Rowena Hurst, Kristin Garvey, Sarah Hellerstein, Katie Pape, Nicole Deering, Annie Roesler, Maureen O'Keefe, Aimee Tiger, Darsi Tedesco, Kestrel Dunn and Cheryl Beaudoin: your students breathed life into this unit. We are immensely grateful.

The team at Heinemann that supported us every step of the way are unparalleled in their time and care. Abby Heim carried the weight of this entire project on her shoulders with grace. Elizabeth Valway and Shannon Thorner took our words and our art and created a masterpiece. Our editors, Tracy Wells and Felicia O'Brien, lent their eyes for precision. We are thankful for their thoughtful questions and keen advice that helped sharpen our teaching and writing of this project.

We would like to thank all our senior leaders at the project, Laurie Pessah, Mary Ehrenworth, Emily Smith, Audra Robb, and Colleen Cruz, for continuing to support us and this work in schools across the country and the world. Your vision, advice, and tenacity bring us all energy and resolve to doing our very best work, always.

Lastly, Valerie and Amanda would like to thank Lucy for steering the ship that resulted in joyful, engaged learning. We are grateful for your guidance and willingness to mentor us into being the best writers and teachers we can be.

—Lucy, Amanda, and Valerie

Contents

Registration instructions to access the digital resources that accompany this book may be found on p. ix.

An Orientation to the Unit

WELCOME TO *PLAYING WITH PHONICS*—the final unit of phonics study in the kindergarten year. As the title suggests, this unit is designed to be a whimsical, experimental, joyful—and most of all, fun—conclusion to your kindergartners' first year of phonics instruction. This unit hinges on the big themes of experimentation and celebration. Throughout the unit, students are encouraged to use their knowledge of phonics to experiment and explore the sounds they hear in words and the sounds they want to write. Then, the unit explicitly celebrates the vast phonics knowledge students have acquired during their action-packed kindergarten year by making students the teachers.

Even as the end of the year rapidly approaches, engagement and excitement are sure to run high during this unit. From the very first session, you'll have kids barking, mooing, and oinking with excitement as the unit launches with a celebration and exploration of animal and invented sounds. Besides being tremendously fun and silly, this experimentation with sound helps students continue to hone several essential phonics skills. At this point in the year, many of your students will be reading conventional text. Still, it is critical that your phonics instruction provides students with ample opportunities to hone their phonological awareness, and these animal-sound sessions do just that in a playful way that students are sure to love. From here, students are encouraged to start listening to all of the sounds they encounter—in their reading, their writing, and the world around them—in new, more sophisticated ways. It is in Bend I, "Playing with Sounds," that students are first introduced to blends. They'll learn to think about not only what sounds letters make, but the instances in which those sounds are changed, muted, or manipulated by neighboring letters. Blends become the focus for the remainder of Bend I, as students bring their new learning about blends into all of the reading and writing work that they do.

As students delve deeper into this exploration of sound, this unit challenges them to tackle longer words and to begin thinking about the sounds that they hear in these words in word parts or phonograms, rather than by single letters. The unit suggests several entertaining and inventive ways that students can further engage with the sounds they hear in words and work to record as many of these sounds as accurately as they can.

Beautiful poetry is woven into many of the sessions across the bends in this unit. As children work to read, perform, write, and revise, this poetry provides authentic opportunities for students to use their phonics knowledge in context. Students use their knowledge of rhyme to create their own silly strings of words which they eventually transform into poetry. Poetry provides yet another outlet for students to hone their phonological awareness as they play with and manipulate word parts and sounds to make rhyming.

The unit culminates with children designing and executing their own phonics projects that are celebrations of their learning. They'll investigate phonics concepts that they have learned over the course of the year and will prepare to teach about them to others. Students will be thrilled for the return of a celebration that mirrors the "ABC School" celebration that closed out Unit 2, *Word Scientists*, as they get the chance to play teacher to their stuffed animals and peers alike.

This "accordion-style" bend was written to be flexible and responsive to the needs of your students who may engage in several phonics projects as you close out your year.

OVERVIEW OF THE UNIT

Bend I begins by inviting students to "horse-around" with a wide variety of animal sounds and other invented noises. Not only is this work wildly fun for kindergartners, but it continues the essential phonological awareness work they have engaged in all year. While many kindergartners are reading conventional text by this time in the year, this critical phonological awareness must not fall by the wayside, because it is closely linked with future reading success. As children move from animal and invented sounds to exploring the sounds and sound effects they encounter in books, they continue to hone their phonological awareness while beginning to think about the sounds they hear and write in new, increasingly sophisticated ways. In Session 2, children learn about consonant blends and are introduced to a new, invaluable tool—the "Blends and Digraphs" chart. Quickly, children begin to tackle trickier blends such as *tr* and learn to differentiate this sound from the digraph *ch*.

Beginning in Session 3, you and your class will dive into an exploration of poetry that provides students with new and inventive ways to apply their growing phonics knowledge. As students explore works of poetry such as Georgia Heard's "Forest Orchestra," they think carefully about the sounds the poet recorded and how the poet intended for the poem to go as they prepare to perform their poetry in front of others. As with any performance, this poetry showcase provides an authentic way for students to celebrate sounds in favorite poems and practice these poems repeatedly. As Bend I continues, students work within a variety of structures to practice orchestrating their phonics content knowledge—including their new learning about blends. For example, students play "Guess the Covered Word" and work on revising their own writing.

At the beginning of Bend II, "Writing Longer Words," students begin to experiment with "magic spells." Conjuring references to famous "magic spells," such as Cinderella's "bibbidi-bobbidi-boo" and Harry Potter's "wingardium leviosa," this part of the bend encourages students to tackle long and winding strings of sounds and to contemplate how to record these sounds. As students embrace these long, made-up words, they will have to employ their phonics knowledge to come up with reasonable spellings, and they'll have to branch out from copying words from the word wall and other go-to spelling techniques. This playful, imaginative work helps our youngest and newest spellers to be brave, jump in, and record as many sounds as they possibly can. Playing with longer words also provides ample opportunities to try out more efficient and sophisticated spelling strategies. It is during their work with "magic spells" that you will help students progress from spelling words letter-by-letter to encouraging students to look for familiar parts within words and transition to spelling part-by-part.

Finally, students turn this experimentation into inquiry, as they scour books such as *Bark, George* by Jules Fiefer; *The Book With No Pictures* by B.J. Novak; and books from the Elephant and Piggie series by Mo Willems to see how the authors of these texts use sound effects in their writing. Soon, these books become mentor texts, as students transition to adding sound effects to their own writing. As students continue to build their phonological awareness, they also add to their knowledge of snap words—continuing to build a repertoire that will support both their reading and writing.

In Bend III, "Playing with Phonics Poems," children will delve deeper into their work with poetry. The bend launches with a continued emphasis on phonological awareness skills as students leverage their knowledge of word parts and sounds to read and create silly little rhymes. In Session 10, children will build silly rhymes by starting with the name of someone special to them. You'll help your class to create an entire "storehouse of rhymes" as children are introduced to important phonograms that will further facilitate their reading and writing as they practice using these phonograms to spell new words part-by-part. Students later transform these silly rhymes into full-fledged poetry by combining their phonics knowledge with inspiration from mentors.

As Bend III continues, students are given more opportunities to take advantage of the performative aspect of poetry—reading and acting out various poems in a reader's theater format. In Session 12, students return to their own poetry to revise using their new learning about blends and digraphs. Following this revision work, students are introduced to the poetic device alliteration—allowing students to further tinker with the sounds they include and record in their poetry. Bend III culminates with a well-deserved celebration when children transform the classroom into a poetry café!

Bend IV, "Phonics Projects," is a culmination not only of the work of this unit, but of all the phonics work children have engaged in during their kindergarten year. This final, project-based bend is designed to be "accordion-style" in structure, in that it works like an accordion, stretching as much, or as little, as needed to fill the gaps in both in time and in your students' phonics learning from now until the end of the year. Use this bend to identify and support additional phonics concepts your students are ready to explore, or perhaps concepts they need to review.

Over the course of this bend, students learn about and execute phonics projects which allow them to synthesize and orchestrate the vast array of phonics knowledge they have acquired during the course of this fast-paced kindergarten year. Conducting these phonics projects pushes students to look at words through the lens of the various phonics characteristics present in these words. The beginning of the bend introduces students to the concept of a phonics project and guides them—with the help of the "How To Do a Phonics Project" anchor chart—through the concrete steps of engaging in this kind of work. In Session 15, students begin by launching an investigation into the letter *I* and sort words that contain the letter *I* by the various sounds this letter can make. Once again, students revisit phonological awareness concepts, while also practicing how to be flexible when reading and writing words—using all that they've learned about phonics to solve them.

Later in Bend IV, students are invited to expand their phonics projects—for instance, the class moves from examining just the letter *I* to investigating all of the vowels in various words. In Session 20, students reach a critical step in the process of creating a phonics project—it is time for them to teach others! This is truly a moment of celebration of all of the amazing phonics work students have done all year. Students who may not have been able to identify a single letter or match it to its sound at the start of the year will now independently teach their classmates about a phonics concept.

As you review all of the phonics content students have worked on throughout the year, you'll coach into kids' rug clubs and guide students to choose a phonics concept on which to focus their phonics project on and eventually teach others about. You'll prompt children to consider not only what they will teach, but how they will teach it by reviewing the various structures students have used to learn about phonics all year long. Students may choose to lead a shared reading session or coach their peers through a round of "Guess the Covered Word." Move through this bend with eyes wide open—noticing which individual students and clubs might benefit from repeated exploration with which specific phonics concepts and make a plan to adjust this final bend to meet the needs of your students as the end of the year approaches.

It's likely that you'll have some time left in your school year after you finish this unit. To respond to the gap between the end of this unit and the end of your year, we suggest engaging students in another round of phonics projects, and perhaps another round after that, if you have time, using the same steps as in Bend IV. It's likely there are additional phonics concepts you'd like to teach, either because your students are ready for new work or because there is work they need to revisit. Or, there might be topics in your school's curriculum you have yet to cover. We recommend continuing to draw on the "How Do a Phonics Project" chart as students move through this work. You'll find if/then teaching suggestions on the online resources that work like an accordion, stretching to accommodate your students' needs and the time you have left. ❀

GETTING READY

We've written this unit with the intention of trying to keep materials to a minimum. As in the previous units in this series, you will need a class set of whiteboards with markers and erasers, as well a system in place to distribute these easily.

Knowing that this will be the last phonics unit of the kindergarten year, we have designed *Playing with Phonics* to be exactly that—playful. To help set this lighthearted tone, you'll want to gather a few props for your connections and demonstrations. For example, you'll want something to use as a magic wand (such as a pointer) when you demonstrate making pretend "magic spells" in Session 6, and you'll want to set the scene for the poetry café in Session 14 by donning a beret (or a dramatic hat) and scarf.

This unit incorporates beautiful poems into the instruction to allow children to use their growing phonics knowledge in context. Students will read Georgia Heard's delightful poem, "Forest Orchestra," focusing their attention on animal sounds and how they are written—and then they'll join in the fun and perform the poem. Arnold L. Shapiro's poem "I Speak, I Say, I Talk" is woven through several sessions across the unit. You may also want to draw upon books from your classroom library that include sound effects and dialogue, such as the Elephant and Piggie series by Mo Willems, *Bark, George* by Jules Fiefer, *The Book with No Pictures* by B.J. Novak, *The Rain Stomper* by Addie Boswell, and *Doggies: A Counting and Barking Book* by Sandra Boynton.

You will be working with pictures in a number of sessions—for example, to help students begin to think about how to play with sounds in Session 1, to introduce students to alliteration in Session 13, and to help kids compare and contrast vowel sounds in Session 16. We have provided images in the online resources and the Resource Pack that you can print out to use. ❀ ▭

You'll also use picture cards for sorting, and we recommend that you use a pocket chart to display these cards. The word sort in Session 15 is a little different—in that one, you'll help students launch their phonics projects by investigating the letter *I*, and you will demonstrate using real-world objects whose names contain the letter *I* (such as a triangle from the math center, a photo of a birthday party, milk, ice cream, rice, and a push pin). For the word sort for this session, you may wish to cut the product name from the packaging to use in the pocket chart.

As students approach the end of this unit, they will be preparing a shared reading to teach Mabel what they have learned in their phonics project. To help them prepare, you'll want some Wikki Stix to allow students to highlight the words they want to focus on.

This unit makes fairly light use of video, but you will want to use it if you can. In Session 6, you'll set the scene for students to work with pretend "magic spells" by showing a YouTube video clip of Cinderella's fairy godmother casting a magic spell. In Session 19, students demonstrate all that they have learned in this unit by presenting their phonics projects. Using your cell phone to make short videos of their presentations is a great way to share their learning with their families.

Of course, you aren't teaching phonics in a vacuum, so you will want to take opportunities to help kids transfer their new phonics knowledge to their independent reading and writing. You will want to make sure to have the usual materials to support their reading and writing work, such as pens, highlighter pens, markers, Post-it notes, blank paper, and sentence strips. Often in this unit, you'll ask kids to bring their writing folders or reading baggies to apply their learning to their workshop work.

ONLINE DIGITAL RESOURCES

Resources that accompany this unit of study are available in the online resources, including all the charts, word cards, songs, and poems shown throughout *Playing with Phonics*.

To access and download the digital resources for *Playing with Phonics*:

1. Go to www.heinemann.com and click the link in the upper right to log in. (If you do not have an account yet, you will need to create one.)

2. Enter the following registration code in the box to register your product: UOSPH_HYSC7

3. Enter the security information requested.

4. Once you have registered your product it will appear in the list of My Online Resources.

(You may keep copies of these resources on up to six of your own computers or devices. By downloading the file, you acknowledge that they are for your individual or classroom use and that neither the resources nor the product code will be distributed or shared.)

Playing with Sounds

Playing with Sounds
Hearing and Recording Letters to Match

PHONICS INSTRUCTION

Phonics
• Recognize and use blends to write sound effect words.

Word Knowledge
• Say a word slowly to hear the sounds in it.
• Make a first attempt to spell an unknown word.

High-Frequency Words
• Learn new words (*come*, *are*, *too*, *love*).
• Develop strategies for learning new words.

IN THIS SESSION

TODAY YOU'LL teach students that readers and writers play with sounds, listening carefully to those sounds so they can record them with letters.

TODAY YOUR STUDENTS will begin playing with phonics. They will imagine the noises that different animals and vehicles might make and listen to their invented noises carefully, trying to hear all the sounds in a noise and write it down so that others can read the writing and make the noise the way the writer imagined.

MINILESSON

CONNECTION

Rally students for the start of a new phonics unit by likening it to getting a wrapped gift. Then announce the title of the unit with great fanfare and get kids wondering about how the unit will go.

As students assembled on the rug, I made sure that each partnership had their whiteboard and marker.

"Kindergartners, today we start a brand-new phonics unit. Don't you love, love, *love* getting into a brand-new unit? It's a little like when you get a present. You get the box, all wrapped up." I pretended to hold a beautifully wrapped box, one with ribbons on top. "You know it will be something new, something special, but you don't yet know what it is." I shook the imaginary box. "You can't help peeking . . ." I opened a corner of the imaginary box, then set it aside to talk to the class.

"In a second, I'll tell you about the new unit, but first we need a bit of drumroll." Raising my hands above my knees, as if the knees were a snare drum, I said, "Hands ready to become snare drums and give us a drumroll?" I looked to see that the kids were similarly poised, and then announced with great pizzazz: "Our new phonics unit will be—drumroll please!" Then I said, reading from an imaginary paper as if I were announcing the winner at the Academy Awards, "Playing with Phonics."

Sitting back in my chair, I repeated the title of the unit, as if I were voicing what the kids must be thinking: "Hmm, . . . playing with phonics. *Playing? Playing* with phonics?

"You must be wondering how a person *plays* with phonics. I mean, you can picture playing with a basketball. You bounce it, you throw it, you shoot baskets with it." I acted out all three as I spoke, playing up the drama as I spoke. "You can picture playing with a toy truck. You drive it, park it, load it up. But how do you play with /b/ /b/ or /ch/ /ch/?"

❧ **Name the teaching point.**

"Today I want to teach you that people who love letters and sounds (and every avid reader and writer *loves* letters and sounds) like nothing better than inventing totally cool, amazing sounds and figuring out ways to put those sounds on paper."

TEACHING

Let kids know that when you read about animals, you almost pretend to *be* the animals. Show a picture of a puppy and pose the questions, "What is he saying? How do you write *that*?"

"I know I am a grown-up, and in the evening after supper, after the dishes are done, I'm supposed to do my work. I'm supposed to pay the telephone bill and make dentist appointments and things like that. But because I'm like you—I love nothing more than reading and writing—I often end up poring over books. Last night I read a couple of great books about animals. And what I do when I read about animals, is that I almost pretend to *be* the animals. For example, I found this picture of a puppy looking at her person, and I just knew the puppy was saying, "Errrrrrrr. Errrrrr." And I knew if no one patted him, he was going to get up and shake his head and go . . ." and I made a doggy sound, "Arrrrrooo!" "But here is my challenge. How do you spell 'Arrrrrooo!'?" I again made that dog-shaking-his-head sound.

Model how you spell the noise made by a dog. Say the noise, listening for all the sounds, and write what you hear in a speech bubble. Reread and keep going until you have written out the noise.

"Will you watch how I try to spell that sound? I have a *lot* of animal pictures, and I'm thinking that maybe all of you can use phonics to capture the sounds that these creatures make. Of course, you need to write the sounds in such a way that someone else who hasn't heard *you* make the sound can read what you have written and bring that animal to life. We can add speech bubbles to the pictures by using Post-it notes." I placed a Post-it note, with a speech bubble in the middle of it, right onto the dog picture.

"Here goes. First, I need to make the dog sound. Arrrrrooo. Let me say the dog sound again slowly, trying to catch the first sound. Arrrrrooooo. Okay, the first sound is /ar/." I put my invented spelling *Ar* into the speech bubble. "Let me reread

FIG. 1–1 A teacher introduces the work of the bend by making the sounds a dog begging would make and inviting students to join in.

In addition to being highly engaging and great fun for kids, working with sound effects here offers a deeper opportunity. According to Merriam-Webster, onomatopoeia is "the creation of words that imitate natural sounds." Without an agreed-upon conventional spelling for most of these words, writers must truly play with sounds across entire words, using all they know about letters to capture those sounds.

what I have so far and then say the noise again, listening for the next part. Arrr-roooo. It sounds like the next part is /rooo/. Let me write that." I added to the label.

"Can you read this label with me and bring this pup to life?" I pointed under the word as a chorus of "Arrroooo's" erupted on the rug. "It worked! I wrote the sounds I heard as letters, and you could read what I wrote!"

ACTIVE ENGAGEMENT/LINK

Display two photos of animals as well as a photo of a race car. Ask partners to choose one of the photographs, act out the sound the animal or car makes, and write that noise on their whiteboard.

"Are you game to try this on your own? Here are two animals—and for those of you who prefer cars, I've given you an alternate photo as well. Will you and your partner start with one of these and begin dramatizing the sounds? You might each have a different idea of the sound, but see if you can learn from each other and agree—or decide on two sounds if you need to. Then take that sound (or those sounds) and try to write it on the whiteboard. You'll need to work hard to get the exactly right letters, so someone else can read what you write and make the sound you want. Work together to decide which letters make the sound, and then one of you will do the recording on the whiteboard. Do your best to get all of the sounds, because in a minute you will be switching boards with the other partnership in your rug club, and you want to make sure they can read what you have written!"

Note that one of the photos shows elephants calling to each other. The other photos were chosen with an eye toward tomorrow's session. The photos need to channel kids into recording "grrr" or "crrr" or both, as the next session builds off the subtle differences between those sounds. That's the reason for the car crash, which otherwise doesn't exactly fit into your teaching!

As kids worked, I coached the partnerships. I first coached them to say and hear sounds in the animal noises they were making. "Say the animal sounds slowly. What sounds do you hear?" Then, I coached partnerships to check what they wrote. "Run your finger under each letter as you read back the animal sound. Do you have all the letters you need?"

After a bit I voiced over, saying, "If you have captured the sound from one of these photographs, try another."

Have partners read the recordings of another partnership. The writers listen to the noise their readers create, checking whether it matches what they intended. If not, they can revise.

"Partners, now comes the challenge. Give your whiteboard to the other partners in your rug club. Don't tell them how *you* want them to read what you have written. Let them use the letters only and see if they make the sound you tried to represent. If they don't, add more letters or make some of the letters big or do whatever you need to do to try to make sure your writing leads them to make the sound you want."

FIG. 1–2   Noisy pictures to help students make and record sounds.

As the kids did this, I listened and then said, "Holy cow! What wonderful and varied sounds, elephants and lions and cars, oh my! Let's do a symphony share of all of these sounds. I'll be the conductor of the orchestra, which is all of you. When I point my baton (which is what the conductor's stick is called)," I used the eraser end of the pencil and pointed it toward the gathered students, "will you and your partner read the sound that is written on the whiteboard you are holding?"

I brought Mabel front and center to listen, and pointed my baton toward the first partnership.

FIG. 1–3 Partners swap whiteboards and read the animal sounds their partner wrote.

RUG TIME

Distribute nonfiction books with animals in them. Encourage clubs to act out and record animal sounds from these books.

I lifted up a bin of nonfiction books. "Do you remember our 'Learn about the World Books' from the very beginning of kindergarten? I realized that so many of them are about very noisy animals."

I opened one of the books and said, "Some people think books are quiet. But look here! Does this frog look quiet? She looks *really* noisy. I know some people think frogs make the sound 'ribbit,' but oh no. The sound some frogs make is, 'Quonk, quonk, quonk.'" I gestured for kids to join in and then picked up a new book. "This isn't a quiet book either—look at these crickets! When they rub their legs together, they make the sound, 'chirp chirp chirp chirp!'" I made the sound, rubbing my arms together to mimic the legs of a cricket.

I quickly distributed books for kids to share, and pens. "When you and your club get a book, open it up quickly and find a page that is *especially* noisy. Once you choose, act it by making the sound with your club. When you come up with a sound you think really fits that page, write it on a Post-it. We can pretend like these Post-its are speech bubbles, or you can even draw one yourself! You'll then add the Post-its you make to that page of the book. You might have time to do a few. There are blank Post-its inside the front covers of these books."

FIG. 1–4 One club writes the sound "woosh" next to the ocean to represent the noise the waves make.

POSSIBLE COACHING MOVES

▶ "Say it slowly. Try making the sound down your arm to help you really hear each part of it. What do you hear?"

▶ "Read what you wrote—exactly. Are you missing any sounds?"

▶ "I love the way you keep repeating the sound and listening to it in your mind. I do the exact same thing!"

▶ "This is such important work."

After a bit I said, "If you finish one, do another. Just leave the finished speech bubble on the page you chose, like a bookmark, and we can attach it to the page later. That way other kids can read not just the pictures but the sounds!"

Channel clubs to read each other's sound effects, paying careful attention to see if the reader reproduces the sound the writers had in mind. If not, coach the students to add more clues.

After a few minutes, I said, "Find a club near you and trade books, so that they can read what you have written, as exactly as they can. Here's the thing: you want to listen to how they read what you wrote, using that as a way to test what you wrote. Do they make the sound you had in mind? If not, do you need to add some letters? To underline parts, or make them bold? Revise your sounds and test the new draft with another group. Ready? Go!"

As the writers shared their sounds with each other, I coached to make sure they weren't just exchanging their printed sounds, but that instead the writers were listening closely to how others read what they'd written and using that as feedback toward revision.

SHARE • Animals Speak! A Shared Reading

Lead the class in a shared reading of "I Speak, I Say, I Talk" by Arnold L. Shapiro, and then channel students to read a stanza of the poem with their partner.

"Grown-ups also do the same kind of work that you all have been doing today—trying to find the words to capture the noises that animals make. I thought maybe we could read and reread a famous poem that a poet named Arnold Shapiro has written about the noises that animals make.

"Follow along while I read this, and then you'll have a chance to listen to some others reading this." I read the poem. Then I played a recording of children reading the poem, and invited the class to join in.

"Let's try reading this in parts," I said. "How about if the kids on this side of the room," and I gestured toward the left half of the meeting area, "join me in reading the name of the animal, and the kids on the other side, you join in reading the sound the animal makes? So it'll go like this." I acted out the back and forth of one group reading "Cats" and the other group responding with "purr."

"Before we read it as a group, will you try to read it—just you and your partner? You won't be able to read all the words, but see what you can do. How about if the front part of this room, you work on the first half this poem, and the kids sitting behind this line, you work on the second part of this poem? I'll be ready to read the last stanza, as the parts are called. I'll read it one more time, first."

I Speak, I Say, I Talk
by Arnold Shapiro

Cats purr.
Lions roar.
Owls hoot.
Bears snore.
Crickets creak.
Mice squeak.
Sheep baa.
But I SPEAK!

Flies hum.
Dogs growl.
Bats screech.
Coyotes howl.
Frogs croak.
Parrots squawk.
Bees buzz.
But I TALK!

Monkeys chatter.
Cows moo.
Ducks quack.
Doves coo.
Pigs squeal.
Horses neigh.
Chickens cluck.
But I SAY!

EXTENSION 1 • Reading Books Aloud with Sound Effects

Set up students to listen to a read-aloud of a book that has sound effects. Pause at the sound effects and model carefully reading through them. Direct partners to read some sound effects.

"Readers, you already know that some authors play with phonics like you do by thinking about the sounds things make and writing them carefully, so other people can read them. Mo Willems, does this type of playing all of the time in his books, like in this one, *Knuffle Bunny*.

The main character Trixie is just a baby, so she doesn't know words yet. Whenever she wants to talk, she makes all kinds of sounds! Let's read this book and try to make out what Mo Willems thinks she sounds like. Work with your partner to write on a Post-it what you think she might say."

Partners read *Agg-le. Aggle* and *Flllaaagggle. Flaggle. Klabble*. Then the class talked about what Trixie might be saying. When we reached the part where Trixie's mom asks, "Where's Knuffle Bunny?" I paused and said, "Look at Trixie's face here! It looks like she'd want to say, 'Dad, I told you so!' If you wanted to write 'I told you so' in Trixie baby talk, what sound effects would you write?"

The class called out all sorts of baby sound effects.

"I heard someone say it would be 'Kababble paggle raggle!' Quick—grab your paper and work with your partner to try to get that down on the page. I said the sounds as kids worked to write them. "Here's the trick. Will you pass what you have written to someone else and see if that person can read what you have actually written?" We continued doing similar work for a few more minutes.

EXTENSION 2 • Learning New Snap Words: *Come, Are, Too, Love*

"Friends, Mabel has something in her trunk for us to read." I unrolled four new snap words—*come, are, love*, and *too*—and attached them to the easel. "New snap words from Mabel for us to learn. Let's use the steps we know to help us learn each word." I gestured toward the "How to Learn a Word" anchor chart.

"Let's start with this one." I held up the *come* word card. "*Come*. Now study it. Tell your partner what you notice. How many letters does it have? What does it start and end with? What sounds do you hear in the word?

We chose Knuffle Bunny *because it is a favorite in kindergarten. If you don't have this book, any book with fun sound effects will do. Some of our favorites are* Bark, George *by Jules Fieffer,* The Book with No Pictures *by B. J. Novak,* The Rain Stomper *by Addie Boswell, and* Doggies: A Counting and Barking Book *by Sandra Boynton.*

FIG. 1–5 Students work to read and revise each other's sound effects.

"Ready to spell the word *come*? Hold your imaginary pen in your elephant trunk and write *come* on the rug. Check each letter to make sure it's right." Kids checked, and I continued on.

"Now let's use it! Let's make some sentences with the word *come*. *Come* to school and meet Mabel. Can you *come* to the park? You try!"

We proceeded through each step with the words *are*, *too*, and *love* before hanging them on the word wall and recruiting students to add them to their pouches.

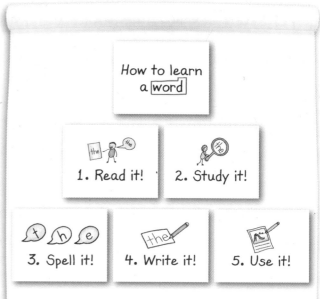

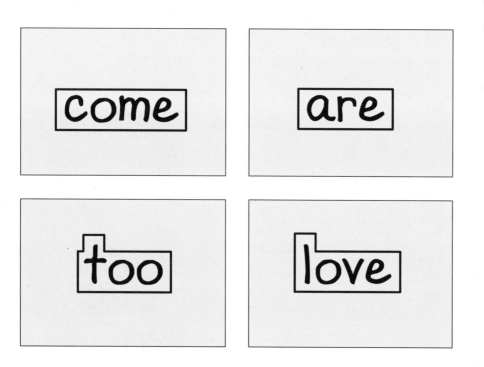

Listening for the Sounds that Are "Hiding in the Edges" of Blends

IN THIS SESSION

TODAY YOU'LL teach students that readers and writers listen carefully to all of the details of sounds, so they hear every sound, including those that are hiding in the edges of blends.

TODAY YOUR STUDENTS will look at photos, and imagine and then write the sound effects, paying more attention to the start of the words and listening carefully to see if there might be a sound hiding (a blend).

MINILESSON

CONNECTION

Compliment children on inventing noises but let them know that you have noticed that lots of the animals (and even the trucks) seem to make the same sound: /rrr/.

"You created quite a kingdom yesterday! This room was filled with the sounds of elephants stampeding and lions roaring. This classroom came to life with *your* inventions!

"I have one concern though about the sounds you created. It seemed like you had a lot of animals (and ever some cars) making the same sound. It looked like this, on paper." I turned to the whiteboard and quickly jotted:

Rrrrrrrrrrrr

I gestured toward the picture of the giant lion and said, "You had this guy making that sound," I pointed at the picture of the puppy, "and *this* guy making that same exact sound. The thing is, a lion's roar and a puppy's growl actually sound pretty different. Right now, can you make a roar for this lion?" The kids roared. "Now can you make a growl for this puppy?" The kids did that as well. "They are different, right?"

GETTING READY

- ✔ Display the photos of a puppy and a lion that were used in Session 1, as well as the photo of the race cars, at various locations around the classroom.

- ✔ Be prepared to play recordings of animals making sounds, such as a bear growling and a horse galloping. A link to the sound of a bear growling is available in the online resources.

- ✔ Display an enlarged copy of the "Blends and Digraphs" chart.

- ✔ Prepare a baggie of noisy pictures for each rug club.

- ✔ Have whiteboards, Post-its, dry erase markers, Post-its, and pens available for each student.

PHONICS INSTRUCTION

Phonological Awareness
- Hear both sounds in a blend.

Phonics
- Recognize and use the blends chart to learn consonant blends.

Word Knowledge/Solving
- Say a word slowly to hear the sounds in a blend.
- Use known blends to generate other words that begin with that blend.
- Use knowledge of blends to read words.

"Today I want to teach you that you need to listen carefully to all of the details in a sound, so you don't miss any of the sounds that may be hiding. It's sometimes easy to miss that there is more than one sound blended in. In the sound /grrr/, it is easy to miss the starting *g*, but it's there."

TEACHING

Make a noise in which the first consonant is swallowed up by the more dominant consonant in the blend. Coach students to identify all of the sounds, pointing out that they missed the more hidden consonant. Let them know the author blended the letters to get a just-right sound.

"I'm going to play a recording of an animal sound and we're going to listen carefully, for *all* the sounds, even some that might be hiding. When you have an idea of what letters you'd use to capture this sound, give me a thumbs up. Don't say anything though." I played a recording of a bear growling.

I thought aloud. "Hmm, . . . when I listened really carefully, I heard /grrrrr/. I think this is how I'd write it." I turned to the whiteboard and jotted the letters *GR*. "I mostly heard that /rrrrr/ sound, but when I listened super-carefully, I was able to hear the /g/ that was hiding. Was that what you thought, too?" Students nodded. "It can be hard to hear the /g/ sound, but it's there!"

ACTIVE ENGAGEMENT/LINK

Listen to a recording of galloping horses. This time, ask students to talk about what letters they would use to represent all the sounds, even the letters that may be hiding.

"Let's listen to more sounds together before you go off to do this work in your rug clubs. Here are some horses, running on a dirt road. Listen up!" I played a recording of horses galloping.

"Make the noise of the galloping horses!" The students made their own versions of the sound. "What sounds did you hear?"

Nodding, I said, "I agree. I hear, 'glop-glop, clippity clop.' Is that how you hear it? If we are going to write *g-l-op*, what are the first sounds? Listen carefully while I make the sound: /g/ /g/ /g/ *glop* . . . Turn to your partner and tell them what you hear." I gave students a moment to talk and then called them back. "Wait! It isn't just a /g/ sound at the beginning, is it? I hear /gl/ . . . /g/-/lllllll/. Do you hear the /l/ sound that is sort of hiding? What letters blend together to make this sound?" I called on Stephen, who told me to write a *g* and an *l*. "Does that look right? What do the rest of you think?" The class agreed. I quickly wrote the rest of the word, *glop*.

"Now, 'clippity-clop.' Listen carefully to the beginning, and say it with me: /ccccc-lllll/, *c* and *l*, right?" I quickly wrote *clippity-clop*.

You may think that you are teaching kids how to represent the call of the wild, but actually you are using the animal sounds as a forum in which to teach the most important concepts about blending—and one of those is the fact that often the dominant sound overrides the other, resulting in kids spelling gr with just the r or st with just the t. There are other dominant letter sounds as well.

You'll probably notice that writers will record the most salient sound in a blend. Here, you'll offer kids some quick practice hearing and recording both sounds in blends at the beginnings of words.

"Do you see how we listened carefully to the beginning part? There sometimes are sounds hiding in words and we want to be able to uncover them."

Introduce the blends chart to children and let them know it can help them to figure out what letters make up a blend. The chart can also help them read and write words with blends.

"I want to show you something that can help you! You might remember using this chart during reading workshop. This is a chart of different blends. Just like your ABC chart helps to remind you how letters sound, this chart will help remind you how different blends sound, with a picture that starts with that blend. So, for the /sc/ blend, you see a picture of a scarf. /Sc/-/arf/. At the start of that word you hear /Sc/ and the letters that make that blend are *s* and *c*. So, when you come to another word that has /sc/ in the beginning like *scarf*, you can think, 'Oh, it has /sc/ at the beginning just like *scarf*. It begins with an *s* and *c*.' Let's read the blends chart together now." I pointed to the blend and we read the keyword and then made the sound of just the blend. "Scarf. /sc/."

RUG TIME

Display pictures and ask set students to make the associated noises, then point out that many produced blends. Help students write those sounds, not omitting the less dominant consonant.

"Now you're going to have a chance to do this same kind of work with your partner! In a minute you'll have a bunch of pictures to choose from, but for now let's all start with that race car picture again." I showed the picture of the race cars from Session 1. "Remember, it takes off at the start of the race and then it hits another car! Think about the sounds that car might make when it hits a car. When you're inventing your own sounds, make sure you say the sounds first. Together, slow down how you say the sound to really listen to the beginning and see if there are any sounds hiding, to hear if there is a blend. You each have your own whiteboard and marker. Make the sound together, then each of you should try and get the exact letters down on the page!"

After a bit, I said, "I heard many of you said the word *crash* was the sound the car would make. Let's talk about the first sound in *crash*. Did you hear the *c* and the *r*? Wow! You are hearing both sounds in these blends." I turned the class's attention to the blend chart. "Look here! /cr/ is on the blends chart."

I distributed a baggie of images to each rug club. "Choose one of these pictures and imagine all the noises in the pictures. Then, write those noises on your whiteboard. Listen extra carefully to the beginning of each word so you can see if any sounds are hiding."

If you are using the reading units, your children will have seen this chart in Unit 3: Bigger Books, Bigger Reading Muscles. If this chart is new to your students, you may wish to spend just a little more time going through it to help them become familiar with it quickly.

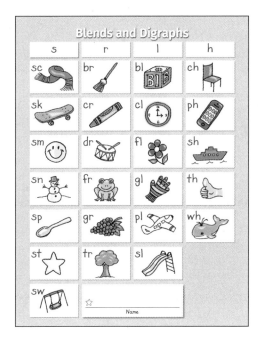

POSSIBLE COACHING MOVES

▸ "Say it slowly and listen to the first two sounds."

▸ "Say the beginning part of the word. Listen carefully for that first sound."

▸ "What two sounds do you hear at the beginning?"

▸ "Write down the first two sounds you hear."

SHARE • Revising the "Blends and Digraphs" Chart

Invite students to draw pictures of words that begin with blends to add to the "Blends and Digraphs" chart.

"I was looking at the 'Blends and Digraphs' chart again, and I'm not sure that it has the best pictures. I mean, there is a picture to go with every blend on here, but I'm wondering if we can make the pictures more interesting or exciting. Can you take a little time and look them over with your partner and see if you can think of some pictures that might be more interesting for kids?"

As the kids worked, I said, "If you think of improvement ideas for our 'Blends and Digraphs' chart, can you make a new Post-it with a sketch showing what you recommend and come and stick it on my 'Blends and Digraphs' chart?"

EXTENSION 1 • Listening for Blends in Words

Channel partners to read the pictures that match _s_ blends in the "Blends and Digraphs" chart. Say a word that starts with one of the _s_ blends and ask students to match the picture to the blend.

"As you know, this blend chart can help you remember the letters that you blend to make two sounds. Will you read the pictures with your partner that represent all the blends that start with _s_? Touch each picture and say the blend together!" Students read down the list with their partners.

"Great work! Now I'm going to say a word that starts with one of these blends, and you figure out which two letters make that sound. Ready? _Small_. When something is tiny, it is very _small_. _Small_. Point to the picture and the blend that starts the same as _sm-all_ on your 'Blends and Digraphs' chart.

"Did you find it? What was it?" Students called out _smile_. "_Smile_. _Small_. Yep, those two words start the same, /sm/. The letters _s_ and _m_ blend to make /sm/. That will help me write the word _small_.

"Okay, you ready for a harder one? Sky! The bird was flying in the sky! Sky. Point to the picture that starts like _sky_. Which blend can you hear? Find it on the blends chart."

I did this with a few more words and had students practice saying the blends and comparing the sounds at the start of words. "Now let's try some animal sounds. What if a snake made a sound like this: _slip, slip, slip_? Or this: _smooth, smooth_? What if it made this sound: /st/ /st/?"

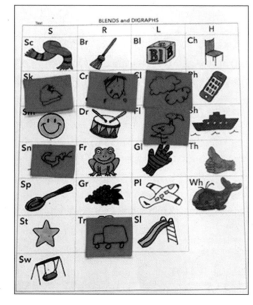

FIG. 2–1 Students revise the "Blends and Digraphs" chart with new picture icons.

FIG. 2–2 A student points to the _sk_ blend on the "Blends and Digraphs" chart.

EXTENSION 2 • Using the "Blends and Digraphs" Chart to Record Beginning Sounds

"Writers, the work we did today with blends is not just going to help you capture the sound effects, it is also going to help you go from being a so-so speller to being a *super* speller. Learning to hear and to write those blends in words is a big deal. It is going to be super-important that from this day on, whenever you write, you keep a blends chart near you. Let's practice right now.

"I'm going to say a word that may or may not start with a blend, and will you record the letters at the start of the word? It might be a single consonant, or it might be a blend. You ready?

"Step. I take a step forward," I did so, demonstrating how I took a step. "Step. /St//ep/," I repeated, empha-sizing the sounds at the start of the word.

I watched while children wrote on their boards. After it seemed most of the children had recorded a letter or two, I said, "Hmm, . . . /st/-/ep/. I hear two sounds at the start of that word. Let's look at the blends chart. Oh, /st/-/ep/ sounds the same at the start as /st/-/op/. So, it starts with the blend *st*. Does that match what you have?"

We proceeded through listening to and writing the sound/sounds at the start of more words: *glue*, *dream*, *crab*, *sport*, *blanket*.

FIG. 2–3   Kindergartners record beginning blends for various words.

EXTENSION 3 • Listening Closely to Words Beginning with *tr-* and *ch-*

"Friends, at lunch today, I was given half a cupcake. I thought, 'What a treat,' and then I thought of you. I thought, 'I've got to tell my kids about that word: *treat*.' Will you say the word and try to figure out how kids sometimes mess up the first sound in the word *treat*."

The kids said *treat* to themselves as I wrote the word on chart paper. "It is spelled *t-r-e-a-t*, but lots of kids say *and* spell it incorrectly. This is how kids sometimes spell the word." I wrote the incorrect spelling.

We talked about the fact that some people pronounce *treat* like *chreat* and spell it that way. "Let's try some other words," I said. "On your whiteboard, write *tr* and then *ch* and then *t*. I'll say a word, and will you and your partner point to the letters that you think are at the start of the word?" One at a time, I said the words *treasure*, *cheat*, *tractor*, *turn*, *champion*, *turtle*, *chirp*. After kids pointed, I wrote the word on the chart paper. We then talked about any misconceptions.

FIG. 2–4   A student points to the beginning sounds /tr/ as the teacher says the word *tractor*.

Reading Poetry with All You Know

GETTING READY

✔ Display the first stanza of "Forest Orchestra" by Georgia Heard.

✔ Have different-colored highlighters to mark a different line of the poem for each rug club to read.

✔ Distribute one complete copy of "Forest Orchestra" to each rug club.

PHONICS INSTRUCTION

Phonological Awareness
• Isolate initial blends in words.

Phonics
• Recognize and use blends at the beginning of words.

Word Knowledge/Solving
• Use knowledge of blends to read and write words.

IN THIS SESSION

TODAY YOU'LL teach students that when readers are reading sound words—or any words—it's important to use what they know about blends and digraphs to read word parts.

TODAY YOUR STUDENTS will practice reading and rereading an animal sound poem, looking closely across the words to read them just as they were intended.

MINILESSON

CONNECTION

Let students know that phonics has applications outside of school. Tell them about how Georgia Heard researched animal sounds and then made a book to teach other people about those noises.

"Everyone, I want to remind you that this work you have been doing—this work of listening so hard to sounds and trying to capture them on paper—this is phonics! It feels so much like playing it can be easy to forget that we are doing real thoughtful work! And it's not just kids who do phonics work.

"A famous poet named Georgia Heard wanted to learn all about animal noises, so she spent a long time listening to animals, so she could write a book all about the sounds they make. Georgia learned that the loudest animal noise of all is made by a shrimp no bigger than your pinky that lives at the very bottom of the ocean. Isn't that crazy?! Mabel, you'll be glad to hear that scientists are actually studying all the different sounds that elephants make, too, and creating an elephant dictionary full of their words! Wow, poets and scientists study animal noises too! This work isn't just for kids in school—it's very important work in the world."

Name the teaching point.

"Today I want to teach you that just like it's fun to play with sounds and try to capture them on the page just as they sound, it's also important to try to read the sounds that others write just the way they are meant to be read."

TEACHING AND ACTIVE ENGAGEMENT/LINK

Share a poem by Georgia Heard with students. Show them how she made the poem, by playing the noise of one of the animals and then have the class read that part of the poem.

"Georgia Heard actually gave us a poem from her book about animal noises, just for us to work with! It's called 'Forest Orchestra' and it's about animal noises in a forest. She worked really hard to capture the sounds that different animals make and put them on the page, so that others could read them and make the same sounds. When she was working on her poem, she listened *so* hard and tried to get the right letters to put the sounds she heard on the page. Then she would reread what she wrote, listen to the animal noise again, and if it wasn't quite right, she'd say, 'No, that isn't quite it. Let me listen harder,' and then she'd try again. Let's take a look at the first part of the poem now." I displayed just the first stanza.

"I think she really wanted her readers to have the fun of reading animal noises out loud, so it actually sounds like the forest. Let's read the first part of her poem now. We'll read the rest in just a few minutes. You're going to need to use all you know about blends and digraphs to help you read this!" I took the lead, began to read about the first four animals and the kids joined in.

> Forest Orchestra
> By Georgia Heard
>
> MAMMALS
> RED FOX: ow-wow-wow-wow   ow-wow-wow-wow   ow-wow-wow-wow
> AMERICAN RED SQUIRREL: muk-muk-muk   muk-muk-muk   muk-muk-muk
> CHIPMUNK: chip-chip-chip   chip-chip -chip   chip-chip-chip
> WHITE-TAILED DEER FAWN: bleat-bleat-bleat   bleat-bleat-bleat bleat-bleat-bleat
>
> INSECTS
> COMMON TRUE KATYDID: ch-ch ch-ch   ch-ch ch-ch   ch-ch ch-ch
> BOLL'S GRASSHOPPER: tst-tst-tst-tst-tst   tst-tst-tst-tst-tst   tst-tst-tst-tst-tst
> LINNE'S CICADA: zeger-zeger-zeger   zeger-zeger-zeger   zeger-zeger-zeger
>
> BIRDS
> OVENBIRD: teacher   teacher   teacher
> EASTERN TOWHEE: Drink-your-TEA   Drink-your-TEA   Drink-your-TEA
> HAIRY WOODPECKER: peek   peek   peek
> BLACK-THROATED BLUE WARBLER: Please-please-SQUEEZE-me   Please-please- SQUEEZE-me Please-please-SQUEEZE-me
> BLUE-GRAY GNATCATCHER: pzzzz   pzzz   pzzzz
> BLACK-CAPPED CHICKADEE: chick-a-dee-dee-dee   chick-a-dee-dee-dee   chick-a-dee-dee-dee
> AMERICAN ROBIN: Cheer-up, cheerily   Cheer-up, cheerily   Cheer-up, cheerily

MAMMALS

RED FOX: ow-wow-wow-wow   ow-wow-wow-wow   ow-wow-wow-wow
AMERICAN RED SQUIRREL: muk-muk-muk   muk-muk-muk   muk-muk-muk

When we got the chipmunk I paused, and said, "Hey! I see a digraph we know! /ch/ Let's make the sound of the chipmunk, ready, 'chip-chip-chip'. Read with me!"

CHIPMUNK: chip-chip-chip   chip-chip-chip   chip-chip-chip

We continued. When we reached the last line in the stanza, I paused again. "Whoa, now she is telling us about the sound the white-tailed deer fawn makes. This is new to me. Anyone else? Let's look closely at the first part of the word. It starts with a blend, *bl*. Let's say it together: /bl/. Great! Now, help me by making that first sound and I will help us with the ending of the word. Ready? *Bleat-bleat-bleat*," I read running my finger underneath the word as I read.

WHITE-TAILED DEER FAWN: bleat-bleat-bleat   bleat-bleat-bleat   bleat-bleat-bleat

"We sound just like a little forest! I love that this poem is called 'Forest Orchestra'—an orchestra is made up of musicians playing instruments and so it's like you are all making the music of the forest! Let's read this again, but this time different rug clubs can take different lines. I'll highlight one line of the poem for each rug club." I quickly highlighted each line of the stanza in a different color for each club, giving some lines to more than one club so that every club would have a chance to perform. "Before you rehearse your line with your partner, let's read the stanza again, together." We reread the stanza about mammals giving students a chance to practice and reread.

"Now, I want you to practice your part with your partner, rehearsing just your line. Read it just the way you think Georgia was hoping. You can even act out being that animal, if you'd like. Then we'll read the poem as a class. Your club can read your line when we get to it."

I coached in as the students rehearsed, helping them to speak the line together as a club, and also do some quick acting out of the animals.

Read the first stanza again, this time pointing to each line and having the club(s) assigned to that line read it. Reread it. Then read it once more as a whole class.

"Okay, are you ready, my forest orchestra? I'll point to each line and the club or clubs assigned to that line will read it. Let's read the title all together!" I pointed to each line and the clubs read the poem.

"Let's try it once more, even better! Ready?" Each club, in turn, read its line.

"Now, let's read it all together, the whole stanza about mammals, from the top! See the forest in your mind as you read." The kids joined in reading the stanza again.

As an alternative to highlighting, you could mark each line with a Post-it to assign the line to a rug club or two.

FIG. 3–1   A teacher leads students in reading "Forest Orchestra." Each part is outlined in a different color so that rug clubs know which part to read.

RUG TIME (CLUBS)

Lead the class in a shared reading of the remaining portion of the poem. Distribute the whole poem to clubs and have them read it together.

I pointed to the last two stanzas of the poem, about insects and birds, and turned toward the class. "There aren't just mammals in the forest. There are insects and birds, too! Let's read the rest of the poem together, remembering to read through all of the sounds in each word. I bet these extra animal sounds will make it sound even more like a forest in here!"

As we read through, I paused at the words *drink* and *please* to draw students' attention to the blends at the beginning. We made the sound of the blend and then carefully read through the rest of the word, including all of the sounds written. I then distributed a copy of the entire poem to each club. "Readers, now that you and your club have your own copy of the *entire* poem—mammals, insects, and birds—reread it once together, so in a minute we can play with it."

Let clubs know that they'll be performing the entire poem and that they can make the decision to act out the animals, add in new animals, whatever they'd like to help bring the poem to life.

"This is awesome! Now I'm going to give your club a chance to make the poem you own and really bring it to life. There are so many things you can do! You can have each member of the club read a different line, or stanza, and act it out. Or you can have half the club read half the poem and then other half read the rest. Or your whole club can read the whole poem, together. Make this poem your own and bring it to life. You'll probably want to try reading it a few different ways to see which you like the best!"

POSSIBLE COACHING MOVES

▶ "Make a plan with your club. How do you plan to read together?"

▶ "Read the animal sound just as it's written. Look across each part of the sound."

▶ "Let's take a moment to check. You said, _____. Did you leave out any sounds?"

▶ "Now that you've read it once, read it again and really sound and act like the animal."

SHARE • Performing Poetry (CLUBS)

Set up clubs to perform for one another, then read the whole poem together again. Tell students they'll take home copies of the poem, so they can read and perform it with their families.

"In a minute, you'll get the chance to share how you've made the poem your own. I'll set up clubs to watch each other perform. Watching club, be sure you do something to celebrate after the performance. You might snap or make a fun animal noise. After one club performs and you celebrate, then the other club can have a turn."

After each club had some time to perform, I said, "All animal voices up high. Let's read and enjoy it one more time, all together." We read through the poem and then I said, "I'm going to send a copy of this poem home with you tonight, so you can keep having fun playing with phonics with your families!"

EXTENSION 1 • Classrooms Make Sounds, Too! Poetry Writing

Lead the class in an interactive writing of a poem. Coach students to hear and write the sounds in blends.

"Friends, I was thinking Georgia Heard must have spent *a lot* of time in forests before writing 'Forest Orchestra.' We spend a lot of time in our classroom, so I bet we could write a poem called '*Classroom* Orchestra.'" I flipped to a piece of chart paper with the title written across the top.

"Close your eyes. What do you hear?"

"The clock!" a few kids called.

"Oh yeah, I hear it, too. Let's try to make the sound the clock makes. Click tick, click tick, click tick. Sounds a bit like that, huh? Now, let's do the writing." I turned back toward the easel. "*Clock*. That's the first word we need to write. Cllllllock.

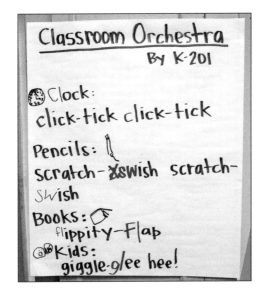

FIG. 3–2 One class's version of "Classroom Orchestra" written during interactive writing. Students shared the pen for the words and sounds that begin with blends.

I think I hear a blend at the start. See if you can write that word on your whiteboard." As students began writing, I invited one student up to write the *cl* for *clock*. Once she sat back down, I finished the word, *clock*.

"Now we have to write the sound the clock makes. *Click tick, click tick*. Let's write *click* first. Clllick. Wait! *Click* starts with the same sound as clock! *Click*. *Clock*. Try to get the whole sound down on your board. *Click*!" I again invited a student up to write the blend.

We finished the poem, stopping on a few words beginning with blends so that one student could share the pen while the rest practiced writing the words on their whiteboards.

Note, you could just as easily write a class poem about the playground or lunch room, if your students might find more inspiration for sounds by thinking of noisier spaces.

EXTENSION 2 • The "What's the Blend that You Hear?" Song

Remind children of a song that helped them hear first sounds in words. Revise the song so that students can practice hearing the blends in words.

"Do you remember the 'What's the First Sound that You Hear?' song?" I hummed a few bars of it, to the tune of "London Bridge Is Falling Down." "Since you're already so good at hearing the first sound in words, I thought we'd revise it so that it's called, 'What's the Blend that You Hear?' Join me when you can!"

I started singing to the tune of "London Bridge Is Falling Down":

What's the blend that you hear, that you hear, that you hear?
What's the blend that you hear in . . . crow, crow, crow?

I paused, giving the students a moment to think.

/cr/ is the blend that you hear, that you hear, that you hear!
/cr/ is the blend that you hear in . . . crow, crow, crow.

We continued singing a few more times with a few different animal names beginning with blends: *spider*, *clam*, *skunk*, and *snake*.

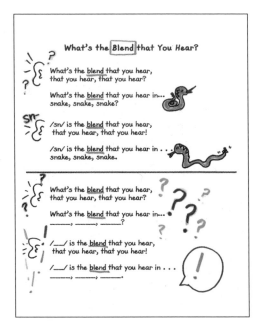

What's the Blend that You Hear?

What's the blend that you hear, that you hear, that you hear?

What's the blend that you hear in... snake, snake, snake?

/sn/ is the blend that you hear, that you hear, that you hear!

/sn/ is the blend that you hear in . . . snake, snake, snake.

What's the blend that you hear, that you hear, that you hear?

What's the blend that you hear in... ____, ____, ____?

/__/ is the blend that you hear, that you hear, that you hear!

/__/ is the blend that you hear in . . . ____, ____, ____.

Playing "Guess the Covered Word" with Poetry

IN THIS SESSION

TODAY YOU'LL teach students that blends alone won't help readers read words; they need to read the blend and also think, "What would make sense here?"

TODAY YOUR STUDENTS will read a poem and figure out the animal sounds in it by using a combination of checking initial blends and cross-checking for meaning.

MINILESSON

CONNECTION

Let the class know that their animal sounds have been so convincing that the principal thought there were actual animals in the classroom.

Once the class was gathered, I leaned in as if to impart something very serious. "Friends, after school yesterday, the principal came into our classroom and started looking around—under my desk, in the closet. I had no idea what she was looking for! I asked her, and do you know what she said?" I paused for extra drama. "She said, 'Are you keeping any animals in your classroom? Some teachers and kids have said that it sounds like a forest in here!'

"I guess the animal noises you've been creating and reading have tricked people in our school into thinking *actual* animals were living right here in our classroom! I didn't tell her anything. But then I started to wonder, 'Have we been having *so* much fun with animal noises that we forgot we are studying phonics?'

"So last night when I went home, I thought hard about what the most important thing is that I can teach you that will help you read blends. I kept thinking and thinking, and I finally realized that one thing you need to know about reading blends is that sometimes when you read, you don't *see* the

GETTING READY

✔ Display the first stanza of "I Speak, I Say, I Talk" by Arnold L. Shapiro. Cover the ending part of the words *snore*, *creak*, and *speak* with Post-its to show only the initial blends.

✔ Provide each student with a whiteboard and dry erase marker.

✔ Distribute copies of "I Speak, I Say, I Talk" by Arnold L. Shapiro to each student.

✔ Give each partnership a copy of the "Blends and Digraphs" chart.

PHONICS INSTRUCTION

Phonological Awareness
• Isolate initial blend sounds in words.

Word Knowledge/Solving
• Use knowledge of blends to read unknown words.
• Generate new words using specific blends.
• Read checking that the blends we say look right and make sense.

blend. You mess up. When you were reading the sound of the fawn bleating, did some of you find that you read the letters one way and then you had to go back and read them another way? Because that happens *all the time*."

❖ **Name the teaching point.**

"Today I want to teach you that blends alone won't help you read words. Readers read blends and think, 'What would make sense here?' and then read through the whole word to check."

TEACHING

Lead students in a shared reading of a familiar poem, stopping at a partially covered word. Model cross-checking the blend and thinking about what would make sense.

I directed children's attention back to the poem "I Speak, I Say, I Talk." "Remember a few days ago, when we first started this unit, we read a poem by Arnold Shapiro called 'I Speak, I Say, I Talk'? Now that we've done some work with blends, let's read the poem again." I displayed the poem with Post-its covering the endings of several key words, revealing only the blends at the beginning.

When we got to the line "Bears sn_____," I stopped and asked, "Bears /sn/? What do bears do?"

"Snore! Growl!" Students called a few varied answers.

"Wow! It sounds like you are thinking about what would make sense, what sound a bear would make. Let's also remember to use the blend to help figure this word out: /sn/. Hmm, . . . if the word starts with the *sn* blend, can it be *growl*?" Students called out no, that it couldn't. "Okay, let me think. I wonder if it could be /sn/-/ore/? That would make sense, bears do snore when they sleep! And I can hear the /sn/ at the beginning. Let's take a look." I removed the Post-it to reveal the word *snore*, and I reread the line.

"Did you see how as I read, when I got to a word with a blend, I thought about what would make sense *and* I checked to make sure the blend matched? That helped me make sure I was reading exactly what was written!"

ACTIVE ENGAGEMENT/LINK

Continue shared reading of the poem, giving students an opportunity to try to figure out, and then write, what the partially covered words might be.

"There are more words covered, so let's keep reading! This time, when we get to a covered word, will you write on your whiteboard what word you think is under the Post-it? Don't forget to think about the blend at the beginning of the word, *and* what would make sense. Ready?"

I Speak, I Say, I Talk
by Arnold Shapiro

Cats purr.	Flies hum.
Lions roar.	Dogs growl.
Owls Hoot.	Bats screech.
Bears sn▊▊	Coyotes howl.
Cr▊▊ cr▊	Frogs croak.
Mice squeak.	Parrots squawk.
Sheep baa.	Bees buzz.
But I SP▊▊	But I TALK!

FIG. 4–1 The teacher covered words that begin with blends with Post-its. She chose to leave the blends uncovered so that students use meaning and visual cueing systems to word-solve as they read.

Crickets cr____.

"Hmm, . . . what would make sense here? What sound might crickets make? Cr . . . ? Write your guess!"

I quickly circulated the rug area, as students wrote *creak*, *cry*, and other various sounds. I made sure to coach any students whose guess didn't start with the blend *cr-* by pointing back toward the poem.

"Some of you guessed *creak* and some *cry*. Both of those would make sense! Let's check." I uncovered the word *creak* and I ran my finger under the word, lingering at the end of the word this time.

"Creak!"

I nodded. "Yes, let's reread that line." We continued on.

Mice squeak.

Sheep baa.

But I SP____!

"'But I /sp/ . . .' Hmm, . . . what would make sense here? Write it on your boards."

Once again, the class wrote their guesses and after just a few moments we uncovered the word, revealing *speak*. We then reread the stanza all the way through without pausing.

I Speak, I Say, I Talk
by Arnold Shapiro

Cats purr.
Lions roar.
Owls hoot.
Bears snore.
Crickets creak.
Mice squeak.
Sheep baa.
But I SPEAK!

Flies hum.
Dogs growl.
Bats screech.
Coyotes howl.
Frogs croak.
Parrots squawk.
Bees buzz.
But I TALK!

Monkeys chatter.
Cows moo.
Ducks quack.
Doves coo.
Pigs squeal.
Horses neigh.
Chickens cluck.
But I SAY!

RUG TIME

Distribute copies of the entire poem to partnerships and direct them to read with their partner, using the first initial sounds as well as meaning if they get stuck.

"Readers, I have good news. That wasn't the end of the poem. There are two more stanzas to read! I'll pass out a copy for you and your partner to read together. As you read, especially if you get stuck, you'll want to read the first sound, or sounds if there is a blend, and then think with your partner, 'What would make sense here?'"

I passed out copies of the poem to partnerships. I coached partnerships as they read the words with blends, reminding them to make the sound of the blend and think about what would make sense.

After a few minutes, I called the class back together to read some lines with blends together. I pointed to a line and we all read, "Chickens cluck, Flies hum, Dogs growl, Frogs croak," and so on.

POSSIBLE COACHING MOVES

▶ "Make the first two sounds and think about a word that would make sense."

▶ "You said the blend. Now think, 'What word would make sense?'"

▶ "Could it be _____? Try it, see if the beginning looks right and makes sense."

▶ "Does that make sense? Try another word."

SHARE • Blends and Digraphs Charades

Teach students how to play blend chart charades by acting out a picture from the chart and having their partner guess which blend it is.

"I thought I could teach you an acting game. It's called charades and it's going to help us get to know the blends chart well. Here's how you play. One partner will look at the blends chart pictures and pick one to act out. The other partner will look across the chart and guess which blend their partner is acting. You'll want to make the sound of the blend when you guess."

"Let's do one together. I'll act, you guess. Ready?" I quickly crouched on the ground and started hopping like a frog as the class looked across their chart and quickly guessed, "Frog!" We made the sound /fr/ together before partners began playing on their own.

EXTENSION 1 • Name Five! Generating More Words with Blends

Channel students to brainstorm five new words that begin with the blend _dr-_. Then ask them to brainstorm five more each for the blends _bl-_, _sc-_, and _sl-_.

"Readers, Mabel wants to know more words that use the blends on our chart! I thought, as we line up for lunch, you all can help Mabel think about _more_ words with blends.

"Mabel wants more words that start like _drum_. She says she wants five! If you have a word like _drum_, put your thumb up! Samir, what word are you thinking?"

"_Dress!_"

"What do you all think? Does that start with the same blend as _drum_? Yup! Great. Come whisper it in Mabel's ear and line up! Who else has one? Let's listen to Raj. If you agree, make the hand signal for agree!"

"_Drip!_"

"Come, whisper it! Who else? Stephen, Marilyn, and Gayle! Listen to their words and then come up and whisper it in her ear!"

We continued with collecting five words that went with _block_, five that went with _scarf_, and five that went with _slide_.

FIG. 4–2   A student acts out _tree_ during "Blends Charades."

The dr- blend is one of most difficult to identify. Don't be surprised if children hear /j/, /ch/, /tr/ or other sounds at the beginning of words like dream or drink. As always, repeated practice with the dr- blend in reading and writing supports children to use it conventionally in time.

Recruit partners to do some seesaw reading, with one partner reading aloud and the listening partner checking to make sure each word was read correctly.

I called for students' attention in the midst of reading workshop. "Readers, you are doing such amazing work today. And I just wanted to point out that readers don't just think about word beginnings and blends during phonics workshop, they think about that stuff *all the time*! Readers always need to pay attention to the letters and sounds and think about if what they are reading makes sense. You've done such a great job in using the beginning sounds at the start of words to help you read. Paying close attention to the letters and sounds is important, but remember, your reading needs to also make *sense*.

"During partner reading today, do a little seesaw reading with your just-right books. When the first partner finishes the page, the listening partner can give a quick signal to say, 'Yep, looks right *and* makes sense' or 'Oops, check that again' if it doesn't! Can we read and help each other do this in your *own* books?" The children nodded, and I signaled for them to begin partner reading.

Revising Writing to Capture All the Sounds in Words

GETTING READY

✔ Display a child's drawing of a chicken with a speech bubble, that reads "ck ck."

✔ Display the "Blends and Digraphs" chart.

✔ Give each student a whiteboard and dry erase marker.

✔ Print *We Can Fix It*, a book written by a child that intentionally leaves out blends. Display page 1 of this book.

✔ Distribute a pen and a copy of either page 2 or page 3 of *We Can Fix It* to each partnership.

✔ Prepare to add a new page to *We Can Fix It*.

✔ Distribute a sentence strip to each partnership.

PHONICS INSTRUCTION

Phonological Awareness
• Isolate the initial blend in a word.

Phonics
• Study the blend chart to learn all of the blends.

Word Knowledge/Solving
• Use knowledge of blends to edit writing.
• Use blends to read and write.

IN THIS SESSION

TODAY YOU'LL teach students that when writers want make sure to capture all the sounds in a word, they say the word slowly, listen very carefully, and then add any letters that are missing.

TODAY YOUR STUDENTS will work to edit a piece of writing by identifying and fixing words that begin with blends but are spelled incorrectly. Students will also use words beginning with blends to make signs to encourage good practices in the classroom.

MINILESSON

CONNECTION

Show students a picture drawn by a child, with labeled animal noises. Read the noises, then ask students to discuss if they agree with what was written, or if they would make any changes.

"Friends, I have something to show you. Last night my little cousin came over and I told her about all the work that you were doing to write down the just-right noises made by different animals. She got so excited that she made an entire book full of animals and labeled all their noises. Let's read it together and see if we agree with the way she wrote the sounds. If not, we can fix them up." I displayed the first page of the book on the document camera.

I pointed at the speech bubble attached to the chicken. "ck-ck-ck," we read. "Hmm, . . ." I looked at the class. "/Ck/ /ck/ /ck/. Is that what chickens say? Thumbs up if you agree. Thumbs sideways if you disagree." Many children had their thumbs sideways. One called out, "Cluck! Cluck cluuuuuck."

"Oh, goodness, friends. Cluck. Cllllllluuuuuccckkk. My cousin got a good start, but there is a lot she didn't hear, right?

"Let's try to help. Let's say the noise very slowly and listen carefully. Then we can add letters we think are missing. Cllllluuuuuccckkk. /Clllll/—wait a minute. I hear the *c* that she wrote, but isn't there something else? /Clllll/ . . . turn and talk. What sounds do you hear at the start? Use the blend chart to help you."

The class talked, and students agreed we needed to add an *l* next to the *c*. I wrote the *cl* in the speech bubble attached to the chicken.

"Clllluuuuccccckkk . . . I hear a vowel. Which one? What do you think?" Kids said, "*U*!" I wrote that in the speech bubble after the *l*, and then I wrote the rest of the word and repeated, "Cluck!"

"It can sometimes be hard to hear all the sounds in a word—especially a sound word like *cluck*!"

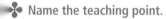 **Name the teaching point.**

"Today I want to remind you that capturing sounds onto the page isn't easy. Sometimes you do your best, then later you reread, and you think, 'Whoops. I can do better!' Then, you revise."

TEACHING

Tell students that the child also wrote a book and she needs some help with hearing blends. Get the class ready to help reading through the blends chart.

"It's been really fun to try to capture the sounds that animals make. This feels more like phonics *play* than phonics work. I want to continue playing with sounds, but you know, all this play with sounds should actually make your spelling *work* better. The way you corrected my little cousin's animal noises got me thinking that maybe you could use your skills to correct her writing, too.

"She has been learning phonics from her big brother, and she has some things a little mixed up. I think she doesn't really hear blends that well. It has been like she only heard the /rrrr/ not the /grrrr/ or the /crrrr/.

"Can I show you her persuasive writing and will you help her fix it up? It is long—she is like you, she loves writing books—so maybe if we all work together on one page, I could then give some of you her second page and some of you her third page, and you can work with a partner and try to help her.

"Before you do that, you want to make sure you are ready to be a Professor of Blends? Let's first read through the blends chart together and then we'll do a super-quick check to be sure you're ready."

Together we read through the blends chart, then I held up a picture card with a picture of grass. "When I play outside I like to run in the *grass*. Grass." I said the word slowly. "Whisper to your partner. What sounds do you hear at the start of the word? What letters make those sounds? Use the 'Blends and Digraphs' chart to help you. Yes! You hear /gr/ and you need *g-r*. Okay, one more. Here is a picture of a drink. I like to drink water when I'm thirsty. Drrrrriiinkkk. What sounds do you hear at the start? Whisper to your partner. Yes! /dr/, *d-r*. Okay, you are warmed up! You're ready to help for sure!"

Demonstrate fixing up part of the child's book by showing students how you say the word slowly and listen for all the sounds, especially at the start.

"Okay, here's the first page of her book. This book is trying to persuade her classmates to put the caps on the glue sticks. A lot of them are forgetting and then she can't make any art projects! Here's what she wrote on the first page." I displayed the first page.

> There is a poblem. Kids aren't putting caps on the gue.

"Hmm. . . . she did her best, but do you already see some words that might need fixing, where it seems like she didn't hear the blend? Let's read through the story; stop me if you see a word we need to fix."

> There is a poblem.

Hands went up. "There is a poblem?" I paused and look confused. "That doesn't sound right, does it?"

"Problem!" someone yelled out.

"Oh, problem. That makes *much* more sense. Okay, we need to help fix up this word. *Problem*. Prrrroblem. Hmm, . . . okay. I hear a *p* and then something else. Prrrrr. Prrrrr. *R*! I hear an *r*. "I added the *r* after the *p* and reread the sentence. "Wow, that looks much better and it makes *way* more sense."

ACTIVE ENGAGEMENT/LINK

Set up students to help you fix another word that is spelled incorrectly and missing part of the blend.

"Let's keep helping. I'll read the next sentence and you stop me if you see another word we need to fix."

> Kids aren't putting caps on the gue.

Hands shot up. "On the *gue*? What does that mean?" I paused, leaving space for students to think. "Oh wait, she must mean *glue*! The glue in our classroom is always missing caps. That would make sense! Looks like we need to help again. Will you say the word very slowly to your partner, listen for all the sounds, and try to write that word on your whiteboard the way you think it should be spelled?"

As students worked, I listened in and coached, helping them to say the word slowly and use the "Blends and Digraphs" chart if needed.

FIG. 5–1 Page 1 of *We Can Fix It*

After a few minutes, I gathered them back. "It seems a lot of you are saying that you hear GlIIIl . . . GlIIIl . . . at the start. Just like *glove*, right? So, you need *g* and *l*." I added the *l*. "*Glue*!

"Remember, writers, any time you want to make sure to capture all the sounds in a word—or in an animal noise!—you need to say the word slowly, listen very carefully, and see if you need to add any letters that are missing."

RUG TIME

Distribute the next two pages of the story to different partnerships and involve them in helping to fix up words that are spelled incorrectly.

"I have the rest of the book here. Remember, she is trying to convince her classmates to put the caps back on the glue sticks so she can make art. I'll give some of you page 2 and some of you page 3. Read it together and look for words that need fixing. I'll come around and coach you."

After a few minutes I gathered students and showed how I had fixed each page on my copy of the book. Students checked their work and fixed anything they had missed. Then we read the corrected version together.

Teachers, you'll notice that page 3 has more errors and words than page 2. You'll want to be strategic about which partnership gets which page.

FIG. 5–2   Pages 2 and 3 of *We Can Fix It* to distribute to partnerships

POSSIBLE COACHING MOVES

▶ "Put the page between you. Read it together. If you see any words you need to fix, be sure to stop."

▶ "Let's read it together. I'll read it with you. Look for anything you need to fix."

▶ "Say the word slowly. Use the blends chart to help you."

▶ "Fix it up. Add in any letters she forgot!"

▶ "Read to make sure it looks right and makes sense."

There is a problem. Kids aren't putting caps on the glue.

All of the glue sticks are drying up! We can't do our art work.

Please put the caps on the glue so we can make pretty things for our friends.

SHARE • Listening for Blends as We Add More to Writing CLUBS

Recruit the class to help you add one more page to your cousin's book containing a tip. Have the class listen for words with blends and signal when they hear them.

"Friends, you are also such responsible community members, so careful to make sure the glue caps are on tightly. I was wondering if we could make my cousin's book even better by leaving little tips for her readers." I taped a new piece of writing paper to the easel. "So, maybe this page should start, 'Here are some tips.'" I quickly wrote it across the page. "Hmm, . . . what should our next words be? What tips could we leave?"

As the class talked, I listened in, collecting their ideas.

"Writers, I heard you saying we could write, 'Press the cap down until you hear a click' and 'Don't let them dry up!' and 'Place them back in the baskets' and "Keep our classroom clean!" These are wonderful tips. You and your partner each have a sentence strip. Will you and your rug club write the extra tip for my cousin and then we will put all the tips on this page when we are finished? Who will write 'Keep our classroom clean'?" I then gave out to each group the task of writing any tip they'd like so we could add them to the book.

"As you write your tip, remember to listen to the words that have a blend at the start to write all the sounds you hear. Also, remember, to use the word wall to help you with your snap words!"

EXTENSION 1 • Fixing Up Blends in Your Own Writing

Challenge partners to read a piece of their writing, check to make sure all sounds were captured, and that each word makes sense. Encourage them to make corrections as needed.

"Writers, you worked so hard to help my little cousin fix up her writing, and I think that now you are ready to help each other! Will you and your partner choose one person's writing to put between you and read it together, checking to make sure the writer has captured *allllll* the sounds in a word. Read each word and think, 'Does it make sense? Does it look right? Does it sound right?' If you think 'No! It doesn't make sense' or 'It doesn't look right,' then fix it!"

As students worked, I circulated, and coached the whole class, voicing over the work they were doing, clarifying and extending the directions I had already given.

FIG. 5–3 Rug clubs work together to write another page for *We Can Fix It* as their teacher coaches them.

POSSIBLE COACHING MOVES

▶ "Say the word very slowly together and listen for *all* the sounds. Then, make sure you write down letters for all the sounds you hear."

▶ "Be especially careful to listen for the sounds at the start of the word."

▶ "Remember that sometimes there can be a sound hiding! Use your blends chart to help you."

EXTENSION 2 • Making Up Important Persuasive Signs with Words that Start with Blends

Show picture cards of words that start with blends, and have partners whisper the letters in each blend to each other. Then channel each partnership to use some of those words to make signs.

"Let's do a super-quick review of blends! I'll say some words that start with a blend. You say the word, listen for the sounds at the start of the word, and figure out the letters that make the blend at the start. Ready?" I said the first word. "*Swing*. 'I played on the swing.' *Swing*. What blend do you hear at the start of *swing*? Whisper the blend and letters in that blend to your partner.

"*Swing* starts with /sw/ and the letters that make /sw/ are *S* and *W*. Ready for another?" Quickly we progressed through the rest of the picture cards for *stairs*, *glasses*, *cry*, *friends*, *drink*, *slide*, and *clean*.

"Now, let's make some important signs for our school to give other students tips and suggestions about how to keep our school safe and clean. You can use some of these words to help you make some signs. I'll leave the picture cards up here, so you can see them. Try to think of a few things you could say on a sign that could help our community fix some problems that we have seen. Then write them down on your paper on your clipboard the best you can." I coached in and helped as students wrote their sentences. I especially supported them in saying the words that begin with blends slowly and listening for the sounds at the start.

"Oh, listen to this important sign! 'Play nice. Don't make friends cry!' We should hang that sign somewhere everyone can see."

FIG. 5–4 Writers are coached to fix up their own writing by thinking, "Does it make sense? Does it look right? Does it sound right?"

FIG. 5–5 Students make persuasive signs for their classroom and school using their knowledge of blends as they write.

Dear Teachers,

In this second bend, students will delight in creating pretend "magic spells," sound effects, and animal noises, while you teach them strategies for spelling words—first letter by letter, then part by part, encouraging them to draw on their knowledge of snap words to help them write the words they want to include in their writing.

You'll begin in Session 6 with a little magic, as you play a video clip of Cinderella's fairy godmother singing a song with a "magic spell" in it: "Bibbidi bobbidi boo." With the playful tone set, you'll show students how to play with sounds and capture them accurately in their writing. You'll play around with a few sounds until you make up a pretend "magic spell," then you'll say it over and over again, showing how you listen to each sound until you can write it down in a way that can be read by others exactly the way you intended. Then you turn it over to your students to try. Partners will write "magic spells" together, then rug clubs will meet to check each other's work to see if they can read all of the "magic spells" the way they were meant to be read.

As you move into Session 7, you'll teach students that they when they want to write a word they've never seen before, maybe even an invented word, they don't just spell it letter by letter. They can sound out the word part by part and rely on the word parts they already know. You'll return to the fairy godmother's magic spell, "Bibbidi bobbidi boo," to demonstrate how to sound out and spell *bibbidi* part by part, then your students will practice this work to spell *bobbidi*. Then during rug time, rug clubs will return to their "magic spells" from Session 6 to practice writing each other's spells part by part, and in an extension, you will teach them how to transfer this work from magic words to real words.

In Session 8, you'll remind students about the power of snap words, this time to help them find word parts they can use to spell and read even more words. You'll show kids how you can take the snap word *all* and add a new letter to the beginning to make new words: *ball, call.* Then students will practice with the word *will*, replacing the initial *W* with other consonants and blends to spell new words, such as *bill, mill,* and *still.* They will continue this work with their partners during rug time, then they'll cement their new learning by teaching their new words to another partnership.

Bend II concludes with Session 9, in which you'll teach students that they can use snap words and blends to make sure people can read what they write. You'll demonstrate how students can figure out how to write a particular word, such as *run*, by reviewing their snap words and finding one (*fun*) with a similar-sounding word part that can help. Then, with your guidance, students try this work with a longer word, such as *crayon*, that they wish to write. They'll review the snap words they know to find those with similar-sounding word parts, then draw upon those to figure out how to write their word. Then during rug time, students will liven up a piece of their writing from writing workshop by adding sound effects, using today's strategies and all that they know to help them write their sounds as accurately as possible. Finally, the bend concludes with a little celebration, as students read their writing aloud within their rug clubs, celebrating each writer's work with animal noises and sound effects.

All the best,
Lucy, Amanda, and Valerie

Magic Spells

IN THIS SESSION

TODAY YOU'LL teach students that when writers want to include pretend magic words in a story, they play with sounds until they create a combination that sounds right, then they say the word slowly and record the letters for each sound they hear.

TODAY YOUR STUDENTS will create pretend magic spells and write them down, listening carefully to the sounds and writing what they hear in such a way that they can be read by others exactly as intended.

MINILESSON

CONNECTION

Let students know that another way to play with sounds is to use them to make magic spells. Show a bit of a clip of someone singing a magical spell to illustrate your point.

"Class, I've told you before, the work you have been doing is serious work. Grown-ups play with sounds and letters just like you do. Grown-ups figure out how to add sound effects—like screeches and roars and pops and bangs—to stories. To do that, they play around with sounds.

"And sometimes grown-ups play around with sounds to make nonsense words and magic spells, like *hocus pocus* or *abracadabra*. If you don't believe that grown-ups play around with sounds to make magic spells, think about the movie *Cinderella*. In that movie, a fairy godmother points her wand, says a magic spell, and changes a pumpkin into a carriage. She says 'Bibbidi bobbidi boo!' Writers invented those magic words. Let's listen to a bit of it." I played the clip of the fairy godmother singing.

"In Harry Potter, there are tons of magic spells, too. One of them goes like this: 'wingardium leviosa!' J. K. Rowling, the *very* famous author of the Harry Potter books, sat at her desk, just like you all sit at your desks, and she invented those magic spells."

GETTING READY

✔ Before the lesson begins, distribute a whiteboard and marker to each student, so students have them in hand when it's time to use them.

✔ Cue a video of Cinderella's fairy godmother singing a magic spell. You'll play to 0:43. A link to the video is available in the online resources.

PHONICS INSTRUCTION

Phonological Awareness
- Hear and connect rhyming words.

Phonics
- Blend consonant sounds to make a consonant cluster.

Word Knowledge/Solving
- Write words letter by letter, by blend, by word part.
- Use a blend to generate more words that begin with the same blend.

❖ **Name the teaching point.**

"Today I want to teach you that if you want to write a story that has pretend magic (and pretend magic spells) in it, you can play around with sounds until you come up with something that sounds just right! Then you figure out how to put those sounds onto paper."

TEACHING

Think aloud about how magicians come up with magic words. Demonstrate creating a magic spell, emphasizing how you find a sound you like and then listen carefully to figure out how to write it.

"So, if you want to write a story with pretend magic in it, how would you go about creating a magic spell? First, you'll need to play around with sounds. When magicians were coming up with the word *abracadabra*, I bet they started out with *abba dabba*. Then they probably thought it needed something more, so they played around with some different sounds. Maybe they went to *abba cabba* and then *abba cabba dabba* and so on until they finally settled on *abracadabra*.

"I'm going to try to create a pretend magic spell right now to turn you all into little magicians." I held my pointer like a wand. "First, I have to put some sounds together. Let's see . . . *kalamoo*! No, that's not magic-sounding enough. *Kalamazoom*! That's better, I'll try and write that one down."

I said the word a few times slowly. "Kaaalllaaammmaaazooooom. I hear the /k/ sound in the beginning. That could be a *C* or a *K*. I'm going to put a *K*. /k//a/. /a/—that's *a*." I wrote the *a* next. I went through the entire word, stretching it out slowly, listening for each sound, and writing a corresponding letter on the board.

Recap the process that you go through when you say a word slowly, chunk by chunk, recording one part and then rereading it and saying the next part of the word.

"Did you see how I did that? I tried putting different sounds together until I came up with some magic-sounding words that I liked. Then I said the words slowly, listening for sounds I knew and then writing the letters on the board."

I waved my magic wand over the children's heads and said, "Kalamazoom, Kalamazoom, bish bah boom. I think I did it. I've turned you all into magicians!"

FIG. 6–1 Teachers lead students as they create pretend magic spells.

ACTIVE ENGAGEMENT/LINK

Channel children to get started making their own pretend magic spells. Help them use blends and sound-letter knowledge more broadly to capture the sounds they select on their whiteboards.

"Now magicians, you're ready to give it a try! Take out your own magic wands. It's okay if they are invisible! Now turn to your partner and try and come up with some magic spells together. Maybe you want to come up with a spell to help Mabel fall asleep. Or a magic spell to help you learn your snap words—or to turn the milk in the cafeteria into chocolate milk!"

I moved around the rug, listening to the silly sounds and imaginary words my students were coming up with and pushing them to try adding or replacing sounds to the words they were coming up with.

After most partnerships had created their own magic spells, I told the class, "Okay, now take out your whiteboards. It's time to write your magic spells! Say your spell slowly with your partner and try to write down all of the sounds that you hear." I moved around, encouraging students to give it their best attempt, even if their spells were super-long or difficult to sound out. "Remember that if you want to write a story that has pretend magic spells in it, you can play around with sounds until you come up with something that sounds good, then listen carefully to every sound so you can write your magic spells down!"

POSSIBLE COACHING MOVES

▶ "What a cool magic spell! Could you make it even longer?"

▶ "What other sounds could you add into your magic spell?"

RUG TIME CLUBS

Ask clubs to read each other's pretend magic spells. Set up the writers to listen and see if the magic spell sounds the way they intended. If not, revise!

"Magic spells are great if you know how to say them, but when you write a story that has pretend magic and pretend magic spells in it, you'll need to write the words in a way that others can read. So, for rug time today, work with the other partnership in your club to see if they can read the magic spell you came up with. You might realize you need to add some more letters to help your friend read your magic spell the way you intend it to be read. If you need to fix it, you can do that right there on your whiteboard!

"Once you have written your pretend magic spell and shared it with your rug club, try writing another. Perhaps all four of you in the club want to try one on your own. I'll distribute some more whiteboards, so you can try writing your own spell. Remember to write it, then reread it, checking that you have all the letters and sounds you need."

After a few moments I said, "Writers, would you make sure that your magic spells record every sound, in every beat? Clap the beats of your magic spell, and make sure you've recorded every sound in each part. Even made-up words need vowels and blends, too, so be sure you listen for those!"

FIG. 6–2 A student works to record her magic spell, writing it part by part.

I moved around the rug, attempting to read the students' magic spells and pointing out parts that could use more sounds.

SHARE • Kid-Created Magic Spells

Have students wave their wands and say their magic spells into the air. Then read some magic spells together.

"Fabulous work today, magicians! Will everyone shout their magic spells into the air?" The students shouted out their magic words.

"Some of you came up with a magic snap word learning spell! That spell is really going to come in handy tomorrow when we learn four new snap words. Let's test it out right now and see if it works. Are you ready to hear it?" I waved my wand and said, "Snapelaroo!

"What else might we need a magic spell for in school? Maybe we need one for . . . lining up? Turn and tell your partner, how would that magic spell sound?"

As the class began to make up spells, I listened in and collected ideas.

"Whoa! I heard so many spells for lining up! What about this one?" I held out my arm and pretended to have a wand in my hand. "Let's see if this spell works. What would you all do if I said . . . 'Line-ius Up-ius!'" I waved my hand over the class and they started to make their way to line up.

I walked over to the line with them and said, "It worked! Who knew that magic would help us line up?"

The class giggled from the line and I said, "We have new spells for learning snap words *and* for lining up. Let's see if we can come up with some more magic later on."

FIG. 6–3   Students make their way over to line up after the teacher says the magic spell, "Line-ius Up-ius."

EXTENSION 1 • Make a Magic Word

Give Mabel some letters and explain to kids that the letters she's holding in her trunk can combine to make a magic spell.

"Look at what I found in Mabel's trunk!" I opened an envelope and placed the letter tiles contained within on the document camera: S, O, O, A, A, T, P, R.

"Hmm, . . . these letters don't look like a magic spell, do they? But I bet if we rearrange them, we can make up our own spells to help Mabel sleep! Some rug clubs have whiteboards and others have the letters on magnetic boards. I am going to try a spell, and as I make it, help me read it!

"STA-PA-ROO!" the class called as I built a spell.

The children then made their own spells and I coached them to use all the letters and read back what they spelled. I also reminded students to rearrange the letters to make new spells. The blends I helped students to make were *tr-*, *pr-*, *st-*, and *sp-*.

"There are so many cool spells that I think will help Mabel. Let's write the best ones down and leave them near her bed. When you finish writing, we will read them and post them, here, next to her bed!"

FIG. 6–4   A teacher models "Making Spells" using letter cards in a pocket chart.

EXTENSION 2 • Listening for Patterns and Predicting the Outcome

Chant a playful rhyme to give students an opportunity to practice listening for patterns and predicting the ending.

"Kindergartners, it's time to line up for lunch. As we line up and walk down the hallways, I have a chant for us to chant that is like a game! Are your ear muscles strong enough to recognize the pattern and guess the next word? Start by snapping a beat for me." I snapped 1, 2, 3, 4, and then began the rhyme.

> *Spat*, *spit*, *spot*, and *spin* . . .
> Guess the next word, try to win?
> *Grat*, *grit*, *grot*, and _____.

"*Grin!*"

> *Grat*, *grit*, *grot*, *grin* . . .
> Guess the next word, try to win?
> *Chat*, *chit*, *chot*, and _____.

"*Chin!*"

EXTENSION 3 • Blend Equations

Explain how blends can be like addition. Add two letters together to make a blend, then recruit students to think of words beginning with that blend.

"Sometimes, when you are learning something new, it can help to look at that thing in a completely different way. We have been learning about blends during word study time, and during math time we have learned about adding. But I've been thinking . . . blends and blending are sort of like what you do when you are adding. Wait a minute! Math?! During word study time?!"

I showed kids the first blend equation:

$s + l = sl$

We read each "equation" like this: "/s/ plus /l/ equals /sl/." Then we took away the math and did just the sounds, like this: /s/ /l/ /sl/.

As we read the first equation I said, "Let's come up with some words that start with *sl*. See if you can fill your whole hand, one word per finger, with words that start /slllll/ like *slllllllide* or *sllllow*. You try!"

Student worked with partners to come up with as many words that start with /sl/ as possible. I walked around and coached, "Is that a real word or a nonsense word?" "Can you think of any other words that start with /sl/?"

We followed these steps for the rest of the equations:

$f + l = fl$

$s + n = sn$

$d + r = dr$

$s + p = sp$

FIG. 6–5   A student produces words that begin with the blend *sl* after reading a blend equation.

Activating Word-Part Power to Write Longer Words

IN THIS SESSION

TODAY YOU'LL teach students that writers don't just spell new words letter by letter; they sound out the word part by part and rely on word parts they already know.

TODAY YOUR STUDENTS will return to the magic words they made up in the previous session and write them again, this time part by part. You will remind them of what they know about clapping out syllables and listening for the first sound and the word part they know in each syllable.

MINILESSON

CONNECTION

Tell students that when they want to write a very long word, it takes too long to write it in a letter-by-letter way. Hint to them that there is a better way to do this.

"Writers, I watched some of you writing pretend magic spells yesterday and want to give you a tip. If you are going to write a long magic spell (or really, any longish word), it is hard to write it if you go in a letter-by-letter way. For example, to spell the word *Supercalifragilisticexpialidocious* in a letter-by-letter way, you'd need to go /s/-/u/-/p/, just to get *sup*. And to spell the whole word like that—/s/ /u/ /p/ /er/ /c/ /a/ /l/ . . . whew, that would take ages! There is a better way to figure out how to write words that you don't know."

✤ **Name the teaching point.**

"Today I want to teach you that when you want to write a word you've never seen before—maybe even an invented word—the easiest way to spell that word is part by part. You can break the word into syllables and then spell each syllable, thinking about the ending part of that syllable."

GETTING READY

✔ Be prepared to write a multisyllabic word on the easel or whiteboard where your entire class can easily see it. We use *Bibbidi Bobbidi Boo* as the example.

✔ Distribute a whiteboard and dry erase marker to each student.

✔ Have your set of magnetic letters to spell out a series of words leading up to the secret word of the day.

PHONICS INSTRUCTION

Phonological Awareness
- Hear, say, and clap syllables.
- Hear the ending phoneme in a syllable.

Phonics
- Recognize and use VC and CVC phonograms.

Word Knowledge/Solving
- Use phonograms to help spell words.
- Use known words to spell unknown words.

TEACHING

Involve the students in helping you spell a made-up word part by part, clapping out the syllables and spelling each syllable, using what they know about onset and rime to help.

"Do you remember the video clip we watched the other day—the one with the fairy godmother singing 'Bibbidi Bobbidi Boo'? So how would we write that? Hmm, . . . *Bibbidi Bobbidi Boo* is three words. Let's write the first word together. *Bibbidi*. First, we can clap out the syllables. *Bib-bid-i*. Okay, so we know the first syllable is *bib*. What's the first sound? Yes, /b/, so I'll write the *b*. Now let's use our word-part power to figure out the rest. /b/-/ib/, /b/-/ib/. What is that word part? That's right, it's /ib/. I'll write that part now." I added *ib* to the *b* on the board.

FIG. 7–1   A teacher leads the class in reading *bibbidi*.

"So, we have the first syllable done, *bib*. Let's do the second syllable. *Bibbidi*. What is the second syllable?

"Bid!

"That's right, it's *bid*. The first sound in *bid* is . . ." I waited for kids to say /b/, then I wrote a *b* on the board. "Now listen for the word part. *Bid*. /b/-/id/. Say that with me. /Id/, that's another word part!" I added *id* to the word on the board.

"Look at that! We almost have the whole word." I pointed to each syllable as I read, "bib bid. Bibbid . . . eee. In this word the *i* makes the sound /eee/, so I'll quickly add that. Now we have the whole word, *bibbidi*!"

ACTIVE ENGAGEMENT/LINK

Set up students to spell and write another made-up word, part by part.

"Now try to do the next word with your partner. *Bobbidi*. Clap out the syllables first." As the students clapped I voiced over, "*Bob-bid-i*. You got it!"

"Now start with the first syllable. *Bob*. Figure out the first sound and then the word part." I listened in as students said the word and wrote the letters on the board as they worked. "I heard a lot of you say it starts with the sound /b/, so I wrote the *b* up here. A lot of you also figured out the word part -*ob*. I'll write *ob* on the board too. So now you have the first syllable: *bob*. Keep going to figure out the rest of the word.

"Oh wow, a few of you noticed that this syllable is the same as in *bibbidi*. *BibBIDi*, *bobBIDi*. They are the same. I'll write that up now! The last part is *boo*, like a ghost! I'll quickly write that up here too.

"Okay, let's read the whole thing together." I pointed to each word as we read, "Bibbidi bobbidi boo!"

RUG TIME CLUBS

Ask partners to write the magic words they invented in the previous session, part by part. Remind them to clap the syllables and listen for the first sound and the word part they know in each syllable.

"Now you're ready to try this out on your own. Quickly, turn to your partner and remind each other of the magic words you came up with yesterday. If you can't remember, that's okay. Make up a new one now!"

"Now that you all remember your own magic word, write them again on your whiteboards. Try and follow the steps we just used today. Clap your word into syllables and listen for the first sound and the word part you know in each syllable. Then write it down on your whiteboard."

A few partnerships needed extra support doing this work, and I stayed close by to help them. For other groups, I voiced over, "If you have finished writing out your word, try and write out a new magic word!" I pulled the word *at* off of the word wall. "See if you can come up with a magic word that has the word *at* inside of it!"

Set up one member of the rug club to say their magic word and cast a pretend spell on the rest of the rug club, so that they will now all write the first member's magic word on their whiteboards.

"You really put your word-part power and your vowel power to use today. I'm glad you haven't forgotten about them! Now let's use your magic words to cast a spell on your rug club! Are you ready to try?" The kids nodded excitedly.

"Great! Rug club member 1's, stand up with your marker, but keep the cap on," I said, holding my own marker in my hand. "This is no longer a marker, it's your magic wand. Member 1, take your wand and quickly cast a pretend spell on your rug club with your magic word, like this," I said, waving my marker around ceremoniously. "Bibbidi bobbidi boo! Once all of your rug clubmates are under your magic spell, they will start to use all that they know about words and sounds to record *your* magic word on their boards. Give it a try!"

One member from each club began saying their magic word to their clubmates, as I listened in. I reminded these students to repeat their magic words several times for their classmates. Then, I coached the kids who were writing to break the magic words into word parts to help them spell these.

SHARE • Secret Word of the Day

Challenge students to figure out the secret word of the day. Introduce a snap word, then change vowels, blends, and rimes to make new words until students figure out the word.

"Friends, we have to do one more thing today. There's a secret word of the day, and you need to figure it out. It's a magical word. As soon as anyone says the magic word of the day, all of us need to flutter magic dust into the air like this." I demonstrated sprinkling magic dust.

▶ "Clap the word into syllables. What is the first part?"

▶ "Say the first part. What is the first sound? Write it!"

▶ "You've written the first part. Clap the syllables of your word again! What it the next part? Listen for the sounds in the second part."

▶ "Stretch that part down your arm. What sounds did you hear at the end?"

▶ "Reread your spell. Did you forget any sounds?"

"It won't be easy to figure out the magic word," I warned. "You'll each need your whiteboard. I'll give you clues. You'll need to write other words to figure out today's secret word. Start by writing the word *hat*. I wore a *hat* on my head. Hat." All of the students did so while I built the word *hat* with magnetic letters in front of them. "Now change the *a* to an *i*. What word do you have now?"

"*Hit*!" the kids yelled out.

"Yes, *hit*, like I *hit* the ball. You're on the track of figuring out the secret word. Let's keep going!"

We progressed in this way, building *hip*, *clip*, *trip*, *drip*, *grip*, and *grad* with students writing each word on their whiteboard. Then I said, "There's one more clue. Once you figure out the last and final word, that's today's secret word. Ready? Change the blend *gr* to the blend *gl*. What word do you have? Say it out loud, then write it on your whiteboard."

"*Glad*!" the kids yelled out and I fluttered my fingers, sprinkling magic dust all over the meeting area and the kids.

"Yes! I'm so *glad* you all came to school today!" I sprinkled more magic dust. "That means I'm super-happy. Try to use the secret word in a sentence with your partner and if you hear it being used, sprinkle down magic fairy dust!" Magic dust sprinkled all over the meeting area as kids tried out using the secret word.

"Friends, don't forget. All day whenever someone uses the magic word, we all sprinkle magic! This is so much fun. I'm so *glad* we get to play with phonics together!"

FIG. 7–2   Students search for magnetic letters to build the magic word of the day.

EXTENSION 1 • Transferring Today's Work from Magic Words to Real Words

Explain that the work kids did writing magic words can help them spell long and tricky real words. Demonstrate how you transfer that work to a tricky word: *hippopotamus*.

"The work you did today—writing those magic spells—actually has magic power to help you as a writer and a speller. If you can spell *bibbidi bobbidi boo*, well then you can spell anything! That gives you amazing spelling power. I'll show you.

"Let's think of a crazy long word—a real word this time. Here's one: *hippopotamus*. You know how to help me spell it, right? You just clap it out—or clap it in your mind if you don't really want to sit there during writing time, clapping away. Here's how that goes: Hip-po-pot-a-mus." I clapped each syllable as I said it.

"Then you spell the first part, remembering word-part power: /h/-/ip/, *h-i-p*, *hip*!

"Reread and say the next part: hip-po—po, /p/-/o/, *p-o*. So, now we have *hippo*.

"Now write that and say the next part: *Hippo—pot*." And so on.

"It's a long and tricky word, right? But we didn't give up. We listened to all the sounds in the word, thought about what came next, and wrote down each sound that we heard. So, when *you* want to write a long and tricky word, don't say, 'I can't do that, it's too long!' Instead say to yourself, 'If I can write magic spells, I can spell any word, especially long ones!'"

EXTENSION 2 • Interactive Editing: Using All that You Know

Channel students to fill in the missing letters on signs that Mabel made, drawing on all they know about blends and digraphs, snap words, and letter-sound knowledge to do this work.

"Writers, Mabel made a couple of signs for the classroom and needs help editing it. She left lines for letters that she needs to make her sign more readable. Can we help her?

"Here is her sign. This is what she wanted to say, 'Throw your paper in the garbage can. Put your clipboards away. Keep our room neat and clean.' Can we help her fill in the letters that she is missing, so that we can hang these signs up and others can use them?"

I coached the students to hear and use the blends and digraphs that they know, their snap words, and letter-sound knowledge in the middle and ending parts of words. After the students helped with making and editing the sign, we read it back.

"I am going to hang this up. Before I do, would you all like a copy of this for your reading book baggies? You did help Mabel make this important sign, *and* it has some super-long words that you now can read! What a challenge!

"When you work on your own signs and letters, remember, use *all* that you know to tackle and write the words!"

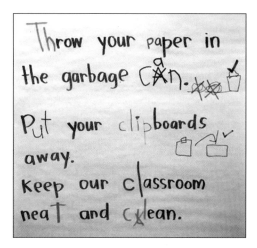

FIG. 7–3 One class's persuasive sign made with interactive writing.

Learning New Snap Words to Write Even More Words

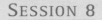

GETTING READY

✔ Prepare a list of potential snap words for you to look over and choose from.

✔ Have chart paper and a marker to write your four snap words: *all*, *ball*, *had*, and *will*.

✔ Display the "How to Learn a Word" anchor chart from Unit 1, *Making Friends with Letters*.

✔ Distribute a whiteboard and marker to each student.

PHONICS INSTRUCTION

Phonological Awareness
• Hear and divide onsets and rimes.

Phonics
• Recognize and use VC and CVC phonograms.

Word Knowledge/Solving
• Use phonograms in snap words to write new words.

High-Frequency Words
• Learn new words (*all*, *ball*, *had*, *will*).

• Develop strategies for learning new high-frequency words.

• Read high-frequency words in continuous text.

IN THIS SESSION

TODAY YOU'LL teach students that writers can learn new snap words, which will often give them word parts that they can use to spell and read even more new words.

TODAY YOUR STUDENTS will learn four new snap words and use them to make other words.

MINILESSON

CONNECTION

Remind students about using words they know to find word parts to help them write new words. Have them use their magic words to inspire them for learning new snap words.

"Magicians, you invented such lovely magic formulas the other day. Let's hear them again and admire them. When I point my magic wand to your rug club, will your club say one of your magic words?" I pointed my marker (my pretend magic wand) to one rug club and then another, sometimes repeating their incantation to give it extra power and pizzazz.

"Holy moly, these are great! Let's see if we can use these magic words to make something magical happen. Do you remember the work you did earlier, when you took words that you already know, and you used them to help you get word parts that helped you write other words? I'm thinking that it would be really, really great if you had even more snap words that you can use to write other words.

"So, would you be game to use your magical formulas to help all of us learn some new snap words? Are you willing? I can pick snap words that will be especially great for our unit. Okay?

"Give me a minute to choose." I pretended to look over a long list of snap words, scratching my head, furrowing my brow as I hemmed and hawed my way to super-special choices. As I worked I made squeals of delight when I settled on one choice or another. I said, "Yes, yes!" and "Oh, good one," as I found great choices.

"Just you wait until you see these snap words," I said, tickled over the choices. I went to the backside of the easel, wrote them on chart paper in such a way that no one could see me do this, then flipped the page around, showing the four new words in all their glory: *all*, *ball*, *had*, *will*.

"Before we read them, let's use your secret formulas to turn your minds onto high, so you'll learn these words so well you can use them even today, even tomorrow. In your club, you are going to need to pull close together, to say your magic words together, saying them over and over, and as you do, sprinkle your fingers so the magic drops over the tops of your heads. Like this," I said, and did a little demonstration saying, "Bibbidi bobbidi boo . . . Snapelaroo! Now, you'll get some magic going, so your brains become super-strong."

The kids did that, and then we read the words together: "*All*, *ball*, *had*, *will*."

❖ **Name the teaching point.**

"Today I want to remind you that when you are learning new snap words, those new words will often give you word parts that you can use to spell and read more and more new words."

TEACHING

Remind students about the process of learning a new snap word. Guide them through the process to help them learn the new snap word, *all*.

"The first new snap word you'll learn today is *all*. Look at *all* of us. We are *all* sitting on the rug! Let's do *all* the things on our chart." I pointed to the "How to Learn a Word" anchor chart and led the class quickly through the steps.

I pointed to the first snap word, *all*, that I'd written on the chart paper. Students read then studied *all*, and they noticed it had one small letter and two tall letters that were the same.

"Now, I see three letters—let's chant them. *A! L! L!* Now write it in the air with your finger. Write it on your knee with your finger!

"Next, cover, write, and check it. Look at it and take a picture with your brain, because I'm going to cover it. You ready?" I covered the word with my hand. "Now write it!" I signaled for the class to write it on their whiteboards. After a moment, I uncovered the word. "Check that your word matches. Does it look right? If you need to fix it, draw a line through it, just like you do during writing workshop, and write the whole word again above it." I scanned students' whiteboards as they wrote the word.

FIG. 8–1   A teacher leads the class in shared reading of the "How to Learn a Word" chart.

"Now, let's *use* the word in a sentence. Hmm, . . ." I paused to invite the class to think along with me and we shared some examples of sentences.

Repeat one club's magic word to give the class the power to look at the snap word and see new words they can make with it.

"Now comes the real magic. Let's borrow Gayle and Dani's magic word for learning snap words: 'Snapelaroo!'" I repeated sprinkling imaginary magic dust over all of us. "With this magic power, can anyone see new words we can make with this snap word, *all*?

"We can make more words with *all* if we use our alphabet chart and blends chart. If I put a *b* in front of *all*, the new word is . . . *ball*! If I put a *c* in front of *all*, the new word is . . . *call*." I wrote those words on the chart paper, near the word *all*. "Will you try some others, and try some blends, too?"

Soon we had a long list of *all* words, including *small* and *stall*.

ACTIVE ENGAGEMENT/LINK

Channel partners to work through the process of learning a new snap word. Challenge them to find the word part in this new snap word that they can use to make other words.

"You all try it with a new word: *will*. Let's say our magic formula, snapelaroo!

"Say it in a sentence: I will write new words! You will write new words!

"Now talk about the letters and say the letters with your partners. Go!

"Write it in the air and on your leg!

"Now, with your charts and whiteboards, see what words you can make with *will*. Remember how to look for the word part inside of *will*!"

Kids wrote words like *bill*, *ill*, *mill*, *still*, *spill*, *till*, *sill*, *grill*.

"Wow, everyone, get your fingers ready and say our magic word that helps us learn new snap words! Snapelaroo!

"You found a lot of words to write, like the word *will*. We see this word a lot in our reading and use it a lot in our writing, don't we? I am going to add *will*, *all*, and *ball* to our word wall because they *will* help us a lot in our reading and writing. They *will* also help us write other words or word parts!"

RUG TIME

Give each partnership in the club another word and coach as they go through the steps to learn the word and try to make new words with it.

"So, in your partnerships I am going to give you each a word to study and make new words. See if you can use the word parts to spell new words. Remember, first study the letters and how you might use the word in a sentence. Then practice writing it. Then think about what other words can you make. Follow the 'How to Learn a Word' chart.

"Here's your new word—*had*. Write that down on your whiteboard: *h-a-d*. When you're ready, start learning that new snap word with your partner, and then see how many words you can write on your boards with *had*."

POSSIBLE COACHING MOVES

▶ "Use the word in a sentence, 'She had . . .'"

▶ "Write it in the air, then write it on your boards. Check it with the word."

▶ "What word can you make? Use your chart."

▶ "Try the *gl* like in *glove*, with the *ad*."

SHARE • CLUBS

Set up each partnership in the club to teach the other partnership their new words, including other words that can be made with those words.

"Partners, let's come back together. I think it is now time for you to teach each other your new words. First teach your snap word, and then show them all the other words that you made with it!

"So, we have *ball*, *all*, and *will* up on the word wall. Now let's add *had*." I gave all four new words to students to add to their pouches.

EXTENSION 1 • Reading Magic Spells with Snap Words: *Ball, Will, Had*

Read a magic spell that Mabel wrote using new snap words.

"Everyone, gather quick! Mabel made a magic spell out of our snap words! She read today's snap words, then took off the beginning sound and added some blends to the beginning." I displayed the spell under the document camera. "Here's her first one. It's long, but I think we can read it. Try to read it with your partner!"

Frall frall frally, frill frill frilly, frad frad fraddy a do!

"Mabel says we can keep it and add it into our book baggies, so we'll have books and magic spells to read.

"Here's another. Mabel took out the *fr* and put in *sk*. Try it to read it with your partner and see what that would sound like."

FIG. 8–2 Students reading Mabel's magic snap word spells with their rug club.

Skall skall skally, skill skill skilly, skad skad skaddy a do!

"Some of us could put this fun spell in our baggie. Here's one more that Mabel made. This one uses a few blends. It's truly a challenge to read, want to try?"

Frall frall frally, skill skill skilly, chad chad chaddy a do!

"We can choose which ones we want for our book baggies so that during reading workshop we can read not just our books, but we can also read our magic spells!"

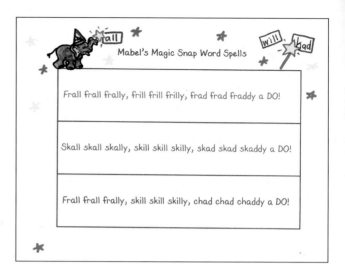

Mabel's Magic Snap Word Spells

Frall frall frally, frill frill frilly, frad frad fraddy a DO!

Skall skall skally, skill skill skilly, skad skad skaddy a DO!

Frall frall frally, skill skill skilly, chad chad chaddy a DO!

EXTENSION 2 • Reviewing Snap Words with a Magic Spell

 Channel students to identify, spell, and write snap words using a playful magical spell.

"Before we go home today, I thought we could sing this magical spell and guess which snap word it came from. Are you ready? When you know, just shout out the word and then we will chant the letters and write it on our hands with our fingers.

"Ala-ka-zee Ala-ka-zit! The word I'm using is the word . . .

"*It!*" the class called.

"Yes, the word is *it*. Now spell *it*!" I said, and kids responded, "*I-t*, it!

"Write it with your finger on your hand and on your knee! Are you ready for another one? Here goes! Ala-ka-zee Ala-ka-zent! The word I'm using is the word . . .

"*Went!*"

"Spell it! Write it—on your arm and on your foot! Time for one more. Ala-ka-zee Ala-ka-zay! The word I'm using is the word . . .

"*Day! Play!*"

"Wait, first spell and write *day*! Then we will do *play*!

"I made five little baggies that have this magic spell and five snap words in each one. Tomorrow, for reading workshop, if some of you want to add this mini-baggie to your book baggie to read, you can borrow them. Then the next day, we will give them to five other friends in the classroom!"

48

Using Snap Words and Blends to Add Sound Effects to Our Writing

IN THIS SESSION

TODAY YOU'LL teach students that when writers want to write with words that sound like real talk, they can use snap words and blends to make sure people can read what they write.

TODAY YOUR STUDENTS will use snap words to help them make other words that the teacher can add to her writing. They will add more sound effects to their own writing, using snap words and a blends chart to help as needed, and will celebrate their work so far with a showcase of noises after each writer has read.

MINILESSON

CONNECTION

Let students know that they can add sound effects to their own writing and show them some examples of texts with sound effects.

"Kindergartners, in the first part of our unit, you wrote the sounds that animals and trucks make. Now, you've been writing the sounds that magicians make. Before we end this part of our unit, I want to tell you that you can also add the sounds that *you* make into your writing, and into your reading.

"I know you have been writing persuasive letters and speeches and signs, trying to make the world a better place. You have been asking people to please stop running in the halls, and you've been telling people to stop throwing stuff on the floor.

"Now I want you to know that you can use your knowledge of phonics to add sound effects into your own writing. Authors do that. Let me show you."

I showed them examples of the books we had looked at earlier in the unit that had sound effects as well as books with dialogue in speech bubbles.

GETTING READY

✔ Gather several books that include sound effects and dialogue, such as the Elephant and Piggie series by Mo Willems, *Bark, George* by Jules Fieffer, *The Book with No Pictures* by B. J. Novak, *The Rain Stomper* by Addie Boswell, and *Doggies: A Counting and Barking Book* by Sandra Boynton.

✔ Select a prop to use as a magic wand.

✔ Prepare a Post-it with the word *all*.

✔ Students need their writing workshop folders and a pen or pencil.

PHONICS INSTRUCTION

Phonics
• Recognize and use CVC and VC phonograms.
• Recognize and use blends at the beginning of words.
• Recognize that words have phonograms that appear in many words, including high-frequency words.

Word Knowledge/Solving
• Use known word parts to solve unknown larger words.
• Use known word to spell unknown words.

"You can do that, too! Get out your writing, then tell your partner what you might add. Be sure to say the exact sounds you'll add! Point to the place in your writing where you will add it.

"Oh, Sarina is going to write *Shhhhhh* on her sign telling people to be quieter in the library. And Neil is going to write *Please* in speech bubbles on his sign telling people to put the caps back on the markers. And Nadia is going to write 'put the books back on the shelf!'"

❧ Name the teaching point.

"But here is a tip for you. Today I want to teach you that if you want to write with words that sound like real talk—words that beg and boom and whine and whisper—you need to make sure people can read what you write. And to do that, it helps to remember that there is magic power in the words you know by heart."

Teachers, in addition to the books we suggested earlier that you might show students as examples of books that have interesting, fun noises, the Elephant and Piggie books are a great choice to show dialogue here. The books are written entirely in dialogue within speech bubbles. You'll also want to show sound effects written in interesting ways. The Princess in Black series by Hale features a princess that fights monsters. During each fight, there are sound effects ("Twinkle twinkle little smash!").

TEACHING

Explain a bit more about what you mean by snap words having magic power.

"You don't believe me that these words have magic power?" I waved my hand at the word wall, indicating the words on it. "Well, part of the magic is that this looks like about twenty words, but it is actually zillions more. Watch!" I held up a magic wand. "This is my magic wand. With my magic wand, I shall use a snap word to *make* other words."

I put a Post-it on the board that had the word *all* written on it. "Now I'll wave my wand and say the magic words: Kalamazoo, Kalamafoo, Blend it up, Rightaroo!!" I stuck a Post-it that had *st* written on it on the magic wand and held the wand next to the word *all* so the two Post-its were side by side. "What new word have I made? Whisper to your partner. Yes! The word is *stall*! Like a horse sleeps in a stall or stall like stop moving . . . When I don't want to take a bath, I stall for time—just kidding. I love to take baths! Do you see how just a snap word and a little blending magic made a new word?"

Demonstrate how you use your knowledge of a snap word to help you figure out how to write a word you want to add to your writing.

"So now let me show you how I can use the magic of snap words to help me add words that sound like real talk to my writing. I am working on a sign to get people to be more careful on the stairs. I want them to stop running because running on the stairs is so dangerous. I decided I'll draw a big speech bubble and write 'Don't run!'" I displayed a sign with a big speech bubble and the word *Don't* inside. "I've already written *Don't*. Now I need to write *run*. I'm not sure how to spell it.

"Help me do some magic, please. Look at the word wall and think if there are any snap words that are like *run*. Are there are any snap words that have any of the same word parts as *run*?" The students quickly located and pointed to *fun*. I took the word *fun* off the word wall and put it under the document camera.

"Okay, so let's say *run* very slowly and think about what parts in *run* are the same as in *fun*.

"Rrrruuuunnnn." We all said it slowly and the kids agreed that *un* was the same. "Rrrruuuunnnn," I said again slowly. "I hear /r/ at the start and then I hear /un/. Like /un/ in *fun*. If I take the head off *fun* and lasso up that little word part at the end, I get *un*. And now, I can do magic and put the *r* right in front of *un*. Ready to do magic with me?" I waved my wand and chanted "Kalamazoo," and then I stuck a Post-it with an *r* over the *f*. "So rrrrrrruuuuunnnnn . . . *R*." I wrote *r* on the paper. "Ruuuunnn. *U-N. R-u-n*. Let me reread to make sure. Don't run!"

ACTIVE ENGAGEMENT/LINK

Set up students to draw on their knowledge of a snap word to help them figure out how to spell another word they can add to their writing.

"Okay, now let's say you are working on a sign to help people keep the room clean and you want to write 'Pretty please, put away your crayon!' *Crayon* is a very tough word, but we can do it! Let's see if we can use snap word magic. Look at the word wall. Crraaayyyon. Are there any words on the word wall that sound at all like *craaaaayon*?" I looked at the word wall, too. The kids were quiet as they read through. To scaffold them, I read a few of the words aloud, deliberately including a few I knew would be helpful: "*is, day, play, on, be*."

Some of the kids started calling out, "Play!" Others noticed that *on* could help.

"Hmm, . . . are you saying that you think we could do magic with two snap words: *play* and *on*? *Playon* isn't a real word but it sounds kind of like *crayon*." I put the words *play* and *on* under the document camera. "What stays the same? What changes? Talk to your partner and try to write the word *crayon* on your whiteboard. Squeeze your brains. You can do it!" I listened in and coached as students worked, reminding them to think about what parts stayed the same and listening carefully to hear all the sounds that would get added.

After a few minutes, I gathered students to me. "Ccccrrrrayyyoon. Hmm, . . . first I hear /cr/. That's a blend I know!" I wrote *cr* on paper under the document camera. "Craaayyyonn. /Ay/ is like /ay/ in *play*. So, I need *a-y*." I wrote those letters down. "Crrraaayyyon. *On*. *On* is a little word! It's a snap word." I added *on*. "Craaayyyoon. *Crayon!*" I said a magic word to celebrate, "Kalamazoo, kalamafoo, blend it up, rightaroo! We did it!"

RUG TIME

Channel partners to help each other add sound effects and dialogue to their writing, reminding them to use snap words and the blends chart as needed.

"Writers, each of you is going to get the chance to add sound effects and real talk to your writing now. You'll get to help your partner. Choose one piece of writing and put it in between you. Then help the writer to add sounds or real talk.

FIG. 9–1   Valerie displays snap words from the wall to channel students to use familiar word parts to spell other words.

We chose the word crayon *to help students practice using known words to spell new words. You could pick any word that would give this practice to your students.*

POSSIBLE COACHING MOVES

▶ "Say the word you want to write really slowly. Is there a familiar word part in it?"

▶ "Look at the word wall. Are there any snap words that have the same word part as the word you want to write?"

▶ "Chop the head off your snap word to find the word part, then use the blends chart to find the right blend to go with it."

▶ "You might need to use more than one snap word to help you—like we needed both *play* and *on* to help us write *crayon*."

Use snap word magic and the blends chart to help you! After you help one partner add a sound or some real talk to their writing, switch! You can keep switching until you have worked on all of your writing pieces!"

I listened in and coached as students worked.

"Friends, remember when Nadia wanted to write, 'Put the books back on the shelf'? She used *look* to help her to spell *books*! She kept the *ook* and put *b* at the start. So, *B-o-o-k* and then she added *s* at the end. *B-o-o-k-s*. Books! I think that calls for a big 'Aarrrroooo!' Let's all 'Aaaaarrroooo' for Nadia!"

SHARE • Celebrating Our Writing with Sound-Effect Cheers

Have students read their writing aloud to others in their rug club, and have students make a celebratory animal noise after each writer finishes.

"Friends, this work is not easy and it's a big deal! All of your playing has taught you to make your writing so much more exciting and important. Everyone will want to read it, the way they want to read Mo Willems's writing and Arnold Shapiro's writing and Georgia Heard's writing and the writing of all of the authors that we know and love. So now it's time for you to share and celebrate your wonderful writing with your club.

"Each of you will read your writing aloud, and we need to celebrate this beautiful writing. Because we are playing with phonics and fun noises, instead of clapping after someone finishes reading aloud, your rug club will get to choose a noise you want to make to celebrate each writer. It can be a real noise or a made-up noise, but everyone in the club will make the *same* noise. So, Mimi might read her sign to us and then our whole club could go 'Arrrroooooooooo!' to celebrate. Talk as a club and decide who will go first and what noise you will all make. You can make a different noise for each writer. Get started!"

As I walked around, I listened to writers reading their work and students playing with sounds.

"Cockadoodle doo!" crowed one club after Jeremy finished.

"Eeep—eeep—eeep—eeep," I heard another club chant.

"Blurf, blurf!"

"HOOOOONNNNKK!"

FIG. 9–2 Kindergartners revise their writing to include speech bubbles, taking extra care to use the word wall and blends to write words and sounds.

Dear Teachers,

While Bend II was all about playing with sounds, in Bend III students will play with sounds in a new way—through poetry. The bend launches by appealing to children's silly side, while you teach them the serious work of using their knowledge of onset, rime, blends, and digraphs to write poems that sound right and make sense. Session 10 begins with silly poems, as you demonstrate how to invent a character and generate words about that character that rhyme with the character's name. Students join in the fun, thinking of new rhyming words using consonants and blends. Rug clubs take this work a step further, creating their own characters and writing rhyming poems about them, and in an extension, you will introduce four new high-frequency words: *go*, *so*, *no*, and *by*.

In Session 11, you'll help students increase their storehouse of rhymes by teaching them how to create more words for their rhyming poems by changing the onset of a word. Partners will generate a list of words using the rimes *-ick*, *-ell*, *-uck*, *-ow*, and *-og*, noting that the ends of rhyming words sound and sometimes look the same. They will use those words to write short rhyming poems. During the share, students will share their poems with the class, while listeners act them out.

In Session 12, you'll encourage students to revise a poem they wrote earlier, and you'll teach them that they can play around with it, revise it, coming up with new words and new ideas. One way to do that is to use blends and digraphs to come up with more rhyming words and then think, "What else could I add to this poem?"

You'll introduce students to the poetic device alliteration in Session 13. You'll model alliteration with a single consonant, then with a blend. Then students will try this work themselves, writing tongue-twisters, first using consonants and then blends. Then students will work with their rug clubs to write tongue-twisters based on a picture card that you give them.

The bend concludes with Session 14, in which you teach students that real poets don't write silly rhymes and tongue-twisters, but instead write about the things that matter to them. You'll set the scene at the beginning of this session by introducing the idea of being in a poetry café (as you don a beret and scarf for extra effect). You'll demonstrate the difference between a silly rhyme (from the beginning of this bend) and a real poem, and once students have figured out how silly rhymes and real poems are the same and different, they will work with their rug clubs to choose a topic that matters and create a poem, drawing on all of their phonics knowledge. The session—and this bend—ends with a poetry café celebration, in which student-poets share their work within their rug clubs and consider the phonics work that went into their poems, as well as the meaning of the poems about things that really matter.

All the best,
Lucy, Amanda, and Valerie

Writing Silly Rhyming Poems

GETTING READY

✔ Have a sheet of chart paper ready so you can write a poem.

✔ Distribute whiteboards and dry erase markers to each student.

✔ Distribute name cards to each rug club.

PHONICS INSTRUCTION

Phonological Awareness
• Hear and generate rhyming words.
• Hear and divide onsets and rimes.

Word Knowledge/Solving
• Use phonograms to spell words.

High-Frequency Words
• Develop strategies for learning high-frequency words.
• Learn new words (*go, so, no, by*).

IN THIS SESSION

TODAY YOU'LL teach students that writers can use their knowledge of onset, rime, blends, and digraphs to write poems that sound right *and* make sense.

TODAY YOUR STUDENTS will draw on all they know about onset, rime, blends, and digraphs to create short rhyming poems. They will decide on a character for the poem, choose words that rhyme with the character's name, then create the lines of a poem that both rhyme and make sense.

MINILESSON

CONNECTION

Continue playing with phonics by creating a little rhyme. Let students know that another way to play with phonics is through poetry!

"Writers, readers, do you want to continue playing with phonics—or are you ready to stop all this playing around and do some plain ol' work? Which? Do you want our phonics vacation to keep going, for us to have *more* phonics fun? You do?

"Okey-dokey. Hokey-mokey!

"Hold on, I'm getting an idea for how we could play around with phonics next. Okey-dokey, hokey-mokey—that's poetry!"

❖ **Name the teaching point.**

"Today I want to teach you that writing poetry is another way to play with sounds. When writing rhyming poetry, writers use all they know about words and word parts to write poems that sound right *and* make sense."

TEACHING

Show students one way to create a silly rhyming poem: invent a character and think of things about the character that rhyme with the character's name.

"Sometimes poems rhyme, sometimes they don't. For today, let's work on writing rhyming poems. One way to do that is to start by inventing a character (a person or a pig or even Mabel). Then you think, 'What does my person, or my cat, my pal, have or do?' It works if your character says, has, or does something that rhymes with that person's name, like this." I wrote the beginning of the poem on chart paper.

My pal Pete

Has two . . .

"What? Has two . . . what?"

The kids chimed in that "he has two feet." I added that to the poem and pressed on a bit, continuing to recruit their input on upcoming rhyming words.

My pal Pete

Has two feet

I hope you . . . (meet)

My pal . . . (Pete)

Involve students in generating more words that rhyme with the character's name, first by using consonants and then by trying out initial blends. Create a list of the words generated.

"Let's come up with some other ideas," I said. "What else rhymes with Pete? Let's come up with more words that we can use in the rest of this poem. Can you take the final sound in Pete and try out these consonants to see if any of them produce new words? *H, B, S.*"

Kids came up with *heat*, *beat*, and *seat*.

Then I coached students to try a few blends and digraphs: *sw, gr, tr, ch*. We soon had this list of words: *sweet, greet, treat,* and *cheat*.

Note that we're working with a name that has a long vowel. You could decide to focus on a character with a VCV name, if you prefer. Even though we haven't focused a unit of study on long vowels, we decided not to avoid long vowels because we know kids work with both long and short vowels all the time.

Let the kids chime in their ideas. The little rhyme suggested here needn't be the one you and your kids produce! You are just soliciting rhyme. This could just as well read, "My pal Pete has very fat feet. Still he is sweet, my pal Pete." There are lots of other equally fun alternatives. You could also start with a CVC name like Sam or Pat.

While this bend begins with silly, rhyming poetry, rest assured that later in the bend, students will be reminded that these little rhymes don't represent the full power of poetry.

ACTIVE ENGAGEMENT/LINK

Reread what you've written so far and push students to add another rhyming line or more to the poem.

"So, writers, I'll give each of you a whiteboard and marker. I'll repeat what we have written, and will you and your partner get ready to add another line or two onto it? Write your line on your whiteboard and then I'll take *all* the lines you write and make one great big class poem up here."

The kids worked, and as they did, I circulated, incorporating as many of their lines as possible into one giant class poem about Pete. We soon had two more verses:

My pal Pete

Can't be beat

I love to greet

My pal Pete

My pal Pete

Is a treat

He is very sweet

My pal Pete

Writing this poem out while the kids watch and wait is probably not worth the time it takes. You might scrawl it on your clipboard and just read it to the class, and then later write it so the kids can read it. Otherwise produce an abbreviated version.

RUG TIME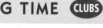

Set up clubs to write their own silly rhyming poems, beginning with inventing a character. Channel kids to choose character names that are easy to find rhyming words for.

"Writers, now it's your turn to write your own poem about your pal or your cat or your worm or your pig. To do this, work with your club to decide who the character will be in your poem. What will his or her name be? For this to work, it is easiest if your pal has a one-syllable name." I distributed name cards to students and channeled them to choose one together.

"After you decide on a name, jot words that rhyme with your character's name on your whiteboard. Those are the words you can use at the ends of the lines in your poem. And I'm going to give you a trick for doing that. You take your pal's name—let's say, Brad—and you walk Brad along the alphabet like this: Brad, *ad* (that's a word), *bad* (that works), *Dad* (that works!), *fad, mad, pad, sad*.

"That's a way to come up with *a lot* of words that you can use in your poem. Get started doing that, then get started making up your poem—saying it into the air. You just have three or four minutes, so work like the wind!"

SHARE • Reciting Poems to Identify Rhymes

Have students recite their poems aloud to the class. Encourage students to make noises—such as snaps—after each rhyming word.

"Friends, can we hear some of your poems? And class, every time we hear a rhyming word, let's all snap. Show me your best snaps!" The class approximated. I called on clubs to read. This was one of their poems:

My cat Jack

Has a pack

He likes to quack

He wears a sack

He sees a crack

Jack!

EXTENSION 1 • Introducing New High-Frequency Words: *Go*, *So*, *No*, and *By*

 **Guide students through the familiar steps of learning new high-frequency words, using the "How to Learn a Word" chart.**

"Mabel gave us four new words, words that you read a lot, words that we might like to use in our poetry! Let's turn them into snap words!" I displayed our "How to Learn a Word" anchor chart.

I held up the word card *go*. "First we *read* it!" Students read the word chorally multiple times as I pointed underneath it.

"Now, let's *study* it. Turn and tell your partner what you see."

"Now, *spell* it. Spell it softly, like a whisper into your hand. *G-O*. Then spell it and cheer it.

"Now *write* it!" Students wrote the word *go* with imaginary markers on the rug.

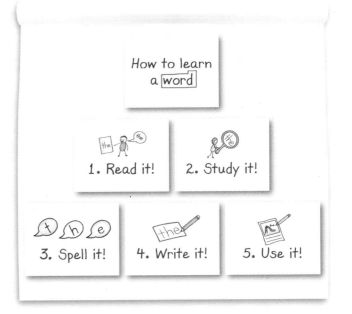

"Last step—*use* it! Share a sentence with your partner." I circulated, listening in and providing support where needed.

We repeated the steps to learn the words *so*, *no*, and *by*, then I said, "Friends, I just noticed something. *Go*, *no*, and *so* all rhyme. Let's read them together." We read them and then I continued, "That's making me think, are there any snap words that rhyme with *by*?"

The class looked across the word wall before shouting out, "*My*!" I agreed and then added the words to the word wall and the children added them to their snap word pouches.

EXTENSION 2 • Sorting Rhyming High-Frequency Words

 Propose that students sort the snap words in their pouches into piles of snap words that rhyme.

"Friends, we've already discovered a few of our snap words that are wonderful to use in our poems because they rhyme: words like *go*, *no*, and *so*! I wonder how many other snap words rhyme? Work with your partner—pick a snap word and then read across your other snap words, listening for words that sound the same at the end. When you find two—or more—words that rhyme, make a pile. How many piles do you think you can make?"

Partners read and sorted their snap words into piles, while I circulated, leading some students toward snap words that rhyme with other snap words I'd already taught: *can*, *me*, *day*, *my*, and *go*.

FIG. 10–1 A teacher leans in to coach a student as they sort snap words that rhyme.

Building a Storehouse of Rhymes (-*ick*, -*ell*, -*uck*, -*ow*, -*og*)

IN THIS SESSION

TODAY YOU'LL teach students that writers can write rhyming poems by changing the onset of a word, creating a number of rhyming words.

TODAY YOUR STUDENTS will generate a list of words using the rimes -*ick*, -*ell*, -*uck*, -*ow*, and -*og*, noting that the ends of rhyming words sound and sometimes look the same. They will use those words to write short rhyming poems.

MINILESSON

CONNECTION

Reveal a poem written by Mabel, featuring new rimes. Highlight the rhyming words as you read, pointing out that words that rhyme sometimes have the same endings.

"Writers, come quickly. Mabel is excited to share a poem she wrote!" I turned to the class mascot, who was propped up near me with a poem in her trunk.

"As I read Mabel's poem, can you snap your fingers for the words that rhyme, just like yesterday? I'll highlight the rhyming words in the poem." I placed the poem under the document camera, highlighting the rimes each time kids snapped their fingers.

"Writers, I'm noticing something. These rhyming words you heard—*pick*, *lick*, *sick*—don't just sound the same. They also look the same. Turn and tell your partner what part looks the same in the words *pick* and *lick* and *sick*." As children talked, I called out, "What other words could they have used?

"Yes, all of those rhyming words end with the same word part: -*ick*. The first letter is changing, but the rest of the word is the same. And look, Mabel found two other words that rhyme—*tell* and *well*—because they both end with the same word part, -*ell*."

GETTING READY

✔ Print the poem "At the Ice Cream Shop" and roll it up, nestled in Mabel's trunk.

✔ Be ready to highlight the rimes in "At the Ice Cream Shop" when you display the poem to the class.

✔ Prepare to record words that rhyme with *cow* on chart paper.

✔ Distribute whiteboards and dry erase markers to each partnership.

PHONICS INSTRUCTION

Phonological Awareness
• Hear and generate rhyming words.
• Segment onsets and rimes.

Phonics
• Recognize and use common phonograms (-*ick*, -*ell*, -*uck*, -*ow*, -*og*).

Word Knowledge/Solving
• Use phonograms to help spell a word.
• Change the beginning blends in words to make new words.

High-Frequency Words
• Study high-frequency words by finding rhymes for them.

I turned back to the stuffed elephant. "Mabel, you did some very important wordplay to write this poem. You didn't just play around with hearing rhymes, you also worked hard to spell those words well."

♣ **Name the teaching point.**

"Today I want to remind you that writers use lots of rhyming words to write fun poems. Remember, one way to make rhyming words is to change the first part of a word but keep the last part. Oftentimes, words rhyme if the last part in both words is the same."

TEACHING

Produce words that rhyme with _cow_, acknowledging that some words are spelled like _cow_, but do not sound the same at the end.

"Let's do what Mabel did when she wrote her poem about the ice cream shop with the words _pick_, _lick_, and _sick_, words that all have the same ending. I've been thinking that you could write poems about animals—like a chick, a duck, a cow, or a dog—and do the same work Mabel did to invent some brand-new rhymes.

"Let's take one of those animals—say, a cow—and find some new rhyming words you can use later to write another poem." I wrote _cow_ on chart paper, then continued. "Remember, if you can't think of a new rhyming word, you can try taking just the word part _-ow_ and walk along the alphabet, trying out different letters, to see if you can make a new word, like this: _cow—dow? fow? gow? how?_ Yes, _how_ is a word!

"Now that we have a whole list of words that rhyme with _cow_, we can say a quick little poem—I could even write it down later! Listen and watch how I try to use as many of our rhyming words as I can. Each time I use one, put your thumb up in the air."

> The cow
>
> Doesn't know how
>
> To bow.
>
> Oh, wow!

"I used a lot, right? Now, I could write that poem down as well. That might be fun to read later!"

Of course, you won't bother distinguishing between a rhyme and a rime with your children. Instead, we'll have a little phonics fun of our own. The message here is that new words can be spelled using familiar parts, in this case, phonograms.

At the Ice Cream Shop
By Mabel

Which one is best I cannot tell.
It is so hard to pick!

I think to help me choose one well,
I'll give them all one lick.

Uh-oh! Now, I'm starting to feel sick!

ACTIVE ENGAGEMENT/LINK

Set up partners to think of words that rhyme with *duck*. Remind students that they can walk through the alphabet if they have difficulty thinking of rhyming words.

"Now it's your turn. Will you and your partner take the duck, and see if you can think of words that rhyme with *duck*, just like we did for *cow*? You can work with your partner to make a list of rhyming words and then come up with a quick little poem about a duck!

"Remember, you can walk *duck* through the alphabet to come up with rhyming words and write them down on your whiteboard. Then, in just a few minutes, we'll be able to say a poem about a duck, using the words that you came up with." I moved around the rug, coaching as needed, and I listed the *-uck* words that students were coming up with on my clipboard. Soon I called the group back together.

"Can I share the list of words you came up with? If you see a word that's on your whiteboard, give it a check mark and put your thumb up! I saw *muck*, *luck*, *tuck*, and *yuck*. You came up with so many!"

Encourage partners to create a short rhyming poem with the words that rhyme with *duck*, trying to use as many rhyming words as possible.

"Now with your partner, come up with a quick little poem, trying to use as many of these as possible. You don't have to write it, just say it!

"Listen to one that I heard,

> The duck
> Needs some luck
> Because she's in the muck.
> Oh yuck!

"So good! You heard all those rhyming words!"

FIG. 11–1 Words that rhyme with *cow* collected on the easel

Brace yourself—you can certainly anticipate at least one child using the phonogram -uck to write a less savory word on their boards. Plan to say something like, 'That does rhyme but isn't the best for our class chart," and then simply move on very quickly. Don't take offense that the kids enjoy this—it's a pretty universal thing to do.

RUG TIME

Invite partnerships to use the collection of rhyming words to write their own rhymes on a whiteboard.

"We've generated so many words to help us! You've practiced making rhyming words and saying little poems and rhymes with them. Now it's time to roll up your sleeves and write some new little rhymes about these animal friends. Pick one of these animals, or choose another if you want, and make a quick list of words that rhyme. Then say your rhyme out loud and finally write it down." After kids had generated a few words that rhymed, I revealed a few ways they could start their rhymes.

- I know a duck . . .

- My pal, the cow . . .

- I know a chick . . .

- I love my dog . . .

FIG. 11–2 A student walks his fingers along the alphabet chart to find words that rhyme with *duck*.

POSSIBLE COACHING MOVES

▶ "Try starting with one of those first lines. Now what three words could you say next that end with one of the rhyming words? Like 'She has a . . .' or 'She loves . . .'"

▶ "Try it one way, then another."

▶ "Read what you've written so far. Then say some following sentences that end with another rhyme."

▶ "Read your poem and listen. Do any of the words sound the same at the end?"

▶ "Try to get the beats right so each line is the same."

"And then think, 'What does my duck or chick or cow do, or say, or have, or say, that uses one of the animals' rhyming words?' Talk with each other and try to think up a poem. If you think of one, tell it to your friends and write it on your whiteboard, super-fast before you forget it. Then keep the poem going!"

We soon had a poem factory going in the classroom, with lots of less-than-perfect poems.

FIG. 11–3 A student helps her rug club by recording the club's rhyme.

My small cow
has chow
and now
can not bow
Wow!
What a fat cow.

My dog
can jog
to a hog
on a log
in the fog.

PLAYING WITH PHONICS

SHARE • Reading and Acting Out Our Rhymes

Encourage a member of each club to read their club's rhymes out loud, while the rest of the students listen and act out what they hear.

"Young rhymers, chanters, and rappers, let's read some of your rhymes out loud and then act them out. Karim, you're up first. Come on up and read your club's rhyme about the little cow. All of us will listen, and we will imagine what's happening and then use our bodies to act it out."

Karim started to read his poem:

> My small cow
> has chow
> and now
> can not bow
> Wow
> What a fat cow.

The kids and I started to put actions to his words. We made faces and gestures to show how we wanted something to eat, and then we pretended to eat *a lot* and made our faces and body look large!

"Let's read and act one more. Harriet, come on up."

> The little duck
> stepped into muck.
> Yuck!
> What bad luck!

Soon we were all pretending to be little ducks stuck in the mud.

EXTENSION 1 • Play the Rhyming "Name Game"

When the class was lined up to walk down the hall, I reminded them of a familiar rhyming game—"The Name Game"! "Friends, you remember 'The Name Game' song, right? The end of your name stays the same, and you change the beginning—but this time, we'll use some blends we know to change the beginning. Let's practice with Mabel. I'll say a blend and we can sing 'The Name Game' song with her *new* name. Ready? /Sp/."

"Spabel!"

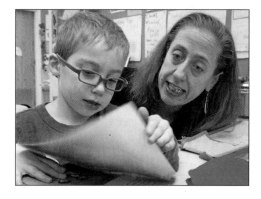

It's possible that some of your students might point out that some words end the same as cow, *but don't rhyme with* cow, *such as* tow *and* low. *Acknowledge their noticing!*

The little duck
stepped into muck.
Yuck!
What bad luck!

Make sure to hold onto a copy of one of these poems to use in tomorrow's minilesson. You may also want to collect all of your students' whiteboards to type up their poems for tomorrow's rug time, when students will be revising these rhyming poems. If you do not want to save your students' rhymes, we have provided some of these rhymes in the online resources to use as an alternative.

"Spabel, Spabel bo-Babel, Banana Fanna Fo Fabel, Me Mi Mo Mabel. Spabel!"

"Let's try it with /br/ . . ."

"Brabel!"

"Brabel, Brabel bo-Babel, Banana Fanna Fo Fabel, Me Mi Mo Mabel. Brabel!

"Mabel, Spabel, Brabel. They all rhyme! Ready to try with your own name?"

When the class agreed they were, I progressed through some blends: *st-*, *gr-*, *fl-*, *sk-*, *sw-*, *bl-*. Each time, the class called back with the rhyme of their own name.

EXTENSION 2 • Snap Word Rhyming Race

 "Friends, who's in the mood for a race? I'll bet you are—but instead of running a race, we're going to have a rhyming word race. Are you game? Get with your club and get out your snap word pouches. I'll distribute whiteboards and markers."

I quickly got kids set up, then continued. "The race will be to see which club can make the most words that rhyme with our snap words. When I say go, you'll look at your snap words, think of as many rhyming words as you can, and write them down on your whiteboards. Keep going until I say 'stop,' then we'll see which club made the most words. But here's the deal—they have to be *real* words, not made-up words.

"Are you ready? Get set? Go!"

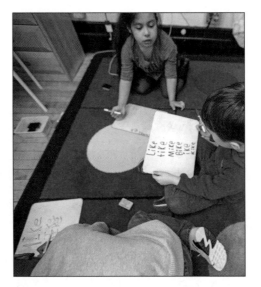

FIG. 11–4 Kindergartners race to list words that rhyme with *like* on their whiteboards.

The Name Game

Katie!

Katie, Katie, bo-Batie

Bo-na-na fanna, fo-Fatie

Fee fi mo-Matie

Katie!

(Repeat with any child's name substituting the first letter with a B or F or M)

The number of rhyming words that kids can generate are almost endless, so the winner will be the rug club that gets all four kids working like the wind to jot rhyming words for several different snap words. Think what you might do with the list the class generates; it can be an important resource for later reading and writing.

SESSION 12

Revising Rhymes Using Blends and Digraphs

IN THIS SESSION

TODAY YOU'LL teach students that writers can revise their poems by coming up with even more rhyming words using blends and digraphs.

TODAY YOUR STUDENTS will revise their rhyming poems by generating more rhyming words using blends and digraphs. They'll use generated words to add onto existing rhymes.

MINILESSON

CONNECTION

Chant a rhyme written by Mabel. Invite students to reread it, drumming the beat on their knees. Point out that Mabel made rhymes using a blend—and students can do the same.

"Poets, chanters, can I share a little rhyme that Mabel and I made last night?" I read the rhyme.

"Can you picture it? A cow that doesn't know how to move slowly? That means, it must be a cow that goes super-fast! Have you ever heard of such a thing? Listen, also, Mabel made up a beat to go with the poem. Listen!" I tapped as I read.

> My cow (tap-tap)
> doesn't—know how (tap-tap-tap)
> she—can go (tap-tap)-tap
> sl—ow (tap-tap)

My cow
doesn't know how
she can go--
slow!

GETTING READY

✔ Display the rhyme "My Cow" written by Mabel.

✔ Print and display "At the Ice Cream Shop" by Mabel and prepare to revise an enlarged copy of the poem.

✔ Display one of your students' poems that you shared in Session 11 or "The Little Duck" rhyme and prepare to revise with the class.

✔ Post the "Blends and Digraphs" chart where all students can see it.

✔ Distribute a whiteboard, dry erase marker, and a copy of one of the animal rhymes, "My Small Cow" or "My Dog" from Session 11, to each partnership.

PHONICS INSTRUCTION

Phonological Awareness
• Hear and generate rhyming words.
• Segment onsets and rimes.

Phonics
• Recognize and use common phonograms.
• Recognize and use blends and digraphs.

Word Knowledge/Solving
• Change the beginning blends and digraphs in words to make new words.

"Will you try to get the beat? Tap your knees and read with me." We brought two beats to each line, even the last one. "Do you notice anything interesting about our little rhyme? Yes, it has *two* different rhymes! *Cow* and *how*, *go* and *slow*.

"That's right! We put two rhymes in. We also used a blend—to make the word *slow*. It got me to thinking, we could revise our little ditties. We could try and make them longer."

❖ **Name the teaching point.**

"Today I want to teach you that after you write a poem, you can play around with it, revise it, coming up with new words and new ideas. One way to do that is to use blends and digraphs to come up with more rhyming words and then think, 'What else could I add to this poem?'"

TEACHING

Reread Mabel's poem, recalling which words rhyme, then make new rhyming words using blends and digraphs. Orally rehearse new stanzas for the poem with these new words.

"Let me show you what I mean. Here is the little poem that Mabel made for us yesterday. Let's reread it to remember." I read the poem aloud, lingering over the last word in each line to emphasize the rhyme.

"If we wanted to help Mabel revise it, we could suggest parts that she could add. First, we need to remember which words rhyme. Do you remember? Oh, right: *tell* and *well* rhyme and so do *pick*, *lick*, and *sick*. Now, we want to add more to the poem.

"Let's use what we know about blends and digraphs to help us make new rhymes." I pointed toward the "Blends and Digraphs" chart that hung on the easel. "This could help! We first need words that rhyme with *tell* and *well*. And we need real words, not nonsense words.

"Look over the blends chart. If you see one or two that can be added to *-ell* to make a word, put your thumb on your knee. I'm going to look as well."

I began saying aloud words—some real, some nonsensical—by adding blends from the chart in front of the *-ell* phonogram. When I said *smell*, *spell*, *swell*, and *shell*, kids signaled that they were words. I nodded. "Yep, we can add any of these rhyming words into our poem."

I looked across them. "Hmm, . . . I bet we could easily use *swell* and *smell* in a poem about ice cream! Let me try . . ." I said out loud a couple of versions:

> I had to leave the ice cream store
> Because of the strong smell.

**At the Ice Cream Shop
By Mabel**

Which one is best I cannot tell.
It is so hard to pick!

I think to help me choose one well,
I'll give them all one lick.

Uh-oh! Now, I'm starting to feel sick!

FIG. 12–1   Valerie and a student lead the class in reading Mabel's poem "At the Ice Cream Shop."

PLAYING WITH PHONICS

I went outside, took a deep breath
and started to feel swell.

Or:

I didn't feel swell.
No, not at all.
The ice cream store smell
Was not a ball!

"Let's ask Mabel which one she likes." I made Mabel raise her trunk at the first one. "Did you see how we created more rhyming words and more parts we could add to Mabel's poem?"

ACTIVE ENGAGEMENT/LINK

Reread another poem, noting which words rhyme. Recruit partners to produce rhyming words using blends and digraphs, then channel students to orally write new stanzas.

"Let's give the same work with the rhyme that Harriett wrote yesterday. First let's read it aloud and think about which words rhyme."

The little duck
stepped into muck.
Yuck!
What bad luck!

"*Duck*, *muck*, *yuck*, and *luck* rhyme. With your partner, go through the blends chart and find as many words that you think rhyme with *duck* and *luck*. When you find one, right it down on your whiteboards and hold it up!"

"Wow, I see *stuck* and *cluck*, *pluck* and *truck*. Turn and tell your partner, how could we add on to this little rhyme here, with these new words?"

As kids worked, I listened in, voicing over a few options. "Oh, I'm hearing funny ones like,

Don't stay stuck!
Go get a truck!

"Keep going. Look at the 'Blends and Digraphs' chart if you need ideas. Try another one!"

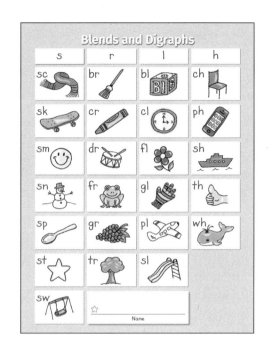

RUG TIME

Direct partnerships to reread a poem from Session 11, underlining words that rhyme. Coach them to produce more rhyming words, using these to revise one of the poems.

"I have some rhymes that could use some revisions. Could you and your partner help out!?" I distributed a poem from Session 11 to each partnership, as well as a whiteboard and dry erase marker. "Partners, start by rereading these rhymes together and underlining the words that rhyme." After a moment I said, "You'll want to come up with more rhyming words, and one way is to use the blends and digraphs charts. Make sure they are words you know! If they are, write them down on your whiteboards to keep track and then use those words to add to the poem you are helping to revise."

> ### POSSIBLE COACHING MOVES
>
> ▸ "Say the blend with the part that is going to make the rhyming sound."
>
> ▸ "Go through all the blends. Keep saying them and thinking, 'Is that a word I know?'"
>
> ▸ "Is *stog* a word? Nope, but good try at looking for one! Keep searching."
>
> ▸ "Say your poem out loud first."
>
> ▸ "Go on to your next poem when you are finished."

After students had a few minutes to revise at least one rhyme I said, "After you add to the rhyme, be sure to reread from the beginning. You'll want to listen to hear if you like what you added. If you don't, you might try to add in another way."

SHARE • Adding a Beat to Poetry

Reread a poem aloud, then encourage students to listen to the rhythm of the poem by tapping the beat on their knees.

"Writers, now that you've revised your poems, we should put a beat to them!" I turned our attention back toward Harriett's little duck rhyme. "Let's do that with Harriett's poem about the little duck. I'll read it once, so we can remember how it goes. Join me if you'd like!"

The little duck
stepped into muck.
Yuck!
Oh, what bad luck!

You'll find rhyming poems in the online resources for students to revise. You could of course choose to use some of your students' actual rhyming poems from Session 11 and disregard the rhymes we have included. You students will love revising their peers' poems!

When students add their parts, it could be as simple as one or two more rhymes. Some students may add more. Remember, you can coach students to continue and practice in another poem. Look out for partners who are not working together or one partnership in the team who is overpowering the other. In that case, perhaps each partner could work on separate poems. You can decide and coach partnerships in the ways that would be most supportive for your students.

FIG. 12–2 Students revised their rhyme from the previous day by underlining the rhyming words first and then adding another stanza using new rhyming words that begin with a blend.

Please don't stay stuck!
Go get a truck!

"This time, let's give it some rhythm and tap in out on our knees. Ready?"

The litt-le duck (tap-tap tap tap)
stepped in-to muck. (tap-tap tap tap)
Yuck! (tap)
Oh-what bad luck! (tap-tap tap tap)

Please-don't stay stuck! (tap-tap tap tap)
Go get a truck! (tap-tap tap tap)

After we read one poem with rhythm, I set students up to try adding rhythm to one of the poems they wrote with their partner.

EXTENSION 1 • Rhyme Up at the End of the School Day

Challenge partners to produce two rhyming sentences at the end of every school day.

"Starting today and for the next week, when you line up to go home, you will also 'rhyme up.' Make two lines, so you end up with a partner, and I'll call out a topic. Then I'll be the tollbooth and before you and your partner can walk past me, you'll need to produce two rhyming sentences that go with our topic. Our topic today is something you can say about food. Here are a few examples to get you thinking."

I love food
When I am in the mood

I hate peas
They make me sneeze

EXTENSION 2 • Finishing the Rhyme

Create a few rhyming poems of your own, leaving the last rhyming word for students to figure out.

"Chanters, rhymers, and rappers, let's make some fun rhymes up as we line up for gym class! I'll start it off and you fill in the rhyme."

We heard the bell,
So we lined up well,
We headed down the hall
Please, no one . . .

"Fall!" Kids called out.

"Good one. I have another! Listen carefully."

Oh, what luck,
Has finally struck!
We are on our way
To go and . . .

"Play!"

When you are at the mall
You should see the wall
It's over the by the /st/ . . .

"Stall!"

When you drink milk, be careful.
Try and keep still.
Don't be a pill.
Try not to . . .

"Spill!"

Alliteration

Playing Even More with Blends

IN THIS SESSION

TODAY YOU'LL teach students that writers can include alliteration in their poems—using a series of words that begin with the same sound, as opposed to ending with the same sound, as in words that rhyme.

TODAY YOUR STUDENTS will use picture cards to generate words that begin with the same consonant or blend and then use those words to write alliterations.

MINILESSON

CONNECTION

Teach students about alliteration by playing a word game. Give clues about how the word starts and a word that the mystery word rhymes with, and let students guess the mystery word.

"Let's play a word game. I'll give you a clue and you try to guess the word! Ready? My word starts like *big* and rhymes with *cat*."

"*Bat!*"

"You got it. *Big bat*! Here's another: my word starts like *green* and it rhymes with *pass*."

"*Grass!*"

"Yes! *Green grass*! Last one: my word also starts like *green* and rhymes with *nose*! Here's a hint . . . the green grass . . ."

"*Grows!*"

GETTING READY

✔ Print picture cards of Mabel, a star, a pen, and a tree.

✔ Have a stack of blank Post-its ready,

✔ Distribute Alliteration picture cards and Post-its to each rug club.

PHONICS INSTRUCTION

Phonological Awareness
- Segment onsets and rimes.
- Generate words with the same initial sound or blend.

Phonics
- Recognize and use initial blends.

Word Knowledge/Solving
- Use onsets in known words to generate other words with the same onset.
- Use known words to write unknown words.

High-Frequency Words
- Review high-frequency words.

"The green grass grows and grows and grows! That sounds cool," I repeated it with an emphasis on the initial consonants, "and feels funny to say! This kind of wordplay has a fancy name. Poets call this 'alliteration.' That's the word for when many words start with the same first sound! You may have heard people call them 'tongue-twisters.' I'm wondering if we might make more alliterations (did you hear that—if we *might make more* alliterations)!"

♣ Name the teaching point.

"Today I want to teach you that when poets play with words, they don't just play with the sounds at the ends of words, they also play with the first sounds. They can create tongue-twisters by putting together a whole bunch of words with the same beginning sound, like when they write 'The green grass grows and grows.'"

TEACHING

Model alliteration using a consonant. Then model alliteration again, this time with other words that begin with a blend.

"Let me show you another one. Let's say I wanted to try one about Mabel." I held up a picture card of Mabel. "I could write:

Mabel listens to music on misty Monday mornings.

"Do you see how I thought about *lots* of words that start with the letter *m*? Do you hear all the /m/ sounds?" I held up a picture card of a star. "What if I wanted to play with the word *star*?

"You hear the blend at the start? I could think about other words that start with /st/. Can you help me think of some?" I took out Post-its to get ready to write words that begin with *st-*. "Here are a few: *stamp*, *still*, *string*, *stare*, *stand*, *stop*, *stay*, *strong*, and *stiff*.

"You can write *stink*!" One of the students shouted. I wrote it down to show that I valued their thinking.

"Now if I want to try and play with the word *star*, I can pick other words to help write something." I read across the words, pointing out that *stamp* and *stiff* might be hard to use in a poem about a star, but *stand*, *still*, and *stare* could work well. I laid the word cards out in order of how I might use them. I pointed to each word as I read.

Stand still, as you stare at the stars.

"Phew, that's a lot! I did it! Now I could just write in the other words." So I did on the easel. "Let's reread what I wrote!

"If I wanted to do a different one about stars I could choose different words." I selected *strong* and *stay*.

The strong stars stay in the sky.

"Do you see how I'm just playing with words here? It doesn't rhyme; instead there are a few words that start the same way."

ACTIVE ENGAGEMENT/LINK

Recruit students to write an alliteration with words starting with a single consonant. Then challenge students to do the same with words beginning with a blend.

"How about we try a poem about a pen?" I said, holding a picture card of a pen. "First, we need to think about words that start with /p/. Are you ready? Turn and talk to your partner and try to list as many *p* words as you can. Count them on your fingers."

I jotted some of their suggestions on Post-its. "Let's read the words you came up with." I gestured for students to read the Post-its with me. "*Pink*, *pretty*, *pig*, *perfect*, *pat*, *panda*, *puppy*, *pass*, *presents*, *pick*. We have so many to play with! Pick a couple with your partner and create a little tongue-twister about the pen."

As kids created alliterations, I listened in. "Here is one that I heard: 'The pink pen made a perfect pig.' And listen to this one, 'I picked the pretty pen to draw a puppy.' Here's one more, 'The pig took the pen and gave it to the panda as a present!' That's a lot of *p*'s!

"Want a challenge?" I held up a picture of a tree. "Try to make one about a tree." I wrote *tree* on a Post-it and placed it under the picture. "Say as many words with the blend *tr* at the start!" I gave partners a moment or two to talk, then continued. "Here are some I heard: *tricks*, *trunk*, *truck*, *treats*, *trim*, *try*, *train*, *trip*. Now try and say something fun about a tree!"

I listened as partners spoke, then said, "Listen to all the /tr/ words in this one I heard: 'Trees have trunks,' and 'Take a trip on a train to see the trees,' and 'Trick or treat, it's a tree!' and 'Hey, truck, watch out for the tricky tree!'"

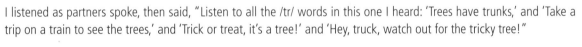

 **RUG TIME** CLUBS

Distribute picture cards to rug clubs. Challenge students to write alliterations using the first sound (consonant or blend) of each item in the picture cards.

"Rug clubs, in your baggie are pictures of things that would be fun to play with and use to write tongue-twisters! One person in the club will pick a picture from the baggie and put it in the center of the club. You'll then write on a Post-it what it is.

FIG. 13–1 One teacher's alliteration beginning with the word *star* modeled for students on the easel.

"Together, you will write words on Post-its that start in the same way. Then, you and your partner can come up with a tongue-twister to tell the other members of your rug club. When both partnerships have said their tongue-twisters, put the word back into the baggie and the next person in your rug club gets to choose one."

I passed out baggies that had pictures inside. I had some pictures of words that started with just a single consonant, like *cake*, *horse*, *rainbow*, and *watermelon*. Then I had other pictures that were of things that had blends at the start, like *crown*, *flower*, *dragon*, *globe*, *snowman*, and *stop*.

You might choose to create baggies for specific clubs. If you have some clubs who are particularly strong at generating, reading, and writing words with blends, you might choose to put only picture cards with words that start with blends in their baggie. You might also place a digraph option in the baggie for an extra challenge!

> ## POSSIBLE COACHING MOVES
>
> ▶ "What other words start with . . . ?"
>
> ▶ "Read across all of the words. Which can go together to make an alliteration?"
>
> ▶ "Say the word in the picture. What sound or sounds are at the start? Do you know other words that begin that way?"
>
> ▶ "Reread your tongue-twister. Do you have lots of words that sound _____ at the start?"

SHARE • Leading a Symphony Share

Lead students in a symphony share of alliterations. Direct listeners to count the number of words that begin with the same sound.

"We have some fun alliterations to listen to and read to each other! Rug clubs, Mabel has a magic wand, and when she points to you, and says, 'Bibbidi bobbidi boo,' will you stand up and say one of your alliterations to us? First show us the picture card. Then, the rest of us, every time we hear a word that starts the same way, let's hold up a finger, so we can count how many words start the same way."

I helped Mabel wave her wand over the first club. "Stand up, rug club. Hold up the picture card and your starting word for your alliteration work." The club showed a picture of snow, so I directed the class to listen for words that start with /sn/.

Each time students heard a word that began like *snow*, they put up a finger. I waited for kids to try raising their finger first and then I would raise mine in confirmation. If kids missed one, after the fact I would say, "Wait, read that one again. I think we missed one. Read yours again but this time put extra stress on the words that sound the same at the start!"

FIG. 13–2   One rug club generates words that begin with the same blend as *flower* to create their own alliteration.

EXTENSION 1 • Using Blends to Change Snap Word into New Words

With a blend on a Post-it at the end of a pointer, recite a spell and place the pointer at the start of snap words, changing them to new words. Use those to create alliterations.

I stood near the word wall and waved my pointer as I said, "This magic wand can turn words we know into new words." I waved my wand over the class and stuck a Post-it to the end with the blend *sp-* written on it.

"I have a new spell for us. I'll say it once and then you can say it with me."

After we repeated the spell together, I placed my pointer in front of the snap word, *got*, so that the *sp-* Post-it masked the *g*. "Now we have . . ."

"*Spot!*" the class called.

I directed one student to record *spot* on a Post-it. We chanted the magic spell again, then collected new words that start with *sp-*. We turned *like* into *spike*, *in* into *spin*, *will* into *spill*, *it* into *spit*, and *went* into *spent*.

"We have all of the words that begin /sp/. Let's make a quick alliteration! Read across the words and make one with your partner."

After we shared a few alliterations such as, "Don't spill spit on your rug spot," and "Spin toward the spike," I asked partnerships to pick a blend and turn their finger into a magic wand that changes snap words into another word. Partners gathered words and created an alliteration of their own.

EXTENSION 2 • Revising Poems to Include Alliteration

Model revising one line of a rhyming poem to include alliteration. Then, have the student practice with the next line before prompting students to revise their own poems.

"Friends, wouldn't it be a great idea to revise some earlier poems so that they include rhymes *and* alliteration? Let's try with that poem from the other day—do you remember the one about my pal Pete?

"That's an alliteration: *pal*, *Pete*. I could even add another /p/ word to describe Pete. My *something* pal Pete. I could say 'my pink pal Pete'! That's weird. Or, how about 'my perfect pal Pete'? I like that!"

My perfect pal Pete

FIG. 13–3 A teacher changes *play* to *stay* using the blend *st* on the end of a pointer.

Students then helped revise the next line, "Has two feet." Students generated a list of words that start with /f/ and we revised the poem, adding one or two of those words before *feet*:

Has two fat fancy feet.

"Do you remember this rhyme? See if you and your partner can revise it for her by adding alliteration. Read it once and decide how to revise each line."

The little duck
stepped into muck.
Yuck!
What bad luck!

I collected some of the revisions partners made and shared them with the class.

Writing Real Poetry Using All of Our Phonics Knowledge

IN THIS SESSION

TODAY YOU'LL teach students that real poets write about things that matter to them, using words to help readers feel what they feel about those topics.

TODAY YOUR STUDENTS will write poems by thinking about the topics that matter to them most and then rehearsing, recording, and celebrating real poems about these topics.

MINILESSON

CONNECTION

Tell students you'll be playing an imagination game and pretend that your classroom is actually a poetry café.

"Poets, today we are going to play an imagination game. When I say the magic spell, we won't be in our classroom anymore. We'll be in a poetry café! Close your eyes."

As the class closed their eyes, I began to recite the magic spell, "Bibbidi bobbidi, abracadabra, hocus pocus, *pow*!"

I left a moment of silence, quickly donning a beret and wrapping a scarf around my neck. "Wow, poets. Open your eyes and look! Instead of desks there are tables." I made sure to play up the drama of pretending, so the class would delight in playing along. "And, oh! Smell the air! It's smells like coffee and hot chocolate."

As the class was sniffing the air and giggling I said, "Look! There are even microphones for celebrating poetry!" I held up paper tubes.

GETTING READY

✔ Set the scene for a poetry café by wearing a beret or another hat and a scarf.

✔ Gather paper tubes or something similar to use as pretend microphones.

✔ Prepare a rhyme, "My Cow,"' and a poem, "Apple" by Nan Fry, on large paper. Display them side by side.

✔ Distribute whiteboards and dry erase markers to each club.

PHONICS INSTRUCTION

Phonological Awareness
- Hear and generate rhymes.
- Segment onsets and rimes.

Phonics
- Recognize and use blends and digraphs.
- Recognize and use VC and CVC phonograms.

Word Knowledge/Solving
- Use phonograms and blends and digraphs to help spell a word.

"Now that we are in a poetry café, I have something serious to tell you, poets. Listen closely and carefully." I leaned in as if to impart a super-important secret.

♣ Name the teaching point.

"Today I want to teach you that the fun little rhymes and tongue-twisters we've been writing aren't the most important work that poets do. Poets write about things that matter very much to them, and they try to find exactly the right words and exactly the right sounds to say what really matters. They can work for days and months even to come up with the perfect way to say something that is too big for regular words."

TEACHING

Read a rhyme from earlier in the bend and then read a poem. Have students name how they are the same and how they are different.

"Poets, it is important that you think about the similarities and the differences between the little rhymes we've been writing and poetry at its finest. I'm going to reread a little rhyme we wrote the other day and then, I'm going to read you a real poem. Will you think about how these are sort of the same, and how they are also very different?" I revealed Mabel's little rhyme "My Cow" from Session 12 and the poem "Apple" by Nan Fry, both written on separate pieces of large paper, hanging on the easel side by side.

"Do you remember Mabel's little rhyme 'My Cow'? I'll read it aloud." After I read the rhyme, I displayed a poem by Nan Fry.

"Now, here is the poem by Nan Fry.

"Turn and talk with your partner about how these are alike and how they are different." I listened in to partnerships, reminding them to name both similarities and differences. I then regained the class's attention.

"You were noticing that the rhyme and the poem were both about something; they each had a topic. One was about a cow; the other was about an apple. The authors of the rhyme and the poem also thought carefully about how to write words. They used parts of words they know," I pointed to the ending of *cow* and *how*, "and blends at the start of words." I pointed to the beginning of *slow* in the rhyme and then to *star*, *crunch*, and *snow* in the poem.

"You *also* noticed how different the real poem is from 'My Cow.' Authors of real poems write about things that are most important to them in ways that make the reader see things in a new way or make them feel a certain way. They also write in a different way than writers of little silly rhymes. When writers write silly rhymes, first they make lists of words whose parts are the same, and then they use those words to create their rhyme.

"Poets work differently. They pick the words that match the feeling their topic gives them. They try out lots of words and phrases until they find the ones that sound just right to their ears. Then, once they have picked the *perfect* words and their poem sounds just right, they write those perfect words using what they know about beginning and ending parts.

"The thing is, up until now, we've just been having fun with words, playing around with them, trying them out in different and fun ways. We haven't been writing from the heart. We haven't been writing about things that matter."

ACTIVE ENGAGEMENT/LINK

Channel partners to generate topics for poems by thinking of things that matter and telling them to each other. Have students orally rehearse their poem into a pretend microphone.

I looked around and continued, "Since we have been transported here, to this poetry café, I think it's time for you all to write some *real* poetry instead of silly rhymes and tongue-twisters.

"First, you'll need a topic—something that really matters to you. Gather some ideas on your fingers of the things you care about most." After half a minute I said, "Turn and tell the person next to you about things that matter to you, the things that are close to your heart. As you're listing, you might think, 'Which one of these do I want to write a poem about?' Give me a thumbs up when you both have a topic!" I gave students a few moments to talk.

POSSIBLE COACHING MOVES

▶ "Remember, poets try to choose perfect words. Is that the word you want there?"

▶ "What feeling do you want people to have? What words and phrases will help readers or listeners have that feeling?"

▶ "How will you show readers that this matters to you?"

"I heard you saying you might write poems about baking cookies, members of your family, bikes, even about Mabel. She does matter to us.

"Poets, hold up your imaginary microphone." Once everyone had one in hand I said, "Now, how might that poem go? Practice some of the phrases into your microphone. Remember, this is just a first try. Poets try out lots of words in all sorts of phrases before they get their poem just right."

RUG TIME (CLUBS)

Challenge rug clubs to choose a meaningful topic and to create a poem. Encourage them to say the poem aloud several times, trying out different words to say what they really mean.

"Poets, move toward your rug club. You'll want to decide together on something that matters to *all* of you. Once you decide, you'll want to work together to say and write a poem on your whiteboard. You might want to say the poem once or twice, deciding on the perfect words, before you take turns trying to write each part. You might not get it exactly how you want it—that can take weeks—but see if you can work together to write a poem that really *matters* to each of you.

"Here is one tip: as you start to write, use everything you've learned about sounds that letters make, word parts, and snap words to help you write your ideas down."

After a few minutes I called the class back together. "Poets, in just a few minutes we are going to celebrate these poems. Before we do that, read your poem aloud and make sure you've used the words and phrases you want to make listeners feel what you feel about your topic, about something that matters to you. As you're rereading, you can revise words or phrases, like poets do, making sure you've chosen the perfect ones for your poem."

SHARE • A Poetry Café Celebration of Poems and Phonics

Channel students to don pretend poets' clothes and then set up each member of a rug club to celebrate their poem twice: first celebrating phonics work and then celebrating meaning.

I held up Mabel who was now also wearing a beret. "Mabel thinks that while we are still in this poetry café, we should celebrate our poems. But first, let's keep our imagination magic strong. Poets, get your beret in your hand and whisper the color of it into the air as you place it on your head. Then think, what else do you want for your poetry celebration outfit? A scarf around your neck? Some cool, colorful glasses? Or something else entirely that your poet-self has dreamt up!" Kids took a quick moment to dress themselves in their imaginary poets' outfits.

"Now that you're looking snazzy, it's time to celebrate with our rug clubs. You'll want to sit in a circle around your café table." As clubs moved to sit in little circles, I quickly distributed one cardboard tube microphone to each club.

POSSIBLE COACHING MOVES

▶ "Say your next phrase or sentence. Write each word carefully!"

▶ "Is there a part of that word you can write in a snap?"

▶ "Is there a tool in the classroom that can help you get that word down?"

Don't worry if students don't have a lot of time to write and revise their poems. It's true that crafting a complete poem takes a lot of revision and a lot of time! The idea is that we want students to feel the difference between writing a little rhyme and writing a poem.

"You're each going to get to celebrate your poem—*two* times. That's right, poets. Each club will read their poem twice. The first time you read your poem, you'll celebrate the phonics work you did to write your poem. You'll have to hold your poem up for all of us to see as you read, and then you'll show us where you used a word part you knew, where you wrote a blend or used vowels—anything you worked on as you wrote out each perfect word!

"Then, you'll read your poem a second time. This time we will simply close our eyes and feel your poem, picturing your words in our minds so that we learn about something that matters to you. When a poet finishes their turn, it's a custom to give that poet snaps instead of clapping your hands." I modeled snapping my fingers and some of the students joined in to practice.

"The only thing this Poetry Café of ours has been missing is the sound of poetry in the air! Let's fix that." Mabel pointed to one club with her trunk. "Let's have the first club come up so we can celebrate."

FIG. 14–1   Students celebrate their poetry with their classmates and Mabel.

Dear Teachers,

This culminating bend of the unit brings together all that your students have learned about phonics and focuses their efforts on phonics projects. Session 15 launches the bend with a project investigating the letter *I*. You'll teach students that when someone wants to begin a new project, they gather the materials they wish to study—in this case, words that contain the letter *I*. You'll guide students into sorting these words into piles: long *I*, short *I*, and other sounds. Then you'll return to a familiar text, Arnold Shapiro's lovely poem, "I Speak, I Say, I Talk," and students will find words containing *I* in the poem, then sort them into categories as you did during your demonstration. Students continue their study more independently by working with their rug clubs to gather and sort even more *I* words.

You'll engage students' attention in Session 16 with three phonics games that help them compare and contrast the different sounds that the letter *I* can represent. After you've introduced all three games, partners will choose one of the games to play together, and before moving to another game, they will stop and think about what they are learning about the letter *I*. At the end of the session, you'll lead a symphony share in which partners share with the whole class what they have learned while playing the phonics games.

Students will apply this knowledge to their reading in Session 17, when you remind them that vowels can make more than one sound. You'll teach them that when they get to a word that sounds strange when they read it, they can check whether that word has a vowel such as *I* that makes more than one sound, then try reading the word another way to see if that makes more sense. You'll read a few lines from a familiar text, Arnold Shapiro's "I Speak, I Say, I Talk," only this time, you'll deliberately misread the words containing the letter *I*, reading short vowels as if they were long, and vice versa. You'll show how you stop yourself at the confusing word, then try pronouncing that letter *I* a different way—discovering the right way to pronounce the word. Then you'll continue on, encouraging the children to stop you when you make a mistake and to help you figure out how to fix that mistake. Partners will then apply this learning to their reading, as partners choose a book from their book baggies to read to each other, helping each other correct any mistakes they might make. You'll remind kids at the end of the session that they now have a new way to solve tricky words, and that they should remember to draw on all that they know when they get stuck.

Now that you've walked through a phonics project investigating the letter *I* together, it's time for kids to work more independently in Session 18. You'll begin by showing them they can use the process they learned for the letter *I* investigation to embark upon phonics projects with other vowels. You'll start by gathering words containing the letter *U* and sorting them, then you'll read aloud from "I Speak, I Say, I Talk," as kids help collect and sort them words into those containing a long *U*, short *U*, and other sounds. Then you'll launch rug clubs on their own investigations as you give each club a different vowel as the focus of their phonics projects. Students will mine their books for words containing their vowel and sort those words, then share their learning with the class.

The sharing will carry over into Session 19, when you begin preparing kids for the end-of-the-unit celebration. You'll inform your students that Mabel wants to learn what they know about phonics, so you will help them get ready to become teachers themselves. You'll show them how to prepare a little lecture about their vowel, then you'll read Nan Fry's beautiful poem "Apple," and show students how you would mark the poem for shared reading. Now rug clubs will plan their teaching by choosing a familiar poem or song to plan their shared reading and highlight words containing the vowel in their phonics project. Finally, rug clubs will teach Mabel what they have learned about their letter. We recommend that you video kids' teaching on your cell phone if you can—it's a delightful way to share your students' learning with their families.

And finally, the celebration for the unit—and the entire kindergarten year—arrives in Session 20. Again, your students will be teaching what they know, but this time they will choose from all of the phonics content they learned over the course of the entire school year. You'll remind students about the different topics they learned over the year and encourage rug clubs to choose one. As clubs begin their planning, you'll be there to help guide them in their planning. Once the planning is done, you'll bring out Mabel—and your children will bring out the stuffed animals or action figures they brought with them to school—and you will welcome them all back to ABC School. Clubs will teach their topics to their toy friends as you move from group to group.

Finally, Mabel brings the unit to a close with a cheerful song to celebrate all that your students have achieved—in this unit, and in the entire kindergarten year.

All the best,
Lucy, Amanda, and Valerie

Launching Phonics Projects
Investigating the Letter I

GETTING READY

✔ Gather items whose names contain the letter *I* (such as a triangle from the math center, a photo of a birthday party, milk, ice cream, rice, and a push pin) and put them in a sack. Photocopy or cut out the product name from the packaging to place in your pocket chart. Alternatively, print pictures of these items.

✔ Set up a pocket chart for a three-column word sort. Add the title "The Different Sounds of *I*" to the chart, and label the three columns "Long *I*," "Short *I*," and "Other *I* Sounds." You will need this chart in Session 17, so be sure to keep it once it's complete.

✔ Prepare to begin building the "How to Do a Phonics Project" anchor chart.

✔ Display the poem "I Speak, I Say, I Talk" by Arnold L. Shapiro.

✔ Have a stack of blank Post-its available for you and for each rug club.

✔ Distribute a whiteboard and marker to each rug club.

PHONICS INSTRUCTION

Phonics
• Discover different vowel sounds for the letter *I*.

Word Knowledge/Solving
• Use a predictable process of collecting and sorting to learn more about letters and sounds.

High-Frequency Words
• Learn new words (*has*, *as*, *her*, *him*).
• Develop strategies for learning new high-frequency words.

IN THIS SESSION

TODAY YOU'LL teach students that when people launch a project about an object—such as a project about a letter or a sound—they begin by collecting those objects, then organizing them into logical categories.

TODAY YOUR STUDENTS will launch into an investigation of the letter *I*. They will collect and sort words containing the letter *I* by studying a variety of items. Doing this work will help them learn how to launch into any kind of phonics project and will support vowel flexibility.

MINILESSON

CONNECTION

Explain that you have been looking at the calendar and you were worried because there is so much left to teach. But then Mabel gave you a fantastic idea—phonics projects!

"Friends, Mabel and I have been talking about how fast this year has been moving. Whoa—there are only a few months left of school! You have already learned sooooo much. Show Mabel and me your reading and writing muscles!" Kids flexed their muscles.

"But here's the thing. There is also so much more to learn this year! Mabel and I were talking about that and she gave me this great idea. Since you are getting older and becoming stronger readers and writers, maybe you are ready to take on some phonics projects. We could study something really interesting about phonics for about a week and then the next week, we could take on a new phonics project.

"So, we might investigate a really interesting letter like *G*, or we might study words that have two words inside them (they are called contractions—*can't* is an example). Each week we could tackle a new phonics project. We could learn that one thing, and then maybe we could even teach other people what we learn!

"I've chosen a really interesting and fun letter for our first project. Are you ready to see which one it will be? Everyone, give me a drumroll! The letter is . . . *i*!"

Name the teaching point.

"Today I want to teach you that when you're going to launch a project about a letter or a sound, the first thing you do is collect words that have that letter or sound. After you get a big pile of those words, it makes sense to sort them into groups that go together."

TEACHING

Explain how collecting and sorting letters and sounds is similar to collecting and sorting other collectibles, such as toy cars and trucks.

"I know that you all have lots of fun projects at home. Maybe some of you have a project going with Beanie Babies or Hatchimals or with ribbons and barrettes, or with books, or with cars and trucks.

"Right now, let's pretend we are doing a project involving toy cars and trucks. If I had that project, I'd start by collecting as many of those little cars and trucks as I could. I'd have some with doors that open and shut, and some with those huge tires. Picture yourself collecting cars and trucks." I ran my hands over an imaginary pile of them, sitting before me.

"What would you do next?" I let kids think and then said, "I don't know about you, but I'd probably sort them. Maybe I'd make a pile of race cars, and another pile of . . . hmm . . ."

Youngsters chimed in, and I agreed. "Yes, construction vehicles! Bulldozers and tractors and all. Good idea. And there'd be a pile of cars for families, right?

Know in advance that this cars-and-trucks project weaves through this bend. You'll be teaching kids how to do a phonics project, and you'll suggest that there isn't a lot of difference between a project with something like cars and trucks and a project with something like vowel flexibility! Though, for now, the kids still think this is a project about the sounds of one vowel.

A single-page version of this chart is available in the Resource Pack.

"The important thing is that when you have a project about letters and sounds, it is a lot like a project with cars and trucks. First you collect a bunch of things and then you sort them, putting them into groups that go together. Then you can study those groups."

Explain the process of making a phonics project about the letter *I*. Show students some products whose names contain the letter *I* and recruit students to sort them by sound.

"We start our letter *I* project by collecting words that have an *I* in them." I put a large sack on my lap. "I've actually been gathering some stuff for our project, and I thought you could help me look at what I've got so far." I started taking objects out and setting them next to me. "These things came from a search I made for words that had an *I* in them," I said. I showed an empty carton of *ice* cream and a push *pin*. "Here's an empty jug of *milk*. And a triangle from the math center." Then I pulled out a package of *rice* and a photo of a birthday party.

Teachers, if you don't want to gather up the actual ice cream cartons and milk jugs, you can find photos of these items in the Resource Pack. However, we do encourage you to bring in the actual products if you can—it adds to the fun. Be sure to use the actual logos, though— don't simply write rice on an index card. This teaching needs to be rooted in a real-world application.

"Let's say these words one more time. As we do, think about what kind of sound the *I* makes. Let's sort by putting the objects and pictures that make the same *I* sounds together. Our pocket chart has three columns: one for words that have a long *I*, /ī/; a column for words with a short *I*, /ĭ/; and a column for words with other *I* sounds. Are you ready to sort?" Kids nodded, and I said, "Let's start with our first word: *rice*. What kind of *I* sound is in *rice*? Rice. Riiiiiiice. That's right—it's a long *I* sound." I placed the package label for *rice* into the "Long I" column of the pocket chart.

I help up a triangle from the math manipulative bin. The class listened to the *I* sound in the next word, *triangle*. Many suggested the object went in the same column, but I tested it out. "*Triiiiangle, riiice*. Those do sound the same, you are right. They both have /ī/.

"Does anything else go there?" The class pointed out *ice cream* and we said the word slowly. *Ice cream* joined the "Long *I*" column.

"What about *pin*—/p/-/ĭ/-/n/? Does that sound like /r/-/ī/-/s/—*rice*?

I let the children make those sounds. "No? It sounds different? So, I will put that in the column for words that have a short *I* sound, like the sound in *pin*." We noted that *pin* and *milk* went together in the "Short *I*" column.

I held up the photo of a birthday party. The kids were stumped by *birthday*. "It doesn't sound like any of them. You can't even hear the *I*," one child said.

"Sometimes letters don't make the sounds you expect," I said. "*I* doesn't make the long or the short sound in *birthday*. Let's put it in the column for 'Other *I* Sounds.'"

ACTIVE ENGAGEMENT/LINK

Continue collecting and sorting words, this time by reading a familiar short text.

"This is a great start to our project, but we need to collect more words! Let's collect *I* words from poems and songs that we know." I placed the first stanza of "I Speak, I Say, I Talk" by Arnold L. Shapiro under the document camera. "Let's reread this poem. And when we find the letter *I*, let's put a Post-it next to it!"

Kaylee's hand shot up. "I see the letter *I*! It's in the title!"

"Hooray! Let me put a Post-it here! Let's keep reading. As we read together, if you see a word, give me a thumbs up!" I read aloud and marked the words with *I*'s that the children noted.

"You found *lions*, *crickets*, *mice*, *pigs*, *chickens*, *flies*, and *neigh*. And we can't forget that we found another *I*," and I pointed to the final lines of each stanza. "I'm just going to jot the words, quickly on these Post-its, so that we have a little collection of *I* words. Now with your partner, will you talk about how to sort these words into our chart? Tell each other where each word should go. Use *rice* and *pin* to help you. Go!"

As students talked, I frequently sent one child up to move the Post-it words into the proper column on the pocket chart. Soon, the class had noted how to categorize more words and had noted that *neigh* did not go in the long or short category—it was another "other" word.

If you don't have a document camera, you can find another way to enlarge the poem.

If students don't notice a word with the letter I on the first read, that is fine. Let it go. You can always decide to do a second read and help highlight the words that they missed. You also don't need to find and sort all of the I words. A few is fine. And you could leave the poem with a rug club or a small group to find more later.

The Different Sounds of I		
Long I	**Short I**	**Other I Sounds**
• Rice	• Pin	• Birthday
• Triangle	• Milk	• Neigh
• Ice Cream	• Crickets	
• I	• Pigs	
• Lions	• Chickens	
• Mice		
• Flies		

The "Other I Sounds" column is an important one to have in this sort. It reminds students that they will find words that don't always fit. This also provides an opportunity for you to assess student understanding of phonics.

"Now, we need to collect more!"

RUG TIME (CLUBS)

Send clubs to different areas of the room to keep collecting words for the I project.

"So, I've given each club a little stack of Post-its. Will you and your club head out into our classroom, searching for more I words?" I gave each rug club directions on where to look for their I words, such as in their book baggies, in their writing folders, on the word wall, or in the shared reading basket of books.

As clubs collected I words, I moved around the room, coaching students as needed.

Gather clubs back and ask them to read and sort their I words.

"Clubs, come on back to the rug! Bring your Post-its and your newfound words! With your clubs, on one whiteboard, put your words into groups based on the sound that the I makes. Go ahead. Reread your words and put them into groups."

POSSIBLE COACHING MOVES

▶ "Slow down. Read that page again. Is there a word with the letter I?"

▶ "Don't forget to write it down on your Post-it."

▶ "What word are you writing down? Say it first."

▶ "Take out another piece of writing. Look for more words."

▶ "Say the word slowly. What word has the same I sound?"

SHARE • Adding Categorized Words to the Class Collection

Have clubs add their categorized words to the class collection. Read through the list of words in each column together to check that the words are all sorted right.

"We have more I words for our collection! Before you and your rug club put your materials away, let's see all of our new words and add them to our class collection. You and your partners, add your I words to the class list up here. If it makes the /ī/ sound as in *rice*, put it here in the 'Long I' column. If it makes the /ĭ/ sound as in *pin*, place it here in the

'Short *I*' column. And if you are not sure, or if it makes a different sound, put it here, with *birthday* and *neigh* with the 'Other *I* Sounds' words."

As students place their words in the chart, encourage them to say the word with the anchor word, rice or pin. Help them emphasize the /i/ sound. The other kids can raise thumbs up when they agree. This helps keep everyone engaged and thinking.

After a minute, I said, "Let's read all of the words in each group to make sure we agree they go together. Read with me." We read each group of words, switching any words that didn't belong.

"Look how we started our first project! Tomorrow we will keep thinking more about letter *I*."

You will refer back to "The Different Sounds of I" chart later in this bend, so be sure to keep it on display after this session.

EXTENSION 1 • Learning New Snap Words: *Has*, *As*, *Her*, and *Him*

 Guide students through the familiar steps of learning new high-frequency words, using the "How to Learn a Word" chart.

"When Popeye's muscles get bigger, he doesn't stop eating spinach. Oh, no. He eats *more* spinach to make his muscles stronger! Your reading and writing muscles are strong, that's for sure. Do you know what you need more of to make them stronger? *More* snap words!"

I taped index cards with the words *has*, *as*, *her*, and *him* written on them to the easel. I displayed the "How to Learn a Word" chart and invited kids to read it with me.

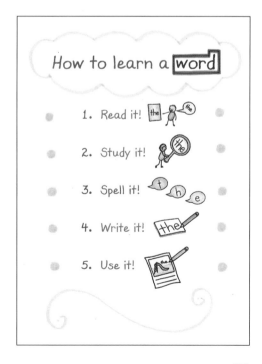

"Let's learn this word first." I pointed to the word *has*. "First, *read* it!" I pointed under the printed card as the students chorally read the word.

"Now, *study* it. Turn and tell your partner what you see.

"Now, *spell* it. Spell it softly, like a whisper into your hand: *h-a-s*. Now, spell it and cheer it.

"Now, *write* it!" Students wrote the word *has* with imaginary markers on the rug.

"Last step—*use* it! Share a sentence with your partner." I circulated, listening in and providing support where needed.

We repeated the same steps to learn the words *as*, *her*, and *him*, then I said, "This snap word—*him*—is special. This one can help us with our phonics project! If we were going to sort *him*, should we sort it with *rice*, *pin*, or does it sound completely different?"

The class agreed we would sort it with *pin*, and we added the four new words to the word wall. Then, I passed out small copies of the word cards, and students quickly added them to their snap word pouches.

FIG. 15–1   A teacher coaches students as they use "The Different Sounds of *l*" chart to rehearse what they learned.

EXTENSION 2 • Rehearsing to Share Our Phonics Project with Families

Remind students the goal of a project is to learn something about the topic. Set partners up to role-play talking to someone at home about what they learned about the letter *l* today.

"Friends, we are about to pack up. Before we do, I want to remind you that the big goal of doing a project is to learn stuff. Right now, will you pretend that you are home and someone in your home has asked you what you learned today? Pretend you want to tell them something you have learned about the letter *l*. What would you say? One of you can get the chance to be the person at home who asks, 'What are you learning?' and one of you can pretend to be the kid answering. Ready? Partner 1, you start by asking, 'What did you learn at school today?' And Partner 2, you answer. If you have time, switch!"

Comparing and Contrasting Words with the Letter *I*

IN THIS SESSION

TODAY YOU'LL teach students that to learn more about a letter sound, they can compare and contrast how that letter sounds in different words.

TODAY YOUR STUDENTS will match picture cards with long *I* and short *I* words and then play a game, trying to find two short *I* or two long *I* picture cards that make a match.

MINILESSON

CONNECTION

Explain that projects often involve collecting things and thinking about how they are similar and different. Use a real-life topic as a way to recruit kids to look at similarities and differences between short-vowel sounds.

"Friends, when people are really curious about something, they keep studying it—they keep thinking about it. Like people who study toy cars and trucks. They don't just study them for one day. They study them for lots of days, trying to learn more.

"If we had our car and truck collection here, I bet we'd want to start playing with them!" I paused as if to pick up an imaginary car. "I could take this bulldozer here and 'rrrrrr' it across a huge pile of dirt, scooping up the dirt to move it. If you had a whole set of trucks and ambulances and race cars, which would you pick to play with? What would you do with it? Tell your partner."

The kids talked and then I said, "I heard terrific ideas! Some of you'd have races, and I even heard one of you say she'd use a truck to carry her pretend horses on a trip. Here's the cool thing: if you have a project going, whether it is about vehicles or about letters and sounds, one thing that you do is you play with the things you are collecting. That's true for vehicles and it is true for letters and sounds."

GETTING READY

✔ Print pictures of a pig, lion, and cricket, and place them in a baggie.

✔ Hang an empty pocket chart near the rug.

✔ Prepare a baggie for each partnership containing several long *I* and short *I* picture cards for the "Sound Match" game.

✔ Prepare a baggie for each partnership containing a picture of a scene and two different-color markers for the "Where Am I?" game.

✔ Introduce the "Old MacDonald Had an /I/!" game.

✔ Be ready to add another point to the "How to Do a Phonics Project" anchor chart.

PHONICS INSTRUCTION

Phonological Awareness
• Hear the difference between the short *E* sound and the short *I* sound in words.

Phonics
• Contrast short and long vowel sounds in words.

Word Knowledge/Solving
• Use a predictable process of playing with words to learn more about letters and sounds.

• Use short *I* phonograms (*it*, *ip*) and blends and digraphs to make new words.

❧ **Name the teaching point.**

"Today I want to teach you that when you have a project going, and you take some time to 'just play,' you end up learning from that play. That's true if your project involves collecting race cars, and it is true if your project involves collecting words that have the letter *I* in them. You play with the cars or the words, and either way, you end up learning!"

TEACHING

Introduce phonics games children can play to help them learn about the letter *I*. Begin with an easy game that involves producing long and short *I* words to insert into a familiar song.

"Friends, I'm going to show you a few different games quickly, so you have lots of time to play and learn. Listen closely.

"The first game you might choose to play is a singing game. It's called, 'Old MacDonald Had an *I*.' Instead of having a cow or a duck, he has things with a short *I* or a long *I*. Let's play—see if you can join me."

> Old MacDonald had a farm,
> *E, I, E, I, O*
> And on that farm he had a . . . ship!
> *E, I, E, I, O*
> With an /ĭ/, /ĭ/ here and an /ĭ/, /ĭ/ there
> Here an /ĭ/, there an /ĭ/, everywhere an /ĭ/ /ĭ/
> Old MacDonald had a ship,
> *E, I, E, I, O*

"Okay, so we gave Old MacDonald a short *I* word. Now if Player 2 were to go, you'd have to think of a word with a long vowel—a long *I*. It's your turn, so as we keep on singing, start getting an idea in your head . . ." We started singing again:

> Old MacDonald had a farm,
> *E, I, E, I, O*
> And on that farm he had a . . .

I let my voice drop out and the class called out words like *ice cream*, *bike*, and *kite*. We finished singing the song, this time making the verse support the long *I* sound. "You take turns with a partner and the things on the farm always go with a short *I*, then with a long *I*, then with a short *I*, and so on."

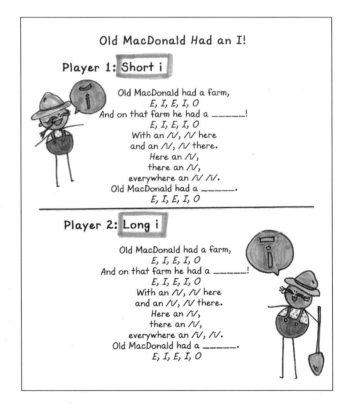

Teach your children another phonics game, "Sound Match"—a game in which they match picture cards that share the same vowel sound in the same place in each word.

"Are you ready for game two? It's called 'Sound Match.'" I held up a baggie of picture cards. "This is a matching game, kind of like matching socks after they come out of the dryer. When you match socks, you want to put the red sock with the red sock—and not with the blue sock. In this game, instead of matching socks, you'll match words that have the same vowel sounds in the same place in the words. So, for example, you'll match words that have short *I* in the beginning of the word, like *iguana* and *igloo*. You can also match words that have a short *I* in the middle of the word, like *pig* and *lip*. You can also match words with long *I* in the beginning of the word, or the middle."

"So, let's say I am Player 1. I pick two cards," I said as I picked two cards out of the bag and held them up.

"Ah, it's a pig. Pig. /P/-/ĭ/-/g/. I hear a short *I* in the middle. Let's see if this other card is a match! Dinosaur. Diiiinosaur. Is there an *I* in the middle? Yes. But are both *I*'s matching, either two short *I*'s or two longs *I*'s?" The students shook their heads no. "You're right! Both *dinosaur* and *pig* have an *I* in the middle, but *lion* has a long *I* and *pig* has a short *I*. So those two do not match." I turned the cards over so their pictures no longer showed.

"Now Player 2 has a chance to pick a card to see if he can make a match." I called a student to be Player 2 and asked him to pick two cards. I had guided him toward *pig* and the card with a picture of a *gift*, knowing it would be a match with *pig*. "Do your cards match?" I asked. He said each word slowly and nodded his head. "You're right! They both have a short *I* sound in the middle."

Explain the third phonics game, "Where Am I?"—a game in which students examine a scene and find words with a short *I* and words with a long *I*.

"All right, friends, I can see you squirming—ready to play—but there is one more game to tell you about. This one is called 'Where Am I?' It is a bit like 'Where's Waldo?'" I placed a scene under the document camera.

"To play this game, you and your partner have to find pictures in this scene that have a short *I* in them, and pictures that have a long *I*. You'll find a picture, like this carton of *milk*, and then you'll circle it and label it: *milk* (short *I*). You might even choose to use one color marker for all of the short *I* words and one for all of the long *I* words."

ACTIVE ENGAGEMENT/LINK

Channel partners to choose one game to play. Coach partnerships as they get started playing the new game.

"You and your partner have three games to choose from." I revealed a chart with the names of each game.

You might choose to take a moment to show kids any picture cards that might be tricky for them to figure out what the image is. For example, if you have a picture of whisper, lip, *or* iguana, *you could quickly hold up the cards and share with the class. Then again, you could choose to leave this as a challenge for some kids, giving them the opportunity to figure out what the image could be, knowing it has to have a short or long I sound. Some students may say, "lizard." Others maybe "animal." "Both do have an I sound in the middle. Let your students approximate.*

"Meet with your partner and decide which you'll play first. You can decide the same way you decide which games to play first on your reading playdates. Once you've decided, you'll find the materials you'll need for each game up here." I pointed to the front of the rug where I laid out piles of materials for each game.

"Here's one last tip. Remember to pause now and again to think about what you're learning about the letter *I* as you play. When you're ready, take what you need and get playing!"

Kids found space on and near the rug and started playing. I circulated, helping partnerships who needed extra support to get up and running.

RUG TIME

Direct partners to name what they are learning so far about the letter *I* and then have them choose a second game to play.

I stood near the rug and called the class's attention. "Before you switch and play another game, take a moment to think what you are learning about the letter *I* as you play. After you've talked with your partner about what you're learning, put your materials away and choose a different game! Ready? Go!"

SHARE • A Symphony Share of the Letter *I*

Lead a symphony share in which partners name the things they learned by playing with the letter *I*.

"Friends, quickly clean up and come back to the rug." Once the class was settled I continued. "You did a lot of playing! I wanted to take some time for you to share what you've learned as you were playing. What are some ideas you're having about the letter *I*? Turn and share them with your partner."

As partners shared what they learned, I coached in, helping partners who were stuck think back to their game playing. I prompted, "Which parts of the game were tricky? Which parts were easy? What does that make you think about *I*?"

After a few moments I called the partnerships back together. "Let's do a symphony share of our letter *I* learning! When Mabel points her wand at you, share what you've learned. If you're a listener, make sure you're gathering up all of your friends' learning, so we can use it when we continue our project tomorrow."

Mabel started pointing at partnerships and each shared. They said things like, "*I* sounds different ways," "There are lots of words with long *I* in the middle," and "You have to say words slowly to hear how the *I* sounds."

FIG. 16–1 A teacher uses a fancy pointer to lead a symphony share.

"From now on, you'll always know that when you have a project going, and you can take some time to 'just play around' with your project and you'll end up learning from that play!" I added another point to our anchor chart.

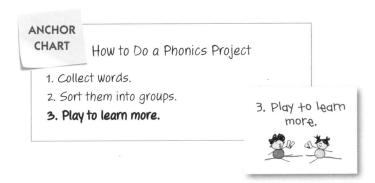

ANCHOR CHART — How to Do a Phonics Project

1. Collect words.
2. Sort them into groups.
3. **Play to learn more.**

3. Play to learn more.

EXTENSION 1 • Playing "Sound Match" to Compare Short *I* to Short *E*

Add short *E* cards to the game students played earlier, "Sound Match," so they can practice distinguishing between short *I* and short *E*.

"Kindergartners, I was thinking you could play 'Sound Match' again. This time, I'll give you and your partners baggies with some short *I* picture cards and some short *E* picture cards. You'll have to work with your partner, listening carefully to the vowel sounds so you can decide if the word has a short *I* or a short *E*. Let's practice together."

I pulled out two picture cards, showing mittens and a web. "Can you and your partner say each word slowly and decide if the vowel sounds in each word match?"

Kids shook their heads, showing that the cards didn't match. We repeated the process with *web* and *leg*. Once the class agreed that we had found a short *E* match, I distributed cards so they could continue playing.

EXTENSION 2 • Speed Sort

Recruit students to speed sort their picture cards, sorting them into long *I* and short *I* columns as quickly as possible and then reading down each column to check.

"Letter *I* investigators, here are your cards back. Let's see if you and your partner are ready for a speed sort!!

"Partner 2, you go first this time. Take the cards and as quickly as possible, read them out loud and sort them into two columns, long *I* and short *I*. When you are finished sorting, you and your partner can read down each column together

to check that each word belongs. If one doesn't, you'll have to move it. Then Partner 1 can speed sort. Remember to say the word as you sort the card.

"Ready? Sort!"

EXTENSION 3 • Minute Words

Challenge students to make as many words as they can in one minute with a short *I* word part.

"Readers, writers, over the last few days you have learned about blends and you have learned about the short and long *I* sound. Let's put all the knowledge together. You'll need a whiteboard. As soon as you get it, make some word parts that start with a short *I*. Like here is one." I wrote on the whiteboard.

ip

"Then I'm going to ask you to imagine yourself building a LEGO guy, and you have *ip* as the body. Use a consonant, blend, or a digraph as the head and attach it to the body. Then the job is to make as many words as you can in one minute. The trick is, it has to be a word. Let's try it together right now."

ip

~~stip~~ (I crossed that one out–not a word)

slip

chip

ship

sip

"And we could keep going with more *ip* words! Are you ready to try this? For now, I'll give you a word part—how about *it*? Add consonants, blends, and digraphs. See what words you can make! You have one minute. Go!"

Being Flexible When You Read *I* Words

IN THIS SESSION

TODAY YOU'LL teach students that when readers get to a word they aren't sure about, they check whether that word has a vowel that makes more than one sound, and if it does, they try reading the word another way to see if that makes more sense.

TODAY YOUR STUDENTS will read in partnerships and draw on all they know to solve tricky words, paying particular attention to vowels, such as *I*, that can sound more than one way.

MINILESSON

CONNECTION

Celebrate how big the phonics project has become. Ask partners to read the *I* words and remind them that some letters, like the letter *I*, make more than one sound.

"Readers, look at how big our project is getting. Our collection is *huge*! This morning, Mabel started reading all our words. She was worried at first that she wouldn't be able to read all of them. And then I said to her, 'Mabel, if you forget how the *I* sounds, you can use *rice* and *pins* to remind you.' Then she zipped through the list of words.

"You want to try it now with your partners? Go ahead, activate that vowel power, and read as many words in our collection as you can!" I gave kids a few moments to read through the pocket chart of *I* words.

"Readers, what you just did is so powerful! Not just because you used your super powers, but also because you are using what you know about letters to help you read! And one thing you know is that some letters, like the letter *I*, have more than one sound! That means that letter might sound like the *I* in *rice* or like the *I* in *pins*, or it might sound different," I said as I pointed to the third column.

PHONICS INSTRUCTION

Phonological Awareness
• Hear the difference between the short *I* sound and the long *I* sound in words.

Phonics
• Contrast short and long vowel sounds in words.

Word Knowledge/Solving
• Use a predictable process of using what you have learned when you are trying to learn more about letters and sounds.

• Use different sounds for the same vowel to read words.

High-Frequency Words
• Review high-frequency words.

♣ **Name the teaching point.**

"Today I want to teach you that when you are doing a phonics project and are learning a lot about letters and sounds, you need to use all that you've learned as you read and as you write."

TEACHING

Read a poem as if you were a novice reader, deliberately messing up reading an _I_ word. Show how you reread, substitute a different sound for the vowel, and test for meaning.

"Let's pretend that I'm a little kid, reading the poem 'I Speak, I Say, I Talk' for the first time. If I mess up, remind me of what to do, so we can use what we've been learning." I read the first two lines. As I read _lions_, I misread it with a short _I_ sound.

> Cats purr.
> /Lĭ-yunz/ roar.

"Nooooooooo!" the class roared. "It's _lions_!"

"Wait, wait! /Lĭ-yunz/," I said again, once again making the short _I_ sound. "That isn't a word. That doesn't make sense or sound right to me either! So, you know what I have to do? I have to try it again. I have to try a _different_ sound for _I_. I'll read it again—see if I do better."

I read it again with the correct, long _I_ sound. "Well? Does it sound better? Does it look right, and make sense? Yes, it does!"

ACTIVE ENGAGEMENT/LINK

Continue to pretend to be a kid, reading the poem and making mistakes when you read _I_ words. Set up students to coach you to read the word another way to fix your mistakes.

"I am going to keep pretending. Will you all pretend to be the teacher and remind me what to do? Tell me to stop if something sounds strange or if you think I need to try a different sound." Then I leaned closer to the group, "But don't tell me the word!

"Ready to play teacher?" This time as I read, I read _crickets_ with a long _I_ sound.

> Owls hoot.
> Bears snore.
> Crī-ckets creak.

This lesson is teaching students about vowel flexibility. It is helping them to understand that while they get stronger at word solving using phonics, they still need to check that what they read makes sense. Sometimes trying on different vowel sounds while thinking about what the text is about helps students to orchestrate all the sources available to them.

This type of practice also helps students understand their role as an active reading partner.

"No!!" kids howled.

"Are you telling me to stop? Should I try it again? Okay, let me try another sound for *I* and think about what makes sense. /ĭ/. *Crickets*. Does that make sense, sound better, and look right? Yup!

"Thank you for reminding me to try it again! After this, I'm going to try to remember always that when a word sounds weird or odd, I have to stop and try it another way. Let's keep playing." This time, when I came to this part, I read *pigs* with a long *I*.

> Ducks quack.
> Doves coo.
> /Pīgs/ squeal.

"Try it again!" kids called out.

"How? Any suggestions?"

"With the /ĭ/ sound like in *crickets*! Think about what makes sense!"

"Okay, give me a thumbs up if I do it well. *Pigs!*" Kids gave me a thumbs up. We then read on. "Makes sense and looks right."

"Readers, that was fun to pretend. You all are great teachers! You know a lot about the sounds of the letter *I*. It was helpful for you to make me stop and try a different sound that the letter *I* makes."

Let your kids know they can be teachers for real with each other and themselves. If a word doesn't sound right, they can coach their partner (or themselves) to try reading the word a different way.

"When you are reading with your partners, you read for real! But remember, you can be teachers with each other. If something doesn't look right, sound right, or make sense, remember to remind your partner they too need to stop and try it again. Sometimes thinking about what makes sense and trying a different sound out can help you!"

RUG TIME

Set up students to start reading in partnerships. Partner 1 starts reading, and Partner 2 is the teacher who coaches if Partner 1 gets stuck or makes a mistake. Then they switch roles.

"It's time for you to use what you've learned as you read from your book baggies. You game? Let's have Partner 1 start. Pick out a book you haven't read in a long time and read it with Partner 2. Partner 2, you be

FIG. 17–1 Partners read together using their knowledge of vowels to word solve.

the teacher. If Partner 1 messes up, use our chart of ways to help solve words from reading workshop. And remember, one way for a reader to fix things up is to try reading the word, giving some letters a different sound. Go ahead, start reading.

"Readers, don't forget, when Partner 1 finishes her book, it's Partner 2's turn. Partner 1, you will turn into the teacher."

Bring out the "We Are Super Readers" word-solving chart you made in Super Powers (Unit 2 of the kindergarten Units of Study for Teaching Reading) to help students with word solving.

SHARE • Be Flexible and Use All You Know When You Solve Tricky Words

Remind readers to be flexible when trying to read words with letters that make more than one sound. Ask students to teach someone in their rug club how they solved a tricky word.

"Remember our imaginary truck project? You could imagine that once you've learned so much about those cars and trucks, you'd want to use what you've learned. Before the project, you might have all of the cars and trucks jumbled, but as you learn more you'd want the race cars to race each other and see who wins. You'd want the construction vehicles to help with construction. Maybe they are on a construction site, helping build.

"The whole point of all of this work is that when you learn new information, you have to use that new information! In our phonics project, you are learning that as you read you need to be flexible. That means you can't expect for things to always be just one way. You can't say, 'The letter / always sounds like this.' We know that's not the case, and it won't help you get unstuck if you think that way. You have to draw on all that you have learned about letters and the different ways they can sound to figure out how to read words in a way that makes sense and sounds right." I added to the anchor chart.

ANCHOR CHART

How to Do a Phonics Project

1. Collect words.
2. Sort them into groups.
3. Play to learn more.
4. **Use what you've learned.**

4. Use what you've learned.

"Right now, will you find a word that was tricky for you today? Put your finger on it. Okay, now turn to someone in your club other than your partner and teach that person how you tried to figure out that tricky word. Listeners, if you hear that someone tried to read a word a few different ways to find the way that made sense and sounded right, give that person a snap. Go!"

EXTENSION 1 • Play Snap Word "Dribble and Shoot"

✳ **Remind students about a snap word game they have played before, in which one partner chants and spells a snap word and the other indicates whether the word is spelled correctly.**

"Readers, do you remember the snap word game, 'Dribble and Shoot'? It's been a little while since we played it, so I'll remind you how it goes. You'll work with your partner—Partner 1 will say a snap word, then Partner 2 will pretend to dribble a basketball as you say each letter, then say the whole word when you shoot the ball into the basket. If you've spelled it correctly, Partner 1 will yell, '*Score!*'

"Okay, now are *you* ready to play? Partner 1s, think of a snap word. Don't just choose a super-easy one! Pick one that is tricky for you. Then dribble and shoot! Partner 2s, listen carefully so you can hear if your partner spells it correctly or needs your help. Ready? Go!"

EXTENSION 2 • Squeezing a Little More Practice into the Day

Challenge students to make use of each precious minute of the school day. Give them ideas for ways they can practice their phonics knowledge, even when they only have five minutes.

"Readers, writers, we have five minutes before the bus comes. When you are deeply involved in a project, like our phonics project with the letter *I*, you use any extra moments you've got to do stuff with the project. So, let's use these precious minutes. How about if those of you on this side of the room take a stack of cards and you play 'Sound Match' with the letter *I*, and those of you on this side of the room, work in twos or threes to make new game boards for the rest of us to play new rounds of 'Where Am I?' You'll need to think of a scene, to embed objects that have a long and a short *I* in it. And if some of you would be willing to make a 'Where Are U?' variation, I have a feeling that before long, we could use a scene with long and short *U* objects hidden in it. Anyone willing to work on that?

"Okay, guys, you've got five minutes. Get started!"

FIG. 17–2   A student creates a scene for "Where Are U?" featuring bubbles, a brush, a rug, a tube, and a tub.

Learning Even More

Investigating Other Vowels

TODAY YOU'LL teach students that when readers learn a lot about one letter or sound, often they are really learning more about a *group* of letters or sounds. To check if those ideas make sense, they can test them by studying other letters or sounds in the group.

TODAY YOUR STUDENTS will check to see if what they have learned about the letter *I* can apply to other vowels. As a class they will collect and sort *U* words, and in rug clubs, students will collect and sort words with other vowels.

GETTING READY

✔ Be ready to alter a copy of "How to Do a Phonics Project" anchor chart to show how a project could be about anything.

✔ Prepare to add a note to the unaltered version of "How to Do a Phonics Project" anchor chart.

✔ Set up a pocket chart for a three-column word sort. Add the title "The Different Sounds of *U*" to the chart, and label the three columns "Long *U*," "Short *U*," and "Other Sounds *U* Makes." Collect photos of objects to sort.

✔ Display the poem "I Speak, I Say, I Talk," by Arnold Shapiro.

✔ Distribute large Post-its to each rug club.

✔ Assign one of the remaining vowels (*A, E,* or *O*) to each rug club, and give each club a piece of chart paper with three columns labeled "Long *A*," "Short *A*," "Other *A* Sounds" for their assigned vowel.

PHONICS INSTRUCTION

Phonics
• Recognize the difference between the long *U* sound and the short *U* sound in words.

Word Knowledge/Solving
• Use a predictable process of adding to your letter *I* project to learn more about letters and sounds.
• Use a predictable process to learn more about all of the vowels (*O, E, A*).

High-Frequency Words
• Study the word wall to learn more about long and short vowels.

MINILESSON

CONNECTION

Remind students that they are learning how to do a project, which could be about anything—not just about letters and sounds. Recap what they've learned in ways that are universally relevant.

"Kindergartners, we've been thinking so much about that letter *I* that we haven't talked for a while about the whole idea of projects—that we can make projects for ourselves about cars and trucks, or projects about horses, or Pokémon, or letters and sounds, or *anything*. Let's think about whether everything we have learned is true for our pretend project on cars and trucks.

I edited our "How to Do a Phonics Project" anchor chart.

ANCHOR
CHART

How To Do a ~~Phonics~~ Project ∧about
Cars and Trucks

1. Collect ~~words~~ ∧cars and trucks.
2. Sort them into groups.
3. Play to learn more.
4. Use what you've learned.

"Yes, I bet if you had a project going about cars and trucks, or about horse collections, or hair bands, this is how you'd make a project for yourself."

Explain that there is one more step people can do when developing a project. That last step is to make their project more encompassing by collecting more, including more.

"But now I want to suggest one last thing that I think you would do with your toy cars and truck project. I think you'd make it bigger.

"There are lots of ways you could make it bigger. For example, you might get interested in real cars and trucks—you might want to go to a car race (with real cars) or you might want to look at the advertisements to buy cars and see what they cost. Or you might get interested in other vehicles—perhaps motorcycles. All of those are ways to make your project bigger, and that is what happens in life. You start out studying toy cars and you end up studying motorcycles too, and bicycles.

"The same thing happens when you start out studying the letter *I*. You end up wanting to make your project bigger. How could we do that? Turn and talk." I gave kids a moment to talk.

"You are right, friends. You've been studying just the letter *I*, but that letter is part of a group of letters called . . ."

Kids chimed in to say, "Vowels!" I held up the red magnetic letters that were vowels. "You know vowels. You've got vowel power. Pretend you've got your vowel shields in hand and let's cheer the vowels."

"*A, E, I, O, U!*" we cheered.

"So, yes, *I* is part of a group of letters. And that means that you can ask yourself this question: 'Might the things we learned about the letter *I* help us know the other vowels better, too?'"

This session is to start helping your kindergartners to learn how to transfer what they have learned about one vowel to the others. You may decide that, after this unit, you want your class or a small group to study any one of these vowels longer. That is, of course, possible if you believe that your students need an extended phonics project about vowels.

Name the teaching point.

"Today I want to teach you that when you learn a lot about one thing, like trucks or a letter, often you are really learning more about a *group* of things. To check if the ideas you learned about one letter (or one truck) are true for other letters (or trucks), you can study more things and test your ideas against those new things."

> **ANCHOR CHART**
>
> How to Do a Phonics Project
>
> 1. Collect words.
> 2. Sort them into groups.
> 3. Play to learn more.
> 4. Use what you've learned.
> **5. Add to your project.**

5. Add to your project.

TEACHING

Remind students of what they learned from investigating the letter *I* and then begin to investigate another vowel—*U*. Collect and sort *U* words.

"Remember you learned that *I* makes several different sounds. You have to be careful when you read a word with the letter *I* because you might read it as if it made one sound, when actually it makes another sound. You also learned that if you read a word and it doesn't make sense, it helps to try reading letters like *I* in another way to see if then the word—and the sentence—*will* make sense.

"So, our question is: is all that true for other vowels? Does the letter *U* make different sounds, and do you have to be careful when you read a word with a *U* in it? Do you sometimes need to try reading *U* words in a few different ways to find the way that makes the most sense? Hmm, . . . thumbs up if you think what we learned about *I* will be true also for *U*. Thumbs sideways if you disagree. Oh, lots of you think that it will be the same! Let's check to find out! Let's investigate *U*.

"Remember, we started investigating *I* by gathering *I* words and sorting them. So, let's gather some *U* words and sort them. I have some that I've been collecting." I rummaged in my bag and dumped items on the floor. "Here's a label from a package of *cups*. Some *cubes* from our math center. Here's a bottle of *glue*."

I pulled out more stuff. "I've also got a pack of *gum*. And here's the package my *ruler* came in. And here's the label from some *purple* paint.

"Let's read all these objects one more time and as we do, think about which words have similar *U* sounds. Ready?" I led the class in reading the items. "Let's start by making a group of words in which the *U* sounds like it does in *ruler*. I placed a title onto the top of the pocket chart—'The Sounds of *U*'—and made a column containing the label, 'ruler.' I labeled it 'long *U*.'"

I picked up the glue bottle and led the class in listening to the *U* sound within it. "Ruuuuuuler. Gluuuuuuue. Those sound the same, right? They both have uuuuuuuuuuuuuuu." The class nodded. Ruuuler. Gluuuue. Those sound the same in the middle! I hear /o͞o/. Sometimes the long *U* sounds like /o͞o/."

"Does anything else go there?" The class pointed out *cubes*. "Everyone, let's say them slowly and check. Ruuuuuuuler. *Cube*. They are quite the same. The u in *cube* sounds more like /yoo/. But yes, it is still a long *u*, even though they aren't quite the same." *Cubes* joined the long *U* column.

"What about *cups*? Does that sound like /r/-/uuuuu/-/ler/?"

I let the children make those sounds. "No? Different? So, I will make another column for words that have an /ŭ/ sound that is like the sound in *cups*." We noted that *cups* and *gum* went together and labeled them short *U*.

"How about *purple*?" I asked.

"*Purple* is weird," someone said, and others nodded.

We all said the word a few times and I labeled the last category "Other *U* Sounds." "Just like the letter *I*, sometimes *U* doesn't make the sound you expect," I said. "It doesn't make the long or short sound in *purple*. Let's put it in a column for other sounds."

ACTIVE ENGAGEMENT/LINK

Continue collecting and sorting words, this time by reading a familiar short text.

"This is a great start to our project, but we need to collect more words! I know! Let's do the same thing we did for the letter *I*. We can collect *U* words from songs and poems we know. Let's reread the poem 'I Speak, I Say, I Talk.'" I displayed it under the document camera. "Let's be on the lookout for *U* words. Signal when you see one and I'll mark it with a Post-it." We read the poem aloud and marked the words with *U*s.

Teachers, of course long U is more complicated than this. Next year in first grade, your students will delve into studying long U in even more depth and will sort and categorize long U words by sound, learning, for example that in the word huge the letter U makes the sound /yoo/, while in the word June the letter U makes the sound /oo/. For now, our big focus is that students understand that U words can make different sounds, so they will need to be flexible when they get to those words and try reading them different ways to find the way that makes the most sense. More precise work on each vowel will come later.

Later the kids will study r-controlled vowels, which will illuminate the spelling of purple, but for now, that is more than they need to know.

I Speak, I Say, I Talk
by Arnold Shapiro

Cats purr.
Lions roar.
Owls hoot.
Bears snore.
Crickets creak.
Mice squeak.
Sheep baa.
But I SPEAK!

Flies hum.
Dogs growl.
Bats screech.
Coyotes howl.
Frogs croak.
Parrots squawk.
Bees buzz.
But I TALK!

Monkeys chatter.
Cows moo.
Ducks quack.
Doves coo.
Pigs squeal.
Horses neigh.
Chickens cluck.
But I SAY!

"With your partner, will you talk about how you'd sort our collection of words?" I asked. As the kids worked, I jotted the marked words—*purr, squeak, ducks, quack, squeal, cluck, squawk,* and *buzz*—onto Post-its. "Use *ruler* and *cups* to help you. Go!"

Soon, the class had categorized the words and I had moved the Post-its. We noted that many of the *U* words did not go in the long or short category—they were *Other* words.

FIG. 18–1 "The Different Sounds of *U*" pocket chart from one kindergarten classroom.

The Different Sounds of U		
Long U	Short U	Other Sounds U Makes
• ruler	• cups	• purple
• glue	• gum	• purr
• cubes	• but	• squeak
	• ducks	• quack
	• cluck	• squeal
	• hum	• squawk
	• buzz	

"What do you think so far? Is the letter *U* a lot like the letter *I*? Does it make different sounds, and do you think you have to be careful reading *U* words and be ready to try them a few ways? Tell your partner what you are thinking and why." I gave kids a moment to talk.

"So, it seems you all think the letter *U* is a lot like the letter *I*. But we still have other vowels to check!"

RUG TIME CLUBS

Set up each club to investigate a different vowel by reading in their book baggies to collect words with that vowel and then sort those words into long, short, and other sounds.

"Let's check the rest of the vowels. I'll give each club a different vowel and some large Post-its. You can start reading in your book baggies and collect words that have that vowel. Write the words you find on a Post-it. Once each person has found a few words, start sorting as a club. See if you can make three piles—the long sound, the short sound, and other sounds that the vowel makes. You just have four minutes to do this, so get started! This club, you've got the letter *A*. These two clubs—you've got the letter *E*. And these two clubs—you have the letter *O*. See if those letters are like *I* and *U*."

Once clubs had collected half a dozen Post-its, I gave each club a piece of chart paper with three prelabeled columns (for example: short *E*, long *E*, other sounds of *E*) and channeled them to sort their words—and their Post-its—into those columns.

It might feel overwhelming at first to have each club on a different vowel. Don't worry. Try it out. You can always scale back to one if you need to. This will give your students a more complex task that asks them to transfer what they are learning. It is a more interesting task as well. Your students will feel stimulated and more excited to share.

SHARE • Leading A Shared Reading of Clubs' Charts CLUBS

Channel clubs to lead the class in a shared reading of their charts. Lead a final discussion about how the letter *I* project can help them learn to read and write more words.

"Let's share the results of your findings. Let's start with the letter *E*." I posted the chart made by the letter *E* club and handed a pointer to a member of that club. "Will you lead us in a shared reading of your chart?" To the class, I said, "And as we all read through each column of words, let's check whether we all agree that the words in that column all contain a long *E*, or a short *E*, or some other sound of *E*."

We read through the words in each column, pausing occasionally to discuss whether the word in question had been sorted correctly. We did the same for the chart for the letter *A* and the chart for the letter *O*.

"Now you've had a chance to see lots of different words with vowels in them. So, what do you think about the way vowels sound? Turn and talk." Soon the class had agreed that all the vowels, like the letter *I*, made different sounds.

Nodding, I confirmed, "So you are all in agreement that vowels all act in similar ways. Our letter *I* project is going to help us read and write so many words!"

EXTENSION 1 • Collecting More Words with Different Vowel Sounds

Set up kids to collect more words as they are on the way back from an activity out of the classroom.

"Friends, on the way back from art, let's collect more words and then add them to our charts to see if they are long vowels, short vowels, or other. I'll give each of you a Post-it. You can look at the bulletin boards, the writing in the hallway, or signs or anything, and when you find a word you like, try to read it, then jot it down and we'll sort it when we get back!"

EXTENSION 2 • Adding to the ABC Chart

Challenge students to study their ABC charts and to add pictures to it, so that every vowel on the chart has pictures of objects with a short-vowel sound and a long-vowel sound.

"Kindergartners, the information we learned about letters today just about knocked my socks off! All vowels make at least two sounds." I pointed toward a copy of the ABC chart that I attached to the easel.

POSSIBLE COACHING MOVES

▶ "Slow down. Read that page again. Is there a word with your vowel?"

▶ "Don't forget to write it down on your Post-it."

▶ "To sort, I'd say each word slowly. Think whether the vowel says its own name, or is it short? Or other?"

"I was looking across the ABC chart, and I realized that our ABC chart only has *short*-vowel sound words on it. The *I* only has a picture of an igloo on it. We need to revise it! Maybe the *I* needs a picture of an igloo *and* ice cream or an ice cube or an icicle. Any of those would work."

I distributed some small Post-its to the class. "Look across your ABC chart and think about how you can revise the vowels so that there is a picture of something with the short-vowel sound *and* the long-vowel sound. That will help make this tool even more useful when we are reading and writing."

EXTENSION 3 • Snap Up Some Vowels

Encourage partners to review their snap words together and talk about which sounds the vowels in their snap words make—long, short, or something in between.

"Kindergartners, I got an idea just now. I'm wondering if you and your partner could read through the words in your snap word pouch and think and talk together about the vowels. Some of those words will be long vowels, some will be short vowels, and some will be in between. Right now, will you get your snap word pouch out? This time, as you read through each word, talk together about the sound the vowel makes. Try to think of two other words that have similar vowels, used in similar ways."

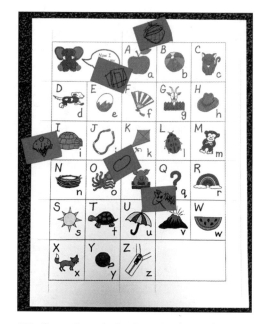

FIG. 18–2 One student's revised ABC chart to reflect long and short vowel sounds.

Sharing All We've Learned about Vowels

Student-Led Shared Reading

IN THIS SESSION

TODAY YOU'LL teach students that when readers and writers know letters and sounds very well, they have the power to teach what they know to others.

TODAY YOUR STUDENTS will work in clubs to plan a short lecture and a shared reading to teach Mabel about the different sounds a vowel makes. Clubs will celebrate all they have learned by teaching the class about their vowel while you make short videos to share this celebration with families.

MINILESSON

CONNECTION

Reinforce to students that what they have learned through doing their project has made them braver readers.

"Readers, you are becoming more flexible in how you solve words. You know that vowels make *different* sounds. When you say a word and it sounds odd to you, you know that you need to try a new sound! And that means that you are no longer the kind of readers who let a lot of letters in a word slow you down or who stop you when you read. You are becoming braver readers! Awesome work, my friends. There is nothing more important."

Tell students that Mabel wants to learn all about what the class learned and that you told her that they could teach her and others.

"Mabel told me that she was watching you collect, read, and sort all these collections of words and said, 'I want to know about that! I want to be able to read all those words too!' I looked at Mabel and said to her, 'But you can! *These* students can teach you. They know how to be teachers. They pretend to be teachers, all the time in reading workshop, on their playdates.' Isn't that right? Don't you?"

PHONICS INSTRUCTION

Word Knowledge/Solving

• Use a predictable process of teaching what you have learned to solidify all learning about letters and sounds (short/long vowel sounds).

• Use knowledge of short and long vowel sounds to plan for teaching.

♣ **Name the teaching point.**

"Today, I want to teach you that when you want to teach others about letters and sounds you are learning, you can say a little bit about what you've learned and then read or write together to show what you've learned."

TEACHING

Explain to students how to teach someone else what they have learned about letters and sounds. Channel students to include both a short lecture and shared reading in their plan.

"I was imagining how you all could teach Mabel what you've learned about letters and sounds. I could imagine if you were teaching someone all you know about a collection of cars and trucks, you might first tell them a bit about what you've learned. You might start by giving a little lecture about it.

"If I were going to teach what I know about the toy front-end loader, I might say, 'This toy front-end loader has a job! It works on construction sites to move things like dirt and cement. It has these *big* wheels to drive right over piles of materials.' Then, I might want to invite the person I was teaching to do some of the work of learning about the front-end loader and other trucks with me. We could play together or study together.

"You could do this to teach Mabel, your little siblings, your friends and family, right? You could come up with a little lecture about what you've learned with your rug club. Then, you could play shared reading, just like you do in reading workshop. This time, your shared reading could be all about the new letters and sounds you've learned about.

"Here's the thing: your friends and family aren't in the classroom with us, so I was thinking we could make some little videos. That way your friends and family can learn from wherever they are and read along with your club to learn more about letters and sounds.

Show students how to make a little lecture and prepare a short text for shared reading by marking words that have the vowel you wish to teach.

"If I were going to teach Mabel about the letter *I*, I'd probably need to start with a little lecture about *I*—just like the little lecture about my bulldozer. I'd want to teach why *I* is special, and maybe give some examples. Maybe I could say, 'The letter *I* is special because it makes lots of sounds. Sometimes it sounds like /ĭ/ as in *igloo*, but sometimes it sounds like /ī/ as in *ice cream*. Sometimes it makes totally different sounds! Like in the word *neigh*, there is an *I*, but you can't even hear it!' What do you think, Mabel? Would that be a good way to start?"

Mabel and the class agreed, so I continued. "Now we need to get our poem ready for shared reading so that our friends and family can do some of the *I* work with us. Could you help Mabel and me get this short text ready for shared reading? Mabel wants to teach people about the letter *I*." I displayed a copy of the poem

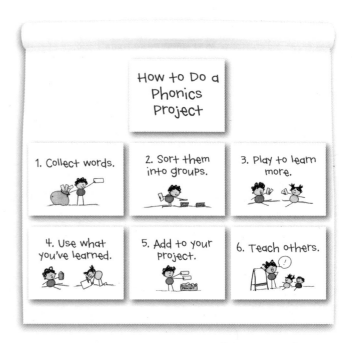

How to Do a Phonics Project

1. Collect words.

2. Sort them into groups.

3. Play to learn more.

4. Use what you've learned.

5. Add to your project.

6. Teach others.

"Apple" by Nan Fry. "I'm going to start reading 'Apple.' You can read along with me. Be thinking which words with *I* should I pop out! I have some Wikki Stix, and I'll put one under the word."

I paused after the word *white*. "Hmm, . . . I am noticing the word *white* has an *I*." I placed one of my Wikki Stix underneath. "When I lead shared reading and we reach the word *white*, I'll want to teach them about this *I*. Hmm, . . . what will I say? Maybe I could say, '*White* has a long *I* as in *rice* or *triangle*.'"

We continued reading, and I repeated the process for the word *bite*. I paused again at *listen* and underlined it with another one of my Wikki Stix. "*Listen* is different than *white* and *bite*."

"It has a short *I*!" a few kids called from the rug.

I nodded and continued. "Yes! So, when I'm teaching here, I might want to tell the people I'm teaching that the *i* in *listen* is a short *I*, as in *igloo* or *pig*." I quickly finished reading the poem as the class signaled me to underline words that have an *I*.

ACTIVE ENGAGEMENT/LINK

Challenge rug clubs to make a plan for their lecture about the letter that they studied in Session 18. Coach students to make sure they cover all the sounds their letter can make.

"Before you begin to plan your shared reading, see if you can work together to decide how your little lecture will go. You'll probably want to teach about the letter you began to study yesterday. You might start by saying, 'We learned about the letter . . .' Then you'll want to think of a few sentences to teach what you've learned and maybe give some examples. Ready, go!"

I quickly circulated the rug to make sure that each club remembered which vowel they were studying and then I coached students to say more about what they had learned by asking questions like, "What examples could you give of short *U* and long *U*? Why is it important to know that vowels make different sounds?"

Encourage rug clubs to plan their shared reading by choosing a poem or song, reading it through, and highlighting the words containing the vowel sounds they want to teach.

After just a minute I called the class back together. "All right, clubs, you are ready to start planning your shared reading." I pointed to some poems in the front of the rug. "Here are some poems and songs you've learned this year. Pick one with your club that has the vowel you are teaching. Before you plan your shared reading, make sure you read it all the way through. Then, start to highlight the words that you'll want to teach Mabel and your family and friends at home about."

Clubs picked poems as I passed out five or six Wikki Stix to each club. Then I began coaching clubs as they planned for shared reading.

Teachers, keep this part brief! There isn't much for students to say in their lecture and we want rug clubs to have time to plan for their shared reading.

POSSIBLE COACHING MOVES

▶ "You found a word with the letter *A*. When you read that word, what will you teach Mabel about it?"

▶ "Does that word have a short or a long vowel? How do you know?"

▶ "Read that line again. Are there any words you should highlight and teach others about?"

▶ "What will you teach when you reach this word, since it's not short or long? That will be important!"

After a few minutes I said, "If you finish highlighting words, start to practice! You'll all want to read the poem or song together. When you get to a highlighted word, pause there and teach what you've learned. You can teach Mabel to listen to the vowel and hear if it's short or long."

RUG TIME CLUBS

Direct rug clubs to teach Mabel what they've learned about their letter by giving a little lecture and leading the shared reading of a short text. Make videos to share with families.

"The moment has come. It's time to teach!" I propped Mabel up on a chair. "Mabel is eager to learn all you've learned during our phonics projects. Your club will want to give your little lecture and then you'll lead us all in shared reading, pausing to teach us about the words you highlighted. I'll make some little videos to share with your family and friends at home." I pointed to one club. "Why don't you come up and teach us first?"

As each club taught about their vowel, I coached their teaching as I made some little videos on my phone to share with families.

SHARE • Encouraging Students to Become Teachers of Phonics CLUBS

Inform students that whenever they have studied something, they can teach it to others. Then, invite toy friends that visited during Unit 2, *Word Scientists*, back to visit.

"Whoa. All of this playing with phonics hasn't just been fun—you've become little phonics teachers! I bet you could do this same teaching with blends and with snap words. I bet you could even teach how to use word parts to write really long words! From now until forever, you'll know that when you've learned a lot about something, you have the power to teach it, just like you did for Mabel today." The class sat up a little straighter.

"As you were teaching, Mabel whispered to me. She thinks it's time for Blue Bear to come back and learn from you. Your toy friends should come back, too! What do you think? Are you game to bring your friends back for one more day of phonics play?" As the class nodded we let Mabel know her idea was a great one. "Make sure to put your friends in your backpack to bring to school tomorrow morning!"

FIG. 19–1   One rug club makes plans for shared reading to teach about their assigned vowel.

POSSIBLE COACHING MOVES

▸ "What is important to know about the letter ____?"

▸ "Give us some examples. You can use the charts in the room to help."

▸ "You highlighted the word _____. Make sure to tell us why!"

▸ "Hold up your poem so we can all read together."

Celebrating Our Learning from Kindergarten

IN THIS SESSION

TODAY YOU'LL teach students that when readers want to teach well, they plan what they will teach and how they will teach it.

TODAY YOUR STUDENTS will work in rug clubs to choose a phonics topic from earlier in the year and plan what about that topic they will teach and what method they will use to teach it. Clubs will hold ABC School and teach their toy friends about their topic.

MINILESSON

CONNECTION

Let students know that today they'll be the teachers again, but this time for their toy friends that they brought to school.

"Friends, will you leave your stuffed animals in your knapsacks, and come over here super-quickly so we can plan ABC School for those friends of yours? Come quickly so we have time to plan!"

As soon as children were in their rug spots, I said, "I want to talk to you about being teachers, because today you are going to be the teachers at ABC School. Yesterday you taught each other. Today, your students will not be kids—they'll be tigers and elephants and bears, and I think I even saw a turtle! But still, I want to give you a few tips about teaching, so you'll be ready to teach them super-well. Here is my tip."

❖ **Name the teaching point.**

"Today I want to teach you that when you are going to teach others about what you know, you need to plan *what* you will teach and *how* you will teach. To plan what you'll teach, you take a topic—say,

---

GETTING READY

✔ Display a list on chart paper of phonics topics students have learned across the year.

✔ Gather phonics tools you've used throughout the school year, such as ABC charts, vowel shields, word-part charts, poems, the "Blends and Digraphs" chart, and so on for students to use.

✔ Provide rug clubs with access to blank paper, whiteboards, Post-its, and markers to use as teaching tools.

✔ Display a copy of Mabel's "Letters and Sounds" song.

PHONICS INSTRUCTION

Word Knowledge/Solving
• Remembering and teaching every phonics principle from kindergarten (letter names/sounds, letter formation, word-part power, short-vowel power, blends, digraphs, snap words, and making poems).

---

blends—and you remember everything you know that your students will want to know. To plan how you'll teach, you think about something fun the students can do that will help them learn."

TEACHING AND ACTIVE ENGAGEMENT (CLUBS)

List the phonics topics you've taught all year. Coach each club to choose one and then plan what they will teach about that topic.

"Friends, I made a list of things you have learned about in our phonics workshop this year, and I'm wondering if each club can choose one of these topics that you can teach. After you choose your topic, you need to think about everything you know related to that topic that you could teach to your stuffed animals. You can just list everything you know across your fingers, or if you want, one person in your club can take notes on what you know, writing down just a teeny tiny note on each thing to remind you when you go to teach.

"Are you ready to look over this list, to choose one topic, and to start remembering everything you know?" I revealed the list of subtopics.

- The names and sounds of letters
- How to write words
- Snap words
- Word power: Making words from *at, it, op* . . .
- Vowel power
- Digraphs
- Blends
- Making poems

"Will you come up and make a check beside a topic after you choose it, so that you don't all plan the same topic? We will want the animals to learn lots of different things! As soon as you have chosen a topic, remind yourselves of what you could teach about your topic. Get started!"

Rug clubs picked topics, and I began to circulate around the rug, coaching students as needed. Many groups decided that to teach well, they needed a tool, such as their vowel shields, some poems we've learned, or the word-part chart. Once they had the tools they needed, students began to rehearse what they might say to their friends in ABC School.

Ask rug clubs to plan how they will teach about their topic and support them by listing some options and then circulating to each club as they make decisions.

After a few minutes I regained the students' attention. "Teachers, now that you know what you will teach, you have to decide *how* you will teach. You'll want it to be fun! You could make some quick

118

picture cards on Post-its and make up a game. You could sing a song to teach or lead your friends in some 'Guess the Covered Word' shared reading. You might want to do some writing or maybe something totally different that you create! You'll only have about five minutes to make your plan and gather your materials, though. Feel free to get anything you think you need from around the room.

"Remember, as you are planning, keep *what* you are teaching—your topic—in mind. Don't let the fun carry you away!"

I coached the rug club who chose vowel power as they made decisions about how to teach. They decided to use a pocket chart for vowel sorting with their animals. Meanwhile, the rug club teaching about blends started making a game board for "Where Is a Blend?" while the rug club teaching word-part power was making picture cards on Post-its to play a game of "Word-Part Match." I quickly continued to circulate, asking clubs how they planned to teach their topic so that their friends would learn a lot.

These are just examples from one classroom, of course. You'll want your students to choose to teach in any way that sounds fun for them and that makes sense! Of course, rug clubs could continue on planning for days. That is not the point here. We simply want kids to draw on not just the content they've learned, but the methods they've learned through, and plan quickly with approximation.

RUG TIME CLUBS

Channel rug clubs to set up their toy friends. Welcome their toy friends to ABC School and then direct rug clubs to begin their lesson plans.

"Teachers, once your materials are prepared and organized, go get your friends! Set them up in a group, so they are ready to learn." Students retrieved their toy friends and propped them up in groups around the rug. I brought out Mabel, so that students could see that she was joining the learning, too.

I began by talking to the students' toy friends and said, "Welcome back to ABC School, students. It's been a long time! Your teachers have learned *a lot* since you've been gone and have worked hard to plan for you."

I then directed my attention back to the class. "Teachers, it's your turn to teach! Remember to talk about your topic and use your tools. You'll then do your lesson plan with your friends. If you finish, switch groups! You can teach another rug club's friends. ABC School has officially begun!"

I crouched down near each club, as if to become a student in their teaching. When needed, I helped by reminding the class to hold up their materials so their "students" could see, to say *what* they were teaching before saying *how* they'll teach, and by helping every student in the rug club have a voice in teaching.

FIG. 20-1 One rug club teaches friends about blends by introducing the blends chart and leading them in a shared reading of a familiar poem.

Inform students that all they've learned about phonics must have made their reading and writing stronger. Teach the class a song about reading and writing well.

"Teachers, scoop up your toy friends and come join me back on the rug." Once the students were settled with toy friends perched on their laps, I said, "That sure was a busy day of teaching and learning! I was thinking as you were teaching that your reading and writing must be so strong! After all, the more you know about letters and sounds, the stronger your reading and writing become."

I pointed toward Mabel who had one more piece of paper rolled up in her trunk. "Look! Mabel has something for us once again. She always knows the perfect time to give us a gift."

I unrolled the piece of paper and displayed the "Letters and Sounds" song under the document camera, so everyone could see. "It's a song! Mabel wrote a song for us as an ending to ABC School. And it's to one of our favorite spell songs, 'Bibbidi bobbidi boo.' Let's sing it together, with our friends."

We sang the song a few times through and gave our furry friends a big hug before dismissing ABC School.

Teachers, this is the end of Unit 5, but it is not the end of your school year. We have left time because we know you need choice about what to teach in the time that remains. It's likely there are additional phonics concepts you'd like to teach, either because your students are ready for new work or because there is work they need to revisit. Or, there might be topics in your school's curriculum you have yet to cover. We suggest engaging students in another round of phonics projects, and perhaps another round after that, if you have time, using the same steps as in Bend IV. We recommend continuing to draw on the "How Do a Phonics Project" chart as students move through this work. We have suggestions for this kind of If … Then … teaching in the online resources.

Word-Part Power

Lucy Calkins, Series Editor

Natalie Louis and Rachel Rothman-Perkins

Photography by Peter Cunningham

Illustrations by Marjorie Martinelli

HEINEMANN ◆ PORTSMOUTH, NH

To my husband, Donald Perkins, for being my superhero on this writing journey and always reminding me that every hour dedicated to creating this phonics curriculum will enrich the lives of so many children.
—Rachel

To Dylan and Luke Nolan, for being the source and the inspiration of my heart power. At home and at work, my greatest hope is that this teaching love is making the world just a little bit warmer and kinder and smarter.
—Natalie

Heinemann
361 Hanover Street
Portsmouth, NH 03801–3912
www.heinemann.com

Offices and agents throughout the world

The authors and publisher wish to thank those who have generously given permission to reprint borrowed materials:

"S and H Put Together Say /Sh/" copyright © 2018 by Joni Boggs. Reprinted by permission of Joni Boggs.

Cataloging-in-Publication data is on file with the Library of Congress.

ISBN-13: 978-0-325-10519-2

Editors: Tracy Wells and Anna Gratz Cockerille
Production: Elizabeth Valway
Cover and interior designs: Jenny Jensen Greenleaf
Photography: Peter Cunningham
Illustrations: Marjorie Martinelli and Kimberly Fox
Composition: Publishers' Design and Production Services, Inc.
Manufacturing: Steve Bernier

Printed in the United States of America on acid-free paper
22 21 20 19 18   VP   1 2 3 4 5

Acknowledgments

AFTER YEARS OF HEARING FROM SCHOOLS that teachers would like the Teachers College Reading and Writing Project to create a phonics curriculum, we finally decided to embark on the journey and we could not be prouder of the result. It is because of our leader, Lucy Calkins, that we felt courageous enough to jump into this project and we believe we have developed instruction that is unlike anything that currently exists in early literacy curriculum. Lucy helped us reimagine phonics instruction, wrote parts of the unit, and guided us through the creation of lessons that are playful, engaging, and have strong and meaningful connections to reading and writing for young children.

This project stands on the shoulders of years of collaboration and learning alongside the entire TCRWP team including our leaders Amanda Hartman, Laurie Pessah, and Mary Ehrenworth; and our writers-in-residence, Kelly Boland Hohne, Katie Clements, and Liz Franco, who together helped us to write many sessions. We are grateful for the support from all of you as we wrote version after version of this unit, making it better with each revision.

We also want to give extra special acknowledgement to former staff developers and mentors to both of us, Enid Martinez and Mary Ann Colbert. Both Enid and Mary Ann have the kind of deep knowledge and teaching skill that we strive to live up to everyday. We are both better for having had the chance to learn from and with them.

Alicia Luick, Lisa Hourigan, and Nancy Brennan were especially willing to pilot these sessions, and their input informed important decisions. Kate Montgomery, Samantha Barrett, and Katie Lindner provided final feedback in the days leading up to publication, helping us to write and teach with greater clarity.

This unit comes to life with illustrated books and songs, picture cards and charts, and other visuals that allow kids to explore, compare, connect to, and remember key phonics concepts in extremely engaging and kid-friendly ways.

Most of this art was created by Marjorie Martinelli who invested talent and care into each drawing. Marjorie also helped us organize the materials for every session. We also appreciate Lisa Corcoran and Suzanne Korn's contributions that brought the little books to life. We smile to know that your children will have chances to read those books during the days and weeks of the unit.

This book could not have happened without all of the literacy experts who have mentored our teaching as well as our work in developing this curriculum. They have been part of our educational journey. First, we are so thankful for the work of Pat and Jim Cunningham, Donald Bear, Tim Rasinski, Isabel Beck, Irene C. Fountas, Gay Su Pinnell, Wiley Blevins, Nell Duke, and Elfrieda Hiebert. We read and reread their writing about phonics to make our own teaching stronger. We are smarter for having learned from such marvelous teachers of teachers.

Joe Yukish read every word of this book and then reread as we responded to his insights. Because of his care and profound kindness, we are sure that our teaching of phonics is more precise and more effective. Joanna Uhry from Fordham University played a crucial role in helping to develop the phonics knowledge that informs the teaching we include in this book. When I (Natalie) studied phonics and the teaching of reading with her, Joanna would come to my classroom and coach into my work with children. This book (and this series) carries her deep knowledge and generous spirit.

How lucky we were that teachers welcomed opportunities to pilot this instruction. We especially want to thank the educators and leaders of PS 39, PS 158, and New Bridges Elementary in New York City for opening up their doors to observe, teach, and reflect with us. Natalie's kindergarten specialty group played a key role as well in the development of the unit. A giant thank you to Lori Barrett, Janis Bui, Melissa Dunne, Peter Falciglia, June Golonka, Bethany Haskins, Grace Marotta, Nicole Mell, Jisun Oh, Liliana

Scamardella, and Alexandra Simmonds. Your willingness to experiment powered this project.

Thank you also to the dedicated team at Heinemann including Abby Heim, Elizabeth Valway, Tracy Wells, Anna Gratz Cockerille, Shannon Thorner, and Lisa Bingen. Your support, organization, care, and the attention to detail you put into the editing and production of these units of study will make them so supportive for teachers. You are the bridge to the classrooms, the reason our words are able to make such an impact on so many children's literacy experiences and your dedication to this process is truly inspirational to us. We hope you know that. Thank you! Thank you! Thank you!

To our families and friends, we say, "You rock!" You were by our sides through the long days and late nights of writing and discussing, making and remaking until we had it just right. Please know that your support gave us the encouragement we needed to keep working. A special thanks to Rachel's dad, Barry Rothman, who illustrated two of the texts in the unit.

Finally, we would like to thank each other. This collaboration was a very special one, and we are grateful for the opportunity to share in the creation of this unit. For a decade we have worked alongside each other at the Project, and even before that we were thought partners. Our own writing and teaching powers have been strengthened by writing this book together, and we are grateful for the chance to brainstorm, teach, and write in each other's company. We hope this book brings you and your colleagues into equally beautiful partnerships.

—Natalie and Rachel

Contents

Registration instructions to access the digital resources that accompany this book may be found on p. ix.

An Orientation to the Unit

THIS UNIT FITS TONGUE-AND-GROOVE with the beloved *Super Powers: Reading with Print Strategies and Sight Word Power*, which is Unit 2 from the kindergarten Units of Study for Teaching Reading. Although you certainly can adapt this unit to teach without its reading counterpart, know it was designed to be taught in conjunction with *Super Powers*. The first session in this phonics unit is designed to follow the first session in the reading unit—it assumes students have been exposed to their first super power: pointer power. We recommend you schedule your reading workshop so that it comes before your phonics workshop each day, so that students can revisit what they learn during the reading workshop while they work on phonics.

This book is full of scaffolds and supports, nudges and shoves for you to use to help your kids progress along pathways toward being conventional writers and readers. For starters, you will want them to use their knowledge of letters and sounds to represent all the salient sounds in words. Don't worry if their knowledge of spelling patterns isn't perfect. What matters most is that they are attempting to use all of their new phonics knowledge in their writing, and that you see evidence that their understanding of phonics features, such as letters, sounds, word parts, and phonograms, is growing.

The unit, then, will align to both your teaching or reading and your teaching of writing, and the work across reading, writing and phonics will combine to push your kids towards the threshold and into the world of conventional reading and writing.

OVERVIEW OF THE UNIT

This unit is composed of three bends, or parts.

Bend I: Writing Power

Bend II: Word-Part Power

Bend III: Word Parts, Snap Words, and Digraphs—Yee-haw!

In the first bend, "Writing Power," your phonics instruction will be in service of moving your class from writing labels to writing sentences during writing time. It's likely that many of your children will already be doing this, especially if you have gotten hold of the individual kindergarten writing unit of study, *Show and Tell: From Labels to Pattern Books* and taught that unit as your second writing unit. By the start of this unit, we hope that most of your children will have graduated from writing one word labels on their drawings and will be writing sentences that are somewhat readable. This bend will be especially helpful for students who still need support to make that leap.

It may seem like a very tall order to expect kindergarteners to write readable sentences at this point in the school year. However, after years—decades, really—of teaching in a huge range of schools, including the most high-need schools imaginable, we are convinced that if you and your children believe they can do this, and if you provide scaffold instruction to help them get there, they can do this. We hope you'll trust us enough to try and see if this isn't more possible than you might have otherwise believed.

You'll start the bend by teaching your children that pointer power has a place in writing workshop, too. You'll teach them to tap the page in preparation for writing, and you'll teach them to slide a finger across the place where they'll be writing a word, stretching the sounds as they do. All of this paves the way for the word-by-word writing they'll be attempting in this bend.

Across the bend, you'll see lots of detailed instruction to help kids to write all of the sounds they hear in a word. You'll teach them to say words slowly, segmenting the words into phonemes. You'll support the process of alternating between hearing an isolated sound and recording that sound on the page. You'll end the bend with an emphasis on rereading in a way that supports cumulative blending and reminds children of the all-important step of checking their work.

The first bend gives way to the second bend, "Word-Part Power," which is, in some way, the true rallying cry of this unit. It is here that kids learn that the phonics workshop will provide them with yet another super power—specifically, word-part power. This is an exciting bend for both teachers and learners, because when kids grasp the power of phonograms, it is as if the whole world of written language opens to them. When they approach a word, even a very long word, they will no longer be without tools to solve it.

At the start of Bend II, you'll teach kids that the little words they know—such as snap words they learned in Unit 2, *Word Scientists*—can give them great power. Although this portion of the unit focuses on phonograms, such as *at* and *it*, a good deal of the payoff for this work will revolve around consonants. That is, any work with onsets (the initial consonant) and rimes (the string of letters that follow the consonant, in this unit, consisting of a vowel and another consonant, such as *at*, *in*, *it*, and *an*) involves a lot of work with the onsets. When your students learn that the words *at*, *in*, *it*, and *an* can be made into lots of other words, and they begin to change *rat* to *mat*, and *mat* to *sat*, they'll build new words with ease as they write. Furthermore, manipulating onsets and rimes in their writing will provide children with added practice in paying attention to initial consonants as they read. This work attending to initial consonants builds on and extends the work of Unit 2, where the focus was more on listening and recording initial sounds during writing. This exposure to onsets and rimes might feel early, but we think it's essential to equipping kids with the tools they need as writers.

You'll rely on a few go-to teaching methods in Bend II. After you introduce students to several snap words that can increase their word-part power, you'll use the activities of making words and sorting words to help students understand how they can combine different onsets and rimes to help them write. As you coach, you'll make sure that you emphasize both the onset and the rime. Chances are that while many of your students are focusing their attention on rimes, the extra practice in onset isolation will benefit your students who are still mastering letter-sound correspondence.

Of course, this work with CVC words and with word parts also helps students become more ready to word solve CVC words, drawing on their knowledge of phonograms. Although for now, many of your kids will only tend to read CVC words when they are reading fairly controlled texts (because those words will be less accessible and predominant in predictable patterned texts), it is a good thing when your instruction marches a bit ahead of students' reading development as your teaching will then enable that development.

That is, this work will help develop the muscles your students will need once they begin actually reading conventionally—which is hopefully just around the corner of this unit.

Expect your students' writing to be filled with words such as *can* and *ran*, *sit* and *run*, *mug* and *man*. Your students may also attempt even longer, more challenging words that contain CVC or closed syllables.

Also in the second bend, the word wall is introduced, and all the words from your snap word collection will be moved to the word wall. This way students will have a tool that organizes the high-frequency words that they are learning to make it more likely they will learn and use those words. You'll continue adding words to the word wall to support children's growing banks of high-frequency words.

In the final bend of the unit, "Word Parts, Snap Words, and Digraphs—Yee-haw!," you'll help kids further expand their word-part power by adding in a few more of the most common VC phonograms. By the end of this unit, children will have been exposed to 10 of the most generative vowel-consonant rimes. This bend is especially powerful, because it teaches children all three ways to read words—by sight, by decoding, and by analogy.

This bend also continues the work of growing the kindergarten bank of high-frequency words. *She* is a perfect word to teach at this time of year, because your children are writing personal narratives in writing workshop—not to mention the fact that Mabel is a she.

You'll introduce digraphs (*sh*, *th*, *wh*, *ch*), pointing out that the snap word *she* begins not just with one consonant but with two consonants. You'll show students how they can combine digraphs with word parts to make even more words. The units ends with a Rime Rodeo! Children get the chance to round up rimes and combine them with onsets—both initial consonant and digraph—to fill the room with newly made words. Yee-haw! Round 'em up!

GETTING READY

Mabel the elephant, the class mascot, continues to play an important role in this unit. Whereas in Unit 2 she was a word scientist, studying the alphabet chart closely, in this unit she joins the class as yet another Super Reader. Because she, like the children, gain a new phonics super power—word-part power, Mabel becomes a braver, more daring speller.

We have tried our hardest to keep the phonics materials you will need to a minimum. We have much respect for the amount of preparation you do each day, and do not want phonics workshop to make your day harder. As in most units, a class set of whiteboards with markers and erasers are primary tools in most of the sessions. We expect you will already have a system in place to distribute the whiteboard materials easily, but if you do not, we recommend you put one into place right away. Many sessions also rely on word cards, available either in the Resource Pack (denoted with 📦) or the online resources (denoted with ✴). You'll notice we do not overly emphasize magnetic letters, despite the fact that we love them. Magnetic letters are a powerful learning tool but they are probably less than ideal for use when kids are working in the meeting area. We suspect you'll use them in your small-group instruction and when you work with individuals as needed.

Earlier we mentioned that in this unit, you will put the many high-frequency words that students are learning onto a word wall. We suggest you disassemble the name wall and remake it into a word wall. Because your students will use snap words more and more throughout this unit, you will want to make sure your word wall is located in a space that you and your students can see easily as they read and write. As you place snap words on the word wall, you will need to decide whether or not to keep your students' names there too. As long as your students are still relying on each others' names as they read and write, you might want to keep their names on your word wall, and then remove them when your students no longer need them as scaffold.

You'll continue to need ways to display your teaching. As in previous units, we recommend a pocket chart that you keep near your teaching area; a way to display work for your demonstrations, such a document camera; an easel to write on, perhaps one that is dry-erase, and blank chart paper. Since you are retiring your snap word pocket chart in favor of placing snap words on the word wall, you can use this pocket chart in other ways to display your teaching.

ONLINE DIGITAL RESOURCES

Resources that accompany this unit of study are available in the online resources, including charts, word cards, songs, and poems shown throughout *Word-Part Power*.

To access and download the digital resources for *Word-Part Power*:

1. Go to www.heinemann.com and click the link in the upper right to log in. (If you do not have an account yet, you will need to create one.)

2. Enter the following registration code in the box to register your product: UOSPH_HYSC7

3. Enter the security information requested.

4. Once you have registered your product it will appear in the list of My Online Resources.

(You may keep copies of these resources on up to six of your own computers or devices. By downloading the file, you acknowledge that they are for your individual or classroom use and that neither the resources nor the product code will be distributed or shared.)

Using Pointer Power in Writing Workshop, Too

GETTING READY

✔ Write "I can write sentences" on chart paper.

✔ Provide each student with a whiteboard and marker.

✔ Make a version of Mabel's "You can do it" sign.

PHONICS INSTRUCTION

Concepts About Print
- Understand that words are written left to right across the page (directionality).
- Understand that words are separated by spaces in print, concept of word.
- Match spoken word to print.

Phonological Awareness
- Say words slowly to hear sounds in words.

High-Frequency Words
- Recognize and use high-frequency words with automaticity.
- Write high-frequency words in continuous text.
- Learn a new word (*can*).

IN THIS SESSION

TODAY YOU'LL teach students that they can use their pointer power to help them write sentences.

TODAY YOUR STUDENTS will work in partnerships to write sentences on whiteboards and read them together.

MINILESSON

CONNECTION

Cement students' identities as Super Readers by suggesting that they are Super Readers across the entire day, in every subject. Rally them to be ready to use their pointer power in a new way.

I stared at the class with furrowed brow. I backed up, sizing the kids up. "Hmm,. . .you know, you all look kind of different." I scratched my head, as if perplexed. "You seem a little taller than you were in our last session, and a little stronger, and a little. . .more super! Wait, now I remember! Today, you transformed from readers into. . . " I left a space, inviting kids to chime in.

"Super Readers!" the class shouted with pride.

"Yes! You're Super Readers now! That must be it! I knew something was different about you.

"You know that the job of a Super *Reader*, like the job of any superhero, never ends, right? Your power sticks with you all day long. I know it isn't reading time, but can you pretend that there were some words written on the rug in front of you, and can you show me how you'd use *pointer power* to read those words?"

The kids stuck out a finger and read the imaginary words, pointing under them. I nodded. "I love it. This isn't even reading workshop, and you are still using your pointer power to read words, one by one. And that is the super-cool thing I want to teach you."

❖ **Name the teaching point.**

"Today I want to teach you that you don't just use pointer power to read. You also use pointer power to write—and to write in ways that help people read your writing."

TEACHING

Recruit students to help you teach Mabel how to use pointer power to write sentences. Explain that Mabel is worried about writing sentences, and rally students to give Mabel a pep talk.

"I know Mabel has been feeling left out. Look, she wants to high-five us for using our super powers. Let's give her a high-five." We high-fived in the air. Then Mabel whispered something to me. "She wants to use pointer power too, and she's thinking that her trunk could really help her point. So, what if you and I showed Mabel how to use pointer power to write, would that be a good idea? Then *all* of us can be using our super powers all day long.

"So, Mabel, come on up here. I'm going to teach you how to use pointer power to write. The first thing you need to do is to write a sentence, all by yourself. You ready for that?"

Mabel shook her head no. She hid her face.

"What do you think she is feeling, kindergartners? Does she think she can only label? That she can only write one word here, or one word there? Do you think she is afraid?"

Mabel nodded. "I think we need to get ready to give Mabel a pep talk, don't you? And we could give that same pep talk to any kindergartner who feels a little worried about writing sentences. What could we say to rally her, to let her know *she can do it*?

"Will the partner sitting near the window pretend to be Mabel? Get yourself looking all scared. Pretend that you think, 'I can only label.' Pretend you are worried that you might mess up, like Mabel is worried.

"And the partner sitting on this other side, think about what you can say to Mabel to cheer her on, to get her to stop being afraid. Remember that when someone is trying to do something new, it can help if they get lots of encouragement. What can you say and do to cheer Mabel along?"

Kids called out ideas. I listened, repeating them and adding to them. "You might say, 'Mabel, you can do it! Just *try*.'" I also said, "You might say, 'Don't be afraid. It doesn't have to be perfect. Just write *something*.'

"I think you are ready to do this now. Will the partner who is pretending to be Mabel, say, 'I'm a little nervous to write a whole sentence'? And then the rest of you, convince her!"

The kids had some fun, pretending to be afraid and cheering the scared writer on, while I listened for a few moments. I reconvened the class, and this time, made Mabel look alert and happy. "All your cheers really helped! Now Mabel's ready to write a sentence. Will you watch how I teach her to write with pointer power?"

Share a sentence Mabel could write. Demonstrate how you use pointer power to point to the place where each word could go. Then, write the sentence, stretching out words and using the snap word pocket chart.

"I'm thinking Mabel might write, 'I can write sentences. I can do it. I will use pointer power.'"

I took out a giant chart-sized piece of writing paper and clipped it to the easel. "Mabel, first it helps if you say the sentence you want to write. You say 'I can write sentences' and touch the paper one time for each word. It's like you use your pointer power to point to the place where each word will go, like this." I said the sentence "I can write sentences" aloud, as I carefully hopped my finger across the page, saying one word each time I touched the paper, so that I was implicitly teaching spacing. When I got to the word *sentences*, I pointed out that it is a long word, but it is only one word. "Did you see how I used my pointer power to point one time for each word?

"We want to write four words."

"Now let's write the sentence." I said, "*I*—that's a snap word!" I wrote it. I reread and said "can" and wrote it quickly, rereading each time with pointer power and inviting children to reread with me. When I came to the next two words, I stretched the first out and, inviting children to chime in with me, wrote the salient sounds as they called them out. I reread what I had written, thought about what came next, and then wrote the last word. I finished by adding a period.

I can rit sentensz.

ACTIVE ENGAGEMENT/LINK

Guide students through the process of rehearsing and writing the second sentence in the air: "I can do it."

"Remember, Mabel also wants to write 'I can do it.' Count how many words she'll be writing in this next part." I repeated it while the class counted. "Four! Four words. Will you help Mabel write that sentence, on your whiteboard? Use your pointer power to point to where those words will soon go and say each word as you point. Ready?" I dictated "I can do it," as the kids pointed.

"Okay, do that again. Get ready to use your pointer power! Say the sentence again and this time, point one time for each word going across the page. Leave a space between your words!"

Remember that segmenting sentences into words can be tricky for some children, especially when they are writing words with more than one syllable. Children often count multisyllabic words as separate words because they are hearing the beats within the word.

Whenever you write in front of your kindergartners, you make a decision about whether to write words conventionally or not.

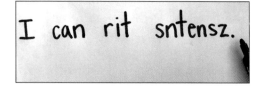

FIG. 1–1 The teacher and students write a sentence to help Mabel feel confident to write. They use their pointer power, the snap word chart, and what they know about sounds to spell words.

"Now start writing the sentence. Point and say and then hear and write the first word. Leave some space. Then point and say, then hear and write the second word."

The kids didn't get too far before I stepped in and said, "Great work," and then I did the same thing they were doing, only I did it on chart paper (quickly). "Remember, anytime you want to write, you can use your pointer power to help you."

RUG TIME

Set up partnerships to write the last line, "I will use pointer power." Coach them as they write the sentence on their whiteboards.

"Okay, everyone, I think you're ready to help Mabel finish her writing. Will you and your partner work together to help her write the last line? You can share a whiteboard and pass it back and forth to write the last sentence for Mabel. Remember, you want to write 'I will use pointer power.' Remember to start by saying the sentence. Then count the words you need to write together. Then point to show where they will go. When you're not writing, cheer your partner on. Tell them, 'You can do it!' and 'Don't be afraid!'

"Get started! I'll come and coach you. If you finish writing that sentence, think of another sentence Mabel could write, and write that one too."

Before I started circulating to coach all the partnerships, I selected one student to do the writing on our chart paper, so that we could read it together as a class during the share. As I circulated I also kept my eye on my special helper and coached her as needed.

POSSIBLE COACHING MOVES

▶ "Reread what you have written so far. What comes next?"

▶ "Say that word slowly. Listen for all the sounds."

▶ "What letter makes that sound? Use the alphabet chart to help you."

▶ "Oh, that's so interesting! Will a /w/ sound come at the start just like /w/ /w/ Wishy Washy? Great thinking to use the name chart to help you!"

▶ "Don't forget to leave spaces!"

After a few minutes, Mabel took a bow. I gathered the students again. "Let's read Mabel's sentences to her!" Together we read the sign we had made to our elephant friend and cheered.

FIG. 1–2   Partners work together to write the next sentence of Mabel's writing.

SHARE

Lead students in a shared reading of Mabel's writing. Restate the teaching point and encourage students to use pointer power to help them whenever they read or write.

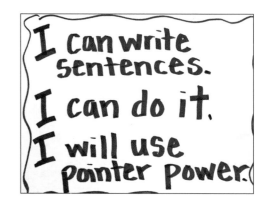

"Impressive. Let's use those powers one more time to read what we've helped Mabel to write." I hung up Mabel's writing, written conventionally now. I used a pointer to point crisply at each word.

"You are Super Readers and Super Writers! Your new super power—pointer power—helped you to write sentences that are easy to read and that include all the words that these sentences need. And, your pointer power helped you to read each word in Mabel's writing. You can use your pointer power whenever you read and write!"

EXTENSION 1 • A Line of Kids Is Like a Sentence with Words

Point out how leaving spaces between words in a sentence is like kids leaving a space between them when standing in line.

"Can you line up for lunch?" I asked the class to line up single file. "Looking at you, it is like you are a sentence. I can use my pointer power to 'read' *you*!" I put out my finger and went down the line, saying each child's name.

"The thing is, it matters when you line up that there is space between you. If you smushed yourself super-close together, I'd have to read you like this," and I tried to smush a few of the kids' names into a garbled smush. "When you write, after one word, you leave a space. Just like in a line." And I again read the names of the kids in the line, with a brief pause between each name.

"Will you try this? Look at the kids in front of you and behind you and use your pointer power to 'read' all your names, leaving spaces in between."

EXTENSION 2 • Brave Writers Include Sentences in Their Writing

GETTING READY

• Students will need a piece of their writing from their writing folders.

Encourage partners to help each other include sentences in their writing.

"You used your pointer power to help Mabel write sentences. She wrote three sentences on her 'you-can-do-it' sign. But your pointer power won't just help Mabel. It will also help you!

"Ready to use your pointer power to add a sentence, or to add even more sentences, to your writing? Partner 1, get out your writing. Read over the page and think, 'What could I add?' Then, use your pointer power to touch where each word will go. Count all the words, and then write them. Partner 2, encourage your partner. Cheer your partner on so they feel as brave writing sentences as Mabel did."

After most students had a sentence written, I channeled Partners 1 and 2 to switch roles.

EXTENSION 3 • Learning a New Snap Word: *Can*

GETTING READY

- Display the "How to Learn a Word" anchor chart.

Introduce a new snap word, and guide students through the familiar process of making a word a snap word.

"Writers, this letter we just helped Mabel write has a word that keeps coming up again in our reading and writing. It's the word *can*. We should turn it into a snap word, so that the next time we want to write it we can all spell it in a snap!

"Let's use the steps we know to help us learn this word." I gestured toward the "How to Learn a Word" chart.

"This word is *can*. I *can* write sentences! First, let's read the word: *can*. Now study it. Tell your partner what you notice. How many letters does it have? What does it start and end with? What sounds do you hear in the word?

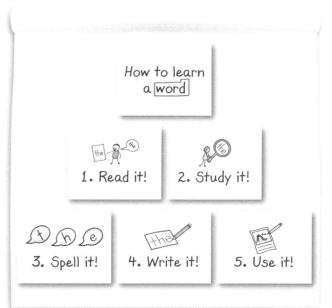

How to learn a [word]

1. Read it!   2. Study it!

3. Spell it!   4. Write it!   5. Use it!

"Ready to spell the word *can*? Get out your imaginary marker and take the cap off. Write *can* on the rug. Spell *can* out loud as you write the letters. Now, write it again. This time, try to write it faster and without looking. Check each letter to make sure it's right.

"Let's use the word *can* in a sentence. Tell your partner as many sentences as you can that use the word *can*. 'I can. . . ' 'Can you. . .?'"

Using Snap Words and Stretch Words to Write

GETTING READY

✔ Display a drawing of a playground that Mabel drew, labeled, and added a sentence to.

✔ Display a drawing that you will add sentences to. An illustrated template for the book about buying apples at the supermarket is available in the online resources. ✱

✔ Have the large alphabet chart in the meeting area. 📦

✔ Distribute a snap word pouch, whiteboard, and marker to each student.

✔ Students will need their writing folders, including a piece of written work that they can add to.

✔ Display the "I can write sentences" chart from Session 1. ✱

PHONICS INSTRUCTION

Phonological Awareness
• Identify and use initial, final, and salient sounds when writing words.
• Say words slowly to identify salient sounds in spoken words.

Letter Knowledge
• Recognize and name all upper- and lowercase letters of the alphabet.
• Demonstrate basic knowledge of letter-sound correspondences by producing the primary or most frequent sound for each consonant.

Word Knowledge/Solving
• Use letter-sound knowledge to spell.

High-Frequency Words
• Locate and read high-frequency words in a text.
• Write high-frequency words in continuous text.
• Learn new words (*to, do*).

IN THIS SESSION

TODAY YOU'LL teach students that when writers want to write a sentence, they use the snap words they know, and they stretch out and write all the sounds of the words they don't know how to spell.

TODAY YOUR STUDENTS will work in partnerships to add sentences to their own written work, using their snap words, saying words slowly to write them, and encouraging each other.

MINILESSON

CONNECTION

Let the class know that Mabel was inspired by their sign and wrote a sentence. Involve the class in reading it.

"Oh my gosh, Mabel loved what you taught her in our last session about writing sentences, and after school she did some more writing." I displayed Mabel's writing. "Look, she's drawn a picture and she has some labels *and* she wrote a sentence! Let's read her writing together. Super Readers, pointer power activate!" All the kids pointed and read:

    I went to the playground.

"Mabel, you wrote a sentence! You can do it! Super Friends, your encouragement really helped!"

"Encouragement helps you write sentences, and pointer power helps, too. Ready to learn another thing that will help you write sentences?"

✤ **Name the teaching point.**

"Today I want to teach you that snap words can help you write sentences. When you want to write a word, you can think, 'Is this a snap word?' If it is, you can get it and write it in your sentence, no stretching needed. If it's not a snap word, you can stretch it out and write all the sounds you hear."

TEACHING

Look at a page of writing and generate a sentence to add. Use pointer power to imagine how the sentence will go. Then, count the words, emphasizing counting multisyllabic words as single words.

"Let me show you what I mean. Last night I went to the supermarket, and there were all these apples. I love apples, so I bought some. I started writing about it." I held up my drawing.

"But now I need help writing sentences on the line. Hmm,. . .what could I write? Oh, maybe I could write *I went to the supermarket*. Let's figure out how many words I need. Count with me. Get your fingers up. *I went to the supermarket.* Oh, I almost counted *supermarket* as four words, but it's only one. That makes five words in total!

"Let me use pointer power to imagine how the sentence will go. Point with me." I hopped my finger across the page, landing on the paper with each word that I said: "I went to the supermarket."

Recruit students to help you write the sentence. For each word, consider whether the word is a snap word or whether it needs to be stretched out.

"It's time to write. For each word, let's think, 'Is this a snap word?' If it is, we can get it from the snap word pocket chart and write it. If it's not, I'll stretch it out and write all the sounds I hear. The first word is *I*. Is *I* a snap word? It is! Marcus, will you grab the word *I* from our pocket chart?

Since supermarket *is four syllables, it would be common this time of year for children to think this is four words or at least to start counting it as more than one word when counting words in sentences. Therefore, we suggest you model counting it as four words and then realize it's one very long word. Then show how you count it only as one.*

"We don't need to stretch this one out because we all know it in a snap. I can just add it to my writing." I attached the card containing *I* to my writing. "Let's reread," I said, knowing that rereading what we already wrote can help children remember what we want to write next.

"'I went.' *Went*. Is *went* a snap word?" Kids called out "No!" "Since it's not a snap word, I need to say it slowly, to stretch it out, and then write all the sounds I hear. Weeennnttt." I recorded *wnt*, using the alphabet chart to help me with writing the *w*.

We continued writing the sentence, each time rereading the sentence after we added a word. "*To*. Is that a snap word?" "Yes," some children called out and spelled it *t-o*. "Guess what, writers, it isn't in our word collection yet, but so many of us have been writing and reading that word that *to* is becoming a snap word! Let's make sure we turn it into a snap word for everyone at the end of phonics workshop, okay?" I knew that *the* was already a snap word in the pocket chart, so I modeled looking to the chart, finding the word, and inserting it into my writing.

When we got to the word *supermarket*, I said, "This is a long one. It's definitely not a snap word. Should I throw my hands up and just give up?"

The kids called out, "No way!"

"Can you give me a little encouragement, so I have the courage to write this word?" Soon the room was filled with a chorus of "You can do it!" and "Try your best to hear all the sounds" and "Say it again and again until you get it."

"Su-per-mar-ket." I clapped out the word. "I hear four syllables. Let me try." I said the first syllable, and recorded the salient sounds using the alphabet chart to help me, then I reread what I'd written and continued in that way through the word. Then I reread the page.

Teachers, you can decide whether to spell went *correctly or with invented spelling. We think that when you are demonstrating how to spell, essentially pretending not to know, you can show kids the process you hope they go through, which will result in invented spellings. You can also do that and quietly alter the product to make it correct. Soon, you will teach* went *as a high-frequency word, but some children are ready to learn it now, which is the reason for our decision in this instance.*

FIG. 2–1 The teacher's supermarket story with words written including sounds that children would be starting to hear and record at this time in the year.

ACTIVE ENGAGEMENT/LINK

Set the kids up to help write another sentence for your writing, using their whiteboards and the high-frequency words from their snap word pouches.

"Will you help me add another sentence to this page? Turn and tell your partner what else I should write."

After only a minute, I called them back. "So many great ideas! You gave me the idea to write 'I got the apples.' Will you help me by writing that sentence on your whiteboard? Don't forget to say the sentence and count the words. Tell your partner how many words. Use your pointer power to plan it across the lines."

A few seconds later, I added, "Now say the first word: *I*. Think, 'Is *I* a snap word?' If it is, and you aren't sure how to spell it, pull it out from your snap word pouch, say it, and then write it in the sentence. If it isn't a snap word, say the word slowly, and write all the sounds you hear. Now reread what you have and keep going. Say the next word." I continued coaching from the sidelines but dropped my tips off as students kept writing.

After most kids had approximated writing the sentence, I modeled a far briefer version of the process, writing it in front of them. "I got the apples. I. . .g /g/ot. . .the. . .apples. Thank you for being my writing partners. You helped me be brave and add two sentences to my writing!"

RUG TIME

Set up partners to help each other add sentences to their writing. Remind students to write any high-frequency words in a snap and to stretch out any words that are unfamiliar.

"Now you're ready to help each other add sentences to your own writing. Right now, will you and your partner choose one piece of writing to add sentences to? Find a page that needs more sentences. Remember to use your pointer power to plan and write the sentences. Partner 1, you'll add sentences first. For each word, ask, 'Is this a snap word?' If it is, you can get the word from your snap word pouch and add it to your writing, no stretching needed, or you can just write it in a snap if you know it. If it's not a snap word, say it slowly, and write all the sounds you hear. Remember to use the alphabet chart if you need it. After you add a sentence to one partner's writing, you can switch and help the other partner. Cheer each other on as you go. Get started. I'll coach."

SHARE

Celebrate students' hard work by directing them to reread their sentences. Then, reread the class you-can-do-it sign and get all the kids to give Mabel a high-five/trunk.

"Super Writers, boy, are you super! You just worked so hard on your own writing, helping each other write sentences. I feel like I should call you Super Partners! You wrote some words in a snap, super quick, without even needing to stretch them. And you said the other words slowly and wrote down all the sounds you heard. And then you wrote so many sentences. They are everywhere in your writing. Right now, will each of you reread your sentences to your partner? Use your pointer power to help you read it. You are Super Readers after all."

After all partners had had a chance to read their sentences, I said. "You know what? The you-can-do-it sign Mabel wrote during the last session helped all of us. I think we should reread it to celebrate and to further activate our new powers. Let's all get our pointers up and ready."

POSSIBLE COACHING MOVES

▶ "Your page has labels. Reread them. Use the labels to help you think about what you want to write on that page."

▶ "Say a lot of sentences before you decide what sentence you'll write first."

▶ "Do you know that word in a snap? If you do, get it out from your snap word pouch and add it to your writing."

▶ "That's one long word! If you don't know it in a snap, say it slowly, and write down all the sounds you hear."

▶ "Use the alphabet chart to find which letter makes that sound."

FIG. 2–2   Partners work together to add sentences to their writing using what they know about snap words and stretching words to hear and record sounds.

Together we read our chart.

I said, "In our previous session, Mabel high-fived us to welcome us to the new work of the unit. I think we need to give Mabel a high-five. Or trunk. Trunks out," I mimed making a trunk as the kids did the same. I held Mabel's trunk out toward them. "Ready? High-trunk!"

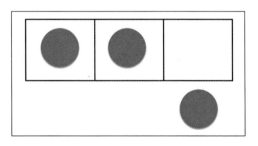

EXTENSION 1 • Hearing *All* the Sounds Across a Word

Remind students about listening to the first sound in a word, then use Elkonin boxes to help them hear the sounds all across a word.

I drew three Elkonin boxes on the board. "Do you remember how earlier in the year, I would say a word, and you'd try to catch the first sound in your mouth and figure out what letter made that sound?" I touched the first box. "I'd say the word *mug*, and you'd catch the first sound. . . " I paused, and students called out /m/, "and then you'd tell what letter made that sound. . .That's right. *M* makes the /m/ sound.

"Since you're so good at hearing sounds at the beginning of words, I thought we could mix things up and listen for letters and sounds that come at other points in the word, like in the middle or the end." I pointed to each box from beginning to end, isolating the sounds in *mug*: /m/-/u/-/g/. "Ready to try it?

"Here's the first one. I see a pen. What's the last sound in *pen*?" I pointed to the last box. I noticed a few kids who needed more coaching, so I said, "Is the last sound /k/-/k/-/k/ or /nnnnn/? You're right. It's /n/. What letter makes that sound? *N*."

We repeated the game a few times. Each time, I pointed to the corresponding sound box. "What is the middle sound in *bat*?" "What is the last sound in *rip*?" "What is the middle sound in *cut*?" "What is the first sound in *pit*?"

EXTENSION 2 • Learning New Snap Words: *To* and *Do*

 GETTING READY

• Prepare to add word cards for *to* and *do* to the word wall.

Introduce two new snap words, and guide students through the familiar process of making a word a snap word.

"Writers, sometimes words become snap words when we don't even mean for them to. We use them so much that we learn them by heart. That happened today when we were writing *I went to the supermarket*. So many of us thought we

Elkonin boxes can help children understand what it means to listen for sounds from left to right.

had *to* in our word collection when we didn't! It is definitely an important word to know by heart, so let's turn it into a snap word for everyone." I turned to the "How to Learn a Word" chart.

I held up the word *to*. "Okay, let's make this a snap word. First, read it!" I pointed under the printed card as the students read the word.

"Now, study it. Tell your partner what you're noticing. Yes, the first letter has a tail and the other is small. Let's count the letters—one, two! The first letter is *t* and the last letter is *o*. The *o* goes with the /o͞o/ sound. /T/ /o͞o/.

"Now, spell it: *t-o*.

"Now let's cover, write, and check it. Quick, take a picture with your brain before I cover it." I covered the word with my hand. "Now write it!" The kids began to work on their whiteboards. After a moment, I uncovered the word. "Make sure it matches and fix it up if it doesn't.

"Now, let's use it. Hmm,. . . " I tapped my temple. "I went to school! Think of some more sentences with your partner." I listened in and coached a few kids. "You might say, 'I went to. . .' or 'We like to. . .'

"You know, friends, there is a word that sounds like *to* and looks like it, too. Do you know what it could be? It's the word *do*. We use it all the time when we say things like, 'It's time to *do* our math' or '*Do* you want to play with me?'"

We repeated the same steps to learn the word *do*.

"Let's lift these words up onto the word wall! Pretend you're lifting *to* up to our pocket chart with me." We all pretended to lift *to* into the air as I put the word on the wall. "*To*!" We finished with our other new word, *do*.

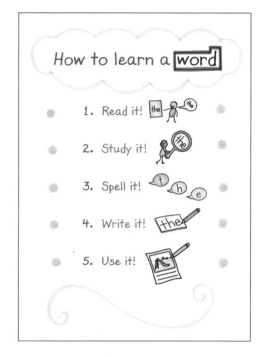

EXTENSION 3 • Practicing Snap Words So We Know Them Inside and Out

 GETTING READY

- Distribute a snap word pouch, whiteboard, and marker to each partnership.

Invite partners to play a game to practice writing their snap words.

"For our snap words to really help you write sentences, you need to know them in a snap. You need to learn them so well that you can write them without even looking at them.

"I've got a game that will help you learn these words even better. I'll give you and your partner a whiteboard. You'll need your snap word pouches. Partner 1, you be the reader. Take a word from your word collection and read it to your partner. Don't show your partner the word! Partner 2, write that word on your whiteboard. See if the word is in your

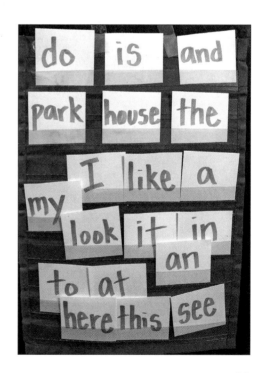

head and you can write it in a snap. If it's not, use the snap word pocket chart to help you. Then, check the word you wrote next to the snap word card to make sure they match. If they match, play again! If they don't match, take a minute to really notice the letters in the word and think about the sounds they make. Then, write the snap word again to make it match. Ready to play?"

After a few rounds, I channeled students to switch roles. I coached in to make sure that students were checking their spelling of their high-frequency words against the word card to be sure each word was spelled correctly.

"Soon, you won't even need these words in your snap word pouches because you'll know them so well!"

Writers Take Risks
Writing All the Sounds in Long Words

IN THIS SESSION

TODAY YOU'LL teach students that writers bravely try to write even long words. They say the words, listening to and writing all the sounds they hear.

TODAY YOUR STUDENTS will work in partnerships to write labels for common objects in the classroom. Partners will share their labels with the class, and students will work together to make sure all labels can be read.

GETTING READY

✔ Prepare to write labels on large sentence strips.

✔ Distribute sentence strips and markers to rug clubs.

✔ For students who may need extra support, you may wish to provide pictures of items in the classroom for children to label, if you think it will be more supportive than simply naming objects for them to label.

MINILESSON

CONNECTION

Focus kids' attention by acting alarmed that Mabel was nervous about writing longer words. Explain that you helped Mabel with a tip—a tip that will help everyone in the class.

"Writers, come quickly to the rug! I'm worried about something. During our previous session, Mabel told me she wanted to label more objects in our room, so we'd know what they were. I thought that was such a kind idea. But guess what she told me? She said she was scared to write some of the words because they were soooo long. She didn't know if she could write all the sounds.

"Have any of you ever felt that way? Have you ever thought, 'I can't write that word. It's too long!'? You have? Then, I want to give you the tip I gave Mabel. It might really help you."

❖ **Name the teaching point.**

"Today I want to teach you that writers don't avoid long words. Instead, they bravely try to write them. They say the long word slowly, listening carefully and writing all the sounds they hear. Then they say the word again, listening for even more sounds. They do this until they hear all the sounds in a word."

PHONICS INSTRUCTION

Phonological Awareness
- Say words slowly to identify salient sounds in spoken words.
- Identify and use initial, final, and salient sounds when writing words.

Letter Knowledge
- Recognize and name all upper- and lowercase letters of the alphabet.
- Demonstrate basic knowledge of letter-sound correspondences by producing the primary or most frequent sound for each consonant.

Word Knowledge/Solving
- Use letter-sound knowledge to spell.

High-Frequency Words
- Recognize and use high-frequency words with automaticity.

TEACHING

Ask students to share words of encouragement with Mabel. Then, share the first label Mabel wants to write with the class.

"Will you help Mabel do this? First things first, give Mabel a little encouragement. Partner 2, will you be Mabel? Look extra nervous. Partner 1, cheer Mabel on! Help her feel brave, so she believes she can write these long words."

The rug filled with cheers of "Don't let that long word stop you!" and "Just take it slow" and "You can always try again" and "You know so many sounds!"

"What do you think, Mabel? Are you feeling a little better?" She nodded. "Okay, great! Your cheers really helped. Mabel, what word do you want to label first?" I held her up to my ear.

"Oh, you want to label the folders? That's a great idea, Mabel. That will help us because our folders always end up in the wrong spots."

Demonstrate for students how you say a word slowly, listening for and recording the sounds you hear. Then, repeat the process, adding more sounds.

I attached a sentence strip to the board. "Since *folder* is a long word with a lot of sounds, we'll probably need to stretch it out more than once. Each time, let's listen for as many sounds as we can. We'll write those sounds on the label.

"*Folder.* Say it slowly with me: *f-f-f-f-ollderrrrr.* Did you catch any sounds? Let's say it one more time: *f-f-f-f-ollderrrr.* I heard the /f/ at the beginning, did you? I know that *f* makes the /f/ sound." I recorded the *f* on the label. "And I heard a /r/ sound at the end. *R* makes the /r/ sound. I'll record that letter at the end of the sentence strip since that's the last sound."

f		r

"Are we done? Not yet! We need to say the word again and listen for even more sounds. Then, we write those sounds where they belong. /f/-olll-/d/-/d/-/r/. Call out the sounds that you hear! I heard /l/ and /d/. Did you? Let's write them. What letter makes each sound?" Soon, our label read:

f	ld	r

"Wow! Saying that long word again and again helped us hear so many sounds in the word."

FIG. 3–1   A label written by the class for a box of writing folders.

Again, we made a decision to write folder *without the* o *because it is likely that many kindergarten children will not hear the sound in that word correctly. In part, that is because vowels followed by the letter* l *can change the sound of that vowel (similar to the r-controlled vowels).*

ACTIVE ENGAGEMENT/LINK

Share another item Mabel wants to have labeled. Coach students as they say the word repeatedly, listening for each sound. Record the letters students hear.

I put my ear down by Mabel's mouth. "Mabel is so excited about that long label you wrote for folders. And she's got something else she wants us to label: the pencils. She said that at the end of the day, there are pencils all over the floor, and the custodians have to keep bending over to pick them up, so they don't get swept into the trash. Mabel thinks that if the pencils are labeled, we'll know where they go, and the custodians won't have to pick up after us anymore.

"Get ready to write this label in the air with your partner. Say the word *pencil* slowly. Say it again. What sounds do you hear? What letters make those sounds?" Many students called out *p* and *n*.

"You heard a few sounds in *pencil*. Say the word again, slowly. Listen for even more sounds."

I recorded the letters students called out on a new sentence strip: *pnsl*.

"Wow! That label is four letters long. You heard four different sounds! Saying that long word again and again really helped you write that word. Let's read with our pointer power, remembering to give it one tap, even though it's a long word."

FIG. 3–2   Writing labels for items in the classroom.

RUG TIME CLUBS

Distribute sentence strips and markers to rug clubs. Channel students to say each word slowly, again and again, hearing and recording all the sounds they hear.

"What is it?" I leaned down close to Mabel. "You've got even more things for us to label? Wow! Mabel wants us to label so many things that I don't think we can label them all as a group. We'd be here all day! I think instead, I'll give you and your partner a sentence strip and name two items that Mabel wants you to label. Say each item one at a time and then say the word slowly, again and again. Record all the sounds you hear in each word."

I distributed a marker and sentence strips to each partnership. I named the following items to label: fountain, sink, counters, computers, whiteboard, paper clips, calendar, bookcase, headphones. Then, I moved from partnership to partnership, coaching in. Occasionally I voiced over with a tip for the whole class.

Smartboard   Calendar
Computer   Shelf door
Elmo   Table   desk   ipad
Chart   Mabel

POSSIBLE COACHING MOVES

▶ "Say the word slowly. Say it again."

▶ "Catch that sound in your mouth. What sound do you hear?"

▶ "What letter makes that sound? Look on the alphabet chart if you're not certain."

▶ "You heard a few sounds in that word. Say it again, slowly, and try to hear more sounds."

▶ "Think about where that sound goes. Does it go at the beginning, in the middle, or at the end of the word?"

SHARE • Reading Labels and Celebrating the Power of Writing More Sounds

Invite partners to share their labels with the class. Rally students to read each label and check the label with the picture to make sure they match. Add missing letters when labels are hard to read.

"Writers, your labels have so many letters. Do you want to test your labels to make sure your classmates can read them? Here's how it will work. I'll call one partnership up at a time. Those kids will show us one of their labels. We'll all read it. Then, we can look around the room and use that to help us read the writing our friends have done."

I called the first partnership up. They held up their label: *papr clps*. "Paper clips!" the class shouted. I asked the class, "Are they correct? Check the picture." The partnership had big smiles on their faces as they pointed to the corresponding object in the classroom.

"You got it! That label was so clear that other readers could read it."

We continued reading each label and checking it with the object in the classroom. When we got to a label that was hard to read, we worked together to add more letters, so everyone could read the label.

If your children will benefit from more meaning support, it may be helpful to have snapped photos on an iPad to be able to scroll through them before showing the labels. This will provide students with support in reading their classmates' labels.

Remember that "hard to read" really has to do with whether that word has some vowels—probably more long vowels—and whether it has the right consonants. So, for example, if a child wrote bks for bookcase, for example, try to get kids to add at least one vowel. Or if a child wrote hos for headphones, I would coach her to hear the salient consonant sounds in the word, so that perhaps the label becomes hdfos.

EXTENSION 1 • Editing Your Own Writing to Add More Sounds in Longer Words

Invite writers to reread their work, checking to see if they included longer words that they could add more sounds to.

"Writers, you did such thoughtful work earlier adding more letters to the labels around our classroom. I think you're ready to do the same thing with your writing.

"Will you pull out a piece of writing from your writing folder? Activate your pointer power and use your pointer power to read each word of your writing. If it's a snap word, write it in a snap. When you get to a long word, reread it carefully. Say the word slowly again and again. Check that you have letters for all the sounds. Add in any letters that are missing. Remember, your alphabet chart can help you." After a minute, I added, "Try another word. Remember to be brave and try writing the long words you really want and need in your story."

EXTENSION 2 • Labeling the Room (and Then Reading the Labels)

GETTING READY

- Provide a rolled-up piece of tape to each partnership for each of their labels.

Channel students to post their labels around the classroom, then ask partners to take a tour of the room to read the labels.

"Readers, I thought I could wait until tonight to put up the labels you wrote, but Mabel is getting impatient. She wants me to put them up right away. I can't do it alone, though. Will you help? I'll give you and your partner a big rolled-up piece of tape for each of your labels. Stick it to the back of your label, and then put your label where it goes in the room."

Two minutes later, when most of the labels were up, I said, "Ready to read them? With your partner, take a tour of all the new labels. Try to find each one. When you find it, use your powers to read the label, working to read all the sounds."

EXTENSION 3 • Learning New Snap Words: *We*, *Be*, and *Me*

GETTING READY

- Display the "How to Learn a Word" anchor chart from Unit 1, *Making Friends with Letters*.

Introduce two new snap words, and guide students through the familiar process of making a word a snap word.

"Writers, do you know what will help you read longer books and write longer sentences? It will help if you know more words in a snap. I've got two new words to teach you. They all go together. Here's the first one." I revealed the word *we* in the sentence "We can read."

"Let's use the steps we know to help us learn this word." I gestured toward the "How to Learn a Word" chart.

FIG. 3–3   The teacher prepares to guide students through the steps to learn a new snap word.

"This word is *we*. *We* can read. First, let's read the word: *we*. Now study it. Tell your partner what you notice. How many letters does it have? What does it start and end with? What sounds do you hear in the word? The *w* goes with the /w/ sound and the *e* goes with the sound of it's name.

"Ready to spell the word *we*? Get out your imaginary marker and take the cap off. Write *we* on the rug. Spell *we* out loud as you write the letters. Now, write it again. This time try to write it faster and without looking. Check each letter to make sure it's right.

"Let's use the word *we* in a sentence. Tell your partner as many sentences as you can that use the word *we*.

"Ready for another word? This word is almost the same as *we*." We repeated the process with the words *be* and *me*, discussing the ways in which all three snap words were similar.

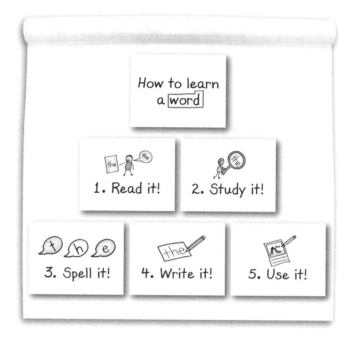

Hearing and Recording More Sounds in Words

IN THIS SESSION

TODAY YOU'LL teach students that writers need to write *all* the sounds they hear in a word, not just the first and last sounds.

TODAY YOUR STUDENTS will write a class letter to Reader-Man, spelling words they don't know in a snap by saying them slowly and writing all the salient sounds.

MINILESSON

CONNECTION

Establish a real-world purpose for writing: to respond to the letter from Reader-Man received in reading workshop. Build excitement around writing a letter back to him.

"Writers, in my family, when I was a kid, my parents taught me that if you get a gift from someone, the polite thing to do is to write a thank-you letter to that person. Like if my grandma gave me a birthday present, after my birthday was over, I had the opportunity to write 'Dear Grandma, Thank you for. . .'

"I'm telling you this because I have been thinking that you could write a thank-you letter back to Reader-Man. I mean, he gave you a pretty amazing gift when he sent you those special power pointers, didn't he? Why don't we work on a thank-you letter to Reader-Man right now? Don't you think that would be a kind and polite thing to do?

"We'll have to put our letter in the mail and send it to Reader-Man, so we won't be there to read it to him. That means we'll have to work extra hard to make sure he can read it without us."

GETTING READY

✔ Prepare to write a class letter to Reader-Man on chart paper.

✔ Distribute whiteboards and markers to each partnership.

PHONICS INSTRUCTION

Concepts About Print
- Understand punctuation has a purpose.

Phonological Awareness
- Say words slowly to identify salient sounds in spoken words.
- Identify and use initial, final, and salient sounds when writing words.

Letter Knowledge
- Recognize and name all upper- and lowercase letters of the alphabet.
- Demonstrate basic knowledge of letter-sound correspondences by producing the primary or most frequent sound for each consonant.

Word Knowledge/Solving
- Use letter-sound knowledge to spell.

High-Frequency Words
- Recognize and use high-frequency words with automaticity.
- Locate and read high-frequency words in a text.
- Write high-frequency words in continuous text.

❖ **Name the teaching point.**

"Writers, I want to give you a tip. To make your writing extra easy for readers to read, you need to write *all* the sounds you hear in the word, not just the first and last sounds."

TEACHING

Recruit students to help you plan out the letter to Reader-Man. Share the version of the letter you'll write, complete with several snap words and a few longer words students will need to stretch out.

"Let's plan out our letter to Reader-Man. Then, we can make the letter extra easy for Reader-Man to read by writing *all* the sounds we hear. Hmm,. . .if you want to thank Reader-Man for pointer power, what might you say? You are going to have to tell Reader-Man why you like pointer power. Turn and tell your partner what you think you might say." I listened in as students generated possible responses.

"Oh my gosh, such great ideas. I heard so many of you say how much you liked your pointer power. I think we can say,

> *Dear Reader-Man,*
>
> *Thank you. We had fun. We like to point.*
>
> *Can we have more powers?*
>
> *Your fans, Class K–234."*

Intentionally only record one letter for the first word. Then, remind students that writers write *all* the sounds they hear. Say the word slowly and write all the salient sounds.

"Let's get this letter started! Usually you start a letter by saying 'Dear So-and-So. That's how I started letters to my grandma. I'll use pointer power to figure out how this first part will go. 'Dear Reader-Man.' That's three words. The first word is *Dear*. I don't know that word in a snap. /d/-/d/-ear. I hear the /d/ sound at the beginning of the word. *D* makes a /d/ sound." I uncapped my marker and added a capital *D* to the page of chart paper, and then said, "Now I need to write *Reader-Man*."

A few kids called out "Stop!"

"Oh," I said, smacking my forehead. "You're right!" I said. "I only wrote the first sound. Reader-Man won't know if that *d* is for *dog* or *dear* or *doughnut*. Let me try again, and this time, I'll write all the sounds I hear." I asked the kids to write it on the rug with their magic pens (their fingers) while I wrote it into our chart-paper letter.

I said the word slowly, stretching it down my arm. "Deeeeerrr. /d/-/e/-/r/. I hear three sounds. Let me figure out which letter makes each sound. /d/ *D*. /e/ *e*. And /r/ *r*." Soon the letter said *Der*.

FIG. 4–1   The teacher writes the first part of the letter children have composed to Reader-Man on the class board.

You could choose to vary this letter. If you do, be sure to keep in mind the phonics principles your students have been exposed to. You'll notice this letter includes words with a few salient sounds, but not so many salient sounds that it would be overwhelming.

"Wow! Reader-Man will have a *much* easier time reading that, because I wrote letters for all the sounds I heard. I can write Reader-Man's name quickly, because his name is on the letter he sent us." I added his name to the chart-paper letter. I made sure to look between his letter and our letter to get the correct spelling of *Reader-Man*. "Now the next sentence is 'Thank you.' I'll write that quickly."

ACTIVE ENGAGEMENT/LINK

Direct students to write the next sentence. Coach them to say each word slowly, hearing all the sounds, and then to name the letter that makes each sound.

"Let's reread what we have so far. Pointer power ready! 'Dear Reader-Man. Thank you.' Will you help me write the next sentence? 'We had fun!'" I distributed a whiteboard and marker to each partnership.

"Use your pointer power to plan out where each word will go: 'We had fun!' How many words? Three!" Touch across your page three times. "Now, write each word. If you know the word in a snap, remember you can write it down on your whiteboard without saying it slowly. Look up at our snap word pocket chart if you need to. If you don't know how to spell the word, say it slowly, stretch it down your arm, and write all the sounds you hear. Get started!"

I coached in as students worked, reminding them to say the word again, slowly, if they had only recorded a letter or two on their whiteboard.

Once kids had a chance to work, I quickly recorded this sentence on our class letter, demonstrating how I heard three phonemes in each consonant-vowel-consonant word. I added an exclamation mark at the end of the sentence. Soon, the letter read:

Der Reader-Man,

Thank you.

We had fun!

RUG TIME

Channel students to write the next two sentences in the letter to Reader-Man. Coach to help them hear more phonemes in each word.

"We need to write the rest of this letter, so we can get it in the mail before lunchtime today—so that Reader-Man can get it soon. Wouldn't it be fun if he wrote back? The next sentence is 'We like to point.'"

POSSIBLE COACHING MOVES

▶ "You've only got one letter, and Reader-Man won't know what word that is. Try it again, only this time, hear more sounds and write more letters."

▶ "Stretch that word down your arm *slowly*. What other sounds do you hear?"

▶ "What letter makes that sound? Check the alphabet chart if you need it."

▶ "If you know that word in a snap, don't sound it out. Just write it quickly on your whiteboard."

▶ "You've got the first and last sounds. Say the word again, and listen for any other sounds you hear. Listen from the beginning and add letters from left to right."

"Try it out. Use your pointer power to plan where each word will go. Then, take turns writing the words with your partner. If you know the word in a snap, write it. Use our snap word pocket chart to help you. If you don't know the word, stretch it out and write letters for *all* the sounds you hear. And encourage your partner if your partner feels stuck or scared."

As students worked, I coached in. I also asked a partnership that had heard and recorded several letters for each word to add their writing to the class letter. After students wrote this next sentence, I recorded that on our class letter. I reminded kids of the next sentence: "Can we have more powers?" and recorded that after students had written it on their whiteboards first. I invited kids to chime in as I stretched out each word and recorded the letters most students could hear and record.

FIG. 4–2   Children work on their whiteboards to help write some of the words in the letter to Reader-Man.

SHARE

Recruit students to help you add a closing to the letter. Reread it, and make a show out of folding it up and putting it in an envelope to send to Reader-Man.

"Our letter is almost done. We just need to tell Reader-Man who wrote it. Let's write: 'Your fans, Class K–234.' Use your pointer power to plan out this part and figure out how many words we'll need."

A few seconds later, I said, "I heard you say we need four words. None of these words are snap words, so we'll have to say them all slowly and work to hear all the sounds. Let's try it with *your*. *Yooorrrr*. /y/-/y/. Catch that first sound: /y/. What letter goes with that sound? *Y*. We can hear more sounds than that! *Yoooor*. Push yourself to hear one more sound in this word. *Yrrrrr*. That's right. *R* goes with the /r/ sound. We don't have a vowel, though. Which one do you think it is? You think it's a *u*?"

We repeated the process for *fans*. I quickly added *Class K–234* to the letter. "Let's reread our letter to make sure it will be super-easy for Reader-Man to read. Here goes." I pointed underneath each word as students read with me.

"Reader-Man will be so excited to get our letter, especially since it will be so easy for him to read! Adding all the sounds you heard really helped. I wonder if Reader-Man will want to be our pen pal. That would be a special treat!"

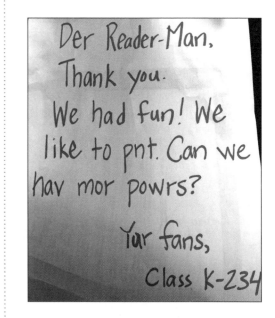

EXTENSION 1 • Using Sound Boxes to Segment a Word into Individual Sounds

GETTING READY

- Draw Elkonin boxes on the board.
- Gather enough circle magnets to move into each box.

Use Elkonin boxes to guide students to listen for all the sounds across a word.

"It can be tricky to hear all the sounds in a word. Remember that you can use these special sound boxes to help you hear and write *all* the sounds in a word. Imagine that I wanted to add to our letter to Reader-Man and say: 'Our pointers are *neat*.' If I wanted to write the word *neat*, I could first say it slow, trying to hear all the sounds. *Nnnn-eeee-tttt*. I think I hear three sounds. Listen, and see how many sounds you hear. *Neeeet*. Three! Great."

I drew three boxes on the board. "What's the first sound you hear in *neat*? /n/-/n/-eat." I touched the first box. "The first sound is /n/-/n/." I moved a circle magnet into the box. "What's the next sound you hear? /n/-eeee-/t/. /ē/ is the next sound." I moved a magnet into the middle box. "Listen for the last sound. /n/-/ē/-/t/." I stuttered the last sound. Kids called out /t/. I moved a magnet into the last box.

"Now we need to figure out the letters that make each sound. *Neat*. /n/-/n/. What letter makes that sound?" Kids called out *n*. I moved the magnet out of the box and wrote an *n* in its place. "What's our next sound? /ē/-/ē/. What letter makes that sound?" Soon all three phonemes in the word were matched to a letter.

"See how these special boxes helped us record all the sounds in a word? Let's try it with another word." I coached students to sound out *love*. The sound boxes ended up looking like this:

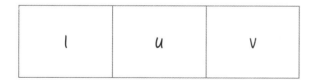

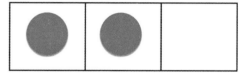

FIG. 4–3 The teacher moves a magnet into the Elkonin boxes, one at a time, as each sound in the CVC word is isolated.

EXTENSION 2 • Punctuation Marks Matter!

GETTING READY

- Make a set of punctuation Post-its® for each partnership by writing a period mark, a question mark, and an exclamation mark on separate Post-its.
- Provide each partnership with a copy of the class letter to Reader-Man.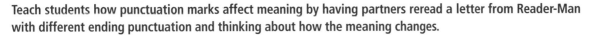

Teach students how punctuation marks affect meaning by having partners reread a letter from Reader-Man with different ending punctuation and thinking about how the meaning changes.

"Writers, I'm not sure if you realized this, but we used some extra-special punctuation marks in our letter today. We used punctuation marks that go at the end of sentences and help readers know how to read writing. This one is a period," and I held up a Post-it with a period on it. "The period tells you to stop and think about what you just read. This one is a question mark," and I held up the question mark Post-it, "and you use it when you want to ask someone something. And this one is an exclamation point," and I held it up. "You use it when you're really excited about something.

"I made a copy of our letter to Reader-Man. Will you listen to how I read it? The punctuation marks will help me figure out how to read each part." I reread the letter, deliberately overemphasizing the parts where I paused or where my voice got really excited or sounded like I was questioning.

"If we mixed up these punctuation marks, the letter would sound really different." I held the question mark Post-it over the exclamation point. "'We had fun?' Reader-Man might think we didn't have fun since we asked a question about it. He'd be so confused!

"I'm giving you and your partner a set of Post-its with each of the punctuation marks on them. I'm also giving you a copy of our letter to Reader-Man. Will you try reading it a bunch of different ways by mixing up the punctuation marks? You could read the first sentence with a period at the end, or an exclamation point, or a question mark." I held up each punctuation mark as I named it. "See if you can figure out which punctuation marks will work best for our letter."

EXTENSION 3 • Playing "I Spy" with Snap Words

 Challenge students to practice reading their snap words with a quick game of "I Spy."

"Super Readers, to use everything that you know to read and write, it is really important you don't forget everything you know. And that's what happens if you don't remind yourself. Things can just slip out of your mind.

"So, I thought we should do some work to remind ourselves of our snap words. We're supposed to know our snap words in a super-quick 'snap!' not in a slow /ssssss/ /nnnnnnn/ /aaaaaa/ /ppppppp/.

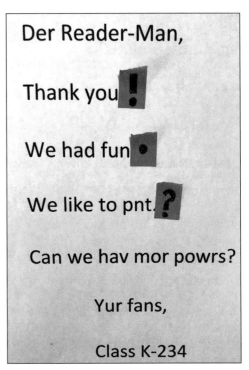

Der Reader-Man,

Thank you **!**

We had fun **•**

We like to pnt. **?**

Can we hav mor powrs?

Yur fans,

Class K-234

"How about if we first read them together?" I moved my pointer through the words on the snap word pocket chart, leading the class in reading them in order, then out of order; quickly and then slowly; in a whisper, then in a squeak.

"Now that we know these in a snap again, let's play a game with them," I said. "You know the game 'I Spy,' right? I'll say, 'I spy with my little eye' and give you a clue, then you'll guess what I'm looking at. Ready to try it? Okay—I spy with my little eye a snap word that has two letters." Children started looking for all the two-letter words.

"You can make a fish fin out of this word. The word rhymes with *fin*."

Kids chimed in with "In!"

"Yes, the word is *in*."

We continued in that fashion with several more words from the snap word pocket chart.

SESSION 5

Using Our Writing Super Powers to Edit and Celebrate Our Written Work

GETTING READY

✔ Ask students to bring their writing folders to the meeting area. You may wish to have them sit on their folders until rug time to avoid distraction.

✔ Print out the letter from Reader-Man and place in an envelope.

✔ Create a piece of your own writing that needs to be edited and place it in your writing folder. Provide a copy of the last page to each partnership. An illustrated template for the book about getting apples is available in the online resources.

✔ Display the "Make Writing Easy to Read" anchor chart from Unit 2, *Writing for Readers*, from the Units of Study in Opinion, Information, and Narrative Writing.

PHONICS INSTRUCTION

Concepts About Print
• Understand that words are written left to right across the page (directionality).
• Understand that words are separated by spaces in print, concept of word.
• Match spoken word to print.

Phonological Awareness
• Say words slowly to identify salient sounds in spoken words.
• Identify and use initial, final, and salient sounds when writing words.

Letter Knowledge
• Recognize and name all upper- and lowercase letters of the alphabet.
• Demonstrate basic knowledge of letter-sound correspondences by producing the primary or most frequent sound for each consonant.

Word Knowledge/Solving
• Use letter-sound knowledge to spell.

IN THIS SESSION

TODAY YOU'LL teach students that writers check their work to make sure it is easy for their readers to read and then they fix it up using their writing super powers.

TODAY YOUR STUDENTS will reread one piece of their writing, checking to make sure they've recorded all sounds in each word. They will then share their work with their rug club in a celebration, in which members of the club read each other's work.

MINILESSON

CONNECTION

Read Reader-Man's response with the class. Build excitement around the idea that students can edit their writing to include more sounds, not just the first and last sounds.

"Writers, you won't believe this, but Reader-Man *already* wrote back! His response was in our mailbox this morning. I couldn't wait for all of you to arrive, so we could read it together. Are you ready?" I made a show of opening the envelope and projecting the letter.

"Read it with me."

> Dear Class K-234,
> I loved your letter!
> It was so easy to read.
> I can tell you worked hard.
> Everyone should read your writing!
> Readerly yours,
> Reader-Man

28　　　　　　　　　　　　　　　WORD-PART POWER

"What a special letter! You know, I think Reader-Man is onto something. You did work really hard on this letter! You work really hard on all your writing. I think he's right that everyone should read your writing. Do you think that before phonics ends today, you could get your writing ready to share with your club in a special rug club celebration?" The kids nodded eagerly. "Oh, good!"

♣ **Name the teaching point.**

"Writers, I want to teach you that before you share your writing with the world, or even just with your rug club, you want to make sure it's easy to read. You can do this by using all of your writing super powers.

TEACHING

Recruit students to help you edit your own writing. Demonstrate how you notice words that only have a few sounds and then stretch those words out, recording all the sounds you hear.

"I want to get my writing ready for the celebration." I rummaged through my writing folder, dramatizing how I looked over a few pieces on the "done" side of my folder to choose the one I wanted to share. "Well, I could share this one. Oh, but I love this one even more. I think this is the best one to share!" I pulled out my book about getting apples that we'd worked on a few days earlier.

"I added a little more to this piece since you saw it last." I read the book to students from the beginning.

(page 1) I wnt to the sprmkt. (I went to the supermarket.)

(page 2) I gt the apls. (I got apples.)

(page 3) They were too heavy for the pr bg. It rpt. (They were too heavy for the paper bag. It ripped.)

(page 4) The al fl on the floor. Erwn looked at me. I was so mbt. (The apples fell on the floor. Everyone looked at me. I was so embarrassed.)

"Will you help me get this book ready? Let me reread a page in my writing, checking to see that I included *all* the sounds in each word, not just the first and last sounds." I posted the third page, which read *They were too heavy for the pr bg. It rpt.*

I started reading the piece aloud, using pointer power to signal under each word. "Looking good so far," I said. At *paper*, I paused. "Hmm,. . .this is supposed to say *paper*, but right now it says *pr*. That's the sound a cat makes, not a paper bag! I know it's missing some sounds because it doesn't have a vowel. Let me say it slowly, this time listening for more sounds. *Paaaaperrrr*. I hear /ā/ after the *p*." I looked up at the alphabet

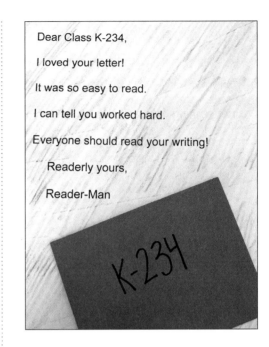

Dear Class K-234,

I loved your letter!

It was so easy to read.

I can tell you worked hard.

Everyone should read your writing!

Readerly yours,

Reader-Man

K-234

FIG. 5–1 Teacher demonstration piece with *paper* edited to include more sounds.

chart. "It must be an *a*." I jotted *pa* above the word. "*Paperrr*. Do you hear another /p/ sound?" Soon, my label looked like this: *papr*.

I repeated the process for *ripped*, recording it as *rpt*.

Debrief, naming the transferable process you just modeled.

"Writers, did you see how I reread each word in my writing, checking to see that I included all the sounds in each word? When I noticed that there were sounds missing in a word, I said the word slowly, listening for even more sounds. I especially listened for sounds in the middle of words. Then, I wrote all the sounds I heard."

ACTIVE ENGAGEMENT/LINK

Distribute an additional page of your writing, and direct students to edit that page to include more sounds.

"Will you help me edit the next page of my writing?" I distributed a copy of the next page to partnerships. "I'll reread it to you, so you know what it's supposed to say, and then will you help me add more sounds to my words so other readers can read it during our special celebration?"

The page read, *The al fl on the floor. Erwn looked at me. I was so mbt*. I read it aloud and then channeled partnerships to reread each word and edit as needed. "If you find a word to edit, you can just put a nice neat line through it and write it the new way right above it. You can use your writing folders as a hard surface while you edit."

FIG. 5–2 Children work together to edit the page of the supermarket book, saying and recording more sounds for the word *apple* and then moving on to other words.

Encourage your students to simply cross a word out and try again, rather than spending precious minutes erasing. This will make it possible for you to assess all their attempts at spelling, editing, and revising. You'll notice that our writing workshop paper has plenty of space between lines and room around the margins, making it easier for young children to write in their edits and revisions.

RUG TIME

Channel students to reread their writing, noticing places where they only included a few letters. Coach them as they say those words slowly, recording all the sounds they hear.

"Writers, my writing is getting easier and easier to read. Thank you so much for helping me edit. Our rug club celebration will be in just a few minutes, so I think it's time for you to get ready. Look through your writing folder and choose the one piece you want to share with your rug club. Got it? Great!

"Now, use your pointer power to reread each word. Check to make sure you've got *all* the letters you need. You can't just have the first and last letter. You'll need to write the other letters as well."

I moved from student to student, coaching in, and I occasionally voiced over with tips for the whole class.

SHARE • Using Partner and Pointer Power (CLUBS)

Hold a rug club celebration. Rally clubs to read their writing aloud to each other, using their pointer power to read each word. Celebrate that students' writing is getting even easier to read.

"Writers, I think this is some of your best work yet. All the hard work that you did to make your writing easy to read will really help your readers. You heard and recorded so many sounds in your words!

"I think we should celebrate all of your hard work during phonics workshop, reading workshop, and writing workshop," I said as I gestured toward the "Make Writing Easy to Read" chart. "Are you ready? Here's how our special celebration will go. Rug clubs, gather close together. Choose one person to go first and put that person's writing in the middle so everyone can see it. If it's your writing, use your pointer power to point to each word. Work together, using partner power, to read the writing, just like when we do partner reading. You'll be able to read each other's writing because you recorded so many sounds. Get started!"

As students shared, I reminded them to put their pieces in the middle, to focus on one piece at a time, and to try and read the pieces with one voice.

After a few minutes, I paused the class. "Wow! I wish Reader-Man could be here to see you now! He'd be so proud, just like you should be proud of your hard work. Your writing is getting easier and easier for your readers to read!"

POSSIBLE COACHING MOVES

▶ "You've got the first sound and the last sound. Say the word again slowly and listen for the sounds in the middle."

▶ "That's a long word, so it will have a lot of sounds and more letters. Say it again and listen for more sounds."

▶ "Uh-oh! That's a snap word. Look at the snap word pocket chart and make sure you spelled it correctly."

▶ "Check the alphabet chart if you need it."

▶ "Once you check one page, turn the page and check the next one."

▶ "Clap the syllables. Say each part and write the sounds you hear in that syllable."

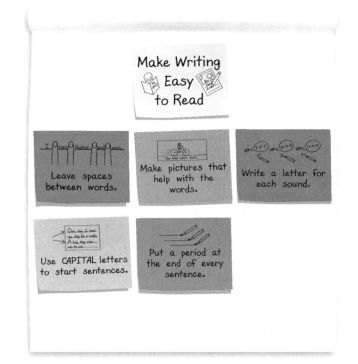

Make Writing Easy to Read

Leave spaces between words.

Make pictures that help with the words.

Write a letter for each sound.

Use CAPITAL letters to start sentences.

Put a period at the end of every sentence.

Dear Teachers,

The second bend of this unit, *Word-Part Power*, kicks off a critical line of phonics work for which this entire unit is named. Whereas Bend I helped tie the reading super powers your students learned in *Super Powers: Reading with Print Strategies and Sight Word Power* to their work as writers, this bend, as well as the bend that follows it, introduces a powerful new phonics super power: word-part power. You'll introduce this power in the first session of the bend and then teach kids ways to activate and strengthen their new power across the remainder of the unit.

Word-part power is the power to use vowel-consonant rimes to generate more and more words. Across the bend, you'll expose students to making words using onsets and rimes. Strengthened by their word-part power, your kindergarten students will be able to take familiar word parts and use them especially within writing workshop. The work begins with familiar sight words that are also rimes in many words. Imagine the thrill of taking a snap word you know well that also happens to be a word part, such as *at* or *in*, and using that word part to build new words with ease. Just knowing the word part *-at* can help kids to write so many consonant-vowel-consonant words: *cat, hat, sat, pat, mat, rat,* and *fat,* among others. Expect to see a lot of these kinds of words in students' writing.

As we wrote in the overview of the unit, you'll rely on a few go-to teaching methods across this bend, mainly making words and sorting words, to help students understand how they can combine different onsets and rimes to help them write. Keep in mind that as you coach students to read and write words, you'll want to help them orchestrate all of their powers, not just their word-part power. They might use their snap-word power to write words they know in a snap, use their sound power to write words without familiar onsets and rimes, and use their word-part power to write words with familiar word parts.

A highlight of this bend is the introduction of an important new tool: the word wall. Up to this point, you've added all the words students are learning to a snap word pocket chart, and it's likely that chart is nearly overflowing. Rather than building the word wall without students, we suggest that you engage them in helping you turn the name wall into a word wall so that they understand how the tool is constructed. We recommend that you leave children's names on the word wall if they are still using each others' names to help them read and write.

Word-part power won't just help students as writers. It will also help them as readers. To help your students use their word-part power to read, the last session of the bend teaches students that when they get to a word they can't easily figure out, they need to activate their word-part power and look for familiar parts they know. In the middle of the bend, you'll coach kids to practice this work in an especially engaging text—a personal narrative written by Mabel. If this exemplar text mirrors the writing your students are doing in writing workshop, it will serve as an additional mentor text for them.

As the bend draws to a close, you'll rally students to co-construct a word-part chart with you to celebrate the word parts they've learned. As the unit progresses, you'll add more word parts to the chart. Expect your students to leave this bend as stronger readers and writers, able to read and write more words because of their word-part power.

All the best,
Natalie and Rachel

Using Word-Part Power

Making Words with Vowel-Consonant Rimes -at and -in

IN THIS SESSION

TODAY YOU'LL teach students that writers use rhyming to hear word parts, and word parts can be used to spell lots of different words.

TODAY YOUR STUDENTS will use whiteboards and word cards to write words using the word parts *-at* and *-in*. They will work on hearing, spelling, and writing new words while helping to write a brief story.

MINILESSON

CONNECTION

Rally the class to the start of a new bend by reminding them that they are Super Readers all day long.

"Friends, today we start a new part to our unit, a new chapter. Before we can do that, I need to check that you're ready for today's work. Will you show me your best superhero pose?" Immediately, the kids flexed their muscles, and some put their hands on their hips. "Oh, whew. I *knew* you were ready! You remember that the job of a Super *Reader*, like the job of any superhero, never ends, right? Those powers stick with you all day long—when you read, when you write, *and* when you study words! That means that right now, you are still Super Readers.

"I'm wondering if you think you are ready to activate a whole new power! How about it? Are you ready?"

GETTING READY

✔ Before you teach this lesson, be sure your students are familiar with the story of Jack and the Beanstalk.

✔ At the beginning of this session, distribute a whiteboard and marker to each partnership.

✔ Have large Post-its, a marker, and a whiteboard to demonstrate making words with rimes.

✔ Distribute an *-at* phonogram card to each partnership during (not before) the Teaching.

✔ Distribute one *-in* phonogram card to each partnership.

✔ Have ready pages of a story with pictures and no words.

PHONICS INSTRUCTION

Phonological Awareness
- Recognize and produce rhyming words.
- Blend and segment the onset and rime of single-syllable spoken words.
- Add or substitute individual sounds in simple, one-syllable words to make new words.

Phonics
- Recognize common phonograms.

Word Knowledge/Solving
- Use various onsets to generate new words with ending phonograms (VC).
- Use familiar word parts including phonograms (*at*, *in*) to spell unfamiliar words.

Recruit students to join you in reciting some familiar poems or rhyming songs, drawing their attention to what makes words rhyme.

The students were ready. "Whoa, with all these growing powers, soon you'll be indestructible! Let's celebrate with a song. You'll see why in a minute, but for now, join in with me if you can." I began singing a song that all my students knew.

"Writers, what we are doing when we sing those songs and say those nursery rhymes is that we are rhyming. We rhyme when we say words that sound the same at the end, like *star* and *are* or *high* and *sky*. Or, like this: 'The *fat cat sat* on the *mat*, and *that* is *that*.'"

❧ **Name the teaching point.**

"Today, as we continue to become more super readers and writers, I want to teach you that rhyming isn't just a fun thing to do in songs and poems and nursery rhymes. It's actually an important part of spelling, of writing words. Rhyming gives you word-part power."

TEACHING

Retell the familiar tale of Jack and the Beanstalk and say that you'll give students magic *words* that will grow and grow. Give students the rime *-at* and begin to teach them to make words with it.

"There's more, though. And this is super-important. Do you remember, in the story of Jack and the Beanstalk, how Jack sold his cow for some magic beans instead of money, and his mom got so mad that she threw them out the window? That night, when Jack was sleeping, a magic beanstalk grew and *grew* outside Jack's window. It turned out those beans were magic. They had special power."

"Well, right now, I'm going to give each of you something—not a magic bean, but a magic *word*. Hold out your hands. Remember the teeny-tiny words we studied in our last unit? They are actually magic. The teeny-tiny magical word I am going to give you can grow and grow into ten words or even more! When I give you and your partner your magic bean—I mean, *word*—don't look at it yet. Just hold your hands around the word so we all look at it at the same time." I excitedly handed each partnership an *-at* phonogram card facedown. "Okay, *look*!" The children turned over their cards. They were a bit surprised that this familiar word could be a magic word. "Yes, it's a word you know—*at*. But here's the thing: *at* can be turned into many words. It can be part of many words."

"You already know how to rhyme words with *-at*." I began an oral poem, not writing anything down. "Pat saw a. . .what?" I gave kids a clue by saying, "/rrrr/"

The kids called, "Rat. She saw a rat!"

I repeated what was becoming the first lines of a new poem, adding a bit: "Pat saw a rat, a rat who was. . . " I gestured to give a clue about the size of the rat. The kids chimed in, "Fat!"

Any poem or any rhyming song will do here, so substitute whatever song your kids know. If you don't have any shared songs or nursery rhymes, you will want to begin introducing some—but meanwhile you can invent silly rhymes such as the one we create in the teaching.

Twinkle, Twinkle, Little Star

Twinkle, twinkle, little star,

How I wonder what you are!

Up above the world so high,

Like a diamond in the sky.

Twinkle, twinkle, little star,

How I wonder what you are!

I kept making the poem, prompting with gestures and initial sounds, until we had added that the fat rat sat on a mat.

Point out that because kids know the *-at* word part, and because they are making words that build on that part, they know how to spell the words they make.

"Here is the cool thing. Not only can you *say* those rhymes, you can use your word-part power to spell them. Let me show you.

"Here's how I can make *Pat* using *-at*. I say both words: *at*, *Pat*. Do you hear that both *at* and *Pat* have *-at* at the end? It takes word-part power to hear that!" I wrote *at* on a large Post-it and stuck it on my whiteboard. "Hold up your *at* card and read it, showing me your word-part power!"

Then I said, "I hear a /p/ sound at the beginning of *Pat*. Let me think about what letter makes that sound. I can look at the alphabet chart to help me if I need it." I made a show of looking at the alphabet chart while many of the kids whispered, "*P*!"

"/P/. That's the letter *P*!" I wrote a *P* on the whiteboard in front of *at*. I reread that initial sound /p/, combining it with /at/.

"Let's all read it—*Pat*!

"Now we said our poem goes 'Pat saw a. . .rat!' So how do we write *rat*? *At*. *Rat*. Do you hear that both *at* and *rat* have *-at* at the end?" I again took out my whiteboard, with the Post-it, ready to write the word *rat*. Some students held up their *at* cards. "Everyone, say the word slowly. . ./r/at, /r/at. What do I need to put here, in front of the *-at* word part? / rrrr/. Check the alphabet chart if you need to." Students called out that I needed an *R*. I wrote the letter *R* and reread the word *rat*.

ACTIVE ENGAGEMENT/LINK

Help the kids to make more words, putting new initial letters at the front of the rime *-at* to make and spell new CVC words.

"You definitely have word-part power because I hardly did anything to help that time. Are you ready to try to use your word-part power to write something else?" I said the first part of our rhyme to the students: "Pat saw a rat who was . . . "

I again gestured to the students to remind them that the rat was fat. "Hmm,. . .I wonder if your word-part power will help you write the word *fat*. Everybody, say the word in two parts, /f/-at. Give me a thumbs up if you think you can use your word-part power to write the word *fat*."

Teachers, here you'll notice that you are still supporting kids in learning letter-sound correspondence. Work with onset and rime actually helps kids listen for the sound of the onset as well as the rime.

The decision to focus on particular short-vowel rimes in this bend—an, at, it, in—is intentional. These are not only some of the most frequently occurring phonograms, but also words unto themselves, so kids already know them. Knowing and being able to use rimes such as at, an, it, and in allows a reader to form more than 500 words.

The kids said the word *fat*, and some gave me a thumbs up to show they heard *at*. "Now it's time to write *fat*." I coached: "Put your *at* card on your whiteboard like mine." I gestured toward my whiteboard. "You have *at*, so now you just need to write the first letter."

As partners worked together to write *fat*, I moved quickly from pair to pair, coaching writers as they worked. Then I called them together and said, "Let's keep going! Use your power to help you write other words in the poem!" I said the poem again: "Pat saw a rat who was fat. It sss. . . " Several students called out "sat!"

Students wrote the word *sat*, while I coached. We then repeated the process with the word *mat*.

> ### POSSIBLE COACHING MOVES
>
> ▸ "Say the word. What sound do you hear at the beginning? Write it."
>
> ▸ "Use the alphabet chart to help you know which letter to write."
>
> ▸ "Write it in front of *at*. It's the first letter."
>
> ▸ "Read the word you made. Put your finger under the first letter. Make the sound. What's the last part? Put them together."

I reconvened the group saying, "Wow, Super Writers. Nice work using word-part power to write so many words!"

Restate the teaching point in transferable language.

"So now you see how rhyming words help you to spell other words. You started with the one magic word—*at*—and now you have a whole story about a rat that sat on a mat. If we had more time, we could write more about that fat rat. We could tell people that the cat saw that rat. That would make the story exciting, right? But for now, instead of writing more and more with the one magic word—*at*—I think you are ready for a second magic teeny-tiny word."

It is easier for kids to write words using phonogram cards and a whiteboard, rather than either medium alone. Using both the cards and the whiteboard helps to accentuate that the consonant is distinct from the word part.

Note that by asking children, "What's the last part of that word?" we are working to counteract the "sound it out" behavior that is the sole go-to strategy for many children when they are reading or writing a word. This prompt begins to develop phonological awareness by getting children to pay attention to the onset and rime in words and not just individual phonemes.

RUG TIME

Invite students to use their word-part power to write a sentence, this time making new words with the rime -*in*.

"This time, will you help each other use this word? Will you work without me to make this new word grow even more words?" The children nodded, solemnly. "For now, hold out your hands so I can give you your next magic word."

I distributed phonogram cards for the next word, *in*, to each partnership, saying, "Don't look at it. Just hold your hand around the word so we all look at the same time." After I'd given a word to each partnership, I called, "Okay, *look*!

"Yes, it's *in*. You and your partner can put *in* on your whiteboard just like you did with *at*," I wrote *in* on a large Post-it and put it on my whiteboard. "And you can use your word-part power to make lots of words. Remember, rhyming can help. Say words that rhyme with *in*. Say the sound of the first letter, then the *in* part! See what word you get! You can even try to make silly sentences like, 'The /p/-in. . .? Has a what? Is where?'" I tried to get them thinking, without taking their fun away.

"The pin has a fin!"
"The pin is in a bin."
"The tin got a win!"

"These are so fun and silly!

"After you and your partner have decided on a sentence, you can start writing it. The alphabet chart is up here if you need it."

SHARE • Interactive Writing to Support Word-Part Power

Engage writers in a quick interactive writing session in which they can practice using *-at* and *-in* to write words for a story similar to one that a child might write during writing workshop.

"Writers, is your word-part power activated? Will you test it out by seeing if you can help me write a story? I'm going to need your help with this story. It's about something bad that my cat did this morning. You got your word parts near?" I pointed to the large *at* and *in* Post-its on my whiteboard. "Let's get started.

"I want to write":

Today my cat ran to her cat bin. But. . .

"You've got to wait to hear the bad part. Can you help me write the start of this story? I'll say it again, and you hold up your power arm if I come to a place where your word-part power can help." I said the first few words of the story, and when I came to the word *cat* I waited to see if the kids picked up that *at* could help with *cat*. Some didn't notice, so I touched the word *at* to clue them in, and soon all the class was signaling. "Use your word-part power to write *cat*," I said, and wrote the start of the story, pretending to copy from their whiteboards for the word *cat*. I reread and elicited their help also with *bin*.

"You ready to write the bad part?" I asked. "It is sort of disgusting, but it is a true story." I repeated the start of the story and added on:

FIG. 6–1   Children think about what letter they could add to the word part *in* to make a new word.

Hopefully kids will grasp that you are referring to a litter box! It is hard to write decodable texts that make maximum sense to kids.

Today my cat ran to her cat bin. But she peed on the mat, not in the bin. "No, Cat! That is not your cat bin," I said.

I said aloud the words "But she peed. . . " and then when I came to *mat* I repeated the word, listening for the word parts in that word. I looked up, as if asking children whether they could use their word-part power to help with *mat*. "Say the word with me: *mat*. Does the word rhyme with *at* or *in*, because if it does, will you point to the word part on your board?" Many children pointed to the *at* and they wrote the word.

We continued in a similar vein.

"Writers, look at how word-part power helps us when we are in writing workshop! When you write, you might hear a word that rhymes with *at* or *in*, and you'll know how to spell it!"

EXTENSION 1 • Blending and Segmenting Onset-Rime

Engage students in a quick listening activity to support phonological awareness and blending.

"Super Readers, before you go home today, I want to make sure you keep your word-part powers strong. You know how some people lift weights to keep their power strong? Word-part power is a funny thing because the way you make it strong is by putting word parts together and taking word parts apart. Some people use a word-part power shake to do this. Watch."

I held out my fist with my thumb up and said "/r/." Then I stretched out my fingers to make my hand flat and said "/at/." I brought the hand and flat fingers together into a downward fist that signaled "Yeah!" or "Got this!" and as I did that, said, "Rat!"

I then did that again with *mat*:
   Fist, with just my thumb up: "/m/"
   Thumb still up but fingers on that hand now outstretched: "/at/"
   Hand and thumb clasped in a fist, which I jerk down toward my side: "mat!"

"Try the word-part power shake with me. Let's do this for *sat*."
   Fist, with thumb up: "/s/"
   Fingers outstretched: "/at/"
   Fist: "sat!"

I did this several more times, saying only the initial letter and the rime, leaving it to kids to blend these into the word. We did this action with *win*, *pin*, *fin*, *bat*, *cat*, and *hat*.

You'll notice that we begin this phonological awareness work with rimes that students are already familiar with. This phonological task, though it seems simple, is vital for the work students will do in the rest of this unit.

EXTENSION 2 • Hearing Word Parts during Writing Workshop

Remind students about using their word-part power with CVC words during writing workshop.

In the middle of writing workshop, I asked for writers' attention. "Writers, when you write today, you might just hear one of these magic word parts—and if so, think to yourself, 'I've got this!'

"If George wants to say his soccer team scored a big win, can you show me with your hands how George might break apart the word *win*?" I made a gesture to show that first he'd record /w/ and then /in/. "Then he can say, 'I've got this!'

"If you want to tell about how you went to the library and *sat* down to read a book, show me with your hands how you can break down that word *sat*. Thumb up for /s/ and other fingers out for /at/. Close your hand into a fist for *sat*." We tried that, and I said, "Yes, and then you can write it, right? You can say, 'I've got this!'"

I continued, doing similar work with other CVC words that the kids had worked with earlier. Then I said, "You want a harder one? What if you want to write about the cold *winter*? *Winter* has two beats. Can you use your word-part power to help spell *winter* so that you can write it?'

"Keep writing, and as you do, make sure to use your word-part power to help you!"

EXTENSION 3 • Generating Rhyming Words Using Familiar Word Parts

Hold a brainstorming session to see how many words students can make with the word parts *-at* and *-in*.

"Those word parts you worked with earlier are extra special because they can help you make words. Not just three words. Not just eight words. Not just thirteen words. No, they can help you make *so many* words. I bet they can help you make more words than there are kids in this class.

"Ready to test that idea with the word parts *-at* and *-in*? Everyone, stand up. Let's try *-at* first. When I point to you, say a word that has *-at* in it, and then sit down. Let's see if you can come up with more words than there are kids in this class. Here goes!" I pointed at the first student, continuing until all students had generated a word. When a student was stuck, I gave clues and encouraged their table groups to help them. "Try adding /h/," I coached one student.

When kids couldn't generate any more *-at* words, I switched students over to *-in* words, and the brainstorming continued.

"Wow! You came up with twenty-three *-at* and *-in* words. That's way more words than there are kids in this class. Those word parts sure are special!"

Making Words with More Vowel-Consonant Rimes

-it *and* -an

GETTING READY

✔ You'll need magnetic letters and a whiteboard to spell words ending in *it* and *an*.

✔ Provide each rug club, and then each partnership, with magnetic letter boards and the letters to spell words ending in *at*, *an*, *it*, and *in*.

✔ Prepare to add word cards for *an*, *man*, *ran*, *pan*, *fan*, *ban*, *it*, *sit*, *bit*, *fit*, *hit*, and *kit* to the snap word pocket chart.

✔ Make enough *at*, *an*, *it*, and *in* cards for each partnership.

✔ Prepare a sign that says *word* to replace *name* on the name wall to change it to a word wall.

PHONICS INSTRUCTION

Phonological Awareness
• Recognize and produce rhyming words.
• Blend and segment the onset and rime of single-syllable spoken words.
• Add or substitute individual sounds in simple, one-syllable words to make new words.

Phonics
• Use common word phonograms to generate new words (VC).

Word Knowledge/Solving
• Use familiar word parts including phonograms (-*at*, -*in*, -*it*, -*an*) to spell unfamiliar words.

IN THIS SESSION

TODAY YOU'LL teach students that they can use snap words they already know—*it* and *an*—to spell many more words while writing.

TODAY YOUR STUDENTS will use letter boards and word-part power to add new consonants to the front of four snap words they already know to make new words.

MINILESSON

CONNECTION

Remind students about the magic words—the rimes—they have learned to make words with, in preparation for teaching them that they can make words with snap words they already know.

"Super Readers and Super Writers, is your word-part power still fully activated? It is? Yes? That's good because word-part power can give you the power to read and write *lots* of words. It's kind of like magic.

"You did that already with *at*. Let's try that magic right now. Take *at*." I pretended to be holding the word card for *at* in my right hand. With my left hand, I pretended to add a letter to the front of *at*, saying, "Add /r/ to /at/ and you get *rat*!

"Let's take that /r/ away. We've got *at* again. Now. . .what should we add?" The kids called out letters and we added various initial sounds to the rime -*at*, doing all of this orally but with lots of gestures.

After a flash round of word making, I said, "These teeny-tiny magic words are making us into word-making machines. We can crank out so many words because we know just these two word parts."

✤ **Name the teaching point.**

"Today I want to teach you that there aren't just one or two magic words. There are actually a bunch of snap words that give writers word-part power. You can take those snap words and use them to make more and more words."

TEACHING AND ACTIVE ENGAGEMENT/LINK

Demonstrate making words with the rime -*it* and practice manipulating phonemes orally, then with magnetic letters, and finally by having students do this work themselves in rug clubs.

"During our last session we found that *at* and *in* are power words. With your word-part power, you can make them into a lot of other words. But there are some other words on our snap word pocket chart that are power words too. Try this one: *it*. Are you ready to do some word magic with *it*? We'll do this by talking, not writing. To start, say the word: *it*."

"It!"

"Add /s/ to *it* and you get. . . "

"Sit!" the kids called.

"Take away the /s/ in *sit* and you are back to. . .*it*. Now add /b/ and you have. . . "

"Bit!" the kids answered. After doing these examples orally, I introduced magnetic letters to this practice, placing the letters for *bit* on my whiteboard.

I nodded, "Take away the /b/ from *bit* and add an *f*. What do you get?" I demonstrated this with my magnetic letters.

"Fit."

"Now let's make the word *hit*. We'll take away the *f*," I said as I took away the letter, "but what letter do we need to add to make *hit*? Say *hit*. Which sound do you hear?"

"/H/!"

"Yes, let's put the letter that makes the /h/ sound in front of *it*. Now let's read it to check to see if it's *hit*."

FIG. 7–1   The teacher demonstrates how to make words with familiar snap words.

Today's teaching method is making words. The teacher starts off with quick phonemic manipulation practice—changing the /s/ to /b/ to make bit. *This is done without looking at print and gets kids warmed up for the manipulation that they'll be doing with their magnetic letters later. Sound work helps kids develop the problem-solving skills they will need to effectively manipulate letters for reading and writing unfamiliar words.*

I repeated this process one more time to ask kids to figure out how to make the word *kit*. "Now it's your turn to use magnetic letters. I'm going to give each rug club a magnetic board with some letters on it. In your club, give each member a number: 1, 2, 3, and 4.

"Rug Club Member #1, find the magnetic letters you need to make *it*.

"Rug Club Member #2, add an *s*. What do you have?

"Rug Club Member #3, take away the *s* and add a *b*, and you have. . .?

"Now, Rug Club Member #4, take away the *b* and add an *f*. What do you have?" We continued in that way through the same list of *-it* words that we'd worked with orally (*it*, *sit*, *bit*, *fit*, *hit*, *kit*), with each club member in turn taking away and adding new letters to make new words.

Ask kids to make another word—*an*—on their magnetic boards and do similar work with it, adding new consonants to the front of the word to make new words.

"Now you are going to use another snap word you already know to help you make more words. Look at the snap word pocket chart and find the word *an*. Rug Club Member #1, make the word *an* on your board. The letters need to be in the right order: *a* first, *n* last.

"We can use the word *an* to help us make more words. I bet we can use the word *an* to make the word *man*. Read the word *an*. Now say the word *man*. What part is the same? What part do you hear at the end of both words?"

"*An*!"

"Yes, now listen for the beginning sound in *man*. Rug Club Member #2, say that first sound, and then find the letter that makes that sound to make the word *man*. Get help from your club members." As children worked, I voiced over, "Remember, you are going to have three letters now!"

Meanwhile, I put together the letters to make the word *man* myself. "Check your word to see if it matches."

I coached the children to make *ran*, *pan*, *fan*, and *ban*.

"Wow! So much word-part power!"

I placed word cards in a pocket chart with the words that were made. "Let's read all of our words again, from the top. Eyes up here!" We read all the words again as I pointed under each one: *an*, *man*, *ran*, *pan*, *fan*, *ban*. "What part is the same in all of these words?" I repeated the same process with *-it*, placing the words that kids made into the snap word pocket chart: *sit*, *bit*, *fit*, *hit*, and *kit*.

It is very important that children are saying the words as they work. Children need to do both the phonemic work (saying the words, isolating the sounds and parts) and the phonics work (matching sound to letter) to be able to write. There should be a buzz in the room during word study (during writing workshop too) as children say words and sounds out loud to help them write.

Early in this work, you'll say the sound and the letter. That is strong scaffolding. In later examples, lighten the prompting to give children more of the work to do.

Restate the teaching point and link the work with words to students' work as writers.

"Wow! You are doing what all writers do when they want to write tricky words. You are using the words you know to help you write so many other words! Your word-part power is getting stronger!"

RUG TIME

Invite kids to use magnetic letters and word cards with the four snap words *at*, *an*, *it*, and *in* to attempt making new words on their own.

"Super Readers, you have been sharing magnetic boards with all the kids in your club. Thanks for such good sharing. Right now, I'm going to hand every partnership your own magnetic board—and to do that, I'm going to ask you to all go to your reading workshop seats, sitting with your partner. I'll pass out magnetic boards and some letters for each of you.

"Here is the challenge: will you see if you can take the letters and make some words of your own? I'll put some word cards on your table that can help you. Start with *at*."

I distributed word cards for *at*, *an*, *it*, and *in* to each partnership and coached children to start by using the first of those small words to make other words on their magnetic boards. As children worked, I voiced over.

"I wonder if you will use your word-part power to make another word out of *at*. Hmm,. . .what letter could you put in front of *at* to make another word?"

One child called out a letter, and I suggested others try it. "Is that a word, or is it just a crazy sound?" I asked. "Try another."

After a few minutes, I voiced over saying, "You might decide to stop working with *at* words and to try *in* or *it* words. You decide. You can use your word-part power!"

While students worked, I voiced over, "You're making so many words. Can I give you one tip? After you make a word, read it, and ask yourself, 'Is this a real word or a fake word?' For example, if I made this word," I put *zin* on my magnetic board, "I can read it using what I know. This word says *zin*. But I want to ask myself, 'Is this a real word or a fake word?' *Zin*, real word or fake word? Have I heard that word before? No! It's probably a fake word. Give your words this same check."

FIG. 7–2   The teacher displays the words made in a large pocket chart.

We encourage you to let kids have a go at this work. Remember that approximation is part of how we all learn.

Kids work will vary. Some will remake the words. Others will play around with the alphabet. Some will create their own words. Expect this variety and be ready to coach.

SHARE • Adding Snap Words to a Brand-New Word Wall

Exclaim your delight at how full the snap word pocket chart has become and propose a new solution: merge the name wall and the snap word pocket chart into a word wall.

"Super Writers, Super Readers, these four special snap words are really helping you. Read them with me: *at*, *it*, *an*, and *in*. You know, pretty soon, you'll have a *ton* of words you can read in a snap. The snap word pocket chart won't be able to hold them all. Before we know it, the chart will be stuffed full!

"I think we should do something about this before it becomes a problem, don't you? Good! We already have a space to hold all of our names. So far this year, our names have helped us learn so much about letters and sounds. We have also had our snap word collections." I walked over to the name wall and I carried our snap word pocket chart over too.

"We have been using this wall to hold our names, and now that our collection of snap words is starting to get so big, I think we could just put them all together and change this name wall into a word wall." I showed the class a sign that read *word*. "What do you all think?"

As kids smiled and said it was a great idea, I said, "I think this will be great too, because just like you use the name wall to help you so much during writing time, I know that you can learn to use the word wall to help you use snap words during writing and reading workshop.

"It's just missing one thing: your snap words. All the words from our snap word pocket chart need to go in the right places on the word wall. Will you help me? I'll hold up a word, and will you shout out which letter it goes under on the word wall?" I started with the four special snap words we'd used that day—*at*, *it*, *an*, and *in*—and then we added the others. Soon, all our snap words were on the word wall.

"This word wall will really help you read and write!"

At this point, you will no longer need a snap word pocket chart. There are so many high-frequency words that it's time for children to begin using the word wall as a tool for using and learning new words. All the words will be put on the word wall from the current snap word collection, and as new words are introduced, they, too, will be added to the word wall.

EXTENSION 1 • Children Learn Word Parts with Songs and Repetition

GETTING READY

- Familiarize yourself with "The Little Word Song."

Sing a song to remind students about all the words they can make with familiar word parts.

"Super Readers, there is a song that has a lot of do with word-part power. You sing it to the tune of 'The Wheels on the Bus Go 'Round and Round.' Listen to me sing a little, and then join in."

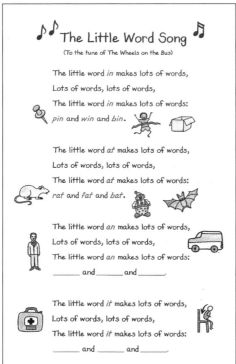

This text is one that could be used for a warm-up to shared reading on other days and eventually put in readers' book bags for independent reading.

We sang with all four of our teeny-tiny words as rimes, repeating each verse several times as more kids sang the last lines of a stanza, and as the class thought of yet new words for those last lines.

EXTENSION 2 • Focus on Rhyming Words by Singing "Down by the Bay"

GETTING READY

- Familiarize yourself with the song, "Down by the Bay."

Give children extra practice with rhymes by singing a familiar rhyming song.

"Have any of you heard the song 'Down by the Bay'? If you haven't, you're in for a real treat! If you know it, sing along with me."

I continued singing the song, substituting in new rhymes using words with word parts we would use throughout the unit. When the kids got the hang of it, I let my voice drop off at the end, so they could fill in the rhyme for me.

Down by the Bay

Down by the bay

Where the watermelons grow

Back to my home

I dare not go

For if I do

My mother will say

Did you ever see a cat wearing a hat?

Down by the bay!

Other rhymes to use:

- Did you ever see a bat get really really fat?

- Did you ever see a man wearing a pan?

- Did you ever see a pin with a really big chin?

EXTENSION 3 • Using the Vowel Chart to Help You Write

GETTING READY

- Students will need their vowel charts.

Remind students that the vowel chart can help them, not only during phonics time, but also during writing workshop.

"Writers, during writing workshop, you all got a chart to help you write words that are easier to read." I held up the vowel chart. "This chart can really help you to remember that every word needs at least one vowel. Now, you have two ways to get more vowels in your words: word parts and the vowel chart. Sometimes you are writing a word and you can't hear a word part that you know.

"Like the other day, Quinn was writing the word *wrestle* because she was talking about what she likes to do with her brother. She tried using her word-part power to hear a word part she knew, but she couldn't. But, she knew that her word needed a vowel, so then she went to the vowel chart and stretched out the key picture on the chart. Like this, /aaaaaa/pple, wr/eeeeee/stle. She wasn't sure, so then she did the letter *e*: /eeeeeegg/, wr/eeeeee/stle. She decided that the *e* in *egg* sounded right and she wrote it in her word.

"Remember that you have two ways now to get vowels in your words: the vowel chart and the word parts that you have been learning."

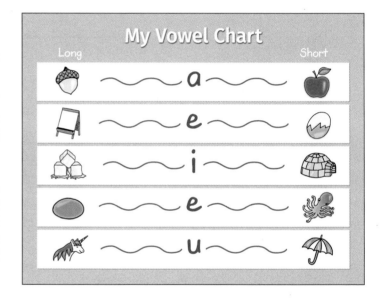

Learning to Hear Rimes in Words

IN THIS SESSION

TODAY YOU'LL teach students that they can develop their word-part power by strengthening their ear muscles and listening for rimes.

TODAY YOUR STUDENTS will use picture cards to sort words into categories based on the end part.

MINILESSON

CONNECTION

Focus kids' attention on today's work by making a comparison between exercising and reading to get strong muscles.

"Do you know any adults who go to the gym or work out at home? They lift weights and do push-ups and do stomach crunches. Why do they do that? To get stronger muscles! Well, you know what? Kids who want to become Super Readers and Super Writers need to work on their muscles, too!"

❖ **Name the teaching point.**

"Today I want to teach you that to have word-part power you need to have strong *ear* muscles. Really! It takes strong ears to hear that *cat* and *mat* both have the same word part: *at*. So, it is really important that you get stronger ear muscles."

GETTING READY

✔ Cue audio clips of everyday sounds, such as a dog barking, a siren, a doorbell, a train whistle, a slamming door, a crying baby, a cow mooing. Links to these sounds are available in the online resources.

✔ Display the picture cards for *rat*, *pin*, *cat*, *fin*, *bat*, *hat*, *chin*, and *win*.

✔ Display the picture cards for *kit*, *sit*, *bit*, *pit*, *hit*, *fan*, *man*, *ran*, *can*, and *van* and distribute one set of these cards to each partnership.

PHONICS INSTRUCTION

Phonological Awareness
- Recognize and produce rhyming words.
- Blend and segment the onset and rime of single-syllable spoken words.
- Add or substitute individual sounds in simple, one-syllable words to make new words.

Word Knowledge/Solving
- Use common phonograms to read new words (VC).

TEACHING

Explain that readers listen to small sounds to develop strong ear muscles, and have kids identify sounds from daily life, then have kids determine which picture cards feature words ending in -at.

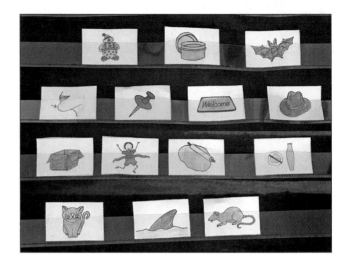

FIG. 8–1 Picture cards of words with the -in and -at word parts are displayed for children to practice using their ear muscles to hear the difference between the words.

"You know who already has strong ear muscles?" I reached behind me and pulled out our stuffed elephant mascot. The children all shouted, "Mabel!" I scrutinized her ears, and said, "Whoa! Those *are* some ear muscles! Look how big they are!

"Over the next few days, you are going to get stronger ear muscles, too. But you don't have to go to the gym to get those muscles—you can get stronger ear muscles right here, in this classroom.

"To get ear muscles that are strong enough to hear that *hit* and *bit* both have *it* in them, you first need to be able to hear and think about even tiny little sounds from the real world. I'll play some sounds, and you listen and try to name the sound you hear. Ready?" I played an audio clip of a dog barking, and then an assortment of other sounds—a siren, a doorbell, a slamming door, a crying baby, a cow mooing, roosters crowing. After each sound, kids called out what they heard.

"How do your ears feel? Bigger? Stronger? Are you now ready to use your ear muscles to hear the different sounds in words?" I put several picture cards of -at and -in words on the easel. "Will you use your ear muscles to hear which of these words have the word part -at in them?

"Sometimes it is hard to know what these pictures are meant to show," I said, "so let me quickly tell you what they are. Then you and your partner say each word and give a thumbs up if the word has *at* in it, and thumbs down if it doesn't."

I showed kids the picture cards, naming what each card showed—*rat*, *pin*, *cat*, *fin*, *bat*, *hat*, *chin*, and *win*—and then we worked on one or two of them together. "Let's say this together," I said, pointing to the picture of the rat. I led the class in this, using the word-part shake to make the sound-segmenting work more concrete.

As they said /r/ and then /at/, I put my thumb up for the initial sound, the rest of my fingers out flat for the rime, and then brought all of my fingers into a fist as I blended the parts into a whole word. "Does *rat* have *at* in it? Yes!" We then tried *pin*, and found that no, it didn't have *at*.

ACTIVE ENGAGEMENT/LINK

Encourage partners to review several picture cards of words ending in -at and -in. Have them give a thumbs up when they find words that end with -at.

"Will you continue on your own, with your partner? Look at the other cards on the easel, then say each word and give it a thumbs up if it has -at in it, or a thumbs down if it doesn't." Students tested the words and determined whether they contained -at.

Many of your students might continue to listen for words that begin or end with the same sound. This is to be expected, because up until this point in the year, we have focused on initial and final sound. Continue to emphasize the difference between words that end the same way and words that rhyme. Including more rhyming texts will help children learn this concept.

RUG TIME

Challenge partners to repeat this process with picture cards ending with *-it* and *-an*, giving a thumbs up when they find words that end in *it*.

"Oh my gosh, you are so good at this, I think you could handle another. Are you ready to try doing this with another whole set of words?" The kids signaled they were ready and I displayed a new set of picture cards for *kit*, *sit*, *bit*, *pit*, *hit*, *fan*, *man*, *ran*, *can*, and *van*. "Let's read through the pictures." We did this to make sure every child knew what word each picture represented.

"This time, will you read these picture cards and listen for which one of these has *it* in it? Let me again help you know what the cards show. We can read them all together once, and then I'll give a set of picture cards to you and your partner, and you both can read them again and give them a thumbs up if they contain *it* and a thumbs down if they don't."

I read through all the picture cards and then said, "Remember, we're looking for words that end with *it*. That means they rhyme with the word *sit*.

"How about *kit*? /K/-/it/. /It/ like *kit*! Yes, thumbs up! Look at the next pictures with your partner. Give a thumbs up if it ends in *it* and a thumbs down if it doesn't."

"Make one pile of words that rhyme with *it* and one pile of words that rhyme with *an*." I came around and coached partnerships as students worked to say each word and listen if the word rhymed with *it* or *an*.

I took note of students who seemed to have a harder time with this, so that I could follow up and offer more additional support in subsequent days.

FIG. 8–2 The teacher coaches students as they work to sort words that have the *-it* part at the end and those that do not.

POSSIBLE COACHING MOVES

▶ "Say the word slowly: /f/—thumb up, /an/—fingers out."

▶ "Does /b/-/it/ sound the same at the end as /f/-/an/?"

▶ "Reread all the words in your pile and double-check that they rhyme with *sit*."

▶ "Listen for the part at the end."

SHARE • Using Rhymes and Rimes to Make Poems

Provide kids with more practice in hearing the sounds in word parts by listening for rhymes in familiar (and less familiar) poems.

"Super Writers, your ear muscles are definitely getting stronger. You are getting better at hearing the sounds in word parts, and you need to be able to hear those sounds to use word-part power. Do you remember that earlier, I told you that rhyming is not just a fun thing for kids to do? It is actually a really important part of spelling, of writing words. I told you that rhyming gives you word-part power.

"When you ask yourself, 'Which of these words end with *-at*?' you are really asking 'Which of these words rhyme?' Listen as I say a little poem, and every time I say a word that rhymes, will you give me a thumbs up?" I recited "Twinkle, Twinkle, Little Star."

"You really could hear the rhymes in that song. Now I'm going to give you three minutes. Work with your rug club to see if you can take all the -an pictures you just sorted and make your own rhyming poem with the words *fan*, *man*, *can*, *ran*, and *van*.

"When you say your poem, the rest of us will give you a thumbs up every time we hear you say rhyming words." I gave clubs a few moments to create their poems and then share them with the class.

"Great work, Super Writers. Your ear muscles are getting stronger by the minute. If you keep practicing, you'll be able to hear even the trickiest sounds in any word! That's going to help you so much when you are writing words. You can use your ear muscles to help and then write using word parts."

EXTENSION 1 • Blending Onset and Rime with a Clip from *Sesame Street*

GETTING READY

- Cue a one-minute video clip from *Sesame Street*. A link to this clip is available in the online resources.
- Have cards to display on your easel: *sad*, *m*, *b*, *ad*.
- Have your phone ready to video your kids.

Reinforce kids' learning about blending onsets and rimes using a clip from *Sesame Street*.

I started a video from *Sesame Street* featuring the two-headed monster. Once the monster appeared on the screen, I paused. "Oh, it's the two-headed monster! This two-headed monster knows how to push the first sound in a word together with the other sounds. He's got word-part power. Watch!" I then played the one-minute video.

"Didn't you love how they used their word-part power to make and then understand a word? I loved how after the monster made the word *sad*, he thought about the meaning and that made him cry." I placed the word *sad* on the easel, so kids would have support when they tried to blend the next words on their own.

"It was so fun to watch those monsters that I thought you could try being two-headed monsters, right now. Maybe I could even make a video of you doing this monster word-part power work." I took out my phone to capture their monster work.

"I already thought of a word that we could use. Let's try this one." I put an *m* card on the easel and left a big space before I placed a card with *ad* written on it.

"Right now, with the person next to you, would you put your heads together, super-close and carefully? Ahhh, now I see a bunch of two-headed monsters."

I then touched the *m* and had kids says the sound, and then touched the *ad* card and had kids say that part. As we did this again and again, I moved the cards together to signal the blending we were doing to read a word.

When the kids finally called out "*mad*," I prompted, "Don't forget to think about what that word means and then act it out like the monster did." My classroom full of angry monsters blustered on the carpet. I then told them we should do it again—this time, with cards reading *b* and *ad*—and I would video them. They were excited to see a video clip of themselves later.

EXTENSION 2 • Reading Words without Pictures

GETTING READY

• Provide each partnership with a small set of word-only cards. Each set should have words with the same ending, either *-in*, *-at*, or *-it*. They will also need a set of matching picture cards.

Challenge readers to match words on their own, without pictures, then ask them to match those words with the pictures that represent them.

"Super Readers, you were so good today at figuring out which of our picture-cards had the *at* sound or the *it* sound that I think you can actually read those words *without pictures*. We have mostly been reading words that have pictures that go with them, but I was thinking that maybe, just maybe, you and your partner have enough word-part power that you could try reading some of these words.

"So, I have here a whole bunch of words that have the word part *-in*. Are there some partners who think you could try reading these words? If you can read some of them, maybe you could put the word and the picture that goes with it together. Let's try it. See this word? Remember, it has the word part *-in*. Can you try to read it? *P-in*! Now, which picture goes with it? Yes, this one, so we can put them in a little pile.

"Do I have some partners who are willing to try this with *-in* words and pictures? Great. How about with *-at* words and pictures?" I'd soon distributed all the word cards and pictures.

After children did this, I suggested that partners work with the others in their rug club, checking to see if they agreed with the matches they had made using their set of word and picture cards.

According to Bradley and Bryant (Bradley and Bryant 1985; Kirtley et al. 1989), before one can expect children to use the "rime" in a word to unlock a new word, they must be able to strip off the onset and tell you what is left. While this lesson mostly involves blending of onset-rime, you might consider teaching this skill to children who are beginning to read more conventionally. This work will be done in Bend III of this unit to help kids learn to use parts of words to read other words.

EXTENSION 3 • A Rhyming Story

Reinforce students' learning about rhymes with a playful rhyming story.

"I have a little story to tell you. It's a rhyming story. See if you can help me fill in the rhyming words.

"Yesterday I went to the *park*.
We had to play fast before it got. . . "

I paused for a second, encouraging students to shout out the word if they knew it. "*Dark*!"

I continued on, "I was having fun on the *swing*.
And then I heard my phone. . . "

The students shouted "*Ring*!" We continued with the rest. At each rhyme, I left a space for kids to fill in.

"It was my *dad*.
He sounded . . . " (*mad*)

"I picked up my pack,
I didn't want to go . . . " (*back*)

Bye park, I *said*.
And went home to . . . (*bed*)

Mix and Make

Making Words with -at, -an, -it, *and* -in

IN THIS SESSION

TODAY YOU'LL teach students that they can put parts of words together to make new words, especially testing combinations of snap words and letters to see which words they can make.

TODAY YOUR STUDENTS will use their word-part power to make as many new words as they can. In rug clubs, they'll combine familiar word parts: -*an*, -*at*, -*it*, and -*in*, with consonants that they know well, making and recording as many real words as they can.

MINILESSON

CONNECTION

Share familiar examples about learning, emphasizing that when you first learn to do something, you do it over and over. Connect this to the way students learned and practiced using word parts.

"Writers, when you first learn something, you do it over and over, again and again—the same thing. Like when you first learned to jump rope, you probably did that over and over and over." I acted it out: jump, jump, jump.

"But as you get better, you can switch things around. You can do one trick, then a different one, then another." I used my hands to show how jump ropers add new twists, like crossing their arms while jump roping.

"The same goes with learning to make words. At first, you learned that you can make a lot of words from the word *at*. You added one letter to *at* and made *cat*, you added a different letter to *at* and made *mat*. You added yet another letter to *at* and made *rat*, and it went on and on.

GETTING READY

✔ Display *at*, *it*, *in*, and *an* phonogram cards on the right side of the pocket chart. Display consonant cards *s, f, m, r, c, w, b,* and *p* on the left side of the pocket chart.

✔ Choose two rug clubs to be in a giant club in a fishbowl and give one club a whiteboard. Give one club a set of consonant cards (*s, f, m, r, c, w, b,* and *p*) and give the other club a set of rime cards (-*an*, -*at*, -*it*, and -*in*).

✔ Pair up all rug clubs to make giant clubs (groups of eight). Give each giant club one whiteboard and one marker, and give a set of consonant cards (*s, f, m, r, c, w, b,* and *p*) to one club and a set of rime cards (-*an*, -*at*, -*it*, and -*in*) to the other.

✔ Make sure each child has a whiteboard and a marker.

PHONICS INSTRUCTION

Phonological Awareness
• Blend and segment the onset and rime of single-syllable spoken words.
• Add or substitute individual sounds in simple, one-syllable words to make new words.

Phonics
• Use common phonograms to generate new words (VC).

Word Knowledge/Solving
• Use familiar word parts including phonograms (-*at*, -*in*, -*it*, -*an*) to read and spell unfamiliar words.

High-Frequency Words
• Write high-frequency words in continuous text.

"Then you did the same with *in*. You added one letter and made *pin*, you added a different letter to *in* and made *fin*, and you added yet another letter to *in* and made *bin*, and on and on.

"That's how learning goes. You learn something once, and then you do it over and over and over—and over again.

"But as you get older and more skilled, and as your ears and your word-part power get stronger, you learn you don't have to do just the one thing you've been taught to do. You can invent new things—you can take some risks and try some things out!"

♣ **Name the teaching point.**

"Today I want to teach you that when you have word-part power, you try putting letters and parts of words together, even without knowing if they will make a word. You explore to see what new words you can make."

TEACHING

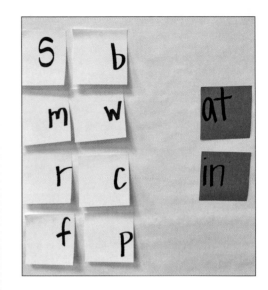

Demonstrate how to use the word parts *-at* and *-in* and a few letters to make a variety of words.

"Friends," I said, and waited for the kids' attention. "Today the thing I need you to realize is that you don't need me! You can take a word part, and you can try all on your own to make some new words with it. You did a little bit of this the other day with your partners in club time. Sometimes when you stick things together, presto! You'll have made a new word. Sometimes, you'll have a nice-sounding thing—like, say, *vin*—but it won't mean anything! But the point is, you have to try.

"So here are two snap words that can give you tons of word power." I pointed to the right side of the pocket chart. "Let's read these: *at*, *in*.

"And beside those, I've listed some of the consonants." I pointed to a list of consonants on the left side of the pocket chart: *s*, *f*, *m*, *r*, *c*, *w*, *b*, *p*.

"What I want you to know is that you can take a word part," and I took the *at* card and moved it toward the center of the page, " . . .and you can take a letter, a consonant, and put them together." I moved the *s* card next to the *at*.

"Let me put these two together and see what I get." I put my finger under the *s* and blended the /s/ with the /at/. "Sat!"

"Now let's invite some friends up to do this work." Children came up to the easel and they chose letters (*f* and *m*) and combined those with the *-at* word part. "Do they make a word?" I asked.

ACTIVE ENGAGEMENT/LINK

Set up two clubs to mix and make words using the letters *s, f, m, r, c, w, b*, and *p*, and the word parts *-an* and *-it* in a fishbowl. Coach the kids making words, as well as the observers.

"Do you all want to play so we can make lots more words?"

"Yes!!"

"Super Writers, will you first get into your rug club?" They did this. "Now watch as two clubs try this out." I distributed cards with the consonants *s, f, m, r, c, w, b*, and *p* to the members of one club. Then I distributed cards with the rimes *-an* and *-it* to the members of the second club. "Stand up," I said to the two clubs of four. The children stood at the front of the room.

"Look at what your card says," I said, "and each one of you, hold up your card and when I point to you, make the sound that your card makes." The four students with consonants made their sounds, one by one, and the four students with rimes read their part.

"Now what, Super Readers and Writers? What can these kids do with their cards?"

The children called out that the kids could make words, and I nodded. "Show us how," I said, and soon a child had engineered things so one club member with a consonant stood arm in arm with a club member with a rime. We all read the word they'd made.

"I'm going to ask these kids to sit back down, this time in a giant club of eight, and ask them to continue trying to make words. Club of eight, I'm going to give you a whiteboard and marker, so that if you make a word, you can write it on your board.

"The rest of us will watch as this club of eight works," I said, "and we might even help." I arranged the one club of eight to function as a fishbowl, with the rest of the students standing in a circle around the central circle, watching. I voiced over as the central club worked, sometimes saying to the outer ring, "Whisper to someone near you what you think she is about to do," or, "Is that a real word or a fake word? Whisper to someone near you."

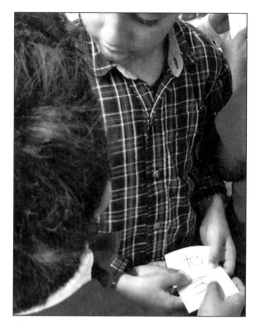

FIG. 9–1 Two children work together to make the word *pin* using their letter and word part cards.

POSSIBLE COACHING MOVES

▶ "Put the letter first, then the part."

▶ "What's the first sound? What's this word (snap word)? Put them together."

▶ "Read the word. Is it a real word?"

▶ "Don't forget to write your word on the whiteboard so you can remember what you made."

▶ "Mix it up and make another word!"

RUG TIME CLUBS

Invite the observing children now to make words themselves with consonants and rimes, while the original fishbowl kids make words with consonants and a new set of rimes.

After watching another club do this work for a bit, the observing children couldn't stand on the sidelines any longer. I invited them to join in the work by saying, "I'm thinking we should *all* do this, right?

"Go back to your rug spots, sit with your own rug club, and I'm going to give everyone a letter or a word part. I'm going to challenge you by giving you four word parts to work with: *-an*, *-at*, *-it*, and *-in*. How many real words can you make?" I paired up the other rug clubs and distributed the consonant cards for *s*, *f*, *m*, *r*, *c*, *w*, *b*, and *p* to one club in each pair, and the *-an*, *-at*, *-it*, and *-in* rime cards to the other club and channeled them to start making words. I gave one child from the two groups a whiteboard and marker and said, "Every time you make a new word, make sure you write it on your whiteboard so that you can save it for our share today."

SHARE • Ways of Writing Words: By Sight, Sound, and Word Part

Channel students to reread all of the words they wrote, then give kids practice in writing a sentence using snap word power, sound power, and word-part power.

"Super Writers, whoever has your whiteboard full of words, will you point under each word while your group reads the word? See if you can read all the words you have written."

FIG. 9–2 Children write a sentence on their whiteboards using what they know about spelling words—by sight, sound, and part.

The kids did that. I then gave each child a whiteboard and a marker. "Let's pretend we are in writing workshop, and we want to write a sentence. We now have three different ways to write words. We can use snap word power, sound power, and word-part power! If you wanted to write to tell the story of when you lost a tooth, you might want to say 'I bit my cookie. My tooth was in my hand!' Right now, write 'I bit my. . .'

"Oh, I hear a word part in *bit*: *-it*." I pointed to the word wall to remind them of *it*. "If we know *it*, we can write *bit*. Think about what sound you hear at the beginning of *bit*." As the kids worked, I reminded them that *my* is a word they know in a snap. "If you forgot it, look at our snap words on the word wall, take a mental picture—'click!'—and then write it and check it." Then I said, "Now you need to add the word *cookie*. Use your sound power to write it as best you can. Reread your sentence now and be sure to use pointer power to help.

"Make space for more words." I then said, "Try writing this: *My tooth was in my hand*." I prompted kids to use their writing powers.

"We need to stop now, but Super Writers, your work during writing time will never be the same again, will it? Tell each other about how you will use your super powers during writing time."

EXTENSION 1 • Shared Reading of *The Cat in the Hat*

- Project a copy of *The Cat in the Hat* for all students to see.

Encourage students to draw on all their powers to read a few pages from a favorite Dr. Seuss book.

"Super Readers, today we worked just with word parts, but to really get word power, you don't just read and write with word-part power. You also use pointer power."

I placed *The Cat in the Hat* under the document camera and the volume in the class rose in an instant. Shouts of, "I know that movie!" and "My preschool teacher read me that book!" created an excited buzz around the rug.

"Super Readers, a lot of you know this book, don't you? Yeah, this is a good one and it is going to take a lot of word-part power for us to read it. It's a good thing we worked on that power in phonics workshop today!

"But readers, to be a *super* reader, you can't just focus on one power at a time. You have to use all the powers you have!

"In reading workshop, you learned about your pointer power and your reread power. Let's use those powers and word-part power together to read a few pages in *The Cat in the Hat*."

We read the first few pages of the book together, carefully pointing to each word, and rereading each sentence to better hear the rhyme and rhythm of the book.

EXTENSION 2 • Practicing Phonemic Blending and Manipulation with a Familiar Song

Sing a familiar song with new words, giving kids a chance to practice the phonemic blending and manipulation they'll need to transfer their knowledge of letters and word parts to their writing.

"Super Writers, let's sing a song that can help us when we want to read and write words with these special end parts. It goes like this. Join in when you are ready." I sang "The Add and Change Song," to the tune of "If You're Happy and You Know It," with kids joining in.

The Add and Change Song
(to the tune of IF You're Happy and You Know It)

If you add an /m/ to /at/ the word is *mat*.
If you add an /m/ to /at/ the word is *mat*. [Welcome]
If you add an /m/ to /at/ the word we made is *mat*.
If you add an /m/ to /at/ the word is *mat*.

If you change the /m/ to /s/ the word is *sat*.
If you change the /m/ to /s/ the word is *sat*.
If you change the /m/ to /s/ the word we made is *sat*.
If you change the /m/ to /s/ the word is *sat*.

If you change the /__/ to /__/ the word is __at.
If you change the /__/ to /__/ the word is __at.
If you change the /__/ to /__/ the word we made is __at.
If you change the /__/ to /__/ the word is __at.

b   c   f   h   p

This add and change song, like phonological awareness songs, is sung without attending to print at first. In the future it might be used as a shared reading.

GETTING READY

- Gather a stack of consonant cards and phonogram cards to distribute to partnerships. Organize the deck to make sure each partnership can make a word with their cards.

Channel partners to make words with onsets and rimes before lining up to leave the classroom, and reward their efforts with a playful gesture.

Just before the class needed to line up for P.E., I grabbed a stack of consonant cards and phonogram cards.

"Super Readers," I said, "I'm going to give you and your partner a consonant or a word part. See if you and your partner can make a word. If you can, line up for P.E. If not, stay here, and I'll hand you another word part."

I handed consonant cards and word-part cards to every partnership. Right away, many partnerships figured out their word. "Go ahead. Line up if you've got a word. Stay here if you need a different word part."

Once every partnership had made a word and lined up, I joined them at the front of the line and asked them to go ahead to the first corner of the hallway. As children passed by me on their way into the hall, I pretended to be the tollbooth. "Pay me with your word!" I said.

Reading Words Letter-by-Part Instead of One Letter at a Time

IN THIS SESSION

TODAY YOU'LL teach students that readers can use their knowledge of word parts to help them read words they don't recognize.

TODAY YOUR STUDENTS will read a text with words containing the parts *-an*, *-at*, *-in*, and *-it* and write sentences using the snap words they already know.

MINILESSON

CONNECTION

Remind students of the work they did in the previous session and of their real purpose in learning everything they have learned so far—to help them read.

"If someone had come into our class during our previous phonics time, they would have seen you shuffling word cards, and they might have thought it was some kind of game. Let's make sure that if a visitor comes to our classroom today, they can take one quick look and know what we're *really* doing. Let's make sure they know that the reason we learn about letters and sounds, the reason we get powers like pointer power and word-part power, is all because we are dying to read. So, let's read, right?"

❖ **Name the teaching point.**

"Today I want to teach you that when you are reading, you can use all of your powers—picture power, pointer power, and word-part power—to read. Your word-part power is especially helpful when you come to a word that you can't easily figure out."

GETTING READY

✔ Display an enlarged version of the book *My Win*, a shared reading text with words containing the parts *-an*, *-at*, *-it*.

✔ Distribute a copy of *My Win* to each rug club.

✔ Set up a pocket chart that will become the word-part chart, and prepare to add the *-at*, *-an*, *-in*, and *-it* phonogram cards to it.

✔ A whiteboard and marker for each student.

PHONICS INSTRUCTION

Word Knowledge/Solving
• Use familiar word parts including phonograms (*-at*, *-in*, *-it*, *-an*) to read and spell unfamiliar words.

High-Frequency Words
• Write high-frequency words in continuous text.

TEACHING

Unveil a book that was left for the class and tell students they can use all of their powers—picture power, pointer power, and especially word-part power—to read it.

"Friends, when I came in this morning, I saw that someone had left a book on my chair. Was it the Book Fairy? She's sort of like the tooth fairy, but she leaves books on your chair instead of money under your pillow. Maybe Mabel left us this book? I'm not sure.

"In any case, I thought that because you all have been working on your reading super powers, maybe instead of *me* reading this book *to* you, you could read it to me and to Mabel. Would you like to give it a try?"

The class nodded, and I reminded them to draw on all their powers. "You have picture power, and you have pointer power. Chances are good you'll also need your word-part power too. Is your word-part power ready and activated?" The kids signaled yes.

Using an enlarged version of the book, model how you combine powers to read the text. Emphasize how using word-part power helps you to read tricky words.

I pointed to the cover of the book. "What do you see on the cover?"

We looked at it and saw a picture of Mabel. "Oh my gosh! It's a picture of Mabel! What might this book be about? She has a necklace on, doesn't she? It's not her name necklace, though—it's a different necklace. What do you think it is?"

Some kids guessed it was a ribbon she'd won. Weighing that idea, I said, "Well, let's read it and find out." We got started by reading the title: *My Win*, by Mabel. "Oh, it looks like Mabel wrote this! Can you believe it? She is a writer like we are!

"Oh, I think you might be right about that necklace. It sounds like the necklace is actually a medal that Mabel won."

I paused. "Let's look at the word *win*. I see a word part that I know. Did some of you see that too? If you don't know the word *win*, you can look at the part you do know," and I pointed to the *in*. "Then you put the first letter together with the word part: /w/ + *in* = *win*." I used my hand to reinforce this, popping up my thumb for /w/, extending my fingers for /in/, and making a fist by my side for *win*.

I turned to the first page of the book and began to read. "Remember you're following along with the pointer. Read with me if you can!" I stopped once I reached the second word. "Looks like I'm stuck. I bet my word-part power can help me here! Let me look for a part I know. . .I know *an*!" I ran my finger under the *an*. "Now I need to blend the /r/. . ./r/ with the /an/. The word must be *ran*! *I ran*."

When you ask students, "What do you see on the cover?" you're inviting them to think along with you—a common move in shared reading. You are modeling for students the kinds of questions that you'll want them to ask themselves when they read their own books independently.

Teachers, you may recognize this work of reading a word as reading "letter-by-word part." Many of your students won't yet be able to use this strategy in their own reading. At this point, most of your students are probably reading their own books by looking at the first sound and using the picture to figure out a word. For now, your instruction in word parts in phonics workshop marches ahead of most of your kids' independent reading.

My Win

I ran.

①

The cat ran.

②

We ran and ran.

③

"I win,"
said Mabel.

④

"I am so fit."
"I am hot too!"

⑤

"Sit with a fan,"
said the cat.

⑥

We sat and sat.

⑦

ACTIVE ENGAGEMENT/LINK

Challenge students in rug clubs to finish reading the book about Mabel and remind them to use their word-part power to figure out any tricky words they encounter.

"Wow. That was good work! Do you want to try reading this without me? I'll give each rug club a copy of Mabel's book, and you can try reading this in your rug clubs. One person points, and then will every reader read with the pointer?" I distributed a copy of the book to each rug club and encouraged them to read and reread the book.

"I see so many of you trying out this work. Remember, you can can use all of your powers—pointer power, picture power, and word-part power—to read. Your word-part power is especially helpful when you come to a word that you can't easily figure out."

RUG TIME • Writing Sentences through Dictation

Introduce students to a sentence they will write through dictation. Coach them as they write the first word, and then channel rug clubs to check each other's words to make sure they are correct.

"I looked through your writing last night and found some sentences that can help us think about using word parts when we write. I thought we might all write one of these interesting sentences.

"Here's our first sentence. One child was writing about when he beat his older sister at basketball and wrote, *I win the game*. Say it with me: 'I win the game.'" I pointed to where the words would go on the page, one space for each word. "Okay, so we're going to write the sentence: *I win the game*. Draw a super-quick picture that matches this sentence." I gave students a few moments to do that.

"Let's write the first word: *I*. Caps off your markers!" While students worked, I voiced over. "*I* is a snap word. Take a peek at the word wall if you need to, then write it in a snap." Then I said, "Check your whiteboards with your rug club! Make sure *I* is correct. Make sure your letter is a capital because it's the first word in the sentence and *I* is always capital when it is by itself as a word. Change it if you need to."

Coach students as they write the remaining words in the sentence.

"Our sentence is 'I win the game.' Keep the word *I* on your board. Don't erase it. Next, you're going to write *win*. It's a word with a part at the end that we know." Kids called out, "In!" "Yes, try it." I coached while students wrote the remainder of the sentence. Once students had written each word, I asked them to first check the word with their rug clubs, then I revealed it on the whiteboard and urged them to check it again.

I accepted *gm* as the spelling for the word *game* because this is where most writers were in their spelling development, but I prompted them to hear the middle sound to encourage the vowel. For writers who recorded only *g*, I nudged them to say the word and hear more sounds. For students who wrote a letter other than *g*, I made a note of needing to do some additional letter-sound correspondence work with those writers.

FIG. 10–1   Children listen as the teacher prompts them to write the second word in the sentence, using what they know about word parts.

"Let's reread our sentence using picture power, pointer power, and word-part power. *I win the game*."

SHARE • Building a Part Chart

Begin to build a part chart that will be added to and referenced throughout the rest of the unit.

I called everyone over to a new chart I made using the pocket chart that once housed the collection of snap words. "What's that?" asked the children. "It's our word-part chart!" I answered. "Let's bring this part of our phonics unit to a close by adding our new word parts to the chart. This way, when you are reading or writing, you can use it to read or write new words. What are the parts we learned this week?"

Children started pointing to the word wall. "Yes, we learned that some of our snap words are word parts. There are two under *A*. What's the first one? That's right, it's *-an*!" I added *-an* and the picture of *ran* to the chart. "Yes, *-an* is a part found in many words like *ran*." I continued with the other three parts, *-at*, *-in*, and *-it*.

You can build this word-part chart using picture cards and phonogram cards so that you can refer to it and build it throughout the rest of this unit and beyond. Other word parts will be added in Bend III.

FIG. 10–2   The teacher builds the word-part chart with the children that will then be on display as a resource for future lessons in phonics, reading, and writing workshop.

BEND III — Word Parts, Snap Words, and Digraphs—Yee-haw!

Dear Teachers,

The last bend in this unit begins with the introduction of a new tool—the letter lasso. After reminding students of the tools that superheroes draw on to solve problems and save the day, you'll show a picture of a special superhero, Word Wonder. "She uses a lasso," you'll say, "but she doesn't use it to capture villains; she uses it to capture word parts!" Then, you'll introduce the letter lasso's special ability. It can lasso up two letters and turn those letters into a word part.

The letter lasso might just be a pipe cleaner, but your enthusiasm will get your students excited about using it in powerful ways. The ability to take a word apart by breaking it into its onset and rime is a prerequisite for the work your students will do in the future using a known word, such as *top* to read an unknown word such as *stopped* or *topple* or even *crop*. By engaging students in this work, you'll help them to see patterns among unknown words.

You'll teach students that they don't have to sit around and wait for you to give them a new word part. Instead, they can use their lassos to round up additional word parts on their own. As the bend progresses, your kids will use their word-part power and their letter lasso to round up five more of the most common phonograms (*-ip*, *-op*, *-ot*, *-ug*, and *-un*). These new word parts will help your students to read and write more and more words.

You'll recruit students to help you turn the rest of the alphabet chart into a part chart. For example, instead of using a *jump rope* in the J box, you'll replace it with *jug*, so that the *-ug* word part has a space. Combining the alphabet chart and the part chart helps to bring together the important work your kids have done across the first three units of kindergarten.

This bend also introduces students to the three most common digraphs: *sh*, *th*, and *ch*. In Session 15, you'll teach students about digraphs, helping them understand that digraphs are two consonants that go together to make one new sound, one that's different from either of the letters that make up the digraph. Learning digraphs will help expand your students' understanding of what can be an onset in a word. Instead of relying on only using single consonants as onsets, students will learn that they can use a digraph, made of two consonants, as the onset in a word. Knowing these three digraphs will allow kids to make so many new words, because they'll be able to combine the digraphs (the onsets) with the ten rimes they've already learned.

We recommend you keep the letter lasso alive across the bend, and that near the end of the bend, you invite students to participate in a rime rodeo, with some playing the parts of cowboy and cowgirl and holding onsets (pretending like they are lassos) and others playing the part of cattle and holding rimes. Marvel as the onsets gallop around the room with their lassos at the ready, trying to round up a rime to make a new word. Once the cowboys, cowgirls, and cattle read the words they've made, invite them to shout out, "Yee-haw!" Be sure to take a step back and admire all the new words they can make and read that they couldn't read a few short weeks ago.

When the unit launched, you shared Mabel's reluctance to write, and your students coached her to be brave and give it a try. As this bend—and unit—come to a close, we suggest you bring things full circle. Set Mabel up to share a piece from one of her stories with the class, and invite students to name the super powers she probably used to help her write. Then, ask them to help you make a sign for the classroom that announces to the world that they have super powers and that they're willing to share the gift of reading with anyone who stops by. Imagine how powerful it would be if the principal popped in, eager to share the gift of reading with your students, or if another class of kindergartners stopped by.

The last session of this unit brings together phonics, reading, and writing workshops so that your kindergartners can understand how they all go together. Expect that your students will leave this unit better prepared to read unfamiliar words by looking for parts they know and equipped to write so many more words than they could a few weeks before.

And, to acknowledge all the growth, you'll invite students to end the unit with a giant "Yee-Haw!" celebrating their snap word power, pointer power, sound power, and, of course, word-part power.

All the best,
Natalie and Rachel

Discover New Word Parts
VC Parts -ap and -ot

GETTING READY

✔ Display the word-part chart that you began in Session 10.

✔ Write the letters *m*, *a*, *p*, *t*, *l*, and *g* on Post-its and the word part *-ap* on a larger Post-it.

✔ Display the superhero Word Wonder with lasso and a cowboy with lasso.

✔ You'll need a letter lasso made with a pipe cleaner, the word card for *lap*, and a magnetic letter board.

✔ Distribute two pipe cleaners and one magnetic letter board with letters to each partnership.

✔ Prepare word cards *map*, *tap*, *lap*, *nap*, *cap*.

✔ Prepare word cards *dot*, *hot*, *got*, *tot*, *jot*, *cot*, *pot*.

✔ Display your word-part chart and prepare to add the *-ap* and *-ot* phonogram cards to it.

PHONICS INSTRUCTION

Phonics
• Segment onset and rime to discover new word parts.

Word Knowledge/Solving
• Use familiar word parts including phonograms (-*at*, -*in*, -*it*, -*an*, -*ap*, -*ot*) to read and spell unfamiliar words.

High-Frequency Words
• Learn new words (*got*, *went*, *was*).

IN THIS SESSION

TODAY YOU'LL teach students that they can make new words by taking off the first letter and adding new letters to the remaining word part. You'll focus on VC word parts: *-ap* and *-ot*.

TODAY YOUR STUDENTS will use pipe cleaner lassos to help them focus on the vowel-consonant combinations that make familiar word parts—including two new ones: *-ap* and *-ot*. They'll add letters to these word parts to make new words.

MINILESSON

CONNECTION

Remind students how to take teeny-tiny snap words like *at* and *in* and make new words. Rally their enthusiasm for the learning ahead.

"Super Readers, today we start a whole new part of our unit. In the part that we already did, you learned that you can take teeny-tiny snap words—words like *at* and *in*—and make so many words from those words. You really have super powers, making all those new words from just a few teeny-tiny words."

I displayed the class word-part chart from Session 10. "Let's remember the power of word parts by looking at our chart, reading a part, and then calling out as many words as we can make using that word part." I touched two or three word parts and we made words by adding letters and calling them out.

"For this next part of our unit, I want to show you that, believe it or not, you have an even stronger power. Ready? This is it, your new power."

Name the teaching point.

"Today I want to teach you that you can take almost *any* short word, and you can take off the beginning and make your own word part. Then you can add different consonants to that word part and make so many words from it."

TEACHING

Demonstrate for students how you take the initial consonant off of a word and make more words with the ending phonogram.

"Let me show you what I mean. We'll start with one short word—but remember, we could do this with almost any short word. Here's the word," I said, and put three large Post-its side by side on the whiteboard: one with an *m*, one with an *a*, and the other with a *p*. Together they spelled *map*.

"Now you can take off the beginning (that's the *m*)." I removed the first Post-it. Then you squish together the last two letters, the *ap*." I placed one *ap* Post-it over the two smaller Post-its that said *a* and *p*. "Now, you can make so many words with the new word part you have made. Watch." I put new Post-its, each holding a different consonant, in front of the rime *ap* and the class read aloud the new words I made: *tap, lap, gap*.

ACTIVE ENGAGEMENT/LINK

Introduce a new tool that will help students capture the word part in a small word—a lasso.

"For you to do this work, I have a new tool for you. Superheroes have tools that help them solve problems and save the day: Batman has a Batmobile, Spiderman has web shooters, Captain America has an indestructible shield. And here is someone who has a lasso that she swings in the air to capture villains, so they can't get away." I held up a picture of Word Wonder. "She uses a lasso," and I gestured toward the lasso in the picture, "but she doesn't use it to capture *villains*; she uses it to capture word parts."

"You are going to get lassos as well." I held up a long, brightly colored pipe cleaner that I twisted in a loop at the top. I swung it in the air above my head and explained, "This letter lasso will allow you to lasso two or sometimes three letters together. You will use your lasso to capture *letters* and make word parts, just like we did when we found the -*ap* in *map*. This tool will help you see that letters belong joined together, almost hugging each other, in a word part." With my hands, I showed that the necessary tool would clasp letters together.

"With your letter lasso, you can make your own word parts. It helps to look for a part with a vowel and a consonant at the end. Are you ready to lasso up your own word part? To get ready, look at this picture of a cowboy lassoing a cow, just like Wonder Woman lassos her villains.

The letter lasso is a tactile tool to engage kids in the work of identifying and isolating known word parts. You might choose to use Wikki Stix in the place of pipe cleaners.

"Hold up your imaginary lasso. Now instead of lassoing a cow or a villain, you get to lasso a word part. Here comes a word!" I took the word card for *lap* and galloped it in front of the meeting area, building excitement for the prospect of lassoing a word part. "Can you lasso up a word part in this word?" I asked, pausing to hold the word stationary for a moment. "Cut off the beginning if that will help you," I said. "What word part do you see in this word? Can you grab it up?" I swung my imaginary lasso and the kids did as well.

I pretended the *-ap* was caught, and said, "Yee-haw! Got you, *-ap*!"

Involve students in making new words, using the word part *-ap*. Distribute a magnetic letter board and two letter lassos to each partnership.

"Let's take this word part and make some new words. I'm going to pass out one magnetic letter board to each partnership and two letter lassos, one for each of you. Your letter lassos need to have the loop at the top, so go ahead and make that loop." I quickly showed them how to make a loop at the top of the pipe cleaner and twist it in place. Let's test them out. We'll make a word, using our lasso to round up the word part and change the first letter to make new words. Here we go!

FIG. 11–1   A student holds Mabel in her Word Wonder costume after making his letter lasso, ready to lasso up word parts.

"Make the word *cap*. I can put the *cap* on the marker. I can put the *cap* on my head. *Cap*." I made the word on my magnetic letter board, so children could use it as a support. "See if you and your partner can find the word part." Some children already started putting their lasso around the part *-ap* as I demonstrated with mine on my board. "You found it so fast since we've been working with that part so much! Now with your partner, see if your letter lasso works. Hold the lasso around the parts, and remove the beginning—the *c*. Now see if you can make the word *tap*. I can *tap* my knee." I did so. "*Tap*. Say it out loud so you can hear the first sound." After kids found the *t*, I prompted them to read the word. "Say the first sound and say the part. Put them together. *Tap*!"

FIG. 11–2   One partnerships' letter board with the letter lasso rounding up the word part *-ap*.

I continued to ask students to make other words that ended in *-ap*, coaching them to say the first sound and then say the part and put them together to read the word. The students made *nap* (I was so tired after I went to the park that I went home to take a *nap*) and *lap* (My cat jumped in my *lap*).

"Super Friends, there are so many words you can make from this super-powerful word part!" I added word cards for *map*, *tap*, *lap*, *nap*, and *cap* to a pocket chart to be read during the share.

RUG TIME `CLUBS`

Set rug clubs up to keep making words and let them know that sometimes they won't make a real word.

"Okay, writers, are you ready to make more words with word parts? I'm going to give you a new word, and you can use the same steps to make new words." I showed students how I made the word *dot* on my letter board. "Will you make the word *dot* on your letter boards? Then use your letter lasso to capture that word part and add different consonants in front of the word part to see if you can make new words. Here are some consonants you might use." I pointed to the letters *h, z, g, t, j, c, p.*

"Help your partner and see if you can make a new word. Some words might not be real—they'll sound silly."

After a few moments, I called children back and shared some of the words they made. "I heard some of you say you could make *hot*." I moved the *h* in front of *-ot.* "It was *hot* in the sun. Some of you said we could make the word *pot*. Put the water in the *pot*. Some people said *zot*. Is *zot* a real word? No, it's a fun made-up word! Your letter lasso is helping you find new word parts that you can use to write other words!" I added word cards—*dot, hot, got, tot, jot, cot,* and *pot*—to the pocket chart.

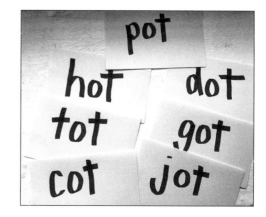

Make sure to define any words that your kids might not know. You can do this defining work through language alone, or you can sketch quick pictures if you think extra support is needed.

SHARE • Using Rhyming Words in Silly Sentences

Set up kids to read all the words they have made, pointing out that these words rhyme and that they all have the same word part. Ask kids to make a silly sentence using at least one of the words.

"Friends, you have made so many words today. Let's read them!" I pointed to the index cards I had put in a pocket chart. Together we read down the list of words ending in *-ap* and I helped students to say first the initial consonant, then the word part, then read the entire word. "/m/ /ap/ *map*! /t/ /ap/ *tap*!" I underlined the *-ap* in each word and continued to do the same for the *-ot* words.

Then I said, "Let's remember that words love to be used. They love to be in sentences. Can you look at these words and come up with a silly sentence for at least one of the words?" There were giggles around the rug as students thought of silly sentences and I shared a few. "Some of you were getting pretty fancy with your sentences. Here is one that I heard that used three of the words we made! *'The tot took a nap in the pot!'*

"Friends, now when you want to write a word that has *-ap* in it or *-ot* in it, the *-ap* and *-ot* word parts can help you. You'll know that part is spelled *a-p* or *o-t*. And when you are reading and see *-ap* or *-ot* in a word, you will know that part says /ăp/ or /ŏt/. And that will help you read the word!" I added the *-ap* and *-ot* phonogram cards to the word-part chart.

a	e	i	o	u
![-an] -an		![-in] -in	![-ot] -ot	
![-at] Welcome -at		![-it] -it		
![-ap] -ap				

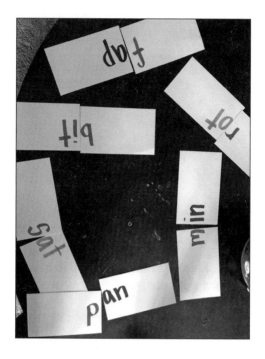

In this phonics version of musical chairs, there are no chairs, but in their place, there is a scattering of phonogram cards, spread around an area that you'll parade around.

EXTENSION 1 • Musical Pairs

GETTING READY

- Distribute the phonogram cards for *-an*, *-at*, *-ap*, *-it*, *-in*, and *-ot* onto tables around the room.

Play a variation on musical chairs in which students match their consonant card with a word part on a table to make a word.

"Readers, writers, we have a few minutes before it is time for math, and I know you are still thinking about your word-part power. That's how it is with Super Readers. Your power stays with you all day long!

"I was thinking of a quick game we could play to let you use your word-part power. To play, I need you all to line up, super-fast, right in front of me, and I'm going to give each of you a letter. When you get your letter, show it to the person beside you in line and see if you can think up some super-fun words that start with your letter. Line up now!"

Once the class had gathered for the parade, I quickly explained the game to them. "You'll start by parading around the classroom singing the alphabet song. Then when I called 'Stop!' you'll all stop where you are and match your letter with a nearby phonogram card on one of the tables. Each of you will say the word that you made, and the rest of the class will decide—is that a real word or a nonsense word? Everyone who made a nonsense word will sit in the meeting area, while those who made real words will parade around again and try to make new words. Are you ready to start?"

EXTENSION 2 • Learning More New Snap Words: *Got, Was, Went*

 GETTING READY

- Prepare to add the *got*, *was*, and *went* word cards to the word wall.

Introduce three new snap words, and guide students through the familiar process of making a word a snap word.

"We really worked our word muscles today, didn't we? I have to tell you, though—my friend is a weight lifter, and she told me that if you really want to get stronger, you can't keep lifting the same amount of weight. You have to keep adding more and more weight when you exercise—that's what makes your muscles stronger. So, let's keep making our word muscles stronger by adding some more snap words to our word wall! Some of you made one of these words today during rug time: *got*!

"Let's turn these words into snap words!" I turned to the "How to Learn a Word" chart.

I held up the first word, *got*. "Okay, let's make this a snap word. First, read it!" I pointed under the printed card as the students read the word.

"Now, study it. Tell your partner what you're noticing. Yes, the first letter has a tail and the rest are small. Let's count the letters—one, two, three! The first letter is *g* and the last part is *-ot*.

"Now, spell it: *g-o-t*.

"Now let's cover, write, and check it. Quick, take a picture with your brain before I cover it." I covered the word with my hand. "Now write it!" The kids began to work on their whiteboards. After a moment, I uncovered the word. "Make sure it matches, and fix it up if it doesn't.

"Now, let's use it. Hmm,. . . " I tapped my temple. "I *got* my coat when it was time to go home! Think of some more sentences with your partner." I listened in and coached a few kids, "You might say, 'She got. . .'

"Very cool sentences. Tyson said, 'I *got* a new cat!' Elva said, 'I *got* sick.'"

We repeated the same steps to learn the words *was* and *went*.

These words have been chosen as sight words during this time of year to support the oral and written language work of the narrative genre that children are doing in writing workshop.

"Let's lift these words up onto the word wall! Pretend you're lifting *got* up to the word wall with me." We all pretended to lift *got* into the air as I put it on the word on the wall. "*Got!*" We finished with our other new words.

EXTENSION 3 • Rereading a Familiar Text to Find and Use Word Parts

GETTING READY

- Display the enlarged version of Mabel's *My Win* book.
- Students need their letter lassos.

Remind students to look for a familiar word part as they reread a text, then challenge them to make new words with that word part.

"Super Readers, let's reread Mabel's *My Win* book, now that we have our letter lassos. I bet we can round up lots of word parts and maybe even see a new one!" I prompted students to use their letter lassos as they read the words with the word parts. I drew a circle around each word part that was underlined.

When we got to *hot*, I paused, giving children a chance to notice a new word part. A few lassos swung in the air. "I see some of you have found a word part! What is it?" "*Ot!*" "Yes, let's read the word. /H/-/ot/ *Hot.*

"Maybe we should try thinking of some words that we can make with the *-ot* word part. What about the letter *d*? Can we make a word using *d* as the first sound with the word part *-ot*? That's right, *dot*! What about the letter *n*? The letter *p*?"

How to learn a **word**

1. Read it!
2. Study it!
3. Spell it!
4. Write it!
5. Use it!

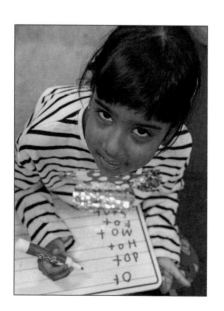

Using Word Parts (-*ip*, -*op*) to Write New Words

IN THIS SESSION

TODAY YOU'LL teach students that to write short words that aren't snap words, it usually helps to say the word, listen for the first sound, then listen for the word part in the rest of the word.

TODAY YOUR STUDENTS will learn to write words letter-by-word-part, segmenting the word into the onset and rime, and then using the word parts they have learned to write the whole word, just as they will do in writing workshop.

MINILESSON

CONNECTION

Rally kids' enthusiasm by reading together a letter from Reader-Man. Channel them to use their letter lassos to identify word parts and add them to the word-part chart.

"Friends, I just received another letter from Reader-Man! He wants to give you some advice. He wrote this letter to Super Writers, so why don't you test out your letter lassos as we read the letter together? Swing your letter lassos in the air to show me you're ready!" Kids made the lasso motion with great enthusiasm, then I continued.

"Terrific—you're all ready! This letter has a couple of words where you can use your letter lasso on new word parts. They are the words that are underlined. When we get to them, you can put the last two letters together to help us read the word." I gestured for students to read the letter along with me.

When we got to the word *quit*, I paused. "Get your letter lassos ready! Remember to look for two letters together—a vowel and a consonant. Do you see a word part?"

Students called out, "-*it*!"

GETTING READY

✔ Enlarge the letter from Reader-Man.

✔ Make sure students have their letter lassos.

✔ Prepare to add the -*ip* and -*op* phonogram cards to the word-part pocket chart.

✔ Distribute a whiteboard and marker to each partnership. Display one set of picture cards for *cop, hop, mop, pop, top, stop*.

✔ Distribute the picture cards for *lip, slip, hip, rip, tip, slip,* and *dip* to each rug club.

✔ Be ready to record words on Post-its and to keep them for the share and for future sessions.

PHONICS INSTRUCTION

Phonological Awareness
• Manipulate the onset and rime of single-syllable spoken words.

Phonics
• Segment onset and rime to discover new word parts.

Word Knowledge/Solving
• Use familiar word parts including phonograms (-*ip*, -*op*) to read and spell unfamiliar words.

High-Frequency Words
• Write high-frequency words in continuous text.

"Lasso up that part. Now, let's blend the first sound and that word part you know together: /qu/-/it/."

"*Quit*! Oh, Reader-Man doesn't want us to give up! Okay, we won't. We will keep reading."

We continued reading on. When we got to the word *tip*, I urged kids to lasso up the -*ip* and use the first sound and the word part to read the word. I pointed out to students that -*ip* was a new word part.

"So, now you discovered the word part -*ip*. Let me add that to our word-part chart." I added the -*ip* phonogram card to the word-part pocket chart. "That should help you read and write other words, like *sip*, *hip*, and *lip*. This is so exciting! Your word-part power is getting stronger and stronger! Let's read to find out the tip!"

We read the next two sentences, lassoing up the -*op* in *hop* and *top*. "Writers, here's a new word part: -*op*! Let's add that to the word-part chart." I added the -*op* phonogram to the word-part pocket chart.

"Oh, writers, this is what we realized in our last session! We made words with the new word parts we learned, -*ap* and -*ot*. Reader-Man knows we are ready to be the kind of writers who write words using word parts and so he wanted to give us more word parts to use. His letter taught us two new ones: -*op* and -*ip*!"

a	e	i	o	u
-an		-in	-ot	
Welcome -at		-it	-op	
-ap		-ip		

We finished reading the letter, noticing and using -*an*.

Dear Super Writers,

Don't quit! Here's a tip!
Use word-part power!
You can spell "hop" and "top."
Use "op"!

Sincerely,
Reader-Man

It is not the time of year when we expect readers to be reading these words with VC parts independently. Therefore, readers will benefit from scaffolds such as underlined word parts, as well as heavy meaning and language support from you.

Notice that although the kids are working with onsets and rimes, their involvement with rimes is strongly supported. Their work with initial consonants is more independent.

"So, Super Readers and Writers, it sounds like Reader-Man wants us to get writing with our word-part power using all these parts we are learning. I think this will really help us, because I do sometimes see kids write the word *sip* this way: *sp*." I showed students by writing *sp* on a Post-it under the document camera. "But that doesn't make a word that makes sense or looks right. If you take off the beginning you don't get a part that you can use to make lots and lots of words. You need to write *sip*, writing the letter for the first sound /s/-*s* and then the letters for the part /ip/ *i-p*." Again, I showed the correct spelling. "With word parts, you can make your writing so much easier to read."

❖ **Name the teaching point.**

"Today I want to teach you that to write short words that aren't on the word wall, it sometimes helps to say the word and to listen for the first sound, then to listen for the word part."

TEACHING

Show students how to use the word-part chart to help them recognize words that have the same ending part.

"If we are in writing workshop and we want to write, 'The balloon is going to *pop*!' I can think, 'Hmm,. . . which word has a part in it?'" I repeated the sentence. "*Pop*! It sounds like. . . " and I searched the part chart for a few seconds, demonstrating how I used the picture to help me read the word part. As I touched the top, I said, "*Top*, that sounds like *pop*."

Segment a word into the onset and rime and write the word letter-by-word-part.

"So, now I can say the first sound /p/ and say the last part /op/." I used my hand gesture to say /p/, with my thumb raised, and then /op/ with my fingers of the same hand, outstretched, and finally, driving my fist down toward my side to connect the first sound with the rime, I said, "Pop."

I got the kids to do this as well.

ACTIVE ENGAGEMENT/LINK

Distribute a whiteboard and marker to each partnership with a set of six picture cards.

"I'm going to give you and your rug club a whiteboard. Here are the pictures." I displayed a few picture cards, each representing a word that ended in -*op*. There were six different pictures. "Let's read them together: *pop*, *cop*, *mop*, *hop*, *top*, *stop*. Since we aren't writing our own stories right now—you'll be doing that later in the day—let's use these pictures to practice the kinds of words we sometimes write in writing workshop."

POSSIBLE COACHING MOVES

▶ "Say the word. Say the first sound. Say the last part."

▶ "You said -*op*. What does that sound like on our word-part chart? *Cat*? *Top*?"

▶ "Write the first letter and then write the part."

▶ "Read the word. Say the first sound and the part. Blend them together."

Ask students to write *-op* words by saying the word, segmenting it into the onset and rime, and using what they know about parts to write the letter and word part.

"Say the word. Then say the first sound and then the word part. Think about which word part that is—you can use the word-part chart to help. Then write the word." I listened in and coached as partnerships worked.

After most clubs had a chance to spell out one word, I said, "Are you reading each word after you make it? Make sure you do!" Children read their words. "I notice you are doing such careful writing work, Super Writers. You said the word you wanted to write, saying the first sound and the part. And you were careful to put those parts together and to make sure the word made sense *and* matched your picture."

As kids wrote *-op* words, I jotted them on some Post-its to be used during the share.

RUG TIME

Set up clubs to make and check the words they make using picture cards with the *-ip* rime.

"Super Writers, you used our letter lasso to discover a new word part, *-op*, and then you used that part to write other words. Are you ready to write words with another word part?"

"Yes!"

"Let's look back at our letter from Reader-Man and reread this word." I pointed to the word *tip*. "It has the word part *-ip*! Here are some pictures of words that end with *-ip*." I showed the pictures as we read them: *lip, sip, rip, dip, hip, slip*. I passed out whiteboards to the students who didn't yet have them.

"I thought you could practice using the *-ip* word part by playing a game of 'Make and Check.' Put the picture cards in the middle of your rug club facedown. Then, turn over the top card, say what the picture is, and then make the word on your board. When everyone is done, turn your board so that it is facing out. Then it is time for the check. Look around the circle to make sure everyone has spelled the word right. Keep going until you have done all of the cards."

As kids wrote *-ip* words, I jotted them on some Post-its to be used during the share.

These types of word-solving prompts are very important for transfer of phonics work to students' independent writing.

POSSIBLE COACHING MOVES

▶ "Say the word you are trying to write. It can help you know what letters to write."

▶ "If your word has some wrong letters, say the word again and remember to use the right word part."

▶ "*Slip* is a tricky one. It is the beginning that you really need to stretch."

▶ "When you finish with the cards, try thinking of some of your own *-ip* words."

SHARE

Read lists of new words that students have made, emphasizing the way the words rhyme.

"Super Writers, you wrote *so* many new words! Now, with your partner, will you read all the new words you wrote?" I gestured to the Post-its I had made from their whiteboard writing. The *-op* words were arranged in one column and the *-ip* words were arranged in another column.

"Start by reading the words that you wrote by lassoing up the word part *-op*. Remember, say the first sound and then crash that into the word part to read the word!" Partners read through the list of *-op* words, then the *-ip* words. "Now you know that writing and reading are so much easier and faster when you use word parts."

Teachers, be sure to save the Post-its from today's share because these words will be used in Session 13.

EXTENSION 1 • Solving Riddles to Keep Our Brains Growing

Focus students' thinking about words with riddles that touch upon beginning and ending sounds, rhymes, and meaning.

"Readers and writers play word games to keep their brains growing. Even grown-ups do crossword puzzles and games like that to keep their brains strong. Let's play a little word riddle game to activate our word-part power. Mabel has a riddle for us."

Because these are phonological awareness exercises involving rhyming and initial sound isolation, the riddles are not written for kids to read.

What word rhymes with *pop*,

Starts with the same sound as *table*,

And is the opposite of *bottom*?

"If you have a guess, put a thumb on your knee! Let's think about the clues we have and solve it together. Hmm,. . .what words rhyme with *pop*? *Hop*, *stop*, *drop*, *mop*? Oh! But that's not all—it also starts with the same sound as the word *table*. *Table* starts with what sound?"

"/T/," students replied.

"It starts with /t/ and rhymes with *pop*. What do you think?"

"*Top*!" the class called out.

"*Top*! Is that the opposite of *bottom*? It sure is! You solved the first riddle! Well done, Super Readers.

"*Top* has a word part that you'll find in lots of words, *-op*. What other words can you think of with *-op*? *Top*. . .*pop*. . .Make a list with your partner." I gave students just a few seconds to come up with some words with the short-*O* rime. Then I echoed a few back.

"I heard words like *hop*, *chop*, *flop*, *cop*! All of those words have the same part at the end, /op/. Ready for another riddle?" I read the next riddle and we solved it using the same process as before.

This word starts like *happy*, *hi*, and *here*,

And it ends like *dot*, *spot*, and *lot*.

It's the opposite of *cold*.

EXTENSION 2 • Making and Using a Word-Part Flip Book

GETTING READY

- Make a word-part flip book from a spiral-bound notebook. With the spiral across the top and the pages hanging down, cut about ten pages into two parts. One part will be a third of the page and the second part should be two-thirds of the page. On the first part of each page (one third), write a different consonant (not *X*). Keep flipping the page to add a new consonant. Then for the second part of the page, write one of the ten word parts you have taught students. Flip the pages and add a new word part on each page.

Demonstrate how students can use a word-part flip book to review word parts and generate new words.

"Friends, I made this word-part flip book. I thought we could use it to practice making and reading words. We can use this flip book to keep our word-part power activated even when we are out here in the hallway."

I then flipped the onset third and kept the rime two-thirds the same. As the children read the words, we were sure to check to see if those words made sense. We often used sentences to test those words.

GETTING READY

- Make a list on chart paper of some of the words that have been generated in your classroom.

Set partnerships up to take turns saying words to each other to write and then read and check them together.

"Are you ready to give your partner a little quiz? It's a way to see if our word-part power is fully activated. Here is a list of some of the words we've been making. Partner 1, look at this list of words." I gestured toward the list of words generated during this session, but these could be a list of any VC phonogram words that have been generated during this unit.

"Choose a word and tell your partner. Partner 2, without looking at the list, try to write the word the best you can. Partner 1, you can help your partner by reminding them to listen for the beginning and the word part.

"Then, together, read the word to check that it looks right. If it's right, switch. If not, fix it, and then switch."

Using Word Parts and Dr. Seuss–like Rhymes to Read

GETTING READY

✔ Prepare to read from *The Cat in the Hat* and make a list of the rhymes that appear in the first couple of pages.

✔ Gather the Post-its from the Session 12 share.

✔ Display pages from *I Can Hop!*, a rhyming book made with *-op* words. Place a Post-it to cover the *op* rime in *top* and *stop* on page 1, leaving the onsets uncovered.

✔ Distribute a copy of Mabel's rhyming booklet, *The Bug Hug*, to each partnership.

✔ Gather the *hop, top, stop, flop, bug, hug, rug, tug,* and *mug* word cards for a word sort into a pocket chart.

✔ Prepare to add the *-ug* phonogram card to the word-part chart.

PHONICS INSTRUCTION

Phonological Awareness
• Hearing, matching, and producing rhyming words.

Phonics
• Segment onset/rime to discover new word parts (*-ug*).

Word Knowledge/Solving
• Use familiar word parts including phonograms to read and spell unfamiliar words.

IN THIS SESSION

TODAY YOU'LL teach students that rhyming words often end in the same spelling—that words that sound the same at the end are often spelled the same at the end.

TODAY YOUR STUDENTS will use their word-part power to read simple rhyming books, while focusing on the fact that words that sound the same at the end are often spelled the same at the end.

MINILESSON

CONNECTION

Rally students' enthusiasm by showing them that one of their favorite authors, Dr. Seuss, has word-part power, just like they do.

"Before when we were reading the different words we made with word parts, I started to feel like we were in a Dr. Seuss book." I pulled out *The Cat in the Hat*. "Look at this book," and I read the title. "Can you hear that Dr. Seuss is using word parts like you do?" I read the first page of the book aloud.

"Listen to more of this book," I said, "and as you listen, see if you can hear the way he uses words that have the same word part, like. . . " and I read off the rhyming words the kids would hear in the first few pages of *The Cat in the Hat*: *play, day, two, do, ball, all, sit, it, bit*. "Dr. Seuss took those words and he made them into a rhyming book. Listen."

I read a few pages from *The Cat in the Hat*. Leaning in and dropping my voice, I said, "Do you think he knew he had word-part power? I wonder if he had a letter lasso, too?"

I paused to give the children a chance to think about Dr. Seuss with a letter lasso. Then I said, "Even if he didn't know that he had word-part power, Dr. Seuss' rhymes have helped children learn to read and write for years and years. They even helped someone as old as me, when I was learning to read. I want to make sure that the rhyming in his books helps you too."

❦ **Name the teaching point.**

"Today I want to teach you that words that rhyme, or sound the same at the end, are sometimes spelled the same at the end. And, when words are spelled the same at the end, they sometimes sound the same—they rhyme. Your word-part power can help you hear and see what is the same in a tricky word, so that you can read and write."

TEACHING

Display a book page with Post-its covering the rime on each rhyming word. Read the page together, asking children to figure out the covered word, then discovering that the rime is spelled the same.

"Here's the exciting thing, Super Readers. Last night after you left, I was taking down the Post-its I had made while watching you write on your boards. I was reading and admiring those words and that made me stop what I was doing. I suddenly thought, 'We can't throw these words out! These words can be made into a rhyming book.'" I scanned the room, wide-eyed.

I thought, "I have a whole room of Dr. Seuss–like writers just waiting to write rhyming books!"

"Do you remember how you started with the word part -*op* and made all these words? *Hop, mop, slop, top, pop, stop, cop.*" I said the list without writing the words down.

"Well, I thought about how I could take those words and then use them to make a rhyming book, just like *The Cat in the Hat*. Do you want me to show you? I made one last night using the words you came up with in our last session." I displayed the second page of the book with the *op* in *top* and *stop* covered with a Post-it. I had left the onset uncovered. I then asked the class to help me read and to follow along with their pointer power in the air—pointing once for each word, as I did the same with my teacher pointer.

We read, "I Can Hop!" I emphasized the word *hop* to make sure children would be able to hear the rhyme/rime. As we read the next line and came to the covered word, I said, "The first letter in this word is *t*, /t/, but what's under here?" I touched the Post-it that covered the word-part *op*.

"Wait! This is a Dr. Seuss–like rhyme, and we know now that when two words sound the same at the end, they are sometimes spelled the same at the end. So, if the first line says, 'I can *hop, hop, and hop*,' then this line must say, 'I can hop to the /t/-/op/, top.' I think that *op* must be under there." A few children nodded yes, and I lifted the Post-it.

I invited the children to think with me as I read the next line, "I stop," doing the same work with the covered word that sounded the same at the end and so might therefore be spelled the same at the end. I was sure to point out that the words sound the same at the end and they are spelled the same at the end, too.

ACTIVE ENGAGEMENT/LINK

Channel partners to read the last two lines, reminding them to look for rhyming words that are spelled and sound the same at the end. Emphasize that this knowledge makes reading books more fun.

I pointed to the last two lines in the book I had made. I underlined the *op* in the words *hop* and *flop*. "It's your turn now. With your partner, use your pointer power in the air to read these lines of my rhyming book. Remember that when a word is spelled the same at the end, it sometimes sounds the same at the end. Use that to help you read, just like I used that fact to help me spell the word."

"Your word-part power was really helping you to read and understand what was happening. That's the really important thing! Because you knew that this was a rhyming book, and because you know that rhyming words are sometimes spelled the same at the end, you could read these words more easily and still have energy left to laugh at what was happening! It was so funny watching that rabbit flop over with his tongue hanging out like that. That's the real reason why word-part power is important. It can help you read and enjoy books!"

FIG. 13–1 The teacher points to the last two lines of the book to signal readers to read, looking closely for the word part *-op*.

Provide partners with a copy of Mabel's rhyming book. Ask partners to read the book together, remembering that words that are spelled the same at the end often sound the same at the end.

"Mabel saw us reading our Dr. Seuss-like rhyming book, and she decided to make her own rhyming book!" I held up a three-page booklet that Mabel made.

FIG. 13–2   Children read the *Bug Hug* book together using the pictures and word parts.

The Bug Hug

The bug was in the rug.

He gave my ear a tug.

He got in my mug.

He gave me a hug.

"Here's the name of her book: *The Bug Hug*. Before I give it to you to read, let's see if we can get our own word part from the word *hug* in the title. Remember how we did that? We took a word and we chopped off the beginning, and

POSSIBLE COACHING MOVES

▶ "Look for a word part."

▶ "Remember this is a rhyming book, so lots of the words will sound the same at the end and may even be spelled the same at the end, too."

▶ "Use the picture to help you."

we used our letter lasso to round up the rest. Let's try that here: *hug*. What should we chop off? Right, the first letter *h*. Let's round up the rest. That's right, *-ug* says /ug/—/ug/ like in /h/-/ug/.

"Will you read the book together now and remember that if a word is spelled the same at the end, it can sometimes sound the same at the end? Use the pictures and your word-part power to help you."

SHARE • Using Word Parts to Spell New Words

Lead children in reading *-op* and *-ug* words from the pocket chart, then challenge partners to use word parts to spell new words. Add the new word part, *-ug*, to the word-part chart.

I arranged the *-op* and *-ug* cards at the bottom of the pocket chart. "You just read so many *-ug* words. Practicing reading can help you write the letters in each word part more easily." I gathered up all of the *-op* words from our *I Can Hop!* book and all the *-ug* words from Mabel's *The Bug Hug* book. "Let's sort them, and as we sort them, let's practice reading them. Remember that you can use the word-part chart to help you remember what parts make what sounds." I pointed to the chart as I said this.

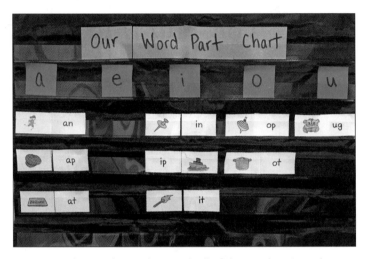

FIG. 13–3   The word-part chart with all of the word parts we have studied in this unit.

I held up *hop*. "Read it. *Hop*." I put it on the left-hand side of the pocket chart. I held up another word: *bug*. "Read it. *Bug*. Does this one go with *hop*? No. Okay, then it goes on this side." We continued through the rest of the words, reading each word and sorting it into the appropriate column.

"Remember that these word parts can help you read and write more and more words. I thought of a couple more words you might try reading and writing using your own word parts. I remembered this song I used to sing when I was little. In the song, the bunny bops the field mice on the head. That's like a little tap. What if we wanted to write the word *bop*? What letters do we need to write the word *bop*? Whisper them in your partner's ear. Use our sorting up here to help you. I heard so many of you say we'd need to use the *-op* word part, and we'd need to write *b-op*. *Bop!*

"Oh, and I was reading a book called *Digging* the other day, and I saw this line in it." I put the sentence on the board. "See if you can read it with me. Get those pointers up in the air! 'The dog dug a hole.' Yes, this word is *dug*.

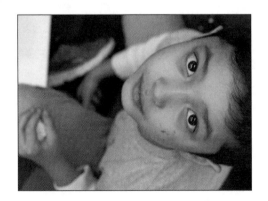

"That was amazing! Learning to hear that words sound the same and knowing that the same sound might mean the same spelling helps us read and write all about dogs and rabbits and field mice."

"Now that we have a new word part, let's make sure that it gets onto our word-part chart." I added the *-ug* phonogram card to the word-part chart.

EXTENSION 1 • Using the Word-Part Chart to Make Real Words

GETTING READY

- Display the word-part chart.
- Have several different consonant cards available to make words using the word-part chart.

Challenge students to make more new words using the word-part chart.

"Look at our word-part chart now! We started off with four different word parts, and now our word-part power is really powering up! There are five new word parts that I added. I know that this chart can help you during reading and writing, but it will only help you if you get to know it better. Let's try using the chart right now to make words. I will hold up a letter and you'll put it with a word part. When you make a word, we decide whether it's a real word, or not a real word. Are you ready?"

I held up the letter *f*. "Let's test this letter with all of our word parts." We said, "*Fan*, real. *Fat*, real. *Fap*, not real. *Fin*, real. *Fit*, real. *Fip*, not real. *Fot*, not real. *Fop*, real. *Fug*, not real." We tried this again with one or two more letters to use as the onset.

EXTENSION 2 • Onset/Rime Crosswords

GETTING READY

- Write one set of word parts horizontally on index cards and write another set vertically.
- Gather magnetic consonant letters.

Teach the class how to build a crossword using onsets and rimes.

"Remember I told you about how adults do word puzzles to help keep their brains strong? I made some cards for us to use to play a new game with our word parts. I have some magnetic letters for us to use as the 'beginnings' of words, and I also put our word parts on cards."

"But, there are two different kinds of cards—ones that go left to right and ones that go top to bottom." I held up the left-to-right version of *-ap*. "Usually letters in words go this way." I traced my finger across the letters from left to right. "But this is a crossword game, and so the words can go either way. They can either go across or down. The biggest challenge to this game is that every new word we make must connect to the rest of the words we have already made. I'll show you how to do it."

I stuck a horizontal *-ot* card to the board. I then picked a magnetic *p* and used it as the onset. Kids called out, "*Pot*!"

I leaned back, looking at the other word parts. I picked up a vertical -in card and placed it under the magnetic p. I put my finger on the p and then moved it down the word. "Pin," the kids said.

"What other words can we add to the crossword? Turn and tell your partner." I gave partners a few moments to talk, then I shared out, "I heard some of you made a word starting with the n at the end of pin. You added the -ap card and made. . . " I placed the -ap card in place. "Nap!" kids called out.

We continued playing until we could not figure out how to add any more onset/rime combinations to our puzzle.

p	o	t
i		
n	a	p

EXTENSION 3 • Partner Dictation: Spelling Quiz

GETTING READY

- Print a small copy of the word-part chart for each partnership.
- Provide each partnership with a whiteboard and marker.

Set partners up to give each other a little spelling quiz. One partner says a word from the word-part chart, and the other partner writes it. Then they read and check it together.

"Are you ready to give your partner a little quiz with some of the words we've been making?" I distributed a small copy of the word-part chart to each partnership.

"Partner 1, look at the chart, choose a word, and read it aloud to your partner. Partner 2, without looking at the chart, write the word the best you can on your whiteboard. Then together check the word, and fix it up if you need to."

Finding Word Parts in the Alphabet Chart

IN THIS SESSION

TODAY YOU'LL teach students that they can find words with the word parts they know, even on the alphabet chart, and they can use those words to write other words.

TODAY YOUR STUDENTS will use words they find on the alphabet chart to write other words with the same word parts.

MINILESSON

CONNECTION

Remind kids about the great work they have done with word parts and let them know that word parts are everywhere—including in the familiar alphabet chart.

"We've been reading words with word parts and writing words with word parts, and it feels like we are using them everywhere, right? Well, I thought so, too. Last night Mabel told me that we missed some words to use for our word-part power—there are word parts hidden in our alphabet chart! She left a little star on the pictures we should read that have word parts. Who knew that the alphabet chart would help us not just with our letters and sounds but also with our word-part power!"

❖ **Name the teaching point.**

"Today I want to teach you that once you have word-part power, you can hear and see word parts everywhere and all of them can help you read and write."

GETTING READY

✔ Display an alphabet chart with stars on words with familiar word parts: *cat*, *hat*, *fan*, *mug*, *fox*, and *zip*.

✔ Provide a whiteboard and marker to each partnership.

✔ Prepare to jot down the words children write with the word part -*un*.

✔ Prepare the alphabet chart that was "invaded" by word parts.

PHONICS INSTRUCTION

Phonological Awareness
- Segmenting and blending onset and rime.

Phonics
- Recognize more common phonograms with a VC pattern.

Word Knowledge/Solving
- Use familiar word parts including phonograms to read and spell unfamiliar words.

TEACHING

Demonstrate how to locate a word on the alphabet chart, generate rhyming words, and then use the word to write other words.

"Let's see what Mabel found. She starred words that contain word parts we can use often." I pointed to the word *cat*. "*Cat*. We sure can make lots of words with the word part in *cat*! I can think of words that have the same part at the end of *cat*—words that rhyme: *sat*, *mat*, *bat*. Join me in saying some rhyming words with this word part." There was a chorus of voices joining me in producing other *-at* words.

"I can write *cat*." I put my thumb up, made the sound /c/, and wrote a *c*. Then I put my thumb up again and made the sound /c/, and the put out my fingers, and said, "/at/." I wrote *at*. I read it. "*Cat*. So now what other word could *cat* help me write? We said *bat*. I know *cat*, so I can take away the *c* and change it to another letter. Let me hear that first sound in *bat*." "/B/," I said "What else could I write?" We said more words.

ACTIVE ENGAGEMENT/LINK

Distribute whiteboards to partnerships to write new words using the word parts in *fan*, *ladybug*, and *zip*.

"With your partner, will you find another one of the pictures that Mabel starred on our alphabet chart? Then write the word that goes with the picture. After you have rounded up the word part from that word, make as many words as possible using your word-part power." I coached students as they made words using the word parts in the starred words *fan*, *ladybug*, *fox*, and *zip*.

RUG TIME

Show the class that there is one more word part hiding in the alphabet chart.

"While you were working, I was looking at our alphabet chart again and I realized that there was one more word part on our alphabet chart. We have not studied this word part yet, and so I thought I might leave the work of lassoing and making words to you and your club.

"I will write the word up here, and will you see if you can find the picture on the alphabet chart that will help you read it?"

I wrote the word *sun* on my whiteboard, then paused for a few seconds until some children were calling out, "*Sun*, *sun*!" I drew a star in the *S* box on the alphabet chart.

POSSIBLE COACHING MOVES

▸ "Once you have used your word part with as many letters as you can to make words, read the list you made and then erase your list. Pick a different starred picture from the alphabet chart and do it again."

▸ "Don't forget to pass the marker back and forth between you. Take turns writing the words you are making."

▸ "Be sure to check that the word you have written is real."

"Good. Now get to it! Round up the word part in this word and then use it to make new words. I can't wait to see what words you make." I observed partnerships as they worked and I wrote down a number of the words they made so that we could refer back to them later in the day.

SHARE

Invite the class to help you use word-part power to transform the alphabet chart.

After a few minutes of work time, I said, "It is amazing, right?! Once you learn word parts, you really do start to hear and see them everywhere. The star in the *S* box reminds us that *sun* has a powerful word part just like *cat* and *hat*. *Fan*, *bug*, and *zip* all do, too."

I sat back, looked at the alphabet chart, and smiled. "You know, at first we used this alphabet chart to learn our letters and sounds, but now we are discovering other ways this chart can be useful. I have an idea. What if we bring our word-part power to the alphabet chart and see if we can transform it into something different, into something that can help us use word power when we write? Do you think that would be fun?"

Then I held up a stack of cards and quickly handed them all out to kids on the rug. Then I called kids up one at a time by the pictures on their cards. So, for the letter *D*, I said, "*Dot*, come up please!" For the letter *J*, I said, "*Jug*, come up please." Students put each card on the correct letter on the alphabet chart.

I then added a mini-chart of the word parts we had studied to the lower right corner of the chart. I also added a photo of Mabel with a lasso to the upper left corner of the chart. I pointed both out to the kids.

Once all of the cards were up, I said, "Look! It's a word-part takeover of the alphabet chart!"

EXTENSION 1 • Revisiting a New Word Part in the Alphabet Chart

GETTING READY

- Prepare to read aloud from the list of -*un* words you gathered during rug time.

Read aloud the -*un* words that students wrote during rug time, and channel partners to spell them to each other. Remind them to check whether each word is real or pretend.

"Remember earlier when we saw another new word part in the alphabet chart? The word *sun* has a word part in it!" I held up my thumb and said /s/, then held out the rest of my fingers as I said /un/. Then I closed my hand into a fist as I blended the two parts together, "/s/-/un/ *sun*. Let me remind you how to write the word *sun*. You break the word into parts using your thumb and fingers. I will write the letters for the sounds you hear." I wrote *sun* on the easel.

"During rug time, you all wrote a whole bunch of words using the word part -*un*. I wrote them down, so now I'll read them out, and you tell your partner how they're spelled. Are you ready?"

Kids nodded their heads. I read out a few of the real words they wrote down—*bun*, *fun*, *gun*, *nun*—and kids spelled them aloud to their partners. I then read out a pretend word, "Here's the last word, *vun*." I saw a few puzzled faces. "Is that a real word, or a pretend word?" Kids agreed that it was pretend.

EXTENSION 2 • Hearing Word Parts Everywhere

GETTING READY

- Make sure that all students can see the word-part chart.

Challenge kids to listen for word parts in some multisyllable words.

"Once you learn word parts, you really can start to hear them everywhere. And, if you can hear them, then you have power to spell them using your word-part power. I found some words in the stories you have been writing. I thought we could practice hearing word parts in these words so that when we are writing, we will be better able to put down the letters we need to make our writing easier to read. Do you want to play? Okay, listen up!"

I made sure the word-part chart was hanging close by. "Okay, remember, you can use the word-part chart to help you listen closely."

I said the following words with a sentence to make sure the kids could make sense of the word.

p**un**ish: "Someone wrote, 'My mom will punish the dog. He ate the last cookie.'"
b**at**tle: "Another child wrote, 'We had a transformer battle. It was a big fight.'"
lipstick: "One kid wrote, 'Sometimes my mom wears lipstick.'"
under: "A piece of writing said, 'I stood under the umbrella.'"
ugly: "Someone wrote, 'I got an ugly haircut. I did not like it.'"

After I said the word and the sentence for each word, I asked the class, "Can you hear a word part in the word I said? Which one? Use the word-part chart."

Studying One Word to Learn about How Letters and Words Work

GETTING READY

✔ Prop Mabel on a shelf next to the *she* word card.

✔ Display the "How to Learn a Word" anchor chart from kindergarten Unit 1, *Making Friends with Letters*.

✔ Prepare to display the *she* word card and the *ship* picture card to the class.

✔ Distribute a whiteboard and marker to each partnership.

✔ Gather the picture cards for *shell*, *soup*, *horse*, *shoe*, and *shark*.

✔ Draw a three-column chart on chart paper, with a sun, a hat, and a girl at the top of each column, respectively.

PHONICS INSTRUCTION

Phonics
• Demonstrate basic knowledge of digraphs (*sh, th*).

High-Frequency Words
• Learn new high-frequency words (*she, he, we, be*).

IN THIS SESSION

TODAY YOU'LL teach students that two consonants can work together to make a single sound—a digraph—and you'll teach them the digraphs *sh* and *th*.

TODAY YOUR STUDENTS will learn two new snap words, *she* and *he*, work with their partners to label pictures with beginning sounds *s*, *h*, and *sh*, and sing a song to help them remember the digraphs *sh* and *th*.

MINILESSON

CONNECTION

Rally students to learn a new high-frequency word—*she*—and teach them that this word has a special feature—a digraph—that will help with reading and writing of other words.

"Super Readers, come quickly! Mabel has a new word that she wants to add to the word wall." I turned to the class mascot, who was propped up on a nearby shelf beside the word *she*, printed on a card.

"Mabel has a word for us." I held the card up to show the class. "Thumbs up if you've seen this word before. Yes, this is the word *she*. It is a word you see in books *and* a word you use in your own stories. Let's make it a snap word so we can *all* read and write it in snap!" I displayed the "How to Learn a Word" chart.

"Let's read this new word in a sentence." I quickly wrote two sentences on the board to convey the meaning of the new snap word. Then, I invited the class to read with me:

Mabel is our friend. <u>She</u> likes to learn about words.

"So, in this sentence, the word *she* is talking about Mabel. *She* is a word you can use when you're talking about your mom or your sister or your friend Mabel! Let's take a closer look at the word *she* and study it. Turn to your partner and tell your partner what you notice."

After a moment, I pulled the class back together, "Some of you noticed the word *he* inside the word *she*." I pointed under the last two letters. "We can make *he* another new snap word and add it to the word wall before phonics workshop is over!

"And some of you noticed this word has one vowel, *e*, and two consonants, *s* and *h*." I pointed to the letters. "And some Super Readers and Writers *also* heard the /sh/ sound at the start of this word. Some of you were going /shhhhh/. Together, those letters, *s* and *h*, are making that special sound, /shhhhh/. Let's spell the whole word. *S-h-e*!

"Now let's cover, write, and check it. Quick, take a picture with your brain before I cover it." I covered the word with my hand. "Now write it!" The kids began to work on their whiteboards. "Now switch and let your partner write it." After a moment, I uncovered the word. "Make sure it matches and fix it up if it doesn't.

"Now, let's *use* it. Hmm,. . . " I tapped my temple. "She is my big sister! Now, you try. Use *she* to make another sentence." I prompted kids to turn and invent a few sentences with a partner, then I called the class back together.

"Mabel, thank you for giving us this snap word to study! We didn't just learn a new word; we also discovered something really cool about how words work! I bet some of you thought the *s* was making that /sh/ sound because most sounds are made with one letter, but no! It's a special sound that *two* letters are working together to make."

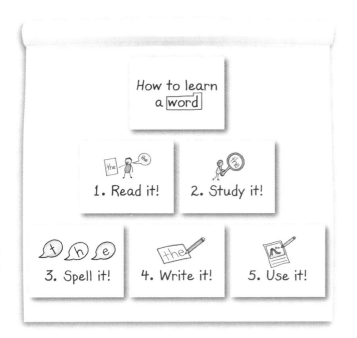

❖ Name the teaching point.

"Today I want to teach you that you can study any one word and learn more about how letters and words work. For example, when you study *she* you can learn about the *sh*—a digraph—two letters that go together to make one sound!"

TEACHING

Guide children in the discovery of how *s* and *h* work together to make one sound and practice writing words that start with /s/, /h/, and /sh/.

"Before we add this word to our word wall, let's study it a bit more to learn about the digraph, the part of this word that goes /shhhhhh/." I put the word card under the document camera and zoomed in. "Hmm,. . .it has a letter *s* as in *see*, /s/, and a letter *h* as in *he*, /h/, but it makes a different sound, /sh/. That's interesting. Those letters work together to make a whole new sound!

"Super Writers, this is an important discovery! Now, when you are writing a story and you hear /shhhhh/ in a word you want to spell, you'll know which letters to put down on the page. . . " I left a bit of space for kids to fill in.

"*S-H*!" students called out.

"That's right, but you're going to have to power up those ear muscles to make sure you *hear* the sound at the beginning of words. Some words will start like *sun*." I quickly drew a sun on the easel. "And some words will start like *hat*." I made a second column and drew a hat at the top of it. "And some words will start like *she*." I made a simple line drawing of a girl in a third column.

"Help me write these words. What sound do you hear at the beginning of *sun*?"

"/Ssssssssss/," students replied.

"We need the letter *s* to write *sun*." I wrote the *s* under the picture of the sun. "Oh! I think we need our letter lassos! Do you hear a word part in *sun*? That's right, *-un*!" I filled in the final two letters. Then, we went on to spell the word *hat* below the second picture.

"Okay, Super Writers, now say the word *she*. What's the first sound that you hear?" I listened carefully as children produced the sound. "Yes, *she* starts with the digraph, /shhhhh/. What letters make that sound?"

"*S* and *h*!"

"Now spell the whole word in a snap, *she*. . . " I wrote the word as the class chanted its spelling. "So, if I wanted to write the word *ship*," I showed the *ship* picture card, "would I start writing it like *sun*, or *hat*, or *she*? Hmm,. . .*ship*?" I left a bit of space to invite more students to think along with me, momentarily ignoring raised hands.

"I hear /shhh/, like *she*, at the beginning of *ship*. Thumbs up if you agree! Can someone come up and write the letters we need at the beginning of *ship*?"

I called a student up and prompted him to write the digraph in the third column. Then, I prompted kids to identify the familiar phonogram and I invited a student to come up and write *-ip* to complete the word.

FIG. 15–1 Partners engage in see-saw writing, taking turns drawing pictures and labeling with beginning sounds /s/, /h/, and /sh/.

While at this point the sounds /s/ and /h/ are very familiar to students, they are being practiced for the purpose of having learners distinguish between the sound of the consonants when they are the onset of a word and the sound of the digraph, the two consonants acting together, as the onset. Until now, writers may have been using the s or the h to represent the /sh/ sound.

WORD-PART POWER

ACTIVE ENGAGEMENT/LINK

Call out a number of words beginning with *s, h,* or *sh* and ask partners to work together to write the letter or letters each word begins with.

"Let's keep practicing, to strengthen those super ears so you can hear and write new words! Quick! Take out one whiteboard to share with a partner. I'll say a word. Then, you and your partner can work together to figure out how to write it. Remember, listen carefully to the first part to decide if it starts like *sun, hat,* or *she.* Here's the first word: *shell*."

"Let's say it together. *Shell.* Listen to that first sound." The kids said /sh/ while some pointed up at the shell picture on the easel. "Check it with your partner. Say both words and make sure the beginning sounds are the same. Then, work together to spell it. Go ahead and write the beginning of that word and then try to write the rest." Then, I wrote the word in the third column on the easel, prompting kids to check their spelling and fix it up if needed.

I went on to call out several more words, including *shell, soup, horse, shoe,* and *shark*. I gradually released the amount of support and coaching to assess what children were able to do with independence.

FIG. 15–2   The teacher sets up for the practice of writing words with *s, h,* and *sh.*

RUG TIME

Set partnerships up for see-saw writing, in which children take turns drawing pictures and labeling with beginning sounds *s, h,* and *sh.*

"Let's do some see-saw. . .writing! I know you see-saw read, taking turns with a partner to read the pages in your books. Right now, let's take turns drawing and writing. Erase your boards so you'll be ready to play." I waited for the students to clear their whiteboards.

"Here's how it works. One partner will draw, and the other will write. So first, I'll say a word, then 'Ready, set, draw!' and Partner 2 will draw it quickly. Then when I say 'Ready, set, label!' you'll pass the whiteboard to Partner 1, who will write the word to label the picture. Let's give it a try!

"The first word is *sock*. I am wearing a black sock on my foot." I held my pant leg up to reveal a black sock, adding a bit of context to support learners. "Ready, set, draw!"

I gave all the Partner 2s about ten seconds to make a quick sketch. Then I said, "Ready, set, label! Partner 1, it's your turn to write. Now, point and read it together. Make sure you listen closely for the first sound!"

I gave the Partner 1s a few moments to finish writing, then prepared students to alternate roles. "This time, partners, swap roles. Partner 1 will draw, and Partner 2 will write. The next word is *shovel*. I like to dig a hole in the sand with a shovel. Ready, set, draw!"

I went on to prompt kids to pass the whiteboard quickly between them, to draw and label words that begin with *s*, *h*, and *sh*, including *hill*, *sand*, and *shop*. I kept the focus of my coaching on the first part of the word, encouraging students to approximate the spelling of the rest of the word.

SHARE • Finding a Digraph in the Familiar Snap Word, *The*

Guide learners in discovering the digraph *th* in the familiar snap word, *the*.

"Guess what, friends? Mabel has another word she wants to teach us." I held up the word card for *the*. "Wait, we already know this word! Maybe Mabel wants us to study it to learn more about how letters and words work? Let's try it! Turn to your partner and tell your partner what you notice about the word *the*." I listened in, and then shared out.

"Many of you noticed that *the* has a *t* and an *h* in the beginning of the word. *Th* is like *sh*—it's another letter pair that goes together to make one sound. Let's all make that sound of *th*, /th/. It feels a little funny to make that sound and looks a little funny, too, with our tongues sticking out! What are some words that start with *th*?" Kids called out *think*, *thorn*, *thumb*, *this*.

"So now we know two digraphs, *sh* and *th*. Let's sing a little song to help us remember how the digraphs work. It's called "The Digraph Song" and it's sung to the tune of 'If You're Happy and You Know It.'"

EXTENSION 1 • Learning Three New Snap Words: *He, We, Be*

 GETTING READY

- Display the *he* word card and the "How to Learn a Word" anchor chart from kindergarten
  Unit 1, *Making Friends with Letters*.

Revisit a new snap word that was discovered during the connection, and guide students through the familiar process of making a word into a snap word.

I displayed the word *he* that we had read during the connection. "Thanks for reminding me that we have a new snap word to learn that we discovered in the word *she*." I turned to the "How to Learn a Word" chart.

"First, read it!" I pointed under the printed card as the students read the word.

WORD-PART POWER

Remember that if a child writes shvl *as a label here, that'd be fine. What we are really looking for in this approximation is the* sh *as the onset.*

The Digraph Song

S and H put together say /sh/
S and H put together say /sh/
They connect to form one sound
Like in sheep and shower
They are letters that together say /sh/

T and H put together say /th/
T and H put together say /th/
They connect to form one sound
Like in this and think.
They are letters that together say /th/

C and H put together say /ch/
C and H put together say /ch/
They connect to form one sound
Like in chin and chow
They are letters that together say /ch/

Teachers, there are two th *sounds in English. One is voiced, meaning you use your vocal cords to make the sound, as in* this *and* that. *The other* th *sound is unvoiced and therefore you do not use your vocal cords, as in* think *and* thank. *You may want to call attention to the difference in articulation, but probably only if there is a confusion.*

"Now, study it. Tell your partner what you're noticing. Yes, it rhymes with *she* and *me* and *we* and *be*! It has two letters—one consonant and one vowel.

"Then spell it: *h-e.*

"Now let's cover, write, and check it. Quick, take a picture with your brain before I cover it." I covered the word with my hand. "Now write it!" The kids began to work on their whiteboards. After a moment, I uncovered the word. "Make sure it matches, and fix it up if it doesn't.

"Now, let's use it. Hmm,. . . " I tapped my temple. "I asked my friend if *he* wanted to play soccer. Think of some more sentences with your partner." I listened in and coached a few kids.

We then quickly wrote *we* and *be*. We used them both in sentences too.

EXTENSION 2 • "What's the First Sound that You Hear?" Song

Invite children to sing a familiar song to practice hearing digraphs /sh/ and /th/ at the beginning of words.

"Remember our song, 'What's the First Sound that You Hear?' that goes to the tune of 'London Bridge Is Falling Down'?" I hummed a few bars to remind students how the song goes.

"Join me when you can. It goes like this":

What's the first sound that you hear, that you hear, that you hear?
What's the first sound that you hear in. . .*shiny*, *shiny*, *shiny*?"

I paused, giving the children time to process.

/sh/ is the first sound that you hear, that you hear, that you hear!
/sh/ is the first sound that you hear in. . .*shiny*, *shiny*, *shiny*.

We continued singing a few more times with different words: *think*, *shiver*, *thumb*.

EXTENSION 3 • Alliteration Game

- Prepare to record words on Post-its.

Brainstorm a list of words that begin with the digraph *sh* and make tongue twisters out of them to reinforce kids' learning about digraphs.

"Everyone, make the sound of the *sh* digraph. Make the sound until you think of a word that starts with that sound: /shhhhhh/-op, *shop*! Your turn next!"

Kids called out a few ideas: "/shhhhh/-oe, *shoe*! /shhhhh/-ort, *short*!"

"Make the sound again and keep thinking of words." I drew a quick picture on a Post-it of each word as the kids called them out: *shell*, *short*, *shiny*, *shark*, *sheep*, *shampoo*.

"Maybe we can turn these into silly tongue twisters. How about this? 'The shiny shark shops for shells.' You see, it's a tongue twister because so many of the words start with the same sound that it makes it tricky to say the sentence. Let's try another one with *short*, *sheep*, *shiver*, and *shower*. Oh, I'm getting a silly picture in my mind. 'The short sheep. . .'"

"Shivers!" "He's in the shower!"

"So funny! Let's say it in a whole sentence. 'The short sheep shivers in the shower!' What two letters does every word in this sentence start with? That's right—*s-h*.

"Now, try saying our tongue twister fast."

We planned to do this work with *th* at another time.

Word-Part Rodeo

Making Words with Digraphs and Word Parts

IN THIS SESSION

TODAY YOU'LL teach students that a digraph, just like individual letters, can be combined with familiar word parts to read and write words.

TODAY YOUR STUDENTS will discover the *ch* digraph and make words with various digraphs, initial consonants, and familiar word parts.

MINILESSON

CONNECTION

Engage students with a tongue twister in which you introduce the digraph *ch*. Channel students to identify a word part and make a new word with a different digraph.

"Friends, when I was your age, my friends and I would compete to see who could say a tongue twister three times without messing up any of the words. It would always make us laugh. Tongue twisters are made by starting almost every word in a sentence with the same sound. Do you want to try one that I made last night?

"Listen. 'I chop cherries, cheese, and chocolate chips for a tasty snack!'

"Can you say that three times fast? Try it!" The class repeated the line, having fun sputtering the words.

"Let's slow it down and listen to the sounds we hear at the start of some of these words." I repeated the sentence, this time emphasizing the digraph *ch*. "Can you hear the sound that's the same at the beginning of *chop* and *cherries* and *cheese* and *chocolate chips*?" I emphasized the words to focus students' ears on them.

GETTING READY

✔ Prepare a tongue twister using the digraph *ch*.

✔ Write the digraphs *ch*, *sh*, and *th* on Post-its, or gather the word-part cards, to demonstrate making words with digraphs and word parts on your whiteboard.

✔ Distribute a whiteboard, marker, and Post-its (or word-part cards) for each of three digraphs (*ch*, *sh*, *th*) to each partnership.

✔ Distribute a set of four phonogram cards (*-ap*, *-ot*, *-op*, *-ip*) to each partnership.

PHONICS INSTRUCTION

Phonics
• Demonstrate basic knowledge of digraphs (*sh*, *th*, *ch*).

Word Knowledge/Solving
• Use common word endings to generate new words (VC).
• Use familiar word parts including phonograms to spell unfamiliar words.

"/Ch/!" the students shouted back.

"Now take a look at the word *chop*." I then hung up the tongue twister. "The first letters in this word look a bit like /sh/ and /th/. This time there's a *c* in front of the *h*. I think we found another digraph—*c* and *h* work together to make a new sound: /ch/.

"And wait, I'm noticing some of you are swinging your imaginary lassos. Did you see the *op* in *chop*? Okay, let's chop off the digraph. I need to make sure I chop off both letters, *c* and *h*." I made a chopping motion and erased the *ch* from my whiteboard. "Let's put a new beginning on this word, another digraph!"

I added the letters *s-h* to the beginning of the word, and the kids read aloud, "*Shop*!"

♣ **Name the teaching point.**

"Today I want to remind you that word-part power can help you make new words. You can chop off the beginning of one word and add another beginning. But here's something new—sometimes you'll need to chop off or glue on not just one, but *two* letters, like the digraph *ch*."

TEACHING

Demonstrate how you make words with digraphs and familiar word parts.

"Now that we know three different digraphs—*ch*, *sh*, and *th*," I stuck a Post-it for each digraph on the top of my whiteboard as I named them, "we can use them to make words using word parts we know. We can activate our word-part power to turn *chop* into *shop*.

"We'll have to lasso up the word part just as we usually do and remember to chop off *both* letters when there is a digraph. Let's try it." I placed the *ch* Post-it in the middle of the board, then quickly wrote the letters *ip* next to it. "Here is the word *chip*. Mmmm, I love chips!

"Watch how I lasso up the word part *ip*." I circled the phonogram. "Now, let's chop off its beginning!" I pulled off the *ch* Post-it, leaving just the phonogram. The class giggled.

"I bet I can make a new word by adding on a new beginning. Let me try *t-h*." I stuck the Post-it with *th* beside the phonogram and read *thip*. "Nope, that's not a real word. Let me try *s-h*." I replaced the *th* Post-it with the *sh* Post-it and read *ship*. "Yes, that's a word!

"So, *chip* can help you spell *ship* by chopping off one beginning and putting on another. Oh, and what if I take away *sh* and add just one letter? Let me try *s*. *Sip*! Let me try *h*. . . *hip*!"

ch Tongue Twister

I chop cherries,
cheese
and chocolate chips
for a tasty snack!

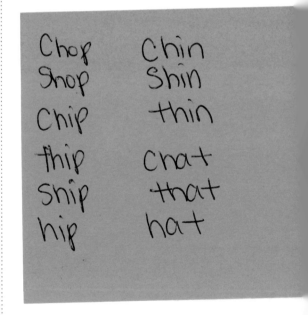

Chop   Chin
Shop   Shin
Chip   thin
thip   chat
Ship   that
hip   hat

ACTIVE ENGAGEMENT/LINK

Distribute a whiteboard with three Post-its, one for each digraph, *ch, sh, th*, to each partnership. Prompt children to make a series of words with different onsets and rimes.

"Now it's your turn! Will you and your partner make the word *chin*? Use the Post-it with the digraph *ch* and write the word part you hear at the end of *chin*. You can check it with mine." I quickly constructed the word on my whiteboard.

Once each partnership had formed the word, I said, "Hmm,. . .what do you and your partner notice about this word? Lasso up the word part you see. Circle it!" After a moment, I voiced over, "I see you lassoing up the ending part, *in*. Now chop off the *ch* and add on a new digraph, *sh*. Put *sh* in front of -*in*. What new word did you make? Say the first sound and then the part.

"*Shin*!" I saw a few puzzled faces, so I reached down and touched the front of my lower leg and said, "This is your shin.

"What if we chop off *sh* and try another digraph? Chop off the *sh* and add *th*. Read the word. Yes, *thin*. It means not thick!

"Wait, now what if we wanted to write the word *tin*? The can is made of *tin*. Chop off the beginning of *thin* and add a new beginning. What letter do you need?" I said, "Listen to the first part of *thin*. Listen to the first sound of *tin*. Put your fingers under the first two letters. Take them away. Change /th/ to /t/."

We went on to manipulate the onset to change *at* to *chat*, *that*, and *hat*.

FIG. 16–1 A partnership's whiteboard with digraph Post-its and a marker to write end parts to make words.

Challenging children to move from chopping off a digraph and then replacing it with a single letter as the onset in a word helps them become more flexible word solvers. This more closely resembles the work kids will have to do in their actual writing.

RUG TIME

Set children up to have a word-part rodeo, matching digraphs to word parts to make words.

"I think with all this lassoing it might be time to have our very own rodeo—but instead of rounding up cattle, we'll round up *words*. We've learned lots of word parts, and now we know about digraphs, so let's practice putting them together to make a bunch of words! Ready for our word-part rodeo?" The kids cheered.

"Okay, here's how it will go. Partner 1 will keep the whiteboard and the Post-its with each digraph—*ch, sh,* and *th.* You'll be the Digraphs." I paused a moment as one student in each pair took ownership of the board. "And Partner 2, I'll give you each a phonogram card, and you'll be the word parts." I quickly distributed one of four phonogram cards (-*ap, -ot, -op, -ip*) to every Partner 2.

"Let's warm up for the rodeo. Digraphs, choose one of your digraph Post-its, swing your lasso, and make the sound of your digraph! Then Word Parts, make the sounds on your phonogram card!" Kids did so.

"Okay, time to start the word-part rodeo. First, stand up and spread out around the room. Digraphs, you can gallop like a horse, swinging your lasso to round up a word part that you can use to make a word—and Word Parts, you can be the cattle moving around the room waiting to be lassoed up." I modeled quickly, galloping then moving slowly across the floor.

"Digraphs, when you see a word part, swing your imaginary lasso and say, 'Got you, -ap!' or 'Got you, -ot!' Then, huddle together to spell the word on your whiteboard. When you've done that, say, 'Yee-haw!' Then set your word part free and round up a new word part to make a different word."

I "galloped" around the room too, supporting children in reading the words they were making.

SHARE • Connecting to Our Writing

Celebrate the words that were made during the rodeo and make a connection to writing.

From the middle of the room, I called for the students' attention. I said, "Wow, what a rodeo! You worked together to round up so many new words. Yee-haw!

"Come back to your rug spots and share all the words you made." While kids shared, I put up a list of words I had just made while listening in, and read them.

"Congratulations on making all these words in our rodeo. Think of all the words you'll be able to write now during writing workshop!"

EXTENSION 1 • Celebrating the Digraph *Ch* with a Song

GETTING READY

- Cue up the short video clip for "Chim Chim Cher-ee" from the film *Mary Poppins*. A link to the clip is available in the online resources.
- Enlarge the new lyrics to the song, and display where all kids can see them.

POSSIBLE COACHING MOVES

▶ "Wait! A word can't have two beginnings! Separate and find an ending part."

▶ "Make sure to read the word and decide if it is a real or fake word."

▶ "When you are done, say 'Yee-haw!' and move to find another match."

Teachers, you may want to do this work with a half or a third of the kids at a time, so that some children are watching and cheering like fans do at a rodeo. Having spectators will help with management for sure, and it will also allow for some of your class to be reading the words that are made.

Play a short video clip of the song "Chim Chim Cher-ee" from the movie *Mary Poppins* **and then teach students the version that you wrote.**

"When I was getting ready to teach you about the *ch* digraph, I thought about how tricky it can be to hear the difference between /sh/ and /ch/. Then I remembered a song from a movie I loved when I was little. The song is called 'Chim Chim Cher-ee' and it is sung by a chimney sweep, who uses the /ch/ over and over in his song. Let's listen!"

I played the ninety-second video clip so kids could become familiar with the tune, then I said, "I wrote more words to help us practice the /ch/ sound. I used some of the words from our tongue twister. Should I teach it to you?" I displayed the lyrics on the easel and I sang the words while pointing to each word with my pointer.

I then invited the class to sing with me.

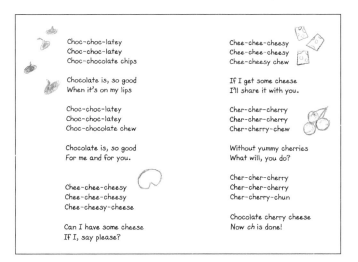

Choc-choc-latey
Choc-choc-latey
Choc-chocolate chips

Chocolate is, so good
When it's on my lips

Choc-choc-latey
Choc-choc-latey
Choc-chocolate chew

Chocolate is, so good
For me and for you.

Chee-chee-cheesy
Chee-chee-cheesy
Chee-cheesy-cheese

Can I have some cheese
If I, say please?

Chee-chee-cheesy
Chee-chee-cheesy
Chee-cheesy chew

If I get some cheese
I'll share it with you.

Cher-cher-cherry
Cher-cher-cherry
Cher-cherry-chew

Without yummy cherries
What will, you do?

Cher-cher-cherry
Cher-cher-cherry
Cher-cherry-chun

Chocolate cherry cheese
Now *ch* is done!

EXTENSION 2 • Using Gestures to Remember Sounds

Introduce gestures that connect to each digraph as a reminder of how the digraph sounds and feels when it is pronounced.

"The digraphs are pretty fun to say, aren't they? You know, like /ch/ /ch/ /ch/. It's fun to make that sound. How many of you think of the word *chop* when we say /ch/?" I made a gesture like I was chopping something with my hand. "Do that with me as we say /ch/. Will that help you remember that /ch/ is the sound for *chop* and is spelled *ch*?" Heads nodded as kids kept chopping and making the sound of the *ch* digraph.

"Also, by chopping with your hand, you can remember that the /ch/ sound is a *quick* sound. You don't hold onto it like this: /chuuu/. Instead, you cut it short—like a little chop: /ch/."

I continued by showing how I put my index finger to my lips and made a continuous /shhhhhh/ sound. I invited the children to join me and see if some *sh* words pop out of their mouth. I then made the /th/ sound, showing students how to make sure their tongues were in the right position, a bit like the feel and sound of blowing a bubble with bubblegum, and made the shape of a bubble with my hands.

You might create a version of this song to teach the sh *and* th *digraphs too!*

GETTING READY

- Have the *sh*, *ch*, and *th* digraph cards ready to display.

Sing a song to give kids practice at the sounds digraphs make.

"The digraphs *sh* and *ch* and *th* are in so many words that it is important to get really good at hearing those sounds. I thought this song could give us the practice we need to help us write these two-letter combinations in our writing. You'll recognize the tune—it's 'Old MacDonald Had a Farm.'"

What is the sound that starts these words: *shirt* and *shoe* and *shell*?
/Sh/ is the sound that starts these words.
Shirt and *shoe* and *shell*.
With a /sh/, /sh/ here.
And a /sh/, /sh/ there.
Here a /sh/, there a /sh/, everywhere a /sh/, /sh/.
/Sh/ is the sound that starts these words.
Shirt and *shoe* and *shell*.

"Shall we sing it again? This time, let's sing it with some new words: *cherries*, *short*, and *think*."

This song can be used for all three digraphs, and you can invite the kids to add in the example words for each digraph. As you sing the song, you may want to flash a card with the sh or th or ch on it so that the children are connecting the sound with the letters.

Using All Your Powers

Snap Word Power, Sound Power, and
Word-Part Power to Write Sentences

IN THIS SESSION

TODAY YOU'LL teach students that when writers want to write a sentence, they use all their powers, especially pointer power, snap word power, reread power, sound power, and sometimes word-part power.

TODAY YOUR STUDENTS will use their writing powers to build sentences and reread their writing, drawing on all that they've been learning in the first three units.

MINILESSON

CONNECTION

Give children a chance to recall and name the writing powers they've been using.

"Writers, you've been working so hard during writing workshop to make sure your stories are easy for you and other people to read. I see you using so many writing powers. Tell your partner which powers you use."

❖ **Name the teaching point.**

"Today I want to teach you that when you want to write up a storm, it helps to think of a word you want to write, and then think, 'How will I write this? Is this a word I'll write in a snap? A word that takes word-part power to figure out? A word to stretch out like a rubber band using sound power?' Writers try all those ways to write words."

GETTING READY

✔ Ask students to bring their writing folders to the meeting area. To avoid distraction, have them sit on their folders until they are needed during rug time.

✔ Print Mabel's story ("I went to the fun pk.") and place into a folder or a booklet. Print the words out and cut them into pieces as shown. Engineer the booklet so that when you close it after reading it, you can pretend that all the words have fallen out of it. 🎇

✔ Create a sign with missing letters that reads "We will _____ to you. It is f_____!" 🎇

PHONICS INSTRUCTION

Concepts About Print
• Demonstrate understanding of the organization and basic features of print.

Phonics
• Identify and use initial, final, and salient sounds when writing words.
• Use letter-sound knowledge to spell.

Word Knowledge/Solving
• Use familiar word parts including phonograms (*un*) to spell unfamiliar words.

High-Frequency Words
• Locate and read high-frequency words in a text.

TEACHING

Guide children through a study of Mabel's writing to see which powers she used to write a page of her story.

"Let's take a look at some of Mabel's writing and see which powers she used to write this sentence." I displayed a page from Mabel's writing and read it to the class.

I went to the fun pk

"Let's read this together and figure out which power Mabel used when she was writing. Snap your fingers if you think she used snap word power, hold your hand up to your ear if you think she used sound power, and swing your imaginary lassos if you think she used word-part power. We'll use pointer power to read. Mabel, did you use pointer power to write?" I made Mabel nod. "So, we know one power she already used—pointer power!

"Let's start reading. 'I. . . '" Readers started snapping their fingers. "Ah, I hear you snapping. *I* is a snap word. Mabel, did you write it in a snap?" I made her nod yes, and we continued on.

"I went. . . " Kids started snapping, and I said, "Snap word power!" We continued reading, naming snap word power for the other words, except for *fun*, when children signaled word-part power was used and *park*, when children signaled that sound power was used.

"Wow, Mabel, when you wrote this page you had to think about what to write and then use *all* of your powers to write the sentence. That's what all writers do. Thanks for sharing your work!"

ACTIVE ENGAGEMENT/LINK

Invite children to help you reconstruct the sentence from Mabel's story using all of the powers they know.

I closed the book, and as I did so, I dropped a cut-up sentence strip on the floor. . . . "Oh no! The words have fallen out of Mabel's book! Can you help me put them back before Mabel finds out? I see a letter: *f*. Oh, and Nicolas just picked up a word part: *-un*. Oh, and here are some snap words. Here is the word . . . *pk*. Is that *park*? Hmm,. . . I think some letters are missing. How can we arrange these words to make a sentence?" I lined up all the words and letter cards to the left of the drawing.

"How did her sentence go?" I tapped the picture. "I went to the fun park," the children said. "First word?" I asked. "*I*!" Children snapped their fingers. I moved *I* under the drawing. "Turn and tell your partner what comes next." As children named the snap words, I moved *went* and *to* next to *I*. "Let's reread the sentence—'I went to the . . .'

"*Fun*!" kids shouted. "I don't see *fun*," I said. Children were swinging their lassos and saying, "Put the *f* with *un*." I moved the letter and word part together next to the word *the*. "Let's blend the first sound and part together to make sure it looks right: /f/-/un/, *fun*!

"So now we have this card left." I held up the card with *pk* on it. "*Park*!" children shouted. "I think maybe we can help Mabel with hearing more sounds in this word. Let's try to read it. Put your pointer power up.

"Let's use sound power: /p/ /k/. Hmm,. . .let's use sound power to hear and write more sounds in this word. Say it slowly." Children were stretching the word and listening for more sounds. "/Rrrr/," said many children. I crossed out *pk* and wrote *prk*. "Great work using your sound power. Now let's reread the sentence and make sure it looks right."

FIG. 17–1 The teacher moves a page of Mabel's book and the words fall off the page, getting all mixed up.

RUG TIME CLUBS

Set clubs up to take turns studying a page of the story that each writer is publishing from writing workshop, noticing the writing powers used to write it—and then fix it up if needed.

"Clubs, you each have your writing folders. Take out the piece you are publishing and find a page you want to check and read to your club members. They are going to help you make sure you've used your powers the best you can." I coached writers to choose their piece and quickly find a page to read.

"Rug club member #1, you will go first. Read your writing, and everyone else in your club will signal the power they think you used to write that word. Remember: snap for snap words, lasso for word-part power, and touch ear for sound power. Here's a tip: as you are reading, if you or a club member realizes you can use a power to make the writing easier to read, just like we did with Mabel's piece, go ahead and fix it! Then switch to the next club member so everyone gets a turn.

"Writers, whenever you are writing you can do the same thing with your writing partner or even by yourself. You can think about what powers you used and if there are any words where you need to use powers to fix it up and make it easier to read."

SHARE • Offering the Gift of Reading to Visitors

Edit a sign you made to celebrate your reading and phonics and to announce that the class wants to give the gift of reading to anyone who comes by the classroom.

"Friends, maybe we should have a sign now that we've been celebrating the gift of reading. Mabel helped me write this sign to hang outside our classroom, so visitors know they can come in to hear us read." I revealed the sign:

We will _____ to you. It is f_____!

"Mabel's sign says, 'We will read to you. It is fun.'" I pointed under each word (or blank space for a word) as I read. "But look! We are missing some important letters and word parts. Will you help Mabel and me with the sign, so people can read it and know to come into our classroom?"

"Yes!"

"We'll need to use our powers. Get your pointer power ready. Let's read this sign together from the beginning. 'We. . .will. . .'" When we got to the first blank, the kids said, "Read" and put their hands to their ears, indicating sound power was needed. "Okay, let's stretch the word and hear the sounds." I recorded the word *read* as children stretched and told me the letter, but I spelled *read* conventionally, because this would be a sign that needed to be read by other readers.

We continued reading and when students reached the last blank, they noticed the word part *-un* missing and added that.

"Readers, now we have a sign for outside our door. Let's bring it outside and hang it up!" We paraded outside the classroom, and a couple of students helped me hold it against the wall next to our classroom door while I taped it. "Let's read our sign together. 'We will read to you. It is fun!'"

"Congratulations, Super Readers and Writers, on using all your powers to read and write. And congratulations on giving the gift of reading to our school, each other, and yourselves! Let's swing our lassos one last time." We did and "Yee-haws" filled the room.

Vowel Power

Lucy Calkins, Series Editor

Angela Báez, Katie M. Wears, and Casey Maxwell

Photography by Peter Cunningham

Illustrations by Lisa Hernandez Corcoran and Marjorie Martinelli

HEINEMANN ◆ PORTSMOUTH, NH

To Eli, our river of dreams. —Angela

To my siblings and Mary Ford, whose words teach love and patience.
—Katie

To my father, who filled my life with books, and got me started down
this path. —Casey

Heinemann
361 Hanover Street
Portsmouth, NH 03801–3912

www.heinemann.com

Offices and agents throughout the world

© 2018 by Lucy Calkins, Angela Báez, Katie M. Wears, and Casey Maxwell

"Dedicated to Teachers" is a trademark of Greenwood Publishing Group, Inc.

The authors and publisher wish to thank those who have generously given permission to reprint borrowed material:

"The Hokey Pokey" © 1950 Sony/ATV Music Publishing LLC. All rights administered by Sony/ATV Music Publishing LLC, 424 Church Street, Suite 1200, Nashville, TN 37219. All rights reserved. Used by permission.

Cataloging-in-Publication data is on file with the Library of Congress.

ISBN-13: 978-0-325-10520-8

Editors: Marielle Palombo, Tracy Wells, and Anna Gratz Cockerille
Production: Elizabeth Valway
Cover and interior designs: Jenny Jensen Greenleaf
Photography: Peter Cunningham
Illustrations: Lisa Hernandez Corcoran, Kimberly Fox, and Marjorie Martinelli
Composition: Publishers' Design and Production Services, Inc.
Manufacturing: Steve Bernier

Printed in the United States of America on acid-free paper
22 21 20 19 18 VP 1 2 3 4 5

Acknowledgments

AMONG KINDERGARTEN TEACHERS' many super powers is the ability to read kindergarten writing. *Vre wun hz a hrt.* "Huh?" most people say. "Everyone has a heart," Kindergarten teachers read, without batting an eye. Kindergarten teachers admire the attempts and picture the possible. Thank you, you miracle-workers, for giving so many children the gift of writing. This unit, we hope, will help your students' messages become clearer to the ordinary civilians of the world too.

This book came to be because Lucy Calkins believed we could write it. Lucy, thank you for seeing us. What an honor to have access to your brilliance, what a gift to have been molded by it. Thank you for being a writing mentor and a challenger, for holding our hands through the dark, for thrusting us toward the light. You steered the ship but let us chart the course.

We are so grateful to Lucy and Natalie Louis for kindling this grand project. They saw a need and filled it, twentyfold. They are innovators of the highest order. Natalie, your magical work with both children and teachers inspires us on a daily basis. You led this project with grace and an incredible sense of humor, and we are forever thankful for your ideas, your kindness, and your willingness to always share your brilliant thinking.

We are especially grateful to the members of the senior staff who co-lead the organization and inspire us with their dedication to helping schools outgrow themselves: Laurie Pessah, Mary Ehrenworth, and Amanda Hartman. Every day, in all of our work, we remember and honor Kathleen Tolan. She always saw our potential and supported us along the way, helping us realize what is possible. We are certain she was with us through the challenging parts and celebrating alongside us when the manuscript was complete.

Our colleagues at the Reading and Writing Project are the best of the best. How proud we are to know them, to learn from them, to grow with them. Rachel Rothman-Perkins and Rebecca Cronin, thank you for the extra time and care you gave to this project. Your beliefs and knowledge are woven through the pages of this series.

When we mention our colleagues and leaders at the Reading and Writing Project, we must also acknowledge the incredible contributions of Kelly Boland Hohne and Katie Clements, who joined us for brainstorming sessions, multiple rounds of drafting and redrafting, and the tons of brilliant revisions that made this book immeasurably better. Heartfelt thanks to Elizabeth Franco, who whispered life into the first pages that shaped all the rest.

This book stands on the shoulders of past staff developers who continue to impact our beliefs about word study. Mary Ann Colbert, Enid Martinez, Elizabeth Moore, and Christine Cook Robson, your anecdotes and wisdom are stitched into our thinking. We would also like to thank Joe Yukish, whose thoughtful feedback always seemed to come at the perfect time.

Our work in word study has been informed by others in the field who have mentored us with their writing, practice, and research. Thank you to Pat Cunningham, Donald Bear, Gay Su Pinnell, Irene Fountas, Donna Scanlon, Kathy Ganske, Marie Clay, and Tim Rasinski.

Finalizing the art and resources that accompany this unit was a giant endeavour that wouldn't have come to fruition without the support of many. Lisa Hernandez Corcoran shared her artistic talents to create the images that will energize this book for the students in your classroom. Lisa was tireless. Through scores of revisions, tedious requests, and last-minute switches, Lisa's only response was *yes*. The results leave us breathless and filled with gratitude. Marjorie Martinelli took on the monumental responsibility of orchestrating the art and resources across this series. Marjorie, we pinch ourselves daily that we have you to beautify our pages. Your attention to detail and generosity astound us. Suzanne Korn and Hillary Andaya graciously gave their time when we called on them to share their expertise. Peter

Cunningham's photographs beautifully represent the smiles, laughter, and joy of the children and classrooms that he has pictured in these pages. We hope that you and your students enjoy the art and resources as much as we do.

We are so grateful to the teachers and children who animated this unit as it was being written and produced. This version of the unit wouldn't exist without the time, help, and feedback from teachers and colleagues. Thank you to Trent DeBerry, Lisa Ultan, and Rachelle Amo for being thought partners and sharing your insights on the manuscript. We would also like to thank Rebecca Pembroke, Rina Britell, and the teachers and students from Barlow Mountain Elementary School, who graciously opened the doors of their classrooms for Peter Cunningham to capture images for this book.

This book received thoughtful guidance from the dedicated team at Heinemann. They knew just when we needed cheering from the sidelines and when to join us for more coaching and support. Marielle Palombo's expertise and attention to detail throughout the editing process left an indelible mark on this book and we are forever grateful. We are especially grateful to Abby Heim and Elizabeth Valway. Their gentle nudges and kind emails helped us reach the finish line with smiles on our faces. Thank you to Shannon Thorner, who provided essential behind-the-scenes support for this series.

Finally, we'd like to thank our personal support systems. *From Angela*: Thank you Mikael, my love, my champion, my partner. You've given me everything I hold most dear. It's all because of you. Mom, thank you for all of the late nights and early mornings. You taught me what a mother's love could do. *From Katie:* Thank you to the mentors and colleagues who influence and support me: Karen DiNatale, Barb Ouderkirk, Tim Cowin, Mary Ford, Josh Block, Eric Byrne, Rachelle Amo, and my family and friends. *From Casey:* Thank you to Scott Maxwell, simply the most supportive partner imaginable, on this and all projects.

With tremendous gratitude and love, it is our sincere hope that this book inspires you and your young learners.

—Angela, Katie, and Casey

Contents

BEND III   Vowels in Bigger Words

Registration instructions to access the digital resources that accompany this book may be found on p. x.

An Orientation to the Unit

YOU HAVE ENTERED that special period in kindergarten when many children are teetering on conventionality in both reading and writing. This is landmark territory. What a magical time! You, and others, can read their writing—mostly. That is because many students are progressing from semiphonetic to phonetic writing.

Linguists call consonants the "noise" and vowels the "music" of language (Bear et al. 2015; Crystal 1987). It is not surprising, then, that early writers attend to consonants as the most prominent features in words. In their writing, they tend to use consonants and only attention-grabbing long vowels at the beginning of words, such as *E* in the word *eat* (likely recorded as *et*). As they move from semiphonetic to phonetic writing, often writers' next big step is working on short vowels, especially in the middle of words.

The authors of *Words Their Way* (2015) describe some markers of this shift from early to middle letter name–alphabetic stage of spelling. They note that during this transition, learners make the leap from partial to full phoneme segmentation. In kids' writing in this stage, you'll often find that consonants at the beginnings and endings of words are present and short vowels are used but confused in monosyllabic words. Vowels in multisyllabic words typically tend to be absent.

Why do vowels pose more of a challenge than consonants? Many researchers attribute this to the way vowels are produced in the mouth. David Crystal (2013), a prominent linguist, invites us to feel for the differences between consonants and vowels:

All the sounds which shut tight or cause a friction sound are consonants. Vowels don't do either of these things. Say I, oo, ah, oh, ee. *Do you notice how open the mouth is? The tongue is moving up and down, backwards and forwards, but it never closes off the mouth completely, and you never get any friction noise.*

Try making the short-vowel sounds in sequence: /ă/, /ĕ/, /ĭ/, /ŏ/, /ŭ/. Your mouth movements vary only slightly. It is no wonder that young children need support noticing the differences among short-vowel sounds. Long-vowel sounds often come quickly to learners because the sound is the name of the letter, but short-vowel sounds can be more puzzling because they lack such a clear letter-sound relationship (Scanlon, Anderson, and Sweeney 2017). As Scanlon, Anderson, and Sweeney note: "For example, for the letter *e*, the short sound is not heard in the name of the letter. Rather the short *e* sounds like the beginning of the name of the letter *a*."

This unit fits tongue and groove with *Bigger Books, Bigger Reading Muscles*, the third book in the kindergarten Units of Study for Teaching Reading. We've built upon the idea of super powers, adding a new one: *vowel power!* Throughout this phonics unit, you will see even more connections to *How-To Books: Writing to Teach Others*, the third kindergarten book in the Units of Study in Opinion, Information, and Narrative Writing. Graphophonic information becomes salient earlier in encoding than it does in decoding. Therefore, the work children do in attending to the medial vowel sound in writing may march ahead of the work they do in reading, where they will attend predominantly to the initial and final sounds of words.

Readers of level C and level D books typically use the beginnings and endings of words along with the pictures to solve words, which is often all they need. To support transfer of key phonics skills, such as attending to individual phonemes and letter-sound correspondence, there are some lessons in this unit where we invite children to search for vowels in the books they are reading. It is *not* cause for alarm when children in this stage are not using all parts of the word, including medial vowels, to read. In fact, surprisingly few CVC words actually appear in level A–D books. However, learning about CVC words is important, because it provides children an opportunity to isolate and manipulate the individual phonemes in words, including the medial vowel. Children will also be able to use this learning when problem solving multisyllabic words, which happens often in writing workshop during kindergarten. In this phonics unit, you'll work with a handful of decodable texts that contain more CVC words than most authentic texts do, so that learners have the opportunity to work with medial vowels in books.

Some students, however, may be ready to begin attending to letters and sounds in the middle of words and will apply these skills to reading as well as writing. Regardless, children's use of inventive, phonetic spelling prepares them for the conventional reading work in their near future. Clay (1993) explains that learning to write letters, words, and sentences helps children visually discriminate details in print, which they will use when reading. It can also provide you with a window into what a child knows about words and how they work, allowing you to nudge them forward within their zone of proximal development. Above all, your students' phonological awareness will develop during writing workshop, where we celebrate approximations and inventive spelling.

Of course, kindergarten students will vary quite a lot in their skill development, and differentiation of instruction will be essential. Remember that this work is always multilevel, and at any given time, you will be coaching students on a range of skills. Just as we support students at different levels in reading and writing workshop, we do the same during phonics time.

OVERVIEW OF THE UNIT

This unit is composed of three bends, or parts:

Bend I: Vowels in Every Word

Bend II: Distinguishing Short-Vowel Sounds

Bend III: Vowels in Bigger Words

The unit opens with a note from Reader-Man, an old friend from phonics Unit 3, *Word-Part Power*, who notices something important: vowels are missing in their writing! Reader-Man then bestows upon the class a new power, vowel power. After all, says Reader-Man, words need vowels to be understood. This launches the class into an investigation leading to the discovery that all words have vowels. At the end of Bend I, you'll return to this idea. You'll tell your kindergartners that it's a writer's responsibility to check that all of their words have vowels, and that they are ready to take on that responsibility.

In the first session, Reader-Man will give your students a new tool—a vowel shield—that functions as a ready reference throughout the unit. It contains pictures that go with the short-vowel sounds and sets children up to study short-vowel sounds across the unit. In Bend I, children will study short *A* and short *I* closely. While all short vowels can sound similar, we start with *A* and *I* because their short sounds tend to be the least frequently confused. Across the bend, your instruction will feature mostly CVC words with short vowels *A* and *I* in the middle. You'll engage in sorting activities that allow children to work with the vowel sounds in isolation, and in shared reading and interactive editing activities that offer the chance to study them in context. You will teach children "robot talk" as a way to segment words into phonemes, the smallest unit of sound in spoken language. Supporting full segmentation of CVC words helps learners isolate the medial vowel sound.

You will also introduce new high-frequency words, *am* and *did*, that further students' study of short *A* and short *I*. You'll add these words to the word wall, alongside two other words, *how* and *you*, that come up very often when writing How-To books. In this bend, these high-frequency words are debuted during extensions, so you'll want to ensure that you get to these particular extensions.

At the start of Bend I, in addition to vowel shields, Reader-Man will give your class an important piece of information: Vowel power grows. After kids have worked with each of the short-vowel sounds, they will be ready to "light up" that vowel on their shields. In Bend I's celebration, Reader-Man sends a note of congratulations and a box of highlighters, and children will highlight the *A* and the *I* and chant the class vowel cheer: "A! E! I! O! U! A, *apple*, /ă/. E, *egg*, /ĕ/. I, *igloo*, /ĭ/. O, *octopus*, /ŏ/. U, *umbrella*, /ŭ/."

As the first bend gives way to the second bend, you'll continue the puzzling work of distinguishing short-vowel sounds from one another. You'll begin sorting short *E* and short *O* along with the previously studied short *I*, and you'll expand your focus to short *U*. The introduction of the high-frequency words *on*, *up*, *fun*, and *get* in Session 10 further supports students in their work with short *E*, *O*, and *U*. Children will also engage in interactive writing and "making words" activities that include all five short vowels. By the end of the bend, Reader-Man will send a new note with his blessing to highlight all of the vowels on the kids' shields, making their entire shield "shine."

In the third bend, students will study vowels in words that are longer than CVC words. This is ambitious, but also realistic work, because most of the words that kids use in their own natural conversation and writing are bigger than CVC words, such as *chocolate*, *celebration*, *playground*, and *basketball*.

In fact, many of your students' names are multisyllabic, and you'll be able to lean on those during this bend, circling back to name study. You'll teach children how knowledge of CVC words is foundational to writing any words they choose. As a callback to Session 1 of the unit, in the first session of Bend III you'll teach students that not only does every word have at least one vowel, but every syllable of every word does, too.

In this bend, you'll work on a variety of activities that involve attending to vowels in bigger words, including segmenting multisyllabic words, exploring other sounds that vowels can make, and revisiting digraphs that were taught in Unit 3. You'll remind children that they have many strategies to help them solve puzzling words when reading and writing, and that they should draw on all that they know, being flexible and persistent. Most of the texts you'll use to support this work are linked to an upcoming special event: your beloved mascot Mabel's graduation! In the accompanying reading unit, *Bigger Books, Bigger Reading Muscles*, the children have a culminating unit celebration where they graduate into stronger readers, so Mabel is taking after her friends here! You'll end your unit with Mabel's graduation celebration, where children will parade with the class mascot and chant their vowel cheer one final time, before inserting their vowel shields in their writing folders so they can always keep their vowel power activated while writing.

GETTING READY

We've tried to keep materials to a minimum. As in the previous units, you will need an accessible alphabet chart and a class set of whiteboards with markers and erasers as well as a system in place to distribute these easily. You will also continue to use sorting jars to support students with categorization.

We also recommend a set of magnetic letters or letter cards that you can use to make words. "Making words" activities can require a great deal of materials preparation. We've tried to find the simplest way to set up this activity while still allowing children to manipulate letters. During the activity in Session 12, we suggest writing each required letter on an index card for the teacher demonstration and a file folder with each required letter written on its own sticky note for students to use. The activity can be done in partnerships to minimize materials. However, you'll want to set up word-building activities in the way that works best for you. Many teachers prefer to give students or partnerships their own set of magnetic letters to use, maybe organizing them

on a cookie sheet. Others have letter tiles or cards with mats for organization and management.

A pocket chart will be helpful to display letter cards and picture cards for sorting, which you will find in the online resources as well as in your kit. All of the sorts in the unit are picture sorts, so be sure to display the picture side of the card to ensure that students are *listening* for the medial sounds in words. In the online resources you will also find printable Elkonin boxes, which are used across this unit to support segmentation and blending of phonemes. You'll want to have counters handy for segmenting as well.

There are some materials that are unique to this unit that we hope will help it to feel special. The vowel shield is a new tool that you'll use nearly every day in phonics workshop. You'll want to have a class set ready to go on Day One of the unit. At the end of Bend I, Reader-Man secretly delivers a box of highlighters to your class. After studying each vowel, kids will get the opportunity to highlight it on their shields, almost like collecting badges of honor. Mabel the elephant plays an important role in *Vowel Power*. She does helpful things, like point out that Y sometimes acts as a vowel, or write texts that contain contextualized examples of vowels that are the focus of instruction. As your class mascot, she'll need her own vowel shield, too, and since she'll be graduating at the end of the unit, she'll also need a little cap to toss and a recording of "Pomp and Circumstance" for her procession, naturally. Across the unit, you'll reveal several letters from Reader-Man, and an invitation from Mable. Starting with these letters in envelopes adds to the excitement, so you'll want to have a stash of envelopes on hand.

One other new material that is utilized in this unit is a set of hand mirrors. Partners can use these mirrors to notice the way their mouths look when they produce vowel sounds to make it easier to distinguish between the sounds.

Your word wall continues to play an important role in this unit. In each bend, you'll add a few words to your word wall, and students will add them to their snap word pouches. While continuing to review snap words from previous units, in this unit you will introduce *am*, *did*, *for*, *fun*, *get*, *how*, *on*, *play*, *day*, *say*, and *you*. You might also notice a few additional high-frequency words that your children are using in writing or that occur frequently in the books they are reading, such as *come*, *have*, and *said*, deciding to introduce these to your class as snap words. This might be done during whole-group or small-group instruction.

We believe that multiple encounters with a word study feature, both in isolation and in context, promote transfer, so we've provided a number of songs, poems, and controlled texts to support your study of vowels in this unit. In many cases, you'll compose or add to these texts with your students during interactive writing or editing. You'll find the books *The Very Bad Day* and *How to Take Care of Your Vowel Shield*, both by Mabel, as well as many other resources, in the online resources (denoted with 👆). Some of these resources are in the Resource Pack (denoted with 📦) as well. Make the most of these texts, remembering that small copies of conventionally spelled familiar texts can easily become reading material during reading workshop. Many of these texts can also become exemplar and demonstration texts in writing workshop.

Interactive writing is frequently used as a method of instruction across this unit. You'll likely want to have correction tape on hand to support writers. Highlighter tape, translucent tabs, and/or Wikki Stix can also help to spotlight words or parts of words.

In one of the extensions in Bend I, you'll use a familiar alphabet book, which fits with the reading work in *Bigger Books, Bigger Reading Muscles*. We reference *A Is for Angry* by Sandra Boynton, but feel free to substitute this with an alphabet book that appeals to the readers in your class.

Often in this unit, you'll ask kids to bring their writing folders or reading baggies to apply their learning to their workshop work. The best test of transfer will be evident in kids' independent reading and writing.

ONLINE DIGITAL RESOURCES

Resources that accompany this unit of study are available in the online resources, including all the charts, word cards, songs, and poems shown throughout *Vowel Power*.

To access and download the digital resources for *Vowel Power*:

1. Go to www.heinemann.com and click the link in the upper right to log in. (If you do not have an account yet, you will need to create one.)

2. Enter the following registration code in the box to register your product: UOSPH_HYSC7

3. Enter the security information requested.

4. Once you have registered your product it will appear in the list of My Online Resources.

(You may keep copies of these resources on up to six of your own computers or devices. By downloading the file, you acknowledge that they are for your individual or classroom use and that neither the resources nor the product code will be distributed or shared.)

Every Word Has at Least One Vowel

TODAY YOU'LL teach students that all words have vowels, and that those vowels help us to read and write clearly. You'll introduce students to the concept of vowel power and to the vowel shield.

TODAY YOUR STUDENTS will search the room to discover that all of the words in the classroom have vowels.

GETTING READY

✔ Print and display Reader-Man's letter to students. You may want to tuck it into an envelope for dramatic effect.

✔ Print and make photocopies of the vowel shield to distribute to students.

✔ Prepare your own vowel shield. You may want to laminate this teacher copy for durability, since you will refer to it often throughout the unit.

✔ Gather small pointers for students to use. You could use the ones that students use during reading workshop or provide Popsicle® sticks.

✔ Gather big books or independent reading books for rug clubs.

✔ Ensure the word *my* is on the word wall from a previous unit.

✔ Prepare to display the *My Win* booklet by Mabel (from Unit 3, *Word-Part Power*).

Do not color or decorate

MINILESSON

CONNECTION

Introduce students to their newest super power, vowel power, and to a special new tool that they will be working to activate as they learn more about vowels—a vowel shield.

"Super Readers, come join me on the rug. A letter from Reader-Man just arrived!" I held up an envelope as students settled in their rug spots. Once everyone had gathered, I began. "Let's find out what Reader-Man wants to tell us!" I opened the envelope and unfolded the letter dramatically. Then I placed it under the document camera and read aloud.

I opened the box beside me and pulled from it a paper shield, covered with vowels and anchor

> Dear Super Readers,
>
> There is a BIG emergency! The vowels in your writing are missing! Words need vowels so they can be understood. There is only one way to fix this. You need...VOWEL POWER!
>
> I have sent you a special box of vowel shields. They can help you make your writing easier to read.
>
> Know this: vowel power grows. When you study each of the vowels on your shield carefully, it will start to shine!
>
> Your friend,
> Reader-Man

PHONICS INSTRUCTION

Letter Knowledge
• Recognize that some letters are consonants and some letters are vowels.

Phonics
• Notice short and long vowel sounds in words and the letters that represent them.
• Recognize and use *Y* as a vowel sound.

pictures. "Making sure your words have vowels—that's an important challenge! Are you ready to power up these shields and to activate vowel power?" The class cheered. "Okay, Super Readers!" I quickly handed each child a vowel shield. Then, I held the tool up high, inviting kids to do the same, and chanted the vowels, "*A! E! I! O! U!*" and the children chanted with me. I chanted again, this time including the short-vowel sounds and keywords. "*A, apple*, /ă/. *E, egg*, /ĕ/. *I, igloo*, /ĭ/. *O, octopus*, /ŏ/. *U, umbrella*, /ŭ/. That will be our vowel power cheer!"

I placed the vowel shield down beside me and leaned forward in my chair. In a serious voice, I went on to say, "If you are going to work hard to learn everything you can about vowels and the sounds they make, you must absolutely know the *most* important thing of all. It's this . . ."

❖ **Name the teaching point.**

"Today I want to teach you that every single word needs at least one vowel. Every label, every name, every snap word . . . they all have at least one vowel."

TEACHING AND ACTIVE ENGAGEMENT/LINK

Distribute pointers and vowel shields, and rally partners to read the room, checking to make sure that each word, each label, contains a vowel.

"Do you believe me? Let's investigate. I'm going to give you and your partner a pointer, and will you use your pointer power to read the classroom? But this time, as you read the words that are everywhere in this room, will you and your partner do a check? Is there a vowel? Look at the words on the walls, on the charts. Who knows, you might even look on your clothes!

"Try to *read* the words you find—and try especially to notice the vowels. Some words might even have *more* than one vowel, but they won't have none. Take your vowel shields with you. They can help you to say the sounds that the vowels make."

The children set about searching the room, finding words taped to the closets, the word wall, written on their partners' shirts, and more. As they worked, I nudged them to look closely at all the letters in their words, name the vowels, and read the words as best as they could.

Recruit students to share their observations about vowels with the class. Emphasize that every word has at least one vowel.

After everyone had located and named vowels in lots of words, I gathered the class back together in the meeting area. "Was I right? Does every word have at least one vowel?" The children began telling tales of the words and vowels they'd found.

POSSIBLE COACHING MOVES

▸ "Check your vowel shield to make sure you're noticing all the vowels in that word!"

▸ "You noticed the vowels! Remember to read the word, too! What would make sense? You can look at the object the word was attached to. That's like using picture power!"

▸ "Sometimes the vowel makes the sound that matches its name, like acorn, /ā/. Sometimes the vowel makes the sound that matches the picture on your shield, like /ă/ in apple."

I called for their attention urgently to share a discovery I'd made while they were talking.

"Kindergartners, eyes on me! I just noticed something!" I invited Eli to hold his foot up, and sure enough, even on the bottom of his shoe, was a word. I read the brand name aloud. "Name the vowels, Super Readers!" As the children called the vowels back, I pointed at them on my vowel shield.

"Yes!" I reiterated. "*Every* word, *every*where, has at least one vowel. My goodness, I think we've proved it! There may even be vowels on the bottoms of our shoes!"

RUG TIME

Channel students to read familiar big books on the hunt for vowels. Coach students as they work.

"Kindergartners, let's look for vowels in books! Do you think it's true that Joy Cowley and all our other favorite authors use a vowel in *every* word on *every* page? I've got some big books here, ones you know. I'll give a book to each rug club," I said, as I distributed them. "Will you read through your book extra carefully and notice if there is a vowel in every word? Read each page, then name the vowels in every word."

Readers of C and D books will tend to rely heavily on pictures and initial consonants (or consonant clusters). While celebrating approximations, you can nudge them to move their eyes to the ends of words as well.

> ### POSSIBLE COACHING MOVES
>
> ▶ "What vowel do you see in this word? Yes, I see it, too!"
>
> ▶ "Oh! That word has two vowels, *I* and *E*. How interesting!"
>
> ▶ "That word says _____. Did you spot the vowel? What sound do you hear that vowel making?"

SHARE • *A, E, I, O, U, . . . and Sometimes Y*

Pretend that Mabel has asked why one of the words in the title of her recent book doesn't include a vowel. Use this opportunity to explain that sometimes Y is a vowel.

Just before I reconvened the class, I began whispering to Mabel in a voice that everyone could hear. "Yes, yes, I'll be sure to tell them. Thanks, Mabel!

"Super Readers, give me your eyes, please." I sat Mabel next to me. "Mabel noticed something while you were working together. 'Pssst! Pssst!' she kept insisting as she pointed to the cover of the book she wrote recently: *My Win*, by Mabel.

"Writers, what do you think Mabel noticed about the word *my*? Turn and talk."

After a minute, I reconvened the class. "You are noticing the same thing Mabel noticed—the word *my* doesn't have *A, E, I, O,* or *U*! So how could it be that every single word has a vowel? Huh!?

"Writers, every word does have a vowel, and here's a secret: sometimes *Y* is a vowel! So that means that the vowel in *my* is *Y*!" We read the title, then moved to the bottom of the cover, where I pointed under the word *by*. "Oh, *by* is like *my*. *Y* is the vowel in that word, too! In both of those words, *Y* makes the /ī/ sound." The class thought of other similar words: *try, fly,* and *why.*

"Before we leave the rug, let's cheer for the vowels one more time because they work so hard in every word!" The children held their vowel shields as I started to sing, and soon they joined me:

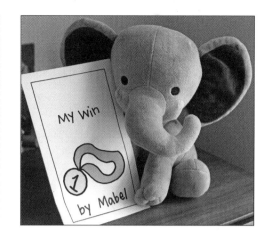

A, E, I, O, U, . . . and sometimes *Y*
A, E, I, O, U, . . . and sometimes *Y*
A, E, I, O, U, . . . and sometimes *Y!*

EXTENSION 1 • Reading the Alphabet Chart for Consonants and Vowels

Engage the class in multiple shared readings of the alphabet chart, sometimes reading only the consonants, and other times reading the vowels.

"Super Readers, you are always learning more about letters and words! You know that some letters are consonants and some letters are vowels, *and* you know that every word has a vowel. Now that you know this, we can read the alphabet chart in different ways. Earlier this year, we read all of the letters on the alphabet chart at once. Well, now that your vowel power is growing, we can have some more fun reading the alphabet chart."

I picked up a pointer and gestured to the alphabet chart on the easel as I said, "The first time, let's read only the consonants together." Then, I used the pointer to direct a shared reading of the consonants on the alphabet chart. We began, "*B, C, D, F, G, H, J . . .*" As we approached each vowel, I slowed down, giving kids a chance to anticipate skipping it.

After reading the consonants together, I led the class in a few readings of only the vowels, inviting a student to join me at the easel to take over the role of pointing to the vowels.

"You know what I just realized? You and your partner read your alphabet charts together in reading workshop. You play and sing with the alphabet. Maybe you will want to read it in different ways, sometimes reading the whole chart, and sometimes deciding to read only the vowels or consonants in reading workshop too!"

Notice that the focus of this extension is recognizing that some letters are vowels and others are consonants. When leading the shared reading, you are saying only the letter name. You might decide to do similar shared reading sessions where you have them say the name of the letter, keyword, and sound.

EXTENSION 2 • Alphabet Book Vowel Hunt

Engage the class in a read-aloud of a familiar alphabet book, encouraging them to stand up or clap when you come to a vowel.

"Readers, earlier in the year we read a whole bunch of alphabet books together. Do you remember all the fun we had with them?" The children looked at each other and back at me as I placed our basket of alphabet books on my lap, and dramatically pulled out one of our favorites, *A Is for Angry* by Sandra Boynton.

"We should read it again, and let's invent a fancy new way to read this alphabet book together! Now that our vowel power is growing, as we read the book, we can give one big clap when we come to a vowel. Before we read our alphabet book, let's get warmed up by cheering for the vowels because they are so important." I gestured to my vowel shield as I started to sing, and soon they joined me:

A, E, I, O, U, . . . and sometimes Y
A, E, I, O, U, . . . and sometimes Y
A, E, I, O, U, . . . and sometimes Y!

After completing the cheer, I read the book aloud to the class, making sure to pause each time we got to a vowel, so that children could celebrate with one big clap.

If you are teaching this word study unit along-side the kindergarten reading unit, Bigger Books, Bigger Reading Muscles, *reading aloud alphabet books and inventing new ways to read them will be a perfect match. During the reading unit, favorite alphabet books are revisited in reading workshop where children think, talk, and play with them to learn more about words and how they work.*

Checking for Vowels in Writing

IN THIS SESSION

TODAY YOU'LL remind students that all words have a vowel, and you'll teach students that writers work hard to make sure that all of their words have vowels.

TODAY YOUR STUDENTS will check a piece of Mabel's writing, and their own writing, for vowels. If vowels are missing, they will add them.

MINILESSON

CONNECTION

Sing a familiar song and celebrate with students all of the once-new things that they now know and understand.

I sang the gathering song, and the children chimed in as they came to the meeting area. "Wow, you really know that song," I said, and sang it again. "We are gathering, we are gathering, on the rug, on the rug . . .

"Do any of you remember way, way, way back to the start of kindergarten when we first sang that song? I sang it and you thought, 'Huh? How does that go?' Now, though, you think, 'I've got this.' Say it with me. 'I've got this!' Say it again, loud and proud. You have mastered that song. *'I've got this!'*

"It's the same with vowels. Do you remember when you were first learning the alphabet and you discovered that some letters are consonants and others are vowels? Can any of you remember thinking 'Huh? Which ones are the vowels?' But now, you know your vowels, am I right?"

"Yeah!" The kids responded. To demonstrate, I turned to the vowel shield and led the class in a choral reading of the vowels, their pictures, and their sounds.

GETTING READY

✔ Prepare to refer to your own vowel shield throughout the lesson.

✔ Print several copies of Mabel's How-To book, *How to Make Jam*. You may want to have it prepared in a folder that matches your class's writing folders.

✔ Equip students with pens or pencils to edit Mabel's How-To book and their own writing.

✔ Read through students' writing folders, using Post-its® to flag pages where you'd like students to check for vowels. (If there's an abundance of examples, you may not need to do this.) Ask children to bring their folders to the rug.

✔ Sing the "What's the Middle Sound that You Hear?" song.

PHONICS INSTRUCTION

Phonological Awareness
- Segment and blend individual phonemes in words.
- Say words slowly to hear sounds in words.
- Isolate and pronounce the initial sound, medial vowel, and final sounds in spoken words.

Letter Knowledge
- Recognize that some letters are consonants and some letters are vowels.

- Use proper letter formation.

Phonics
- Hear and identify short vowel sounds in words and the letters that represent them.

High-Frequency Words
- Learn new words (*how, you*).

"You really can name the vowels! But I think Reader-Man was trying to tell us something about vowels in his letter. Vowel power is a little more complicated than just naming your vowels."

❧ **Name the teaching point.**

"Today I want to teach you that vowel power is more than just knowing what vowels are and recognizing them. When you have vowel power, you *use* vowels to help you write. You can reread your writing and look for the vowel in each and every word. If a vowel is missing, you add it in."

TEACHING

Explain that you've noticed that students sometimes write words with no vowels. Emphasize that studying vowels—and using them in writing—is a sign of growing up.

"Kindergartners, the work you will be doing in the next few weeks will help you really use your vowel power. But it will take work. I'm saying this because after we spent yesterday looking for the vowels on our walls and on our sneakers and in our big books, I decided to look for the vowels in your writing. Reader-Man was right! Lots of them were missing! The real problem is that without those vowels, your beautiful words aren't yet easy to read."

Unveil Mabel's How-To book. Then, reread it to check for missing vowels.

"This is why it is *so* important to check your writing, making sure those vowels are there, in *every* word, even the teeny-tiny ones. Should we start by helping Mabel check her words?" The children nodded. I took out a piece of Mabel's writing. "Mabel is writing a How-To book, just like each of you. Let's check her words to make sure they look right!"

I placed the book under the document camera and read the title aloud, pointing crisply under each word. "How to Make Jam." I paused at the word *jam*. "Ooooh. I see the vowel, A. *Jam*, /j/-/aaaaaa/-/m/. That looks right! I guess we are all done checking for those vowels." I began to put the book away, but students protested, insisting we continue to check the rest.

"You are right! There are vowels in every word, so it will be important to check every word to make sure they are not missing!

"Let's keep going . . ." I turned the page and read aloud:

> First, you gt the berries.

"First you . . . hmm, . . . I'm stuck. /g/-/t/?" I pointed to each of the letters in the word that was missing a vowel. "What does this say? Why is this *so* hard to read?"

"No vowels!" a voice called out.

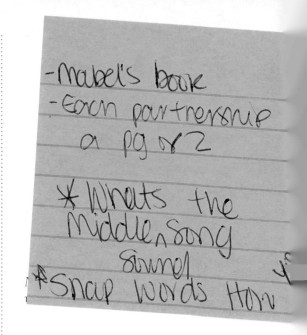

- Mabel's book
- Each partnership
  a pg or 2

⭐ Whats the
Middle ᴧsong
              sound
⭐ Snap words How

How to Make Jam

by Mabel

"That's it! The vowel is missing! But which one? Mabel, what do you want to say?" I let the elephant whisper in my ear. "Oh, the word you wanted to write is *get*? Super Readers, let's help Mabel fix it up. What vowel does Mabel need in the word *get*?" I turned to the vowel shield. "First you *gat*? No. First you *get*? Yes, I agree. We need an *E*!" I quickly crossed out Mabel's attempt, and rewrote the word correctly above it.

I quickly recapped my steps to help students replicate them. "Did you see how we did that? We reread, pointing under each word, checking for vowels. When we saw that a vowel was missing, we jumped into action to say the word and listen for the sound to fix it up!"

ACTIVE ENGAGEMENT/LINK

Channel students to continue rereading their mascot's book, checking for a vowel on every page and adding in the missing ones.

"Right now, will you and your partner check the rest of Mabel's How-To book? I'll pass out the other pages, so you can work together to take a closer look at her words. Check to make sure *every* word has a vowel. If you spot a word that's missing a vowel, cross it out and write the word again on top, adding in the vowel. Then, we can give these pages back to Mabel, so she can fix up her book."

I quickly read the rest of the book aloud, then distributed multiple copies of the remaining pages of the How-To book. I gave some partnerships copies of the second page, some copies of the third page, and others copies of the fourth page. I reminded the children to start by rereading the page they'd been given, then to begin editing it.

I moved around the meeting area, listening in as partners worked to reread the sentence and fix up the words. I coached in with some lean prompts.

Soon, the words in the pages of the Mabel's book were corrected.

Don't prolong the work of isolating and recording the correct vowel. You'll provide students with more opportunities to practice this work in future sessions. Right now, your goal is to relay the message that without vowels, words aren't yet easy to read.

POSSIBLE COACHING MOVES

▶ "Point under the words as you read. Look for the vowel in each one. Remember, every word has at least one vowel!"

▶ "Check your vowel shield to help you remember the vowels."

▶ "Use the shield to help as you listen for the vowel sound. Then, add in that vowel."

▶ "Listen closely. What letter makes that sound?"

▶ "You added a vowel to that word! That will make it so much easier to read!"

Encourage students to locate words with missing vowels. Don't expect students to edit perfectly. During today's session and other sessions, remember the value placed on process, learning, and feedback. Celebrate the words they do find, as well as their approximations when adding vowels to those words.

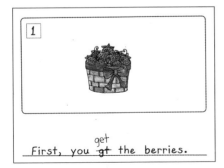

1

First, you ~~gt~~ get the berries.

2

Next, you put ~~thm~~ them in a ~~pt~~ pot.

3

Then, you ~~mx~~ Mix it ~~p~~ up

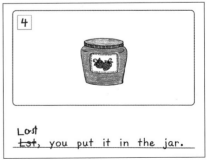

4

~~Lst~~ Last, you put it in the jar.

After a minute or two, I called the group back together. "Quick! Point to a word that you and your partner fixed up!" Kids held up their pages, pointing to words. "Amazing! Just like Reader-Man, you found words with missing vowels, and you worked hard to add in those vowels. I'll give these pages to Mabel later." I collected the pages and made a neat stack.

"You really used your vowel power! There's some big work ahead, but you are ready for it, and your vowel power will get stronger the more you work at it!"

RUG TIME

Channel students to look through a flagged piece in their writing folders to see if they've activated vowel power during writing workshop.

"Let's get started with that work right now. I want you to see what Reader-Man saw in your folders. Open your writing folders and take out the writing with the Post-it on it. Turn to that page. Read it and think, 'Was my vowel power fully activated? Does every word I wrote have a vowel?'

"Put your folder between you and your partner. Then, read the page out loud. Together, check that every word has a vowel. Then, switch to the other partner's writing!

"Share what you found with your partner. You'll probably say things like, 'Yes, I used vowel power,' and then you'll point to words where you had vowels. Or, you'll say, 'No! My vowel power wasn't activated. I didn't have any vowels in this word.'" Partners talked for a minute.

Two minutes later, I voiced over, "Partner 2, if you didn't go yet, it's your turn. If both of you have had a chance, turn to another page and practice again."

While partnerships worked, I voiced over suggestions periodically.

POSSIBLE COACHING MOVES

▶ "Partners, you're a team. Even though you might not be the writer of the piece, your partner needs you to pay really close attention, too. If you're having trouble, stack your pointers on top of each other, so you read the same word at the same time."

▶ "Take care of your partner's heart. Remember that writing is putting your whole heart onto a piece of paper. Be kind as you help your partner fix things, so others can more easily understand what they are writing."

It is important to be strategic when creating an interactive editing piece ahead of time. Monitoring involves knowing when something is right so you can keep going, and knowing when something isn't quite right, so make sure to use the focal feature both correctly and incorrectly in the shared piece. And remember, this instruction might also happen during writing workshop.

You might choose to look through all of your students' folders and flag a page for them to study. If this is the route you choose, look for a page where the student has not written with vowels at all, or has written with vowels inconsistently. You will likely find, however, that your students could do this checking work on any page from their writing folder. If this is the case, flagging a specific page is not necessary.

In reading and writing workshops, you've probably assigned each partner a number. No matter how you've grouped your students, be sure to draw on that same arrangement here.

SHARE • Singing the "What's the Middle Sound that You Hear?" Song

Sing a variation on a familiar song to provide students with repeated practice hearing the medial sound in consonant-vowel-consonant (CVC) words.

"Remember earlier this year when you sang the 'What's the First Sound that You Hear' song?" I hummed a bit of the tune to remind students how it went. "That song helped you get even better at hearing first sounds in words. Well, I changed the song a bit, and I think this new version will help you get better at hearing the middle sound in words, which you'll need to do if you want to include the right vowels in your writing.

"Let's sing it! Join me when you can." I began singing to the tune of "London Bridge."

We continued singing the song a few more times. I alternated between words with short *A* and short *I* sounds to give students practice distinguishing between different vowel sounds: *sap, sip, rip, rap.*

"You heard the short *A* sounds and short *I* sounds in the middle of all those words!"

What's the Middle Sound That You *Hear?*
(To the tune of London Bridge)

___ ___ ___

What's the middle sound that you hear,
that you hear, that you hear?

What's the middle sound that you hear
in ... ____, ____, ____?

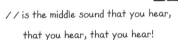

/ / is the middle sound that you hear,
that you hear, that you hear!

/ / is the middle sound that you hear
in ... ____, ____, ____!

EXTENSION 1 • Introducing New Snap Words: *How* and *You*

Introduce two new snap words, and guide students through the familiar process of making a word a snap word for each one.

"Kindergartners, when there are words that keep coming up a lot in your writing, those are great words to make into snap words, so you can just know them by heart forever for the rest of your life. I've been noticing some words that keep coming up in your How-To writing. I want to teach you two of those words today." I held up two cards with our new word wall words—*how* and *you*—written on them, then taped them to the easel.

"You already know how to turn words into snap words. So, let's do it!" I displayed the "How to Learn a Word!" anchor chart and invited kids to read it with me.

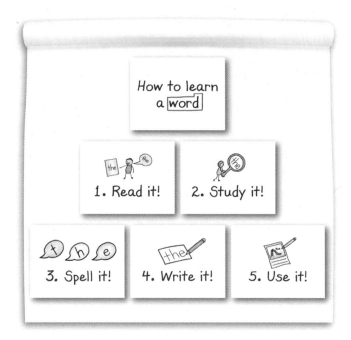

I held up the first word, *how*. "Okay, let's make this a snap word. First, *read* it!" I pointed under the printed card as the students chorally read the word.

"Now, *study* it. I slid my finger under the word from left to right. "How many letters? Yes, three! What letters do you see? Name them to your partner. And you noticed that this word has one vowel! Yes! Every word has at least one vowel.

"Now, *spell* it. Spell it softly like a whisper into your hand. *H-O-W*. Now, let's spell it and cheer it. *H-O-W!* Okay, now you spell it to your partner.

"Here's step 4: *write* it!" I pointed to that step on the chart as I said this. "Let's first write it in the air, writing it the right way. All of you, stand up so you have lots of air around you. You ready?" I wrote in the air and recited the letter formation pathways for lowercase *H*, *O*, and *W*. "You did it! Now write it a few more times, so you really get it into your muscles."

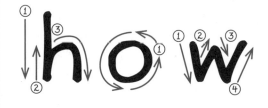

As the children wrote in the air, I wrote the word on chart paper and voiced over the letter formation.

"Now it's time for the very last step—*use* it! Think of a sentence with the word *how* in it. You might say, 'I am going to teach you how to . . .' Or your sentence could be a question like, 'How do . . . ?' Go!" I gave them a minute to share their sentences with their partners and then asked for their attention again.

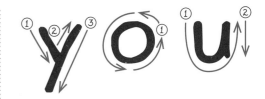

"Now, I want to give you a chance to learn another word by heart. Here's another word that you have been using over and over in your writing. *You!* Let's make *you* a snap word. Look at the chart. What do we do first?" We repeated the same steps to learn *you*.

"Let's cheer for these words as I add them to our word wall." I also made a mental note that, later in the day, I would add small word cards with these new words to students' snap word pouches.

EXTENSION 2 • Providing More Practice with Segmenting and Blending

Use Elkonin boxes to provide students with additional support in segmenting and blending the phonemes in words.

"We've been thinking about how readers and writers are always saying words slowly and thinking really carefully about the sounds they hear in those words. Let's practice that again, and this time let's use our special tool. You've seen it before." I displayed an Elkonin box with three-part sound boxes under the document camera and zoomed in, so the boxes were enlarged. I also had a few counters ready to help with segmenting.

"Now, watch what I do. I'm going to say the sounds that go in each of these boxes. Listen carefully." I broke up the word *bat*, saying the individual sounds separately: /b/ /ă/ /t/. "Will you join me?" Students pointed and said the sounds as I pushed a chip into each sound box. "Now, I'm going to push the sounds together!" I swept my finger underneath the boxes, saying the entire word.

We repeated this with the words *cap*, *sip*, *big*, *sat*, *cab*, and *lid*.

As we continued with the additional words, I prompted students to use their arms to support them with segmenting, while I continued to segment by pushing a chip into each sound box for each phoneme. As I noticed students who would benefit from additional support segmenting and blending, I called them up to try out the Elkonin boxes, allowing me to provide support to them as the entire class continued working alongside me.

Elkonin boxes are a versatile word study tool. They can be used to support the phonological skills of isolating, segmenting, and blending sounds. They are a helpful visual scaffold once a child is able to say a word slowly, stretching out the sounds. It is important to remember to have a box for each sound, not each letter. For example, the word way *would have two boxes because there are two sounds: /w/ and /ā/.*

Recruit students to find places in their own writing to use the new snap words *how* and *you*.

A few minutes before writing time ended, I called for the class's attention. "Each of you, take a moment to find a place where you could use our new snap words in your writing." I removed *how* and *you* from the word wall and placed them under the document camera. "Maybe you already have a place in your writing where you wrote 'I am going to teach you . . .' and you can check how you spelled *you* and fix it up if needed. Or you could write a new sentence, like, 'First you . . .' Maybe you'll make a title for your book and use *how*—*How to Make a Banana Split*. When you write the word once, don't stop! Look for other places in your writing where you might add the words *how* and *you*."

I coached students as they worked, making sure they used the letter formation pathway to write each letter. After a moment I said, "Writers, now you'll know these words by heart forever! When you want to write them, you don't need to stretch them out; you can just write them in a . . . snap! That will help you so much in your writing!"

FIG. 2–1   Editing to add the snap word *you*

Isolating the Short-Vowel Sound in the Middle of Words (-VC)

IN THIS SESSION

TODAY YOU'LL teach students that they can strengthen their vowel power by segmenting the phonemes in words and noticing the differences in the sounds of the vowels.

TODAY YOUR STUDENTS will sort short *A* words and short *I* words that have the same ending sound.

MINILESSON

CONNECTION

Begin with a phonological game to support students with segmenting the individual phonemes in CVC words with short *A* and short *I* sounds.

"Let's play the robot game!" I said. Then, I looked around at the class as if astonished. "Wait, what? You don't know the robot game?! Well, let me teach it to you. I'm going to say a word and then you have to translate it into robot language. Let me show you what I mean. Let's try it with the word *mad*. *Mad*. If I translate the word *mad* into robot language, it'll sound like this." I started making robotic movements with my arms and torso, shifting them as I segmented the sounds, "/M/-/ă/-/d/." The class giggled. "Can you be robots with me? Let's all make the sounds in the word *mad*, one sound at a time. /M/-/ă/-/d/. Yes, that's robot talk!

"Let's try another word: *hip*!" The students acted like robots as they made the sounds. I listened carefully for each phoneme. From some kids, I heard only a distinct beginning and ending sound. "Careful. Make sure to say all the sounds separately: the first sound, the middle sound, and the last sound," I voiced over. "/H/-/ĭ/-/p/," I coached as kids echoed.

"Now let's try another word. Let's do *map*!" Again, I listened and coached as kids acted out robot arms and robot voices while segmenting the sounds.

GETTING READY

✔ Prepare picture cards for today's medial sound sort: *rag*, *bag*, *wag*, *tag*, *flag*, *wig*, *dig*, *twig*, *big*, *pig*. Decide how you'll display the pictures as you sort them. You could tape them to a piece of chart paper, or you could use a pocket chart. You could make the sort more authentic by transferring the sorted pictures to real jars during the share.

✔ Provide students with their own sets of sorting pictures and sorting mats.

✔ Make sure students' vowel shields are handy.

PHONICS INSTRUCTION

Phonological Awareness
• Segment and blend individual phonemes in words.
• Isolate and pronounce initial sounds, medial vowel, and final sounds in spoken words.

Letter Knowledge
• Use proper letter formation.

Phonics
• Hear and identify short vowel sounds in words and the letters that represent them.
• Demonstrate basic knowledge of letter-sound correspondences by producing the primary sounds for each consonant.

High-Frequency Words
• Learn new words (*am*, *did*).

"Kindergartners, when we were saying /m/-/ă/-/d/, I called that a robot game and made it sound silly, but that work is actually super-important. To be able to write with vowels, you have to do a little robot talk in your own mind. If you want to write *map*, you can say /m/-/ă/-/p/ like a robot. And sometimes you have to work hard to hear the vowel in the middle."

♣ **Name the teaching point.**

"Today I want to teach you that your vowel power grows stronger when you listen very closely. You can study the sounds that vowels make and notice how one vowel sounds different from another. Some vowels make a short sound, like /ă/ in *apple* or /ĭ/ in *igloo*."

TEACHING

Celebrate the work students are doing segmenting words. Explain that sorting can help them to distinguish between vowel sounds in the middle of words, and recruit students to help you sort.

"You were really saying your words slowly, segmenting them like robots. That is the first step to fully activating your vowel power. The next thing you need to be able to do is figure out which vowel goes in a given word. And here's the thing—kids everywhere get their vowels confused. They write *K-A-D*, *kad*, when they mean to write *K-I-D*, *kid*—honest!

"Sorting can help you hear the different sounds in words well enough that you can listen to a word like *hip* and know which vowel to write down. You have sorted before.

"The sorting you are going to be doing today will really help to activate your vowel power. More and more, you'll be writing with vowels.

"Quick! Get those vowel shields ready. Let's work to power them up, listening for the sounds short *A* and short *I* make in the middle of words. Help me sort these words. We can say the words like robots to hear the vowel sound in the middle. We'll put the words with /ă/ like *rag* into one jar, and words with /ĭ/ like *wig* into the other jar. These vowels are in the middle of words, so it will take some powerful listening. You ready?" I slipped *rag* and *wig*, the two anchor cards into the pocket chart, starting two columns.

"I'll do the first one, if you help me." I held up a picture of a bag. "This is a bag. Let's use robot talk to hear the vowel and to think about which vowel matches the sound. /b/-/aaaaa/-/g/. Hmm, . . . does the middle of *bag* sound like the middle of *rag* or *wig*? Baaaaag, raaaaag. I think those two middle sounds match!" I placed the bag picture underneath the rag.

"Here comes another word. Get your vowel shields ready! Activate your vowel power!" I held up the picture of *big*. "Does *big* go with *rag* or *wig*?" As I said the anchor words slowly, I pointed to each anchor picture. Students pointed to the wig to show that the middle sound of *fig* matched the middle sound in *wig*.

You'll notice a shift in prompting language in this session. When supporting children with onsets and rimes, as you did frequently in Unit 3, your prompts will often refer to using word parts. In these cases, you might say, "Say the word. Say the first sound. Say the end part." When working on segmenting words into phonemes, as in this session, your prompts should refer to the individual sounds in the word. In these cases, you might say, "Say each sound in the word." Remember that the ultimate goal is flexibility, so you will find yourself coaching in both ways in a class of diverse learners at different moments in every unit.

It is important to remember that students need to be very comfortable with hearing beginning and ending sounds before you ask them to listen for middle sounds. The earlier units supported students with hearing beginning and ending sounds; now that you are moving more explicitly to middle sounds in this unit and beyond, make plans to support students who still need additional help hearing beginning and ending sounds.

ACTIVE ENGAGEMENT/LINK

Recruit students to join you in sorting the rest of the picture cards by determining the medial sound in each word.

"You're listening so carefully to the vowel sounds in the middle of words, and the jars will soon be organized again! Let's keep going with this! I'll show you a card, and you figure out where that word goes."

I held up a picture of kids playing tag. "This is a game of tag. Say *tag*. Turn and talk. Double the strength of your vowel power and work together to figure out where it goes." The students turned to each other and used robot talk to isolate the middle sound.

"I heard so many people saying the word slowly: /t/-/aaaaa/-/g/. And Zoe and Chanel just said, 'Oh! It must go with the rag!' I agree. It goes in the short *A* jar!" I added the *tag* card to the /ă/ column on the pocket chart and quickly held up the next card, featuring a twig. We again repeated the entire process: "Get your vowel shields ready! Turn and talk with a partner. Which jar will the word *twig* go in? /T/-/w/-/iiiiiii/-/g/."

We continued through the rest of the pictures. Students turned and talked and found the medial sound for each picture, and we then added it to the pocket chart in its appropriate category.

When we finished, our pocket chart was organized.

"Wow, your vowel power is getting so much stronger! You've been working so hard to say every sound and figure out which vowel sound is inside of each word. Let's do our vowel power cheer to celebrate!" I gestured to the vowel shield and invited the kids to chant the vowels with me in their loudest, proudest voices. "*A! E! I! O! U!*" we chanted together. Then we chanted again, this time including the short-vowel sounds and keywords. "*A, apple, /ă/. E, egg, /ĕ/. I, igloo, /ĭ/. O, octopus, /ŏ/. U, umbrella, /ŭ/.*"

You'll notice that all of the words in this sort have either an -ag or an -ig ending. Today's work focuses on the middle sound, and we've chosen these words to deliberately draw students' attention to the middle sound.

We encourage you to think about opportunities for movement across your day. The cheers and chants in this unit offer a perfect opportunity for this. Consider having your class help you create movements for the vowel power cheer. This might include a strong vowel power pose at the conclusion of the cheer.

RUG TIME (CLUBS)

Set clubs up to sort pictures again. Nudge children to distinguish between short *A* and short *I*.

"Now I'm going to give your club the same cards. Will you spread out and sort them again, this time on the rug in front of your club? And, if you don't know what a picture is, work together to try to figure it out." I distributed a baggie of pictures to each club. As students worked, I listened in and coached, sometimes saying my tips loudly enough that the whole class could hear.

After a few minutes, I saw that many students were finishing, and I moved them along. "Once you think you've got all your words in the right place, make sure to check them! Say each one slowly, and check to be sure that the middle sound matches!"

SHARE • Hearing Medial Sounds in Words

Guide students as they first read through the list of picture cards in one category, and then read through the list in the other category.

"Oh, you worked so hard today, *and* you helped me organize my mixed-up jars. Let's read all the picture cards we said belong in the short *A* jar and use vowel power to check them. Get your shields ready. Hold your shields high." We chanted /ă/ /ă/ /ă/ /ă/, then read through the list of picture cards in the short *A* column on the pocket chart. I ceremoniously placed those cards in the short *A* jar. Then we held our shields high again. We chanted /ĭ/ /ĭ/ /ĭ/ /ĭ/, then read through the list of short *I* words. I placed those cards in the *I* jar.

After reading through the picture cards in each category, I said, "Wow! You noticed the short-vowel sound in the middle of each word! That helps your vowel power to grow. I also noticed that *-ag* and *-ig* are both new word parts, so that means your word-part power is growing too!'"

EXTENSION 1 • Introducing New Snap Words: *Am* and *Did*

Introduce two new snap words, and guide students through the familiar process of making a word a snap word.

"Kindergartners, when you know the short *A* and *I*, it can help you read and write so many words. And you'll see these vowels everywhere, even in our snap words. Right now, will you look at the word wall and tell your partner if you see any snap words that have the short vowel *A* /ă/ or *I* /ĭ/? You'll need your vowel shields. Say the word aloud and really listen for the vowel. Do you hear /ă/ or /ĭ/?

Notice that these prompts for word solving support sound analysis and are listed from the lowest level of teacher support to the highest. It's important to remember that prompting is a way to support and scaffold learning. To move learners toward independence, it's best to use lean, generalizable prompts.

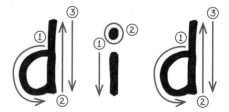

"Wow—*an*, *at*, *is*, *it*—you're finding so many! And today, I want to teach you two more snap words that have the vowel sounds we have been studying." I held up cards with our new word wall words—*am* and *did*—written on them, then taped the cards to the easel.

"Let's turn the words on these cards into snap words!" I displayed the "How to Learn a Word" anchor chart and invited kids to read it with me.

I held up the first word, *am*. "Okay, let's make this a snap word. First, *read* it!" I pointed under the printed card as the students chorally read the word.

"Now, *study* it. I slid my finger under the word from left to right. "How many letters? Yes, two! What letters do you see? Name them to your partner. And you noticed that this word has one vowel! Yes! Every word has at least one vowel. This word has the short vowel *A*. Hold up your shields. Chant the sound with me. /ă/ /ă/ /ă/ /ă/. *Am*.

"Now, *spell* it. Spell it softly, like a whisper into your hand. *A-M*. Now, let's spell it and cheer it.

"Now, *write* it!" I pointed to that step on the chart as I said this. "Let's first write it in the air, writing it the right way. Everyone, stand up so you have lots of air around you." I wrote in the air and recited the letter formation pathways for lowercase *A* and *M*. "Great, now write it a few more times, so you really get it into your muscles." As the children wrote the word in the air, I wrote it on chart paper and voiced over the letter formation pathways.

"Last step—*use* it! Think of a sentence with the word *am* in it. Tell your partner." I gave them a moment to brainstorm, listened in, and then said, "Wow, I hear sentences like these: I am in school! I am six! I am hungry! I am hungry, too!

"Now, I want to give you a chance to learn another word by heart. Here's another word that has one of the vowel sounds we've been studying. *Did*. Shields up. Chant short *I* with me. /ĭ/ /ĭ/ /ĭ/ /ĭ/. This is the word: *did*. Let's make *did* a snap word. Look at the chart. What do we do first?"

We repeated the same steps to learn *did*.

"Kindergartners, let's cheer as I add these two new words to our word wall."

Once we had added the two new words to the word wall, I passed out small copies of the word cards, and students quickly added them to their snap word pouches.

EXTENSION 2 • Singing to Support Vowel Power

Remind children of their vowel power and introduce a game to support phoneme segmentation.

"Writers, let's celebrate our growing vowel power with a new twist on a familiar game!"

As I pointed under the words, I began singing the song "What Are All the Sounds You Hear?" to the tune of "London Bridge," and the children chimed in readily.

I coached the children to listen to the letter sounds at the beginning, middle, and end of the word. We continued singing the song together with additional short *A* and short *I* words, such as *sag*, *rid*, *ham*, and *sick*, and I made a mental note to tuck the song into transitions across the day, perhaps even as a warm-up for writing workshop.

EXTENSION 3 • Building on Segmentation Work with Elkonin Boxes

Segment words again, this time writing the letters as students hear them.

I placed the three-part Elkonin boxes from earlier in the bend under the document camera and said, "Do you remember how we used this tool to help strengthen our ear muscles *and* our vowel power?"

The class nodded their heads in unison as I said, "Today we are going to use this tool again. Are you ready? This time we are going to place a letter in a box for each sound you say and hear."

I modeled for the class by saying the word *mmmmmmaaaaaattttttt* and writing the letter *M* in the first box as I was saying /m/, the letter *A* when I got to the /ă/, and the letter *T* in the final box as I said /t/.

As a reminder, I gestured to the class alphabet chart and said, "Now will you help me? As we say the sounds in a word, you can write the letters for the word in the rug with your fingers, and I will write them up here. Show me your magic writing fingers!"

We repeated this routine with the words *mad*, *had*, *pin*, *zip*, *lap*, and *sit*. To support students who would benefit from additional practice hearing sounds in words and building their letter identification skills, I made a mental note to repeat this extension as a small group in reading or writing workshop.

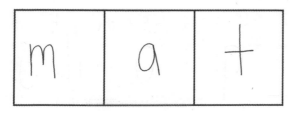

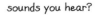

> **What Are All the Sounds You Hear?**
> (To the tune of London Bridge)
>
> What are all the sounds you hear,
>
> sounds you hear,
>
> sounds you hear?
>
> What are all the sounds you hear,
>
> in the word, ____?

Activities that involve blending parts of words or sounds together are especially helpful in supporting students' reading development. Activities that place an emphasis on segmenting are particularly helpful in supporting children as they encode words in their writing.

Previously in this bend, this learning focused primarily on hearing the sounds in words, but this time it includes noting sound-letter correspondences. According to research, phonemic awareness instruction is especially effective when it is coupled with letter work (Literacy Lessons Designed for Individuals, Second Edition, Marie Clay, 2016). This helps children use what their eyes can see to help make letter-sound connections, a fundamental step in learning to read.

Writing Sentences with Short *A* and Short *I* CVC Words

IN THIS SESSION

TODAY YOU'LL teach students that when they want to write a word, it helps to say each sound in the word, listen for the vowel, and then think, "Which vowel makes that sound?"

TODAY YOUR STUDENTS will orchestrate all of their powers, including vowel power, to write sentences with CVC words. Students will take part in a sentence dictation activity that supports flexibility and transfer of phonics skills to writing workshop.

MINILESSON

CONNECTION

Build momentum by inviting the class to help you make new words by changing the medial vowel, initial consonant, or final consonant of a CVC word.

"Hold up your vowel shields, Super Readers!" I leaned backward, as though their mere presence overwhelmed me. "I can feel your vowel power growing stronger! Some tools are so important that superheroes need to have them on hand at all times. Wonder Woman always has her lasso, Batman always has his utility belt, and from now on, you'll *always* have your vowel shields—when you listen to words, and when you write them, too!

"The work you have done, listening for the sounds that vowels make in words, is super-important. But there is another thing you can do because you have vowel power: you can make new words like magic! I think you know that, as you have done it before. You can start with a word you know, like *hat*, and think, 'Let me change around one letter,' and then presto change-o, you have *hit*—a totally different word with a completely different meaning! Just from changing one letter!"

GETTING READY

✔ Display the letters *H, P, A, T, I, S, F*, and *D* on index cards in a pocket chart.

✔ Have chart paper and a marker to build a chart of the CVC words children make.

✔ Prepare whiteboards and markers for your demonstration.

✔ Distribute a whiteboard and marker to each student.

PHONICS INSTRUCTION

Phonological Awareness
• Manipulate individual phonemes to make new words.
• Isolate and pronounce initial sounds, medial vowel, and final sounds in spoken words.
• Segment individual phonemes in words.

Letter Knowledge
• Recognize which letters are consonants and which letters are vowels.

Phonics
• Demonstrate basic knowledge of letter-sound correspondences by producing the primary sound for each consonant.
• Hear and identify short vowel sounds in words and the letters that represent them.

Word Knowledge/Solving
• Use knowledge of short vowel sounds to write words.
• Use familiar phonograms to write words.

High-Frequency Words
• Read and write high-frequency words in continuous text.

I gestured to the pocket chart where the letters *H*, *P*, *A*, *T*, *I*, *S*, *F*, and *D* were displayed and put the letters *H*, *A*, and *T* together in a new row. Many students called out "*hat*!" before I prompted them to read the word. Then I wrote the word on chart paper.

"Let's change the word *hat* to *hit*. Use your vowel power to think about what letter we need to change and when you know, point to that letter."

We'd soon moved the letter *A* back to the top row and brought down the *I*. "Let's try some more!" I changed *hit* to *sit*, inviting students to read and call out the new word after I made it. I coached students through this sequence, changing one word to another: *hat–hit–sit–sat–pat–pit–fit–fat–fad–dad*.

"Wow! Your vowel power sure is getting strong. I think it's time to put it to use to help you write."

❖ **Name the teaching point.**

"Today I want to teach you that when you want to write a word, you can say each sound in the word and listen for the vowel. Then, think, 'Which vowel makes that sound?'"

The word choice in this connection is a deliberate one. The selection of different vowel phonograms will channel learners to attend to the short vowels in the middle of the words. This will help them notice the differences in the sounds of the vowels and match the right vowel to its short-vowel sound.

TEACHING

Demonstrate how you use all of your powers to write a sentence that is easy to read.

"You made so many words!" I said, standing back from the list of words the children had just crafted. "But you know, I'm getting an idea. Words don't like to be all by themselves. They really want to be together in sentences that mean something. Let's use some of these words in sentences that mean something. I'll go first," I said, as I brought the letters *D*, *A*, and *D* to a new row on the pocket chart. "So, if I want to make a sentence with this word, maybe I could say, 'I see dad dig.'

"Let's try *writing* that sentence together. 'I see dad dig.' First, let's figure out how many words are in the sentence." I restated the sentence, putting a finger up for each word. "There are four words. Okay, what's our first word? *I*. You know that word. It's up on the word wall." I wrote the first word on my whiteboard and channeled students to reread it with me.

"What's our next word? *See*. Another snap word!" I wrote the word *see*, and again invited the children to reread with me what we had written so far: "I see."

"The next word is *dad*. Hmm, . . . that word is in the pocket chart! It is also on the word wall." I wrote *dad* quickly, then commented on the medial vowel. "And I hear /ă/ in the middle."

When you begin this work by orally rehearsing

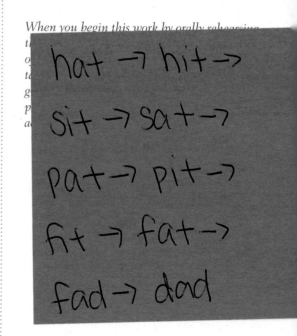

Segment the next CVC word to match medial phonemes to the correct vowels.

"*Dig* . . . I'd better activate my vowel power. I can use robot talk and say each sound in that word to be sure I hear the vowel. /d/ /ĭ/ /g/. I hear /ĭ/ in the middle. Which vowel makes that sound? Yes! *I!*" Soon our sentence was complete, and I channeled students to reread it with me.

"Wow, everyone, your super powers can really help you make some super sentences. They can also help you with all of your writing. Using vowel power to hear the individual sounds in words can really help make your writing easier to read!"

ACTIVE ENGAGEMENT/LINK

Rally students to write an additional sentence on their whiteboards.

I asked the children to get out their whiteboards and markers as I said, "I think you are ready to try to write the next sentence on your own."

Once everyone was ready, I explained, "I am going to say a sentence. Will you combine all your powers to write the sentence on your whiteboards?"

As the class nodded in unison, I widened my eyes with excitement and said the sentence, "Dad has a crab!" As I was saying the sentence, I put one finger in the air for each word, inviting the children to join me in counting the words. Then, I prompted the class to orally rehearse the sentence a few times, and again, raised a finger as they said each word. Before the children began writing the sentence on their whiteboards, I said, "Now, make sure you write one word for each finger."

As children were writing the sentence on their whiteboards, I circulated around the rug area, coaching as needed. After the class finished the sentence, we reread it together, using our pointer power to point under each word. Then we practiced with another sentence: "The crab bit dad!"

RUG TIME

Channel students to use short *A* and short *I* words to compose an additional sentence that extends the story.

"Let's review our story so far," I said. "Can you read along with me?" I read, "I see dad dig. Dad has a crab. The crab bit dad!" Then I said, "Wow! What do you think might happen next? See if you can work with your partner and use all your powers to write another sentence in the story. Think about how dad might have felt or what dad might have done.

"Okay! Turn and talk with your partner about your sentence ideas. Then, work together to write one down. Don't forget to listen carefully for the vowels."

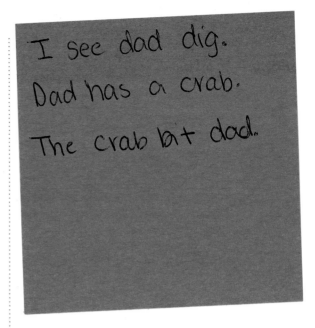

POSSIBLE COACHING MOVES

▸ "When you're done spelling your word, leave a finger space before writing the next word."

▸ "Remember, if it is a word you know, you can write it in a snap."

▸ "Say the word slowly and write each sound you hear."

▸ "Maybe your word-part power can help you."

▸ "That makes sense! 'Dad had a fit!' Now write it down, one word at a time."

As the children worked, I provided coaching as needed. I made sure that each partnership had thought of a sentence relatively quickly, so they could get to work writing it down. In some cases, that meant prompting them a bit.

SHARE • Combining Super Powers to Read Sentences (CLUBS)

Channel students to work in rug clubs to read their original sentences aloud.

"Writers, you used all your super powers to help you write some great sentences to finish our story! I heard a lot of you using vowel p[...]e them, let's celebrate those sentences by reading each one a[...]

"Will you gather t[...] whiteboard in the middle of your club at a time, and use al[...]uzzling word—maybe a word that doesn't include a vowel ye[...]rd to make it easier to read. Get to it!"

I circulated amon[...]en, such as "Dad was mad!" and "Then the crab ran." I coach[...]uch as possible.

Snap word power point

EXTENSIO[...] a Familiar Context

 Revise the clas[...]d to note completed activities, offering repeated enco[...]

Once we had finished with writing workshop, I turned students [...] to the schedule. I prepared our schedule cards with new sentences on the back using one of our new high-frequency words. On the back of the card that read, "We will have our morning meeting," I wrote, "We did morning meeting" and so on, for all the day's activities.

As the class finished sharing, I said: "You know, we already had writing workshop and morning meeting. The schedule should probably show that, right?" I flipped the sentence strips for both previous activities, so the schedule now said "We did morning meeting. We did writing workshop." A few students recognized the word *did* and called out, "Hey, we learned that word yesterday!"

"We sure did! Now that we know that word by heart, we can use it in our schedule. Let's go ahead and read those two sentences!" I pointed underneath the words while students chorally read. "And, later today, we'll go back to our schedule, and we'll make sure that we keep on reminding ourselves of what's coming up, and what we already did!"

EXTENSION 2 • Clapping and Snapping for Consonants and Vowels

Use word wall cheers and chants to reinforce high-frequency words.

I displayed our four new high-frequency words and said, "Maybe we should do a special cheer for our new snap words. We can spell each word out loud, clapping our hands each time we say a consonant and snapping our fingers each time we say a vowel. Let me show you how this special cheer goes." I said the word *did* aloud, then spelled it as I clapped and snapped for the consonants and vowel: *D* (clap) *I* (snap) *D* (clap).

"Are you ready to cheer some of our snap words with clapping and snapping?" The children nodded as many of them began snapping and clapping. "I'll say a word, and then you can spell the word out loud together. Make sure you snap your fingers each time you say a vowel and clap your hands each time you say a consonant."

After doing our special cheer with *am*, *did*, *how*, and *you*, we practiced with a few additional words from the word wall. Then I gave students a couple of minutes to clap and snap their names with partners. Throughout the day, I asked the class to clap and snap words here and there as we encountered them in our work together.

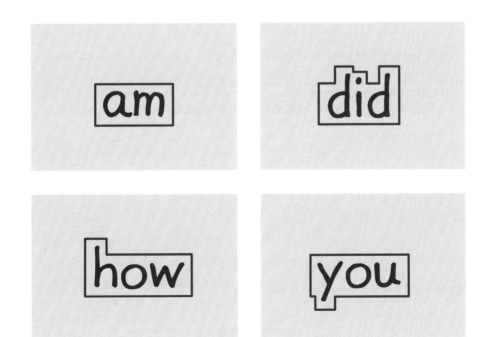

Shared Reading with a Focus on Words with Short *A* and Short *I*

GETTING READY

✔ Prepare a text message from Mabel that says, "My vowel shield is broken!" For added authenticity, you might have a friend send you a text, and change the contact name to Mabel. Alternatively, create a handwritten note from Mabel.

✔ Print a copy of *How to Care for Your Vowel Shield* to display on the document camera.

✔ Have your letter lasso handy to lasso word parts.

✔ Make sure that students have their vowel shields and book baggies.

PHONICS INSTRUCTION

Concepts About Print
• Demonstrate one-to-one match.

Phonological Awareness
• Blend individual phonemes in words.

Word Knowledge/Solving
• Use familiar phonograms to read words.
• Use knowledge of short vowel sounds to read words.

High-Frequency Words
• Read high-frequency words with automaticity.

IN THIS SESSION

TODAY YOU'LL remind students to use all of their super powers to help them read a text.

TODAY YOUR STUDENTS will join you in shared reading and will also read from their book baggies, practicing using all of their powers together.

MINILESSON

CONNECTION

Explain that *super-*, as a prefix, means greater or bigger than. Remind students that to truly be Super Readers and Writers, they need to combine their super powers.

After the children gathered in the meeting area, I leaned in close, as though I was about to divulge a secret. "I think it's time to tell you what *super* really means. *Super-* means greater than or bigger than, like in *super*hero, or *super*star—they're even greater than regular heroes or regular stars. Or even *super*market! A *super*market is bigger than a regular market!" I stretched out my arms to illustrate.

"So, to truly be a *Super* Reader, you need to gather all of your powers!" I mimed scooping up the powers from the reading charts and growing bigger to carry their weight in my arms.

❖ **Name the teaching point.**

"Today I want to teach you that vowel power works with all of your other super powers. When you are reading, you can use *all* your powers to help you."

TEACHING

Reveal an urgent message from Mabel and introduce the shared reading book you will read together.

"Readers, before we go any further, I have some sad news! I got a message from Mabel last night, and you'll never believe what happened!" I placed my phone under the document camera and showed the students Mabel's text message. "I'm going to read it to you." I inhaled dramatically before reading, "'My vowel shield is broken!'"

I looked around as the students gasped. "Mabel broke her vowel shield. As soon as I got the message, I called Mabel and asked, 'How did that happen?' She told me that she had an accident and her shield broke. I was thinking, 'How can we prevent other accidents?' Then, like magic, Mabel said she'd just written a book about taking care of vowel shields!

"Ready to use all of your super powers to read Mabel's book? It's a How-To book, just like the kind you are making in writing workshop! Before we read the book, you'll need to activate your vowel power. Luckily, *you* all still have *your* vowel shields. Ready?" I held up my shield and gestured for students to do the same. We chanted the short-vowel sounds together. "Your vowel power is activated! You're ready to read!!"

Rally students to read Mabel's book with you, using all their super powers to help them. Place special emphasis on the CVC words that contain short *A* and short *I*.

"Mabel's book is called *How to Care for Your Vowel Shield*. Read the title with me." I pointed crisply under each word as students read it aloud. "Mabel told me she *really* wants to make sure that your vowel shields don't break, like hers did. Let's read and learn from Mabel. Use your vowel power and all your other super powers to help you!"

Keep in mind that readers of level C and level D books will rely more heavily on pictures and initial consonants or consonant clusters when reading independently. Nudge them to move their eyes to the ends of words to gather more visual information. Along with the picture, this will often be enough to solve unknown words in their independent books. In this session, you are studying short vowels in the context of reading; but it is not an expectation for readers to use medial sounds while reading independently until around level D/E.

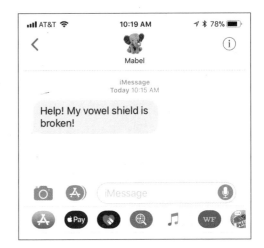

"Let's read the picture. Activate picture power! Oh, Mabel looks so upset with her broken shield. Okay, is your pointer power ready?" We read the first line together, while I pointed crisply beneath each word. I paused before the word *sit*. "Hmm, . . . this word has a vowel in the middle that's in between two consonants. I bet your vowel power can help you read this word. Say each sound. /s/-/ĭ/-/t/. *Sit!* Oh, *sit* also looks right, because I can activate my word-part power and lasso up *-it* in *sit*!" I used my letter lasso to demonstrate.

"Now, use your reread power to make sure this line makes sense. 'Do *not* sit on your shield.' Does that make sense? Oh, that must be how Mabel broke her shield. She sat on it! She is an elephant after all. That makes sense! Let's keep reading."

We read through the next two lines, pausing whenever we got to a CVC word with a short *A* or short *I* sound. The students used their picture power and vowel power to figure out the word *bag*. They used sound power and vowel power to read the word *tag*.

When we read the speech bubble in step 3, I paused at *lose*. "Hmm, . . . this word is interesting. You'll need to put all of your powers to work." The children helped me use picture power, book talk power, and persistence power to figure out the tricky word before reading and rereading the entire sentence.

ACTIVE ENGAGEMENT/LINK

Recruit students to continue to read the shared text. Pause at CVC words, and voiceover to remind students to use all their powers to read them.

"Readers, there is one more page in Mabel's book. Make sure all your powers are ready to use!" I called up Josiah and asked him to use his pointer power to help the class read.

I asked Josiah to keep his finger under the word *big*. "Activate your vowel power. Make sure that word looks right!" Students said the word slowly—/b/-/ĭ/-/g/—and agreed that *big* had a short-vowel sound.

I nudged Josiah to move to the next word and paused as students solved the word *tip*, some using word-part power and others using vowel power. "Oh! Sometimes How-To authors do this. They give an extra helpful tip to readers. It's even written in bold print. This must be a very important step. Let's read this step very carefully."

We paused again at *tap*. "Work with your partner to read the rest of the page the best you can."

"Let's activate our reread power and read this page as a big team. 'Big tip: Tap your shield to activate *vowel power*!' Wow, that's a helpful tip, Mabel! She's teaching us that we can really care for our vowel shields by using them. Of course! Thanks, Mabel!"

Make sure to continue to demonstrate to students how all of their other powers work in this context. All students will benefit from the repetition, and, within your phonics time, it's helpful to show students how they can combine all of their powers while reading.

Be strategic about your choice of students across this session. If you still have a student who is not yet reading with one-to-one correspondence, you might recruit that student to be the pointer.

Remind students that their super powers will be particularly important to reading as books get more challenging.

"Readers, as your books get more challenging, you're going to need to bring every power you have to your reading. There will be new words on every page, and your super powers, now including vowel power, will help you to read them."

RUG TIME

Prepare reading partners up to read books from their baggies together, using everything they know to tackle puzzling words.

"Are you ready to put all your super powers, especially your vowel power, to the test? Get with your reading partner. Partner 1, will you pull out one book you can read together today? Read through your book with your partner. When you get to a puzzling word, remind each other to use *all* your powers to help you, especially your vowel power. Remember to say each sound in a word to figure out what it is. If you finish one book, pull out another one and keep reading."

I moved from partnership to partnership, coaching in as students worked.

SHARE • Singing a Song to Practice Blending Phonemes

Sing a new song to provide students with additional practice blending the phonemes in words.

"Do you remember the song 'If You're Happy and You Know It'?" I asked. "We used to sing it during morning meeting at the beginning of the year." The children nodded expectantly.

"I have a new song to that tune, which I know you're going to love. And, you know what? It will also help us strengthen our vowel power!"

I began singing the new song to the tune of "If You're Happy and You Know It," and I invited the children to join in.

Most of the children raised their hands, and I called on one child who said, "*Tap!*"

For additional practice, we continued singing the song a few more times with other short *A* and short *I* CVC words: *bat*, *sat*, *rip*, *map*, *tag*, and *pig*.

"Wow, I couldn't trick you. Your ear muscles keep getting stronger and stronger!" I said as I pointed to my ear and flexed my arm muscles in the air.

POSSIBLE COACHING MOVES

▶ "Activate your picture power. Think about what would make sense."

▶ "Try your vowel power. Does it help?"

▶ "Use word-part power to find a part you know."

There may not be many CVC words in your students' independent reading books. After they solve words by combining their super powers, you might coach readers to confirm that each word looks right in the middle.

If You Think You Know This Word
(To the tune of If You're Happy and You Know It)

If you think you know this word, raise your hand.

If you think you know this word, raise your hand.

If you think you know this word,

Then tell me what you've heard.

If you think you know this word, raise your hand:

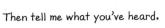

$$/ / - / / - / /$$

(say each phoneme in a word,
i.e., /t/ - /a/ - /p/)

EXTENSION 1 • Beginning a High-Frequency Word Password Routine

 Practice high-frequency words by creating a password system.

When the children returned from lunch, I stood in the doorway with the snap words *how*, *you*, *am*, and *did* written on index cards. Just before they entered the room, I stopped them. Holding up the first snap word, I said in my most official voice: "Wait. What's the password?" The children looked at each other and laughed, unsure of what I meant.

"Sometimes in stories, there are closed doors. If you know the password, you can open the door like magic. In those stories, often the password is 'Open Sesame!' You say it and *poof*!—the door opens and you can pass through. In our class, the password will be one of our snap words. Once you read it, you can pass through the door."

I looked at the first five children in line and held up the card for *how*. "What's the password?" I asked, smiling. "How!" several children in the group called back. I stepped to the side, making space for all of them to walk into the classroom. For the next group, I held up *am*, and repeated my prompt. We continued this way until everyone had entered, and then I taped one of the words—the least automatic—outside the classroom door. Every time children passed through the door, they could encounter and reread the word. I changed the word weekly to reflect their needs.

EXTENSION 2 • Using Different Voices to Read the Word Wall

Do a shared reading of the word wall, taking on different voices for each repetition.

With a pointer in my hand, I moved beside the word wall as I said, "We have been learning new snap words, but it is *also* important to keep practicing all the snap words on our word wall. Let's read our word wall together and change our voices when we do it." I referred students to our "Read the Word Wall!" chart listing different voices.

I invited the children to stand up and said, "Let's read it with a whisper voice!" I cupped one hand around the side of my mouth and started pointing to the words on the word wall. Mimicking my motions, the children cupped their hands around the sides of their mouth, bent down a bit, and chimed in with their best whisper voices.

After reading through the words together in a whisper voice, I exclaimed, "Wow! I can't believe how many snap words you have learned this year. Not only does your vowel power keep growing and growing, so does your snap word power."

After reading the word wall in a scary voice and then a squeaky voice, I said, "Remember to use your snap word power to help you read and write lots and lots of books!"

Read the Word Wall!

Loud like a monster.

Scary like a witch.

Squeaky like a mouse.

Whisper like a secret.

Invent your own.

Editing for Short Vowels *A* and *I*

IN THIS SESSION

TODAY YOU'LL teach students that because words always have vowels in them, writers *check* for those vowels and add or fix them as needed.

TODAY YOUR STUDENTS will participate in interactive editing to check for vowels in every word and fix vowels that don't seem right. They will celebrate their work with the short vowels *A* and *I* by making them light up (highlighting them) on their vowel shields.

MINILESSON

CONNECTION

Tell a story about an essential object that you were responsible for and what that responsibility meant.

"Writers," I began, "When you have vowel power, it's like you have the keys to how spelling goes—and that helps you write *and* read.

"I want to tell you a little story. When I was growing up, I wanted so much to have a set of keys like my mom. She told me that even when I was baby, I always pointed at them and screeched, 'Keys! Keys!' I got older, about your age, and I still asked—a lot—if I could hold her house keys. And she would always say back, 'Oh, no. Not yet. These are just too important!'

"But then, one day, my mom looked me in the eye and told me to hold out my hand. She put the house keys in my palm, and then closed my fingers around them very, very tightly. 'You are ready to have your own set of keys now,' my mom said. 'Remember, these open the doors to our home, so you must never lose them. Keep them with you always, and check that you have them often. You are *responsible* for these keys.'" I paused to let the gravity of the last sentence linger in the air.

GETTING READY

✔ Provide each student with a whiteboard and marker.

✔ Distribute students' writing folders.

✔ Display Reader-Man's letter. You may consider printing it and placing it in an envelope for dramatic effect.

✔ Gather one highlighter per student, and set them in a box outside the classroom door.

PHONICS INSTRUCTION

Phonological Awareness
- Segment individual phonemes in words.
- Isolate and pronounce initial sound, medial vowel, and final sounds in spoken words.

Letter Knowledge
- Recognize which letters are consonants and which letters are vowels.

Phonics
- Demonstrate basic knowledge of letter-sound correspondences by producing the primary sound for each consonant.
- Hear and identify short vowels sounds in words and the letters that represent them (*E, O, I*).

Word Knowledge/Solving
- Use familiar phonograms to write words.
- Use knowledge of short vowel sounds to write words.

"Writers, I'm telling you this because it makes me think of your work. Just like the keys were important to my family, vowels are important to words. Writers are responsible for their vowels!"

♣ **Name the teaching point.**

"Today I want to teach you that you are responsible for your vowels. You can reread each and every word of your writing and think, 'Does this word have a vowel? Is it the right vowel?'"

TEACHING

Set students up for a vowel power check-up. Say words with short *A* and *I* vowel sounds aloud, and channel students to write them. Lead them in checking each word.

"After all the work you've done—sorting words and writing words and moving vowels from one word to another word—my bet is that your vowel power has *really* grown stronger. Let's give your vowel power a checkup! I'm going to say a word—it will be a word that has a short vowel—and will you work your hardest to spell the word correctly? Afterward, you can look back and check to see whether your spellings showed some vowel power or *a lot* of vowel power.

"Get a whiteboard and get ready! Okay, first word: write *tag*. Remember, before you write it, you can use robot talk to say the word slowly and hear all the sounds. Write down all the sounds. Then check that you got the vowel right."

I dictated two other words—*sad* and *big*—and led the class in checking them. "Thumbs up if you put a vowel in every word," I said. "You did it! Hooray! You were responsible for your vowels!"

"Now let's check whether you got the right vowel." I said and wrote each word on the easel. "Tell each other which letters you got right," I said. "Which letters do you still need to work on?

"Writers, it is so important that you make sure your writing is super-easy for readers to read. Vowels really help readers know how to read what you have written, so just like you check your writing to be sure you put your name on your paper, you also need to check to be sure you wrote with vowels, and hopefully, the right vowels!"

ACTIVE ENGAGEMENT/LINK

Channel partners to help each other edit their writing, paying special attention to editing for vowels.

"I bet all of you could do this same work in your own writing. Pull out a piece of your writing from your writing folder. Partner 2, put your writing in the middle. Help your partners be responsible for their vowels! Read each word and ask,

'Does this have a vowel? Is it the right vowel?' If not, say the word slowly so you can hear all the sounds, and then add the vowels you hear."

I coached the developing writers with a range of skills as they worked; some students were rereading labels, while others were rereading sentences.

"Oh! Your writing is becoming easier to read! Always remember that you are responsible for your vowels. As you are writing, be sure to listen for the vowel as you say words to yourself. After you write, you can reread each word and check, 'Does this have a vowel? Is it the right vowel?' If a vowel is missing, say the word again and add in the vowel!"

POSSIBLE COACHING MOVES

▶ "You can use your pointer power to be sure that you are reading every word."

▶ "That word has a part you might know. Activate your word-part power!"

▶ "Be sure to check for vowels on every page of your book."

▶ "Remember to ask yourself if it looks right."

RUG TIME (CLUBS)

Use a new letter from Reader-Man to show students how to reread each word to check that it has a vowel. Emphasize how you say words slowly to hear all the sounds if you notice a vowel is missing.

"Readers, writers, I've been watching your vowel power grow stronger and stronger this entire week. Reader-Man must have noticed, too. Look!" I pulled an envelope from behind the easel and sliced it open. "It's from Reader-Man! Ooh, there are two pages." I cleared my throat and read the first page: "Put your vowel power to the test! Can you fix up my note?" Wide-eyed, I looked up at the children before flipping to the next page. "Hmm, . . . this page is harder to read." I smoothed the page out and placed it under the document camera.

"I think some of the vowels are missing or just don't look right. It is tough to read, but I think I can figure it out. I think it says, 'Pat yourself on the back. Two vowels will be lit up on your shield. Hip hip hooray!' Oh my goodness, everyone! How exciting!" Squeals erupted all around the meeting area.

"Okay, Reader-Man wants us to help him be responsible for his vowels! We'll need to ask, 'Does this have a vowel?' and 'What vowel sound do I hear?' If the word is missing a vowel or if it's not right, we'll need to say the word again slowly, hearing the vowel and adding it in.

"Here goes . . . uh-oh! This first word doesn't have any vowels at all! It's supposed to be *Pat*. Let me say the word slowly, saying each sound carefully so I can hear the vowel. *Paaat*. /p/-/ă/-/t/. I hear /ă/. That's a sound *A* makes. Let me add an *A* to this word."

> Put your vowel power to the test!
>
> Can you fix up my note?

> Pt yourself on the bick. Two vowels will be lat up on your shield! Hp hp hooray!

We continued reading. "Check the next word. Thumbs up if it has a vowel. Thumbs down if we need to fix it." I waited for the children to respond. "Yes, *yourself* has lots of vowels, and it looks right! Let's keep reading."

We got to the word *back*, spelled *bick*. Many kids gave me a thumbs down. "That one doesn't look quite right. Help me say the word we want to help Reader-Man write slowly, so we can hear all the sounds. *Baaaack*. /b/-/ă/-/k/.

"What sound do you hear in the middle, and what letter makes that sound?" I asked. "/ă/. *A!*," the children called back. I changed *bick* to *back*.

We read through the first sentence.

Channel children to edit the last two sentences of the note in rug clubs.

"Ready to edit the rest of Reader-Man's letter? I'll reread it, so we remember what it says. 'Two vowels will be lit up on your shield! Hip hip hooray!'

"With your club, look at each word and ask, 'Does this have a vowel? Is it the right vowel for the word?' If the vowel is missing, say the word slowly, so you can hear all the sounds. Figure out which vowel you need to add."

While students worked, I coached in, prompting as needed.

After listening in, I made their suggested edits on the note, and we reread it together triumphantly.

As we finished the last few words, I noticed something written in tiny print on the bottom of the page, just out of view of the document camera. I slid the paper up and zoomed in on the words, "'Look outside the door!' There must be a special delivery that goes with this special note!" I beamed as I walked over to the door and opened it to find a box of highlighters waiting for their new owners.

POSSIBLE COACHING MOVES

▶ "Check your vowel shield."

▶ "Listen for the sound in the middle of the word. You can use robot talk to hear each sound. Does the middle sound match *apple* or *igloo*?"

▶ "Write the first sound you hear, the next sound, the last sound."

▶ "Does that look right?"

SHARE • Highlighting the Vowels *A* and *I* on Vowel Shields: A Celebration

Celebrate the work students have done with the short vowels *A* and *I* by inviting students to "light up" the *A* and *I* on their vowel shields with highlighters.

I rushed back to the meeting area, highlighters in hand. "Readers, writers, check out what Reader-Man sent us! Now it's time to celebrate! A few days ago, I gave you your vowel shields. All week, you've practiced and learned about the short *A* that says /ă/ and the short *I* that says /ĭ/. I watched you using short *A* and short *I* as you read and as you wrote.

"You are ready to light up the *A* and *I* on your vowel shields! Watch this!" I colored in the *A* on the shield with a highlighter to light it up. I did the same with *I*.

Then, in a loud and proud voice, I held up my shield and said, "*A* lit up. /ă/ /ă/ /ă/. /ă/ /ă/ /ă/. *I* lit up. /ĭ/ /ĭ/ /ĭ/. /ĭ/ /ĭ/ /ĭ/.

"I'm going to give each of you your shield and a highlighter. It's time to light up your *A*! Highlight it like I did. Then, make the short *A* sound. /ă/ /ă/ /ă/." The rug filled with a chorus of /ă/ /ă/ /ă/. "Now you can light up your *I*. Highlight it and make the short *I* sound. /ĭ/ /ĭ/ /ĭ/." The children followed.

"Now that you all have your *A* and *I* all lit up, your shield is starting to shine, just like Reader-Man said it would in his first letter about vowel power!" I said.

Distinguishing Short-Vowel Sound

Dear Teachers,

This bend builds upon the work you've started with distinguishing vowel sounds. In the last bend, you focused on short *A* and short *I*. In this bend, you'll spotlight short *E, O,* and *U,* and then work with all of the short vowels together. CVC words are the primary vehicle for studying these sounds, and you will continue to use robot talk to segment words by phoneme to isolate the medial vowel. To reinforce the work with digraphs introduced in Unit 3, you will, at times, segment CCVC words that contain digraphs. Remember that though these words with digraphs have four letters, they have three phonemes. Using Elkonin boxes will provide students with additional support segmenting and blending the phonemes in words. This versatile tool can be used during whole-group, small-group, and one-on-one instruction. Remember to use a box for each sound, not each letter. Elkonin boxes can help students make letter-sound connections, a fundamental step in learning to read. When coupling Elkonin boxes with letter work, if there are two letters in one box because they make one sound, you can divide that box with a dotted line to show that the two letters make one sound.

You'll begin this bend by featuring short *E, O,* and *I,* and you'll remind your students that studying more vowel sounds will help to strengthen their vowel power. For example, you'll enlist students in sorting picture cards, offering an opportunity to listen for short vowels that can sound so similar in the middle of words.

You'll likely want to keep a class vowel shield handy, perhaps enlarged, and on it, the vowels *A* and *I* will be highlighted from Bend I's celebration, acknowledging that these vowels have been closely studied. Your students will spend Bend II in pursuit of lighting up the remaining vowels on the shield (*E, O,* and *U*) through careful study and practice with short-vowel sounds, both in isolation and in context.

Be open with your students about how similar these short vowels sound, and how practice with them can help them strengthen their ear muscles and write texts that are easier to read. Throughout the bend, you'll work with short vowels in various ways, such as shared reading and interactive writing. During interactive writing, you'll invite children to generate ideas as you listen intently and value all that they say. Because this is phonics workshop, we have carefully planned how the accompanying booklets will go, deliberately offering children the opportunity to encounter particular short vowels at specific times. After the children turn and talk, you'll often find yourself saying, "I heard many of you saying that . . ." and then composing what you've preplanned so that kids can practice precisely what you intended. So that your students can begin to internalize conventional print, be sure that the end product of interactive writing is conventional. Celebrate your writers' approximations and then fix up the words as needed.

In this bend, you'll introduce four new high-frequency words: *get*, *on*, *up*, and *fun*. Reader-Man will once again leave a note for your class, and this time, he will deliver these soon-to-be snap words, which can also help students remember the sounds that short *E*, *O*, and *U* make. Keep in mind that pronunciation can vary from region to region, and that some of the words we suggest featuring may not include the prototypical short-vowel sound when spoken by your students.

By the end of the bend, your children will have read, written, and made monosyllabic words using all of the short vowels. They will be ready to highlight all the vowels on their vowel shields! True to his word, Reader-Man will give students the green light to highlight the entire shield, so that it shines. With their vowel shields fully lit up, and their vowel power activated, your students will be ready for the more challenging vowel work ahead.

All the best,
Angela, Katie, and Casey

SESSION 7

Distinguishing Short *E*, *O*, and *I* Sounds

IN THIS SESSION

TODAY YOU'LL teach students how to identify and distinguish short-vowel sounds of the letters *E*, *O*, and *I* in words.

TODAY YOUR STUDENTS will segment, sort, and read words with short *E*, *O*, and *I* sounds.

MINILESSON

CONNECTION

Make a clumsy entrance to the meeting area, with materials for today's session in your arms. Drop the picture cards to set students up to sort by listening for the vowel sounds.

I stumbled into the meeting area, struggling to hold all the objects in my arms. I held three jars stacked on top of one another, steadied by my chin, a handful of picture cards, and the class vowel shield between my teeth. Out of breath, I slowly dismantled my pile. I rested the vowel shield near the pocket chart and then used the same hand to line the jars up underneath. I turned to the children with my arms full of picture cards.

"Can someone help me with these . . .? Oh no!" I spilled the picture cards all over the floor.

"Oh, kindergartners!" I huffed. "Your vowel power has grown so strong that you're ready to study some new vowels. That's why I had so much stuff in my hands!" Some children scurried to help pick up the scattered cards, but I quickly scooped them into a mound in the middle of the circle.

"I'll need your help to organize these later. For now, leave them in a pile and look up here!" I moved back to the easel and picked up the vowel shield. "You've worked hard to hear and read and write

GETTING READY

✔ Gather sorting jars, picture cards (as shown in the Teaching and Active Engagement/Link), your vowel shield, and a pocket chart.

✔ Make sure students have their vowel shields.

✔ Distribute the first verse of "Hickory Dickory Dock" and a marker or pen to each rug club.

✔ Have a few index cards on hand to record words

PHONICS INSTRUCTION

Phonological Awareness
- Isolate and pronounce initial sounds, medial vowel, and final sounds in spoken words.
- Segment and blend individual phonemes in words.

Phonics
- Hear and identify short vowel sounds in words and the letters that represent them (*E, O, I*).
- Demonstrate basic knowledge of letter-sound correspondences by producing the primary sound for each consonant.

Word Knowledge/Solving
- Use knowledge of short vowel sounds to write words.
- Record digraphs to write new words.

Session 7: Distinguishing Short *E, O,* and *I* Sounds

39

short *A* /ă/ and short *I* /ĭ/ vowels. Hold up your vowel shields!" Pointing to the highlighted *A* and *I*, I said, "Wow, those vowels really shine!

"But with only those two vowels lit up, your shields look a little . . . lopsided. Let's work to make these other vowels light up, too." I ceremoniously pulled two picture cards out of my pocket—the egg and the octopus—and slipped them into the pocket chart above the jars, forming two columns. "Dun-da-da-da!"

♣ **Name the teaching point.**

"Today I want to teach you that, as your vowel power grows, you'll need to know more vowel sounds to help you read and write well. Remember that sometimes *E* makes the short sound /ĕ/ and sometimes *O* makes the short sound /ŏ/."

TEACHING AND ACTIVE ENGAGEMENT/LINK

Add a third column on the pocket chart to review short *I* and chant its sound before chanting the new vowel sounds, short *E* and short *O*.

In a new column, I slipped the igloo picture card into the pocket chart. "You know this short-vowel sound really well! Let's review it!" I pointed to the card and the kids chanted, "/ĭ/ /ĭ/ /ĭ/!"

"Yes! Short *I* makes the /ĭ/ sound, like in *igloo*. Now let's chant the other vowel sounds in the pocket chart." I touched the egg card and said, "*E. Egg* /ĕ/!" clearly, and the children repeated me. Then I touched the octopus card and said, "*O. Octopus* /ŏ/," and the children did the same. "Ooh! I feel your vowel power growing already!"

Spread out the spilled picture cards on the rug and direct students to take one card each. Channel students to partner up and read their cards together.

"Okay, let's make our ear muscles really strong and listen for the vowel sounds on these cards," I pointed to the cards on the floor, "*and* clean up this mess!" I spread the cards out across the rug so that they were within reach of all the children.

"In a minute, when I say 'Go!,' will you grab the closest card and keep it a surprise until you meet with your partner? Ready to do that super quickly? Go!" Once every child had a card, I directed them to share those cards with their partners. "Now get shoulder to shoulder with your partner and say the name of the picture on each of your cards. When you say those words, will you try to say each sound in the word slowly, listening for the vowel in the middle of that word? Think, 'Does it sound more like *egg* /ĕ/, *octopus* /ŏ/, or *igloo* /ĭ/?' You'll do that with one partner's card, then with the other partner's card. Now . . . *go!*"

Partners read their picture cards to each other while I circulated, clarifying any words children had confused. The children holding the picture of a *pot* thought the word was *pan*, and the partnership holding *pet* thought it was *puppy*.

There's no need to exactly re-create this scene. The important thing is that students know you are carrying so many materials because they are ready to increase their vowel power, and that you drop the picture cards, thus giving students an authentic reason to help you sort them later.

To support students in really working on hearing the medial vowel, this sort includes many words that have matching initial and final consonants, forcing the use of the vowel for sorting.

Sort the picture cards on the pocket chart.

Once I reconvened the class, I said, "Let's do this like a symphony. I'll point to a partnership. Then, together, say your word and match it to the word on the pocket chart that has the same sound in the middle. Thumbs up when you are ready!"

Like a conductor, I pointed with an imaginary baton to ready partnerships, and I nudged them to compare their cards to the anchors, as in, "*Ten* /ĕ/. *Egg* /ĕ/." I always followed each attempt with "Check it!" and waited for the children to repeat the anchor picture to be sure of a sound match. As each partnership sorted, I coached with prompts and reminders as needed.

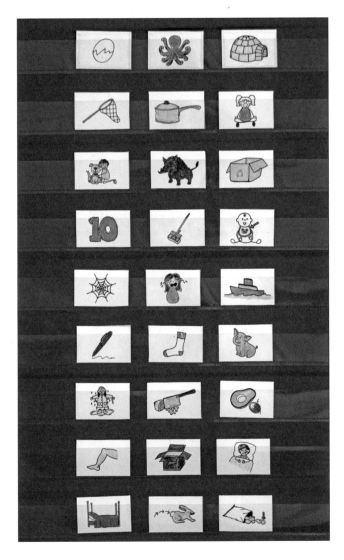

RUG TIME (CLUBS)

Recruit students to hunt for words with short *E, O*, and *I* sounds in a familiar song.

"Super Readers, let's find some words to add to our sort! Let's hunt for vowels in a song that I think you know well." I quickly distributed the first verse of "Hickory Dickory Dock" and a few index cards to each rug club. "Read the song together, and when you notice a word that has a short *E, O*, or *I*, circle it. We'll collect those words in our short-vowel jars along with the picture cards!"

As the children worked, I circulated among them, especially supporting the kids who were hunting and pecking for short-vowel words, rather than reading the song and noticing them in the midst of reading.

As soon as each club had found and circled a word or two, I recorded their findings on index cards and together, we sorted the words under the corresponding columns on the pocket chart.

SHARE • Shared Reading of Sorted Picture Cards and Words

Lead a shared reading of the sorted picture cards and words. Organize the picture cards into their corresponding short-vowel jars.

"Wow, you listened really closely and noticed *E* /ĕ/, *O* /ŏ/, and *I* /ĭ/ in so many words! You're on your way to lighting up more vowels on your shield. Let's get an extra vowel power boost by rereading our whole sort."

We read down each column, saying the picture name, then the sound. I left the anchor pictures in the pocket chart but collected each picture card and word card as we read them. When we reached the bottom of the column, I dropped the set of cards into its short-vowel jar.

"Whew, thanks for helping me clean that up, Super Readers! Your vowel power definitely grew today. One more chant before we go: *E!* /ĕ/ /ĕ/ /ĕ/. *O!* /ŏ/ /ŏ/ /ŏ/. *I!* /ĭ/ /ĭ/ /ĭ/."

EXTENSION 1 • Practice Segmenting and Blending with Elkonin Boxes

Use Elkonin boxes coupled with letter work to provide students with additional practice segmenting and blending sounds in words.

I placed the three-part Elkonin boxes from earlier in the unit under the document camera and said, "Do you remember how we used this tool to help strengthen our ear muscles *and* our vowel power?"

POSSIBLE COACHING MOVES

▶ "Be sure to read every word, so that your reading makes sense."

▶ "You see that vowel in the word? Read the word and listen to check that it makes the same short-vowel sound as the anchor picture."

Hickory Dickory Dock

Hickory dickory dock,

the mouse ran up the clock.

The clock struck one,

the mouse ran down.

Hickory dickory dock!

If you have started the reading unit, Bigger Books, Bigger Reading Muscles, *your children will likely already have this song inside their book baggies, since it is one of the recommended Shared Reading texts. If that is the case, you might just ask children to bring their copies to rug time. If this song is new to your children, be sure to sing it with them before asking them to hunt for short vowels.*

The class nodded their heads in unison as I said, "Today we are going to use this tool again! Are you ready? Just like we did last time, we will place a letter in each box for each sound you say and hear."

I modeled for the class by saying the word *bbbbbbooooooxxxxx* and writing the letter *B* in the first box as I was saying /b/, the letter *O* when I got to the /ŏ/, and the letter *X* in the final box as I said /x/.

I asked the class to say each sound separately with me as I pointed under the corresponding letter. "Now let's blend the sounds together again to make the word." I ran my finger under the letters in the boxes as we all said the word *bbbbbbooooooxxxxx* again.

As a reminder, I gestured to the alphabet chart and vowel shield and said, "Now will you help me? As we say the sounds in a word, you can write the letters for the word in the rug with your fingers, and I will write them up here. Show me your magic writing fingers!"

We repeated this routine with the words *chop*, *wet*, *ship*, *ten*, *shop*, and *chip*.

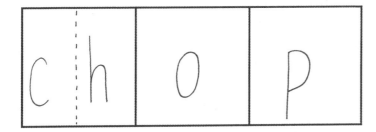

EXTENSION 2 • Singing to Support Listening for Medial Vowel Sounds

Introduce a song that supports children in noticing the medial sound in words.

"Writers, let's celebrate our growing vowel power."

I began singing the song "What's the Middle Sound That You Hear?" to the tune of "London Bridge," and the children chimed in quickly. For the first round, I selected the word *bet*.

I coached the children to listen to the middle sound in the word, prompting them to use robot talk as needed. We continued singing the song together with additional short-vowel words, such as *rag*, *rip*, *beg*, and *pop*, and I made a mental note to tuck the song into transitions across the day, perhaps even as a warm-up for writing workshop.

Remember that when you are coupling Elkonin boxes with letter work, if there are two letters in one box because they make one sound, you should divide that box with a dotted line to show that the two letters make only one sound.

What's the Middle Sound That You Hear?
(To the tune of London Bridge)

___ ___

What's the middle sound that you hear,

that you hear, that you hear?

What's the middle sound that you hear

in ... ___, ___, ___?

/ / is the middle sound that you hear,

that you hear, that you hear!

/ / is the middle sound that you hear

in ... ___, ___, ___!

When selecting words, you might decide to use some of the picture cards from sorts the children have engaged in across this unit. You might also consider having the song and picture cards available for students to use independently or with a partner at other times in the day.

Identifying and Editing for Short *E*, *O*, and *U* Sounds

TODAY YOU'LL teach students that writers work hard to tell short-vowel sounds apart, especially *E*, *O*, and *U*. They can say each part of the word, listening closely for the vowel sound so they can then write it.

TODAY YOUR STUDENTS will engage in a shared reading to practice identifying short *E*, *O*, and *U* sounds within connected text. They will also practice distinguishing vowel sounds as they edit their own writing and sing a song.

GETTING READY

✔ Display the book *The Very Bad Day*, with small Post-it notes covering selected vowels.

✔ Prepare to distribute students' writing folders, pens, and pencils.

PHONICS INSTRUCTION

Phonological Awareness
- Isolate and pronounce initial sound, medial vowel, and final sounds in spoken words.
- Segment individual phonemes in words.

Phonics
- Demonstrate basic knowledge of letter-sound correspondences by producing the primary sound for each consonant.
- Hear and identify short vowel sounds in words and the letters that represent them (*E, O, U*).

Word Knowledge/Solving
- Use knowledge of short vowel sounds to read and write words.
- Use familiar phonograms to read and write words.

MINILESSON

CONNECTION

"Would you believe I was almost late to school this morning? It might sound silly, but I had trouble finding a matching pair of socks! I searched through my dresser drawer for two socks that matched but it was a *huge* mess! So, I decided to dump all the socks onto the floor and work to pair them all up, matching one striped sock with another striped sock, one flowered pink sock with another flowered pink sock. I had to be careful not to get any mixed up! After all, I didn't want to come to school wearing one purple sock and one yellow polka-dotted sock!" The class giggled.

"You might be wondering why I'm going on and on about socks. Well, I realized something as I was working carefully to match my socks together. I realized that writers need to do that careful work, too. Except instead of matching socks, they match sounds with letters.

"Writers don't worry about mixing up their socks, but they do worry about mixing up their vowels, especially in words with /ŏ/ like *hot*, and /ŭ/ like *hut*.

✤ **Name the teaching point.**

"Today I want to teach you that, as writers, you need to work hard to tell vowel sounds apart, especially short *O* /ŏ/, and short *U* /ŭ/, and sometimes short *E* /ĕ/. You can say each part of the word, listening closely for the vowel sound. Then, you can write the vowel that makes the sound."

TEACHING

Cover the short vowels in a shared reading text. Demonstrate solving words and then figuring out the covered vowel.

"First, we'll practice this with someone else's writing, then we'll try it with yours. That means we get to read a new book together! It is called *The Very Bad Day*, and it is about one kindergartner's tough day. Don't worry, there's a happy ending! I've covered up some of the short vowels. Watch how I listen carefully to figure out which vowel is covered."

I read the title and turned to the first page. I searched the picture, which showed a child tumbling out of bed, and reacted to it. "Oh no!" Pointing under the words, I began, "I . . . /f/ . . . Hmm, . . . in the picture, he fell out of bed, so I think this page says 'I fell out of bed." I kept my finger under *fell*. "*Fell* makes sense and sounds right. What vowel do I expect to see in the middle?" I thought aloud, and I signaled the kids who offered help to give me a moment to think. "I'm going to need to activate my vowel power!

"I'll say each sound: /f/-/ĕ/-/l/. I hear /ĕ/. Hmm, . . . is that like *egg* /ĕ/, or *umbrella* /ŭ/? They sound so similar."

I tapped my chin as I considered this, then looked at my vowel shield. "*Fell* /ĕ/. *Egg* /ĕ/. I think it's *E*!" I quickly recorded the letter *E* on the Post-it in the middle of the word. "Now I need to check it."

Many kids nodded in agreement as I pulled off the Post-it to reveal the letter *E* as I'd expected. "I was right! Okay, I'll keep reading!"

I repeated the steps for the word *bed*, first asking, "What would make sense and sound right? What vowel do I expect to see?" then segmenting the word and listening closely for the medial sound. Once again, I modeled carefully, distinguishing between similar vowel sounds before landing on one. After writing in the vowel and checking it, I turned to the children.

The Very Bad Day with short vowels covered up on pages 2 and 3.

"Did you see how I said each sound and listened closely for the vowel? It can be puzzling to tell the vowel sounds apart. I think I can feel my vowel power growing when I work hard at it!"

ACTIVE ENGAGEMENT/LINK

Recruit partnerships to figure out the masked vowels in the rest of the book.

"Now it's your turn, Super Readers and Writers! Activate your vowel power and figure out which vowels are covered in the words on the next page!"

I turned the page, and as we read the picture together, I commented, "Oh no! He got a cut! He really is having a bad day, like the title says. Well, you've activated your picture power. Now you're ready to read the words. Activate your pointer power!"

I pointed as we read *I* together and then stopped at *got*. "You can use sound power to say the beginning sound. What would make sense and sound right?" Several children responded, "*Got!*"

"*Got* makes sense, and it sounds right and looks right at the beginning and end. Now, if it is *got*, what vowel do you expect to see in the middle? It's one of our snap words, so you might be ready to just name the vowel. If not, activate your vowel power! Turn and talk with your partner!"

We continued through the book this way, reading and quickly stopping to solve the covered words in partnerships. I called children up to record the covered vowels, before checking the text. During each of the turn-and-talks, I coached in as needed.

POSSIBLE COACHING MOVES

▶ "Try robot talk. Say each sound."

▶ "Does the vowel sound more like *octopus* /ŏ/ or *umbrella* /ŭ/? Or maybe *egg* /ĕ/? They can be easy to mix up."

▶ "You need a vowel next."

▶ "Does it look right?"

"So, remember, kindergartners, you can work hard to tell vowel sounds apart! You can say each sound in the word, listening closely for the vowel sound. Then, you can write the vowel that makes the sound."

The purpose of word study is to become a more flexible, fluent problem solver when reading and writing connected text. Thus, you may present your learners with the option of using vowel power or word-part power. In today's lesson, the aim is to emphasize vowel power, knowing you have the option to return to this learning to reinforce word-part power.

RUG TIME

Channel students to edit a piece of their own writing.

"You can do this in your own writing! It's easy to get short-vowel sounds mixed up. They sound so similar. But if you listen closely and say each sound in the words you want to write, those words will be easier for others to read. Get to it! Open your folders and take out the piece of writing you were last working on. Read each word and think about the vowels inside. If a word doesn't look right, you can say each sound and listen carefully, then fix the spelling above it. Your vowel shield can help you remember the sounds that go with each vowel."

POSSIBLE COACHING MOVES

▶ "Say your word. Now say each sound you hear. You can use robot talk to help you hear each sound in the word."

▶ "Listen to the sound of the vowel. Does it sound more like *octopus* /ŏ/ or *umbrella* /ŭ/ or *egg* /ĕ/?"

▶ "Check your vowel shield. Does that sound match the letter?"

SHARE • Variation on a Familiar Song to Reinforce Short Vowels

Sing a song that helps children practice the vowel sounds. Start with a familiar version, then introduce a variation.

After the children stashed their writing away, I reconvened the class by humming "Old MacDonald." Some children began humming the familiar tune with me, and others started singing the song aloud.

"I have a new version of that song, and I think it can help us tell the vowel sounds apart. I think," I leaned in closer, "it can help us grow our vowel power! Let's use it to study the short *U* sound first."

I started singing, and the children joined in quickly:

> Old MacDonald had a farm
> AEIOU.
> And on that farm, he had a *duck*
> AEIOU.
> With an /ŭ/ /ŭ/ here and an /ŭ/ /ŭ/ there,
> Here an /ŭ/, there an /ŭ/,
> Everywhere an /ŭ/ /ŭ/.
> Old MacDonald had a farm
> AEIOU.

"Now let's sing to study the short *O* sound. Try hard to hear the difference between the *O* /ŏ/ and the *U* /ŭ/."

> Old MacDonald had a farm
> AEIOU.
> And on that farm, he had a *fox*
> AEIOU.

Because of differences in common regional pronunciations of the words dog *and* hog, *we chose* fox *for the verse with short O. You might note that if the farmer has a fox, it's likely an uninvited guest. Feel free to substitute any farm animals that will allow you to practice prototypical short-vowel sounds in this song.*

With an /ŏ/ /ŏ/ here and an /ŏ/ /ŏ/ there,
    Here an /ŏ/, there an /ŏ/,
    Everywhere an /ŏ/ /ŏ/.
    Old MacDonald had a farm
    AEIOU.

"Wow, when you sing that song, I can really hear how *fox* /ŏ/ and *octopus* /ŏ/ sound different from *duck* /ŭ/ and *umbrella* /ŭ/! It's helping your vowel power grow!" We sang the song a few more times, using it to distinguish among all of the short-vowel sounds. We sang *cat* for /ă/, *hen* for /ĕ/, and *pig* for /ĭ/.

Notice the use of engaging songs, poems, and chants across this unit. These play an important role in building phonological awareness and phonics skills. They also support engagement and play. You might recall a similar version of this song from Pat Cunningham, a mentor for many in the literacy world.

EXTENSION 1 • Writing Sort to Practice Distinguishing Vowels

Use whiteboards to engage students in a writing sort to practice distinguishing between short *E* and short *U* sounds.

Once the children had gathered at the rug, I had a few students help me distribute a whiteboard and marker to each child. I held up my whiteboard and demonstrated drawing a vertical line down the middle of the board, prompting the class to do the same thing. Then, I wrote an *E* on the top of the left side and a *U* on the top of the right side, asking the children to prepare their boards in the same way.

"We are going to make your vowel power grow by doing a special kind of sort. I'll say a word. You'll repeat the word and listen closely for the vowel sound. If you hear /ĕ/, write the word on the left side under the *E*, and if you hear /ŭ/, write the word on the right side under the *U*." After I demonstrated with the word *hut*, I supported the children as they participated in the writing sort with the words *pet, gut, wet, met, but, vet,* and *nut*.

After I said a word, I supported some children by prompting, "Say each sound. Listen for the vowel sound in the middle of the word. Robot talk might help you."

When we finished with the writing sort, I exclaimed, "Your vowel power is *really* growing. Let's use it to help read the words in our sort." After the children used their pointer power to read down each column, I said, "Your vowel power is definitely growing. Let's do a chant before we go! *E!* /ĕ/ /ĕ/ /ĕ/. *U!* /ŭ/ /ŭ/ /ŭ/."

EXTENSION 2 • Playing a Game to Practice Distinguishing Vowels

For additional practice reading CVC words and distinguishing vowels, engage the class in a variation on a familiar singing game.

"Let's play a few rounds of 'One of These Words Is Not Like the Others.' Do you remember that game from *Sesame Street*? We've played it before." I hummed a few bars, and the children nodded. "Let's sing it together." I began the song, and soon the children were singing along with me.

> One of these words is not like the others,
> One of these words just doesn't belong,
> Can you tell which word is not like the others
> By the time I finish my song?

Before this extension, you may wish to review the Sesame Street *song, "One of These Things Is Not Like the Others." A link to the song is available in the online resources.*

"Can you tell me which word has a different vowel from the others?" I placed four pictures on the easel. "Here are the words: *ten*, *leg*, *pig*, and *bed*. When you think you've figured out which word doesn't belong, put a thumb up." I paused a moment to give kids time to think about all four words. Then, I prompted partners to turn and share their answers with each other.

"Let's come back together and share." We sang the verse once more to focus everyone's attention. Then I signaled for the class to shout out their guesses. "*Pig!*" they chorused. "Why?" I asked. "Why doesn't *pig* belong?"

One student explained, "*Pig* has an *I* in the middle, and the other words have an *E*."

"Yes! Three of the words have a short *E*, /ĕ/ in the middle, but *pig* has a different vowel sound: short *I*, /ĭ/. Turn and talk with your partner about another word that *does* belong with *ten*, *leg*, and *bed*." There was lots of chatter, and after a minute, I asked for ideas. Students suggested that *get*, *wet*, *men*, and *bell* would all belong in the short *E* group.

"Let's play another round. Ready?" We sang the verse again, and this time, I placed four more picture cards on the easel without saying them aloud: *box*, *bag*, *sock*, *mop*. "Now, turn and talk with your partner about which word doesn't belong. Say each word aloud and listen carefully for the vowel sounds. Go!"

After sharing their responses, students explained why *bag* didn't belong in the group and then brainstormed other words that did. We played the game with a few more sets of words.

Vocalizing Vowel Sounds to Notice Differences

GETTING READY

✔ Make sure students have their vowel shields.

✔ Prepare one baggie for each rug club containing a whiteboard, marker, and a small pile of the short-vowel picture cards that were sorted in previous sessions.

PHONICS INSTRUCTION

Phonological Awareness
• Isolate and pronounce initial sound, medial vowel, and final sounds in spoken words.
• Segment individual phonemes in words.

Phonics
• Demonstrate basic knowledge of letter-sound correspondences by producing the primary sound for each consonant.
• Hear and identify short vowel sounds in words and the letters that represent them.

Word Knowledge/Solving
• Use knowledge of short vowel sounds to write words.
• Record digraphs to write new words.

High-Frequency Words
• Write high-frequency words in continuous text.

IN THIS SESSION

TODAY YOU'LL teach students that they can notice how each vowel feels when vocalizing it, and that can help them distinguish vowel sounds when writing.

TODAY YOUR STUDENTS will practice spelling words on picture cards and writing sentences, paying close attention to how the vowel sounds feel when they are vocalized.

MINILESSON

CONNECTION

Pretend to be a singer warming up for a performance. Liken it to the way writers can chant vowel sounds to prepare for writing.

"Kindergartners, have you ever heard a singer prepare for a performance? Before they go on stage in front of a big audience, singers do warm-up exercises with their mouths and vocal cords—the parts inside the throat that make sounds."

I rose gracefully from my chair, chin up, eyes closed, trying to do my best impression of a distinguished vocalist. I raised one hand in the air and rested the other on my throat and began to sing, "Me me me me me me. La la la la la la." The class giggled, but I persisted. "Ah ah ah ah ah. Oo oo oo oo oo.

"Singers repeat those warm-up sounds again and again, and it gets them ready to sing all the notes in their songs very precisely.

"You know what? Writers can do that, too! To really be ready to write the words in your books, to really know which vowels to use, you can do a little warm-up! Take out your vowel shields!" I pointed to my vowel shield as I sang the short-vowel sounds to the singer's melody. "*E!* /ĕ/ /ĕ/ /ĕ/ /ĕ/ /ĕ/! *O!* /ŏ/ /ŏ/ /ŏ/ /ŏ/ /ŏ/!"

"Try it with me! It's helpful to pay attention to *how* you make each vowel sound." Soon there was a chorus of vowel sounds ringing through the room as we sang each short-vowel sound together in succession.

❖ **Name the teaching point.**

"Today I want to teach you that, as your vowel power gets stronger, you'll start to notice that different vowels feel different in your throat or your mouth when you say them. You can make your vowel power even stronger by not only *listening* for vowel sounds, but also *feeling* for vowel sounds."

TEACHING AND ACTIVE ENGAGEMENT/LINK

Invite students to chant the vowel sounds with you, calling their attention to the way the sounds feel as they are vocalized.

"Let me show you what I mean." I held up my vowel shield and pointed to the *O*, beginning to say the sound in a stretched way: "/ooooooooo/ . . ." Students joined me. "Now freeze! Oh my! I'm looking at all of you, and I see that your mouths are open and round, like the shape of an *O*! Everybody, trace the *O* with your finger!" I demonstrated for students, showing them how I could trace the shape of my mouth as I produced the short *O* sound, /ŏ/.

We continued. I pointed to the *E* on the vowel shield, again allowing students to chant the short-vowel sound, then feel for the shape of their mouths. "Interesting. When I make the sound /ĕ/ /ĕ/ /ĕ/, my mouth opens a little and stretches back. Let's see if that's true for you, too." I prompted kids to make the sound of short *E*, paying attention to the way their mouths opened and pulled back.

I next pointed to the *I* on the vowel shield, and students quickly started chanting the /ĭ/ sound. "Turn and face your partner. See if you and your partner can figure out what your mouths do when you make the /ĭ/ sound." I walked around as a chorus of chanting began on the carpet, and I noticed students giggling as they felt for the shape of their mouths. I voiced over: "I think you noticed it! I heard Quinn telling Anny, 'Look at how my mouth opens, but only a little bit . . .'"

As I circulated, I prompted partners to move on to do the same with the short *A* and short *U* sounds. Then, I called the group back together. "So, we've noticed that every time we make a different vowel sound, our mouths do different things. That can actually come in really handy when you're writing. Sometimes, if you're writing, and it's tricky to figure out the sounds in your words, you might think about not only what you hear, but also what you feel in your mouth. That can help you spell so many words!"

Notice that, today, we are giving children yet another entry point into work with vowels. We are also making this work multisensory. Some children will be able to notice vowel sounds easily. For others, it may be easier to feel the difference as vowel sounds are produced. Both methods are effective ways for students to distinguish sounds.

Channel students to write the words that match a set of picture cards. Coach them to listen and feel for vowels.

"Let's try this out right now!" I quickly distributed baggies to each rug club. I had prepared them in advance with whiteboards, markers, and a pile of picture cards in each. "We're going to play a little spelling game. First, put your pile of picture cards in the middle. One of you is going to turn the top card over, and everybody's going to try to spell the word on that card. Then you can check each other's spelling, and maybe even give each other tips to write even better!"

As I walked around, I coached students on both spelling and group process. I noted that students were working on a range of phonics skills—some were distinguishing vowel sounds, while others were striving toward segmenting words or recording initial and ending consonants. I coached accordingly.

This is a complicated task for kindergartners that requires skill in both phonics and the social-emotional realm. If you feel like your kids need more scaffolding with the social challenges, you could try setting times and voicing over instructions for each step to the entire class. If you let go of the reins, though, you may be surprised at the degree to which kids can take charge of their own learning.

POSSIBLE COACHING MOVES FOR WRITING

▶ "Say it slowly. How does your mouth feel when you make that sound?"

▶ "Does that sound match any of the pictures on the vowel shield?"

▶ "What sound do you hear? Write the letter down. Use the alphabet chart (or vowel shield) to help you."

POSSIBLE COACHING MOVES FOR GROUP PROCESS

▶ "Try taking turns. Who's going to turn the card over next?"

▶ "What a great tip! Don't tell that to me; tell that to your friends in your rug club."

▶ "Try saying something like, 'Can I give you a suggestion?'"

▶ (Whispering) "Do you have a different idea about what that letter should be? Tell the others!"

SHARE • Writing a Sentence with Short-Vowel Words

Support students as they write a sentence using one of the words from their pile of picture cards.

After the children had had multiple opportunities to practice spelling the words on the picture cards, I called them back together. Once everyone was ready, I said, "Let's use one of the words in your word pile to practice writing a sentence on your whiteboards." I bent down and picked up a picture of a ship. "This ship is red."

As I said the sentence again, I put one finger in the air for each word, inviting the children to join me in counting the words. Then, I prompted the class to orally rehearse the sentence a few times and write it on their whiteboards. As children finished, I prompted them to use their pointer power to reread their sentences.

After a few moments, I reconvened the class and said, "Before we put everything away, let's celebrate everything we learned today by doing our vowel power cheer." I pointed to my vowel shield and we chanted, "*A! E! I! O! U! A*, *apple*, /ă/. *E*, *egg*, /ĕ/. *I*, *igloo*, /ĭ/. *O*, *octopus*, /ŏ/. *U*, *umbrella*, /ŭ/."

EXTENSION 1 • Using Vowel Power to Construct a Text

Use interactive writing to construct a reminder poster for the classroom, inviting students to share the pen for words with short vowels.

"Kindergartners, I was thinking about ways to keep our classroom safe and special, and I thought we could write a reminder together. Remember, to make our reminder easy to read, we will need to make sure we activate our vowel power."

I gestured to some scraps of paper on the floor. "Writers, what could we say to remind each other to put trash and wrappers in the garbage can?" The children talked briefly with their partners, and then I called them back together, knowing ahead of time that what we would write would offer them the opportunity to practice short vowels.

"Yes! Many of you said something like, 'Pick up the trash!' That's a helpful reminder! Let's write it, and later we can tape it by the garbage can."

I planned the sentence by raising one finger each time I said a word and inviting the children to join me. Before I began writing the message, I reminded them, "We'll have to make sure to write one word for each finger."

I paused before the word *pick*. "Hmm, . . . *pick*. Writers, activate your vowel power! Every single word needs a vowel. Say *pick* slowly and listen closely for the vowel sound." In unison, the children chorused the word. "*Pick*. What sound do you hear in the middle? Lean and whisper it to your partner.

"Writers, eyes on me. *Pick* has the /ĭ/ sound in the middle, just like *igloo*. Everyone, write *pick* on the rug in front of you." As the rest of the class spelled the word on the rug, I worked with the child who was writing *pick* in the class text. Then, I continued constructing the text with the children, making note of the two snap words and prompting the children to help me with the short vowel and digraph in *trash*.

> Pick up the trash!

"Let's reread our reminder!" I pointed under each word as the children read. "Every single word here has a vowel! This reminder sign is going to help us keep our classroom clean. Remember to activate your vowel power when you are in writing workshop!"

EXTENSION 2 • Playing "Name That Vowel"

Hold up a series of CVC word cards with the vowel covered by a Post-it. Say the word aloud, then challenge partners to figure out the correct vowel.

I prepared a set of five index cards. I wrote a word on each: *pet, bib, bun, top,* and *sag*. Then, using small Post-its, I covered the vowel in each word.

"Let's play 'Name That Vowel!' I'll hold up and say a word. The vowel will be covered, and it will be your job to *name . . . that . . . vowel!*

"Ready?" I held up *pet*. "*Pet*, as in, 'A dog is a kind of pet.' Name that vowel! Turn and talk." The children whispered with their partners. When I signaled for them to come back together, I slowly unveiled the vowel. "Let's check it. Name that vowel!"

"*E!*" the class chorused back. Next I held up *bib*. "*Bib*, as in, 'The baby is wearing a bib.' Name that vowel! Turn and talk." After the children tried it, I again revealed the vowel. "Check it. Name that vowel!"

"*I!*" they responded. We continued playing with *bun*, *top*, and *sag* to practice with all of the short vowels. We played the game with other CVC words here and there throughout the week while waiting for kids to gather on the rug or line up to go to lunch.

SESSION 10

Introducing New Snap Words

On, Up, Fun, *and* Get

IN THIS SESSION

TODAY YOU'LL teach students that readers can use snap words to help them remember vowel sounds. You'll introduce four new snap words featuring short *E, O,* and *U* to help them solidify those vowels in their repertoires.

TODAY YOUR STUDENTS will practice using the "How to Learn a Word" routine to learn four new snap words and write dictated sentences that include those words.

GETTING READY

✔ Prepare an envelope from Reader-Man containing a note and the snap words *on, up, fun,* and *get.*

✔ Display the "How to Learn a Word" anchor chart from Unit 1, *Making Friends with Letters.*

✔ Distribute a whiteboard and marker to each student.

MINILESSON

CONNECTION

Unveil a letter from Reader-Man along with four new high-frequency words: *on, up, fun,* and *get.*

"Super Readers, gather at the rug quickly today. We have a new letter from Reader-Man, and it's heavier than usual!" I winced at the envelope's thickness before tearing it open and placing the note on the document camera.

After reading the letter, I turned back to the envelope to find four new high-frequency word cards for *on, up, fun,* and *get.* I clipped them to the easel.

"These are written on the same kind of paper as our other snap words, and I *have* seen them in a lot of books, but what could Reader-Man mean

Dear Super Readers,

I am sending you 4 words.
They are in lots of books.

They can become snap words
AND they can help your vowel power grow.

You are almost ready
to light up your whole shield!

Your friend,
Reader-Man

PHONICS INSTRUCTION

Letter Knowledge
• Use proper letter formation.

Phonics
• Recognize and use short vowel sounds at the beginning of words.

High-Frequency Words
• Write high-frequency words in continuous text.
• Read and write high-frequency words with automaticity.
• Develop strategies for learning new high-frequency words.
• Learn four new words (*on, up, fun, get*).

when he says that they can help your vowel power grow?" I puzzled for a moment before kids' voices filled the silence.

"They have *E*, *O*, and *U* in them! We need to light up those vowels!" Several children held up their vowel shields and pointed to the letters that were decidedly unhighlighted.

"Oh, yes," I said. "We'd better get to work turning these words into snap words then!"

♣ **Name the teaching point.**

"Today I want to teach you that you can lean on certain words to help you remember your short-vowel sounds. When you turn them into snap words, you'll always have those helpful words with you."

TEACHING

Follow the familiar sequence for turning a word into a snap word. Call attention to the short vowel within the word.

"Let's turn these words into snap words, like Reader-Man said!" I displayed the "How to Learn a Word" anchor chart and invited kids to read it with me.

I held up the first word: *on*. "Okay, let's make this a snap word. First, *read* it!" I pointed under the printed card as the students chorally read the word.

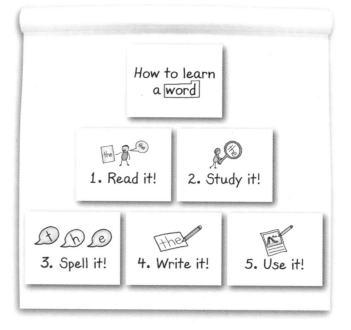

"Now, *study* it. It has two letters. What letters do you see? Name them to your partner. And you noticed that this word has one vowel, *O*. Yes! It is one of the vowels we've been studying closely this week.

"Now, *spell* it. Spell it softly, like a whisper into your hand. *O-N*. Now, let's spell it and cheer it. *O-N! On!* Okay, now spell it to your partner."

"Here's step 4: *write* it!" I pointed to that step on the chart. "Let's first write it in the air, writing it the right way. All of you, stand up so you have lots of air around you. Ready?" I wrote-in-the-air and recited the letter formation pathway for lowercase *O*, "Bump back and travel all the way around." Then, I did the same for lowercase *N*, "Line down. Back up. Bump around and down. Now write it a few more times so you really get it into your muscles."

After a few seconds, I said, "Okay, sit down. Pull the cap off your marker. Write *on* on your whiteboard. Spell it aloud as you write the letters. Write it three times." As students wrote the word *on* on their whiteboards, I wrote the word on chart paper and voiced over the letter formation pathway.

"Now will you check to see if you already know the word by heart? Can you write it without looking? I'm going to cover up the word. Erase your whiteboards. Then write the word on your whiteboard again. Say the letters as you write them." After everyone had a chance to try this, I said, "I'm going to uncover the word. Did you get each letter right? Check it!"

"Now it's time for the very last step—*use* it! Think of a sentence with the word *on* in it. You might say, 'I am sitting *on . . .*' Go!" I gave them a minute to share their sentences with their partners and then asked for their attention again.

ACTIVE ENGAGEMENT/LINK

Repeat the high-frequency word study sequence with additional words, *up*, *fun*, and *get*.

"Now, let's learn another one of these words by heart. Reader-Man sent us the word *up*! It can help us remember the short *U* sound. Up! Let's make *up* a snap word. Look at the chart. What do we do first?"

We repeated the same steps to learn *up*. Next, we learned *fun*, and the children noticed the *U* in the middle of the word, rather than the beginning, as in *up*. *Get* came last, where kids also commented on the *E*'s position in the middle of the word.

"Now that these words are snap words, we can lean on them to help us remember the short *E*, *O*, and *U* sounds!"

RUG TIME CLUBS

Use dictation to practice writing the new snap words in context.

"You practiced using our new snap words in your talk, and now you are ready to use them when writing sentences! After all, if they are going to help your vowel power grow, you'll need to practice as much as possible! I'll say the sentence, and you can write it on your whiteboard. Work in your rug club so you can check in with your partners."

> <u>Get up on</u> your feet!
>
> Let's have some <u>fun</u>!

"Here's the first sentence: 'Get up on your feet!'" I nudged writers to use the snap words on the easel if they needed help with the first three words. Children said the rest of the words slowly and wrote the sounds they heard.

For the introduction of these high-frequency snap words, we've drawn on research by Marie Clay. When you introduce new snap words using this routine, you're incorporating three ways of remembering—visual, auditory, and tactile (see it, say it, make it). Keeping this in mind whenever you work with high-frequency words will surely pay off!

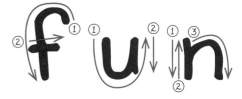

During activities like this and throughout your day, it's important to remember the role of inventive spelling. Your goal is to support learners in using all they know about letters and words to make their writing easier to read, while celebrating approximations and recognizing that the learners in your classroom will be at various stages of spelling development.

"Ready for the next sentence? 'Let's have some fun!' Go!" The children wrote and checked in with their partners as I coached them.

SHARE • Celebrating New Snap Words

Include the new snap words in the class vowel cheer. Add them to the word wall.

"Let's listen to the sentences we just wrote and get up on our feet! The snap words that Reader-Man sent us *did* help us grow our vowel power! We should do our vowel cheer to celebrate! I held up my vowel shield and right on cue, the children did the same. We chanted, "*A! E! I! O! U! A, apple, /ă/. E, egg, /ĕ/. I, igloo, /ĭ/. O, octopus, /ŏ/. U, umbrella, /ŭ/.*

"Ooh, maybe we should add to our chant, just for today! Let's add our new snap words to the vowels they'll help us read and write. *E, get, /ĕ/! O, on, /ŏ/! U, up, /ŭ/! U, fun, /ŭ/!* We continued chanting as I paraded the new words to the word wall. I made sure that these new words were added to students' snap word pouches later in the day.

EXTENSION 1 • Practicing High-Frequency Words

Use word wall cheers and chants to reinforce high-frequency snap words.

"I have a new cheer for our snap words. It's called Blast Off! We can spell each word out loud, starting near the floor and standing up a little higher as we say each letter, finally jumping into the air as we say the whole word. Let me show you how this special cheer goes." I said the snap word *fun* aloud, then crouched down and placed my hands near my feet. I stood up a little higher each time I said a letter—*F-U-N*—jumping up at the end, saying, "*Fun!* Blast off!"

"Let's all try it! Go ahead and stand up. Now, crouch down like a ball near the floor. I'll say a word, and you can spell the word out loud together, standing up a little bit each time you say a letter. Make sure you say the whole word at the end, and don't forget to blast off with a jump!"

After cheering with *on*, *up*, *fun*, and *get*, we practiced with a few additional words from the word wall. During transitions, I remembered to use the Blast Off cheer to reinforce snap words and have some fun!

In this session and across your day, it's important to compliment students' instant recognition and quick writing of known high-frequency words. It's also important to clarify that when students slow down to problem solve a puzzling word, they'll need to speed back up afterwards, as all of this supports reading and writing fluency.

EXTENSION 2 • Using New Snap Words to Write a Pattern Book

Once interactive writing time rolled around, I took out the book I had prepared and placed under the document camera. I pointed to the cover and said, "This is a book called *Fun at School*. It is about different things we play with at school." I turned to the first page. Some students called out, "Hey! That's Kenta in the block area!" Kimora said, "Whoa! We know some of those words!"

"We do know some of these words! Let's start with a little quiz. Everybody point to the word *get*! Now, everybody show me *the*! Can you point to *fun*?" Students pointed along, and I said, "Let's read the whole thing together." I pointed underneath the words and read the first page. Many students, knowing the snap words, could read along with me. To support their orchestration of reading strategies, I pointed to the picture when we got to the word *blocks*.

I turned the page, revealing a photo of students working with connecting cubes. "We're going to keep the pattern going. What will go on this page? Turn and talk with your partner." I gave students a moment, then called them back together and said, "Let's say this page together." As we said "Get out the connecting cubes. It is fun!," I held up a finger for each word.

"Now it's time to write the words! *Get* . . . *get* . . . everybody look at the word wall. Say the letters while I write them." Students said *G-E-T* while I wrote the word. "Let's do the same thing for *the*." We continued in this manner, with students spelling the snap words aloud as I wrote them. On later pages, I released the scaffold and channeled more engagement by having students write the words on each other's backs, with imaginary markers on their hands, and with their fingers on the carpet.

On the last page, we added a pattern break: "Kindergarten is so much fun!"

To get ready for this extension, take photos of hands-on items from the classroom: various math manipulatives, blocks, books, or toys could work well. Glue these photos onto the pages of a blank book. Write on the first page of the book: "Get out the blocks. It is fun!" This will establish the pattern for the book, which you'll develop with students. Prepare to display the book with a document camera.

Using Interactive Writing to Build Ownership and Support Transfer

GETTING READY

✔ Prepare to illustrate a blank book or print the ready-made illustrated version of *How to Gather at the Rug* in preparation for interactive writing.

✔ Students will need their writing folders.

PHONICS INSTRUCTION

Concepts About Print
- Understand punctuation has a purpose.

Phonological Awareness
- Segment individual phonemes in words.
- Isolate and pronounce initial sound, medial vowel, and final sounds in spoken words.

Letter Knowledge
- Use proper letter formation.

Phonics
- Demonstrate basic knowledge of letter-sound correspondences by producing the primary sound for each consonant.
- Hear and identify short vowel sounds in words and the letters that represent them.

Word Knowledge/Solving
- Use knowledge of short vowel sounds to write words.
- Use familiar phonograms to write words.

High-Frequency Words
- Write high-frequency words in continuous text.

IN THIS SESSION

TODAY YOU'LL teach students that they can draw on everything they have learned about how to identify and make use of vowels to make their writing easier for everyone to read.

TODAY YOUR STUDENTS will engage in an interactive writing session, during which you'll coach them to listen for the vowel sound in every word, then work hard to think about what vowel they should write.

MINILESSON

CONNECTION

Remind students how much their vowel power has grown, and warm up with a familiar phonological game to support segmenting individual phonemes in CVC words.

After the children gathered at the meeting area, I leaned in with a grin and said, "Let's use the robot game to help us warm up our vowel power! I've picked words that will activate your vowel power as we notice and say the vowel sound in the middle of each word.

"Let's say the word *met* using robot talk!" I said, as I made robotic movements with my arms and torso and segmented the sounds, /m/-/ĕ/-/t/, inviting students to join me in saying each sound in the word.

"Robot talk is a lot of fun, and it *really* helps us to activate our vowel power and strengthen our ear muscles. Let's try another word: *pen*!" Students acted like robots as they made the sounds. "Make sure to say all the sounds: the first sound, the middle sound, and the last sound," I coached. I segmented the word, /p/ /ĕ/ /n/, as many kids echoed. We continued warming up our vowel power with the words *pet*, *dug*, *top*, *tag*, *rot*, and *rug*.

"Kindergartners, playing the robot game is not only fun, it is also super-important. Sometimes you forget to use your vowel power when you are writing. Doing a little robot talk in your own minds might help you activate your vowel power when you're writing. This is a *really* important responsibility, because your vowel power makes your writing easier for everyone to read."

❖ **Name the teaching point.**

"Today I want to teach you that you are responsible for using your vowel power. It is important to try your best to listen for the vowel sound in every word, then use your vowel power to think about what vowel you should write."

TEACHING

Establish an authentic purpose for writing by creating a How-To text to teach next year's kindergartners the routine for gathering at the rug.

"Writers, not only do you know a lot about short vowels, you also know a lot about kindergarten. Maybe we could write a How-To book together, and I can save it to share with next year's kindergarten students. Before we get writing, turn and tell your partner things about our class that you could teach to new kindergarten students. Maybe you could help them learn our routines. I'll listen in." The children talked briefly, and then I called them back together, knowing ahead of time that what we would write would offer them the opportunity to practice their vowel power within continuous text.

"Yes! Many of you said something like, 'We should teach new kindergarten students how to gather at the rug!' That would be really helpful for any kindergartner! Let's write it together, and maybe we could even hang it up in our room as a reminder for us. And I'll make sure to save it to share with my new kindergarten students next year!"

Before moving to the construction of the text, I placed a blank How-To booklet under the document camera and wrote "How to Gather at the Rug" on the title page, reading each word aloud as I wrote it. We quickly practiced touching and telling which step would go on each page of the booklet. I made sure to emphasize using a teaching voice and quickly sketched an illustration for one step on each page of the booklet.

Interactive writing supports students as they transition from emergent readers and writers to conventional readers and writers. Notice that this work supports oral rehearsal and oral language. It's important to build in time for composing a text before moving to the construction of the text.

Use interactive writing to construct the How-To text, inviting students to share the pen on CVC words that contain a short vowel.

After finishing the sketches for each step, I returned to the first step and ran my finger around the picture as I rehearsed the sentence aloud: "Walk to the rug." I wrote the first three words and paused before the word *rug*. "Hmm, . . . *rug*. Writers, activate your vowel power! Every single word needs a vowel. Get those shields ready. Hold them up. Say *rug* slowly and listen closely for the vowel sound." In unison, the children chorused the word. "*Rug*. What sound do you hear in the middle? Lean and whisper it to your partner." I took note of what the children said, chose one child to come to the easel and share the pen, and then reconvened the class.

"Writers, eyes on me. *Rug* has the /ŭ/ sound, just like *umbrella*. Everyone, write *rug* on the rug in front of you." As the rest of the class spelled the word on the rug, I worked with the child who was writing *rug* in the class text, supporting conventionality as needed. To support letter formation, I prompted the student with the letter formation path for each letter. I also nudged her to add a period at the end of the sentence.

I repeated the same process with the second step on the second page of the booklet, inviting a different child to join me at the easel. I coached the children to use their vowel power for the words *spot* and *sit*.

"Let's reread our first two steps!" I pointed under each word as the children read. "Every single word here has a vowel! This is going to help everyone remember how to gather at the rug!"

ACTIVE ENGAGEMENT/LINK

Construct the text on the final page of the booklet, giving children the opportunity to share the pen on additional words that contain a short vowel.

"Writers, we need to finish our How-To book!" I ran my finger over the picture on the final page and said, "Quick! Turn and tell the person next to you what we could say!" I listened in and then brought everyone back together.

"Wow! So many of you said, 'Have fun learning!' Let's write it, and make sure that every single word has a vowel!"

I wrote the first word, and we reread it before gearing up for the second word. "*Fun*. That's one of our new snap words and it has a short vowel in it." One child came up to write *fun* in the class text, and others said each letter aloud while he wrote it and I coached into conventionality.

"Writers, *fun* has a *U* in the middle, just like *umbrella*! And it sounds like you have a lot of fun learning, so we can add an exclamation mark at the end." I added the last word and the punctuation, and we reread the sentence with big feeling.

Interactive writing sessions often have a predictable structure that moves seamlessly from composition and rehearsal to construction. During the construction of the text is when you'll share the pen with a student. Notice that you did most of the writing, sharing the pen for clear examples of CVC words that contain short vowels. Because interactive writing supports students as they transition from emergent readers/writers to conventional readers/writers, the end product of interactive writing is conventionally correct. Reference word study resources as appropriate and engage the children on the rug as well as the one at the easel.

Level C texts, which many kindergartners are reading at this time, can contain varied punctuation, while most level A and B texts contain only periods. This is a chance to encounter this new work together, and rereading with big feeling supports fluency.

"All of those words have vowels in them! Remember, writers, every single word has at least one vowel in it, and if you make sure to use vowels whenever you write words, people will be better able to read your writing!"

RUG TIME

Channel students to listen for the vowel sound in every word, then work hard to think about what vowel they should write as they work in their writing folders.

"Let's get our writing folders out and get started. As you are writing, you can make your writing easy to read by listening for the vowel sound in every word and thinking about what vowel you should write. Open your writing folders and take out a piece of writing you are still working on. Reread what you have written so far and then keep writing. As you are writing, make sure your vowel power is fully activated and that every word has a vowel. You might use robot talk to help you hear the vowel sound."

I circulated to support writers, providing lean prompts as needed.

SHARE • Coaching Partners to Read Their Writing

Invite partners to play the echo game with their own writing, in which one writer reads their writing by pointing to each word and the partner echoes.

"Put your writing between you and your partner. Then, get ready to play the echo game. Partner 1, point under each word and read a page out loud. After you read the page, your partner can echo you, reading the page again while you point under each word. After you have read your whole book, switch roles."

After a few minutes, I voiced over, "Partner 2, if you haven't read your writing to your partner, it's your turn to read and let your partner echo you. If both of you have had a turn, get out another book from your writing folder and play again."

EXTENSION 1 • Distinguishing Vowels in Dictated Sentences

Engage students in a dictation activity in which they will distinguish between /ĕ/, /ŏ/, and /ŭ/ sounds when writing sentences on whiteboards.

As I gathered students at the carpet, I asked some to help me distribute the whiteboards and markers to the class. Once everyone was ready, I exclaimed, "Let's put your vowel power and your snap word power together to help you make your writing easier to read. I think your pointer power and word-part power might also help you. I'm going to say a sentence, then will you combine all your powers to help you write it on your whiteboards? Are you ready?"

POSSIBLE COACHING MOVES

▶ "Say it slowly. What do you hear in the middle?"

▶ "Does it sound like _____ or _____?"

▶ "Does that look right?"

▶ "You need a vowel next."

▶ "Remember that you can use robot talk to help you hear the vowel sound."

▶ "Could word-part power help you?"

In reading and writing workshops you might have assigned each partner a number. However you've grouped your students, be sure to draw on that same arrangement here.

As the class nodded in unison, I said the sentence, "Look at my pet." As I did, I put one finger in the air for each word, inviting the children to join me in counting the words. Then, I prompted the class to rehearse the sentence a few times orally, and again, raise a finger as they said each word.

Before the children began writing the sentence on their whiteboards, I prompted, "Now, make sure you write one word for each finger." As children were writing, I circulated around the rug area coaching as needed. To support spacing and one-to-one matching, I said, "When you're done spelling your word, leave a finger space before writing the next word." If it was a snap word, I said, "Remember, if it is a word you know, you can write it in a snap." For some students, I provided support for spelling the CVC word by saying, "Say the word slowly and write each sound you hear." Sometimes I also said, "Maybe your word-part power can help you."

After the class finished writing the first sentence, we reread it together, using our pointer power to point under each word. Then we practiced with another sentence: "I am on the bus."

EXTENSION 2 • Practicing Segmentation with Robot Talk

Play the robot talk phonological game to provide additional practice segmenting the phonemes in CVC words.

"Do you want to play the robot game again?" I asked as the students smiled and began using their arms and torso to act like robots.

"Let's try it with the word *top*. *Top*. Let's say it using robot talk!" I said. I made robotic movements with my arms and torso and segmented the sounds, /t/-/ŏ/-/p/, inviting the students to join me.

"Robot talk is a lot of fun, and it *really* helps us strengthen our ear muscles. Let's try another word. *Vet*!" The students acted like robots as they made the sounds. I listened carefully for each phoneme. "Make sure to say all the sounds: the first sound, the middle sound, and the last sound," I coached. I segmented the word, /v/-/ĕ/-/t/, as many kids echoed.

We continued using robot talk with the words *dot*, *tug*, *sun*, *net*, *cup*, and *box*. As we played the game, I gradually removed the scaffolds of my voice and coaching.

Making New Words by Changing Vowels and Other Letters

IN THIS SESSION

TODAY YOU'LL teach students that they can use their vowel power to make words using all of the short vowels they have learned. ✒

TODAY YOUR STUDENTS will practice making words by changing one letter of a word to make a different word. Students will celebrate their learning in this bend by "lighting up"—highlighting—the remaining vowels on their vowel shields.

MINILESSON

CONNECTION

Celebrate the fact that students have vowel shields filled with vowels that they now know.

"Super Readers and Writers, grab your vowel shields and come to the meeting area!" I waited as students walked over and placed their vowel shields in front of them on the rug. Once they were all sitting, I asked them to hold up their shields. I marveled at how much stronger the vowel power in the room felt.

"You've only been using your vowel shields for a little while, but I can already feel the glow of your vowel power getting stronger!"

Provide students with added practice in chanting the vowel sounds.

"I think that your vowel power has gotten so strong because you've been practicing so much! Let's do another quick round of practice so we can make it even stronger."

I chose Juliette to come up and lead the vowel power cheer. The other students held up their vowel shields, with some pointing to each letter as we cheered for it. "*A! E! I! O! U!*" we chanted together.

GETTING READY

✔ Make sure students have their vowel shields.

✔ Prepare for each partnership a file folder containing small Post-its with each of the following letters: *A, E, I, O, U, L, P, B, G,* and *J*.

✔ Write the above letters, as well as the following words, on index cards to be placed in the pocket chart: *lip, lap, lag, bag, big, beg, bug, jug, jog*.

✔ Print Reader-Man's letter and place it surreptitiously in the highlighter box in a corner of the room. ✺

PHONICS INSTRUCTION

Phonological Awareness

• Manipulate individual phonemes to make new words.

• Segment individual phonemes in words.

• Isolate and pronounce initial sound, medial vowel, and final sounds in spoken words.

Phonics

• Demonstrate basic knowledge of letter-sound correspondences by producing the primary sound for each consonant.

• Hear and identify short vowel sounds in words and the letters that represent them.

Word Knowledge/Solving

• Use knowledge of short vowel sounds to write words.

• Use familiar phonograms to write words.

Then we chanted again, this time including the short-vowel sounds and keywords. "*A, apple, /ă/. E, egg, /ĕ/. I, igloo, /ĭ/. O, octopus, /ŏ/. U, umbrella, /ŭ/.*"

"Now that your vowel power is so strong, let's do something fun with it."

♣ Name the teaching point.

"Today I want to teach you that, when your vowel power gets really strong, you can make tons of words. You'll find that, by just changing the vowels in words, you can do amazing things, like turn *big* into *beg* or even *bug*."

TEACHING AND ACTIVE ENGAGEMENT

Invite students to participate in the construction of an initial word with a short vowel, in preparation for making lots of words with different vowels.

"Get ready to work with your partners." I quickly distributed to each partnership a file folder containing Post-its with the letters *A, E, I, O, U, L, P, B, G,* and *J.* As students were getting set up, I placed the same letters on small index cards into the pocket chart. I also prepared each whole word we would make on an index card, ready to display in the pocket chart.

"Let's get started! Let's see what kind of magic your vowel power can work!" I pointed to my top lip as I said, "I'm thinking of the top part of your mouth. Yes, your lip." I said the word *lip* slowly. "You can make this word! Work together to spell it on your folders." I watched as students moved three Post-it letters down, noticing who spelled automatically, who used a word part, who segmented the word slowly, and who was not yet matching letters and sounds.

"You did it! Look up here and check that your word is like mine." I spelled *lip* letter by letter in the pocket chart. "What's the word, kindergartners?" Students called out "*Lip!*" and I placed the index card displaying the entire word into the pocket chart.

Channel students to make more words as you add to the collection in the pocket chart.

"Let's see what other words we can make if we change the vowel. Partner 1, do what I do, and then read the word. Partner 2, your job is to check your partner's work and offer help if needed." I removed the *I* and put an *A* in its place and watched as students did the same with their Post-its. "What word did we make?" Once I'd heard that students had figured out the word, I added *lap* to the pocket chart.

"This time, let's keep the vowel and change a consonant. Partner 2, it's your turn. Partner 1, you're the checker this time." We continued with the rest of the words in our collection: *lag, bag, big, beg, bug, jug, jog.* Students took turns, alternating roles. Each time we worked with a word, I repeated the procedure. I made sure to say the word and invited students to spell it, read it, and check it. Then I showed the new word, letter by letter, in the pocket chart before adding the index card with the completed word to the collection. If I anticipated that a word might be unfamiliar, I made sure to use it in a sentence before nudging children to spell it.

You could distribute whiteboards with these letters on Post-its, instead of file folders, or use magnetic letters in trays. The point is to have a stable surface on which to work. Asking the kids to write each letter would slow things down and be less effective.

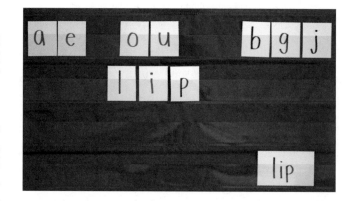

LINK

Restate the teaching point and link the work students did making words to their ongoing work as writers.

"Let's reread the words that we just made." I pointed to each word on the pocket chart, and students joined in with me as we read it chorally.

"Oh, my goodness, kindergartners! Look at how strong your vowel power is! You can make so many words when you write. Knowing this could help you during writing workshop. When you have vowel power, you know that changing the vowel changes the whole word!"

RUG TIME

Set students up to practice making more words with their partners.

"Are you ready to try it on your own?" I demonstrated clearing the pocket chart, and students joined me, moving their Post-its to the bottom of their file folders.

"I see everybody's ready, and now it's your turn! I'm going to give you a chance to make more words with these letters. See how many you can make with your partner! One big tip I have is to start by making one word and then see if you can change one letter—it could be the middle letter or the first letter or even the last letter—but change one letter and see if you can make a new word. Then keep going! You'll know it's a real word if you can use it in a sentence that makes sense. You can try making some of the words we just made together, or you can try making your own words. Have fun!"

SHARE • Celebrating Our Work by Highlighting Vowels *E*, *O*, and *U* on Vowel Shields

Search unsuccessfully for a new letter from Reader-Man to build suspense for the letter to come.

As the children were finishing up with their partners, I took my place at the front of the meeting area and began mumbling audibly. I checked my watch and searched the easel, only to look back at my watch again, frustrated. "It should be here by now. It should be here," I repeated to myself, loudly enough that everyone could hear.

"What's the matter?" Grace called out, sensing that something wasn't quite right.

I reconvened the class and sighed, "Well, kindergartners, it's just that . . . I was watching you make so many *new words* on your own because you could tell *all* of the vowel sounds apart, and I thought that Reader-Man would have noticed by now."

POSSIBLE COACHING MOVES

▶ "What could you change to make another word?"

▶ "Oh, you want to change the middle letter? What will you change it to? What kind of letter do you think you need? A vowel? Okay, get your vowel power ready then!"

▶ "Try changing the middle sound. What word do you get?"

▶ "Read the word by saying the sounds slowly, then push them together."

▶ "I see that you made a word! Read it with your partner. Is it a real word or a made-up word?"

Be aware that students might do this work in many different ways. Some will make lots of new words, some might make one or two new words, others might make nonsense words, and still others might not yet grasp this concept. Understand that there is learning in this type of approximation. Even if it looks like kids aren't yet understanding, major steps toward understanding happen when they make these attempts!

Find Reader-Man's letter and celebrate students' growing vowel power by highlighting the rest of the vowels on their shields.

Just then, something caught my eye in the back of the room. It was a bright red envelope sitting inside the box of highlighters that Reader-Man had delivered at the end of our last bend.

"Oh! I didn't think to check there. Of course, it's here!" I rushed over and grabbed the bin, then returned to the meeting area. "Reader-Man *did* notice! Look!"

I placed the letter under the document camera and read it.

"You did it, Super Readers and Writers! Let's do our vowel power cheer: "*A! E! I! O! U! A*, *apple*, /ă/. *E*, *egg*, /ĕ/. *I*, *igloo*, /ĭ/. *O*, *octopus*, /ŏ/. *U*, *umbrella*, /ŭ/!"

After a raucous rendition of the cheer, I said, "Now close your folders and take out your vowel shields!" I distributed highlighters to the children and watched as they colored in the remaining vowels on their shields triumphantly.

Dear Super Readers,

You have studied each vowel. You have listened closely to tell vowel sounds apart. Your vowel power has GROWN and GROWN again! It is time for your whole shield to shine!

There is still more to learn about vowels. Light up all of the vowels on your shield so you are ready!

Your friend,
Reader-Man

Dear Teachers,

In this bend, the work progresses from vowels in mostly CVC and monosyllabic words to vowels in longer words. This shift is especially important because most of the words that students write are not CVC words. Their How-To books include words like *careful* and *elevator*, and this bend channels them to use their growing vowel power to write even the biggest words they wish to express through their writing. Celebrating risk taking and approximations is important and allows us to reinforce why writers write—because they have a message to share with others.

You'll begin the bend with Mabel, who has noticed something special about her name—it has more than one vowel! Until now, the words you've worked with in this unit have been monosyllabic, with only a single vowel. You'll share a secret with Mabel—and the class—that circles back to the beginning of the unit: not only does every word have at least one vowel, but every syllable in every word has at least one vowel! This sends children on a hunt through a very special note from Mabel and focuses the work of the bend on identifying vowels in bigger words.

That special note is an invitation to Mabel's graduation, which frames the storyline of this final bend. We expect that Mabel's graduation will occur shortly after your students' graduation in the reading unit *Bigger Books, Bigger Reading Muscles*, so your students can teach Mabel a bit about being a graduate. If you have not taught *Bigger Books, Bigger Reading Muscles*, you might want to add more context about graduations into the early sessions of Bend III.

We define bigger words as those that have more letters than the CVC words you've worked with in previous bends. Identifying short vowels in bigger words provides an opportunity to revisit words with digraphs like *thin* or *shop*, words with phonograms like *sick* or *clock*, and, of course, multisyllabic words like *closet* or *pumpkin*.

As you shift from monosyllabic words to multisyllabic words, the way you support segmenting will shift as well. In the first two bends, you often coached readers to say each sound in the words they wanted to write, segmenting phoneme by phoneme. Now, in multisyllabic words, you can coach writers to segment by syllable, as it is simply too inefficient to segment words like *graduation* by phoneme.

In bigger words, you are also apt to find more than just *short* vowels. In Bend III, you'll acknowledge a fact that children already know: vowels can make more than just the short sound. Though they may not have used the term, long vowels are in your kindergartners' bones. Because the sounds of long vowels match their letter names, long vowels tend to be comfortable territory for young writers. You'll explore the concept of long vowels in a session featuring new high-frequency words: *play, say,* and *day.* Know that long vowels are a word study concept that children will study in greater depth in kindergarten Unit 5, *Playing with Phonics* and in the first-grade Units of Study in Phonics. You'll also briefly note that vowels can make sounds other than long and short. For example, the schwa sound, which is frequently heard in unstressed syllables, is among the most common in the English language. The first *A* in the word *away* the makes the schwa sound, as does the *O* in *parrot.* Toward the end of this bend, you'll introduce another high-frequency word that does not have a short vowel—*for. For* is taught during Session 18, Extension 1, so you'll want to make time for this extension.

Essentially, Bend III broadens the applications of vowel power. Students' work with CVC words laid the foundation for the work they will need to do with longer, less predictable words. The goal is for readers and writers eventually to move back to using word parts, as knowing word parts is more efficient than spelling phoneme by phoneme. Toward the end of the bend, you'll teach a session that emphasizes knowing oneself as a writer and supports flexibility with writing strategies. Writers speed up and write snap words or word parts when they can, and also slow down when they need to, writing some words or parts of words, sound by sound.

The unit culminates with Mabel's graduation ceremony. The children will make signs, using all they know, with an emphasis on everything they know about vowels, to cheer Mabel on as she graduates. The celebration is for Mabel, but it is also for you and your students, to marvel at how much they've grown as writers and readers. Congratulations!

All the best,
Angela, Katie, and Casey

Every Syllable Has at Least One Vowel

GETTING READY

✔ Provide Mabel with her vowel shield and an envelope with a graduation invitation in it. Prepare to display the invitation for the class and use a highlighter to mark the vowels.

✔ Distribute a copy of Mabel's invitation and a highlighter to each rug club.

PHONICS INSTRUCTION

Phonological Awareness
• Hear, say, blend, and segment syllables in spoken words.

Letter Knowledge
• Recognize that some letters are consonants and some letters are vowels.

Phonics
• Recognize *Y* as a vowel sound.

High-Frequency Words
• Spell high-frequency words with automaticity.

IN THIS SESSION

TODAY YOU'LL teach students that not only does every word have a vowel, but every syllable in a word has at least one vowel as well.

TODAY YOUR STUDENTS will read a special invitation from Mabel, both as a whole class and in rug clubs. They will clap syllables and confirm that each syllable has at least one vowel.

MINILESSON

CONNECTION

Share Mabel's discovery that bigger words can have more than one vowel.

Before the class gathered in the meeting area, I outfitted Mabel. She held her vowel shield, with all vowels now highlighted, and an envelope. With Mabel in my lap, I gathered the children.

"Super Readers and Writers, Mabel has some big news! She was doing some writing last night, and she noticed something special about her name." I took the envelope from between Mabel's feet, placed it under the document camera, and read it aloud.

"Mabel realized that her name has *two* vowels!" I pointed under the *A* and the *E* in *Mabel*. "She felt proud because a lot of the words we've been studying lately, like *cut* and *sit*, only have one vowel. Well, of course!" I said back to Mabel. "You see, kindergartners, Mabel's name is bigger than the words we've been studying, and bigger words usually need more vowels. And then I told Mabel a secret. You need to hear it, too." I leaned in close.

✤ **Name the teaching point.**

"Today I want to teach you that not only does every word have at least one vowel, every syllable does, too!"

TEACHING AND ACTIVE ENGAGEMENT/LINK

Remind students that syllables are the beats in a word. Demonstrate clapping the syllables in Mabel's name and noticing the vowels in each syllable.

"When Mabel heard that, she got so excited! She immediately wanted to investigate, but I convinced her to wait for you—because learning this can help you *and* Mabel strengthen your vowel power.

"Remember that syllables are beats in a word. We used to clap for each syllable in your names during our name study, right? Let's clap for the syllables in Mabel's name and hunt for vowels inside each one."

I pointed under the word *Mabel* on the envelope. "Here is Mabel's name. Let's clap the syllables. *Ma-bel*. Two syllables! Let's find the vowels. There has to be at least one vowel in every syllable. Let's look." I gave the kids time to clap and check the word.

"Yes! *Ma-* . . . there's an *A* in the first syllable, *-bel* . . . and an *E* in the second syllable." I highlighted the vowels as I talked. See, Mabel? Every syllable in your name has a vowel!"

Reveal an invitation from Mabel and read the first sentence together. As a class, clap for every syllable and notice the vowels in each syllable.

"We need to investigate this further. But first, I just can't wait to find out what's in the envelope! Aren't you all curious, too?" The children nodded, and I made Mabel clap her feet to show her excitement.

After opening the envelope and placing the letter under the document camera, I read it.

"Oh, Mabel, congratulations! That *is* exciting news." The class began applauding for Mabel, and I made Mabel do a little bow before stashing her behind the easel.

"Now, let's be sure that every syllable in every word has at least one vowel."

We reread the first sentence together. "We know that *Mabel* has two syllables, and that there is an *A* in the first syllable and an *E* in the second syllable. Next word: *is*!" We clapped one time, and the class identified the vowel, *I*. I highlighted it.

Mabel is graduating!

You are invited.
Come to the celebration!

Mabel's graduation parallels the children's graduation in Bigger Books, Bigger Reading Muscles. *If you aren't teaching this reading unit concurrently, or if your children are new to the concept of graduation, you might want to offer a bit more explanation here.*

"Oh, *graduating* is a big word. I'm already guessing that it has a lot of syllables. Let's clap the syllables together. *Grad-u-a-ting*. Four syllables!" With the highlighter, I underlined the first syllable as I said "*Grad-*," and prompted the children to name the vowel in the syllable. After highlighting the *A* in the first syllable, I underlined the remaining three syllables and said, "With your partner, name the vowels in each of these syllables. Turn and talk."

I gave the children a moment to name the vowels in each syllable, then I called them back together and shared what I wanted them to notice. "Yes! *Grad-* has an *A*, *-u-* has a *U*, *-a-* has an *A*, and *-ting* has an *I*." I highlighted the vowels as I said each syllable. "Whew! What a big word. So many syllables, so many vowels!"

The purpose of this session is to expose learners to the concept that every syllable contains a vowel. Know that you will return to this across the remainder of the bend and beyond, so use today's exposure to rally the children and create excitement, always celebrating approximations.

RUG TIME (CLUBS)

Distribute a copy of Mabel's invitation to each rug club. Reread the next sentences and channel students to notice the vowels in each syllable.

"Kindergartners! I just noticed that there are more copies of the invitation under this one!" I uncovered a stack of papers on the document camera. "Aw, Mabel wanted to be sure that all of you could see this up close. There are enough for every rug club!" I quickly distributed the invitations and some highlighters.

"The next sentences say, 'You are invited! Come to the celebration!' Rug clubs, sit close together and find that part on your invitation. Reread with me." The children did that, and then I directed them, "Clap the syllables and check for vowels in each syllable. Highlight the vowels you find. Remember, bigger words need more vowels!" I circulated as the children worked together, and I reread the sentences to the children, as needed.

"Kindergartners, I think you've proved it! Not only does every word have at least one vowel, every *syllable* in every word has at least one vowel!"

Mabel is graduating!

You are invited.
Come to the celebration!

POSSIBLE COACHING MOVES

▶ "That sentence says _____. Say the first word. Clap the syllable(s). Find the vowels in each one."

▶ "That's a long word! It must have more vowels!"

▶ "Clap for each syllable. Which vowels do you see?"

▶ "I'll clap for each syllable first. Then you try."

SHARE • Revisiting the Name Chart and the Letter Y

Hunt for vowels in every syllable in a name on the class name chart. Revisit the use of Y as a vowel.

"This must be true in names, too!" I placed the name chart on the easel and located Mrs. Wishy-Washy. I said the first word, then clapped for each syllable. "*Wishy. Wish-* . . . There's an /ĭ/, *I* in that syllable . . . /ē/ . . . Hmm, . . . wait. Where's the vowel in the second syllable?" I asked, holding my finger under the *Y*.

"It's the *Y*! . . . and sometimes *Y*!" several kids sang back, recalling our cheer from Session 1.

"Oh yes! *Y* is the vowel in this syllable. And it sounds like the letter *E*. How interesting!"

Next, I said and clapped the second word in Mrs. Wishy-Washy's name. "*Washy. Wash-* . . . There's an *A* in that syllable . . . /ē/ . . . there's a *Y* in that syllable. It's true! There is at least one vowel in every syllable of Mrs. Wishy-Washy's name!"

Channel children to clap for syllables in their own names and notice the vowels in each syllable.

"Now try your name! Say your name. Clap the syllables. Check for the vowel in each syllable. There might be more than one vowel in each syllable, but there can't be none! You can look at the name chart for help."

All at once, the rug filled with a chorus of names and clapping. I listened in, marveling at numbers of syllables and numbers of vowels.

"Kindergartners, this is so exciting! Bigger words mean more vowels and stronger vowel power!" We closed our session with our vowel power cheer: "*A! E! I! O! U! A, apple,* /ă/. *E, egg,* /ĕ/. *I, igloo,* /ĭ/. *O, octopus,* /ŏ/. *U, umbrella,* /ŭ/!"

If Mrs. Wishy-Washy is not on your class name chart, feel free to write her name on a sentence strip.

EXTENSION 1 • Playing Snap Word "Simon Says"

 Channel students to practice their high-frequency words by playing a follow-the-directions game.

I quickly distributed whiteboards and markers to students and announced that we would be playing a game of "Simon Says." "I know we've played this game a ton, so I'm just going to quickly remind you of the rules. Remember, your job is to listen really carefully to the directions. If you hear 'Simon says,' then make sure you follow the directions. If you don't hear 'Simon says,' do *not* follow the directions."

We began the game. "Simon says, 'Pick up your marker.'" I continued, "Simon says, 'Take the cap off your marker.'"

"Write the word *fun*." Some students proceeded to write the word. "Remember, you have to listen really carefully!" Of course, though, everybody stayed in the game.

"Simon says, 'Write the word *fun*.'" I gave students a moment, then said, "Simon says, 'Hold your boards up and check your work!'" As students checked their work, I displayed the word *fun* from the class pocket chart.

We continued playing, practicing words from both this unit and previous units, for several more minutes.

EXTENSION 2 • Finding Vowels in Multisyllabic Words

"Let's test our idea about there being at least one vowel in every syllable with some great big words." I asked kids to suggest a word, and I wrote one of the words they called out on the whiteboard.

Once I had a word on the whiteboard, I recruited kids to clap the syllables, and as they did, I followed them by marking the syllables using Wikki Stix. Then I asked kids to work with partners and check whether there was at least one vowel in every syllable.

I continued this with another word or two, and then suggested partners do that work on their own, this time, trying it out with big words in a book or on the walls of the classroom.

Remember that you could offer some words to work with, but you might be surprised at what kids offer when you give them this invitation!

If you don't have Wikki Stix on hand, a regular highlighter or different-colored marker would also work.

Segmenting Bigger Words by Syllable

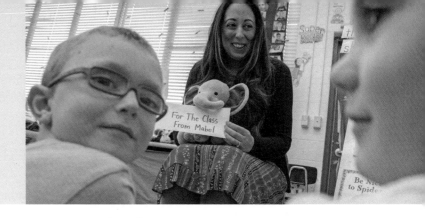

IN THIS SESSION

TODAY YOU'LL lead an interactive writing session to help students transfer the idea that each syllable in their writing will have at least one vowel.

TODAY YOUR STUDENTS will share the pen with you during interactive writing, then write the final sentence of the class text with their rug clubs.

MINILESSON

CONNECTION

Demonstrate and explain how to modify robot talk to accommodate bigger, multisyllabic words.

Using my robot voice, I called the class together by clapping my first word: "Kin-der-gart-ners! Come . . . to . . . the . . . /r/-/ŭ/-/g/."

When the class joined me, I continued in robot mode. I clapped the syllables of the multisyllabic words, spoke most high-frequency words completely, and segmented the CVC words. "Wel-come . . . to . . . phon-ics work-shop. To-day . . . will . . . be . . . /f/ /ŭ/ /n/!"

Snapping myself out of it, I smiled and said in my regular voice, "Writers, now that we are studying bigger words, our robot talk needs to change. You see, it just takes too much time to say /k/ /ĭ/ /n/ /d/ /r/ /g/ /r/ . . . ugh! See? I'm already losing track!" I sighed.

"I wanted to say *kindergarten* in robot talk, but it just doesn't work. That word is too big."

GETTING READY

✔ Refer back to Mabel's invitation from the previous minilesson.

✔ Be ready with a marker and paper to compose a response to Mabel's invitation using the document camera.

✔ Make sure correction tape is handy to use for interactive writing.

✔ Equip students with whiteboards and markers for rug clubs.

✔ Prepare an envelope for the class RSVP.

PHONICS INSTRUCTION

Concepts About Print
- Understand punctuation has a purpose.

Phonological Awareness
- Isolate and pronounce initial sounds, medial vowel, and final sounds in spoken words.
- Segment individual phonemes in words.
- Hear, say, blend, and segment syllables in spoken words.

Letter Knowledge
- Recognize which letters are consonants and which letters are vowels.

Phonics
- Demonstrate basic knowledge of letter-sound correspondences by producing the primary sound for each consonant.
- Hear and identify vowel sounds in words and the letters that represent them.

Word Knowledge/Solving
- Use familiar phonograms to write multisyllabic words.
- Use knowledge of short vowels to read CVC words.

High-Frequency Words
- Write high-frequency words in continuous text.

✤ **Name the teaching point.**

"Today I want to teach you that writers can use syllables to help them write bigger words. They can clap out the syllables, and then make sure that each syllable has a vowel. That makes their writing much easier to read!"

TEACHING

Demonstrate clapping the syllables in big words to help with hearing all the sounds.

Holding up Mabel's note from the day before, I blurted, "Oh, writers! I forgot to tell you! I noticed that there was a little more writing on the back of Mabel's invitation.

"It says, 'Please respond.' What should we tell Mabel? We should write back soon. That's only polite when you get an invitation. What should we say? Turn and talk!"

The children shared ideas. I called the class back together and suggested a response I'd cobbled together from listening to their ideas, while also trying to give the class practice writing both monosyllabic and multisyllabic words. "Many of you said something like, 'Yes! Congratulations, Mabel!'" I clipped a piece of paper to the easel and said, "Can you join me in listening for and writing all the sounds? If we get to a longer word, let's clap for syllables and write the sounds we hear.

"So, let's remember what we want to say. Hmm, . . . the first word we want to write is . . ."

The kids chimed in that the first word was *yes*. "We don't need to clap syllables for that word, do we? There is only one syllable. Let's use robot talk to listen for the sounds: /y/ /ĕ/ /s/." I wrote *Y*, then paused. I made the sound of the short *E*, "/ĕ/," and asked students to activate their vowel power. I glanced at my vowel shield and murmured, "*Egg, /ĕ/*," then wrote *E*, and finally, *S*. Rereading, I said, "*Yes*! Now, let's check that there is at least one vowel in every syllable." I clapped one time. I tapped the *E* so that the children could see me checking for a vowel.

"Next word: *congratulations*. Oh my. That's a big word. What should we do to tackle that word?" Some children suggested we break it into syllables, and I nodded and clapped the syllables as I said, "Con-grat-u-la-tions." Then I repeated the first syllable: "*Con*- Do you hear *on* in there? I do!" I recorded that first part of the word. "Now let's check that I have a vowel in that syllable . . . *O* . . . check!"

I continued segmenting the word by syllable. When I got to the last syllable, I said "/shŭnz/" and recorded it conventionally as *-tions* in front of the children. As I did so, I casually commented, "And this is how that ending usually looks in books," knowing that the letters weren't likely to match kids' expectations for the sounds. As usual, I remarked on the vowels. "Do I have vowels in this syllable?" and, after scanning, confirmed, "Yes! Did you see how, when I got to a bigger word, I clapped the syllables to help myself? Then I wrote the sounds I heard.

Notice that the end product of this message should be conventional. The final syllable of congratulations *should be recorded quickly to keep the focus on using syllables to segment words without veering off on a tangent about surprising word endings.*

"The last word is *Mabel*. That's on our name chart. I'll write it quickly, but I'll still make sure I included vowels in every syllable." I clapped the two syllables and checked them for vowels, then reread.

Yes! Congratulations, Mabel!

ACTIVE ENGAGEMENT/LINK

Compose and construct a second sentence for the RSVP using interactive writing, giving children the chance to write a multisyllabic word.

"Writers, we have lots more space. What else should we tell Mabel about joining her celebration? Quick! Turn and tell the person next to you what we could say.

"Many of you said that we should tell Mabel how we feel about her graduation. Let's write 'We are excited to come.' *We*. That's a snap word. I'll write it quickly on the paper, you write it on the rug, then check it with mine! *W-E, we*," I spelled aloud. We followed the same steps with *are*.

When we got to *excited*, I paused. "*Excited*. That's a big word. We can clap the syllables to help ourselves." Together, we clapped and segmented the word by syllable. "*Ex-ci-ted*."

The class wrote the word on the rug while I invited one child to write it at the easel. I nudged that child to include a vowel in every syllable. She approximated the word: first writing *xidid*, then adding an *E* to the beginning of the word after my prompt, before stepping back from *exidid*. "You did it! You made sure to write a vowel in every syllable!" I responded. "Let me show you how that word looks in a book." I quickly covered the word with correction tape and wrote it conventionally on top.

"Let's reread what we have so far. 'We are excited . . .' The next word is *to*. It's a snap word! Write it quickly on the rug while I write it up here."

When we got to the word *come*, another child joined me at the easel while the rest of the class worked at the rug. The student at the easel segmented the word by phoneme, while others recorded a part they knew, and a few knew the word's conventional spelling. At the easel, I complimented all the sounds the child heard and wrote *come* conventionally before rereading the entire sentence with the class. "Wow, bigger words really do have more vowels!"

Yes! Congratulations, Mabel!

We are excited to come.

Yes! Congratulations, Mabel!

We are exidid to cum.

Yes! Congratulations, Mabel!

We are [excited] to [come].

Remember, always, to honor approximation. The goal here for students is not total conventionality. The children will be using inventive spelling as they problem solve. The goal is that students try a new method for hearing more sounds in longer words, and include more letters when they write, thus growing closer to conventional writing. The language you use as you rewrite the words conventionally should be supportive and encouraging.

RUG TIME

Dictate a closing to the RSVP note, and invite students to write it on whiteboards with their rug clubs, giving them an opportunity to spell single-syllable and multisyllabic words.

"Okay, now we need to tell Mabel who this is from. Let's give her a little extra love, too. Let's write, 'Hugs and kisses, Kindergarten.'" I distributed whiteboards to rug clubs. "Taking turns with your rug club friends, write the end of our note."

As children wrote, I circulated among them, coaching in with lean prompts.

"Writers, look at all those big words that you wrote! You really used syllable clapping and robot talk to help you hear all the sounds. I'll write the last part of our letter back to Mabel. You can use my writing to check yours."

SHARE • Rereading to Support Fluency

Conduct a shared reading of the message the class wrote and place it in a special envelope to deliver to Mabel.

"Can you use all your super powers to read the message we wrote to Mabel? Let's make sure everything makes sense and looks right before we send it back." I pointed crisply under the first word and began reading the message aloud as the children chimed in. After reading the first line, I paused, pointed to the exclamation marks and said, "Let's reread that part again and make our voices match the feeling."

After rereading the first line, we continued reading the rest of the message together. To support rereading and fluency, we read the message together one more time.

When we were finished reading, I reached behind the easel and pulled out a large manila envelope. "We need to send our message to Mabel, so she knows we will be at her graduation celebration. I think it would be fun for Mabel to get this in the mail. Let's put it in the mail so she can see it in her mailbox. She will be so surprised." Gently, I folded up our message and placed it in the envelope. I thought aloud as I wrote on the front of the envelope, "For Mabel, from Kindergarten." I assured the class I would deliver our message to Mabel's mailbox that afternoon.

> ### POSSIBLE COACHING MOVES
>
> - "Say the first syllable and write the sounds you hear. Be sure there is a vowel. Then do the next syllable, and the next."
> - "You need a vowel in that syllable. Say it again. Which vowel do you hear?"
> - "Activate your vowel power!"
> - "Try it! What would look right?"

Remember to consider pacing during interactive writing sessions. Notice the decision in this case for the teacher to write the snap words and to share the pen when problem solving a variety of unfamiliar words. This keeps things moving while focusing students' efforts on the specific work of the session.

EXTENSION 1 • Reviewing CVC Words and Short Vowels

Sing a new song to provide students with additional practice reading words with short vowels.

"Let's play a new singing game with our vowel shields. As you sing the letters, you'll use your vowel power to read words. It goes like this." I held up a shield, pointing to each vowel as I sang to the tune of "Bingo Was His Name-O."

I wrote *sip* on the whiteboard and held it up. "Will you read this word?"

"*Sip*!" the kids shouted out, some pointing to the letter *I* on their vowel shields.

We sang another few verses, each time reading other short-vowel words, such as *peg*, *chat*, *cot*, *thin*, and *mug*.

While reading the words, I sometimes paused and said, "Wow! You worked so hard to notice the short-vowel sound in the middle of each word, and I also noticed that some of you are using word-part power." After our final round, I reminded students that vowel power and word-part power can help them read and write.

EXTENSION 2 • Reviewing CVC Words during Transitions

Transition students to new activities by asking them to read a CVC word that is written on a whiteboard.

As we got ready for choice time, a small group of children gathered near the choice board to move their name cards. As they began to walk away, I said: "Wait! I need one last thing from you!"

They momentarily looked confused. I wrote the word *lid* on the whiteboard and said, "First, I need you to read this word!" They read the word quickly and headed to their center. I looked out at the rest of the class and said, "Get ready! It's time to use your vowel power to practice reading words before going to centers."

As groups of students made their selections for choice time, I wrote additional words, such as *did*, *red*, *sip*, *cab*, and *cob* on the whiteboard and prompted them to read the word before going to their centers, sometimes prompting them to notice a word part in the word. I made a mental note to repeat this activity during other transition times, sometimes using snap words.

The Vowel Shield Song
(Sing to the tune of "Bingo")

There are five vowels on our shield

And they can help us read...

A-E-I-O-U

A-E-I-O-U

A-E-I-O-U

Will you read this word?

Distinguishing Short-Vowel Sounds in Bigger Words

GETTING READY

✔ Prepare for group sorting using your pocket chart and picture cards with short *A* words, short *I* words, and short *U* words.

✔ Prepare baggies for rug clubs with sets of the above picture cards in each.

PHONICS INSTRUCTION

Phonological Awareness
- Say words slowly to hear sounds in words.
- Isolate and pronounce initial sounds, medial vowel, and final sounds in spoken words.

Phonics
- Hear and identify short vowel sounds in words and the letters that represent them (*A*, *I*, *U*).

IN THIS SESSION

TODAY YOU'LL teach students that they can strengthen their vowel power by distinguishing among vowels in bigger words.

TODAY YOUR STUDENTS will sort short *A* words, short *I* words, and short *U* words, saying each word slowly and matching words with the same short-vowel sounds in the middle.

MINILESSON

CONNECTION

Create excitement by singing a familiar song, placing an emphasis on noticing short vowels in bigger words.

As the children gathered in the meeting area, I gestured to the vowel shield, and said, "Let's activate vowel power with our vowel power cheer!" In unison, the class chanted, "*A, apple,* /ă/. *E, egg,* /ĕ/. *I, igloo,* /ĭ/. *O, octopus,* /ŏ/. *U, umbrella,* /ŭ/."

"We've been talking about bigger words with more than one syllable. But some words with only one syllable are also bigger because they have more letters and sounds than the three-letter words we've been studying, like *hat* and *mop*.

"Let's sing one of our favorite songs, and this time, let's try it with bigger words. This will make your vowel power even stronger!"

I began singing the familiar song to the tune of "London Bridge," and the children chimed in.

What's the middle sound that you hear, that you hear, that you hear?

What's the middle sound that you hear in . . . *glass, glass, glass*?

My voice lowered and I let the children lead in the response:

/ă/ is the middle sound that you hear, that you hear, that you hear!
/ă/ is the middle sound that you hear in . . . *glass, glass, glass*.

"We hear /ă/ in the middle of *glass*. Let's sing the song again. We'll say each new word slowly to help us notice the vowel sound in the middle. This will help us strengthen our vowel power." We continued singing the song together with additional words, such as *snug*, *still*, and *stuck*.

"Wow! Noticing vowel sounds in bigger words will *really* help you in writing workshop!"

❖ **Name the teaching point.**

"Today I want to teach you that to strengthen your vowel power, you'll need to notice vowel sounds in bigger words. It will help to say the word slowly, listening for the vowel sound in the middle."

TEACHING

Invite students to listen for short-vowel sounds in bigger words, matching words with the same short-vowel sound in the middle.

"You were really saying your words slowly, noticing the vowel sound in the middle. This will help you use your vowel power in bigger words and be able to figure out what vowel you should write.

"Sorting will help you hear the different vowel sounds in bigger words. This will really help make your writing easier to read, especially when you're writing bigger words. You have sorted before, and the sorting you'll be doing today will really help you because more and more, you'll be writing bigger words and you'll want to figure out which vowel is in each word.

"Quick! Let's activate our vowel power. It will help us listen for the vowel sound in the middle of bigger words. Help me sort these words in the pocket chart. We can say these words slowly to hear the vowel sound in the middle." I gestured to the columns in the pocket chart and said, "We'll put the words with /ă/ like *apple* in this column, those with /ĭ/ like *igloo* in this column, and words with /ŭ/ like *umbrella* in this column. These vowels are in the middle of the words, so it will take some powerful listening. Ready?" I slipped the three anchor cards into the pocket chart, starting three columns.

Begin to sort the picture cards into the pocket chart columns.

"I'll do the first one, if you'll help me." I held up a picture of a rocket blasting off. "This is *blast*. A rocket can blast off. Let's say the word slowly to hear the vowel and to think about which vowel matches the sound. *Blllaaasst*. Hmm, . . .

Connecting today's session to writing workshop supports students in transferring what they are learning in word study to their independent writing. Students will benefit from consistent language during all word study sessions and across the day.

Notice the teaching decisions guiding today's sorting demonstration: placing the anchor cards at the top of the columns, explaining the word study principle with consistent language, saying each word and placing it next to the anchor cards. Explicitly modeling these behaviors supports students with the routine of sorting.

does the middle of *blast* sound like /aaaaa/pple/, /iiiii/gloo/, or /uuuuu/mbrella/? Blllaaassst . . . aaaaapple. I think those two sounds match!" I placed the blast picture underneath the apple.

"Here comes another word. Get ready!" I held up a picture of a fish. "This is a fish! Does *fish* go with *aaaaapple*, *iiiiigloo*, or *uuuuumbrella*?" As I said the anchor words slowly, I pointed to each anchor picture. Students pointed to the igloo to show that the middle vowel sound in *fish* matched the initial vowel sound in *igloo*.

ACTIVE ENGAGEMENT/LINK

Begin sorting picture cards together by determining the medial short-vowel sound in each word.

"You're listening so carefully to the vowel sounds in the middle of words. Let's keep practicing! I'll show you a picture and you figure out where that word goes."

I held up a picture of a brush. "This is a brush. Say *brush*. Turn and talk and say it slowly to figure out where it goes." The students turned to each other and said the word slowly to notice the vowel sound in the middle of the word.

"I heard so many people saying the word slowly. And Landon and Keegan just said, 'Oh! It must go with the umbrella!' I agree." I added the brush card to the /ŭ/ column on the pocket chart and quickly held up the next card, featuring a picture of someone clapping. We again repeated the entire process. "Turn and talk with a partner. Where will the word *clap* go? Say it slowly." After the students shared their responses, I placed the *clap* card with *apple* and *stamp*.

"Wow! Your vowel power is getting so much stronger with bigger words! Let's do our vowel power cheer to celebrate!" I gestured to the vowel shield and invited the kids to do the cheer in their loudest, proudest voices. In unison, the class cheered, "*A, apple, /ă/. E, egg, /ĕ/. I, igloo, /ĭ/. O, octopus, /ŏ/. U, umbrella, /ŭ/.*"

RUG TIME CLUBS

Set rug clubs up to sort the remaining picture cards. Nudge children to distinguish between short *A*, short *I*, and short *U* sounds in bigger words.

"Before I give your club some picture cards, let's review some of the pictures." I placed a few of the picture cards with unfamiliar vocabulary under the document camera and discussed their meanings with the class. Then I said, "You are ready to sort all these picture cards. Decide if they go with short *A*, short *I*, or short *U*. Remember that you can use your vowel shield, *A, apple, /ă/. I, igloo, /ĭ/. U, umbrella, /ŭ/.*"

POSSIBLE COACHING MOVES

▶ "Listen for the letter vowel sound in the middle."

▶ "Say it slowly. What do you hear in the middle?"

▶ "Check it with the anchor card. Does it match?"

▶ "Do those words sound the same in the middle?"

▶ "Does it sound like _____ or _____?"

I distributed a baggie of picture cards to each club. As students worked, I listened in and coached, sometimes saying my tips loudly enough so the whole class could hear.

After a few minutes, I saw that many students were finishing, and I moved them along. "Once you think you've got all your words in the right place, make sure to check them! Say each one slowly, and check to be sure that the middle sound matches!"

SHARE • Hearing Medial Short-Vowel Sounds in Bigger Words

Sing a familiar song, placing an emphasis on noticing short *E* and short *O* in bigger words.

"Now that we've sorted bigger words, let's sing our "What's the Middle Sound That You Hear?" song again and see just how much our vowel power has grown. This time, we'll listen for short *E* and short *O*." I began singing the song once again to the tune of "London Bridge."

What's the Middle Sound That You Hear?

What's the middle sound that you hear, that you hear, that you hear?
What's the middle sound that you hear in . . . *stem, stem, stem*?

My voice lowered and I let the children lead in the response:

/ĕ/ is the middle sound that you hear, that you hear, that you hear!
/ĕ/ is the middle sound that you hear in . . . *stem, stem, stem*.

While singing the song, I paused and prompted children to say the word *stem* slowly, noticing the vowel sound in the middle.

"A stem is the long part of a plant. We hear /ĕ/ in the middle of *stem*. Let's sing the song again. We'll say each new word slowly to help us notice the vowel sound in the middle." We continued singing the song together with additional words, such as *rock, chest, vest,* and *block.*

Before closing the day's workshop, I gestured to the vowel shield, and said, "Let's do our vowel power cheer one more time together!" In unison, the class chanted, "*A, apple, /ă/. E, egg, /ĕ/. I, igloo, /ĭ/. O, octopus, /ŏ/. U, umbrella, /ŭ/.*"

When you are engaging your class in song activities to support phonological and phonemic awareness, remember that these are also times for you to informally assess your learners. Notice what skills your students need additional support with and make intentional plans to support those skills.

EXTENSION 1 • Singing a Song to Locate Short Vowels in Words

Sing the "Beginning Middle End" song to practice locating short-vowel sounds in words.

"Remember the 'Beginning Middle End' song?" I hummed a bit of the tune, which was the same as "Frère Jacques," to remind students how it went. "That song helped you get even better at hearing sounds in words, and it can also help us with our vowel power. We've been studying vowel sounds in the middle of words lately, and it's important to remember that vowels can be found in other places in words, like the beginning and end. Singing this song will help us hear vowel sounds wherever they are in words.

"Let's sing it! Join me when you can."

I prompted to the children to say the word *it* slowly. I said, "When I snap, tell me where you hear /ĭ/. Beginning, middle, or end?" I paused and snapped my fingers in the air. In unison, the children replied, "Beginning!"

We sang the "Beginning Middle End" song a few more times with words such as *crack*, *check*, *inch*, *otter*, *sun*, *alligator*, and *up*. As we sang, I prompted children to say the word slowly, listening to where in the word they heard the short-vowel sound.

Beginning, Middle, End
(to the tune of Frère Jacques)

Beginning middle end.
Beginning middle end.

Where is the sound?
Where is the sound?

Where is the /m/ in man?
Where is the /m/ in man?

Let's find out!
Let's find out!

(Substitute /m/ in man with other words and sounds)

EXTENSION 2 • Singing a Familiar Song to Practice Hearing Medial Vowels

Sing "What's the Middle Sound That You Hear?" to provide students with repeated practice hearing the medial sound in bigger words.

"You know the song 'What's the Middle Sound That You Hear?' so well." "That song can help you practice hearing the middle vowel sound in bigger words, which you'll need to do when you're writing bigger words.

"Let's sing it again! Join me when you can."

What's the Middle Sound That You Hear?

What's the middle sound that you hear, that you hear, that you hear?
What's the middle sound that you hear in . . . *drip*, *drip*, *drip*?

My voice lowered and I let the children lead in the response:

/ĭ/ is the middle sound that you hear, that you hear, that you hear!
/ĭ/ is the middle sound that you hear in . . . *drip*, *drip*, *drip*.

We continued singing the song a few more times with words such as *stack*, *bump*, *gas*, *tack*, *check*, and *thick*. If the meaning of a word was unfamiliar to the students, I provided students with the meaning of the word and used it in a sentence.

Vowels Make More Than One Sound

IN THIS SESSION

TODAY YOU'LL remind students that vowels can make more than one sound, and that those sounds are represented by the same letter.

TODAY YOUR STUDENTS will sort words that feature both long *A* and short *A*. They will practice vocalizing the different vowel sounds and focus on how these vowels feel and sound.

MINILESSON

CONNECTION

Find a new letter from Reader-Man containing new snap words to study. Note that vowels can make more than one sound.

As the children gathered in the meeting area, they noticed a new envelope from Reader-Man sitting on the easel.

"Oh, my goodness, readers! Reader-Man has been here again. There must be something important in there!" I gingerly opened the envelope and revealed a new letter from Reader-Man.

I reread the word *growing*, emphasizing the *O*. "*Groooowing. Ooooctopus*. Those two *O*s sound different, don't they?" I continued pointing

> Dear Super Readers,
>
> I see your vowel power growing as you use more vowels in bigger words!
>
> Did you notice that some of those vowels sounds are different from the ones on your shield?
>
> Vowels really can be puzzling. Luckily you have your shields to light your way!
>
> Your friend,
> Reader-Man

GETTING READY

✔ Prepare an envelope from Reader-Man, containing a letter, word cards (*play*, *day*, and *say*), and a set of picture cards (as shown in the Active Engagement/Link) for sorting.

✔ Provide mirrors to students so they can see the shape of their mouths when pronouncing different vowel sounds.

✔ Display the lyrics to "Rain, Rain, Go Away." You may also want to photocopy the song to give to students for independent reading time.

PHONICS INSTRUCTION

Phonological Awareness
- Say words slowly to hear sounds in words.
- Segment individual phonemes in words.

Letter Knowledge
- Use proper letter formation.

Phonics
- Hear and identify short vowel sounds in words and the letters that represent them (*A*, *O*).
- Distinguish between long and short vowel sounds.

High-Frequency Words
- Read high-frequency words with automaticity.
- Read high-frequency words with endings.
- Learn three new words (*day*, *play*, *say*).

under the highlighted words, and as a class, we compared those words to the corresponding short-vowel picture words on the vowel shield. "Reader-Man was right!"

♣ Name the teaching point.

"Today I want to remind you that vowels can make more than one sound. Sometimes, vowels make a short sound, like in the words we've been studying. Sometimes vowels make a long sound, which is the sound that matches their names."

TEACHING

Reveal the words that Reader-Man has sent, notice the vowel sounds, and check to see if the information in his letter is accurate.

I shook the envelope, and three word cards fell out: *play*, *day*, and *say*. "Reader-Man gave us these words. I'm wondering if these are the kinds of words that he's talking about. I wonder, if we studied these words carefully, would we find that they make those different sounds that he mentioned?"

I placed each card into the pocket chart and read it aloud as I did so. I then reread the words slowly to set students up to analyze their sounds. "Hmm, . . . *Plaaaaayyy* . . . *apple*. *Daaaaaayyy* . . . *apple*. I don't hear a short *A* in *play* or *day*. *A* is making a different sound in these words. It is saying its own name. *Saaaaaayyyy* . . . *apple*. A different sound there, too!

"Okay. Say each sound in *play* with me." We used robot talk to hear and investigate the vowel sound, saying "/p/ /l/ /ā/." I observed, "The *A* sound in this word matches its name. I guess Reader-Man gave us those words for a reason! He gave us those words because he wanted us to remember that sometimes vowels make long sounds that match their names." We investigated again with the words *say* and *day*.

ACTIVE ENGAGEMENT/LINK

Sort a collection of picture cards based on whether the vowels in the words make the short *A* or long *A* sound.

"I bet Reader-Man left some more work for us. He probably wants us to practice a lot with these different sounds that vowels can make!" I again shook the envelope, and a pile of picture cards fell out.

"Now, you're going to make your ear muscles super strong by thinking about whether you hear the short *A* or the long *A* sound when you read each of these pictures." As I said each sound, I placed the anchor cards at the top of our pocket chart: *apple* for the short *A* and *say* for the long *A*.

I held up the first picture card: a rat. "I'm going to do what we always do when we do a sort like this. I'm going to say this word with the pictures at the top and think, 'Which one does it go with?'" I modeled while thinking aloud. "*Apple*. *Rat*." I said the words slowly, making sure to isolate the vowel sounds as "I did so. "I hear that short *A* in both of those

In this session you're using the selected words to return to the concept that vowels can make more than one sound. Later, you will return to these words, turning them into snap words.

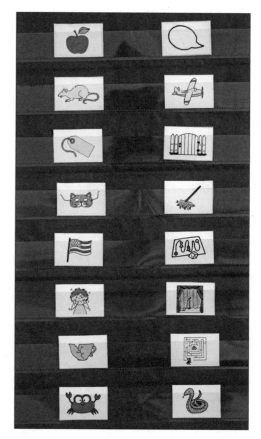

Your class sort could go in a different order, of course. Just make sure that each word ends up in the correct column.

words. I'm just going to check to be sure. *Say. Rat.*" Again, I said the words slowly, isolating the vowel sounds. "Those sounds don't match. *Rat* goes with *apple.*" As I said the words one last time, I made sure again to isolate the vowel sounds. I placed the picture card in its appropriate column.

"What about this one?" I said, as I held up the card with a picture of a plane. "*Plane. Apple.*" As I said the words, I isolated the vowel sounds. "No, those don't match. *Plane. Say.* Yes, those vowel sounds match." I put *plane* in the long *A* column.

We continued sorting the remaining words, and I quickly released the scaffold, so that by the time we had finished the first few words, students were simply saying the sounds themselves and pointing to where on the pocket chart the pictures fit.

By the end, the pocket chart contained all the sorted words.

When we had finished sorting all of the pictures, we read through each column.

Restate the teaching point and connect to students' ongoing writing work.

"I think you've done exactly the work that Reader-Man wanted you to do, and I bet that your vowel power is stronger now! Remember that you can use it when you're writing! Every time you hear /ă/ or /ā/, you can record it by writing an *A*. The letter *A* makes both of those sounds!"

After finishing a sort, you'll want to reinforce the habit of checking by rereading the pictures. This is also a time to reflect on how the pictures are sorted and connect the learning to reading or writing workshop.

RUG TIME CLUBS

Channel students to vocalize the words from the sort, this time thinking about where sounds are produced and how sounds feel as they are spoken.

"We've talked before about how you can actually *feel* the difference among the vowels when you say them. When we say /ă/, it feels a certain way in our throats. When we say /ĕ/, we can sort of feel a little pushing feeling. We can distinguish between short and long vowels the same way. Short vowels feel a certain way in our mouths, and long vowels feel a different way in our mouths.

"We're going to practice a bit with this. I'm going to give every rug club a mirror. Your job is to practice saying the words that we just sorted, and, while you're doing that, see if you and your rug club can feel and see the differences in the vowel sounds while you say the words."

Students picked up their mirrors and got to work. As students worked, I walked around and coached in as needed.

After a few minutes, I called the class back together, and we quickly debriefed. "One way to notice the different sounds that vowels make is to think about how they sound and what you hear. The other thing that you might notice, though,

POSSIBLE COACHING MOVES

▶ "Say the word slowly. What does your mouth do?"

▶ "When you say (*gate*), does your mouth feel different from when you say (*van*)?"

▶ "Do you feel the sound that you're making? Does it feel like a long *A* or a short *A*?"

Notice that this work harkens back to previous sessions where you channeled students to both listen and feel for vowel sounds. You are again inviting students into this multisensory work, but, this time, students are being coached to distinguish long- and short-vowel sounds.

is that different vowel sounds feel different when you say them. So, when you're thinking about long and short vowels, you might also notice and think about how they feel."

SHARE • Studying the Different Ways a Vowel Can Sound

Read "Rain, Rain, Go Away," listening for the different ways that the vowel *A* can sound.

Once I'd gathered the students back together, I displayed the song "Rain, Rain, Go Away" on the document camera. "Some of you might know this poem. It's called 'Rain, Rain, Go Away,' and it's actually a song that some people sing on rainy days to wish the rain away. The other day my nephew Sam and I were singing it. When we read it, you'll notice lots of different sounds that the vowel *A* can make!"

We engaged in a quick shared reading of the song, and, once we'd finished, I went through and highlighted the words with an *A*, naming them aloud as we went through: *rain, away, again, another, day, Sam, wants,* and *play*. "I'm noticing that all of the words have the letter *A* in them, but they all make different sounds. I read the highlighted words slowly again, stretching out the vowel sound each time.

"Did you all hear what I heard? The vowel *A* actually makes many different sounds—not just long and short sounds— and they're all spelled with the letter *A*! Now, when we're writing, we can make sure to be on the lookout for *all* of the different sounds that *A* makes, and we can record those sounds with an *A*."

After we finished our work for the day, I provided students with small copies of the poem for their book baggies.

EXTENSION 1 • Learning High-Frequency Words *Play*, *Say*, and *Day*

 "Reader-Man sent us three new words earlier. You use them a lot in your writing, and they are in lots of the books we read. Let's turn them into snap words!" I displayed our "How to Learn a Word" anchor chart.

I held up the word, *play*. "First we *read* it!" Students read the word chorally multiple times as I pointed underneath it.

"Now, let's *study* it. Turn and tell your partner what you see."

I quickly called the students back together. "Now, some of those letters are vowels, and one of them is even a funny, sometimes-vowel letter. Which letter is that? Which letter is a vowel?" Students responded chorally, and I continued our study of the vowels in the word. "The *A* and the *Y* together make that /ā/ sound. Say it with me." This time, as we read the word, I swept my finger underneath it, emphasizing the vowel sound at the end.

"Now, *spell* it. Spell it softly, like a whisper into your hand. *P-L-A-Y*. Now, spell it and cheer it."

Rain, Rain, Go Away

Rain, rain, go away
Come again another day
Little Sam wants to play.

How to learn a word

1. Read it!
2. Study it!
3. Spell it!
4. Write it!
5. Use it!

"Next, *write* it!" Students wrote the word *play* with imaginary markers on the rug.

"Last step—*use* it! Share a sentence with your partner." I circulated, listening in and providing support where needed.

We repeated the steps to learn the words *say* and *day* before I added the words to the word wall and the children added them to their snap word pouches.

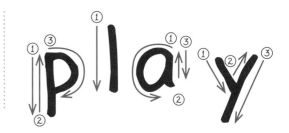

EXTENSION 2 • Adding Inflections to Snap Words

 Work with high-frequency words in isolation to add the *-ing* ending.

Just before the children lined up for lunch, I removed the words *play*, *say*, *do*, and *look* from the word wall.

"We've talked a lot about how syllables in every word have a vowel. There's a special syllable, though, that joins words at the end. And, no surprise here, it has a vowel!" While facing the children, I held an index card with the *-ing* ending in my left hand. "This special syllable is /ing/." I tapped the *I* to highlight the vowel in the syllable. "It hangs out at the end of words. Let me show you what I mean." With my right hand, I moved the *play* word card in front of the card for *-ing*.

"*Play-ing*. *Playing*," I read, blending the two parts together. To give the word context, I used it in a sentence, "I was *playing* in the park.

"Let's try it with another one." I took away the word *play* and replaced it with *say*. "Remember how we did that? Read the snap word and add the ending." I gave students a moment to do so, then gestured for students to say the word aloud. "You've got it! The word is *saying*. Can you hear what I am *saying*?"

I continued with the words *do* and *look* before reminding readers, "Remember, you know your snap words, even when they have special endings!"

EXTENSION 3 • Exploring Other Long Vowels

Conduct an oral sort using words in the classroom that contain short and long *O*.

As the children lined up for lunch, I began a short *O* / long *O* oral sort using items from around the classroom.

I pointed to the clock in the classroom, which was labeled. With my pointer under the *O*, I said, "*Clock*. Is the vowel short like in *octopus*, or long like in *open*?" I nudged the children to check by comparing the words: "*Clooock, ooooctopus. Clooock, ooooopen.*" Many children called back, "*Octopus!*"

"Yes! *Clock* has a short *O* like the beginning of *octopus*," I replied.

"Let's try another word! *Soap*. Is the *O* short or long?" I held up the labeled soap bottle from the sink area as I spoke. The children talked with their partners, once again comparing the new word to *octopus* and *open*. "You're right! *Soap* has a long *O*, like *open*," I said.

We continued sorting with other classroom objects, such as *box*, *closet*, *coat*, and *block*.

I made a mental note to practice with different vowels on other days, using words such as *table* and *bag*, *sign* and *bin*, and *seat* and *pens*.

Becoming More Automatic with Digraphs

IN THIS SESSION

TODAY YOU'LL teach students that they can use their knowledge of digraphs to help them solve puzzling words when reading. You will help readers notice digraphs at the beginning of words, and prompt them to use this knowledge along with their vowel power and other super powers to read.

TODAY YOUR STUDENTS will engage in a shared reading session where they practice using their knowledge of digraphs along with their vowel power and other powers. Students will also transfer today's learning to reading the books in their book baggies.

MINILESSON

CONNECTION

Create excitement by singing a variation of a familiar song, placing an emphasis on digraphs and short vowels, and making words with magnetic letters.

As the children gathered in the meeting area, I organized magnetic letters on the easel. I placed *S*, *H*, *C*, *T*, *I*, and *N* in a row, and slid *C* and *H*, then *I* and *N* in a new row, with space between the onset and the rime. "Let's sing one of our favorite songs! This time, let's try it with words that have more letters. After all, we are studying bigger words now!"

I began singing the familiar song to the tune of "If You're Happy and You Know It," and the children bopped their heads along to the melody.

If You Think You Know This Word

If you think you know this word, raise your hand.
If you think you know this word, raise your hand.
If you think you know this word,

GETTING READY

✔ Prepare to display and manipulate magnetic letters (*S*, *H*, *C*, *T*, *I*, and *N*).

✔ Display the illustrated "Hokey Pokey" song. Highlight digraphs with highlighter tape and cover with another page so that you can reveal one line at a time.

PHONICS INSTRUCTION

Phonological Awareness
- Blend and segment the onset and rime of single-syllable spoken words.
- Segment and blend individual phonemes in words.
- Isolate and pronounce initial sounds, medial vowel, and final sounds in spoken words.

Phonics
- Demonstrate basic knowledge of letter-sound correspondences by producing the primary sound for each consonant.
- Identify digraphs in words.
- Hear and identify short vowel sounds in words and letters that represent them.

Word Knowledge/Solving
- Use knowledge of digraphs to read and write words.
- Use knowledge of vowel sounds to read words.

Then tell me what you've heard.
If you think you know this word, raise your hand:
/ch/-/in/.

"*Chin*!" many children called back. I nodded and slid *-in* over to meet *ch-*. "That's right, when you put *ch-* together with *-in*, you have *chin*!" I pointed to my chin to illustrate. "It is important to remember that sometimes two letters make one sound. Those are called digraphs. And, don't forget everything you have learned about word parts and short vowels! Combining your powers will help you solve puzzling words.

"Let's try with another digraph." I slid *ch* up as a unit and then pulled *sh* down into the row with *-in*, again leaving a space between the onset and the rime.

If you think you know this word, raise your hand.
If you think you know this word, raise your hand.
If you think you know this word,
Then tell me what you've heard.
If you think you know this word, raise your hand:
/sh/-/in/.

"*Shin*!" the children responded, some a little unsure of the unfamiliar word. "Yes, *shin*!" I said, pointing to the lower part of my leg. We played one more time with the word *thin* before I commented, "When you know digraphs and vowels, you can read so many big words!"

♣ **Name the teaching point.**

"Today I want to remind you that some letters go together to make one sound, like *C* and *H* in *chin*. When you see a digraph at the beginning of a word, remember that those letters make one sound."

TEACHING

Engage the class in a shared reading of an illustrated song that contains beginning digraphs and short vowels.

I gestured to the easel and said, "Let's use all our powers to learn a new song. This is a song that will help us with digraphs in bigger words." I pointed crisply to the title and read it aloud, "The Hokey Pokey." Many of the children called out, "I know that song from PreK!"

"Let's have fun singing and solving some words together! I've highlighted some digraphs with our special tape. When we get to those words, we can look at the picture and think, 'What would make sense and sound right here?' Then, we can get our mouths ready by saying the beginning sound. Combining our powers will help us read bigger words."

The Hokey Pokey

You put your thumbs in, you take your thumbs out.
You put your thumbs in and you shake them all about.
You do the hokey pokey and you turn yourself around,
    that's what it's all about.

You put your chin in, you take your chin out.
You put your chin in and you shake it all about.
You do the hokey pokey and you turn yourself around,
    that's what it's all about.

You put your shoulder in, you take your shoulder out.
You put your shoulder in and you shake it all about.
You do the hokey pokey and you turn yourself around,
    that's what it's all about.

94

I started reading using a singsong voice and paused when I got to the digraph that I'd highlighted with tape.

You put your thumbs in, you take your thumbs out.

"Readers, let me tell you a secret. I highlighted these letters because they are a digraph, and you know the sound it makes." I pointed to the illustration at the end of the line before pointing to the word and said, "/th/ *thumbs*." Then, I quickly slid my finger to the end of the word, noting the short vowel after the digraph. "What's the vowel sound after /th/?" I asked. The class responded with a choral short *U* sound. "Yes, /ŭ/." I read the whole word slowly. "*Thumbs*. That makes sense, sounds right, and looks right. Now, let's reread together!" I pointed under the words as we sang together:

You put your thumbs in, you take your thumbs out.
You put your thumbs in, and you shake them all about.

We continued until we got to the next word with a highlighted digraph, *shake*. Then, we worked together to solve it, using the picture to think about what would make sense and getting our mouths ready by saying the beginning sound. Then, I slid my finger under the word, demonstrating that readers should always check their reading after they solve a word. "This word has a long *A* sound after the /sh/ sound at the beginning."

Finally, we sang the entire verse together, making sure to include the actions.

You put your thumbs in, you take your thumbs out.
You put your thumbs in, and you shake them all about.
You do the hokey pokey and you turn yourself around,
That's what it's all about.

ACTIVE ENGAGEMENT/LINK

Invite students to notice digraphs at the beginning of words and get their mouths ready to make one sound.

"Readers, there is another verse to this song! Let's sing it together and use all our powers to help us solve bigger words." I pointed to the first word and invited the children to begin reading, stopping when we got to the word with the digraph highlighted.

You put your chin in, you take your chin out.

"Put a thumb up if you know what you think the word might be." Some of the kids put their thumbs in the air right away. I tapped the illustration at the end of the line and said, "Get your mouth ready by saying the beginning sound. When I snap, say the word." I snapped my fingers and the children said, "*Chin*!"

While you aren't yet pushing readers of level C and level D books to attend to internal parts of words when reading independently, sliding your finger across the word to the ending solidifies directionality and offers exposure for those who might be ready.

We went through the process of checking it and noticing the short vowel after the digraph. Then we sang the entire verse with accompanying actions, pausing at the word *shake* to notice the digraph and get our mouths ready.

> You put your chin in, you take your chin out.
> You put your chin in, and you shake it all about.
> You do the hokey pokey and you turn yourself around,
> That's what it's all about.

Remind students that today's learning can help them with bigger words when they are reading and writing.

"Readers, you used all your powers to help you read the song, and you remembered that when you see a digraph, it helps to get your mouth ready. Remembering that sometimes two letters make one sound will *really* help you solve bigger words."

This time, leave the digraph in the word shake *unhighlighted, still pausing to prompt the children to notice the digraph at the beginning. Highlighting parts of words is a scaffold that readers won't have when they're reading their books independently, so be sure to plan at least one place for this scaffold to be released.*

RUG TIME

Set reading partners up to read books from their baggies together, using everything they know to tackle puzzling words.

"Are you ready to practice using all your super powers to help you with bigger words? Get with your reading partner. Partner 1, will you pull out one book you can read together today? Read through your book with your partner. When you get to a puzzling word, remind each other to use *all* your powers to help you, and if you notice a digraph that makes one sound, get your mouth ready. If you finish one book, Partner 2 can pull out another one and keep reading." I circulated to support readers, giving lean prompts as needed.

SHARE • Revisit a Song to Practice Blending Onsets and Rimes

Revisit the song from the connection to provide students with repeated practice blending onsets and rimes, emphasizing digraphs and short vowels.

"Wow! You're using *all* of your powers to help you solve bigger words! Let's close our phonics workshop by singing 'If You Think You Know This Word' again."

I began singing the familiar song to the tune of "If You're Happy and You Know It," and I invited the children to join in.

If You Think You Know This Word

If you think you know this word, raise your hand.
If you think you know this word, raise your hand.

POSSIBLE COACHING MOVES

▶ "Think about the cover to get your mind ready to read."

▶ "Look at the picture and think about the story to help you."

▶ "How does this story go?"

▶ "Get your mouth ready."

▶ "What could help you figure that out?"

▶ "Check it."

If you think you know this word,
Then tell me what you've heard.
If you think you know this word, raise your hand:
/sh/-/ip/.

Most of the children raised their hands, and I called on one child who said, "*Ship*!"

For additional practice, we continued singing the song a few more times with other words: *chair*, *shell*, *sheep*, *chop*, *chick*, *show*, *ship*, *think*, *shed*, *check*, and *thick*.

"Wow, your powers are getting stronger and stronger," I said as I pointed to my ear and flexed my arm muscles in the air. "This is going to help you solve lots of bigger words!"

EXTENSION 1 • Reading a Poem to Practice Blending Word Parts

Read the poem "Put Them Together" to provide students with repeated practice blending word parts.

I pointed to an enlarged poem on the easel and exclaimed, "Readers, let's celebrate solving bigger words with a new game!"

As I pointed under the words, I began reading the poem, and the children chimed in readily.

Put Them Together

It begins with /ch/
and it ends with /ip/.
Put them together,
And they say _____. (*chip*)

I coached the children to blend the word parts together, making sure to talk about the meaning of any words that might be unfamiliar to the class. We continued reading the poem together with additional words, such as *chair*, *shell*, *thorn*, *shed*, *chain*, and *shark*. I made a mental note to tuck the poem into transitions across the day, perhaps even as a warm-up for shared reading.

Put Them Together
It begins with _____
and it ends with _____.
Put them together,
And they say _____.

Provide students with more practice segmenting and blending sounds by using Elkonin boxes coupled with letter work, with an emphasis on digraphs at the beginning and end of words.

I placed three-part Elkonin boxes under the document camera and said, "Do you remember how we used this tool earlier to help strengthen your powers? We can also use it to help you with digraphs and bigger words!"

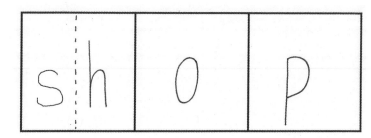

The class nodded their heads in unison as I said, "Today we are going to use this tool again. Are you ready? Just like we did last time, we'll place a letter in each box for each sound you say and hear. If there are two letters that make one sound, we'll divide that box with a dotted line. This will help you with digraphs and bigger words."

I modeled for the class by saying the word *shop* slowly. I wrote the letters *SH* in the first box as I was saying /sh/ and making a dotted line between the *s* and *h*, the letter *O* when I got to the /ŏ/, and the letter *P* in the final box as I said /p/.

I asked the class to say each sound with me as I pointed under the corresponding letter. "Now let's blend the sounds together again to make the word." I ran my finger under the letters in the boxes as we all said the word *shop* slowly again.

"Now will you help me? As we say the sounds in a word, you can write the letters for the word in the rug with your fingers, and I will write them up here. Show me your magic writing fingers!"

We repeated this routine with the words *chop*, *ship*, *chip*, *thin*, *chin*, *chat*, and *shed*.

Flexibility with Vowel Power, Word-Part Power, and Snap Word Power in Writing

IN THIS SESSION

TODAY YOU'LL teach students, through interactive writing, how to use all of their super powers flexibly to write a text, and then engage students in a shared reading of that text.

TODAY YOUR STUDENTS will practice slowing down and speeding up as needed when writing, employing their sound power, vowel power, word-part power, and snap word power as needed.

MINILESSON

CONNECTION

Share a story about baking using new versus familiar recipes, and explain the parallels to being flexible when writing, either slowly and carefully or quickly and automatically, depending on the need.

"Kindergartners, I thought of you yesterday. I was making a batch of cookies using a new recipe. I'd never made them before. While I followed the recipe, I added each ingredient very carefully. I measured everything out a little at a time. I worked slowly, bit by bit.

"It's different when I make my grandma's special cookies. My family and I have made them for years. I don't have to measure; I just toss in the ingredients quickly and move on to the next step. Sometimes, I don't even need to look back at the recipe because I just know the next step by heart!

"It reminds me a lot of writing. Sometimes writers need to write slowly, going sound by sound. Other times, they are ready to write words more quickly, going part by part. And other times still, writers can write whole words in a snap, without stopping at all."

GETTING READY

✔ Prepare to display the book *How to Graduate*.

✔ Have correction tape available for use during interactive writing.

✔ Distribute whiteboards and markers to rug clubs.

PHONICS INSTRUCTION

Phonological Awareness
- Isolate and pronounce initial sounds, medial vowel, and final sounds in spoken words.
- Segment individual phonemes in words.

Letter Knowledge
- Recognize which letters are consonants and which letters are vowels.
- Use proper letter formation.

Phonics
- Demonstrate basic knowledge of letter-sound correspondences by producing the primary sound for each consonant.
- Hear and identify short and long vowel sounds in words and in the letters that represent them.
- Identify digraphs in words.

Word Knowledge
- Use familiar phonograms.
- Record digraphs to write new words.

High-Frequency Words
- Write high-frequency words in continuous text.
- Learn a new word (*for*).

✤ **Name the teaching point.**

"Today I want to teach you that writers are flexible. They speed up or slow down, and use the powers they need, to write even the biggest words as best as they can."

TEACHING

Share Mabel's request for information about what to do during her upcoming graduation and invite students to brainstorm steps to write in a book for her called *How to Graduate*.

"Writers, Mabel whispered something to me earlier. She's never been to a graduation! Her graduation celebration is very soon, and she doesn't know what's going to happen, or what it will be like. I told her not to worry, that we could help. After all," I paused to flash my proudest smile, "you *are* graduates!

"Since we know so much about graduating, we should write a How-To book for Mabel!" I revealed a book with the illustrations already drawn across four pages:

I pointed under each word as we read the title together. "Writers, look at the pictures on each page and plan each step. Remember to use a teaching voice. Turn and talk to your partner." I turned pages as they rehearsed what to write in the How-To book and then reconvened the class.

This is a reference to the reading unit of study Bigger Books, Bigger Reading Muscles, *where the children have a graduation ceremony toward the end of the unit. If you have not taught that unit with your students, take a little time to make sure they understand what a graduation is.*

This interactive writing text also supports the popular kindergarten unit of study for writing workshop, How-To Books: Writing to Teach Others. *During this writing unit, children write steps across pages to teach others through their pictures and words.*

Demonstrate flexibility in writing the first page of the book *How to Graduate*, **slowing down or speeding up and using different super powers, depending on the word.**

"I'll write the first page. As I do, I'll make sure to be flexible, using the powers I need to help me write as best as I can. Sometimes I'll need to slow down and go sound by sound, using sound power and vowel power. Sometimes I'll be able to speed up and use my word-part power or snap word power!

"A lot of you said that the first page could go like this: 'Step 1. Stand up tall in line.' *Stand*. That's a big word. It starts with /s/ /t/ . . . I can use my sound power for that." As I said the sounds, I wrote the *S* and *T* on the page. "/st/-/and/! Wait! I know that part! I can speed up. Activate word-part power!" I wrote *-and* quickly and then put my finger under the *A* to demonstrate checking for a vowel. "Activate vowel power!

"The next word is *up*." I gasped. "That's a snap word! I can speed up again and write that right away. 'Stand up . . .'" I reread.

"*Tall*. /t/. I have sound power for that," I narrated as I wrote the letter down. "/all/! I don't have to say every sound, I know that word part. Activate word-part power!" My pen zipped across the page to finish the word. "*Stand up tall . . . in*. Another snap word! I don't need to stop. I have snap word power!" I wrote *in* on the page quickly.

"The last word is *line*. "Hmm, . . . I need to slow down and go sound by sound for this word, and I'll activate my vowel power to be sure there is a vowel inside. /l/-/ī/-/n/. That *I* has the long sound; I hear its name." I wrote each letter as I said its sound and added an *E* at the end to make it conventional, saying casually, "This *E* is silent, and it's what makes the *I* a long vowel.

"Writers, did you see how flexible I was as I wrote? I didn't just use one power. I used all the powers I needed to help me write as best as I can!"

ACTIVE ENGAGEMENT/LINK

Engage students in interactive writing of the next page.

I turned to the next page of the book. "Now it's your turn! Let's write the next page together. Lots of you said that this page could say, 'March to the music.' That makes sense," I agreed, as I touched the picture.

"We need to write *march*. Everyone, say it: *march*." The children obliged. "Which powers do you need to write this word? Do you need to go sound by sound, or is there a part you know? Take out your imaginary pens and write *march* on the rug. Be flexible with your powers!"

As the class wrote the word on the rug, I called one child up to write the word in our book. I reminded her to say the word again and write it as best as she could. She began sound by sound, recording *MR*. I nudged her to listen for a part she knew, and she said /ch/ and wrote the matching digraph quickly. "You sped up!" I responded. "Now, activate vowel power!" When she noticed that the word was missing a vowel, she said the word again, then looked back at me, puzzled. "That vowel is hard to hear, isn't it? Let me show you what the word looks like in a book." I swiftly covered the word with correction tape and wrote *March* conventionally on top.

We continued this way for the last two words on the page. For each word, I coached one child at the easel, while the rest of the children practiced by writing with their fingers on the rug.

"Writers, you slowed down when you needed to, saying each sound. You used vowel power to make sure your words had vowels. You sped up and used word parts or snap words when you could. How flexible!"

RUG TIME

Recruit students to write the next two steps, one at a time, on whiteboards in their rug clubs.

"We need to finish this book and get it to Mabel, so she can learn about graduating!" I urgently distributed whiteboards and markers to rug clubs. "Write the next sentence with your rug clubs: 'Throw your cap.'"

As the children wrote, I coached in as needed.

As rug clubs were finishing with the sentence, I wrote it on page 3 of our book. Then I signaled for their attention and turned the page of our How-To book. "Ready for the last step? 'Hug each other.' Write it with your rug club!"

Once again, I circulated and coached writers, before writing the final sentence in our book. "Oh, writers! Thanks for making this book," I said as I reconvened the class. "It is really going to help Mabel feel ready for her big day!"

SHARE • Shared Reading of the Interactive Writing Text

As a class, read *How to Graduate* to Mabel to help her prepare for her ceremony.

"Mabel? Mabel?!" I searched the room, calling for our stuffed elephant. When I located her, I sat her in my lap, looking at the children. "Mabel, the kindergartners can teach you how to graduate! They wrote this book just for you!"

I led the class in a shared reading of *How to Graduate*. When we finished reading, I turned to Mabel. "Now do you feel ready for your graduation ceremony, Mabel? It's coming so soon!" I made Mabel reach up and toss an imaginary cap in the air. "I think she's ready!" I smiled.

Notice that this series presents students with a balance of reading and writing in isolation and in context. This supports flexible use of developing skills and concepts and transfer to reading and writing workshop.

POSSIBLE COACHING MOVES

▶ "Say the word. Do you need to write it sound by sound, or is there a part you know?"

▶ "How do you write /th/? What sound is next?"

▶ "Activate vowel power! Check that there is a vowel in every word."

▶ "Does it look right?"

Introduce a new snap word, and guide students through the familiar process of making a word a snap word.

On the easel, I rested the envelope that Mabel left for us on the first day of the bend. "Writers, we've been writing notes back and forth a lot in the past few days. There is a word that we keep using, and it comes up in lots of books, too. I think you are ready to know it by heart." I pointed to the word *for* on the envelope and then held up a card with the new word wall word written on it, which I taped to the easel.

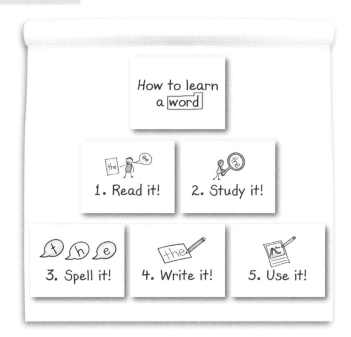

"Let's turn this word into a snap word!" I displayed the "How to Learn a Word!" anchor chart and invited the children to read it with me.

I held up the word *for*. "Mabel made this invitation *for* us. First, *read* it!" I pointed under the printed card as the students chorally read the word.

"Now, *study* it. How many letters? Yes, three! What letters do you see? Name them to your partner. Now, let's notice the vowel. It's *O*. It isn't making the short sound, like *octopus*, is it? It isn't making the long sound, like its name, either. Interesting! Sometimes vowels can make more than two sounds!

"Now, *spell* it. Spell it softly, like a whisper into your hand. *F-O-R*. Now, spell it and cheer it. *F-O-R*!

"Now, *write* it! Let's write it in the air. Everyone, stand up and be safe, leaving space around you." I wrote-in-the-air and recited the letter formation pathways for lowercase *F*, *O*, and *R*.

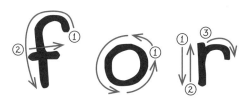

"Last step—*use* it! Share a sentence with your partner." I circulated, listening in and providing support where needed.

"Writers, before we add this word to the word wall, I think there is one more place that we should use our new snap word." I placed *How to Graduate* on the easel. "Since we wrote this book *for* Mabel, maybe we should officially dedicate the book to her by writing that on the inside front cover. Lots of authors dedicate their books to special people in their lives who inspire them to write." I opened the book and thought aloud, "For Mabel." I invited one student up to write it in the book while the rest of the class wrote it in the air one last time. Before we ended, I added *for* to the word wall and the children added it to their snap word pouches.

EXTENSION 2 • Dedicating More How-To Books

Offer repeated encounters with the high-frequency word *for*.

I opened to the dedication pages of a few of the class's favorite books and read them aloud.

"Writers, you've made so many How-To books. Your folders are practically bursting with books, all waiting to teach readers about so many topics! I bet you had people in mind as you were writing. Maybe they are people who are special to you, and you want to give your book to them as a gift. Maybe they are people who need to know what you are teaching.

"Right now, will you pull out a few of your books, ones you've worked especially hard on, and get ready to dedicate them? As you hold one of your books, you might think, 'Who is this for?' or 'Who needs to read this?' Once you know who, you can use our new snap word *for* to dedicate your book. On the inside front cover, you can write, '*For . . .*' and then the person's name, just like in your favorite books. Use the word wall if you need to!"

Mabel's Graduation and a Celebration of Vowel Power

IN THIS SESSION

TODAY YOU'LL teach students that writers keep their vowel power activated all the time, always staying on the lookout for vowels in their writing and checking that every syllable of every word has at least one vowel.

TODAY YOUR STUDENTS will use their vowel power and other super powers to write celebratory signs for Mabel's graduation and read each other's signs when participating in the ceremony.

MINILESSON

CONNECTION

Process to the meeting area to practice for Mabel's upcoming graduation ceremony. Marvel at how students' vowel power has grown since the beginning of the unit.

I stood in the middle of the classroom and signaled for the children's attention. Humming "Pomp and Circumstance," I waved the children into line behind me. We paraded to the meeting area in time with the song and sat down.

"Kindergartners, today is Mabel's graduation day. It's so exciting! I haven't seen Mabel yet today," I explained, glancing all around. "She must be getting ready. Do you know what she told me? She is planning to wear her cap *and* her vowel shield to the celebration!

"When Mabel said that, I realized that *you* also have a lot to celebrate. Your vowel power has grown and grown and *grown*. Not only do you use vowel power when writing small words, you use vowel power even when writing the biggest of words. You use vowel power all the time!

GETTING READY

✔ Prepare large paper and marker to write a graduation sign and for students to make celebratory graduation signs.

✔ Hide Mabel with a graduation cap and her vowel shield under a cloth until revealing her for the graduation ceremony. If you don't have a graduation cap for Mabel, you can find instructions online for making a simple one out of paper.

✔ Prepare to play "Pomp and Circumstance" for the graduation ceremony. A link to the song is provided in the online resources.

PHONICS INSTRUCTION

Concepts About Print
- Understand that words are separated by spaces in print, concept of word.
- Understand punctuation has a purpose.

Phonological Awareness
- Hear, say, blend, and segment syllables in spoken words.
- Isolate and pronounce initial sounds, medial vowel, and final sounds in spoken words.
- Segment individual phonemes in words.

Letter Knowledge
- Recognize which letters are consonants and which letters are vowels.

Phonics
- Demonstrate basic knowledge of letter-sound correspondences by producing the primary sound for each consonant.
- Hear and identify short and long vowel sounds in words and the letters that represent them.

Word Knowledge/Solving
- Use familiar phonograms to write words.

High-Frequency Words
- Write high-frequency words in continuous text.

"This is such a big day for all of us. Often at graduations, people make signs to show how proud they are of the graduates. We should make signs for Mabel—and each other—and hold them up during the celebration. So that everyone can read the signs, you'll need to use all you've learned to help make your writing easy to read."

♣ **Name the teaching point.**

"Today I want to teach you that writers keep their vowel power activated all the time, always staying on the lookout for vowels in their writing. Now and forever, they can check that every syllable of every word has at least one vowel."

TEACHING

Model making a sign to support Mabel at the graduation celebration.

"Hmm, . . . let me think about what could go on a sign for Mabel that shows how we feel about her hard work. I want the words to make her smile as she is walking in her graduation ceremony. I also want *all of you* to see the sign and remember that we are proud of each other, too!

"I think I'll say, 'We are so happy for you!' If Mabel—and all of you—are going to read this sign today, I'd better make sure to keep my vowel power activated the whole time I'm writing!"

I began writing on a large piece of paper. "I'll make my writing bigger than usual since this is a sign. *We.* I'll write that in a snap and then check that I included a vowel in every syllable. Join me by writing the word on the rug." I wrote the word quickly, clapped once for the single syllable, and pointed under the *E.* "That's a long *E* that sounds like the name of the letter. I'll keep my vowel power activated as I move to the next word, *are.*" Again, I wrote the snap word quickly and double-checked for the vowels, as the children did the same on the rug.

"The next word is *so.* That's a small word, just one syllable. I'll write what I hear. /s/ /ō/. Try it on the rug as I try it on the sign. Oh, that's a long *O.* Its sound matches its name." I wrote the letters, then held my finger under the *O* and nodded at the class to exaggerate my vigilance in checking for vowels.

"*Happy.* That's a bigger word. Let's clap the syllables together!" We clapped twice. "There will definitely be more than one vowel. *Hap-,*" I recorded the first three letters and continued, "*-py,*" recording the last two letters. As I wrote the *Y,* I made sure to comment, "*Happy* sounds like *Mrs. Wishy-Washy* at the end. *Y* is the vowel in that syllable!"

We reread what I'd written so far before moving on. "*We are so happy . . . for you!* Two of our newest snap words!" I peeked at the word wall before writing both words swiftly and checking for the vowels inside them.

"Writers, did you see how I kept my vowel power activated the whole time I was writing? As I was writing, I was on the lookout for vowels. After I wrote, I checked that every syllable in every word had a vowel."

You are inviting children to write for an authentic purpose, keeping meaning making front and center. Remember that instruction at all levels should support meaning making. This will provide children with motivation to use everything they know to make their writing easy to read.

Remind students how vowel power can also help them solve words when they are reading.

Then I invited students to read the whole sign with me. When I got to the word *happy*, I stopped and asked students for help, inviting them to listen closely to the sounds.

"Yes!" I said when they read the word *happy*. "If the vowel were an *O*, the word would be *hoppy*. And if the vowel were an *I*, the word would be *hippy*. Knowing the sounds that go with each vowel can help you solve words. So, your vowel power helps you read, too!"

Finally, we read the whole sentence again with expression.

ACTIVE ENGAGEMENT/LINK

Recruit children to make their own signs, reminding them to use vowels in their writing.

"Now it's your turn, writers! Think, 'What will I write to Mabel—and all the kids in our class, too—to wish them congratulations?' Turn and talk to your partner!"

Lovely sentiments filled the space, and I named some aloud when I reconvened the class. "Kindergartners, how caring you are! You are so proud of how much everyone's vowel power has grown. I heard kind wishes like, 'You did it!' and 'Hooray for Mabel and for us!' and 'Congratulations to everybody!' and 'We all have vowel power!'

"Let's make those signs! It's almost time for the graduation ceremony to begin. You'll need to use all that you've learned as you write, making sure to keep your vowel power activated so everyone can read your caring words."

I distributed large pieces of paper to the children and they spread out around the classroom to make their own signs. I coached in as they worked.

After a few minutes, I called for their attention. "Writers, your vowel power sure has grown! You worked hard to keep your vowel power activated the whole time you were writing!"

> **POSSIBLE COACHING MOVES**
> ▶ "Activate your vowel power!"
> ▶ "Can you use word-part power there?"
> ▶ "That's a snap word. Check the word wall!"
> ▶ "What a big word! Try clapping the syllables."

RUG TIME

Channel students to edit their writing with their partners, supporting each other to keep their vowel power activated.

I reconvened the children in the meeting area with their signs. "Writers, these signs will be published today, in just a few minutes! Lean on your partners to help you edit. Decide who will go first, then put your sign between you and your partner. Read the sign together, making especially sure there are vowels in every syllable. Keep your vowel power activated when you switch to the other partner's writing!"

As partners worked, I whispered in, nudging children to coach each other. I reminded them to use all they knew about making writing easy to read, in addition to focusing on using vowels.

POSSIBLE COACHING MOVES

▶ "Remind your partner about spaces between words!"

▶ "Remind your partner to check for punctuation at the end of the sentence. Does she need a period or an exclamation mark?"

▶ "Remind your partner to activate vowel power!"

SHARE • Celebrating Mabel's Graduation

Unveil Mabel, dressed in a graduation cap, and set students up as spectators in her graduation ceremony. Invite students to cheer Mabel on by holding up the signs they made.

"Writers, it's time!" I directed students to clear the meeting area. As they returned their pens to their tables, I quietly located Mabel, whom I'd covered with a small blanket and stashed away earlier.

In the center of the room, I waited until all curious eyes were on me. I raised my secret package and pulled away the fabric to reveal Mabel, clad in her new graduation cap and vowel shield. "Dun-da-da-da!" I sang. The class broke out in applause for Mabel.

I quieted the students, then silently ushered the children into two rows on the sides of the meeting area, seated and facing each other, to form an aisle. "You can rest your vowel shields against your legs. Shine your vowel power toward the middle of the aisle, so Mabel can feel it as she walks through. Hold your signs up high, so she and your friends can see them, too! As Mabel is passing by, you can read each other's signs out loud to cheer her on," I whispered.

In a more official voice, I said, "Our graduation ceremony is about to begin." I turned on "Pomp and Circumstance" and started to march through the aisle, holding Mabel on my shoulders, as the children shouted encouragement from the sidelines.

I turned around and walked back through and motioned for the children to get up and follow me. We paraded around the classroom, vowel shields in the air.

Parade around the classroom, singing some favorite cheers from the unit. Toss imaginary graduation caps and channel students to store their vowel shields in their writing folders.

"Super Readers and Writers, Mabel just requested that we do our vowel cheer. Ready?" We launched into our familiar cheer a few times, as we walked in a line around the classroom. "*A! E! I! O! U! A, apple, /ă/. E, egg, /ĕ/. I, igloo, /ĭ/. O, octopus, /ŏ/. U, umbrella, /ŭ/!*"

As we continued our procession, I began to sing another familiar song to the tune of "Bingo Was His Name-O" with a new twist. After the second or third round of singing, the children picked up on the words and joined me.

We made our way back to the meeting area and I turned off the music. Remembering the How-To book that we wrote for Mabel, I motioned for everyone to grab the imaginary caps on their heads. I tossed Mabel's cap, and the kids did the same. Then I passed Mabel around for anyone who wanted to give her a hug.

"Your vowel power is so strong now." I distributed writing folders to the children. "Store your vowel shields in here. That way, your vowel power can stay with you always."

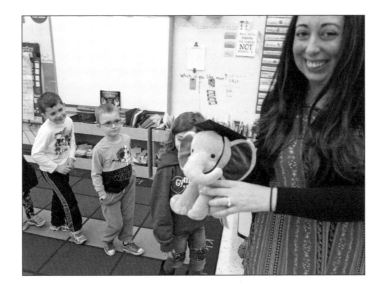

Vowel Shield Celebration
(Sing to the tune of "Bingo")

There are five vowels on our shield

They help us read and write.

A-E-I-O-U

A-E-I-O-U

A-E-I-O-U

Our shields are shining bright! Yay!

Making Friends with Letters

Lucy Calkins and Natalie Louis

Photography by Peter Cunningham

Illustrations by Marjorie Martinelli

HEINEMANN ◆ PORTSMOUTH, NH

Dedicated with great gratitude to Patricia Cunningham. We thank you for your friendship, your decades of brilliant work, and above all, for your generosity. —Lucy and Natalie

Heinemann
361 Hanover Street
Portsmouth, NH 03801–3912
www.heinemann.com

Offices and agents throughout the world

Cataloging-in-Publication data is on file with the Library of Congress.

ISBN-13: 978-0-325-10517-8

Editors: Tracy Wells and Anna Gratz Cockerille
Production: Elizabeth Valway
Cover and interior designs: Jenny Jensen Greenleaf
Photography: Peter Cunningham
Illustrations: Marjorie Martinelli and Kimberly Fox
Composition: Publishers' Design and Production Services, Inc.
Manufacturing: Steve Bernier

Printed in the United States of America on acid-free paper
22 21 20 19 18   VP   1 2 3 4 5

Acknowledgments

THIS WAS THE FIRST BOOK that we wrote in the new phonics series, and as such, it was the most challenging of all. We invented the structures, methods, and principles that undergird the entire series while working on this book. To do that, we worked shoulder-to-shoulder with the entire community of primary-level educators at the Teachers College Reading and Writing Project, and especially closely with a small team that included Rachel Rothman-Perkins, Rebecca Cronin, Allyse Bader, Marie Mounteer, Shanna Schwartz, and Valerie Geschwind.

The book required a score of drafts, as we revised our way to a voice, a design, a plan. To move through that process, we worked especially closely with the Project's team of writers, including Katie Clements, Kelly Boland Hohne, and Liz Franco. We spent two weeks of the summer holed up, writing and rewriting our way to decisions about how the entire series would go. Hareem Atif Khan was a part of this group as well.

Once we'd fashioned a through line for the unit, it required lots of field testing, and again the whole organization joined us in that work. On many Thursdays, we headed to a nearby school, PS 180, to try out minilessons and small groups, and then afterwards we gathered to rethink and reinvent. Thanks to the teachers at PS 180 who opened their classrooms to us, and again, to the entire team of primary staff developers for helping us learn our way into the methods you see in these pages. We extend a special thank you to Natalie's Kindergarten Specialty Group: Lori Barrett, Melissa Dunne, Peter Falciglia, June Golonka, Bethany Haskins, Grace Marotta, Nicole Mell, Jisun Oh, Liliana Scamardella, and Alexandra Simmonds, for their thoughtful discussions, their willingness to test parts in their own classrooms, and their insightful feedback.

Each session and each extension in these phonics units required an extraordinary amount of vigilant detailed attention. When one change was made it often required a domino sequence of other changes. No one was more helpful in this work than Emma Coufal Bemowski, who gave tireless loving care to every page of this book. We brim with gratitude to her. Emma was assisted in this work by two other brilliant colleagues, Mary Ann Mustac and Sara Berg. They, too, read each page, making sure that every item that you will need in a session is included in the Getting Ready list and that each session builds on the one before it. Samantha Barrett read this book from the viewpoint of a teacher and made careful adjustments to the seemingly small details that make a huge difference in classrooms.

Because Natalie and I were pulled between this book and others, we especially relied on Marjorie Martinelli's careful help with materials. She went way above and beyond to support the artwork that accompanies this book, and we are so grateful to her. Her talent radiates throughout the pages of this entire series. Those of us who work alongside Marjorie are equally grateful for her personality—her calmness, her grace, her willingness to move heaven and earth to be helpful.

This entire effort stands on the shoulders also of colleagues throughout the nation who have taught us about phonics. We are grateful to Tim Rasinski, who read a very early draft of this and other books and gave us his thoughtful counsel; Donald Bear, who has been our teacher for years; Lori Hellman, who has helped us with supporting English language learners; and the late Marie Clay. This book is dedicated to Patricia Cunningham—a decision that we made right from the start. Before we even began this project, I asked Pat whether she'd prefer we go to great lengths to reinvent her work, pretending that it wasn't rooted in her wisdom, or could we be public and upfront about the fact that this first unit was built on the foundation of her brilliant name study teaching. Pat could not have been more gracious, encouraging us to do as professionals do which is to build on the knowledge base of each other. Pat was the person who pioneered the idea of teaching letters and sounds to kids through name studies. Her influence runs far deeper than just that, however, and we are grateful for it all, and especially for her friendship.

We also thank the other leaders at TCRWP. More than anything, we thank Mary Ehrenworth, Laurie Pessah, Amanda Hartman, Emily Butler Smith, and Audra Robb for their friendship and dedication. We are heartened to work alongside them, gaining energy from their passion and love.

Thank you as always to Peter Cunningham, photographer extraordinaire, who has an unparalleled way of capturing each and every child engaged in the work so that both the child and the work come alive on the page. These books would not be what they are without Peter's touch. Thank you as well to the schools who opened their doors so we could photograph or videotape their children and teachers, including New Bridges Elementary, Ridgebury Elementary, Barlow Mountain Elementary, PS 9, PS 39, PS 40, PS 58, PS 116, PS 139, PS 158, PS 267, and PS 347.

It is impossible to put into words that care that every one of our partners at Heinemann invested into this effort. Abby Heim and Lisa Bingen parent the whole endeavor at Heinemann. We are sisters. We work shoulder to shoulder, finishing each other's sentences, anticipating each other's requests. The seamless partnership with Lisa and Abby is what makes these books and all our Heinemann publications the accomplishment that they are. Abby and Lisa, like all of us at TCRWP, are part of a team of people who care every bit as much as they do. Elizabeth Valway, our fabulous production editor, and her intrepid team deserve all of our gratitude. They take rough documents and transform them into the beautiful texts you hold in your hands, in record time, as if by magic. Anna Gratz Cockerille plays a senior editor role, functioning often like a co-author as well as an editor. She gave this book in particular a great deal of time and energy, helping to write and rewrite sessions, and making sure the overall organization and sequence were rock solid. Tracy Wells has edited a dozen Units of Study books and she lives and breathes these units. Her knowledge of the form, design, language, and of the people, too, makes her an invaluable editor. Beth Moore gave us her wisdom and attention to detail in early iterations of this unit. Shannon Thorner, editorial associate, takes care of hundreds of details so that the editorial team can do their best work. She has taken a particularly active role in placing the photos you see in the pages of these books.

Finally, thanks to all of you, our readers. You bring this work to life. We are immensely grateful to be on this journey with you.

All the best,
Lucy and Natalie

Contents

BEND III   Using Star Names to Write

Registration instructions to access the digital resources that accompany this book may be found on p. xi.

An Orientation to the Unit

ALTHOUGH HUMAN BEINGS don't experience the metamorphosis that characterizes the life of a caterpillar, the transformation that happens during their kindergarten year is no less astonishing. Many of your children start their year holding books upside down and backwards and making letters that look like squiggles, and they end the year reading and writing for their own important purposes. Phonics instruction is at the center of this transformation.

Your children come to school primed to learn their ABCs. For both the youngsters and their parents, there isn't anything more central than "learning the ABCs." Your kids will be gung ho for this unit of study, and your teaching will be designed to build on their energy. You'll teach concepts of print, phonemic awareness, the alphabetic principle, and sound-letter correspondence during this upcoming unit, and all day long too. When your kids sign in at the start of the day, when they join in singing, "Make new friends, but keep the old …," when they huff and puff to blow the little pig's house down, and when they notice their name written above their coat hook, they'll be developing the skills and knowledge that are central to this unit. The focus of this first phonics unit, then, will be supported across the whole day, and will be supported in a zillion ways.

Over the course of this unit, you'll immerse your children in letters and sounds, rhyme and word play. Your kids will grow in leaps and bounds, and it will be important for you to see and focus on that, and to not worry that their knowledge will be incomplete and full of holes and gaps, misconceptions, and half-baked ideas. That is how every learner learns, and your job will be to celebrate the messy and brilliant learning that your youngsters do. Your job is not to teach towards mastery or to expect mastery.

This unit supports a variation of Patricia Cunningham's beloved "Star Names" unit. We send our thanks to Pat for her brilliant work helping a world of teachers tap into the power of children's own names as their first reading material and as their first source of letter-sound knowledge. We've kept the spirit of Patricia Cunningham's name study work, and altered many of the details.

Before the start of the school year, your class is just a list of names. But really, one shouldn't say *just*, because each name brings with it a person. As you get to know each quirky individual and as the class gets to know each other, those names become a group of friends, each person bringing his or her unique personality, his or her own stories, ideas, and spirit. Meanwhile, each precious friend also brings to life another name, a name with letters and sounds in it. The totally cool and amazing thing is that those letters—the letters in the names of the people in a classroom—can be put together to make the alphabet of letters. Those letters hang at the front of the room, and they also make their way into signs, jokes, songs, messages, letters, and books.

"We're people who love, love, love to read and write," you'll convey to kids. "To read and write, we need alphabet letters and we need friends who want to learn about those letters with us." This unit combines the two—friends and letters—by suggesting that your class list can be a source of phonics review and study. Through a study of each others' names, children can study letter formation, letter-sound correspondence, syllables, and the like.

On almost every day throughout the unit, the class will study another name. This makes the unit extra personal in more than one way. Because the unit revolves around the names of the children in your class, the unit is inevitably more homemade than most units. In this beautiful culturally diverse, idiosyncratic world of ours, there is absolutely no way you could begin to predict the names on your class roster. Because of this, this unit can only suggest a sequence of sessions and provide you with transferable templates for how those lessons might go. You'll need to bring your own children into your unit plans, tailoring each lesson to your class list.

The way that the unit unfolds is that you'll use your children's names, and the letters in those names, to teach phonics concepts. You'll draw names from a "Star Jar," doing some quiet machinations so that you control the sequence of names and in that way, channel your class to study letters in a sequence that roughly matches one that we argue for in *A Guide to the Phonics Units of Study, Grades K–1*.

M S T N A R L D F I V P K X E B Z J O C H U W G Q Y

We discuss the details of this sequence in the *Guide*, but for now, know that the sequence front-loads letters that will give kids good mileage in their writing. This sequence also front-loads letters whose sounds are in the letter's names—as is the case for *M*, *S*, and *T* and is not the case for *U*, *W*, *Y*, and *H*. With an exception or two, the sequence also front-loads letters for which you can say the letter for a long time and still be making that letter's sound (as in *M*, *N*, and *S*, but not *T*, *B*, *J*, and *W*). The sequence we recommend also spreads out letters that are easily confused because they are associated with similar sounds, such as the *P* and *B*. Vowels are dispersed, with the easier and highest utility vowels taught first.

 You'll see in the online resources we've provided detailed advice on how you can sequence all the names in your classroom. Please study those directions before you start this unit. There are lessons midway through the first bend, for example, in which you teach kids whose names start with the same letter. You will need to anticipate that lesson (and that way of covering all your names) and to save the appropriate names until then. Know that whenever we suggest you teach a name that begins with a particular letter, if you have no child whose name starts with that letter, you can skip ahead to the child whose name starts with a letter we recommend next or soon afterwards in the sequence. You may also create a reason to teach names that are not in the classroom: your name, your principal's name, the name of your class fish. That's your call.

Over the course of this unit you will build a name wall which will eventually contain all of the names in your class. In future units, this name wall will become a word wall. Make sure that the names (and later, the words) you place here are large enough to be seen from across the room.

You'll notice that every day's phonics workshop lasts just 15–20 minutes and is structured like a miniature reading or writing workshop. There is a micro-lesson (a very short minilesson) that follows the architecture of

minilessons, and a semi-independent work time. To save time, this work time is generally carried out entirely on the rug, with kids working with partners or with larger "rug clubs." We give more specifics later in this write-up on how to set up these social structures for this first unit. You can also read more about them in *A Guide to the Phonics Units of Study, Grades K–1*.

For each day, we've also written a detailed description of several extensions that you may want to teach sometime across the day. Some of these are extremely quick—a little ritual you can use, a song you can sing, a game you can play when your class walks down the hallway, eats a snack, or packs up to go home. You might decide to combine the workshop and an extension, making phonics time itself closer to half an hour, but we think it is ideal if the extension comes later in the day, or even at the start of the next day, as your kids' phonics development will be best supported if phonics weaves throughout the day. The extensions are generally optional, although we think a few are critical.

For example, you will not want to miss the extensions in this unit that provide explicit instruction designed to introduce letters. In many of these, you feature a star name. Direct, explicit instruction in the letters is really important. "Here's the letter. Here's the sound it makes. Here's how you make it. Listen to these words and signal which ones start with this letter, which ones don't." Keep this letter instruction brief. It is potent, packed with invaluable work, but needs to be brief so that you can have room in your day for all the other work your kindergartners need.

OVERVIEW OF THE UNIT

This unit is composed of three bends, or parts.

Bend I: Studying Peoples' Names Can Help You Get to Know Each Other—and the Alphabet

Bend II: Learning Your Own Name by Heart

Bend III: Using Star Names to Write

Bend I launches the name study with a session revolving around a stuffed elephant, a class mascot named Mabel. We decided to teach the name of a class mascot first rather than highlight a single child in that way, and we also want to start the year by studying the letter *M*. Children will be able to use *M* immediately in their stories (to label themselves, *me*). *M* is also a continuous sound: children can say the letter for a long time and still be making the sound /m/ (unlike, for example, the letter *T*). You can, of course, name your mascot something else, but we recommend choosing another name that starts with an *M*. We vote for *Milo* or *Mikey* as alternatives. Your mascot will be a very important presence throughout your phonics workshop, helping to make all of your teaching more engaging.

You'll see that we devote several days to the work with the first letter, *M*, and less time to others. The reason for the prolonged time with the first letter is that children are learning how to learn about letters, and developing their understanding of the alphabetic principle. As the unit unfolds, you'll see that we devote only one day to a letter—which, granted, is a lot less than the letter-a-week that some programs suggest. Know first that you can always devote another day to anything you teach, based on the needs of your students. And secondly, know that there are many, many opportunities for students to consolidate, review, and apply the early knowledge of letters that they develop during the first month or two of school. Unit 2, *Word Scientists*, revisits the alphabet, focusing on it for a large part of that unit. So, don't worry if each and every child does not master the alphabet before this unit ends.

The name study that is launched in Bend I doubles as both a way to create community in your classroom and as a way to introduce kids to the letters of the alphabet while also helping them develop critical concepts such as concept of letter, word, and an ability to hear, segment and manipulate sounds. There is a lot of support for phonological and phonemic awareness woven into all you teach.

The second bend continues the work begun in Bend I, only with a new emphasis on kids learning their own names, including the letter formation pathway that will help them to write their own names quickly and properly. Bend III, the final bend, returns to the work begun at the start of the book, continuing to teach more letters, but with a new emphasis on using what students have learned in order to write.

Recurring throughout this unit—and every unit—will be an attention to high-frequency words. You'll refer to those as "snap words" because these are words that kids will want to read and write "in a snap." The unit highlights snap words that are on the Dolch list of most frequently used words, including *me*, *a*, *the*, *I*, *like*, and *my*. Many of those words are abstract for young children. Therefore you'll want to be sure to also teach some concrete words that are specific to your class. If your children seem head over heels for

cats—add *cat* to the list of snap words. *Mom* and *dad* definitely belong there. Don't swamp the high-frequency words with too many concrete words, but mixing a few of these words in will make the entire collection of words mean more to your youngsters.

The "snap words" that are taught in this unit include two one-letter words: *I* and *a*. Don't be alarmed if your children do not seem to master these words yet. Think about what an abstraction the word *a* is! Then, too, until children have a firm command of the alphabet and a knowledge of letter-sound correspondence, you can't really expect them to retain what you teach about high-frequency words. So, you can expect that some of your children will begin to use those words "in a snap," while others are still doing some of the foundational learning that will allow that to happen shortly.

GETTING READY

First and foremost, we strongly urge you to choose a stuffed animal mascot who will accompany your phonics teaching throughout the year. Such a mascot can make your phonics workshop beloved by your students, and that matters tremendously. We originally proposed a mascot for this first month of kindergarten only, as a way to launch this unit's name study without highlighting one particular child's name. We were totally smitten by children's affection towards the mascot we proposed, the elephant you'll soon meet named Mabel. It was immediately clear that Mabel made a major difference in helping children feel at home with phonics.

You can, of course, bring in your own favorite creature and bestow on him your own favorite name. We've built some story line around Mabel, and the fact that she is an elephant (sometimes she thinks about the sounds in the word *elephant*, for example) so there is an advantage with staying with an elephant, but mostly there won't be important consequences to you choosing another animal. If you are head over heels in love with chimps or giraffes, go for it! As mentioned earlier, if you decide to choose a different name for your mascot, you might look for a name that begins with *M*, as we recommend this letter to launch the name study. We spent as much time naming Mabel, and Rasheed, our first grade mascot, as parents do with their first-born, and we hope to see Mabel and Rasheed showing up soon on all the lists of "Most Popular Names for Newborn Babies!"

As this is the first unit of the year, they'll be some set-up required to create or organize the phonics materials you will use. Many of these materials extend across units, so this work will be well worth it. Following is a list of the materials that are most fundamental to the unit, and that we recommend preparing in advance. Note that many of these are available on the online resources (denoted with ✣) and some are in the Resource Pack (denoted with 📖) as well, so be sure to register your book and access those materials before you begin.

- **Name chart:** Prepare a class name chart, with all of your students' names and, if you wish, their pictures. You can refer to this as needed before kids' names get added to the name wall.

- **Name wall:** This might look like a traditional word wall with the alphabet letters in order on the wall with space for names underneath each letter. You will fill this in over the course of the unit by placing students' names/pictures underneath the first letter of their names. The name wall should be visible from the whole classroom. This name wall will be turned into the class word wall after this unit.

- **Star names:** Each student in your class will have his or her name featured as a Star Name. Prepare for this by writing each child's name on a sentence strip and attaching a photo. You may find the template in the online resources helpful. ✣

- **Star Jar:** Find a large opaque jar that can hold all the star names for all of your students. You will draw one or more names from the Star Jar each session to teach the first letter of the name.

- **Pictures for letter sorts:** Create picture cards for letter sorts by printing the pictures onto cardstock and cutting them apart. For letter sorts, you'll need a number of pictures that start with the desired letter and several pictures that start with other letters that students already know. You'll place a mix of both types of cards into a baggie for each partnership. You may wish to copy the sets onto different colors of cardstock, so that when stray cards slip into their neighbor's set they are easy to spot. ✣ 📖

- **Pictures for letter books:** Throughout this unit, you'll make class letter books containing a number of pictures of objects starting with the same letter. On the online resources, you'll find a cover for each letter book (one per letter) as well as pictures for each letter that you can print out. To make a class letter book, you may choose simply to print

out the pictures and staple them with a cover, or you may choose to print out a letter-book template that you can glue the pictures into. ✣

- **Elkonin boxes:** We recommend that you use Elkonin boxes to help students listen for the sounds in words. Elkonin boxes are a series of drawn boxes, usually three, with each box representing one sound, or phoneme, in a word. To use Elkonin boxes, a child listens to a word and moves a token into a drawn box for each sound or phoneme. You can create these with actual boxes, but it's just as easy and effective to draw a set of boxes on a whiteboard or paper and have students move a token, or even tap each box to represent individual phonemes.

- **Name baggies:** Before Bend II, you'll need to prepare a name baggie for each student. Prepare a name baggie for each child, containing the child's name on an index card, letter tiles cut from paper (one tile for each letter in the child's name, with the uppercase letter on one side and the lowercase letter on the other), and the child's picture. Prepare a similar name baggie for Mabel. ✣

SOCIAL STRUCTURES

This is your students' first-ever phonics unit, and presumably, they are starting their first-ever reading and writing units as well. So, in this unit, you'll need to usher students into ways of working that will last across the year, and beyond.

We assume you have read *A Guide to the Phonics Units of Study, Grades K–1* and you have learned from that resource about how your phonics time will unfold each day. In a nutshell, you'll give a micro-lesson that channels kids into some active and interactive work that they do first with more and then less scaffolding. All of that work is done "on the rug," as we are referring to the meeting area.

One of the social structures to which you'll introduce your students is partnerships. Plan to assign your students to a partner early in the unit so that they know with whom to work during collaborative times. There is no need for partners to be ability-based at this point in the year, so there is no need to do any kind of assessment before assigning partners. You might take a day or two, though, to get to know your students and to think about their personalities before you partner them up. (You'll see we don't assign partners until Session 2 of the unit.) We recommend that you assign students the same phonics partner as reading partner, or writing partner, or even the same partner for all of these. It's a lot for a kindergartner at the start of the year to get to know three different partners!

In Session 10, you'll introduce students to a second social structure: rug clubs. You'll teach them how to turn to another partnership on the rug to create a small group of four to five students. As with partnerships, there is no need for clubs to be ability-based. Seat partners hip to hip, and seat the four children who will comprise a club in such a way that they can easily turn and work with each other—we imagine one set of partners constitutes half the club and they sit in one row, the other half of the club are the partners who sit in the row behind. Sometimes children will be asked to work in hip-to-hip partners, sometimes in clubs, and occasionally as the year unfolds, there will be days when you decide to elongate work time and to send kids back to their work spots.

Meanwhile, *Small Groups to Support Phonics* will help you support informal, short-lived small groups that will buttress and extend this curriculum and provide you with an opportunity to provide more assessment-based instruction, especially to outliers who are either less or more skilled. Those small groups are most apt to occur outside of phonics time, during your reading or writing workshop. Some may happen during intervention time.

ONLINE DIGITAL RESOURCES

Resources that accompany this unit of study are available in the online resources, including all the charts, word cards, songs, and poems shown throughout *Making Friends with Letters*.

To access and download the digital resources for *Making Friends with Letters*:

1. Go to www.heinemann.com and click the link in the upper right to log in. (If you do not have an account yet, you will need to create one.)

2. Enter the following registration code in the box to register your product: UOSPH_HYSC7

3. Enter the security information requested.

4. Once you have registered your product it will appear in the list of My Online Resources.

(You may keep copies of these resources on up to six of your own computers or devices. By downloading the file, you acknowledge that they are for your individual or classroom use and that neither the resources nor the product code will be distributed or shared.)

Studying Peoples' Names Can Help You Get to Know Each Other—and the Alphabet

BEND I

To Learn a Name Well, It Helps to Do Things with the Name

GETTING READY

✔ Before this session, prepare a class name wall. This might look like a traditional word wall with the alphabet letters in order on the wall. It should be visible from the whole classroom.

✔ Prepare a class name chart, with all of your students' names and, if you wish, their pictures.

✔ Choose a stuffed animal for the class mascot. We chose Mabel, the elephant. She is today's star name.

✔ Write your mascot's name on a sentence strip in large, clear handwriting. Add a picture of the mascot inside a star shape.

✔ Bring handfuls of magnetic letters to the start of your minilesson.

✔ Place objects whose names begin with *M* near you.

✔ Make cards that can be strung together for your mascot's name necklace.

PHONICS INSTRUCTION

Concepts About Print
- Recognize that spoken words are represented in written language by specific sequences of letters.
- Use one's name to learn about words.

Phonological Awareness
- Hear and say syllables.
- Identify and produce groups of words that begin with the same sound (alliteration).

- Identify the initial phonemes of spoken words.

Letter Knowledge
- Recognize uppercase and lowercase letters.
- Recognize the names/sounds of letters.

IN THIS SESSION

TODAY YOU'LL teach students that when readers and writers really want to learn a new friend's name, they study it in different ways so that they can remember it.

TODAY YOUR STUDENTS will learn a sequence of activities that they will use in future sessions to learn the names of all kids in the class. Together, you and the class will read the class mascot's name, count and study the letters, and cheer the spelling of the name.

MINILESSON

CONNECTION

Rally students to see themselves as people who read and write and therefore need to know an armful of letters and sounds. One way to learn letters is by studying names.

"Today is a *big* day! It's the very first day of kindergarten! Starting today, and every day after today, you are going to be *reading* and *making* lots of books. To do all of that reading and writing, you'll need some stuff—not just books and paper and pens—but you will also need these . . . " I held up a big scoop of magnetic letters "You are going to need letters and sounds to make and to read all kinds of words!

"The other thing we'll *all* need is friends. For us to all be friends with each other, we need to know each other's names. Will you quickly tell someone sitting near you your name and say hello?" The kids turned to practice a little turn-and-talk. "Now, look back at me! This time, can you tell that person three things that you absolutely love? Go ahead, quickly tell each other some of the things you love!

"I am already getting to know you better! Everyone, this is Georgina and she loves puppies! This is José and he loves Pokémon cards! Names are so important! Names tell us who is here today, they tell us where to hang up our coats, they show us where our table space is. Knowing your name and the names of your friends will help you a lot this year!

"Quick—whisper your name into your hands like a secret." They did. "Now, when I count to three, shout your name as loud as you can: one . . . two . . . three!" The kids shouted. "Oh my goodness, so many beautiful names!

"Guess what else? I've made a chart with all of our names. This is our class name chart." I pointed to a chart I had made with each child's name and picture. "Soon we'll add these names to our name wall." I gestured to the name wall, with letters as placeholders but without any names.

"Let's work together to look closely at one new friend's name." I reached behind the easel and pulled out a stuffed elephant who would become our class mascot. "This is Mabel. And," I said, holding up a sentence strip on which I'd written the name, "this is her name: *Mabel*. Her name is going to be our star name for our very first day. In the next few weeks each of you will have a turn having your name as the star name."

❖ **Name the teaching point.**

"Today I want to teach you that when you want to really, really learn a new friend's name—like you will want to learn Mabel's name—it helps to do stuff with that name so you remember it, so it almost becomes part of you."

TEACHING AND ACTIVE ENGAGEMENT/LINK

Introduce the star name by teaching children a replicable sequence of steps to study a name. Name each step, then follow it, to help kids begin to learn the routine of studying a star name.

I held up the strip with Mabel's name and picture on it and showed the class. "This word is *Mabel*. Let's notice some things about this word, the name of our stuffed elephant."

I led the way. "Let's read her name first. Then we can count and name the letters in her name." The class chimed in to read *Mabel* and then counted the letters. I pointed crisply under each letter as I led the children in counting from start to end. "One, two, three, four, five. Wow! There are *five* letters in the name *Mabel*.

"Let's look at all of the letters and notice if some are the same or if all of the letters are different." I slid my finger slowly beneath the word to guide kids to study the shape of each letter along with me. "Are any of these letters the same? Are there two of any letter?" Some children called out "no" and I agreed. "You are right. None of the letters in the name *Mabel* are the same. There are five different letters in the name *Mabel*.

Teach this first lesson straight from your heart. Your connection today is a love song, and its purpose is to create community, to generate energy. Your kids will need your full and whole-hearted attention. As you teach today's lesson, think about how important it is that your kids absolutely adore this part of their day. You are establishing tone, and that is a big deal. You will want your teaching to be as different as possible from the teaching that accompanies a plodding, dull phonics workbook.

The reason to count the letters is to reinforce kids' knowledge of what a letter is, as opposed to a word. For extra support with this concept, you might cut each of the letters apart, to show the difference between the word and its individual letters.

"What else can we notice?" I stared at the word, showing how I study it. "Hmm, . . . put a thumb up when you're noticing something else about the letters in this word." I gave the children just a moment to study the word. "Is anyone noticing something about the size of the letters in the word?" Nodding, as if agreeing with their observations, I said, "Yes, three of the letters are taller," and I pointed to *M*, *b*, and *l*. "Two are smaller." I pointed to *a* and *e*.

Point out that each letter has its own name. Then, show kids how to cheer each letter to spell the name out loud, using their bodies to show tall, small, and hanging letters.

"Guess what! *Mabel* is our elephant's name, and each of the letters in the word *Mabel* has *its* own name. That's pretty cool. Let's cheer the name of each of the letters that make up the word *Mabel*. Ready? I'll show you how.

"Stand up right in your rug spot and watch what I do. Then, you'll join me." I stood up, signaling for the children to stand as well, and cupped my hands around my mouth to say, "Give me an *M*!" As I did this I held my arms straight over my head in a way that I knew would come to represent all tall letters.

I helped the kids to cheer back, "*M*!"

"Give me an *a*!" This time I bent my arms at my elbows, holding my arms against my chest, and I scrunched down to signal a small letter.

"Give me a *b*!" I modeled, making my arms tall over my head again and pointed to the *b* on the card. "*B* is a tall letter. See how it reaches way up high?"

The kids echoed *b*.

"Is the next letter tall or small?" I pointed under the lowercase *e* and the kids answered, "small." We used our posture to show that there is a small letter and moved on to the *l*.

"What's that spell? *Mabel*!"

Say the name of the first letter of Mabel's name and the sound that it makes. Give examples of other words that start the same way.

"We counted that there are five letters in the name *Mabel*. Let's just look at the first letter in this name: *M*. And *m* goes /mmmm/ . . . *Mabel*. That's the sound that *M* makes: /mmmm/ . . . *Mabel*. What are some other words that start that way? /Mmmm/ . . . *mom*. Oh, that's a good one! /Mmmm/ . . . *me*. Do you hear how these words all sound the same at the beginning? Mmmmom, mmmme, Mmmmmmabel." Children chipped in ideas.

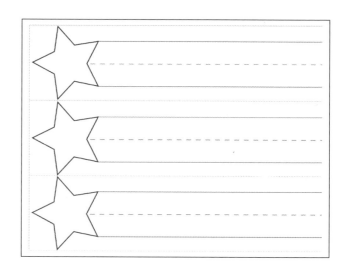

After you ask a question, leave silence into which kids will do their own thinking, supplying their own mental words. Know that kids will see you thinking, and that model will be an influential one.

For letters that dip below the line, such as g or y, you can hang one arm down at your side.

There is a lot of demonstration in this first session. As time goes on and students get more adept at knowing how to study words, you will turn a lot of this work over to them and you'll do more voicing over to coach. But at the start, you'll likely need to take the lead. Be sure to do this in such a way that students are with you. Do your best to be as engaging as possible.

RUG TIME

Invite children to work with a partner to <u>find items in the classroom with the same initial sound as the name of the class mascot.</u>

"Let's see if there are other things in our classroom that start the same way as Mabel's name, with that letter *M*. Will you and the person beside you join hands and go and find something in the room, say its name, and then check if it matches the beginning of *Mabel*? Do they start the same way? Go!" I listened in and coached kids to point to objects in the classroom, saying the word and comparing it to Mabel's name.

Connect w/ ext-2

SHARE • Making a Name Necklace for Today's Star Name

Reconvene kids' attention and rally them to again celebrate the star name by assembling the letters into a name necklace for the class mascot and posting the name onto the name wall.

"One, two, three, eyes on me!" I sang, and once I had everyone's attention, I said, "Hurry back to the meeting area." Then I said, "Let's make a name necklace for our star of the day! I'm going to give out special cards, one for each letter in Mabel's name." I distributed cards to five kids, then held up the class elephant. "The first letter in Mabel's name is an *M*. Who has the *M*?"

As children brought the letter cards forward, I strung them onto a piece of yarn and rallied the class in a cheer for each letter. "Give me an *M*!" The children responded by cheering back, "*M*!" We continued through the name. After the last letter was strung, I tied the necklace around Mabel's neck and announced, "Three cheers for Mabel! Hip, hip, hooray!

"Let's add Mabel's name to the name wall. Where should we put her name? Which letter should she go under?" I waited for a moment, and a couple of students said, *M*! I nodded and pointed to the *Mm* heading, then I ceremoniously attached the sentence strip with Mabel's name and picture underneath it.

EXTENSION 1 • "Willoughby Wallaby Woo"

GETTING READY

- Copies of "Willoughby Wallaby Woo" are available in the Resource Pack.
- A link to a video of "Willoughby Wallaby Woo" is available in the online resources.

Teach students a silly song that they will revisit often throughout this unit and beyond.

"I want to teach you a really silly song! It goes like this." I held Mabel and sang the first verse to the kids.

POSSIBLE COACHING MOVES

▶ "Oh, you pointed to a book. Say it! /b/-book! Now check it with Mabel's name . . . /m/-*Mabel* . . . nope, sounds different. What else can you try?"

▶ "Hmm, . . . I wonder if /m/-mirror starts the same way! Check it with /m/-*Mabel's* name . . . /m/-*mirror*, /m/-*Mabel*. Does it match? Yes! What will you point to next?"

▶ "You're stuck? Try this." I pointed to a marker. "Say the word slooowly . . . now check with the beginning of /m/-*Mabel*. Say /m/-*marker*. Say /m/-*Mabel*. Do they sound the same?"

This process should be super-quick and fun. It should feel like the cheers at halftime in a football game.

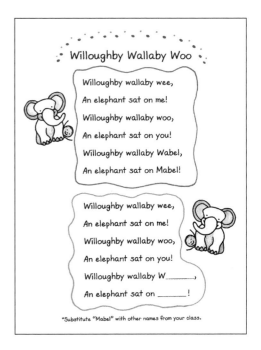

Willoughby Wallaby Woo

Willoughby wallaby wee,
An elephant sat on me!
Willoughby wallaby woo,
An elephant sat on you!
Willoughby wallaby Wabel,
An elephant sat on Mabel!

Willoughby wallaby wee,
An elephant sat on me!
Willoughby wallaby woo,
An elephant sat on you!
Willoughby wallaby W_____,
An elephant sat on _____!

*Substitute "Mabel" with other names from your class.

"Salima, will you hold Mabel? Now let's sing it again!"

Willoughby wallaby woo,
An elephant sat on you!
Willoughby wallaby Walima,
An elephant sat on . . .
"*Salima*!"

Salima passed the elephant to someone else and the class brought that name into the song.

Willoughby wallaby woo,
An elephant sat on you!
Willoughby wallaby Watricia,
An elephant sat on . . .
"*Patricia*!"

We continued to play with several different names.

This song gets kids working on rhyming and initial phonemes, and can be used throughout the unit with other kids' names.

EXTENSION 2 • Identifying *M* Items for the Class Mascot

GETTING READY

- Select a small basket or box for the class mascot to "sleep" in, and gather several objects that begin with the letter *M*.

Act out tucking the class mascot into bed with items that start as her name starts. Hold up items and ask students to determine whether they start with the same sound as *Mabel*.

"Friends, we have to put Mabel to bed before we leave for home! You know how some kids like to snuggle with teddy bears when they go to bed?"

"Well, Mabel doesn't like to snuggle with teddy bears. She likes to sleep surrounded by *M* things, with things that start the same way as her own name. I have this nice shoe box for Mabel to sleep in. Do you think we can find some things for her to snuggle with in her new bed?" The kids agreed. I held up a magnet from the whiteboard. "Let's check to see if Mabel will want this magnet. Say it—/m/ *magnet*. Check it with Mabel's name—do they sound the same? *Magnet*, *Mabel*."

I coached the kids to say both words. "Listen to the first sound. Are they the same? Yes! We can give her this magnet for tonight." I put it in the basket.

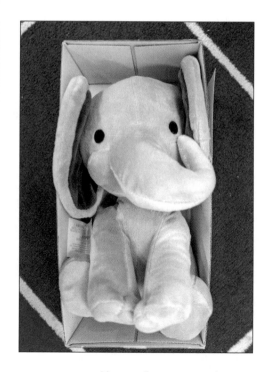

"Let's try something else. How about this pencil? Try saying it to yourself—does *pencil* start the same way as *Mabel*?" The kids tried saying the words, comparing the initial sounds. "What do you think? Will she want this pencil? Does it start the same way as her name?" The kids yelled, "*No!*"

EXTENSION 3 • Creating a Predictable Chart with Class Names

GETTING READY

- Prepare to create a class name chart on chart paper.

Begin a class name chart by writing each class member's name in a sentence and adding the sentence to the chart.

"Since we will be spending a lot of time learning each other's names, let's work together to make a few charts that help us remember how to introduce ourselves. I wrote the first two sentences already. Let's read them together." I gestured for kids to read along if they could as I pointed to each word and read the sentences I had written.

My name is Mabel.

My name is . . .

I called on a few more children and asked for their names to add to the chart. After the chart had five sentences on it, we read it aloud together. I asked each child whose name was in a sentence to come up and point to the words in the sentence as the class read.

I promised to start a second chart tomorrow with five more names on it.

Later that day, I added pictures next to the names on the chart.

We decided against creating one giant chart with a sentence for each child. Long lists of sentences can become too much to read in one sitting. Too much return/sweep can be tricky for beginning readers.

After you have created charts with sentences for each child's name, you might consider stapling them together and creating a big book of names.

Names—and Words—Can Teach Us Letters and Sounds

TODAY YOU'LL remind students that when readers and writers really want to learn a new friend's name, they study it in different ways so that they can remember it.

TODAY YOUR STUDENTS will study a second star name, one that begins with the same letter as the name the class has already studied. You will guide kids to study the name as they did yesterday: read the name, count and name the letters, observe the shapes and sizes of the letters, cheer the name, note the first letter and sound.

GETTING READY

✔ Today's star name should be a student's name that begins with the same letter as your class mascot. We use *M*, for Mabel. If no students' names begin with *M*, choose a name beginning with a different consonant from early in the sequence of recommended letters.

✔ Before this session, choose a large opaque container for a Star Jar. For each child, make a paper strip with the child's name and photo and a star drawn around the photo, as you did for the class mascot. Develop a system to secretly manipulate the contents so you draw the intended name.

✔ Decide on rug spots and on partnerships for the class. Likely you'll use the same rug spots and partnerships as reading, or writing.

✔ Find cards for the *M*/not-*M* picture sort. Organize into one baggie for each partnership.

✔ Prepare an Elkonin box to help students isolate the first sound in words.

✔ Prepare to create a class *M* book. Use the templates provided to make a class booklet, into which you can paste pictures of Mabel and items beginning with *M*. Or, print a cover for your book and simply staple the pictures and the cover together to make the book.

PHONICS INSTRUCTION

Concepts About Print
• Use one's name to learn about words.

Phonological Awareness
• Hear and say syllables.
• Identify and produce groups of words that begin with the same sound (alliteration).

• Identify the initial phonemes of spoken words.

Letter Knowledge
• Recognize uppercase and lowercase letters.
• Recognize the names/sounds of letters.

MINILESSON

CONNECTION

Lead children in the "We Are Gathering" song, then pull a name from the Star Jar, telling kids the first letter in the name. Later show the sentence strip conveying the star-name child.

I signaled for children to join me in the meeting area by singing the "We Are Gathering" song, which they learned during reading workshop. I ushered them to their same rug spots from reading workshop, sitting alongside their reading partners, who would also be their partners for phonics time.

When they were all assembled, I reached over to the shelf where Mabel lay "napping" and

Our Gathering Song
● We are gathering.
● We are gathering.
● On the rug.
● On the rug.
● Everyone is here now,
● finding their own space now.
● We are here.
● We are here.

whispered, "Mabel . . . Mabel . . . Wake up! The kids are here! It's time for Star Name. Your favorite!" I lifted Mabel gently from her resting spot, pretending that she had awoken.

Then I turned to the children and said, "Mabel and I have something super-exciting to show you today. This is our Star Jar. All of your names are in this jar." I held up a container and tipped it so kids could see the colorful stars inside. "When it is Star Name time, we will pull out a new name or two to study, and we'll study that name just like we studied Mabel's name. That name or those names will be our star name for the day."

I sang the first verse of the "Guess the Name" song to the tune of "The Farmer in the Dell."

> Can you guess the name?
> Can you guess the name?
> Hi-ho, the derry-o
> Can you guess the name?

I reached into the jar and dramatically pulled out one of the paper stars. I peeked at the name and whispered, "It starts with . . . an *M*!"

I looked at the name, but I didn't show it to the class. To give students a hint, I sang the first line of a new verse of "Guess the Name." When I reached the second line, I gestured for students to join in to sing the rest of the verse.

> It starts with an *M*
> It starts with an *M*
> Hi-ho, the derry-o
> Can you guess the name?

A couple of the children shouted out guesses. I turned the sentence strip over, revealing it to the class, and said, "Today the star name will be . . . *Mike*! Let's get ready to study Mike's name."

♣ **Name the teaching point.**

"Today I want to remind you that when you want to learn a new friend's name—like we will want to learn Mike's name—it helps to do stuff with that name, so you remember it, so it becomes part of you."

TEACHING

Explore the star name by coaching children through the replicable strategy of reading the name, counting and naming the letters, studying and talking about the shapes, sizes, heights of the letters.

I showed the class a sentence strip with Mike's name and photo on it, then taped it to the easel. "This word is *Mike*. Let's notice some things about this special word—the name of our friend." I gestured to Mike, who waved, and the class cheered.

This teaching point is almost identical to yesterday's—that is very unusual. Providing a similar teaching point today will solidify yesterday's brand-new routines with repeated practice. Establishing the star name routine will allow students to concentrate on the letter of the day, rather than on figuring out new routines.

Today, you'll guide students through the same sequence of steps as you did yesterday to study the star name: counting the letters, noticing the size of the letters, cheering the name of each letter, and studying the first letter. After this sequence, invite children to notice whether all of the letters are different from each other or whether some are the same. This work is crucial because it helps your kindergarten kids look extra closely at letters to distinguish one from another.

"Let's count how many letters are in the name *Mike*." I pointed under each letter as kids chimed in, counting along with me. "Wow! There are *four* letters in the name *Mike*.

"What else can we notice? Look closely and give a thumbs up when you notice something else about the letters in this word." I gave the children just a moment to study the word. "Oh, we could think about the size of those letters, right? Thumbs up if you noticed something about the size of the letters in the word. Two of the letters are taller" (I pointed to *M* and *k*) "and two are smaller" (I pointed to *i* and *e*).

"There's one more thing we might do to learn the name *Mike*. Let's look at all of the letters and notice if some are the same or if all of the letters are different." I covered the letters in Mike's name with a blank sheet of paper and slowly revealed one letter at a time, guiding the kids to study each letter along with me. "None of the letters in the name *Mike* are the same. There are four different letters in the name *Mike*."

Point out that each letter has its own name. Then, show kids how to cheer each letter to spell the name out loud, and how to use their bodies to show if a letter is tall, small, or hanging.

"This word is our friend's name: Mike. Remember that each of the letters in the word *Mike* has its own name. Let's cheer the name of each of the letters inside the word *Mike*. Ready?

"Stand up right in your rug spot and cheer with me." I stood up and cupped my hands around my mouth to say, "Give me an *M*!" I added, "It's a tall letter, so let's make it tall," and I held my arms up high straight over my head, signaling a tall letter, and kids followed along.

"Give me an *M*!"

"*M*!" the kids cheered back.

We cheered the remaining letters together. "The last letter of *Mike* is *e*. What's that spell? *Mike*!"

Say the name of the first letter and the sound that it makes. Give examples of other words that start the same way.

"Let's just look at the first letter in this name. This is the letter *M*. And *M* goes /mmmm/, *Mike*. *M* goes /mmmm/ like in *Mike*. /Mmmm/ . . . *Mabel*. /Mmmm/ . . . *mom*. Oh, that's a good one! /Mmmm/ . . . *me*.

"Do we have any other kids in *this* class whose names start the same as Mmmmmike and Mmmmabel? Let's look." I pointed to the class name chart and read through a few of the names. "Mmmmike, Fffrancisco. Nope, not the same. Hmm, . . . Mmmike, Mmmary. Oh, *Mary* has that same sound too!"

Be prepared to respond if students notice any other attributes of the letters in the name you study.

In 2016, at the National Reading Recovery Conference, trainer Mary Fried spoke about how very beginning readers need to be taught how to move left to right through words. If children are having trouble with this concept, you may consider using a 3 × 5 blank index card to uncover letters from left to right to help guide the eyes of your kindergarten children.

Again, this is meant to feel like a cheer at a football game. Be a cheerleader. Move quickly.

ACTIVE ENGAGEMENT/LINK

Channel students to recap some of the ways they've learned to study a friend's name.

"Friends, in the last two days, we have learned so many things we can do to learn a friend's name. Would you turn and tell your partner some of the things you might do the next time you are learning a friend's name?"

While students talked, I listened in to partnerships, nodding agreement and offering brief reminders.

After a few moments, I gathered the class back together. "You all are becoming name study experts already! I heard you saying that to study names, you count the letters, notice the shape of the letters, cheer the names of the letters, and notice whether the letters are all different or whether some are the same."

Summarize what the class has learned thus far, emphasizing the transferable lessons.

"You have already looked closely at the names of two new friends: Mabel and Mike. And both of those names start in the same way, with the letter *M*, which makes the /m/ sound. When you're reading your books or when you are out in the world, you can keep a lookout for other *M* words. When you find one, say a silent *M* cheer to yourself!"

RUG TIME

Demonstrate for students how they might sort picture cards to find more words that start with the /m/ sound.

"Now that you know so much about the letter *M* and the sound it makes, /mmm/, let's find some other things that start with the letter *M*, like *Mike* and *Mabel*. I have some picture of things, some of them start with /m/ *M* and some do not. When I hold one up, will you and your partner read the picture and then give me a thumbs up if it starts with /m/ *M*? Give me a thumbs down if it does not." I held up picture of a monkey, and said, "Monkey. Will you and your partner read the picture to each other? Say 'monkey,' and then decide to give this a thumbs up if it starts with an *M* like *Mabel* and *Mike*, or a thumbs down if it doesn't." I gave children time to do this, and then continued, "Yes, Mmmmonkey starts with *M*. Let's put it in the *M* pile."

I held up a picture of a bear. I said, "Bear." I again coached students to say the word themselves—to "read" the picture—and then students signaled with thumbs down to show that no, this did not start with an *M*. I said, "B-b-b-bear." I touched the first box on the left of the Elkonin box I had drawn as I said the /m/ sound. "Mmmmmabel. They don't sound the same. B-b-b-bear is not *M*, it starts with *B*. *Bear* goes in the Not-an-*M* pile."

Remember, your primary aim is to teach letter sounds. So be sure to say the letter sound along with the name when you invite children to sort.

Invite children to work with partners to sort a stack of pictures into *M* and Not-an-*M* piles.

"You are so good at this that I'm going to pass out stacks of pictures, one stack for each partnership. With your partner, read each picture and ask yourself, 'Does this word begin with a /m/-*M* or not /m/, Not-an-*M*?'" As I said this, I pointed to the first square of an Elkonin box I had drawn. "In front of you, you'll make two piles: a /m/-*M* pile and a Not-/m/ pile. Are you ready, partners?"

I passed around the pictures for partners to sort through and coached partners in sorting. After a few minutes, I called out. "Would you and your partner go through your /m/ *M* pile and read each word aloud to yourselves, and check to make sure that they all sound the same?"

After they had time to do this, I sang, "Stop, look, and listen!," waiting to check that I had kids' focus. "Show me your favorite *M* picture. What words did you find that start with the /m/ sound just like *Mike* and *Mabel*? Whoa, *monkey*? *Mom*? *Mug*?"

I pulled out a blank book and wrote a capital *M* on the cover. "We can put all of the /m/ *M* pictures together and make an *M* book. Read the pictures with me as I glue them into our book. Let's make sure each one starts with the /m/." Before I began, I slipped some pictures into the pile that did not begin with *M* so that students would have the opportunity to point out that those did not belong.

I led the class in saying the name for each picture along with me. I asked them to gesture with a thumbs up or a thumbs down to signal if the picture belonged in the *M* book. Then, I quickly glued each *M* picture into the book.

I reached for two more pictures from behind the easel. "I know what can make this book even better." I revealed the pictures of Mabel and Mike. "We can put *Mabel* and *Mike* in the book. What do you think?" The class cheered, and I glued their pictures into the book.

SHARE • Practicing a Letter Name and Sound

Post today's name onto the name wall, then introduce your class to a song that you will sing to celebrate each star name and practice letter name and sound.

I added Mike's name to the name wall beneath Mabel's. "Three cheers for Mike! Hip, hip, hooray!

"Now, I want to teach you a special song to celebrate today's star name. It's called the 'Star Name Celebration Song.' We can sing it every time we learn a new name! It goes to the tune of 'Old MacDonald Had a Farm.'" I hummed a little bit of the tune and then invited the children to join in when they could.

"Soon we'll study and sing everyone's name. I can't wait to find out which friend we'll get to know next!"

You will be making more letter books like this in future sessions, so you may want to plan ahead now. To save time later, make several blank booklets now out of plain paper—perhaps a dozen or so. Gather pictures of items for kids to sort by their initial letter; presort them by letter into separate baggies if you have time, being sure to include several in each pile that do not start with the same initial letter. You might also want to select a bin to hold your letter books.

When you sing this song, in the section that starts "With a . . . ," be sure to make the letter sound rather than say the letter name.

EXTENSION 1 • "Willoughby Wallaby Woo" with a Star Name

Remind children about the "Willoughby Wallaby Woo" song and sing it this time with today's star name.

"Class, remember that silly song we learned yesterday?" I began to sing:

> Willoughby wallaby woo,
> An elephant sat on you!

"Will you join me? Get ready for the silly part when I add a new name! See if you can figure out whose name it is!" The class joined me as I sang the verse.

> Willoughby wallaby *wike*
> An elephant sat on . . .

"*Mike*!" the kids yelled, and I gave them a thumbs up. I continued to sing, adding on yesterday's verse using the name *Mabel*.

Think about how much you love returning to old favorite songs. Your kids will love that too. After all, kids like yours are insisting on Mom and Dad rereading Goodnight Moon *every single day for months on end! So know that harkening back to yesterday's extension will be comforting for kids. Return to any song you introduce, and do so often, whether we mention that song in an extension or not.*

EXTENSION 2 • Tucking More *M* Items into Mabel's Bed

Bring back the class mascot to engage your students in repeated practice of identifying initial sounds.

"Friends, let's tuck Mabel into bed before we leave! Remember, she likes to sleep surrounded by *M* things. Yesterday we gave her this /m/ magnet. What else could we put in Mabel's bed? Work with each other to give me some suggestions." I voiced over as the students discussed. "Oh, I just heard /m/ marker—she will definitely like that! Do you think we should put this soap in her bed?" The kids yelled out, "That is not an /m/ thing!"

Learning to Own Letters

GETTING READY

✔ Gather some magnetic letters and letter formation cards, making sure one of the letter cards has the letter *M*.

✔ Be ready to display the "How to Learn a Letter" anchor chart.

✔ Make sure that all children can see the name wall.

✔ Select a book for each partnership. These can be any high-interest books from your classroom.

✔ Gather Post-its® for students to use and place them on the cover of each high-interest book you choose.

PHONICS INSTRUCTION

Concepts About Print
• Understand the concepts of letter and word.

Phonological Awareness
• Identify and produce groups of words that begin with the same sound (alliteration).
• Identify the initial phonemes of spoken words.

Letter Knowledge
• Recognize and name all upper- and lowercase letters of the alphabet.
• Recognize the names/sounds of letters.
• Use efficient and consistent motions to form letters.

Word Knowledge/Solving
• Make connections between names and other words.

IN THIS SESSION

TODAY YOU'LL teach students that when readers and writers want to know a letter well, they name it, sound it, write it, and use it to make lots of words.

TODAY YOUR STUDENTS will try these steps using letter *M*. You'll say the same steps to write the letters in the same way each time, thus creating a pathway that will help students internalize the letter formation.

MINILESSON

CONNECTION

Point out that to read and write with letters, kids need to feel as if they own them. They need those letters to be in their back pockets.

I invited students to the meeting area by singing the "We Are Gathering" song. When everyone found their spots, I began. "Writers, readers, when we met the other day, I told you that to read and write *lots* of books, you'll need not just books and paper and pens, but also these." I held a big scoop of magnetic letters in my hands, letting them fall from my hands like a dramatic waterfall. "I told you that you are going to need all these letters and sounds so that you can make (and read) tons of words!

"But here's the truth. It isn't enough for you to be able to grab armloads of these letters. You actually need to *own* each of these letters. You need each of these letters to be . . . " and I slid a letter into my pocket, " . . . in your back pocket." I slapped my pocket several times.

❦ **Name the teaching point.**

"Today I want to teach you that to own a letter, to know that letter so well that you have it in your back pocket, ready to use whenever you read or write, it helps to do some things with the letter. It helps to name the letter, sound it, write it, and to use it to make lots of words."

TEACHING AND ACTIVE ENGAGEMENT/LINK

Provide children with practice in naming and sounding the letter you are helping them to "own."

"Let's try this work together." I posted a card containing a capital and lowercase *M* onto the easel. "*M* is the first letter in Mike's name"—I pointed to the *M* in *Mike* on the name wall—"and also the first letter in Mabel's name." I moved my finger to the *M* in Mabel's name.

"Let's say the name of this letter together." I pointed to the giant *M* that I had placed on the easel. "Everybody point to the letter and say it with me." I nodded as the class pointed and called out "*M*." "Let's whisper its name." I whispered, "*M*" and nodded encouragingly for children to whisper. "Let's shout the name!" I let the kindergartners yell out, "*M*!"

"Now that we know the *name*, let's *sound* it together. *M* says, 'Mmmm,' like in *MMMabel*. *M* says /mmm/ like in *MMMike*. Everyone sound it with me: /mmm/. Let's stretch the sound even longer, mmmmmmmmm. Let's do it again, this time adding Mabel's name. /mmmmmmmm/ *MMMMMabel*."

Channel children to write the capital version of the letter several times with invisible markers, first in the air and then on the carpet, repeating the letter formation pathway each time.

"Now that we can name the letter *M*, and we can sound the letter *M*, let's *write* it! We can write this letter in two ways. We can write it uppercase, or capital, like this one." I pointed to the uppercase *M* I'd displayed at the start of the minilesson and also to the capital *M* on Mabel's necklace. "Or we can write it small—or lowercase—like this *m*." I pointed to the small *m* that I'd displayed at the start of the minilesson. "Try it with me! Let's all write the capital *M*, writing in the air! Everyone, arms out in front of you." I voiced over the letter formation pathway as students wrote in the air, "Line down! Back up! Slanted line down. Slanted line up. Line down!

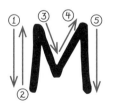

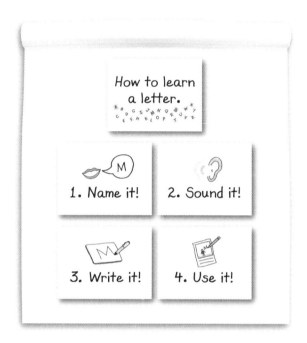

Note that in your first two sessions, you essentially taught kids how to come to know—to own—a name. Now you are zooming in and helping them to come to know—to own—a letter.

You'll definitely want kids to engage in whole-arm invisible writing along with you. The large physical actions will help them. You'll probably want to follow the letter formation pathways exactly unless your school has another version it prefers. The important thing is that whatever language you use to say the way you write the letter, you stay consistent with that language throughout your teaching of letter-sound work.

"Let's write it again! Capital *M* goes like this." I once more led the kids in making the capital *M* using the letter formation pathway. I invited the kids to make the letter three times with me. Each time we did this, more students joined in. "Say the sound that letter makes with me, ready? /Mmmmmm/—*M* says /mmmmm/.

"Now let's write it on the rug with invisible markers!" I wrote the letter on my easel whiteboard, making sure to use consistent strokes and keep my language the same. "I am going to start high." I pressed my marker at the top of the board. "Then, capital *M* goes like this—Line down! Back up! Slanted line down. Slanted line up. Line down!

"With your make-believe marker, will you write capital *M*? I'll watch. Remember: start high on the page. Line down! Back up! Slanted line down. Slanted line up. Line down!" I scanned the meeting area, watching as children made the strokes to "write" the capital letter.

Introduce the lowercase letter and repeat this process of model writing with the lowercase version of the letter, repeating the letter formation pathway each time.

"Now let's write the lowercase *m*." I pointed to Mabel's name tag and the letter *M* on the name wall and said, "The capital *M* and the lowercase *m* have the same name, *M*, and the same sound, /mmmm/, but they look different. Watch me first." I turned my body away once more and held my arm out in front of me. "I start a little lower. Then, line down! Back up. Bump around. Bump around and down.

"Let's do it in the air together. Don't start as high as the first time. Start a little lower." I repeated the letter formation pathway: "Make this be your best small *m* ever! Let's go: Line down. Back up. Bump around. Bump around and down." The students copied my movements. "Nice job. Try again." And I coached kids to do this two more times.

"Now I am going to write the small *m*!" I got my invisible marker ready and put it on the invisible chart paper. "I'll put them together because they are a team. Watch me! I start a little lower. Then, line down! Back up. Bump around. Bump around and down.

"Your turn. Magic paper out? Make-believe marker ready? Use your hand as pretend paper and make the lowercase *m*, the small one. Start lower than the big *M*. Line down. Back up. Bump around. Bump around and down. Beautiful! Write it again!"

Channel students to read the letter _M_. Remind them of the sound _M_ makes and invite them to use the sound.

"Now writers, you have written the _M_ lots of times. Try reading it. /Mmmm/. That's the sound you make when food is good, isn't it? Mmmm!" I rubbed my stomach and mmm-ed contentedly, inviting kids to follow. "What sound do you make when food is good?" The kids "mmmm-ed."

"That sound can also be the noise you make when you want to say, 'Don't do that!' I shook my head, meaning _no_, and said, "Mm-mmm." Then I added, "Try that with me. Shake your head when you do it." I leaned forward, inviting kids to follow suit, shaking their heads and saying, "Mm-mmm."

Sum up and help support transfer by helping students imagine times they would write the letter _M_.

"Congratulations, readers, writers. You now _own_ the letter _M_. You can put it in your back pocket and pull it out whenever you need it. So, writers, if you wanted to write a book about your family, and you drew a picture of yourself, and you wanted to label yourself with the word _me_, what would you write?"

The kids called out, "_M_!"

"Yes, _M_ for /m/-_me_. And if your mom asked you what treat you wanted on a hot summer day, and what you really wanted was a _milkshake_, what would you write? Yes, _M_ for /m/-_milkshake_."

RUG TIME

Organize students into partnerships and give each partnership a book. Invite partners to search for words that begin with _M_ in their book. If time allows, have partnerships swap books.

"Writers, readers, yesterday we wrote a book together, and we filled it with _M_ things. We tucked Mabel into bed in her shoebox with _M_ things. Today, I was thinking that maybe you'd like to read a book, and to see if you can find words in that book that begin with the letter we have in our back pockets. The letter is _M_!

"I'm going to give you and the person next to you a book. Will you read the book together? If you see something on one of those pages that starts with an _M_, will you mark that part with a Post-it? There are Post-its stuck onto the covers of each of the books." As students worked, I added, "Make sure you'll be able to see your Post-it when your book is closed!"

The children worked for a bit and then I sang, "Stop, Look, and Listen," to get their attention. "Okay, friends, hold your books up in the air!" A few students began arguing over who could hold up the book. "Look at the way Tymel and Jessica are holding their book together." I motioned for students to look at the partnership. "They each have a hand on one side of the book. That's teamwork! Can everyone try that with your partner? Amazing!

"Now we are going to trade books. When you get a new book, see if you can go to the parts of the book that your friends have marked and see if you can find the *M* word that they marked. This isn't easy work, so when I hand you your book, get started!" I quickly grabbed the books students were holding up and passed them to new partnerships.

SHARE • Finding Initial Sounds in Words and Pictures

Share the words that two partnerships found, highlighting that some students found words in the text starting with *M*, while others found something in a picture that started with the /m/ sound.

"Kindergartners, you did some hard work today searching for *M* words in your books! Kim, can you come up and show the class the word you and your partner found?" Kim came up and pointed to the word *me*. "Wow, you found the word *me*! And Abbie, you put your Post-it next to something different, didn't you? Can you come up and show the class?" Abbie came up and pointed to the picture of a mom in her book. "You're right, *mom* does start with the /m/ sound! Learning our letters and sounds can help us read the words *and* the pictures in our books."

EXTENSION 1 • Putting Mabel's Name Necklace Back in Order

GETTING READY

- Before this extension, shuffle the letters on the class mascot's name necklace, so they are in the wrong order.

Invite students to help put Mabel's name necklace back in order. Set them up to talk in pairs. Remind them to study her name on the name chart if they need help.

"Kindergartners, come quickly, I need your help! Mabel was so excited about her name necklace that she spent all night playing with it. But when she went to put it back on, she couldn't remember the order of the letters. She put them back on all out of order! Can we help her put her name necklace back in the right order? Let's look at her name on the name chart to help us." I pointed to Mabel's name on the chart and then back to her jumbled name on her necklace. "Hmm, . . . turn to someone next to you. What should we do first to fix Mabel's name?" I listened in as students talked.

"I was listening to you all talk, and I heard Corrie say we need to move the *M* to the front." I took the letters off of Mabel's necklace. "Corrie, can you come up and string the *M* back where it belongs?

Wow, thank you! I know Mabel really appreciates that help!" Other students came up one at a time and helped put the rest of Mabel's name back in order. Some children could not say the name of the letter when they wanted to move it but they could point to it or describe what it looked like.

"Thanks for your help, everyone! Let's read Mabel's name together now that we have the letters in the right order." I pointed to the letters as we read them, moving left to right across the word. We repeated this a few times, and then I ceremoniously strung Mabel's necklace around her neck.

EXTENSION 2 • Reading a Picture Book to Practice Rhyming

GETTING READY

- Before this session, choose a book with a simple rhyme pattern that is easy to hear. We use Mem Fox's *Time for Bed*.

Read a rhyming picture book, leaving space for students to fill in rhyming words based on the pattern of the story.

"Class, I brought a book to read to you today. Most kids love this book so much, they join in while I'm reading it. Even if you've never read this book before, I bet you'll be able to jump right in. You will know when it is your turn because I will lean my head toward you and wait for you to say the word that goes in that part. Are you ready?"

I began to read, "It's time for bed little mouse, little mouse," and I emphasized the second *mouse* to signal that word was important. I continued reading, "Darkness is falling all over the . . . " I stopped before the rhyming word *house*, and I again tilted my head toward the children. When no one called out *house*, I read the word, then continued. I continued to pause at the end of each couplet, and soon children were guessing rhyming words.

Trust in the process of repeated practice here, even if your students aren't guessing the rhymes. Try not to do too much explaining and resist the urge to post the rhyming words up on the easel so that children can study their spelling similarities. Remember, the focus of your teaching at this point in the unit is phonological awareness, so here you invite children to listen to sounds in words.

By Studying Names, We Can Learn More Letters

GETTING READY

✔ Prepare to pull a star name from the Star Jar beginning with the letter *S* or another easy initial consonant that children will be able to use to spell lots of other words.

✔ Locate cards for the *S/not-S* picture sort.

✔ Draw an Elkonin box, a rectangle divided into thirds.

✔ Prepare the "Let's Study a Name!" anchor chart.

PHONICS INSTRUCTION

Concepts About Print
• Understand the concept of *first* in written language.

Phonological Awareness
• Connect words by sounds.
• Identify the initial phonemes of spoken words.

Letter Knowledge
• Recognize and name all upper- and lowercase letters of the alphabet.
• Recognize the name/sound of letters.
• Understand that there is a relationship between sounds and letters.

IN THIS SESSION

TODAY YOU'LL teach students a secret that can help them learn many letters: for a lot of letters, when you know the letter's name, you know the letter's sound.

TODAY YOUR STUDENTS will engage in a name study of a child's name that begins with letter *S* to learn this letter and the sound it makes. During rug time, they will do a card sort to find pictures that begin with an *S* sound. They'll also search the classroom for items that begin with *S*.

MINILESSON

CONNECTION

Tell children that one reason it is so cool to learn letters is because this lets them write more things.

While singing the "We Are Gathering" song, everyone found their spots. "Writers, you have learned to write letter *M*'s, and yesterday I actually saw some *M*'s cropping up in your stories. I saw an /m/-*McDonald's* in Tony's writing, and am I right that David, you had a picture of macaroni? And you labeled it with an *M* because you heard the /m/ sound, right?

"But friends, here's the thing. Your writing will be pretty wacky if the whole story has to be filled only with words that begin with *M*. Suppose you wanted to write this," and I pretended to write in the air as I said, "At the movies, I asked Mom for money for a snack.

"If you only had *M*'s, you'd have to say that you asked /m/-Mom for /m/-money for a mmmack. That'd be silly! So, writers, I am pretty sure you agree that I have to teach you a lot *more* letters, really soon. *And* you have to start learning letters on your own, without me even teaching you. So, let's study another star name and see if that star name can teach you another letter."

Lead children through the now-familiar steps of a star name study, doing this extra quickly to save time for a deeper study of the initial consonant.

I led the class in singing the "Guess the Name" song to the tune of "The Farmer in the Dell," as I pulled another star name from the jar. The name was *Salima*.

Can you guess the name?
Can you guess the name?
Hi-ho, the derry-o
Can you guess the name?
It starts with an *S*
It starts with an *S*
Hi-ho, the derry-o
Can you guess the name?

"What do you notice when you study the name *Salima*?" I asked. "Turn and tell your partner"

"Some of you noticed that Salima's name has a lot of small letters. Nod if you noticed that." I nodded along with children. Others noticed Salima's name has an *m* in it, wow! Mabel and Mike's letter is inside Sali-mmmma's name. Thumbs up if you noticed that!"

Help the class cheer the star name, briskly, and discuss what they notice when they study the letters.

"Are you ready to cheer this word? Everyone, stand up and give me an *S*!" I stretched my arms high in the air, to indicate the tallness of the letter, urging children to follow suit.

"Give me an *a*!" I crouched down low to show the *a* was a small letter. Give me an *l*! Stretch back up high!" We did this, and then cheered the rest of the letters together. "What's that spell?"

"*Salima*!" We all cheered together. "Now that we've gotten to know Salima's name, let's use her name to help us get a new letter in our back pocket." I slapped my pocket. I wrote uppercase and lowercase *S*'s on my whiteboard easel.

 Name the teaching point.

"Today I want to teach you that when you learn the letter *S*, you learn a secret that will help you learn tons of other letters. This is the secret: for many letters, when you know the letter's name, you can figure out the letter's sound."

Note that the star name part of this session is done in the connection, so that the rest of the minilesson can help kids grasp the new letter—in this case, S. Kids will learn a second star name during an extension to today's lesson. You need to pick up the pace to get through your whole class!

We chose the name Salima because it begins with a consonant that is particularly accessible, in that the name of the letter helps to say its sound.

POSSIBLE COACHING MOVES

▸ "Yes, there are six letters. Can you spot the two that are the same?"

▸ "Do you recognize any letters you know inside Salima's name?"

▸ "Are there some tall letters, some small letters? How many are tall?"

TEACHING

Guide children through the steps of making friends with a new letter. Begin by naming it, sounding it.

"So, class, what is the name of this letter?" I pointed to the uppercase and lowercase *S*. The class chimed in that it is an *S*. "Yes, and *S* makes the /s/ sound, let's all make the letter *S*'s sound together, ready?" The students made /s/ sounds. As they did so, I cupped my hand behind my ear, listening. "You are right. The letter name ends with the letter's sound.

"Let's learn this letter so we have it in our back pocket," I said. "Hello class, I'd like you to meet . . . " and I pointed to the letter. The class chimed in "*S*." I cupped my hand behind my ear, the gesture suggesting that I wanted to know the letter's sound. They said /s/, so I added, "/s/-*Salima*, /s/-*snake*, /s/-*Stegosaurus*, /s/. The letter *S* makes the /s/ sound, so any time I hear the /s/ sound at the beginning of a word I know it starts with /s/ *S*."

Move children into writing the capital letter, writing in the air as you voice over the letter formation pathway.

"Before we can own the letter *S*, let's practice making it the right way." I guided students through writing the letter *S* in the air as I voiced over the letter formation pathway. "To write the letter, bump around, slide down, bump around the other way and stop.

Because this is still very early in kindergarten, kids need repeated practice naming the letters in a word and clarifying what a letter is in contrast to a word. Repeated study of the shapes and sizes of letters helps solidify these concepts.

"And guess what? Lowercase *s* is written the same way, just a little smaller. Let's try the *S* again, this time, making it smaller, so it's lowercase." I voiced over the same letter formation pathway as students wrote in the air.

"Let's do it again! This time, take out your magic paper and make-believe pen and get ready to write the *S* on the rug. What color is your make-believe pen? Green? Red? Glittery? Whisper your color to your friend! Now we're ready to write the first part of Salima's name, the capital *S*. Bump around, slide down, bump around the other way and stop." I led children through this another two to three times. "Your *S*'s are /s/-spectacular. They're /s/-super /s/-superb!"

The letter S is the first letter students have learned that is made almost the same way in its capital and lowercase forms, so it makes sense to emphasize this point here. Be sure to point this out for the other seven letters that fall into this category when you teach them (C, O, U, V, W, X, and Z).

ACTIVE ENGAGEMENT/LINK

Help children use the letter's sound to think of other words that start with the same sound, then add the name to the name wall.

"Let's use the /s/ sound of the *S* to think of more /s/ words! *S* makes the sound /s/ like the hissing of a snake. Let's hiss like snakes using /s/, /s/, /s/, /s/, /s/. What other words begin like this? /s/-*Salima*?" We soon had a list: /s/-*silly*, /s/-*slide*, /s/-*spaghetti*, /s/-*superhero*." I encouraged the children to shout out other words that began with the /s/ sound.

I added Salima's name and photo to the name wall under the *Ss* heading and led the class in the "Star Name Celebration Song."

Salima, Salima is a star
Clap, clap, clap, clap, clap
Salima's name starts with *S*
S, S, S, S, S

With a /s/ /s/ here and a /s/ /s/ there
Here a /s/ there a /s/
Everywhere a /s/ /s/
Salima, Salima is a star
/s/ /s/ /s/ /s/ /s/

RUG TIME

Show picture cards and have students listen for the words that start with *S*. Then give a stack of picture cards to sort.

"Now that you know the letter *S*, you can find *S* words everywhere. Let's try it!" I have some pictures of things; some of them start with /s/-*S* and some do not. As I said this, I pointed to the first box in an Elkonin box I had drawn to help children isolate the first sound.

"When I hold a card up, read the picture and then give me a thumbs up if it starts with /s/-*S*, or thumbs down if it does not." I held up picture of a snail. Most of the kids gave a thumbs up. "*Snail* starts with /s/-*S*. I'll put *snail* in the S pile. I held up a picture of a goat. Many thumbs turned down. "Tell your friend why." After children talked, I said, "*G-g-g-goat* does not start like /s/ *Salima*. *Goat* goes in the Not-an-*S* pile.

"Now, get together with the friend next to you, your partner for today. In a minute, I'm going to pass out some pictures, one set for each partnership. With your partner, read the picture and ask yourself, 'Does this word begin with an /s/-*S* or Not-an-*S*?' In front of you, you'll make two piles: an /s/-*S* pile and a Not-an-*S* pile. Are you ready, partners?"

After a couple of minutes, I called out. "Would you and your partner hold up some of your /s/-*Salima* words? What words did you find that start with the /s/ sound like *Salima*?" The kids held them up and said the words they represented. "Whoa, *soup*? *Socks*? *Sun*? These are all terrific /s/ words."

Channel kids to walk around the room finding objects that start with *S*.

"We have two more minutes in our phonics workshop. Can you and your partner for today hold hands and go around this room, seeing if you can find things that start with the /s/ sound? When you get to something, touch it and say its name and listen for the /s/ sound. You might also find some things that start with /m/-*M*."

POSSIBLE COACHING MOVES

▶ "Can you read that picture? A pumpkin? Is *pumpkin* an /s/-*S* word? Let's see: /p/-/p/-/p/-*pumpkin* . . . /s/-/s/-/s/-*Salima*. Do they sound the same? No? Then put that in the Not-an-*S* pile."

▶ "Interesting! You found a /m/-*Mabel* word? *Mmmmountain*? That's so smart! Let's show everyone. Maybe we can make a new *M* pile for words what begin with /m/."

▶ "Can you think of other words that start with *S*, like *Salima*?"

SHARE • Introducing the "Let's Study a Name!" Chart

Remind children that charts are helpful for remembering steps in a process. Introduce the "Let's Study a Name!" chart that will help children remember how to study names.

"Class, I noticed that when you came into the classroom today, you knew how to unpack. I didn't have to tell you to hang up your coat, put away lunch, or come to the rug for meeting—you did it without asking me for help.

"I was thinking that because we are studying star names every day, maybe we could have a chart that reminds us of how to study star names. Does that sound like a good idea? Then we could just pull a name from the jar and you all could study it without me even telling you what to do." I put up the "Let's Study a Name!" chart. I pointed to each bullet and read them aloud, then gestured for kids to read the steps along with me.

EXTENSION 1 • Studying a *T* Star Name

Guide students to study a new star name, using the "Let's Study a Name!" chart to remind them of the steps.

"Let's use our new chart from earlier to help us study another star name." I led the class in singing the "Guess the Name" song as I reached into the Star Jar and pulled out the name *Tymel*.

"Okay, what do we do first?" I asked the class, pointing to the first bullet on the chart. "Read it!" The students responded. We read Tymel's name together. "What's next?" I asked, pointing to the second line. "Count the letters!" We counted the letters together on our fingers. "Okay, time to study the letters! Tell your partner what you notice about the letters in Tymel's name.

"You noticed a lot about the letters in Tymel's name! I heard some of you talking about this letter, here," and I tapped on the *y*. "This letter has a hangy-tail. We'll talk about that more when we cheer Tymel's name.

"Let's think about the letter and sound that /t/-*Tymel* starts with. *Tymel* starts with the letter *T*. *T* makes the /t/ sound. I hear /t/ at the beginning of /t/-*Tymel*. Let's make *T*'s sound together, ready?"

"/t/ /t/ /t/," the class said together.

"Yes, the letter *T* has the /t/ sound, just like in /t/-*toast* and /t/-*turtle*.

Because T is a stop-consonant, model the "shortness" of the /t/ sound. This is not "tuh" but /t/. Correct the kids if they make a "tuh" sound as some are sure to do.

"A time to cheer Tymel's name! Give me a *T*! Give me a . . . a . . . hey! Wait a second. The letter *y* isn't just small. It has a hangy-tail." I pointed to lowercase *y* in Tymel's name. "See that tail?" I bent down and let one arm hang low to indicate a tail, nodding for children to repeat my movement as they "gave me the *y*."

"Give me an *m* . . . " we cheered the remaining letters together. "What's that spell?"

"*Tymel*!" We all cheered his name together. "Now that we've gotten to know Tymel's name, let's use his name to help us get a new letter in our back pocket." I slapped my pocket. I wrote an uppercase and lowercase *Tt* on my whiteboard easel.

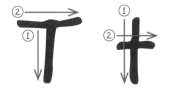

Move children into writing the capital letter, by writing in the air.

"Now we're ready to write. Stand up tall like me and raise your arm up high because this letter is a tall letter. It's the start of Tymel's name, so the *T* is a capital *T*." Standing with my back toward the children to model, I walked through the letter formation pathway, leading the children to practice by writing a *T* in the sky while chanting the pathway with me. "Let's start high. Line down! Line across the top. Let's do it again. Say it, all together: Line down. Line across the top. One more time: Line . . .

"Kindergartners, wait a minute." I pointed to the lowercase *t* on the card I had posted at the start of the lesson. "Does this lowercase *t* match the *T* at the start of Tymel's name? No! They look different. How?" Children said the capital letter has a line that goes across the *top*, whereas the lowercase *t* has a line that goes across the *middle*.

"Get ready to make the lowercase *t*. The lowercase *t* is just as /t/ tall as the capital *T*, so stand up tall again." I modeled, raising my arm high, standing with my back to the children. "Watch this. Straight line down. *Little* line across *the middle*." I emphasized the words to model the difference in the letter formation pathways for the lowercase and capital versions of the letter. The children practiced as we repeated the letter formation pathway. "Uppercase *T* and lowercase *t* look different but they both make the /t/ sound."

I added Tymel's name and photo to the name wall under the *Tt* heading and led the class in the "Star Name Celebration Song."

Tymel, Tymel is a star
Clap, clap, clap, clap, clap
Tymel's name starts with a *T*
T, T, T, T, T
With a /t/ /t/ here and a /t/ /t/ there

Here a /t/ there a /t/
Everywhere a /t/ /t/
Tymel, Tymel is a star
/t/ /t/ /t/ /t/ /t/

EXTENSION 2 • Gathering More Pictures for *M* and *S* Books

GETTING READY

- Have a labeled bin for your class letter book ready.
- Prepare more pictures to sort into *M* and *S* letter books.

Introduce a bin to keep in the classroom library to hold the letter books the class makes together. Show pictures of items and ask partners to decide if they belong in the *M* book or the *S* book.

I pulled out a bin labeled "Letter Books" and placed it next to me as I held up the class *M* book we had made. "We are going to learn so many letters and make so many letter books, I thought we should make a bin for them that we can keep in our class library. Should we have Mabel put the first book in the bin?" I turned to Mabel and asked, "Mabel, would you do the honors?" I picked Mabel up and pretended to have her put the *M* book in the bin.

"Earlier, you sorted pictures and made a pile of pictures of things that started with *S*. I thought we could make a book for letter *S*, just like we did for letter *M*. Can you all help get more pictures for both of these books?" The students nodded, and I continued, "I'll hold up pictures, some of which we looked at earlier. Will you and your partner say the name of the item and say whether it starts with /s/-*S* or /m/-*M*? Then we'll add it to the right book."

I added the pictures to the books, with the students' help. When we were finished, I added them both to the bin and placed the bin in the classroom library. "We'll keep these books in the library, so you can read them during reading workshop."

EXTENSION 3 • Revising Writing with the Help of a New Letter

During writing workshop, demonstrate how you might revise the story from this session's connection, this time using the new letter children have learned.

"Class, I'm so glad we now have a new letter to use in our writing, the letter *S*. We can use our new letter to fix up our story about asking Mom for a treat at the movies. Do you remember our story? We started by saying, 'At the movies, I asked Mom for money for a snack.'" On my whiteboard, I quickly sketched two stick figures and said, "This is Mom, and this is me, going to the movies. What letter can I write next to Mom? What letter does *Mom* start with?" I paused a beat, allowing kids to suggest I label Mom with an *M*. I recited the letter formation pathway as I wrote the *M*, "Start high on the page. Line down, back up, slanted line down, slanted line up, line down." I repeated the process for the *M* in *money*.

If you notice most of your writers are not using the letters M *and* S *to label their writing, this would make a nice mid-workshop teaching point during writing workshop. If you notice only a handful of writers who have yet to include these letters, you could teach this extension as a small group during writing time.*

"But friends, here is my snack. What letter should I use here, to label the /s/ snack? Say the word with me. What sound do you hear at the start? Let's say it again and listen to the letter at the start of *snack*." The kids chimed, "*S*!" I recited the letter formation pathway as I drew the *s* to label the snack. "Bump around, slide down, bump around the other way and stop."

Channel students to study their writing, looking for things in their sketches they could label with an *M* or an *S*.

"Right now, take a look at your writing. "Do any of you think you might need an *M* on your page? If you have a drawing of yourself on the page, you might write *M* for *me*. Or, you might need to label /M/ for *Mom*, or /m/ for *monkey bars*. Put up your thumb if you see something you could label with *M*." I saw a few thumbs go up.

"Now check your writing again. Is there something you could label with *S*? Maybe you have a /s/ swing in your piece of writing, or a /s/ sidewalk. Thumbs up." Again, a few children signaled, and I said, "Fabulous! I can't wait to see."

Syllables Can Help Readers and Writers Tackle Long Words

GETTING READY

✔ For today's star name, select a name with multiple syllables—ideally one from early in the suggested letter sequence, one beginning with an easier initial sound, but not to worry. Today's focus is on segmenting the syllables (or parts) of the word, rather than the initial sound. You'll return to initial sound teaching after this lesson.

✔ Display and prepare to add to the "Let's Study a Name!" anchor chart. 👆

✔ Gather a mix of beautiful books, ideally big books, out to disperse among rug clubs.

PHONICS INSTRUCTION

Concepts About Print
• Use one's name to learn about words and make connections to words.

Phonological Awareness
• Count, pronounce, and segment syllables in spoken words.
• Identify the initial phonemes of spoken words.

Letter Knowledge
• Recognize and name all upper- and lowercase letters of the alphabet.
• Recognize the names/sounds of letters.
• Understand that there is a relationship between sounds and letters.

IN THIS SESSION

TODAY YOU'LL begin by teaching students another star name. You'll then teach that writers can say any word and hear the beats in it—the syllables. Doing this helps to read and write longer words.

TODAY YOUR STUDENTS will clap and stomp the beats of names and words as you guide them, and then they will stomp and clap the beats in words they find in their books.

MINILESSON

CONNECTION

Rally kids to the work of today by choosing a new star name—this time, one with more syllables than previous star names.

"Readers and writers, today we'll jump right in by choosing today's star name. Join me!" I began to sing the "Guess the Name" song to the tune of "The Farmer in the Dell" and gestured for students to join me.

Can you guess the name?
Can you guess the name?
Hi-ho, the derry-o
Can you guess the name?

I reached into the jar and dramatically pulled out a name, peeked at it, and whispered, "It starts with . . . an *N*!" I deliberately pulled out a name that I had preselected for its three syllables. I sang the second verse, again gesturing for kids to join in:

It starts with an *N*
It starts with an *N*

Hi-ho, the derry-o
Can you guess the name?

"Today the star name will be . . . " And I revealed Natalia's name card, taped it to the easel, and pointed to it as I read it. "Natalia. This name is *Natalia*." I signaled for children to read it with me, "Natalia!"

Coach children to note the attributes of the name: counting and naming the letters, noticing if any are the same, noting which are tall and which are small.

"Remember yesterday when Tymel was our star name? You used the chart to remind you how to study his name." I gestured toward the chart as I spoke. "Let's try that again. With your partner, read Natalia's name, then count the letters." I listened as kids talked.

After a minute, I voiced over, saying, "Some of you said that Natalia's name is long—longer than Mike's! You are right. Seven letters! Now, study the name. To do that, try pretending you're touching each letter. You can do this in the air, pretending to touch the name even if it is up here on the easel." I gestured to kids to get their fingers in the air, pretending to touch the name card.

"Are some of the letters the same? Is every single letter different?" Then I turned to the kids and said, "What do you see?" After hearing from a few, I said, "So some of you noticed that *Natalia* has three tall letters and four small ones. And she has three of the same letter!"

Encourage kids to do a super-quick cheer while still sitting, so they have time to think about the syllables of the name.

"Let's make our cheer be super-quick so we have time still to think about the beats to this lovely long name. Can you cheer with me, all together?" I sat tall and cheered, signaling for the kids to read the letters and join me. "*N*!" I reached up above my head, then pointed to the next letter and recruited the kids to call "*a*" while we scrunched down in our seats. We continued through the word.

♣ **Name the teaching point.**

"Today I want to teach you another secret. When you go to write a long word or a long name, it helps to first say the name (or the word) in a way that lets you hear the beats—the syllables. Writers can say any word and hear the beats in it, hear what people call the *syllables* of that name or that word."

TEACHING

Explain the larger concept of beats—of rhythm—to set the stage for syllabication work. Practice singing and drumming some familiar songs to give students practice hearing different rhythms.

"Class, I think I need to teach you something about drumming. Turn your knees into a drum, your hands into drumsticks, and try to drum along with me. I'll drum in one way, you try to drum the same as I do." I drummed in a slow even pace: *dum, dum, dum, dum*, leaving time for students to echo-drum. I started a different rhythm by drumming in double beats: *dum-dum*, pause, *dum-dum*, and the students echoed. Then, I changed the rhythm again: *dum, dum-dum, dum, dum-dum*.

"Each of these different ways of drumming has a different beat, a different rhythm. Songs have different rhythms too. Listen to the rhythm of 'Hickory Dickory Dock.'" I sang the song, then I drummed the rhythm of the song to emphasize the beats. "It is different than the rhythm of 'Old MacDonald Had a Farm.' Let's sing that, then we'll try drumming the beats." Together, we sang and then drummed the beats to the song.

Explain that words have beats, and those beats are called *syllables*.

"I'm teaching you this about the beats in music because words have beats too. So when I want to write about nachos in my story, I first say the word *nachos* in a way that lets me hear the beats of the word: *na-chos*. We can do that with *Mabel* too. Try it with me: *Ma-bel*. I first say the word *Ma-bel* in a way that lets me hear the beats in the word. That way I can write first 'Ma' and then 'bel.' *Ma-bel*."

If most of your kids know the names of letters and can call out all the letters, then you can do the cheer in the way described here. If many of them need more support recognizing and naming the letters, a call-and-response cheer might be better, where you call, "Give me an N!" and the kids echo, "N!"

Some students will have difficulty hearing and drumming the rhythm in songs, and when a whole class is drumming on their knees, it may not sound at all like "Old MacDonald Had a Farm." That's okay—it's the act of trying this that will help them understand syllabication.

"Here's the thing: by Thanksgiving or maybe even earlier than that, you are going to want to write using totally cool long words like *spaghetti* and *dinosaur*. You might even write *Tyrannosaurus rex* soon after that. And to be able to write these long words, you need really strong muscles for hearing the beats in a word. Like: Ty/ran/o/saur/us."

Return to today's star name. Coach kids to listen for the syllables in the name, clap and stomp them, and then compare today's name with an earlier star name.

"How about if we do this important new work with Natalia's name? Let's all say her name together and listen for the syllables. Ready, everyone say, Na-tal-ia!" The kids joined me in saying her name this way. "Try it with each other, without me. Be sure to say it beat by beat."

"Now let's clap it out together, one clap for each part of the name. Ready?" We clapped together, "Na-tal-ia!" I led the kids in clapping her name several times.

"Now let's see if we can stand and stomp her name too. Ready? We're going to use both feet. Go for it!" The kids stomped the syllables on the rug.

"Earlier some kids were noticing that Natalia's name *looked* a lot longer than Mike's, that it had more letters. Let's find out—does it also *sound* longer than Mike's? Which name has more beats? Try saying and clapping the beats with your partner. Start with *Mike*." I coached kids to say and clap each name. "So, what do you think? Yep, Mike's name sounds shorter too—only one clap—but Natalia's name is longer, with three claps."

ACTIVE ENGAGEMENT/LINK

Invite children to clap the beats in their own names, and in some of their friends' names.

"Now that we have learned to clap the beats in Natalia's name, I bet you are wanting to try clapping the beats in your own name and in your friends' names. Right now, take a look around the rug, find a friendly face, say that friend's name and then clap the beats. Then do another."

As kids got started clapping their own names and a friend's name, I cheered them on. "Try to clap as many names as you can. If you don't remember a name, ask that person their name. Then maybe you can clap that name together."

Explain that all words have beats, and that clapping the beats in words can help students with their writing.

"But we know it's not just names that have syllables, it's all words! I was reading this book," I held up a book from our class library, "and I saw an alligator. I might want to write a story about an alligator—but . . . but . . . *alligator* is a long word!

"Here's the thing. If I want to write the word *alligator*, it helps to hear the beats in it, the syllables. 'Al-li-ga-tor.' You can try this anytime you are writing, especially when you are writing a long word."

We are tackling such long multisyllable words so early because teaching kids that long words have beats gives them a way to tackle words that otherwise might seem intimidating. We want kids to be fearless with words. And remember, we are not teaching for mastery, we are teaching for approximation—and for fun! This lesson, after all, allows for stomping and parading, so what could be wrong with that?

Syllables are also a way to teach the phonological awareness skills of blending and segmenting. Teaching kids that a word can have more than one beat can help them understand the idea that one word has many sounds that need to be combined or listened for to read and write them.

This month, most kindergartners will progress toward labeling with first consonants only—so spelling alligator *may seem ambitious. But this is a lesson in hearing sounds, and it is easier to hear the larger sound unit of syllable than to hear the smaller unit of phonemes. Kids will need time to master the skill of listening for syllables, so the more opportunities they have to practice this orally, the more success they will eventually have. Meanwhile your teaching is providing early support in hearing phonemes, as well as essential help to the kids with stronger letter-sound knowledge who are ready to record more sounds in long words.*

Debrief in ways that accentuate the transferable work that kids have learned.

"Class, this is one more way we can get to know not only our friends' names, but any words in the world. We can listen for the beats, maybe even clapping or stomping them, and compare words to see which ones are longer or shorter.

"Let's add this to our 'Let's Study a Name!' chart so we don't forget. I'm going to add this right under 'Read it' so that from now on, it will be the second step we take when studying a name. We will read the name and then clap and stomp its syllables."

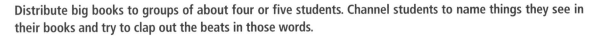

RUG TIME (CLUBS)

Distribute big books to groups of about four or five students. Channel students to name things they see in their books and try to clap out the beats in those words.

"Writers, you've gotten so good at seeing things—at seeing things that start with letters you know, like *M, S, T, N*, and others, too, and now you can also hear the beats in the words. I'm going to give groups of about four of you a big book to look through. Will you open to a page, name something in the picture, and then clap the beats in that word? Do that work for as many words as you can."

I passed out our beautiful books. After kids worked a minute, I said in a voiceover, "Maybe there is an alligator in your book, or a marshmallow. Whatever you see, try to say that word and to hear the beats in it. Then if you ever want to put that word or those things into *your* books, you'll be ready." I coached while students worked, celebrating approximation and modeling clapping parts of words.

POSSIBLE COACHING MOVES

▶ "Point to something! Oh, do you know what that's called? It's called a strawberry. Say the word, *strawberry*. Now try clapping out the parts!"

▶ "Hmm, . . . that seemed like too many claps. Watch me do it—gi-raffe. Now you try again."

▶ "Oh, you found a bunch of one-clap words? *Bug. Leaf. Sun.* Wow! I wonder if you can find any more!"

SHARE • Finding Beats in a Syllables Parade

Reconvene the class's focus and post the star name on the name wall. Invite students to march out the beats in each name on the name wall to celebrate the work of today.

"As we put Natalia's name up on the name wall today, let's have a syllables parade by marching to the beat of the names on our name wall. Stand up and get ready to march right in place."

I added Natalia's name to the name wall under the letter *N* and I gestured for the kids to chant and march in place, "Na-tal-ia! Na-tal-ia!" Then I pointed to the other names on the name wall, and the kids chanted and marched to the beats in these. When we were done with the names, I started calling out other multisyllable words: *Bicycle. Roller coaster. Videogame.*

"Writers, I can already tell that in the blink of an eye, you're going to be ready to write stories about totally cool long words like *Tyrannosaurus rex* and *magician*. Then I'll say, 'Fab-u-lous!'" and I clapped the beats as I said this.

EXTENSION 1 • Syllables Band

GETTING READY

- Gather enough percussion instruments—drums, maracas, rhythm sticks—to have one for each child. (Everyday objects such as cups, bins, and pencils can work as instruments too!)

Pass out percussion instruments. Give students a moment to play with their instruments, then guide them to make some music together by playing the beats, or syllables, in words.

"Class, I was thinking it would be really fun to make some music together today." The class cheered as I passed out drums, maracas, and rhythm sticks, one per child. "Remember, if you didn't get the instrument you wanted today, that's okay! Try it out this time, and next time you can try a different one." I encouraged students to play with their instruments for a few minutes.

"Stop, look, and listen!" I sang, and asked everyone to put down their instruments for just a moment. "Remember earlier we learned a secret to help us write loooong words?"

"You can clap them!" a student called.

I nodded and continued, "You're right—you can clap out the syllables, or the beats, in the words. Well, guess what? Clapping and stomping aren't the only way to make beats. You can drum them, shake them, and tap them too!

"Should we try it together right now? Pick up your instruments. Try your own name first!" The class erupted in the sound of students shouting their names and instruments being played. After a minute I called students' attention back to me.

"Now let's try other words. I will say a word and we can all sound out the beats using our instruments. Let's try Mabel, Ma-bel," I said as I tapped my drum two times, encouraging the class to do the same. We went through a few more names and familiar words together.

I invited students to shout out long words we could break into parts, and soon these became long and complicated— *ridiculous*, *caterpillar*, *Tyrannosaurus rex*, *spectacular*, *Mom*, *abracadabra*.

I gestured for the class's attention and said, "That was awesome! You came up with some fascinating words, and you really heard those beats!"

Coach children through writing the capital and lowercase letter *N* in the air. Recite the letter formation pathways for these letters as children form them.

"Kindergartners, during writing time today I realized something. We didn't have a chance to write a capital *N* so we have this letter in our back pockets and can use it." I pointed to a capital *N* that I had written on my whiteboard. "Let's do this now. You ready? Line down, back up, slanted line down, line up." I repeated the letter formation pathway as I drew the letter in the air, encouraging the students to try it with me.

"Now get out those make-believe markers and let's write the *N* on the rug in front of us." I grabbed a marker and modeled for students on the whiteboard as I repeated the letter formation pathway out loud. The children drew their *N*'s on the rug, then in their hands. "Nice writing capital *N*, friends! Oh! /n/-nice work, did you hear that? Remember the letter *N* goes with /n/ /n/ /n/. Say it with me this time!"

I pointed to a lowercase *n* I had drawn on the whiteboard and said, "Kindergartners! Does this lowercase *n* look like the capital *N* we just drew?" Students chimed, "Noooo."

"You're right, the capital and lowercase *N* look different, and we have to know both to use them in our writing. We need the uppercase for words like names, and the lowercase for words that are not names, like *nuts* and *nibble* and *nose*.

"Let's practice writing the lowercase *n*." I encouraged students to practice along with me as I drew the *n* in the air and said the letter formation pathway, "Line down, back up, bump around and down." We practiced the lowercase *n* a few more times together.

Return to a familiar story to demonstrate how students might use the letter *N* in their writing.

"We now have a new letter to use in our writing. We could use our new letter to add to our story about asking Mom to help us get some candy at the movies. Remember, this is my mom, and this is me, going to the movies." I pointed to the sketch from the previous day. "Now we can add a snack that starts with /n/. Hmm, . . . does *licorice* work? /l/-/l/-*licorice*. No. Does *KitKat* work? KitKat /k/-/k/. No. How about *nachos*? /n/-/n/-*Natalia*, *nachos*. Yes!"

I drew some nachos and repeated the letter formation pathway to myself as I labeled my sketch with the letter *n*.

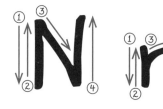

Though it's not necessary to belabor the upper-case/lowercase point right now, it's not too early to introduce this concept with this simple explanation of names or not-names, which you'll expand upon later.

EXTENSION 3 • Singing the Alphabet Song

GETTING READY

- Copies of the Alphabet song are included in the Resource Pack.

Wrap up today's work by leading the class in singing the alphabet song. Point to each letter as the class sings.

"We have a few minutes to sing a special song together that celebrates letters. I bet I don't even have to teach most of you this song because you've probably heard it pretty much your whole life. It's the alphabet song. Sing along with me if you know it!"

I pointed to each letter as we sang the song together. "*A, B, C, D, E, F, G, . . .* "

Sing the song two more times, this time emphasizing the letters the class has learned so far: *M*, *S*, *T*, **and** *N*.

"Beautiful singing! Let's sing it one more time together. But this time, when we get to the four letters we have already learned—*M, S, T,* and *N*—will you shout those letters extra loud and jump up and down, too? Ready? Try it with me":

    A, B, C, D, E, F, G!
    H, I, J, K, L, ***M, N****!*
    O, P,
    Q, R, ***S, T***
    U, V, W
    X, Y, Z
    Now I know my ABCs
    Next time won't you sing with me?

"Whoa, that was tricky! Let's try it one more time. Again, jump up and shout when you hear any of the letters we've learned so far—*M, S, T,* and *N.*"

Singing this song reinforces and implicitly teaches letter names. Be sure to point to each letter as the class sings to help students practice one-to-one match.

Comparing Two Names that Both Start with the Same Letter

GETTING READY

✔ For today, choose two star names beginning with *R, D, F, P,* or *B.* If you don't have two, you could use the name of a familiar teacher or book character. If you have more than two, teach all three.

✔ Create enough sentence strips to distribute to pairs of children. Half of the strips should have one name on them, half, the other.

✔ Display the "Let's Study a Name!" anchor chart.

✔ Prepare a sentence strip with Mabel's name on it for each pair of children.

✔ Distribute a copy of your story (just pictures) to each partnership so kids can add labels.

PHONICS INSTRUCTION

Concepts About Print
• Use one's name to learn about words and make connections to words.

Phonological Awareness
• Connect words by the sounds.
• Count, pronounce, and segment syllables in spoken words.

Letter Knowledge
• Make connections between words by recognizing letters.
• Recognize the names/sounds of letters.

IN THIS SESSION

TODAY YOU'LL teach students that by studying how two names are the same and how they are different, they learn more about names.

TODAY YOUR STUDENTS will compare and contrast two star names that both begin with the same letter. Then they will compare their own name and their partner's name. This gives students added practice talking and thinking about letters.

MINILESSON

CONNECTION

Draw two names beginning with the same consonant from the Star Jar, sing the "Guess the Name" song, then channel children to use the anchor chart to study one of the names.

I took hold of the Star Jar, holding it ceremoniously in both hands as I sang the first stanza to "Can You Guess the Name?"

Then I pulled out a name, as usual, but this time, two names were stuck together. The kids saw me stare curiously at what I'd drawn from the jar. I looked at each of the name cards, and then I sang the second verse of the "Guess the Name" song, emphasizing the pronoun *they*.

They start with an *R*
They start with an *R*
Hi-ho, the derry-o
They start with an *R*

By now, some children were already pointing at Rebecca and Roman. I nodded, gesturing to the two-star children, and I pinned their star names, written on sentence strips complete with their photos, onto the easel.

"Friends, this has never happened before. Two names with the same letter on one day! Wow. That's a lot to learn. Do you think it is too much?" With a dubious tone in my voice, I pressed. "Do you think we have enough brainpower to learn *two* names?" The kids were adamant: "Yes!"

"Okay," I said, "but we'll need to help each other to get this done. Would you be willing to divide up the work to help us study these names a little faster?"

I gave a sentence strip containing one of the two names that I'd pulled from the Star Jar to each pair of children in the first row, and then I gave a sentence strip containing the second name to each pair of children in the second row. In this way, I made sure that the children in row one could learn one name with the person beside them and could eventually compare the name with the children behind them.

"Right now, study the name that I've given you, either Rebecca or Roman."

As the kids worked, I voiced over the steps from the chart. "Whether you are studying *Rebecca* or *Roman*, you can read the name, and clap it out. Re-bec-ca! How many claps was that? Three! Rebecca's name has three parts. How about Roman's?" After most of the partners had done this, I said, "You can count the letters, right? And you can study them. Are there tall letters? Small ones?"

❖ **Name the teaching point.**

"Today I want to teach you that when you want to get to know something really well—and this is true whether you want to get to know things, or names, or really any words—it can help to look at a few of those things and to think 'How are these the same, and how are they different?'"

TEACHING

Help partners understand what it means to think about ways things are similar and different by channeling them to discuss ways their shoes are like and unlike their partner's shoes.

"I'm wondering if you know what I mean when I say you can look at two things and think, 'How are these the same? How are they different?' Let me show you. Will you and your partner put your shoes beside each other—you don't have to take them off, just move your feet so your shoes and your partner's shoes are beside each other." After the kids did that, I said, "So now . . . will you look at your shoes and think, 'How are these kind of the same?'

Teachers, your frequent references to the anchor chart will remind kids to use the chart to guide their work. This will set them up to work with names (and eventually other words) with independence later.

"Let me show you what I mean. Rebecca and Roman, will you come up here, and put your shoes near each other?" The two stood side by side at the front of the class. "Now I'm going to look at your shoes and think how they are the same. Hmm, . . . well, they both have laces to keep them on. They both have a rubber bottom that looks like it would help when the ground is slippery. But, there are ways these shoes are different. They are different colors. And Rebecca's have a top that goes up higher on her ankle.

"Will you and your partner take a minute and think 'How are our shoes the same? How are they different?'"

The kids did that. "As you talk about ways your shoes are the same and different, you become sort of experts on shoes. Looking so carefully like that makes you into an expert."

Now channel students to work with a partnership who studied a different name and to think between the two star names, talking about ways those names are similar and different.

"Let's try studying today's star names—*Rebecca* and *Roman*—in ways that help you think what is the same about these two names and what is different. The partners in front of and behind you have a different name on their sentence strip. Put your names alongside each other so you can compare the names. First, you might notice things that are the same. You might say, 'They both have . . . ' and show your friends what you see. Get started!"

As the kids laid out their sentence strips and talked between them, I listened and celebrated what I heard them doing.

"Writers, eyes back here," I said. "Your minds were on fire just now. I love the way you worked really hard at this. You didn't just look one time and say, 'I see one thing that is the same' and then be done. No way!"

ACTIVE ENGAGEMENT/LINK

Distribute a sentence strip with Mabel's name on it to each pair of children, then have the children consider how Mabel's name and the star names are similar and different.

"Wait," I stopped in my tracks. "What is that sound?" I listened, as if on high alert to what in truth was an imaginary sound. I rushed to Mabel's bed and leaned over her, saying, "Were you calling something, Mabel?" I leaned down as if to hear her better, cocked an ear, listened, and then stood to report what I'd heard to the class.

"Mabel is asking, 'What about me? Why aren't you looking at *my* name?' I think we'd better not leave her out. Right now, will you and your partner take the name you have been studying and talk about how it is the same as Mabel's name, and how it is different?" I distributed sentence strips that contained Mabel's name so the kids could lay these side by side and talk between them.

As the kids compared the name on their sentence strips—*Roman* or *Rebecca*—with Mabel's name, I coached into their work.

POSSIBLE COACHING MOVES

▶ "I notice that some of you are finding tall letters in both names! How cool."

▶ "You are seeing the same letter in both names. Smart work."

▶ "Wow! Some of you are already talking about what is different in the two words."

▶ "I see some of you pointing at the names as you talk about them."

▶ "Such smart work. Some of you are listening to the beats in the two names."

Guide students through the letter formation pathway for *R* and encourage them to add this letter to their back pockets.

"Writers, one really cool thing about studying names this closely is that this is a way to get more letters in your back pocket. You can use all these names in your writing! I started a story last night about my rabbit, and I wonder if you and your partner could help me label it? I have copies for you. Writers, always remember that names can help you know letters. If you are writing a book about a rattlesnake, and you draw a snake, and you want people to know this is a /r/-*rattlesnake*, you can say the name /r/-*Roman*, and hear the beginning sound: /r/, /r/. The letter *R* makes the /r/ sound in those words. Do you hear the /r/ /r/ /r/ in *rattlesnake*? Try saying it with me, /r/ /r/ /r/-*rattlesnake*. If you know *R*, you could put an *R* in your story to tell your readers what kind of snake you are writing about.

To make an *R* quickly, it will help to practice it. Let's do the capital *R* together. Get your fingers ready to draw it in the air." I repeated the letter formation pathway a few times as I drew the letter *R* on the whiteboard. Students followed along, drawing the *R* in the air. "Line down, back up, bump around, slanted line down."

"Remember, you can use names to help you. Rebecca and Roman's names can help you label my rabbit. See what else you can label in my story."

After practicing the capital *R* together, we moved on to the lowercase *r*. I drew the *r* on the board as students practiced on the rug. "Line down, back up, tiny turn and stop."

Sing the "Star Name Celebration Song" and add the new names to the name wall.

"Now that we have that *R* in our back pockets, let's sing the 'Star Name Celebration Song' and get both of these beautiful names up onto the name wall!" I altered the song to include both names at the same time.

Rebecca, Roman they are stars
Clap, clap, clap, clap, clap
Their names start with an *R*
R, R, R, R, R
With a /r/ /r/ here and a /r/ /r/ there
Here an /r/ there an /r/
Everywhere an /r/ /r/
Rebecca, Roman, they are stars
/r/ /r/ /r/ /r/ /r/.
Clap, clap, clap, clap, clap

EXTENSION 1 • More Star Names: The Letter *L*

Choose two more names that begin with the same letter for the class to study.

I brought out the Star Jar and reached inside, grabbing two new names to study. I sang the "Guess the Name" song once again, emphasizing the pronoun *they* as we draw out two names. This time we sang "They start with an *L*."

The class began to look around and a few students started to point at Lucas and Lisa, and I said, "You are getting the hang of this so quickly. Yep, *Lucas* and *Lisa* are our new star names! When I hand you one of their names, work with your partner to study it. Don't forget to use the chart!" I handed out a sentence strip with one name written on it to each partnership. Half of the class worked on studying Lucas's name and the other half worked on studying Lisa's name.

As the students worked, I voiced over the steps from the chart. After a few minutes, I invited one partnerships to work with another to compare the two names.

After students had compared the two names, I gathered the class back together. "Wow, friends, you noticed a lot about these two names! They certainly have some differences, but one thing they have in common is that they start with the same sound, /l/. Can you /l/-listen to the /l/ sound? /l/ /l/ /l/. Both /l/-*Lucas* and /l/-*Lisa* start with the /l/ sound. The letter *L* makes the /l/ sound in both /l/-*Lucas* and /l/-*Lisa*. What other words start with that /l/-*L* sound? Hmm, . . . /l/-*laugh* and /l/-*leaf* and /l/-*library*! All of those are *L* words because they start with the *L* sound—/l/-*lovely* work, friends!"

You will need to work quickly to introduce more star names and letters before Bends II and III. We suggest continuing to teach one or two—or more—names at other times in the day to make this happen.

EXTENSION 2 • Making a Class *R* Book

GETTING READY

- Prepare to distribute pictures and cards, some starting with an *R* and some not.
- Plan on making an *R* book comprised of *R*-pictures.

Invite children to work in partnerships to sort pictures into *R* or Not-an-*R* piles.

"Earlier we figured out that clocks make a /t/-/t/ sound. And when the food looks good, we make an /mmmmm/ sound. So what letter goes with a /rrrrrr/ sound?"

The kids all made growls with the /r/ sound and named some animals that made those sounds.

Nodding, I said, "I am going to pass out some new pictures to you and your partner today. Just like we did with the letters *M* and *T*, you can read the picture and decide, 'Does this word begin with a /r/-*R* or does not begin with *R*?' Sort the pictures into two piles."

I coached as they sorted.

"Stop, look, and listen," I sang after most of the students had finished sorting. "Will you and your partner hold up the *R* pictures you found today? Show me the words that sounded like /r/-*Rebecca*. *Rainbow*, *rose*, *rat*! So many terrific *R* words!"

Create a class *R* book by adding the pictures that start with *R*.

I pulled out a blank book and wrote a capital *R* on the cover. "We can put all of the /r/-*R* pictures together to make an *R* book to go with our *M* and *T* books. Read the pictures with me as I tape them into our book. Help me make sure it starts with /r/."

After we read each picture together, I quickly taped them into the book. "And we can't forget about Rebecca and Roman," I said and added pictures of Rebecca and Roman.

We added the *R* book to the letter books bin along with the *M* and *S* books.

EXTENSION 3 • Using Manipulatives to Hear Syllables

GETTING READY

- Gather some math cubes (or other small, hard objects) and a bucket to help kids hear syllables.

Set students up to clap syllables in a few names. Reinforce this work by dropping math cubes into a bucket to emphasize each syllable.

"Remember the other day when we found the beats in songs and in names? For example, we found the beats in *Gre-go-ry*. Let's reread all the names on our name chart and drum out the beat in each name." I pointed, and the kids drummed with their hands on their knees.

"Let's keep practicing hearing the syllables, the beats, in our names." I held up some math cubes and a small bucket. "Each time we clap a syllable, I'll drop one of our math cubes into the bucket, like this." I dropped a cube into the bucket to show how this would sound. "Try some with me. Let's do Lisa's name. *Li-sa*. You clap, while I drop the cubes." As I said each syllable, I dropped a cube into the bucket. "One more time," I said, and I gestured for the kids to clap along again as I dropped two cubes into the bucket to represent each beat.

Teachers, if you notice that many of your students are struggling to clap out the syllables in names and words, using manipulatives can be a supportive scaffold. Here we are using manipulatives to help kids "see" segmented sounds. To encourage engagement, you might hand out a set of math cubes to each partnership and let students drop cubes along with you. If only a few students still need more support with this skill you may consider teaching this lesson in a small group.

Then I tried a few of the class's favorite words, like *Tyrannosaurus rex* and *fabulous*. I invited a few children to come up and drop the cubes into the bucket once it seemed most of them were catching on.

"Now let's try it the other way around. I'll say the name in parts, and you put the parts together to say the whole name. Ready?" I dropped three cubes in the buckets as I said, "*Mar-i-gold*."

"*Marigold*!" The class shouted. I continued on in this way, segmenting a few other multisyllable words and encouraging the class to blend them together. "*Kin-der-gar-ten*."

Vowels Are Special Letters

IN THIS SESSION

TODAY YOU'LL teach students that there are two kinds of letters, consonants and vowels.

TODAY YOUR STUDENTS will learn the names of the vowels, and they will practice finding vowels in the star name for today, in the other star names that were already studied, and in words around the classroom.

MINILESSON

CONNECTION

Choose a star name from the Star Jar that begins with a vowel and move quickly through the star name routine.

"Writers, come quickly." Once the kids had all gathered, I pointed to Mabel who was holding a star name card in her trunk. "Will you look at that? Mabel already pulled the star name out of the Star Jar!"

I looked at the name and sang the second verse of the "Guess the Name" song.

It starts with an *A*
It starts with an *A*
Hi-ho, the derry-o
It starts with an *A*

"Today's star name is *Ava*! Let's go through the steps quickly, as we've been doing, to

GETTING READY

✔ Choose a star name that begins with a vowel. We chose *Ava*.

✔ Display the "Let's Study a Name!" anchor chart.

✔ Prepare to show students your organized set of magnetic letters in their container. Ideally, your vowels will be one color and your consonants another.

✔ Invite your principal to join you in leading the final song, as a way to end the first bend of the first unit.

PHONICS INSTRUCTION

Concepts About Print
• Understand left-to-right directionality of print.

Letter Knowledge
• Recognize and talk about the sequence of letters in words.
• Understand that some letters represent consonant sounds.
• Understand that some letters represent vowel sounds.
• Recognize the name/sound of letters.
• Use efficient and consistent motions to form letters.

study Ava's name." As partners studied the names, I voiced over, reminding them to go through the steps on the "Let's Study a Name!" chart.

Pretend that your class mascot is whispering to you, telling you a secret about the name's sounds. Point out that the letter *A* goes with more than one sound.

I pretended Mabel was talking, saying something to me so quietly that I had to lean in to hear her whisper. "What's that?" I asked. "I can't hear you." I asked the class to be extra quiet, so I could really listen.

I nodded at Mabel, then said to the class, "Mabel just told me something really important. She said, 'The name *Ava* starts with *A*, and the word *apple*,' Mabel's favorite fruit, 'also starts with *a*. But the *A* in *Ava* goes with a different sound than the *a* in *apple*.'" I paused for dramatic effect, then emphasized, "/ā/-*Ava*. /ă/-*apple*. The letter *A* goes with more than one sound."

♣ **Name the teaching point.**

"Today, I want to teach you another secret about letters: there are two kinds of letters. Some letters are called vowels, and some letters are called consonants. This is important because almost every single word is made with both kinds of letters—some consonants and some vowels. Vowels are special letters that make more than one sound."

Don't worry if your students can't use these academic terms accurately or at all. This is the first of many exposures to these concepts.

TEACHING

Teach children the set of vowels by showing them your organized magnetic letters case. Teach that vowels are red, and consonants are blue as a way to differentiate between the letters.

I held up my whole container of magnetic letters so that the children could see into the twenty-six letter compartments. I asked, "What do you notice about the red and blue letters?" I paused for a second to invite children to think with me and then continued. "You probably noticed that there are many more blue-letter containers than red-letter containers. Let's count the red-letter containers."

I nodded and said, "There are only five red letters, and those are the vowels." I pulled one vowel at a time from the magnetic letter container and named each one as I set them in a line at the top of the board. I asked the students to name each vowel again along with me.

Note that if you have a set of magnetic letters in which vowels are not a different color, you'll need to adapt this lesson. We recommend using a set of letters in which vowels are differentiated in some way, so that children can easily identify them. You might find or make some letter cards in which the vowels are a different color, for example. However, we also know that because real words in text are not color coded, this scaffold needs to be taken away for real reading and writing transfer to happen.

"Knowing about these red and blue letters gives us another way to look at names, and at any words, really. We could look for and name the vowel/consonant pattern that makes up names. For example, Ava's name goes, vowel-consonant-vowel." I chanted it with a little rhythm and bopped my head too. "Do you want to join in with me?" We chanted the name again.

"Let's try it with Mabel's name." We named the letters and then the vowel/consonant pattern. "Consonant-vowel-consonant-vowel-consonant."

Review that vowels make more than one sound. Point out that the long-vowel sound is the letter's name.

"Kindergartners, do you remember when we studied Salima's name, and we learned the secret that for many letters, when you know the letter's name, you know the letter's sound?"

The children nodded, and I continued, "Well, for vowels, these special letters that make more than one sound, the letter name is *one* of the sounds the vowel makes. But each vowel makes another sound, too. And people who know a lot about words know both of the sounds that vowels make."

ACTIVE ENGAGEMENT/LINK

Set children up to practice learning about consonants and vowels by having them name the vowel/consonant pattern in the names that are already on your name wall.

"As a way to learn even more about these special kinds of letters, I thought we could go back to some of the names we have already studied and name the vowel/consonant pattern in those names. I bet there are all different kinds of patterns in our names. I'll point to a name on the name wall. Read the name with your partner and then try naming the pattern."

Quickly recap a few of the patterns in the star names.

"Let's name the pattern in Mike's name together. First, let's say the letters." We did this, and then we chanted, "Consonant, vowel, consonant, vowel."

"*Karen*!" We said the letters, and then said, "Consonant, vowel, consonant, vowel, consonant."

We named patterns in a few more names in this way.

"Now that you know about vowel/consonant patterns, you can find them in words all around you."

RUG TIME

Set children up to search the room with a partner, finding words to study and to identify their vowel/consonant patterns.

"There are so many words all around the room, and now that we know there are two kinds of letters—consonants and vowels—and that all words are made up of a mixture of these two kinds of letters, we can look at words differently. I thought it would be interesting to find words around the room to study in this new way. Take your partner's hand and find words around the room to study. First, say the letters in the word. Then, say the vowel/consonant pattern. Off you go!"

I coached partnerships as they did this work around the room.

You might question, and rightfully so, whether children at the start of kindergarten are ready for the concept of long- and short-vowel sounds. Today, you plant the seeds for this concept, but most children won't really grasp it until much later. So, it's not necessary to linger over this part. Just mentioning that vowels are special letters that make more than one sound is enough.

POSSIBLE COACHING MOVES

▶ "Don't forget to try naming the letters first if you can. Then name the pattern."

▶ "The vowels are up here all together on the board. There are five of them."

▶ "Be on the lookout for any vowel/consonant patterns that are the same."

▶ "You might also notice when vowels make a sound like the letter's name, and when they don't."

SHARE • Celebrating the Bend with the Alphabet Song

Congratulate students on all they have learned so far. Then, lead them in several rounds of the alphabet song, encouraging them to learn the song as well as they know their own names.

"Kindergartners, today ends the first part of our very first unit. You have already learned so, so much, and you'll keep learning even more star names and letters. As a way to celebrate, I thought we'd sing a song together that most of you already know as well as you know your own names. What better way to celebrate all you are learning about letters than with this favorite song that is all about letters?

"Today, we have a special guest coming to lead us in singing this song." I gestured for the principal to come in from the hallway.

"Readers, writers," he said, "I heard you have learned so many letters and that you are experts at singing the alphabet song. How about we sing it together while your teacher points to the letters?"

The class chimed in as we made our way through the song. We sang a few more times, each in different ways, such as quickly, then slowly, then in silly voices. Then I invited some children to point to the letters as the principal and I led the rest of the class in singing a few more rounds of the song.

"Kindergartners, you are getting to know that song so well. When you get home tonight, would you teach it to your parents, your brothers, sisters, cousins, grandparents, anyone you can find? Let's share our love of letters with the world."

Of course, it is totally optional for you to invite the principal to join. Having the principal or other special guest lends an air of gravitas to this turning point in the unit but is not necessary for the work of this celebratory share.

Make this your own. Some teachers add musical instruments. Others invite students to stand up when their letter is sung. You might also take a video of one of the renditions to share with parents.

EXTENSION 1 • Writing the Letter *A*

Practice writing the vowel letter that students learned today, first the uppercase, and then the lowercase.

"Ava, thank you so much for helping us to learn about the two kinds of letters—consonants and vowels! Now, let's practice writing this first vowel, so we can put it in our back pocket with the other letters we have studied.

"Let's start with the capital *A* first, because names begin with a capital letter." I then turned my back and looked over my shoulder as I wrote the letter on the board. I voiced over using the letter formation pathway for *A*. "Slanted line down. Slanted line down. Little line connecting." I did and said it again, with some kids joining.

"Try it with me! Let's all write it! Arms out in front of you. Slanted line down. Slanted line down. Little line connecting." I repeated the letter formation pathway each time we wrote the capital *A*. I led the kids in writing the capital *A* three more times.

Model making the lowercase version of the letter in the air in front of the students, then lead them to sky-write this version as well.

"Let's write a lowercase *a* next. Watch me first." I turned my body away a little and got ready to sky write the lowercase *a*. "Start a little lower than the big *A*. Bump back around. Line up. Line back down.

"Do this in the air now. This is the lowercase *a*." All the kids got their arms ready. "Here we go!" I voiced over the letter formation pathway each time. The kids wrote in the air.

"Looks like we have another letter in our back pocket, class!"

EXTENSION 2 • Introducing "Apples and Bananas" to Practice Vowel Sounds

GETTING READY

- Post the five vowels on your easel using magnetic letters. Or, create letter cards for students to flash each time they sing a different vowel sound.
- Teach students the "Apples and Bananas" song. A link to the song and a printout of the lyrics are available in the online resources.

Teach students a song to help them practice manipulating words and hearing long-vowel sounds.

"Class, remember how earlier we learned that the *E* makes two different sounds? We also learned the rest of the vowels do, too. They have a short sound and a long sound. One way to remember which is which, is that the long sound is the one that sounds like the name of the letter. The long sound for *A* is /ā/ and the long sound for *E* is /ē/, *I* is /ī/, *O* is /ō/, and *U* is /ū/. Cool, huh?

"I want to teach you a silly song today called 'Apples and Bananas.' In this song, we will use the long-vowel sounds. Don't worry, you will catch on quickly. Let me show you!" I started singing "Apples and Bananas."

 Apples and Bananas

I like to eat, eat, eat, apples and bananas
I like to eat, eat, eat, apples and bananas

I like to ate, ate, ate, ayples and banaynays
I like to ate, ate, ate, ayples and banaynays

I like to eat, eat, eat, eeples and baneenies
I like to eat, eat, eat eeples and baneenies

I like to ite, ite, ite eye-ples and ban-eye-eyes
I like to ite, ite, ite eye-ples and ban-eye-eyes

I like to oat, oat, oat, oaples and banonoes
I like to oat, oat, oat, oaples and banonoes

I like to ute, ute, ute, uuples and banunus
I like to ute, ute, ute, uuples and banunus

Dear Teachers,

This will be a favorite part of the unit because now, at long last, each child gets a chance to study his or her own name. You'll channel kids to think about all the letters in their names and to learn to write all of those letters efficiently, following a pathway you'll teach. You'll introduce the idea that there is an easier, more efficient way to make letters, and you'll help students begin to internalize the letter formation pathways for at least the letters in their own names. You'll introduce a metaphor for students learning to write their names automatically—they are learning to write their names by heart, just as they know how to do other daily activities by heart, such as zipping their coats.

To support the work of this bend, you'll need to spend some time gathering a name baggie for each child. We think you'll find that the baggies are well used and worth the effort. In the baggie, put the child's name on a sentence strip and also cut into individual letters to make letter tiles. Each letter tile should have the uppercase letter on one side and the lowercase on the other. For Session 9, you'll need to insert a name map showing proper letter formation for each letter in children's names. You'll see detailed instructions on how to do this in that session. You will also want to include a picture of the child's face. You'll need to make a baggie for your class mascot as well, which you will use in demonstrations. You may find that kids will end up wanting to make similar baggies for their family members' and pets' names.

You'll note that the sessions themselves in Bends II and III do not teach new star names. Of course, there is no way you will have gotten through your entire class list in Bend I, so it will be important for you to continue to teach new star names—along with letters of the alphabet—throughout the unit. Therefore, star name work continues in the extensions in Bends II and III to provide you the opportunity to teach all the remaining letters of the alphabet. As we describe in the "An Orientation to the Unit" section, we suggest following the recommended sequence for teaching letters as much as possible:

M S T N A R L D F I V P K X E B Z J O C H U W G Q Y

If your students are tiring of star names, or if you have an especially large class, you can teach new star names in multiples at a time, especially if some of the names start with the same letter. We recommend you stay close to the name study protocol you've used thus far, guiding kids to follow the steps on the "Let's Study a Name!" chart, teaching the letter formation pathway for writing the new letter, and then making a letter book to add to the letter books bin. By the end of this unit, you will want to have completed your class list of names and ideally created star names for empty letters on your name wall. For these, you might draw on other teachers in the school, or characters from books. In Bend III, you'll see a session that can help you teach the name of a character from literature for a letter that isn't supported by the names on your class list.

You will want to establish a whiteboard routine for your class. For each child, you'll need a whiteboard, a dry-erase marker, and either a dry-erase eraser or a sock that can double as both an eraser and a place to store each child's dry-erase marker. Some people use Velcro dots to attach a sock (with a marker inside) to the back of each miniature whiteboard with a Velcro dot for storage. Many teachers store these in bins, with one bin for each row of students. For example, if students are sitting in rows of eight, there are eight whiteboards in a bin so that "row leaders" can quickly fetch the whiteboards for their row when it is time. You will want to set aside some time at the beginning of the unit to practice this routine, being explicit about the procedure for distributing whiteboards and about the importance of holding the dry-erase marker in the dominant hand and putting the sock-eraser on their nondominant hand.

All the best,
Lucy and Natalie

Learning Your Own Name by Heart

IN THIS SESSION

TODAY YOU'LL teach students that it is important to know get to know their own name by heart. One way they might do this is to study their name in the same way they studied star names.

TODAY YOUR STUDENTS will start to learn their names by heart by doing all the things they have done in past sessions to study a name: read it, clap and stomp the beats, count the letters, study the letters, and cheer it.

MINILESSON

CONNECTION

Rally the class to the work of this new bend by explaining the concept of what it is to know something by heart. Illustrate by pointing out that kids know the class mascot's name by heart.

"Last night, when I was lying in bed, thinking about what I could teach you today, for some reason I started singing our gathering song. As I sang, 'We are gathering, we are gathering, on the rug . . . on the rug . . . ' I thought to myself, 'Our whole class knows that song *by heart* now.' Am I right?" The kids nodded, and I pressed on. "Can you each sing that with your partner?"

Before the song was over, I reconvened the class, and said, "Then I thought, 'I think my kids *also* know the name *Mabel* by heart.' Do you? Can you spell *Mabel* by heart? Try it." I led the class in a chant of *M-A-B-E-L*. "Do you know how to spell *Mabel* by heart so that you can whisper-spell it all on your own, without my help? Try it!" I demonstrated for them, whispering into my cupped hands.

GETTING READY

✔ Display the "Let's Study a Name!" anchor chart.

✔ Prepare a name baggie for each child, containing the child's name on an index card, letter tiles cut from paper (one tile for each letter in the child's name, with the uppercase letter on one side and the lowercase letter on the other), and the child's picture. Prepare a similar name baggie for Mabel.

✔ Bring Mabel to the rug with her name baggie to demonstrate how to reconstruct her name.

PHONICS INSTRUCTION

Concepts About Print
• Construct one's name accurately with letter cards.
• Use one's name to learn about words.

Phonological Awareness
• Count, pronounce, and segment syllables in spoken words.

Letter Knowledge
• Recognize and name all upper- and lowercase letters of the alphabet.
• Recognize and name letters in words.

"Do you even know how to write the first letter in Mabel's name? Without looking up here, will you write an *M* with your finger on the rug? If you know another letter from her name, write that too."

I gave students a moment to do this, and then continued, "See—I was right. You definitely know Mabel's name by heart. That's a great thing."

Turn toward the work of today, suggesting it's a really big deal for kids to know their own names by heart.

"Last night, I also started to think, 'Isn't it important for the kids in my class to also know their *own* names by heart?'"

♣ **Name the teaching point.**

"Today I want to teach you that it is super-important to know your own name *by heart*. And the way you get to know your own name by heart is by doing all the stuff with your own name that you have done to turn other kids' names into star names."

TEACHING

Quickly lead kids through a recap of what it is they have learned to do to get to know a star name. Help them refer to the chart and do all the steps on it with the name of the class mascot.

"Let's first remember what we do to learn any star name—we'll do all those things with Mabel's name. Then, here is the exciting part—I'm going to give each of you your own star name baggie, and each and every one of you will do all those things—only this time, with *your own name*. You ready for this?

"First: let's look at our chart. Read it with me." I pointed to each line and read, and gestured for the kids to chime in.

"Okay, let's do those things with Mabel's name." I pointed to *Read it* and signaled for the class to do it without instructions from me. The students read, "*Mabel*." I pointed to *Clap and stomp the beats* and signaled for the class to do this. I pointed to *Count the letters* and then to the *M* in *Mabel*. I began counting, "one," and the class continued counting all the way to five. I said, "Now, will you and your partner study the letters together? Tell each other three things you notice." I held up my hand and pointed to three fingers to show they'd be listing the things across their fingers. They did this. Then I led them in a cheer, showing the tall and small letters.

The theme of this will be the idea that one can come to know things by heart, so play that up. Touch your heart as you say that phrase and do that continually throughout this lesson.

You might pause here for dramatic effect, as this whole bend revolves around kids coming to know and be able to use their own names by heart.

Let's study a name!

Read it.

Clap and stomp the beats.

Count the letters.

Study the letters.

Cheer it!

ACTIVE ENGAGEMENT/LINK

Recruit everyone's help getting each name baggie to its owner. Ask children to read the name on a baggie and to pass it toward its owner.

I continued, "Now you'll have a chance to do all these things with your very *own* name. I've got a name baggie prepared for each one of you, with some really great stuff inside. Let's get them passed out to everyone. Will you help me?" Children nodded, and I continued, "When you get a name baggie, will you first read the name, and then pass it on toward the owner? Every time you touch a name baggie, try to read the name, then keep passing it in the direction of its owner. We'll keep passing until everyone has gotten their baggie."

I held up Mike's baggie. I read, "*Mike*," and I passed it to a nearby child, coaching her to also read *Mike*. Then I said, "Would you all help get this baggie to Mike? Read the name, and then pass it in Mike's direction. Let's keep passing these out. When you get your baggie, don't open it yet. We'll wait until everyone has gotten their baggie."

Channel kids to lay their name baggies in front of them and to then do all the things with their own name that they have learned to do with star names. Refer to the "Let's Study a Name!" chart.

"Put your baggie on the floor in front of you," I said. I held up Mabel's baggie. "Mabel's baggie has two kinds of things in it." I held up each thing as I showed it to the class. "Mabel has her whole name on a name card, and she has each letter of her name on a letter tile. The letter tiles have the capital letter on one side and the lowercase letter on the other side.

"And guess what? You all have those things in your baggies, too. Right now, will you take out just the name card from your baggie? Put it on the rug right in front of you." Once all the children had done this, I continued, "Now, begin to get to know your name by heart. Use our chart to help you remember all the things you can do. If a step is hard for you right now, ask the person next to you for some help and I will be around to help too. Get started. Learn your name by heart. Mabel and I will be watching."

Recap students' work and reiterate the refrain of this bend: the importance of learning things by heart.

"Oh my goodness! Writers, you have done so many things with your names. You are well on your way to learning your names by heart."

The process of distributing names in this way offers practical experience in word solving for your students. It may take a while, and so, you may decide to only pass out ten names or so this way, distributing the rest as quickly as possible. You may also want to make sure that there is a picture of the child clearly visible in each baggie to support name reading.

POSSIBLE COACHING MOVES

▶ "See if you can point to the parts of your name as you read it. Which letters make the sounds you are reading?"

▶ "Try clapping the breaks in your name."

▶ "Touch each letter as you count it."

▶ "If cheering your name is hard, you can sing the alphabet song to help you remember the name of a letter."

RUG TIME

Launch rug time by using the class mascot to demonstrate how to use the name card to put the letter tiles in the correct order to spell a name.

"I see a few of you peeking into your baggies at your letter tiles. Are you ready to figure out what you can do with those? Mabel is really curious about her letters, too." I pantomimed Mabel taking the letter tiles out of her baggie. I placed them on the easel, purposely out of order. I made sure the letter *M* was turned to the capital letter side, and the rest were lowercase. I looked at them with a confused expression and then pretended to have Mabel whisper in my ear. "Friends, you know what Mabel just told me? She realized those are the letters in her name, all mixed up. She wants to try to put them in the right order."

I took out Mabel's name card and fastened it to the top of the easel. I pretended to talk to Mabel. "Mabel, you can use your name card to help you put the letters in the right order." Then I turned to the class. "Would you all help Mabel as well?"

We proceeded letter by letter to put the letter tiles in order, and we named each letter as we did.

Channel students to try this work, using their name cards to put the letter cards of their own names in the correct order.

"Now, would you all try this? Make sure your name card is on the rug in front of you. Then, take out your letter tiles. Use your name card to put the letters in the correct order."

Once students had done that, I said, "Here's a tip as you get started: check to make sure the first letter of your name is flipped to the capital side, just like Mabel's is."

As students worked, I checked to make sure everyone's letter tiles were in the right order, and I corrected as needed. I checked that children were using the capital letter side of their first letter tile to start their names. I voiced over, "Be sure to use the lowercase letters in the rest of your name."

Challenge students to put their letter cards in order *without* the scaffold of the name card. Demonstrate with the class mascot to set up this work.

After most of the students had finished putting their letter tiles in order, I said, "Look what Mabel can do now. Watch closely because then you can try doing this." I pantomimed Mabel taking away her name card and messing up the order of her letter tiles. "Let's see if Mabel can put her letters in the right order, without her name card, and without our help."

With my help, Mabel pulled the letter *M* from her pile, and for a moment laid it sideways where the letter belonged. I had her pull back, look at what she'd done, and then move the letter right-side up. Proceeding in a similar way, making somewhat silly mess-ups that she self-corrected, Mabel proceeded to lay more of her tiles out without looking at the correct spelling of her name. She got stuck over the sequence of the last two letter tiles, so I had Mabel pull out her name card, study it, put it aside, and then complete her name. "Mabel, you did it!"

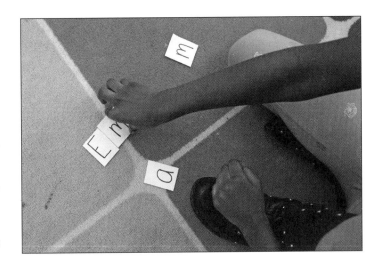

Channel the kids to do the same with their names, trying to do so without the support of the name card, only drawing on the name card if they are stuck.

"Can you try messing up your letters and then putting them in order again, without looking at your name card?" I asked. "Only look at your name card if you need help."

As students worked, I coached them, reminding them to use what they knew about the letter sounds in their names to put the letters in order, and to check their name cards if needed.

SHARE • Teaching Each Other Our Names

Invite partners to teach each other their names, as a way to solidify the idea of knowing their own names by heart.

Once much of that work was done, I said, "Now you really truly know your names by heart. When you really know something by heart, you can teach it to someone else. Would you and your partner take turns teaching each other your names? Be sure to say the names of the letters as you work together."

After a few minutes, I reconvened the class. "We could work a lot longer, teaching each other our names, but we have other work to do today. The good news is that you'll be doing cool stuff with your names all week, and soon, we'll begin to learn each other's names by heart too.

"Put your letter tiles and your name card into your baggie and I'll collect them. We have to keep them in great shape because we have a lot more work to do with them. So, make sure to put all of your letters and your name card away carefully. Cheer the letter names for the tiles in your name as you put them back into the baggie to make sure you have all of your letters."

The next session begins with you distributing these baggies to kids, so consider collecting all the baggies from each row of kids at the end of today.

EXTENSION 1 • Making Name Necklaces

GETTING READY

- Prepare a baggie for each child containing materials to make a name necklace: a string long enough to slide over the child's head, and letter tiles with holes punched in two top corners.

Remind students about the name necklace the class made for the mascot and explain that each of them will get to make their own name necklace. Hand out materials, and coach as students work.

"Remember back to the beginning of school—when you met Mabel? Do you remember how we made that special name necklace for her? Well, a few of you were asking, 'Hey, what about me? I want a name necklace too!' And you know what, you're right—we should all have name necklaces!

"I'm going to give you a bag with all the materials you need for your name necklace. When you get your bag, carefully take out your letters and put them in order. When you get them in order, start to string them onto your name necklace. When you are finished, I will come around and tie your necklace."

I passed out baggies to each student. As students worked, I moved around the rug, noticing which students still needed support to put their names in the correct order. I coached in quickly, while also tying the necklaces of students who had finished.

"Once your necklace is made, put it on—and then read each other's name necklaces. As you make a sound in someone's name, try to point to the letter that makes the sound. If you don't know the name of a letter in someone's name, ask about it."

This extension is engaging and highly motivating for many children, but it does require a great deal of preparation. Please consider it optional, and feel free to skip it if you are short on time or resources. This could also become a choice for choice time. During free play time, different groups of children could take turns making their name necklace. If you want to have children wear these necklaces as part of your end-of-unit celebration, be sure every child gets a chance to make one before Session 17.

POSSIBLE COACHING MOVES

- "Look at your name on the bag. Does it look the same?"
- "Which letter comes first? Now what comes next?"
- "Can you make the sound of each letter as you put it on the necklace?"

EXTENSION 2 • Reading the Name Wall

Teach students how to read the name wall, then lead them to read it in a few different ways.

"Readers, you are not just learning each other's names, you are learning to read! Let's all read the names on our name wall, only let's read it like this: we'll first read the letter: *M*. Then the name, *Mabel*. Then we'll say the letter sound, /m/. So it will sound like this: *M, Mabel,* /m/. You ready?" I used my pointer to point at individual names as we read them, and I reminded children to stay with me if they read ahead or lagged behind.

"Now let's reread the name wall, only this time, will you read it in a squeaky mousey voice?" We did the same thing.

"Does someone have an idea for another way we could read this?" I asked, and soon we tried that way.

This is the way the alphabet chart will be read in Unit 2: first the letter name, then the representative word, then the letter sound. There will be empty letters on your name wall at this point, so just skip letters that do not have names attached to them yet. This will be the first of many times you'll guide students to read the name wall. Teaching them to do it today with fewer names is a more manageable introduction than waiting until the wall is filled.

Pick a new name from the Star Jar. Sing the "Guess the Name" song, then guide students through the steps to study the name using the "Let's Study a Name!" chart.

I held up a new name and sang the "Guess the Name" song with the class. Then we read through each step on our "Let's Study a Name!" chart.

Teach students to write the letter correctly, voicing over the letter formation pathway while students practice writing the letter with invisible markers several times.

Then we followed the steps to write the new letter. I recited the letter formation pathway while students wrote the letter in the air, then on the carpet, then on their partner's hand with invisible marker.

Sing the "Star Name Celebration Song" and post the name on the name wall.

We wrapped up our time together by singing the "Star Name Celebration Song" and posting the name on our name wall.

Learning to Write Names by Heart
Your Muscles Can Learn to Write Letters Quickly

GETTING READY

✔ Before this session, prepare a name map to add to each child's name baggie. Use the letter formation pathway font in the online resources, or write the name on a sentence strip and use numbers and arrows to show proper formation of the letters. You might use different colors for each step to help children see the pathway more clearly.

✔ Prepare an additional name map with arrows for each student's writing folder.

✔ Bring Mabel's name baggie to the rug and prepare to show her name map. Focus on the capital letter *M* and use a marker to draw the letter.

PHONICS INSTRUCTION

Concepts About Print
• Write one's first name with all letters in accurate sequence.

Letter Knowledge
• Recognize some letters and state their names, especially letters in children's names.

• Recognize the name/sound of letters.

• Use efficient and consistent motions to form letters.

IN THIS SESSION

TODAY YOU'LL teach students that it is super-important that they learn to write their own names fast. You'll also teach that if they practice this over and over, their muscles will learn to do this.

TODAY YOUR STUDENTS will use a name map showing the correct pathway to write each letter in their names to practice the first letter in their names and then, during rug time, the rest of the letters.

MINILESSON

CONNECTION

Tell a story about a time or two when writing your name was especially important. Explain that people write their names in tons of places, as a way of declaring ownership.

When all of the children had gathered, I said, "Have you ever been to the beach and seen kids use a stick or their hand to write their names in the sand? I used to do that. I'd take a big stick and write my name," I paused and quickly jotted my name on my chart paper, then continued, "as a way to say to the world, 'I am here!'

"I used to write my name on all kinds of stuff. Once, my aunt gave me a special book, so I put my name on the inside cover to make sure everyone knew it was mine.

"Artists sign their names on their paintings. And sculptors—people who make frogs and people out of stone—they even sign their names *in the stone*. And, authors sign their names on their books. People wait in line to get their favorite author's autograph.

"So yes, it is *super*-important for each of us in this class to know how to write our own names."

❖ **Name the teaching point.**

"Today I want to teach you that it is super-important to learn to write your own name fast—and, more than that, it is important that *your muscles* learn to write your own name."

TEACHING

Show kids how muscle memory works, then invite them to demonstrate a few activities that their muscles can do by heart. Point out that their muscles can learn to write their names by heart.

"Here is something amazing: People's *muscles* can learn things by heart." I paused for dramatic effect. "It's true, let me show you. Raise your hand if you know how to hop." Hands shot up. "Really? All of you know how to hop? That's terrific, let me see it. Stand up in your spot and hop!

"How about spinning a fidget spinner? Do some of you know how to do that? Hold an imaginary fidget spinner and show me how you do that.

"Here's another. Do some of you know how to zip up your coat or your sweatshirt? With an imaginary zipper, show me how to do it. Pretend the zipper isn't even started, it isn't on the track yet."

The kids did all these things. "I'm not sure you realize it, but each of those activities takes a bunch of complicated steps. Like the zipper—first you have to get the little box-thing in your hand and then you bring it over to the zipper-track, right? And you have to set things up, so the zipper will be on its track, right? Then you hold one end down and pull the other up. That's a lot of steps!

"My point is that if you are good at zipping your coat, you do all those tiny little actions *by heart*. Your muscles know how to do them. You don't even think about them because your muscles have done them so often that you know them by heart. Well, in the same way, you need to learn to write your name and your muscles need to learn to do that by heart."

Review the path to write the letter *M*. Introduce a map that shows the path to write a letter.

"You already learned to write some letters. Like the capital *M*. Let's write it together." I gestured for kids to join me as I wrote in the air and recited the letter formation pathway for capital *M*: "Line down, back up, slanted line down, slanted line up, line down.

"Here's the thing. Each letter in your name has its own path, just like the *M* does. I can't tell each of you the pathway for all the letters in your name right at this moment. But I can give you a name map to follow so you can learn to write your own name. And if you write your name about a million times over and over, your muscles will learn to do this by heart.

Just as automaticity in reading leads to fluency and comprehension, automaticity in writing leads to fluency and meaning making.

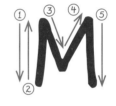

"I'll show you how to read and follow your map by showing you what I did for Mabel. When Mabel was just learning to write her name, I gave her this map of her name." I showed the kids Mabel's name map. I asked the class, "What do you notice?"

"It has arrows and numbers," one child called.

"Let me show you how I follow this name map. For now, I'm going to work on just the first letter, capital letter *M*. I'm following the map to write with my finger—my imaginary pen. You'll do that with your name in a minute." I put my finger on the number one and then demonstrated how I followed the arrow in the proper direction. I continued following numbers and arrows to complete the letter. As I did this, I said, "Number and then slide along the arrow. Number and then slide."

Demonstrate how to read and follow the letter map again, this time writing the letter *M* with a marker to show the path that you followed.

"Let me try this again, only this time, instead of using my imaginary pen, I'm going to use a marker. I'll follow the name map again. Hmm, . . . where is number one?" I found the first number, noticed the direction of the arrows, and showed students how I made the mark. I continued to use the map to write the rest of the letter with a marker.

"So, writers, you'll have a chance to practice this a whole bunch with your own names. The more times you make the letters in your names, the more your muscles will learn to make those letters by heart. And the easier it will be to write your name everywhere—on the beach and on foggy mirrors, and especially in your stories."

ACTIVE ENGAGEMENT/LINK

Point out that within each name baggie, you have included a name map showing how to make the letters in each child's name.

"Right now, will you open your name baggie. Inside you'll find the map showing how to make the letters in your name. For now, do like we've done with Mabel and just think about the first letter in your name. Find out where to start making that letter, and follow the arrows, drawing the letter with your imaginary pen in the air."

I gave the children a moment to do that, and as they did, I kept an eye out for children who needed more help. Then I said, "Show your partner how you do this. Watch each other make the first letter of your names."

Once many of the kids had made their letter once or twice, I said, "Now remember. To help your muscles how to make your first letter by heart, your hand needs to make it about a million times. So try it again, this time on the rug. Use your map, and make sure to follow the numbers and arrows."

You'll need to decide on routines for distributing name baggies. You won't have time to repeat yesterday's long process, so you might simply hand kids their name baggies as quickly as possible and ask them to sit on them until it's time to use them. Or, you might organize these into bins for each row, and ask row leaders to quickly pass them out.

Invite children to continue practicing the first letter of their names and let them know this is something they can do all the time.

"Writers, one cool thing about knowing how to make your letter is that you can practice it anytime. At dinner, you could write it with your finger on the table. While you wait for a bus, you could write it, with your imaginary pen, on the bus stop bench. It's like leaving a secret mark wherever you go."

RUG TIME

Channel students to use their name maps to write the rest of their names. Coach them as they work.

"Oh, look at this! I can't believe my eyes. Some of you are moving on to write the other letters in your names and you are doing that without me even telling you to! What an amazing group of workers we have in this classroom.

"Writers, go for it. Follow your name map and write the other letters of your name. Do it as many times as you can to help your muscles learn it!"

As students worked, I circulated, helping those that needed it to follow their maps and correctly write the letters in their names.

Don't worry if you aren't able to make sure that each and every student in the class is forming the letters in his or her name exactly right during this rug time. Today is an introduction. There will be plenty of opportunities to help your students fine-tune the letter formation of their names going forward. The truth is, you can coach in to letter formation including anytime during the day when children are asked to write their names.

SHARE • Setting Up to Write Names during Writing Workshop

Set students up to continue writing their names across the day at school and at home. Be sure that you've put a name map into each child's writing folder.

"Now writers. We have to stop. I know, I know, you don't want to stop practicing your names. Here's the good news. I've put a name map in each of your writing folders so that you'll have it near you when you write. From now on, you can write your name for real, with pens, whenever you have writing time. You are definitely going to want to put the author's name—your name—on each of your writing pieces. And, if you draw a picture, at school or at home, what will you add to your picture? Yes! Your name!"

EXTENSION 1 • Writing Giant Letters in the Sky

Ask students to spread out around the room in partnerships. Then, have them take turns writing their names in the air in giant letters, using their name maps for support.

"Writers, do you remember that earlier today, I told you that you are soon going to be able to write your name by heart, using muscle memory, just like you can hop on one foot or zip your coat?

"Some scientists have said that the best way for you to get your name into your muscles' memory is to draw your name in *gigantic* letters that are as big as you are.

"So right now, I'm going to ask you to work with your partner. First, the two of you find a place in the classroom where no one will bother you, where you can make your name in giant letters. Go ahead, spread out with your partner." I waited until children were ready. "Decide on one partner to be the writer, and the other to be the teacher." The children did that, and I continued, "Teachers, hold up the name map for your partner, high up so your partner can see it. And then, writers, will you follow the map and write the first letter of your name in the air, making the letter as tall as you are?"

Once the kids did that, I called out, "Do that again. Your muscles need to learn to do that by heart!" Again, after a minute, I called out, "Go on to the next letters."

After a bit, I asked the kids to swap so the "teachers" had a turn to be the writers.

This extension also works well done outside with sidewalk chalk.

EXTENSION 2 • Labeling Coat Spots

GETTING READY

- Prepare a big card for students to write their names on and a marker for each student.

Offer students an authentic purpose for writing their names: labeling the spots where they hang their coats.

"Writers, before you go home, don't you think it would be a good idea to label the spot where you hang your coat? I'm giving you a big card and a marker. When you get these tools, will you follow your name map and write your name on this card? Get started!

"If you finish early, write your name on your writing folder. Your name should be all over your stuff."

Of course, it may be too early in the school year for coats where you live, or you may live in a climate where students don't need coats. If that's the case, you can invite students to label any spot in the classroom where they keep their personal belongings.

EXTENSION 3 • Introducing a Star Name

Pick a new name from the Star Jar. Sing the "Guess the Name," song then guide students through the steps to study the name using the "Let's Study a Name!" chart.

I held up a new name and sang the "Guess the Name" song with the class.

We went through each step on our "Let's Study a Name!" chart.

Teach students to write the letter correctly, voicing over the verbal pathway while students practice writing the letter with invisible pens several times.

Then we followed the steps to write the new letter. I recited the verbal pathway while students wrote the letter in the air, then on the carpet, then on their partner's hand with invisible marker.

Sing the "Star Name Celebration Song" and post the name on the name wall.

Star Name Celebration Song

(to the tune of Old MacDonald had a Farm)

_____, _____ is a star

Clap, clap, clap, clap, clap

_____'s name starts with a ____

___, ___, ___, ___, ___

With an /_ / /_ / here and a /_ / /_ / there

Here a /_ /, there a /_ /

Everywhere a /_ / /_ /

_____, _____ is a star

/_ / /_ / /_ / /_ / /_ /

We wrapped up our time together by singing the "Star Name Celebration Song" and posting the name on our name wall.

When you have time, either as part of this extension or later on, have students help you sort pictures to create a letter book for this letter, as you did before. Depending on how much time you have, you can have students sort pictures in partnerships or groups, or you can simply hold pictures up and ask them to call out or give a thumbs up if the picture belongs in the letter book. The latter will be the faster way.

Owning Letters and Teaching Them to Others

GETTING READY

✔ Bring Mabel's name baggie to the rug, and make sure students have their name baggies.

✔ Before class, assemble whiteboards and related supplies. Be ready to distribute a whiteboard and marker to each rug club.

PHONICS INSTRUCTION

Letter Knowledge
- Recognize the name/sound of letters.
- Distinguish between uppercase and lowercase letters.
- Use efficient and consistent motions to form letters.
- Recognize and use beginning consonant sounds and the letters that represent them.

Word Knowledge/Solving
- Say a word slowly to hear any sound.

IN THIS SESSION

TODAY YOU'LL teach students that one way to make sure you really own the first letter of your name is to teach it to others.

TODAY YOUR STUDENTS will work in rug clubs to practice teaching the first letter of their names to each other.

MINILESSON

CONNECTION

Rally students to today's work—to own the letters in their own names. Demonstrate how to do this by tracing and calling out each letter in your class mascot's name.

"I've been seeing you write your name on your writing. That is great. It is as if you really *own* your name and all its letters and the way to make those letters. When you really own something, you walk through the world with that thing—whether it is swimming or playing the piano or writing your name—and you can say to the world, 'Don't worry. I got this!' For example, I think I've learned to write Mabel's name. Watch . . . "

I took out Mabel's name card from her name baggie and hung it on the easel. I touched the *M* in Mabel's name, and traced it with my finger. Then I called out, "*M*!" and said, "I've got this!" I did the same with the other letters in Mabel's name.

"Now it's your turn. Take out your name card. Trace each letter in your name, like I did with Mabel's letters and call out the name of that letter. If you know that letter, say, 'I've got this!'

"It's so cool to know your name by heart. Your name can help you do more and more things as a reader and a writer. And that is what I want to teach you today."

❖ **Name the teaching point.**

"Today I want to teach you that once you know your name by heart, you *own* the first letter (and maybe even other letters) in your name. When you own a letter, you can even *teach* what you know to others!"

TEACHING

Invite one student to help demonstrate teaching her first letter to the rest of the class.

"Jessica, can you come up here? Jessica, do you know the first letter in your name so well you could tell us about it, you could teach it to us?" Jessica said yes. I continued, "*Jessica* starts with a *J*. Letter *J* makes the /j/ sound at the beginning of *Jessica*. Let's all say it together. /j/-*Jessica*.

"Let's watch Jessica write her letter." I gave Jessica a marker, and she drew a *J* on the easel while I said the letter formation pathway. "Line down and hook up. Line across the top. Now, would you all give this a try? Jessica, write the *J* again, and this time, all of you follow along with your imaginary pens on the rug in front of you."

The class did this, while I voiced over the letter formation pathway again, and then I said, "Jessica, could you teach us some *J* words? Let's think of words that start in the same way as your name. Whisper a few you know to me."

Jessica shared her words with me, and I asked her to tell them to the class. "*Jellybeans* and *jar*." I asked the rest of the class to think of words they knew that started with *J*, and I gave them a couple of minutes to share their words in partnerships.

I called on another couple of children to teach their letters to the class.

ACTIVE ENGAGEMENT/LINK

Allow students to practice teaching the first letter of their names to each other. Coach students who need extra support, including those whose names may follow the patterns of various languages.

"Are you all ready to be the teachers and teach your friends about your first letter? Let's do it! You're going to stand up and walk around the rug, introducing yourself to each other. Pretend you are grown-ups at a work meeting, just meeting each other for the first time. Say, 'Hello, my name is . . . ' and then say your name. Shake hands, like this." I shook a student's hand as I spoke. "After you say your name, say the first sound in your name, then say the letter, like this, 'My name is Mabel, /m/ *M*.' Let's give it a try!"

I walked around with the students, modeling the process with my own name a few times.

Don't worry about leaving enough time for kids to call out each letter in their name. Allow them time to call out just a few, knowing that this will be enough for them to grasp the idea.

If you have students who need more support with this activity, you may wish to choose their names as examples. Make sure to explicitly connect the letter sound with each new letter that is introduced and give students an opportunity to make the sound several times. Listen in carefully to students' articulation. For sounds like /j/ it is essential that students say /j/ and not /juh/ or /jah/. You can direct children's attention to the way the sound feels in their mouth to scaffold sound making even more.

"One, two, three, eyes on me. Kindergartners, can I pause you for one minute?" I waited until everyone had turned to face me. "I have to tell you something so special that I just found out! Javier was introducing himself to Corrie. He said 'My name is /h/ Javier. My first letter is *J*.' And Corrie said, 'Wait, wait, I'm confused, I thought *J* made the /j/ sound!' And Javier said, 'But in my name it makes the /h/ sound!' And you know what, they are both right! A lot of times the *J* makes the /j/ sound like *jump* and in Javier's name it makes the /h/ sound.

"That's actually because in Spanish, *J* makes the sound /h/. I'm so glad you could teach us that, Javier and Corrie! That really makes me think about how important it is to always ask someone how to say their name when you meet them. You can learn so much!"

The students continued to move around the rug, teaching each other the first letter of their names. I coached in to support a few students as they did this work. A few minutes later, I called the students back to their spots.

Remind students of today's learning: that when you really own the first letter of your name, you can teach it to others.

"Wow. I didn't know if it was possible this early in the year, but here you all are, beginning of kindergarten, and you are already teaching the class! You've shown that you really own the first letter of your names—you own those letters so well that you can teach them to each other. I think you are ready to take this work to the next level."

You will likely run into similar sound variations like this one with Javier. That is one of the lovely things about studying names, the opportunity to learn about different pronunciations of letters, and different cultures. However, working with names that come from various languages can feel tricky, since we want to make sure students learn the English sounds of each letter. Explain to students why some names begin with different sounds—the name may come from a different language or may begin with a digraph. This allows students to value that all names are special. This also helps students begin to gain an awareness that not all words will follow the same rules, and that is amazing. For names that don't have the primary sound for a letter, you will probably want to introduce that name with other names that begin with the same letter and not worry too much about the difference in sound.

RUG TIME

Form clubs of four or five students to teach each other how to write the first letter of their names, with students taking turns writing on a whiteboard while the others write in the air or the rug.

"We are going to work in 'rug clubs' today. That means you will be in a group of four or five. Let me show you what I mean." I moved around the rug, showing partnerships how to turn toward each other, forming little groups of four or five students. Once all the kids were sitting in a club, I set them up to work. "Okay, now that you are in your club, you will each get a chance to be the teacher in your club. We have something else that's new today, we're going to work with these handy tools, whiteboards and markers." I held up a whiteboard and a marker. "We'll use these a lot in phonics time from now on. If I hand you the whiteboard, that means you go first. Teach your group all about your first letter and then show them how to write it. Everyone else will write it in the air or on the rug. Maybe the teacher can think of words that start with your letter. After you teach your letter, pass the whiteboard to the friend next to you and let them try it."

I passed out whiteboards and markers to one student in each group that I felt could demonstrate this with success. As students began to teach, I moved around the rug, mostly helping to manage the process and support groups as they took turns with the whiteboard.

SHARE • Hearing All of the Sounds in Names

Work with the whole class to hear salient sounds in the names of the mascot and a few children. Teach a visual scaffold, touching your arm at different points to represent sounds across a name.

"Our names have other letters in them too. We can use our names to help us get even more letters in our back pockets, and then eventually, to learn to write them by heart. First, we have to practice hearing the sounds across a whole name, not just the first sound.

"Try saying this name using a stretching-out technique that first-graders often use to stretch out words as they write. You ready? Let's try it with *Mabel*." I put my left hand high up on my right arm and said, "*Ma-bel*." As I reached the /b/ sound, I slid my hand to the middle of my arm. And, as I got to the /l/ sound, I slid my hand to my wrist.

"Now, let's clap the name. That can help us to hear all of the sounds in *Ma-bel*." I clapped each syllable as I said this, and then I led the class in clapping the name a few times. Then, I wrote *Mabel* on my whiteboard easel, saying the salient sounds as I got to them.

We repeated this process for a few more names in the class.

Suggest that hearing more sounds will come in handy when kids want to write. Use the sounds in one child's name as an example and talk about all the labels that one child can now write.

"I'm so glad that we helped Mabel hear the /b/ sound and the /l/ sound in her name. Now she can write with more than just the letter *M*. She can also write *bubblegum* with a *B* and *lollipop* with an *L* in her story about the candy she loves. Mabel could also teach these letters to a friend to help that friend learn even more letters and the sounds they make.

"The good news is that because you are pushing yourself to hear more of the sounds in your name, *all* of you have a lot more letters that you can use now as you write. Tell the person next to you which letters in your name will be especially helpful to you as you write."

This share gives the day's teaching scope. It will be beyond the reach of some of your kids—some are still working on hearing the first letter in a word—but the work of this share will be helpful for kids who are more proficient.

Sliding your hand down your arm in this way is a visual scaffold to help students hear the sounds in the beginning, middle, and end of words. You can return to this often to help students stretch out words to hear all of their sounds.

EXTENSION 1 • Making Name Collages

GETTING READY

- Set up magazines and catalogs at tables, so children can search for items that begin with the same sounds as their names.
- Provide a sheet of construction paper to each child.

Coach children to create a collage of objects that begin with the same sound as their own name, highlighting that every name can help to spell other words that start with the same sound.

"You know that you can use your name to help spell other words, right? In a few minutes, you'll have some time to make something special to help people spell. Each of you is going to make a collage to help other people use your name to spell other words. At each table I've placed some magazines and catalogs for you to look through, so that you can find pictures and words that start with the same sound as your name. When you find a picture, you can cut it out and glue it onto your construction paper. Later, we'll display these for everyone to enjoy.

I sent each group off to tables to begin searching for pictures and words. As students worked, I circulated and coached them.

When a student's name begins with a letter that makes a sound that is from another language, such as Javier, explain to the student that because their name is special, they can decide how to do this project. Javier may choose to find pictures that start with the /h/ sound, like his name, or he may want to use pictures that begin with J, like jellybeans. Celebrate how much students can learn when names make different sounds.

POSSIBLE COACHING MOVES

▸ "Look at the pictures and say the words that go with the pictures. Listen to the first sound. Does it sound like your name?"

▸ "Say the word that goes with your picture really slowly. What do you hear at the beginning? Now say your name slowly. Do they sound the same?"

▸ "Oooh, look at this page. I see a word that starts like your name. See if you can figure out which one it is."

EXTENSION 2 • Practicing Salient Sounds in Names

Remind students of a way they sang the alphabet song, popping up when their first letter was sung. Invite them to extend this work by popping up when they hear any of the main sounds in their names.

"Class, earlier we sang the alphabet song and each of you popped up when your letter was sung—Lisa, you popped up when we sang the *L*. I thought we might sing it again right now, and this time, will you pop up *whenever* you hear one of the main sounds in your name? So class, Lisa will need to pop up not only when we sing *L*, but also when we sing *S*." We sang the song as I pointed to each letter on the name wall.

Encourage students to draw on all of the letters in each other's names as they write. Give a few examples to illustrate this.

"Now that you are getting to know all of the letters in your name, you can also help other people think of words that start with those letters. You become the class expert on all of the letters in your name, not just the first letter. So, Lisa's name could help us to write /l/-*lollipops*, but the *S* could also help us to write /s/-*sandwiches*."

"During writing workshop, if anyone needs help writing a particular sound, you can ask others at the table to help. And you can help each other using not just the first letter in your names, but all of the letters. If José needed help writing about *nasty noodles*, Natalia could help him with the *N*, but so could Ben." I emphasized the /n/ sound.

Pick a new name from the Star Jar. Sing the "Guess the Name" song, then guide students through the steps to study the name using the "Let's Study a Name!" chart.

"Let's get another name from our Star Jar. This time, as we learn the new name, we'll listen not just for the first sound, but for as many sounds as we can hear."

I drew out another name, a short, simple name that I had prepared. I began to sing, "It starts with a *B*." The kids joined in and figured out this was *Ben*.

"Okay, before we race ahead here and start stretching out more sounds in Ben's name, let's make sure we go through all the steps to study his name first. We don't want to miss anything important—that wouldn't be fair to Ben or his name!" I gestured toward the "Let's Study a Name!" chart and we quickly went through the steps as a class.

Teach students a technique to help them stretch out sounds using today's star name: touching their arms at different points while they say the sounds they hear in the word.

"Whew, great work! Now friends, can you try to really hear all the letters in *Ben*? Stretch out his name using the technique that first-graders use. Touch the parts of your arm as you say the sounds in his name." I put my left hand high up on my right arm and stretched out the name "Bbbbbeeeeeeeennnnnn" as I touched first my shoulder, then the middle of my arm, then my wrist. "What sounds did you hear in Ben's name? Turn and tell your partner."

I listened in and then voiced over. "Did you hear that /n/ sound at the end? Me too! Okay, Ben, can you come up and help us with your name? Everyone, say Ben's name slowly as he underlines it with his finger. Make sure to stop when you get to the letter that makes the /n/ sound." I helped Ben run his finger under his name and pause at the letter *n*.

Teach students the fast way to write today's letter, while you voice over the letter formation pathway.

"Okay, friends, get your imaginary markers out. Let's learn Ben's letter, *B*. Ben is going to trace the *B* on his name, and the rest of us will do it in the air." I said the letter formation pathway out loud as Ben began to trace. "Line down. Back up. Bump around. Bump around. And now, let's practice the *n* in Ben's name. Ben, you trace it up here while everyone else does it in the air." I recited, "Line down, back up, bump around and down."

Add Ben's name to the name wall and sing the "Star Name Celebration Song."

"Before we stop today, let's make sure we get Ben's name up on the wall. Sing with me." The class joined in on the "Star Name Celebration Song" to the tune of "Old MadDonald."

> Ben, Ben is a star
> Clap, clap, clap, clap, clap
> His name starts with a *B*
> *B, B, B, B, B*
> With a /b/ /b/ here and a /b/ /b/ there

"Class, we should stop. I heard that we have ravioli for lunch. Wait a minute. I just thought about something. We can stretch out *ravioli* like we stretched out *Ben*. Try it. /r/," I said, putting my hand high on my arm, waiting for the class to do the same. I modeled saying *ravioli* slowly, then I said it again, this time calling out the salient sounds and modeling, touching each part of my arm as I did so.

"What do *you* like best to eat? Tell your partner—only this time, say it slowly, listening for the sounds and touching your arm as you go. What sounds really pop out at you in each word?"

Using Names to Build New Words
Exploring Rhyme

IN THIS SESSION

TODAY YOU'LL teach students that when they know words by heart, they can use parts of those words to make new words. You'll teach them that changing the first sound in a word to a different sound produces a rhyming word.

TODAY YOUR STUDENTS will practice changing the first letter in familiar names to make new words.

MINILESSON

CONNECTION

Rally students around the idea that being silly and playing with names is a fun way to learn more.

"I heard the silliest song the other day, and thought it would be so perfect for our class. Guess what the song is called? 'The Name Game Song!' That's perfect for us since we are learning all about names. I'll play you a bit of it." I played the chorus of 'The Name Game Song' by Shirley Ellis for the class.

We listened to the song and I giggled along with the class. "I bet we could sing this song with lots of different names. Should we try it with Mabel's name?"

We sang the song together, with the YouTube version in the background: "Mabel, Mabel, bo Babel, banana fanna fo Fabel, Fee Fi mo Mabel . . . Mabel!"

"That song is so fun! And it really gets me thinking about more things we can do with our names."

GETTING READY

✔ Cue up the chorus of "The Name Game Song" by Shirley Ellis. You'll play from 1:48 through 2:22. A link to this video is available in the online resources. Copies of "The Name Game Song" are included in the Resource Pack. 📦

✔ Write the name of one student in each rug club on a whiteboard. We recommend choosing names that begin with consonants. Have these and markers ready to distribute to each club.

PHONICS INSTRUCTION

Concepts About Print
- Use one's name to learn about words and to make connections to words.

Phonological Awareness
- Recognize and produce rhyming words.
- Hear, say, and clap syllables.
- Change the beginning phoneme to make a new word.

Word Knowledge/Solving
- Use the letters in names to read and write other words.
- Change the beginning sound or sounds to make and solve a new word.

♣ **Name the teaching point.**

"Today I want to teach you that when you know your name by heart (or actually, when you know *any* word by heart) you can use parts of it to make new words. You can make real words, and you can make silly pretend words, too."

TEACHING

Demonstrate how changing the initial sound in a name creates words that rhyme with that name.

"Let me show you what I mean. We know Mabel's name starts with the letter *M* /m/." I wrote Mabel's name up on the board. "But what if we played around with Mabel's name a little? What if we took off the *M* and changed it to a *B*? Hmm, . . . it's not /m/-*Mabel* anymore, now it's . . . " I left space for kids to think about this, and a few chimed in, "*Babel*!" I nodded, "Yes, it is /b/-*Babel*! We made a new name!

"And you know what else? *Mabel* and *Babel*, those rhyme! If you change the first letter in a word to make a different word, you make rhyming words.

"Let's try another one." I erased the *B* and wrote *L*. "Not /m/-*Mabel* or /b/-*Babel* anymore, now it's . . . "

The kids called, "/l/-*Label*!"

I nodded, "Yes, *label*! And this time we made a real word. Do you see how all we did was change one letter and we made a funny name, *Babel*, and a real word, *label*? And the words we made all rhyme—*Mabel*, *Babel*, *label*. Can you make more words that rhyme with *Mabel*? Try it now with your partner."

The kids all started talking at once. I listened in to their conversations and nodded as they talked. I corrected one partnership, "Oh, I see you tried to change two sounds in *Mabel* to make a new word. You said, 'La-dle.' Those words are similar, but they don't quite rhyme. You can use the beginning sound you came up with, /l/, but keep the rest of the word the same, -*abel*. Put those together and you get *label*. See how *Mabel* and *label* rhyme?"

ACTIVE ENGAGEMENT/LINK

Encourage students to practice changing the initial sound with another name.

"Let's try it with a different name. Yesterday we read *Pete the Cat*. Why don't we use Pete's name?" I wrote *Pete* on the board. "/p/-*Pete*," I said.

"Okay, what happens if I erase this *P* and make it an *S*?"

"*Seat*!" a few kids shouted.

Teaching
Mabel
Babel
Label

write on board - replace 1st letter

ActiveEng./Link
Pete the Cat
Own name w/ partr
"D" P

You can invite students to come up with rhyming words as they do in this session at any time of the day, such as when they are lining up for recess or waiting to go home at the end of the day.

Spelling doesn't matter at this point. Of course, the word seat *won't be spelled correctly if you erase the* P *and make it an* S, *but there is no need to point this out to kids. You're simply encouraging them to practice with onsets and rimes.*

"Yes! /s/-*seat*! Now turn to your partner; what other words can you make with the name *Pete*?" I listened in as the kids came up with new words that rhyme with *Pete*. I voiced over the words that some partners had come up with to provide a scaffold for other partnerships. "Oh, *Pete*, *beat*, that's a cool one!"

Channel the class to do similar work with their own names, working with a partner.

"Now will you and your partner take a moment to play around with your own names? Say your name, then put a new letter in the front of your name. Try these letters," and I named some consonants from the name wall.

I listened a bit and then shared a few with the whole class. "These are great! *Dahlia*, *Bahlia*, *Mike*, *hike*. *Daniel*, *Faniel*."

For students with longer names, like Georgina, *you might suggest they try this with only part of their names, otherwise the rhyming work gets too complicated.* Georgina *might find rhymes for* George *or* Georgie, *for example.*

RUG TIME

Organize children into rug clubs and distribute a whiteboard to each club with a name written on it. Coach children to practice doing this same work with the name on their board.

"I can tell you are ready to try this with other kids' names. When you get in your rug clubs, I am going to hand each club a whiteboard with one name on it. If it's your name, you get to be in control of the marker today. See how many new words your club can make just by changing the first letter in your name. Remember, they might be real words, or they might be pretend words. If you have the marker, write these words down as your club works."

I passed out the whiteboards to students whose names were written on them, and I handed each a marker. I coached as clubs worked, making new rhyming words using the names written on the board.

POSSIBLE COACHING MOVES

▶ "Look up at the letters on our name wall. Which letter comes next? Try that letter."

▶ "Say your name first to help you get the sound right, then say the new word like this: *Natalia*, /h/-*Hatalia*! Now you try."

SHARE • Celebrating the Bend with a Name Parade

Encourage students to share one rhyming word—real or pretend—for their own names.

After the kids had some time to come up with words, I brought them back together. "On the count of three, everyone shout one new word that you came up with today using your name. Like Mabel might say '*Babel*!' or Ben might say, '*hen*!' Put your thumb on your knee when you're ready. One, two, three!" The kids shouted out their words.

"Whoa, that's a lot of silly words and some real ones too," I said, acting as if I were almost falling over, I was so overwhelmed by all their work.

Set students up to stage a name parade. Ask them to line up behind you. Call out names and ask students to stomp the beats. Change the names' initial sounds to make new names.

"Today is a big day, boys and girls, because we've reached the end of another bend, or part, of this unit. We've done a lot of work getting to know our own names by heart, and now we are ready to move on to learning other letters and even words by heart.

"But for today, let's celebrate! How about a name parade? You line up behind me and I'll call out one of your names. Then we'll stomp the name, saying the parts as we parade to it.

"But wait, there's a twist! After we stomp the name, I'll call out a letter we can add to the beginning of the name to make a new name. Then we'll stomp that new name. Let's try it in our spots before we make our parade."

I demonstrated, "*Ava*!"

With my urging, the class repeated "*A-va, A-va, A-va*," stomping in their spots.

I called "*M*," and demonstrated, "May-va, May-va, May-va!"

I called "*T*" and we stomped "*Tay-va*."

"We are ready for our parade! Row one, line up behind me." When they were all lined up, I called, "Row two, it'll be your turn to line up."

We stomped and paraded to as many names as we could fit into the time we had. We ended with the name *Mabel*.

Another way to celebrate the work of this bend is to make a large name book with the class. You can call it an autograph book. Prepare a piece of chart paper for each letter, and place these around the room. Ask children to circulate, writing their names, leaving their autograph, on their first letter's page. Then, to extend this work, ask them to write their names on the pages for each letter in their names. For example, Ben would write his name not only on the B page, but also on the E and N pages. Have students circle the letter in their name that matches the letter of the page. So, Ben would circle the E in his name when he writes his name on the E page. This celebration sets up the work of Bend III nicely. In Bend III, the children use class names to help them write other words. The autograph book can serve as a resource for that work.

Dear Teachers,

This final bend of the unit cycles back to where you began, allowing you to return to letters and names that you haven't yet taught and moving through those quickly. You'll decide whether this bend is one you can teach in approximately a week, or whether your students need you to slow down a bit and explicitly teach each and every letter. The down side of that trade-off is that if your teaching proceeds too slowly, your children will be reading and writing without the advantage of instruction that could help them do both. It may make more sense to teach the most high-utility, high-frequency letters, words, and concepts and to do so fairly quickly, knowing that your instruction will review and consolidate later.

You will want to get through all of your class names and most, if not all, letters in this bend. To that end, Session 15 will be a favorite session. In this session you will add beloved characters to the name wall. You will probably teach a variation of this lesson over the course of a few days to teach the remaining letters on your name wall. For any letter that has no star name, be sure to find a name that is meaningful to your kids to help them learn that letter name and sound. (Kids could even vote as a class.) You may want to start brainstorming character names for tricky letters. We found the *X*, *Y*, and *Z* were especially hard. For *X*, we came up with *Max* (of *Max and Ruby*) or *X-men*; for *Y*, *Yoda* or *Yertle the Turtle*; and for *Z*, *Zazu* (from *The Lion King*) or *Zorro*.

There may be some esoteric names that you decide you won't address just now, and that's your decision. We don't think you need to feel terribly uneasy about leaving a few gaps in your teaching because "coverage" has always been a myth. That is, you can grant equal amount of time to every letter in the alphabet, but that by no means suggests that your kids will have learned every letter—or even been present in school (or attentive in class) when every letter is taught. Keep in mind that Unit 2, *Word Scientists*, focuses on the alphabet, and children will have lots of opportunities to learn about any letters that they don't yet control by the end of Unit 1.

Another emphasis of this unit is that kids need to use the letters they are learning about as they write. In Bend III, you'll encourage your students to transfer what they are learning about letters and words into their writing. You will teach your students to use the names and letters they have learned to add labels to their writing. There is not a huge focus on this, however, because we know this is the message of your writing workshop. The important thing is that kids understand that the only reason to learn letters and sounds is to use them, and that it is okay for them to approximate their way toward mastery.

This bend also contains a few sessions that focus on snap words—revisiting and using the snap words that kids already have, as well as extending their list by learning new words. You will introduce six high-frequency words, or "snap words," in this bend, because writers need more than just letters in their back pockets—they should have whole words in there too. You will want to display these words somewhere visible in the classroom, but don't add them to the name wall just yet, because there will be a chance for this in Unit 3.

A word about snap words. You will not want all of your snap word teaching to focus exclusively on words from the Dolch list, from Frye's high-frequency word list. It is true that those words are incredibly important—they dominate what kids read and write, and some are irregular enough that they are best learned by heart rather than figured out, but those words are also abstract. Kids don't fall head-over-heels in love with words like *from* and *an* and *these*. So, you will also want to mix in a small number of concrete words, based on your knowledge of your class. What do your kids love most? You will see that in this unit, we teach *Mom* and *Dad*, neither of which belong in a traditional list of high-frequency words. We hope you also teach *friend* or *cat*, based on your class.

If you worry that this unit ends by pronouncing the kids to be far more accomplished than they are, don't worry. All of us role-play our way into being the readers, writers, and learners we hope someday to be. Proclaiming your kids to be experts in the alphabet and to be the kinds of people who walk through life differently because they are readers and writers is a bit like calling them writers when they are still just labeling scrawls that have a vague semblance to a dog. It's called education. It's what we are here on earth to do.

All the best,
Lucy and Natalie

Labeling Things in the Classroom

GETTING READY

✔ Place Mabel face down on the floor in a visible location.

✔ Prepare two blank index cards and some tape to label Mabel's bed.

✔ Prepare some fabric or a piece of paper to create a tent for Mabel.

✔ Gather giant Post-its and pens for each rug club to use to label the room.

PHONICS INSTRUCTION

Concepts About Print
• Use one's name to learn about words and to make connections to words.

Phonological Awareness
• Hear and say the beginning phoneme in words.
• Hear and say the same beginning phoneme.

Letter Knowledge
• Recognize and name letters in the environment.
• Use efficient and consistent motions to form letters.

Word Knowledge/Solving
• Say a word slowly to hear any sound.

IN THIS SESSION

TODAY YOU'LL teach students that writers can use the letters they know to help them write anything they want.

TODAY YOUR STUDENTS will label areas and objects in the classroom by isolating the initial sounds in words and using the names they know to write the letter that goes with that sound.

MINILESSON

CONNECTION

Tell a story about a different classroom with many labels to motivate children to use letters they know to label things.

"Writers, yesterday I visited Mrs. Rogers's first grade. I found a coat on the playground that belonged to one of her kids. When I brought it to Mrs. Rogers, she said, 'Will you hang it up in the closet?' and when I went to do that, you won't believe what I saw. Her closet has a big sign on it.

"You know how every McDonald's has a sign that says 'McDonald's,' even though we could tell it is McDonald's without that sign? Well, in Mrs. Rogers's first grade, they have a sign that says 'Closet,' even though I could sort of tell that was the coat place even without the sign. But I loved that sign.

"In fact, I thought, 'Hey, why don't *we* have a sign like that?'

"But then, Kindergartners, when it was time for me to leave her room, I confess I didn't walk straight out. I sort of spied on her class. (I know, I was being a bit sneaky . . .) Let me tell you what I saw."

In a loud whisper, I said, "I saw another sign in her room, on the sink! Honest! It said . . . "

The children said—in a whisper—"sink."

Nodding, big-eyed, I said, "True story. And her block area had a sign that said, . . .

"Yep, you got it—it said 'blocks.' So, my spy-trip gave me an idea for what we can work on for the rest of this unit, because today starts the last part of our first unit. We still have a few more names to study, don't we?" I gave a thumbs-up signal to the children who had not yet been featured as star names. "But I think from now on, we need to not just learn star names, but also to *use* them. We can use the names we know"—and I pointed to the children and the name wall—"to help us write labels just like the first-graders do."

♣ **Name the teaching point.**

"Today I want to teach you that when you want to label something—*anything*—you can use the names you know to help you figure out how to write that label. You say the thing you want to write sl-ow-ly, and you listen for sounds. When you hear a sound, you can think, 'Who has *that* sound in their name?' Then you write that letter!"

TEACHING

Pretend to be startled to see that the class mascot slept in an awful location the night before, using that situation to recruit the class to help label her bed. Show kids how to use the name wall to help.

"Friends, this is *huge* news. Because that means that from now on during phonics time, you won't just be learning names, you'll also be using all those names to write tons of stuff. Phonics time will almost become another writing workshop! Isn't that cool?

"Writers—that's what I should really call you, right? I thought we'd start by doing some writing together right now. I was thinking we could write a label for—wait! Oh no." I stopped in my tracks and stared in shock at Mabel, face down on the floor. "*Look* at what I am seeing. What a disaster!"

I pointed to Mabel. "Mabel is sleeping on the hard floor! Can you believe it? She must have fallen out of her bed last night, and our custodian didn't see her or maybe he didn't know where to put her. We *definitely* can't let that happen again! Anytime she needs to go back to bed, people need to know where her bed is. What can we do to help people know where Mabel's bed is?"

The kids called out suggestions, including the idea that we could label her bed. Nodding, I said, "We can label her bed. That way, everyone who comes into our room will know where Mabel belongs. Will you help do that?"

Say the word you'll write, and then ask students to say the word, slowly, to hear all the sounds.

"Let's label Mabel's bed together. To write *bed* or any word, we need to say the word slowly, like a turtle, so that we can hear the sounds in that word." I swept down my hand my arm to illustrate stretching out the word. "B-b-b-e-e-e-d-d-d. Try it without me." The kids said *bed* so quickly it was hard to hear the sounds.

I reminded them, "Slow like a turtle. Watch me. B-b-b-e-e-e-d-d-d. Now you try saying the word slow as a turtle." This time, students said the word a little slower.

Demonstrate how you compare the initial phoneme in the word you're writing to names on the name wall to determine what letter makes the first sound. Coach students to do the same work.

"To write it, we need to say it again. B-b-b-e-e-e-d-d-d. I hear the /b/ sound, don't you? That's the very first sound my mouth makes when I say the word." I touched my ears and then my mouth as I said this.

I gestured toward the name wall. "Hmm, . . . I wonder if there's someone in this room whose name could help us? Now we need to figure out the letter that goes with that sound." I said. "Watch me first. I'm going to hear the sound, then match it to the first sound in a friend's name. Does b-b-b-ed start the same as Mmmmmabel and Mmmmmike?" As I spoke, I touched Mabel's and Mike's names on the name wall. I shook my head, "No."

"I'll try another one. Does b-b-b-ed start the same as Rrrrroman and Rrrrrebecca?" This time several kids called along with me, "No!"

"Test a few with your partner. Does b-b-b-ed start the same as Georgina? Or Lisa?" I let students talk for a moment.

"Wow! Some of you are saying that b-b-b-ed starts the same as Ben. Let's get Ben to help us spell *bed*. Ben, what letter should we use to spell *bed*?"

Ben called out that we needed to start the word with a *B*. I nodded and said, "Thanks Ben, and guess what? Even if Ben wasn't here today, he could have helped us. We could have found his picture on our name wall under the letter *B*, and we would have known that *bed* starts with *B*." I gestured to the name wall.

Show students how you write the first letter, reciting the letter formation pathway as you write. Ask students to write the letter on the rug as you repeat the letter formation pathway.

"Ben's name starts with the letter *B*. Ben, would you watch us make the letter, and make sure we are doing it right?" To the class I said, "Let's all make the letter together." I raised my arm to write in the air, and kids did likewise. I formed the letter in the air, saying the letter formation pathway as I did. "Line down. Back up. Bump around. Bump around!" Then, I channeled students to write a lowercase *b* on the rug, and then on their knees. "Long line down. Back up a scootch. Bump around." I repeated the letter formation pathway each time.

Touching your ears and your mouth is a cue for children that they can use their ears and the feel of a letter in their mouths to help them hear sounds and write letters in words.

If you don't have a student in your class whose name starts with a B, you might decide instead to label her mat or some other thing that belongs to Mabel and starts with the same letter as a child in your class. Be sure then to alter the story used here.

"I'll write *b* on the label now," I said, as I wrote the lowercase *b*, again saying aloud the letter formation pathway as I wrote it.

"Some of you might already be hearing more sounds in the word *bed*." I said the word slowly, and then I wrote the *e* and the *d* to complete the word *bed*. "Let's read what we have written." I put a finger under the word and read "*bed*" one more time, then I taped it to Mabel's bed.

If you want a correct label for display, you can fill in the missing letters at any point.

ACTIVE ENGAGEMENT/LINK

Invite students to help you label another item for the class mascot. Remind them to use the name wall for help figuring out how to write the word.

"I love fixing stuff up for Mabel, don't you?" I said. "I'm wondering if maybe we could make something else for her. Hmm, . . . oh! I know." I pulled out a piece of fabric. "Maybe later you could help me make a tent for Mabel. That way she won't fall out of bed." The class agreed.

"But wait! That means we'll have to label Mabel's tent, too." I taped another index card to the easel. "Ready to write *tent*? First, say the word slowly like a turtle so you can hear all the sounds." I listened as the kids sped through the word and said, "Say it really slowly: t-t-t-e-e-e-n-n-n-t-t-t." The kids said it again, a little slower.

"That was sooooo sslllllooooowwww! That must mean we're ready to write the first sound, /t/ /t/ t/. Let's see, do we have someone whose name can help us write that sound?"

"Tymel!" a few kids called.

I turned to the name wall and pointed. "Whoa! Some of you think *tent* starts the same as *Tymel*. Let's check! Ttttent. Ttt-tymel. Say it with me!" I encouraged the class to repeat *tent* and *Tymel*, putting extra emphasis on the beginning sound.

"You're right! The first sound in *tent* sounds the same as the first sound in *Tymel*. That must mean we need a letter *T*." I pointed to the first letter in Tymel's name.

Invite a student to write the first letter of the word for the label. Say the letter formation pathway as the student writes the letter.

I invited one child to write the letter *t*. "Patricia, will you come write the *t* in the word *tent* for us? Make sure to write it in lowercase because *tent* is not a name. Can you all help by writing it with your make-believe marker? Let's remember how to write lowercase *t*." I held my pointer finger up. "Line down. Little line across."

Patricia wrote the letter *t* on the blank label, and I finished the word by filling in the *ent*. "Great! Let's read what we wrote." I pointed under the word as we read "tent" in unison.

Again, this is entirely optional to add the rest of the letters to the label at this moment. Your teaching needs scope, and modeling writing the whole word may be helpful if some are ready.

Set students up to work in rug clubs to label areas and objects in the classroom.

"This is a great start, but I am still thinking about Mrs. Rogers's classroom, and all of the labels her students made, and I'm realizing we haven't labeled so many of the things in our classroom.

"I was thinking, if a few of you work together, maybe you can come up with some things that could be labeled in this classroom. Maybe one group of you might decide to label the block area, or one group might want to label our coats, or even our door. And then you can use all of your names and all that you know about letters to help you with the job.

"I'll pass out some giant Post-its and pens to each rug club. But first, decide as a club what you want to label." As students discussed, I began passing out the Post-its and pens.

"Now you can work together to figure out how to write that word. When you think you've got it, write it on your club's Post-it."

As students finished writing their labels, I sent them to post their labels in the correct spots around the classroom. Soon the groups were working on a second or a third label.

Teachers, please note that these labels will most likely not be spelled conventionally. We want students to know that we value their approximations and we want them to feel ownership over the things in their classroom. We also want to be sure that the labels in the room are helpful to students as readers and writers. For this reason, we have chosen to use a temporary method of labeling, Post-its. Later, you will take down all of these labels and use more sounds to make new and improved labels. However, you may want to take a few down earlier and use interactive writing to work together to write the words conventionally. We have written up a way this could go in an extension to this session.

SHARE • Choral Reading the Name Wall

Remind students how to read the name wall: first say the letter, then say the name, then say the letter sound. Demonstrate with the name of the class mascot.

"Writers, I think you are realizing how important it is to have a lot of letters in your back pocket! I'm looking at our name wall and realizing that we have helped each other learn so many letters. Let's read the name wall together as a way to celebrate all of the letters we know.

"Remember, we read the name wall like this." I demonstrated with Mabel's name. I pointed to the letter *M* and said, "*M, Mabel, /m/.*" Then, I moved to the start of the alphabet and gestured for the students to join me in saying all the letters and names on the name wall in our usual way: saying the first letter, then reading the name, and making the sound of the first letter.

Then, we read the name wall a few more times together in silly voices.

For the names that begin with a sound that does not match that grapheme in English, you might add in an extra phrase to acknowledge the difference in that name. You might say, "I, Isabel, the I sounds like the letter I in Isabel." Or, "J, Javier, the J makes the /h/ sound in Javier."

When you read names that begin with letters that have more than one sound, such as vowels, use the same sound as the name. So, you might read, "A, Abe, /ā/; A, Abbie, /ă/."

EXTENSION 1 • Interactive Writing to Revise Labels

GETTING READY

- Gather cardstock, tape, and markers to make a few new labels.

Continue to label the classroom through interactive writing.

"Class, remember how we started labeling our classroom earlier? Well, those Post-its are just not sticky enough! They keep falling off. I couldn't find the one that said *bookshelf*. It must have fallen off! Let's work on making some new labels together, using thicker, stronger paper and tape to make sure they really stick this time.

"Let's start with the bookshelf. Hmm, . . . " I began to think out loud. "I'll say it slowly first: b-b-b-ook-sh-elf. What sound are you all hearing first? Let's check the name wall . . . /b/ /b/. Whose name can help us with this sound?"

"*Ben*!"

"Oh yeah, /b/-*bookshelf*, /b/-*Ben*. They both start with the letter *B*. Ben, can you come on up and help us write the lowercase *b*? Everyone else, get out those imaginary pens and get ready to write it in the air."

As the class wrote the *b* in the air, and Ben wrote it on the piece of cardstock, I voiced over the letter formation pathway, "Long line down, back up a scooch, bump around!" I looked down and noticed the *b* was written backward. I wrote the *b* correctly on a Post-it and placed it above Ben's backward *b* (which was a *d*).

"Let's look at this *b* closely, what did you get right? Yep, long line down, back up a scooch, and bump around. Great. Now can you write the *b* again, so it looks like this one?" Ben crossed out his backward *b* and wrote it correctly above. I coached into correct letter formation to help him do so. "Nice job!" I quickly wrote in the rest of the word *bookshelf*.

I led the class to make a few more labels in this way, calling on students whose names began with the first letter to help start the label, correcting as needed, and filling in the rest of the word.

If you already have labels up in your classroom, you may find new reasons to add even more labels to the room (i.e., parents are coming tomorrow for a writing celebration and need to know where the materials are).

EXTENSION 2 • Introducing a Star Name

Pick a new name from the Star Jar. Sing the "Guess the Name" song, then guide students through the steps to study the name using the "Let's Study a Name!" chart.

I held up a new name and sang the "Guess the Name" song with the class.

We went through each step on our "Let's Study a Name!" chart.

Teach students to write the letter correctly, voicing over the letter formation pathway while students practice writing the letter with invisible markers several times.

Then we followed the steps to write the new letter. I recited the letter formation pathway while students wrote the letter in the air, then on the rug, then on their partner's hand with invisible marker.

Sing the "Star Name Celebration Song" and post the name on the name wall.

We wrapped up our time together by singing the "Star Name Celebration Song" and posting the name on our name wall.

In Bends II and III, the last extension of most sessions will be a star name/learn a letter extension. You will want to get through all of your students' names and introduce most, if not all, letters of the alphabet before the end of this unit. Continue following the suggested sequence of introducing letters.

Learning More Words by Heart

IN THIS SESSION

TODAY YOU'LL show students that it's important to learn other words in a snap, not just their name. You will introduce students to a new series of steps—the steps to learn a word, a process they can follow anytime they want to learn to read and write a word in a snap.

TODAY YOUR STUDENTS will move through the steps to learn a word to learn the word *me* by heart. Then, during rug time, they'll learn the words *a* and *the* by heart.

MINILESSON

CONNECTION

Ask writers to bring their writing folders and a pen to the meeting area. Invite them to look through their writing pieces to find places where they could write their names.

"Writers, when you come to the meeting area today, bring your writing folders and a pen or a marker. I have something huge to tell you. Let's sing 'We Are Gathering' in a super-fast way so we can get started." As the kids located their folders, I led the class in singing "We Are Gathering" at double speed.

"This is what I want to tell you, writers. When you were at lunch yesterday I got a chance to look at the writing in your folders, and you know what I saw? Some of you did a super-smart thing. Beside the pictures of you, doing stuff, some of you wrote your name to show it was you, like this." I held up a page of my writing that had a picture of me watering my garden. I'd labeled the picture with my name to show it was me. "Do you see how this picture has my name on it? But it's not there to tell that this is my piece of writing. My name is there as a label, to show that this is me on this page, watering my garden.

"Right now, will you look through your writing and if you have written your own name as a label on one of your pictures to show the picture is you, show your partner. If you haven't yet done that, show

GETTING READY

✔ Ask students to bring their writing folders and a pen to the meeting area.

✔ Bring some of your demonstration writing, preferably as a three-page chart-sized booklet. Have at least one drawing labeled with your name, and one labeled with the word *me*. On another page of your writing, include the words *a* and *the*.

✔ Prepare snap word cards with the words *me*, *a*, *the*.

✔ Prepare the "How to Learn a Word" anchor chart.

✔ Prepare a pocket chart to display snap words.

✔ Prepare to show one student's piece of writing and have large Post-its ready to label items.

PHONICS INSTRUCTION

Concepts About Print
• Understand the concept of a word.

Letter Knowledge
• Recognize and talk about the sequence of letters in a word.

High-Frequency Words
• Locate and read high-frequency words in text.
• Develop strategies for learning high-frequency words.
• Learn to read and write new words (*me*, *a*, *the*).

your partner a place where you *could* do it. You can even make the label now. Make sure you write your name the right way, so you are giving your muscles practice.

"Great, you all wrote your names so quickly, in a snap!" I snapped my fingers. "I can tell you are all learning to write your names by heart."

❖ **Name the teaching point.**

"Today I want to teach you that people don't just know how to write their own names by heart, in a snap. They also learn to write other words by heart, in a snap."

TEACHING AND ACTIVE ENGAGEMENT/LINK

Introduce students to a process they can move through whenever they want to learn a word by heart.

"One of the words people learn by heart is sort of like your name. It is the word *me*." I pointed to the word card with *me* that I had posted on the easel. "Right here, right now, I'm going to teach you the word *me*, so you know it by heart. That is, so you have it in your muscle memory, so you can use it in a snap anytime you write." I snapped my fingers as I said this.

"Whenever you want to learn a word so well you know it in a snap, you can use these steps." I revealed a new chart, "How to Learn a Word." I pointed to each step in the process as I read it aloud. Then, I read through the steps again, and gestured for children to read along with me.

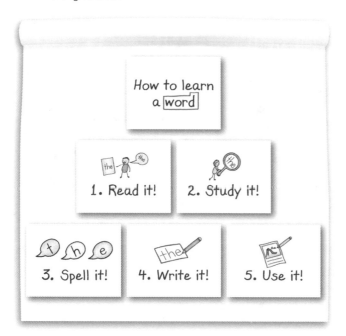

This protocol is drawn from research in phonics, especially the work of Diane Snowball and Wiley Blevins. Those of you familiar with our reading and writing units of study will no doubt notice that this protocol has been slightly altered from the protocol that is used in those units to help kids make any word a snap word. We've added step 1: Read it! and step 5: Use it! to incorporate more recent brain research about what it takes to learn and to retrieve knowledge, especially Wiley Blevins's work, A Fresh Look at Phonics (2017).

Coach students as they read the word. Then, channel students to study the word and name a few characteristics of the word.

"Let's try the first step," I said, pointing to the first number on the chart and then to a place in my demonstration writing where I'd written *me*. I read the word, *me*, and then gestured for students to join me as I read it a second time.

"Now we need to study the word." I pointed to the chart as I said this. "You're pros at studying names, so now study this word in the same way. Notice how many letters there are, how many are tall and small, and name the letters. Quickly turn and tell your partner what you see. Make sure that you are studying the sounds in the word. So the letter *M* goes with the sound /m/ and the letter *E* goes with the sound /eeeee/."

Coach students through the rest of the steps, culminating in students using the new word in their writing.

"Ready for our next step? Let's spell the word. Try it with *me*: *m-e*. Let's do it again." I lowered my voice, so the class could spell the word without as much support. "Now tell your partner, how is the word *me* spelled?"

"Here's step 4, write it!" I pointed to that step on the chart as I said this. "Let's first write it in the air, writing it fast. All of you stand up so you have lots of air around you. You ready?" I wrote in the air and recited the letter formation pathway for lowercase *m*, "Line down, back up, bump around, bump around and down." Then, I did the same for lowercase *e*, "Little line out, bump back around and stop. Great, now write it a few more times so you really get it into your muscles."

After a few seconds, I said, "Okay, sit down. Pull the cap off your imaginary marker. Write *me* on the imaginary paper you have in front of you on the rug. Spell the word aloud as you write the letters. Write it three times."

As students wrote the word *me* on their imaginary papers, I wrote the word on chart paper and voiced over the letter formation pathway.

"Now will you check to see if you already know the word by heart, if you can write it without looking? I'm going to cover up the word. Write it on your hand with your imaginary pen. Then write it on your partner's hand. Say the letters as you write them."

After each partner had a chance to try this, I said, "I'm going to uncover the word. Did you get each letter right?

"Now it's time for the very last step—use it! Each of you take a moment to find a place where you could use this word in your writing. Maybe you already have a picture of yourself that needs a label, so you can add the word *me*. Or maybe you will draw a new picture of yourself and will label it *me*. When you write the word once, don't stop! Look for other places in your writing where you might add the word *me*. Off you go!"

It helps to provide context and a visual, in this case, your sketch of yourself along with the written word, as you are teaching new words. Providing a picture and showing students the word in your writing will help them to grasp the word's meaning and understand how it's used.

I coached students as they worked, making sure they used the correct pathway to write each letter. After a moment I said, "Writers, some of you noticed something smart. The same sketch could be labeled *me* or with your name. When you can write both words by heart, you'll be able to make that choice as a writer.

"We'll be learning more words by heart, more words you'll know in a snap. For now, let's keep these words in a special place so we can use them anytime we are reading and writing." I placed the word *me* in a pocket chart I had prepared especially for snap words.

In Unit 3, Word-Part Power, *when your name wall becomes a word wall, you'll add these snap words to the word wall. For now, we recommend you keep the name wall for names only, and display snap words in a pocket chart, as we do here.*

RUG TIME

Guide students to learn two more words they'll need to know by heart: *a* and *the*. Show them these words in your writing and refer to the "How to Learn a Word" chart as students work.

"Writers, the word *me* is a word you'll use about a zillion times in your writing. There are a couple of other words that you'll probably use about a zillion and one times in your writing! You might remember these words from writing workshop: they are *a* and *the*. These are two words you can use a lot when you label."

I turned to a new page in my writing, where I had sketched a picture of me playing at the playground. I had written "<u>a</u> slide" and "<u>the</u> swings," with the snap words underlined.

The way you approach this rug time will depend on whether you have already taught the words a *and* the *in writing workshop. If students have already learned these words, you can keep this rug time to a quick review. Or, you might ask students to look for places to add all three words to their writing.*

I gestured to the "How to Learn a Word" chart and said, "I'll read these words first, then you read them with me." I read each phrase as I pointed to the words in my writing, emphasizing the snap words. Then I said, "Now, study them with your partner. Because there are two words, you might compare them with each other, just like we compared Rebecca and Roman's names."

Next, I led the students in spelling both words, first all together with me leading, and then in partnerships. Then, I pointed to step 4 on the chart, and showed students the correct way to write first the word *a* and then the word *the*. I invited them to try writing these words first in the air, and then with invisible pens on the carpet while I modeled writing them on the easel and voiced over the letter formation pathway for each letter.

I said, "Soon, you'll have a chance to try step 5, which is to *use* these words. Congratulations on learning another couple of words by heart!" I added the words to our snap words pocket chart.

Keep in mind that your snap word list is yours to develop. We recommend of course including all of the snap words kids learn in these sessions. But you can add other words you feel will be helpful for your writers. You will probably also want to add a concrete word or two—that is, a word that represents something very real and very important to your children. You don't want to only teach the Dolch list, as kids probably won't care about words like of *as much they'll care about words like* mom. *Consider teaching* mom *right alongside of* a *and* the.

SHARE • Making Plans to Add New Words to Writing

Share a page of student writing and demonstrate ways the writer might add today's new words to his writing. Then, invite partners to share ways they might add new words to their own writing.

"Kindergartners, you've just learned not one, not two, but *three* new words you can use to add even more to your writing. Let's take a look at a page from one of Roman's books. On this page, Roman is writing about a day at the park where he climbed a tree higher than he'd ever climbed before." I pointed to the tree and said, "This is the tree Roman climbed, not just any old tree. Roman could label it, '*the* tree.'" I wrote these words on a large Post-it and added it to Roman's page. "Roman could use *a* to label some of the other things on the page. He could write '*a* flower, *a* bird, or *a* cloud.'" I pointed to these things in Roman's drawing. "And of course, he has to label himself! Here, he could write *me*." I pointed to where Roman had drawn himself.

"Take a moment now, and plan some of the things you might add to your writing, especially now that you know the words *me*, *a*, and *the*. Tell your partner what you might write."

FIG. 13–1   Adding words to Roman's book

EXTENSION 1 • Using New Words to Revise Classroom Labels

Gather a few classroom labels. Explain that you could add to them as a class now that you've learned some new words. Guide students to practice the new words while you write them.

I took down a few of the labels from around the room and brought them to the meeting area. I held up one label and asked, "Friends, do you recognize this label from our classroom?" A few students recognized that this was the label from the door.

"I brought this label over because I realized we could add to it! Now that the words *the* and *a* are snap words for you, meaning you know them in a snap, we can have those words in our classroom labels too. This isn't just 'door,' it's *the* door, right? So, let's fix it together!"

I pointed to the word *the* on the snap word pocket chart and said, "Will you all spell the word *the*? Now will you show me how to write it in the air?" I watched as the students wrote the word in the air. Then, I added it to the label in front of the word *door* as I voiced over the letter formation pathway for each letter.

"Now we can read our new label together, 'the door.'" I read it a second time, so students could follow along. "That's so much better. Mike, will you go stick this label back where it belongs?"

We revised a few more labels together, adding the words *the* or *a*.

EXTENSION 2 • Snap Word Hunt

GETTING READY

- Prepare to display the lyrics to the familiar song "Willoughby Wallaby Woo" to the class, possibly using a document camera.
- Print out the nursery rhyme "Jack and Jill" if you want to practice snap words again.

Explain that snap words are helpful not just in writing, but in reading too. Display the lyrics to the familiar song, invite children to read them with you, and point to the words as they do.

"I'm so glad we learned those three snap words today. They are really going to help you with your writing. And you know what, they can also help you in reading! Those snap words are in tons of songs, poems, and books. Now that you know them, you will probably start to see them everywhere.

"Here are the words to 'Willoughby Wallaby Woo.' Let's try and find our new snap words in this song! Let's read the words together, and if you notice a snap word, give a thumbs up."

We chanted "Willoughby Wallaby Woo" together. As we did I pointed to each word. Students began noticing the snap words and putting up their thumbs.

Invite partners to share the snap words they saw in the poems with their partners.

"Quickly, tell your partner which snap words you saw!"

You might do this same work with "Jack and Jill." This nursery rhyme will give your students a chance to find the snap words a and the.

As partners talked, I underlined the snap words in the poems. "Wow, you guys found the word *me* in 'Willoughby Wallaby' right away. And you saw *a* and *the* in 'Jack and Jill'! I'm going to underline these words, so we always remember where to find them.

"I bet you can find these new snap words in tons of books. Keep an eye out this week and see how many you can find!"

EXTENSION 3 • Introducing a Star Name

GETTING READY

- Prepare a new name to add to the name wall.

Pick a new name from the Star Jar. Sing the "Guess the Name" song, then guide students through the steps to study the name using the "Let's Study a Name!" chart.

I held up a new name and sang the "Guess the Name" song with the class.

We went through each step on our "Let's Study a Name!" chart.

In Bends II and III, the last extension of most sessions will be a star name/learn a letter extension. You will want to get through all of your students' names and introduce most, if not all, letters of the alphabet before the end of this unit. Continue following the suggested sequence of introducing letters.

Teach students to write the letter, voicing over the letter formation pathway while students practice writing the letter with invisible markers several times.

Then we followed the steps to write the new letter. I recited the letter formation pathway while students wrote the letter in the air, then on the carpet, then on their partner's hand with an invisible marker.

Sing the "Star Name Celebration Song" and post the name on the name wall.

We wrapped up our time together by singing the "Star Name Celebration Song" and posting the name on our name wall.

Writing New Letters with Help from Friends

IN THIS SESSION

TODAY YOU'LL teach students that sometimes, to write everything they want to write, writers need to be brave and write letters they've never used before. One way to do that is to ask a friend whose name starts with the sound they want to write.

TODAY YOUR STUDENTS will help label a class book. To write new labels, they'll isolate a word's initial sound, then will check for a classmate whose name starts with the same sound and will elicit help from the classmate in writing the letter. They'll practice hearing middle and ending sounds to add to their labels.

MINILESSON

CONNECTION

Place a name tag with each child's name at his or her rug spot. Call the class to come to the rug to find their special gift. Instruct students to put on their name tags to label themselves.

Before calling the class over to the rug, I said, "Kindergartners, when you head over to the rug today, you're going to see something special waiting for you."

The class gathered, finding name tags waiting for them at their rug spots. I told them, "When you find your special gift, stick it carefully on the front of your shirt."

After most children had placed the stickers on themselves, I said, "Now you are all labeled! Let's read these labels. Everyone all together, read out your name!"

The class read their name tags out loud in unison. "That was beautiful! And the great thing is, you can use all these beautiful names to help you write all kinds of things."

GETTING READY

✔ Prepare adhesive name tags with each child's name and place in the meeting area at children's rug spots You may also prepare a tag that reads "Ask me about the letter _____."

✔ Have ready demonstration writing, preferably a book you have written that you also use to demonstrate in writing workshop. Here, we use "All About the Playground."

✔ Set up a couple of students to share stories with the class that highlight letters the class has not yet learned.

✔ Gather students' writing folders and ask students to bring these to the meeting area.

PHONICS INSTRUCTION

Concepts About Print
• Use one's name to learn about words and to make connections to words.

Phonological Awareness
• Identify the initial phonemes of spoken words.
• Hear salient sounds in words.

Word Knowledge/Solving
• Recognize and find names.
• Use the letters in names to read and write other words.

♣ **Name the teaching point.**

"Today I want to teach you that to write all the exciting things you want to write, you sometimes need to be brave and write with new letters that you've never used before. One way to do that is to ask a friend whose name starts with a sound you need to help you out."

TEACHING

Use a shared piece of writing to demonstrate how one might use names to add to their writing. Elicit a story from one student, and draw on other students' names to help label.

I pulled out our "All About the Playground" book from writing workshop. "Let's look at our class book that teaches all about the playground. This idea of using all of our beautiful names to write could help us add to our book. Let's start a new page. We might write a page that's all about ways to get hurt on the playground. We could make a pretty gross and fascinating page about the bloody cuts and bumps kids sometimes get."

The class agreed.

"Gosh, if you wanted to write about all of the cuts and bumps kids get at the playground, you'd need a whole lot of sounds and letters!

"Let's try this out together." I turned to the next page in our playground book. "Who in here has gotten hurt on the playground before?" A majority of the hands shot up in the air. I called on Francisco to share his story.

"I fell off the monkey bars and got a huge cut on my leg, right here!" he exclaimed, touching his leg.

"Oh no! That sounds so painful!" I said. "So, getting a cut is one way kids might get hurt on the playground." I sketched a picture of a boy falling off the monkey bars. I drew an arrow, pointing to his leg. "I want to add a label here, *leg*," I said the word slowly, then said the initial sound, "l-l-l-eee-g-g-g, /l/ /l/."

"Now, let me see if I can find someone's name to help me write the sound I need, /l/." I looked at the labels of each child and paused when I reached *Lisa*. "Lisa! Those words start the same, /l/ *leg*, /l/ *Lisa*. But we haven't studied Lisa's letter yet. Lisa, would you remind us the first letter of your name? Oh, an *L*? Could you come show the class how to make that letter?"

Lisa came up and drew an *L* on the easel. I watched her, and then said, "So you make a line down, then a little line out. Let's all try that." I drew an *L* next to the picture of the cut on Francisco's leg.

To make this teaching work, you'll need to choose a letter that the class hasn't studied yet and that matches a student's name. Feel free to alter this example if your class has already learned the letter L. As noted in the Getting Ready, you might want to set a couple of students up beforehand to tell stories about things that start with letters the class has not yet studied.

FIG. 14–1 "All About the Playground," showing *leg*

ACTIVE ENGAGEMENT/LINK

Elicit a story from another student to add to the class book. Set students up to work in partners to isolate the initial sound in a word, and then to think of a classmate's name with the same sound.

"Let's do another one. Who else has had an accident on the playground and can teach us something to add to this page?" I called on Tymel. "One time I was on the swings, and I got my finger stuck in the chain. I got a bad pinch."

"Whoa, Tymel, I'm glad you are okay!" I drew a picture of a boy sitting on a swing, with an arrow pointing to his hand. "So, a *pinch* is another way kids might get hurt on the playground. Now we have to write the word *pinch*. Work with your partner. Stretch out the word *pinch* and see if you can figure out who in the class could help us write the first sound. When you and your partner have figured it out, touch your nose!"

I listened in and then selected a partnership to share. "Mary, who did you and your partner think could help us with this letter?"

"Patricia!"

"Let's say it together, /p/ /p/-*Patricia*, /p/ /p/-*pinch*. Awesome! You know who else could help us with this word? Pete the Cat, from our favorite books!"

I asked Patricia to come up to the easel to show the class how to write the letter *P*. I guided students to write the letter in the air, while I recited, "Line down, back up, bump around." I repeated the letter formation pathway as I wrote the letter to make the label in the class book.

FIG. 14–2   "All About the Playground," showing *pinch*

"So remember, as Francisco and Patricia helped us to learn today, anytime you aren't sure what letter to use for a label, you can think of the sound you need, find a friend's name with the same sound, and *voilà*! You'll know what letter to write. You can even ask that friend for help making the letter, if you need to."

For now, because students are using each other's names for help making labels, it's fine if they use uppercase letters to write. What is most important is that they are drawing on friends' names to write more. There will be plenty of opportunities to teach into uppercase and lowercase letters throughout this unit and the next unit too.

RUG TIME

Channel students to try today's work in their own writing. Remind them to ask friends for help if they don't know the letter that a sound makes. Coach them as they work.

"I think it's a perfect time to add some more labels to our own writing. You have all your friends sitting around you right now. When you want to label something with a letter you've never written before, just lean over and ask a friend whose name starts with that letter to give you some help.

"Okay, take out one of your stories from writing workshop and find a part of your picture that you can label. Remember to say the word slowly and listen for the first sound, and other sounds too."

SHARE • Hearing More Sounds and Adding More Letters to Labels

Invite children to read some of their labels to each other. Then, set them up to work with a partner to hear more sounds and add more letters to one of their labels.

"Writers, get together with your partner now, and show off some of the work you did today. Show each other two places where you used a letter you didn't know yet to make a label. If you didn't do this in two places, show where you are planning to do it."

After kids had talked for a minute, I said, "While you were working earlier, I noticed that some of you didn't stop after the first sound in words. You kept on going, listening for sounds that came in the middle, and even at the end of words. You used friends' names to help you write the letters for those sounds. For example, if Lisa were making a label for the word *bump*, she could use Ben's *B* to help her, and also Mike's *M* and Patricia's *P*.

"Right now, would you work together to add more letters to your labels? Each partner, choose one of your labels you think you could add to. Work together to hear more sounds in that word and figure out what the letters could be. Use friends' names if you need to. Make sure you both get a turn. Off you go!"

EXTENSION 1 • "Hickety Pickety Bumblebee"

Teach students a chant that can be done often throughout the day that celebrates and reinforces name study.

"Friends, I want to teach you a little chant we can do, now that we know so much about the names in our class. It's called 'Hickety Pickety Bumblebee.' Let's practice it with Mabel first.

Hickety Pickety Bumblebee, won't you say your name for me?

This is an engaging name chant to weave in throughout the day. It can be used during transitions, as a morning greeting, while waiting for lunch. You could even chant it together while walking in the hallway.

MAKING FRIENDS WITH LETTERS

"Let's try that part together!"

The kids chanted.

  Hickety Pickety Bumblebee, won't you say your name for me?

I held Mabel in my lap and said, "My name is Mabel." Then I said, "You say back, 'Your name is Mabel.'" THe kids did just that.

"Okay, here's the next part."

  Let's all whisper it. Mabel! (very soft)
  Let's all clap it. Mabel! (with two claps)
  Let's all stomp it. Mabel! (with two stomps)
  Let's all shout it! Mabel! (very loud)

We went through each part of the song with Mabel's name and then continued with a few more names from the class. I promised we would get to everyone's name by the end of the week.

EXTENSION 2 • Reading the Name Wall to Warm Up for Writing

Guide students to read the name wall in the usual way and explain to them that they can read the name wall anytime as a warm-up for writing.

"Friends, earlier today, when I watched you using your own names and your friends' names to help you label more parts of your writing, I thought about how helpful all of the names on our name wall really are. We've practiced reading the name wall before, so you know how to do it. Let's read the name wall together now."

I pointed to each letter on the name wall and gestured for children to join me as I read the letter name, pointed to the face of the child and said the name, and then made the letter sound. "*A, Abe, /a/, B, Ben, /b/, . . .* " Soon more voices were joining in and we read our whole name wall.

"Now, would you read the name wall with your partner, quiet as a mouse, and as you do, would you think about some new labels you might add to your writing that have the same sounds as some of these beautiful names?"

When students had finished, I said, "Writers, you can warm up for label writing every day by reading our name wall."

Pick a new name from the Star Jar. Sing the "Guess the Name" song, then guide students through the steps to study the name using the "Let's Study a Name!" chart.

I held up a new name and sang the "Guess the Name" song with the class.

We went through each step on our "Let's Study a Name!" chart:

In Bends II and III, the last extension of most sessions will be a star name/learn a letter extension. You will want to get through all of your students' names and introduce most, if not all, letters of the alphabet before the end of this unit. Continue following the suggested sequence of introducing letters.

Teach students to write the letter, voicing over the letter formation pathway while students practice writing the letter with an invisible marker several times.

Then we followed the steps to write the new letter. I recited the letter formation pathway while students wrote the letter in the air, then on the carpet, then on their partner's hand with an invisible marker.

Sing the "Star Name Celebration Song" and post the name on the name wall.

We wrapped up our time together by singing the "Star Name Celebration Song" and posting the name on our name wall.

When you have time, either as part of this extension or later on, have students help you sort pictures to create a letter book for this letter, as you did before. Depending on how much time you have, you can have students sort pictures in partnerships or groups, or you can simply hold pictures up and ask them to call out or give a thumbs up if the picture belongs in the letter book. The latter will be the faster way.

Favorite Characters Can Become Star Names

IN THIS SESSION

TODAY YOU'LL teach students that they can turn any name into a star name, using what they've learned so far about how to study a name.

TODAY YOUR STUDENTS will move through the steps to learn a name using the name of a favorite character from a book. Then, they'll work in small groups to study a new set of star names, this time moving through the name study steps with greater independence.

MINILESSON

CONNECTION

As a way to open your name study to names outside your classroom, tell a story about how you and the class mascot realized that it might be good to have other friends join the name wall too.

"Friends, the other day after you had all gone home for the night, Mabel and I were sitting here looking at the name wall. We were smiling as we thought about all the friends we have on our wall.

"As we studied the wall, we noticed we still have a couple of blank spots. But the thing is, we don't have anyone in the class whose names begin with these letters. So Mabel and I had an idea.

"We thought that it might be nice to include some other friends, not just the kids in our class but maybe friends from around the school or from the books that we read. What do you all think? Should we make our name wall into a collection of other friends too?"

GETTING READY

✔ For today's star name, choose a character's name that begins with a letter for which you don't have a class name. We chose Wishy-Washy (from the book *Mrs. Wishy-Washy*, used in the shared reading plan for *We Are Readers*) because we have found that many classrooms have no names beginning with a *W*.

✔ Display the "Let's Study a Name!" anchor chart.

✔ Prepare to have today's star name and picture on a sentence strip for the name wall.

✔ Prepare name cards and pictures for star names not yet studied, or for a variety of popular characters. We recommend choosing characters that your class is familiar with and names that can fill empty spots on your name wall.

PHONICS INSTRUCTION

Concepts About Print
- Use names to learn about letters and words.

Phonological Awareness
- Identify and produce groups of words that begin with the same sound (alliteration).
- Count, pronounce, and segment syllables in spoken words.

Letter Knowledge
- Recognize and name all upper- and lowercase letters of the alphabet.
- Recognize the name/sound of letters.
- Recognize and use beginning consonant sounds and the letters that represent them.
- Use efficient and consistent motions to form letters.

✤ **Name the teaching point.**

"Today I want to teach you that you can turn any name into a star name—your brother's name, your best friend's name, even your favorite character's name! All you have to do is study it using all that you know from our class name study work."

TEACHING AND ACTIVE ENGAGEMENT/LINK

Ask the class to recall the steps for studying star names. Read, clap, count, study, and cheer.

I made sure the "Let's Study a Name!" chart was close enough for students to read. "Let's try remembering how to study a star name. Name the steps with me." I pointed to each step as we read.

"You are definitely star name experts. It should be no problem for you to study this tricky name we have today."

Reveal the star name, and guide the class to study the new name the same way they have learned to study other names.

"Mabel and I noticed this blank space, for the letter *W*." I gestured to the blank space under the letter *W* on the name wall. "And we thought, maybe one of our favorite characters, Mrs. Wishy-Washy, could join our wall." I placed a sentence strip on the easel with *Wishy-Washy* written on it and a picture of Mrs. Wishy-Washy.

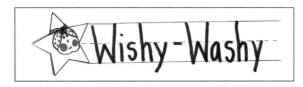

"I can already see some of you starting to study the name: *Wishy-Washy*. I didn't even say get started and you have started already! Put one finger up if you can say *one* thing that you notice about this name. Put two fingers up if you can say *two* things that you notice! Whoa, really? Can anyone say *three* things that you're noticing?"

Pointing to the chart again, I said, "Would you work together to turn *Wishy-Washy* into a star name for our name wall? I will walk around reminding you and admiring your work, but you and your partner should do this work mostly on your own. You can decide the order of things you do to study the name, but they are all important, so be sure you try them all. Are you ready? Go!

"*Wishy-Washy* is a pretty cool name! Did anyone notice the *two* capital *W*'s?" Some students nodded. "Yeah, me too. And that line in the middle—that's called a dash, whoa! So much to study with this name!"

You may want to repeat a variation of this lesson, or the extensions that follow, with other letters for which you don't have student names. For any letter that has no star name, be sure to find a name that is meaningful to your kids to help them learn that letter name and sound.

POSSIBLE COACHING MOVES

▶ "Reading this name is trickier than reading other names because it has two parts. Try reading each part on its own."

▶ "If you get stuck counting so many letters, work with your partner. Help each other keep track of all the letters."

▶ "Use the chart. What can you do next?"

▶ "You might compare the two parts of the name as a way to study the letters."

▶ "Yes, that little line in between the words is tricky. Do you have any ideas about why that might be there?"

▶ "You are ready to cheer it? Great! Do that with your partner."

Help students get the letter *W* in their back pockets. First, coach them to practice the letter sound. Then, coach them to write the letter in the air using the letter formation pathway.

"So, class, today's star name letter is the letter . . . " I left a pause, and the students chimed, "*W*!" I continued, "That's right, *W*! *W* makes the /w/ sound. Can you make the *W* sound, /w/?" I cupped my hand behind my ear to indicate I was listening for the letter sound. Students responded, "/w/." I continued, "Shout the *W* sound!" and students did so. Then I said, "Whisper the *W* sound." Students did this as well. "You got it. *W* makes the /w/ sound like at the beginning of /w/ *whisper* and /w/ *window* and /w/ *watermelon*.

"We've got this letter's sound, now we are ready to get this *W* in our back pockets! Let's practice the capital *W* first. Imaginary pens up! Now, slanted line down, slanted line up, slanted line down, slanted line up.

"Let's try the lowercase *w* on the rug. It looks just like the capital only a little smaller. Slanted line down, slanted line up, slanted line down, slanted line up."

After students had done this, I said, "Time to add this new star name to our name wall!"

Add the new name to the name wall and rally the class to join you in singing the "Star Name Celebration Song."

I added Wishy-Washy's name to the name wall and led the class in singing the "Star Name Celebration Song":

Wishy-Washy is a star
Clap, clap, clap, clap, clap
Wishy-Washy starts with a *W*
W, *W*, *W*
With a /w/ /w/ here and a /w/ /w/ there
Here a /w/ there a /w/
Everywhere a /w/ /w/
Wishy-Washy is a star
/w/ /w/ /w/ /w/ /w/

Recap the purposes for learning new letters, then rally the class to study more names to be able to use more and more letters in their writing.

"Writers, I'm so glad that we are including other friends on our name wall. That's just the kind of class we are. But listen, there are still a few names that we haven't studied yet. Raise your hand if your name has not been studied yet."

After a couple of children raised their hands, I said, "See? We still have friends in this class that we need to get onto our name wall. And the more friends we get on our name wall, the more letters we'll have in our back pockets. And the more letters we have in our back pockets, the more letters we can use to write all kinds of fascinating things."

If, at this point, you have already introduced all of the star names in your class, you can alter this lesson to have students studying more character names during rug time instead.

RUG TIME

Set students up to work in small groups to study another set of star names.

"So I was wondering if you could do name studies with your partner today. We have our chart that tells us what we can do to study a name, and I'm going to ask you to work with your partner. That way we can get all of our star names up onto our name wall. We have three kids in our class whose names start with the same letter! Let's study them now." I reached into the Star Jar and pulled out three new names—*David*, *Dahlia*, and *Daniel*. I held up the names and we sang the "Guess the Name" song together:

> They start with a *D*
> They start with a *D*
> Hi-ho, the derry-o
> They start with a *D*

"You four partnerships on this side of the rug will study David's name, you four in the middle can study Dahlia's name, and you four on this side can study Daniel's name." I handed out name cards to each partnership. Then I pointed to the "Let's Study a Name!" chart. "Okay, class, you know what to do! Let's turn these names into *star* names!"

I moved around the rug, supporting students as they moved through the steps on the chart. After a few minutes, I paused the group. I quickly led them in sounding the letter *D*, and in writing the uppercase letter in the air as I recited the letter formation pathway: "Line down, back up, big bump around!"

Then, we did the same for the lowercase *d*. "Bump back around and stop, line up, line back down."

After a few moments I called for the class's attention. "One, two, three, eyes on me," I sang. "Friends, you did a great job studying our star names! Did you notice one thing that /d/-*David*, /d/-*Dahlia*, and /d/-*Daniel* have in common?" From around the room I heard calls of /d/ /d/ /d/. "That's right, they all start with the /d/ sound. The letter *D* makes the /d/ sound. Whisper that sound into your hand. Now, turn to your neighbor and ask, 'How do you /d/ /d/-do?' Any time you hear a word that starts with /d/, you can write a *D*. /D/-*dinosaur*, /d/-*dump truck*, even a stinky /d/-*diaper* all start with the letter *D*!"

Add the new names to the name wall and sing the celebration song for all of them.

I posted the three new names on the name wall and led the class in singing the "Star Name Celebration Song." I gestured for students to join me.

> David, Dahlia, and Daniel are stars
> Clap, clap, clap, clap, clap
> Their names start with a *D*
> *D*, *D*, *D*, *D*, *D*
> With a /d/ /d/ here and a /d/ /d/ there
> Here a /d/ there a /d/
> Everywhere a /d/ /d/
> David, Dahlia, and Daniel are stars
> /d/ /d/ /d/ /d/ /d/

"Wow, we are really starting to fill in this name wall! I can't wait until we have names up here for every kid in this class and for every letter in the alphabet. How cool will that be?"

SHARE • Singing the Alphabet Song to Practice Letter Names

Sing the alphabet song, asking students to raise their hands when their first letter is sung. Sing it a second time, asking them to raise their hands for all of the letters in their names.

"Let's sing the alphabet song to end our phonics time today. The first time we sing it, when we sing the letter that your name starts with, raise your hands up high in the air, as if you are saying 'That's me.'" We did this.

Then I said, "Let's sing it again, but this time, throw your hands high whenever we sing the name of *any* letter that is in your first name. So those of you with lots of letters, like Jeremiah and Patricia and Francisco, you will be thrusting your hands up in the air a lot! You ready?" We sang again, while I pointed to the letters on our name wall.

Point out an empty spot on the name wall and suggest that a favorite character whose name starts with that letter could join the wall.

"Class, I noticed we have another empty spot on our name wall." I pointed to the letter *O* and then continued. "We have no friends in our class with names that begin with the letter *O*. I was thinking, maybe we could invite another of our favorite characters with an *O* name to join our name wall. What do you think?" Many kids nodded, and I held up the book we had been reading earlier, *Olivia* by Ian Falconer. I continued, "Olivia's name starts with *O*. Maybe we could ask her?"

Lead the class in doing some shared writing to compose an invitation to the character, asking her to join the name wall.

"I was thinking. If we want to invite her to our name wall, we could write her an invitation, like when you invite someone to a party." I flipped to a blank page of chart paper and a grabbed a marker and began to think aloud.

"Hmm, . . . I wonder what we should write first on this invitation. We probably have to say who it is for, like, we might start, 'Dear . . .'"

A few kids called out, "Dear Olivia!"

I gave a thumbs up and continued, "Great idea, let's start the invitation with 'Dear Olivia.'" I wrote *Dear* on the chart paper and then turned to the class. "That says *Dear*. See, it starts in the same way as *David*, *Dahlia*, and *Daniel*. Now let's write Olivia's name." I invited the class to say the name with me, listening for the first sound and naming the first letter. I invited a student to come up to the easel and write the *O*, then I invited the rest of the class to write the letter in the air. I recited the letter formation pathway, "Bump back and travel all the way around." After the students wrote the *O*, I quickly wrote the rest of Olivia's name.

We continued using shared writing to compose a letter to Olivia.

When we were finished with our letter, I promised the class I would get the letter in the mail to Olivia that afternoon.

At a later time, reveal a response from the favorite character agreeing to join the name wall. Read the letter, then lead the class in adding the name to the wall.

The next morning, I unveiled a sealed envelope to the class. "Look! I think Olivia has written us back! Should we open it?"

"Yes!"

Dear Olivia,

Would you like to join our name wall? We need someone with an O name.

We really like your books. Thank you!

From,
Our Class

I opened the envelope and pulled out a letter, along with a name card with Olivia's name and picture on it. I put the letter under the document camera and read it aloud to the class.

The class cheered, and I added Olivia's name to the name wall.

EXTENSION 2 • Reading a Surprise Letter to Add to the Name Wall

GETTING READY

- Write out a letter from Harry (the Dirty Dog) to display to the class.
- Prepare a star name sentence strip with Harry's name and picture.
- Place both items in an envelope.

"Kids, come quickly, I got a letter in my school mailbox today and it is addressed to our whole class!" I placed the letter under the document camera, and read it aloud, pointing to each word. I paused so that kids could read some of the words they knew along with me.

I showed the class the sentence strip with Harry's name and picture.

I said, "Well, what should we do? Should we let Harry onto our name wall? Turn and tell your partner what you are thinking." I listened in as students shared. Then I called on a few students to share their responses.

"Yes, because we don't have any *H* names!"

"Yes, because he asked nicely!"

"No, he's dirty!"

Dear Room 104,

I heard that you invited Olivia to your class name wall. I feel sad because you didn't invite me.

Can I be on your wall too?

Here is my name card and picture. Please use my name!

From,
Harry (the dirty dog)

"Okay, class, I think we should take a vote. Who thinks we should add Harry to our name wall? Raise your hands. Who thinks we shouldn't?" I announced, "The majority of you said yes, let's add him to our wall. I agree! After all, we need his letter to be able to write words like /h/-*horse*, and /h/-*hamburger*, and /h/-*holiday*. I bet a lot of you will want to write about those things in your stories."

I placed the name card and picture on the name wall, and I gestured for children to join me in singing the "Guess the Name" song for Harry.

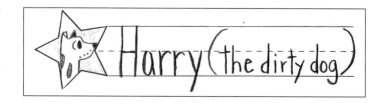

EXTENSION 3 • Making Books for New Letters

GETTING READY

- Prepare materials to make new letter books for the letters the class studied in the session. ✶

Divide the class into two groups and give each group a different set of picture cards to sort according to their initial sounds to make two more letter books for the class.

"Let's make some books for our new letters—we need a *W* book and a *D* book for our letter books bin. I have some pictures here, and I was thinking I could give one group of you pictures to sort for the *W* book. Meanwhile, I'll give another group of you some *D* pictures to sort for our *D* book. Then we can add the two new books to our library."

I organized the students so they were sitting in two small circles on the rug. Then, I handed the pile of pictures to one student in each group.

"Okay, Dahlia and Mike, I gave you each a pile of pictures. Hold each picture up for your group so everyone can say the word together slowly. Then Dahlia, ask your group if it is a /d/-*D* word or not a /d/-*D* word. And Mike, you ask your group if it is a /w/-*W* word or not a /w/-*W* word. Then you can make two piles in front of you. This is *big* work—but I know you can do it!"

I moved between the two groups, reminding them to say each word slowly and listen for the first sound. When each group had separated their pictures into two piles, I picked up the piles and asked the class to move back to their rug spots.

Collect the cards the students sorted and use them to create two new letter books for the class. Correct errors so the whole class can learn from them.

"Let's make this *D* book first!" I quickly read through each picture from the *D* pile Dahlia's group had sorted and glued them into the *D* book. "Oh, /d/-*dinosaur*, that goes in our *D* book for sure! /f/-*flower* . . . Hmm, . . . how did that sneak into this pile? We better add that to our *F* book." I went through the same process for the *W* book.

"Whew, that was awesome work! Our bin of letter books is getting so full!"

You might decide that the format of this extension, with students working in two separate groups, is too complex for your class at this point in the school year. In that case, you can create these letter books as you've done before, having the class sort the pictures in partnerships.

Learning Even More Words by Heart

IN THIS SESSION

TODAY YOU'LL teach students a few more words they'll need to know how to read and write in a snap: *I*, *like*, and *my*.

TODAY YOUR STUDENTS will progress through the word-learning protocol to learn the words *I*, *like*, and *my* by heart. They'll learn each word with increasing independence. During the share, they'll help to begin a predictable chart using today's snap words.

MINILESSON

CONNECTION

Sing an iconic song about making new friends and celebrate the friendships that students have made with each other. Point at children and have the class call out each other's names.

I posted a few lines from the song, "Make New Friends (but Keep the Old)." I said, "Friends, there is a song that I love. It goes like this." I gestured to the chart paper where I had written the words, and I sang:

> Make new friends, but keep the old,
>
> One is silver and the other gold.

"Can you sing it with me?" We sang the song several times, as I pointed to the words. "Don't you love the words, 'make new friends, but keep the old'? That's what we have done. Some of you were friends before you even came to kindergarten. You've kept those friendships and made so many new ones too.

"We're coming to the end of this big huge lovely unit that has been all about making friends—friends with each other, with our whole class! Let's read the class. Instead of pointing at words, I'm

GETTING READY

✔ Write the first two lines of the lyrics to "Make New Friends (but Keep the Old)" on chart paper.

✔ Display the snap word pocket chart.

✔ Prepare word cards for *I*, *like*, and *my*.

✔ Distribute a whiteboard and marker to each student.

✔ Display the "How to Learn a Word" anchor chart.

✔ Prepare a predictable chart.

PHONICS INSTRUCTION

Concepts About Print
- Understand the concept of a word.

Letter Knowledge
- Recognize and talk about the sequence of letters in a word.
- Use efficient and consistent motions to form letters.

High-Frequency Words
- Develop strategies for learning high-frequency words.
- Locate and read high-frequency words in a text.
- Learn to read and write new words (*I*, *like*, *my*).

going to point at *you*, and let's read the names of everyone in the class." As I pointed to each student, everyone shouted his or her name. In this way, we "read" the class.

Suggest that kids have also made friends with the alphabet and with snap words and use that as a segue to suggest that they need to learn new snap words.

"Here's the thing, kindergartners. We've also made friends with the alphabet, haven't we? Let's read the alphabet, while we sing its song." We sang the alphabet song and I tapped the letters on the name wall as we did so.

"We've made friends with words, too, some words that you now know in a snap. Those words are like old friends. Let's reread the words that you now know in a snap."

I pointed to each of the words on our snap word pocket chart, including *me*, *a*, and *the*. We read them together and I used each in a sentence. "I love the way you already know these words. They are old friends. But now you know that song," and I sang the lines again, emphasizing "Make new friends."

❖ **Name the teaching point.**

"Today I want to teach you that kindergartners should go through their days making new friends. They make new friends during recess, and at lunch, and during reading workshop. And it's not just important to make new people-friends, it is also important to make new word-friends."

TEACHING AND ACTIVE ENGAGEMENT/LINK

Display three new snap words. Guide children in reading the words and suggest that this particular group of words can help them to write whole sentences.

"To write books and songs and poems and stories, I know you are going to want to make friends with lots and lots of words. For today, I chose a few that can help you write a whole lot." I pointed to the three words I had posted on the easel: *I*, *like*, and *my*.

"Let's read the words together." I read them first, as I pointed to each one. Then, I led the class in reading them a few more times.

I studied them intensely for a moment, and then said, "You know what? I think these words could even help us to write whole sentences! We could write, 'I like my dad,' or 'I like my toy.'" I quickly jotted these sentences on my easel whiteboard.

I like my dad.

I like my toy.

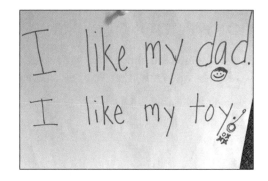

Channel students to progress through the protocol for learning snap words. Guide them through each step to learn the first word.

"Let's go through our steps for learning these new words together." I pointed to the sentence. "The first word is a really special word: *I*. It is just one letter—the capital letter *I*! Let's all stand up together and make the shape of the *I*. Nice! Now let's turn *I* into a snap word!"

"First we have to read it," I said, as I pointed to the first step on the chart. I guided students to read it, first on the word card, and then in the sentences I had written.

I pointed to the next bullet and said, "Time to study the word. Hmm, . . . " I drew my fingers along the capital letter *I*. "What are you noticing?"

"It's just one letter!"

"It's really tall!"

"Yes, the word *I* is just one letter *and* it's always a capital! You'll see lowercase *i* in words like *ice* and *igloo*, but when *I* is by itself to make the word *I*, it'll always be capital.

"Okay, let's spell it together. *I* is spelled *I*! Say that with me: *I*. Easy peasy!"

You could decide to teach another snap word alongside these three, particularly if there is a word that has been coming up often in kids' writing. If you taught mom *earlier, you might not want to leave out* dad*! Additionally, teaching a word like* dad *in this session would enable students to put all four words into a sentence today.*

I quickly distributed a whiteboard and marker to each student, then I continued. "Now, let's write it! Watch me first." I wrote the letter on my easel whiteboard, voicing over the letter formation pathway as I did so, "Line down, line across the top, line across the bottom. Now, take out your whiteboards and take the caps off your markers. And go ahead, write *I* on your whiteboards. When you finish, hold up your whiteboard so we all can see!" I voiced over the letter formation pathway again while kids wrote.

As students held up their whiteboards, I noted to myself who needed more support with their grip or letter formation. After a minute, I continued, "Fantastic. Now erase those whiteboards and set them down in front of you and get those caps onto those markers. It's time for the final step: Use it! Listen to me use the word *I* in a sentence." I said dramatically, "*I like to read.*"

"Can each of you say your own sentence with *I*? Just say it into the air. You might start with 'I like' as I did."

After the kids had said their sentences, I continued, "I heard Mike say, 'I like Legos.' And Daniel said, 'I am five.' So many great *I* sentences!

"Let's learn another word or two and then you can *really* use these words—wait and see!"

Channel students to follow the steps to turn the next word, *like*, into a snap word. This time, decrease the amount of support you give.

"This is the word *like*." I pointed to the word card. Then, I read the two sentences I had written earlier, emphasizing the word *like*.

> I like my dad.
>
> I like my toy.

"Read the word with me!" I pointed to the word card, and then to each sentence as students read them. "Great! Now let's study it. Turn and tell your partner something you notice about the word *like*."

After students had talked for a moment, I said, "I heard some of you say that *like* has four letters and that it starts with an *L* just like Lisa's name. That's true! And yes, the first two letters are lines, almost. The letters go tall, small, tall, small, don't they?

"Ready for our next step? Let's spell the word. *Like* . . . *l-i-k-e, l-i-k-e, l-i-k-e* . . . *like*! Try it with me. Let's do it again." I lowered my voice to a minimum so the class could spell the word without me. I kept watch for any students who appeared to be having trouble.

Ask students to write the word a few times, saying the letter names aloud as they write. Then, cover the word, and rally students to practice writing and checking it multiple times.

"Let's practice writing the word *like*. Remember to spell the word aloud as you write it." I modeled how I said "*Like, l-i-k-e*" while I wrote the word. "Get out your whiteboard. Uncap your marker. *l-i-k-e*. Make sure the letter matches the letter name you're saying. Then read it. Check that everything is there." I coached students as they wrote the word *like* three times on their whiteboards.

"Okay now, erase your whiteboards. You are going to write it again, but this time, I'll cover the word. Check to see if the word is already in your head, if you already know it by heart." I covered the word card *like* and the sentences containing the word. "Write the word *like* on your whiteboard. Whisper the letters to yourself as you write them."

I gave students a few seconds to write, and then I said, "I'm going to uncover it. Check each letter. If your word doesn't match what is up here, then erase the whole word and make it again." I asked students to erase the word and write it again from memory two more times.

Set students up to use the snap word. Introduce them to a game where they generate sentences using the word. Coach partnerships as they generate sentences.

"Let's *use* the word *like*. With your partner right now, try to make as many sentences as you can. You might say, 'I like my . . . ' or 'I like . . . ' and then keep going. You could even ask a question such as, 'Do you like . . . ?' And it doesn't just have to be about you. You could say, 'My sister likes . . . '"

I moved around from partnership to partnership as students worked, offering support.

I gathered students back. "Oh my gosh! You all are really able to take some words—like just the few number of words we have taught you—and you make them say such important things. I heard kids telling each other, 'I like you.' Could anything be more important? I wish I could have captured all of what you said.

"I heard someone else say, 'Oreo cookies look like panda bears.' Isn't that interesting? It's not just 'I like . . . ' but it's comparing two things. There are so many great ways to use this word."

When students notice a missing or misplaced letter and go to correct it, make sure they are not just inserting a letter into the word. If students write l-i-k for instance, you'll want them to rewrite the entire word instead of just adding an e at the end.

Once a snap word is learned, kids sometimes think it's the only form of the word. Coach students to use variations of the word by modeling these variations, such as likes, liking, *or* liked.

POSSIBLE COACHING MOVES

▶ "Oh, your mom likes bananas. We add an *s* when we are talking about someone else. What else? 'My mom likes . . . '"

▶ "I heard you say 'I like' a whole bunch of times. You are getting so good at making up sentences that start that way! Try a different beginning, 'My brother likes . . . '"

RUG TIME

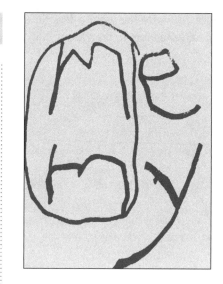

Guide students to turn the word *my* into a snap word.

"Writers, I have one more word for you that I know you'll use all the time in your writing. It's the word *my*." I pointed to the word card, and then to the sentences, and said, "Here it is in our sentences."

> I like my dad.

> I like my toy.

I read each sentence out loud, emphasizing the word *my*, and then I encouraged the class to read them with me. "Now, will you study that word with your partner to try and turn it into a snap word?"

I listened in as students studied the word, voicing over some of what they noticed. "Oh, it does look like the word *me*. What is the same between those two words and what is different?"

I continued to voice over each next step to learn a word as I pointed to it on the chart. "Make sure you spell it! When you are ready, write *my* on your whiteboards." When rug time was almost over I said, "Time to try and use the word *my* in a sentence. Tell your partner what you came up with!"

As students did this, I added the new words to our snap words pocket chart.

SHARE • Creating a Predictable Chart with Snap Words

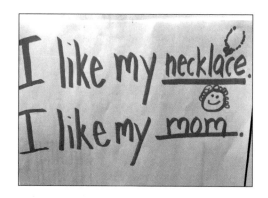

Create a predictable chart together using the sentence stem "I like my _____."

"The words *I*, *like*, and *my* are important for so many reasons. One reason is that you can use them to learn more about your friends.

"I wrote the start of a sentence up here on this piece of chart paper. It says, 'I like my _____.'" I turned to Mabel and asked, "Mabel, how would you finish this sentence?" I listened as she whispered in my ear. "Oh, you like your necklace. Yeah, I like it too. Okay, Mabel wants to write, 'I like my necklace.'" I reread each word and then quickly wrote *necklace* in the blank. I drew a picture of a necklace next to it.

Then I called on a student to help with the next sentence. "Emma, do you have something you like? How would your sentence go?"

"I like my mom."

I wrote the sentence on the line and did a quick sketch. "Let's all read it together, 'I like my mom.'"

I called on a few more children to contribute and then promised to check in with the rest of the class later so they could add their sentences to the chart too.

Today is the last day for star name work before the end of the unit. If you haven't featured all of your students yet, aim to do so before the next session, the final celebration of the unit.

EXTENSION 1 • Building Sentences

GETTING READY

- Gather the snap word cards for *I*, *like*, *my*, and *necklace* and place them in a pocket chart.
- Have a few more blank cards ready to add words.

I pointed at the words *I like my necklace* I had set up in a pocket chart and told the class, "I wrote out the first sentence from the chart we made together earlier on cards. This is Mabel's sentence. Will you read it to me?" We read the sentence together, as I pointed to each word.

"Guess what? We can use most of these cards to make the second sentence on our chart, 'I like my mom.' That was Emma's sentence. Hmm, . . . what words do we already have up here that can help us build the second sentence? I see *I*." I took the word card with *I* and moved it down to the next row on the pocket chart. "I like my mom," I repeated the sentence. "What other words do we already have up here that I can move down?"

"*Like*!" David called out.

"Great, David, will you come move the word *like* into our new sentence?"

I called another student to move the word *my* down as well. I read the cards, "*I like my . . .* " and I tapped the empty space after the word *my*. "We need a new card for the word *mom*." I wrote *mom* on a blank card and placed it in the pocket chart to finish the sentence.

We built a few more of our sentences together this way.

EXTENSION 2 • Making a New Book for the Classroom Library

Rally children to help you create a pattern book for the classroom library, using the sentence starter "I like." Invite children to come up and write the snap words.

"I was thinking, we have a lot of books with patterns in our class library. Some have the pattern 'I went'; others have patterns like 'On the farm . . . ' or 'At the zoo.' I was thinking we could make a class book with a pattern, a pattern that could help teach people all about our class. All of the pages could start with the pattern 'I like.'

"I'll go first. I like reading." I wrote the sentence on a blank page of the large book I had prepared, and I and drew a quick sketch of me reading a book.

"Now, you all think of something you really like to add to our book. Turn and tell your partner something you like." I listened in while students talked.

After a minute, I said, "Daniel said, 'I like puppies.' So do I! Daniel, will you come up and help us write the first two words in that sentence?" I handed Daniel the pen. "As Daniel writes the words *I like*, everyone else can practice writing it on their whiteboard."

When Daniel had finished, I encouraged the class to check whether their words matched Daniel's.

"Now, what sound do you hear at the start of the word *puppies*? /p/, that's it, write the lowercase *p* right there on the line." Daniel did this, while I voiced over the letter formation pathway, and then I filled in the rest of the word. I asked the class to read the sentence out loud together.

EXTENSION 3 • Introducing a Star Name

GETTING READY

- Prepare a new name to add to the name wall.

Pick a new name from the Star Jar. Sing the "Guess the Name" song, then guide students through the steps to study the name using the "Let's Study a Name!" chart.

I held up a new name and sang the "Guess the Name" song with the class.

We went through each step on our "Let's Study a Name!" chart.

Teach students to write the letter, voicing over the letter formation pathway while students practice writing the letter with an invisible marker several times.

Then we followed the steps to write the new letter. I recited the letter formation pathway while students wrote the letter in the air, then on the carpet, then on their partner's hand with an invisible marker.

Sing the "Star Name Celebration Song" and post the name on the name wall.

We wrapped up our time together by singing the "Star Name Celebration Song" and posting the name on our name wall.

Let's study a name!

Read it.

Clap and stomp the beats.

Count the letters.

Study the letters.

Cheer it!

SESSION 17

Walking through Life Differently
A Celebration

IN THIS SESSION

TODAY YOU'LL teach students that now that they know letters and the sounds they make, students will walk through life differently—as readers.

TODAY YOUR STUDENTS will apply all that they've learned about letters to read labels around the room and read books, and they will celebrate the hard work they've done and the knowledge they've acquired over the course of this unit.

MINILESSON

CONNECTION

Ask students to read all of the names on the word wall, and then to find names with different characteristics, such as names that start or end with a certain letter.

"Readers, writers, today is the last day in our unit. We've got all your names up on our name wall! How lovely, looking up at all those names!

"On every other day, we have thought about a few of your names. For today, we can think about *all* of your beautiful names. First, let's read all of your names on our name wall, and let's stomp the beats as we do."

After we did this, I said, "Wow, that sounded like a parade! Now let's see what other things we can notice about our names. How many names do we have that start with an *R*? Don't say, just think. In a minute I'm going to ask you to whisper your answer to your partner." After a moment, the kids exchanged counts, and I confirmed the answer, asking those children whose names started with *R* to stand and take a bow.

GETTING READY

✔ Have your set of magnetic letters on hand to review letters' names and sounds with students.

✔ Select a few students who already love books, and set them up to be reading books on the rug while other kids are reading the room.

✔ Display the anchor chart "We Are Readers!" from Unit 1 *We Are Readers* from the Units of Study for Teaching Reading.

✔ Write a note from Mabel that says, "Congratulations!" and put it in an envelope placed Mabel's hand.

PHONICS INSTRUCTION

Concepts About Print
• Use one's name to learn about words and to make connections to words and to other names.

Letter Knowledge
• Recognize and name all upper- and lowercase letters of the alphabet.
• Recognize the name/sound of letters.
• Understand that some letters are consonants and some letters are vowels.

Word Knowledge/Solving
• Recognize and find names.

I continued asking children to check or notice things about our class names—things like noting the number of kids with names that started or ended with certain letters. We noted names that had letters with tails, such as Mary and Tymel. We noted that all names began with an uppercase letter and had lowercase letters for the rest of the name, such as Ava and Kim.

"The amazing thing is that you have learned not only to say each other's names, but to spell each other's names, too." I held up a pile of magnetic letters and let them slide from my hands in the same dramatic way I had done at the start of the unit. "When we started the year, these were just plastic things. Now you know these letters by name, and by sound.

"Let me show you how much you know," I said, and held up a few of the magnetic letters, each time asking kids to read the letter, to make the letter's sound, and to point to someone whose name started with that letter.

❖ **Name the teaching point.**

"Today I want to teach you that once you know letters and their sounds, you walk through life differently. You see words everywhere."

TEACHING

Remind students about how much they've grown as readers and writers and explain how this growth means that they walk through life differently now.

"I should take a picture of each of you today and send it home for your parents to put in their collection of special stuff. Do some of your parents save things that show you growing up? Do some of your parents keep things that remind them of the big growing-up days in your life—like maybe a picture of your first birthday party, or a lock of hair from your first haircut, or your baby outfit from when you were teeny tiny? Or maybe some of your parents have a mold of your foot or your hand when it was teeny.

"Lots of moms and dads and grandparents, too, save things that remind them of the big growing-up days.

And you know what? Today is one of those days. Because from this day on, you will walk through your life as a different sort of person because *anytime* you see letters, you'll stop and say, 'I know you.'

"If you walk past the door with the sign that says, 'Principal's Office,' you won't just see a door. You will see letters. And if it is our principal's office and the letters start like this—'Mr. . . . '—you won't just walk on by. No sir. You'll say 'Huh? That's the principal's office! And I know how to start the word *principal*: /p/ /p/.' You'll think, 'Why does that sign start with an *M*, not *P*?' And maybe you will think, 'Does it say, *My* principal?' and maybe if you work at it, you'll read on and realize it actually says Mr. Ellis—that's why there is an *M*, for *Mister*.

"But my point is that now that our first unit is over, you will walk through your life differently. Let's try it right now. You ready to walk through this classroom differently?"

ACTIVE ENGAGEMENT/LINK

Take students on a walk around the classroom, asking partners to read the labels to each other. Urge them to ask each other questions and work out labels that may be particularly challenging.

"Let's take a tour of the classroom to read the labels. Some you may know right away, and some of you might need to work on the word a little. Partners, will you quietly read the labels you see to each other? If you're unsure about a label, ask each other questions—look really closely at the letters and figure out the sounds that go with those letters. Remember to think about what would make sense. I believe that together, you can figure them all out. Are you ready?"

I took my pointer and as a class, we walked around a portion of the room. I pointed at each label, and partners worked together to read the labels. I often asked the class to read a label to themselves, to whisper what it said to their partner, to talk about their questions.

RUG TIME

Channel partners to continue reading the room. Encourage students to read books, drawing on their knowledge of letters and sounds to look at the content of books differently.

"Readers and writers, I love what I am seeing. Right now, will you and your partner pick up a pencil and pretend it is a pointer, and will you continue to read the room, only this time without me helping you? Mosey around the room, reading the labels and the names and the snap words and the poems and anything you see."

After a bit of time, I engineered a few kids to be sitting on the rug, reading words from a book (or finding letters they recognized). I called the whole class over to observe. "Look what I see. When these girls were reading the room, they realized that meant reading books, as well as labels. Will all of you find a book? This time, when you look at the book, try to notice letters and words. Try to see differently because you know letters and sounds." I referred to the "We Are Readers!" chart.

Celebrate students' hard work with a congratulatory note from a friend, a reminder of the work they've accomplished, and a rendition of the alphabet song.

I looked over at Mabel and channeled the children to notice her as well. She was holding an envelope, which I opened with great trepidation. "What might this say?" I asked. I drew out the letter and showed the class that in large letters, she'd written them a message:

Congratulations friends!

I helped the class to read the message. "Congratulations, indeed! Mabel is right—you should feel very proud of all the hard work you've done—and of all the knowledge you now have about letters and sounds. Pat yourselves on the back—stand up and take a bow! Now, let's celebrate your achievements with the alphabet song." I concluded our celebration by leading students in one last rendition of the alphabet song.

Mabel sang the loudest of all.

As an alternate way to celebrate the work of this bend, you might channel students to use all they've learned about letters and sounds to create and label a banner, sash, or crown with their name to wear at the "We Are Readers" parade that marks the finale of the reading unit. The banner, sash, or crown could include their name and sounds from their pictures of things that start with sounds from their name.

After the parade, kids could share what is on their sash, banner, or crown with someone else to show what they have learned in this phonics unit.

Small Groups to Support Phonics, Grades K–1

Lucy Calkins, Emma Coufal Bemowski, Rebecca Cronin, Christine Holley, Laurie Pessah, and Sarah Picard Taylor

Photography by Peter Cunningham

Illustrations by Marjorie Martinelli

HEINEMANN ◆ Portsmouth, NH

Heinemann
361 Hanover Street
Portsmouth, NH 03801–3912
www.heinemann.com

Offices and agents throughout the world

Cataloging-in-Publication data is on file with the Library of Congress.

ISBN-13: 978-0-325-10532-1

Editors: Tracy Wells and Anna Gratz Cockerille
Production: Elizabeth Valway
Cover and interior designs: Jenny Jensen Greenleaf
Photography: Peter Cunningham
Illustrations: Marjorie Martinelli and Kimberly Fox
Composition: Publishers' Design and Production Services, Inc.
Manufacturing: Steve Bernier

Printed in the United States of America on acid-free paper
22 21 20 19 18 VP 1 2 3 4 5

Dedication

The pages of this entire series brim with lessons we learned from the Teachers College Reading and Writing Project's own sons and daughters, nieces and nephews. We are especially grateful to those who wrote stories and poems, who helped us practice small groups and minilessons.

This book is dedicated to:

Thomas Cockerille

Aidan Elizabeth Hohne

Maggie Taylor

Joseph and Alanna Brennen

Nico and Sam Cruz

Brody and Hannah Pollack.

Acknowledgments

THIS BOOK STANDS ON THE SHOULDERS of decades of work at the Teachers College Reading and Writing Project and of the entire organization's efforts to think and rethink methods for leading small groups. The entire staff of the Project meets every Thursday to rethink our best ideas, and to push ourselves to outgrow assumptions and methods so they go from good to great. The small groups in this book and the ideas about small-group instruction in general are very much the product of the electric, surprising, deep thinking that we all did together. For that reason, we thank the entire organization.

We especially want to acknowledge the profound influence of Kathleen Tolan, our late Senior Deputy Director. Kathleen nudged us all to ask the question, "Who is working the hardest in our small groups?" and to help us think about ways to lead small groups that allow kids to be active and interactive and we, as teachers, to listen, watch, and coach responsively.

Mo Willems once said that the art of writing a picture book involves working endlessly so as to give the impression that you just whipped off the book, sending it to print when the ink was still wet. We hope these small groups read as if they just flowed naturally from us. In truth, each of the sessions has been drafted and revised, piloted and rethought, written and rewritten. Each has gone through a process that involved well over a dozen drafts and often well over a dozen people. And even after a small group was done, there was yet more work as the art and the extensions were developed, the photographs taken and placed.

We'd like to thank the teachers at Hartland North Primary, CH Bird Elementary, Anna C. Scott Elementary, Quaker Ridge School, Safety Harbor School PS 11, PS 267, PS 116, PS 158, PS 172, PS 58, PS 52, PS 9, PS 45, and PS 22 for their help with all this. We were lucky to work with some talented literacy coaches at these schools including Gina Newmann, Trina Lester Luna, Lisa Feldner, and Lillian Ruffo. We thank, also, the principals who especially opened their doors to our camera, including Jane Hsu, Medea McEvoy, Deanna Marco, Lisa Bonello, Jamie Palladino, Rebecca Pembroke, and Maria Martinez.

Various coauthors played particular roles. Rebecca Cronin took a lead role especially in the first half of the book, with support from Emma Coufal Bemowski. Sarah Picard Taylor gave especially generously of her time, and provided extra help with inventing sessions, and with photographs, videos, artwork, and the rest. Laurie Pessah took the lead role in organizing the videos. Lucy helped develop and record our ideas on small groups and took the lead role in revising the small groups. Christine Holley's deep knowledge of phonics was a resource especially in the second half of the book.

A huge team of colleagues helped to write and rewrite these sessions. Thanks go especially to a team of TCRWP writers: Kelly Boland Hohne, Liz Franco, and Katie Clements. They each wrote and rewrote many small groups. Their help was absolutely precious. The brilliance of Shanna Schwartz and Amanda Hartman is embedded in everything we do. A team of brilliant colleagues helped us whittle this project down from 120 rough drafts to 70 clearer ones, and to work across those 70 groups to build in more consistency. That team included Katy Lindner, Sara Berg, Carl Ciaramitaro, Nour Jalloul, Amy Luczak, Megan O'Connell, and Mary Ann Mustac, who also brought her prodigious organization skills to the work of helping to organize all of this, and we thank her.

Meanwhile there is the art, and for that we have so many people to thank. First and most of all, Marjorie Martinelli has led that department of this work and we are indebted to her. Kim Fox, Lisa Corcoran, Hannah Arlone, Hannah Tolan, Hilary Andaya, and Graham Holley each made gigantic contributions.

In the midst of all the drafting and revising, our partners cheered us on and whisked us away for a quick dinner or walk in the park. Adam, Graham, Jerry, John, Rob, and Tony are the reasons we could lean in to this important project.

Once the book was semicompleted, the incomparable Joe Yukish, who has been an instructor in Reading Recovery, gave us feedback on every session. Then our brilliant senior editor, Anna Gratz Cockerille, took over, helping to trim each session, to turn bits into summary, to make sure all the voices cohere. The book was pushed through the finish line with the grace and brilliance of Kate Montgomery, Marielle Polombo, and Tracy Wells.

Finally, a magical team at Heinemann led by Abby Heim, with Elizabeth Valway's prowess every present, and Shannon Thorner's eye for detail, worked to take Peter Cunningham's pictures, everyone's art, and to bring all the pieces together onto the page. Whew. What a team effort. What a gift of love.

And now, the best part. YOU take all of this, and add your pacing, your choices, your wise coaching, your laughter and . . . and . . . your children's imagination and their curiosity and their laughter and their burgeoning skills.

Contents

An Orientation to
Small Groups to Support Phonics

YOU WILL WANT TO LEAD small groups to support your children's phonics. You'll presumably lead these during your reading and writing workshops, and the groups will feel a lot like the small groups that you already lead to support your youngsters' development as readers and writers. These groups will help you support students' transferring all that you teach during phonics time into their reading and writing, and they will also allow you to provide the individualized, assessment-based support in phonics that your youngsters need.

The groups that we have included here are meant as exemplar. You'll develop your own groups. I hope that the information included in *A Guide to the Phonics Units of Study, Grades K–1* will let you in on the guiding principles that inform methods of small-group instruction. I suggest you read (and reread) Chapter 4, "Small-Group Work in Phonics," from the *Guide* as you use this book.

You'll see that this book is organized into sections that are roughly correlated with stages of phonics development and with the content of the kindergarten and first-grade phonics units. Chapter 1, "Phonological and Phonemic Awareness, Letter Knowledge, and Concepts About Print," offers small-group sessions that can support your children's burgeoning understanding of letters, sounds, and concepts of print. These groups roughly correspond to the work of kindergarten Unit 1, *Making Friends with Letters*, although you may well have children in late kindergarten who can use this support. Next, Chapter 2, "Letter-Sound Correspondence, Hearing and Recording Sounds," offers small groups that can help your children grow stronger in their letter-sound correspondence. Those small groups can help to ground the work that is introduced in kindergarten Unit 2, *Word Scientists*, and you will have children who benefit from you returning to this content long after that unit is completed. Chapter 3, "Blends and Digraphs," will support your children's growing understanding of these phonics features. The content that is taught in

these groups has a place in kindergarten Unit 3, *Word-Part Power*, and Unit 5, *Playing with Phonics*. Chapter 4, "Short Vowels and Long Vowels with Silent E," provides a range of instruction to support students' ongoing understanding of vowel sounds and patterns. Many units spotlight work with vowels, and this chapter especially supports concepts introduced in kindergarten Units 3 and 5, and in first-grade Unit 2, *The Mystery of the Silent* E. Chapter 5, "Endings, Contractions, and Possessives," corresponds to work introduced in first-grade Unit 2 and Unit 3, *From Tip to Tail*, and Chapter 6, "Long-Vowel Teams, Diphthongs, and *R*-Controlled Vowels," to first-grade Unit 4, *Word Builders*, and Unit 5, *Marvelous Bloopers*. Chapter 7, "Snap Words," offers small groups that will help children who need additional work shoring up their bank of high-frequency words.

The final two chapters, Chapter 8, "Strategies for Writing Words Correctly," and Chapter 9, "Strategies for Reading Words Correctly," are chapters that support work that is ongoing across units and that are especially intended to support children's transferring their phonics work to their reading and writing.

Although each of these chapters has special ties to particular units of study, the groups are designed to help you support children's work with that content, and we know children will be continuing to work with content long after you have taught it. Some first-graders, for example, may still need more letter-sound support. We mention the way that chapters correlate to work that is introduced in certain units only to give you a sense of the logic that undergirds the organization of this book. We also do this to help you find small-group lessons that correspond to your whole-class instruction so that you can support students during and after you introduce particular concepts.

You will not progress through this collection of small-group lessons in a chapter-by-chapter fashion, but will instead dip in and out of these chapters in ways that respond to your children's needs and interests.

As discussed in the *Guide* in Chapter 4 "Small-Group Work in Phonics" and in Chapter 5, "Assessing Your Students' Phonics Development," you'll have many sources of information on which to draw to help you choose the small groups that will best support particular children's needs. In Chapter 5 of the *Guide*, you'll find implications for instruction for each assessment, along with recommendations for small-group instruction based on what you learn about your children as you score the assessments.

MANAGEMENT AND MATERIALS

Our goal as we worked on this book was to make your life easier. We have tried to use minimal materials, and to reuse many of these. When possible, we have tried to do the legwork for you. You'll find lots of tools in the online resources (denoted with ✥) and the Resource Pack (denoted with 📖).

We give some tips for preparing and managing materials for small groups in the *Guide*, and we'll reiterate them here so you have this information handy. When leading small groups, we find it is best to only distribute materials when it is time for kids to use them. So if the small group starts with you channeling kids to review something in partners, with each partner holding a chart, we recommend you distribute those charts at the start of the group. Then, if you want the kids to attend to you for two minutes, collect the papers that partners are holding, and perhaps write on a whiteboard to give the kids a visual focus. Midway through the small group, if you want kids to focus on their work and not be all-eyes-on-you, materials can help kids shift their focus.

Generally, you will want enough materials so that kids can work with partners on whatever work you're asking them to tackle. If they are editing a hypothetical child's writing or sorting some words, providing only one set of materials for two partners guides children to work together in a way that channels them to articulate their thinking to each other. You'll then be able to listen and to decide whether and how to coach.

THE ARCHITECTURE OF YOUR SMALL GROUPS

We recommend that within a five- to seven-minute small group, you include some, but not all, of the following component parts. You'll see that we often combine parts or skip them altogether, depending on what the topic and activity call for. You'll find detailed descriptions of each of these parts in the *Guide*.

- **Rally:** Convey the reason for the teaching that you are about to do, building students' commitment to the work and their sense of how it will fit with their ongoing work. This usually involves saying a few sentences.

- **Activate Phonics:** Involve students in a quick warm-up that gets them doing some work that reminds them of prior phonics learning. For example, students may work in pairs to reread a vowel chart. Try to decentralize this warm-up so as to make them all active.

- **Launch:** Detail the work students will do to engage with the phonics principle. Then the kids get started.

- **Work Side by Side:** You might play an active role, supporting students' work.

- **Challenge:** You might intercede to either lift the level of the work all students do or you may channel students to continue work with less of your support.

- **Teach toward Tomorrow:** Explain ways the work of the small group can affect students' ongoing work as readers or writers and channel them to apply the phonics principle to their ongoing reading and writing.

At the end of many phonics small-group lessons, you'll see a box that overviews other supports. These boxes contain three categories of supports: replications, extensions, and related lessons from elsewhere in the curriculum that could provide additional support to the members of your small group.

- *Replicate:* Here you'll find suggestions for ways you can teach a similar small group, with new phonics content. For instance, if you've just taught a small group on writing with digraphs, you'll find a suggestion for how you could reteach that lesson using a new text to support writing with blends. The texts and materials you need to do that replication are often included in the online resources.

- *Preteach* ▼: You may find yourself in the midst of teaching a group and realize that one or more students don't yet have the prerequisite skills to participate successfully in the group. If you've just begun the group, you might want to send the child back to his independent work. On the other hand, if you are well into the group, you might just let that child continue to participate. Either way, plan to meet with the child again to provide more foundational support. In the Preteach section, we list resources you can draw upon, including sessions and extensions from units, to help you plan this kind of instruction. Note that we code these resources as such. "Gr 1, Unit 2, Sess. 3, Ext. 1: Watching Out for Words with a Long *A* Sound and Silent *E*" indicates Grade 1, Book 2, Session 3, Extension 1.

OTHER SUPPORTS

Replicate: You can replicate this group as you teach new high-frequency words. Add new words to children's word pouches and invite them to try this exercise so that they get practice reading and using the new words in the context of a sentence.

▼ **Small Group 46:** "Learning Words in a Snap"

▼ **Gr K, Unit 1, Sess. 16, Ext. 1:** Building Sentences

▼ **Gr K, Unit 1, Sess. 16, Ext. 2:** Making a New Book for the Classroom Library

▲ **Gr K, Unit 2, Sess. 6, Ext. 2:** Making a Class *R* Book

An example of the "Other Supports" from Small Group 47.

• *Extend* ▲: The *Extend* suggestions provide additional supports or added challenge for teaching the same phonics concept. For instance, you might follow up a small group in which students sort words with different long-vowel patterns with a lesson that asks students to draw on that knowledge to engage in some shared editing. These are coded in the same way as the preteach resources.

Keep in mind that everyone need not stay with a small group for the entire time. Sometimes, you'll begin a group by checking in on what students already know, as when you ask children to read over a list of words containing digraphs. If you note early in the group that one of the children you've gathered seems to have aced these, you might send that child off to read or write while you teach the remaining children.

We wish you all the best as you use this book. We hope it helps you to provide engaging, targeted instruction to help you meet each and every one of your students where they are, and help them realize their full potential.

Warmly,

Lucy, Laurie, Rebecca, Christine, Sarah, and Emma

Phonological and Phonemic Awareness, Letter Knowledge, and Concepts About Print

CHAPTER 1

A Beats Walk
Syllable Segmenting

BEST TAUGHT TO

- Children who are still consolidating their concepts of print
- Children who do not yet chime in when the class is rhyming
- Children who have trouble clapping the beats in each other's names

BEST TAUGHT DURING

- Writing workshop
- Choice time
- Intervention time

GETTING READY

✔ Ask students to bring their backpacks to the small group.

✔ Prepare the "Take a Beats Walk" chart.

ACTIVATE PHONICS: Invite students to clap to show the beats in the names of the things in or on their backpack.

"You've been hearing and clapping and stomping the beats in your names, right? How would you do that for the name *Mabel*?"

After kids clap and stomp for Mabel, lead them in doing the same for the names of the group members.

LAUNCH THEM: Invite students to clap syllables to the items in their backpacks. They'll point to an item, say its name, and clap its beats.

Speaking in a stage whisper, tell the children, "Here's a secret. Pull in close." Then say, as if this is the greatest secret imaginable, "You can hear the beats in the names of *anything*. Honest."

To show them what you mean, say, "Open up your backpacks. Will you touch a part of your backpack or reach into it and bring out something?" Then add, "Say the name of what you touched." The kids may say *zipper*, *pocket*, *snack*, *sweatshirt*.

"Now will you clap, stomp, or snap the beats to that word? Like if you touch the pocket of your backpack, you could say and clap *pocket: pock* (clap) *et* (clap). Then, find more parts to your backpack or things in your backpack and clap the beats to those things.

"Are you ready to try it in partners? Do the same thing with all the stuff in your backpacks. Go ahead."

Encourage children to continue pulling objects out of their backpacks or touching parts of their backpack, saying the word and clapping the beats for each object.

If kids look to you for support between each item they touch, point to and read aloud the steps in the chart and visibly pull yourself back, away, saying, "I'll just watch as you keep doing this."

CHALLENGE THEM: Disperse kids to do a "beats walk," syllabicating as they touch items throughout the classroom.

"You can hear the beats—they are really called *syllables*—in the name of anything and everything. Let's test that out by seeing if you can hear the beats in the names of things in this classroom. In a moment, you and your partner will have a chance to do a 'beats walk.' To do a beats walk, you touch something, and you say the name of what you've touched and clap or snap the beats." Demonstrate this by touching some nearby items and clapping the beats. "*Chair:* one clap. *Ta-ble:* two claps.

"You ready? Off you go."

In this small group you don't explain the rationale for syllabication, which is to develop phonemic awareness. It is important for students to hear the syllables in words but explaining the rationale for this would be confusing for them.

If kids run out of objects in their backpacks, they can do this with items of clothing they are wearing.

FIG. 1–1   Students clap to show the beats in the names of the things in or on their backpack.

FIG. 1–2   Vincent claps the beats in items around the room.

TEACH TOWARD TOMORROW: Remind students that this work is important for them to continue doing.

"This may not seem like it will help you write, but it will. Saying words in parts will help you hear more sounds in the whole word. This will help you be ready to write lots and lots of words. If you want to write *Mabel*, you can say her name in beats—Ma/bel. Then you can try and write the letters for /Mā/ and the letters for /bəl/. So, as you go through your day, remember you and your friends can have fun saying words and clapping the beats and you'll become better writers as you do it."

OTHER SUPPORTS

Replicate: Go on a rhyme walk. Follow the same steps as the beats walk, this time inviting children to produce rhymes (real and nonsense words) for objects around the room: *book/took*, *wall/ball*, *nose/toes*.

Blending Syllables

ACTIVATE PHONICS: Say each child's name in syllables and ask the group to put the parts together to say the name.

"I thought about you last night as I was making a peanut butter and jelly sandwich. Do you know how to make a peanut butter and jelly sandwich? You need all the parts: bread, peanut butter, and jelly. But to make it a sandwich, you need to smoosh all the parts together. Can I tell you something special?"

Lean in close to the group to show how important this is. "It's the same with words. Especially when a word is long, you can break the word apart, and then you can smoosh the parts back together to say the whole word. Let me show you what I mean. Let's try this with a long word. I'm going to say and clap each beat, each syllable. Then, I'll smoosh the beats back together to say the whole word."

Demonstrate for students using any long word, such as *lollipop*. Say the word in syllables—"lol-li-pop"—while clapping the beats. Then, make a gesture to show smooshing the syllables back together, rubbing your palms against each other. Say the word *lollipop* smoothly with the syllables back together.

"Do you see what I mean? You say and clap the beats—talking almost like a robot—and then you smoosh the beats, the syllables, back together and say the whole word again.

"Do this with each other's names. Say your partner's name in beats, then smoosh the beats together and say your partner's whole name."

LAUNCH THEM / WORK SIDE BY SIDE: Invite students to do this same thing with picture cards.

"It's a cinch with your names, but it can get harder. Let's try this out with some picture cards. I'll give you and your partner a stack. One partner will pick up a card and without showing the picture, say the word in beats like a robot. Then the other partner will smoosh the beats together and say the whole word. You can look at the picture to check."

BEST TAUGHT TO

- Children who are still consolidating their concepts of print
- Children who do not yet chime in when the class is rhyming
- Children who may be starting to label initial sounds in their writing

BEST TAUGHT DURING

- Reading workshop
- Choice time
- Intervention time

GETTING READY

✔ Prepare photo cards with two-, three-, and four-syllable words. We have provided photo cards with the following images:

  ✔ Two-syllable words: *cupcake, birthday, brownie, rabbit, flashlight*

  ✔ Three-syllable words: *basketball, dinosaur, butterfly, banana*

  ✔ Four-syllable words: *watermelon, caterpillar, alligator*

TEACH TOWARD TOMORROW: Remind students that this work is important for them to continue doing. Remind them to try this work as they read independently.

"When you get back to your reading spot, remember that when you get to a long word, you can say it in parts, like a robot, and then smoosh those beats together into one word. I'll leave you to get started."

OTHER SUPPORTS

▼ **Gr K, Unit 1, Sess. 6, Ext. 3:** Using Manipulatives to Hear Syllables

---

POSSIBLE COACHING MOVES

▶ "Say the word in beats."

▶ "Smoosh the word together."

▶ "Does that sound like a real word?"

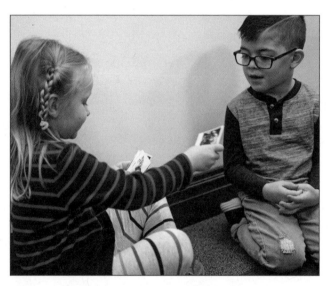

FIG. 2–1   Eleanor says the word in syllables and Joseph blends the syllables back together.

SMALL GROUP 3

Letter Lunch
Phoneme Manipulation

LAUNCH THEM: Invite students to play with sounds. Hold up a letter, introduce the letter name and sound, then demonstrate how you can make new words by changing initial phonemes.

"Friends, it's time for Letter Lunch! We can all take turns pulling a letter out of this pouch. We'll use the letter to make silly names for all the foods in your lunch. To do this, we'll change the first sounds in the names of our foods, so they start with that letter's sound.

"Let me show you how it goes. I'll pull a letter out of this pouch and show it to the group. Don't worry, you'll all have a turn to choose the letter. What letter did we get?

"Right, the letter *P*!

"And what sound goes with the *P*?

"Yes, /p/!

"Okay, let's try it. I see some of you have a cookie in your lunch. Let's change the word *cookie* to start with /p/. *Cookie, pookie!*

"And what would we call this apple?

"Right, *papple!*"

WORK SIDE BY SIDE: Invite children to look through their lunches and manipulate the initial phonemes in the names of their foods.

"That's so silly! Look through your lunches and try to make all your foods start with the sound /p/. Then someone else can choose another letter!"

BEST TAUGHT TO

- Children who need practice manipulating sounds
- Children who need practice rhyming
- Children who need practice with letter-sound knowledge

BEST TAUGHT DURING

- Lunch, snack, or choice time

GETTING READY

✔ Gather a few magnetic letters or letter cards in a pouch. Consonants that children already know will work best.

Continue encouraging children to take turns pulling out letters and changing the names of their foods to start with each letter's sound.

> ## POSSIBLE COACHING MOVES
>
> ▸ "You have a *banana*, and you changed it to *mamama*. Close, you changed so many sounds in the word to /m/. If you changed only the first sound, the /b/, what would it sound like? Right, *manana!*"
>
> ▸ "*Orange* is a tricky one. You are trying to take away the /ō/ sound at the start, but that makes a word that's hard to say. What if you add a /t/ at the start without taking away the /ō/? You'd have *torange*, right!"
>
> ▸ "Oh *crackers*, that's a tricky word, because it has the /k/ and the /r/ sounds stuck together at the start. You could take both sounds away to make the word *dackers*." (For an extra challenge, or if students are ready to manipulate blends, you could coach them to say *drackers*.)

TEACH TOWARD TOMORROW: Encourage children to continue playing with letters and sounds in this way at school and at home.

"Friends, you can *play* with letters and sounds anytime. Do any of you think you could teach this game to someone in your family and play it at dinner? That would be so cool! If you do that, tell us about it tomorrow."

OTHER SUPPORTS

Replicate: You may decide to play different versions of this game, such as Robot Lunch, where students are encouraged to say all their foods in robot talk, breaking apart words and emphasizing all the sounds they hear. For example, instead of *pancake*, a child might say /p/ /ă/ /n/ /k/ /ā/ /k/.

Versions of this game can be played at different times of the day, including choice time.

If students cannot identify the name of the letter or the sound associated with it, teach them these. You might say, "This is a P. The sound /p/ goes with P." Or, you might refer students to the alphabet chart if there is one nearby. If students haven't brought a lunch, you might encourage them to pair up and take turns or use other objects entirely.

FIG. 3–1   Tucking in word play during snack time. This child is about to eat *Mogurt*!

Sorting Letters with Mabel

RALLY THEM: Explain that letters are similar to Beanie Babies: people who don't know them might think they are all the same, but experts know they aren't. Experts can sort letters based on how they look.

Gather the group and say, "When you are a little kid, it can be hard to tell the letters of the alphabet apart. They all just look like sticks and squiggles. When you start to be an expert on the alphabet, you realize that if you look closely, you can see that the different letters actually look different."

"Did you know some people who don't know anything about Beanie Babies don't really notice that the bear and the dog are different? They just say, 'They are all Beanie Babies.' But *you* know that the bear is completely different than the dog, right?"

"It is the same with letters. They actually are completely different."

LAUNCH THEM: Encourage students to explore magnetic letters and make observations about their features.

Lay out the magnetic letters on the table and say, "Let's take a look at these letters! Tell each other what you notice about them."

Observe as students take out letters and begin to play with them. Encourage their play and exploration and help put words to what they are noticing.

WORK SIDE BY SIDE: Channel students to begin sorting letters in different ways.

After a few minutes of this, say, "Mabel loves letters so much. You know how some people have a special jewelry box and they put all the bracelets in one compartment and all the necklaces in another? Or they have a tool box, and they put all the long nails in one place and the screws in another? Well, Mabel thinks we should make a jewelry box," or you could say a *tool box*, "for letters. She isn't sure how to sort them. Maybe the letters with tails go in one spot and the tall letters in

BEST TAUGHT TO

- Children who are not yet showing interest in learning letters
- Children who are not noticing different features of letters during the "Learn a Letter" routine
- Children who are able to name only about half the letters of the alphabet

BEST TAUGHT DURING

- Choice time
- Reading workshop
- Intervention time
- Writing workshop (if necessary)

GETTING READY

✔ Gather at least two sets of magnetic letters. If you have a magnetic letter set that comes in a divided box, you can use that box for this small group. If your magnetic letters are in a tub or a bag, you will want to gather a bunch of small boxes or a larger box with compartments to encourage the children to sort their letters in different ways.

✔ Set Mabel on the table next to the magnetic letters.

✔ Prepare a copy of the "Sorting Letters" chart.

another? Can you all work with your partner to try to sort your letters in a system that you think would make sense? Then you can explain your system to Mabel and see what she thinks."

Sorting Letters	
Sort by...	Examples...
Tall	h t
Short	e o
Curves	c s
Straight Lines	t l
Slanted Lines	w v
Holes	o a
Tails	j g
Dots	i j

Give the children a few minutes to sort letters by features.

"The thing is, Mabel wants to know your thinking. As you sort, will you say the name of the letter and talk about it by name, so she can follow what both of you are doing? Don't just say, 'This one goes here.' Say, 'This *G* goes here because it has a tail.' If you don't know the name of the letter, you can work together to figure that out."

OTHER SUPPORTS

▼ **Gr K, Unit 2, Sess. 1, Ext. 3:** Noticing Letter Features

▶ "You found two letters that are the same! That letter is called *S*. *S* is a curvy letter."

▶ "Those *O*'s do look like eyes. There's a hole in that letter!"

▶ "That letter has three sticks. That letter is the letter *F*."

FIG. 4–1 Partners work together to sort letters by features.

Forming Capital and/or Lowercase Letters

RALLY THEM: Talk up the importance of forming letters fast so that readers can read their stories.

"You've all been working so hard on your writing! And you've been adding letters so that people can read your writing. I brought you here today to practice writing a really important letter, one you will probably use *all* the time in your writing. It's the letter *R*.

"You'll need the letter *R* if you are writing a book about /r/ robots, /r/ rain, or /r/ rabbits. Yep, this is an important letter for sure."

LAUNCH THEM: Coach students to study the letter and then to make it, following the pathway with invisible ink, on the rug, and in the air.

"Let's look at this letter *R* together for a minute. What are you noticing about it?

"Oh, you see the straight line down? If you cover this line it looks like a *P*? You're right! What else?" Gather observations about the letter.

"Now let's write the letter *R* together. I will write it on my whiteboard while you use your finger to write it on the rug. Line down, back up, bump around, and a slanted line down."

Make sure that students are following along and doing each step with you. Repeat this a few times. Encourage the students to say the pathway along with you.

"Now let's stand up and write a giant letter *R* in the air. Start with your finger all the way up like this. Line down, back up, bump around, and a slanted line down."

WORK SIDE BY SIDE: Coach students to write the letter on their whiteboards.

"Now write the letter *R* on your whiteboards. Write it as many times as you can. Line down, back up, bump around, and a slanted line down."

BEST TAUGHT TO

- Children who consistently form letters incorrectly or inefficiently. Make sure children are not being taught differently by occupational therapy or other support teachers.

BEST TAUGHT DURING

- Writing workshop
- Choice time
- Intervention time

GETTING READY

✔ Choose one focus letter for the session, one that the students consistently write incorrectly. Print the letter formation pathway card for that letter or review the formation pathway prior to coming to the group.

✔ Gather whiteboards and markers for each student and for yourself.

✔ Consider preparing a tactile medium for students to practice forming the letters, such as a tray of sand or salt or a gel-filled plastic bag.

Students can practice writing the letter in a variety of tactile mediums. Many teachers choose to use sand or salt trays or bags filled with gel. The act of forming the letter this way helps students commit the letter to muscle memory. Writing the letter without looking helps with this, as well.

TEACH TOWARD TOMORROW: Remind students of the pathway before sending them off. Encourage them to find places to write the letter in their writing.

"Whenever you need to write the letter *R*—which will probably be a lot—don't forget to follow the pathway like we did together. Line down, back up, bump around, and a slanted line down!

"When you go back to your writing spot, look over your writing and your drawing. See if there is anything that needs to be labeled with the letter *R*. If you find something, write it in! /r/ *Rainbow*, /r/ *recess*. Those start with *R*. Label them! Try to write *R*'s all over the place."

OTHER SUPPORTS

Replicate: You can replicate this group for any other capital or lowercase letters students need support with. Depending on the level of support needed, you might teach students two letters at a time instead of just one.

▲ **Gr K, Unit 1, Sess. 9, Ext. 1:** Writing Giant Letters in the Sky

▲ **Gr K, Unit 2, Sess. 9, Ext. 3:** Write Lowercase Letters

SMALL GROUP 6

The Words Fell Out of the Book!
One-to-One Correspondence

LAUNCH THEM: Reread a favorite book and explain that Mabel's copy fell apart.

"Readers, do you remember this book from reading workshop? It's one of your favorites, isn't it? Can we read it together to remind ourselves of how it goes? Join me when you can." Read the book aloud, letting your voice drop off as students read along with you.

Lunch

BEST TAUGHT TO

- Children who are working on concepts about print (concept of word, one-to-one correspondence)
- Children who are approaching level A or B books

BEST TAUGHT DURING

- Reading workshop

GETTING READY

✔ Bring Mabel to the group.

✔ Select a very familiar shared reading text. We use the book *Lunch*, though you can use any familiar shared reading text.

✔ For each page of the book, create a baggie containing the picture and two copies of the text (one cut into individual words and one full sentence) from that page.

"Something so silly happened last night. Mabel was reading her copy of this book, and all the words and pictures fell out. She couldn't put them back together, so she gathered them all up in these baggies hoping you could help her."

WORK SIDE BY SIDE: Give each partnership a baggie containing a picture and the set of words from that page. Invite them to reconstruct Mabel's version of the book.

"I'll give you and your partner a baggie that contains the words and pictures from one page of Mabel's book. I'll also give you a copy of how the sentence on that page is supposed to look. Will you work together to put the words back in the right order? I'll put a copy of the book right here, too, if you need it."

POSSIBLE COACHING MOVES

▶ "Look at the picture first. What does this page say? Okay, now where is the first word you need?"

▶ "Which word comes next? Match it with the word on the page."

▶ "Reread your sentence. Make sure the words are in the right order."

▶ "Hmm, . . . something doesn't look quite right. Point to the first word in the sentence. Now point to your first word. Do they match?"

When partnerships finish reconstructing one page, have them reread the sentence.

OTHER SUPPORTS

Replicate: You can replicate this group with any other familiar text. You might consider choosing a book with longer sentences that includes more high-frequency words children could use as anchors to rebuild the sentences.

When distributing pages, keep in mind students' needs. For example, some students will need the page with just three words, while others may be ready to approach the pages with more words or pattern shifts.

If partners complete their page quickly, hand them a bag with a new page to work on, possibly one with more words or a pattern break.

FIG. 6–1   Students check to see if they put the words back in the right order.

Make It Match
One-to-One Correspondence

RALLY THEM AND ACTIVATE PHONICS: Rally kids to join in a shared reading of a letter from Reader Man that encourages them to strengthen their pointer power.

"Super Readers, come quickly, Reader Man left a note with your names on the envelope. Let's read it together. Everyone read with me!"

Place the letter so the children can all see it, and read it aloud, pointing to each word as you do. You might ask one child to rest a finger on top of yours and read the letter together in this way.

Dear Readers,

Your reading powers are getting stronger!

The more you use them, the stronger they get.

Here are some cards with words for you to read.

You can use them to strengthen your pointer power.

Good luck,

Reader Man

LAUNCH THEM: Distribute a color dot card to each student and channel students to use their pointer power to read their cards.

Draw the color dot cards out of the envelope. "Whoa, cool! Let's see the words Reader Man left you to strengthen your pointer power." Distribute one card of colored dots to each student.

BEST TAUGHT TO

- Children who are working on concepts about print (concept of word) but are not yet using one-to-one correspondence
- Children who are using one-to-one correspondence but still get tripped up on multisyllabic words

BEST TAUGHT DURING

- Reading workshop

GETTING READY

✔ Ask students to bring their pointers and book baggies. If they do not have pointers, make some using Popsicle® sticks with googly eyes, glitter, or star stickers on the end.

✔ Write the names of all the children in your group on an envelope. Inside the envelope, enclose a letter from Reader Man, along with one color dot card for each student.

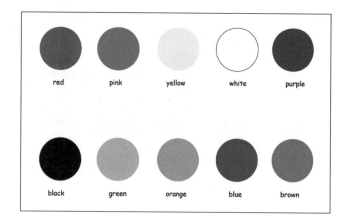

red   pink   yellow   white   purple

black   green   orange   blue   brown

POSSIBLE COACHING MOVES

▶ "You pointed twice, but there's only one word. Try it again."

▶ "Let's count the words on this page together. One, two, three, four words. This one is a long word but we only pointed to it once. Now you try on the next page!"

▶ "See the space between the words? When you get to the space, get ready to tap. You don't need to tap again until after the next space."

"Oh, these are color words. Reader Man must have given you these to help you practice pointing to each word, one point for a word. Some of these words are long, and some are short, but they each get only one tap. Look at the color, then point to the word below it and read. As you read, be sure to point to each word just once. Even if a word has more than one beat, it still gets one tap."

Coach students as they work and voice over important observations. "Yes, *purple* has two beats, but it's just one word, so you only point to it one time. Try it again with one tap for each word."

CHALLENGE THEM: Direct students to take out a book from their book baggie. Encourage them to point to and count the words on each page prior to reading.

"Now here's some *big* work. Take out a book from your book baggie, and let's test your stronger pointer power. Open up to the first page in your book and point to each word on the page. You don't even have to read them yet—just point to each word and count how many are on the page. Once you've pointed to and counted the words on the page, use your pointer power to read the page. Then, keep going until you've used your pointer power to read the entire book."

TEACH TOWARD TOMORROW: Encourage students to go back and continue strengthening their pointer power as they read their books.

"Nice work strengthening your pointer power today! Go back to your reading spots and try this with some more books. First point

FIG. 7–1 Tommy tests his pointer power in his own book.

Make sure students also choose books with some two-syllable words, so children can practice their pointer power.

to each word, count how many words there are on the page, and then read! You might even teach your partner how to do this during partner time, so your partner can have stronger pointer power, too."

OTHER SUPPORTS

Replicate: You can replicate this group by creating other pages of pictures that readers can use to practice pointer power. For example, you might make a page of different modes of transportation and arrange the pictures starting with one-syllable words and increasing to multisyllabic words. You could have a boat, a car, a truck, and a bus, and then add a scooter, a helicopter, and a motorcycle. You could also create a page with princesses, action figures, or anything else that would grab children's interest. We have created some for your use, available in the online resources.

Learning the Letter *V*

RALLY THEM AND ACTIVATE PHONICS: Read the alphabet chart and remind children of the routine they use to learn letters.

"I brought you here today because you are ready to learn a new letter. Let's get ready by reading the alphabet chart."

Guide students to read the alphabet chart. Have one child point to each letter on the chart while you lead the group in first saying the name of the letter, then naming the picture, then making the letter's sound.

Asking students to isolate the first sound in the keyword picture on the alphabet chart will help them be able to use this tool to find the letter sound independently.

As students say the sound for letter V, correct those who add the schwa sound to the end of the letter V. The sound is /v/, not /vuh/. This is also true when they say other letters. Adding the schwa sound will cause difficulty when children record sounds in writing and blend sounds when they are reading.

Remind students of the "How to Learn a Letter" chart. "You've already learned so many letters. You followed the same steps each time you learned a letter.

"For today, I've chosen a letter that is a little tricky. You kind of know it, but you don't quite own it yet." Write the letter on your whiteboard.

WORK SIDE BY SIDE: Coach students through the steps to learn a letter, naming it, sounding it, writing the uppercase and lowercase, and using it by generating words that start with the same sound.

"Are you ready to own this letter? First, we need to name it. This is the letter *V*. Can you say *V* and point to it on alphabet chart? Wow, *V* is way down at the end of the alphabet chart, isn't it? Lots of kids find the letters down there to be harder. It's going to be great for you to totally own it."

BEST TAUGHT TO

- Students who need support with letter-sound identification

BEST TAUGHT DURING

- Reading workshop
- Writing workshop
- Intervention time

GETTING READY

✔ Bring an alphabet chart.

✔ Make sure the "How to Learn a Letter" chart is visible.

✔ Provide a whiteboard and a marker for each child.

✔ Bring a counter like a Unifix® cube, and an index card with three boxes drawn on it for each child.

✔ Choose words to use during this lesson that have the target sound at either the beginning, middle, or end of the word. We provide a list of possible words for each letter in the online resources.

Point to the next step on the "How to Learn a Letter" chart. "Ready to sound it? Use the picture on the alphabet chart to help you. Look at the picture, say the word, and grab the first sound. /v/- /v/- *volcano.*

"Yes, the sound /v/ goes with the letter *V.* Say the sound, /v/ /v/. Say it again and think about how your mouth goes, /v/ /v/. Yep, that's it."

Hand a whiteboard and marker to each child. "Ready for the next step? Write *V!* Watch me first. This is the capital *V.* Slanted line down, slanted line up. This is the lowercase *v.* Slanted line down, slanted line up. You notice they are the same shape, but different sizes. Good noticing! Now, try it on your own whiteboards. Write a big one and a little one. Remember to start at the top." Repeat the pathway as students write the letters.

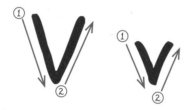

"Here's the last step: Use it! What other words do you know that start with the /v/ sound? Turn and tell your partner.

"Let me say some words, and will you give a thumbs up if they start with a /v/ sound and a thumbs down if they don't?" Share several words with students: *lettuce, vacuum, love, fox, valentine, vehicle, bed.*

CHALLENGE THEM: Invite students to identify whether the letter sound is at the beginning, middle, or end of the word.

Hand a Unifix cube and an index card with three boxes drawn on it to each student. "Want to try something harder? When I say a word that has *V* in it, it will be up to you to figure out where the /v/ sound is in the word—at the beginning (like *vacuum*), in the middle (like *giving*), or at the end (like *love*). Put the cube on the card in the place you hear the sound."

Say several words and observe your students to see who needs help placing the /v/ sound. You might say: *voice, have, arrive, vest, violet, above, glove, over, wave, river, lava, even.*

"Now that you have—*havvvvve*—the letter *V* in your back pockets, you can use it whenever you write, and you can look for it whenever you read. Get back to reading (or writing) now and be on the lookout for the letter *V* in your books."

OTHER SUPPORTS

Replicate: You can use this session to teach any letter. See the online resources for a chart to support teaching other letters. ✴

FIG. 8–1 Students listen for the targeted sound at the beginning, middle, and end of a word.

Playing with Letters and Sounds

RALLY THEM AND ACTIVATE PHONICS: Let students know that one way to get to know letters and sounds as well as possible is to play with them. Sing the alphabet chart to warm up.

"You are working so hard to learn all the sounds that go with each letter. I want to tell you that this doesn't have to feel like hard work. One way that you can get to know letters and sounds well is to *play* with them!

"Before we play, let's warm up by singing the alphabet chart to the tune of 'Row, Row, Row Your Boat.'"

LAUNCH THEM: Dramatically reveal a set of magnetic letters you've brought for children to play with. Demonstrate a few ways to play with the letters that channel children to make letter sounds.

"Look at all of these lovely letters I have here with me." Dramatically dump out the container of magnetic letters.

"I thought we could spend some time playing with them. Let me show you some of my favorite ways to play with letters, and then you and your partner can pick the way you want to play or make up your own way to play. One thing I like to do is pretend that letters are rocket ships. When they blast off and fly around, they make their letter noise. Watch."

Pick up the letter *T* and hold it on the floor like it is a rocket ship about to blast off. Zoom the rocket ship around as you make the sound for *T* and then bring it back to earth: "/t/ /t/ /t/ /t/ /t/ /t/ /t/ /t/ /t/."

"Or, I like to pretend letters are boats and they each make their sound. Sometimes I pretend the letters are race cars making their sounds."

Hold the letters *L* and *C* close to the edge of the table as if they are at the starting line of a race. Move the *L* forward, making the letter sound "/l/ /l/ /l/." Then move the *C* quickly forward to meet

BEST TAUGHT TO

- Children who are just learning about letter sounds
- Children who do not seem interested in learning about letters

BEST TAUGHT DURING

- Choice time
- Snack or lunch time
- Intervention time

GETTING READY

✔ Bring a copy of the alphabet chart.

✔ Gather magnetic letters into a bucket. The consonants *M*, *T*, *D*, *C*, *K*, *L*, *R*, and *P* work especially well. Include several of each, if possible.

✔ Prepare a baggie with several consonant letter cards for each child to take home.

the *L* in the race, "/k/ /k/ /k/." Continue the letter race, alternating making the sounds of each letter until reaching the finish line at the other end of the table.

"I also like to pretend that letters are like action figures who can talk to each other. They each make their sound." Hold the *M* and the *D* and face them toward each other. Say "/m/ /m/ /m/ /m/ /m/ /m/." Make the letter sound, with a cadence that feels like speech, and make the *M* jump as it talks to the *D*. Then, do the same with the letter *D:* "/d/ /d/ /d/ /d/ /d/."

"Sometimes I can make the letters be animals. You might try this, too. You can figure out what they say and do. Will you and your partner think about which way of playing with letters you want to try first and get started? Go for it!"

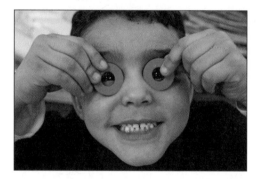

CHALLENGE THEM: Ask students in the group to teach someone else in the group what game they played and coach their friends as they play.

"Okay, here's a super-fun challenge! Get with someone you haven't played with yet and teach them your way of playing with the letters. You might make them people, or animals, or you can make them a kind of vehicle. Be sure to coach them if they need help making the sounds."

TEACH TOWARD TOMORROW: Remind kids that learning their letters can be fun. Give them a baggie with some letter cards and invite them to keep playing with letters at school and at home.

"Friends, remember that learning letters and sounds is hard work, but it can be fun! We can *play* with letters and sounds. I have a baggie of letter cards for you to take home. You can play with letters at home or at other times of the day. I'll check in with you soon to see how you are playing with those letters. See you soon!"

OTHER SUPPORTS

Replicate: Play with vowels. Follow the same steps for this group, focusing only on vowels.

POSSIBLE COACHING MOVES

▸ "If you're not sure what sound goes with that letter, check the alphabet chart!"

▸ "Oh, the letters are racing. What sound is that *P* car going to make? Not /puh/—/p/. Try again! Do it with me. /p/ /p/ /p/ /p/. Get that race car moving!"

▸ "See if your partner can think of a different way to play. Will your letters be animals next?"

FIG. 9–1   Vincent turns the *S* into a snake.

Picture Sort with Initial Sounds

RALLY THEM: Rally children around the importance of having letters in their minds.

Display the lowercase letter *H* with the keyword picture from the alphabet chart and say, "Writers, some of you are confused about this letter *H*. If you are writing about your pet, you need to be able to say *hamster* and then think, 'Yes, *hamster*, /h/ is like *hat*.' In your mind, you need to see the letter *H* so you can pop it onto your page. If you are writing about your *house*, you need to think, '*house* /h/. That's like /h/ *hat*,' and then see that *H* and pop it onto your page.

"Let's do some work with these letters so you can have them in your minds. Make the lowercase *h* in the air with your magic pen. Follow along with me. Line down, back up a bit, bump around and down. Now make it big in the air with your arm. Line down, back up a bit, bump around and down."

To support kinesthetic learning, you could encourage students to form the letter with a material such as pipe cleaners, Wikki Stix, or string if you have any of these handy. This is valuable enough that it's worth the trouble!

"Can you guess these words that begin with *H*?"

Model or show a few examples of things that start with *H*. For example, you might:

- Stand and hop. "Yes! *Hop* starts with *H*."

- Hold out your hand and wiggle it. "Yep, *hand*. *Hand* starts with *H*."

- Touch your hair. "*Hair* starts with *H* too."

BEST TAUGHT TO

- Children who have trouble isolating initial sounds and matching sounds to the letters that represent them

BEST TAUGHT DURING

- Writing workshop
- Intervention time
- Choice time

GETTING READY

✔ Choose two letters, based on your assessment of the letters students need. Cut out the letter and picture keyword squares from the alphabet chart for the letters you'll teach.

✔ Prepare picture cards for each letter. For this lesson we have chosen the letters *B* and *H*. Alternatively, you could collect a set of objects beginning with each of the letter sounds and use the objects for the sort.

✔ Prepare two jars for each partnership, labeled with the letters for sorting. You may also use baggies or envelopes for the sort.

✔ Provide pipe cleaners, Wikki Stix®, or string (optional).

Elicit other suggestions from kids. You might prompt them to suggest words such as *head*, *heart*, and *happy*.

Lead the group through the same steps with the letter *B*. Examples might include *big*, *board*, *back*, *button*, *belt*, *baby*, and *bed*.

"Now let's do some sorting with these letters so you can really get them in your minds. Scientists have jars of things in their laboratories—a jar for sand, a jar for rocks. You are like scientists, but you are *word* scientists. Let's make a jar for things that start with *B* and a jar for things that start with *H*."

LAUNCH THEM: Distribute picture cards and jars to each partnership and coach as they sort picture cards with words that start with *H* or *B*.

Distribute a stack of pictures and two labeled jars to each partnership.

"You each have a set of pictures in front of you. Some of them go in the *B* jar, and some of them go in the *H* jar. What sound goes with the letter *B*? That's right, /b/, like /b/ *ball*. And *H*? /h/, right, /h/ like *hat*."

Point to each picture keyword as you say the sound.

"Pick up one picture at a time, say the name of what's in the picture, and then say the sound it starts with. You can use the picture keyword to help you."

If students are unfamiliar with the pictures, take a minute to teach into the vocabulary. You can hold up each picture card and say, "This is a hose. Say hose. A hose is something you use to water your plants."

> ### POSSIBLE COACHING MOVES
>
> ▶ "Say *bone*. Say *bat*. Do they start the same?"
>
> ▶ "Say *hug*. Say *hat*. Do the beginning sounds match?"
>
> ▶ "Say the word. Say it again slowly. *Bone, b-b-bone*. What's the first sound?"
>
> ▶ "/h/ *hose*. Does that go with /b/ *ball* or /h/ *hat*? Say /h/ *hose*, /b/ *hose*. Which sound the same?"

TEACH TOWARD TOMORROW: Encourage partners to check their sort and celebrate having more letters in their minds.

"Let's read through the pictures together now and make sure we have them in the right jar. *Hug, hose, hat, bone*. Oops, how did *bone* get in there? Let's move it over to the *B* jar. Great!

"Now you have all of the pictures in their correct jar and most of all, you have these letters in your mind! If you want to write *boot*, what letter will you put on the page?" When the kids called out *B*, I shook their hands and said, "Congratulations!"

OTHER SUPPORTS

Replicate: You can do this same sort with different letters. To adjust the difficulty, consider the following:

- Start with two obviously contrasting sounds like /b/ and /h/, where the letter sounds are made in different parts of the mouth.
- Move on to sort sounds that are more difficult to distinguish such as /b/ and /p/, or /v/ and /f/, and/or look for children that might be having a challenge with particular sounds like these.
- Move to sorting three or four sounds at a time.
- Include words that do not belong in either category (oddball words).
- Have students generate other words that could be added to a jar.
- Sort for ending sounds.

Using the Alphabet Chart to Label Pictures in Favorite Books

BEST TAUGHT TO

- Children having difficulty with letter sounds (possibly indicated on the letter-sound identification assessment)
- Children who are not yet labeling in their writing

BEST TAUGHT DURING

- Reading workshop
- Choice time
- Intervention time

GETTING READY

✔ Cut an alphabet chart into individual letters and pictures and distribute a baggie of them to each partnership.

✔ Choose a familiar, beloved book containing pictures for students to label. Alternatively, you may choose to use a piece of demonstration writing or student writing from writing workshop.

RALLY THEM AND ACTIVATE PHONICS: Explain why you've gathered students together. Then, lead them in identifying letters and sounds on the cut-apart alphabet chart.

"You've all been doing the big work of saying words slowly and catching the first sound that you hear. Sometimes, though, when you hear that sound, it's tricky to figure out which letter goes with that sound. The alphabet chart can help you when you are trying to match letters to sounds."

Distribute cut-apart letters and pictures from the alphabet chart to each partnership.

"I'm giving each partnership a stack of letter and picture cards from the chart. Will you and your partner spread these cards out in front of you and then read each one? Touch each one and say the letter's name and the sound that goes with it.

LAUNCH THEM: Channel children to match the letters and keywords from the chart to parts of children's bodies and then to pictures in a book.

"Now we can use these letters to label things. Like this letter, *L*." I pointed to the picture. "*L*, *ladybug*, /l/. I could stick it here, right?" and I put it on my leg. "/l/ *leg*, right?

"Where could we put this one? It's the letter *N*. First, we had better remember the sound it makes. Let's look at the drawing. It's a nest, /n/ *nest*. The letter *N* has the sound /n/. So, where does it go? On your *mouth*? Turn and tell your partner. No, /m/ *mouth* doesn't match with /n/ *nest*.

"How about your *hair*? Turn and tell your partner. That doesn't work either. /h/ *hair* doesn't match /n/ *nest*.

"How about your nose? Turn and tell your partner. Yes! /n/ *nose* starts with the same sound as /n/ *nest*.

"We aren't really going to stick this on your nose, but we *could* label your whole body, couldn't we? That's fun, but the real place where we need letters is in books, not on our bodies! Let's try to use these letters in one of our favorite books. Let's find a picture that you and your partner can label."

Open the book to a spread with lots of details to label, and direct partners to label items on one of the pages.

"Can you two work on this side together, and notice things on that page? And you two work on this side and notice things on this page? Then can you use your letters to label those things? You will have to share the letters, so ask another partnership if they have a letter you need. You might need to use the picture on the card to figure out the sound that the letter makes and check to make sure the first sounds match."

FIG. 11–1   Partners work together to spread out and name the letter and sound for each card.

> **POSSIBLE COACHING MOVES**
>
> ▶ "*Leash* does start with /l/. Hmm, . . . which letter makes the /l/ sound? Let's check the picture icons. /l/ *cat*. No, not that one. /l/ *volcano*. What do you think? No?. /l/ *ladybug*. /l/ *leash* . . . What do you think?"
>
> ▶ "Try saying the name of the picture that goes with the letter. Now say the name of what you see in the book. Let's check if they match. Say *fan*. Say *fence*. Do they match? Do they sound the same at the beginning?"

TEACH TOWARD TOMORROW: Remind readers of the usefulness of the alphabet chart and encourage them to use it during reading workshop.

"I'm going to leave you here, so you and your partner can keep working together. Go to another page and keep studying the pictures in the book closely and choose something in the picture and catch the first sound. Then, you can use your letters to label it.

"And one more secret—just as you used the pictures and letters from the alphabet chart today to label the pages in books, you can use this when you write during writing workshop. You can use the full alphabet chart when you label your pictures in your writing."

FIG. 11–2   Tommy uses the picture on the card to figure out the sound that the letter makes.

Matching Magnetic Letters to the Alphabet Chart

BEST TAUGHT TO

- Children who are struggling to locate letters on the alphabet chart
- Children who are not yet identifying many letters
- Children who are not yet labeling their writing

BEST TAUGHT DURING

- Writing workshop
- Choice time
- Intervention time

GETTING READY

✔ Distribute an alphabet chart to each partnership.

✔ For each partnership, mix up a set of twenty-six lowercase magnetic letters and place in a bag.

✔ Ask students to bring their writing folders to the session.

RALLY THEM: Rally students around the importance of using the alphabet chart as a reading and writing tool.

"You know how grown-ups use special tools for their jobs? Like how a doctor uses a stethoscope and a construction worker uses a hammer? Well, as you become stronger writers, you will need to use some important tools as well. One tool you already have is the alphabet chart! The alphabet chart is a super-helpful tool for readers and writers. It shows you how to write capital and lowercase letters. It also helps you remember the sound that goes with each letter. Let's spend some time really getting to know the alphabet chart. This will help you find letters quickly when you need to know the shape of the letter or the sound that goes with that letter."

LAUNCH THEM: Distribute magnetic letters and alphabet charts and set up students to match the magnetic letters to the letters on the alphabet chart.

"Here is a set of magnetic letters and an alphabet chart for you and your partner. You'll choose a magnetic letter from your set and match it up to the same letter on the alphabet chart. Before you place the letter on the chart, say the letter's name and the sound that goes with it. Watch me first."

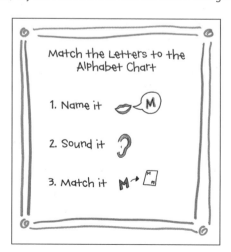

Match the Letters to the Alphabet Chart

1. Name it
2. Sound it
3. Match it

Choose a magnetic letter, say its name, and look for its location on the alphabet chart.

"This is the letter *T*. It goes with the sound, /t/. Now I find where it goes on the chart. Hmm, . . . oh, here it goes. Now it's your turn, go ahead, and with your partner, match up all of your magnetic letters to the letters on your alphabet chart."

CHALLENGE THEM: Encourage students to transfer the magnetic letters from the alphabet chart to their writing.

"Now take out the writing from your writing folder. Let's see if you can use some of these letters from the alphabet chart to add labels into your writing. Point to a picture you've drawn, say the word slowly, and listen for the first sound. Then, find that letter on the alphabet chart. When you find it, take it off the chart and place it on your writing."

Give students a few minutes to do this, and coach them as they do.

"Great! You all have a few letters placed onto your writing. And now we need to make sure those letters stay there. The best way to do that is to write those letters! One at a time, lift each letter up and write it on your page, right where it goes."

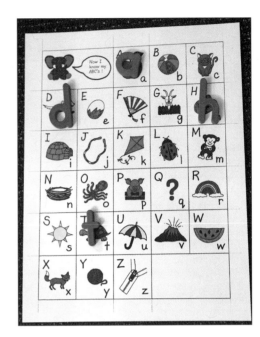

TEACH TOWARD TOMORROW: Remind students of the importance of the alphabet chart and encourage them to continue using it as a tool for reading and writing.

"Writers, whenever you write, you can use the alphabet chart to help you label your writing. Remember to point to a picture you've drawn, say the word slowly, and listen for the first sound. After you find that letter on the alphabet chart, then write it onto your page. Right now, take the book where you added labels to your writing and go teach your writing partner how to add *more* labels to their writing!"

POSSIBLE COACHING MOVES

▶ "That's the letter *V*. Look toward the bottom of your chart to find that letter."

▶ "That's *S*. It has the same sound as the first sound in *sun*, /s/. Do you see the *sun* on the alphabet chart?"

OTHER SUPPORTS

▲ **Gr K, Unit 2, Sess. 5, Ext. 2:** Singing and Writing the Alphabet by Heart

---

Tap It! Identifying Beginning Sounds

BEST TAUGHT TO

- Children who need more practice isolating initial sounds and identifying the letter that represents that sound

- Children who have difficulty using the alphabet chart when they do not know which letter matches a sound in a word they are trying to write

- Children who are not yet labeling initial sounds in their writing

BEST TAUGHT DURING

- Writing workshop

GETTING READY

✔ Select a class story or familiar mentor text with pictures that students can label. We use our text about a trip to the farm.

✔ Bring an alphabet chart and a pointer (such as a Popsicle stick or the eraser end of a pencil) for each child.

✔ Ask children to bring their writing folders.

✔ Prepare a copy of the "Tap it!" chart.

RALLY THEM AND ACTIVATE PHONICS: Explain why you've gathered students together. Then, ask them to point to the letters in their names on the alphabet chart using pointers.

"You have all been working hard to say words slowly, catching the first sounds in words and figuring out the letter that goes with that sound. The alphabet chart can be a really helpful tool for readers and writers to use when you are trying to match letters to their sounds. Let's get ready for some letter-sound work by using these pointers to find letters quickly on the alphabet chart."

Distribute an alphabet chart and a pointer to each child.

"For now, use your pointer and tap all the letters in your name."

WORK SIDE BY SIDE: Channel writers to use the skills they have practiced in phonics workshop to label the illustrations in a class story.

"In phonics, we've been focused on saying words slowly and listening for sounds. Let's practice that with the pictures in our class story of our trip to the farm. I'll point to something in the picture. Then will you and your partner take your pointer and point to the letter that goes with that sound?"

Tap a picture, then voice over the steps as children follow along.

"Say *duck* slowly. Catch the first sound, /d/. Go to the alphabet chart. Is it /t/ like in *turtle*? Does it match? How about /r/ like in *rainbow*? Does that match? No way! Tap the letter that matches the first sound in *duck*, /d/. *Duck*, *dog* (referring to the icon on the alphabet chart). They match!"

LAUNCH THEM: Channel partners to choose more illustrations in the class story. For each word, ask them to isolate the initial sound and then find the corresponding letter on the alphabet chart.

"Now will you work with your partner? Will one of you tap something in this same picture of our trip to the farm? Then, both of you can say the word and listen for the first sound, then find and tap the letter (or keyword picture) that goes with that sound."

CHALLENGE THEM: Invite students to take out their writing folders and encourage them to add more labels to their writing.

"Hey, I have an idea! Why don't you use these pointers and alphabet charts and work on your own writing? Each of you, get out the writing you have been doing and point to something in your picture. Then tap the letter that goes there. And then, make that letter on the page."

TEACH TOWARD TOMORROW: Celebrate writers getting more words into their writing. Encourage the rest of the class to do the same.

"I am so thrilled to see how many words you are getting into your writing. This was such an important day for you. Can I tell the other kids about it?"

If you are teaching this group in the middle of writing workshop, call for the attention of the rest of the class.

"Can I have everyone's eyes over here? Today has been a huge day for this small group of writers, and I just wanted to tell you about the important work they have started to do. They aren't just making pictures as writers anymore. They are using their alphabet charts to match the sounds they hear to letters and getting way more labels into their writing. Now, they've turned into much more grown-up writers. They write with *letters* as well as pictures. I'm going to ask them to hold up their writing, and any of you who are near enough to see it, take a look. Admire those letters. And writers, I'm hoping some of the rest of you begin to do this, too, because it is huge and important work."

OTHER SUPPORTS

Replicate:

- This group focuses on isolating and identifying *initial* sounds. You can also do this with *ending* sounds in words.
- You can replicate this group in reading workshop. Select an emergent storybook and do the same work with the illustrations.
- ▼ **Gr K, Unit 2, Sess. 1, Ext. 2:** Learning a Letter

FIG. 13–1   Arwen uses her pointer to locate the letter she needs to label her picture.

Writing to a Storybook Character (to Practice Initial Sounds)

BEST TAUGHT TO

- Children who are not yet labeling their writing
- Children who need more support with isolating initial sounds and matching sounds to the letter that represents them
- Children who need more practice with letter formation

BEST TAUGHT DURING

- Reading workshop
- Writing workshop

GETTING READY

✔ Have a blank page of paper on a clipboard for writing to a character.

✔ Ask children to bring their book baggies and small Post-its®.

✔ Bring an alphabet chart for each partnership.

✔ Choose one emergent storybook that students know very well. We use *Caps for Sale*.

RALLY THEM: Invite children to help you write a letter to a favorite emergent storybook character.

"Readers, each time we read our book *Caps for Sale*, I think about the peddler and those monkeys. I thought we could write a letter to the peddler, warning him about those tricky, tricky monkeys. Would you help?"

LAUNCH THEM AND WORK SIDE BY SIDE: Invite children to help you isolate and record initial sounds. Share the pen with one child as the others record letters on whiteboard.

"We should start our letter with *Dear Peddler*. Let's start our words at the top, left side of the page."

Make two horizontal lines to represent the two words you'll be writing. Point to each line as you work on that word.

"Let's say *Dear*, and let's listen for the first sound, /d/, *Dear*. Can you and your partner tap the letter on your alphabet chart that goes with this sound?

"Great. Now, can someone write the letter on this first line? The rest of you, write the letter on your whiteboards."

After a child writes the letter *D*, fill in the rest of the word on the first line. Then, follow these same steps to write the word *Peddler*. Say the word, isolating the initial sound, and ask a child to point to the letter on their alphabet charts. Recruit one child to write the first letter on the second line on the chart paper and ask the others to write the letter on their whiteboards. Then, fill in the rest of the word on the chart. Don't expect them to do that on their whiteboards.

<u>Dear</u> <u>Peddler</u>,

"What should we tell the peddler? Turn and tell the person next to you.

"I heard you say we should tell him, 'Watch out for the monkeys!' Let's count the number of words we will need to write."

Lead the children in counting the words in the sentence, and then write five horizontal lines, one for each word. They can do the same on their whiteboards. Invite the children to say the sentence with you as you tap on each line to orally plan what you will write. Write the words *Watch out* on the first two lines, then recruit children to help with the next word.

"Help me with the word *for*. Say it slowly, then say it again, and catch the first sound. Give me a thumbs up if you hear the first sound. Yes, it's /f/. What letter goes with /f/? Can you and your partner tap it on your alphabet chart?

"Now, write it." While students write on their whiteboards, one child can write on the shared text. Once the child writes the letter *F*, quickly fill in the rest of the word. Say the sound for each letter as you write it.

"Let's read what we have so far. 'Watch out for . . .' The next word is *the*. That's a snap word! Would you all write the letter on your whiteboards? I'll write it up here, while you all write it in a snap."

Invite another child to record the initial sound in *monkeys* as the rest of the children write the word on their whiteboards. Fill in the rest of the word. Then, invite children to join you as you read the whole letter.

<u>Dear</u> <u>Peddler</u>,

<u>Watch</u> <u>out</u> <u>**f**or</u> <u>the</u> <u>**m**onkeys</u>.

CHALLENGE THEM: Encourage students who are able to record initial sounds to listen and record more sounds. Coach them as they say each word slowly, hearing and recording the salient sounds.

"Oh! We have to warn him that they will get his caps. We can write, 'They will get your caps!'"

Listen in as the children count the number of words in this sentence, then make five horizontal lines to plan for each word. Write the word *they*. Guide children in writing the initial sound in the word *will*, as before.

Invite children to try recording more sounds they hear in the word on their whiteboards.

"Once you write the first sound, say the word again and listen for more sounds. *Wiiillll*. What sound do you hear at the end? /l/ Write the letter that goes with /l/."

Continue this process with the words *get*, *your*, and *caps*.

Dear Peddler,

Watch out for the monkeys.

They will get your caps!

Ask the children to read the letter with you and invite them to sign their names.

FIG. 14–1   Eleanor labels the Troll in _The Three Billy Goats Gruff._

TEACH TOWARD TOMORROW: Invite students to take out emergent storybooks and label things in the pictures.

"I'll get this letter to the peddler right away. Thank you for your help, writers! You said words slowly and caught the first sounds, and then wrote the letters that went with those first sounds. That's the same work you can do anytime you write.

"You know, I just had a _big_ idea! Why don't you take a book you love from your book baggie? Here are some Post-its you can use to label the pictures, so you can continue practicing hearing sounds and writing the letters that go with those sounds. Take an alphabet chart if you need one."

OTHER SUPPORTS

Replicate: Once students become proficient at isolating and identifying initial and final sounds, you can have them do this same work, listening for more sounds in words. You might say, "Let's say it slowly and listen for more sounds. _Peeddlerr._ Let's reread and listen for more sounds. What letter goes with that sound?"

▼ **Gr K, Unit 1, Sess. 12:** Teaching, Active Engagement/Link, and Rug Time

---

This will work best if students label a book with engaging pictures. An emergent storybook will work better than a leveled book.

When children read emergent storybooks, they are relying heavily on the pictures and memory of the story to "read" and reread every day. Engaging kids in an interactive writing session and inviting them to label the illustrations in their books offers the opportunity to work with letters and sounds. Some children can write the words from the story such as "Trip, trap . . . , following the model of today's work.

Popping Out the Caboose Sounds

LAUNCH THEM: Ask students to identify not only the initial sound in a word, but also to pop out the final sound.

"I know that many of you love to play with trains, right? I brought a toy train to our group today, and I was thinking that maybe we could label its cars and its different parts so that everyone can learn about trains when they play. Can you help me?

"This car is called a tank. Let's write the word *tank* together. First, we need to say it slowly.

"What sound to you hear at the beginning? Say the word again, really stretching it out. Right, there is the /t/ sound at the beginning, /t/ *tank*. Point to the letter that makes that sound on your alphabet chart.

"Right, letter *T*. I'll write *T* to label the /t/ *tank*." Write the *T* on a Post-it.

"Now, let's listen for more sounds in *tank*. Say its name and *pop* out the ending sound. Put out your arm, put your hand at the top and slide it down to your wrist as you say the word."

Demonstrate sliding your hand down your arm as you stretch the word *tank*. Emphasize the final sound.

"Do you hear the /k/ sound at the end? Me, too. Point to the letter that makes that sound on your alphabet charts. Right, it's the letter *K*. Let's add that letter to our label."

Add the letter *K* to the Post-it to label the tank with *tk*.

WORK SIDE BY SIDE: Channel students to label the parts of the train. Remind them to say the words slowly and to isolate the beginning and then the ending sounds.

"The cars of this train need labels, too. Here is the engine, and the boxcar, and the caboose."

Distribute a drawing of a train and a few Post-its to each partnership.

BEST TAUGHT TO
- Children who are typically writing with initial sounds and not yet including other sounds

BEST TAUGHT DURING
- Writing workshop
- Intervention time

GETTING READY
- ✔ Bring pens and Post-its for each partnership and yourself.
- ✔ Bring a toy train or print a photograph of a tank car.
- ✔ Print one train drawing and an alphabet chart for each partnership.
- ✔ Ask students to bring their writing folders.

"Work with your partner to write labels for all of these cars on Post-its. Remember to say the word slowly and make sure you listen for the beginning sound. Then say the word again and listen for the ending sound."

TEACH TOWARD TOMORROW: Remind writers of the importance of hearing and recording beginning and ending sounds. Encourage them to do this in their writing.

"Writers, words are a lot like trains. Every word you write has a sound at the beginning—the engine—and a sound at the end—the caboose. When you write a word, make sure that you not only catch the beginning sound, the engine, but also the last sound, the caboose!

"Writers, will each of you take out the piece you are working on now? Reread your writing and make sure that you have recorded the beginning, engine sounds *and* the ending, caboose sounds in your words."

POSSIBLE COACHING MOVES

▶ "Say the word slowly. What is the beginning sound you hear?"

▶ "Say the word again slowly and pop out the caboose sound."

▶ "Check the alphabet chart. What letter goes with that sound?"

OTHER SUPPORTS

▼ **Gr K, Unit 2, Sess. 10, Ext. 3:** Listening for Ending Sounds in Shared Reading

▲ **Gr K, Unit 2, Sess. 12, Ext. 3:** One of These Words Is Not Like the Others (Ending Sounds)

If a child writes an initial or final letter that is far from accurate, you might direct her to the alphabet chart and help her to choose a letter sound that is closer to the correct one. But what's most important is that kids are engaging in the process of saying the word, stretching it, isolating sounds, and attempting to match the sound to a letter. So, for example, if a child writes a K for caboose, that child is succeeding in the work at hand.

FIG. 15–1 Students hear and record final sounds in words.

Labeling with More Sounds

RALLY THEM: Introduce an authentic purpose for writing—helping solve the problem of kids not using the writing center. Suggest a shared writing project that could help.

"Writers, I've noticed a problem, and I'm hoping you can help. Our writing center is filled with cool tools, but kids are only getting *paper* from the writing center. The cool tools—the Post-its and pens and revision strips and staplers—are all sitting there unused, even though those tools could help kids make their writing *a lot* better.

"I was thinking it might help if we added *labels* to the tools, reminding kids of all the tools they can use."

WORK SIDE BY SIDE: Invite students to help you write labels. Emphasize that if they stretch words out slowly, they can include more letters and make their labels easier to read.

"Will you help write labels for all these tools?" Pull out a basket of writing tools (such as Post-its, colored pens, revision strips, and a stapler). "It will be important to make the labels easy to read. To do that, it helps to stretch each word out, perhaps down your arm. Say the word slowly, down your arm, trying to hear all the letter sounds.

BEST TAUGHT TO

- Children who need additional support hearing more sounds in words

BEST TAUGHT DURING

- Writing workshop

GETTING READY

✔ Bring a basket of tools from the writing center (such as Post-its, colored pens, revision strips, and a stapler).

✔ Gather blank envelope labels or small Post-its and pens for each partnership.

✔ Distribute an alphabet chart to each partnership.

✔ Print a copy of the "Say it. Slide it. Hear it. Write it." chart for each child.

"Let's try the first one together, then you'll try some on your own." Hold up a stapler. "Stretch this word down your arm a bunch of times. *Staaaappllerrr*. *Stapler*. *Stapler*.

Show kids what you mean by saying a word slowly and drawing your hand down the parts of your arm, your shoulder, the inside of your elbow, and the inside of your wrist, moving down your arm as you say each sound in the word.

"Now let's write it. Say the word again and listen for the first sound. *Stapler*, /s/. Tell your partner what letter goes with that sound."

Write the letter *S* on a label. "Now, say the word again. Tell your partner what other sounds you hear."

Add the other sounds students say to the label.

LAUNCH THEM: Set partnerships up to write additional labels for objects. Coach them as they say each object's name slowly, hearing and recording all the sounds they hear.

"This label will be a *big* help to the other kids. Will you and your partner work together to make a lot more labels? Take turns choosing an object from the basket. Say the name of that object slowly, stretching it down your arm. Do that a bunch of times so you can hear all the sounds. Then, write the sounds you hear. I'll give you special labels, so we can stick them onto the tools when we are finished."

While students stretch the word down their arm, make some quick assessments. Who says the entire word by the time they're at their elbow? Who moves down their arm so quickly it's clear they aren't isolating individual sounds? Noticing how students stretch words will give you some ideas for how to coach.

If the children have been hearing and recording initial and final sounds, chances are they will now begin to hear the middle sounds in words. So, if after hearing the /s/ in stapler, they then hear the final /r/, you can go ahead and write these letters, leaving spaces for the middle letters. You can then invite them to say the word again to see if they can hear any middle sounds. Point to the empty middle space to imply that there are more letters to add. Then add them in after students say the sounds.

> **POSSIBLE COACHING MOVES**
>
> ▶ "Say the word slowly. What sounds do you hear in the beginning, middle, and ending of the word?"
>
> ▶ "Say the word slowly and try to pop out the vowel. *Pens*. /p/-/ĕ/-/ĕ/-/ĕ/-/nz/."
>
> ▶ "Check the alphabet chart. What letter goes with that sound?"

CHALLENGE THEM: Challenge children to test each label by seeing if others can read it. Help them add additional letters to the labels that are hard to read.

"Put all the objects into the basket, removing the labels. Ready to test these labels? One partnership will show a label, and the rest of you will see if you can read it so you figure out which object matches that label. If it's tricky to figure out, you can add more letters so that everyone in the class can read the label."

Celebrate labels that are easy to read. When labels are tricky to read, you could say, "Let's all say this word slowly. What other sounds do you hear that we should add?" Tape the labels back onto the objects.

FIG. 16–1   Using more sounds to label tools in the writing center.

TEACH TOWARD TOMORROW: Remind students to listen for and record multiple sounds in words whenever they write.

"Writers, whenever you write, you can make your labels and sentences easier to read by saying each word slowly and listening for all the sounds you hear in each word. Try this out in your writing today!" Distribute copies of the "Say it. Slide it. Hear it. Write it." chart for children to keep with them as they write today and every day.

OTHER SUPPORTS

Replicate: You can extend this group by including high-frequency words you have taught. You might guide children to write labels such as, "The stapler" or "This is the word wall."

▲ **Gr K, Unit 2, Sess. 10, Ext. 1:** The World, Like Your Own Writing, Is Full of Labels

---

Be a Word Wizard!

Writing More Sounds

BEST TAUGHT TO

- Children who are able to match most letters and sounds
- Children who are able to label with initial sounds and possibly more but are not doing much labeling in their writing
- Children who are not writing left to right

BEST TAUGHT DURING

- Writing workshop

GETTING READY

✔ Make a word wizard kit for each child, including a wand and stickers. Make the wizard wand from a Popsicle stick, adding a star sticker or glitter paint at the end. For the stickers, you might choose to print the Magic Label Stickers, or make your own from regular address labels by placing a dot on the left side of the stickers.

✔ Bring an alphabet chart for each student.

✔ Prepare a copy of the "Be a Word Wizard!" chart.

RALLY THEM AND ACTIVATE PHONICS: Explain why you've gathered students together. Then, encourage them to activate their letter-sound knowledge with magnetic letters.

"Writers, I called you here today because you have something in common as writers. You are working every day to make amazing pictures in your writing. Now, you all are ready to do more and more labeling of the things in your pictures.

"Let's get ready for some labeling work by practicing naming letters and saying their sounds. I'll give you all a handful of magnetic letters, and you can pick one up and say its name and make its sound."

LAUNCH THEM: Gather the writers and present word wizard labeling kits with a flourish. Invite students to become word wizards and add more labels to their writing.

"I have a special kit that can help you get more and more words into your writing. It's a word wizard kit, and it will help all of you to become word wizards!

"In each of your kits, you have a wizard wand and some Magic Label Stickers. You'll use your wizard wand to tap on something in your picture that you plan to label, and you'll write your label on your Magic Label Stickers. You'll see the stickers have a dot on the left side. You put a sticker on the place you tapped your wand. Once you've done that, you'll touch the dot on the sticker and say the word slowly, moving your wand across the sticker as you say it. This will help you to hear all of the sounds in the word. Last, write the sounds you hear on the sticker. Then you'll be ready to tap something else and add another label.

Be a Word Wizard!

1. Tap it!
2. Stick it!
3. Slide it!
4. Write it!

"Ready, word wizards? Get out your wands and open your writing up to a picture that still needs labels. Look at the picture and tap a part you will label." After each student has tapped a picture and said the word he or she wants to write, encourage students to place a label sticker next to the image. "Now that you have your label stickers placed, it's time to get labeling! Say the word you are going to write and write down the sounds you hear. Use your alphabet chart to help you if you need it."

FIG. 17–1 Tommy uses the word wizard wand and label stickers to label his writing.

"The reason you write labels in your writing is so that other people can read what you wrote. So, word wizards, let's put your labels to the test! Turn to your partner and see if you and your partner can read the labels that you wrote today."

TEACH TOWARD TOMORROW: Send writers off with their word wizard labeling kits, and encourage them to add more words to all of their books.

"Writers, I know you are itching to write some more in your books. You can go back and keep going on your writing, using your new word wizard kits. Don't forget to add more words to *any* writing you do. See if you can write at least five labels on each page!"

OTHER SUPPORTS

Replicate: Once children are labeling with initial, final, and other salient sounds, and they have learned some high-frequency words, they are ready to move from labels to sentences. You can replicate this group to support sentence writing. To do this, teach children to use their "wizard wands" to touch where they plan to write each word in their sentences as they orally rehearse them. Then you can teach them to rehearse each sentence again and this time draw a "magic line" with their pencils for each word they plan to write. Then they go to it!

▼ **Gr K, Unit 2, Sess. 2, Ext. 1:** Turning the Classroom Into an Alphabet Chart

▲ **Gr K, Unit 2, Sess. 6, Ext. 2:** Use Snap Words to Add Sentences Into the Class Letter Books

As students work on their labeling, be sure you pull back and let them work on one label after another without always checking with you. Be on the lookout for their spelling stages. If they are labeling with initial and final consonants, you can coach into this by writing the first and last letters on a label, leaving a gap in the middle. For example, you could write the word storm *like this:* s_____m. *Then, slide your finger across, pausing at the empty space and asking, "What else do you hear in the middle?"*

Coach students to practice reading each other's labels by looking at the picture and using the sounds to determine what the label says. If, at this point, students notice that their label needs additional sounds to be readable, encourage them to write down those sounds as they hear them.

POSSIBLE COACHING MOVES

▶ "Say the word slowly and slide your finger across the label. Now write the sounds you hear."

▶ "Say the word _____. What sound do you hear in the beginning of the word? Write the letter that goes with that sound. Keep going. Listen for more sounds."

▶ "Say the word again. Listen for more sounds."

▶ If students say the incorrect letter name, say, "Let's check the alphabet chart. Say ___, say ___. Do they match?"

▶ "Reread your label. Listen for more sounds."

Clean Up Your Sounds
Eliminating Extra Letters

BEST TAUGHT TO

- Children who are adding a schwa sound to their letters and putting extra sounds in their writing

BEST TAUGHT DURING

- Writing workshop

GETTING READY

✔ Prepare a piece of example writing in which some of the words have extra sounds.

✔ Bring an alphabet chart.

✔ Ask students to bring their writing folders and pens to the group.

RALLY THEM AND LAUNCH THEM: Compliment students on the work they have been doing in their writing to hear and record sounds. Share a student example that includes extra sounds.

"Writers, can I just give you all a compliment? You have truly been writing up a storm. I was looking through your writing folders last night, and I could tell you have been working hard to say words slowly and put down as many sounds as you can when you write. That's not easy work!

"You know, I realized, you have been working so hard to put down your sounds that sometimes you're actually putting down *too many* sounds! Can I show you what happens when you put down too many sounds?

"This is a piece from one of last year's kindergartners. She was writing about her dog.

FIG. 18–1

"Let's try and read some of her labels. *T-A-L-U*. /t/ /ā/ /l/ /ə/. *Tail-uh*. Whoa, I think she meant *tail*. Will you read this? *L-E-G-U*. /l/ /ĕ/ /g/ /ə/. *Leg-uh*. Huh? What do you think she was trying to write, *leg*? And over here she made another word, *sit-uh*. I wonder what she was trying to tell the dog to do? *sit*? I think so too, but she actually told the dog to sit uh!

"I think I figured out what happened, and it might be the same thing that's happening to you sometimes. When she said the word *tail* slowly, she said it like this: /t/ /ā/ /l/ /ə/. Then instead of just writing the *L*, she wrote down a *U*, too. She did the same thing with *leg*, /l/ /ĕ/ /g/ /ə/, and *sit*, /s/ /ĭ/ /t/ /ə/. She was adding extra sounds to her letters! The sound is /l/, not *luh*, and /g/, not *guh*, and /t/, not *tuh*. She needs to clean up her sounds and letters."

WORK SIDE BY SIDE: Channel kids to produce consonant sounds without adding a schwa sound.

"Let's practice saying a few of the letter sounds together and work really hard to make the sounds crisp and clear."

Point to consonants with stop sounds (such as *B, C, D, F, G, J, K, P,* and *T*) and letters with continuous sounds (such as *L, M, N, R, S, V, Z*) on the alphabet chart, and channel students to say the sound associated with each letter. If students produce the schwa sound attached to the letter say, "Try that one again. The sound isn't /kə/, it's /k/."

CHALLENGE THEM: Channel students to apply this to their writing, saying sounds crisply and then checking for extra sounds in their writing.

"Get out your writing and turn to a page where you need to add words. Say the words slowly and catch the first sound. Make sure you say the words crisply."

TEACH TOWARD TOMORROW: Send students off with a reminder to pronounce their sounds crisply and clearly.

"Don't forget, when you say your letter sounds, today and every day, say them crisply and clearly. Like the letter *B*. It's not *buuuhhh*, it's . . ."

Pause a beat for students to respond, "/b/."

"And over here you don't say *tuuuhhh*, you say . . ."

Again, pause a moment so students can respond, "/t/."

"I think you've got it! Off you go!"

FIG. 18–2   A student points to the extra sounds.

If you know the specific letters for which students are adding the schwa sound, certainly choose those.

POSSIBLE COACHING MOVES

▸ "Catch the first sound. Make it crisp. *Ball*, /b/, not *buh*."

▸ "Listen for the last sound. That sound is /f/. Say the sound with me."

▸ "Can you check the way you spelled that?"

▸ "Say this word again, making all of the letter sounds crisp. Do you hear the extra sound?"

Remember Blends and Digraphs!

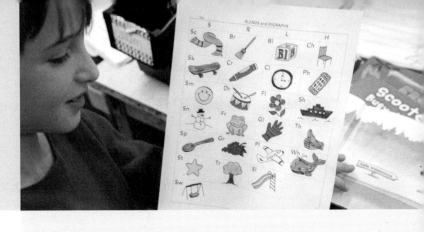

RALLY THEM: Tell the writers a story about a time you forgot to do something and explain that students often forget to use blends and digraphs. Set them up to study these using the chart.

"Writers, do any of you have the same problem I have? Sometimes even when I *know* how to do something, I forget. For example, a couple of days ago, I was trying to sprinkle a little salt on my food, and it came pouring out in a huge pile. I had to wash my hamburger off under the faucet. Crazy, right? But I wasn't going to waste my burger. I told myself, 'Next time, be careful to sprinkle just a *little* bit of salt.'

"But you know what I did last night? I reached for the salt shaker, started to sprinkle a little and . . . Yep! You guessed it. It came pouring out again. I forgot to be careful. I forgot to do what I know.

"I'm telling you this because you *know* about these letters." I held up a "Blends and Digraphs" chart. "Am I right—you know these?

"But here's the thing. You all—each of you— forget to use them. It's the same as my salt shaker—you forget to do what you know. So, I was thinking you could become a little club of people who help each other remember to use what you know."

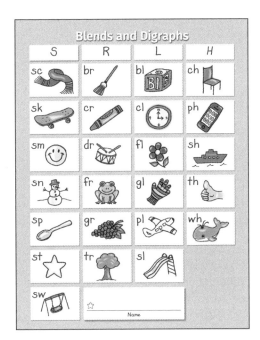

BEST TAUGHT TO

- Students who are not writing with blends and digraphs or are using them incorrectly

BEST TAUGHT DURING

- Writing workshop

GETTING READY

✔ Bring a copy of the "Blends and Digraphs" chart and a copy of the "Find and Fix Spelling Mistakes" chart.

✔ Bring a sheet of pictures that kids can use to practice identifying initial sounds.

✔ Provide each partnership with a copy of Gerty's writing for every partnership and some colored pens.

✔ If you can, find a page from each child's writing where that child has struggled with blends and digraphs. Place a Post-it on that page.

"For starters, will you turn your brain on super-high and really study this chart? You have two minutes to read these over and make sure you know the blends and digraphs and the sounds they make."

ACTIVATE PHONICS: Ask the kids to identify the sound at the start of the words shown in several photos. Use this sheet to check on the children's command of these.

"Let me show you this sheet now, so you can test yourself and can see how many of these you know. I'm going to show you five pictures. Super-quickly, would you write down the sound at the start of each of these words on your whiteboard?" Encourage students to say each word out loud to determine whether or not the word starts with a blend or digraph and if so, which blend or digraph it is.

Show children the sheet with the following photos: sun, cherries, truck, thirteen, sheep.

"You see that you mostly know these, right, even though you sometimes forget—just like I did with the salt. After this, after you write a piece of writing, will you check it to make sure you have used the blends and digraphs that you know?"

LAUNCH THEM AND WORK SIDE BY SIDE: Ask children to put their knowledge of blends and digraphs to work by helping your neighbor Gerty to correct a piece of writing.

"To practice checking over writing for blends and digraphs, I thought maybe you could help my neighbor, Gerty. She made a book about the important information she learned at the zoo. She needs a good editor. I made copies for every pair of you to share. For now, I'll read her writing while you follow along. If you and your partner see that she's forgotten a blend or digraph, underline the mess-up and then later, you can come back and write the word correctly.

"Here's the first page. Follow along as I read: 'Fish and sharks swim in the sea. They splash in the water.'

Read the whole sentence through twice. Don't read until you reach an error and then pause while the kids all correct that error before you resume reading. Finish the page.

"Oh, my goodness, I see you've found places to correct already. Get to it, editors! Fix this page and all the other pages, too."

CHALLENGE THEM: Ask partners to work together to edit another sentence. Raise the challenge by asking them to read the sentence on their own, using the picture for support.

"You're really helping Gerty edit her writing. Will you read the next sentence together, and help her fix up places where she didn't use the right blend or digraph? Use the picture if you need help figuring out a word."

Give students several minutes to work, and coach in as needed. Help them read words if they are stuck.

"If you are nearly finished, will you and your partner show another partnership what you fixed and see if you all agree? If not, talk it out until you are sure you have corrected her writing. Soon, we will be able to put a copy of Gerty's book in your book baggies. Gerty will be thrilled!"

We chose to include the word sun to give children the opportunity to determine whether a word has a digraph or not.

Resist the instinct to teach right now. Use this opportunity to glean information from your students that you can keep in mind as you coach later. If one student needs particular support, launch the other students into their work and then support that one student.

Fiss and sarks swim in the sea. They splach in the water.

FIG. 19–1   The first page of Gerty's book about the zoo.

POSSIBLE COACHING MOVES

▶ "You heard the digraph at the end of the word. What letters go with that sound? Check the digraph chart."

▶ Does that sound right? Check the picture. What could that word be?"

▶ "Say the word. What sound do you hear in the beginning (or at the end)? What two letters go with that sound?"

▶ "You're right, -ch is a digraph on our chart. But does it belong at the end of that word? Which digraph would go better there?"

TEACH TOWARD TOMORROW: Remind students that they can always do this work in their own writing. Invite them to work on a page of their writing with errors in blends or digraphs.

"Writers, this work with Gerty's writing will help you with your own writing. You'll see I've marked a page of your writing with a Post-it at the top. When you get back to your seat, reread that page of your writing. Look for any blends or digraphs you may have forgotten."

FIG. 19–2   Shyla edited her writing using both her purple pen and pink strips to spell more words correctly.

OTHER SUPPORTS

Replicate: This session can be adjusted to support either blends or digraphs. See the online resources for sample practice texts. ✳

▼ **Gr K, Unit 3, Sess. 15:** "Studying One Word to Learn about How Letters and Words Work" (introduction to -sh/-th)

▼ **Gr K, Unit 3, Sess. 16:** "Word-Part Rodeo: Making Words with Digraphs and Word Parts" (introduction to -ch)

▼ **Gr K, Unit 3, Sess. 16, Ext. 2:** Using Gestures to Remember Sounds

▲ **Gr K, Unit 4, Sess. 7, Ext. 1:** Practice Segmenting and Blending with Elkonin Boxes

Find and Fix
Spelling Mistakes

1. Read slowly

2. Find Mistakes

3. Fix them

Capturing Both Sounds in a Blend

BEST TAUGHT TO

- Children who are not yet capturing both sounds in consonant blends when reading

BEST TAUGHT DURING

- Reading workshop

GETTING READY

✔ Prepare one set of consonant magnetic letters for you and one for each student. These will help students practice the blends they struggle with in their reading. You might consider focusing on *L* and *R* blends, such as *gr*, *cr*, and *cl*, *bl*. Many students struggle with these. If students will be practicing the *L* and *R* blends, each set should include *G*, *R*, *B*, *L*, and *C*.

✔ Print a set of illustrated sentence cards for each partnership.

RALLY THEM: Let students know that today's work will be on blends. Remind them that a blend is made of two consonants, and when you say the blend you have to capture both sounds.

"In a few minutes, I'm going to suggest that we do something *funny* using blends. Before we do that, let me remind you about blends."

Put up two fingers as you say, "Remember that a blend is made of two consonants." Tap each finger and say, "And when you say the blend you have to capture both sounds. It's tricky work, but so important."

LAUNCH THEM: Invite partners to practice saying all of the sounds in a blend by adding blends to articles of clothing they are wearing.

"Okay, here is the funny thing I said we would do. Let's try talking in blends. Let's say we want to use the *bl* blend to say 'hi' to each other."

Place the magnetic letters *B* and *L* in front of you, so each student can see them. Touch each letter and say its sound. Then, sweep your finger under the letters as you say the blend.

"The letter sounds are /b/ and /l/. When I put them together, the sound is /bl/. So instead of saying 'Hi Kevin,' I might say, 'Bli Blevin.' Let's all say 'hi' to Leah in this way. 'Bli Bleah!'

I see a crab.

I like to use crayons.

The grass is green.

I like grapes.

I brush my teeth.

I like bread.

"Now you try. Tell your partner what you are wearing using blend talk! You might say, 'I'm wearing a blirt, blants, and bloes.' Funny, right?"

As partners tell each other all the things they are wearing, remind them they can say one thing after another, and they don't need to check with you for confirmation.

"The thing is that talking in blends is not just fun, it also helps you practice saying all the sounds in a blend. Saying all the sounds in a blend is important when you read words with blends in your books."

Give each partnership their set of consonant letters.

"Let's try this again, but this time, you decide which blends to use. Work with your partner and the letters I'm giving you to make another blend. Practice reading the blend together, being sure to say each letter's sound. You might sweep your fingers under each letter to help you. Then, name what you are wearing again, this time using the new blend."

As partners play, prompt them to continue forming new blends and using these to say their articles of clothing. You might also prompt them to name objects they see around the room if they are tiring of naming their clothing.

CHALLENGE THEM: Ask students to work in partnerships, taking turns reading from a set of illustrated cards with blends.

"Now, I'm going to give each partnership a few cards. Partner 1, you will read the sentence on the card. Use the picture to help you, and remember to capture both sounds in any blends you see. Partner 2, you will listen to see if Partner 2 captured both sounds in each blend. If not, you can help. Then, switch roles, and read another card."

TEACH TOWARD TOMORROW: Remind students that any time they come across a blend, they need to capture both sounds. Set up students to read their independent books, alert for blends.

"Awesome! Remember when you are reading and you come across a blend, you need to say both sounds. You might need to back up and reread. And when you are writing, and you want to spell a blend, remember to write both consonants. You can go back to your reading now!"

OTHER SUPPORTS

▼ **Gr K, Unit 5, Sess. 22:** "Listening for the Sounds that Are "Hiding in the Edges" of Blends"

▼ **Gr K, Unit 5, Sess. 2, Ext. 2:** Using the "Blends and Digraphs" Chart to Record Beginning Sounds

▲ **Gr K, Unit 5, Sess. 5:** "Revising Writing to Capture All the Sounds in Words"

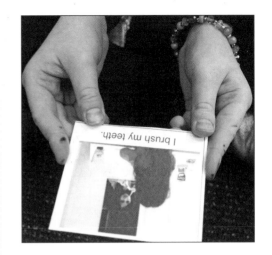

Shared Reading with Blends and Digraphs

BEST TAUGHT TO

• Children having trouble reading with blends and digraphs

BEST TAUGHT DURING

• Reading workshop

GETTING READY

✔ Prepare two sets of picture cards.

✔ Choose a short text for shared reading that contains blends and digraphs. We use "Brooms" by Dorothy Aldis.

✔ Have the "Blends and Digraphs" chart nearby.

RALLY THEM AND ACTIVATE PHONICS: Use a metaphor to illustrate the concept of "letters that stick together." Channel partners to generate lists of blends and digraphs they know.

"Readers, today I want to remind you that some letters are like peanut butter and jelly. They stick together. Like the letters *S* and *H*. They stick together and make the sound /sh/. This sound is at the start of words like *shy* and *shout* and *short*. It's at the end of words like *wish* and *flash* and *push*. What a lovely sound! The /sh/ sound is a digraph.

"And remember, there are also letters that go together like peanut butter and jelly, but in sort of a different way. They stick together, but you can still hear each letter's sound. Like the letters *S* and *T*. They make a blend that sounds like /st/. You can hear this blend in words like *star* and *stick*."

To create a model for kids' work, hold up your whiteboard, and draw a line down the middle. In one column, write *sh*. On the other, write *st*. Then, distribute whiteboards and markers to each student.

"I'll give you a moment now to work with your partner to think of more letters that go together like peanut butter and jelly. Draw a line down the middle of your whiteboard, like I did. On one side, write letters that are

50

SMALL GROUPS TO SUPPORT PHONICS, GRADES K–1

digraphs, that go together to make one sound, like *sh*. On the other side, write blends, letters that go together but still keep each letter's sound, like *st*."

After a couple of minutes, pause the students even if they are still working. "Share your lists. As you read through your lists, will you say the sound that goes with the letters and say a word that starts with that sound? If you aren't sure whether something is a blend or a digraph, talk about it."

LAUNCH THEM: Channel students to listen to a list of words and then say the blend and/ or digraph they hear in the word, along with the letters that make that sound.

"So, writers, my question is this: How well can you hear blends and digraphs in words? I'll give you and your partner a set of photo cards. Say the word that matches the picture on the card, and then say the blend or digraph you hear in the word. It goes like this:

"If you and your partner see a picture of a *crayon*, you would say *crayon*, then you would say the sound of the blend, */cr/*, and then the letters, *C-R*. Try a few."

Hand a stack of picture cards to each partnership and help children as needed to say the blend or digraph and to name the letters that make it up.

Smile (/sm/, S-M)	*Brown (/br/, B-R)*
Block (/bl/, B-L)	*Shadow (/sh/, S-H)*
French fries (/fr/, F-R) (/ch/, C-H)	*Stapler (/st/, S-T)*
Thirteen (/th/, T-H)	*Clip (/cl/, C-L)*

WORK SIDE BY SIDE: Rally students to join you in reading an unfamiliar poem, raising two fingers when they see a word with a blend or digraph.

"You are great at that! You are ready to listen for the sounds of blends and digraphs in a text. First, just listen to this beautiful poem, 'Brooms' by Dorothy Aldis. Then we can reread it and think about blends and digraphs." I read the poem, adding the obvious gestures when the trees swept the sky, swishing and sweeping it.

"Let's read it again. This time, let's really enjoy the sounds the blends and digraphs make. They add so much to this poem. When you hear a blend or digraph, hold your two fingers up together to show you heard some sticky letters."

During this reading, point under each word as you lead the children in reading the poem. Emphasize the blends and digraphs with your voice as you read.

Brooms
by Dorothy Aldis

On stormy days
When the wind is high,
Tall trees are brooms
Sweeping the sky.
They swish their branches
In buckets of rain
And swash and sweep it
Blue again.

"Great job noticing the sounds of the blends and digraphs! They are sticky letters, right? Yes!

"Let's read it one more time, and this time, when we get to those words with blends and digraphs, say those beautiful words loud and proud, and make sure when you say the sound that it matches those sticky letters."

During this reading, let your voice drop on words with blends and digraphs so kids can read them without as much support.

TEACH TOWARD TOMORROW: Ask partners to read the poem together. Then, channel them to read their just-right books, watching out for blends and digraphs.

"Okay, everyone, will you put this poem between you and your partner and reread it aloud? When you see a blend, remember to make the sound of each letter. When you see a digraph, remember to make the new sound of those two letters together. Then, shift to a just-right book. As you read, watch for those sticky letters, blends, and digraphs."

OTHER SUPPORTS

▼ **Gr K, Unit 3, Sess. 15:** "Studying One Word to Learn about How Letters and Words Work" (introduction to -sh/-th)

▼ **Gr K, Unit 5, Sess. 2:** "Listening for the Sounds that Are 'Hiding in the Edges' of Blends" (introduction to blends/blends chart)

▲ **Gr K, Unit 3, Sess. 15, Ext. 3:** Alliteration Game (support for sh but can be replicated for other digraphs and for blends)

POSSIBLE COACHING MOVES

▶ "You are adding an extra sound after the B. It is /b/, not buh. And /l/, not luh. Otherwise the word black would go like this: buh-luh-ack-uh. It's not that, it's black."

▶ "Hold your two fingers up when you get to a blend or digraph to remind yourself of the special way to read those sticky letters."

▶ "I love that when you were stuck just then, not sure what this word said, you went back and reread and got your mind onto the story again. That is just what readers do. When you are stuck, you think, 'Let me reread and get the story in my mind.'"

Solving Missing Letters
Blends and Digraphs

RALLY THEM AND ACTIVATE PHONICS: Introduce today's work, then have kids whisper-read the blends and digraphs chart to a partner.

"I have a treat for this group today. You get to play a game called 'Solving Missing Letters.' Instead of me doing the covering up like I do when we play other games, you'll get to do it! You'll be covering up and working with blends and digraphs, so you'll need to use all you know about them.

"To get ready, will you whisper-read the 'Blends and Digraphs' chart with your partner?"

LAUNCH THEM: Set partnerships up to read a familiar nursery rhyme and then to hide the consonant blends and digraphs in that rhyme.

"I am going to give each partnership a different nursery rhyme. These are nursery rhymes you all know well."

Distribute a nursery rhyme and marker to each partnership and show students the "Solving Missing Letters" chart.

FIG. 22–1 Students play "Solving Missing Letters"

BEST TAUGHT TO

- Children who are solving words letter by letter
- Children who need support solving for blends and digraphs in their reading. For example, you might teach this to readers moving to level D books, which contain more words with initial blends, to remind them to attend to the first two letters rather than just the first letter.
- Children whose writing shows they need help hearing and recording the sounds in blends and digraphs

BEST TAUGHT DURING

- Reading workshop
- Writing workshop
- Intervention time

GETTING READY

✔ Print a copy of the "Blends and Digraphs" chart for each partnership.

✔ Select two familiar nursery rhymes that contain blends and digraphs. We chose "The Itsy-Bitsy Spider" and "Twinkle, Twinkle, Little Star." Place the nursery rhymes in sheet protectors so that you can reuse them.

✔ Prepare a copy of the "Solving Missing Letters" chart.

✔ Bring a dry erase marker and eraser for each partnership.

As children play this game, they practice attending to challenges presented by higher levels of text. In level D books, they'll need to attend to initial blends, not just initial consonants. Then, in level E books, they'll need to attend to the short vowels in the middle of words. When they move to higher levels, they'll need to attend to vowel teams. This game is a lively way to introduce or reinforce the new work children will need to do as their texts increase in sophistication.

Don't be alarmed if students cover up parts of words that are not blends or digraphs. Remind them to check the blends and digraphs chart and check their work.

"Here's a little chart to help you remember what to do. First, read your nursery rhyme with your partner once all the way through. Next, find all the blends and digraphs, and then cover them with your dry erase marker. Help each other, and make sure you find them all. Remember, they are often at the beginnings of words, so check those parts carefully. Get to work!"

As partners work, remind them to refer to the "Blends and Digraphs" chart as needed, and to keep working without checking with you for reassurance each time they cover a blend.

CHALLENGE THEM: Invite partnerships to switch nursery rhymes and to figure out the missing blends and digraphs in each other's rhymes.

"Okay, friends, time to switch! Trade nursery rhymes on which you've covered up blends and digraphs with another partnership. When you get your new nursery rhyme, start reading it with your partner. Try to figure out the missing blends and digraphs. When you figure them out, go ahead and write them in, right above the marked-out spot. Use the 'Blends and Digraphs' chart to help you."

"Okay, let's all read both of the nursery rhymes together and check that your work makes sense and looks right. When we come to a blend or digraph, give a thumbs up."

TEACH TOWARD TOMORROW: Remind students of the importance of being alert to blends and digraphs when they read and write.

"This is important reading and writing work. When you are reading or writing, and you come across words that have blends or digraphs, make sure you notice both the letters in that blend or digraph. For example, there is a big difference between reading the words *fog* and *frog*! You wouldn't want to read, 'The duck swam up to the fog,' when the words really say, 'The duck swam up to the frog.' You'll want to be sure you notice both letters at the beginnings of words like *frog* so that what you read makes sense and looks right. I'll leave you here to keep working."

FIG. 22–2   A student solves the missing blends.

OTHER SUPPORTS

Replicate: This session can be replicated using other nursery rhymes to support students in working on a variety of different phonics principles:

- For example, when working on short vowels, you might replicate this session using "Hickory Dickory Dock," "Jack and Jill," "Lucy Locket," or "To Market, to Market."
- When working on ending digraphs, you might use "The Mulberry Bush."
- When working on vowel teams you might replicate with "I'm a Little Teapot," "Little Bo Peep," "Row, Row, Row Your Boat," "Rain, Rain Go Away," or "One, Two, Buckle My Shoe."
- And for inflectional endings, you might use "It's Raining, It's Pouring," or "The Itsy Bitsy Spider."
- See the online resources for additional practice texts. 👆

POSSIBLE COACHING MOVES

▶ "Start by reading the whole rhyme with your partner. Listen carefully for what might be missing."

▶ "Say the word slooooooowly. Stretch it out and really listen to all the sounds. What could those missing letters be? Write them in."

▶ "Reread the whole thing and see if what you wrote in makes sense."

Tricky Spelling Patterns
dr- and tr-

BEST TAUGHT TO

• Students who frequently misspell *dr-* or *tr-* word beginnings

BEST TAUGHT DURING

• Writing workshop

GETTING READY

✔ Bring whiteboards and markers for each child in the group.

✔ Make a set of picture cards for each partnership.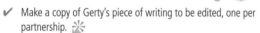

✔ Make a copy of Gerty's piece of writing to be edited, one per partnership.

✔ If you can, flag pages in students' work that contain *dr* and *tr* misspellings. Kids will need their writing and colored pens for editing.

✔ Print a copy of the "Find and Fix Spelling Mistakes" chart.

RALLY THEM: Let students know that some beginning blends can be especially tricky to spell. Tell kids about two tricky sounds. For each sound, give an example of a word that has that sound, and show a common spelling mistake for that sound.

"Writers, I have been looking over your writing, and I see that the beginnings of some words are especially tricky. You are spelling them the way they sound, but that's not the way they look in a book. So, I wanted to help you with some blends that are tricky for lots of people.

"Let me show you what I mean. Let's all say the word *drum* slowly and listen to the beginning sound. *Drum. Drum.* At the start of the word, many people hear a /j/ sound, but the word *drum* does not have a *j* at the start of the word. Here's how it is written."

Write *drum* on your whiteboard. Point to the letters as you reference them.

"The *dr* blend can sometimes sound like /j/ or /jr/, so you have to be super-careful when you hear /j/ or /jr/ at the start of a word because it might actually be /dr/ and spelled *dr*.

"I have one more tricky word part to tell you about. Say the word *truck* with me slowly, listening to the beginning sound. *Truck. Truck.* Many people hear /ch/ at the start of that word, but *truck* doesn't start with a *ch*. It starts with *tr*. It looks like this."

Write *truck* on your whiteboard, below *drum*. Again, point to the letters as you reference them.

FIG. 23–1   Helping students pronounce and write some blends.

"You have to be very careful with that *R*. Lots of words that actually start with the blend *tr* might sound like a /chr/."

LAUNCH THEM: Dictate words that have those spelling patterns, coaching kids to use the keywords you shared to help them figure out how to spell each dictated word on their whiteboards.

"Okay, take out your whiteboards and your markers. I am going to give each partnership a set of cards, and you'll say the words together and then write them on your whiteboards. Some of these words will have one of these tricky sounds that are easy to mess up. For words where you hear a /j/ sound at the start, you'll have to think, 'Does the word start with the letters *dr*, like *drum*, or does it start with *j*?' For words where you hear a /ch/ sound at the start, you'll think, 'Does it start with *tr*, like *truck*, or does it start with *ch*?' I'll leave these keywords on my whiteboard to help you."

Distribute the set of word cards to each partnership, and coach students as they work.

CHALLENGE THEM: Set up partners to correct a piece of writing that makes some of these common spelling errors, then read the corrected version together.

"I need your help. I have a piece of writing that my neighbor Gerty wrote, and it has some of these sorts of spelling mistakes. Will you and your partner get together and help Gerty fix up her mistakes?"

FIG. 23–3   Gerty's writing

Coach students while they work. Once they have corrected several mistakes, invite partners to reread the corrected version.

FIG. 23–2   Valerie coaches students to write some tricky first sounds.

Don't worry if students don't spell the vowel patterns or the word endings correctly. Keep today's focus on coaching them with these tricky beginning blends. If writing the whole word is taking students a long time, channel them to just record the starting sounds, or to whisper the starting sounds to their partner.

POSSIBLE COACHING MOVES

▸ "Say the word again very slowly. Listen carefully to the beginning sounds. Does the word *trip* start like *drum* or *truck*?"

▸ "Does it look right to you? Does it look like the way you've seen that word in a book?"

I went with my mom to get a treat. We got ice cream. We sat under a tree with lots of leaves to eat our treat. I looked at my cone and saw a drip. Then I saw a big drip. "It's melting," I said. Mom stopped eating. "Drink up the drips!" she said. I did. I liked getting a treat with Mom.

TEACH TOWARD TOMORROW: Remind writers to be especially alert to these sounds. Leave them working on some pages in their writing you've flagged with these sorts of mistakes.

"Writers, I've flagged some pages in your writing that I think you could fix up using the work we did here. Will you and your partner help each other fix up the one page I've given each of you, and then, each of you, keep going with your writing? Remember to be especially alert if you are listening for the sounds in a word and you think you hear one of those especially tricky sounds. Use the keywords to help you figure out how to spell that word. I'll come back and look at your writing a little later."

Leave a copy of the "Find and Fix Spelling Mistakes" chart so that students can see it. You might remind them of the steps as you do so.

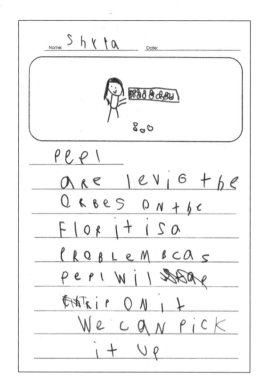

FIG. 23–4   A student's edited piece of writing.

OTHER SUPPORTS

▼ **Gr K, Unit 5, Sess. 2, Ext. 3:** Listening Closely to Words Beginning with *tr-* and *ch-*.

Building Words
Short-Vowel Rimes

BEST TAUGHT TO

- Children who are spelling letter by letter and are not using word parts to write
- Children who need support blending onsets and rimes

BEST TAUGHT DURING

- Writing workshop

GETTING READY

✔ Prepare letter cards with the consonants *S*, *F*, *B*, *P*, and *L*, and phonogram cards *-in*, *-an*, *-op*, and *-it* for each partnership. ✋

✔ Gather a set of high-frequency word cards for each partnership: *see*, *look*, *I*, *the*, *is*, and *at*. ✋

✔ Prepare a copy of the "Building Words" chart. ✋

✔ Ask children to bring their writing folders to the group.

RALLY THEM: Use a familiar toy as an analogy to words. They both contain parts that you can crash together to make something new.

"Have you ever played with LEGO® people? When I play with them, my favorite thing to do is to take a head from one person and a body from another person and crash them together to make a new person.

"Words work the same way. Words don't have heads and bodies, but they are made up of word parts you can crash together to make new words.

"What are some word parts that you could crash together to make new words?" Listen as students call out familiar phonograms.

LAUNCH THEM: Set partnerships up to make words using word parts. Rally them to read each word they make to check whether it's a real or a pretend word. Coach in as students make words.

"Ready to try making words? I'll give you and your partner a bunch of word parts and some letters. Work together to make words by putting the word parts and letters together. After you make each word, read it and check whether it's a real word or a pretend word. Then repeat. See if you can use all of the letters and parts."

Distribute cards with consonants and familiar phonograms to each partnership: *S*, *F*, *B*, *P*, *L*, and *-in*, *-an*, *-op*, and *-it*. Show students the "Building Words" chart to remind them how to make words.

FIG. 24–1   Ashwara at work building words.

"After kids start assembling, point out that some of them have made nonsense words. "Here's a tip. All these letters and word parts can fit together to make actual words. Try new combinations to find more words.""

Once students have done this, invite children to reread all the words they made to their partner.

CHALLENGE THEM: Invite children to make sentences using the new words they've generated and a set of high-frequency words.

Distribute a set of high-frequency word cards (*see*, *look*, *I*, *the*, *is*, and *at*) to each partnership.

"Are you game for an added challenge? Remember, words love to be in sentences. Try putting your words together with these snap words to make sentences. For example, you could make the sentence 'I see the fan.' Work with your partner and see how many sentences you can make."

Prompt students to read their sentences aloud to their partner as they create them, and to unmake and remake new sentences.

TEACH TOWARD TOMORROW: Channel students to return to their writing, remembering that when they write, many words are made from word parts they know.

"I know you want to return to your own writing. As you do that, remember that many of the words you write are like LEGO people. They are made of parts, many of them parts you know, that you can crash together. Many words even have words you know in a snap. Thinking about words as made of parts will help you be able to tackle even the biggest, hardest words."

Leave a Post-it note reminder showing a toy figure head + body and the parts of a word (for example, you might write *c* and *at* in the two parts of the figure). If possible, print the image we have provided in the online resources. 🖐

OTHER SUPPORTS

Replicate:

- This session can be replicated for other short-vowel phonograms such as *-ub* and *-ut*.
- You may also want to replicate it to include VCC phonograms that end in blends and digraphs, such as *-ock*, *-ash*, and *-ick*.
- This session can also be replicated for CVCe phonograms. For this replication, you can use phonograms, such as *-ape*, *-ope*, and *-ute*.

All of these phonogram cards can be found in the online resources. 🖐

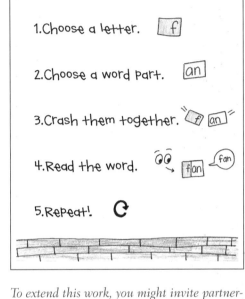

To extend this work, you might invite partnerships to generate their own beginning sounds and word parts. They could add new word parts that would help them to make more words, or they could generate new word parts for another partnership to use.

POSSIBLE COACHING MOVES

▶ "Try crashing some parts together. Do they make a real word?"

▶ "Take that pretend word and see if you can change it into a real word."

▶ "What other word can you make with the same beginning but with a new ending? Or keep the same ending and try a new beginning."

Interactive Editing
Short Vowels

BEST TAUGHT TO

- Students who omit short vowels in their writing

BEST TAUGHT DURING

- Writing workshop

GETTING READY

✔ Print a short-vowel chart for each partnership.

✔ Bring a writing sample that includes short-vowel errors. You may use ours or substitute your own piece. Print copies for each partnership. ✶

✔ Print a copy of the "Find and Fix Spelling Mistakes" chart. ✶

✔ If possible, flag a page from each child's writing in which that child has omitted vowels.

ACTIVATE PHONICS: Explain why you've gathered students together. Then, have partners read the vowel chart together.

"Writers, you all know that vowels are so important in writing because every word needs at least one vowel. Let's activate our vowel power right now."

Hand each partnership a vowel chart. "Try reading the vowel chart with your partner. We can read the first vowel all together. *A, /ă/ apple*. Now read the rest of the vowels with your partner."

LAUNCH THEM AND WORK SIDE BY SIDE: Invite students to help correct a piece of sample writing with missing vowels.

"Now that your short-vowel power is activated, you are ready for some important work. My nephew Sam doesn't have a writing workshop at his school. I told him about the fun you have writing stories, and he sat down and wrote his own story about when he played tag and he ran really fast and fell down. But Sam doesn't have a writing partner. Would you be willing to be his partner and help him with his story?

"As I read his writing, hold up a thumb when you notice he has some fixing to do. Watch for whether each word has a vowel."

Distribute the piece to each partnership and read the first page aloud, encouraging the students to point under each word.

"I saw some thumbs up when I read this word, *tag*. Will you and your partner see if you can help Sam fix *tag*? Because you are right, it is missing a vowel.

"Here is a whiteboard and a pen for each of you. Will one partner write the word *tag* the right way on your whiteboards and the other fix it on your copy of the book?"

SMALL GROUPS TO SUPPORT PHONICS, GRADES K–1

FIG. 25–1   Sam's story

If needed, whisper to one child in each partnership to cross off the misspelled word *tg* on the writing sample and to rewrite it including the vowel.

CHALLENGE THEM: Ask partners to work together to edit the next pages.

"Keep going with your partner. Read over the next two pages together. Look for places where Sam forgot to use short vowels, and then fix those places. Use the 'Find and Fix Spelling Mistakes' chart if you need a reminder of what to do."

POSSIBLE COACHING MOVES

▸ "Say the word. What sound do you hear in the middle?"

▸ "Check the vowel chart. Is it /ă/ as in *apple* or /ĕ/ as in *egg*?"

▸ "Reread what you wrote and check the vowel. Does it look right?"

TEACH TOWARD TOMORROW: Coach students to use vowel power to edit their own pieces of writing. Remind students that they can do this work whenever they write, rather than waiting to edit.

"Ready to give this a try with your own writing? Open up your writing folder and pull out the writing page I marked for you. Reread your writing, checking each word to make sure you have a vowel. If a word is missing a vowel, fix it up. Use the vowel chart if that will help. Cross it off and rewrite it the correct way."

FIG. 25–2   WIllma edits her own writing.

"Then can you check other pages of your writing and your partner's writing, making sure every word has a vowel and that the vowel looks like it is the right one?"

OTHER SUPPORTS

▲ **Gr K, Unit 4, Sess. 2, Ext. 2:** Providing More Practice with Segmenting and Blending

▲ **Gr K, Unit 4, Sess. 3:** "Isolating the Short-Vowel Sound in the Middle of Words (-VC)" (focus on /i/, but you could adjust to focus on other vowels)

▲ **Gr K, Unit 4, Sess. 4:** "Writing Sentences with Short *A* and Short *I* CVC Words"

▲ **Gr K, Unit 4, Sess. 6:** "Editing for Short Vowels *A* and *I*"

▲ **Gr K, Unit 4, Sess. 8, Ext. 1:** Writing Sort to Practice Distinguishing Vowels

Hearing and Recording the Right Short Vowel

RALLY THEM AND ACTIVATE PHONICS: Emphasize the importance of vowels. Give students picture cards for *CVC* words, asking them to record the vowel. Channel them to work independently, then to check their work.

"Writers, I know you have been studying vowel power during phonics time. But here's the thing. Vowel power is super-important when you write because *every* word needs at least one vowel. To make your writing easy for people to read, you need to use the correct vowel. You wouldn't want to say, 'The fire was *hat*' when you meant 'The fire was *hot*.' Your readers would be so confused!

"But using the correct vowel can be tricky for tons of reasons. One reason is that it can be hard to hear the difference between those short vowels, right? Let's see which of these sounds are especially tricky for each of you.

"I'm giving each of you a half-sheet of paper numbered one through five and a small stack of picture cards. Will you jot each word down quickly, one word next to each number? Make sure not to look at each other's work. If you finish early, you can come up with some other words I could have asked you to write for each vowel."

Take notes as students record for each of the following picture cards: *bat*, *bed*, *pig*, *fox*, *bug*, *van*, *dog*, *ten*. It is not important for kids to get through all eight cards. Just be sure they get through the first five cards, attempting to spell a word for each vowel.

"Great, now let's check these words. I'll write them on my whiteboard and will you and your partner check your words? Find the ones that don't match mine."

Spell each word aloud as you write it. Help children as needed to find spellings that don't match yours.

"Some of these are a little confusing, right? It becomes a little easier if you think about how your mouth goes for each of the sounds. To do this, say /ă/ as in *apple*, and /ĭ/ as in *igloo*. Can you feel how each sound feels different in your mouth? How's it different?

BEST TAUGHT TO

• Students who are omitting short vowels or are using them incorrectly in their writing

BEST TAUGHT DURING

• Writing workshop

GETTING READY

✔ For each student, number half-sheets of paper from 1 to 5 and print picture cards for *bat*, *bed*, *pig*, *fox*, *bug*, *van*, *dog*, and *ten*.

✔ Bring pencils, colorful pens, and a copy of the vowel chart for each partnership.

✔ Print a copy of the "Find and Fix Spelling Mistakes" chart.

✔ Print the story to be edited, or select your own piece that has vowel errors, and make one copy per partnership.

✔ If you can, flag a page from each child's writing where that child has omitted or confused vowels.

Children will agree that they open their mouth more for the short A. "You are getting good at this. I'll say a word and you repeat it, feeling the vowel in your mouth. Then tell me if it is an opened mouth /ă/ or a back-of-the-throat /ĭ/."

Say the following words and ask students to repeat them: *rat*, *sit*, *flat*, *smash*, *into*.

"Here's a trickier one. Try the short E sound. It's sort of in between in your mouth. Say that sound in *bed* or *peg*."

"Ready to try a few words? I'll say them, and then you say them a few times, feeling them in your mouth. See if you can choose the vowel."

Say the following words and ask students to repeat them: *hit* (back of the throat), *mat* (open mouth), and *egg* (in between).

"We could keep going with the other vowels, but the point is that when you are writing, it helps if you take some time to try to hear and feel which vowel sound you are writing."

LAUNCH THEM: Recruit the kids to help your neighbor Gerty correct a piece of writing with short-vowel errors.

"Now that you're getting better at figuring out which short-vowel sound you hear in a word, I thought maybe you could help my neighbor, Gerty. She wrote a story last night and she needs help with short vowels. Can you use your short-vowel power to help her?

"I've made copies for each partnership to share. I'll read Gerty's writing while you follow along. Then, work with your partner to help her fix up her vowels.

FIG. 26–1   Gerty's story

We recommend you refrain from altering this activity so it resembles a whole-class spelling test. Instead, channel students to work with their word cards with independence while you shift from observing one to observing the next. Use this time to assess, not to teach.

"Page 1 says, 'One day I went to a big park. I ran up and down a big hill with my family.'"

"Here are some colorful editing pens. Get to work helping Gerty! It goes for a couple of pages. When you see a word that needs vowel help, cross it out, and work together to write the word correctly right there on the page. Use the 'Find and Fix Spelling Mistakes' chart to remind you what to do."

When you finish, you can pair up with another partnership, compare your work, and see if you agree. If you don't agree, you'll need to talk it through so Gerty doesn't get different directions from each of you! That would be confusing!"

TEACH TOWARD TOMORROW: Direct students to reread a page of their own writing that you flagged, editing to make sure that each word has the correct short vowels.

"Writers, this work with Gerty's writing should help you with your writing, today and every day. You'll see I've marked a page of your writing. Can you reread that page of your writing, checking that you've included short vowels when needed and doing a bit of fixing up? Then, when you've fixed up that page, continue with your writing, but keep these tricky short vowels in mind as you work."

OTHER SUPPORTS

▲ **Gr K, Unit 4, Sess. 2, Ext. 2:** Providing More Practice with Segmenting and Blending

▲ **Gr K, Unit 4, Sess. 3:** "Isolating the Short-Vowel Sound in the Middle of Words (-VC)" (focus on *All*)

▲ **Gr K, Unit 4, Sess. 7:** "Distinguishing Short *E*, *O*, and *I* Sounds in Words"

▲ **Gr K, Unit 4, Sess. 8:** "Identifying and Editing for Short *E*, *O*, and *U* Sounds"

▲ **Gr K, Unit 4, Sess. 8, Ext. 1:** Writing Sort to Practice Distinguishing Vowels

Find and Fix Spelling Mistakes

1. Read slowly

2. Find Mistakes

3. Fix them

POSSIBLE COACHING MOVES

▶ "Say the word. What sound do you hear in the middle?"

▶ "Check the vowels chart. Is it /ă/ as in *apple* or /ĕ/ as in *egg*?"

▶ "Reread what you wrote and check the vowel. Does it look right?"

Middles Matter
Reading Short Vowels

BEST TAUGHT TO

- Children who are not looking closely at the whole word—especially the middle letters

BEST TAUGHT DURING

- Reading workshop

GETTING READY

✔ Collect word cards, one set for each partnership: *lamp, lip, pen, pin, pan, stick, snack,* and *sock.*

✔ Bring a few Post-its to cover up the middles of the words on the index cards.

✔ Print a copy of "Clouds" by Christina G. Rossetti.

✔ Ask children to bring their book baggies.

RALLY THEM: Use an analogy to highlight the importance of paying attention to the middles in words.

"I was making a sandwich the other day, and I couldn't decide what to put in between the two pieces of bread. I mean there are so many choices: ham, tuna, cheese . . . What do you like in your sandwiches? Quickly tell your partner.

"Imagine if your sandwich only had bread. That wouldn't even be a sandwich! What's in the middle really matters, doesn't it?

"That got me thinking of the work you are doing as readers. You've gotten really good at looking at the beginnings and endings of the words you read. Now you are ready to also look closely at the *middle* parts of words. I mean, without the middle there wouldn't even be a word!"

LAUNCH THEM: Ask kids to read sets of words that have the same beginning and ending parts, but that are different in the middle. Point out that the middle of a word really matters.

Display the words *lamp* and *lip* on index cards. Cover the middle parts of the words—the *am* in *lamp* and the *i* in *lip*.

68

"Let's look at these two words. With the middles of these words covered, they look like they could be the same word. They start the same and they even end the same. But they aren't the same at all. Look!"

Remove the cover to reveal the middle letters. "Now read these two words with your partner. Look closely at the middle letters. Move your eyes across the word and say the whole word.

"Yes, the words are *lamp* and *lip*. Do you see now how the middle part really matters? If you don't look at it, you could say the wrong word and then get all confused when you read.

Distribute word cards to each partnership. "Let's try another set of words. Here are three words that start and end the same way. See if you can work with your partner to read them all. Remember, pay really close attention to the middle parts!"

Coach partners as they read the words *pen*, *pin*, and *pan*, this time with the middle parts uncovered.

Repeat the process with one more set of words.

WORK SIDE BY SIDE: Read aloud a poem and intentionally make errors on middle parts of words. Invite children to follow along and coach you as you read to cross-check for meaning.

"It's clear that the middles matter! When we read together and you forget to check all the parts of the word, I'll sometimes whisper, 'Try again!' But you don't need me to whisper to you. When you read words in a sentence, the sentence will tell you to try again. When a word doesn't make sense, it's almost as if there's a little whisper in your ear saying, 'Pssst . . . try again!'

"Let's practice with this poem. I'll pretend to be six years old. Will you pretend to be my teacher? If something doesn't make sense or the word doesn't look right, will you whisper to me, 'Try again'? Okay, here I go . . ."

Read the first two lines of the poem aloud. Substitute the word *hill* with *hotel*:

When coaching kids to read the middle part of the word, remember that it is important not to disrupt the directionality. Proficient readers problem solve words by working left to right across the word, breaking it up part by part, not letter by letter.

"Clouds"
by Christina G. Rossetti

White sheep, white sheep,
On a blue **hotel**,

"Oh! I hear you whispering, 'Try again! Try again!' You're right, *hotel* doesn't make sense here. Let me try again. This time, let me make sure to check all the parts of the word, especially the middle."

Reread the two lines. Slide your finger under the word *hill* to demonstrate checking the middle of the word.

"*Hill* . . . that looks right all the way through. 'White sheep, white sheep, on a blue hill.' The clouds in the sky are like sheep on a hill. I get it now! That makes sense. Thank you, teachers!"

Read the next two lines. Substitute the word *still* with *stool*. Again, pause so children can point out the error, and demonstrate stopping to fix the word.

When the wind stops
You all stand **stool**.

"Partners, you can be each other's teacher, too. Read the rest of the poem together, and if something doesn't make sense or look right, stop your partner and say, 'Try again!'"

TEACH TOWARD TOMORROW: Invite children to return to their reading. Remind them to pay attention to the middles of words, and to check themselves when a word doesn't make sense.

"You look ready to get going on some reading! Be sure to check the whole word from start to end, and remember, the middles matter. Right now, take out one of the books from your baggie and start reading on your own. You don't need a teacher or a partner to whisper, 'Try again!' When you read words in a sentence, and something doesn't make sense, you can tell yourself to try again. Get started!"

OTHER SUPPORTS

Replicate: You may, on another day, do similar work with more challenging sets of words.

Clouds
By Christina Rossetti

White sheep, white sheep,

On a blue hill,

When the wind stops,

You all stand still.

When the wind blows,

You walk away slow.

White sheep, white sheep,

Where do you go?

POSSIBLE COACHING MOVES

▸ "Try again! Go back and reread."

▸ "Slow down and try that word part by part. Look closely at the middle."

▸ "Great, you are checking the middle part of that word. Now, you have to think about the sound that the vowel makes. Try the vowel two ways and see which one sounds right."

▸ "Remember to cross-check by thinking about what would make sense here. What is happening in the poem? Does that word make sense?"

Solving Missing Letters
Short Vowels

RALLY THEM AND ACTIVATE PHONICS: Introduce today's work, then have kids whisper-read the short vowel chart to a partner.

"I have a treat for this group today. I called you together because you are ready for more challenges in your reading and writing. You are getting so good at reading and writing the beginnings and endings of words. Today, you get to play a game that will help you get stronger at tackling the middle parts of words. It's called 'Solving Missing Letters.' Instead of me doing the covering up like I do when we play other games, you'll get to do it! You'll be covering up and working with short vowels, so you'll need to use all you know about them.

"To get ready, will you whisper-read the short vowel chart with your partner?"

Asking students to read the chart with a partner rather than all together is a small way to encourage independence and allows you to observe one partnership, then swing over to observe another.

LAUNCH THEM: Set partnerships up to read a familiar nursery rhyme and then to hide the vowels in that rhyme.

"I am going to give each partnership a different nursery rhyme. These are nursery rhymes you all know well."

Distribute a nursery rhyme and marker to each partnership and show students the "Solving Missing Letters" chart.

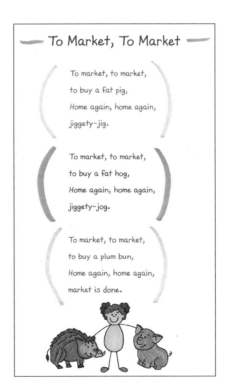

— To Market, To Market —

To market, to market,
to buy a fat pig,
Home again, home again,
jiggety-jig.

To market, to market,
to buy a fat hog,
Home again, home again,
jiggety-jog.

To market, to market,
to buy a plum bun,
Home again, home again,
market is done.

BEST TAUGHT TO

- Children who are beginning to read at level E, when attending to middle parts of words becomes more important
- Children who are confusing short vowels when they are attempting to solve words in reading
- Children who are confusing short vowels in their writing

BEST TAUGHT DURING

- Reading workshop
- Writing workshop

GETTING READY

✔ Print a copy of the vowel chart for each partnership.

✔ Select two familiar nursery rhymes that contain words with short vowels. We chose "Hickory Dickory Dock," "Jack and Jill," "Lucy Locket" and "To Market, To Market." Place the poems in sheet protectors so that you can reuse them.

✔ Prepare a copy of the "Solving Missing Letters" chart.

✔ Bring a dry erase marker and eraser for each partnership.

"Here's a chart to help you remember what to do. First, read your nursery rhyme with your partner once all the way through. Next, find all the vowels, and then cover them with your dry-erase marker. Help each other, and make sure you find them all. You'll need to listen closely to hear the short vowel sound. Remember, they are often in the middles of words, so check those parts carefully. Get to work!"

As partners work, remind them to refer to the short vowel chart as needed, and to keep working without checking with you for reassurance each time they cover a vowel.

CHALLENGE THEM: Invite partnerships to switch nursery rhymes and to figure out the missing vowels in each other's rhymes.

"Okay, friends, time to switch! Trade your nursery rhyme with the covered up short vowels with another partnership. When you get your new nursery rhyme, start reading it with your partner. Try to figure out the missing short vowel. When you figure them out, go ahead and write them in, right above the marked-out spot. Use your vowel chart to help you."

POSSIBLE COACHING MOVES

▶ "Start by reading the whole rhyme with your partner. Listen carefully for what might be missing."

▶ "Say the word sloooooowly. Stretch it out and really listen to all the sounds. What could that missing letter be? Write it in."

▶ "When you're done, reread the whole thing and see if what you wrote in makes sense."

As children play this game, they practice attending to challenges presented by higher levels of text. In level E books, they'll need to attend to the short vowels in the middles of words. When they move to higher levels, they'll need to attend to vowel teams. This game is a lively way to introduce or reinforce the new work children will need to do as their texts increase in sophistication.

Don't be alarmed if students cover up parts of words that are not short vowels. Ask them to say the word again and listen for the vowel sound. Remind them to check the short vowel chart and check their work.

"Okay, let's all read both of the nursery rhymes together and check that your work makes sense and looks right. When we come to a short vowel, give a thumbs-up."

TEACH TOWARD TOMORROW: Remind students of the importance of being alert to vowels when they read and write.

"This is important reading and writing work. When you are reading or writing, and you come across words that have vowels, make sure you listen closely. For example, there is a big difference between reading the words *cat* and *cut*! You wouldn't want to write or read, 'I wore my *cut* dress to the party,' when the words really say, 'I wore my *cat* dress to the party.' You'll want to be sure you use or say the right short vowel so that what you read makes sense and looks right. I'll leave you here to keep working."

FIG. 28–1   Students cover the vowels in poems.

OTHER SUPPORTS

Replicate: This session can be replicated using other nursery rhymes to support students in working on a variety of different phonics principles:

- For example, when working on ending digraphs, you might use "The Mulberry Bush."
- When working on vowel teams, you might use "I'm a Little Teapot," "Little Bo Peep," "Row, Row, Row Your Boat," "Rain, Rain Go Away," or "One, Two, Buckle My Shoe."

▲ **Gr K, Unit 4, Sess. 3:** "Isolating the Short Vowel Sound in the Middle of Words (-VC)" (focus on short *A* and short *I* sounds)

▲ **Gr K, Unit 4, Sess. 7:** "Distinguishing Short *E*, *O*, and *I* Sounds"

▲ **Gr K, Unit 4, Sess. 8:** "Identifying and Editing for Short *E*, *O*, and *U* Sounds"

▲ **Gr K, Unit 4, Sess. 8, Ext. 1:** Writing Sort to Practice Distinguishing Vowels

Making CVC Words

BEST TAUGHT TO

- Students who are not writing with short vowels at all or are using incorrect short vowels

BEST TAUGHT DURING

- Writing workshop

GETTING READY

✔ Gather whiteboards and markers.

✔ Gather short-vowel chart (one for each partnership).

RALLY AND ACTIVATE PHONICS: Tell the writers a story about a time when having the wrong vowel sound changed the meaning of a word you wrote.

"Writers, I have got to tell you a story about something silly that happened to me yesterday. Before I left for work, I wrote a shopping list for my brother to get supplies for the birthday party we're throwing this weekend. I put all kinds of things on the list: potato chips, cookies, and plates and cups. When I got home, I checked in to make sure he got all the right supplies—but, do you know what happened?

"I looked in the bag and there were the plates, the chips, the cookies—but no cups! Instead there were all sorts of caps! There were baseball caps, skiing caps, even caps for a party, but no cups. When I asked my brother about it, he said, 'But you didn't ask for cups—you asked for caps.'

"I looked back at the shopping list and he was completely right! Instead of writing *C-U-P-S*, I wrote *C-A-P-S*. I couldn't believe it! I forgot to check the vowel in my word.

"I'm telling you this, because this is something that can trip writers up all the time—not just in shopping lists, but in stories, too. This is why it's so important to make sure we know and use all of our sounds in our writing."

LAUNCH THEM: Channel children to make simple CVC words, changing one letter at a time.

Distribute a whiteboard and marker to each child.

"Let's do some work on listening for all the sounds in words together. I'll say a word for you to write, then you can change one part of it to make a new word. Be sure to listen closely to all the sounds, especially the short-vowel sound.

"Will you start by writing the word *cap* on your whiteboard? 'I can wear a cap on my head.' *Cap*. Now see if you can change one letter to make the word *map*. 'We used a map last week to help find a new park.' *Map*. Be sure to check each sound to see which part of the word will change."

Channel students to continue working to change one letter to make the following words: *cap*, *map*, *mop*, *top*, *tip*, *sip*, *sit*, *set*.

> ### POSSIBLE COACHING MOVES
>
> ▶ "Use the Elkonin box. Touch the squares for each sound you hear, then write the letters to match."
>
> ▶ If a child uses an incorrect short vowel, say "Good guess, but that word would say *stap* and you wanted to say *stop*. Say the word slowly to figure out which part of the word you would change."

CHALLENGE THEM: Coach students to use their knowledge of letter sounds, particularly short-vowel sounds, as they work on their own pieces of writing.

"Writers, get out a piece of your writing that you are working on. Think carefully about which sounds each word needs as you go. Pay extra-close attention to the short-vowel sounds and use your short-vowel chart if you need to. This will make your writing easier to read and help you avoid silly mix-ups, like mine with the cups."

TEACH TOWARD TOMORROW: Remind writers of today's work of listening closely to each sound in words and then rally them to continue this in their future writing.

"Whenever you're writing, from tomorrow all the way through the rest of your life, you can do this work of listening closely to the sounds in the words you are writing. As you are writing, think carefully about which short-vowel sound each word needs as you go."

> ### OTHER SUPPORTS
>
> **Replicate:** You can follow this same routine with students who need support listening for ending sounds, blends and digraphs, or CVCe patterns. See the online resources for additional word lists to use when making words. ✸

Listen for kids isolating each sound of the word to find which part they need to change: beginning, middle, or ending. Students may benefit from using Elkonin boxes during this activity to provide a physical cue to identify the sound/letter they must change.

Expect that some words will be unfamiliar for students. Don't worry about word meaning here, but rather push students to hear each sound, particularly the vowels. If needed, you may want to provide students with a chart of short-vowel sounds to reference as they work.

FIG. 29–1   Students write the words on their whiteboards.

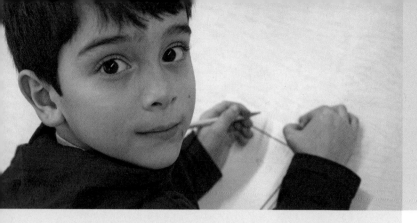

Interactive Editing

CVCe Words with Long Vowels

BEST TAUGHT TO

- Students who know the differences between long- and short-vowel spelling patterns, but make spelling mistakes

BEST TAUGHT DURING

- Writing workshop

GETTING READY

✔ Bring a copy of the vowels chart for each partnership.

✔ Prepare a copy of the "Find and Fix Spelling Mistakes" chart.

✔ Gather some things around the room that contain long- and short-vowel sounds—such as tape, pen, dice, lunches, notes, clips, and blocks. Words that contain one syllable will work best.

✔ Prepare a copy of a student's writing to be corrected for each partnership. We recommend placing the writing in page protectors so that you can use it again.

✔ If you can, place a Post-it on a page of each student's writing where he or she has made a long-vowel spelling error.

ACTIVATE PHONICS: Ask the kids to identify the vowel pattern in items around the classroom. Use this to check children's command of long vowels.

Distribute a vowels chart to each partnership.

"We've been doing a lot of work with vowel sounds. Let's refresh our memory of long and short sounds. I gathered some things from around the room that contain a long or short vowel." Quickly name the objects as you place them in front of the students. "Will you and your partner point to an object and say the word? Then, point to the vowel sound you hear in the middle of the word on your vowel chart. Last, you'll write the word. Ready? Here we go."

As children point to vowel sounds and write the words, observe them and coach them as needed.

"Nice! I can see that you mostly know these, right? You activated your long-vowel power to point to and spell the sounds. Today we are going to practice, so that you always remember to activate your long-vowel power. Sometimes when you are doing your own writing, you forget to activate your long-vowel power and you forget to spell the long vowels with patterns like CVCe."

LAUNCH THEM AND WORK SIDE BY SIDE: Ask kids to help your neighbor correct a piece of writing using their knowledge of long vowels, especially those with the CVCe pattern.

"Now that your long-vowel power is activated, would you be willing to help my neighbor Gerty with her writing? She wrote these pages to explain how to get started in writing workshop. She forgot to use her long-vowel power!

"i've made copies for each partnership to share. Read her writing together. If you see a word where she's mixed up the vowel spelling pattern and it looks wrong, will you circle it on her paper? Then later, you can come back and write the word correctly."

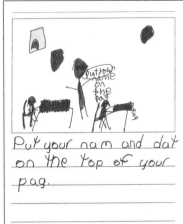

FIG. 30–1   Gerty's writing

If students need support reading the text, offer to read it along with them. When you get to a word that is spelled incorrectly, first read it the way it is written. For example, you might read page 1 as: "Today during writing, tak out your folder . . . *tak* out your folder? Hmm, . . . that doesn't make sense, I think she meant to write *take*."

CHALLENGE THEM: Ask partners to look back through the student work and correct the words they've circled.

"Ready to be an editor with your partner and help this writer fix up any places where she didn't use the long-vowel patterns she knows?"

POSSIBLE COACHING MOVES

▶ "I love that you heard the long-vowel pattern in this word (*take*) and wrote it. Such alert thinking!"

▶ "Listen for the vowel sound. Is it a short sound or a long sound?"

▶ "Oh, does this word need an *E* at the end to make it look right and to help us remember to say the long vowel?"

▶ "Think about the long-vowel endings you know, like -*ake*, -*ane*, -*ame*, -*ate*."

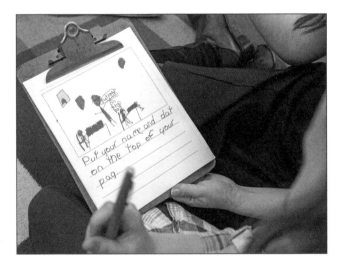

FIG. 30–2   A student edits Gerty's writing.

"Now that everyone is mostly finished, will you and your partner show another partnership what you fixed and see if you agree? If not, talk it out until you are sure you have corrected her writing."

TEACH TOWARD TOMORROW: Get students started editing their own writing. Remind them they can do this work whenever they write, rather than waiting to edit.

"Writers, this work we did today with another student's writing will help you with *your* writing. You'll see I've marked a page of your writing with a Post-it. Can you reread that page of your writing, checking that you've included long-vowel spelling patterns when needed? Remember that all syllables need vowels! From now on, you can be your own editor, checking your writing as you go."

 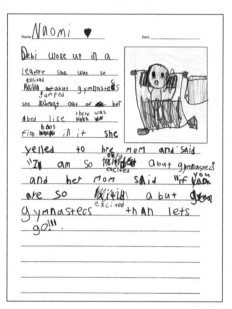

FIG. 30–1   Naomi edits her book about gymnastics.

OTHER SUPPORTS

Replicate: Follow the same steps as this interactive editing small group, this time focusing on a different vowel. We have provided student writing samples with a focus on long *I*, long *O*, and long *U* in the online resources.

▼ **Gr 1, Unit 2, Sess. 3, Ext. 1:** Watching Out for Words with a Long *A* Sound and Silent *E*

▲ **Gr 1, Unit 2, Sess. 1, Ext. 2:** Supporting Transfer to Writing Workshop

▲ **Gr 1, Unit 2, Sess. 3, Ext. 2:** Transferring Learning from Phonics Workshop to Writing Workshop

The Case of the Silent *e*

RALLY THEM AND ACTIVATE PHONICS: Invite children to play teacher with their partners and read the vowel chart.

"Readers, remember when you were in kindergarten and you loved to play pretend school? I bet you pretended to be a teacher and your friends were the students."

Provide a vowel chart to each partnership.

"One of you can be the teacher and the other will be the student. If you are the teacher, hold up the chart, point to the letter, and ask your partner to say the long-vowel sound, then the short-vowel sound. Then switch."

LAUNCH THEM: Read a text aloud, incorrectly pronouncing words with -VCe as words with short vowels, and channeling students to help you fix up your reading.

"You all are really good at playing teacher! Now, can you be *my* teacher? Teach me everything you know about the silent *E*. Remember, you can use the chart to help you."

Provide a copy of "The Case of the Silent *e*" anchor chart and a "Be the Teacher" sign to each partnership.

"I'll read this poem and you be my teachers as I read. Pay close attention to how I read those sneaky silent *E* words. If I read a word with the

Animals Make Me Smile
By Christine Holley

A lion has his mane.
A zebra has her stripes.
Be careful of a bumblebee
who may leave you with some bites.

A snake can be quite scary.
A hippo can be too.
But just enjoy the time you have
when you see them at the zoo!

BEST TAUGHT TO
- Children who have difficulty reading CVCe words in text

BEST TAUGHT DURING
- Reading workshop

GETTING READY

✔ Prepare a long- and short-vowel chart and a copy of "The Case of the Silent *e*" anchor chart. If you are teaching Grade 1, Unit 1, "Building Good Reading Habits" from the Units of Study for Teaching Reading, you might want to print the "Oops" sign (see "Be the Teacher" games sign template in Session 10 in those online resources.) Alternatively, plan to channel kids to signal errors with a thumbs down.

✔ Print the poem "Animals Make Me Smile."

wrong vowel sound, hold up your 'Oops!' sign (or give me a thumbs down)—and then you can help me fix it up."

Hold the poem "Animals Make Me Smile" so that the children can see it while you read it aloud. When you get to a word that has a VCe pattern, make common mistakes, such as:

- saying the short-vowel instead of the long-vowel sound

- pronouncing the *E* when it should be silent

Each time students notice a miscue, prompt them to teach you to notice the VCe part in the word: "Teach me! What part should I notice in this word? How should I read it?"

WORK SIDE BY SIDE: Channel partners to read the poem once more together.

"Now that you helped to make sure my reading made sense, will you and your partner reread this poem together? Remember to pay close attention to that sneaky *E*."

TEACH TOWARD TOMORROW: Encourage students to be their own teachers and pay close attention to words that end in *E*.

"You were really good teachers today! Thanks for teaching me about the silent *E* and reminding me to look for that pattern in the words I read. Remember, be on the lookout for the sneaky *E*. When you see words with an *E* at the end, check that your reading makes sense and sounds right, too."

OTHER SUPPORTS

▼ **Gr 1, Unit 2, Sess. 5, Ext. 1:** Reviewing Short- and Long-Vowel Sounds

▼ **Gr 1, Unit 2, Sess. 3, Ext. 1:** Watching Out for Words with a Long *A* Sound and Silent *E*

▲ **Gr 1, Unit 2, Sess. 8, Ext. 1:** Sorting Long *U* Words

FIG. 31–1   Sophie teaches Rebecca about silent *E*.

Building Words
-VCe Phonograms

ACTIVATE PHONICS: Set students up to work in partnerships to read through a pile of familiar phonograms.

"You all are starting to really know and use parts of words! That means you can use them to read and write more and more words."

Distribute familiar phonogram cards -*ane*, -*ate*, -*ake*, -*ame*, -*ate*, -*ave*, -*ipe*, -*ive*, -*ove*, -*ole*, -*one*, -*ope*, -*ute*, -*uve*, and -*ule*.

"I've given you and your partner a stack of word parts. They are all parts that have a silent *E*. See how fast you and your partner can read through the pile.

The goal is for students to decode and spell letter-by-part, rather than one letter at a time.

FIG. 32–1 Solal and Elin making words with long vowel patterns.

BEST TAUGHT TO
- Children who are spelling letter by letter and are not using word parts to write
- Children who need support blending onsets and rimes

BEST TAUGHT DURING
- Writing workshop

GETTING READY

✔ Prepare letter cards with the onsets *C, H, T, M, CR, SH, FL, GR, ST* and phonogram cards -*ane*, -*ate*, -*ake*, -*ame*, -*ate*, -*ave*, -*ipe*, -*ive*, -*ove*, -*ole*, -*one*, -*ope*, -*ute*, -*uve*, and -*ule* for each partnership.

✔ Gather a set of high-frequency word cards for each partnership.

✔ Prepare a copy of the "Building Words" chart.

✔ Ask children to bring their writing folders to the group.

LAUNCH THEM: Set partnerships up to make words using the onset and phonogram cards. Rally them to read each word they make to check whether it's a real or a pretend word.

"Ready to try making words? I'll give you and your partner a bunch of letters and some blends and digraphs. Work together to make words by putting the letters and the word parts together. After you make each word, read it and check whether it's a real word or a pretend word. Then try another one. See if you can use all of the letters and word parts."

Distribute the following cards with consonants, blends, and digraphs to each partnership: *C, H, T, M, CR, SH, FL, GR, ST*. Show students the "Building Words" chart to remind them how to make words.

"I see some of you have made nonsense words. Here's a tip. All these letters and word parts can fit together to make actual words. Try new combinations to find more words."

Once students have done this, invite children to reread all the words they made with their partner.

CHALLENGE THEM: Invite children to make sentences using the new words they've generated and a set of high-frequency words.

Distribute a set of high-frequency word cards (*see*, *look*, *I*, *the*, *is*, *like*, *there*, *a*, *in*, *go*, *can*, *we*, *on*, *you*, *do*, *have* and *at*) to each partnership.

"Are you game for an added challenge? Remember, words love to be in sentences. Try putting your words together with these snap words to make sentences. For example, you could make the sentence 'I like cake.' Work with your partner and see how many sentences you can make."

Prompt students to read their sentences aloud to their partner as they create them, and to unmake and remake new sentences.

TEACH TOWARD TOMORROW: Channel students to return to their writing, remembering that when they write, many words are made from word parts they know.

"I know you want to return to your own writing. As you do that, will you remember to use the word parts you know as you write lots of words. Thinking about words as being made of parts will help you be able to tackle even the biggest, hardest words."

OTHER SUPPORTS

▼ **Gr 1, Unit 2, Sess. 4:** "Word Detectives Practice Their New Skills: Making Words with Phonograms"

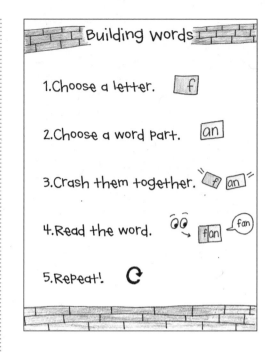

POSSIBLE COACHING MOVES

▶ "Try crashing some parts together. Do they make a real word?"

▶ "Take that pretend word and see if you can change it into a real word."

▶ "What other word can you make with the same beginning but with a new ending? Or keep the same ending and try a new beginning."

To extend this work, you might invite partnerships to generate their own beginning sounds and word parts. They could add new word parts that would help them to make more words, or they could generate new word parts for another partnership to use.

Making Words

-VCe Patterns

RALLY AND ACTIVATE PHONICS: Tell the writers a story about a time when having the wrong vowel sound changed the meaning of a word you wrote.

"Writers, I have got to tell you a story about something silly that happened to me yesterday. Before I left for work, I wrote a note to remind myself to get a cape for my costume. At the end of the day, I checked my note—but, do you know what happened? It said, 'remember to buy a cap'. I thought, 'What?! Why do I need a cap?' Then, I realized I really meant to write the word *cape* because I need a cape for my costume. Wow, that silent *E* is really important. Without it I wrote the wrong word!"

"I'm telling you this because this is something that can trip writers up all the time—not just in shopping lists, but in stories, too. This is why it's so important to make sure we know and use all of our sounds in our writing."

LAUNCH THEM: Channel children to make simple CVCe words, changing one letter at a time.

Distribute a whiteboard and marker to each child.

"Let's do some work listening for all the sounds in words together. I'll say a word for you to write first, then you can change one part of it to make a new word. Be sure to listen closely to all the sounds, especially the short vowel sound.

FIG. 33–1 Ryan, Alexandra, and Aaryan make new words with -VCE phonograms.

• Children who have difficulty writing CVCe words

BEST TAUGHT DURING

• Writing workshop

GETTING READY

✔ Gather whiteboards and markers.

"Will you start by writing the word *lane* on your whiteboard? 'Don't drive your car in the bus *lane*.' *Lane*. Now see if you can change one letter to make the word *mane*. 'A lion has a beautiful *mane*.' *Mane*. Be sure to check each sound to see which part of the word will change."

Have students continue working to change one or two letters to make the following words: *cane, cape, shape, shake, make, take, tame, game, shame, lame, late,* and *date*. You might say a sentence for each word so students can hear the word in context.

CHALLENGE THEM: Coach students to use their knowledge of letter sounds, particularly long vowel sounds, as they work on their own pieces of writing.

"Writers, get out a piece of your writing that you are working on. Think carefully about which sounds each word needs as you go. Pay extra close attention to the long vowel sounds and the silent *F*. This will make your writing easier to read and help you avoid silly mix-ups, like mine with *cap* and *cape*."

TEACH TOWARD TOMORROW: Remind writers of today's work of listening closely to each sound in words and then rally them to continue this in their future writing.

"Whenever you're writing, from tomorrow all the way through the rest of your life, you can do this same work. You can use words you know to spell other words just by changing some of the letters."

OTHER SUPPORTS

Replicate: You can follow this same routine with students who need support listening for ending sounds, blends and digraphs, or vowel teams. See the online resources for additional word lists to use when making words. ☀

Listen for kids isolating each sound of the word to determine which part they need to change: the beginning, middle, or ending.

Expect that some words will be unfamiliar for students. Don't worry about explaining the meaning of each word here. What's most important is that students check each sound.

Studying Contractions

BEST TAUGHT TO

- Children who have been introduced to contractions but who need support using them in their writing and/or decoding them in their reading

BEST TAUGHT DURING

- Writing workshop
- Reading workshop

GETTING READY

✔ Print a chart with common contractions and the words that make them up, one for each student.

✔ Find a familiar book that contains words that can be made into common contractions. We chose *Frog and Toad Are Friends* by Arnold Lobel, pages 25 and 26.

RALLY THEM: Point out the advantages of writing informally with contractions.

"You're working hard to make your stories come alive—by adding dialogue! Today I want to teach you a tip to make your dialogue sound more like real talk. When people talk, they often push their words together and speak with contractions.

Switch your voice tone to show the difference between a stuffy, formal tone and an informal tone as you say: "For example, you probably wouldn't tell your mom, 'I do not like to eat asparagus. I will not eat it.' Instead, you'd say, 'I *don't* like asparagus. I *won't* eat it.' See how the second way sounds more realistic?"

LAUNCH THEM: Introduce a chart with contractions on one side and words that make up the contraction on the other. Channel kids to talk in partnerships about guidelines for contractions.

"Here is a chart with contractions on one side and the words that make up those contractions on the other side. Read them with your partner.

"Study these contractions and the words in them. Talk to each other about what you notice. How do these words change from two little words to one word?"

CHALLENGE THEM: Share out some of what students noticed. Then challenge them to look at a page from a familiar book and find words that could be changed into contractions.

"Most of you remembered that to make a contraction, you smoosh two words together to make one word. Then, you add an apostrophe, this little mark here, in place of the missing letter or letters.

"Guess what a couple of you noticed? This partnership noticed that in these contractions, it's the vowel in the second word that disappears. See that? When *do not* becomes *don't*, the *O* in *not* goes away. When *she is* becomes *she's*, the *I* in *is* goes away."

"Will you try to put these ideas about contractions to use? I'm going to read a page from one of our favorite books, *Frog and Toad Are Friends*. I'll show you the page, so you can follow along. As I read it, keep an eye and ear out for words that could become contractions. Watch me first."

> *"I am feeling much better now, Toad,"* said Frog.

"Wait, I already see two words in this very first line we could make into a contraction. See these words: *I am*? We could make those *I'm*. So, Frog would say, '*I'm* feeling much better now, Toad.'"

"I'll keep reading. Would you put your thumb up when you hear words that could become a contraction and we can all try it?"

> *"I do not think I need a story anymore."*

"I saw lots of thumbs up. What did you notice? Tell your partner.

"Right, the words *do not* could become *don't*. So the sentence would say, "I *don't* think I need a story anymore. That sounds more like people would talk, right? Here, take this book in the middle of the group and keep reading to the end of the next page to see if you can find any more words that could become contractions."

TEACH TOWARD TOMORROW: Tell children that they now are becoming experts and can teach their friends what they know.

"Wow! You are becoming experts on contractions. Will you teach your friend what you've learned about contractions? Each of you gets to keep this contractions chart so you can use it to explain to your friends."

OTHER SUPPORTS

Replicate: Children can study contractions with words that drop the first two letters of the second word. Consider showing the following contractions: *I have*→*I've*; *she will*→*she'll, I will*→*I'll, can not*→*can't*. You might also show *will not*→*won't* as an outlier.

▼ **Gr 1, Unit 2, Sess. 14:** "The Case of the Words in Disguise: Investigating Contractions" (please don't teach this until the class encounters this unit—you'll spoil the fun!)

▼ **Gr 1, Unit 3, Sess. 16:** "Making Contractions with *Not*"

▲ **Gr 1, Unit 3, Sess. 16, Ext. 1:** Using Contractions to Act Out a Song

---

POSSIBLE COACHING MOVES

▶ "Which letter disappeared in each contraction?"

▶ "This little mark is an *apostrophe*. What was there before?"

▶ "Let's cross out the letters that go away. Hmm, . . . what do those letters have in common?"

Writing the Tricky *-ed* Ending

BEST TAUGHT TO

• Students who frequently misspell *-ed* endings

BEST TAUGHT DURING

• Writing workshop

GETTING READY

✔ Bring a whiteboard, marker, and eraser for yourself.

✔ Print out the student piece of writing to be corrected. Make one copy per partnership.

✔ Print a copy of the "Find and Fix Spelling Mistakes" chart.

✔ If you can, flag pages in students' writing that have spelling mistakes with *-ed* endings.

RALLY THEM: Remind students that the *-ed* ending can be tricky to spell. Help them to hear that the ending may sound different, but is still spelled with *-ed*.

"Writers, I have been looking over your writing and I see you are spelling some words the way they sound, but that's not the way they look in a book. So, I want to help you with a tricky type of ending.

"This tricky ending is one you've seen all over your books whenever something is happening in the past, like when yesterday someone *looked* or *wanted* or *played*. All those words end with the exact same spelling, with an *-ed*. That signals it happened in the past. Write, *looked*, *wanted*, and *played* on your whiteboard.

"But here's the tricky part: if you try to spell the end of those words like they sound, you might be fooled into spelling the end of those words without an *-ed*, even though you know that an *-ed* should be there. Remember, the *-ed* ending can sound like /d/, /t/, or /id/. Now that you're hearing more and more sounds in words as you write, all of these different ways *-ed* sounds can cause you to make mistakes when you write."

LAUNCH THEM: Set up partners to correct a piece of writing that makes some of these common spelling errors, then read the corrected version together.

"Okay, I need your help with something. I have a piece of writing that my neighbor wrote about a trip she took in the past. Will you and your partner get together and fix the mistakes?"

Distribute the sample writing to each partnership. Place the printout of the "Find and Fix Spelling Mistakes" chart at the center of the group so everyone can see it.

> I walkt to the store with my mom. "Can I have a treat?" I askt. "No more treats," she yelld. She pulld me over to the fruit aisle. I was happy, but I fakt being mad. The treat I wantid was a mango. My mom said, "Eat healthy foods." She watcht me as I pickt out a fruit to eat. I said, "Thanks, Mom," and smild when she lookt away.

Coach as students work. Remind them to keep going; they don't need check with you after they correct each mistake. Once partnerships finish, set them up to compare their corrections with another partnership.

TEACH TOWARD TOMORROW: Let students know you have flagged some pages in their writing with these sorts of mistakes and encourage them to fix up their own writing.

"Writers, you're spotting these spelling mistakes like champs! I've flagged some pages in your writing that I think you could fix up using the work we did here. Will you and your partner help each other to get started and then keep going with your writing? Remember to be alert if you are sounding out a word and you think you hear one of the tricky sounds. Use the keywords I've written on my whiteboard to help you figure out how to spell that word. I'll come back and look at your writing a little later."

  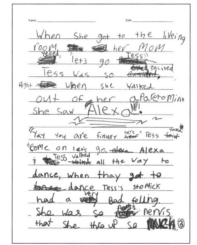

FIG. 35–1 Addison's edited independent writing

OTHER SUPPORTS

▲ **Gr 1, Unit 3, Sess. 3, Ext. 3:** Singing about How the *-ed* Ending Represents Three Different Sounds in Different Words

▲ **Gr 1, Unit 3, Sess. 3, Ext. 1:** Words Ending in *-es* Make Different Sounds, Too!

▲ **Gr 1, Unit 3, Sess. 3, Ext. 2:** Pluralizing Words Using *-s* and *-es* Endings

▲ **Gr 1, Unit 3, Sess. 4, Ext. 1:** Writing Words that End in *Y*

▼ **Gr 1, Unit 3, Sess. 3:** "Investigating Different Sounds that *-ed* Makes in Different Words"

Interactive Editing
Word Endings

BEST TAUGHT TO

- Children who are not writing with endings at all or are using them incorrectly

BEST TAUGHT DURING

- Writing workshop

GETTING READY

✔ Provide a whiteboard and marker for each student.

✔ Print a copy of the piece of writing to be corrected for every partnership.

✔ If you can, flag a page from each child's writing where that child has struggled with endings.

✔ Gather colorful editing pens.

RALLY THEM: Remind children that endings matter in books they read, and those they write, and even in actual words. Point out this is especially true of action words.

"Endings matter. Whenever we read great stories, we can't wait to get to the ending to see what happens, right? And we sometimes talk after we finish a book about how it could have ended differently. We did that with *Jabari Jumps*. You thought about how differently things would have been for Jabari if he hadn't jumped off that diving board.

"You know, endings matter in the stories you write, as well as in the stories you read. And—here is my point for today—they matter in the *words* you write, too.

"Endings on action words show *when* something happened. So, if we use the word *jump*, 'I jumped' means I already did it, but 'I am jumping' means I am doing it right now. See how those endings are so important?"

ACTIVATE PHONICS: Invite children to take turns acting out action words and inviting others to add inflectional endings to these actions.

"Here, I'm giving each of you a whiteboard and a marker? Will each of you take a turn showing us an action—like, you might hop—and everyone else will write that action with as many sensible endings as they can?"

You can expect children to act out words such as *jump*, *skip*, or *walk*. If they need help thinking of words, whisper a few, such as *talk* or *point*. If your students are ready for an added challenge, give them a word such as *sit* with an irregular past tense.

"Great! You worked hard to add endings that make sense, like -*ed*, -*ing*, and -*s*. Some of you knew that for some words, you have to add an extra consonant before the ending. Like for *hop*, you add a *P* to make *hopping* and *hopped*."

CHALLENGE THEM: Distribute to each child a page of student writing that contains errors in endings. Ask partners to edit separate pages and then compare their work.

"Could you and your partner each try to edit Gerty's writing, and when you are done, compare your corrections to see if you agree?"

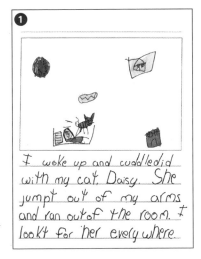

❶ I woke up and cuddledid with my cat, Daisy. She jumpt out of my arms and ran out of the room. I lookt for her every where.

❷ Then I saw her runnin, jumpng and scratching on the coach.

❸ I went into the kitchen and put down some food. She came runngn in and gobbledid it up!

❹ I called out, "Oh now I see. She didn't want to cuddle because she want'd food!"

FIG. 36–1   Gerty's book about her cat

TEACH TOWARD TOMORROW: Debrief, by explaining again, why endings matter. Prompt students to pay attention to endings in their own writing.

"Can I stop you, even if you haven't finished? You've done a great job helping Gerty with her endings. Where else do you suppose you could look to find endings to fix? Yes, in your own writing! I've marked one page of your writing with a Post-it. Take a look. Make changes with your editing pens if you need to fix an ending."

OTHER SUPPORTS

▲ **Gr 1, Unit 3, Sess. 3, Ext. 1:** Singing about How the -*ed* Ending Makes Three Different Sounds in Different Words

▲ **Gr 1, Unit 3, Sess. 2, Ext. 2:** Using What You Know about Words to Predict the Right Endings

▼ **Gr 1, Unit 3, Sess. 2:** "Getting to Know Some Common Endings"

▼ **Gr 1, Unit 3, Sess. 3:** "Investigating Different Sounds that -*ed* Makes in Different Words"

FIG. 36–2   Aaryan and Evan editing for word endings.

If you do not have time to mark students' writing ahead of time, have them check their own writing for endings they need to fix.

Sorting and Reading Words with -*ed* Endings

RALLY THEM AND ACTIVATE PHONICS: Remind students that the -*ed* ending has more than one sound. Have students correct you as you misread words with -*ed* endings.

"Readers, when you were little toddlers you probably said things like 'I jump-id on the trampoline,' or 'I wish-id for a pony.' But then you learned that you should be saying 'I *jumped* on the trampoline,' or 'I *wished* for a pony.'

"One thing that is very tricky about words that end in -*ed* is that the -*ed* can sound like /d/, /t/, or /id/. For words that end with a /t/ or /d/ sound, like *start* or *need*, the -*ed* ending sounds like /id/, and adds an extra syllable, as in *started* or *needed*. Other words with the -*ed* ending like *played* or *looked* have the /d/ or /t/ sound at the end of the word, which does not add an extra syllable.

"Now that you're first-graders, you already know this when you're talking. But, a funny thing happens to some first-graders: they sometimes make mistakes with -*ed* endings when they *read*. They say, 'The girl jump-id over the puddle,' when they know that word should sound like *jumped*!

"Let's warm up your -*ed* ending ear muscles. I will say some -*ed* ending words and I'll pretend that I'm just learning. You'll call out the correct way to say those words. Ready to try?"

Say the following sentences, intentionally adding an extra syllable by mispronouncing the -*ed* endings. Pause so kids can say these words correctly.

"I look-id both ways."

"I stopp-id for ice cream."

"I like-id the red one."

"I sail-id on the ocean."

"I play-id a fun game."

BEST TAUGHT TO

- Students who are mispronouncing the -*ed* ending sound when they are reading

BEST TAUGHT DURING

- Reading workshop

GETTING READY

✔ Prepare a set of word cards for each partnership with the words *looked*, *stopped*, *liked*, *started*, *sailed*, *added*, *played*, and *counted*.

✔ Print a copy of the example story for each partnership.

LAUNCH THEM: Set up students to read and sort a set of *-ed* ending word cards. When they are finished, invite them to check their work.

"Here is a set of cards with *-ed* ending words for each partnership. Practice reading these words together and listen very carefully to what the *-ed* sounds like at the end of each word. Sort the words into two piles based on the sound you hear at the end. Make one pile for words that end with the /d/ or /t/ sound and another pile for words that have another syllable at the end and end in the /id/ sound."

CHALLENGE THEM: Set up kids to read *-ed* words in context and to self-correct if needed. Prompt them to try reading the endings of those words another way to see if that way makes more sense.

"Readers, you are going to come across lots of words that end in *-ed* as you read. It's an ending that gets added on to lots of words, especially action words that say what happened in the past. I *look* at the book now. I *looked* at the book yesterday. I *stop* playing now. I *stopped* playing last night. See how the *-ed* ending tells us the action happened in the past?

"That *-ed* ending is going to come up so much in the books you read. You've got to be ready to try to read the word a few different ways, if the way you read it first doesn't make sense or sound right.

POSSIBLE COACHING MOVES

▶ "First read the word. Listen to the ending."

▶ "Does that make sense and sound right? How do you know?"

▶ "Read through the words in that stack. Do they all end with the same sound?"

▶ "The *-ed* ending in that word sounds like /t/. Look . . . /t/. *Looked*. Okay, say the whole word now."

This explanation does not mean students are meant to master past-tense grammar. Rather, the aim is to illuminate for students the context in which they will come across words with -ed endings while reading and why these words are important.

❶ I walked into the kitchen. Something smelled terrible. I looked at the stove. Nothing was cooking.

❷ I looked in the fridge. It smelled okay.

❸ Then I opened the garbage can. "Yuck!!" I yelled.

❹ I pulled the garbage out. Now, I liked the way the kitchen smelled.

FIG. 37–1 Gerty's story about her smelly kitchen

"Now that your -*ed* ending ear muscles are all warmed up, let's try making sure you are also thinking about what makes sense. I've got a story that my neighbor Gerty wrote, about a time when something smelled bad in her kitchen. I'll give each partnership a copy. With your partner, read these pages out loud, paying extra attention to the words with -*ed* endings. If you read an -*ed* ending word and it doesn't make sense or sound right, try it another way. Partners, listen to one another read each word with an -*ed* ending, and make sure it sounds right."

TEACH TOWARD TOMORROW: Remind students to be alert to -*ed* words when they are reading and to try words another way if they don't sound right or make sense.

"Of course, the really important work is that you try this in your own books. Remember that -*ed* at the end of words can have more than one sound. When you see a word that ends in -*ed*, read the first part of the word and then think about what would make sense and sound right to help you to read the end.

"If it doesn't make sense or sound right, if you hear yourself adding that /-id/ syllable when it should not be there, fix it up by trying to read it the other way, and see if that sounds right."

FIG. 37–2   Kyle and Mason read side by side, monitoring for -*ed* endings.

You might snap a picture of a set of cards, sorted into the two groups according to their sounds, then print this for students to keep in their book baggies.

OTHER SUPPORTS

Replicate: This group can be repeated with another text. You can select a piece of example writing, as shown here, or a favorite text with plenty of -*ed* endings. A selection that works particularly well is from *Frog and Toad Are Friends*, pages 4–7.

▲ **Gr 1, Unit 3, Sess. 3, Ext. 3:** Singing about How the -*ed* Ending Makes Three Different Sounds in Different Words

▼ **Gr 1, Unit 3, Sess. 3:** "Investigating Different Sounds that -*ed* Makes in Different Words"

What's the Rule?
Adding -ing

BEST TAUGHT TO

- Students who need support spelling words with *-ing* endings
- Students who have command of conventional vowel use and are ready for a challenge

BEST TAUGHT DURING

- Reading workshop
- Writing workshop

GETTING READY

✔ Print or make cards with the following words: *putting, clapping, eating, hopping.* ✂ 📦

✔ Prepare a copy of the "What's the Rule?" chart. ✂

✔ Print or make word cards with pairs of base words and words with *-ing* endings added, one set for each partnership and one set for yourself. ✂ 📦

✔ Print word cards with base words and room for students to add an *-ing* ending, two to three cards for each student. ✂ 📦

✔ Ask students to bring their writing folders.

✔ Bring Post-its to mark students' writing.

RALLY THEM: Show students four words and sing the song "One of These Things Is Not Like the Others." Ask students to consider which word does not belong in the group and why.

Sing the song, "One of These Things Is Not Like the Others." You may need to sing it twice—once to remind kids of the lyrics, and again to have them sing along with you.

Show the word cards with *-ing* endings.

Putting	Eating	Clapping	Hopping

"One of these words is not like the others. Can you see which one? If you aren't sure, look at the middle parts of the words.

"I hear some of you saying *eating*. Quickly, tell your partner why that word doesn't belong in this group.

"I agree, all of the other words have double consonants in the middle, but *eating* does not."

LAUNCH THEM: Invite students to sort words based on how they look with the *-ing* ending added.

"You all know that you can take an action word like *hop* or *run* or *jump* and add an ending to it. You can say, 'Yesterday I *hopped*,' or 'Today I am *hopping*.' You can say, 'Yesterday I *jumped*,' or '*Today* I am jumping.' But this can be tricky, because for some words, like *hop*, you have to double the last letter before you add the ending. But for other words, like *jump*, you *don't* have to double the last letter. You can just add *-ing*. And it's tricky to know when to do which, right?

"Now, I could just tell you the rule. But here's the thing—the best way to learn a rule like this is to figure it out and explain the rule yourself. You can do it!

"I'm going to give each of you a set of words. On each card, you'll see a base word, and the word with the -*ing* ending added. Try to sort them into two groups based on how they look with the -*ing* ending added. Think about the work we just did figuring out that *eating* did not belong in the group.

"Make sure you say the pair of words aloud as you work."

WORK SIDE BY SIDE: Ask students to look over the sort and to consider a rule for when words need to have the consonant doubled before the ending.

"Okay, so now you need to do the most important step in sorting, which is to look over the words in one category and figure out why they might all be in that category. You might say something like, 'For words that are like _____, you *usually* double the last letter before you add -*ing*.' I say *usually* because there can be exceptions.

"Here's a tip: notice whether each letter is a vowel (V) or a consonant (C) and see if that helps you.

"Hmm, . . . for the word *hop*, where the letter does get doubled, the base word goes consonant, vowel, consonant. Hmm, . . . is that how the other words in that category go, too? Talk to your partner.

"So maybe we could say that usually for CVC words, you double the last C (consonant) before you add -*ing*. Let's check the words we sorted to see if this rule works.

"Yep, it works for all of the words we put in the double column."

CHALLENGE THEM: Give students some cards with base words written on them and room to add *-ing* endings. Have students write the *-ing* endings and then add the words to the sort.

"I have a stack of base words that need endings. I'll give each of you two or three words. Will you add *-ing* to your words? Think about whether you need to double the last consonant or not. Then, add the word to our sort in the category where it goes."

Give each student a few of the following word cards: *walk*, *tap*, *sort*, *fan*, *get*, *run*, *keep*, *play*.

TEACH TOWARD TOMORROW: Remind students that when they write a word that ends in *-ing*, they can think about today's sort and consider if the word needs a double consonant before the ending.

"The sorting work you did here will help you when you write an *-ing* word. You can think, 'Hmm, . . . does the base word end in CVC or not? If it does, I probably have to double the consonant before adding the *-ing*.'

"I'll snap a picture of our sort and give you a copy, if you think that would be helpful to you. Here's a Post-it. If you check and fix an *-ing* ending in your writing, will you mark that page with the Post-it so later I can see what you tried? Head back to your writing!"

OTHER SUPPORTS

▲ **Gr 1, Unit 3, Sess. 2, Ext. 3:** Adding *-ing* to CVCe Words

▼ **Gr 1, Unit 2, Sess. 12:** "The Case of the Letter Twins: Using Double Consonants to Solve Multisyllabic Words" (Don't teach this until the class encounters this unit—you don't want to spoil the fun!)

POSSIBLE COACHING MOVES

▶ "You're not sure if that word would have its last letter doubled? Check the words that are in the category for doubling the last letter. Is the word like those words? Does it have a CVC pattern?"

▶ "You've written the ending. Where should that word go in our sort?"

▶ "With your partner, read all the words in that category and check that everything belongs."

SMALL GROUP 39

Solving Missing Letters
Inflectional Endings -ing and -ed

RALLY THEM AND ACTIVATE PHONICS: Introduce today's work, then have kids work in partners to add inflectional endings to known words.

"I have a treat for this group today. You get to play a game called 'Solving Missing Letters.' Instead of me doing the covering up like I do when we play other games, you'll get to do it! You'll be covering up and working with endings, so you'll need to use all you know about them.

"To get ready, will you write these three words on your whiteboards: *play*, *look*, *jump*. Now, work with your partner to add the *-ed* and *-ing* endings to these words. For example, next to *play* you can write *played* and *playing*. Get started!"

After each partnership has written the new words, have them check the words on their whiteboard with the other partnership and correct any misspellings.

LAUNCH THEM: Set partnerships up to read a familiar nursery rhyme and then to hide the inflectional endings in that rhyme.

"I am going to give each partnership a different nursery rhyme. These are nursery rhymes you all know well."

Distribute a nursery rhyme and marker to each partnership and show students the "Solving Missing Letters" chart.

"Here's a little chart to help you remember what to do. First, read your nursery rhyme with your partner once all the way through. Next, find all the *-ed* or *-ing* endings and cover

BEST TAUGHT TO
- Children who are not reading or writing the inflectional endings on the ends of words
- Children who are confusing familiar words with inflectional endings

BEST TAUGHT DURING
- Reading workshop
- Writing workshop

GETTING READY

✔ Select two familiar nursery rhymes that contain words with inflectional endings. We chose "The Itsy Bitsy Spider" and "It's Raining, It's Pouring." Place the poems in sheet protectors so that you can reuse them.

✔ Prepare a copy of the "Solving Missing Letters" chart.

✔ Bring a dry erase marker and eraser for each partnership.

makes sense. I've got a story that my neighbor Gerty wrote, about a time when something smelled bad in her kitchen. I'll give each partnership a copy. With your partner, read these pages out loud, paying extra attention to the words with -*ed* endings. If you read an -*ed* ending word and it doesn't make sense or sound right, try it another way. Partners, listen to one another read each word with an -*ed* ending, and make sure it sounds right."

TEACH TOWARD TOMORROW: Remind students to be alert to -*ed* words when they are reading and to try words another way if they don't sound right or make sense.

"Of course, the really important work is that you try this in your own books. Remember that -*ed* at the end of words can have more than one sound. When you see a word that ends in -*ed*, read the first part of the word and then think about what would make sense and sound right to help you to read the end.

"If it doesn't make sense or sound right, if you hear yourself adding that /-id/ syllable when it should not be there, fix it up by trying to read it the other way, and see if that sounds right."

FIG. 39–1 Kids cover missing letters for their partners.

OTHER SUPPORTS

Replicate: This group can be repeated with another text. You can select a piece of example writing, as shown here, or a favorite text with plenty of -*ed* endings. A selection that works particularly well is from *Frog and Toad Are Friends*, pages 4–7.

▲ **Gr 1, Unit 3, Sess. 3, Ext. 3:** Singing about How the -*ed* Ending Makes Three Different Sounds in Different Words

▼ **Gr 1, Unit 3, Sess. 3:** "Investigating Different Sounds that -*ed* Makes in Different Words"

You might snap a picture of a set of cards, sorted into the two groups according to their sounds, then print this for students to keep in their book baggies.

POSSIBLE COACHING MOVES

▶ "Start by reading the whole rhyme with your partner. Listen carefully for what might be missing."

▶ "When you're done, reread the whole thing and see if what you wrote in makes sense."

Apostrophe+*S* Shows Possession

RALLY THEM: Tell students a story about a mix-up that Rasheed had because his lunch was not labeled.

"Friends, Rasheed needs your help. Today he left his lunch in the classroom while we were all out at recess and . . . someone *ate* it! Another teacher had her lunch in the same fridge and took Rasheed's lunch by accident. He was so hungry, poor Rasheed! Why didn't she check whose lunch it was?"

LAUNCH THEM AND WORK SIDE BY SIDE: Explain that the apostrophe has different uses and demonstrate how to use it to show possession. Invite children to help you label Rasheed's lunch.

"Luckily, Rasheed was able to get some lunch from the cafeteria, but he doesn't want someone to accidentally take his lunch again. Do you think we could help him label his lunch to make sure this never happens again?

"There's a special way we write words when we are trying to show that something belongs to someone or something. So, if we want to write that this is Rasheed's lunch and not Mia's lunch or the principal's lunch, we write Rasheed's name and then make a special mark before adding the *S*."

Write Rasheed's name on a Post-it and pause dramatically before explaining the apostrophe.

"This mark is called an apostrophe. I am sure you've seen this mark before when you are reading. It has two jobs: it can be used for a contraction, like when *do* + *not* make *don't*. And, it can be used to show that something belongs to someone. Let's make that apostrophe together."

Gesture for the kids to put their arms in the air and make an apostrophe.

"Start way up high and make a little curve in the air. Remember to stay up high the whole time. Okay, now we're ready to make this label for Rasheed's lunch. Let's read this word: *Rasheed*!

"Now let's add apostrophe *S*. Put that apostrophe up high, and now add an *S*!"

BEST TAUGHT TO

- Students who need support spelling words with apostrophe+*S* to show possession
- Students who are confusing the use of the apostrophe when they are reading

BEST TAUGHT DURING

- Reading workshop
- Writing workshop

GETTING READY

✔ Gather Post-its and markers for yourself and each student.

✔ Make sure each student has his or her writing folder.

Add the apostrophe *s* to Rasheed's name on the Post-it and ask students to read it with you: "Rasheed's." Add the next word and invite the kids to read the whole label with you: "Rasheed's lunch."

"What would it look like if you were going to label *your* lunch? Write it in the air quickly.

"Now look at your writing folder. It's labeled with your name. Take a marker and change it to show that it's yours by adding an apostrophe *s* to your name."

CHALLENGE THEM: Invite students to find things around the classroom that belong to someone and label them with an apostrophe *s*.

"I bet there are all kinds of other things we could label with the apostrophe *s* to show they belong to someone or something, like Fernando's mittens or Oscar's chair or Black Panther's suit!

"Here are a bunch of Post-its for each of you. Will you go around the room and label things that belong to someone?"

Send the children off to label things in the room. After students have labeled a few things, gather them back together.

TEACH TOWARD TOMORROW: Restate the teaching of the day and encourage them to be on the lookout for the apostrophe+*S* in their own reading and writing.

"Great job labeling things with the apostrophe *s*. I bet we will have fewer mix-ups in our classroom now! Remember, an apostrophe can do two things—it can make a contraction, and it can be used to show that something belongs to someone."

This concept is not taught in the phonics units of study because we know most kids pick it up on their own through repeated exposure in independent reading. However, some children may need this direct small-group instruction to highlight the meaning behind apostrophe+S.

FIG. 40–1   Joanne with her labeled water bottle.

Long-Vowel Teams, Diphthongs, and R-Controlled Vowels

CHAPTER 6

Try It Many Ways

Spelling with Long Vowels

BEST TAUGHT TO

- Students who are confusing commonly used long-vowel patterns when spelling unknown words

BEST TAUGHT DURING

- Writing workshop
- Intervention time

GETTING READY

✔ Prepare picture cards that feature words with both CVCe and CVVC patterns, like *cake, rain, face, rope, coat, sheep,* and *leaf*.

✔ Bring a vowel team chart.

✔ Print the "Try It Many Ways" chart.

✔ Bring whiteboards, markers, and erasers for yourself and for each partnership.

✔ Ask students to bring their writing folders to the group. You might bring special colored editing pens as well.

RALLY THEM: Remind students of a familiar reading strategy, "Try it a few ways," then suggest they can do this to spell words with long vowels.

"You already know that when you are reading, and you are trying to figure out the vowel sounds in a tricky word, it helps to try the vowels two ways, checking for the right sound. Well, I want to remind you that when you *write* a tricky word, it also helps to try it two ways, checking that you've got the vowels right. Remember, when you need to spell a word with a long vowel, you'll either need to add a silent *E*, as in *make*, or you'll need to write a vowel team, like in *rain*.

"The trick is to make sure your words look right. Imagine sticking a zebra's head on a kangaroo's body! It just wouldn't look right. The same is true for words. Think about all the times you've read the word *rain*, for example, like in the nursery rhyme 'Rain, rain, go away.' It would look wrong if you put a silent *E* instead of the vowel team *AI* and wrote *rane*."

Jot *rane* on your whiteboard, then quickly cross it out.

"When you are spelling, you need to always be asking, 'Does that look right?' and thinking about other times you may have seen that word."

ACTIVATE PHONICS: Quickly study several picture cards, helping children isolate and name the long vowel in each word.

"I will give you each a few picture cards. Say aloud the word for each picture and listen for the vowel sound with your partner. You'll be able to do this pretty quickly because each of these words has a *long* sound, and you'll hear that vowel's name shine through."

Pass out the picture cards, including words that feature both CVCe and CVVC patterns, like *cake, rain, face, rope, coat, sheep,* and *leaf*. Listen while partners say the words and listen for vowel sounds.

"What vowel sound do you hear in the word *rope*? Say it slowly and listen: *roooooooope*. I hear the long *O*, too. One way to write long *O* is with a silent *E*, and another way is with the vowel team *OA*."

LAUNCH THEM AND WORK SIDE BY SIDE: Demonstrate spelling a word using both a CVCe and CVVC pattern, before deciding which version of the word looks right.

"Now, let's label a few of these picture cards to practice spelling words with long-vowel sounds. Then, let's check to make sure the pattern we use looks right."

Hold up the cake picture card.

"*Cake* . . . I hear /ā/ as in *make*. What can you do to spell that long *A* sound? Yes, that's right, you can try a vowel team. Which vowel team can represent a long *A* sound?"

Wait for students to offer their ideas, then continue. "Right, some of you said the vowel team *ai* makes the long *A* sound."

Write *caik* on your whiteboard.

"Hmm, . . . does that look right? Why don't you try it another way? This time, use a silent *E* instead."

Write *cake* on your whiteboard.

"Which one looks right? Have you ever read this word before?"

Pause so students can mull this over, then continue. "Yep, the second one—C-A-K-E—I agree! *Cake* looks right with this pattern, using silent *E*."

Erase your whiteboard, and repeat these steps using a word with a long *A* that is spelled with a vowel team, like *rain*.

CHALLENGE THEM: Invite students to continue spelling words using long-vowel patterns in partnerships.

Spread out the picture cards in front of the group, and hand a whiteboard and marker to each partnership.

"Right now, will you and a partner work side by side to spell some of these other words? Remember to try to write it on your whiteboard a few ways, using the patterns you know. Then, decide which word looks right. Circle the word that looks right and cross out the word that doesn't."

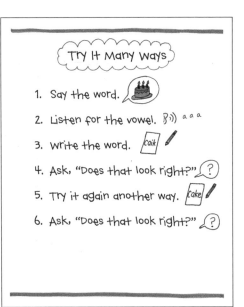

Try It Many Ways

1. Say the word.
2. Listen for the vowel. ᵃ ᵃ ᵃ
3. Write the word. caik
4. Ask, "Does that look right?" ?
5. Try it again another way. cake
6. Ask, "Does that look right?" ?

Of course, your students may not yet have a sense for what looks correct. Even if your students think that caik looks right, encourage them to try it another way. They may get it right, they may not, but the purpose of this small group is to give students another strategy to draw upon. If students cannot decide whether caik or cake looks right, you might also encourage them to think about the snap words they know that rhyme with the word they're trying to spell. The snap word make might help them figure out the right way to spell the word cake.

POSSIBLE COACHING MOVES

▶ "Listen for the vowel you hear in the word. Add silent *E* at the end to make that vowel long."

▶ "What vowel teams make that long-vowel sound? Try one in the middle of that word. Then, check if it looks right."

▶ "Long *E* is sometimes made with *EE* and other times with *EA*. Try it both ways and decide which way looks the way it would in a book."

TEACH TOWARD TOMORROW: Set students up to apply this work to their own writing, editing words with long vowels.

"Now, take out your writing and reread, listening closely for words with long-vowel sounds. When you hear one, stop and check the word. Ask, 'Does it look right?' If it doesn't, try the word with a silent *E* or with a vowel team on your whiteboard. Then, if you need to, fix up your writing with your editing pen."

If children need more support locating their mistakes, you might flag a page of their writing that has mistakes with long vowels.

  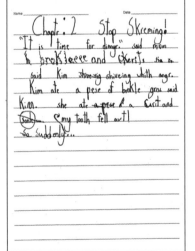

FIG. 41–3   Talia's edited book, *Tooth Trouble*

OTHER SUPPORTS

Replicate: If students need more support with specific long-vowel patterns, you can follow this same routine for one long-vowel sound at a time.

▼ **Gr K, Unit 4, Sess. 3:** "Isolating the Short-Vowel Sound in the Middle of Words (-VC)" (focus on *A*/*I*)

▼ **Gr K, Unit 4, Sess. 7:** "Distinguishing Short *E*, *O*, and *I* Sounds in Words"

▼ **Gr 1, Unit 2, Sess. 2:** "Word Detectives Look Closely to Find Patterns in Words: Sorting Long and Short Vowels"

▼ **Gr 1, Unit 2, Sess. 9:** "Investigating Words with a Long *E* Sound: An Introduction to Vowel Teams"

▲ **Gr 1, Unit 2, Sess. 4:** "Word Detectives Practice Their New Skills: Making Words with Phonograms" (Make CVCe words with the vowel *A* and use phonogram patterns to sort the words.)

▲ **Gr 1, Unit 4, Sess. 3:** "Digging Up Discoveries about Vowel Teams: An Inquiry" (introduces other vowel teams such as *AI*)

FIG. 41–1   Emma supports students to activate phonics.

FIG. 41–2   Children spell each word a few different ways and decide which one looks right.

Spelling with Diphthongs
ow and *ou*

BEST TAUGHT TO

- Students who need support with recognizing the sound of diphthongs in the words they want to write and recording them with accuracy

BEST TAUGHT DURING

- Writing workshop

GETTING READY

✔ Gather word cards for the sort. For the *ow* and *ou* diphthongs, you'll need *cow, cloud, brown, found, growl, shout, crowd, couch, crown, pouch, how,* and *mouth.*

✔ Print a copy of the two-column charts for each partnership and one for yourself.

✔ Prepare picture cards with pictures of words that have the *ow/ou* diphthong.

✔ If you have time, flag student work that needs editing for the *ow/ou* diphthong spelling pattern.

RALLY THEM AND ACTIVATE PHONICS: Remind students that diphthong sounds can be made in different ways. Warm up by reading and sorting words where the /ou/ sound is spelled in different ways and quickly sort ten /ou/ sound words.

"Writers, I know you are working on getting stronger at using vowel teams in your writing, and I have a very important reminder. Remember that one tricky thing about using vowel teams is that the vowel team sound can be spelled in more than one way. Let's warm up by reading two words containing vowel teams in which the same sound is spelled differently." Read the two words in the headers of the two-column chart.

cow	cloud

Provide each partnership with a two-column chart and a set of picture cards of words that have the *ow/ou* diphthong.

"Whoa! Do you notice the different ways to spell the /ou/ vowel team sound! Here are some more words with the /ou/ sound. Will you work with your partner to quickly sort these word cards? Put each card in the column that matches the spelling of the /ou/ vowel team sound."

LAUNCH THEM AND WORK SIDE BY SIDE: Show students that to spell a word with a diphthong sound, they might need to try the word a few ways. Set them up to practice spelling a few /ou/ diphthong words.

"When you want to spell a word and you hear the sound a vowel team makes in that word, you might need to try it a few ways, using what you know about different ways to spell the sound of that vowel team. Then you can think about how you might have seen the word spelled and see which way looks right." Remove the sort cards from the two-column chart and set them aside.

"Let's practice spelling a few words with the /ou/ sound together. Let's start with the word *frown*. What sounds are at the beginning? Yes, I hear the /fr/ too. What sound is at the end? That's right, an *N*, but now I have to think about the sound of that vowel team in the middle."

Stretch out the word *frown* so that children can hear the /ou/ diphthong.

"There are two ways that part of *frown* could be spelled."

Record each possible spelling in the corresponding column on your copy of the chart.

"We could spell the /ou/ sound of the vowel team using *ow* as in *cow*: *frown*.

"We could spell the /ou/ sound of the vowel team using *ou* as in *cloud*: *froun*.

"Now we need to think . . . which way looks right? Hmm, . . . are you thinking the first way? Yes? Have some of you seen that word *frown* before?"

Draw a star next to the correct spelling and cross out the incorrectly spelled word.

"You try one. How about the word *count*? With your partners, could you try spelling that word two ways?" Record what students say under each column. "Now let's check, which one looks right? Yes, *count*!" Again, draw a star next to the correct spelling and cross out the incorrectly spelled word.

CHALLENGE THEM: Set partners up to look at pictures of diphthong /ou/ words and spell and write the words on their charts. Push them to try different ways of spelling the word and choose the way that looks right.

"I have pictures of other words that contain an /ou/ vowel team sound. Will you try spelling the words containing the /ou/ vowel team in the pictures? You can try them each way and see which looks right, writing each attempt on your dry erase board, or you might just know the right way and be able to write it once. Try working on your own for a few minutes, then you can share."

Distribute the /ou/ diphthong pictures to each student and invite them to begin writing the words on their dry erase boards.

FIG. 42–1   Mark and Cate sort words with diphthongs.

TEACH TOWARD TOMORROW: Remind students that whenever they want to spell a word with a diphthong sound, that sound can be made in different ways, so they might need to try spelling the word different ways to see which way looks right.

"Of course, the really important thing is that you try this work in your own writing. I've tagged a few pages where I think this work can especially help you. Work with a partner and put one writing piece at a time between you. Then read over a tagged page and listen for words that have the /ou/ vowel team sound or any vowel team sound that you might need to fix. Try writing it a few different ways on your board and then decide which looks right. When you're done with that page, go back to your seats and try this work in other parts of your writing on your own."

OTHER SUPPORTS

Replicate: If students need support with other diphthongs, you can follow these same steps using different word and picture cards. We have provided word and picture lists for *oil* and *oy* as well as *aw*, *au*, and *al* in the online resources. ✳ 📦

▼ **Gr 1, Unit 4, Sess. 3:** "Digging Up Discoveries about Vowel Teams: An Inquiry"

▼ **Gr 1, Unit 4, Sess. 6, Ext. 1:** Creating Individualized Linking Charts for Vowel Teams

▲ **Gr 1, Unit 4, Sess. 8:** "Using *OU* and *OW* to Learn New Snap Words"

▲ **Gr 1, Unit 4, Sess. 9, Ext. 2:** Reminding Readers to Watch Out for Vowel Teams *OU* and *OW* in Reading Workshop

---

POSSIBLE COACHING MOVES

▶ "Say the word slowly. Do you hear the sound of a vowel team in that word? Which one?"

▶ "What are ways you know to make that vowel team sound? Try out spelling the word using some of those ways."

▶ "What are three ways you could spell that word? Circle the one that looks right to you."

▶ "Even if you think you already know which one is the best way to spell it, try both ways to be sure."

Solving Words with the Vowel *E*

RALLY THEM AND ACTIVATE PHONICS: Remind readers that it's important to be flexible problem solvers. Guide children to read a set of words, some with short- and some with long-vowel sounds.

"Readers, tell me something. If you are in a minilesson and I say, 'Turn and talk,' but your partner is absent that day, do you just sit quietly?

"No, you solve the problem: you might join another partnership, or you might find someone else whose partner is absent, or you might work with a teacher. Problem solving is important everywhere in life, in reading too. When you get to a problem word, what do you do?

"Yes, you try to solve it, maybe by trying the word another way, maybe trying different vowel sounds—because you know vowels have more than one sound."

Distribute a stack of cards with words containing a short *E* or a long *E* sound to each partnership.

"I've given you and your partner a stack of words. They are all words with *E* in them, but in some words, it makes the long *E* sound, like in *seat*. In others, it makes the short *E* sound, like in *bed*. It also sometimes makes some other sounds that aren't really long or short. Tricky, right?

"Will you whisper-read the words together? You'll probably end up reading some of these a couple of times, trying them one way and then another way."

POSSIBLE COACHING MOVES

▶ "Don't forget, readers have to be problem solvers. If the word doesn't sound right, try the vowel sound another way."

▶ "Use what you know about vowel teams to help you. You don't have to sound out each letter."

▶ "Try both a long- and a short-vowel sound to go with that vowel team."

BEST TAUGHT TO

• Students who need support with reading short and long *E* vowel sounds

BEST TAUGHT DURING

• Reading workshop

GETTING READY

✔ For each partnership, prepare a set of index cards of words with the short and long *E* vowel sound. We use the following: *feather*, *wheel*, *forget*, *bread*, *beast*, *beak*, *get*, and *feel*.

✔ For each partnership, make a copy of a short text, such as a poem, for shared reading that includes many words with long *E*. We use the poem "Recess Race" by Christine Holley.

✔ Ask children to bring their book baggies to the group.

LAUNCH THEM: Channel students to read an unfamiliar poem in partnerships, trying words (especially those with *E* vowels) one way and then another when they need to do so.

"If you aren't sure which way to read a word, the meaning in the text often helps. Now, with your partner, read this poem, 'Recess Race' by Christine Holley. It's about some kids playing at recess, just like you do. If you come to words that sound wrong or don't make sense, try a different vowel sound."

> ## POSSIBLE COACHING MOVES
>
> ▶ "Try the vowel sound another way. Is it long or short?"
>
> ▶ "Go back to reread. Think about what's going on, then get your mouth ready for the vowel sounds."
>
> ▶ "When you are stuck, think, 'Let me reread and get the story in my mind.'"
>
> ▶ "Reread and check—does that make sense? Does it look right? Does it sound right?"

Give children a few minutes to attempt to read the poem. Then, lead them in reading it again, all together, letting your voice drop off when you get to words with *E* vowel sounds.

TEACH TOWARD TOMORROW: Reinforce that when reading, it's important for students to be flexible problem solvers, trying words another way if something is not right.

"Readers, when you can't read a word, try reading the vowel another way, then another way. Stay right here, pull out your book baggies, and keep reading."

Expect that the words will cause some difficulties, and hope above all that the child tries the word one way, then another way. You are not looking for perfection but for readers who are willing to be flexible and to try. If you are going to praise, be sure to praise the child's flexibility more than correctness.

Recess Race

By Christine Holley

Who's on my team?
Meet me on the yard.
Move your feet fast.
Run! Run! Run!
I can feel the sweat.
We can defeat them.
Recess is the best!

It is tempting in a shared reading to just read the text to the kids. Remember, don't do all the work for them. Let them problem solve together.

OTHER SUPPORTS

Replicate: If children need more support transferring long- and short-vowel work into their independent reading, consider replicating this group for other long-vowel patterns. In the online resources and the Resource Pack, you will find poems that focus on:

- long *A:* "Fish Cake"
- long *I:* "Sky Bird"
- long *O:* "Don't Forget"
- long *U:* "Ruby the Mule"

We have also included the word cards to use during the Activate Phonics portion of your replicated session.

▼ **Gr 1, Unit 2, Sess. 1:** "Word Detectives Investigate Tricky Words" (introduces silent *E*)

▼ **Gr 1, Unit 2, Sess. 1, Share:** To Figure Out a Mystery Word, Word Detectives Try a Vowel Two Ways

▼ **Gr 1, Unit 2, Sess. 2:** "Word Detectives Look Closely to Find Patterns in Words: Sorting Long and Short Vowels"

▼ **Gr 1, Unit 2, Sess. 9:** "Investigating Words with a Long *E* Sound: An Introduction to Vowel Teams"

Reading Words with *R*-Controlled Vowels

BEST TAUGHT TO

- Children who have already been exposed to the concept of *R*-controlled vowels and need more practice reading them

BEST TAUGHT DURING

- Reading workshop

GETTING READY

✔ Print a copy of the poem "Stars" for each child and one for yourself.

✔ Gather the *R*-controlled vowel picture-word cards *star*, *bird*, *dark*, and *turn*.

✔ Gather pencils and Post-its for each child.

RALLY THEM: Invite children to be your teachers, explaining that teachers must figure out *how* to help to be most effective.

"Readers, I thought today we'd do something a little different. I thought that, I'd be the six-year-old kid who needs help with reading and spelling, and you can be my teacher.

"But here's the thing. You may not realize it, but teachers need to decide which kinds of things will be useful to teach about reading."

SIDE BY SIDE: Read a text aloud, incorrectly pronouncing the words with *R*-controlled vowels and channeling students to think of how to help you improve.

Give each child a copy of the poem "Stars" and a pencil.

"I'll read. Remember, you're the teacher, and I'm the kid who needs your help. As I'm reading, watch what I do and don't do, and think about how to help me improve my reading."

Pick up the text and read it aloud. When you get to a word that has an *R*-controlled vowel pattern, read it slowly, part by part, like your students might do when they attempt unknown words. Include miscues by using the short-vowel sound for medial vowels rather than the correct *R*-controlled vowel sound:

Stars

There are stars
in the sky.

The birds
turn and fly
in the dark
night sky.

There are stars	/st/-/ă/-/rs/
in the sky.	
The birds	/b/-/ĭ/-/rds/
turn and fly	/t/-/ŭ/-/rn/
in the dark	/d/-/ă/-/rk/
night sky.	

FIG. 44–1 A child begins her sort after reading the poem.

LAUNCH THEM AND WORK SIDE BY SIDE: Encourage students to discuss the errors you made. Then, remind students about *R*-controlled vowels, channel them to read some picture-word cards, and recruit them to read the poem to their partners.

Play the role of a young reader and ask, "Teachers, how was that?" Then ask students to talk with partners about what they noticed. Students may say that you said the words wrong or you said the short-vowel sound when you weren't supposed to.

"It's sounding like I have trouble with words that contain vowels and an *R*, am I right? These are mess-ups that *lots* of kids make. My six-year-old self isn't the only one—a lot of you do, too! Let's make sure you know about *R*-controlled vowels."

Show the kids some picture-word cards (*star*, *bird*, *dark*, *turn*) that have the *R*-controlled vowel underlined.

"Here are some of those words that I mess up *all* the time. Try reading these words. When you see the *R* after the vowel, heads up, that's an *R*-controlled vowel, which means you should probably try it a few different ways to figure out what sounds right." Have each child read each word.

"Now try reading the poem to your partner. Take turns, so each of you gets a chance to be the reader and the listener. If you're the listener, and you hear that your reader partner needs to try a word with an *R*-controlled vowel again a different way, hold up a sideways thumb to signal your partner to reread the word. Okay, go!"

CHALLENGE THEM: Challenge students to generate other words containing *R*-controlled vowels and to sort them according to their sounds.

"Can you come up with other words I should practice with?"

Place the *star*, *bird*, and *turn* picture-word cards in the center of the group. Then distribute Post-its to each student.

"These three words will be keywords. Think of some other words that are like each of these keywords and write each word on a different Post-it."

As students generate additional words, coach them to place their words in a column beneath the keyword that has the same spelling pattern as their new word.

OTHER SUPPORTS

▼ **Gr 1, Unit 5, Sess. 2:** "Investigating *-ar*, *-er*, and *-or*"

▼ **Gr 1, Unit 5, Sess. 5, Ext. 1:** The Many Sounds of *-ear*

▼ **Gr 1, Unit 5, Sess. 6:** "Learning Many Spelling Patterns for the /air/ Sound"

POSSIBLE COACHING MOVES

▶ "Remember to try reading the word a few different ways and listen for which one sounds right."

▶ "One word goes on each Post-it. Do a quick drawing to help people know what word that is."

▶ "If you are stuck, look at the words we already have. Choose one and think of words that rhyme with it. So, let's take *star*. What else rhymes with *star*? *Car*, *bar* . . . Hmm, . . . those words would be good ones for me to practice, too. Pick another keyword and try thinking of words that rhyme with it."

Writing Words with *R*-Controlled Vowels

RALLY THEM AND ACTIVATE PHONICS: Give students a quick quiz to determine what they know about writing words with *R*-controlled vowels. Note which students need specific support.

"Let's warm up your writing muscles! I'm going to read a few words, and will you write them on your whiteboard?

"Star. Dirt. Butter."

Note which students write the *R*-controlled vowels accurately, which choose the wrong vowel, and which omit the vowel entirely.

BEST TAUGHT TO

- Children who omit *R*-controlled vowels (*frst* instead of *first*)
- Children who substitute the incorrect vowel when writing words with *R*-controlled vowels (*berd* instead of *bird*)
- Children who have already been taught Bend I of Grade 1 Unit 5, *Marvelous Bloopers: Learning through Wise Mistakes*

BEST TAUGHT DURING

- Writing workshop

GETTING READY

✔ Gather whiteboards, dry erase markers, and erasers for each student and for yourself.

✔ Print the *butter* word card.

✔ Make a set of *R*-controlled vowel word cards for each partnership, including *car*, *dare*, *barn*, *part*, *scare*, *her*, *were*, *fern*, *cheer*, *skirt*, *bird*, *fire*, and *tire*.

✔ Ask students to bring their writing folders and pens.

LAUNCH THEM: Remind students of what they know about writing words with _R_-controlled vowels.

Show the correct version of the words on a whiteboard.

"Here's _star_, _dirt_, and _butter_. These words all have those bossy _R_'s. Remember how you learned that the letter _R_ is so bossy that word scientists—linguists—call the vowels near it '_R_-controlled vowels'? That's because the _R_ is easy to hear, and it's hard to hear the vowel.

"I noticed that when you write words with these bossy _R_'s, sometimes you leave out the vowel entirely! You'll go to write _dirt_—_d-i-r-t_—and you'll write _d-r-t_ instead. Or, you'll write the wrong vowel because it's so hard to hear—like if you wrote _d-e-r-t_ by mistake.

"Even when the _R_ is bossy, you still have to remember to include a vowel in every syllable. You might also need to try out a few different vowels until you get the word right."

WORK SIDE BY SIDE: Distribute a stack of word cards to each partnership, and coach them as they take turns reading and writing the words.

"Ready to try this? I'm giving you and your partner a stack of words. Partner 1, you'll read first. Pick up a word card and read it to your partner without showing it. Partner 2, write the word on your whiteboard. Then, check the word. If your partner forgets something, give a tip. You might say, 'Do you have a vowel?' or 'I don't think that looks right, could we try another way?' After you try one word, switch roles."

TEACH TOWARD TOMORROW: Channel students to edit their writing for words with _R_-controlled vowels. Set them up to write words with _R_-controlled vowels accurately as they go.

"Writers, let's go back into your writing. Before you do anything else, will you reread your writing and be on the lookout for places where you wrote words with that strong, controlling _R_? Make sure all those syllables include at least one vowel and try out other vowels if the word doesn't look right. Then, keep writing. Take your time when you get to a word with a bossy _R_, so you can make sure it's right. Off you go!"

OTHER SUPPORTS

▼ **Gr 1, Unit 5, Sess. 2, Ext. 1:** Helping Rasheed Fix His Bloopers

▼ **Gr 1, Unit 5, Sess. 2, Ext. 2:** Helping Rasheed Get the Vowel Right

▼ **Gr 1, Unit 5, Sess. 2, Ext. 3:** "Mind Reader" Game

▲ **Gr 1, Unit 5, Sess. 1, Ext. 1:** Support Transfer to Writing Workshop

---

POSSIBLE COACHING MOVES

▶ "Check that word. Does it have a vowel?"

▶ "Try that word again with another vowel."

▶ "It's hard to hear that vowel because the _R_ is so controlling. Say the word again, slowly, to see if you can hear it."

▶ "There's a blend/digraph at the beginning of that word. What other letter(s) make that sound?"

FIG. 45–1   Children reread and edit their writing after practicing a few words with partners.

Learning Words in a Snap

BEST TAUGHT TO

- Children who are unable to identify previously taught high-frequency words (in context or in isolation)

BEST TAUGHT DURING

- Writing workshop
- Reading workshop
- Intervention time

GETTING READY

✔ Select one snap word that students are struggling to read or write, and write it on an index card. For this lesson we have chosen the word *the*.

✔ Choose a page from any book that contains many instances of the snap word.

✔ Print the "How to Learn a Word" chart.

✔ Distribute a whiteboard and marker to each student.

✔ Ask children to bring their book baggies and writing folders to the group.

✔ Bring Post-it notes and pens for each student.

RALLY THEM: Explain to students how important it will be for them to own the word *the*.

"I brought you all over here to give you some more practice with a very special snap word. I've chosen a word that you will really want to own because you will see it in tons of books, and you will definitely use it all the time in your writing."

Hold up the card with the word *the* written on it. "This is the word *the*. *The* is such an important word to know. Researchers have studied all the words in the English language and do you know what they found? The word *the* is used more than any other word!"

Show a page of a book with many instances of the word *the*. "Look! Just on this page, the word *the* is here about a zillion times! Whoa, that is one powerful word. So, we definitely want to make *the* a word you know by heart."

LAUNCH THEM: Coach students through the process to learn a new word.

"I know you have studied this word before, but it's not quite a snap word for you yet. So today let's make *sure* it becomes a snap word for you. Let's go through the steps for learning a word on our 'How to Learn a Word' chart, but this time let's make sure you really pay extra attention during the spell-it stage."

"First, *read* it: *the*. Read it with me: *the*. I swam in *the* pool. Now will you *study* it? Remember, pay extra attention. What are you noticing about the word *the*? Tell your partner three things you notice.

"Great! I heard some of you say that it has three letters. Others noticed two of the letters are tall, and one is small. Time to *spell* it: *t-h-e*. Everyone together: *t-h-e*. Use your squeaky mouse voices now: *t-h-e*. Use the magnetic letters and make the word *the*.

"Take your finger and try to *write* it on the rug. Let's say the pathway for each letter together: Letter *t*. Line down, little line across. Letter *h*. Long line down, back up a bit, and bump around and down. Letter *e*. Little line out, bump back around and stop."

CHALLENGE THEM: Cover the word, and then ask students to try writing it. Invite them to check their words against the word card, then look for the word in books and writing.

"Here's a challenge. I'm going to cover the word card. Would you write *the* on your whiteboards, without looking?"

Give students a moment to do this. "Now, I'll uncover the word card. Check your word against the word *the* on the card. Does yours look the same? If not, try to figure out what is different. Then, cross it out and write it again. Write it as many times as you can!

"Remember how I told you that the word *the* is the most frequently used word in books? Well, let's put it to the test. This partnership, will you go on a snap word hunt? Take out the books in your baggies and I'll give you a Post-it note and a pen. Make a tally mark each time you find the word *the*.

"And this partnership, take out your writing folders. Try and find the word *the* in your writing."

FIG. 46–2 A teacher leads kids through the "make it a snap word" routine.

FIG. 46–3 Students practice learning the word *some*.

Snap Words

Prompts for Students		Big Thinking
• "Write that helpful sentence on the back of your word card." [Karate is fun]	**Read it.**	• Put it in sentences that are personally meaningful to the child, (e.g., "Karate is fun.")
• "Say the word, say the parts."	**Study it.**	• Graphophonemic analysis to study. was /w/ /ǝ/ /z/
• "Spell the word. (th-e) (th-e)."	**Spell it.**	• "Aural" memory can aid in learning, prompt kids to spell with a rhythm.
• "You know that word. It's a snap word. Try writing it on the desk. Do you know it now?" [write it bigger, write it faster, write it lots of times]	**Cover, write, check it.**	• Muscle memory aids learning, have kids write lots of ways. • "Coach between attempts and correct version, "This is your try. What do you notice about the difference?"
• "You know play, what word could that be?" • "Is there a snap word that could help you spell that word? Use the word wall!"	**Use it.**	• Use words to make and read other words. • Use in oral language (I use). Sentence frame. You use.) • Use in writing – teacher-made dictation with words, read in our made sentences.

FIG. 46–1 Teacher chart with prompts. This chart is for your instruction, to prompt children as they move through the snap word routine.

If children do not have many instances of the word the *in their writing, coach them to add the word. You might say, "Maybe you already have a label that says* swings. *You can write* the *before it, and then it will say* the swings. *Try it out now."*

TEACH TOWARD TOMORROW: Remind students that if they ever forget how to spell the word, they can find it up on the word wall.

"Now you have this snap word in your back pocket! Keep a lookout for this word in your books and make sure you are spelling it correctly in your writing. If you ever forget how to write the word *the*, just look up on the word wall under the letter *T*. Do you see it? Go point to it on the word wall as you walk back to your table."

OTHER SUPPORTS

Replicate: Use this same routine to teach other high-frequency words, starting with the earliest ones, such as *I* and *like*.

▲ **Gr K, Unit 2, Sess. 10, Ext. 2:** Snap Word "Simon Says"

▲ **Gr K, Unit 2, Sess. 14, Ext. 1:** "Guess My Rule"

Building Sentences with Snap Words

RALLY THEM AND ACTIVATE HIGH-FREQUENCY WORDS: Channel kids to read their snap word collections, noticing which words they read fluently and which they are still unsure of.

"You all are starting to really know your snap words! That means you can read and write them in a snap."

Distribute a set of high-frequency cards to each partnership. "I have a set of snap words for you two, and another set for you two. Would you read them together now?"

LAUNCH THEM AND WORK SIDE BY SIDE: Channel students to build sentences using the snap word cards and some small toys.

"Now that you know so many snap words, we can use them to make sentences! Spread all your words out in front of you. We're going to make some sentences that go together, that are all about one thing, so they can go into a book. How about a book about toys?"

Set a small toy (or picture card) within each partnership's array of high-frequency words. Use one partnership's set of words and toy to model a quick example.

"Watch me so you can see how this might go. I could start with the word *I*. I . . . what? How about *see*? Now, this toy train could come next. *I see train*. No wait, we need one more word. I'll add the word *a* before the train, and I have a sentence: *I see a train*.

FIG. 47–1 Tommy points and reads the sentence he built.

BEST TAUGHT TO

- Children who are still working on one-to-one correspondence
- Children who are not yet recognizing or using previously taught high-frequency words
- Children who could benefit from more practice with pattern recognition and syntax clues

BEST TAUGHT DURING

- Reading workshop
- Writing workshop

GETTING READY

- ✔ Prepare a set of familiar high-frequency word cards, one for each partnership. If the students are in early stages of reading development, we suggest words such as *I*, *me*, *like*, *the*, *a*, *look*, *at*, *see*, *this*, *is*, *here*.
- ✔ Have ready the "How to Learn Word" chart.
- ✔ Gather some small toys or picture cards.
- ✔ Bring some blank word cards and pens.

"Now it's your turn! Think about how you could use your snap words and the toy I've given you to make a sentence."

Some possible sentence starters:

- I like . . .
- Look at the . . .
- I like the . . .
- I see the/an/a . . .
- This is the/an/a . . .
- Here is the/an/a . . .
- It is the/an/a . . .
- Is it the/an/a . . .
- It is in the . . .
- Is it in the . . .
- I see a ___ in the . . .

"Let's read our sentences together. Remember to point under the words as you read."

How to learn a word

1. Read it!
2. Study it!
3. Spell it!
4. Write it!
5. Use it!

Take this time to note which words students are reading fluently and which words they are still unsure of. If the whole group needs more practice with a specific word or two, quickly take them through the steps on the "How to Learn a Word" chart. If only one child needs help with a word, keep that child working with this group and then plan to meet with that child individually to learn the word at a later time.

Be sure to find some way to record the sentences that students build, so that you can turn them into a book. You might, for example, snap a picture of each sentence and then print these images, turning them into a book for students' book baggies.

POSSIBLE COACHING MOVES

▶ "I see you're not sure where to start. What if you started with the word *look* or *here*?"

▶ "Read your sentence so far. What could come next?"

▶ "Point under each card as you read your sentence."

▶ "There are some words that seem to go together. If you use the word *it*, you might need the word *is* next for your sentence to make sense."

▶ "Read your sentence together. Does it make sense? What might you need to add (or take away)?"

CHALLENGE THEM: Invite students to make more sentences, this time with more independence. Encourage them to use invented spelling to add words to their sentences.

"Mix up your words again and let's try some more sentences. This time, you don't need to use the toy. You can make up sentences about anything. Choose a word to start with, then choose the words to follow. If you want to use a word in your sentence that isn't in your word cards, you can write the word you need. I have some blank cards for you to use.

"I'll leave you here to keep making sentences. Think about what you want to say and build your sentences. Don't forget to reread each one to your partner."

OTHER SUPPORTS

Replicate: You can replicate this group as you teach new high-frequency words. Add new words to children's word pouches and invite them to try this exercise so that they get practice reading and using the new words in the context of a sentence.

▼ **Small Group 46:** "Learning Words in a Snap"

▼ **Gr K, Unit 1, Sess. 16, Ext. 1:** Building Sentences

▼ **Gr K, Unit 1, Sess. 16, Ext. 2:** Making a New Book for the Classroom Library

▲ **Gr K, Unit 2, Sess. 6, Ext. 2:** Making a Class *R* Book

If time allows, you may choose to challenge students with this additional task. You may also decide to do this work as a quick follow-up on another day.

Using Snap Words to Make Books

BEST TAUGHT TO

- Children who are not yet recognizing or using previously taught high-frequency words when writing or reading
- Children who could benefit from more practice with syntax clues

BEST TAUGHT DURING

- Reading workshop
- Intervention time

GETTING READY

✔ Prepare a set of high-frequency word cards for each student. Here are some words you might include in the set: *the*, *is*, *has*, *can*, *here*, *a*, *an*, *it*, *look*, *at*.

✔ Bring some blank cards.

✔ Print pictures for each page of a book. We have provided some for you to use, or you may use your own.

RALLY THEM AND ACTIVATE PHONICS: Use a metaphor about storing items in a book room to explain what it means to store high-frequency words. Read the word wall together.

"I gathered you here for some practice using your snap words to make stories. You know how we have a book room (or storage closet) where we can store books and take them out when we need them? Well, the word wall is a place where we store snap words. We take words from there whenever we need them! Let's remember the words we have stored on our word wall by reading through them together." Read them together. Listen to kids as they read the word wall. Make a note of any words that they may need more practice with. You can use Small Group 46 to teach these words.

LAUNCH THEM: Show students some pictures and let them know that they'll make a book to read using the pictures and some high-frequency words pulled out of storage.

"Here are some amazing pictures. They all show an eagle. In this picture, it has a fish in its claws. And here, the eagle is in mid-flight!

"Let's together turn these pictures into a book. We can pull some of the words we need from storage, from our word wall—we don't need to stretch it out and listen for the sounds. We can just grab it for our writing."

Distribute the high-frequency word cards to each student. "Here are some snap words on cards—you can see which of them you might pull from storage to use. (Of course, our book is also going to need words that *aren't* snap words, so I'll help you write some of those.) Also, I'll give each partnership one of these eagle pictures. Say out loud some other words you might need to put on the page with that picture, and then try your best to write them on these blank cards." If you feel that it will take too long for students to write the words or that they are not ready to do this, just write the words for them quickly.

WORK SIDE BY SIDE: Have partnerships use the high-frequency word cards and other words to make sentences to go with their pictures.

"Okay, you've got a bunch of great words that we could put in this book about the eagle—*eagle*, *fish*, *claws*, *flying*, *wing*. So, now, we need to start making the book!

"With your partner, move your cards around and try to make some sentences to go with your picture. For example, I might look at this picture and say, 'The eagle is flying.' Oh, I used two snap words in that sentence! *The* and *is*. Look, I can pull them right out of storage and put them in the sentence. *The* eagle *is* flying.

"Try building a bunch of sentences using your word cards. First, build a sentence and place it under the picture to match. Point under the words and reread it with your partner. Then pick the words up and put them in your pile to make the next page. I'll be leaning in from one partnership to the next to coach you and take photos of the sentences you build for our book.

"In a minute, each partnership will build and read one or two of your sentences, and we'll all get to hear the book we've made. Okay, this partnership can start."

"Here is the eagle. The eagle has a fish. The eagle is flying. It has wings. Look at the eagle!"

TEACH TOWARD TOMORROW: Remind students that using high-frequency words will help them to read and write in a snap.

"I know people will love this book and learn a lot, too! I'll take pictures of your other sentences and make them into a book. Then we can copy it and put it in our library and your book baggies. Remember to use snap words from the word wall to help you write your stories."

OTHER SUPPORTS

Replicate: You can replicate this session with different images and additional high-frequency words to create other books. See the online resources for images to use to write a similar book about sharks.

▼ **Small Group 47:** "Building Sentences with Snap Words"

▲ **Gr 1, Unit 1, Sess. 10, Ext. 1:** Practicing Snap Words during Shared Reading

▲ **Gr 1, Unit 1, Sess. 10, Ext. 2:** Practicing Snap Words during Partner Reading

▲ **Gr 1, Unit 1, Sess. 12, Ext. 1:** Play "Dribble, Dribble, Shoot"

POSSIBLE COACHING MOVES

- "Try starting with *Look*. '*Look* at the . . .'"
- "Can any of these snap words help you write that word you are trying to write?"
- "'Has a fish.' Hmm, . . . that doesn't make sense. *Who* has the fish? I think you'll need to add a word or two for your reader to understand."

FIG. 48–1 Kids read the page of their book together.

Snap Word Checkup

BEST TAUGHT TO

- Students who need extra help learning previously taught high-frequency words

BEST TAUGHT DURING

- Reading workshop
- Writing workshop

GETTING READY

✔ Provide a snap word pouch, a "Snap Word Checkup" chart, and a "Say it. Make it. Spell it. Say it." chart for each student.

✔ Gather word-making materials, such as Wikki Stix, pipe cleaners, string, beads, or any other flexible materials for children to build words with.

RALLY THEM AND ACTIVATE PHONICS: Invite children to do their own snap word checkup, creating a pile of snap words they know well and a pile of ones they are still learning.

"How many of you go to the doctor for a checkup? Well, today you are going to be your own doctor. You are going to give yourself a special kind of checkup—a snap word checkup.

"I'll give each of you some tools to do this checkup, like doctors have. You'll each get a snap word pouch and a snap word checkup chart. You'll dump out all of your snap words and read them one by one. If you know the word in a snap, put the card in the 'strong' side on your 'Snap Word Checkup' chart. If you don't yet know it in a snap, put it in the 'working on' side."

LAUNCH THEM: Introduce children to a set of materials they can use to build the words they are working to learn. Then, invite them to work in partnerships to build these words.

"Great! Now that you've separated your cards into two piles, take a moment to congratulate yourself on all the words you know. Once you've done that, let's dig in to the 'working on' pile. We're going to do some work today to help you learn those words, so you know them in a snap. We find that most students are honest in their self-assessment. If you have a student who places all of their words in the "strong" pile, encourage them to read them out loud and support them as they sort.

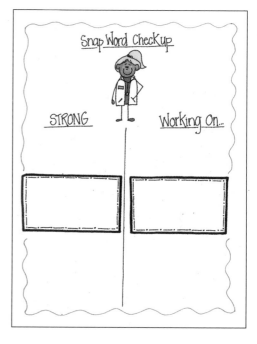

"Here are some steps that have helped many kids to learn snap words, so they know them forever. I'll give each of you a chart, so you can use it to help you remember the steps."

"Take the first word from your 'working on' pile and put it in the first rectangle on your chart. Step 1 is 'read it.' Go ahead and read the word you are working on."

Place the word-making materials in the center of the group, so students can choose from them.

"Step 2 is 'make it.' Move your word card to the next rectangle. Researchers who study how kids learn agree that it really helps kids to learn words to actually *make* the words you are trying to learn using materials like these. Here, we have Wikki Stix, pipe cleaners, beads, and string. You can choose the materials you want to work with and build some of the words you're working on. Build the snap word so it looks like it does on the card."

Encourage children to say the letters out loud as they build their snap words.

"Now, after you make the snap word, spell it out loud—that's step 3. If you're ready to do this, you can move your snap word card on the chart. Make sure to point under each letter as you spell it. If you need help with a word, ask your partner.

"Step 4, move your card, and say it. If you feel like you've gotten stronger with that snap word, pull another card from your 'working on' pile and repeat the steps. If you feel you still need a bit more practice with the word, you can practice it again, or you can put it in the bottom of your 'working on' pile to try again another time."

Coach as partners work through the steps. If both partners don't know the snap word, supply the word and have them say it back. Then they can move forward with the routine. Ideally, students will get to work on three to four snap words before you wrap up the group.

TEACH TOWARD TOMORROW: Remind students that this is important work that they can do at any time.

"Let's stop there for today. Great work, word builders! Take the 'Snap Word Checkup' chart with you. Remember that you can always give yourself the snap word checkup to make sure that you are growing stronger with your snap words. If you need some extra practice learning a word, you can follow the steps from today, and remember that it helps to build it."

OTHER SUPPORTS

Replicate: You can repeat this group as students add more high-frequency words to their collection and need more practice with new words.

▲ **Gr 1, Unit 1, Sess. 13, Ext. 3:** Word Wall Practice: Speed Writing

Of course, if you don't have time to print the chart for each partnership, students can make piles without the chart. But having the chart reinforces the self-assessment work that students are doing.

If time is tight, you can leave the group to work, so you can get another group going or monitor the rest of your class. Tell the children to set words aside if they get stuck. Come back to wrap up and help children with any words they couldn't solve on their own.

Where, Oh Where, Is Mabel?

Reading Prepositions in a Snap

BEST TAUGHT TO

- Students who are reading longer texts that may include prepositional phrases and who could use support

BEST TAUGHT DURING

- Reading workshop

GETTING READY

✔ Choose a level C book that contains at least one preposition. We chose *Ethan's Cat* by Johanna Hurwitz, the demonstration text from kindergarten reading Unit 3: *Bigger Books, Bigger Reading Muscles*.

✔ Bring the class mascot and a box she can fit in.

✔ Gather small Post-its in two different colors. On one color, write *Mabel*, *jumps*, *runs*, *sits*, *sleeps*, *the*, and *box* on separate Post-its. On the other color, write *in*, *on*, and *off*.

✔ Bring a camera to take photos to make a book for students.

RALLY THEM AND ACTIVATE PHONICS: Invite children to join you in reading from a familiar book that contains prepositional phrases.

"Readers, you've been reading harder books! They don't just say, 'This is a ball.' They also say where the ball is, like, 'The ball is on the grass.'"

"Here's a great one, *Ethan's Cat* by Johanna Hurwitz. Let's read some and see if it tells where things are. Join me when you can." Read a few pages of the book, letting your voice drop off as children join you.

"Did you see how it says, 'over the fence,' 'under the bush,' and 'up a tree'? It tells where the cat is."

LAUNCH THEM: Invite children to help make a book about Mabel that includes prepositional phrases.

Place Mabel and the box in the center of the group. "Today Mabel asked if we would write a book about her! In our book, let's tell where she is, like Johanna Hurwitz did for Ethan's cat. Here are some words that can help you."

Distribute sets of Post-its with the three prepositions (*on*, *in*, *off*) and some sentence words (*Mabel*, *jumps*, *runs*, *sits*, *sleeps*, *the*, *box*) each written on a Post-it. Ask students to quickly read the words with their partners. Help any children who are stuck on a word.

"You can make sentences about Mabel with your Post-its. I'll get you started." Arrange Post-its to make *Mabel jumps _____ the box*, leaving an empty space for a missing word.

"Now, here is the next step. Can one of you take Mabel and have her jump in, on, or off the box?"

"Whoa, it looks like Mabel jumped *off* the box! What word should we put in the sentence?"

Invite one student to choose the Post-it to fill in the blank space. "Great, now read the sentence with your partner. Does it sound right? Does it look right?"

CHALLENGE THEM: Invite partners to continue arranging the Post-its to make sentences about Mabel. Take photos of Mabel and students' sentences for a book for students to keep.

"Readers, can you work with your partner and make more pages for Mabel's book? You might start your sentence just like we did: *Mabel jumps*. Or, Mabel might do something else on your page. I'll give you some Post-its to make other words. She might sit, or run, or even sleep! Be sure to explain *where* she does these things. When you finish, let Mabel follow your directions and put her *on* the box or *in* the box or *off* the box. Let me know when you are ready, and I will take a picture of Mabel and the sentence you made."

FIG. 50–1   Kylie and Nastia put Mabel in the box.

FIG. 50–2   Mabel's book

OTHER SUPPORTS

Replicate: You can replicate this group with other common prepositions such as *under*, *over*, and *above*.

▼ **Small Group 46:** "Learning Words in a Snap"

▼ **Small Group 51:** "Snap Words Help Readers and Writers"

▼ **Gr K, Unit 1, Sess. 16, Ext. 1:** Building Sentences

Snap Words Help Readers and Writers

BEST TAUGHT TO

- Children who are approaching or have recently begun reading level D books

BEST TAUGHT DURING

- Reading workshop

GETTING READY

✔ Prepare an envelope of word cards for each child containing these words:

   ✔ 1 card each: *am, day, at, did, for, fun, get, how, up, you, all, are, as, ball, by, come, has, had, go, will*

   ✔ 2 cards each: *went, to, on, play, ran*

   ✔ 3 cards each: *I, the*

     Although many of these words will be in children's pouches, they will need multiples of some words, so it may be best to print new sets for this activity.

✔ Choose a level D book that contains many snap words.

✔ Bring Post-its and a pen for each child.

✔ Prepare a copy of the "Building Sentences" chart.

✔ Bring a camera to take photos to make a book for students.

RALLY THEM: Let kids know that a page full of words in a book is actually easier to read than they think, because most of those words are snap words.

"Sometimes when you turn the page of a book and look at what you will read next, do you think to yourself, 'Whoa. That's a *lot* of words!'?

"Here's the thing. When you see so many words, it actually may not be as hard as it looks at first glance. Because *often*, many of those words are snap words! And you can read them in a snap."

ACTIVATE PHONICS: Have partners whisper-read a set of snap words, dividing them into words they know and words that are still hard. Then read a page of a level D book together to reinforce that many of the words are snap words.

"I put together a special envelope of snap words for each one of you. Take out the words and start whisper-reading through them, and as you read, make two piles." Use your hands to illustrate the two piles. "One for words you *know* in a snap, and one for words that are still a little hard. You'll read some words twice, because I have made more than one copy.

Resist the temptation to teach into the snap words that students think are still a little hard. Take note of these and address this at another time. Also, be alert for times when a child lingers on a word and doesn't move on. Instead of helping the child now, coach that child to put that word into their "still a little hard" pile and move on.

If students struggle to read more than 70% of the words you give them, you might consider going back to teach Small Group 46, "Learning Words in a Snap."

This work is meant to be quick, just fifteen or twenty seconds long. Don't worry about whether students spot all the snap words on the page. They'll get the point that snap words are everywhere after they point to a few.

"See? You already know a lot of these words! And your books are full of these words. Let's read a page together and *see* how many of these words are actually easy-peasy snap words."

Read a page of a level D book together. Ask students how many snap words they found, and then invite them to share some examples. Note again that snap words are all over the books they're reading.

LAUNCH THEM AND WORK SIDE BY SIDE: Demonstrate how to make sentences using the snap words. Show kids that they can write an additional word for the sentence using a blank card.

"Why don't we work together to write a book with tons of these snap words, just like the ones in your baggies? Writing a book with lots of these snap words will help you get even more familiar with them, which will help you to read the books in your baggies. And instead of writing it with the pen, let's write it with our snap word cards. It should be about something fun. Hmm, . . . playing at recess?"

Use a student's set of word cards to demonstrate.

"Let me show you how you do this. Let's make a sentence for a book about recess out of these words. We should start the sentence with a person. How about . . . *I*?"

Slide the *I* word card into the first place of the sentence, then recruit the student whose cards you are using to help you choose words to continue the sentence.

"Great, you chose the word *went*, and I added *to* and *the*. So far, we have *I went to the*. What could go next? Hmm, . . . what do you do when you're at recess?

"*Swings*! That word isn't in your envelope, so you can write it on a Post-it. /sw/ /ing/ /s/. Go ahead and write that.

"You heard the blend, then the *-ing*, and then the *S*. Great! Now reread and see if you have a whole sentence."

FIG. 51–1 Sarah coaches Aubrey and Simone to read and write with snap words.

The emphasis within this section is on getting students to read and write with snap words. Because of that, you might decide to accept students' attempts at spelling the extra words in their sentences that are not snap words.

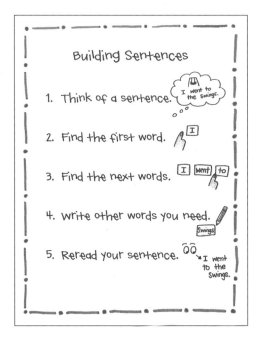

Building Sentences

1. Think of a sentence.
2. Find the first word.
3. Find the next words.
4. Write other words you need.
5. Reread your sentence.

CHALLENGE THEM: Invite children to make more sentences about recess. Coach them to reread the words often, prompting them to make sure their sentences make sense and sound right.

"Can each one of you make more sentences about recess? Make them all be about the same person—I—so they go together. Remember you can add any other words you want to your sentences using extra Post-its. You can make lots of pages! I think you'll see that you can use a *lot* of these snap words. As you build your sentences, say the snap words and move them. Make one sentence and then another. Each sentence will be a page for our book. Remember, you can use the 'Building Sentences' chart to help you as you work."

POSSIBLE COACHING MOVES

▶ "What will your sentence say?"

▶ "What is the first word?"

▶ "What word could go next? And after that?"

▶ "Reread. Point under the words."

"Let's read all of the sentences you came up with and hear how the book will go! I'll snap some pictures of your work and later we can add this book to your book baggies."

TEACH TOWARD TOMORROW: Reinforce the notion that books are full of tons of snap words and then send students off to read independently.

"This work of making your own books with lots of snap words will help you to *read* your books that have lots of snap words. Readers, will you go back into your books now and read them? If you get to a page that has a lot of words, say to yourself, 'I've got this! There are probably a ton of snap words here.' Get started."

OTHER SUPPORTS

▼ **Small Group 47:** "Building Sentences with Snap Words"

▲ **Gr 1, Unit 1, Sess. 10, Ext. 1:** Practicing Snap Words during Shared Reading

▲ **Gr 1, Unit 1, Sess. 10, Ext. 2:** Practicing Snap Words during Partner Reading

▲ **Gr 1, Unit 1, Sess. 12, Ext. 1:** Play "Dribble, Dribble, Shoot"

Teachers, this may seem like writing work, but the process of getting kids to cobble together sentences out of high-frequency words, adding in a few additional words, will really help them to see how the books they are reading are mostly comprised of high-frequency words. In addition, you've been strategic about which words you give students to work with to make these sentences, so they are getting practice reading and rereading some of the most common snap words.

Earlier your students made attempts at spelling the extra words in their sentences that are not snap words. You accepted their approximations to keep the focus on snap words. However, if you are photographing these sentences for a book in your classroom library, you will want to correct any misspelled word by writing it again on a Post-it and putting it in place of the approximated Post-it. Do this after the kids have left the group.

Clearing Up Snap Word Mix-Ups

RALLY THEM AND ACTIVATE PHONICS: Set partnerships up to quiz one another using the word wall.

"I called you over near the word wall because there are so many snap words you are starting to know so well that you are ready to learn some more! Will you quiz each other to see which words you do and don't know? One partner will point to words on the wall and the other partner will read. After five words, switch." Give a pointer to one child in each partnership and suggest that the pointer-child point and the other child read.

To make this work especially exciting, you might consider distributing flashlights instead of pointers.

LAUNCH THEM AND CHALLENGE THEM: Channel partnerships to choose a set of confusing words to study. Suggest different ways they could study the words, coaching in as they work.

"Come on back. You are ready for the next step, and you can now put a little elbow grease toward learning the harder words, the more confusing ones.

"For example, sometimes you want to write *from*, but you write *for*! I want you to work to clear up those mix-ups for yourselves and your partners. You and your partner pick a set of confusing words and really work on mastering that set.

Channel partnerships to choose a set of words to study, or distribute words strategically based on needs.

"You decide what to do to learn these words. Maybe you'll trace the words, write them a few times on your whiteboard in different colors, write a song, or put them in sentences. Maybe you'll write the word on a note card and then cut it up letter by letter and put it back together like a puzzle. Look at our chart, 'Clearing Up Snap Word Mix-Ups' to get some ideas about how to study your words. You decide!"

BEST TAUGHT TO

- Students who miscue when reading commonly confused high-frequency words or who are writing the wrong high-frequency word in their writing

BEST TAUGHT DURING

- Reading workshop
- Writing workshop

GETTING READY

✔ Provide a pointer or flashlight to each partnership.

✔ Print the "Make It a Snap Word" and "Clearing Up Snap Word Mix-Ups" charts.

✔ Gather materials for students to practice writing snap words: whiteboards, markers, erasers, note cards, pens, and scissors.

✔ Prepare sets of words cards in baggies or paper clip each set together.

   ✔ Set 1: *for, from, of*

   ✔ Set 2: *there, them, then*

   ✔ Set 3: *when, where, what, with*

   ✔ Set 4: *was, saw*

   ✔ Set 5: *on, no*

   ✔ Set 6: *who, how*

TEACH TOWARD TOMORROW: Invite partnerships to teach each other how they will remember the tricky words.

"Friends, let's come back together and teach each other. Partnership 1, tell us how you will remember your words."

The partnership studying *there*, *them*, and *then* may say:

- "They all start with *t-h-e*, so you have to look at the last letter."

- "*Then* is a time-telling word, like the word *after*. You don't write 'Them I went home.' You write 'Then I went home.'"

The partnerships studying *was* and *saw*, and *on* and *no*, might say:

- "They are flipped!"

- "You have to say the word and think about the first sound. Then you will know which word it is!"

- "I've got a song! I *was* not scared when I *saw* the bumblebee. I *was* excited when I *saw* the bumblebee."

OTHER SUPPORTS

▲ **Gr 1, Unit 3, Sess. 9, Ext. 3:** Practicing Confusing Snap Words: *Then* and *Than*

We recognize that many word study experts would not teach two similar high-frequency words at the same time. We've chosen to group these words together for this session because the focus is on usage, not on learning the word for the first time.

FIG. 52–1 Kids at work clearing up their mix-ups.

Making Phrases with Snap Words

ACTIVATE PHONICS: Direct partnerships to warm up by reading some familiar high-frequency words.

"Readers, no matter what sport, athletes always warm their muscles up before they play. Will you and your partner warm up your reading muscles by reading a few words you've been learning to read in a snap? If you find one that's tricky to read, put it off to the side."

Distribute a set of familiar snap words to each partnership and observe as students quickly read through them.

RALLY THEM AND WORK SIDE BY SIDE: Explain to students that there are a few common phrases that are made up of snap words; show examples.

"Guess what? There are actually some really common phrases, things we say all the time, that are made up of snap words. You could call them 'Snap Phrases.' Here are some." Quickly arrange the cards on the floor, making a drumroll noise, and form the phrase: "Because I said so." Use tape to stick the words together.

"Here's a phrase people say a lot: 'Because I said so.' You might ask, 'Why can't I stay up late?' and some grown-up says, 'Because I said so.' How many of you have heard that phrase? And look—it's made of all snap words.

"Here's another one. Drumroll, please! 'Could you go . . .'" Tape the words together.

"Have you heard this? 'Could you go get my blanket? Could you go get me a giant bowl of ice cream?' 'Could you go' is a phrase you see a lot—and it's made of snap words."

LAUNCH THEM: Coach students as they work together to construct familiar phrases out of snap words.

"There are a lot more phrases like this. Will you and your partner work together to make some? Use your set of word cards. When you find a set of words that go together in a phrase, tape them together."

BEST TAUGHT TO

- Students who need support reading high-frequency words with automaticity
- Students who are not yet reading fluently

BEST TAUGHT DURING

- Reading workshop
- Intervention time

GETTING READY

✔ Prepare one set of familiar snap words for each partnership, containing these words:

  ✔ 1 card each: *could, come, get, it, it's, about, time, when, will, here, so, are, she, came, home, because, top, bottom*

  ✔ 2 cards each: *you, and, from, there, said, to, over*

  ✔ 3 cards each: *go, we, I*

✔ Gather tape, whiteboards, markers, and erasers for each partnership.

✔ Print a copy of Carl's story for each student.

Students might make the following phrases:

- could you go
- come and get it
- it's about time
- when will we go
- from here to there
- so there you are

- she said to go
- we came home
- because I said so
- over and over
- from top to bottom

FIG. 53–1   Partners working on putting together phrases

CHALLENGE THEM: Direct students to write the familiar phrases they created. Partner 1 reads a phrase and Partner 2 writes it on the whiteboard. Then, students check the phrase and switch roles.

"You're learning to read these phrases in a snap. You can also *write* them in a snap, too. Ready to try? Flip the new phrases you made over so you can't see the words. Partner 2, pull out a phrase and read it. Partner 1, write it on your whiteboard. Then you can check it. I'll listen in and coach you. Go!"

TEACH TOWARD TOMORROW: Reinforce the notion that students can read *entire phrases* in a snap by channeling them to do some shared reading. Then, send them off to read independently.

"You can read and write these phrases in a snap! Here's a little story I wrote. Let's read it together. Notice how when you come to those phrases, you can just read them in a snap."

"Back to your reading, and remember that if you see phrases like this in the future, don't read them word by word. Read them in a snap!"

POSSIBLE COACHING MOVES

▶ "What's the first word in that phrase? Try to get a mental picture of that word. Now write it fast, in a snap!"

▶ "Reread that phrase. When might you use that phrase? Tell your partner."

Dinner was ready. **"Come and get it,"** Carl's dad said. All of the kids came for dinner. Carl's dad said, **"There you are! Could you go** and wash your hands?"

"Why do we have to wash our hands?" Carl asked.
"Because I said so!" said his dad.

Strategies for Writing Words Correctly CHAPTER 8

Making an Editing Checklist

BEST TAUGHT TO

- Children who do not recognize the miscues in their writing

BEST TAUGHT DURING

- Writing workshop

GETTING READY

✔ Have a copy of "My Editing Checklist" on hand.

✔ Print the criteria from "My Editing Checklist" onto sticky labels that students can use to create personalized checklists. If you cannot print onto labels, cut up the editing checklist and students can use glue to build their own.

✔ Give each student a blank piece of paper to create an editing checklist.

✔ Gather enough colored pens for every student; we use purple.

RALLY THEM: Rally kids to take the job of checking their writing seriously.

"Yesterday I watched you reread your writing to check it. You were just flying through your pages going, 'Good, check! Check! Done!' So, I wanted to talk to you more about what it really means to check your own work. When you check your writing, it doesn't go like that. Instead of 'Read it . . . check! Done!' what you want to do is say to yourself, 'I want to get better at _____. I'm going to really work hard at _____.' Then, when you're checking your work, you look for ways to work on that thing you've chosen as a goal."

LAUNCH THEM: Show students a list of phonics principles they might work on in their writing. Ask them to decide on a short list of goals for themselves and to then make their own checklist.

"When I do this, I look at my own writing and think, 'Which are the biggest challenges for me?' I might start to read my writing and notice . . . 'Oh, here is a snap word that isn't spelled right. Oh, here's another snap word that looks wrong. And here's another. Wow. I *really* need to work on spelling my snap words.'

"Or I might notice that some of my words don't have vowels, and I might decide I need to work on recording *all* the sounds I hear in words.

"Will you, right now, look over this editing checklist and look through your own writing and start thinking: Which of these are the biggest challenges for me? What do I really need to work on? You might ask your partner to look at your writing and help you choose the one or two things you want to put on your checklist. In a minute you are going to create your very own editing checklist, with the things that *you* really want to work on.

"Now, build a tool—a checklist—to help you remember your big challenges. I put each of the items from the Editing Checklist onto these sticky labels. Since you have decided what you will work on, you can pull the labels off and stick them onto the piece of paper I give you, to make your own checklist. Stick the labels in order from what you need to work on the most at the top, to what you need work on the least at the bottom. Then you'll get the chance to check your writing. Go to it!"

CHALLENGE THEM: Set writers up to use their checklists to help them edit their writing. Ask them to point out a hard spot and tell their partners how they tackled it. Celebrate their efforts.

"Get started checking your writing. Really read your writing and think, 'I want to get better at my goal. How can I fix my writing?' You can use these purple pens to help you make your writing better."

> ### POSSIBLE COACHING MOVES
>
> ▶ "Start with one item on your checklist. Read each word, thinking about that item, then go on to the next item on your list."
>
> ▶ "Hmm, . . . blends are tricky. Here's a tip: Read each word of your writing out loud and really listen for the beginning sounds of each word. If it sounds like there might be more than one sound at the start, it could be a blend. The 'Blends and Digraphs' chart could help you."
>
> ▶ "If you say a word aloud, you can hear the beats. Then check that you have a vowel in each beat, each part, of the word."
>
> ▶ "You're checking for digraphs? Amazing! Have you found any yet that you had to fix? Remember there are digraphs in words like *the*, *there*, *with*, and *she*. Keep looking."
>
> ▶ "Check the next page!"

After students show some confidence navigating their checklists, pull them together. "When you're working on something challenging, it's powerful to share the hard parts with each other. Will you put a dot in the margin in places that were really hard to fix?"

Then, after a minute, "Talk to someone near you about what you did in those hard parts. Help each other.

"This is not easy work. You should feel proud of yourselves. Give yourselves a fist pump and in your head, say, 'I rock!'"

My Editing Checklist

	I put spaces between my words.
	I wrote a letter for each sound.
	I wrote CAPITAL letters to start every sentence.
	I put a punctuation mark at the end of every sentence.
	I spelled my snap words right.
	I noticed and spelled blends and digraphs.

Use this time to look over students' writing with each of them, noticing a page or two that will be worth attending to, and nudge the children to notice spelling miscues and set goals. If a child's goals are far afield from your hopes for her, you can alternatively coach the child toward goals you believe will pay off.

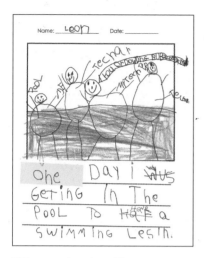  

FIG. 54–1   Leon's writing

TEACH TOWARD TOMORROW: Reinforce the importance of checking writing to make sure others can read it. Send students off with their individualized checklists to use as they keep writing.

"Now the job is to think about these things *while* you write! Keep these checklists with you and push yourself to work on these things today as you do some new writing."

Writing Longer Words, Part by Part

RALLY THEM: Celebrate that children have been brave to write a longer word, and then show kids that writing it syllable by syllable rather than letter by letter is their new job.

"Holy moly, it's so exciting for me to see you writing these huge, long words in your writing. I saw one of you write *skateboard* yesterday! It takes bravery and determination to write long words like that—wow!

"Here's a tip: If you want to get better at writing long words, don't stretch-write them by thinking letter by letter. Instead, think syllable by syllable. As you write each syllable, remember each one needs a vowel."

ACTIVATE PHONICS: Tell students a multisyllabic word or two and ask them to say the words, clap the beats, say the syllables. Then ask the kids to write the word, syllable by syllable.

"You are all going to need to concentrate and chop that word up with your ear. You'll need to say it a few times to hear the familiar pieces to chop. Ready? Let's try with some harder, longer words. Take the word *wonderful*. Whisper it. Cup your hands up around your mouth and whisper it to your partner."

Repeat the word *wonderful*. Encourage kids to clap the beats and say the syllables: *won-der-ful*.

Pass out whiteboards and markers. "Okay, now that you've said the word syllable by syllable, will you write that word the same way? Write

Writing Longer Words

1. Say it
2. Clap the beats
3. Say the syllables   won-der-ful
4. Write the syllables   wonderful

BEST TAUGHT TO

- Students who are using multisyllabic words in their writing, but not recording a vowel in each syllable

BEST TAUGHT DURING

- Writing workshop

GETTING READY

✔ Ask students to bring their writing folders and a pen.

✔ Distribute a whiteboard and marker to each student. Also have your own set.

✔ Print a "Writing Longer Words" chart for each student.

the first syllable you heard, *won*, then the next, *der*, now the last, *ful*. Remember, each syllable needs a vowel."

Write the word correctly on your own whiteboard and have kids check to see how close they were to the correct spelling. Some children may spell *won* as *one*. If so, point out that this is another way to spell this syllable, but in the word *wonderful*, the spelling is *won*.

"Wow, that was fabulous! Let's try it with the word *fabulous*." Give kids another chance to try it with their partners. *Fab-u-lous*. Repeat the process used for *wonderful*.

CHALLENGE THEM: Ask children to say the words, clap the beats, and say the syllables. Then ask the kids to write the word, syllable by syllable.

"Try it in your own writing right now. Take out a piece you are working on. Check your quick sketch and say what you were planning to write next. When you get to one of those longer words, say the words, clap the beats, say the syllables, and write it syllable by syllable. Be sure each syllable has a vowel."

TEACH TOWARD TOMORROW: Remind children that they need to get into this new habit of listening for beats they hear, rather than stretching out a word letter by letter.

"Writers, I feel like you got yourself into a new habit today. You've got to keep doing this whenever you write. Rather than writing letter by letter, write the syllables you hear. It can help you spell more words correctly, and you'll be able to write those longer words a little more quickly."

Send students off with a copy of the "Writing Longer Words" chart or a Post-it reminder with the word *won-der-ful* on it.

OTHER SUPPORTS

▲ **Gr 1, Unit 3, Sess. 11, Ext. 2:** The Vowel Inspector Is Coming!

▶ "Clap the word. What's the first syllable? Write that down. What's the next syllable? Write that. What's the last syllable? Write that, too."

▶ "Remember to put a vowel in each syllable." *Or,* "Remember every syllable needs a vowel."

▶ "Say it syllable by syllable. Do you know another word like that to help you get started?"

FIG. 55–1   Christine coaches kids to spell longer words.

Don't Just Sound It Out
Using Many Strategies to Spell Words

RALLY THEM: Tell a story to make the point that people need different tools for different jobs. Suggest it is equally important to use different tools as spellers.

"Readers, let's pretend you and I are cleaning. Pretend we have some tools: a sponge, a mop, and a vacuum cleaner. I'm going to describe a few cleaning jobs, and you can tell me which tool you think would be the best for each job." Describe a few cleaning jobs. Give students a moment to consider which tool would be the best for each, and then invite them to share their thinking. For example:

- "I dropped the milk carton and the milk spilled all over the kitchen floor."
- "A bunch of kids dragged dirt across the living room carpet."
- "I spilled a few drops of orange juice on the counter."
- "There's dog hair all over the sofa."

"You all are really good at choosing the right tools for different cleaning jobs. My point for today is that you need to do the same when you are writing. I've noticed that some of you tend to use the same strategy over and over, no matter what. Whenever you go to spell a word, some of you always try to sound it out, while others always check the snap word wall. Using the same way all the time is like using a vacuum cleaner for every cleaning job, and you wouldn't use a vacuum cleaner for spilled orange juice! When you are cleaning and when you are spelling, you need to think, 'Wait, which tool would be the best one for *this* job?'"

ACTIVATE PHONICS: Share a chart to remind children of the strategies they know to spell words.

In the middle of the group, place a small version of the "Ways to Spell Words" chart with strategies students know for spelling words.

BEST TAUGHT TO

- Students who are only relying on one spelling strategy in their writing

BEST TAUGHT DURING

- Writing workshop

GETTING READY

✔ Prepare a copy of the "Ways to Spell Words" chart.

✔ Gather a whiteboard and marker for each student in the group.

✔ If you can, find a page from each child's writing where that child has lots of misspelled words. Stick a Post-it on that page with a number written on it to signal how many need to be fixed.

✔ Print a mini-copy of the "Ways to Spell Words" chart with an example word for each strategy for each student.

"Will you and your partner read over each of these strategies? Talk with your partner about which strategies are helpful, and which ones you sometimes forget to use."

LAUNCH THEM: Call out words and ask kids to decide which of the strategies they would use to spell each word.

"For now, let's *not* work on spelling words. Let's just work on choosing the right *tool* for the job. I'll call out a few words, and you tell the person beside you which spelling tool you might use.

"How about the word *the*? I went to *the* supermarket."

Give children a moment to talk, then continue, "I heard you say the way to go is to use your snap words—to spell the word *the* in a snap. I agree! You don't need to sound out *the*!"

Continue calling out words. Say each word in a sentence to provide context. Give students a moment to share with a partner which spelling tool they would use for each word. You might call out words such as:

caterpillar *(write it part by part, or listen for syllables)*

stay *(use a word you know: day or say)*

when *(use snap words)*

hippopotamus *(write it part by part, or listen for syllables)*

CHALLENGE THEM: Set students up to spell each of the words you said aloud, using the tools they picked to help them. Then, direct them to use the spelling tools to edit their own writing.

"So now, will you do some spelling? I'll call out the words again, and each of you, try to spell them on your whiteboard using the spelling tool you picked. When you've written the word, compare it with the person next to you and see if you agree on the spelling. If you don't, talk it out."

Call out the same list of words as above. Coach students as needed as they write the words and as they compare words with each other.

"So, writers, will you now go to your writing? You'll see I put a Post-it on a recent page of your writing that could use some spelling attention. I wrote the number of words that need help on the Post-it. As you work to spell these words correctly, think first, 'Which spelling tool will I reach for?'"

As students work, coach them to identify words they could correct and to choose a spelling strategy that makes sense.

There may be other strategies you could add to this list if you have already taught them. For example, in time you will want kids to spell with an awareness of prefixes, suffixes, and inflectional endings and to draw on meaning as a source of help. For now, you probably haven't taught these strategies—and this session is not the occasion for doing so.

TEACH TOWARD TOMORROW: Reiterate the importance of choosing the best strategy when trying to spell a particular word.

"Head back to your seat. Remember: don't use the vacuum cleaner to clean up spilled orange juice! Choose the tool that's best for the job—and when spelling words, that isn't always to just 'sound it out.'"

You may wish to leave students with a mini-copy of the "Ways to Spell Words" chart with an example word for each strategy.

FIG. 56–1   Kids busy at work spelling the best they can using the strategy that works best for each word.

OTHER SUPPORTS

Replicate: If you are finding kids having trouble relying on a repertoire of strategies as they spell, you can revisit this with a focus on more explicit teaching into one or two strategies from the chart.

▼ **Gr K, Unit 1, Sess. 5:** "Syllables Can Help Readers and Writers Tackle Long Words"

▼ **Gr 1, Unit 2, Sess. 3:** "Word Detectives Use the Patterns They've Learned to Write New Words: Interactive Writing"

▼ **Gr 1, Unit 2, Sess. 16:** "Tracking Down the Look-Alike Word Part: Using Analogy to Solve Words"

▼ **Gr 1, Unit 3, Sess. 11, Ext. 2:** The Vowel Inspector Is Coming!

Study and Learn from Your Mistakes

BEST TAUGHT TO

- Children who make a similar type of error in in their writing (such as omitting letters from three-letter blends, choosing the incorrect long-vowel pattern, or using the wrong homophone)

BEST TAUGHT DURING

- Writing workshop

GETTING READY

✔ Write a sentence that contains an error commonly made by the students you gathered together. We use: "I spay water on my sister."

✔ Ask students to bring their writing folders.

✔ Distribute Post-its to each child.

✔ Bring a purple, red, or green pen.

RALLY THEM: Share an example of computer programmers learning from their errors to illustrate the importance of children studying and learning from their writing mistakes.

"You know the games and apps that people have in their phones? Well, those are all designed by computer programmers. The programmers type in code, which looks like a bunch of letters and numbers, and that code tells the computer how to make the games. Sometimes, the programmers make mistakes—and when they do, the games don't work right, and the programmers have to study their code to figure out what mistakes they made. But you know what? The programmers actually *like* when this happens. Because when they study those mistakes, they learn how to write code that's even better.

"I'm telling you this because it makes me think of your writing. It's tempting to quickly fix your mistakes and then just move on. But to become even better at spelling words, you have to work like a computer programmer. You have to study your mistakes, using everything you know about phonics to help you."

LAUNCH THEM AND WORK SIDE BY SIDE: Recruit students to help you find mistakes in your writing. Demonstrate how you study a mistake and learn from it, drawing on phonics knowledge.

"Help me try a bit of this in my writing. First, let's read it and think, 'What words don't look right?'"

Display a sentence that contains a common error and read it aloud.

I spay water on my sister.

"Did you find a word that doesn't look right? *Spray* looks wrong to me, too. I think some of you already see what's wrong. But instead of just fixing it up and moving on quickly, let's really study it. First, let's figure out which part of the word looks wrong: the beginning, middle, or end. The ending looks right to me. That's one of our vowel teams, *ay*. I think it's the beginning that looks wrong: *sp*.

"So now that I know which part of the word looks wrong, I can think, 'What do I know about letters and sounds that might help me fix the beginning of this word?' Can you all do this, too? Tell your partner what you are thinking.

"Some of you are saying that there is a sound at the start of this word that I forgot to write. Listen as I say the word slowly and see if you can hear what sound I'm missing. /spr/-/ay/. /spr/. /spr/. Oh, yes! I am missing /r/." Cross out the word and rewrite it: *spray*.

"So, what did I learn from this mistake? Well, the next time I write this word, I'll need to remember that *spray* starts with three letters at the beginning: *S-P-R*. I'll also need to remember to always listen for *all* the sounds at the beginning of words."

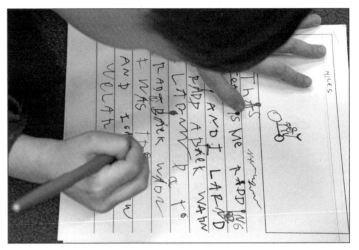

CHALLENGE THEM: Set students up to reread their own writing, notice their mistakes, and study them. Coach them to draw on their knowledge of phonics as they study their mistakes.

"Ready to try this with your writing? Pull out your current piece and study the first page, asking, 'What words don't look right?' Here are some Post-its for each of you. Stick a Post-it next to any words that don't look right.

"Now choose one of those words to study. Notice which part of the word is wrong: the beginning, the middle, or the end. Then, use what you know about letters and sounds to fix it up! You might have to try a few different things until it looks just right, then write the word correctly above it with a colorful pen. Finally, pause and think, what can I learn from this mistake?"

TEACH TOWARD TOMORROW: Celebrate what students learned from studying their mistakes. Encourage students to always do this moving forward.

"Wow, writers! You learned so much from studying your mistakes. Will you share one of your mistakes with your partner, and tell your partner what you learned?"

OTHER SUPPORTS

▼ **Gr 1, Unit 5, Sess. 1:** "Studying Bloopers with *R*-Controlled Vowels"

▲ **Gr 1, Unit 5, Sess. 7:** "Sharing and Learning from Our *Reading* Bloopers"

POSSIBLE COACHING MOVES

▸ "Which part looks wrong: the beginning, the middle, or the end?"

▸ "How else could that part go? What other letter goes with that sound?"

▸ "Check the room. Is there a chart that can help you figure out that word?"

▸ "There's another word that sounds like the word you wrote but it is spelled differently."

▸ "What did that mistake teach you?"

▸ "You got it. Now look at the next word you found. Try and fix it up."

CHAPTER 9

Strategies for Reading Words Correctly

Check the Pictures *and* the Letters

RALLY THEM: Remind children that yes, readers rely on meaning to make a guess at a word, but then they look at the first letters to check the guess.

"Readers, I am so excited to have you here with me in this little circle. I notice that as you read, you look at the picture and you think about what the book is saying. You are ready for the next step now. After you use the picture to guess, think, 'Does the first letter match my guess?'"

LAUNCH THEM: Invite the children to help you solve a tricky word. Coach readers to use the picture, then to look at the first letters of their guess to check it.

Hold up a copy of a level C book, such as *Mouse Has Fun: Picnic* by Phyllis Root, and open to a page with picture support. "Let's try this together. 'Mouse finds cookies. Mouse finds apples. Mouse finds . . .' Hmm, . . . this next word is tricky. Let's check the picture, right? I see Mouse in the picture. He found more *food*!

"Now what do we need to do? Yes! We need to check the letters. Oh, it's a letter *B*. So, it can't be the word *food*, but it seems to be a kind of food that starts with /b/. What do you think it is? 'Mouse finds *bread*?' That makes sense with the picture and it matches the first letter!"

If you are using *Lunch* from the online resources, you might pause when you get to the word *cheese*, and say, "I see a cat with a bunch of cheese. He got more food! Could the word be *food*?"

CHALLENGE THEM: Invite children to open their book baggies and start reading while you move from reader to reader, coaching them to use the first letter in addition to the picture.

"Now it is your time to read! Remember to not only look at the picture but also check the letters. Ask, 'Does the first letter match the sound of my guess?'"

BEST TAUGHT TO

- Children who can read level A and B books with independence, but when they try a level C book, they look at the picture and make meaningful guesses, but they don't look at initial letters. (For example, the text is *van* but the child reads *car*.)

BEST TAUGHT DURING

- Reading workshop

GETTING READY

✔ Ask students to bring their book baggies to the group.

✔ Find a page in a level C book in which you can use the meaning and the picture to guess a challenging word, then use the letters to help you double-check. For example, in *Mouse Has Fun: Picnic* by Phyllis Root, the challenging word might be *bread*. We have also provided the book *Lunch* as an optional text to use with this group.

✔ Print the "Check Your Reading" bookmark. ⚡

POSSIBLE COACHING MOVES

▶ "What other words might this be?"

▶ "What is the first letter in the word?"

▶ "Get your mouth ready to make the first sound in that word."

▶ "Find that letter on the alphabet chart to help you figure out what sound it makes."

TEACH TOWARD TOMORROW: Remind students to continue checking the pictures and to be sure they check the first letters in words, also.

"Friends, keep checking the picture *and* double-checking with the first letter to make sure your guess looks right. Remember, you can always use an alphabet chart to remind you of a letter's sound!"

OTHER SUPPORTS

Replicate: This group can be replicated with students reading their books to each other, taking turns playing the role of coach. They can use an alphabet chart or their Super Powers chart to help them.

Replicate: This group can be replicated to also help readers attend to the *final* letters in words. You can coach them in a similar way, but you will want to say, "Check the first letter *and* move your eyes to the end of the word."

You may decide to leave students with a copy of the "Check Your Reading" bookmark as a reminder.

Moving Your Eyes to the End of the Word

RALLY THEM: Remind readers of the game "Guess the Covered Word," an adaptation of an activity by Patricia Cunningham, to help readers pull together information and read the ends of words.

"Ladies and Gentlemen, get ready to play 'Guess the Covered Word'! Do you remember playing this game? It's a game that reminds you to look across all parts of words, and check that words make sense, sound right, and look right. You have been doing such a good job using the picture and the first letters to solve tricky words that now you are ready to move your eyes to the end of the word and check that your guess looks right *all the way to the end of the word*.

"Do you remember the rules? When you get to a covered word, think, 'What would make sense and sound right in the sentence?' Then, you'll make some guesses and I'll write them down. Then, we'll uncover the word, so you can look all the way to the end of it and check your guesses."

LAUNCH THEM: Invite children to read the text with you. Coach readers to use the picture and first letter(s) to read covered words, then to check their guesses against the final letters.

"This poem is called 'Going to School.'"

Invite the children to read along with you. Point under the words as you do.

Going to School

I put on my sh____.

"Let's guess the covered word! What might this word say?"

Jot the children's responses on your whiteboard. "You guessed *shirt*, *shoes*, and *ship*. Let's check if these guesses make sense and start with the /sh/ sound. The word *shoes* starts with the /sh/ sound, and it makes sense that you put on your *shoes* to go to school. The word *shirt* also starts with /sh/

BEST TAUGHT TO

- Children who can read level C books with independence but don't always attend to the last part(s). (For example, the text is *stairs* but the child reads *steps*.)

BEST TAUGHT DURING

- Reading workshop

GETTING READY

✔ Choose a poem or level D book as your teaching text. Find and cover the endings of words, leaving the letters up to the first vowel uncovered. We use the poem "Going to School."

✔ Bring a whiteboard and a marker.

✔ Ask the students to bring their book baggies.

and it makes sense that you put on your *shirt*. Hmm, . . . could the word *ship* fit here? I agree that *ship* does start with /sh/, but does it make sense? Would you put on your *ship* to get ready for school? I agree, that's silly! No, *ship* doesn't fit here.

"Think about your guess. What letter do you expect to find at the end of the word?"

Pause and give the children a moment to think. Then uncover the word *shoes*. "What's the word? Yes! It must be *shoes*. It couldn't be *shirt*, because *shirt* ends with the /t/ sound and the last letter in this word is the letter *S*, so it must be *shoes*."

Continue the game with the words *backpack*, *mother*, and *bike* then reread the whole poem together.

CHALLENGE THEM: Invite children to read from their book baggies. Coach them to use the pictures and the first letter(s) to make a guess, and then to move their eyes to the ends of words.

"Now it is your time to read! Remember to look at the picture and think about what makes sense and to also check the letters. Don't forget to move your eyes to the end of the word and check those letters, too."

TEACH TOWARD TOMORROW: After a few minutes of reading and coaching, remind readers that this is something they should always do.

"Readers, keep checking the picture and using the first letters and moving your eyes to the end of each word. It's so important to check the last letters to make sure your guess looks right all the way to the end. I am going to go coach some other readers. Keep reading!"

OTHER SUPPORTS

Replicate: If readers need more practice, you can replicate this with any level D book or with poems you love. Remember to carefully choose the words you cover up, so that kids can use meaning to guess the word. Then they will have to check the letters to see what is actually written on the page. It works best when there are a few different words that could make sense in place of the covered word. In addition, you can replicate this with level E or F books, coaching kids to guess the covered word while checking the word part by part, including the internal parts.

You might choose to cut the Post-its to the exact size of the word you are covering so that readers can also use the size of the word as they make guesses.

POSSIBLE COACHING MOVES

▶ "Move your eyes to the end of the word. Does that last letter match the ending sound of your guess?"

▶ "If that word was *cat*, what letter would you expect to see at the end of the word?"

Going to School

I put on my shoes.

I put on my backpack.

I kiss my mother.

I get on my bike.

I am off to school!

We recommend using the version of this poem without the pictures for this activity. Later, you can distribute this illustrated version for students to keep in their book baggies.

You've Got to Double-Check!

RALLY THEM: Celebrate students' efforts at figuring out tricky words. Guide them to look all the way across the word to make sure their guess makes sense and looks right.

"I gathered you all here, because I'm noticing that sometimes when you read, the word you say makes sense, but it doesn't always match the word on the page. I want to show you how to match your reading to what's on the page."

LAUNCH THEM: Tell students you're going to pretend to be a younger reader. Set them up to follow the words closely as you read and to stop you if you make an error.

"Right now, I'm going to read like my neighbor Gerty might read. Watch me read and follow the words as I read. Look all the way across the words. If you see me read something that doesn't match the letters on the page, put your hand up and say 'Stop!' Then I'll try to fix up my error by looking all the way across the word more carefully."

Show the students pages 2–3 of *The Beach House*. Read the text but substitute the word *backyard* for *beach* and then *stay* for *sleep*.

> *Dad said to Emma and Matthew, "We are going to the beach [backyard] for two days."*

BEST TAUGHT TO

- Children who guess words based on meaning, but do not cross-check them with their phonics knowledge

BEST TAUGHT DURING

- Reading workshop

GETTING READY

- ✔ Choose a book at your students' instructional reading level. Select a few words to read incorrectly, but that would make sense in the text. We use the book *The Beach House* by Jenny Giles.

- ✔ Ask students to bring their book baggies to the group.

- ✔ Prepare a copy of the "Check it!" chart.

- ✔ Prepare Post-it notes to leave behind with students in the group, saying: "Does it look right?"

"Readers, I see you with your hands up like stop signs. What should I do? *Backyard* makes sense! You could go to the backyard. I looked at the picture and made a guess. Oh, but that word doesn't look like *backyard*, though. If it were *backyard*, I'd see /ack/ in the middle. I don't see that in this word. You're right. I need to fix my mess-up.

"Hmm, . . . I'll try to solve that word a different way. Let me look at the word more carefully. I'll look across the whole word for any parts I know. I'll take the word apart and crash it back together. Let's see, there's that /ea/ and /ch/. Crash it with me! *Beach*. Reread with me, 'We are going to the *beach* for two days.' That makes sense and it *looks* right. Sounds right, too. Let me keep reading. Get ready to coach me."

> *"Oh good," said Matthew, "Where are we going to sleep [stay]?*

"Oh, I see you with your hands like a stop sign again. *Stay* makes sense—they need a place to stay at the beach. What should I double-check? Help me to look at the parts of the word."

The children are likely to encourage you to look at the first two letters: *sl*. If they don't, you can say, "Hmm, . . . let's look at the beginning of the word. . . . It is /sl/, so the word can't be *stay*. /Sl/ . . . *sleep*. That makes sense and it matches the word on the page! Yes, it does look right!"

CHALLENGE THEM: Prompt students to cross-check meaning and visuals in their own books. Help students recognize all of the word parts they know when they look across a word.

"Now it is your turn to read from your baggie. Don't forget that when you get to a tricky word and you try to figure it out, your guess has to make sense *and* match the letters on the page. If you're not sure how to solve the word, try searching for parts you know. After you know some parts, try the whole word again, then keep going."

TEACH TOWARD TOMORROW: Remind readers that when they come to a tricky word, their guess has to make sense *and* look right. Leave them reading while you coach other readers. Offer a reminder Post-it.

"Readers, remember that when you come to a tricky word, your guess has to make sense *and* look right. Your guess has to match the word that is on the page. It's always important to double-check yourself using another strategy."

Give students a reminder Post-it that says, "Does it look right?"

"Keep this Post-it to remind yourselves to ask 'Does it look right?' and to try looking carefully at the parts and crashing them together. Keep it in your book baggie so you can use it when you read. Once you are remembering, 'I need to guess a word that makes sense *and* looks right,' you won't need that Post-it anymore."

OTHER SUPPORTS

▼ **Gr K, Unit 4, Sess. 8:** "Identifying and Editing for Short *E, O,* and *U* Sounds"

▲ **Gr 1, Unit 2, Sess. 16:** "Tracking Down the Look-Alike Word Part: Using Analogy to Solve Words"

POSSIBLE COACHING MOVES

▶ "Check that."

▶ "Does that make sense? What could help you figure out that word?"

▶ "You're going to look for parts? Oh, nice strategy. Let's see if it helps you figure out that word."

▶ If they try three times and cannot figure it out, "Could that word be . . . ?"

▶ "Reread to make sure it makes sense and sounds right."

FIG. 60–1 Emerson reads while Siena listens and coaches her partner.

SMALL GROUP 61

Using Snap Words to Read Longer Words

RALLY THEM AND ACTIVATE PHONICS: Activate students' knowledge of snap words by giving partnerships a set of words to read through quickly.

"You've been working so hard to read big, long words—they can seem scary, but they're actually not! Long words are like a long train—the train has different cars, just like big words have different word parts. Big words are made up of word parts and sometimes little words that you know in a snap."

Distribute a set of snap words to each partnership.

"To help you remember some of those snap words and word parts, will you and your partner read through this set of words together?"

This warm-up is meant to be quick, with partners taking a few seconds to read each word. If you notice students have difficulty with a word, you might step in and read it yourself, or you could put the word card aside, saying, "That's not yet a snap word for you, but it will be soon."

LAUNCH THEM: Write a long word on each partnership's whiteboard and distribute these. Channel partners to work together to read the word, using words or word parts inside the word to help them.

Distribute a whiteboard on which you have written the word *handstand* to each partnership.

"I've written a word on your whiteboards. If you know the word right away, don't shout it out. Instead, take a close, careful look at the word for parts you know." Don't worry if children are able to decode the word more quickly than you anticipate. The true purpose here is to help readers locate known words and word parts inside of other words. Practicing with a word that children can already read can help them more readily apply this strategy to unfamiliar words.

BEST TAUGHT TO

- Students who need support in solving tricky words while reading.

BEST TAUGHT DURING

- Reading workshop

GETTING READY

✔ Make a set of about ten familiar snap words for each partnership. Possible words include *an*, *and*, *will*, *all*, *out*, *in*, *at*, *she*, *look*, and *like*.

✔ Write the word *handstand* on a whiteboard for each partnership.

✔ For each student, make a copy of "Mabel's Handstand" that includes the long words you'll teach today.

✔ Give each student a marker or pen.

"This word is like a long train—it has in a row other words and word parts you know in a snap. Look for them! Use them to help you read the long word." Listen in as children find words and parts they recognize: *an*, *and*, *hand*, or *stand*.

"You found a bunch of little words hooked together, like *an* or *and*, and *hand* and *stand*. And some of you found parts like /st/, a blend you know!" Draw boxes around each of the parts of words on your whiteboard to highlight the known parts, like linked train cars, and draw wheels below them. "Look! A train of little words and parts you know that helped you read this big, long word: *handstand*."

CHALLENGE THEM: Explain that it is even easier to read long words when they are in a sentence. Guide students to read long words using a story about the class mascot.

"Here's the thing. It is even easier to read these big, long words when they come in sentences. As you read, you can think about what would make sense in the story and look for words or word parts you know.

"You will have a chance to try this now. I'm giving each of you a page from Mabel's story about the day she learned to do something new. Remember to check the picture and think about the story, because that can also help you figure out the tricky words. Mabel did us a favor, and the long words are written in bold."

"Look at my **handstand!**" I shouted. I did not **fall.**

I can **spin** like a **windmill!** "**That** was fun!" I said.

"As you read it, when you get to one of those big long bold words, take a careful look at the word for parts you know. Use your marker to put a box around the parts or words you know inside of the word, just like I did with the word *handstand*.

"You can work with your partner to think about what would make sense *and* look for parts you know, as you are reading Mabel's writing." Prompt partners to do more than read the word outright, taking the time to locate known parts.

POSSIBLE COACHING MOVES

▸ "You think it says ____? What little word would you expect to see inside of ____? Find it."

▸ "Use the word wall. Are there snap words that could help you? Can ____ help you read a word like this?"

▸ "This word starts with a digraph. Check the 'Blends and Digraphs' chart."

▸ "Start at the beginning of the word and look for words or parts you know."

As students read through the remainder of the page, point out how they could use more than one snap word to solve longer words, like *in* and *will* to figure out *windmill*. As they locate known parts, highlight them on your own copy.

FIG. 61–1 Emma coaches a reader.

"Look at my handstand!" I shouted. I did not fall.

I can spin like a windmill! "That was fun!" I said.

TEACH TOWARD TOMORROW: Remind students of today's work, using words they know to solve long words, and then rally them to try this in their reading.

"Ready to give this a try in your own reading? Remember when you come to a word that is tricky, you have a few strategies that can help you. You can think about what makes sense, and you can also see if the word is like a train, a line of little words or word parts together. Take out a book and start reading."

OTHER SUPPORTS

Replicate: This group can be replicated with other words.

▼ **Gr K, Unit 3, Sess. 6:** "Using Word-Part Power: Making Words with Vowel-Consonant Rimes: *-at* and *-in*"

▲ **Gr 1, Unit 3, Sess. 14, Ext. 2:** Using Snap Words to Help Read Other Words

Putting the Parts of a Long Word Together

BEST TAUGHT TO

- Students who are having difficulty solving multisyllabic words
- Students who are still solving words letter by letter, rather than part by part

BEST TAUGHT DURING

- Reading workshop
- Intervention time

GETTING READY

✔ Print a page of snap words for each partnership: *out*, *best*, *and*, *going*, *but*, *my*, *play*, *on*, *wait*, *her*.

✔ Write four multisyllabic words on sentence strips: *outstanding*, *butterfly*, *playground*, and *container*. Plan to distribute one or two of these words to each partnership.

✔ Bring a pair of scissors for each partnership.

✔ Ask students to bring their book baggies.

RALLY THEM: Compare the work readers do to solve multisyllabic words to the work of solving a jigsaw puzzle.

"Thumbs up if you have ever worked on a really big jigsaw puzzle. You might spread out all the pieces, and think, 'Oh boy, I'm not sure I'll ever figure this out!' But when you take a careful look at each of those pieces, you discover how one fits with the next, and the next, and the next . . . and before you know it, you've solved it. You see the *big* picture!

"Big, long words are a lot like jigsaw puzzles—they're made up of a bunch of smaller parts. You can search for the parts you know, fitting one part with the next, to solve them."

LAUNCH THEM AND ACTIVATE PHONICS: Review ten familiar snap words that feature common phonograms, blends, endings, and vowel combinations.

"The word wall is filled with words that can help you find parts inside of bigger, longer words. When you look across a long word, you can think, 'Do I know a snap word that has some of the same parts?' You find parts you know inside that big word, and then you fit those parts together to read the whole word.

"Let's read a few snap words that are especially helpful, so you'll be ready to use them to solve some bigger, longer words."

Distribute the page with the list of snap words to each partnership.

"Work with your partner to read these words. Take turns pointing to the words and reading them. Help each other as you work."

If students have difficulty reading these words with automaticity, consider reviewing the word wall in any of these inventive ways from the extensions in Bend III of *From Tip to Tail: Reading across Words*, Unit 3 in the Grade 1 Units of Study in Phonics:

- When You Need to Relearn a Snap Word
- Play "I Spy" with the Word Wall
- "Guess My Rule" with the Word Wall

WORK SIDE BY SIDE: Guide students in using familiar snap words to identify known parts in the multisyllabic word *outstanding*.

"Now, let's use these snap words to read some really long words. I hunted for one of the biggest, longest words I could find. Ready for it?"

Display the sentence strip with the word *outstanding*.

"Don't worry about reading the whole word just yet. Instead, help me find smaller parts that are similar to words you know. You can use *any* word you know to help you, but the snap words you just read will be especially helpful."

"Right now, work with your partner. Which words could help you to read parts of this big word?"

Give students a few minutes to work, and coach them as they do.

"I'm hearing you say that you see a whole snap word right at the start of this big word, *out*."

Cut the first three letters off of the word *outstanding* to isolate the first part.

"Some of you noticed that the snap word *best* has a part that looks the same as the next part of this big word. Can you all spot it? The end of *best* looks the same as this part, *S-T*. The word *best* can help us remember to make the sound of this blend, /st/."

Cut off the blend, *st*, then repeat these steps to help children identify snap words that can help them to read other parts of the long word, like *and*, and *ing* at the end of *going*. Cut off these parts of the long word as you discuss them, so that you have four word parts: *out*, *st*, *and*, *ing*.

"Wow! So many little pieces. We can put these parts together to make a big, long word. Help me solve it. I'll put all of these cut-up pieces side by side, and I'll crash the parts back together. *Out-st-and-ing*, *outstanding*! We used *four* snap words to help us solve this word. Outstanding word-solving work, readers!"

CHALLENGE THEM: Set partners up to locate known parts across other multisyllabic words, and to cut the multisyllabic words into parts to help them read these words part by part.

"Ready to try it with another big, long word? Look across the word from beginning to end to find the parts that look the same as other words you know. Here's a hint: these snap words will help you! When you find a small part inside

POSSIBLE COACHING MOVES

▶ "Start from the beginning. Is there a part you know?"

▶ "Take a closer look at this part."

▶ "Use the word *wait* to help you with the middle of this word. What sound is this vowel team making?"

▶ "This word ends in the same way as the word *her*."

▶ "Crash those smaller parts back together to read the whole word."

the big word that you can read using one of the snap words you know, cut out that small part. Keep going until you've cut the whole word into small parts you can read. Then, you can crash the word back together to read the whole thing at the end."

Give each partnership another multisyllabic word or two, such as *butterfly*, *playground*, and *container*, along with a pair of scissors.

TEACH TOWARD TOMORROW: Remind students that they can use this strategy anytime they are reading when they see big, long words in their books.

"You can do this work anytime you come across a big, long word in your books. You won't actually cut up those words like we did, but you can break them apart in your mind by looking across the word from beginning to end to find parts you know. And remember, the words on our word wall can help you! Take out your book baggies and try it right now. When you see a big, long word in your book, stop and think, 'Do I know a snap word that looks the same?'"

OTHER SUPPORTS

▲ **Gr 1, Unit 2, Sess. 16:** "Tracking Down the Look-Alike Word Part: Using Analogy to Solve Words"

▲ **Gr 1, Unit 3, Sess. 15:** "Using Snap Words to Help Make and Read Other, Longer, Trickier Words"

Word Scientists

Lucy Calkins, Rebecca Cronin, and Allyse Bader

Photography by Peter Cunningham

Illustrations by Marjorie Martinelli

HEINEMANN ◆ PORTSMOUTH, NH

To two former colleagues who are with us still; Mary Ann Colbert and Enid Martinez. —Lucy

To Nonnie. For your unconditional love, quiet strength, and ongoing support. —Rebecca

To the loves of my life; Ray, Charlotte Rae, and Eli. —Allyse

Heinemann
361 Hanover Street
Portsmouth, NH 03801–3912
www.heinemann.com

Offices and agents throughout the world

The authors and publisher wish to thank those who have generously given permission to reprint borrowed material:

"I'm A Little Teapot" written by Clarence Kelley and George Sanders. Copyright © 1939, renewed 1967, Marilyn Sanders Music LLC. All rights reserved. Protected under international copyright conventions.

Cataloging-in-Publication data is on file with the Library of Congress.

ISBN-13: 978-0-325-10518-5

Editors: Marielle Palombo, Tracy Wells, and Anna Gratz Cockerille
Production: Elizabeth Valway
Cover and interior designs: Jenny Jensen Greenleaf
Photography: Peter Cunningham
Illustrations: Marjorie Martinelli and Kimberly Fox
Composition: Publishers' Design and Production Services, Inc.
Manufacturing: Steve Bernier

Printed in the United States of America on acid-free paper
22 21 20 19 18 VP 1 2 3 4 5

Acknowledgments

WE FIRST WANT TO THANK the amazing group of co-authors with whom we worked on the Kindergarten Units of Study in Phonics series: Rachel Rothman-Perkins, Angela Báez, Casey Maxwell, Katie Wears, Amanda Hartman, Valerie Geschwind, and especially Natalie Louis, who has played a leadership role in this series. We are so grateful for the collaboration and support throughout this journey of reimagining the teaching of phonics.

This unit wouldn't have been possible without support from the community of educators who comprise the Teachers College Reading and Writing Project's faculty. We are especially appreciative of the primary staff developers who helped us develop and test the ideas in the unit in classrooms across the country. A special thanks to Elizabeth Franco who brought her magic touch to our final sessions even while she was working on her own units. Emma Bemowski worked tirelessly to support this book in endless ways, and we thank her for her attentiveness and wisdom. Katie Clements is a whiz of a writer and she lent us a hand in a few key moments. Our friend and colleague Celena Dangler Larkey spent hours listening to our thinking and sharing her own. Celena's DNA is very much a part of this book. The amazing Mary Ann Mustac reread the final manuscript, bringing her astute judgement to it.

We have tried to make every detail of this unit be worthy of you, the teachers, who will bring the unit to life, and to do that we tapped the talents of people with artistic talents. Marjorie Martinelli brought TCRWP's rigorous standards for excellence to each of the pictures on her alphabet charts, charming us all with her pig in its pen and her goat near its gate. With help from Kimberly Fox, Hilary Andaya, and Hannah Tolan, Marjorie has helped us to bring a set of amazing tools, charts, and illustrations to you.

Thank you to Andre Martins and Peter Cunningham for capturing the children's work with this unit on film. Your talents bring so much life and beauty to this book.

We are also so very grateful to the members of the senior staff who co-lead the organization and continue to inspire us: Laurie Pessah, Mary Ehrenworth, Amanda Hartman, Colleen Cruz, Emily Butler Smith, and Audra Robb.

Our knowledge has grown like an oak tree, over years and years. Many of the early growth rings in our knowledge base happened in the company of three people who were staff developers at the Project years ago, and who are still with us. We thank Enid Martinez, Mary Ann Colbert, and Christine Cook. A special thanks to Joe Yukish, who was both our colleague and our teacher for years, and who returned to read through each page of each of our units, discussing fine points with us. We acknowledge also that all that we do continues to exist in the wake of the late Kathleen Tolan.

This book stands on the shoulders of decades of work by experts in the field of literacy. These people are our heroes and mentors and we realize that their knowledge and generosity helps teachers around the world nurture lifelong readers and writers. We are especially grateful to Pat Cunningham, Donald Bear, Lori Hellman, Tim Razinski, Irene Fountas, Kathy Ganske, Gay Su Pinnell, Isabel Beck, Afreida Hiebert, and especially the late Marie Clay.

We know that the work we do wouldn't be viable without the spirit, and energy, of the many administrators, literacy coaches, teachers, and children whom we learn alongside. Many thanks especially to the kindergarten teachers at William Greenacres School, Quaker Ridge School, William O'Schaefer, Parkville School, and PS 164. Special thanks to the school community at PS 180 for opening their doors and sharing their children with us on many occasions as we thought through the structures of the workshop and taught together.

We work side-by-side with the team at Heinemann. Abby Heim is part of our family. We couldn't imagine life without her steady support and her great wells of attentiveness to details. How lucky we are that her standards match our own! Big thanks to the production team, led by Elizabeth Valway. This has been a slightly new genre for us—the chance to work with color was an opportunity that we needed to grow into and we thank you for your patience with us. And a very special thank you to our editors, Tracy Wells, Anna Gratz Cockerille, Karen Kawaguchi, and Marielle Palombo for your attention to detail, your writing talent, and for your commitment to helping make this curriculum be as clear and cohesive as possible. We are so thrilled that Lisa Bingen will now bring her famous spunk to the effort to bring these units to teachers throughout the world.

Thank you to our families and friends. We will be forever grateful for your patience and encouragement as we worked through weekends, holidays, early mornings, and late nights.

Finally, we would like to thank each other. The brainstorming, collaboration, and support we shared made this book better. Rebecca and Allyse would especially like to thank Lucy for the opportunity to write with her. The leadership, wisdom, and energy you bring to every project is truly inspiring. Lucy, in turn, would like to thank Rebecca and Allyse. This book was the first one finished in the series, and in many ways, this book taught us all to fall in love with Mabel, with phonics, with this beautiful project of ours. Your bottomless well of perseverance and your contagious enthusiasm made the work irresistible.

Thank you!
Lucy, Rebecca, and Allyse

Contents

Registration instructions to access the digital resources that accompany this book may be found on p. xii.

An Orientation to the Unit

THE FIRST FEW MONTHS of kindergarten are high season for your students' phonics development, and many parts of your day will work in alignment to further this development. Your students will learn phonics during the twenty minutes a day that are allocated explicitly and specifically to phonics study—but they will also learn phonics when they sign in every morning as part of your attendance, and when you read aloud the agenda for the day, your pointer tapping across the print as you read left to right, top to bottom, saying one word for each patch of print. They will learn phonics when they sing rhyming songs, chime in on familiar nursery rhymes, and most of all, when they grow to see themselves as people who label and write stories and all-about books. Throughout the whole day, your teaching will support your students' phonological and phonemic awareness and their knowledge of phonics, while also helping them develop early reading and writing skills, understandings, and habits.

We've developed this unit so that it can be taught alongside units of study in teaching reading and writing, or alongside any balanced literacy classroom. We anticipate that most of you will want to get the additional writing unit, *Show and Tell: From Labels to Pattern Books*, a book that has been written to align with this unit and to help children take all-important steps to use phonics as they write. If you teach using the TCRWP Units of Study for Teaching Reading, the reading unit that we imagine you are teaching alongside this unit is one that is merely summarized in the *If…Then…Curriculum: Assessment-Based Instruction* book within the series. However, your teaching of reading can rely on any other curriculum and you'll still find it easy to teach *Word Scientists*.

It is all-important that you keep in mind that supporting phonics means reading aloud to kids, immersing them in rhyme and story and information books, singing with them, writing with them, and providing time and instruction to support their writing.

Keep in mind that most of your children's learning will occur on many fronts at once. As you immerse your kids in the alphabet, in poems and songs, in stories and information books, and as you invite them to mess about—playing and inventing, talking and questioning, and approximating reading and writing—they'll make progress toward learning many early literacy concepts. *A Guide to the Writing Workshop: Primary Grades, A Guide to the Reading Workshop, Primary Grades* as well as *A Guide to the Phonics Units of Study* will help you to teach early literacy concepts through your shared reading, interactive writing, and the rituals and habits of your day. Your explicit direct teaching of phonics will be important, but it won't be responsible for all that your students learn.

For now, it is helpful for you to know that there are three primary goals to this unit, and your teaching in each of these dimensions will build upon prior instruction in Unit 1:

- Letter knowledge and letter-sound correspondence
- Phonological awareness
- High-frequency words

OVERVIEW OF THE UNIT

This unit is composed of three bends, or parts.

Bend I: Studying the Alphabet and the Alphabet Chart

Bend II: Using the Alphabet to Write

Bend III: Studying and Using High-Frequency Words to Write and Read

In each bend, you'll introduce songs, games, poems, and nursery rhymes that you'll revisit again and again to support phonemic awareness and early reading concepts. You'll also introduce songs and games that can help you teach letters and high-frequency words; these, too, will be revisited throughout the unit and the year.

In Bend I, you'll rally kids to become word scientists. As such, they'll do what scientists do: they'll look closely, and they'll notice and note, question and invent. The first thing that you invite kids to study will be the alphabet chart, and this whole-class focus on the alphabet chart will rally your students to consolidate what they have already learned about letter-sound correspondence, to learn the letters they may not have secured during your first unit, and above all, to begin using all of this knowledge as they label their pictures within the writing workshop. As Rollanda O'Connor writes in *Teaching Word Recognition*, "Perhaps the most powerful demonstration of the alphabetic principle is during activities where children segment words into all of their constituent sounds, represent each sound with a letter of the alphabet, and then read the word back. In other words, the most powerful way to demonstrate the alphabetic principle is by showing children how to spell simple words" (pp. 49–50). That work is at the heart of the writing workshop, and *Units of Study in Opinion, Information, and Narrative Writing* can guide that portion of your instruction. This phonics unit makes it likely that all of your students will have the skills and knowledge they need to be fully engaged in the writing workshop, progressing from labeling pictures to writing sentences, learning to write in such a way that they and others can read their writing. This is the progression that your children will make during the fall of their kindergarten year.

Early in Bend I of this unit, children are invited to study the alphabet chart, noting keywords and their corresponding letters, examining upper- and lowercase letters, and sharing their observations. Your teaching will help them understand how the alphabet works—the relationship between keywords and initial sounds. We know that sometimes children simply memorize the letter, keyword, and sound so they can chant the alphabet along with their classmates. However, to develop a command of the alphabetic principle, they need to understand the tool and its relationship to their growing letter-sound knowledge.

There is a lot of research connecting the development of phonological awareness and knowledge of the alphabet. In their 2001 article, "Critical Components in Early Literacy—Knowledge of the Letters of the Alphabet and Phonics Instruction," Janice Wood and Bronwyn McLemore note:

The single best predictor of first-year reading achievement is the child's knowledge of and the ability to recognize and name the upper- and lowercase letters of the alphabet (Adams 1990; Honig 1996; Riley 1996). Stahl (1997) found that knowledge is still the strongest predictor of reading success in fourth grade. A child with automatic, accurate recognition of letters will have an easier time learning about letter sounds and word spellings than a child who does not know the letters of the alphabet.

In the first bend of this unit, children will continue to study letter formation, again reviewing and consolidating what they learned earlier and building upon that knowledge. You'll lead children to be aware of the features of lower- and uppercase letters to help them differentiate one letter from another.

Throughout this bend, you will help students to fully engage in their investigation of the alphabet chart. In one session, students will compare several alphabet charts, thinking about how they are the same and different. The actual goal in that work is not for your youngsters to delve into a genre study of alphabet charts, but instead, for children to notice the different ways that a letter-sound correspondence can be illustrated through word pictures on different charts. That becomes a highly engaging way for them to reinforce their command of letter-sound relationships and gain flexibility in their application of the alphabetic principle. As they do this work, you'll encourage them to ask questions. "Why is there a sandwich in the *h* box?" a child might ask, but then will realize that the sandwich is actually a hamburger. This sort of inquiry will engage students who are more and less proficient in their knowledge of sound-letter correspondence (who among us doesn't find it fascinating to compare and contrast alphabet charts?) and meanwhile, it provides authentic, engaging reasons for the classroom community as a whole to become engrossed in a whole-class study of letter-sound relationships.

As Donald Bear, lead author of *Words Their Way*, points out, "Many phonics, spelling and vocabulary programs are characterized by explicit skill instruction, a systematic scope and sequence, and repeated practice. However, much of the repeated practice consists of drill and memorization, so students have little opportunity to discover spelling patterns, manipulate word concepts, or apply critical thinking skills. Although students need explicit skill instruction within a systematic curriculum, it is equally true that 'teaching is not telling'" (Bear et al., 5). In this unit, students manipulate, invent, discover—and as a result, learn.

Your teaching will vitalize this bend in other ways. For example, in one session you'll point out that scientists look at things in the world and think, "There's got to be a better way," and then they make inventions. Just as the Dustbuster® was invented when someone looked at full-size vacuum cleaners and thought, "There's got to be a better way to clean up little spills," you'll teach students that they can invent better ways to do things, too. You'll invite them to look at the pictures that illustrate the letters on their alphabet chart and to think, "There's got to be a better way." One child might decide that a ball is just too boring as the picture depicting a *B*, so he or she might decide to substitute *Batman* or *butterfly*. Energy will be high as kids oust the *egg* from one chart and replace it with an *elephant* and make other similar substitutions.

Bend II of this unit reminds youngsters that the only reason that the alphabet chart—actually, the alphabet itself—matters is that children can use it to help them write and read. In this bend, you'll help kids listen for the sounds in words and record them as best they can. The unit begins with a focus on helping kids to stretch words, isolating the initial sound, and then matching that sound to a letter and recording the letter. Throughout this bend, you will be teaching students to stretch segment words to hear phonemes (ffffuuunnn) before moving them to segment each individual phoneme (/f/ /ŭ/ /n/).

Be on the lookout for how your students are forming the first letter sound in words. Say to them, "Watch my mouth," and then say the sound yourself. You may need to say, more specifically, "Watch my lips. They are pressed tightly together when I say /mmm/." It may be helpful to carry a compact mirror with you, so that students can see themselves say the letter sound.

Your invitation to write will be an opportunity for you to assess your students' skills and understanding. Watch closely to see which students can stretch out a word and hear the individual phonemes that make up the word. Which students can isolate sounds? Which can match sounds to letters? You'll continue throughout this bend to help students identify letters, to write letters using the suggested letter formation pathways, and to read the letters they write, blending them. This bend, then, gives students opportunities for practice and gives you opportunities for feedback that guides their practice.

Bend II quickly shifts from recording first sounds to recording all the salient sounds in a word, including—but not limited to—the ending sounds. Traditional phonics programs progress from initial to final sounds, and that progression makes sense if the focus is on reading and students are reading many CVC words. Your students, on the other hand, will also be participating in a writing workshop where they write more complex words, such as *recipe* and *bicycle* and *caterpillar*, and when students attempt to write words such as those, they are as apt to hear medial sounds as final sounds. The proper guidance is to say, "Say the word slowly, and record the sounds you hear." Throughout this work, you'll be linking phonemic awareness to students' knowledge of letter names and sounds.

Bend III, the final bend of this unit, focuses on helping students develop their knowledge of high-frequency words (HFW, or "snap words," as we often refer to them with students), and their command of the words you will have already taught. Note that in the prior two bends, students already learned a few high-frequency words, and they spent a bit of time reviewing their list. Students need to learn new high-frequency words continually, and this bend will not be the first time in this unit when you spotlight the importance of students expanding the bank of words that they know in a snap. This bend is unlike the earlier ones in its treatment of this topic, because the entire storyline of this bend will focus on the topic of high-frequency words.

The reason we place so much emphasis on high-frequency words is simply because these are the words children will encounter most often when reading and use most often when they are writing. As Patricia M. Cunningham writes in the second edition of *Phonics They Use: Words for Reading and Writing*:

> *There are some words you don't want students to have to decode while reading, or invent the spelling of while writing—the frequently occurring words in our language. Of all the words we read and write, it is estimated that approximately 50 percent is accounted for by 100 highly frequent words. As soon as possible, children should learn to read and write these words.*

In this bend, you'll give each of your students their own snap word collection. You'll want to convey to kids that this is a cherished word collection, so we recommend that you give them little cloth pouches to contain these words, if you are able to, although we know you may need to use baggies. Across the bend, you'll help kids to recognize these high-frequency words, even when they are written in varied fonts, and you'll help kids use these words in their reading and writing.

Note that throughout this unit, we expect you to continue to dedicate much of your bulletin board space to a name wall. In addition, you'll have a spot on your wall for your snap words. While your collection of snap words is still small, you may not want to disperse them among all the letters of the alphabet as in a traditional word wall. You'll see we channel you to go from a small snap word display to an alphabetic word wall toward the end of this unit.

Be sure that your snap word collection contains some of the words that are especially concrete and beloved to your kids. If your class of children adores the Mets or soccer, you will want those words up there on the snap word wall. Their names will already be there, and that, too, sends a message. This is particularly important because in Bend III, you will help students add a few of the more challenging words to their word bank: *in*, *it*, and *an*. These words can be tricky for children, because they are abstract functional words. We chose them purposefully to set students up for the teaching of onset and rime, which will occur in *Super Powers*, Unit 3 in the Units of Study for Teaching Reading series. In this bend, we bring back the song "The Name Game" and sing it with snap words. This, also, is done in preparation for rime work in Unit 3.

The bend ends with Word School, in which students demonstrate all that they have learned by teaching their high-frequency words to their stuffed animals. Children prepare for Word School by reviewing the process they use to learn new words, as well as favorite snap word games and songs, so they are prepared to teach the high-frequency words they know in the next session. Word School is held on the final day of the bend. Children teach their stuffed animals all the high-frequency words they know, then send their animals off to sleep with a lullaby filled with snap words.

GETTING READY

By now, your children will have settled into the routines and structures of your classroom and curriculum. Students will already demonstrate more independence, distributing whiteboards, negotiating with a partner, and sharing materials. If you have not had success with students doing these tasks with independence, now is the time to ensure these routines become solid.

Evaluate your daily routines to make sure they are as efficient as they can be.

Take a minute to evaluate your systems and think about ways you can make these daily routines more efficient. Perhaps it becomes one student's job to hand out the alphabet charts, while the child at the end of each row of kids gets the whiteboards for his or her row, making sure the boards have erasers and a marker attached—a child-size sock is a great eraser and also stores the marker inside. Whatever you choose, keep the routine consistent.

You will see that in Bend II it is helpful if children bring their writing folders and a pencil with them when they come to the rug. You may want to ask students to sit on their folders until you tell the class to take them out.

Collect the necessary teaching materials.

For this unit, you will need some basic materials to support your teaching and student's learning. You will find some of them in the Resource Pack (denoted with ⬛) or in the online resources (denoted with ✳).

- **Mabel, the class mascot:** By now your students have fallen in love with Mabel, so it's only appropriate that Mabel becomes a word scientist along with your kids in this second unit. Mabel will help launch the unit, so if you have the resources you might want to dress her up a like a scientist—have some fun! Maybe you have a special lab coat that Mabel can put on during the first session.

- **Large class alphabet chart:** The class alphabet chart will be the focal point of your workshop. Keeping the large class alphabet chart accessible will be important. It may be tempting to place it on a bulletin board across the room where you have more wall space, but you will be pointing, singing, chanting to that chart each and every day, so be sure it's close. Think of it as extension of your arm! ⬛

- **Small alphabet charts:** You will also need small copies of the class alphabet chart for each of your students. These alphabet charts will be used every day, so we suggest laminating them for extra durability. They will be most convenient for you if they are kept in a small bin next to your easel for easy distribution and collection. The online resources also include alphabet charts containing different pictures—one with foods and another with animals. These are used for a few sessions to help students have flexibility with reading different alphabet charts and to develop an understanding for how these charts work, so print these in mind for partnership work. ✳ ⬛

- **Alphabet pocket chart:** You will assemble an alphabet pocket chart for Session 2. You'll return to this tool in your small-group work. We are confident you will find lots of ways to use this resource.

- **Snap word pocket chart:** We suggest starting to collect snap words in a special pocket chart in Session 3. We find it difficult for children to locate words on an alphabetized word wall early in the year. They will be able to find words in the snap word pocket chart if you collect them in the order that you introduce them. You may wish to title your pocket chart something like, "Our Snap Words," and begin filling it with the high-frequency words that students learned in Unit 1, *Making Friends with Letters* (*the, my, like, me, a, I*). We suggest keeping the snap word pocket chart close by your meeting area, so students can read the snap words frequently. You'll also want to have on hand some blank index cards for adding some concrete words (such as *mom, dad,* and *cat*) to this pocket chart. In Unit 3, *Word-Part Power,* you will move the snap words out of the pocket chart and create a word wall as your students' knowledge of high-frequency words outgrows the storage capacity of your pocket chart.

- **Snap word pouches:** In the first session of Bend III, Mabel gives each student a special word collection pouch full of the snap words students have been studying in Bends I and II. Learning these new words deserves a little extra hoopla, so we suggest cloth pouches or even little velvet bags, if you can—although you can use more modest containers like baggies if you need to. Whatever you choose to use, make sure to create some drumroll so that kids understand the importance of these containers—and their snap words. You may wish to keep all of the students' snap word pouches in a bin close by the easel for easy distribution and collection just like you do with the alphabet charts.

Plan for partnerships, rug clubs, and small groups.

We assume you have read *A Guide to the Units of Study in Phonics* and you have learned from that resource how your phonics time will unfold each day. In a nutshell, you'll give a micro-lesson that channels kids into some active and interactive work that they do with more and then less scaffolding. All of that work is done "on the rug," as we are referring to the meeting area.

- **Establish partnerships:** We recommend that you assign students the same phonics partner as reading partner, or writing partner, or even the same partner for all of these. Your routines will work more smoothly when kids know for sure who they work with when it's time for collaborative work.

- **Establish rug clubs:** In Bend II you'll match up partnerships to form rug clubs. You'll teach partners how to turn to another partnership on the rug to create a small group of four to five students. Seat partners hip to hip, and seat the four children who will comprise a club in such a way that they can easily turn and work with each other—we imagine one set of partners constitutes half the club and they sit in one row, the other half of the club are the partners who sit in the row behind. Sometimes children will be asked to work in hip-to-hip partners, sometimes in clubs, and occasionally as the year unfolds, there will be days when you decide to elongate work time and to send kids back to their work spots.

- **Plan small groups:** Meanwhile, *Small Groups to Support Phonics* will help you support informal, short-lived, small groups that will buttress and extend this curriculum and provide you with an opportunity to provide more assessment-based instruction, especially to students who are either less or more skilled. Those small groups are most apt to occur outside of phonics time, during your reading or writing workshop, unless your school has another time in the day designated for intervention.

Plan ways to bring more joy into your classroom.

Students learn best when they are enjoying themselves, so make every effort to reinforce the idea to kids that learning can be fun. We have built joy into this phonics unit, and there are two particular areas in which you can emphasize the joy of learning:

- **Sing songs and read poems aloud:** A principal once said, "It is easy to pick out the best kindergarten rooms by just walking down the hallway—you hear children singing—learning is joyful!" The extensions are loaded with poems and songs that can be printed. These will give you a great start collecting shared reading material for the unit of study, *Super Powers,* in the Units of Study for Teaching Reading. Although some of us find it intimidating to sing, it's important to get over that self-consciousness for the sake of the kids. Belt it out! When using the poems, songs, and chants with the whole class, make sure the copy is enlarged by either writing the words on chart paper or by placing them under a document camera. You will want all eyes on one text.

- **Celebrations:** You will not want to miss the special celebrations that mark the end of each bend. Students will bring in their own stuffed animals from home to celebrate the first and last bend with ABC school and Word School. Many teachers find it helpful to have a few stuffed animals of their own on standby in case a student forgets his beloved animal at home.

Ensure access to a selection of high-quality books and make plans to support transfer and protect reading and writing time.

Students learn letters and sounds for the express purpose of writing and reading. We can't stress enough the importance of a daily writing workshop in which kids use invented spelling to capture their own important ideas on the page. Children learn phonics also to read, so make sure to provide access to a good supply of high-quality books, especially emergent storybooks and alphabet books. In addition to using these books in a few sessions and extensions, be sure to provide students with lots of protected reading time to read and browse these books during reading workshop and other times of the school day to support transfer.

ONLINE DIGITAL RESOURCES

Resources that accompany this unit of study are available in the online resources, including all the charts, word cards, songs, and poems shown throughout *Word Scientists*.

To access and download the digital resources for *Word Scientists*:

1. Go to www.heinemann.com and click the link in the upper right to log in. (If you do not have an account yet, you will need to create one.)

2. Enter the following registration code in the box to register your product: UOSPH_HYSC7

3. Enter the security information requested.

4. Once you have registered your product it will appear in the list of My Online Resources.

(You may keep copies of these resources on up to six of your own computers or devices. By downloading the file, you acknowledge that they are for your individual or classroom use and that neither the resources nor the product code will be distributed or shared.)

Studying the Alphabet and the Alphabet Chart

We Are Word Scientists

GETTING READY

✔ Bring the class mascot, Mabel, to the meeting area.

✔ Distribute one small alphabet chart to each student.

✔ Display large class alphabet chart on the easel.

PHONICS INSTRUCTION

Phonological Awareness
- Identify and produce words that begin with the same sound.
- Identify the initial phonemes of spoken words.

Letter Knowledge
- Recognize features of letters.
- Recognize and name all upper- and lowercase letters of the alphabet.
- Recognize the order of the alphabet.

Phonics
- Demonstrate basic knowledge of letter-sound correspondence by producing the primary sound for each consonant.

IN THIS SESSION

TODAY YOU'LL teach students that they can study and talk about the alphabet chart, just like scientists study special objects.

TODAY YOUR STUDENTS will study the alphabet chart in partnerships, noticing different features of letters, including upper- and lowercase, and the similarities and differences between them. They will also begin to talk about keyword pictures and letter sounds.

MINILESSON

CONNECTION

Rally kids to become word scientists, to think about what scientists do, and to imagine doing those things when studying words. Highlight the work of looking closely.

"Writers, readers, today you begin a new unit in our phonics workshop. Starting today, you will be . . . " I leaned forward and lowered my voice into a whisper: " . . . word scientists!

"How many of you have *some* ideas about what scientists do?" I waited for the kids to signal yes. "Oh my gosh, turn and tell each other what you think scientists might do!"

The room erupted into talk. I listened for a moment, then said, "Holy moly—I heard you say that scientists collect stuff, and then they study what they collect. That reminds me of something I learned about the first person who went up in a spaceship to the moon, the first astronaut. He brought collection bags with him—he collected soil and rock from the moon and put the things he collected into his bag, so when he came back to earth, he could dump the bag out onto his desk, and then start studying all the things he collected.

"Scientists are like that. They collect stuff, and then they study what they collect. Some scientists can spend an hour or even a week studying a bug. You'll see them hunched over a rotting log, or peering into the crack in a sidewalk, enthralled by all that lives in that log or in that sidewalk crack. They notice every little thing.

"I'm wondering if you might want to study *letters* and *words*, like scientists study bugs and rotting logs and other things in the world. You game? That means you'll need to look closely, to really notice a lot of things—just like scientists do."

Build excitement for the new unit by making Mabel become a word scientist.

I picked up Mabel and sat her in my lap. "Mabel wants to be a word scientist, too! She loves *looking* closely at letters . . . " I tilted Mabel's head down to peer at some print, "and *listening* closely to sounds," I said, cocking Mabel's ear. I then pretended Mabel was saying something to me. "What's that, Mabel? You can't wait to get started? Me too! Let's get ready to study letters and words together!"

Suggest that kids need copies of the alphabet chart. Demonstrate how you read it, naming the letter and the corresponding picture, and then making the letter's sound.

"As word scientists, I think you need a copy of the alphabet chart, which is a really important tool for readers and writers." I distributed a copy of the alphabet chart to each partnership. "You'll be studying this chart every day, so protect it. Hold it carefully.

"This alphabet chart includes all the building blocks that make up all the books and pages and stories—all that is written in English (and many other languages). It will be the key that helps you study writing and understand what it means.

"It's going to be super important for you to learn to read this alphabet chart. I'll show you how to read it, and you'll get to study this chart closely. Pretty soon you'll know it by heart.

"You read the alphabet chart like you read the name chart. Watch me read just the first few letters." I read letter, keyword, sound, pointing as I did. "A, apple, /ă/. B, ball, /b/."

Pausing to name what I'd just done, I asked, "What do we read first, in a square?" I repeated: "A, apple, /ă/."

The kids chimed in that first, we read the name of the letter, then the picture, and finally the sound.

Keep the class alphabet chart somewhere easily accessible.

Note that you can draw kids in and rev up their energy by talking more quietly, as well as by talking loudly. There's nothing like a whisper to make little kids wiggle with excitement. It is helpful for even young kids to have some understanding of the way curriculum unfolds, which is why we take the time to tell kids that they are in a new unit now, and to give them a sneak preview to the unit.

You may be thinking that the alphabet chart is not new for your kids—why all the fuss over it? We recognize that you presumably distributed alphabet charts during writing workshop a week or two ago, and your classroom probably has one displayed. But it can be easy to not look closely at something that is there all the time, and there is a lot of helpful sound-letter work to be done with an alphabet chart.

You will want all eyes on the large class alphabet chart during the teaching and active engagement. It may be helpful to have students place their small copies on the rug in front of them or have them sit on their charts and pick them up again during rug time.

"You got it! Right now, will you point to each letter on your chart while we do all those things? We'll say the name of the letter, then read the picture, and then make the sound that goes with that letter." We read the alphabet together row by row.

❖ **Name the teaching point.**

"Today I want to teach you that, just as scientists study rocks and oceans and creatures that live in rotting logs or in cracks in the sidewalk, *word* scientists study the alphabet chart, looking closely at it. Word scientists notice lots of things on the alphabet chart."

TEACHING

Demonstrate looking closely at the alphabet chart, noticing lots of things. Channel students to look closely at the first box—the letter *A*—on the alphabet chart and to tell each other what they notice.

"Let's all study the alphabet chart, even Mabel." I placed Mabel on my lap. "Word scientists, look closely with me." We stared at the chart.

"Scientists notice the things regular people just walk right past. So let's look closely at just this first box," I said, pointing to the *A* box on the alphabet chart. "Tell your partner what you notice."

Reconvening the class, I said, "I agree. I see the letter *A*. Some of you noticed there are two *A*'s. Thumb on a knee if you saw that." Many so indicated. "The first is a capital *A*, and the second is a lowercase *a*. Can you say that word? *lowercase*. Some people call it 'little *A*,' but as word scientists, you use the fancy name for it, right? *Lowercase*."

Ask students to discuss why they think the alphabet chart features specific pictures. Then, explain that each picture represents a word that begins with the corresponding letter's sound.

"Here's my question: Why are there pictures all over this chart? Why is there an apple here? I mean, I like apples, but why isn't it a peach? Or a tomato? Talk with each other and try to solve this mystery."

My eyes roamed ahead on the chart. "And why a dog beside the *D*? Turn and talk."

The kids talked, and after a bit, I called them back. "So, you are saying that the picture always shows a word that starts with that letter? Maybe? Hmm, . . ." Then, as if I just got an inspiration, I said, "Wait! We're scientists, and scientists test things out, so let's do that. Let's test out whether each picture matches the sound that goes with the letter. Let's take a letter and check out whether the picture starts with that letter's sound."

The kids called out a letter and we tested our theory. "R! We know R goes with the sound /r/ like Rebecca's name, and the picture here is a rainbow. /r/ Rebecca. /r/ rainbow. Yes, that one works!

"I heard someone else shout out S. S goes with the sound /s/ like Salima. Let's see if the S word on the alphabet chart starts with that same sound. /s/ Salima. /s/ sun. That one works, too!"

Discuss why the picture icon of a fox is next to the letter X on the class alphabet chart.

"But wait!" I pointed to the picture of the fox. I looked a bit confused and said, "A fox next to the letter X? That doesn't make sense. Fox starts with the sound /f/." Some students agreed while others looked a bit puzzled, so I continued.

"But there has to be a reason why this fox is with the letter X. X goes with the sound /x/." I quickly drew Elkonin boxes—a rectangle divided into three boxes—on the whiteboard. I stretched the word fox, sliding my finger into each blank box for each phoneme. As I did this I asked students to point to the box where they heard the X. "So, do you think you could figure this out? Turn and talk."

I leaned in closely, and after just a few moments, shared out the students' discovery that the sound of /x/ comes at the end of fox.

"So, we have to remember that fox ends with /x/. It is the only picture on the alphabet chart not like the others. That's an important observation!"

ACTIVE ENGAGEMENT/LINK

Return to the theme of the class as word scientists, this time encouraging the class to notice and share interesting things they find on their alphabet chart.

"Let me remind you that scientists notice teeny-tiny interesting details, the things that any ol' person would just walk right past, because that helps them understand more. They say, 'How interesting!'

"You and your partner can have some time now to study your alphabet chart, noticing and talking about interesting things. Point out the things you notice. For example, I notice that the capital A has only straight lines and the lowercase a has curves.

"You ready? Right now, take out your alphabet charts and work with your partner to notice interesting things."

To solidify the concept that children are word scientists, and to encourage their early ideas about the alphabet chart, give them a chance to share some of their observations.

As children noticed and talked, I channeled them to say, "I notice . . . " and to talk about what they see. I asked, "What surprises you about that?"

Elkonin boxes are a versatile word study tool. They can be used to support the phonological skills of isolating, segmenting, and blending sounds. They are a visual scaffold that can be used once a child is able to say a word slowly, stretching out the sounds. It is important to have a box for each sound or phoneme, not each letter. For example, the word way *would have two boxes because there are two sounds: /w/ and /ā/. Remember, think sounds, not letters!*

Your kids might notice things like these. Add in your own as well!
- *"I saw that the capital* M *is pointy, but the lowercase* m *is round."*
- *"The* b *and the* d *look almost the same, but the round parts are on different sides."*
- *"I see the pictures, and they make the sound of the letter. Like* dog *makes /d/."*
- *"Some of the capital and lowercase letters look the same, like capital* O *and lowercase* o."

Invite partners to investigate their favorite letters on the alphabet chart. Encourage them to look closely at the shape and size of the letter and at the picture.

"Word scientists, remember that scientists notice things that other people walk past. Scientists see a moth, hanging from a leaf, and they notice an ant, carrying something bigger than it is. They notice that some rocks have lots of different colors in them, and that water turns to ice when it's really cold. So to be a word scientist, you need to look closely and notice everything you can on the alphabet chart.

"I'd start by finding one letter you especially like—maybe it's the letter at the start of your name—and then notice everything about that letter. Is the letter curvy or straight or both? What other letters does it look like? What picture is in the box? What other words start with that sound? Ready to do some intense noticing? Get started!" As kids worked, I coached them to talk about what they noticed.

After a minute, I said, "Try noticing a letter you don't know very well. What can you learn about it? Can you think of words that start with that letter? That end with it?"

After a bit, I convened the class. "Wow, word scientists, I heard lots of great findings! For example, I heard someone say the capital *F* has no curves, and the lowercase *f* has a curve. High-five your partner!"

FIG. 1–1 Two children poring over the alphabet chart.

SHARE • Choral Reading the Alphabet Chart

Demonstrate how you read the alphabet chart. Rally students to read the class alphabet chart, naming the letter and the corresponding picture, and then making the letter's sound.

"To celebrate the fact that you are becoming word scientists, who will be studying this alphabet chart like scientists study things like rocks and oceans, let's read this one last time," I said. "For now, all eyes up here. Read with me." I led the class in a choral reading of the alphabet chart.

"Now will you and your partner read the chart on your own? Help each other." After listening to them do this, I convened the class and said, "Some of you are making the sounds longer than they actually are. Like this one," and I pointed to the *B*, "is not *buh*. It is just this /b/ /b/ /b/. And this one?" I pointed to the *D*. "It's not *duh*," I said, accentuating the *uh* sound at the end. "It's /d/. Let's try it again together."

Asking students to read the alphabet chart will strengthen their knowledge of sound-symbol correspondence and help them use this tool with independence. This activity will also support children's knowledge of concepts about print, such as left-to-right directionality, one-to-one match, and return sweep.

EXTENSION 1 • Sing the Alphabet Chart in a Different Way

Lead students in singing the alphabet song as they point to each letter on their alphabet charts, then have students do it on their own. The third time, sing the alphabet song to a different tune.

"I have a song for you. It is one that some of you already know. Listen—and join with me if you know the song." I began to sing the alphabet song, "A, B, C, D, E, F, G . . . "

"Will more of you join in this time," I said, "and this time, as we sing, will you point to the letter on your alphabet chart?" We sang the alphabet again.

Try to find opportunities across your day to chant, sing, and read the alphabet chart, so that students get lots of exposure to the letters, key words, and sounds, and develop early concepts about print.

"Now the hard part! Will you and your partner sing this *again*, this time without me? Be sure to touch the letters as you sing!

"Now let's have some fun! Let's change the tune of how you sing it. Listen to me hum the song 'Row, Row, Row Your Boat,' and then will you sing the alphabet chart to that tune? Ready? Listen closely." I hummed the tune and then invited the students to hum alongside me. "Now, let's try to sing the alphabet song to 'Row, Row, Row Your Boat.' I'll start. Join in when you ready!"

EXTENSION 2 • Learning a Letter

Use the "How to Learn a Letter" routine to teach a new letter and encourage students to use this routine to teach themselves letters.

"Word scientists, something really terrific happened today. Some of you spotted letters on the alphabet chart that you don't know very well. The really cool thing is that I saw you realizing that you don't need *me* to teach you every letter. You can teach *yourselves* letters you don't know!

"Let's look at one of the letters that most of you don't quite know yet." I held up the *V* and said, "Word scientists can't just shrug their shoulders and say, 'Oh well, I don't know that one.' Instead, you can teach yourselves that letter. You can continue to use the 'How to Learn a Letter' routine to teach yourself a letter." I displayed the chart and read the steps.

"First, we need to name the letter. So, this is the letter *V*. Wow, *V* is way down at the end of the alphabet chart! Now we need to learn its sound. Look at the picture, say its name slowly so you hear the first sound, the /v/ sound. /V/- /V/- volcano, *V* makes the sound /v/. Now write it. Remember to start at the top." I said the letter formation pathway as the students wrote the letter in the air. We did the same for the lowercase letter. "Now use it. What other words do you know that start with the /v/ sound? Turn and tell your partner." I listened in and heard students say words like *van*, *vegetable*, and so on.

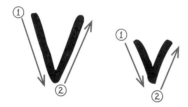

"Let me say some words, and will you give a thumbs up if they start with a *V* and a thumbs down if they don't?" I did that.

"All those steps helped us learn the letter! You can do this anytime you want to learn a new letter!"

Choose a letter that most children don't know. You can continue to use the "How to Learn a Letter" routine after today to reinforce more letters.

To make this work more sophisticated, you could invite students to discriminate whether the letter sound is at the beginning or end of the word. "I'll say a word. Give me a thumbs up if the V is at the beginning of the word and a thumbs down if the V is at the end of the word."

Teach students some ways that word scientists describe features of letters. Invite partners to study the alphabet chart together and talk about some of the letter features they notice.

"Writers, today you looked at the alphabet, and you talked about what you noticed. Talking about letters isn't always that easy, though, because it's not like they are wearing clothes and you can say, 'Notice the letter wearing the polka dot shirt,' or 'I have questions about the letter that has on that coat with the fuzzy collar.'

"Word scientists do, however, have ways to talk about letters, and you started to learn about that earlier this year when you were studying names. I'll remind you of some of the ways that word scientists talk about letters, and then you can try talking about letters, even though they are naked.

"Will you and your partner pull out your trusty alphabet chart, so you can be studying the letters as we talk?"

I waited. "So, one thing you already know is that some letters are tall, and some are small. Show your partner some tall letters, and, if you can, say their names." I let kids do that. "Show your partner some small letters and, if you can, say their names."

"Here is something else you can say about letters: Some letters have holes, some don't. Talk with your partner about holes or no holes, and if you can, say the letter's name when you talk about holes.

"How about this: straight lines and curvy lines? Again, talk about what you notice, and if you can, say the letter names.

"I notice you are talking mostly about the top line of your alphabet chart. Will you talk about the bottom line, too? Go letter by letter and talk about whether the letter is tall or small, has holes or no holes, straight or curvy lines—and notice if the letter has a tail, too. Get started!

"Come back together, let's do this bottom line together, because these are super hard letters.

"Now, time is almost up, but will you look at the letters in your name and talk about those letters, talking like word scientists?"

Understanding How the Alphabet Chart Works— Keywords and Initial Sounds

GETTING READY

✔ Prepare your alphabet pocket chart, leave out picture-letter cards for *A*, *S*, *D*, and *G* and several other picture-only cards. Scatter the picture-only cards for those letters around the floor.

✔ Distribute class alphabet charts to each student.

PHONICS INSTRUCTION

Phonological Awareness
- Identify and produce words that begin with the same sound.
- Identify the initial phonemes of spoken words.
- Match words with the same beginning sounds.

Letter Knowledge
- Recognize and name all upper- and lowercase letters of the alphabet.
- Recognize the order of the alphabet.

Phonics
- Demonstrate basic knowledge of letter-sound correspondence by producing the primary sound for each letter.

IN THIS SESSION

TODAY YOU'LL teach students that the pictures on the alphabet chart can help them remember the sound that goes with a letter.

TODAY YOUR STUDENTS will look at the picture, say the word, really listening to the first sound, and find the letter that goes with that sound on the alphabet chart.

MINILESSON

CONNECTION

Rally the children to help solve a problem: some pictures from the class alphabet pocket chart were knocked off. Can the class help reconstruct the alphabet pocket chart?

"Word scientists, come quickly! Something has happened to our alphabet chart! Mabel got so excited about our alphabet chart that she decided to play with it last night. But guess what? She accidentally knocked some of the pictures out of our pocket chart!" I showed children that the pictures were scattered around the floor. I collected them, and said, "Well, it's a good thing we spent yesterday studying this chart so closely. We're just going to have to help Mabel put it back together.

"Are you game for helping? We'll take the pictures, one by one, and figure out where each goes." Holding up the picture of an apple, I said, "Let's start by reading this picture. It's an apple, right? How do we figure out where this apple goes in the pocket chart?"

Hands shot up, but I gestured for kids to lower them. "I know this one is easy, but watch how we figure it out so you can do the same to figure out the other letters as well." I said the word slowly, "apple, apple," and said, "I'm listening for the first sound in this word, can you hear it?" I said, "apple, apple," then said, "Say the word slowly. Listen for the first sound. /ă/-/ă/-apple.

"This picture helps me figure out the sound of the letter that's in that box. /ă/-/ă/ goes with the letter *A*."

I placed the apple picture underneath the *Aa* on the alphabet chart.

♣ **Name the teaching point.**

"Today I want to teach you that the pictures on the alphabet chart can help you remember the sound that goes with a letter. You look at the box with the letter and picture, and you say the name of the picture slowly and catch the first sound of that word. That is the sound that goes with that letter."

TEACHING

Tell a story about other kids who had a hard time hearing the first sound in a word. Do this in a way that makes your kids feel capable and shows them how to listen to initial sounds in a word.

"Let me tell you a story of something that happened in a different kindergarten classroom. A little girl was writing a story, and she went to her teacher and asked, 'How do you spell *Santa*?' The teacher said to the little girl, 'Say the word s-l-o-w-l-y and listen for the sounds that you hear.'

"So, the little girl said, 'Ssss-anta' over and over. Then she said to the teacher, 'I got it! I hear . . . ' and she said 'Ssss-anta,' one more time. Her teacher thought she was listening for the sounds and hearing /s/ /s/. But then the little girl said, 'I hear "ho ho ho."'"

The kids giggled, and I continued, "Friends, Santa *does* say 'ho ho ho.' But when the teacher told that little girl to say *Santa* slowly and to listen for the sounds, she meant that the little girl needed to listen for the sounds in the *word Santa*. She meant, 'Say "Ssss-anta" slowly, and listen for the first sound in the word.' She hoped the little girl would listen, and then put the letter that goes with that first sound right onto her paper.

"Let's help that little girl hear the sound at the beginning of *Santa*. To do this, catch the sound you hear at the start of the word in your mouth, and think, 'What letter goes with that sound?'" I quickly demonstrated how I listened for the beginning sound in the word *Santa*. I said, "Ssss-anta, /s/, S. *Santa* starts with letter *S*."

Rally kids to use their abilities to hear initial sounds to reconstruct the alphabet pocket chart.

"Will you use those listening skills to reconstruct our broken alphabet chart?" I held up a picture of a sun, and the kids chimed in, saying "sun."

"You're right—it's a sun. Let's say the word slowly and see if we can hear the very first sound." I gave them a few seconds to do that, then joined in, saying "*Ssss-un*. /s/ like *Santa*, right? /S/ *sun*. Let's get this sun back where it belongs!" I placed the picture of the sun underneath the *Ss* in the alphabet pocket chart. "/S/ sun goes with the letter *S*."

As you work with the alphabet chart, pay close attention to the pronunciation of the sounds and words. Be careful you or your students are not adding additional phonemes to sounds (/d/ not "duh"). Pay extra attention to your pronunciation of egg *and* igloo, *because a different pronunciation can yield an inaccurate sound. (*Egg *might yield a long* a *and* igloo *might yield a long* e *if you are not careful.)*

Many children memorize the letter, keyword, and letter sound (A, apple, /ă/) when chanting the alphabet chart. However, they will be unable to use the keyword to identify the letter sound if they can't say and hear the initial sound in the word.

"How about this one?" I held up the picture of the dog. "*D-d-dog*. Say it with me. *Dog*." I said *dog* into my cupped hand, miming that I was holding the /d/ sound in my cupped hand. I invited the kids to do the same. "What sound are you hearing?"

Soon we were placing the dog picture underneath the *Dd* in the alphabet pocket chart. I said, "Up you go, little dog, back where you belong!"

ACTIVE ENGAGEMENT/LINK

Continue to prompt students to say the name of the picture dropped from the alphabet chart, to isolate the first sound, and to match that sound to the appropriate letter on the alphabet chart.

"We have quite a few more pictures to put back. Can I get your help with this? I'll hold up a picture, and you and your partner can figure out the sound. You have to be able to catch that first sound to figure out what sound goes with that letter." I held up the picture of a goat. "Turn and talk with your partner. When you know where it goes, point to the place on our alphabet chart."

After the students decided where the picture went, I said, "The goat helps you figure out the sound that goes with the letter *G*: /g/," and placed the picture in its spot. As I did, I said, "Get back up there, little goat! You belong next to the *G*."

I repeated this routine a few more times with more pictures.

RUG TIME

Channel students to hear initial sounds with the pictures on the alphabet chart.

"We talked earlier about how scientists really look closely at things. They'll study the way some birds, like pigeons, walk like this," and I did my best pigeon imitation, " . . . and they open up flowers to see what's inside them. You are word scientists, so that means you need to look closely, too. Let's do some noticing with these alphabet charts. Ready?"

I quickly distributed an alphabet chart to each student. "Get together with your partner, then take turns being the word scientist. For now, the partner on the window side of our meeting area—you're Partner 2, and you'll be the word scientist. Thumbs up if you are Partner 2." The kids signaled. "As word scientists, you will study the alphabet chart and choose a letter—but don't tell your partner which letter you have chosen. Do that now." I gave the children half a minute to do that.

"Robert, come up with your alphabet chart and do this," I said. "Have you thought of a letter?" He nodded. "Now, look at the picture that goes with your letter and say that word, really listening to the first sound. Like this," I said, and pointed to the *E*. "*Egg*, *eeeeggg* /ĕ/. Do you hear how I said *egg* slowly, so I could hear and say the first sound?"

POSSIBLE COACHING MOVES

▶ As students say the word, coach them to draw out the first sound so they can clearly hear it being enunciated. Do this with them once or twice, but then remove your scaffold, say, "Do it yourself this time."

▶ "Say the word together slowly. Now catch the first sound."

▶ To the partner who needs help, say, "Can a name help you?"

▶ Suggest that students who know lots of letters and sounds think of other words that start with a sound.

Robert chose a *T* with the key word *turtle*. I said to him, "Look at the picture and say the word slowly, listening for the first sound. Do it with me: *T-t-t-t-turtle* /t/."

Then I said to the class, "Pretend you are Robert's partner and guess what letter goes with that sound."

One child guessed that it was a *K*, so we compared it to a student's name. "*Kyla* starts with *K*; /k/-/k/-*kyla* sounds different than /t/-/t/-*turtle*." Another child guessed the letter was *T* and Robert nodded his head to confirm that the letter he chose was *T*.

"Partner 2s, do you have your letter chosen? Say the word that goes with it, and the first sound, so your partner can guess the letter." As the students worked, I moved around and coached each partnership. I reminded them to take turns and play a few rounds.

FIG. 2–1   A word scientist guesses and locates the letter *G* for *goat*.

SHARE • Alphabet Aerobics

Wrap up today's work by inviting students to chant the alphabet one more time with movement.

"Let's end today by chanting the alphabet one more time. This time, let's get up and move. As you say the letter, twist your body to the left, toward the window. Then, as you say the picture, twist to the right. And now the best part—throw your hands above your head as you say the sound! I'll show you the moves—watch me." I said the usual "*A apple* /ă/," but this time did a twist, twist, hands-in-the-air sequence to accompany the chart. "Ready for some alphabet exercise? Let's go!"

If you're not going to have time to get through the whole alphabet, focus on the second half. Lots of kids learn the first half the alphabet way better than the second half!

FIG. 2–2   Encourage students to use their bodies to learn.

EXTENSION 1 • Turning the Classroom into an Alphabet Chart

Explain that the class is going to make the whole classroom into one giant alphabet chart. They'll do this by labeling as many items as possible with their first letter.

"Word scientists, I visited another kindergarten classroom and guess what I saw? Their rug was an alphabet chart! Yes, each square had a letter and a picture, and kids were sitting on the alphabet chart! At first, I wished that we had an alphabet chart rug, but then that got me thinking that we can make our whole classroom into one big alphabet chart. We can hang letters all around the room to help us learn our letters and sounds. Are you up for It?

"I thought we could start labeling a few things in the room together, and then you and your partner can walk around the room labeling the rest.

"How about the books? What letter do I put on the books? Hmm, . . . *books* starts with the /b/ sound. Oh, *book* starts like *ball*. That's the letter *B*." I wrote a large *b* on a Post-it and placed it on the shelf of books.

"Let's try this one together. What letter do I put on the rug, /r/? Turn and tell your partner." I gave kids a moment to talk, then said, "I heard lots of us say *R*, like in *rainbow*. Let me write an *R* on this Post-it and label the rug." I placed the Post-it on the rug.

"Right now, I'm going to give you and your partner a bunch of Post-its. Work together to look around the room and find objects, then label those things with the first letter of the word, like we did with *books* and *rug*."

If your classroom does have a rug alphabet chart, you can warm up by having students notice the letter they sit on. Then think about how fun it would be if the entire classroom was one big alphabet chart.

FIG. 2–3   Encourage students to find new things to label.

EXTENSION 2 • Letter Books for Letters *F* and *H*

GETTING READY

- Make your own pages for letter books by downloading clip art or gathering pictures from a magazine. You will want to have about six pages with pictures of things that start with *H* and six pages of things that start with *F*. (Use your assessment to determine letters your children still need to learn.)

Recruit the class to help make more letter books like the ones from the previous unit. Today, ask them to help you sort pictures to create two letter books, one for *F* and one for *H*.

"Yesterday, some of you spotted letters on the alphabet chart that you don't know very well. I saw a bunch of you talking about these two letters," and I wrote *Ff* and *Hh* on the whiteboard. "They are important letters, so I wonder if you'd be game to make letter books to help you learn those letters? Remember how you made other letter books?" I held up some of their books. "We only made a few of those books, and it'd be great to have some more for our library. I've started a shelf for alphabet books, and only a few of them are written by our class.

"I have some pictures of things—some of them start with /h/-*H*, some start with /f/-*F*, and some might just be pictures that don't go in these books at all. Let's work together to sort these pictures so we can put them in our books. When I

14

hold one up, read the picture so you can name what it shows, and then call out whether it goes in the *F* book or the *H* book. I tapped the floor to show where I would place the pictures to go in the *F* book and tapped another spot indicating where I would place the pictures for the *H* book.

"After we sort this pile of pictures into those that start with /f/-*F* and go in this book, and those that start with a /h/-*H* and go in that book, we can make the books. If a picture starts with a different letter entirely, speak up!"

I held up picture of a fish, and kids said *fish*. I told the kids to point to the book that this belonged in and they did. "Let's check it by saying the word again, and the first sound and the letter. Like this: *fish* starts with /f/, *F* like *fan*." I referred to the keyword on the alphabet chart.

I held up a picture of a house. Many kids responded and pointed, and again I asked them to check it by saying the word, the first sound, the letter, and the keyword. "*House* starts with /h/-*H* like *hat*." I continued.

After a bit, I pulled out a blank sheet of paper and wrote a capital and lowercase *F* on it to make the book cover. "Let's start with our *F* book." I picked up the pile of pictures that we'd decided started with an *F*. "Read the picture with me, and let's double-check to make sure each of these items starts with /f/."

After students checked each picture, I quickly stapled the book cover page and the picture pages together to make the *F* book. We then continued this process to make the *H* book.

"Let's add these books to our alphabet shelf. And I'm hoping many of you will read these books during reading time."

EXTENSION 3 • The "What's the First Sound That You Hear?" Song

Teach children a song to help them hear first sounds in words. Use the name of the class mascot as the first example, then repeat the song with the names of a few of the children in the class.

"Let's sing a song that can help us get even better at hearing first sounds in words. It's called 'What's the First Sound that You Hear?' and it goes to the tune of 'London Bridge Is Falling Down.' You probably know it already." I hummed a few bars to remind students how the song goes.

"Join me when you can. It goes like this:

What's the first sound that you hear, that you hear, that you hear?
What's the first sound that you hear in . . . Mabel, Mabel, Mabel?"

I paused, giving the children time to process.

"/m/ is the first sound that you hear, that you hear, that you hear!
/m/ is the first sound that you hear in . . . Mabel, Mabel, Mabel."

We continued singing a few more times with different names of kids in the class.

Be sure to say the letter sound and the letter name when you set up this work to promote letter-sound correspondence.

Learning Snap Words to Write about What We Notice

GETTING READY

✔ Display the "How to Learn a Word" anchor chart from Unit 1 *Making Friends with Letters*. 🖐️

✔ Prepare word cards for high-frequency words: *at*, *look*, *see*. 🖐️ 📦

✔ Distribute whiteboards and markers to each student.

✔ Distribute a few Post-it notes, a pencil, and an alphabet chart to each student. 🖐️ 📦

✔ Prepare a pocket chart with the title "Our Snap Words," and fill with the word cards for *a*, *I*, *like*, *me*, *my*, and *the*. Prepare to add the word cards for *at*, *look*, and *see*. 🖐️ 📦

PHONICS INSTRUCTION

Phonological Awareness
• Count, pronounce, blend, and segment syllables in spoken words.

Letter Knowledge
• Recognize and name all upper- and lowercase letters of the alphabet.
• Recognize the order of the alphabet.

Phonics
• Demonstrate basic knowledge of letter-sound correspondence by producing the primary sound for each letter.

High-Frequency Words
• Develop strategies for learning high-frequency words.
• Recognize and use high-frequency words with automaticity.
• Learn new words (*look*, *at*, *see*).

IN THIS SESSION

TODAY YOU'LL teach students that readers and writers can turn words they will read and write a lot into snap words by reading, studying, spelling, writing, and using the words.

TODAY YOUR STUDENTS will learn three new snap words as they practice a five-step process for turning any word into a snap word. Students will use snap words to write their observations about the alphabet chart.

MINILESSON

CONNECTION

Rally kids to mark an alphabet chart with observations to share with another kindergarten class. Explain that they can write words and draw arrows to point out what they notice.

"Word scientists, the kindergarten class across the hall is anxious to know what you all noticed on the alphabet chart—and to show you what they noticed, too. So, I'm thinking that maybe you could mark up your alphabet charts with things you notice, and they could do the same with their alphabet charts. Then we could send them our charts, and they could send us theirs. We can study the things they found interesting, and maybe we'll end up seeing more. Fun, right?

"You can use Post-its to tell the kids in the other class what you notice. You can write 'Look!' and use an arrow to point to the thing you want the kids to notice, or even 'I see . . . ' and again, use an arrow to point. I know you have seen a lot of interesting things on your alphabet charts, so you'll probably be writing these things over and over."

❖ **Name the teaching point.**

"Today I want to teach you that when you know you will need to use a word over and over—like if you want to tell another class 'Look!' or 'I see' over and over—that's a good time to learn the new word so that you can use it easily, in a snap."

TEACHING

Give an example of what kids might point out on the chart, and suggest words kids can use to share observations. Remind them of a routine that you'll revisit often for learning high-frequency words.

"I'm wondering what I want the other kids to notice," I said, and studied the alphabet chart. Pointing to the capital and lowercase *W*'s, I said, "These look almost the same! But *these* don't," and I pointed to the capital and lowercase *E*'s.

Turning to the class, I said, "Do you see how I first found something interesting on the alphabet chart? Now watch how I write a note to mark what I found, so I can remember to share it." I wrote "Look at" on a giant Post-it, and then I made an arrow to the letters I'd noticed.

"I could write something different to show other things I notice," I said. "This time I wrote 'I see' and a smiley face, with an arrow pointing to the picture of the cat. He is so cute! And *cat* makes the /c/ sound.

"To write notes like that, you need to be able to write *look*, *at*, and *see*, and even to write sentences, like 'Look at this' or 'I see that.' Let's make sure all of you learn to write these words in a snap. Whenever you want to learn a word really well—so well you know it in a snap—you can go through some steps. You'll remember this chart from our last unit." I revealed the "How to Learn a Word" chart from *Making Friends with Letters* and gestured for kids to join me as I read through each step in the process.

You're not only teaching kids a few high-frequency words. You are teaching them how to go about learning to recognize and spell a word with automaticity, and you are teaching kids the power that comes from "just knowing" a bank of commonly found words.

Many researchers agree that across this year, your children should learn about fifty high-frequency words, and that learning needs to be distributed across the year with many opportunities to revisit. The snap words we're suggesting you highlight are accessible ones that will prove to be very useful for students who are in this unit and in the aligned writing workshop units. Part of the goal is to help kids see the payoff from learning these words by heart.

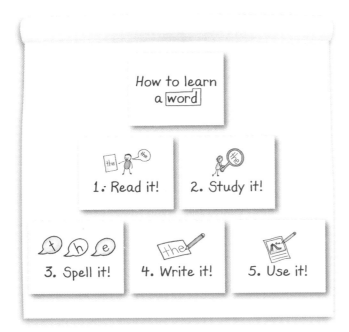

Coach students as they go through the steps for learning a word. Channel them to read the word, then to study it, drawing on the work they did in the previous unit.

I wrote the word *look* on chart paper. "Are you ready to learn the word *look*?" I pointed to the first bullet on the chart. "Read *look*."

Moving to the next bullet, I said, "Now we need to study the word. You're pros at studying things closely. Remember how you studied the letters on the alphabet chart and noticed a ton about them? Ready to study the word *look*?" I covered the word with an index card and slowly revealed one letter at a time, guiding the kids to study and check each letter along with me. I reminded them they could talk about the letters—noticing if they are tall or small, have holes or no holes, and so forth.

After a minute, I called students back. "I agree with what you noticed. There are four letters in the word *look*. There are two tall and two small letters. And you are right that the word has two *O*'s. They have holes in them, right?"

Coach students to spell the word repeatedly. Then, direct them to write the word on their whiteboards while looking at it. Then ask them to try writing the word again without looking at it.

"Ready for our next step? Let's spell the word. *Look* . . . l-o-o-k, l-o-o-k . . . *look*! Try it with me. Let's do it again." I lowered my voice, so the class could spell the word without me. I kept watch for any students who appeared to be having trouble with this.

"Here's step 4. We need to write it." I quickly handed out whiteboards and markers. When everyone had them, I said, "Start writing the new snap word *look*, l-o-o-k. Spell it out loud as you write the letters. Then, cover it with your hand, and spell it again. Now, erase the word, and this time try to write it faster and without looking up here. Then erase and spell it again. Write it five times. Each time, check each letter."

ACTIVE ENGAGEMENT/LINK

Repeat the high-frequency word studying sequence with additional words: *see* and *at*. As much as possible, recruit students to do more of the work.

"Let's learn two more words, and then you can use all the words to write notes to the other kindergarten class. Here's another word that you'll use over and over again. This is the word *see*."

I repeated the "How to Learn a Word" sequence with the additional words: *see* and *at*, moving through the same four replicable steps—read, study, spell, and write, still saving the last step (in which students use the word) for rug time.

Today, you'll support the last step in the routine—using the word—during rug time.

Remind students about the importance of snap words, and tell them how snap words will help them in their ongoing reading and writing work.

"Word scientists are always learning more words they will use again and again. Now we know *see*, *look*, and *at*—three very important words for scientists. And earlier this year, you learned some other words, too, didn't you?" I brought forward word cards for *I*, *me*, *the*, *my*, *like*, and *a*. "Let's read all these words," I said, and I used a pointer to direct a shared reading of the words. We read them several times, in different sequences and at varying speed.

"You know what I just realized? We can make these into sentences, or at least the start of sentences." I showed students how I could shuffle the words around to construct sentence starters: "Look at the . . . " and "I see a . . . " I asked the students to read each phrase with me.

RUG TIME

Channel students to use their new snap words to make note of things they notice on their alphabet charts. They'll share their marked-up alphabet charts with each other and with another class.

"You know some words to use to point out things you notice for the kindergartners across the hall," I said. "But before you can point out the things you see, you need to study your alphabet chart really closely. Are you going to look at your alphabet chart like this?" I said, making a sweeping glance past my copy of the chart. The kids chimed in to say, "Noooo!" and soon they were studying the chart more carefully.

"Maybe you'll notice a picture that you don't think makes sense," I said. "Maybe you don't know what something is meant to be, or you don't know why it is beside that letter. Or maybe you'll notice a letter where the lowercase letter is nothing like the capital letter.

FIG. 3–1 A student notes observations on their alphabet chart.

It would be preferable if kids make interesting observations—but even just noticing cute pictures still gives them opportunities to use their new high-frequency words, and that is the real purpose of this lesson.

POSSIBLE COACHING MOVES

▶ "If you aren't sure how to write that snap word, look at it again, study it, then close your eyes and see it in your mind. Then write it and check it."

▶ "Say the letters as you write."

▶ "Look at the word and check the letters. Does it look the same?"

▶ "What do you notice about the alphabet chart? What do you think others might find interesting? Go ahead and mark that with a snap word and an arrow!"

▶ For kids who are ready for more of a challenge, you might say, "See if you can write a whole sentence. 'I see a dog.' or 'Look at the sun.'"

"Whatever you notice, use your Post-its to point out what you see to the other kids. You might write 'Look!' or you might write 'I see . . .' and put an arrow. If you wonder about something, you could make a question mark." I wrote one on the board as a model.

SHARE • Creating a Class Snap Word Chart

Explain that just as scientists have special places to store their collections, the class needs a special place to store words they know.

"Will you show a partner what you noticed? Use your notes to remind you of what you discovered when you studied the alphabet chart. Scientists do this all the time." I listened in as students shared.

Convening the class, I asked if the kids would send their charts to me, and I made a stack of them. "I'm so excited to share these with the kids across the hall!

"Word scientists, have you ever been to a museum and seen science collection displays? Sometimes scientists put all of the things they study in a box, with a special spot for each thing." Some kids chimed in that yes, they saw a butterfly display at the Museum of Natural History. One shared that she had a rock collection. I nodded. "Sometimes scientists even have empty spots in their collection boxes, so they'll have room to add new things to their collection." I shared a few pictures of science collection boxes.

Reveal a pocket chart that will be used to display all of the snap words that kids are learning. Add the words the class learned today to the chart.

"I'm asking you about this because I've made a place where we can store things we collect, too. Only we're not collecting butterflies and rocks, but words." I pointed to a pocket chart that was labeled, "Our Snap Words."

Then I said, "I already put the snap words you learned earlier in this place, and I was thinking we could add today's words, too. Will you read the words that are already here?"

The children followed my pointer and read me, *a*, *the*, *I*, *like*, and *my*, and soon we'd added the

FIG. 3–2 Making a display can make it easier to study the objects in a collection. Word scientists can also make displays of their word collections.

words from today: *see*, *look*, and *at*. I pretended each word was a fragile butterfly or a precious stone as I added each card to the pocket chart.

"Word scientists, this is the way we can keep our words together, so we can read them every day. Let's read them all right now." I led the class in a shared reading of the snap words.

EXTENSION 1 • Practicing High-Frequency Words with a Poem

GETTING READY

- Gather all the snap words from the pocket chart: *a, at, I, like, look, me, my, see, the.*
- Display an enlarged version of the poem "I Look Closely."

Provide students another opportunity to practice their new snap words with a shared reading of the poem "I Look Closely."

"Readers, it's important to read your snap words often so that you will be able to read and write these words in a snap. When I point to the word in our chart, will you read it, spell it aloud, and then read it again?" We quickly reviewed each word.

"Once you know a collection box full of words, those words help you to read other things—stories, letters, even poems." I revealed a poem on the easel. "Let's read this poem. I'll read it, and if you see a snap word up here, a word you know in a snap, put your thumb up."

I pointed under the words as I read the title: "I Look Closely." I scanned the carpet to see many students giving a thumbs up and I said, "You know these two words, right?" I pointed to *I* and *look*.

"Before we read on, let's stop and think: What might this poem be about? Think about the title, look at the pictures. Turn and talk with your partner."

After half a minute, I continued. "I agree. I think this poem will be about looking closely, but not at letters and words like word scientists, but at things in nature."

I started reading, and each time I read a snap word, I said it with an extra punch, signaling to students to notice the word.

"Word scientists, this time, will *you* read the poem? I'm sure I'll hear many voices because you can read so many of the words. Ready, let's get to it!" The class read the poem. I listened for who was able to read the snap words.

I Look Closely

I look at the sky.
I see the clouds.

I look at the trees.
I see the leaves.

I look at the flowers.
I see a bee!

Throughout this unit, look for opportunities to return to previously taught high-frequency words in continuous text. You may also want to take this opportunity to add a concrete word to your word wall—a word like soccer, *if many of your students are obsessed with soccer. You don't want the entire word wall to be overtaken with functional words that don't have concrete meanings for kids.*

EXTENSION 2 • And the Winner Goes to . . . ! Marking Favorite Pages in Alphabet Books

Invite partners to read through alphabet books, reading the letters, looking at the pictures, and figuring out what they represent.

"You've been finding amazing things in alphabet charts. Look what else you can study!" I triumphantly placed a basket, brimming with alphabet books, into the middle of the meeting area. Distributing these among the kids, I said, "Can you believe what treasures these are? Go ahead, you can look at them."

I gave the kids some time to *ooh* and *ahh*. Noticing that few of them were actually reading the books from cover to cover or in any alphabetic sequence, I said, "I love, love, *love* that you are actually reading these. Holy moly, that is so grown-up! Will *all* of you do that? Put the book between you and a partner, and will you take turns reading? One of you reads the letter, then you both look at the pictures and try to figure out what the picture is on that page. Then the next person reads the next page. Go!"

After kids did this work, I said, "Oh my gosh, watching you just gave me another idea. I saw one of you *singing* your book. That was such a brilliant idea! Maybe a bunch of you would want to read your ABC book by singing it.

"How about trading books with another partnership so you get a new book?"

Rally students to select their favorite pages and award the winning page a special blue ribbon.

"I'm afraid we need to end, but before we do, I'm going to give each of you a blue Post-it. Did you know that at dog shows or horse shows, the winning dog or the winning horse is given a blue ribbon? Blue means champion. It's the same at car races. The fastest car gets a blue ribbon.

"When you get your blue Post-it, that is for the winning page, the champion page. Will you and your partner decide which page is your very favorite, and put your blue ribbon Post-it on that page?

"If the two of you can't decide, if it is a tie, I can give you a second blue ribbon Post-it."

EXTENSION 3 • Use the Alphabet Chart to Clap and Blend Syllables

Invite students to practice clapping the beats in the names of the pictures on the alphabet chart. Start by having students warm up by clapping the beats in their own names.

"Word scientists, I thought we could use some more practice listening to the beats in words. I was trying to think of a fun new way to practice, and then I thought, 'Oh my gosh! Why don't we use the pictures on the alphabet chart?' Before we start, let's warm up—clap out the beats in your name."

After kids did that, I continued. "Yes, you remember how to do it with your name, but now let's try it with pictures. When I point to a picture, clap the beats. Ready? Let's practice a few together, and then you'll play with your partner."

I pointed to the apple on the alphabet chart and said, "Now, let's practice clapping the beats we hear." We all clapped the syllables. "Yes, two claps or two beats in the word *apple*." We practiced with a few more pictures.

"Now, I will give you and your partner an alphabet chart. One partner will point to a picture, and the other partner will clap the beats. Then switch. Ready, go!"

Model segmenting syllables by saying the beats in words. Invite students to blend the syllables back together and say the whole word.

"Wow! You are getting so good at clapping the beats in words. I think you might be ready to do some new listening work. I am going to say the beats in the word separately, and then you have to put them all together and think what the word is. Let's try it with a name first. I'll say the beats, and when you know whose name it is, put a thumb on your knee. Jess-i-ca. Let's all say the name. Jessica!"

After some practice with two-syllable words, I invited the class to blend syllables of some multisyllabic words from the alphabet chart: *ladybug*, *octopus*, *volcano*, and *watermelon*.

If students need more practice with clapping the beats in words, kids can walk around the room, touching things in the room and clapping out the syllables in that item's name: fish, *one clap;* scissors, *two claps.*

Comparing Different Alphabet Charts

GETTING READY

✔ Gather different alphabet charts.

✔ Enlarge the animal-themed alphabet chart to display alongside the original alphabet chart.

✔ Prepare one food-themed alphabet chart for each partnership.

PHONICS INSTRUCTION

Phonological Awareness
- Count, pronounce, blend, and segment syllables in spoken words.
- Identify and produce words that begin with the same sound.
- Match words with the same beginning sounds.

Letter Knowledge
- Recognize and name all upper- and lowercase letters of the alphabet.
- Recognize the order of the alphabet.

Phonics
- Demonstrate basic knowledge of letter-sound correspondence by producing the primary sound for each letter.
- Associate the long sound with the letter name for the five major vowels.

IN THIS SESSION

TODAY YOU'LL teach students that readers and writers understand that different alphabet charts all work in the same way, and that students can use any alphabet chart to help them read and write.

TODAY YOUR STUDENTS will compare and contrast different alphabet charts, noticing how the letters and pictures go together in each.

MINILESSON

CONNECTION

Tell a story about how you discovered there are many different alphabet charts, and explain that the class will study some of these in addition to the chart they already know.

"Word scientists, come quickly! I found something I can't wait to show you. Last night, when I was planning for our phonics time, I didn't have our alphabet chart with me. So, I searched for alphabet charts on my computer. A whole bunch of them popped up!"

I held up several different alphabet charts. "Look at this one. Every letter is illustrated with a different animal." I picked up Mabel. "And Mabel, it has a picture of an elephant on it.

"I had no idea there were so many different alphabet charts. I think we need to study not just our class alphabet chart, but some of these other alphabet charts, too. It will help us to develop our reading and writing muscles! Are you game?" I flexed my biceps.

❖ **Name the teaching point.**

"Today, I want to teach you that to really understand how an alphabet chart works, you can compare different alphabet charts. It helps to figure out what is the same and what is different on more than one alphabet chart, so you can use *any* alphabet chart to help you read and write."

TEACHING

Demonstrate looking closely and comparing two alphabet charts, noticing what is the same and what is different.

I placed an enlarged copy of the new alphabet chart—one featuring animals for every letter—next to an equally large copy of the original alphabet chart. "Let's all study these two alphabet charts. Mabel, you can join us too." I put Mabel on one child's lap.

"Word scientists, let's first look at just the first boxes on the two different alphabet charts," I said, pointing to the *A* boxes on the alphabet charts. "Will you tell the person near you what you notice? What is the same? What is different?"

After a minute, I called the class back together. Nodding, I said, "I agree. They both have the capital letter *A* and the lowercase *a*. Thumb on a knee if you noticed they have different pictures." All of the children placed a thumb on their knee. "Our alphabet chart has a picture of an apple on it, and this other one has a picture of an alligator.

"An alligator? Does an alligator belong in an *A* box? Let's check. Say the words with me." I lengthened the initial sound of each word to accentuate it. "*A-a-apple. A-a-lligator*. Yes, they match!"

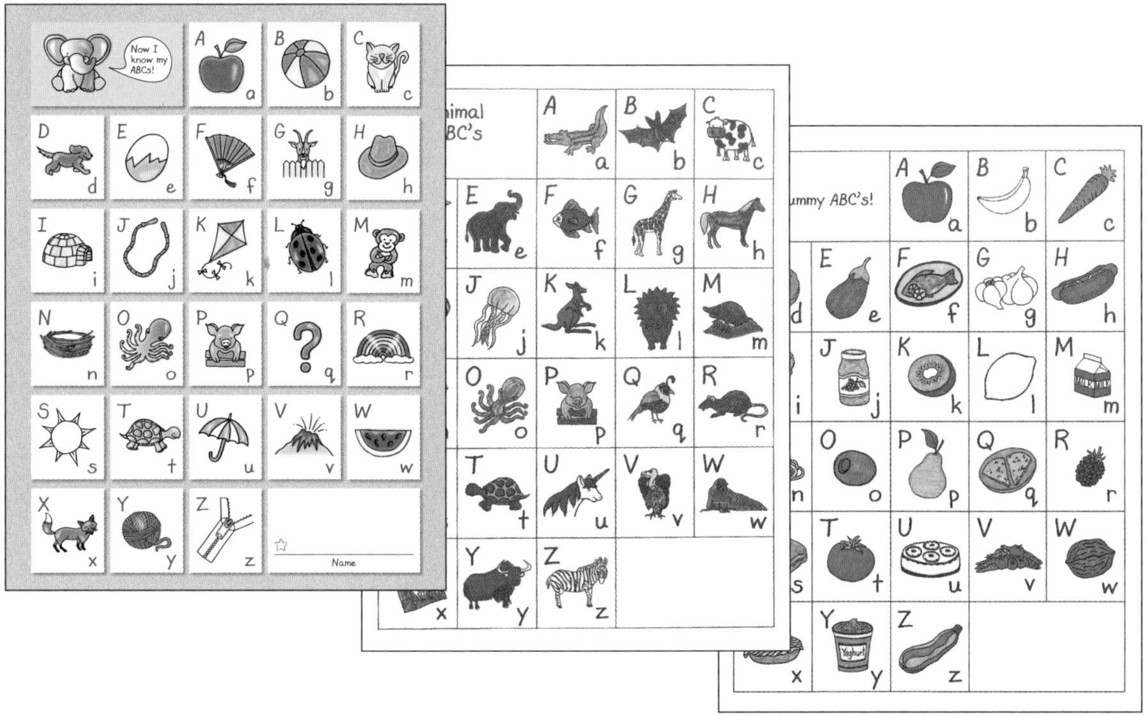

FIG. 4–1   Different versions of alphabet charts

In many classrooms, students learn to read just one alphabet chart. Although the anchor of one familiar chart is important, it can be a hindrance to students' flexibility when learning letters and sounds to only be exposed to one chart. In this session, students will see and use a variety of alphabet charts that they can use as a resource in reading and writing workshop.

Ask students to figure out if the different alphabet charts work the same way as the class alphabet chart, where each picture represents a word that begins with the corresponding letter's sound.

"We already figured out how our class alphabet chart works. Each picture is always a word that starts with that letter, except for the picture of the fox. I wonder if this other alphabet chart, this new one, works the same way? Word scientists, can you test this out? Study the charts and talk with your partner."

The room buzzed and then I said, "I heard some of you studying the box with the elephant, Mabel's box." I pointed to the *E*. "Does this elephant picture on the new alphabet chart belong here with the *E*? Let's check. Say *elephant* and listen to the first sound." The kids said, "*elephant, /ĕl/ /ĕl/ /ĕl/*." Nodding, I said, "It works!"

ACTIVE ENGAGEMENT/LINK

Invite the students to continue comparing the pictures that are used on two different alphabet charts, suggesting they do that for the letters in their names.

"Word scientists, will you continue this research with your partner? You might look at the first letters in your names and see whether there is a picture on both alphabet charts of something that starts like your name starts. Or start with the second row and check those letters. Maybe you'll find some letters that have the same pictures on both alphabet charts."

After a few minutes, I convened the class. "Wow, word scientists, great research! I heard some of you find that on the two charts, the pictures showed the exact same thing, which is the sound that goes with that letter. Am I right that you figured out that both of these alphabet charts work in sort of the same way?

"Word scientists," I said, "the important thing is you can use both of these alphabet charts to help you read and write."

RUG TIME

Distribute two alphabet charts to each partnership—the familiar one they've used thus far in the unit, and a different, unfamiliar one. Lead them in reading the familiar chart together.

"It's time for Rug Time. How are your word scientist muscles? Are you game for more of this thinking work? For more looking closely?"

The children nodded, and I said, "Then I have really important work for you to do. I'm going to give each partnership two alphabet charts. These are precious, so hold them carefully. One of them is a copy of our class alphabet chart, like the one you held the other day, and the other is another alphabet chart—a whole *different* chart."

I distributed the alphabet charts—the class alphabet chart and the food-themed chart—and then asked partnerships to study the class alphabet chart first. "Let's start reading this together." We read, "A apple /ă/, B . . . " and my voice grew quiet while the kids continued, mostly in sync. I chimed back in at a few key points.

Ask partners to read the familiar alphabet chart again, then the unfamiliar chart. Explain that to do this, they'll need to figure out the pictures. Finally, ask them to compare the charts.

When they finished, I said, "That was great reading together! Will you and your partner read that chart again, only this time, whisper it just to each other? Then read your next alphabet chart," the food alphabet chart, "which will be a lot harder because you'll need to figure out the pictures."

As I noticed children finishing with both charts, I asked kids to compare the two charts and notice places that were the same on both charts. After a bit I said to the whole class, "Now will you notice things that are *different* on both charts?"

SHARE • Using Questions to Grow New Ideas about Alphabet Charts

Share some of the questions you overheard while partners were working with the alphabet charts, and invite the class to reason some answers together.

"Word scientists, I love that you have not only been noticing things, you have also been asking questions. Did any of you find pictures that made you go 'huh?'" I asked, and kids shared some of the things they wondered.

One partnership said, "We found a cake in the *U* box." We all looked and sure enough! A cake in the *U* box. "What could the author of this chart have meant for that picture to be?"

The kids had no clue, so I asked, "Have any of you heard of upside-down cake? I think that's what this is." I explained that pineapple upside-down cake is a special kind of cake. I continued responding to confusions, such as "The *X* has a picture of something on a bagel. What could it be? It's *lox*—that is salmon, a type of fish. The word *lox* ends with the letter *x*."

Kids also found that the *i* had an igloo on one chart, and ice cream on the other. Nodding, I pointed out that some letters represent more than one sound. "The letters *a, e, i, o,* and *u* are special letters. They all represent more than one sound. They all represent the sound of their names—like *i* does in *ice cream*—but they also say another sound, like *i* does in *igloo*. Vowels are really important. Let's keep an eye on them and notice how they work.

"Whew, there's a lot to notice on these alphabet charts! Good studying."

The theme-based alphabet charts have a few pictures that represent the less common sound that goes with a letter (e.g., long I in ice cream). Children were introduced to the idea that letters can represent more than one sound in the first unit, Making Friends with Letters. *This will provide another opportunity to expose children to these sounds.*

FIG. 4–2 Students share a noticing about the picture icons for the letter *G*.

If the soft sounds of C and G did not come up during the name study, you might bring it up during this share. You could point out that the giraffe on the animal alphabet chart represents another sound for the letter G. You might also explain that celery *could have gone on the food chart and introduce the soft sound of the letter C.*

EXTENSION 1 • Alphabet Aerobics Accentuating Vowel Sounds

Invite students to join you in chanting the alphabet chart, giving particular emphasis to the vowels.

"You know we can't go a day without chanting the alphabet chart. Let's stand up and have some alphabet exercise. This time, let's really think about how the letters *a*, *e*, *i*, *o*, and *u* are special letters. The vowels are really important because every word has vowel sounds! Let's give them some special attention as we chant the alphabet chart. We'll say the letter, the picture, the sound like we do, with a twist, twist to the other side, and then hands in the air, but when we get to one of the special letters—the vowels—we will sing out their (short) sounds. Another thing that makes vowel sounds special is that they are made with an open mouth, which makes them good for singing." I sang each short vowel sound. Then I continued doing the movements as I said, "So here's how we'll do it this time: A, *apple*, /aaaaaa/; B, *ball*, /b/; C, *cat*, /k/, D, *dog*, /d/ then . . . E, *egg*, /eeeee/. Ready to try it?"

EXTENSION 2 • Sorting in Ways that Support Hearing First Sounds

GETTING READY

- Make a set of about fifteen pictures in a baggie for each partnership. About half of the pictures should represent things beginning with the same letter. Label the baggie with that letter.

"Word scientists. I'm not sure if you have ever been in a scientist's work area, called a laboratory. In many laboratories, there are tons of collections. Let me help you imagine what a lot of scientists' laboratories look like. Usually there is a big work table. That is where the scientists put all the things they are studying, whether leaves, or rotting logs, or bugs.

FIG. 4–3   Scientists organize the items they study. Word scientists can organize the words they study, too.

FIG. 4–4 Start off with some whole-class sorting if your students need more support with isolating first sounds.

FIG. 4–5 Encourage students to first read their picture cards and then begin sorting and isolating first sounds.

"Then on the walls around that table, there are often shelves full of things the scientists want to study. On those shelves, scientists have a lot of jars. In one jar, they might have seashells, or pig feet, or bird nests, or dog poop. Really—scientists find *everything* interesting.

"But here is the thing. Each jar is for one kind of thing, and each jar has a label. In a scientist's laboratory, you wouldn't see a jar labeled 'Junk' that had one pig's foot and one piece of dog poop and one dead goldfish in it. Each jar contains just one kind of thing.

"I have some alphabet jars, but I'm afraid that my jars have gotten all messed up. Like this is supposed to be a jar of pictures of things that start with a *D*, but I think I've got some other stuff mixed in here. Not dog poop, but pictures that really go in other jars. So, I'm wondering, can I give you and your partner a jar that is labeled, and will you make sure that everything in that jar actually goes there? Be very, very careful to make absolutely sure of what you are doing, because remember, this is science!"

As partnerships began to finish, I asked them to trade jars with a neighboring partnership, so they could continue sorting.

EXTENSION 3 • Using Themed Alphabet Charts to Practice Clapping and Blending Syllables

Provide partners with practice in listening for syllables by having them clap the syllables of words on different alphabet charts. Then have students practice blending syllables with a different chart.

"Word scientists, I thought we could use some more practice listening to the beats in words. We had so much fun doing this with the pictures on our class alphabet chart, why don't we try it with one of these new charts?

"I'll hand you and you partner the food-themed alphabet chart and you can work together to clap the beats in each word." I coached partnerships as they worked.

"Now let's do some of our new listening work." I placed the animal chart on the easel. "I am going to say just the beats in some words on the animal alphabet chart, and then you have to think what the word is. Listen to me say the beats. When you think you know the word, don't call it out, put your thumb up." I glanced at the alphabet chart and said, "Tur-tle." Thumbs shot up, and I called on a student who responded, "Turtle!"

I continued to segment syllables with two-syllable words from the alphabet chart, such as *zebra* and *walrus*. After I saw that they were able to do this, I continued with three-syllable words: *iguana*, *kangaroo*, and *elephant*.

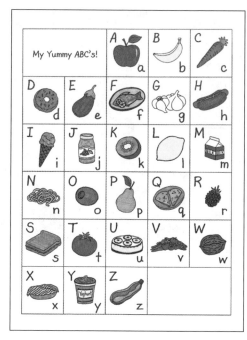

SESSION 5

Reconstruct a New Alphabet Chart

IN THIS SESSION

TODAY YOU'LL teach students that to figure out the first letter in any word, word scientists might say that word slowly and try to catch the first sound. Then, they think about what letter goes with that sound.

TODAY YOUR STUDENTS will work in groups to reconstruct an alphabet chart by taking pictures and matching them to an alphabet chart with letters only.

MINILESSON

CONNECTION

Tell kids that you found a bunch of unlabeled pictures that belong on an alphabet chart and recruit them to help match the pictures to the letters.

"Word scientists, earlier I told you about how I found a bunch of different alphabet charts on my computer. Well, when I was searching online for alphabet charts, I also found all of these pictures meant to go on an alphabet chart, but they don't have letters on them. They're lonely. They want to go on an alphabet chart with their letters. I was going to ignore them and keep on searching for complete alphabet charts, but then I remembered that, as scientists, you all have a talent for studying things that are puzzling and figuring out how things go together. So I'm wondering, would you be willing to help me figure out where each of these pictures belong?"

Many of the kids nodded, and I said, "I knew it! It's going to be hard work, but you are up for the challenge, right?" Again, the kids signaled their willingness to give this a go.

"The hard part will be taking a picture—like this one," I said, holding up the dolphin picture card, "and figuring out where it would go on the alphabet chart. I have all these possible pictures," and I showed the kids pictures of a queen, a person doing yoga, a windmill, and so forth, naming what

GETTING READY

✔ A copy of the picture-only ABC grid.

✔ A few cut out picture cards from the picture-only ABC grid; we used dolphin, queen, yoga, windmill.

✔ Set up a few tables with letter-only alphabet charts and cut up picture-only cards.

PHONICS INSTRUCTION

Phonological Awareness
- Identify and produce words that begin with the same sound.
- Identify the initial phonemes of spoken words.
- Match words with the same beginning sounds.

Letter Knowledge
- Recognize and name all upper- and lowercase letters of the alphabet.
- Use proper letter formation.

Phonics
- Demonstrate basic knowledge of letter-sound correspondence by producing the primary sound for each letter.

High-Frequency Words
- Recognize and use high-frequency words.

they were. "We'll need to figure out the first sound, so we can figure out the letter that goes with that sound. Then you'll need to find that letter on the alphabet chart.

We suggest naming a few picture cards that are apt to give students the most trouble with identifying. You can choose the picture cards you would like to model with (like exercise and yoga).

"Figuring out the first letter in a word is something you need to be able to do to match up these new pictures to their letters on the alphabet chart, and yes, also to read and to write."

♣ **Name the teaching point.**

"Today I want to remind you that when you want to figure out the first letter in a word, you say that word super slowly, so you can really catch the first sound. You have to be quick, and grab just that very first sound before it slips past you. If you don't know the letter that makes that sound, you hold onto it, and check a completed alphabet chart."

TEACHING

Using pictures from the alphabet chart, lead students in isolating the initial sound of a word and then finding the letter that makes that sound.

I held up the picture of a dolphin, then said, "Let's try it with this cute little dolphin. We have to figure out what letter *dolphin* starts with. Remember, say the word super slowly and listen for just the very first sound. When you hear that sound, catch it!"

The class isolated the first sound "/d/-/d/-dolphin." We repeated that word a few times. "Did you catch that first sound?" The kids all said the /d/ sound. Many also called out "*D!*" and I cautioned, "I asked for the *sound*, not the letter. What is the sound at the start of *dolphin*?" The class made a /d/ sound.

"For a moment, pretend none of us knew what letter made that sound," I said. "Watch how I'd figure it out." I turned to our class alphabet chart. I started with letter *A*, and I read the letter and said the letter sound. I did the same for *B* and *C*, then "/d/ *D*. Aha! *Dolphin* starts with /d/, the letter *d*. *Dolphin* starts like *dog*."

ACTIVE ENGAGEMENT/LINK

Set students up to try this work with more independence. Show them a picture, and ask them to say the word slowly, catch the first sound, and share their thinking with their partner.

"You ready to try this on your own? I'm not going to do the work this time. I'll show you a picture and say the name of the picture super slowly, then you'll catch the first sound and *whisper* to your partner what letter you think matches this picture. You ready?"

Note that the teaching point and the work of this session are similar to those of Session 2, in which students learned to catch the first sound of the picture word to help place pictures back in the pocket chart. In this session, kids revisit this work, with the added challenge of matching pictures on the alphabet chart to the letter without the support of the picture icon.

During writing time, kids will be labeling their drawings, and this work with letter-sound correspondence will be immensely helpful. As kids are writing, you'll be able to assess which ones are hearing sounds all the way across words, because their labels will show that. These students are likely ready to progress from labels to sentences.

I held up a picture of a *windmill*. "Say the word slowly, /w/-/w/-windmill. Catch the first sound. What letter goes with that sound? If you don't know the letter, you can use the alphabet chart and find the picture that starts like *windmill*."

"I heard many of you say *windmill* starts with the letter *w*." I pointed to the *w* on the alphabet chart. "Let's check. *Watermelon*. *Windmill*. They start the same."

I showed the class several more pictures, and voiced over to remind kids to just whisper when they thought they knew the first sound.

RUG TIME

Set students up to work in groups to reconstruct a broken alphabet chart. Remind them to catch the first sound in the picture to match pictures to corresponding letters on the alphabet chart.

"You're getting so good at this! I thought I'd give you a chance to try this on your own. You'll work in groups to put the broken alphabet charts back together. You game?" Students nodded, and I continued, "Each group will work with an empty alphabet chart, to put the pictures back with their letter."

On a few tables around the room, I had set up some empty alphabet charts, along with the picture pieces.

"Today, rather than working with a partner, you will work in groups, because we have lots of pictures to put back on those broken charts. You willing? I actually have the picture pieces and alphabet chart on the red table, if you two partnerships want to work on that alphabet chart. And do you two partners want to work on another chart?"

In that way, I dispersed many of the kids to tables, leaving just two sets of partners who might need more support to work on the carpet, reminding kids, "You'll have to decide which picture goes with which letter."

FIG. 5–1   A small group works together to put the broken chart back together.

Today we suggest creating rug clubs. There are a few sessions throughout the remainder of this book where we ask small groups of kids—two or three partnerships—to join together to make a club. We suggest making these clubs strategic, so you can coach and prompt kids at their readiness level. At other times, you may find it appropriate to make heterogeneous groupings. As the unit progresses, these clubs should be flexible, and any time we suggest working with a partner, you might choose instead to have students work in clubs, and vice versa.

SHARE • Writers Know Their Alphabet and Snap Words

Remind students that writers need to know both their alphabet and their snap words. Lead kids in reading the alphabet chart out of order. Then lead kids in a reading of the snap word chart.

"How fabulous! You've got most of those pictures back on an alphabet chart where they belong! Let's leave them where they are for a minute, right on the middle of our tables, and let's gather back together in the meeting area."

"Let's chant the alphabet chart," I said. "Since you're getting to know the alphabet chart so well, I bet you can read it out of order." I pointed to the chart. "Say the names of the letters reading *down* the columns of the chart. Ready?" I led the class in reading the alphabet chart top to bottom, one column at a time.

"Friends, we've been acting as if the alphabet chart is the only tool we have—but actually, writers also need other tools. Of course, you'll want to know all of the letters and sounds on the alphabet chart in a snap, but you're also going to want to make good use of your new snap word chart. Let's practice reading the snap word chart. I'll point to a word and you can read, spell, and say the word again. *Me, m-e, me.* You ready?" The class and I did a choral reading of the words on the snap word chart.

EXTENSION 1 • Reading the Alphabet Chart with Sounds Only

First, lead the class in reading the alphabet chart in a familiar way. Then, teach the class another way to read the alphabet chart, with sounds only.

"Readers, you already know how to read the alphabet chart in a very specific way, a way that word scientists would use. Let's read the chart together in that scientific way. Remember, we say the letter, the picture, then the sound: *A, apple, /ǎ/.*" I led the class in that type of reading of the alphabet chart, pointing to each letter and picture as we read.

"Now let's read it another way. It's a little tricky—are you up for the challenge?" The class agreed, and I continued. "This time, we will read by just saying the sounds. Listen." I pointed to each letter as I said the sound: /ǎ/, /b/, /k/, /d/. "Ready to try it?" We went on reading the alphabet chart in this way. Again, I pointed to the letters as students said the sounds.

EXTENSION 2 • Singing and Writing the Alphabet by Heart

This activity will support letter knowledge, the order of the alphabet, and letter formation. Blank alphabet charts are available in the online resources.

Lead the kids in singing the ABCs to a different tune. Then, give each student a blank alphabet chart to fill in. Coach them to sing the ABCs if they find themselves stuck on a letter.

"It's super important to know the alphabet really well, so let's sing it together. Let's sing it to the tune of 'Happy Birthday.'" We sang the alphabet to this alternate tune.

"Now let's keep thinking about the alphabet and the way it goes. This time, instead of singing the alphabet, you'll write it. I'll give you a blank alphabet chart. Fill in the lowercase letters—we need lots of practice with those. If you get stuck, try singing the alphabet to help you get unstuck. Ready to get started?" I coached the children with letter formation as needed as they wrote the alphabet chart.

EXTENSION 3 • Reviewing Snap Words with Movement

Teach students an engaging way to review snap words: by acting out sports moves while saying and spelling the words.

"Let's have some fun reviewing our word collection, so we really know these words in a snap. Let's get some exercise as we review our snap words and our names.

"We can start with snap word *basketball*. When I point to a word, first, say the word. Then, pretend to dribble a ball as you spell the word." I pantomimed dribbling a ball." Then, say the word again, and . . . shoot!" I jumped up and shot a basketball into an imaginary hoop. "Ready?"

I held up the word *like*. I gestured for the class to join me as I said, "*Like*." Then I said, "Dribble as you spell, *l-i-k-e*!" I did this along with the kids. "Now, say the word again, and shoot. *Like!*"

I continued leading the class in reviewing snap words and names taken from the name wall in this way, varying the sport each time. We threw a football, hit a hockey puck, and so on.

Patricia Cunningham recommends frequently returning to newly taught high-frequency words in different ways after they have been taught. Be sure kids are active, productive, with the words—doing something with them. Chanting high-frequency words in this manner is a favorite.

Adding Pictures to the Alphabet Chart

✔ Each student will need an alphabet chart.

✔ Display the animal-themed alphabet chart.

✔ Have Post-its and a marker to draw new pictures for the alphabet chart.

✔ Display the class alphabet chart.

✔ Provide students with about six small Post-its each and a pencil.

PHONICS INSTRUCTION

Phonological Awareness
- Identify the initial phonemes of spoken words.
- Identify and produce words that begin with the same sound.
- Match words with the same beginning sounds.

Letter Knowledge
- Recognize and name all upper- and lowercase letters of the alphabet.
- Identify the order of the alphabet.

Phonics
- Demonstrate basic knowledge of letter-sound correspondence by producing the primary sound for each consonant.

High-Frequency Words
- Recognize and use high-frequency words.
- Write high-frequency words in continuous text.

IN THIS SESSION

TODAY YOU'LL teach students that word scientists notice when something can be improved, and they invent solutions to make things better.

TODAY YOUR STUDENTS will make new pictures for their alphabet charts to inspire them to use their charts more often when reading and writing. Students will generate words that have the same first sound.

MINILESSON

CONNECTION

Encourage kids to think about common inventions that have made their lives easier. Tell them that each invention was created by a scientist who saw a problem and invented a better way to solve it.

"Do any of you have one of those little vacuum cleaners—the handheld ones you can use to suck up little spills? I think they call them Dustbusters®?" A few kids nodded.

"And maybe some of you have seen those suitcases that come with wheels on them. You have? Some of you even have backpacks with wheels."

"What not everyone realizes is that those kinds of things, like tiny vacuum cleaners, and bags with wheels on them, are inventions. The way that the world got those things is that a scientist saw a regular vacuum cleaner, a regular suitcase or backpack, and said, 'Wait a minute—there has *got* to be a way to make this thing work even better.' Then the scientist invented a solution to improve these things, to make them better."

❖ **Name the teaching point.**

"Today, I want to teach you that scientists study things in the world—like rotting logs and stars and even alphabet charts, too. Sometimes when scientists study something, they say, 'I have a better idea,' and then the scientist becomes an inventor."

TEACHING

Explain that as word scientists, students can decide to improve their alphabet charts. Suggest that they might substitute pictures they prefer for selected letters.

"I'm telling you this because the other day, you realized that sometimes, when kids get an alphabet chart and they look at the pictures that are supposed to help them know the sounds that the letters make, they think, 'Huh? That is a crazy picture.' I know the other day when we looked at the picture of a cake that was supposed to work for the *U*, we thought, 'What?!' And earlier, when we were studying the animal alphabet chart, I don't know if you saw the picture for *R*, but I did. Look at it now: a mouse! I thought, 'Huh? *Mouse* starts with /m/ /m/ *M*. Why is there a mouse on my *R*?'

"I realized the person who made that alphabet chart probably meant that picture to be something bigger and fiercer than a mouse—something that starts with /r/ . . . "

A few kids, following me, called out, "A rat!"

Nodding, I said, "A rat does make sense for the letter *R*. But you might think, 'I don't want a rat on *my* alphabet chart.' You might think, 'I don't even like rats.' And you might wish that your alphabet chart had a cute little rabbit, not a rat, for the *R* picture.

"So, word scientists, if you have found a picture you don't like on your alphabet chart and you are a scientist who invents ways to make things better, what can you do?"

The kids called out that they could fix it. I nodded. "You can invent a solution. You can decide to draw a rabbit instead of the rat on your alphabet." I did just that on a Post-it. Showing it to the class, I said, "Now we need to find where that *R* is," I said. "Help me look for it."

"I think *R* is in the middle of the alphabet chart." I pointed to a row in the middle of the chart and ran my finger along the line of letters until we reached the *R*, and I stuck the new rabbit Post-it right smack on top of the rat. "Bye, bye, rat!" I said.

"Let's check to be sure this is where the rabbit goes. Say *rat*. Say *rabbit*. *Rat, rabbit*—they both start with the same sound. I can put my rabbit on the *R*."

ACTIVE ENGAGEMENT/LINK

Channel partners to practice inventing a new picture for the letter *B*. Share some of the students' responses.

"I bet you guys have been looking at the alphabet chart and thinking about other pictures that aren't the best. I mean, this one is sort of *bo-ring*, isn't it?" I pointed to the picture of a ball in the *B* box. "Remember, scientists look at things as they are and think, 'I have a better idea!'

"Let's invent something more interesting to illustrate the *B*. Tell your partner a more interesting picture that could go with the /b/ sound. Turn and talk!

"I've been thinking about your great ideas. I was talking to one partnership about the word *banana*, and at first we were thinking that would go nicely with the apple on our *A*. But then we realized— bananas are great when they are fresh. But if we were to keep that banana on our chart for weeks and weeks, the smell of rotten bananas is pretty awful!" I paused a moment for kids to laugh at my silly comment, then continued on. "So, let's think of other ideas. A couple of you suggested *butterfly*. José said *Batman*. Do they both make the right sound? Let's check: /b/ *butterfly*, /b/ *Batman*. Yes, they both make the /b/ sound. Let's vote on which picture you think would make our alphabet chart super cool." The class voted, and we added Batman to our class chart.

"I have a feeling that you are just bursting to put some of your own pictures on the alphabet charts."

RUG TIME

Set kids up to read their own alphabet charts and invent ways to make the pictures better. Coach them to make sure they match the first sound of the word with the letter.

"Kindergartners, it's time to make your own alphabet charts even better! For each letter, think, 'Is this picture okay, or could I choose a better one?' If you decide to invent a better picture, make sure the sound of the thing you pick really works for that letter. Draw it as carefully as you can, so that people know what you drew.

"Word scientists, take out your alphabet charts, and I'll come around with some Post-its for each of you. Then get to work!" As students worked, I coached them to listen closely to the sounds and make sure the picture word sound matched the letter sound.

SHARE • Sharing New and Improved Alphabet Charts

Encourage partners to read their alphabet charts aloud to each other, highlighting the new changes they have made to the pictures and words.

"Will you share with your partner what you have so far on your new and improved alphabet chart? Read your whole alphabet chart to each other. Remember, we read like this: *A apple /ă/*. But you may not have an apple in your box anymore—be sure to read it with the pictures you added. Ready, turn and share!"

After a few minutes of partner sharing, I dismissed the students, a row at a time, to place their improved, personalized alphabet charts inside their writing folders.

If a child places a picture on the incorrect spot on the alphabet chart, this is a valuable opportunity for teaching. Help the child isolate the beginning sound, and work together to find its correct spot on the chart.

You can encourage students to add more pictures to their alphabet charts as you reinforce more letters and sounds during writing workshop small groups and conferences.

EXTENSION 1 • Dancing to the Alphabet Song

Invite kids to join you in singing the ABC song a new way—with a dance.

"Let's end by singing the alphabet song," I said, and I led the class in a raucous rendition of the ABC song. I pointed to the alphabet chart while we sang.

"Did you know that people dance to that song? Stand up and I'll teach you how the alphabet dance goes. You take two steps to the left as you sing *a, b, c, d*, and then clap on the last letter. So it's step left, *a, b*, step left, *c, d*, and clap on the *d*. Then two steps to the right, *e, f, g*, then clap. Then back to the left, *h, i, j, k*, clap on the *k*. Back to the left, *l, m, n, o, p*, clap. You got it? Ready to do the Alphabet Hustle? Let's go!"

a, b, c, d (clap on the *d*)
e, f, g (clap)
h, i, j, k (clap on the *k*)
l, m, n, o, p (clap)
q, r, s (clap)
t, u, v (clap)
w, x (clap)
y and z (clap)
Now I know my (clap on *my*)
ABCs (clap)
Next time won't you (clap on *you*)
Sing with me! (clap, clap, clap)

EXTENSION 2 • Use Snap Words to Add Sentences into the Class Letter Books

 Continue the work from an earlier session by helping students to write words and sentences for the *H* letter book they made several days ago.

"Word scientists, a few days ago we made some more letter books. Now we have a whole bunch of them. They have pictures on each page, but . . . but . . . no words! I love books that have pictures *and* words, don't you? Let's add some words. We can tell readers what to look at, right?"

We quickly warmed up by reading the snap word chart.

I held up the *H* book we had made a few days ago. "Let's work together to add words to this book."

"Okay. Let's look at this *H* book." I opened to a page with a picture of a house and showed that page to the kids. "Will you tell each other what we could perhaps write on this page?" I tapped the pocket chart of high-frequency words, including *I*, *like*, *my*, *me*, *see*, *look*, *at*, *the*, and *a*.

Looking at the collection of words in the pocket chart, I mulled to myself, "Hmm, . . . maybe it could go, 'I see a house'."

Soon, with the kids' help, I'd written, "Look at the house." I pointed out that the first word in the sentence starts with a capital letter. We continued sharing the pen, with individuals coming to the front to write the words they knew on the page, while other children wrote the words with magic (imaginary) pencils on the carpet in front of them.

EXTENSION 3 • One of These Words Is Not Like the Others

GETTING READY

- Before this extension, familiarize yourself with the song "One of These Things Is Not Like the Others" from *Sesame Street*. A link to this song in available in the online resources.
- Gather some picture cards. You will need groups of four words, three that start with the same sound and a fourth that starts with a different sound.

Set up a game in which students choose a word that is different from the others in the set. Begin by teaching a song that introduces the game.

"Let's play a little game today that will help you listen to sounds in words. It has a little song that goes with it. I learned this song on *Sesame Street*. It goes like this." I began singing.

One of these words is not like the others,
One of these words just doesn't belong.

Can you tell which word is not like the others
By the time I finish my song?

"It's a song *and* a game! Let's play! Tell me which word is different from the other words. Ready?"
I placed four pictures on the easel. "Here are the words: *cat*, *cop*, *can*, *doll*. When you think you've
figured out which word doesn't belong, put a thumb up." I paused a moment to give kids time to
think about all four words. Then, I prompted partners to turn and share their answer with each other.

"Let's come back together and share. Ready?" I recited the verse once more, as some kids began to
chime in:

One of these words is not like the others,
One of these words just doesn't belong.
Can you tell which word is not like the others
By the time I finish my song?

Then, I signaled for the class to shout out their guess. "*Doll*!" many of the kids called out.

I nudged them a bit further. "But why? Why doesn't *doll* belong?"

"Because it starts with *D* and the other words start with *C*," one student explained.

"Precisely! Three of the words start with the letter *C*. I need your help to tell me another word that could join the group.
Say into your hand another word that would belong. Pop your thumb up once you say it." I gave kids a moment to
respond. I nodded, "Yes, words like *candy*, *carpet*, and *candle* could all go in this group. *Kangaroo* also starts with the
/k/ sound, but that one starts with a *K*. Sometimes the /k/ sound is a *C* and sometimes it's a *K*."

"Let's play another round. Ready?" I sang the verse again, this time calling out four new words. "*Fish*, *food*, *dog*, *four*."
Then, I prompted the class to turn and share their answers with a partner before sharing aloud.

"Now explain why *dog* doesn't belong." Kids answered, and I gave them a thumbs up. "Yes, the word *dog* starts with
/d/ *D*, not /f/ *F*. Now, tell your partner another word that would fit with these *F* words."

We played the game with a few more sets of words.

Using the Alphabet Chart with Increasing Automaticity

GETTING READY

✔ Distribute alphabet charts to each student.

✔ Gather a stack of picture cards.

✔ Create a plan for your rug clubs, putting together two partnerships of students at the same readiness levels.

✔ Prepare stacks of picture cards for each rug club.

✔ For tomorrow's celebration, ask kids to bring a stuffed animal or action figure to school. To make sure all kids feel included in the celebration, be sure to have some extras on hand in case children forget.

PHONICS INSTRUCTION

Phonological Awareness
• Identify and produce words that begin and end with the same sound.
• Identify the initial and final phonemes of spoken words.
• Match words with the same beginning sounds.

Letter Knowledge
• Recognize and name all upper- and lowercase letters of the alphabet.

Phonics
• Demonstrate basic knowledge of letter-sound correspondence by producing the primary sound for each consonant.
• Identify and use beginning and ending sounds when writing words.

High-Frequency Words
• Recognize and use high-frequency words.

IN THIS SESSION

TODAY YOU'LL teach students that they need to be able to use the alphabet chart with automaticity. To find a letter to write a word, they need to say and hear the sound in the word and quickly find that letter on the chart, checking to make sure that the letter matches the sound.

TODAY YOUR STUDENTS will work in rug clubs for the first time. In groups of around four, they'll use picture cards to say, hear, and then locate the appropriate letter on an alphabet chart.

MINILESSON

CONNECTION

Tell a story about someone needing to find a tool quickly, so that the person could carry on with important work rather than wasting time searching for the tool.

"Writers, readers, I thought about you last night while I watched my dad making dinner. He was making spaghetti, so he needed a pot. Do you think he went looking in the bedroom for the pot? In the bathroom? When it came time to cook the spaghetti, do you think he had to get on his hands and knees to peer under the sofa, wondering if the pot could be there?

"No! That pot was right beside the stove, and he knew just where it would be. He reached for it without hardly looking at all!

"And when he had to pick up that steaming hot pot to drain the water out of the spaghetti, how long do you think it took him to find the pot holders?

"Yes! About two seconds.

"I'm telling you this because, just like my dad needs tools when he cooks, you need tools when you write. And, like my dad, you need to know where to find things *fast*. If you need to know what an *S* looks like, you don't want to search high and low before you find that *S*."

You'll see a bit of gender education embedded in these lessons! Let's bring up our young boys so they expect to help with the cooking.

♣ **Name the teaching point.**

"Today I want to teach you that, just as cooks benefit from knowing just where the pot holders are, writers benefit from knowing where the letters and sounds are that they'll need to write. Writers have to be able to find the letters and sounds they need *fast*."

TEACHING AND ACTIVE ENGAGEMENT/LINK

Channel students to practice finding letters quickly that match certain sounds. Show several picture cards and ask students to point to the letter of the first sound of each word on their alphabet charts.

"If you are writing about your collection of superheroes, and you want to write the name *Wonder Woman,* you don't want to have to go looking, looking, looking for the letter that makes the /w/ sound, so you can label your drawing of Wonder Woman. You don't want to have to look for your *W* like this . . . " and I sang my way through the whole ABC song with a tired note in my voice as I inched through the chart.

I quickly passed an alphabet chart to each student. "So I'm going to give you one minute only—sixty seconds!—to study the alphabet chart. Pay special attention to the second half of it, because I am pretty sure most of you are more confident about the first half. Notice where the letters are, because in a minute, I'm going to ask you to show me that you don't have to search high and low to find a letter."

I waited a minute, then continued. "You ready? Where would you go to get help writing about a *puppy*? Point to where you'll get the help you need." Most kids pointed to the letter *P* on their alphabet chart.

I gathered a stack of picture cards. "Now let's try it with some pictures. You can say the word, and then point to the letter that makes the first sound of that word on your alphabet chart."

I held up a picture of a car. "Say the word, and find the letter that makes the first sound." I waited as they pointed to the letter on their alphabet chart. "Yes, *car* starts with a *C*. Let's try another one." I held up a picture of a spider. "Quick, find the letter for that first sound!"

We continued with more pictures, increasing the speed as we went. "You're getting faster at this," I said. "Do you know why?"

"Practice!" students shouted.

"Yes!" I said. "The more you practice, the faster you'll get! If this is hard for you, if you aren't sure yet how to find a particular letter when you need it, I'll work with you later, so you can do this quick as a wink."

Have rug club members take turns being the teacher, holding up picture cards as the other members listen for the first sound and find the letter that makes that sound.

"Today you'll work not just with your partner, but in a rug club. That means partnerships will be joining together and working in a club." I quickly told which students to join together.

"I'll give each club a stack of picture cards. Could you take turns being the teacher? The teacher in your club will hold up a card, and the rest of you will find the letter that starts that word as quickly as you can. Are you willing?" The students agreed.

I distributed a stack of picture cards to each club and said, "You'll have to decide who will be the teacher first. Then work as quickly as you can."

Prompt students to play the same game, this time listening for the final sound.

"The alphabet chart doesn't just help you with the first sound in words, but it also helps you listen to the sounds in any part of the word. Now, friends, go through your picture cards again, and this time will you listen for the *last* sound in each of the words? Say the word, say the last sound, then find it on the alphabet chart."

I quickly demonstrated listening for the last sound in a word. "What's the last sound in this word?" I said, holding up a picture of a hat. "Yes, /t/. And what letter is that?" Students shouted out a resounding *T*. I reminded kids that sometimes last sounds are tricky, so if they were confused about a sound, like the /sh/ in *fish*, they should just place that card to the side.

POSSIBLE COACHING MOVES

▶ "Say the word. Grab the first sound. What letter goes with that sound?"

▶ "Check if you were right. Say *car*, say *cat*. Do they match?"

▶ "Can you think of other words that start with that sound?"

▶ For students who may need more of a challenge you might say, "I've included some extra pictures for you, and you'll need to think about the letters that represent more than one sound," and include pictures of things beginning with long vowels or soft/hard *g* and *c*.

SHARE • Reading the Alphabet Chart Out of Order and Practicing Snap Words

Remind students that writers need to know their alphabet. Challenge partners to read the alphabet chart in a different order.

"Word scientists need to know each letter of the alphabet chart quick as a wink. The other day we read the alphabet chart from top to bottom. You said the names of the letters reading *down* the columns of the chart. I thought you could do this with your partner today. Partner 1, will you read down the first column, and then Partner 2, read down the second column? Then keep taking turns until you're done."

It is important for students to be able to identify letters quickly and accurately out of order. You can continue doing this kind of reading of the alphabet chart and then move to having the students just say the sounds of the letters.

Remind students that writers also need to know their snap words. Lead kids in a reading of the snap word chart, then cover it and test their memories.

"Friends, we've been acting as if the only tool you'll need is the alphabet chart—but actually, writers also need other tools. Of course, you'll want to find your way around the alphabet chart easily, but you're also going to want to make good use of your snap word chart. Let's practice first reading the snap word chart, then we'll practice using those snap words in a snap. You ready?"

The class and I did a choral reading of the words on the snap word chart. Then I said, "Usually, you won't need to look at the chart, because those words should be in your mind—that whole chart should be in your mind. I'll cover it, and you can test whether it is.

"Let's say you were writing a book about your lion collection and you wanted people to look at your lion's mane. Tell your neighbor how you'd spell *look*." After they did, I removed the card from the snap word chart and asked kids to check their spelling. We then did that with a few more words.

"So, writers, now you have two tools that you can use just as easily as my dad uses pots and pot holders when he is cooking!"

EXTENSION 1 • Lowercase Letter-Sound Practice

GETTING READY

• Prepare a stack of all twenty-six lowercase letter cards.

Show students the lowercase letter cards, one by one, and invite them to make the sound that goes with each letter.

"Word scientists, you have become experts at using the alphabet chart. Just today, I noticed Hanna saying a sound and finding the letter on the alphabet chart without even looking at the pictures for help. Hanna just knew the letter in her head, so she wrote it lickety-split. It was impressive word scientist work! So, I was thinking, you word scientists are ready for something more." I gathered the students close and whispered, "I have a new challenge if you are willing!"

I pulled out a stack of cards containing only the lowercase letters, and I fanned them out. "Look at this—all twenty-six letters are here. But wait, something is missing!" I held one card for the class to study. "Notice that this card looks a bit different than the alphabet chart. There is no picture and no capital letter. So what if I challenge you to say the sound that goes with the letter without using the picture? Would you be able to do it? Wow, this will certainly be hard work! Are you up it?" The class agreed.

This is an exercise that assesses students' letter-sound accuracy and speed recognition.

I held up the lowercase *a* and the class said /ă/. If the students named the letter instead of saying the sound, I prompted for the sound only. We proceeded through the remainder of the alphabet.

"Ready for a challenge?" The children cheered, and I shuffled the cards. "Say the sound that goes with each letter." We continued saying the sounds of the letters, this time out of order.

EXTENSION 2 • Getting More Words into Your Writing—and Beloved Words into Your Snap Words

Challenge students to label the pictures in their writing that do not yet have labels. Urge them to say each word slowly, listening for and recording the sounds they hear.

Knowing that nothing matters more than that kids are using the alphabet chart—and their knowledge of the alphabet—as they read and write, I asked students to pull out their alphabet charts and their writing, and to reread all the writing they had done in the writing workshop. "Use your finger as a pointer, and point under the words you have written," I said.

"Now find something you have drawn that doesn't have even one little word beside it, and right this minute, write a label for that picture. Say the word slowly. Use your hands to help you stretch the word out. Hear the first sound and use your alphabet chart to pop that sound right onto your paper. If you hear more sounds, write them down, too."

"You have five minutes. Right now, see how much writing you can get done. Help each other. Make sure everyone at your table is getting words onto their papers."

As children worked on their writing, I studied what they were working on and settled on two or three concrete words that they especially needed as writers—and that could help them feel especially connected to the snap word collection. In a class in which many kids are writing about their dogs, I would add *dogs* to the snap word collection. If many are writing about pets, that would be the word I'd choose. Don't flood the snap word collection with high-utility concrete words such as these, but know that adding a few to that collection helps kids feel attached to the entire list.

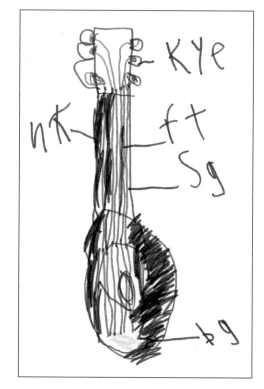

FIG. 7–1   A student adds labels to their picture.

EXTENSION 3 • Sing "Who Has a Word that Starts (Ends) with _____?"

Give kids another opportunity for letter-sound practice by singing a song about the sounds at the beginning (or end) of words.

"Writers, now that you are using the alphabet chart to write, it's super important that you get to know not only the names of the letters, but also the *sounds* that those letters make. There's a song that I love that helps people know the sounds the letters make. Can I teach it to you? If you know the song 'Skip to My Lou,' it uses the same tune. It is called 'Who Has a Word that Starts With . . . ?' and you'll see that there's a part in it where kids have to call out a word.

"It goes like this." I modeled the first verse.

> Who has a word that starts with /d/,
> Starts, starts, starts with /d/?
> Who has a word that starts with /d/?
> *Dance* starts with *D*.

"I think you get the idea." I continued, "If you have a word, put a thumb on your knee. Sing along with me and think of a word. Let's do it!"

> Who has a word that starts with /d/,
> Starts, starts, starts with /d/?
> Who has a word that starts with /d/?

This time I gestured to a student, signaling with a thumb, who called out, "Dinosaur!" and then I sang the last line of the stanza,

> *Dinosaur* starts with *D*.

We then sang the song a few more times with several different letters.

Vary this to focus on the sounds that words end with, if your kids are able to stay with you for that.

ABC School

TODAY YOU'LL teach students that when word scientists become experts in their ABCs, they can teach others everything they know.

TODAY YOUR STUDENTS will demonstrate their learning from this bend by teaching the ABCs to their stuffed animals—first individually, teaching the first letter of their animal's name, then working in rug clubs to teach all that they know about letters and sounds.

GETTING READY

✔ Make sure students have their stuffed animals with them on the rug. You may want to have a few extra stuffed animals or action figures for kids who do not have one.

✔ Distribute to each rug club a small alphabet chart, small whiteboard and marker, and something that can be used as a pointer (such as a Popsicle® stick).

✔ Print out class alphabet charts for each student to take home.

PHONICS INSTRUCTION

Phonological Awareness
• Identify and produce words that begin with the same sound.
• Identify the initial phonemes of spoken words.

Letter Knowledge
• Recognize and name all upper- and lowercase letters of the alphabet.
• Recognize the order of the alphabet.
• Use efficient motions to form letters.

Phonics
• Demonstrate basic knowledge of letter-sound correspondence by producing the primary sound for each consonant.

MINILESSON

CONNECTION

Celebrate becoming word scientists who are ready to share their findings with others.

While kids were still sitting in their workplaces, I said, "Today we end one of the chapters in our Unit of Study on being word scientists. You'll still be word scientists for one more week, one more chapter, but you won't be studying the alphabet next week. That chapter is over for now.

"I thought we should celebrate all that you have learned. The reason I suggested you might want to bring your stuffed animals to school today is that it is good to invite some friends to a celebration, right?

"So, if you brought a little friend with you, bring your friend to the meeting area with you and let your friend squish in beside you on the rug. Share your friend with kids who didn't bring one." I gave Mabel to a child who seemed especially in need of a friend.

Once the kids and their stuffed animals had gathered, I said, "Mabel shouldn't be the only stuffed animal who knows the alphabet, right? I think we *all* need to know our ABCs. So, let's have ABC School, and teach all the other stuffed animals the ABC song. Let's teach them the regular way."

We sang enthusiastically: "A, B, C, . . . "

"Now let's teach them how to sing the ABCs to the tune of 'Row, Row, Row Your Boat.' You might want to warn our furry friends that this is a little tricky. You can whisper that if you want." We continued with the song.

♣ **Name the teaching point.**

"Today I want to teach you that once you become an expert in something—like your ABCs—you can teach others *everything* you know. It's important for everyone to know their ABCs!"

TEACHING

Suggest that word scientists can teach their stuffed animal the ABCs, starting with the first letter in their name.

"Sam, I see you have a young friend with you, and I bet he wants to learn his ABCs. What's this little guy's name?

"Blue Bear."

"Nice to meet you, Blue Bear." I shook Blue Bear's paw. "Class, what do you think Blue Bear would especially like to learn? Do you think he'd like to learn the letter at the start of his name?"

The class was enthusiastic about that idea, so I said, "Whenever you teach somebody something, you have to first think, 'Hmm, . . . what do I know that I could teach? And what might my student want to learn?' Sam, will you cover Blue Bear's ears for a minute while we think about what we could teach him about the letter at the start of his name? We don't want to confuse him."

Sam covered Blue Bear's ears, and the class chipped in ideas about what we could teach the bear. I nodded at their ideas. "Good thinking," I said. "I'll bet he'd love to learn all about the first letter of his name! He probably doesn't even know what a *B* looks like. Or that the capital *B* is different than the lowercase *b*! Let's make an capital *B* in the air so we are ready to teach it to him."

The kids wrote both a capital and a lowercase *B* in the air. "Do you think we should tell him words that start with a *B*?" I asked, and partners shared ideas for what those words could be.

"Sam, can you bring Blue Bear up here, so he can go to ABC school?" I said. Once Blue Bear was seated at the front of the meeting area, Sam, the class, and I proceeded to teach him as much as we could about the letter *B*. I gave Sam a copy of the alphabet chart and said, "Sam, maybe you should tell him about the things that are in the *B* box." Sam pointed to the letter. "This is the *B*." I encouraged him to keep going. "This is the big, um, the capital *B* and lowercase *b*. And this is a butterfly . . . like /b/-/b/-butterfly."

ACTIVE ENGAGEMENT/LINK

Repeat the process with the class, releasing the amount of scaffolding you are providing.

"Do we have some other stuffed animals who would like to learn their ABCs?" I asked. "If you have a stuffed animal with you or near you, will you learn that animal's name and decide what letter you want to teach that animal? Then teachers—that's you, class!—cover the ears of your little friends for a moment and plan with your partner. Think about what you can teach your stuffed animal about his or her letter. Help each other think of lots of words that start with that letter."

After children had a moment to plan, I channeled them to begin teaching. "One of you will need to hold your stuffed animal, and the other will be the teacher. If the stuffed animal doesn't understand, make sure he lets the teacher know that he's confused!"

POSSIBLE COACHING MOVES

▶ "What sound goes with that letter?"

▶ "What sound do we say when we see that letter?"

▶ "What other words start with that letter?"

▶ "You might want to show her how to make that letter. Write it in the air."

▶ "Do you want to teach him another letter? Can you hear another letter in his name?"

▶ For kids who need more of a challenge, you might say, "Now that you've taught the first letter, can you teach your friend other letters in her name?"

RUG TIME CLUBS

Rug clubs play ABC School with their club members and stuffed animals, demonstrating everything they have learned about the alphabet chart.

"Teachers, eyes up here," I said, and let the class know I was talking to them. "So far you've been teaching one student at a time, but these stuffed animals want to be in a class, like you all are. They want to sit with other kids and learn. So, in each rug club, will you meet and think about what you could teach *all* your stuffed animals? Look over the alphabet chart, and think about what your students need to learn. They may not know the alphabet song. They probably don't know very many letters. So, you all can decide what to teach them.

FIG. 8–1   Mabel wants to see what everyone has learned.

"I'll give you some things that you need to be teachers. I can't give you each an easel, but I'll give you a whiteboard and an alphabet chart, and I think you'd better have a pointer, too.

"Will you take turns being the teacher, and the rest of you, can you hold your students up in a nice line? Be sure to teach your students everything you know about letters and sounds." As I handed out the whiteboards, I said, "Okay, teachers, get teaching!" I coached as the children taught, and every few minutes, I suggested that a new child take on the role of teacher.

SHARE • Practicing ABCs at Home

Give your students alphabet charts to take home to continue to play school.

"Time is up!" I said. "Wait, wait, Mabel wants to tell me something." I brought her up to my ear and listened intently. "Mabel is saying that her animal friends want more school. They are *mad* that school is over. They are saying 'No fair! We need more time to learn our ABCs.'

"Hmm, . . . what can we do? Say, I have an idea! It is asking a lot of you, but might you be willing to teach your stuffed animal more ABCs at home? *If* you'd be willing, I have some alphabet charts that I was going to give to teachers at the other schools . . . but I guess I could tell those teachers we need them and give them to you.

"If you had an alphabet chart to bring home, would you be willing to teach ABC school at home? Would you?" The kids insisted they would, and I pretended to reluctantly bestow on them my precious alphabet charts. "Do any of you have little sisters or brothers, or cousins, or neighbors? Because I bet they would like to go to ABC school, too!"

POSSIBLE COACHING MOVES

▶ "Remember to tell your students how to make that letter" (letter formation pathway).

▶ "Sing and chant the alphabet song with your class."

▶ "Have your stuffed animals try to write the letter on the board. You will have to help them hold the marker!"

▶ "Tell your students other words that start with that sound, and then invite them to think of new words."

▶ For students who are ready for more of a challenge, you might suggest that they invite their animal friends to identify other sounds in a word besides the first and figure out those letters. Or they might ask their friends to change the first sound in a word (e.g., *cat*) to make a rhyme.

Dear Teachers,

This bend signals a major shift in the unit. You'll put your full teaching force into sending the message that your youngsters can use all they know about letters and sounds and the alphabet to write in ways that others can read. You may feel a little unsure about moving from a focus on teaching letters and sounds to asking kids to use that knowledge to write. You may find yourself wanting to say, "Wait—let me check which of them have full control of letter-sound knowledge first." You may want to get out the letter maps and reteach kids how to write letters the proper way. Our advice to you is this: fear not. Go forward. Remember that in life, too, you often learn on the run, as you use new information. For those of you who are new to the Units of Study in Opinion, Information, and Narrative Writing, Units of Study for Teaching Reading, or Units of Study in Phonics series, you probably feel sometimes as if you are changing the car tire while driving down the highway. You may say, "How I wish I had known everything I needed to know before I got off the starting block!" But the truth is that learning just doesn't happen that way. It doesn't happen that way for you, and it won't happen that way for your youngsters.

So as you shift from Bend I to Bend II, put your full force behind that shift. The best possible way for kids to apply what they are learning—and learn what you hope they are learning—is for kids to be using all you teach as they write. The bend begins with you sending kids the message that they don't just *study* the alphabet chart, they *use* it. To write, your students will need to say a word slowly, segmenting it into its constituent sounds, and then recording the sounds they hear. At the start of Bend II, many of your students will mostly hear and record initial consonants, but you'll encourage them to record more sounds. As the unit progresses, they'll also record snap words, and doing so will be a major step toward helping them write longer labels (such as *the pencil*) as well as sentences (such as *I see the pencil*). In the middle of Bend II, you'll add to students' collections of snap words, helping them to learn the words *here*, *look*, and *at*, before helping kids use these words as they write.

As Marie Clay says, writing slows the reading process down—so children can discover how letters go together to make words, and how words go together to make sentences that tell a story. This is ambitious work, but it's also exciting work, and you are not asking your kindergartners to master any of it. You are asking them to delve in, to approximate. There are many more opportunities over the upcoming year when you'll return to the content that you teach in this bend and reteach it. So, for now, your intention is to invite kids to join in as best they can. As Patricia Cunningham writes in *Phonics They Use*, "Accepting a variety of writing—from scribbling to one-letter representations, to invented spellings, to copied words—is the key to having young children write before they can write. Without the attitude of acceptance, the very children who most need to explore language through writing will be afraid to write."

Although this unit focuses in a sense on the alphabet chart, your students will actually turn to that chart less often as the unit unfolds. Increasingly, they'll have command of letters and sounds and be able to draw on their internalized alphabet charts—that is, on their knowledge.

You will also observe your students progressing from labeling pictures with a single letter to labeling with several letters. As soon as kids are labeling a picture of the sun with *sn*, they are ready to write sentences, not just labels.

On the other hand, if some of your students are not labeling with beginning consonants, you can lead small groups to address that. Turn to the book, *Small Groups to Support Phonics* and draw on the plans there. Know in advance that we've designed many of the small groups to fit tongue-and-groove into the teaching in this unit, requiring only a minimal amount of setup for you.

As you teach this bend, always remember that you are inviting kids to approximate. Be ready to celebrate their efforts!

All the best,
Lucy, Rebecca, and Allyse

When You Know the Alphabet Chart Really Well, You Can Use It to Write

IN THIS SESSION

TODAY YOU'LL teach students that writers learn the alphabet to help them write words.

TODAY YOUR STUDENTS will label items in pictures, first by thinking of a word that names the picture, listening for the first sound in that word, thinking about which letter goes with that sound, checking the alphabet chart, and then writing the letter.

MINILESSON

CONNECTION

Remind students of how much they learned about the ABCs in the last bend, and rally their enthusiasm for studying the alphabet chart in a new way—as a tool to help them write.

"Readers, writers, I loved seeing you teach the alphabet chart to all those stuffed bears and rabbits and unicorns the other day. I was *amazed* at how much you all have learned in just a few weeks of school. The great thing about learning your ABC chart is that once you really know it well, you can use it to write labels and signs and books. Pretty soon you'll be using these . . . " and I let a handful of magnetic letters cascade from my hands, " . . . to write books that will go right here on our library shelf. Maybe we'll even end up with books by Blue Bear and Mabel as well as by all of you!

"So today, we start a whole new part of this study. You will still be word scientists, looking closely at the alphabet chart, but from this day on, you'll be looking at it to help you *write*."

❖ **Name the teaching point.**

"Today I want to remind you that when you want to write a word, you start by figuring out the first sound in the word. Remember that to do that, you say the word s-l-o-w-l-y, starting with the first

---

GETTING READY

✔ Have a few magnetic letters on hand to preview a tool that students will be using soon.

✔ Display pages from a book about Blue Bear and Mabel (or a stuffed animal of your choosing) that you will be writing on.

✔ Distribute an alphabet chart to each partnership.

✔ Provide whiteboards and markers for each student.

PHONICS INSTRUCTION

Concepts About Print
- Recognize that spoken words are represented in written language by specific sequences of letters.

Phonological Awareness
- Identify the initial phonemes of spoken words.
- Say words slowly and identify salient sounds in spoken words.

Letter Knowledge
- Recognize and name all upper- and lowercase letters of the alphabet.
- Use proper letter formation.

Phonics
- Demonstrate basic knowledge of letter-sound correspondences by producing the primary sound for each consonant.

High-Frequency Words
- Recognize and use high-frequency words.
- Write high-frequency words.

sound so you catch that first sound before it slips past you. Then you find that sound on the alphabet chart and write it on your paper."

Blue bear is the name of a stuffed bear we imagine a child brought for ABC school. You can choose any name/animal you want to keep kids engaged with the storyline.

TEACHING

Remind students of an earlier lesson that helped them say and listen to initial sounds in words. Explain that listening to first sounds in words is a big deal. Use the word *hi* as an example.

"Do you remember last week when I told you the story of that little girl who wanted to write *Santa*, and her teacher told her to say the word slowly and listen to the sounds she heard? That little girl thought the teacher meant she should listen for the sounds Santa makes, but no, the teacher was telling her that if you want to write *Santa*, you need to say 'Sssssanta' really slowly and try to hear the first sound. Can you try to do that now?"

The kids said "Santa" and heard the *S*. I nodded, "Good listening. It may sound funny that listening to the sounds in a word is a big deal. I mean, I say 'hi,' and you hear the sounds. The sounds say what?"

The class repeats, "Hi."

I nod. "Yes, you heard the sounds in *hi*, but let me tell you the tricky part. To write *hi* in your own story, you need to know what sound comes first in that word. And that actually isn't the easiest thing to figure out.

"To get better at *hearing* the first sound in *hi*, try saying the word into your hand. Your hand can take that sound up toward your arm like this," I said, using my hand almost as a conch shell. "Say *hi* and try to hear just the first sound." I said "Hi, hi, hi, /h/, /h/" into my cupped hand, holding it right beside my mouth, and invited the kids to do the same.

I drew a rectangle on the whiteboard and divided it into two boxes and said, "Stretch the word *hi* with me." As we stretched the word, I pointed to the first box and the class said "/h/." I pointed to the second box and the class said the long *i*, "/ī/." "Let me stretch the word *hi* again," I said as I pointed to each box.

After saying and listening to "hi," many kids agreed that the first sound was /h/. "So now, do you need to look at the alphabet chart to find the letter that makes that /h/ sound, or do you just know it?" Many of the kids called out that it was an *h*.

Throughout this session the focus remains on generating and recording only beginning sounds, so you may choose not to record the other letters in the word at this moment. If you do write the whole word, record the remaining letters quickly without much fuss.

Holding up a book with images of Blue Bear and Mabel waving at each other, I said, "So if we wanted to write a story, we could make Blue Bear and Mabel meet each other. Here's one way to show that someone is talking." I pointed to Mabel's speech bubble and wrote *Hi* inside it.

Recruit students to add to the story by saying the first sound in the word, then match it to the correct letter on the class alphabet chart. Use the words *good morning* as an example.

"Do you want to help write the story of Mabel and Blue Bear? I have Mabel saying 'Hi,' so now I want them to say something else. If Mabel says, 'Hi,' Blue Bear should probably say something back, right? What do you think Blue Bear will say? Turn and tell your partner." I gave partners just a moment to speak.

"Oh, Blue Bear could say 'Good morning!' back. That would make sense. Now say each of those words s-l-o-w-l-y, so you catch their first sounds before they slip past you. If you need to find a sound on the class alphabet chart, you can do so, but you probably know it in your mind. Once you have it, tell your partner the letters we should write."

Page 1

I made a speech bubble coming from Blue Bear's mouth and wrote *G* after we confirmed *G* was the first letter in *good*, and then I quickly filled in the rest of the word. Then I did the same for the word *morning*. For each of the letters, I voiced over the letter formation pathway. Then I reread, pointing to each word as I did so.

ACTIVE ENGAGEMENT/LINK

Rally the students to join you in writing. Engage students in hearing the first sound and then using the alphabet chart to find the letter. Explain that writers don't just know the alphabet, they *use* it.

I handed out an alphabet chart to each partnership and said, "Let's keep telling the story of Mabel and Blue Bear." I ran my finger over the picture searching for other things to label. "Let's start by labeling them with their names. *Blue Bear* is two words." I tapped the page twice where I planned to label as I said, "Blue Bear. Will you say *Blue*, catch the first sound, figure out what letter you need?" Kids did so.

"Yes, we need a *B* for *Blue*. We need to make sure that it's a capital *B*, because it's someone's name, right? Everyone put your finger on the capital *B* and trace it as I write." I said the letter formation pathway, "Line down, back up, bump around, bump around!" I quickly wrote the rest of the word. "Let's read what we have so far," and I pointed to the word as we read. We repeated the process for *Bear*.

"Now we need to label Mabel. You know her name—it is on our name wall. What is the first sound you hear in *Mabel*?" Some kids called out "/m/," and others called out "*M*!" I said, "Yes, the first sound is /m/, and the letter that says /m/ is *M*." I labeled Mabel's picture with an *M*.

You will inevitably have students that will hear and can record more sounds in words. For today keep your focus tight on just first sound, but if students call out that they hear more sounds, support that by saying something like, "Yes, there are more sounds. Good listening."

I flipped to page 2 of the story. It showed Mabel giving Blue Bear a present with a heart. I pointed to the empty speech bubble and said, "Mabel wants to say 'love.' How would you start to write the word *love*? Listen to the first sound, catch it, and tell me what letter that is." When kids called out "*L*!" I wrote the word in the speech bubble and said, "Yes! Now let's keep going in our book."

We continued quickly through the rest of the book in this manner, with students isolating the first sound and matching it to a letter, then I wrote the initial letter and then quickly wrote the rest of the word we chose for each speech bubble. We talked briefly about how surprised we were about Blue Bear's reaction to the gift.

Page 2

Page 3

Page 4

When we completed the story, I said, "You don't just *know* the alphabet chart, you *use* it. You use the alphabet chart to help you write your own stories and songs and books."

Keep an eye on time during this part of the lesson. Your aim is to keep the work on each page of the book quick, so that students say a word, catch the first sound, figure out what letter it makes, and write it, all in under a minute. If you notice this work is running long, you can pause after a few pages of the book and pick it up again at another time.

Invite students to write their own stories about their favorite characters. With each label, reinforce the process of saying the word slowly, isolating the first sound, and checking the alphabet chart.

"Are you ready to make your own story?" I started to hand out the whiteboards and markers. "You could draw Mabel and Blue Bear, like we just did, or you can draw the stuffed animal you brought to school the other day. Or draw Mrs. Wishy-Washy, or anyone else from our books. Ready, everyone? Draw!" I scanned the class to ensure everyone sketched quickly so we could get to the important work of writing.

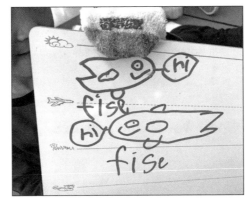

FIG. 9–1   Fish saying, "Hi."

"Now, whomever you drew, label that person's name! Say the name slowly, and catch the first sound. If you need to use the alphabet chart to write it down, do so. If you hear more sounds, record them too."

I urged the students to add what their character might be saying. I said, "If you drew Mrs. Wishy-Washy, she might be putting the pig in the tub and saying 'in.' Figure out what your people are saying! Then say the word slowly, catch the first sound, find it on the alphabet chart, and then write it down."

As students began to work, I coached, giving frequent reminders not to erase their boards so they could share their work in a few minutes.

SHARE • Adding More Snap Words to Our Writing

Channel students to share their writing in ways that invite partners to do some reading. Rally students to reread their snap words and use those snap words to write.

"Share what you have written with some kids near you. Don't just tell them what your picture and your words say—let them try to read your writing first. Don't forget to take turns."

After a few minutes, I called the children back together and said, "You're really using the alphabet chart and writing up a storm. I saw some of you used our snap words in your writing! That is so terrific. Before we end today, will you and your partner each read the list of snap words to each other, making sure you can read them in a snap?" I gave students a few moments to do so.

FIG. 9–2   The teacher supports this student with labeling the parts of his picture with beginning and ending sounds.

In Session 16, "Bringing Our Writing to Life" (in Unit 1 Launching the Writing Workshop of the kindergarten Units of Study in Opionion, Information, and Narrative Writing), students learned to add speech bubbles to enhance their stories. However, if students are having trouble thinking of things the characters might say to one another, you might prompt them to label parts of the person or the setting.

"Hearing you read all those snap words got me thinking. I bet we could add snap words to our writing, too!" I opened to page 2 of our class story about Blue Bear and Mabel. "Should Mabel also say 'Look' and point to the present? We can use our snap words to write *look*, can't we? Write *look* with your imaginary pencil on the rug in front of you while I write it up here." Soon, we'd added *look* to our class book.

"Could you do this same thing in your own writing? Reread your writing. Is there a place where you could add a snap word? Add in a snap word if you can!"

EXTENSION 1 • Use Letters, Sounds, Snap Words, and Pictures to Share Your Ideas about Books

FIG. 9–3   "Mabel and Blue Bear talking to each other. Hi, bye bye, see ya."

GETTING READY

- Distribute a couple of Post-its and a pencil to each student.
- Distribute a few books for students to read.

Encourage students to share meaningful moments in their books by leaving Post-it notes for the next person to read their book.

"Writers, I love that you are writing up a storm during phonics time *and* during writing time. I was thinking that you probably want to be writing during reading time, too. So will you get out your book baggies and choose a book that is really interesting, a book you'd love to show to someone else and talk about with them?"

I waited a minute for kids to choose a book from their book baggies. "Now find a part in the book that makes you think or feel something—a part that might make you sad, or happy, or mad, or it might make you go 'huh?' Put your finger on that page to hold your spot, as I come around and hand each of you a couple of Post-its.

"Now that you know your letters and sounds, and you have all these snap words that you can write in a snap, you can mark up your books with Post-its, just like the big kids do in this school. So, put one of your Post-its on that page, and then write a message to other people who might read the page about something you find interesting.

"You can write words, like *wow* and *huh?* and *oh no* and *happy*. Or you could draw faces—like smiling faces or mad faces or 'huh?' faces—any kind of face. Don't tell your partner what you are going to make in your book. Just make it, keeping it a secret. If you are writing *sad*, remember to say the word slowly and write down the sounds you hear. Same with if you are writing *huh?*

"After you mark one page, find another page that makes you think or feel something and leave a Post-it on that page, too. You just have a few minutes and then you'll be sharing your writing and your thinking with someone."

EXTENSION 2 • Support Word Writing—Today and Every Day

Rally students to read their writing from today and write more words on the pages. Challenge them to use all that they know about letters and sounds to write more words from this day forward.

"When you were at gym today, I took a peek at your writing, and you won't believe it, but there are some of you who didn't have *any* letters, any words, on your writing! That can't happen. You are writers now, and word scientists, and you *all* know how to use letters to spell your ideas.

"So, writers, will you get out your writing super-fast? Read what you wrote today and make sure you have *lots* of words on your pages. Help each other to get more words on your pages. And after this, from this day forward, during writing time, use all you know about writing with letters and sounds to write words."

EXTENSION 3 • Write Lowercase Letters

Explain that writers use lowercase letters most of the time, saving capital letters for special uses. Write capital letters on the board, and challenge students to write the lowercase versions of those letters.

"Word scientists," I said. "You've been working to hear and record more sounds. Let's make sure we are also thinking about which kind of letter is the right one to use in different places. You know there are two kinds of letters, right— capital (or uppercase letters) and lowercase letters. Most of the time when we write, we use the lowercase letters. We save the capitals for special times—like the very first letter of your name or the start of a new sentence.

"Since we use the lowercase letters the most, let's practice them a little more. I'll write a capital letter up here, and will you see if you can write the lowercase version of that letter on your whiteboard?"

I made a capital *F*, without naming the letter. "Without saying anything, will you think, 'What letter is that?' and find it on your alphabet chart?

"Now make the lowercase version of that letter on your boards." I gave children a moment to do that.

"Remember, when you write, you usually use the lowercase version of a letter. If you forget how to write the lowercase version, you can always use your alphabet chart to check."

POSSIBLE COACHING MOVES

▶ "This is the capital *F*. Look, here it is on the alphabet chart. Now try and make the lowercase *f*."

▶ "Let's all make the lowercase *f* together. I'll tell you the letter formation pathway and write it on my board, and you follow along on your board."

Writers Use What They Know about Letters to Label Their Writing

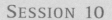

IN THIS SESSION

TODAY YOU'LL teach students to use what they know about letters and sounds to listen for and write more sounds in words.

TODAY YOUR STUDENTS will label items in their writing, listening and recording more sounds in the words. Students will understand that some letters they want to write may already be in their mind.

GETTING READY

✔ Make sure students bring their writing folders to the meeting area with a pencil.

✔ Display the class story from Session 9.

✔ Select a student writing piece that has the opportunity to add lots of labels, or use the example we provide.

PHONICS INSTRUCTION

Concepts About Print
- Recognize that spoken words are represented in written language by specific sequences of letters.
- Understand that words are written left to right across the page.
- Match spoken word to print.

Phonological Awareness
- Identify the initial and final phonemes of spoken words.
- Say words slowly and identify salient sounds in spoken words.

Word Knowledge/Solving
- Identify and use initial and final sounds when writing words.

High-Frequency Words
- Recognize and use high-frequency words.
- Write high-frequency words in continuous text.

MINILESSON

CONNECTION

Recruit students to reread the class story. First, only read the words. Then, emphasize how readers need to read the words and pictures and think about what's going on, and reread to demonstrate.

"Writers, today will you bring your writing folders with you? Hurry, we have a lot to do!" Once the children had settled, I said, "Earlier, I told you that you needed to know letters and sounds really, really well so you can use them to write, and during the last session you did that. Let's read the story you wrote yesterday, as a class." I touched each of the words and the class joined in as we read the words.

Once we'd read the words on page 1 aloud and started reading page 2, I paused. "Wait a minute! We are forgetting what we know about reading. We need to read the words *and* the pictures—and we need to ask, 'What's going on?' Let's reread, and this time, do your best reading." This time, we read—and read *into*—the words and the pictures.

"Mabel and Blue Bear are saying 'Hi' and 'Good morning' to each other. They seem happy to see each other."

We read the words, and then said, "Mabel even gives Blue Bear a present and says 'love' to him. She is happy because she loves her friend."

We again read the words and then said, "Blue Bear is mad. He doesn't like the present. We don't know what it is, but he does *not* like it. He is mad."

"Now Mabel is mad, too. She stomps off, saying 'bye' to Blue Bear. I think her feelings are hurt because he didn't like her present."

When we reached the end, I said, "Whew! This is a sad story, isn't it? But the great thing is, you can look at the pictures and read the words, and you can put together a whole story in your minds. That's why writers use words and pictures to put their ideas on the page.

"I want to give you a tip that will help you write even more words on your pages. Here it is."

♣ **Name the teaching point.**

"Today I want to remind you that writers use letters and pictures to put their ideas on the page. Then other people can read what's on the page and figure out what it says."

TEACHING

Extol the alphabet's usefulness to writers. Channel kids to help one child record a few words to accompany her drawing. Emphasize only using the alphabet chart when it is needed.

"Do you remember the other day when you taught your stuffed animals the ABCs? That was fun! But you know that you didn't do that just for fun. You aren't learning the alphabet just to teach it to your stuffed animals, are you? You're learning the alphabet, so you can write books and labels and songs.

"Writers use their knowledge of letters and sounds to add the words that will help readers understand what they have written. Writers decide what they want their writing to say, and they figure out which word to write first. Then they say that word really s-l-o-w-l-y, listening for the first sound. Often, they'll know just what letter goes with that sound, so they'll write it down, without even using the alphabet chart. Then they reread their writing, and try to hear more sounds.

This time, read just the words on the page and nothing more. You are going to correct yourself and do some rereading.

Page 1

Page 2

Page 3   Page 4

"Let's help Kiera do that work with her writing about her toy horses. She's drawn one big horse and a baby horse, and there is something on the ground over here but I am not sure what it is. Kiera, can you tell us what you want your writing to say? Then we can help you to make sure you have the words written to help everyone read your writing."

Kiera pointed to the big horse and the baby horse, and she said, "That's the mother horse, and that's the baby horse." She pointed to the stuff on the ground and added, "That's hay for them to eat."

Nodding, I said, "Okay, writers. Do you have your muscles ready? Kiera first wants to tell her readers that this is a mother horse and a baby horse, and this is hay. So, first we'll start and say the first word really slowly. Say the word *mother* slowly, listening for that very first sound. Don't let it slip past you! See if the letter that makes that sound is already in your mind, so that you don't even need to use the alphabet chart to help you."

We heard the /m/ at the beginning, and kids called out that the letter *m* made that sound. "Wow, you didn't even need the alphabet chart for that one. You already have it in your mind." After recording the *m*, I asked kids to reread it and see if there were more letters they heard in *mother*.

I said the word *mother* repeatedly, accenting the final sound; the students heard the *r*. I wrote the rest of the word, emphasizing the /r/ at the end of the word as I recorded the *r*.

We then also labeled *baby horse*, *soft mane*, and *yellow hay*. The students heard several sounds for each word. Each time, I celebrated how students had so many sounds and letters in their minds that they didn't need to check the alphabet chart.

ACTIVE ENGAGEMENT/LINK

Invite partners to write words that could be added to one student's writing. Encourage them to use their alphabet charts only if needed.

"I'll bet that you, too, have more things you can say about your writing. Who thinks they have more to tell their readers? Thumbs up if you do!" Thumbs shot up around the room, and I continued.

FIG. 10–1   Kiera's writing

FIG. 10–2   Students writing with beginning sounds. *M* for *moon*. *S* for *stars*.

We imagine that you will use a piece of student work from your own classroom in this session—children are often inspired by the work that other learners have done.

You can decide whether to record words with inventive or conventional spelling. The really important thing is that you teach kids the sense of agency and confidence that allows them to know that writing words is within grasp for them. To make sure they see this as doable, you can't be too far beyond them. If many of your kids are not yet hearing more than initial sounds in words, you may want to model with inventive spelling—but if you are uncomfortable leaving something up on display that contains incorrect spelling, you can remove this once you have shown them the process of saying a word slowly, listening for sounds, recording them, then returning to the word to listen for yet more sounds.

Students have been working on stretching sounds in words since the start of kindergarten, and this has been especially highlighted in Session 10, "Stretching Out Words to Write Even More Sounds" in the Unit 1 of the kindergarten Units of Study in Opinion, Information, and Narrative Writing, Launching the Writing Workshop. *Today, nudge your students to write more sounds in individual words, and note that many students may be ready for much more writing. Invite these students to write longer two- and three-word labels like* my doll *or perhaps even simple sentences.*

"Terrific! You can work in pairs—the writer sitting on this side," I said, pointing to my right. "You are going to be Partner 1, and you'll go first. Will you bring out the writing you have been working on during writing workshop? You and your partner will first read over any of the words that you have written. Put your finger under those words and read them. Read the picture, too, and talk about what is going on. After you read what you have *already* written, will you work together to get some more writing onto your page? See if you can write more words without looking at the alphabet chart!" As the kids worked, I moved around the room, coaching students who needed more support and voicing over comments to support all writers.

You may have some children whose drawings are not representational enough for them to recall the content they hoped to represent. You can usually coach these youngsters to say what they wished their writing showed. You may need to feed them some ideas. "Is this your Lego man? Is it a fireman? Perhaps it wasn't originally a fireman, but good enough: onward. Say 'fireman' and listen for the first sound."

RUG TIME

Encourage partners to switch roles, with Partner 2 rereading his or her writing and adding more words with the help of Partner 1.

"I know, Partner 2, you are hankering to work on your writing. Again, start by rereading any writing you already have on your page. Put your finger under the words you have written, just like I put my pointer under the words when we read as a class. Then the two of you can work together to try to get more writing on your page. Don't forget to listen carefully to hear the first sound. Use your snap words if you can."

As the children worked, I circulated, noticing students who could hear more than initial sounds and helping them to do so, channeling students to write *the* or *a* when an article was called for: *the bad guy*, *the weapon*.

SHARE • Reading Aloud to Club Members and Friends

Channel students to read their writing to their rug clubs.

"Writers in this row, will you and your partner share the writing the two of you did with the partners sitting behind you? And writers in this row, do the same. Start with Partner 1's writing, and will you point as you read it? Then go to the next writer, and the next."

After children shared for a bit, I said, "Writers, now I am *really* sad that your stuffed animals aren't in school any longer, because they missed out on this! It would be so great if you could put your turtle or your rabbit on your lap and read your writing to your little pal, right? Tonight, would you teach your stuffed animal that knowing the alphabet is all well and good, but the really important thing is that you *use it* to write? By this point, you know so many letters and sounds in your head that you only needed to look at your alphabet chart once in a while."

POSSIBLE COACHING MOVES

▸ "I noticed that some of you are rereading what you have written before you write more!"

▸ "So many words on a page. Wow! Can you add some more?"

▸ "Say the word slowly and listen for more sounds. What letter goes with that sound?"

▸ "Can you add more words to make longer labels? Can you add a snap word?"

▸ For kids who need more of a challenge, you might say, "Don't stop! You can write the whole sentence to match the picture. Say the sentence, count the words, now write."

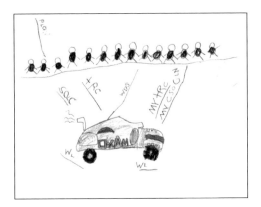

GETTING READY

- Display signs containing only letters to the class. 👆
- Distribute a whiteboard and marker to each partnership.

"Writers, as we walk to lunch today, will you keep your eyes open to notice whether we pass any writing in the hallway, because I've been thinking that just like you write words on your drawings, the people who made this school wrote words on our building!"

The kids noted words in the hallway.

Later, back in the classroom, I said, "When we walked down the hall today, you noticed how many things *grown-ups* label. Here are some labels I saw yesterday, on my way home from school. See if you and your partner can figure out what these signs are saying.

FIG. 10–3   Many signs out in the world are labeled with letters.

"Yes, I think you could read some of these signs, but it was a little tricky to read them all because they have just one letter. I think we could improve these labels by adding more sounds. Want to try?"

I distributed each partnership a whiteboard and marker. "Pick the sign you like the best, and then try to add more sounds. If I pick *McDonald's*, for example, what are the other sounds I hear? There is certainly more than just the /m/ sound in *McDonald's*. Say the word slowly and write more sounds. After you have improved one label, try another.

"Today, will you notice writing that you pass on your way home from school? And you might even add writing in your house, if you see things that should be labeled with sticky notes."

EXTENSION 2 • Snap Word "Simon Says"

GETTING READY

- Gather enough whiteboards and markers for you and for each student.

Give kids additional practice in writing snap words with a game of "Simon Says."

"Writers, I see so many of you using your snap words in your very own writing! I promise that if you practice writing them more and more, you won't even need to look at the snap word pocket chart anymore! You will just have them in your mind. Let's play the 'Snap Word Simon Says' game to get those words into your mind. Are you ready?

"Kindergartners, to play this game, you have to listen closely to what Simon asks you do—and then do it! But if I don't say *Simon*, then don't follow the direction." The kids were excited to start. I said, "Simon says, get a whiteboard and a marker. Each of you needs your own."

Once kids had their whiteboards and markers ready, I said, "Simon says, write the snap word *the* in the middle of your board." I demonstrated, and then asked students to follow my example. Then we erased our boards. "You're really listening carefully to what Simon says!

"Simon says write the snap word *like* really big on your whiteboard. Use our snap word collection if you need help spelling *like*." After everyone had written something, I prompted students to hold up their boards for "Simon" to do a quick check.

"Okay, now write the snap word *like* really small." As some students began to write, I laughed and said, "WAIT! I didn't say . . . " and the kids shouted back, "'Simon says!'"

We continued the game for several rounds. I prompted students to write snap words big, small, in the top corner, in the bottom corner, write the word twice, write it all lowercase, all capital, and so on.

This game is traditionally called "Simon Says." However, you might find it even more engaging for your students if you use your name instead of Simon's, calling the game "Ms./Mr. . . . Says."

EXTENSION 3 • Listening for Ending Sounds in Shared Reading

GETTING READY

- Display a familiar nursery rhyme or poem, such as "Jack and Jill."

Encourage students to listen to the sounds at the ends of words, particularly the /əl/ sound, through shared reading of a familiar nursery rhyme.

"Word scientists, you can listen closely to the sounds in words as you read, too." I revealed a poem on the easel. "Thumbs up if you recognize this poem." I pointed under the words as I read the title.

"Let's get started listening for the /l/ sound, like the sound you hear at the end of *Mabel*. What's important to know about this poem is that the /l/ sound is not at the beginning of words like *lll-ollipop*, but at the end like *Mabe-lll*.

"Each time you hear the ending sound /l/ in a word, do a silent cheer." I waved my hands in the air. "So, we can take a closer listen to that word."

I read the title. "Jack and Jill." I looked up and noticed a few hands waving in the air. I announced, "Yes, my hands are cheering, too! I hear the /l/ sound. Let's double-check that it's at the end of the word. Say it together. *Jill*. Now slowly, / Ji-/lll/. I hear the /l/ at the end of the word. Now let's write the letter for that sound in the air."

We continued reading, stopping, and listening at *hill*, *pail*, *fell*. We silently cheered and wrote *L* in the air each time.

"Now, reread this poem with your partner and listen closely for /r/ sound at the end of words. Anytime you and your partner hear the /r/ sound at the end of a word, clap. Then double-check by saying the word slowly and checking the ending letter."

As the students began to read the poem, I coached partnerships to listen closely to the ending sounds, check the letters, and then write them in the air.

I called the class back together after a few moments and said, "Word scientists, listening closely to ending sounds is hard work. All of this listening work will help you to read and write. The only way we will get better at this is with more practice!"

Learning to read happens much more easily for kids who have phonological awareness. To problem solve tricky words, kids need to become adept at blending phonemes, the smallest sound units in words. The foundational skills involved in this revolve around phonological awareness—not phonics itself. That is, the first step is for kids to work with sounds, even before they work with the symbols that match those sounds. This shared reading supports that work, and also supports kids learning to segment, or to hear individual phonemes in a word, which is something they need to do to write.

Jack and Jill

Jack and Jill
went up the hill
to fetch a pail
of water,
Jack fell down
and broke his
crown,
and Jill
came tumbling
after.

Learning New Snap Words

IN THIS SESSION

TODAY YOU'LL teach students that readers and writers can turn words they will write a lot into snap words by reading, studying, spelling, writing, and using the words.

TODAY YOUR STUDENTS will learn three new snap words as they practice a five-step process for turning any word into a snap word. Students will use the snap words to make and read simple phrases and sentences.

MINILESSON

CONNECTION

Share the observations another kindergarten class made when they studied the alphabet chart, and suggest learning new snap words.

"Kindergartners, we got a package! Come quickly." Once the children had gathered, I opened the package, with great fanfare, knowing that it was the alphabet charts that I pretended were sent to us from the class across the hall. "Now we'll be able to see what those kids noticed when they looked at the alphabet chart," I said. "This will be so interesting!"

"They sent one big alphabet chart, so let's look at this one together, and then I'll give you and your partner each a chart to look at." I displayed a large chart, one that held many signs that said things such as, "This is an *f*" (fan), "This is a *g*" (goat), and "Here is an *r*" (rainbow).

I pointed to the first phrase: "This is an *f*," and said to the kids, "I can read what they wrote, but most of you don't yet know the words they've used on their alphabet chart. They must have learned some different snap words than we learned!"

GETTING READY

✔ Mark up a few alphabet charts with Post-its (e.g., "This is an *f*" and "Here is a *g*") and draw an arrow to something on the chart, as if done by another kindergarten class.

✔ Display the "How to Learn a Word" anchor chart.

✔ Prepare word cards for high-frequency words: *this*, *is*, and *here*.

✔ Distribute whiteboards and markers.

✔ Prepare baggies with copies of each snap word card, ten picture cards of your choice, any concrete words in your collection, and a few blank cards for each partnership.

PHONICS INSTRUCTION

Concepts About Print
- Recognize that spoken words are represented in written language by specific sequences of letters.
- Understand that words are written left to right across the page.
- Understand that words are separated by spaces in print, concept of word.
- Match spoken word to print.

High-Frequency Words
- Recognize and use high-frequency words.
- Locate and read high-frequency words in a text.
- Write high-frequency words in continuous text.
- Learn new words (*here*, *is*, *this*).

"That is so cool! They made Post-its about things they noticed on the alphabet chart, too, but they used different words. I think we should learn those words, too! What do you think?" The students agreed.

"First, let's warm up. Remember that lots of people, before they start something, do a quick warm-up to get ready for it. Let's warm up by reading our words." I pointed to the pocket chart. "I will point to a word from our word collection box, and let's all read it. Then let's spell it, and read it again."

We reviewed our snap words. "I think we are ready to learn some new words!"

❖ **Name the teaching point.**

"Today I want to teach you that anytime, you can decide to learn some new words, and if you learn them really well, then when other kids write those words, you can read them in a snap—and you can read and write with them, too. Your reading and writing goes faster when you know words in a snap."

TEACHING AND ACTIVE ENGAGEMENT/LINK

Support your kids to progress through the steps detailed in their "How to Learn a Word" chart, referring to the chart to help them eventually do so independently.

"Let's learn the words that the other kindergartners wrote on their alphabet charts: *here*, *this*, and *is*."

I displayed the "How to Learn a Word" chart prominently on the easel. The kids joined in reading the chart as I pointed under each word.

Coach students as they read the new snap word. Then, channel students to study the word, drawing on the work they did in Bend I, Session 3. Help them name a few characteristics of the word.

I held up a large Post-it that I pretended had come from one of the other kindergarten alphabet charts and said, "Someone wrote an arrow next to this rainbow and wrote the sentence, 'Here is a rainbow.'" I underlined the word *here*. "Are you ready to learn the word *here*?" I pointed to the first bullet on the chart. "Read *here*."

Moving to the next bullet, I said, "Now we need to study the word. Ready to study the word *here*?" I placed the word card on the easel. I covered the word with an index card and slowly revealed one letter at a time, guiding the kids to study and check each letter along with me. I reminded them they could talk about the letters—whether they are tall or small, curves or no curves, and so forth.

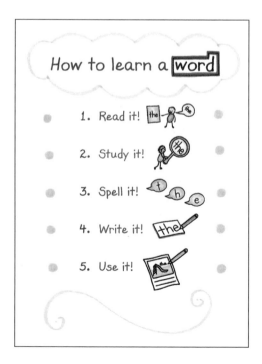

How to learn a **word**

1. Read it! *the*
2. Study it!
3. Spell it! *t h e*
4. Write it! *the*
5. Use it!

After a minute, I called students back. "I agree with what you noticed. There are four letters in the word *here*. There are one tall and three small letters. And all of the letters have curves."

Coach students to spell the word repeatedly. Then, direct them to write the word on their whiteboards. Cover the word and ask them to try writing the word again.

"Ready for our next step? Let's spell the word. *Here*, *h-e-r-e*, *h-e-r-e*, *here*! Try it with me. Let's do it again." I lowered my voice so the class could spell the word without me. I kept watch for any students who appeared to be having trouble with this.

"Here's step 4: we need to write it. Will you spell *h-e-r-e* aloud as you write the letters?" I began to hand out whiteboards and said, "Once you get a marker, start writing the new snap word *here*, *h-e-r-e*. Spell it, cover it with your hand, and spell it again. This time try to write it faster and without looking. Then erase and spell it again. Write it five times, and each time, check each letter."

I repeated the same high-frequency word study sequence with the words *this* and *is*, moving through the same replicable steps. "The last step of *using* these new snap words will happen during rug time.

"Whenever you are reading, there will be words you read again and again. And whenever you are writing, there will be words you write again and again. Word scientists are always collecting more of these words. Now you know *this*, *is*, and *here*. Knowing those words will help you read and write more and *more*!" I added word cards for *this*, *is*, and *here* to our snap word pocket chart.

RUG TIME

Invite students to rehearse and make simple phrases and sentences with the snap word and picture cards.

I quickly distributed a baggie containing snap word cards. Your collection will include *I*, *a*, *me*, *the*, *like*, *my*, *look*, *at*, *see*, *this*, *here*, *is*, and any concrete words that you selected, based on your knowledge of your class. I also distributed several picture cards, and a few blank cards to each partnership. "Word scientists, you know the reason why we learn so many snap words is so we can *use* them! I thought you might want to make some sentences, so I have given you some snap words written on cards, and you can line up these cards to make sentences.

"You'll see some cards are blank, so you can write more words if you need them. Or, if you want, I also gave you some picture words—like this elephant. The word *elephant* isn't written out, but I bet you can name it, right?

"So will you and your partner take a few minutes and make a bunch of sentences using the word cards? You can use the picture cards, too, to write sentences like, "Here is a robot," or "Here is a turtle"—or you can make some of your own cards. But you only have two minutes to work. Go!"

As the kids worked, I worked on the easel at the front of the room, to model for any children who might need a little extra help in knowing what to do. I picked up the word *me* and placed it next to the elephant picture card. I pointed to the two cards and muttered, "Me elephant—that doesn't sound right . . . " I then put the *me* card back into the collection.

"I think I'd better start with a few snap words. What if I take *here*, *is*, and the word *the* . . . ?" I lined up the snap words and read what I had put together. "Wow, I have a sentence! Read it with me."

Voicing over as children continued to work, I said, "Work together. Make sure that the sentences you put together make sense and sound right. Try more than one sentence if you have time!"

You may have a child who notices that the first word in the sentence isn't capitalized but should be. If that happens, you should confirm that sentences should always begin with a capital letter, but explain that for today, you are using the cards you have, which only have lowercase letters. Provide a similar rational for ending punctuation.

SHARE • Reading Snap Words in a Different Order

Add new words to the snap word collection and invite a "snap word reader" to lead the class in a shared reading of snap words.

"Let's add our new snap words to our collection.

"You've learned a lot more words," I said. "Let's read them all." I handed the big pointer to one child who led the class in a shared reading of all the snap words. She did this in order, so I said, "Wow, this is too easy for you!" I removed all of the cards from the pocket chart and placed them in a different order.

The snap word reader pointed to the snap words in the new order and the other students read along. I encouraged her to do that one more time, picking up speed. When the student had finished a few rounds, I changed the order of the words again, and she passed the pointer to a new snap word reader.

When we had finished, I placed the word cards back in order so that students could easily find words when they needed them.

EXTENSION 1 • Using New Snap Words to Turn a Letter Book into a Pattern Book

Continue the work from Session 2 Extension 2, "Letter Books for Letters *F* and *H*," by helping students to use their new snap words to turn their letter book into a pattern book.

I held up a letter book we had made earlier in the unit. "Word scientists, are you up for a challenge? Now that you know so many snap words, I think we could make our letter books even fancier. Will you help me turn one of our letter books into a pattern book using our new snap words?

"Let's work on this *F* book." I opened to a page with a picture of a fish and showed that page to the kids. "First, we have to figure out how the pattern will go. Will you tell each other what we could perhaps write on this page?" I tapped the snap word pocket chart—including the new words *here*, *this*, and *is*. Soon, with the kids' help, I'd written a sentence on that page. "This is a fish."

I turned the page to a picture of a fox. "Help me plan this page. This is a pattern book, so each page will start the same way." I tapped the page as we orally planned the sentence: "This is a fox."

"Let's say it again and count how many words it has. 'This is a fox.' Four words! Will you all write this sentence on your whiteboard while I add it to our book? The first word in a sentence starts with a capital letter. Great! First, tap where you'll write each word. Now, let's say the first word that we'll write: *This*. Spell it. *T-h-i-s*. Now write it on your board. Check each letter to make sure it matches the word *this*." We worked together saying and spelling the snap words aloud and stopping to listen for the sounds in the word *fox*.

After we finished writing we reread the book. "Nice work writing *and* reading, word scientists."

EXTENSION 2 • Knowing Snap Words Changes Your Reading

Give students a tip about how knowing snap words can help their reading, then lead them in reading the words to "The Teapot Song" as they sing along.

"Readers, today we're going to read a poem called 'The Teapot Song,' but before we read it, I want to give you a little tip. Now that you know so many words by heart, it can sometimes help to just look through the page before you read it and check if you see any of your snap words. If you see any snap words in this poem, put a thumb up. That way, when you get to that word when you are reading, you can read it in a snap."

The Teapot Song

I'm a little teapot,

Short and stout.

Here is my handle.

Here is my spout.

When I get all steamed up,

Hear me shout;

Just tip me over

And pour me out!

I pointed under the words in the poem, moving left to right before I started reading. I scanned the carpet to see many students giving a thumbs up, and I said, "You know some of these words, right?" I pointed to *here*, *is*, *my*, and *me*.

I then sang the song, inviting the students to join in when they could. We sang the song a second time, this time lowering my voice, as more children joined in to "I'm a Little Teapot."

EXTENSION 3 • Adding Snap Words to Writing

 Channel students to use snap words to extend their writing.

"Word scientists, nothing matters more than that you are using what you are learning as you read and write. Right now, will you and your partner work together to read our snap word collection?"

After students read the words, I said, "Wow! You've learned so many words. What matters most, though, is that you *use* what you're learning. Will you pull out your writing and reread all the writing you did on that piece? Use your finger as a pointer and point under the words you have written.

"Now find something you have drawn that has one word beside it, and right this minute, see if you can add some snap words to that label. You might write *the* toy, *Look!* a toy!, *here is a* toy, *I see a* toy, or *this is a* toy. You have five minutes. Right now, see how much writing you can get done!"

FIG. 11–1   Adding the snap word *my*

Listening to the Ends of Words Matters

IN THIS SESSION

TODAY YOU'LL teach students to say words slowly, all the way to the end, because hearing and recording more sounds helps someone else read your writing.

TODAY YOUR STUDENTS will write longer words listening for all the sounds they hear. Students will learn that sometimes it helps to make a line, say the word slowly, and then write the word on the line.

GETTING READY

✔ Make a classroom label with the letter *D* for *door*.

✔ Distribute a whiteboard, marker, and baggie of short/long-word picture cards to each partnership.

MINILESSON

CONNECTION

Remind writers that word scientists notice little things, then extend the storyline of the unit by pointing out that they also *listen* to little things. Recall that students learned to listen to first sounds.

"Word scientists, remember how I once told you that scientists notice little tiny things, that they study tiny plants growing in the crack of a sidewalk, and legs on insects that live in rotting logs? Well, today I need to tell you something else. Scientists not only look closely, they also listen closely.

"Remember the other day, I told you that it can be hard to hear the *first* sounds in words? We said 'hi' into our hands and tried to really hear that super quiet /h/ sound in *hi*. And we said 'love' and heard the first sound in that word. Let's try it now!"

I led the class in saying "love" into our hands and hearing the /l/. We said "mad" and heard the /m/. "You see what I mean? Word scientists need to not only *look* closely, but to also *listen* closely."

PHONICS INSTRUCTION

Concepts About Print
* Understand that words are written left to right across the page.
* Understand that words are separated by spaces in print, concept of word.
* Match spoken word to print.

Phonological Awareness
* Say words slowly to identify salient sounds in words.
* Identify the initial, medial, and final phonemes of spoken words.

Word Knowledge/Solving
* Identify and use initial and final sounds when writing words.

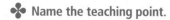

"Today I want to teach you that when you want to write a word, you need to listen not only for the first sound, but also for the other sounds you hear. Sometimes people don't hear the last sound, because they don't listen for it. It helps to really listen for the last sound, so you can *write* the last sound."

TEACHING

Explain to kids that earlier in the year, when they labeled the room, they did this with only initial sounds. Help them now to point to objects and say their names, accentuating the final sound.

"Writers, I collected some of the labels that you made long, long ago when you were new to kindergarten, and what I noticed is that most of you only wrote the first letter on your label. Like you labeled this . . ." and I pointed to the door, "with a *D*, which is a terrific start. But I'm thinking you can listen really closely to the word *door*, and maybe you'll hear even more sounds. Say 'door' into your hand and this time, listen as closely as you can to the ending sound. Door. Door."

Kids called out that they heard an *R*. I added the rest of the letters to the label, emphasizing the /r/ as I wrote the letter *r*.

"Writers, before you can write the last sounds in a word, you need to say and hear them. Will you work on saying the names of things in such a way that you really pop out the ending sound? Like this: boar-/d/! ru-/g/!

"Let's try a few more together. I'll point to something, and can you try to say what this is, making sure you say and hear the ending sound?"

I pointed to a few objects around the meeting area and we said them together, popping out the final sound. Boo-/k/, chai-/r/, penci-/l/.

ACTIVE ENGAGEMENT/LINK

Rally the kids to roam the classroom, looking at objects as they did earlier in the year, but this time saying and hearing at least the first and final sounds.

"Will you head off around this room, saying the names of things that you see? Notice things you couldn't see from the rug. This time, try to hear not just the first sounds in a word, but also more sounds. To do that, say the name of the object twice. Say it once to catch the first sound, then say the name again to pop out more sounds all the way to the end.

"Let me show you what I mean. Nicole, can you be my partner?" Nicole came up to the front and we modeled for the class, pointing to an object and popping out the first sound—/t/-able—and then the final sound—tab-/l/."

As students become more proficient with isolating sounds at the beginning of a word, teach them to listen for more sounds in words. We want to move students toward the important work of full segmentation. The next step of this work is to isolate sounds at the end of words.

FIG. 12–1 Students practice saying the word slowly and popping out the last sound they hear in the word.

"Make sure that you say and hear the first and the last sound in every word. You'll probably even hear some of the middle sounds, which will be totally cool.

"Okay, walk around the room with your partner and see how many words you can say, hearing sounds all across the word."

RUG TIME

Challenge partners to write more words together. Students choose a picture card, say the word slowly, and record all the sounds they hear on a whiteboard.

"Word scientists, you were doing some super close listening, weren't you? I heard words like *computer* and *whiteboard*. Those are some big words with lots of sounds!

"I was wondering if you want to learn a grown-up way for writing super-duper hard and long words. Would you like to learn that? You would? It's going to take some writing muscles—show me your muscles. It is also going to take some *ear* muscles, because you are going to have to do some serious hearing. Are you game?" They were.

"Okay. I have some pictures in this jar. I thought, just for fun, you might want to try to write some really tricky words. But, here is the thing: there will be lots of sounds to say and hear. Sometimes it helps to make a line as you say the word slowly, and then you can write the word on that line.

"Let's try it together with this word." I showed the kids a picture of a dinosaur. "First, you say the word, and as you say it, you make a line for the word. Like this."

I said "dinosaur," and as I spoke, wrote a line. Then I said, "Then you repeat the word, and write any sounds you hear down on the line. Watch:

"Dino . . . di . . . /d/ /d/ /d/," and I wrote *D* on top of the left side of the line. Then I said "Dinosaur. Di-no-saur. /n/ /n/," and I added an *N* on the line after the *D*. I repeated the word again, this time emphasizing the final sound, and recorded an *R*.

"You ready to try? You and your partner will need a whiteboard and an envelope of picture cards. Some are super hard. Pull a word out and try it. If you don't know what it is, try another."

After kids worked for a while, I suggested they each share their favorite word with the rest of their rug club. "See if you can work together to hear even *more* sounds in that word," I said.

Traditionally, phonics instruction in early kindergarten emphasizes the first and final sounds only, but keep in mind that usually that instruction revolves around kids' reading, not their writing, and most of their reading is relying on CVC words. On those words, it makes sense for kids' focus to be on initial and final sounds. But if the child is labeling a marker or computer, they may be apt to hear salient sounds in the words.

SHARE • Sing "What's the Last Sound that You Hear?"

Sing a song to practice identifying the last sound in a word.

"Remember the song we sang to help us get even better at hearing first sounds in words? It was called, 'What's the First Sound that You Hear?' Let's change it to 'What's the *Last* Sound that You Hear?'" I hummed a few bars of "London Bridge Is Falling Down" to remind students of the tune. "Join me when you can."

What's the last sound that you hear, that you hear, that you hear?
What's the last sound that you hear in . . . Mabel, Mabel, Mabel?

I paused, giving the children time to process.

/l/ is the last sound that you hear, that you hear, that you hear.
/l/ is the last sound that you hear in . . . Mabel, Mabel, Mabel!

We continued singing a few more times with different names from kids in the class.

EXTENSION 1 • Beginning, Middle, End Song

GETTING READY

- Display the lyrics to "Beginning, Middle, End" on chart paper, with large Elkonin boxes to segment phonemes at the bottom of the chart.

Teach a new song to practice listening for sounds in different parts of a word: "Beginning, Middle, End."

"Friends, Mabel has a favorite song for saying and hearing sounds in words. Let's learn it so we can sing it for her."

"It helps to use your whole body to do this work." I demonstrated as I said, "Move your hands from your shoulder to elbow to wrist to figure it out: /m/ /ă/ /n/. Tap your shoulder if you hear the /m/ at beginning, elbow if you hear it in the middle, or wrist if you hear it at the end." The kids signaled they heard it at the beginning. I pointed to the first Elkonin box to signal beginning sound.

We sang the "Beginning, Middle, End" song a few times, changing the place of the sound we were listening for. As we sang, I segmented the word, pointing to the Elkonin boxes on the chart.

The focus of this unit is to have students identify and isolate beginning and ending sounds, to stretch words to hear sounds, and to record those sounds in their writing. This song provides an invitation to segment individual phonemes in words.

78

EXTENSION 2 • Help Mabel Write a Letter

GETTING READY

- Display an enlarged version of Mabel's letter to Blue Bear.
- Display the class alphabet chart.

Recruit students to complete words in Mabel's letter by listening for final sounds.

"Mabel asked us for a special favor. She has been using her alphabet chart to write up a storm, too! She wrote a letter to Blue Bear, but she wants us to help her reread and listen for more sounds so she can add those to her writing. Think we should help?" The class looked willing.

"Here is her letter." I pointed under each word as I read Mabel's letter to the class.

Dear Blue Bea__,

You are my bes__ frien__. Let's have a playdate after schoo__ today.

Love,

Mabel

"Wow, Mabel has really been using her alphabet chart to write, and I can tell she's been using snap words, too. Let's help her out with the tricky work of listening and writing ending sounds, too.

"It says, 'Dear Blue Bea__.' Let's say 'bear' together, listen all the way to the end. Bea/rrrr/. Yes, I hear it too, /rrrr/. Quickly find the letter that says /rrrr/ on the alphabet chart. If you already know it, write it in the air while the rest of us search the alphabet chart.

"Oh yes, bea/rrrr/, like /rrr/rainbow. That's the letter *r*. Should it be the capital or lowercase? Yes, lowercase because it's at the end of the word. Each of you, write your best lowercase *r* in your hand. José, come quickly to write it in Mabel's letter."

We continued to fill in the rest of the ending sounds in Mabel's letter. When we finished we reread the letter, paying special attention to the ending sounds we had recorded.

"Mabel thanks you! I will be sure to deliver this to Blue Bear, so they can have that playdate."

EXTENSION 3 • "One Of These Words Is Not Like the Others" (Ending Sounds)

GETTING READY

- Before this extension, familiarize yourself with "One of These Things Is Not Like the Others" from *Sesame Street*. A link to this song is available in the online resources.
- Gather sets of picture cards. You will need groups of four words, three that end with the same sound and a fourth that ends with a different sound.

"Let's play our little game that helps us think about sounds in words. Remember the one I learned from *Sesame Street*? It goes like this." I began singing.

One of these words is not like the others,
One of these words just doesn't belong.
Can you tell which word is not like the others
By the time I finish my song?

"Tell me which word is different from the other words. I am going to make it a little harder. Ready?" I placed four pictures on the easel. "Here are the words: *dog, bag, pig, man*. When you think you've figured out which word doesn't belong, put a thumb up." I paused a moment to give kids time to process. Then, I prompted partners to turn and share their answers with each other.

"Let's come back together and share. Ready?" I recited the verse once more, as some kids began to chime in.

Then, I signaled for the class to shout out their answers. The kids called out different words. "Listen closely." I read the picture cards, exaggerating the ending sounds this time.

"Man!"

"But why? Why doesn't *man* belong?"

"Because it ends with /n/ and the other words end with /g/," one student explained.

"You got it. Three of the words end with the /g/ sound, the letter *g*.

"Let's play another round. Ready?" I sang the verse again, this time displaying four new pictures: bat, pot, fan, rat. Then, I prompted the class to turn and share their guesses with a partner before sharing aloud.

"Now explain why *fan* doesn't belong. Yes, the word *fan* ends with /n/ *n*, not /t/ *t*."

80

Listening for Sounds All across the Word

IN THIS SESSION

TODAY YOU'LL teach students to listen for and write sounds across words. You will teach them to say the word slowly, listening for not just the first sound, but stretching and recording all the way to the end of the word.

TODAY YOUR STUDENTS will write labels, listening and recording sounds using a shared story, and then transfer their learning to their own writing.

MINILESSON

CONNECTION

Pose a question about why pictures on the alphabet chart appear with the first letter of the word. Then explain how all the sounds in a word matter—and why.

"Word scientists, here is my question. Why is the dog here?" I pointed to the *D* square on the alphabet chart, "and not here?" I pointed to the *G* square, to the sound at the end of *dog*. "And why is the ball here?" I pointed to the *B* square, "and not here?" and I pointed to the *L* square, representing the sound at the end of *ball*. I stared at the alphabet chart, as if fascinated by the question, waiting for my meaning to dawn on some kids. After a half minute, I developed my question.

"Yesterday, we talked about how important it is to listen not only for the beginnings, but also for the endings of words. That's important, because sometimes we act as if only the first sound matters!

"Let's stretch the word *dog*, stretch it down your arm and listen closely for the sound hiding at the end. Yes, d/ŏ/gggg." I tapped my wrist to signal the ending sound. "We heard a sound at the end— it's the /g/ sound. Listening all the way to the ends of words helps you write more sounds, and when you write more sounds, others can read your writing. They don't even need the picture—they can read your letters."

GETTING READY

✔ Prepare a sketch to demonstrate how to label with words and sentences. 🌿

✔ Distribute whiteboards and markers.

✔ Make sure students bring their writing folders to the meeting area with a pencil.

PHONICS INSTRUCTION

Concepts About Print
- Understand that words are separated by spaces in print, concept of word.

Phonological Awareness
- Identify the initial and final phonemes of spoken words.
- Say words slowly to identify salient sounds.

Word Knowledge/Solving
- Identify and use initial, final, and salient sounds when writing words.

High-Frequency Words
- Recognize and use high-frequency words.
- Writing high-frequency words in a continuous text.

♣ **Name the teaching point.**

"Today I want to teach you that when you write, some words will be words that you know in a snap, and you just write those. Other words will be ones that you say s-l-o-w-l-y all the way to end, working to hear and record all the sounds. That way people can read your writing without even needing the picture. They read your letters."

TEACHING

Elicit children's help labeling a drawing, saying each word slowly, isolating sounds, and writing.

"I have this drawing that one of the kindergartners made last year. It's a picture of her doll house's tiny kitchen, but she never finished it. Let's do some writing for her. We can start with labels for her pictures and then write a sentence, just like you all can do in your own writing."

I pointed to the picture of a miniature kitchen and said, "Here's the table with a tiny cup on it. Do you have your muscles ready? What do you want to label, for starters?" Soon we were saying the word *cup* slowly, listening for sounds. After the students wrote and read *cup* and *table*, I pressed on.

Tell children that once they are able to record several sounds in a word, they can write sentences. Help them do so, shifting between writing snap words and listening to the sounds in other words.

"Writers, once you are writing with a couple sounds for a word—at least a first and a last sound—you can write more than just labels beside items in your pictures. You can actually write sentences, or complete thoughts about your pictures. What might this writer want to say about her miniature kitchen? Let's help her write a sentence. Turn and talk about your ideas."

I listened as children talked and soon reconvened the class. "So, let's help her write, 'See my little cup and table.'"

The class began by coaching me to write *see* and *my* in a snap. "*Little* will be harder," I said, but we can do it. "Show me your big ears for listening to sounds!" Soon we'd recorded the sentence.

ACTIVE ENGAGEMENT/LINK

Encourage students to continue labeling the picture with beginning and ending sounds, and also to record another sentence, using snap words as well as invented spelling.

"There are so many tiny things in the picture—so much more to label! Would you be willing to label more items in the picture?" I distributed whiteboards and markers as I continued, "After you have more labels, you can try writing a sentence that this writer might want to add under her picture."

FIG. 13–1   Notice the students that record beginning sounds and nudge them to write salient sounds. Some students may be recording vowels.

FIG. 13–2   Nudge other students to write sentences with snap words they know.

I asked students what else they saw. "I see a coffee cup. It's like my mug," one said.

"Mug!" I repeated, pouncing on the word that would be within reach for them. "Can you write the sounds you hear in *mug* on your whiteboard?" I asked, drawing out the word slowly. I wandered around as students said the word aloud and wrote the letters they heard. "What sounds do you hear?" I asked. After each sound that students shared, I asked what letter they'd written. "Great! If you hear the /m/ sound, you write the letter *m*. Keep listening all the way to the end of the word.

"Okay. Label more stuff!" I said. Students were soon writing *pot*, *pan*, *mop*, *sink*, *oven*, *refrigerator*, and *microwave*. I encouraged them to hear as many sounds as possible.

"Writers, now that you are writing with several sounds in a word, I bet people could read your writing even if you were writing a sentence at the bottom of the page instead of just a label. Talk to your partner, decide what you want to say, and write a sentence." As children worked, I congratulated some for rereading often and for using snap words.

You will certainly find that children are more likely to spell words like pan *and* mop *conventionally, while their attempts to write longer, harder words like* refrigerator *will be far from correct. You'll want to celebrate their approximations, noting the sounds that they are recording accurately, and keeping an eye open for students who may need extra support in hearing the salient sounds in the words.*

RUG TIME (CLUBS)

Channel students to apply what they have been practicing to their own writing—listening for and recording sounds across a word.

"I know this isn't writing time, but aren't you itching to work on your own writing instead of writing about that other kid's drawing? Will you meet with your rug club first? Get out your writing folders and show your rug club whatever writing you have been working on recently. Talk together about whether you have just a few words on your writing, or a lot of words, and talk to someone about what you could write today. If you haven't yet written sentences in your writing, find a place on your paper where you can do so, and get started right this second while we are all here."

As children worked, I coached them to say each word slowly to themselves, listening carefully to each sound all the way across the word. I encouraged other writers to add more words to the page, making longer labels and simple sentences to match their pictures.

"Word scientists," I said, "can someone share a word that you are writing, what sounds you hear in it, and what letters you are writing?"

One student shared that she was writing the word *elephant*. She pronounced the word slowly, and said that she heard /l/ and wrote *L*, and she heard /t/, and wrote *T*.

"I hear those sounds, too!" I said. "Does anyone hear any other sounds?"

"The /f/ sound is in the middle," said another student.

POSSIBLE COACHING MOVES

▶ "I notice the way you keep saying that word again and again, hearing more sounds each time."

▶ "You can write that little line for your word and then put what you hear at the start of it. Listen more and see if you can put something at the end of it, too."

▶ "You know that word in a snap! You don't need to copy from the snap word list. Just write it as best you can, and then check it."

▶ "Let me see if I can read this. I'm going to put my finger under the first word. Does it say . . . ?"

▶ "Write a sentence. Say it out loud, then write it word by word."

▶ For kids who need more of a challenge, you might say, "Say the word again. What sound do you hear in the middle of the word?"

"I hear that, too!" I said. "Do others hear it? *Elephant*. Sometimes it can help to ask someone else to listen for more sounds. Ask your partners if they hear any other sounds in your words, okay? Go!"

SHARE • Celebrating with an Alphabet Parade

Invite students to celebrate their hard work with a parade around their writing while you all sing the ABC song. Vary the singing by putting the same words to other familiar tunes.

"What great writing! Let's celebrate the hard work you have done with an ABC parade around your writing. Marco, you'll be the leader, and you parade in and around the room, so you all can pass your writing and admire it, while all of us sing the ABC song. Ready, let's go!"

After we sang the alphabet two or three times, I called out, "Now, let's chant the alphabet! First, come together and let's do it together." We chanted the alphabet once while standing in a clump, then continued the parade, this time with the chant as our marching music. "How about we chant and add our movements? Twist, twist, hands in the air," I called, and we continued.

EXTENSION 1 • Label Favorite Storybooks

GETTING READY

- Display a storybook with pictures labeled only with initial letters.
- Prepare a Post-it that records the salient sounds of the name of a picture.
- Provide emergent storybooks, Post-its, and pencils for each student.

Recruit students to label emergent pictures in a favorite storybook, listening for all the sounds they hear in a word and recording those sounds with letters.

"Word scientists, do you remember earlier this year, we started to look inside our old favorite storybooks and label the pictures with beginning sounds just like this? Here in the book *Carrot Seed*, we labeled the letter *C* right next to the carrot. Well, look at my new label." I replaced the letter *C* Post-it with *crt*. "On this Post-it, I drew my label line and listened closely to all the sounds, all the way across the word. I even practiced writing in all lowercase letters.

Teachers, you may have facilitated a minilesson during reading workshop in the first kindergarten unit from the Units of Study for Teaching Reading, We Are Readers, in which students labeled their favorite storybooks with beginning sounds. Today we want to connect and extend this earlier work.

"Partners, roll up your sleeves, grab your old favorite storybook, and get started writing labels, listening all the way across the word, and then writing all the letters for the sounds you hear."

EXTENSION 2 • Sing New Snap Words

 "Today, we'll sing our snap words to help us remember them. But before we do that, let's read all of the snap words." We did a choral reading of all the snap words in the pocket chart, then I continued. "Now let's sing our snap words! Let's start with the little snap word *is*. We can sing *is* to 'Twinkle, Twinkle Little Star.' Listen and join me when you're ready. It goes like this":

I-s, i-s, i-s, is
I-s, i-s, is, is, is.
I-s, i-s, i-s, is
I-s, i-s, is, is, is.
I-s, i-s, i-s, is
I-s, i-s, is, is, is.

"Now, we can sing *here* and *this* to 'Row, Row, Row, Your Boat.'" I hummed a few bars of the tune.

H-e-r-e, here.
H-e-r-e, here.
H-e-r-e, here, here, here.
H-e-r-e, here.

EXTENSION 3 • Adding Concrete Words to the Snap Word Collection

 "Writers, many of you have been asking how to spell *house* and *park*. I know that you are always writing about the things and places that matter to you. I can add these important words to our snap word collection, so they are here when you need them."

Teachers, you can decide if you progress to the "How to Learn a Word" routine with these words. These words are not typically included on high-frequency word lists; they are what Patricia Cunningham considers "concrete" words. Many high-frequency words do not hold meaning. The purpose of adding just a few words like these will help writers feel more connected to their collection of snap words.

Dear Teachers,

There is nothing more joyful than kindergarten and one big part of that is your children's discovery of the power they get from knowing a handful of words in a snap. They will progress from writing letters to writing sentences! What could be more exciting than that?

In the first session of this bend, Mabel gives each student a special word collection pouch full of the snap words students have been studying in Bends I and II. You may be wondering, why not just a baggie? High-frequency words are very important and we recommend that you give them an extra drumroll by giving children little cloth pouches to hold their snap words. This extra hoopla is entirely optional. In the end, we leave these materials decisions up to you.

Early in the bend, you'll want to teach children a few snap words that are actually not included in the Dolch or Fry lists of words that are frequently found in children's books. Teach them words that will be close to their hearts, choosing just a few concrete words to teach just as you will teach words such as *at* or *to*. The reason to do this is that you are teaching children what a word is, and also, that it's grand to know a word well. It will be easier for children to understand these lessons for words like *Mom*, *soccer*, or *The Mets*. Your students' names are already prominently displayed, and you will want to treat those as snap words of a sort as well (although it is not critical that kids spell all their names correctly). If your students pass a McDonald's every day on the way to school, have the McDonald's sign included in your snap word collection.

At the launch of this bend, you will also introduce students to a new batch of high-frequency words, and these new words will be more abstract and therefore harder for kids to learn than words like *Mom, look,* or *me*. Specifically, you will teach them *it, in,* and *an*. These teeny-tiny words are not only important because they are used frequently in the books your children will soon read, but also because they are common phonograms that can be used to make other words. Once you have taught these words to your children, be sure that they spell them accurately during the writing workshop.

As you wind down the bend, you'll pass the baton to your students to take charge of their own learning and teach everything they know about snap words to others. Your kindergartens will be eager to compose a class letter to their stuffed animals, through an interactive writing session, inviting them to "Word School." They will then make lesson plans for what and how they will teach their stuffed animals about their collection of snap words by reviewing the repertoire of games, songs, and poems they learned throughout this bend. Even though you may feel a little nervous letting them do such grown-up work, remember that the highest level of learning anything is being able to teach others what you know. It's a good time to informally observe and make small-group plans for those students who may not be learning high-frequency words as quickly as the others.

All the best,
Lucy, Rebecca, and Allyse

SESSION 14

Keep Your Word Collection Close, So You Can Grow, Study, and Use It

IN THIS SESSION

TODAY YOU'LL teach students that readers and writers continue to grow their snap word collections.

TODAY YOUR STUDENTS will learn three new snap words as they perform a five-step process for turning any word into a snap word. Students will receive their own snap word collection to study and use in their reading and writing.

MINILESSON

CONNECTION

Rally kids' enthusiasm for the work of this bend—and for their future work as readers and writers.

"Writers, readers, gather close because today is a big day. Today is the start of the very last part of our unit. In four days, we're going to have a great big celebration for the ending of this unit.

"I think we should spend these last few days making sure you have the tools that you need to write and to read as best you can."

Draw parallels between the collection boxes that scientists keep and the word collections your kids will keep. Help kids get invested in the idea of constantly adding to their collections.

"Earlier, I showed you the collection boxes that some scientists have: some keep moths and butterflies in those boxes, all carefully labeled; some keep rocks, again with labels for each rock. But the point is, those people don't just *keep* moths or rocks in special collections. The point is, they are always *adding to* those collections.

GETTING READY

✔ Display the word cards for *the, at, I, me,* and *a.*

✔ Prepare one set of word cards for *an, in,* and *it* for each student.

✔ Display the "How to Learn a Word" anchor chart.

✔ Distribute a whiteboard and marker to each student.

✔ Write two sentences from Mabel to display: "Mabel is an elephant." and "Look in my bag."

✔ Prepare snap word pouches with previously taught high-frequency words for each student. Ideally, pouches are fancy— a cloth pouch—although Ziplock bags are an option.

PHONICS INSTRUCTION

Concepts About Print
- Recognize that spoken words are represented in written language by specific sequences of letters.

High-Frequency Words
- Recognize and use high-frequency words.
- Develop strategies for learning high-frequency words.
- Learn new words (*it, in, an*).

"Scientists walk in the woods, hum-de-hum, having a nice day, maybe with their dog or their sister, and all of a sudden, they are on their hands and knees peering at the soil or at a leaf. The people with them think, 'Have you gone nuts? Get up!' but the scientists will say, 'Wait, wait, I just saw a really cool rock that I need to collect.' Pretty soon, those scientists will have filled their pockets with so much stuff that their pants will practically be falling down!

"I'm telling you this because *word* scientists are no different. You walk through life, hum-de-hum, reading and writing and having a dandy time, and then all of a sudden you are stopped short, saying 'Hold it, hold it, I've just seen something I've got to collect!'

"And if you are a word scientist, the things you collect are . . . yes, you guessed it: words! Over the next few days, I'm going to help you collect quite a few new snap words—more than most teachers say kids your age can possibly learn. But I think you are special, and I can't resist showing you these cool words."

✦ **Name the teaching point.**

"Today I want to remind you that as important as the alphabet chart is, it is not the only tool that you rely on to read and to write. No way! You also need snap words. People who read and write a lot are always adding to their collection of snap words."

TEACHING

Stir up excitement about studying the class's collection of teeny-tiny words. Review the snap words students already know by working with a partner to spell them.

"I was thinking that many of you like teeny-tiny trucks and teeny-tiny horses and teeny-tiny houses. So, I was thinking, you might like a few teeny-tiny words. Would you?

"Actually, you have a few teeny-tiny words already." I gestured to the collection of the teeny-tiny words they already "owned": *the*, *at*, *I*, *me*, *a*.

"To get yourself ready for a few more teeny-tiny words, read these to your partner and spell them. If you are brave enough, try closing your eyes and spelling them, just for fun. Help each other."

Distribute three new words—words that actually double as phonograms, which will be studied in the upcoming unit, but don't tell that to the kids. Create a drumroll around this.

After the kids did that, I said, "If you hold out your hands, I'll give you more teeny-tiny words. Don't look at them until everyone has their words."

I distributed these words to all the kids: *an*, *in*, *it*. "Okay, look! Don't you love them?!"

We have chosen these three words because they are also phonograms. In the upcoming unit Word-Part Power, *students will learn to put consonants in front of these words to make new words, so these will become super important and beloved. Don't stint on your affection for these little words!*

Lead students in studying these new words, following the familiar protocol: read the word in context, study its features, spell it, write it (without looking, if possible), check it, then use it.

"You will need to study these one by one, so they are really truly yours. Let's start with the word *it*. Oh my gosh, oh my golly, I love it, love *it*. Did you hear that? I used *it* in a sentence. You try it: 'I love it, love it, love it!' Now let's follow our 'How to Learn a Word' chart to really learn this word." I pointed to the second bullet.

I wrote "I love it!" on the whiteboard. "Let's read our new word in this sentence together: I love *it*! Now let's study *it*. With your partner, take out your imaginary magnifying glass and study this teeny-tiny, lovely word like it is a prized butterfly. What do you see?" Turn and talk.

I quickly summarized what I heard students say. "You're right, two small letters, a vowel, and the consonant *T*—your letter, Tymel!"

We continued moving through the steps, spelling and then writing the word several times on whiteboards.

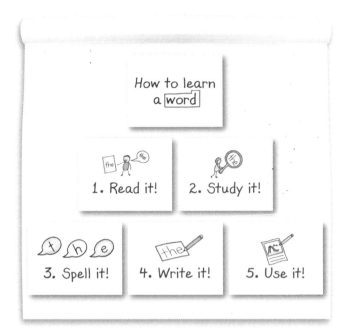

ACTIVE ENGAGEMENT/LINK

Invite partners to repeat this process with the snap word *an*. Coach students as they follow the steps on the anchor chart to learn the word so that they can write it.

"We learned the word *it*, but we have two more little words to learn: *an* and *in*. How about if I help you with one of them, and then I become invisible and watch you study the third word, just you and your partner without me? Is that okay?

"So, we need to learn *an*. Let's look at our chart again to remember how to learn a word." We reread and remembered that first we needed to read the word in a sentence. "Hmm, . . . a sentence." Then I caught sight of Mabel, holding two things in her trunk. I looked at the items and said, "Oh, great! Mabel seems to have two sentences for us! One for *an* and one for *in*."

I displayed the sentence containing *an*: "Mabel is an elephant."

"Can you all read it?" The kids read the sentence. Then I said, "Now you need to study *an*." I enlarged the word. "Pretend you have your magnifying glasses. Tell your partner what you see. I'll whisper some hints about the kinds of things you could see."

I whispered, tucking in my comments about what kids should look for as they talked: How many letters? Vowels? Consonants? Tall or small? Holes, bumps, tails? Like other words? Not like other words?

Then I said, "Show me you can spell it aloud, and then remember to take mental pictures of the word, so that you can write it without looking." After kids wrote the word on their whiteboard, I coached them to check it, fix it by rewriting if need be, and to repeat.

RUG TIME

Rally students to repeat this process once more with the word *in*, this time with even greater independence.

"Okay, now you need to do the steps for the third teeny-tiny word independently. Mabel has the sentence, and we can read it together—then you are on your own!" I read the sentence with the kids: "'Look in my bag.'

"Huh? That seems like a secret message to us. We're going to need to look in her bag, but first will you go through the steps on the 'How to Learn a Word' chart to learn this word, *in*? Study, spell, and write the word *in* on your whiteboards a bunch of times."

SHARE • The Gift of a Special Snap Word Pouch

Create excitement around the start of a new bend by distributing to each student a special bag—a snap word pouch—in which they can keep all their high-frequency words.

Once the kids had done some work with it, I called for their attention. "You ready to do what Mabel's sentence told us to do? Who can read it?" A child came forward and led the class in reading "Look *in* my bag."

I opened Mabel's bag, and, as if mystified, pulled out what everyone soon realized were snap word pouches—one for each child.

"Oh my goodness, oh my goodness! So now, we'll be able to keep our collection of snap words right near us. Remember how my dad had to look under the sofa for the pot holder, because his tools weren't near him when he was cooking? With these special snap word pouches, you won't have to look under the sofa for the spelling of your snap words." I handed out the pouches and asked students to put their new teeny-tiny words (*it*, *an*, *in*) into their bags with the rest of their snap word collections.

"Let's end today by each of you reading your collection of words to someone near you. Go!" As the kids got started, I recruited a few to read their collection of snap words to Mabel.

FIG. 14–1   Try to give your kids a fancy pouch!

We suggest storing the pouches in a bin close to the easel for ease of distribution each day.

EXTENSION 1 • "Guess My Rule"

 GETTING READY

- Distribute a snap word pouch to each partnership.

Rally students to play a game of "Guess My Rule," in which they take turns grouping words according to similarities and guessing each other's grouping rules.

"Let's play a game called 'Guess My Rule.' Here's how you play. You make a group of words by thinking about what's the same about all the words in the group. (That is the rule.) And then others try to guess your rule. Let's have one try together."

I took the words *the* and *see* out of the pocket chart and placed them on the easel. "Look really close. How are they the same? Don't shout out! Keep the rule in your head so everyone can think. When you are ready to guess my rule, put a thumb on your knee."

After a few moments I said, "Okay, turn and tell your partner what my rule is. How are they the same?" I heard them say, "They both have three letters."

"Yes!" I said. "They both have three letters. Let's try another one." I took out the words *a* and *an*. Kids immediately started talking with their partners about how both words started with the letter *A*.

"You've got it!" I said. "Ready to play with your rug club? I will hand out a snap word pouch to each partnership. Spread out the words. You can take turns putting the words in groups, and your partner can guess your rule."

There are a number of ways you can prompt students to sort the words for the "Guess My Rule" game:

- *number of letters*
- *beginning sounds letter*
- *ending sounds letter*
- *same letter in each word* (is, this, like)

EXTENSION 2 • Read Snap Words in Different Voices

 Invite students to read the snap word collection in different voices.

"Word scientists, each of you has your own collection of words, but we can't forget that snap words live right here in our snap word pocket chart.

"Let's have some fun reading our snap words. Let's use different voices to read the words. Like watch this: I could read the words in my squeaky mouse voice." I demonstrated, and the students giggled. "Or how about my big giant voice, or even my scary monster voice? There are so many ways! Think of a fun voice to try with your partner."

I quickly coached each partnership to pick a way to read their snap word collection and then return to their reading.

EXTENSION 3 • Play a Game Of "I Spy" with Snap Words

Invite students to play a game of "I Spy" with snap words, in which one player gives a clue that prompts others to guess which word it is.

"Kindergartners, I have another snap word game! Let's play 'I Spy.' It will help us to find words in our collection quickly. It's important we use the snap word pocket chart to find words quickly, so we don't waste a second when we are reading and writing!

"Let me tell you how to play. One partner studies the snap word collection and chooses a word—but doesn't tell the others which one it is. Then they say, 'I spy with my little eye a word that . . . ' and gives clues to help others guess. People often say, 'It starts with the letter . . . ' or 'It has two letters . . . '

"Let's play it once together," I said. "Bryce, will you come on up here and go first? This time, tell me your word so I can help."

Bryce chose the word *see*, and his first clue was, "It's a word with only small letters." One child guessed that it was *in*. I said, "*In* has two letters, but that is not his word. Bryce, give them another clue." Bryce's next and final clue was "The word has three letters." That clue led kids to guess the word *see*.

I then prompted students to use the class snap word collection to continue the game. The game continued for several rounds, with me giving voice-over coaching to remind kids that a helpful clue was, "This word has . . . " or "It starts with . . . "

Recognize Snap Words When the Font Is Different

IN THIS SESSION

TODAY YOU'LL teach students that they can read snap words no matter what—even when they look a bit different.

TODAY YOUR STUDENTS will study and sort the snap words into piles. Students will notice how capital and lowercase letters, size, and different font do not change how they read the snap word.

MINILESSON

CONNECTION

Help kids invest in the idea that a word is a word, no matter how it appears. Tell a story about how changing your shoes doesn't change who you are.

As children settled in their rug spots, I bent over and peered down at my shoes. "Some days, I like to wear my sneakers, and other days I like to wear my sandals. For fancy parties, I like to wear my sparkliest party shoes. But if it's raining outside, I almost always put on . . . " I trailed off, inviting the students to chime in.

"Rain boots!" the class filled in.

"Yup! You guessed it—my rubber rain boots! You see, no matter what shoes I have on, I'm still *me*! I'm me with sparkly party shoes and I'm still me outside with rubber rain boots. Words are like that, too. They are the same, no matter how they're dressed and no matter where they are."

❖ Name the teaching point.

"Today I want to teach you that your snap words—the words you know by heart—sometimes get changed around a little bit, and they can be tricky to recognize. Word scientists always know that word is still a word, even if it looks a little different."

GETTING READY

✔ Gather three emergent storybooks with the same high-frequency words in the title. Two should be capitalized and the third should not. We chose *The Three Billy Goats*, *The Gingerbread Boy*, and *Harry the Dirty Dog*.

✔ Prepare a few snap word cards in different fonts. Place one of these different cards over each snap word in the snap word pocket chart, and distribute the additional word cards (with other fonts and some capitalized) around the room.

✔ Prepare a list of all the snap words on the chart for each partnership.

PHONICS INSTRUCTION

Concepts About Print
• Recognize that spoken words are represented in written language by specific sequences of letters.

Phonological Awareness
• Say words slowly to identify salient sounds in words.

Letter Knowledge
• Recognize and name all upper- and lowercase letters of the alphabet.

High-Frequency Words
• Recognize and use high-frequency words.
• Write high-frequency words in continuous text.

TEACHING

Tell the story of a student who discovered that the same snap words can look quite different when they are capitalized or written in a different font.

"I was reading with Makayla yesterday, and she did some great word scientist work that I just have to share with you. She was looking closely at one of her storybooks and she made a *huge* discovery."

I placed *Harry the Dirty Dog* and *The Gingerbread Boy*, two familiar emergent storybooks, on the easel. "Look closely and see if you can also find what Makayla discovered." I paused for just a moment. Then, I said, "Zoom in on the words in the title. Makayla found something that was the same. When you see it, put a thumb on your knee." I paused as the students scanned the covers.

I pointed under *the* in the title of the first book and then the second book. "The, *t-h-e*, the. It is still the, even if it starts with a capital letter."

I placed *The Three Billy Goats Gruff* next to the other books on the easel. I pointed under *The*. "The, *t-h-e*, the. Word scientists know that a word is still a word, even if it looks a little different."

ACTIVE ENGAGEMENT/LINK

Reveal the snap word pocket chart that contains snap words in different fonts and cases. Lead the class in reading the snap words that look a little different.

I revealed the snap word pocket chart with snap word cards in different fonts and cases. "Look at our snap word collection! It got changed around a little bit. The words might be a little tricky to recognize—but you know these words by heart. Word scientists, let's read our snap word collection together."

I placed my pointer on the first word. "Word scientists, look closely at each word. Remember, a word is still a word, even if it looks a little different." The children followed my pointer and read each word. I pretended to be confused when we reached each word that was capitalized.

When we finished I said, "Wow, you really *do* know these words by heart!"

Send partners on a snap word scavenger hunt. Remind them that if they know a word by heart, they can read it, no matter where it is and what it looks like.

"A word is a word, no matter where it is or what it looks like. *T-h-e* is always *the*, and *l-o-o-k* is always . . . " I trailed off, inviting the children to chime in: "*look*!"

"You know, I had a *big* idea this morning—I could send you on a snap word scavenger hunt! A scavenger hunt is a game where you have to go around and find a list of funny things. Earlier, I placed a bunch of snap words that look a little funny all over the room. You and your partner can go around and point and read them. Work together to try to find every word from our snap word chart—the snap words are your list!"

I gave each partnership a snap word checklist and a pencil and sent them off, a few at a time, to read the words around the room, checking them off on their lists as they did.

I moved from one partnership to the next, listening in as students read each snap word. I coached in, prompting students to try reading the words together. "Can you each read the word together like we do in shared reading? You could take turns, too—you read to her, then you read to him. Does it look like a word you know?"

After a few minutes, I called partners back to the meeting area.

SHARE • Recognizing Snap Words, No Matter How They Appear

Restate the big teaching point of the day and read the snap word collection.

"Nice work, word scientists. When you look closely, you don't get tricked! Remember, you need to look closely at words. You can ask yourself, 'Does this look like a word I know?' It might be a snap word that looks a little different.

"It was really fun to find and read snap words all over the room, but the really important place you need to find and read them is in books! Will you and your partner work together to find snap words in a book? If you look closely, you can spot snap words that look a little different." I passed an emergent storybook to each partnership and coached as they searched for snap words.

EXTENSION 1 • When Do Writers Use Capitals?

Explain that capitals are used for proper nouns and at the beginning of sentences. Channel students to consider whether to use uppercase or lowercase letters in their writing.

"Word scientists," I said, "you've been working to hear and record more sounds. Let's make sure we are also thinking about which kind of letter is the right one to use in different places. You know there are two kinds of letters, right? Uppercase, or capital letters, and lowercase letters. Most of the time when we write, we use the lowercase letters. We save the capitals for special times—like the very first letter of your name or the start of a new sentence.

"This is hard work, so let's practice it. I'm going to say something, and I'd like you think about whether it's just a normal time, and we can use lowercase letters, or whether it's a special time, like the very first letter of your name or the start of a new sentence, and you need to use capital letters.

"Here's the first one. What if you wanted to write *Mabel*? /M/-Mabel. *M* makes the /m/ sound. Think about what kind of letter you need at the beginning of a name. Now write Mabel's name." Most kids wrote *Mabel* with a capital *M*. "You're right. You need a capital letter for a special time like the beginning of a name."

I gave students a few more examples to practice with: the word *marker*, their own name, and the sentence *I like you*.

"Writers, you're really thinking about whether you should use a lowercase letter, like writers do most of the time, or whether it's a special time and you need a capital letter."

EXTENSION 2 • Labeling Choice Time Centers

GETTING READY

- Have Post-its, strips of paper, and pencils available for students to label their favorite things.

Recruit students to label objects in their favorite play areas or choice time centers.

"I was looking around the classroom and noticed that we have always labeled the same old things, like the table, chair, and books, and I was thinking we should label the things you all really love! Let's label our choice time centers. Wouldn't it be neat if we could go into our favorite play center and label everything we love to play with?" The students looked back with wide eyes, already thinking about where they loved to play.

"I love the kitchen center." I grabbed the basket of food and picked out my favorite dinner to make. I picked out rice, vegetables, and the hot dog and placed them on a plate. I said, "There! Now that I have the dinner I always like to make, I can grab my pencil and some paper and start writing all the words.

"I could just write a one-word label for all the food on the plate—like *food*. But I know so much more about words, I can push myself to write a two-word label, or maybe even an entire sentence! I think on the top of my menu, I will write, 'This is my restaurant.'

"Let's all write that sentence quickly. I will write it up here on the paper, and you can write it with your imaginary pencils on the rug. 'This is my . . .' Ready? Write those snap words super-fast, and I will write them here on the menu!" When we got to the word *restaurant*, we listened for all the sounds we heard in the word and recorded '*rstrnt*.'

"Do you see how we can have so much fun writing while we are playing, too? Like if you are in blocks, you can write, 'This is my block tower,' or in art, 'Here is my masterpiece!' I think you get the idea. Who's ready to label their play area? I have Post-its and strips of paper you can choose. Just get playing and labeling your favorite things!"

FIG. 15–1   Stella is excited to show off her choice time label.

Interactive Writing
An Invitation to Word School

GETTING READY

✔ Prepare for interactive writing by setting up a document camera or chart paper on an easel.

✔ Make sure students bring their writing folders to the meeting area.

✔ Provide Post-its for students to mark their best work.

PHONICS INSTRUCTION

Concepts About Print
- Recognize that spoken words are represented in written language by specific sequences of letters.
- Understand that words are written left to right across the page.
- Make return sweep at the end of a line of text.
- Understand that words are separated by spaces in print, concept of word.
- Match spoken word to print.

High-Frequency Words
- Recognize and use high-frequency words.
- Read high-frequency words in continuous text.
- Write high-frequency words in continuous text.

IN THIS SESSION

TODAY YOU'LL teach students that they can use snap words for real-life purposes, like writing a letter to a friend.

TODAY YOUR STUDENTS will help compose a class letter inviting their stuffed animals to attend "Word School," through an interactive writing exercise. Students will reflect on their writing and select a final writing piece to share with their stuffed animal in two days' time at "Word School."

MINILESSON

CONNECTION

Propose that the students write a letter inviting their stuffed animals back to school to attend "Word School."

"You've learned so much about words, let's invite your friends back to Word School. They can be the students, and *you* can all be the teachers! Doesn't that sound fun?"

I put a hand over my head. "Oh no! There's a problem. How will all those fluffy friends know to come to our Word School? We need to write them an invitation and send it right away. Do you think you could help me write it? After all, you know *so* much about letters and words! You will? Wonderful!"

✿ **Name the teaching point.**

"Today I want to teach you that writers don't just learn letters and words, they *use* them to communicate. You can use snap words you know to write messages in a snap!"

TEACHING

Compose an invitation, using interactive writing to practice snap words.

"Let's not waste a minute. We'll need our word collection to write words we know in a snap." I pulled over the pocket chart of snap words. Then, I put a piece of paper under the document camera and uncapped a black marker. "Should we say, 'Can you come to school this Friday?' Oh, I hear a snap word from our collection in that sentence. Did you hear it? Listen again, 'Can you come to school *this* Friday?'"

"This! This!" voices piped up.

"Yes! Can you find the word *this* in our word collection?" I turned to the snap word pocket chart as kids pointed toward the *this* card. I tapped on the word. "*This*! *T-H-I-S*. I'll need a volunteer to help me write that word." I wrote the start of the sentence and called up a child to fill in the snap word, *this*. "Everyone else, spell that word with a finger on the rug. Write it in a snap!" I watched as kids traced the letters. "Now let's check. Does it look right? *T-H-I-S*! Yes, it looks right! Well done." Then, I quickly filled in the next word and we reread the sentence together.

Can you come to school **this** Friday?

"Let's tell them how much fun it will be. We can write, 'It is going to be fun!' Say it with me . . . " We echoed the sentence, and I recruited the class to listen for the snap words *it* and *is*. "Now let's find those words on the snap word pocket chart. Then, we can write them in a snap." I tapped the words on the pocket chart, and we spelled them out loud.

I called up a child to start the sentence, coaching him to start with a capital and space his words, while the rest of the class traced the words on the rug. Then, I filled in the rest of the sentence before I invited the class to reread with me.

Can you come to school **this** Friday?

It is going to be fun!

"Oh! We can tell our stuffed animals that we will show them the words in our pouches! Let's add, 'You can look in my word pouch.' Listen for the snap words and then you can help me write them in a snap!" I repeated the sentence, emphasizing the words, "You can *look in my* word pouch." "Quick, turn and tell your partner what words you heard that you know in a snap!" I gave partners a moment to share.

"I heard lots of you say that we'll need the words *look* and *in* and *my* to write this sentence." I invited a few children to come up and fill in the snap words as I wrote the sentence.

FIG. 16–1   Share the pen with students at the snap words.

You'll want to keep this interactive writing lesson moving at a quick pace. There are several opportunities for kids to practice using snap words from their collection to write. However, if you notice that you are running short on time, you may decide to fill in the rest, rather than asking for more volunteers.

We went on to record a final sentence, pausing at the words *here* and *at* to practice another pair of snap words.

Can you come to school **this** Friday?

It is going to be fun!

You can **look in my** word pouch.

Be **here at** 9!

ACTIVE ENGAGEMENT/LINK

Reread the invitation that the class composed together. Invite students to signal each time they read a snap word.

"Let's read our invitation together to make sure it makes sense and sounds right. And let's look and listen for snap words. As we read, whenever you see or hear a snap word we've learned, give a thumbs up! Ready?" I led the class as we reread the whole text together, pointing out the snap words as we read each line.

"Thank you for your help, writers! You used words you know how to write in a snap! That's the same work you can do any time you write, especially during writing workshop! I'll make a copy of our invitation. Then, you can send it home so your stuffed animals won't miss the big day!"

RUG TIME

Encourage students to reread their writing and select their best writing piece to share at Word School.

"You know, I just had a *big* idea! When your friends come for Word School on Friday, you could show off all the snap words in your own writing! I bet you could look in your folders and find a piece that really shows your best work. Then, you can read that piece to your special visitor. Quick! Find just one book in your folders that you can read to your stuffed animal."

I gave students a moment to look through their folders and pull out one piece of writing. I voiced over, "Choose your very best writing—the piece that shows off lots and lots of snap words! Then put that piece on top of your folder and close your folders up."

"Writers, eyes up in one . . . two . . . three!" I got students' attention. "Wow! Everyone chose a book from their folders to share at Word School. Right now, let's get ready to share those pieces on Friday. Work with your partner, and take turns reading and checking your words. You can use the words in our collection to fix up snap words in your writing that don't look right." I pointed to the pocket chart. "Get started, partners—oh, I mean, word professors!"

I moved from one partnership to the next, listening in as students worked to reread their pieces to one another. I coached in, prompting students to check snap words. "Oh! I spy a snap word on that page. You used the word *here*! Check it on the pocket chart. Does it look right?" After a few minutes, I called partners back together.

SHARE • Reviewing Snap Words in Preparation for Word School

Ask students to point out snap words they used in their writing. Then, ask students to flag their selected pieces with a Post-it, so they are ready to share them during the celebration.

"Will you hold your books way up high, so we can all see your impressive work?" The children held up their writing. "Thumbs up if you used lots of snap words in your writing! Really, you did? Prove it! Quick, find and point to a snap word in your book!" Kids leafed through their pages, pointing at words in their writing. "Oh, wow! Is that the *only* place you wrote a snap word? No? There's more? Quick, find another word! Whoa! Can you spot another? Find it!"

I fell back in my chair, as if stunned. "Wow! Absolutely phenomenal work, word scientists. I can't wait for you to share your books with our visitors at Word School! Will you stick a Post-it on top of your book, so you remember that this is the piece you'll read to your stuffed animal on Friday? Then, put it back in your folder."

EXTENSION 1 • Playing with Patterns

Rally students to compose a variety of sentences with snap words and picture card words.

I held up a snap word pouch and a stack of picture cards. "Writers, these fifteen snap words can help you write more and more. I bet you can put them together in lots of different combinations to write about these picture cards now." I placed a picture of a slide on the easel. "I could put these words together . . . " I placed the *look*, *at*, and *the* word cards in front of the picture on the easel as I read, "Look at the slide. Or . . . " I placed another group of word cards in front of the picture and read, "This is a slide."

"Take out your snap word pouches, and I'll give you some picture cards. Work together with your partner and make as many different sentences with snap words and pictures as you can."

Possible patterns students might make include:

I like . . .
Look at the . . .
I see the/an/a . . .
This is the/an/a . . .
Is this the/an/a . . . ?
Here is the/an/a . . .
It is the/an/a . . .
Is it the/an/a . . . ?
It is in the . . .
Is it in the . . . ?
I see a ___ in the . . .

EXTENSION 2 • Sing New Snap Words

 Sing spellings of snap words to familiar tunes.

"Let's sing our new words to help us remember them. We can sing a song to the tune of 'Twinkle, Twinkle, Little Star.' Listen and join me when you are ready."

I-n, i-n, i-n, in.
I-n, i-n, in, in, in.
I-n, i-n, i-n, in
I-n, i-n, in, in, in.
I-n, i-n, i-n, in
I-n, i-n, in, in, in.

"Let's sing one of the words we learned when we first became word scientists: *see.* We can sing it to the tune of 'Jingle Bells.'" I hummed a few bars before I started to sing. "Join me when you can."

S-e-e, s-e-e
S-e-e spells *see*
s-e-e (pause), *s-e-e*
(pause) *s-e-e* spells *see*

EXTENSION 3 • Reviewing Snap Words with Movement

 Teach students to review snap words by acting out sports moves while saying and spelling the words.

"Let's have some fun reviewing our word collection, so we really know these words in a snap. Let's get some exercise as we review our snap words. Everyone, spread out a bit so you have room to move.

"We can start with baseball. When I point to a word, first, say the word. Then, pretend to hit a baseball as you spell the word." I pantomimed swinging a baseball bat. Then, say the word again, and . . . hit the ball!" I pretended to take a big swing. "Ready?"

I held up the word *it*. I gestured for the class to join me as I said, "It." Then I said, "Swing your baseball bat as you spell, *i-t*!" I did this along with the kids. "Now, say the word again, and swing: *it*!"

I continued leading the class in reviewing words in these ways, varying the sport each time. We kicked a soccer ball, swung a tennis racket, and so on.

Making Lesson Plans
What Will We Teach Our Stuffed Animals about Snap Words?

✔ Select a word from the snap word pocket chart to teach to Mabel.

✔ Display the "How to Learn a Word" anchor chart. 🖐

✔ Make sure partners have their snap word pouches.

✔ Display the "Ways to Teach Snap Words" chart. 🖐

✔ Invite students to bring a stuffed animal to school tomorrow for the Word School celebration.

PHONICS INSTRUCTION

Concepts About Print

• Recognize that spoken words are represented in written language by specific sequences of letters.

• Understand that words are written left to right across the page.

• Understand that words are separated by spaces in print, concept of word.

• Match spoken word to print.

High-Frequency Words

• Recognize and use high-frequency words.

• Locate and read high-frequency words in a text.

• Develop and use strategies for learning high-frequency words.

• Learn a new word (*and*).

IN THIS SESSION

TODAY YOU'LL teach students that when you know something really well, you can pass that knowledge along by teaching it to others.

TODAY YOUR STUDENTS will make plans for teaching others the snap words they have learned. Students will review favorite snap word games and songs, so they are prepared to teach the snap words they know in the next session.

MINILESSON

CONNECTION

Invite kids to review the list of snap words by reading them in different voices.

"Our word collection keeps growing—look at all the words you know in a snap! Let's read all of these words to keep them strong in our brains. First, let's read them in a soft, whisper voice." I dropped my voice to a hush. "Ready? Here we go . . . " I led the class in a choral reading of the word list in a whisper.

"Now let's read it like big, hungry dinosaurs. Ready?" We reread the list in loud, ferocious voices.

"Scary! Word School begins tomorrow, so I think we'd better practice acting and sounding like word professors." I sat up tall in my chair, adjusting my posture, and folded my hands in my lap. "Let's read our words one more time, using our most proper professor voices. Shall we? Let's begin . . . ahem . . . " I led the class in one final reading of the snap word list.

"You have practically turned these words into best friends! You know them *so* well!"

♣ **Name the teaching point.**

"Today, I want to teach you that when you know something really well, you can pass that knowledge along by teaching it to others."

TEACHING

Suggest that students use the familiar routine for learning words to teach words to others. Then, demonstrate with the class mascot.

"You've not only learned new words, you've also learned *how* to learn a word. We have a word routine to help us." I clipped the chart to the easel. "You can use these same steps to teach a word to a friend. When we teach a word," I touched each step on the chart, "we can read it, study it together, and point to the letters to spell it. Then, we can help our friend write it and use it in a sentence."

"Let's invite Mabel to Word School." I reached over and propped up the elephant beside me. "Welcome, Mabel. We know it's a day early, but we're all playing teacher to get ready for tomorrow!" I turned back to the class.

I pulled a word from the pocket chart. "Mabel, this is the word *look*. Can you study it with me? What do you notice?" I leaned in as if listening to a response. "Mmm-hmm, . . . uh-huh, . . . Yes, it does have four letters! And yes, there are two *o*'s in the middle. Let's spell it!" I pointed to each letter. "*L-o-o-k—look*! Now let me show you how to write it." I took Mabel's trunk and traced the letters on the card to form the word. I voiced over the letter formation pathway as I traced. Finally, I used it in a sentence. "I like to *look* for seashells at the beach! Now you know this word, Mabel! Look!"

> ### POSSIBLE COACHING MOVES
>
> ▶ "Remember the steps. Use the chart to follow the routine."
>
> ▶ "Study the word! Ask your partner to say what he or she notices about the word."
>
> ▶ "Spell it together. Then, write it on the rug with your finger."

ACTIVE ENGAGEMENT/LINK

Set partners up to play teacher, using the word routine to teach snap words to each other.

"Now it's your turn to play teacher. Pull out a word from your snap word pouch and teach it to your partner. Use all the steps for learning a word to teach it. Then, switch!" I prompted partners to decide who would play teacher first and

signaled for students to begin. I moved quickly around the meeting area, observing children at work and coaching in as needed.

RUG TIME

Display and review a menu of ways students can teach their stuffed animals snap words.

"Okay, professors, it's time to plan your lessons for Word School tomorrow. Your students will be here, and they'll be so excited to learn all about snap words. Remember all the ways we have for learning new words!" I pointed to the "Ways to Teach Snap Words" chart that offered a menu of word activities. "Make a lesson plan! What words will you teach? What games will you play? What songs will you sing?"

Invite partnerships to review their snap word collections. Discuss their plans for how they will teach their stuffed animals at Word School.

"Take out all of your words and read them with your partner. Then decide what you'll teach your stuffed animal." I prompted partners to begin reviewing their word collections. Then, I moved from one pair to the next, coaching students to plan and practice.

SHARE • Sharing Lesson Plans for Word School

Review ways that students plan to teach their stuffed animals snap words during Word School.

I called the group back together. "Excuse me, word scientists, give me a thumbs up if your lessons are planned for tomorrow. Are you ready to teach your students everything you can about snap words?" The kids nodded enthusiastically.

I turned back toward the chart. "Let's count up all the ways we'll teach our furry friends. Put a finger up if you plan to teach your class how to spell a snap word!" Kids held up fingers. "Put another finger up if you think you'll play a game, like 'I Spy' or 'Guess My Rule.'" I held up two fingers. "Put another finger up if you'll show off the snap words in your writing. Will any of you sing your students a song?" I held four fingers up in the air. "Wow! You have *so* many ways to learn and teach new words! I can't wait for Word School!

"Don't forget to bring your stuffed animal to Word School tomorrow!"

POSSIBLE COACHING MOVES

▶ "What game might you play with your furry friend tomorrow? Play a round with your partner to practice!"

▶ "Is there a song you can sing to teach your student some snap words? Sing it together to rehearse!"

▶ "Play with patterns. Use your word cards to make some sentences that follow a pattern."

▶ "Reread the piece of writing you chose in the previous session and show your partner the snap words you used."

EXTENSION 1 • Making New Words with Initial Sounds and Phonogram Snap Words

Demonstrate how to make new words by adding initial sounds to phonogram snap words.

"Kindergartners, I have some exciting news to share about our snap word collection." As soon as the students were seated, I explained my new finding. "When I was telling everyone to *sit* on the rug I realized something special about that word *sit*. Listen carefully when I say /s/it, *sit*. Do you hear a teeny-tiny word we know? Yes, the word *it* is hiding inside the word *sit*. So that made me wonder, could some of our teeny-tiny words help us make other words? Want to give it a try?

"Let's try with the word *an*. Listen to me say the word—give me a thumbs up if I make a new word, and thumb sideways if I make a silly made-up word."

I wondered aloud, "What first sound can I say in front of *an* to make a new word? Oh, I know, what about /p/-an, *pan*?" The class gave me a thumbs up, signaling it was a new word. "Now listen to this one: s/-an, *san*." I scanned the room to see most thumbs sideways. "You're right—*san* isn't a real word. You're getting the hang of this! Let's keep going. I wonder what other words we can make?"

I continued to generate real and made-up words with the snap words *an*, *it*, and *in*.

This extension focuses on listening to word parts. This activity will help prepare students for the word work that will begin in the third kindergarten Phonics unit, Word-Part Power.

EXTENSION 2 • Playing with Snap Words Like We Play with Names

Sing the "The Name Game" song with phonogram snap words and identify the real words that get generated.

"Remember when we were studying names and we sang this song together? 'Mabel, Mabel, bo Babel, banana fana fo Fabel, fee fie mo Mabel . . . Mabel!'

"That song is so fun! And it really gets me thinking about more fun things we can do with our snap words. Do you think we can sing it with our snap words like we did with our names?" The class agreed. "Let's try singing 'The Name Game' song with *in*. Join me when you can. 'In, in, bo bin, banana fana fo fin, fee fie mo min . . . in!'

"Now try it with *at*. 'At, at, bo bat, banana fana fo fat, fee fie mo mat . . . at!' This is so fun! Did you hear the real words that we made, like *bat* and *fat* and *mat*?

"Let's try singing with more snap words and see if we can make new words." We continued with other snap words that are also common phonograms: *it*, *an*.

EXTENSION 3 • Adding a New Snap Word to Our Collection (*And*)

 GETTING READY

- Write the sentence "I like to read and write" on the board or chart paper.
- Display the "How to Learn a Word" chart and the poem "I'm a Little Teapot."

"Word scientists, we've been having so much fun with our word collection, I think it's time to add to it! I've got a new word to teach you." I revealed the word *and* in the sentence "I like to read and write."

"Let's use the steps we know to help us learn this word." I gestured toward the "How to Learn a Word" chart.

"This word is *and*." I pointed to the word in the sentence. "I like to read *and* write. First, let's read the word: *and*." I wrote the word on the whiteboard. "Now study it. Tell your partner what you notice. How many letters does it have? What does it start and end with? What sounds do you hear in the word?

"Ready to spell the word *and*? Get out your imaginary pen, and take the cap off. Write *and* on the rug. Spell *and* out loud as you write the letters. Now, write it again—this time, try to write it faster and without looking. Check each letter to make sure it's right.

"Let's use the word *and* in a sentence. Tell your partner as many sentences as you can that use the word *and*."

"Let's hunt for it in our poem." I displayed the poem "I'm a Little Teapot" on the easel. After we located the word, we read the poem and had the students make a silent cheer when they saw the word.

"Let's add *and* to our snap word collection." I placed the card in the pocket chart and said, "Our snap word collection is getting really full! Let's read them all so we are sure to have them in our back pocket!"

Word School

IN THIS SESSION

TODAY YOU'LL teach students that once you learn a lot about something—like snap words—you can pass it on, you can teach others *everything* you know.

TODAY YOUR STUDENTS will teach their stuffed animals all the snap words they know, then send their animals off to sleep with a lullaby filled with snap words.

MINILESSON

CONNECTION

Celebrate becoming word scientists, ready to teach others what they have discovered through studying words.

"Today is a very important day! Today is the last day of our unit, and to celebrate, we've invited some special friends back to school, so we can share everything we know *now*! First, they came to learn about letters, and now we can teach them about *words*!

"So, if you brought a little friend with you, will you sit that furry friend beside you on the rug? Share your friend with kids who didn't bring one and sit your stuffed animal in between you and a partner.

"Let's welcome our friends to Word School with a little song we've learned." I displayed the lyrics to "I'm a Little Teapot" and we sang the song together.

"Now, let's sing the song again, and this time, let's show our friends all the snap words hiding inside it. When we sing a snap word, let's make our voices a little louder so we can make sure our friends can really hear those words!" We sang the song once more, stressing the snap words as I pointed to each one on the page.

GETTING READY

✔ Have students bring their stuffed animals to the rug.

✔ Display the lyrics to "The Teapot Song".

✔ Make sure partners have their snap word pouches.

✔ Prepare sets of snap words that students can take home with them.

✔ Display the lyrics to "Rock-a-Bye, Baby".

PHONICS INSTRUCTION

Concepts About Print

- Recognize that spoken words are represented in written language by specific sequences of letters.
- Understand that words are written left to right across the page.
- Make return sweep at the end of a line of text.
- Understand that words are separated by spaces in print, concept of word.
- Match spoken word to print.

High-Frequency Words

- Recognize and use high-frequency words.
- Locate and read high-frequency words in a text.
- Develop and use strategies for learning high-frequency words.

"Today I want to remind you that once you learn a lot about something—like snap words—you can pass it on; you can teach others *everything* you know."

TEACHING

Explain that students can teach their stuffed animal the words they've collected, starting with one of the snap words in the shared song.

"Sam, I see you brought Blue Bear back to school. It's great to see you again, Blue Bear." I reached down to shake the bear's paw. "Have you been practicing your ABCs at home? You have? Excellent! I know you have a great teacher at home!" Sam beamed proudly.

"Class, what should we teach Blue Bear next? Let's think, 'Hmm, . . . what do I know that I could teach?' Sam, cover up Blue Bear's ears for a minute so we can plan what we'll teach him next." I scratched my head, as the kids started calling out some suggestions.

"Oh yes, of course! Our snap words." I turned toward the pocket chart collection. "He probably doesn't know what any of these say. Let's take one out and teach it to him. We could read it and spell out the letters, and then take his little paw and trace the letters to write it."

"Sam, can you bring Blue Bear up here so he can go to Word School?" I said. Once Blue Bear was seated at the front of the meeting area, I said, "Blue Bear, we'd like to teach you one of the words we've learned." I turned to the words in the pocket chart and pulled a card out. I held it up. "Will you read this word to Blue Bear?"

"It!" the class shouted.

"This is the word *it*, Blue Bear. Let's spell it for him."

"*I-T*!" voices chanted.

"Sam, will you show Blue Bear how to write those letters?" I held up the card, and Sam took the bear's paw and traced the shape of each letter. "Oh! I bet we could play a word game with Blue Bear, too. Let's play with patterns and make sentences." I took the *it* word card and put it on the top of the pocket chart. Then, I added words from the snap word collection to make a sentence. "Let's read this sentence to Blue Bear."

The children and I read together, "It is in the . . . " and I filled in the last word, "house!"

"Here's another." I rearranged the word cards and invited the class to read the new sentence.

"Here it is in the . . . "

"Park!" I said, completing the sentence.

ACTIVE ENGAGEMENT/LINK

Repeat the process of teaching a word with the class, releasing the amount of scaffolding you are providing by prompting without modeling.

"Do we have some other stuffed animals that would like to learn some words?" I asked. "Decide what word you want to teach that friend. Pull one of the words out of your snap word pouch. Then, teachers—that's *you*, class—cover the ears of your little friend for a moment and plan with your partner. Think about what else you can do to teach the word to your stuffed animal. Help each other think of a song you can sing or a game you can play with your words."

After children had a moment to plan their teaching, I channeled them to begin. "Okay word professors, let Word School begin! Teach a word! Sing a song! Play a game!" I circled the meeting area, listening in and coaching partners.

RUG TIME

Rug clubs play Word School with their club members and stuffed animals, demonstrating everything they have learned about the words in their snap word pouches.

"Word professors, I think your stuffed animals want to be in a class with more furry friends and learn all together. So in each rug club, will you teach *all* your stuffed animals? Remember those lesson plans you prepared in the last session. Get out your writing you fixed up earlier.

"Will you take turns being the teacher, and the rest of you, can you hold your students up in a nice line? Be sure to teach your students everything you know about snap words."

I coached as the children taught, and every few minutes I suggested that a new child take on the role of teacher.

POSSIBLE COACHING MOVES

▶ "Remember to tell your students what that word says. Point to it and read it. Then teach your class how to spell it."

▶ "Have your stuffed animals trace the word on the card to write it."

▶ "Play a game with your class. Maybe you can make word patterns and read your sentences together."

▶ "Read your writing and point to the snap words!"

SHARE • Ending the Unit with a Snap Word Lullaby

Give your students word bags to take home to continue to play school. Then, sing "Rock-a-Bye Baby" to send the stuffed animals off to sleep.

"It's almost time for Word School to be dismissed. Before our friends go home, let's scoop up all these snap words and put them back into the pouch. Then, we can give each stuffed animal a word bag, so they can play word school at home!" I gave students a minute to clean up all their words and put Mabel on my lap.

"Let's end Word School with one last song. Sit your stuffed animal in your lap. If you spot a snap word, make sure you point at it with your little one's paw. Sing with me . . . " I placed the lyrics to "Rock-a-Bye Baby" on the document camera. We sang together, as I pointed to the snap words on the page.

"Boys and girls, I think Mabel is really sleepy after all this word work. Do you think your friends are sleepy, too?" I cupped my ear and leaned in. "Oh yes, I think I hear some of them yawning. Let's rock them to sleep like little babies." I cradled Mabel in my arms and rocked her back and forth, as the students did the same with their stuffed animals. We sang the song one last time to end the unit.

Rock-a-bye baby,

In the treetop.

When the wind blows,

The cradle will rock.

When the bough breaks,

The cradle will fall.

And down will come baby,

Cradle and all.